"I am often asked whether the teachings and techniques of Buddhism continue to be relevant in the present day and age. Like all religions, Buddhism addresses basic human problems. So long as we continue to experience the basic human sufferings of birth, disease, old age, and death, there is no question of whether it is relevant or not. Therefore, I welcome this new English edition of Buddha-Dharma that presents a concise and clear anthology of the Buddha's teachings."

His Holiness, the Fourteenth Dalai Lama

"The New English edition of 'Buddha-Dharma' is an excellent assemblage of the understandings, sayings and doings of Sakyamuni Buddha, drawn in non-sectarian way from both Theravada and Mahayana sources. Reading this book gives one a good introduction to the world of this great enlightened person and his followers, it is a kind of experience of meeting the Buddha, listening to his Dharma, and associating with his Sangha community. I warmly recommend it."

Professor Robert Thurman, Jey Tsong Khapa
Professor of Indo-Tibetan
Studies, *Columbia University*

"The world of English-speaking readers owes deep respect and gratitude to the late Dr. Yehan Numata. It is quite admirable that he dedicated a considerable percentage of his company's profits to the noble cause of propagating the teachings of the Buddha. Along with his grand project of translating and publishing the Taisho Tripitaka in English, 'Buddha-Dharma' is an important part of his selfless legacy. This book is an excellent anthology of Buddhist teachings that will be beneficial for all that would like to deepen their understanding."

Samuel Bercholz, Founder & Editor-in-Chief,
Shambhala Publications

"Due to the generous vows of Rev. Yehan Numata, the life and teachings of the Buddha Sakyamuni are further disseminated to all seekers of the Awakened life. In reading this volume, which draws upon sources from both the Theravada and Mahayana traditions, you will find yourself in the midst of the historical Buddha's lively assembly. And you will recognize in your life the essential humanity of those who practice this intimate Dharma. This volume is an excellent and appealing introduction to Buddha-Dharma."

Wendy Egyoku Nakao,
Zen Center of Los Angeles

"A much needed, comprehensive presentation of the basic teaching of Buddhism, including important Theravada and Mahayana scriptures. Well organized and very readable, this book should appeal to readers who seek to gain an overview of the Buddhist tradition. Perhaps the closest thing to a Buddhist Bible at the present time."

Dr. Taitetsu Unno, Jill Kerr Conway Professor
Professor Emeritus of Religion, *Smith College*

"This gathering of texts called 'Buddha-Dharma' presents just that, the life and actual teachings of the historical Buddha, Shakyamuni. The greater part of it covers the years of Sakyamuni's teachings. The account that emerges is inspiring, in its very humanity that the earnest (and sometimes skeptical) laypeople, Bhikkus, Bhikkunis, were vivid people from all walks of life. The Great Teacher himself is constant, profound, patient, sweet, and occasionally vexed by his complicated followers. This is truly the source-story of Buddhism. It takes us back to the roots, which are perennial and incredibly deep, and all the stronger for their familiar quirkiness. This is our own story, to be lived in and by, in a clear and handy volume."

Gary Snyder, *Pulitzer Prize Winning Writer*

"Drawing from the vast scriptural resources of Theravada and Mahayana Buddhism, this comprehensive anthology offers representative selections of passages on various topics and aspects of Buddhism. The rich and diverse tradition has produced story, myth, legend, parable, metaphor and teachings through which the student of Buddhism can experience the flavor of the Dharma and its spirit of compassion and wisdom. This volume will be indispensable for the study of Buddhist insight and way of life. Its glossary, index, and list of textual sources will greatly assist in navigating this text."

Dr. Alfred Bloom, Professor Emeritus,
Department of Religion
University of Hawaii

BUDDHA-DHARMA

BUDDHA-DHARMA

Revised Second Edition

Numata Center
for Buddhist Translation and Research
2003

First Printing, 2003
ISBN: 1-886439-19-2 (cloth)

First Printing, 2003
ISBN: 1-886439-20-6 (paper)

Library of Congress Catalog Card Number: 2003107221

Published by
Numata Center for Buddhist Translation and Research
2620 Warring Street
Berkeley, California 94704

Printed in the United States of America

TABLE OF CONTENTS

PREFACE

The most authoritative and complete edition of the Buddhist scriptures is called the Taisho Shinshu Daizokyo or Taisho Daizokyo, widely studied throughout the world. It was compiled by various eminent Japanese Buddhist scholars during the Taisho Period (1912-1925) and published in 1924-1934. This 100-volume edition consists of 3,360 works in nearly 12,000 fascicles. All of the texts are in Chinese, either translations from the original works in Indic and Central Asian languages or treatises, commentaries, catalogs and other works by Chinese or Japanese monks and scholars. Taisho Daizokyo is, simply stated, a Chinese language edition of the Tripitaka.

During the difficult work of compiling this monumental collection, the Japanese scholars, led by Professor Junjiro Takakusu, recognized the necessity and urgency of publishing a small collection of selected texts from the Daizokyo translated into Japanese for the general readers in Japan who heretofore had never been able to read or possess a book of Buddhist sutras in Japanese. As a result, the first edition of the Shinyaku Bukkyo Seiten (The Newly Translated Buddhist Scriptures) in concise form was published in 1925 under the editorship of Rev. Muan Kizu, representing the Bukkyo Kyokai (Buddhist Association) in Nagoya, Japan. Because of the length and excessive use of technical terms in the original 1925 edition, Rev. Kizu, with the help of Professors Chizen Akanuma and Shugaku Yamabe, deleted some terms and passages that might not be readily understood by the readers and published revised editions in 1929 and 1976. The length was reduced from 1,626 pages to 720 pages and thereby reducing the price of the book and making it more widely affordable.

The Society for the Promotion of Buddhism (Bukkyo Dendo Kyokai) in Japan and the independently-established Numata Center for Buddhist Translation and Research in Berkeley, California, are involved in the formidable task of translating and publishing the entire Taisho Daizokyo into English. Since it may take a hundred years or more to complete this task, it was decided that an English translation of the 1976 revised Shinyaku Bukkyo Seiten would be a quick and desirable way to provide general English readers with a concise collection of Buddhist scriptures. Thus, the first edition of the Buddha-Dharma was published in 1984.

This present edition is a thorough revision of the 1984 edition, with the addition of an introduction for each of the eight main sections, a listing of original sources for selected passages, the compilation of Sanskrit and Pali names and terminologies, an enlarged glossary, and a definitive index. Also, for this edition of the Buddha-Dharma, the translations of different sections undertaken by various Buddhist ministers in America for the first edition were carefully reviewed for consistency of word use to provide a faithful reflection of the original Japanese text.

Unlike other anthologies of Buddhist scriptures in English, which are arranged according to the various schools or sects with which the texts are associated, the Shinyaku Bukkyo Seiten, the original collection in Japanese, was arranged more or less chronologically, regardless of source, so that readers can appreciate the discourses of the Buddha in the context of his travels in India, from the time of his Enlightenment in Bodhgaya to his demise 45 years later in Kusinagara.

Also, in this edition, the practice of the 1984 edition to use Pali or Sanskrit names or terms corresponding to the original text of the passages, from which translations were made for the Japanese collection, were generally retained. Most of the Chinese texts from which the Japanese translations were made have their source in Sanskrit texts.

Certain forms now in general use and may appear in English dictionaries, such as nirvana, dharma, arhat, atman, etc., were used regardless of the source. As in the first edition, the diacritical marks were intentionally omitted to make the reading easier for general readers. A Pali and Sanskrit word list with added diacritical marks is provided in the back of the book.

The Foreword by Rev. Kyoshiro Tokunaga, written originally for the 1984 edition, acknowledges many Buddhist ministers who contributed their part in the difficult task of translating the Shinyaku Bukkyo Seiten into readable English.

It is hoped that for many readers, the present book would be a good introduction to the life of Shakyamuni, the historical Buddha, and to his wonderful teaching, the Buddha-Dharma.

Editorial Staff,
Numata Center for Buddhist Translation & Research

FOREWORD

During the past decades, literally hundreds of high quality books on Buddhism in English, and other languages, have been published. For Western readers to have an overview of Buddha-Dharma, numerous readable materials are available. For more academically inclined students, there are a large number of the original texts translated into various European languages. Why, then, publish another volume? We believe we have something unique to offer the reading public that justifies this publication.

Buddhist canon as it exists today is very voluminous to say the least. There are several reasons for this. The Buddha lived a long life. Between the time of his Awakenment at the age of thirty-five and the time of his demise at eighty, there were forty-five years during which he continuously expounded the Dharma. The teaching was directed not only to one segment of the population but to all sorts of people. Among his audiences were those of high and low caste, young and old, wealthy and poor, men and women, learned and unlearned, and his own disciples as well as the masters and disciples of other teachings (there were at least six philosophical schools other than Buddhism in India at the time). The Buddha's way of teaching was flexible enough to accommodate all of their spiritual needs in most effective ways.

The Buddhist canon, called Tripitaka, meaning Three 'Baskets' or 'Containers,' is composed of three parts: Sutras, Vinayas and Abhidharmas. The Sutras, meaning 'warps' and, by extension, 'Unchanging Principles,' are sometimes called, 'Buddhavacana' or 'the 'Buddha's Words'. The Vinayas are the combination of precepts and rules of the monastic order. The Abhidharmas are the treatises or commentaries on the Sutras by the masters and scholars. At the time of the first compilation of the canon, which took place only several months after the demise of the Buddha, the Abhidharmas were not included. The canon was a collection of rather simple recitations of the Buddhavacana that the leading disciples had committed to memory and to which all the participating disciples in the council, said to be five hundred in number, had to agree as to their veracity and authenticity. Thus, it was customary to begin the Sutras with the phrase, "Thus Have I Heard."

Later, in the First Century B.C.E., the first written Tripitaka was compiled in the dialect of Magadha. Several more compilations were conducted during the ensuing centuries. A more complete compilation was made in Ceylon using the Pali language. With the passing of time, more Sutras and Abhidharmas were added. What started as a simple Tripitaka gradually increased in volume, especially in the case of the Mahayana school. Most of the Chinese editions have more than 5,000 volumes. As the teaching spread among the Asiatic countries, it had to find expression in different languages, such as, Wigur, Khotan, Tibetan, Chinese, Mongolian, Manchurian, Korean and Japanese. In Japan, among other editions, The Taisho Daizo-kyo (The Taisho Great Storage Canon) which is considered to be the most complete Mahayana Tripitaka, includes Chinese and Japanese masters' treatises and more recent discoveries from Tunhuang. It contains 11,970 fascicles.

When we consider these facts, one can easily envision what an enormous task it is to read and understand thoroughly all of these scriptures. Even merely to browse through them is well nigh impossible in one's lifetime. Many attempts have been made to epitomize the whole of Buddhavacana into a single or a short series of volumes thereby making it available to the general reader. However, most attempts were either too academic and technical for the ordinary reader or not comprehensive enough to encompass the whole gamut of the teaching and did not carry the deeper, inspiring tone of the original Buddhavacana.

Some years ago, Bhiksu Sangharakshita wrote an excellent book, A Survey of Buddhism. As a survey, it gives a lucid exposition of the various facets of the Dharma. In the preface to this book, the author writes to the effect that his utmost concern is to see the teaching as a whole and to see it in sufficient depth to be able to discern the underlying interconnections both within itself and to the spiritual life of the individual Buddhist. I believe this to be the proper stance for a student in pursuit of understanding any religion. All religious experiences are related in that it is at that deep level that one finds the common ground or the basic philosophical and spiritual principles upon which the whole structure of the teaching is based.

In order to delve into the depths of Buddha-Dharma, one has to experience that "feeling" of it; and this cannot be experienced by just reading a compendium or two. Buddha-Dharma can be fully appreciated only when one goes deeply enough to discern the "interconnection." It means that the reading materials should offer substance or "meat" to be savored, and this can be accomplished only when one acquaints oneself with the original words of the sage. By "original," I do not necessarily mean that the materials must be read in the original language or the dialect used by the Buddha. We are not even sure in which dialect or dialects he taught. However, they must be the words uninterpreted by the writer. The interpretation is to be done by the reader. This is the purpose that the present volume intends to serve.

Fortunately for our attempt, there was a prototype that we could follow. It was compiled by such Buddhist scholars as the Reverend Muan Kizu, Professors Chizen

Akanuma, Shugaku Yamabe and others of Otani University of Kyoto, Japan. The book entitled Shinyaku Bukkyo Seiten, the newly Translated (Concise) Buddhist Scripture (referred to as the "New Translation" hereafter), was the answer to our quest for a model volume, short enough to be available to ordinary laity yet comprehensive and detailed enough for the reader to feel the presence of the great person. We adopted freely from it to compile our present English version. We feel most grateful to the aforementioned scholars.

We do not consider the present volume to be complete. Because of the magnitude of the subject matter and of the limited space, some portions have been inadequately treated. Upon cursory reading, one might find some parts even superficially contradicting, especially since there are vast differences between the Theravadan and Mahayanist approaches and interpretations. Even within each school, there are many divergences comparable to the differences one finds between the various denominations of Christianity and those within other religions. In this regard, I suggest that the reader recall the words of Sangharakshita. One must dig deep enough to discover that the bamboo shoots making appearances in different spots in a grove sprout from the same root.

As we send this manuscript to the press, we would like to express our deep appreciation to Mr. Yehan Numata of Bukkyo Dendo Kyokai (The Buddhism Promoting Foundation) for giving us the opportunity to work on this. It was the zeal and the sincerity of that gentleman that motivated us to undertake the project and sustained us throughout the somewhat extended period of preparation of the volume. Personally, I would like to offer my unfeigned thanks to those contributors who gave every spare moment out of their busy professional duties to prepare the materials. They are: the Reverends John Doami, Masami Fujitani, the Reverend Dr. Ronald Nakasone, the Reverends Shojo Oi, Takashi Tsuji, Shodo Tsunoda and Tetsuo Unno. They are ordained Buddhist priests, well versed in Buddhist thought with an excellent command of English and the Japanese languages as well as the reading ability of Chinese texts. My special thanks go to the Reverend Masami Fujitani, an accomplished linguist, for overseeing the Sanskrit and Pali terms, and to Dr. Ichimura for preparing the detailed maps of which we could use only one and an extensive glossary which also had to be shortened due to lack of space. I am deeply indebted also to the Reverend Tetsuo Unno for co-editing the manuscripts and to the Reverend Takashi Tsuji for his constant advice. My thanks also go to the Reverends Ejitsu Hojo, Keizo Norimoto and Junjo Tsumura for their ever encouraging words and to Mr. and Mrs. Robert Lyon for typing and going over the whole manuscript. Lastly, I am deeply grateful to Messrs. Steve Yamamoto and Art Hayashi and the entire staff of MTI Graphics, Inc., who produced this volume, for their kind advice and patience during the final stages of the publication. All in all, I feel the truth of, and am grateful for, Pratityasamutpada, without which this work, however imperfect, could not have been completed.

Gassho,
Kyoshiro Tokunaga
Editor, 1984

ACKNOWLEDGEMENTS

This book is a revision of the 755-page BUDDHA-DHARMA published in 1984. A large number of people were involved in the preparation of the material for the First Edition and their efforts were acknowledged by the editor, the Reverend Kyoshiro Tokunaga. At this time, I wish to thank Reverend Tokunaga for the tremendous job he performed in compiling the translations accomplished by eight Buddhist ministers and publishing an anthology of Buddhist scriptures. What is amazing is that this was accomplished in the face of many obstacles, the most serious of which was severe time constraints. The book had to be published by November 1984, since it was to be used as a commemorative gift on the occasion of the establishment of the Numata Center for Buddhist Translation and Research in Berkeley, California. In order to meet the deadline, he had to exert efforts that went far beyond normal expectations. He had to supervise the translation work accomplished by the Buddhist ministers, most of the editing and all the sundry activities necessary in the book-making process. As the result of the stressful work at an advanced age (in the mid-70's), he ruined his overall health. I cannot thank him enough for the sacrifices he made. He was also destined to make major contributions for the Second Edition.

As can be imagined, many people were also involved in the production of the Second Edition. Above all, it was the Reverend Tokunaga who, it seemed, recognizing the shortcomings of the First Edition, felt duty-bound to rectify the situation. He assisted in the re-editing, the tedious translation of the section on scriptural sources, and in the initial compilation of the index. Sadly, however, the Reverend Tokunaga was unable to have the satisfaction and the pleasure of seeing the results of his self-sacrificing efforts for the Second Edition. He passed away in June of 2001.

For the present revised volume, I wish to thank, first of all, Ms. Kimi Hisatsune, who graciously agreed to assume the huge responsibility of assisting in the overall editing of this valuable work. She is the eldest daughter of the late Reverend Inshu Yonemura, a Buddhist priest who served in the United States from 1927 to 1949. From 1987 to 1991, Ms. Hisatsune was the Associate Managing Editor of "The Pacific World," the journal of the Institute of Buddhist Studies in Berkeley, California. Her goal for this book was to assure that the revision would respect the past efforts of the eminent Japanese scholars who compiled the original anthology, as well as all those who translated and produced the First Edition. New elements of the revision included the addition of introductions to the eight sections of the book, a listing of scriptural sources, the compilation of Sanskrit and Pali names and terminologies, an enlarged glossary, and the production of a definitive index. Ms. Hisatsune spent countless hours on all aspects of editing and on the research and writing of the introductions for the eight sections of the book. The introductory material led to a smoother transition and easier understanding of the section that followed. The production of a useful and comprehensive index also consumed much of her energy and concentration. Words are inadequate to express my appreciation for her dedicated efforts. Mention must be made of the role of Ms. Kimi Hisatsune's spouse, Dr. Clarence Hisatsune, Professor Emeritus of Physical Chemistry, Pennsylvania State University, and Adjunct Professor of Science and Buddhism, Institute of Buddhist Studies, Berkeley, California. I am indebted to him because he carefully read the complete text three times, proofread the manuscript, and provided significant suggestions to the editor.

Many others contributed to this Revised, Enlarged Edition. Valuable ideas and recommendations for revision were made by Charles Niimi. Special thanks go to Dr. Kenneth K. Inada, Distinguished Service Professor Emeritus, SUNY, and Professor Emeritus Dr. Francis Cook, University of California at Riverside, for reviewing the introductory material for the Eight Books and the glossary. I am also grateful to Dr. Taitetsu Unno, Professor Emeritus, Smith College, Northampton, Massachusetts, for his suggestions for general improvement in the quality of the book and post-publication ideas. My gratitude goes to Elizabeth Cook, who helped to create the map showing the area of Sakyamuni's evangelical activities in India, and to Koh Nishiike in the review of the new sections on scriptural sources and Pali-Sanskrit equivalents. Brian Nagata has been most helpful in making contacts and providing administrative assistance.

In addition, for accomplishing the myriad of tasks necessary in producing a major revision of a 750-page book, I am appreciative of the efforts of the following people: Diane Ames, Brian Galloway, Marianne Dresser, Betty Jo Yamamoto, Dr. Eisho Nasu, and the Rev. Tetsuo Unno.

Special mention must be made of the fact that I am also deeply indebted to the Reverend Toshihide Numata, Chairman of Bukkyo Dendo Kyokai (The Society for the Promotion of Buddhism), and Shigeru Yamamoto of the Buddha Dharma Kyokai (Society), USA for providing generous financial assistance for the production of this book, and for their encouragement and unflagging patience. I hope that this book will prove helpful to students, useful to teachers, inspirational to Buddhist lay people, and interesting to general readers. Above all, I remain hopeful that the teachings in this book will help to promote peace and harmony among the peoples of the world by making every man, woman, and child reading the book, a more wholesome and a better person. This was the inspiring vision of the late Rev. Dr. Yehan Numata, the Founder of the Society for the Promotion of Buddhism in 1965.

October 2001   Seishin K. Yamashita, President
                                                 Numata Center for Buddhist
                                                  Translation and Research

GATHA

In the beginningless, endless flow of time
    you meet the Buddha but once.
Therefore, discard your worldly attachments
    and receive the Dharma.

We are all sinking in the sea of suffering
    and our depraved minds tremble in fear.
But the Buddha with his compassion
    shows us the Realm of Purity.

In each ray of light
    innumerable Buddhas reside,
Who by countless means
    work tirelessly to save us all.

The body of the Buddha is pure and serene,
    he radiates light throughout the world
but his Truth is quiet and formless.

The realm of the Buddha is unfathomable
    and his teachings are limitless,
but he speaks with one voice
    and the voice of the Dharma reaches everything.

And all beings attain Enlightenment.
    each according to his capacity,
but all teachings are one.

Many are the joys of the world
    but none surpass the joy of pure peace.
Untainted Dharma is the Buddha's domain,
    from there he views the world with purity of vision.

All the countries of the world
    occupy less space than a strand of hair.
Truly the compassion of the Buddha
    is wide as the open skies.

Our pride is as massive as a mountain
  But the Buddha destroys it with the power of his
  skillful means and wisdom.
He worked tirelessly to realize Buddhahood
  which dispels the darkness of our ignorance.
Pure indeed is the Buddha's wisdom.

In the infinite past
  he transcended the suffering of birth and death.
He teaches the way of purity.
  The Buddha is the lamp of wisdom.

Ah, birth, old age, sickness and death,
  misery and sorrows weigh heavily on the human heart.
But, when one sees the Buddha just once,
  his mind immediately enters the Realm of Purity.

All the countless Buddha worlds
  are filled with his profound virtues.
Here great numbers of untainted Buddha's children assemble,
  always to listen to the voice of the Dharma.
The Buddha is high and lofty
  but he also resides in every speck of dust.

He shows us numerous practices
  and uses means beyond our understanding
to lead all of his children to the Realm of Purity.

Ah, the pure world of Enlightenment, the ocean of virtue,
  all beings blessed with the good circumstances to hear the Dharma
  vow to follow the path
And ultimately realize supreme Buddhahood.

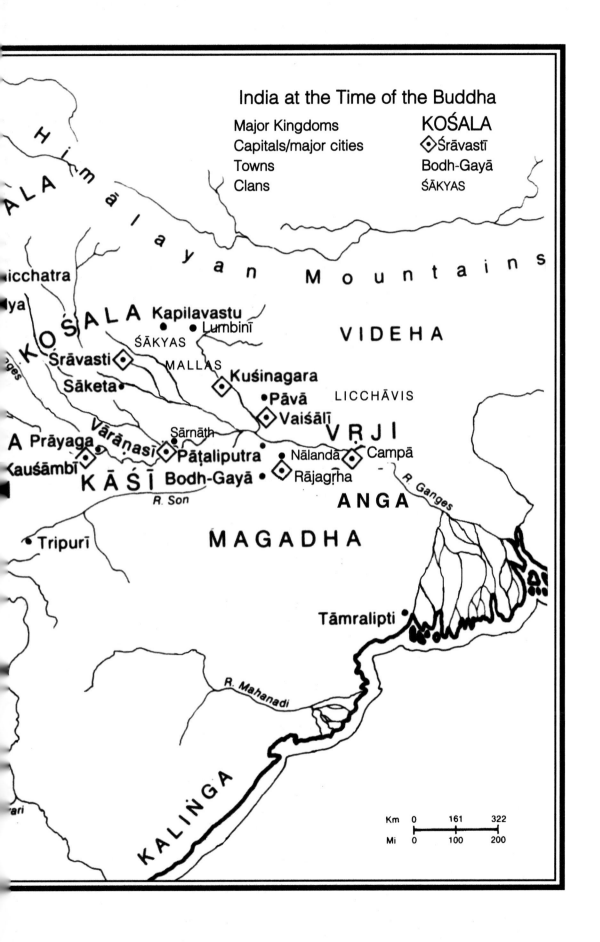

India at the Time of the Buddha

Major Kingdoms
Capitals/major cities
Towns
Clans

KOŚALA
◇Śrāvastī
Bodh-Gayā
ŚĀKYAS

Introduction

Book I begins with the legendary life of the Buddha from the time of his birth to his enlightenment and ends with the establishment of the first monastery by Anathapindika for the Buddha and his disciples at the Jetavana (grove) in Savatthi (Skt: Sravasti), the capital city of the Kosala clan. This ancient city has been identified as the modern twin cities of Sahet-Mahet of Gonda district on the southern shore of the Rapti River.

Inspired by the fabulous stories of gods and celestial beings of the Hindu pantheon narrated from time immemorial in ancient India, the early Buddhist scribes embellished the life story of Gotama (Skt: Gautama) Buddha with fictional and supernatural events, intermixed with historical facts and places, to honor this great spiritual teacher. Thus, the first chapter begins with the Buddha's former life as Sumedha, who vowed to Buddha Dipankara that he would save human beings from delusions that cause them suffering. His good karma earned him rebirth in the celestial realm. Later, he descended from the celestial realm to enter the womb of Queen Maya. After his birth, King Suddhodana tried to prevent the Prince from becoming a monk as prophesied and surrounded him with all kinds of pleasures and luxuries in an attempt to shield him from witnessing the sufferings of life. The legend of the Four Gates symbolizes the young Prince's concerns for old age, sickness, and death, which he eventually discovers. The fourth gate represents the decision he finally made to leave the palace in search of the path that would free him from these inevitable miseries of life.

In spite of the fantastic tales, the historicity of Gotama's life can be found not only in physical traces discovered by archeologists but also from records written by non-Buddhist scribes contemporary to the time of the earliest Buddhist records. Also, two Chinese monks who came to India to study or to collect copies of the Buddhist scriptures (Fa-Hsien in the fifth century C.E. and Hsuan-tsang in the seventh century C.E.) described in detail the holy places pertaining to the Buddha's life they had visited.

Gotama (family name of the historic Buddha) was born in mid-sixth century B.C.E. (the exact date is unknown) in the Lumbini Grove, located between Kapilavatthu and Devadaha, the birthplace of his mother Queen Maya, of the Koliya clan. Although the original vegetation has completely disappeared from the area, the villages at the time of his birth were separated by dense forests that extended from the Ganges River to the Himalaya mountains at the north of the plains. The Lumbini site in Nepal near the Indian border is marked by a stone pillar erected in 249 B.C.E. by King Asoka, the ruler of the Magadhan Empire that encompassed nearly all of present-day India.

According to the Sinhalese (Sri Lanka) tradition, Asoka's coronation took place 218 years after the Buddha's death. For estimating the chronology of the rulers of Magadha and other contemporary figures in the time of the Buddha, his death date is of great importance to scholars. According to the discussion of this crucial point in "The Age of Imperial Unity," v.2 of The History and Culture of the Indian People, edited by R. C. Majumdar (Bombay: Bharatiya Vidya Bhavan, 2nd ed., 1953), the Sinhalese fix the date of the Buddha's death at 544 B.C.E.; the Chinese place it at 486 B.C.E., which was determined by their practice of recording a dot each year after the death of the Buddha. Since the date of the coronation of Asoka can be placed in 269 B.C.E. "with a tolerable degree of certainty," 218 years before this date would be 487 B.C.E. Thus, the above cited source declares that most scholars place Buddha's death within a few years of this date. Most Buddhist scholars have settled on the Buddha's dates as 563-483 B.C.E. However, the readers must be aware that since archeological or documental proofs do not exist to substantiate these dates, scholars have had to choose various available historical dates from which to calculate the probable chronology of the Buddha's life.

The site of the Buddha's enlightenment in Bodhgaya is marked by a large Bodhi tree (pippal, ficus religiosa), and right beside it stands the Maha Bodhi Temple with its massive pyramidical tower. There is no direct evidence that would fix the exact or probable date when this temple was erected. Various traditions ascribe its establishment to Asoka, but the Chinese pilgrim Fa-hsien, who visited Bodhgaya in 409 C.E., did not record seeing this impressive structure by the Bodhi tree. Another Chinese monk, Hsuan-tsang, visited the site in 637 C.E. and described a temple 160 feet in height, which he heard was built by a brahmin on advice given him by the god Shiva. In other words, who ordered its construction is unknown, but it seems likely to have been built in the 6th century before Hsuan-tsang's visit. The physical description recorded in detail by Hsuan-tsang closely corresponds to the present temple.

Bodhgaya is situated six miles to the south of modern Gaya in the state of Bihar, and about 70 miles to the south of Patna, the capital of the present state of Bihar, India. The Neranjara (Skt: Nairanjana) River in which the Buddha bathed himself after his six years of ascetic practices, and just before his enlightenment, is located about 200 yards from the site of the Bodhi tree.

Chapter 3 presents to the reader the Buddha's First Sermon which was delivered to his former companions, who had practiced austerities with him but deserted him when he ceased ascetic practices and took food from the maiden Sujata. The five ascetics became his disciples after hearing the doctrine of the Four Noble Truths and the Middle Path to spiritual liberation, which is the basic teaching of the Enlightened One.

Chapter 1

IN SEARCH OF THE PATH

1. A Former Incarnation of the World-Honored One

In the far distant past, the ascetic Sumedha lamented that people were destined to an unending life of suffering in this world. In order to free himself from this fate, Sumedha performed selfless humanitarian acts. Patiently bearing hardships, he practiced the path with single-minded devotion. At that time the Buddha Dipankara appeared in this world. He expounded the Dharma, pointed out the path, and worked to save people. One day, it was learned that this Buddha was to visit the village of Rammaka. The villagers gathered together, decorated the eaves of their houses, and leveled the roads by pouring sand into water-filled potholes. Just then, Sumedha came into the village, observed this activity, and said, "Even to hear the name of a Buddha is difficult; what good fortune that a Buddha should appear before our eyes here and now!" Filled with joy and in high spirits, Sumedha joined the villagers and threw himself into the task of repairing the roads. But before they could complete their repairs, the Buddha, accompanied by a large number of disciples, appeared in the village. Sumedha believed that now was the very moment that he should make an offering to the Buddha. He untied his hair, lay on the muddy ground, and said, "World-Honored One, for the sake of my happiness and eternal benefit please do not step in the mud but walk together with your disciples over my back." After addressing the Buddha with these words, Sumedha vowed, "Like the Buddha Dipankara, I also vow to burn all my defilements; and after attaining enlightenment, I vow to save all beings from the ocean of delusion."

The Buddha stood near Sumedha's prostrated head, gazed down at him, perceived the vow in Sumedha's mind, and said, "Sumedha, in the far future, you shall beyond any doubt become the Buddha Sakyamuni." Dipankara praised Sumedha's aspiration and then departed.

2. The Birth of the Buddha

(1) From that time, Sumedha gradually practiced the path of the Buddhas, and before long he rose to the rank that leads to Buddhahood. He was born into the Tusita heaven and became a bodhisattva.

The Bodhisattva resided in a land with asoka trees and blooming mandarava and lotus flowers, where parrots, peacocks, and kalavinkas sang their songs. Surrounded by music performed by celestial maidens, he ascended to the Lion's Seat in the Great Hall of the True Dharma, and for the sake of a host of divine beings, he expounded the teaching.

At a gathering one day, the music of the divine beings naturally produced a song: "O Arhat, aeons past under the Buddha Dipankara you attained the enlightenment of the Buddhas.

"You have completed the practices and are filled with wisdom.

"O Arhat, where people have thirsted for water for a long time, quickly descend to the world and pour them water.

"Where the fires of defilement burn furiously, spread out a cloud of compassion and let the rain of the Dharma fall.

"Destroying the demons' ruses and false teachings, reveal the path of the Bodhisattva and save the people of the world."

The Bodhisattva heard this song, and sensing that he must perform a great mission, he vowed to descend to the world of men. The host of divine beings raised their voices in rejoicing and shouted, "Now the Buddha is going to appear in the human world." The Bodhisattva surveyed a multitude of human worlds, and wishing to be born into a household belonging to a noble clan he chose the family Gotama of the clan Sakya.

The king of the Sakya clan, King Suddhodana, constantly performed virtuous acts and governed his people magnanimously. His consort, Queen Maya, was beautiful in appearance, and her heart was pure. She was skilled in various arts and possessed all the merits needed to become the mother of a Buddha.

(2) Then the Bodhisattva, for the sake of the host of divine beings, expounded the teachings: "All of you, first give rise to faith, venerate the teaching, hold the Buddha, the Dharma, and the Sangha in your mind, and attain the path of the sages. Knowing that the world is impermanent and filled with suffering, abide in an egoless mind. With peace in your mind, do not give rise to thoughts of greed. Ceaselessly absorbed in meditation, attain wisdom and, using skillful means, guide those people who are shrouded by the darkness of ignorance.

"Even the marvellous adornments of the celestial world sink down into the lands of suffering when the good fortune that produced these adornments exhausts itself. Even greed is pathetically fleeting. All is as empty as a dream. Greed is never satiated; it is like being parched and drinking salt water.

"Therefore, urging yourself onward, attain the bliss of the uncreated. Should you attain transcendent wisdom, you will then realize fulfillment.

"Study the principles of things; do not become attached to words. Act in accordance with your words, and speak in accordance with your actions.

"Always be aware of your own evil, and do not look at the faults of others. Without your own actions, you will not receive the fruits of the actions performed by others." The Bodhisattva instructed the host of divine beings with these words.

Just when he was about to descend from the celestial world, innumerable divine beings of that world gathered together at the palace in the Tusita heaven and made offerings to the Bodhisattva by playing music. At that time, from the body of the Bodhisattva, light streamed forth, shone on the great three thousand worlds, and dispelled the darkness. The heavens and the earth trembled, and the light of the sun and the moon lost their power. The people were filled with joy, and they became as loving toward each other as parents and their children. The celestial beings residing in the sky sang out,

> For a truly incalculably long span of time, he lacerated his flesh and pulverized his bones. As a reward for this complete practice, the Bodhisattva attains a body that is immovable.
>
> Receiving the helmet of compassion, he dispels the harm done by defilement. Having pity for all people, the Bodhisattva now appears in the world.
>
> Shining forth the light of wisdom, he awakens all those who slumber, and as king of the great thousand worlds, he appears in the world like the sun.

(3) The Bodhisattva at this time assumed the form of a huge white elephant with six tusks and descended from the Tusita heaven. He then passed under Queen Maya's right arm and entered her womb as she slept peacefully. The palace was filled with joy and peace. Auspicious clouds trailed in the sky and enveloped the tiled roofs of the lofty towers.

One day in the last month of her pregnancy, the queen decided that she would like to pass the spring day in a flower garden. Receiving permission from the king and attended by a retinue of ladies-in-waiting, she had herself driven to the Lumbini Grove. The trees were abloom with beautiful flowers that gave off pleasant fragrances; the deep green grasses were like the tail feathers of a peacock and swayed like soft fine silk blown by the wind. The queen took a pleasant stroll; she leaned on the limb of an asoka tree which drooped down because of the weight of its flowers. At that moment, the Bodhisattva was born, suddenly and yet peacefully. Immediately after birth, he took seven steps in each of the four directions and proclaimed, "In heaven above and on earth below, I am the most honored one. I shall dispel the suffering that fills the world."

The divine beings residing in space praised the virtues of the mother, Queen Maya. The Naga king rained down cold and warm water and bathed the body of the Bodhisattva. The great earth trembled and shook with joy. Shortly thereafter, the infant was received by the queen, and since everything proceeded without difficulty, the prince was named Siddhattha (Whose Goal Is Achieved). Seven days after his birth, his mother Queen Maya departed this world and was born in the Tavatimsa heaven, and her younger sister Mahaprajapati assumed the role of compassionate foster mother to the prince.

At that time the sage Asita, who had been living in the mountains near the city of Kapilavatthu, was startled by the auspicious signs that accompanied the prince's birth. He visited the royal palace, taking along with him his nephew, a child named Narada. Asita cradled the prince reverently and gazed down at him for a long time, but soon, choking with tears of sadness, he said, "O king, if this child remains at home, he will become a universal monarch and bring peace to the four worlds. But he will without doubt leave home in search of the path and become a Buddha. I am an old man and shall not be able to hear the teaching of this Buddha; realizing this, I shed tears of sorrow." King Suddhodana heard these words and rejoiced, making offerings to the sage and Narada in a variety of ways.

3. Betrothal to a Princess

From the age of seven, Prince Siddhattha studied languages, mathematics, forensics, astronomy, geography, archery, and so forth under various teachers. The superiority of his intelligence and physical strength repeatedly astonished his teachers.

One year in spring, at a plowing festival, King Suddhodana, leading a party of officials, performed the ritual of plowing with a golden spade. The prince accompanied them, taking leave of the castle. He watched as the farmers plowed the field. He caught sight of a bird that came swooping down from the sky to pick up a worm that had been accidentally dug up by the tip of the plow. His compassionate heart was pained by this sight. He lamented, "How sorrowful! Living beings devour each other in order to survive." Overcome by sadness, he went into the forest at the edge of the field. Sitting down under a jambu tree, thick with foliage, he sank deeply into his thoughts. The prince was nowhere to be seen, so, feeling concerned, people began to search for him. When they stumbled onto him, they discovered a strange thing. While the surrounding trees cast a shadow, the tree under which the prince had sat down cast no shadow. King Suddhodana looked at the majestic form of the prince steeped in thought. Even though the prince was his own son, he praised him and said, "He is like the moon that shines clearly in the sky."

When the prince was nineteen, the king erected palaces for the three seasons of summer, winter, and the rainy season, and he decided that they would be the prince's residences. The waters of the lake lapped the palace stairs, and small waves rippled on the surface. Always the fragrance of the pure lotus hung in the air. That year, the king decided to choose a virtuous princess and make her the prince's consort. His foremost choice was Princess Yasodhara, the oldest daughter of Suppabuddha, the king of the Koliyas, the family of Queen Maya.

Following the customs of the times, they organized a festivity at which the prince would engage with other young princes of related clans in a Selecting a Groom contest. On that day, the princess, dressed beautifully and accompanied by her father, took the seat that had been readied for her. At the festivity, the princes, their hearts beating rapidly, matched their skills with the prince. But there was no one who could equal the prince in the martial arts, whether it be wrestling, archery, or other skills. Amidst the words of praise that rained down on him, the prince and the princess were betrothed; thus was the future queen chosen on this site.

4. Travelling beyond the Four Gates

(1) Following his betrothal, the prince and his princess lived at the palace for nearly ten tranquil years. During that time, however, the prince had deeply contemplated the nature of life, and now the moment for him to leave home in search of the path was near at hand. One day, in the music being performed at the palace, he heard the following verses:

> The music performed by beautiful maidens leads men astray with lust. But the strength of a man free of defilements will enable him to listen to the music as being the words of the Dharma.

> O Arhat, recall those bygone days in which you observed the suffering masses and vowing to save them accumulated virtues for their sake. Now is the time to leave home. With a mind of great compassion, take in those afflicted by the three poisons. Truly, in these three worlds defilements burn like a raging fire. The ignorant are infatuated with youth but are soon shattered by old age, illness, and death. The wise man, in years gone by, met the Buddha and has already become enlightened to the true Dharma.

> The time to rain down the sweet nectar of the Dharma is now!

(2) More and more the prince spent his days in a pensive mood. One day, he thought, "Ultimately, to live as a human being is nothing more than to seek for something. There is a seeking that is good and a seeking that is evil. Evil seeking is to seek in the following way: Although one is a being that undergoes birth and gradual aging, one seeks other beings who undergo birth and aging. Although one has a body that falls prey to illness, withers and dies, sinks into depression, and is stained by defilement, one seeks others who suffer the same. What are some of the things that undergo birth? They are such things as one's wife and children, servants, livestock, and gold and silver. Like oneself, these are things that age, become ill, die, sink into depression, and are stained by defilement. People of this world, although they themselves will eventually wither and die, still seek out those things that also wither and die; moreover, they are attached to and led astray by these things.

"Good seeking is to seek in the following manner: One who undergoes birth, observes the misfortune of those that undergo birth, and seeks the nirvana of unsurpassed calm, which is a Dharma that does not undergo birth. Or, one who ages, becomes ill, dies, sinks into depression, and is stained by defilements, observes the misfortune of those who suffer the same, and seeks the nirvana of unsurpassed calm, which does not age, become ill, sink into depression, or become stained by defilement.

"When I reflect on myself, I too am one of those who seek things that are unworthy. How foolish! From now on, I must seek those things that are freed from depression and defilement."

(3) Again, at one time Siddhattha thought to himself, "My body is extremely handsome and delicate. At my palace, lakes filled with countless lotuses are filled to the brim with water. Flowers in a multitude of colors—blue, red, and white—bloom in all their glory. If the perfume is not from the candana tree that grows

in the country of Kasi, I refrain from rubbing it on my body. I also wear silken undergarments next to my skin, and lower and upper garments and hats made of silk, all from the country of Kasi. Night and day, above my head, a white canopy shelters me from discomforts of heat and cold and shields me from dust, grass, dew, and so forth.

"Moreover, I own three palaces. During the four months of the rainy season, I seclude myself in the Rain Palace; and, surrounded by maidens, I never come down from the palace, which is filled with the pleasures of song, dance, and wine. The servants of other houses are served meals of unhulled rice or sour tasting gruel, but in my house, even to servants, clean white rice is served.

"I live in the midst of such opulence, blessed with a splendid body; however, what is all this for me when I am attempting to awaken? The people of the world are beings who will eventually age; they are vessels that will become ill; they are beings who will, of their own nature, wither and die. Yet, seeing the aged, the sick, and the dead, they view them with distaste. I must not behave like this.

"Right now, I shall abandon the pride of youth, health, and life."

(4) As the prince's mind engaged in a profound struggle, his father the king, remembering the words of the sage Asita who had offered a prophecy regarding the prince, worried profoundly that the prince might leave home to seek the path. One day, he heard that the prince planned to leave the castle and visit the forest, and he ordered his attendants to remove all foul and ugly things from the prince's view. He ordered the attendants to clean the roads, decorate the city, and sweep and clean the garden. The prince, accompanied by his attendants, left by carriage from the East Gate. On the road, he caught sight of a man laboriously shuffling along. The man appeared to be a hunchback; his hair was white; his body was emaciated; and he leaned on a cane. When the prince asked the charioteer what manner of man he was, the charioteer answered, "An old man." The prince said, "Am I going to become like that man?" The charioteer said, "All living beings, whether noble or ignoble, are unable to escape this fate." The prince became distressed, and thoughts of visiting the garden vanished, so he immediately ordered the chariot to return to the palace.

The second time, the prince left the city through the South Gate. He caught sight of a man who had wasted away to the bone. While he writhed in pain in the middle of a rubbish heap and panted, beads of perspiration flowed down his jaundiced skin. The prince asked, "Will I also someday become ill like that man?" The charioteer answered, "No one is able to escape this suffering." Again the prince ordered his chariot back to the palace.

King Suddhodana heard about this and became increasingly distressed. With added severity, he ordered his attendants to clean every part of the city. But when the prince left the city through the West Gate, he chanced upon a procession of people grieving mournfully and bearing a dead man on a bier. The prince sighed and asked, "Alas, in the end, am I going to become like that man?" The charioteer answered, "All living things must inevitably die." Therefore that day again the chariot was ordered back.

On the next occasion, when he left the city through the North Gate, he met a man clothed in a saffron robe, walking along with great dignity. His hair and beard were shaved off, and he was carrying a begging bowl in his hands. When the prince asked the charioteer, "What manner of man is he?" the charioteer answered, "A mendicant who seeks the path." The prince stepped off the chariot, bowed to the man, and said, "What kind of benefits are there for the mendicant?" The man answered, "Observing the transiency of this world, old age, illness, and death, I seek to liberate myself, and abandoning all my relatives, I practice the path now in tranquil surroundings. Guided by the true Dharma, I now restrain my five sensory organs, and with great compassion I protectively guard all people without being stained by the defilements of this world; these are the benefits of the mendicant."

Hearing these words, the prince firmly made up his mind, and thought inwardly, "There is nothing in this world that surpasses this; I must also leave home and study the path." He then bowed reverently to the mendicant, stepped onto the chariot, entered the forest, and spent the entire day in a variety of playful activities.

As dusk approached, he bathed in a lake hidden in the forest. Then he had his attendants fetch his best finery, and he dressed himself. Amidst the exclamations of delight of the court ladies, he boarded the chariot. At that moment, a messenger from the king brought news of the birth of a prince. The prince dispassionately said, "Another fetter that I must undo has been born." Having heard the word rahula (fetter), the messenger reported it to the king; and thus the newly born son was named Rahula. The prince, who had firmly made up his mind to leave home that night, hurried home to the palace and was surrounded by a crowd of happy people. But on the way, a young maiden named Kisa Gotami, who was on the upper story of her palace that looked out onto the main thoroughfare, caught sight of the prince and, filled with delight, recited this verse:

Happy indeed is the father,

Happy indeed is the mother,

Who has such a son.

Happy indeed is the wife

Who waits upon such a husband.

How truly happy!

The mind of the prince was not disturbed by such tender and passionate verses, but because the word for "happy," nibbuta, resembles the word nirvana, he was put in mind of the latter. In gratitude for her unwitting blessing on his new venture, he unfastened a necklace of pearls and presented it to the young maiden; then, urging his charioteer on, he returned to the palace.

5. Leaving Home to Seek the Path

(1) In order to rest from the fatigue of that day's outing, the prince lay down on his jewelled bed. A group of beautiful court ladies tried to comfort the prince by singing and dancing in step with the music. The exquisite quality of their performance and the gracefulness of their forms reminded one of celestial maidens. But now there was no way that even their skillful dancing and singing could affect the mind of the serene prince, who before he knew it fell into a deep slumber. The court ladies saw this and lost their enthusiasm for dancing and singing. They stopped the music and went to sleep themselves. Only the flame of the scented perfume flickered playfully in the hushed night. The prince suddenly awoke from his slumber, sat up in bed, and surveyed the scene surrounding him.

The night was calm, the palace was beautiful, and the incensed light exuded a pleasant fragrance. But how loathsome the sleeping dancing girls appeared! Spittle dribbled from their mouths; they gnashed their teeth and mumbled in their sleep. Their clothes and bodies were in disarray, and they were oblivious to their propriety as women. In groups of two or three, they were in deep sleep. Indeed, the palace that had sparkled in the afternoon had turned into a graveyard. The prince shuddered in disgust and stood up. In his heart, he cried out, "All things are like this scene; in no way can I bear this." He made up his mind to flee the palace at once; he quietly left his room and moved toward the palace gate. He called for his charioteer, Channa, and ordered him to saddle his horse. He then returned once again to the sleeping quarters of the princess and gently opened the door. In the room, scented lamps cast pale shadows in the deep of the night, and there was only the quiet breathing of someone in deep slumber. He thought, "If I hug my child and grieve over this final parting, the princess will awaken and try to prevent my leaving home. Instead of doing this, it would be wiser to see this child after I attain enlightenment." Leaving the palace and mounting his gallant steed Kanthaka, he hurried to the great outer gate of the city. As a precaution against the prince's leaving home, the king had stationed a large number of soldiers at this gate and ordered them to guard it. In addition, the two iron gates were constructed in such a way that even the strength of a thousand men could open them only with great difficulty. But perhaps owing to the agency of divine beings, the guards mysteriously fell asleep, and even those great iron gates swung open without a sound. The white steed Kanthaka ran through the gate like a gust of wind. The time was midnight on the day of the full moon of the fourth month.

At this time, King Mara appeared in the sky and shouted, "O prince, give up your unwise intent of leaving home and go back to the palace abloom with flowers. If you do so, within seven days you will become a universal king who rules the four directions." The prince replied, "O King Mara, away with you! Evil demon, begone with you! Sovereignty over this world is not my goal; my only aspiration is to attain the path." When the prince rebuffed him with these words, King Mara quietly faded in dejection. But he thought to himself, "Now or later, the bird of hatred will someday build a nest in the prince's heart; at that time, I will seize my chance." And from that day, like a shadow that follows a body, he stuck by the prince's side and did his best to obstruct his enlightenment.

(2) The prince, who had left the palace resolutely, thought that he would like to take one last, lingering look at his city, which was gradually fading into the distance; he admonished himself, however, and pressed on. Because of the ferocity of the struggle within his mind, the great earth mysteriously spun around like a potter's wheel and the city appeared of itself in his mind's eye. But with renewed determination, he rode on at full gallop; after riding for seven miles, he reached the banks of the river Anoma at dawn. Urging himself onward, he flew over the river with a single bound.

He lowered himself onto the sand that was beginning to shine brightly, glittering in the morning sun. The prince took off his clothes and gave them to Channa and said, "O Channa, some people serve with their minds but not with their bodies; while others serve with their bodies but not with their minds. You have served me with your body as well as your mind. People fight with each other to serve those of high status who abound in wealth, but they shun those who are poor and of low birth. You alone, however, abandoned your own country and followed me over long distances to this place. Your action is truly admirable!" Unraveling his topknot, the prince held out a gem and said, "Channa, go back now to the palace and offer this to the great king. Convey these words to him, 'The prince wants nothing of the things of the world. People are all fettered by emotions of love and affection, but in the end they are unable to elude old age, illness, and death. Please ponder over this truth and do away with affliction. While the prince has not attained enlightenment, he will not return to the palace.' "

Then he unfastened a necklace, handed it to Channa, and said, "Please offer this to the Queen Foster Mother and say to her that desire is the root of suffering and that I have resolved to sever the root of suffering and to do away with affliction." Again, he handed over a variety of other bodily ornaments and said, "Please offer these to the princess and relate to her that in the world of men, without fail, there is the sorrow of separation; and that the prince has resolved to cut off the root of that sorrow. If she is cast down by the emotion of loving attachment, tell her that she must not sink down into affliction."

Channa broke down and wept and pleaded to be allowed to become a mendicant together with the prince, but he was not allowed to do so. Channa then cried out in a loud voice. The steed Kanthaka followed by bending his forelegs and licking the prince's feet while whining sadly. The prince stroked Kanthaka's head and consoled him with these words, "O Kanthaka, you have accomplished everything that you were called upon to do; there is no reason at all for you to feel sad." He drew out his sword with his right hand, and with his left hand he took hold of his hair, and cut it off. He then flung the hair into the air, exclaiming, "If I am able to attain true enlightenment, let this hair remain suspended in the sky. If I am unable to do so, let it fall to the ground." The hair remained suspended in the sky and did not fall. The divinity Indra caught the hair in a jewelled vessel and placed it in the Tavatimsa heaven. The prince dressed himself in the three garments presented to him by the child of a divinity named Ghatikara and holding a bowl in his hand calmly began to walk forth. In tears

Channa bade farewell to the prince as he faded into the distance. With a heavy heart, Channa returned to the palace. Although he incurred the anger of the whole clan, especially that of the great king Suddhodana and of Princess Yasodhara, Channa faithfully relayed the prince's words.

(3) The prince had now become a humble mendicant. He felt reborn in both mind and body, and with bowl in hand he begged for food at neighboring houses. But at first the prince, who had feasted on lavish meals at the palace, was unable to eat the sour food that he had managed to collect. He went to a spot under a tree and tried to eat but hesitated; without thinking, he was about to throw the food away. But suddenly struck by the thought that he was now a mendicant who seeks the path, he partook of that food with good grace. From that moment on, throughout his life, the prince never suffered over food. The prince then entered Vesali and visited the ascetic Bhaggava to observe the practices of his followers. He observed that they dressed themselves in robes made of leaves and bark of trees and ate tree roots and fruits. At times they ate once a day; at other times, they ate once every two or three days. They worshipped fire and water and lay down in alleyways. The ascetic expounded on the benefits of mortification. He claimed, "Through these practices, in the future, you will be born in the celestial realms." But the prince pressed him with questions such as, "When the bliss of the heavens comes to an end, must we not once again sink back into the world of suffering? Why do you and your followers cultivate the seeds of suffering and seek their fruits?" The ascetic Bhaggava was not able to respond in a satisfactory manner. The prince then thought, "Traders seek treasures and dive into the sea. Kings seek more territories and make war against other countries. These ascetics seek celestial worlds and undergo ascetic practices." In this way the questions and answers continued until nightfall. The prince passed the night there; but he became convinced that these practices were not the true way. The following day he took his leave, and crossing the Ganges, toward the south, he moved toward the neighborhood of Rajagaha. He then visited an ascetic named Alara Kalama, who lived on Mount Sumeru, and asked about the path. "O Kalama, I wish to practice under your teaching." The ascetic answered, "Stay here with me as you wish; this teaching can be attained by anyone in a short time." The prince quickly mastered the teaching.

The prince thought, "When Kalama himself claims that he has attained this teaching, he does not merely believe he has done so. He has no doubt that he has fully realized the teaching." Thinking this, the prince asked, "Kalama, what is the nature of your enlightenment?" Kalama answered by speaking on the state of infinite nothingness. "In the state of infinite nothingness, thoughts of material things are transcended and all existing things are void. This state is the meditative state in which one realizes that only the void exists in infinite nothingness." The prince thought to himself, "Alara Kalama is not the only one who has faith; I also have faith. Not only he, but I, too, possess exertion, right mindfulness, meditation, and wisdom. I shall strive to attain that teaching that, it is said, he has attained." Before long, the prince attained that teaching and went before Kalama and said, "Kalama, is this the extent of the teaching that you claim to have attained?" "This is the extent," answered Kalama. The prince said, "I, too, have attained this teaching." Kalama said, "Friend, I am fortunate indeed to have gained a fellow student like you. The teaching that I have realized, you have also realized. The teaching that you have attained, I also have attained. You and I have attained the same state. Let us, therefore, together guide the disciples."

But the prince thought, "This teaching does not lead to release from delusion. This is not the true and enlightened teaching that is free of greed. Through this teaching one merely attains a state called infinite nothingness." Unfulfilled by this teaching, the prince searched anew for the good. Then, seeking the path that leads to peace, he went to Uddaka Ramaputta and practiced his teaching.

There the prince attained Uddaka's teaching. He discovered that Uddaka's teaching merely led to the realization of a kind of meditative state in which there was neither consciousness nor unconsciousness. He thought, "This teaching also does not lead to release from delusion; this is not the true and enlightened teaching that is free of greed." He thought that if the state of neither consciousness nor unconsciousness were devoid of ego, then even the term "neither consciousness nor unconsciousness" rightfully should not exist. If, on the other hand, there were an ego, then inevitably there must be consciousness. If there were consciousness and one were to become entangled in worldly connections, then attachment would arise. Thinking that this could not be regarded as release, he left Uddaka and once again set out on the road to seek the good.

(4) Spurring himself on this road, the prince entered Rajagaha and went from place to place begging for his food. The people of the city noticed the prince's noble appearance and fought with each other to walk behind him. Because of the commotion, King Bimbisara finally became alarmed. Ascending his palace tower, he saw the prince's majestic appearance in the distance. He followed after the prince in his carriage until he came to the Pandava Hill outside the city. After an exchange of greetings, the king said, "Although you are a mendicant, you are still young; you appear to be a prince of noble birth. If you have the ambition to rule, I would not regret dividing the country in two and offering you half." The prince answered, "I am a prince of the Sakya clan that dwells in the foothills of the Himalayas. Realizing that greed is the root of suffering, I have abandoned all greed and now aspire for the peace of nirvana. That is the only thing I seek."

The king was profoundly moved by the prince's noble mind and said, "If you attain enlightenment, I should like to be the first to be saved by you." The prince silently accepted the king's entreaty and departed. He travelled in a southwesterly direction, crossed the river Neranjara, and entered the quiet forest of Uruvela. This lush and beautifully green forest, situated near the river Neranjara with its shores of pure white sand, became the site for a six-year period of the prince's practice of the bodhisattva path. Shortly after the prince entered the path of the mendicant, his father, King Suddhodana, chose five men, Kondanna and four others belonging to the Sakya clan, and had them follow after the prince. While doing so, they eventually joined the prince and began to undergo spiritual exercises themselves.

6. Ascetic Practices

(1) For the next six years the prince partook of one meal a day, or of one meal every two weeks, or of one meal a month. Crossing his legs, he sat with a dignified posture and did not succumb to rain, wind, or thunder; remaining silent, he never trembled with fear. At times he clenched his teeth, pressed his tongue against his upper palate, and restrained his mind. Perspiration flowed from his armpits just as if he were being pressed down by a man of enormous strength, but his mind did not falter from exertion. His right mindfulness remained undisturbed; and instead of weakening, he was filled with energy and was spurred on by that great suffering. On one occasion, the prince practiced meditation without breathing. When he stopped breathing from the mouth and nose, the breath that had been trapped inside came rushing out of his ears with a tremendous noise. The noise was as loud as that of a blacksmith's bellows. When he went further and stopped the breathing of his ears, violent winds thrust upward against the top of the head; it was like being pierced by a sharp sword. On still another occasion, the violent winds trapped inside caused the head to ache as if it were being stabbed with a broken piece of pottery. At another time, he suffered violent temperatures as if a kitchen knife were being thrust into his stomach, or as if he had thrown his body onto a charcoal fire. And yet the prince's mind never wavered.

Seeing this, one man thought that Gotama had died. Another thought that he would die before long. And still another surmised that the prince had attained enlightenment and had entered the life of a sage.

(2) The prince then made up his mind to intensify his practice and to abstain from eating altogether. The celestial beings were taken aback and shouted, "You must not abstain from eating. If you are determined to fast, we celestial beings will pour fluids into your pores and keep you alive." But the prince unwaveringly rejected their offer. The prince then ate only a small ration of beans, and before long he became emaciated. His arms and legs became like withered reeds, his buttocks like a camel's back, and his spine like a braided rope. His ribs protruded outward like the rafters of a broken-down shack, and the skin covering his head became weather-beaten like a half-ripened gourd that had been scorched by the sun. Only his eyes, set deep in their sockets, sparkled like the stars reflected in a deep well. When he rubbed his stomach, he was able to grasp hold of his spine; and when he rubbed his spine, he was able to grasp his stomach. When he attempted to stand up, he reeled and fell down. The roots of the hair on his head rotted, and his hair fell out in clumps. The prince thought, "No ascetic or mendicant in past worlds, in the present world, or in future worlds has ever undergone, is undergoing, or will undergo greater suffering than this."

(3) Thus the prince undertook practices that were unsurpassed by others in their excellence and that led to the abandonment of desire. He departed from traditional practices. For example, instead of washing his hands after meals, he licked his hands. He refused alms that were offered to him with the words, "Please come in; please take this." Again, he rejected invitations and refused to accept food from houses where dogs were kept or where flies swarmed about. He did not eat

fish or drink liquor; he ate one meal a day or one meal every two or seven days. Gradually, he reduced the amount of food he ate and went without food for half a month. He ate such foods as cereal husk, grain chaff, rice bran, water plants, and rotted nuts and berries. For clothing, he wore burlap, hemp, clothes made of discarded cloth, tree bark, and animal skin. He undertook all manner of ascetic practices of self-mortification: the plucking out of hairs on his head or in his beard, constant standing, constant squatting, lying down on a bed of thorns, rubbing oil on his body and pouring dust on it, parching himself near a fire, immersing his body in water and withstanding the cold, and so forth. In this way the grime of years fell off without being touched. His skin lost its luster and became ashen in color, like the color of a tree with old moss growing on it. He was careful not to take the lives of living creatures, making certain that he did not step on even tiny insects. Having retired from the world, he avoided people, shunning even cowherds, grass cutters, and woodcutters, and retreated deep into the forest.

> (4) Scorched by the sun, numbed by the cold, all alone.
>   In the fearful forest, without clothing or fire,
>   The sage sits in meditation
>   With the radiant light of his ideals.

The prince, moreover, slept at nights in the graveyard, where corpses and bones lay scattered or piled up in heaps. Shepherds' children caught sight of the prince and spat and threw mud at him; or, breaking off a tree branch, they thrust it in the prince's ear. But the prince's mind did not feel any anger toward these children.

Undergoing such ascetic practices, he accomplished that which is difficult to accomplish; however, he was still unable to attain that Dharma that transcends this world. He was unable to achieve divine wisdom. The prince, realizing now that these practices would not lead him to release, that they would not extinguish suffering, and that they would not cause him to attain pure wisdom, decided to seek the path anew.

Chapter 2

ENLIGHTENMENT

1. The Conquest of Mara

(1) The prince's ascetic practices had come to naught. Six years had flowed by in vain. The prince decided that he would no longer fruitlessly mortify his body; he decided to partake of food, nurture his body, and attain release of the mind. After bathing himself in the river Nairanjana, he clung to tree roots and climbed up the river bank; then, with great difficulty, he walked into a neighboring village.

At that time, Sujata, the daughter of Senanipati, a landowner in Uruvilva, had made preparations to make offerings to the tree divinities. She had squeezed the milk of healthy cows, had cooked milk gruel, and had gone into the forest, hoping to offer it to the tree divinities on the day of the full moon of the fourth month. In the forest, she caught sight of an ascetic who was weak and emaciated. Moved by a feeling of reverence, she offered the ascetic her milk gruel and said, "Venerable ascetic, please take pity on me and accept this offering." The prince accepted it and gathered his strength. Thinking that through this he might attain enlightenment, he concluded that there still existed a ray of hope. Kaundinya and the four other ascetics were both dumbfounded and suspicious. They thought that the prince had abandoned his practice; therefore, showing their disdain, they forsook the prince and departed for the Deer Park in Varanasi. The prince, regaining his strength through the offering of milk gruel, made his way to the forest, which was luxuriant with foliage. The land there was flat, and the view in the four directions was clear. Pliant grasses grew beautifully; and in the middle of the forest a huge pippala tree, thick with foliage, spread its branches like a celestial canopy. Beautiful flowers bloomed with a pleasant fragrance. The prince received an offering of kusa grass from the child of a grass cutter who happened to be there and made it his seat. He vowed, "If I am not able to attain enlightenment here, I shall not rise from this seat alive."

(2) The prince believed that this was the time to subjugate Mara. He emitted the light of wisdom from the white curl on his forehead. Mara's palace rattled and shook, provoking great fear. Mara writhed in agony as if he had drunk poison. He then concocted a scheme to throw the mind of the prince into confusion. He dispatched three evil spirits and had them approach the prince. Their robes of fine silk were as light as feathers; flowers adorned their hair beautifully;

they were alluring. The three danced and sang gracefully and beautifully. They tried in every way to seduce the prince. They sang,

Spring comes; spring comes;

The sun's rays provide warmth,

And young buds have sprouted.

O handsome Lord, why do you abandon the pleasures of youth

And seek enlightenment, which lies far away?

You do not look at us, with our beauty—

Us, with whom even ascetics who have retreated

From this floating world have become infatuated.

The prince spoke to the three. He said, "As the reward of your past karma, you now possess the bodies of celestial beings; but before long, you will be assailed by the impermanence of aging and death. Your figures are captivating, but your minds are not true—it is as if a beautiful colored vase were filled with foul-smelling poison. Greed is the source of self-destruction; it is the cause of descent into the realm of evil." At those words, the three evil spirits at once lost their beauty and were transformed into wretched old crones.

(3) King Mara was incensed and immediately assembled one hundred million eight thousand demons; he had them storm the base of the pippala tree, firing their crossbows and brandishing their swords. Heaven and earth were enveloped in darkness, and the sound of the thunder was terrifying. Demons, evil spirits, and their cohorts, all with grotesque appearances, some with the heads of lions, bears, bulls, or horses, some with the heads of human beings and the bodies of snakes—these monsters with bared fangs and glittering claws spewed forth flames of poison, rained down all kinds of weapons, and advanced against the prince.

This was the outbreak of a great battle between the great king Mara and the prince, the savior of this world. In the sky, a thousand stars streaked by; black clouds swirled about; and the great earth and the great ocean, struck by typhoons, quivered like the petals of a flower. Tidal waves rolled across the great sea, and rivers rose up, levelling mountains on which ancient trees one thousand years old had grown in abundance. The vibrations from the blows and the howls were truly terrifying. The whole world was covered over as with a black curtain; the sun lost its light; and the sky was filled with hordes of monsters.

King Mara, at the head of a great army of one hundred thousand, swooped down on the prince from four sides. The gods who up to that time had surrounded the prince and had sung his praises fled in fear. Now there was no one who could save the prince. But the prince thought to himself, "The Ten Precepts that I have practiced for a long period of time are my mighty army; they are the jewelled sword and the stalwart shield that guard my being. Carrying the virtuous practice of these Ten Precepts in my hand, I shall annihilate the army of demons." He remained completely unmoved. Mara lured the wind divinity into creating gale winds, but even the edges of the prince's garments remained unruffled. Urging the rain divinity on, he had torrential rains pour down, but not even dew or droplets of water could wet the prince. He poured down rains of rocks, swords, and fire, but they were all transformed into a crown of flowers; and, changing into scented powder, they were scattered all over the ground. Even the darkness that King Mara shot forth was transformed into the sun's radiance as it neared the prince. The weapons that were hurled at him changed into a celestial canopy. There was nothing that could harm the prince.

King Mara came striding to the front of his army and shouted, "O medicant, what do you seek, sitting under that tree? Quickly take leave; you are not worthy of that Diamond Throne." The prince, however, solemnly pointed to the great earth and said, "In this world encompassed by heaven and earth, I am the only one worthy of sitting on this throne. Only he who is adorned with the roots of merit from the distant past is worthy of occupying this throne. Divinity of the earth, quickly make your presence known and confirm what I say here." And suddenly the great earth underneath the throne opened up, and the divinity of the earth appeared. King Mara's mind was shattered by the thundering roar that accompanied the divinity's appearance. Trembling with fear and without even looking back toward his cohorts, he scampered away into the four directions.

(4) After some time had passed, Mara appeared once more. Changing his tactics, he tried to seduce the prince with honeyed words: "How terrible is the color of your sickly, emaciated face! Truly your death is close at hand. Death is a great part of you; life is only a small part. Live! It is good to live. Live and perform good deeds. Perform pure deeds, worship fire, and your merits will be many. Why do you strive so fruitlessly? The path is hard to tread and difficult to attain."

Without wavering, the prince rebuked Mara: "Demon, slave of sloth, why do you come here? I have no need of merits. Why do you exhort me to live, me, who diligently strive on the path with faith, exertion, and wisdom? Even the river that flows is dried up by hot winds; how should my blood that strives on diligently not dry up?

"Blood dries up, fat melts, flesh wastes away; but the mind becomes all the more pacified. Right mindfulness and wisdom become clear, and my meditative state becomes all the more steadied. In years past, I experienced the utter limits of the pleasures of the five desires. I no longer look to those desires. Behold this pure being! As for you, your first army is lust. Your second army is aversion. Your third army is hunger and thirst. Your fourth army is craving. Your fifth army is sloth. Your sixth army is fearfulness. Your seventh army is doubt. Your eighth army is vanity and obstinacy. Your ninth army is fame and profit. Your tenth army is self-praise and casting aspersion on others. Demon, these are your armies; these are your weapons. But the hero emerges victorious, subjugating these armies, and attains peace.

"Instead of living in defeat, it is far better to do battle and die! But should they go to defeat to Mara's armies even once, mendicants and sages alike will be unable to recognize, know, or practice the path of the virtuous ones. Mara, riding atop a huge elephant, you came leading a whole army. Come, do battle! I shall emerge victorious. You will not throw me into disorder. Although the human and celestial worlds were both unable to destroy your army, I shall defeat your army as a rock destroys tree leaves.

"With a mind that is true and thoughts that are upright, put to rest your desires. I shall travel throughout the world and train numerous disciples. If they train diligently, follow my teaching, and attain desirelessness, in the end, sorrow will be no more."

Mara, seeing that there was nothing to be gained in doing battle, was dejected and sorrowful. "For seven years, I pursued the World-Honored One, but I was unable to find a weakness in the Enlightened One, who abides in right mindfulness. There is a rock that looks like tender meat; birds flock together and try to taste its sweetness but are unable to do so and depart. I am like the bird that pecks at such rocks." Mara was crushed, and with a heavy, heavy heart, he faded away.

(5) In this way, the prince in one day reached the summit, attained tranquillity of mind, and entered into a meditative state.

First, he parted with desire and evil. In the first meditative state, he tasted joy and bliss. He advanced to the second meditative state, and, stopping the uncontrolled activity of the mind, he immersed himself in the bliss of meditation. Advancing to the third meditative state, he entered a state of equanimity and extinguished pleasure and pain, joy and sorrow. Moving on to the fourth meditative state, with a tranquil, pure, unstained, and pliant mind that could not be disturbed by anything, he contemplated his past lives. At the outset of the first night, as he recalled in detail numerous lives of the distant past, he attained the first wisdom, took leave of ignorance, and dispelled the darkness.

Next, he strove to understand the forms of birth and death that people undergo. With a pure, divine eye, he saw scenes of people undergoing birth and death and being borne along the stream in accordance with their actions. "Oh, the ocean of birth and death swirls around and around without end, and people sink into and drift on a boundless stream; nowhere is there any support." He then saw those who accumulate evil, malign arhats, harbor wrong views, and walk around and around on the evil path. He also saw those who accumulate good karma, follow the arhats, hold correct views, and walk on the good path. In the middle of the night, he attained the second wisdom; and taking leave of ignorance, he dispelled the darkness.

Next, with the wisdom that extinguishes defilement, he strove and clearly saw what was suffering, what was the cause of suffering, what was the extinction of suffering, and what was the path that led to the extinction of suffering. Again, he clearly saw what was defilement, what was the cause of defilement, what was the cessation of defilement, and what was the path that led to the cessation of defilement. By virtue of this enlightened wisdom, his mind was freed from lust and ignorance and gave birth to a wisdom that attained emancipation, namely, the wisdom that vows, "Birth has come to an end. I have completed the pious practice. I have accomplished that which I had to accomplish. This is my final birth. After this, I shall never again be born in samsara." At the end of the night, he attained this third wisdom, took leave of ignorance, and dispelled the darkness.

At this time, the great earth trembled with joy, and the world shone brightly. Divine beings, like clouds gathered together, rained down celestial flowers, played celestial music, and sang the praise of the World-Honored One, who, in great joy, recited this verse: "I sought the builder of this house of suffering, but I was unable to find him. The wheel of samsara turned around and around, and I repeated lives of suffering again and again. But you, builder of the house, I see you now. You will not build the house again. All the rafters are broken, and the ridgepole is destroyed. My mind takes leave of craving and attains nirvana."

In this way the prince became a man worthy of receiving offerings from the world. He became a man of true enlightenment, namely, a Buddha. The prince was thirty-five years old. It was the dawn, around the hour that the planet Venus glittered in the morning sky.

(6) In this way, the World-Honored One attained enlightenment at the base of the Bodhi Tree on the banks of the river Nairanjana, which flowed through the forest of Uruvilva. For seven days, he sat motionless and savored the bliss of enlightenment. During the first watch of the seventh day, he meditated, forwards and backwards, on the principle of dependent origination from which all sufferings arise. He perceived that from ignorance arose karmic activity; from karmic activity arose consciousness; from consciousness arose name and form; from name and form arose the six sensory organs; from the six sensory organs arose contact; from contact arose feelings; from feelings arose desire; from desire arose grasping; from grasping arose becoming; from becoming arose birth; and that from birth arose old age and death, anxiety, sorrow, pain, suffering, and anguish. He saw that the whole accumulation of suffering arose in this manner.

Therefore, if ignorance were extinguished without any residue, karmic activity would cease. If karmic activity were extinguished, consciousness would cease. If consciousness ceased, name and form would cease. If name and form were extinguished, the six sensory organs would cease. If the sensory organs were extinguished, contact would cease. If contact were extinguished, feeling would cease. If feeling were extinguished, desire would cease. If desire were extinguished, grasping would cease. If grasping were extinguished, becoming would cease. If becoming were extinguished, birth would cease. If birth were extinguished, then old age and death, anxiety, sorrow, pain, suffering, and anguish would cease. He saw that the whole accumulation of suffering would be extinguished in this manner.

In the middle and last watches of the night, following the same procedure, the World-Honored One meditated, forwards and backwards, on these twelve links of dependent origination. He then entered into the following contemplation:

(7) Originally all dharmas are equal. Their natures are not immutable, and their forms are not differentiated. Originally they are pure entities that are unstained by defilements; therefore, they are equal. Those who practice the path must meditate on the equality of all dharmas; with great compassion as primary, they must broaden their great compassion and contemplate the states of birth and extinction that rule this world. And they must think in the following manner:

In this world, differentiated beings come into being because of clinging to a self. If one ceases being attached to a self, one will not recognize the existence of differentiated beings. All are equal. But ordinary people continually produce wrong views. Because of ignorance, they close their eyes, perform various acts while clinging to a self, and as a result give birth to a self that is subject to birth and death. For them karma is like a rice field, and consciousness is like seeds. Enshrouded in ignorance, they sprinkle the seeds with the water of desire. With a mind attached to a self, they water the seeds and breed more wrong views; this is the process that produces a self composed of name and form.

Because of name and form, the six sensory organs, the eye, ear, nose, tongue, body, and consciousness, are produced. From the six sensory organs, contact arises. From contact, feeling arises. From feeling, desire arises. From desire, grasping arises. From grasping, becoming is produced. From becoming, there is birth. From birth, there is old age and death. Because of old age and death, anxiety, sorrow, pain, suffering, and anguish come into existence. But in the twelve links of dependent origination, there is nothing that comes into existence and nothing that dissipates into nonexistence. Conditions merely come together to produce becoming; and when those conditions dissipate, it turns into nothingness. Ordinary people do not know that the Absolute Truth embodies equality; therefore, they perceive differentiation among the twelve links of dependent origination. If one becomes aware that in truth there are no differentiations such as self and the object to which a self attaches itself, or an agent that produces and objects that are produced, then the three worlds to which one is attached are seen to be only the shadows of a deluded mind, and all attachments cease. Truly these Twelve Links of Dependent Origination all arise out of the mind. This was his contemplation.

In the ocean of the serene mind of the World-Honored One, all things now were reflected as bright images. There are no words to praise adequately this state of mind.

2. Verses in Praise of Enlightenment

(1) At that time, because of the power of the Buddha, the branches, leaves, and trunk of the Bodhi Tree glittered with the seven gems. From his seat, light streamed forth to the ten directions and shone on all worlds everywhere.

Now the Buddha's wisdom was deeper than the ocean and vaster than the sky. Its light shone on worlds enshrouded in darkness. The images of a multitude of worldly objects serenely and immediately manifested themselves in his heart, like the stars in space that cast their images without cloudiness on the great ocean. Innumerable bodhisattvas and gods gathered together like clouds and, relying on the power of the World-Honored One to inspire them, sang praises of his merits:

> (i) The boundless, wondrous Dharma world fills the body of the Buddha.
> Although that world is eternally quiescent, it is the ground of all sentient
> beings; the Buddha came forth now into this world to proclaim this truth.
> The Buddha came forth into this world and established the true Dharma.
> His enlightenment is boundless. With his light he extinguishes our
> suffering and confers on us infinite joy. With his inconceivable power, he

expounds for our sake the teaching of enlightenment. The light of the sun reveals the forms of things; likewise the sun, the Buddha, now reveals for our sake the forms of karma and causes us to enter true meditation.

(ii) For us, who grow arrogant because of the darkness of ignorance and pass through life heedlessly, the Buddha manifests the enlightened teaching. He thereby guides us each to proper aspiration and joy. He serves as the supreme ground for our being and expunges the sufferings of this world. If we wish to see him, he appears before us like the full moon rising up over the mountains.

(iii) In every conceivable way, the Buddha manifests compassion, enters into our being, and pacifies our minds. Those of us with pure eyes of wisdom never tire of gazing at him. When we reflect on his boundless merits, profound joy arises within. This is due to the Buddha's power. Should we reflect even briefly on the Buddha, for aeons a multitude of sufferings fall away. The light of wisdom is infinite; it shines everywhere upon the worlds of the ten directions. He resorts to a multitude of means so that we are able to revere him here and now.

(iv) How wondrous it is that wherever the light of wisdom reaches, the world becomes lucid! People's minds awaken to the path and rejoice. Even one blinded by the darkness of ignorance opens his eyes to the light of wisdom and bows down to this manifestation of the Buddha of purity. Although we have become strangers to the bliss of the sage and have become immersed in the sufferings of the world, because of the Buddha's pure Dharma our minds now rejoice and are serene. All things are like phantom flowers, but the Buddha is the light that reveals the truth. With a beneficent cloud of wisdom, he covers over this world and waters it with the rain of the Dharma. Only the Buddha dries up the ocean of endless suffering; with the skillful means of a great wisdom, he opens up the mind's eye. As with the ocean, there is no end to the merits of his teaching; he listens to all of our wishes and aspirations. Although his voice is gentle, it reverberates like thunder. Because the Buddha expounds the true Dharma, we are filled with bliss. Hearing his voice, our minds rejoice, and the bliss of the Dharma fills our hearts to the brim.

(v) Our evils are grave; not once in aeons have we bowed down to the Buddha. Again and again we underwent birth and death and experienced suffering. In order to save us, the Buddha appeared in the world. Employing various methods, he removes grave evils and evil obstructions and grounds us in the Dharma. Because he praised all previous Buddhas when he underwent spiritual practices for an extremely long period of time, his fame is widespread in this world. Although he sits serenely in meditation, with a power that is indestructible, he appears in all worlds, and people revere his appearance. Adorned with a multitude of perfect virtues, and shining forth throughout the worlds, his light reveals the profound truth.

(2) (Hymn by Samantabhadra) Then the Bodhisattva Samantabhadra received the power of the Buddha and perceived the actions and aspirations of all the people in all worlds. He also perceived the Buddhas of the three worlds. Following this, he said to the vast number of great bodhisattvas who had gathered

together in vast numbers like the ocean, "O children of the Buddha, there is no way to conceive of the arising and cessation of the worlds of the Buddhas nor of the Buddhas' pure wisdom. But relying on the Buddha's power, I shall expound the following gates of the Dharma in order to lead people to enter the ocean of the Buddha's wisdom." And he expounded the Dharma through verses:

(i)   People's minds are boundless; their actions produce all the countries. If people are stained, the worlds are stained. Since their karma is boundless, the arising of worlds is also infinite. If people undergo the practice of Samantabhadra, they will always dwell in a pure world. Their merit will be like that of the Buddha. They will give birth to an infinite number of Buddha countries. Numberless worlds have been born from one moment of thought of the Bodhisattva Samantabhadra. These countries are peaceful even to each and every particle of dust; the mind of the Buddha, like a cloud, protects each and every country. All countries arise from the activity of the mind and present numberless different appearances. At times they are pure while at other times they are foul; their sufferings and pleasures are infinite in their variety. All things constantly change, and they constantly revolve.

(ii)   From the distant past, if one befriends a good teacher and if pure practices persist, along with compassion, Buddha countries will be purified. With an exceedingly pure mind, believe firmly in the Buddha. If the power of patience is not stained, each and every country will be exquisitely adorned.

With a limitless number of methods, producing all countries and responding to the wishes of the people, the Buddha appears in the world. It is difficult to conceive of the Buddha's being; since he has neither shape nor color, there is nothing to which he can be compared. Those who accept the Dharma, however, see his appearance everywhere. The Buddha, employing a variety of skillful means, born out of the full and great ocean of compassion, here and now manifests himself.

(iii) This country is adorned with gems; each gem glitters like a cloud and extinguishes the worldly suffering of beings; it pacifies people with the true way. The lakes are filled to the brim with fragrant water; the flowers' light streams forth in the four directions. The voices of rejoicing are heard from afar. Parapets of gems, rows of jewelled trees, and the sound of clear music are all true and serene. They praise the virtues of the Three Treasures. The nets of gems strike each other and produce the Buddha's voice; from the other shore are heard the teachings of all bodhisattvas and Buddhas, Samantabhadra's practices, and the voice of the Buddha's vows.

(iv)   Although the Buddha manifests his form everywhere in the ten directions, he neither comes nor goes. But because of the Buddha's vow, people without exception perceive him. Although countries enter into each other, they neither increase nor decrease. Although one country fills the ten directions and the countries of the ten directions enter into one country, the world's forms are not destroyed. Even in the particles of dust of all the countries, the power of the Buddha's freedom is seen. His voice reverberates in the ocean of his vow and brings harmony to the people.

(v)   A diversity of trees bear a diversity of fruits; a diversity of countries are peopled by a diversity of inhabitants. Different seeds produce different fruits; like these examples, different actions produce different countries.

Like the Naga king who generates clouds, the Buddha, through the power of his vow, generates all countries.

As the artist produces paintings, the mind produces countries; in each and every thought, it produces numberless countries. Because these countries are sustained by the Buddha, they are pure and devoid of defilements.

One country is made of dirt and is not pure; devoid of light, it is eternally dark. Those who have committed evil live here. Another country is made of dirt and filled with suffering. Those whose good fortunes are scant dwell here. Again, another country is made of dirt and filled with endless suffering. Although it exists for aeons in darkness, light shines upon it like the ocean.

In the world of beasts, countless beings exist. In accordance with their actions in previous worlds, they undergo endless suffering. Those who dwell in the world of the King of Death are perpetually tortured by the suffering of starvation and thirst or pursued up a mountain of fire; they undergo suffering without end.

(vi) Responding to the wishes of the people, the Buddha manifests his being in a variety of ways; however, those who lack the karmic conditions are obstructed by the cloud of defilements and fail to see the Buddha. Another country is filled with the sound of pious practice. The voice of light streaming forth, of bodhisattvas, of ceaseless vows, of the path being practiced, and of the venerable names of the Buddhas of the three worlds are heard.

(3) (Hymn by Maitreya) From the various countries of the ten directions, an infinite number of bodhisattvas gathered together like clouds at this assembly. The Bodhisattva Maitreya saw this and rejoiced; he turned to the great assembly and said, "The dwelling place of the Buddha, the Buddha's Dharma, the appearance of the Buddha in the world, and the arising of the Buddha's country are all inconceivable. When the Buddha expounds the Dharma, he first perceives the minds of the people and in accordance with them he expounds the Dharma; therefore the Buddha employs an infinite variety of skillful means and gates to the Dharma." He expounded the Dharma in verse:

(i) He frees himself from a multitude of sufferings, realizes nonattachment to this world, and purifies the eye of the path. He perceives that there is nothing to grasp onto and realizes that all things eventually die away; thereby, he becomes a Buddha. His mind penetrates to the principle of equality and the teaching of nonduality, and he is called a man who is inconceivable. In the one, he sees the infinite; in the infinite, he sees the one. Things produced by the mind are not real; the wise man, therefore, has no fear.

(ii) Seeing people beset with lust and tortured by foolish suffering, he seeks the path of enlightenment; this is truly the path of the buddhas. Freeing himself from the erroneous views that things exist and that things do not exist, he perceives the true Dharma and expounds a teaching that was not taught in the ancient past. The sage does not destroy any of the realms; he travels to innumerable countries, and without attachment to all things he is free, like the buddhas. For the sake of each and every person, he enters the hell of ceaseless suffering; although he is boiled for an eternity, his mind is as pure as the buddhas'. If one guards the Buddha's teaching constantly without sparing one's body and life and exerts oneself in the practices of patience, one attains the Dharma of the Buddha. Free yourselves from the pleasures of people and gods and, with the mind of Great Compassion, save all people. Perceive your true form. All things are quiescent. Free yourselves from the thought of 'I' and that which is not 'I'. Producing a boundless world, swallow the ocean that contains all sufferings and attain great power.

(iii) If one claims to have perceived the Buddha by perceiving the supreme form of the Buddha, his defective eye is producing delusions. That one is ignorant of the supreme teaching. In no way can people of this world perceive the Buddha's form. Although they may ponder for aeons, they will not be able to perceive the Buddha's power. Form is not the Buddha, and the Buddha has no form. But the Buddha manifests marvellous forms in response to the needs of the people.

The Buddha's true teaching is difficult to comprehend; it transcends all words; it neither converges nor disperses. Its nature is always quiescent. A corporeal body is not the Buddha. If you see this clearly and do not become attached to his form, you will attain the power of freedom and perceive the Buddha.

The body and mind are equal; you are free of both inward and outward obstructions. Your thoughts are constantly true and devoid of all thoughts of attachment. You stream forth light everywhere and shine upon all realms. With the eye of wisdom, you perceive the ground of all things. The one is infinite; the infinite is one. In response to the natures of people, you manifest all forms. And yet your being neither comes nor goes. Moreover, conditionally there exists a diversity of beings. The worlds are all produced by delusion; deluded dharmas lack true nature. Only the Buddha perceives their true form. One who realizes the truth clearly in this way is the one who perceives the master.

(iv) The Buddha extinguishes the ultimate in delusion; he hoists the light of wisdom. He builds the vessel and bridge of the true teaching and saves all those who should be saved. In that prison of birth and death, misfortunes are truly infinite. The sufferings of old age, illness, and death assault people without cease both day and night. The Buddha awakens to the profound truth, and applying the wisdom that employs skillful means, he expunges their suffering. This is the realm of the Buddha. The Buddha is void and quiescent; however, he is not an illusory phantom. Like the blind man who confronts color, you may perceive the Buddha, yet there is nothing to see. Those who become ensnared by illusory forms are unable to perceive the true Buddha. Those who are free of attached thoughts perceive the true Buddha.

The infinite Buddha stretches across space and neither comes nor goes. Worlds come into being and crumble without any absolute ground; just like this, the Buddha's being also fills space.

3. Brahma's Entreaty

(1) Then the World-Honored One, after seven days had passed, emerged from his meditation. From the Bodhi Tree he went to sit under the nigrodha tree. Again,

for seven days, he sat continuously and savored the bliss of enlightenment.

At that time, a brahmin who was known for his habit of scorning everything drew close to the World-Honored One and said, "Gotama, Honored One, what kind of man is a brahmin and what is the teaching that he should practice?" The World-Honored One perceived the meaning of this question and answered with a verse:

> The one who frees himself from evil, refrains from scorning others, drives away defilements, restrains himself, attains the ultimate wisdom, and completes the pure practices is a brahmin.
>
> That man feels no greed or anger toward things of this world and never adds to ignorance.

(2) Again, after seven days had passed by, the World-Honored One left his seat under that tree and moved over to the mucalinda tree. He sat there continuously for seven days and savored the bliss of enlightenment.

At that time, unseasonable clouds appeared and for seven days it rained continually. Cold winds blew and darkness enshrouded all four sides. The Naga king emerged from his palace, covered the World-Honored One with his body, and prayed, "May there not be any harm from cold or heat, from mosquitoes or horseflies, from wind or rain, or from snakes." After seven days had passed, the rain cleared, and there was not even a speck of cloud in the sky. The Naga king then transformed himself into a child and appeared before the World-Honored One. He put his palms together and bowed to the World-Honored One. The World-Honored One said,

> The mind is fulfilled; one listens to the teaching, sees the true principle, and is at peace.
>
> For all living beings, it is also peaceful to keep oneself without anger. Those who, freeing themselves from greed, pull away from worldly desires are also at peace.
>
> To overcome the thought that the 'I' exists is unsurpassed peace.

(3) The World-Honored One, once again, after seven days had passed, arose from his meditation and, leaving his seat under the mucalinda tree, savored the bliss of enlightenment for seven days under the rajayatana tree. At that time, two merchants who had come from Ukkala, Tapussa and Bhallika by name, happened to travel by. A blood relation of theirs who was now in the celestial world urged them as follows: "For the first time the World-Honored One has awakened to enlightenment and remains under the rajayatana tree; therefore offer him barley and honey." They therefore presented themselves before the World-Honored One and said, "World-Honored One, for the sake of our everlasting happiness, please accept this barley and honey." The World-Honored One thought, "Buddhas cannot receive food with their hands. With what bowl should I receive this offering of barley and honey?" The four guardian deities became aware of this and, from the four directions, each presented him with a stone bowl. The World-Honored One made the four stone bowls into one, received the foods, and partook of them. The merchants said joyfully, "World-Honored One, we take refuge

in the World-Honored One and in the Dharma. From now to the end of our lives, please protect us as followers." These were the first followers of the Buddha to take refuge in the two treasures, the Buddha and the Dharma.

(4) Again, after seven days had gone by, the World-Honored One left the rajayatana tree, sat in meditation under the nigrodha tree, and thought as follows: "The Dharma to which I have awakened is truly difficult to awaken to. It is quiescent and unexcelled and difficult to attain through ordinary reason. Deep and profound, it can be known and attained only by the wise. How can the peoples of this world, who are addicted to the pleasures of desire, know such truths as 'All things are born of conditions, and according to conditions they are extinguished' or that of the realm of nirvana where all desires have been extinguished and where defilements have disappeared? Even if I expounded this Dharma, they would not be able to attain enlightenment. I would simply add to my weariness."

The World-Honored One thought in this way and did not consider expounding the Dharma. At that time, Brahma perceived the mind of the World-Honored One and lamented, "Oh, the world perishes and crumbles; the Buddha has no intention of expounding the Dharma." Then, as quickly as a strong young man extends his bent arm, he left the Brahma world and appeared before the World-Honored One. With his robes draped over one shoulder and with his right knee planted on the great earth, he bowed down to the World-Honored One with his palms together and said, "World-Honored One, I beseech you to expound the Dharma. There are those in this world who possess an eye of wisdom that is not stained by filth. If they do not hear the Dharma, they will perish. If they do hear it, they will without doubt awaken to the World-Honored One's Dharma."

After speaking in this way, he continued with the following verse:

In the country of Magadha, till now, the impure teaching of people who were stained was expounded. World-Honored One, may you open the door of immortality.
Like a man who stands atop the summit of a hill and surveys all that lies below, the wise one ascends to the palace of the Dharma and frees himself from sorrow. O wise one, turn your eyes now to those who, drowning in sorrow, are overwhelmed by birth and old age. O heroic one, conqueror in battles, leader of caravans, debtless one, begin your travels throughout the world. If the World-Honored One expounds the Dharma, surely there will be those who will attain enlightenment.

(5) The World-Honored One perceived Brahma's entreaties, and moved by a mind of compassion toward all people he gazed upon the world with the eyes of a Buddha. A diversity of people were reflected in the World-Honored One's eyes: those whose minds were only slightly clouded; those whose minds were heavily clouded; those with keen faculties; those with dull faculties; virtuous people; evil people; those who were easy to teach; and so forth. Again, the spiritual capacities of a diversity of people were clearly reflected in the World-Honored One's eyes, much as in a lake filled with lotuses. In that lake are lotuses that are blue, yellow, red, and white in color. Some lotuses sprout in the water, grow in the

water, and never break the surface of the water. Some lotuses sprout in the water, grow in the water, and remain on the surface of the water. Some lotuses sprout in the water, grow in the water, rise above the water, and are never touched by the water. Then the World-Honored One answered Brahma with a verse:

> O Brahma, thinking it might be futile to teach it, I thought of refraining from expounding the Dharma to the people. But those who have ears to hear will hear and attain faith. I shall open the doors of immortality.

Chapter 3

DISSEMINATION OF THE DHARMA

1. Turning the Wheel of the Dharma

(1) Now the World-Honored One pondered, "To whom shall I expound this Dharma? Who will awaken to this Dharma? Alara Kalama is a learned and wise man with only a faint trace of ignorance; he will awaken to this Dharma." Then, however, the World-Honored One, with his celestial eye, perceived that Alara Kalama had passed away seven days before. The World-Honored One said, "Alara Kalama's death is a great loss. Now to whom shall I expound the Dharma? Uddaka Ramaputta is also a wise and learned man; I shall transmit this Dharma to him." But he learned that Uddaka had also passed away, one day before. He lamented this loss and turned his thoughts to the five mendicants. He thought, "Those five monks attended to me during my practice of ascetic training. They are men of great import; I shall first give the Dharma to them."

The World-Honored One decided thus and set forth from the forest of Uruvela toward the Deer Park of Isipatana near Baranasi.

(2) On his way, the World-Honored One met Upaka, a follower of a false path that espoused an evil way of life. Upaka was struck by the serenity of the World-Honored One's appearance and said, "Your appearance is truly serene, pure, and lucid. As a mendicant, whom did you take as your teacher and what kind of teaching does he impart?"

The World-Honored One answered this question in verse: "I am victorious in battle; my wisdom is superior; I am unstained by all things; I am free of all sufferings; the thirst of lust has been emptied in me; I am perfectly enlightened. This is entirely due to my wisdom; whom shall I regard as my teacher? In heaven and on earth, there is no one who is my equal. I am the Enlightened One of this world; I am the supreme teacher. I alone dwell in pure quiescence. From now on, I shall turn the Wheel of the Dharma in this blind world; here I shall beat the drum of immortality. To accomplish this, I now direct myself to the city of Kasi."

Upaka said, "World-Honored One, do you, of your own accord, call yourself 'the Enlightened One' and 'the Victorious One'?" The World-Honored One replied, "He who has extinguished all defilements and has restrained evil—is not that man 'the Victorious One'?" Upaka said, "Perhaps that is so," and, nodding his head, he departed, taking a different path.

(3) The World-Honored One entered the Deer Park of Isipatana. The five mendicants saw the World-Honored One and said to each other, "Here comes Gotama. He who has abandoned spiritual training and has escaped into a life of self-indulgence comes toward us. We need not prepare a seat for his sake. Let him sit wherever he pleases." But when the World-Honored One drew near the five monks, they forgot their promise to each other. One monk approached the World-Honored One. Another prepared a seat; still another provided water to wash his feet. After the World-Honored One washed his feet and took his seat, the five mendicants turned toward the World-Honored One and addressed him as "Gotama" or "friend." But the World-Honored One said, "You should not address the Buddha by name or with such terms as "friend." I am a Buddha who has attained enlightenment and am worthy of receiving the world's offerings. O monks, listen to me; I shall teach you the path to immortality. If you abide by and follow the Dharma that I am about to teach, before long you will fulfill the aspirations that caused you to leave home and become mendicants. You will be endowed with pure practices, and you will be able to attain enlightenment naturally."

The five mendicants said, "But Gotama, even on an austere path and with terrible ascetic practice, you were not able to attain the true wisdom that excels all others. You have abandoned that spiritual training and have escaped into a life of self-indulgence. How can you have attained that Dharma?"

The World-Honored One answered, "Mendicants, I do not indulge in sloth nor have I abandoned spiritual training. I am truly a Buddha who has attained an enlightenment worthy of the world's offerings. Listen to me; I shall teach you the path that leads to immortality." But the five monks did not acquiesce to the words of the World-Honored One and repeated their previous remarks three times. Finally, the World-Honored One said, "O mendicants, do you recall that I ever spoke in this manner before?" The mendicants answered, "O World-Honored One, no, you did not." "Do you see? The Buddha does not long for a life of self-indulgence nor does he abandon spiritual training. I am truly a man who has attained enlightenment. Listen to me; listen to the Dharma that leads to immortality." Then for the first time the five mendicants decided to listen to the Buddha with wholehearted sincerity.

(4) The World-Honored One said to them, "Mendicants, there are two extreme paths that the mendicant must avoid. The first is a life of foolish pleasures, addicted to base desires. The second is a life of foolish ascetic practices that mortify the self in vain. Mendicants, the Buddha was enlightened by the Middle Path, which is free of these two extreme paths, opens the eyes of the mind, deepens wisdom, and guides all beings to quiescence, wisdom, enlightenment, and nirvana.

"Mendicants, what is this Middle Path? It is the Eightfold Noble Path, namely, right view, right thought, right speech, right action, right livelihood, right effort, right mindfulness, and right meditation.

"Mendicants, this is the Noble Truth of suffering. Birth is suffering. Old age, sickness, and death are all suffering. To have contact with something hateful, to part with someone you love, and not to obtain what you seek are all suffering. In short, to exist as a human being is suffering.

"Mendicants, this is the Noble Truth of the cause of suffering. Thirsting lust produces new life, accompanied by pleasure and greed, resulting in the pleasures of lust in this and that realm. There are three kinds of lust, the lust of passion, the lust for existence, and the lust for nonexistence.

"Mendicants, this is the Noble Truth of the cessation of suffering. Suffering ceases when its cause is removed.

"Mendicants, this is the Noble Truth of the path that leads to the cessation of suffering. It is the Eightfold Noble Path of right view, right thought, right speech, right action, right livelihood, right effort, right mindfulness, and right meditation.

"Mendicants, these Four Noble Truths are a Dharma that has never been expounded before; this is the Dharma to which I have been enlightened. Through this Dharma, I opened the eyes of the mind and gave birth to wisdom and light. Suffering must be understood, and I understood it. The cause of suffering, desire, must be severed, and I severed it. The cessation of suffering must be awakened to, and I awakened to it. The path that leads to the cessation of suffering must be practiced, and I practiced it. Grounded in this Dharma to which I was enlightened, I opened the eyes of the mind and gave birth to wisdom and light.

"Mendicants, as long as the pure and true insight of the Four Noble Truths had not yet arisen within me, I did not proclaim among the various worlds and peoples that I had attained enlightenment. But since such insights have arisen within me, I now proclaim that I have attained enlightenment. Moreover, the following insight arose within me, 'My mind, which has freed itself from bondage, will never be shaken; this is my final birth; for me, there will be no more deluded births.' "

When the World-Honored One had set forth this teaching, one of the mendicants, Kondanna by name, acquired the eye of the Dharma that is free of defilement; he perceived that all things that come into existence perish without fail.

(5) Again, the World-Honored One turned the Wheel of the Dharma. The gods of the earth all shouted in unison, "At the Deer Park of Isipatana at Baranasi, the World-Honored One has turned the unexcelled Wheel of the Dharma that has never been turned in this world by anyone." The voices of these gods reverberated to the worlds of other gods and finally reached the world of Brahma. At that instant, the thousand worlds shook and trembled, and a boundless light that transcended the light of the gods shone upon all worlds.

At that time, the World-Honored One said, "Verily, Kondanna has understood (annasi) this"; therefore he was called Annata Kondanna. He became a disciple who followed the teaching of his master; he perceived the Dharma with great depth, transcended doubt, freed himself from delusion, and attained fearlessness. Without interruption, the World-Honored One spoke on the Dharma to the four other mendicants. These four remaining mendicants—Vappa, Bhaddiya, Mahanama, and Assaji—also freed themselves from defilement and attained the eye of the Dharma that perceives that all things that come into existence perish without fail. And all, like Kondanna, became disciples.

(6) The World-Honored One gathered them together and expounded the Dharma: "Disciples, the body is not the self. If the body were the self, we should

be able freely to change our bodies this way and that. In the same way, the mind also is not the self; we are unable freely to change our minds this way and that."

He asked them, "Disciples, what do you think? Is the body permanent or impermanent?" "It is impermanent," replied the disciples. He asked them, "Are impermanent things painful or pleasurable?" The disciples answered, "World-Honored One, they are painful." He asked, "Can you regard as mine or as my self that which is impermanent, painful, and constantly changing?" They answered, "World-Honored One, we cannot regard it as mine or as my self." He said, "Disciples, the mind is like that. Noble disciples must perceive and hear this same truth; they must give birth to the mind that loathes both mind and body. If you do not attach yourselves to either, you will attain freedom and give birth to the wisdom that is fully aware of this attainment. This is the wisdom that knows that 'birth has come to an end; the pious practice has been completed; that which had to be accomplished has been accomplished; and after this, there will be no other births'. "

The five men heard this discourse of the World-Honored One and rejoiced; they freed themselves of attachment, rid themselves of defilement, and became sages. In this way, there came to be six sages in this world.

2. The Home-Leaving of Yasa

(1) At that time in Baranasi, there was a splendid youth named Yasa, the son of a wealthy merchant. He was the only son of that merchant and consequently was afforded all sorts of luxuries. In the cold season, he was given a winter palace; in the hot season, a summer palace; in the rainy season, a mansion for rain. One night, after he had indulged himself in the pleasures of lust, he fell into slumber for a short while. After a while, when he awoke, under the light of a beautiful solitary lamp, women who had tired of music were in deep slumber, oblivious to any sense of decorum. There were some women who had rolled on their sides atop the lutes; some dancers had drums resting on their necks. There were women with disheveled hair; some dribbled saliva down their chins while mumbling in their sleep. Yasa, who had observed at close hand this scene that resembled a charnel ground, perceived the evils of lust and aroused a mind that was repelled by lust. Crying out, "It is fearful; it is fearful!" he put on his gold slippers and ran out. He proceeded directly to the Deer Park and at dawn hurried toward the World-Honored One who was on the road. The words, "It is fearful; it is fearful!" came from Yasa's mouth. The World-Honored One said, "Yasa, there is nothing fearful about this place. Sit here and listen to my teaching." These words pacified Yasa's deranged mind. Yasa took off his gold slippers and sat at the side of the World-Honored One. The World-Honored One then spoke in orderly fashion on the following: selfless giving, the precepts, birth into the heavens, the defilement and evil of sensual lust, the benefits of freeing oneself from the world of desire, and so forth. After bringing peace to Yasa's mind, he expounded the Four Noble Truths of suffering, its origin, its cessation, and the path leading to its cessation. Just as a pure robe is easily stained by color, Yasa's mind was stained by the color of the teaching, and he gave birth to the eye of the Dharma that perceives that all things that come into existence perish without fail.

(2) The news that Yasa was missing from the palace shocked the members of the clan. Messengers sped off in the eight directions in search of Yasa. The father also personally set off in search of his son. By chance he found himself in the vicinity of the Deer Park, and spying the gold slippers that had been left discarded, he asked the World-Honored One about the whereabouts of his son. The World-Honored One said, "In due time you will be able to meet your son; therefore it will do you good to sit here for a short while." He then expounded the teaching and caused the father to attain the eye of the Dharma that was free of all defilements. The wealthy father rejoiced and repeated the Three Refuges. He said, "World-Honored One, this is a superb event. Like lifting someone up who has fallen, like revealing that which was concealed, like showing the path to someone who is lost, like holding up a light in the darkness and encouraging those with eyes to look at the forms of things, in various ways the World-Honored One manifests the teaching for our sake. World-Honored One, I take refuge in the World-Honored One. Please accept me as a believer who takes refuge from this day forward to the end of my life." In this way, the seeker and the sought both entered the path, for Yasa left home and became a sage.

The next day the World-Honored One, accompanied by Yasa, was invited to his home. He made believers of Yasa's mother and young wife. Following Yasa's example, his four friends—Vimala, Subahu, Punnaji, and Gavampati—left home; a party of fifty friends, encouraged by Yasa, also became disciples of the Buddha. These men followed the teaching of the World-Honored One, practiced according to the Dharma, and attained enlightenment. At this juncture, there were sixty-one sages in the world who had become disciples of the Buddha.

(3) At that time, the World-Honored One addressed his disciples, "Disciples, I have freed myself from all shackles. You have also freed yourselves from all shackles. Disciples, have compassion for the world; for its welfare and happiness, roam throughout this world. Two men, however, should not travel the same route. Disseminate the teaching that is good in the beginning, good in the middle, and good in the end, the teaching that is endowed with both letter and meaning. Explain the practice that is utterly pure and perfect. In the world there are people whose eyes of wisdom are only slightly stained. If they do not listen to the teaching, however, they will be ruined. If they listen to the teaching, they will attain enlightenment. Disciples, in order to expound the teaching, I shall go to Senanigama in Uruvela."

Then Mara suddenly appeared before the World-Honored One and said, "You are bound by every shackle and are tied up with thick bonds. You cannot escape me." The World-Honored One responded to Mara, "I am free of all shackles; you have been vanquished now."

Mara spoke again, "The shackle called the Concentration of Infinite Space is nothing else but greed. I have shackled you with this fetter. Mendicant, you cannot escape me." The World-Honored once again replied, "I am free of greed for the five desires; you have been vanquished now." Mara said, "The World-Honored One knows me" and dolefully faded away.

(4) The World-Honored One dispatched sixty of his disciples in all directions and entered Kappasiya Grove in Uruvela alone. At that time, thirty young men who called themselves the Pleasure Group were enjoying an outing in the grove. Of the group, twenty-nine of the men had wives; for the lone bachelor, they hired a harlot to serve as his wife. The sixty men and women were thoroughly enjoying themselves at this party held in a grove. The harlot waited for her chance and ran away with their beautiful garments and jewels. The members of the party were stunned and ran in search of her, turning this way and that. By accident, they drew near the World-Honored One, who was sitting serenely under a tree. They noticed his radiant appearance and, struck with wonder, asked the World-Honored One about the harlot's whereabouts. The World-Honored One said, "Young men, why do you search for a woman? Which is superior, searching for a woman or searching for oneself?" The young men said, "World-Honored One, to search for oneself is superior." "Young men, then you would do well to sit here; I shall expound that teaching of searching for oneself." Submitting to his words, they sat down by the side of the World-Honored One. The World-Honored One, step by step, elucidated the teaching. He waited for their minds to settle down; then he expounded the Four Noble Truths. The young men all opened their eye of wisdom and became mendicants and disciples of the World-Honored One.

3. Conversion of the Three Kassapas

(1) Then the World-Honored One gradually moved onward and arrived at the banks of the river Neranjara in the grove at Uruvela. At that time in the country of Magadha, there were three brothers called Kassapa, who were all held in high esteem by the people. Kassapa of Uruvela was attended by hundred disciples; Kassapa of Nadi stood at the head of three hundred disciples; and Kassapa of Gaya was accompanied by two hundred disciples. They wore matted hair and were all devotees of fire worship. The World-Honored One went to the place of Kassapa of Uruvela and asked for a night's lodging in the fire chamber. Kassapa brought up the danger from the poisonous dragon that lived in the fire chamber and refused the request. But the World-Honored One persisted and finally entered the chamber. That night, flames spewed out of the windows of the fire chamber; the people were concerned for the welfare of the poor ascetic inside. The next morning, the World-Honored One put that poisonous dragon into a bowl and showed it to the people.

Kassapa was amazed by the loftiness of his virtue and power but continued to think that this mendicant was inferior to him. The World-Honored One remained in the fire chamber and repeatedly manifested divine powers. One evening, a host of gods assembled there to hear the teaching, and because of this, the forest of Uruvela glittered with the light of the gods. Another day, he brought back the fruits of a distant world, and because of this a sweet fragrance filled the grove. On still another occasion, because of the power of the World-Honored One's teaching, firewood would not split apart; fire would not burn; dry dirt appeared from water; and a lake was born in a place without water. Kassapa marvelled at the power of the World-Honored One's teaching but still thought, "This mendicant is not my equal."

The World-Honored One, observing that the time had ripened, admonished him, "Kassapa, you are not an arhat. You have not discovered the path that leads to becoming an arhat. Your teaching is not the path that leads to becoming an arhat." Kassapa was stunned, and on his knees he bowed down at the Buddha's feet and vowed to become a mendicant with the World-Honored One as his teacher. The World-Honored One accepted him, his two brothers, and their one thousand followers as disciples.

(2) The World-Honored One thought, "Now, for the first time, the moment has come for me to realize the promise that I made to King Bimbisara." Together with the three Kassapas, who were regarded as the wise elders of Magadha, and their one thousand disciples, he travelled toward Rajagaha. He climbed up a hill in Gayasisa, and gazing at the fires of the city of Rajagaha that flickered in the distance, he expounded as follows: "Disciples, everything is burning. How is everything burning? Disciples, both the eyes that see and the things that are seen, both the consciousness that sees and differentiates and the sensations that result from this act are burning. In the same way the ears, the nose, the tongue, the body, the mind, their objects of consciousness, and the differentiations and the sensations that occur there are all on fire. Disciples, with what fire are they aflame? They are aflame with the fire of greed, the fire of anger, and the fire of ignorance. They are aflame with the fire of birth, old age, illness, and death, and with the fire of anxiety, grief, pain, suffering, and anguish. Disciples, if the followers of this teaching, seeing and hearing thus, become weary of all things, they will free themselves from passion and give birth to the wisdom that realizes that 'I have attained release.' They will know that 'birth has come to an end; I have accomplished the pious practice; I have realized that which I had to realize. From this moment forward, there will be no more delusive births.'

(3) "Disciples, there are five desires. Each possesses an attractive, charming appearance and the power to seduce and stimulate. The five desires are for the forms seen by the eye, the sounds heard by the ears, the scents smelled by the nose, the tastes savored by the tongue, and the tactile sensations felt by the body. All mendicants who drown in these five desires and remain blind to their evil and who are ignorant of the path that leads one away from such desires are described as people who are immersed in misfortune, are beset with evil, and have fallen into the trap devised by Mara. They are like forest deer that have stepped into a trap and have fallen in; people say of them, 'These deer have fallen into a trap devised by the hunter and are unable to escape.'

"Disciples, if they see the evil of these five desires, know the path that leads them away, and are practicing that path, mendicants will be described as people who are not immersed in misfortune, and who do not fall into traps devised by Mara. They are like the forest deer that have not fallen into the hunter's trap and are able to run away when the hunter approaches.

"Disciples, a deer of the forest is able to roam around freely in the forest and the mountains, and peacefully rise and lie down, because he dwells in an area where the hunter is unable to penetrate. In the same way, when disciples practice meditation, they are called people who have blinded Mara and who have escaped those areas that are assaulted by Mara. In their walking, standing, sitting, or lying down, they are filled with confidence and are at peace.

(4) "Disciples, when I was still a bodhisattva who had not attained enlightenment, I thought thus, 'What is worldly happiness? What is misfortune? How can I escape this misfortune?' Again, I thought, 'In this world, it is happiness that gives rise to pleasure and joy. The fact of this world being a world of impermanence, suffering, and change is a misfortune. If, in this world, one restrains oneself and abandons greed, one escapes this world.'

"Disciples, I sought worldly happiness, and having attained it, I probed for its source. Again, I sought worldly misfortune and probed for its source. Again, I contemplated the path that leads to release from this world, and having attained it I probed for its source. Disciples, when I in this way realized the true nature of worldly happiness, misfortune, and the release from both, I attained supreme enlightenment. Now my mind is unshakable. The wisdom that 'this is my final birth; I shall not be born again' arose within me. Disciples, if happiness did not exist in the world, people would not become attached to the world. Because there is happiness in the world, people become attached. If misfortune did not exist in the world, people would not become weary of the world. Because there is misfortune in the world, they grow weary of the world. Again, if the Dharma that teaches the path to release from the world did not exist, people would not find release from the world. Because such a Dharma exists, they are able to find release from the world." Hearing this teaching, the thousand disciples freed themselves from attachment and gained enlightenment.

4. Bamboo Grove Monastery

(1) The World-Honored One, accompanied by the three Kassapas and one thousand disciples, entered Rajagaha; they stopped at the Suppatittha Shrine, which was located in a bamboo grove on the outskirts of Rajagaha. Their presence was relayed to Rajagaha. The people praised the World-Honored One, saying, "The Buddha is a man worthy of receiving the offerings of the world. He is a man of true enlightenment. He is a teacher to all worlds. He is a paragon for human beings and celestial beings. Having attained enlightenment himself, he expounds in all worlds the Dharma that is perfectly endowed with both letter and meaning."

The king of Magadha, Bimbisara, surrounded by a large retinue, went to the World-Honored One, bowed to him, and sat to one side. The other people also took their seats.

(2) Now many of the people of the country of Magadha doubted that Kassapa of Uruvela, who was considered the wise man of his time, had become a disciple of the World-Honored One. Whether Gotama was to practice under the guidance of Kassapa of Uruvela or whether Kassapa of Uruvela was to practice under the guidance of Gotama was not clear. The World-Honored One perceived this at once and glanced backward at Kassapa of Uruvela; Kassapa perceived his intention and said so that everyone could hear, "World-Honored One, before, in the forest of Uruvela, I worshipped fire and became emaciated from ascetic practices. But now because of the teaching of the World-Honored One, I have come to delight in the

true way, World-Honored One. The World-Honored One is my teacher; I am his disciple." He repeated this twice. For the first time, these words dispelled all doubts.

(3) The World-Honored One expounded the Dharma earnestly in an orderly manner and caused King Bimbisara and a large number of people to open the eye of the Dharma. King Bimbisara said to the World-Honored One, "World-Honored One, once when I was a prince, I had five aspirations. I aspired to be crowned as a king; I wished for a Buddha to appear in my country; I aspired to serve that Buddha; I wished to listen to the Dharma from that Buddha; and I aspired to attain enlightenment. Now all of these aspirations have been fulfilled. The World-Honored One has expounded the Dharma in various ways; it was like raising someone who had fallen, uncovering something that had been concealed, showing the path to someone who was lost, guiding someone with sight to perceive forms, or holding up a light in darkness. World-Honored One, I take refuge in the World-Honored One. I take refuge in the Dharma and the Sangha. From now on to the end of my life, I beseech you to accept me as a follower. I ask you, together with your disciples, to visit my palace tomorrow." And the World-Honored One silently agreed to do so.

The king was overjoyed and returned to the palace; preparations for a meal were carried on throughout the night. The next morning, he informed the World-Honored One of the time of the meal.

The World-Honored One put on his robes, took his begging bowl in hand, and, accompanied by over one thousand disciples, entered Rajagaha. At that time, the ruler of the gods, Indra, assumed the form of a youth, strolled in front of the World-Honored One, and sang:

Leading a retinue of peaceful men, of freed men,

The World-Honored One now comes to Rajagaha.

Leading a retinue of quiescent men, of freed men,

The World-Honored One comes to Rajagaha.

The people saw him and thought, "Who is this youth with such a splendid and graceful appearance?" Perceiving this, Indra sang, "The Buddha is wise and pure and without peer; I am a youth who follows him."

(4) The World-Honored One entered the palace of King Bimbisara and sat down on the seat that was prepared for him. The king offered him food with his own hands. After he thus served him, he also sat down and thought, "Where would be the best place for the World-Honored One to live? It must be a place neither too far nor too near a village; a place convenient for both coming and going; a place accessible to all; a place that is free of crowds in the afternoon and quiet in the evening; a place that is suitable for contemplation and seclusion. Is there such a place?"

After pondering over this, he realized that the bamboo grove would be ideal. Aspiring to offer this park to the World-Honored One, he took up a gold vase, poured water onto the hands of the World-Honored One, and said, "World-Honored One, I wish to offer the bamboo grove to the World-Honored One." The

World-Honored One expounded the Dharma and encouraged the king. After he had returned to the grove, he said to his disciples, "From now on, receiving an offering of a grove will be allowed." And a monastery was built there.

5. Sariputta and Moggallana

(1) In a wealthy family that lived in the village of Narada, northeast of and not far from Rajagaha, there was a youth named Upatissa. He became fast friends with Kolita, who lived in a neighboring village; they often discussed their aims and goals. One day the two friends viewed the throng of people drifting around at a mountain festival and felt deep repugnance. They sought out a quiet place and, gazing down at Rajagaha at the foot of the mountain, steeped themselves in contemplation. They thought, "Those people in bustling crowds, hungering for fleeting dreams, are engrossed in pleasures—how many of them will be alive one hundred years from now? Even while they are captivated by the music played by heavenly Gandhabba musicians, the sadness of human beings will come upon them unrestrained. That city that appears in the distance will someday crumble. What use is it for someone who will crumble to seek something that will also crumble?" The two youths became mendicants together and, entering Rajagaha, became disciples of Sanjaya, who was a renowned ascetic of that time.

Sanjaya had a following of two hundred fifty disciples. Upatissa and Kolita presently attained the same stage as their teacher and were served by their disciples as befitting their position as senior disciples; and they continued to seek the path with great zeal. The two made this pact, "Should one of us attain enlightenment, he will immediately report this to the other."

(2) One morning, a disciple of the Buddha named Assaji made his round of begging in Rajagaha. His dignified appearance caught the attention of Upatissa, who accidentally met him on the road. "Oh, what a noble appearance; if there are men who have attained enlightenment in this world, this mendicant is surely one of them." Upatissa approached Assaji and thought to inquire about the path; then, however, he thought, "This is not the appropriate time; I must wait until he is finished with his round of begging"; and he trailed after Assaji.

After Assaji had finished his round of begging and left the village, Upatissa went up to him and said, "Friend, your body is truly filled with serenity; you are bright and clear and pure. Whom do you regard as your teacher?" Assaji said, "Friend, there is a great mendicant who has left home from the Sakya clan; I am one who follows the teaching of that World-Honored One." Upatissa asked, "What manner of teaching does your teacher hold forth?" Assaji said, "I have only recently come to the teaching; therefore, I am unable to explain it in detail. But to summarize it in one sentence, it can be expressed with the words, 'Dharmas come into existence, dependent on conditions; and dependent on conditions, they cease to exist.'"

Upatissa listened to this teaching and became enlightened to the principle that things that come into existence without fail cease to exist. He spoke of what had happened that day to Kolita, with whom he had made the promise to do so; he also spoke of this matter to two hundred fifty of his friends. Subsequently, following Upatissa and Kolita, they all asked to practice the path under the guidance of the World-Honored One. The two friends spoke about this to Sanjaya. Disregarding their teacher's attempt to stop them, and leading two hundred fifty men, they went to the Bamboo Grove Monastery where the World-Honored One dwelt.

(3) The World-Honored One gazed at Upatissa and Kolita coming in the distance. He said to his disciples, "Disciples, two friends are approaching here; these two will become great disciples of mine." The two friends became disciples of the World-Honored One, and before long they came to be revered as elders among the group of disciples. From that time, Upatissa was called Sariputta and Kolita was called Moggallana. But among the senior disciples, because of this rapid advance, a number of grievances arose. The World Honored One learned of this and said, "Disciples, I made Sariputta and Moggallana elder disciples, but not out of favoritism. Their station was determined by their roots of merit and aspirations from their previous lives. It is unseemly for those who left their homes in search of supreme nirvana to quarrel over positions of rank. You must purify your minds, and, with single-minded concentration, move forward." He then set forth the Verse of Precepts Commonly Taught by the Seven Buddhas:

Do not commit evil; perform a multitude of good acts;

Purify your own mind: this is the teaching of the Buddhas.

(4) After Sariputta and Moggallana became mendicants, the sons of a number of celebrated families in Magadha successively became disciples of the World-Honored One. Because of this, the people reproached the World-Honored One, saying, "Gotama robs parents of their children, wives of their husbands, and houses of their heirs." They spread the following rumors, "A thousand fire worshippers became mendicants; two hundred fifty disciples of the renowned Sanjaya became mendicants; the sons of celebrated families in Magadha became mendicants. Who will be pulled in next?" Some began to sing mocking songs when they caught sight of the Buddha's disciples:

A great mendicant appeared in the city, in the mountains of Magadha.

He dragged in the disciples of Sanjaya.

Whom will he snatch next?

The disciples relayed this to the World-Honored One. The World-Honored One said, "Disciples, these voices will not continue for long; they will fade away after seven days. Disciples, if you go to the city and hear these voices, reply in the following manner:

With the true Dharma, the Buddha guides all beings. What can arrows of jealousy do? People heard this, and soon the mocking voices subsided.

(5) Then the World-Honored One lived in the Boar's Cave on Vulture Peak, which was located northeast of Rajagaha. Sariputta's uncle, the brahmin Dighanakha, seeking to meet his nephew's teacher, came to the World-Honored

One. He said, "World-Honored One, my principle is not to affirm anything at all." The Buddha said, "Brahmin, if you claim not to affirm anything, you must not affirm the principle of not affirming anything." Dighanakha said, "That is so; if I affirm the principle of not affirming, then that would be affirming something." The Buddha said, "Brahmin, there are many like you who, while maintaining negation, do not abandon negation itself; those who are free of that error are few. In the world, there are those who say that they affirm all things and those who say that they affirm one part while not affirming another part. Among all these views, on the whole, the principle that affirms all things is closely related to greed, bondage, and attachment; and the principle that does not affirm all things is only distantly related to them. But in either case, if you firmly attach yourself to any of these principles, enemies will appear and engage in disputes, obstructions will form, and troubles will ensue. Those with wisdom perceive this and abandon those principles.

"Brahmin, this corporeal body is born of mother and father and is sustained by food; it is impermanent and ultimately is destroyed. It suffers, is without a self, and is empty. Perceiving this, you must free yourself from attachments and passions that are directed toward your corporeal body. Furthermore, there are three types of sensations, painful, pleasurable, and those that are neither painful nor pleasurable. These three sensations come into existence in accordance with conditions. They are impermanent and are destroyed; you must not become attached to them. My disciples who follow this teaching reject pleasure along with pain and the state of neither pain nor pleasure, free themselves from greed, and attain release. They live without quarrelling with anyone."

At that time, Sariputta was standing in back of the World-Honored One and was fanning him. He earnestly thought, "The World-Honored One truly sets forth the teaching of freeing oneself from desire." And he was able to free himself from defilement without any lingering traces. The brahmin Dighanakha, who perceived that things that come into existence are without fail extinguished, also attained the eye of the Dharma. He became a follower who, throughout his life, took refuge in the Three Treasures.

6. The Teaching at Bamboo Grove Monastery

(1) At Bamboo Grove Monastery, the World-Honored One frequently imparted the teaching to the disciples. "Disciples, from time to time, three types of celestial sounds reverberate among the gods. First, when a disciple of this teaching shaves off his beard and hair and decides to become a mendicant, a celestial sound arises to reverberate, 'This man is going to do battle with Mara.' Next, when that disciple performs the true practice that becomes the seed of enlightenment, a celestial sound arises to reverberate, 'This man is battling Mara.' Next, when this disciple completely extinguishes defilement and attains enlightenment, a celestial sound arises to reverberate, 'This man has won the battle.' Disciples, from time to time, these types of celestial sounds arise among the gods.

(2) "Disciples, when gods are about to disappear from the celestial world, five types of signs make their appearance. Their garlands of flowers wither; their robes

become stained; from under their armpits, perspiration flows; their bodies give off a foul odor; and they begin to feel dissatisfied with their dwelling place. At that time, the other gods encourage them by saying, 'Friends, you would do well to go to a good place, to attain that which is good, and to stand firmly on that ground.' Disciples, 'a good place' refers to the world of human beings, and 'attaining that which is good' refers to the attainment of faith in the teaching expounded by the Buddha in the world of human beings. When that faith has been firmly settled and is not upset by the teaching of other men, this is called 'standing firmly on that ground of faith.'

(3) "Disciples, if a disciple of mine takes hold of the hem of my robe and follows me, even if he were to trace my footsteps, if his mind is filled with desire and is in disorder, he will be distant from me, and I shall also be distant from him. The reason for this is that he will not perceive the Dharma.

And he who does not perceive the Dharma does not perceive me. On the other hand, even if a disciple is separated from me by thirty-odd miles, if he has freed himself from desire and if he is of a true mind, he will stand beside me.

The reason for this is that he perceives the Dharma; by perceiving the Dharma he perceives me.

(4) "Disciples, I give to those who ask; I am an enlightened being and am always prepared to give. I am an unsurpassed great physician. You are my children; you were born of the Dharma and are heirs to the Dharma. You are not heirs to material wealth. Disciples, there are two types of gifts, gifts of material wealth and Dharma gifts. There are two types of joyful giving, the giving of material wealth and the giving of the Dharma. There are two types of aid, the aid of material wealth and the aid of the Dharma. There are two types of offerings, offerings of material wealth and offerings of the Dharma. The Dharma is always superior to material wealth.

(5) "Disciples, suppose there is a man who floats on a flowing river; he floats downstream pleasantly on a pleasure boat. A man with eyes that see stands on a bluff, sees this boat, and shouts, 'Why do you sail so blissfully down the river? Downstream, waves are rising up; there are whirlpools; there are deep waters where crocodiles and demons dwell; you will surely meet your death there." The man hears that voice and begins to swim to shore by moving his arms and legs. Disciples, the flowing river is the thirst of lust; to float pleasantly refers to attachment to the corporeal body; the deep waters downstream mean the defilement that arises in the lower world. Waves rising up refer to the defilement of anger; whirlpools refer to the five desires; crocodiles and demons refer to women. Disciples, to swim to shore refers to release from bondage; to exert oneself with one's arms and legs refers to spiritual exertion; and the man with eyes that see standing on a bluff is the Buddha.

(6) "Disciples, music is lamentation; dancing shows a disordered mind. Moreover, to laugh with one's teeth showing is childish. Therefore, stop listening to music and stop dancing. If there is something pleasant, it would be well simply to smile.

(7) "Disciples, whether a Buddha appears in this world or not, all things are impermanent. This is an unchanging law. The Buddha is enlightened to this law;

he perceives it and explicitly teaches that all things are impermanent. Whether the Buddha appears in the world or not, the truths that all things are suffering and that all things are devoid of a self are unchanging. The Buddha is enlightened to these truths; he perceives them and expounds them."

Chapter 4

SAKYAMUNI IN HIS NATIVE HOME

1. Mahakasyapa and Narada

(1) On the day Sakyamuni attained enlightenment, a young man named Pippalayana, who lived in the brahmin village of Mahatistha, left home. The manner of his birth was this. His father, called Kapila, was a man of wealth unequalled in the neighboring villages and towns. When Kapila's wife was in the last month of her pregnancy, she took a stroll in their large and verdant garden. While she was resting under the shade of a huge pippala tree, a celestial garment came floating down out of the sky onto the top of that tree. Then her son was born under that tree, so he was called Pippalayana. He grew up amidst luxuries and was taught various arts and sciences. He was intelligent and excelled in eloquence. Even adults marvelled at his abilities. But from the time he was a child, he turned away from the pleasures of the floating world and sought something noble and lofty. Finding it difficult to refuse the urgings of his parents, he married a beautiful maiden named Bhaddakapilani of the Kausiya family who lived in the city of Sagara in the country of Madra in the far northern regions. But the bride also rejected the five desires and aspired to perform pure practices; the two, therefore, took the vow never to share a bed.

After the death of his parents, Pippalayana mourned the transience of life, even that of an insect caught on the tip of a farmer's plow. Bhaddakapilani gazed at the countless insects that swarmed on the sesame seeds that were being pressed and grew weary of the world. After discussing the matter, both left their home and set out on a pilgrimage, heading west and east. Because of his family lineage, Pippalayana was called Mahakasyapa.

(2) When the World-Honored One dwelt at the Bamboo Grove Monastery, he perceived one day that conditions for Mahakasyapa's enlightenment had come to fruition. He then left the monastery, travelling in a northeasterly direction, and sat at the foot of the huge nyagrodha tree that was situated between Rajagriha and Narada. At that juncture, Mahakasyapa felt that he was being pulled by some unknown force; seeking the World-Honored One, he travelled toward the Bamboo Grove Monastery. But by chance he caught sight of the World-Honored One

sitting under the tree in a meditative posture. Believing that this was the great teacher whom he was seeking, he said, "The World-Honored One is my great teacher; I am a disciple of the World-Honored One." The World-Honored One earnestly expounded the teaching of the Four Noble Truths and imparted it to his disciple. Following that, Mahakasyapa practiced the path with great effort and on the eighth day attained enlightenment.

(3) During that period, Narada also became a mendicant. At first, the seer Asita prophesied that Prince Siddhartha would become a mendicant and attain enlightenment. But when he perceived that Siddhartha would turn the Wheel of the Dharma at the Deer Park only after his death, he aspired to have, at least, his nephew Narada experience the good fortune of meeting the teaching of the World-Honored One. He feared that after his death Narada would continue the family name and receive huge offerings and as a consequence would lose the mind that meditates on the appearance in this world of the World-Honored One. He therefore built a house in the neighborhood of the Deer Park and instructed Narada to meditate on the World-Honored One three times a day. Asita then passed away. After his death, as feared, Narada grew attached to the offerings and became negligent about meditating on the World-Honored One.

At that time, the Naga king recalled the words imparted to him by Kasyapa Buddha: "At the time of Sakyamuni Buddha's appearance in the world, you will be able to free yourself from the body of a Naga." Thinking that he must find the Buddha in the world and going to the middle of the river Ganges, he heaped a mound of silver millet into a gold bowl and a mound of gold millet into a silver bowl; then he had two beautifully dressed maidens sing this song:

> Who is the king of kings?
>
> How can we, both the tainted and the untainted,
>   free ourselves from defilement?
>
> What is ignorance? What is carried off by its stream?
> What attainment deserves the name of wisdom?
> What is meant by flowing and not flowing?
> Moreover, how can we attain nirvana?

The Naga king said, "He who awakens to the meaning of this verse and can answer its questions is a Buddha. I am prepared to offer the gold and silver millet heaped into gold and silver bowls and the two maidens to such a man."

(4) But no one, neither mendicants, nor scholars, nor other sundry people, was able to solve this verse. Narada was also unable to solve this verse, disappointing his countrymen; he was finally forced to seek out the World-Honored One and ask him its meaning. The World-Honored One responded with the following verse: "All, from King Mara of the sixth heaven downward, are either tainted or not tainted; if one is not tainted, there is no defilement. Those who are tainted are called ignorant; they are carried away by the stream. That which

extinguishes ignorance is called wisdom; that which abandons the stream is not carried away and is called released."

Then Narada, on the seventh day, went to the river Ganges and conveyed this verse to the Naga king. The Naga king was overjoyed; he asked where the World-Honored One was staying, went to him, and became his follower. Narada also became a disciple and before long attained enlightenment.

2. The Verses of Celestial Beings

(1) Around that time, various gods came to the World-Honored One and sang his praises, or they exchanged questions and answers with the Buddha:

(i) All living beings pass away. Life is brief, and there is no one to shield them. Awakening to the fearfulness of death, they will accumulate those merits that lead to quiescence. Freeing themselves from the world's filth, they will advance toward enlightenment. Time passes; the days flow by; youth abandons everyone and fades away.

If people do not awaken to the Dharma, they will pursue evil teachings. They will sleep without waking up. Awaken them now! If they awaken to the Dharma, they will not fall into evil teachings; their enlightenment will be true, and their path will be straight.

(ii) If they become deluded about the teachings, they will pursue evil teachings. If they do not become deluded about the teachings, they will not fall into evil teachings. If they have pride, the five senses will not be in harmony. If the mind is not pacified, there is no quiescence. Even if they dwell in the forest but are negligent, they will not transcend Mara's domain. If they free themselves from pride and their minds become quiescent, if they unravel bondage with a wisdom that is clear, if they dwell in the forest and are not negligent, then they will transcend Mara's domain.

(iii) If they have children, they are pleased because of the children. If they own cows, they are pleased because of the cows. Pleasure and greed accompany each other. If they have children, they grieve because of the children. If they own cows, they grieve because of the cows. Grief and greed accompany each other. The enlightened man has neither cottage, nor nest, nor connecting thread; he is released from bondage. The mother is the cottage; the wife is the nest; the child is the connecting thread; the thirst of lust is the bond. Now the enlightened man has no cottage awaiting him; he has no nest to return to and no connecting thread; he is released from all bondage. Human and celestial beings of this world and later worlds search for his traces, but there is no way to uncover them. Therefore, in this world, do not commit evils of body, mouth, or mind. Abandon desire, make right your thoughts, and guard your conduct. Do not bring onto yourself sufferings that bring no benefits."

(iv) One evening, the gods of the Tavatimsa heaven visited the Jeta Grove and sang the praises of their own glory. "Those who have not seen the pleasure gardens, the dwelling places of the Tavatimsa heaven, which is known throughout the world for its glory, have yet to know true pleasure." In response to this voice, the other gods answered with these verses:

You are ignorant. Do you not know the Buddha's teaching that all things are impermanent and in flux? Birth and extinction are the nature of all things. Things are born and without fail they are extinguished. When both birth and extinction are transcended, one will attain the true happiness of quiescence.

Dwell with good people; keep company with truthful people. If you know the true Dharma, you will move toward the good and will not drift into evil.

Dwell with good people; keep company with truthful people. If you know the true Dharma, you will learn wisdom from another.

Dwell with good people; keep company with truthful people. If you know the true Dharma, you will know that even in this sorrowful world, there is no real sorrow.

Dwell with good people; keep company with truthful people. If you know the true Dharma, you will shine forth among people.

Dwell with good people; keep company with truthful people. If you know the true Dharma, you will be born in a good country.

Dwell with good people; keep company with truthful people. By knowing the true Dharma, you will attain release from all suffering.

(v)   If you are greedy and negligent, you will not perform the act of giving. If you meditate on merits and possess wisdom, you will perform the act of giving. Greedy people are fearful and do not give; but what must really be feared is the failure to give.

That is because what the wise man fears are the hunger and thirst that the unwise must suffer both in this world and in the next. Therefore vanquish the defilement of greed and perform the act of giving. Merits are truly the docking place for all people in the afterworld. The man who, like a traveler journeying through the wilderness, shares what little he has with another person will never perish while living among things that do perish. He will prosper forever. To give when one has little is superior to giving when one is wealthy. To give with faith is superior to both.

(vi) Faith is a good companion. If you have faith, you will have glory in this world; and in the afterworld, you will be born in a good country. The precepts do not age; faith is the good and peaceful ground; wisdom is man's treasure; merits cannot be taken away.

In the forest, there is a huge assembly; the gods also gather there. We come to this sacred forest in order to gaze upon this Sangha, which is victorious in battle. Disciples, bring peace to and rectify your minds. The wise man, like a driver who grasps the reins, controls his five senses. If you take refuge in the Buddha, you will not go to an evil country. When this body's life ends, you will join the assembly of the gods.

(vii) One celestial being posed a question in verse: "You and your disciples live in the forest, undergo severe practices, and take only one meal each day. Why do you and your disciples have complexions that are so clear?" The

World-Honored One answered, "If one does not grieve over days that have flowed by and does not yearn for the future that is yet to come, one is at peace with that which exists now. Therefore one's complexion is truly clear. The ignorant man, who yearns for a future that is yet to come and grieves over days that have flowed by, withers like a dried reed."

(2) One disciple, aspiring to exert himself in the manner of the World-Honored One, went too far and lost his life. While leaning against a post, he was born in the Tavatimsa heaven as a reward for his good karma although he had not yet attained enlightenment. Celestial maidens sang, danced, and waited upon him. He did not, however, at first believe that he had been born into a celestial world. The celestial maidens brought him a full-size mirror. Peering into it, he saw for the first time that he was in the celestial world. Turning away from this birth into the celestial world, accompanied by celestial maidens who served as his attendants, he came to the World-Honored One and sang this verse: "To be served by celestial maidens is like being haunted by demons that suck my blood. Forest of Ignorance would be an appropriate name for this forest. Where can I find a way out?"

The World-Honored One instructed him with a verse: "If you board this vehicle, which is outfitted with a curtain of right thought and a Dharma driver, and which is guided by the right view, the right path, the fearless ground, a noiseless cart, and contrition, you will peacefully enter nirvana."

3. The World-Honored One Returns to the City.

(1) The tidings that World-Honored One had attained enlightenment spread throughout the countries of India. The one who rejoiced most over this news was his father, King Suddhodana. When he received reports that the prince had perished during his six years of ascetic practice, he had not believed them. Now that the World-Honored One had attained enlightenment and had become a Buddha, the king wished to meet the him on the earliest possible day. The king's messengers, one after another, travelled south. But not one came back. They all sought refuge in the teaching of the World-Honored One and exerted themselves in the practice of the path. They forgot their tasks as messengers; there was no one left to convey his father's inconsolable heart to the World-Honored One. As a last resort, King Suddhodana enlisted the aid of Kaludayin and dispatched him southward, about 500 miles to Rajagaha. Kaludayin was born in the same year as the World-Honored One and was his childhood friend. He answered the king, "If you will allow me to become a mendicant, I shall carry out my duties as a messenger." The king acceded to this wish but fervently ordered Kaludayin to have the World-Honored One return to Kapilavatthu. Kaludayin went before the World-Honored One and listened to the teaching. He became a mendicant and attained enlightenment. On the day of the full moon in the last month of the year, he went before the World-Honored One and attempted with a song to persuade the World-Honored One to return home: "World-Honored One, the trees are now dyed with crimson. Their fruits have ripened. Withered leaves have fallen off, and they blaze forth like flames.

"It is neither too hot nor too cold. It is a time for travelling, a most pleasant season. So that your countrymen can gaze upon the World-Honored One, journey westward and cross the river Rohini.

"Fields are plowed in hope; seeds are sown in hope; traders set sail in hope of finding treasures. May the hope that I have come to pass."

(2) The World-Honored One heard this song and perceived that the moment to instruct his family had arrived. Accompanied by a large number of disciples, he headed for his native home, about 500 miles in a northerly direction. The World-Honored One travelled at a pace covering about 10 miles each day. Kaludayin flew through the sky and arrived at the place where King Suddhodana was to report on the journey of the World-Honored One.

At Kapilavatthu, the people of the Sakya clan were busy with preparations for the return of the World-Honored One. First of all, they cleansed Nigrodha Tree Park and invited the World-Honored One and his disciples there. From the beginning, the Sakya clan was traditionally a proud people, and this resulted in a number of problems. On this occasion, when the World-Honored One took his seat, the elders of the clan, seized by their inbred pride, refused to bow down to the World-Honored One. They said, "Gotama is younger than we are; therefore we need not bow down to him. The younger ones should step forward and bow down to him; we shall stay behind." The World-Honored One perceived their feelings, and in order to crush their prideful minds he ascended into the sky and manifested a divine transformation. King Suddhodana saw this miracle and bowed down at the feet of the World-Honored One. Then the other members of the Sakya clan also bowed down reverently at the World-Honored One's feet. Thereupon, the World-Honored One descended from the sky and took his seat. Surrounded by his kinsmen, he recounted the Vessantara Jataka:

(3) Long ago, King Sivi reigned in the city of Jetuttara in the country of Sivi. The king had a prince named Sanjaya. When the prince came of age, they had him take the daughter of King Madda, Phusati, as his consort and handed the kingdom over to him. Phusati became a favorite of the great king Sanjaya; among all the consorts, she became the foremost. At that time, the god Indra thought, "With this, I have been able to realize nine out of the ten aspirations that I promised in Phusati's former life to fulfill. This time I shall fulfill the promise of a child." In the Tavatimsa heaven, Indra approached a bodhisattva whose life in the celestial world was drawing to a close and urged him to descend to the world of people and dwell in the womb of King Sanjaya's consort Phusati.

At the time of her pregnancy, the queen felt a powerful urge to give freely. She established six locations in order to do this; they were situated at the four gates of the city, the center of the city, and the gate of the rear palace. Every day she aspired to give away six hundred thousand coins. A diviner said, "A bodhisattva who is unflagging in his devotion to selfless giving has entered your womb." The great king was overjoyed and, following his consort's wishes, practiced giving magnanimously.

In the tenth month, the queen received permission from the great king and had her carriage driven to the middle of the city. When they arrived at the area populated by people of the common class, she suddenly experienced labor pains. Entering a hut hastily constructed for the purpose, she gave birth to a bodhisattva. Since he was born in the quarters of the common class, he was named Vessantara. As soon as the prince was born, he asked his mother's permission to distribute freely a bag of one thousand coins. After that, he found joy in giving away his possessions to all beings. But when he was eight, he leaned on a chair and thought, "Everything that I give away originally came to me from some other source. I am not fulfilled by such giving. I must give away something that is mine. If someone wants my heart, I shall take it out and offer it to him. If someone desires my eyes, I shall give him my eyes; if someone desires my flesh, I shall tear out my flesh and offer it to him." Then the great earth trembled, mountains swayed, and auspicious omens appeared in the sky and the ocean. The gods sang the praises of his aspirations. When he was sixteen years of age, Vessantara mastered the various arts and took as his consort Maddi, a princess of the family of King Madda. He rose to the rank of crown prince; and each day he gave away six hundred thousand coins. Soon after that, a prince was born to them; they named him Jali. Then a princess named Kanhajali was born.

Vessantara rode atop a white elephant named Paccaya, who was born at the same time as he. Each day he made the rounds of the six large areas set aside for the practice of giving. This white elephant possessed a mysterious power; he was able to cause rain to fall at will on grounds that had been imprinted with his footsteps.

Now at that time, in the country of Kalinga, there was a long period of drought, which was followed by a famine. The people were plagued by both hunger and thieves. Overcome with suffering, they rushed to the royal palace and vented their anger at the king. The king, on the strength of the power of his merits, by his observance of the precepts, and by his selfless giving, attempted to make it rain, but he was unable to do so. At the urging of the people, the king dispatched brahmins to ask Vessantara for the use of his white elephant. The brahmins who received the king's orders purposefully covered themselves with dust and smeared mud over their bodies. After a long journey, they entered the city of Jetuttara. On the day of the full moon, they spied the prince at the south gate of the city and beseeched him to give over to them the elephant that was the glorious treasure of the country of Sivi, the elephant that had the power to save the world.

The prince thought, "I aspire to offer even my own self; it is an easy matter to offer something other than myself." He immediately dismounted from the back of the white elephant and offered it, together with countless precious objects, to the brahmins. The shock and rage of the city's people when they learned of this gift was extraordinary. They shouted, "We shall be ruined; we shall be ruined!" and berated the prince. The brahmins who were riding on the elephant escaped the city with great difficulty. Anger now turned into a riot, and there was no way the people could be pacified. The desperation of the people finally moved the king; this resulted in the banishment of the prince to Mount Vanka.

The prince, however, rejoiced inwardly because he had performed an act of giving that was difficult to perform. He did not brood over the banishment, and the following morning he intended to take leave of Princess Maddi and go deep into the Himalaya mountains. But the princess objected to the separation and sang the following verse: "The luxuriant foliage of the forest will prosper because of the presence of our children and ring with the sound of pure voices lifted in song.

"The deer will roam together, the peacocks dance; elephants will move in herds through the forest abloom with flowers, and kinnaras sing along with the murmuring sounds of fresh waters.

"Although I abandon the city, the place where the children are will be my home; deep in the mountains, I shall be with you."

Vessantara acceded to the princess's wish to accompany him. He said farewell to his parents. On a carriage drawn by four horses, he took along their two children, and pointing to the mountain paths he set out on the journey. On the road, a brahmin asked for his horses and carriage, and the prince gave them to him. He had the princess take the hand of their daughter, and he himself carried his son on his back.

Hurrying along, they reached Mount Vanka. The mountain was filled with poisonous snakes and wild beasts, but they were all won over by the prince's virtues and lived together in harmony. The prince's household spent seven peaceful months in this manner.

(4) Around that time, there was in the country of Kalinga a brahmin village called Dunnivittha, and there lived a brahmin there called Jujaka. Jujaka was asked by his wife to purchase a maidservant, and he attempted to do so, but he did not have enough money. Thereupon, he attempted to take advantage of Vessantara's charitable spirit. He made a long journey and climbed up Mount Vanka. Spying the prince's consort setting out to gather the fruits of trees, he went before the prince and said, "Like the waters of that great river that fulfills the desires of those who are parched, I believe that the Honored One will, without fail, hand over his two children to me." The prince held down his two children, who were attempting to run away and hide, and gave them over to the brahmin. "Jali, Kanha, please do not hide. Go down the mountain with this brahmin and become his servants. Become the vessels that let me cross the ocean of birth and death. Oh, my children are dear to me; however, enlightenment surpasses my love for my children ten trillion times over." With these words, the prince gazed after his children, who were cruelly bound with wisteria vines and were being taken away into the distance. The brahmin hurried the children along by whipping them over and over. Their skin was torn; blood flowed; and time after time, they both staggered under the blows. By chance, the brahmin stumbled over a rock and fell down. As soon as the bonds loosened around the soft bodies of the two children, they ran back to the prince, crying deliriously. They wrapped their arms around the prince's legs and begged him not to let them be led away. The prince did not utter one word. The children pleaded, "Father, we do not fear death; that is the fate of all beings. Rather we fear for mother. Mother will cry forever and ever. With our loss she will suffer deep sadness, and her tears will flow forever, like a river." The brahmin viewed this scene; then heartlessly and violently he dragged the children away and marched them off. The children said, "Father,

take good care of yourself. All of our possessions, cows, elephants, horses, are all left to mother. May they alleviate mother's grief." Wailing and crying out, the two children were dragged away.

The prince's heart became hot and his whole body shook. Unable to bear it, the prince went into his hut and cried, shedding copious tears. Standing up, he took hold of his sword and pursued the brahmin with the thought of killing him. But in a moment the prince's wisdom restrained his emotions.

The brahmin encountered great difficulties trying to drive the two children down the mountain. Jali escaped his bonds and returned to his father. When the brahmin dragged Jali away again, Kanha, staggering, ran back and threw herself at the prince's feet. She cried out, "Father, please, please, father, please save me!" The prince's mind wavered, and he wept tears of blood. He thought, "This suffering is the result of the thirst of lust; I must abandon lust and attain the mind of detachment." With the light of wisdom, the prince endured painful gasping and sat quietly in meditation.

His consort Maddi had gone deep into the mountains to gather the fruits of trees; she dug for tree roots and returned to the shack at dusk. But she was unable to find her children. She thought of the fearful dream that she had had the night before and, like a crazed woman, ran around in search of her children. The prince remained silent and told her nothing. She searched and searched in a frenzy and at dawn returned to the shack. Thereupon she swooned and lost consciousness; but with the prince's ministrations she revived.

This great and heart-rending practice of selfless giving astonished Indra. Indra, in order to test the resolve of the prince, assumed the form of a brahmin and asked for his consort. The prince could not possibly answer, "Yesterday I gave away my two children; how can I now give away my consort?" Rather, without a trace of attachment, and as if he were tossing out a bundle of one thousand coins, he picked up a jar, poured water on the brahmin's hands, and handed over his consort to him; and she gracefully did the prince's bidding and went with him. This was all done for the sake of perfecting the path. Indra was moved by the prince's resolve and his consort's fidelity, and he manifested himself in his true form as a god and returned her to the prince. The brahmin who had with him the two children Jali and Kanha intended to go to Kalinga, but drawn by this god he went instead to the city of Jetuttara. The two children went to their grandfather. Both the prince and his consort returned home and were received by their country. A large gathering to celebrate Vessantara's selfless giving was held.

The people of the Sakya clan heard this story and were overjoyed as they departed the forest to return home. But not one invited the World-Honored One to share a meal with them the following day.

4. Yasodhara

(1) The World-Honored One took up his begging bowl and went to Kapilavatthu. No one invited the World-Honored One to his house nor did anyone take his bowl and fill it with food. The World-Honored One moved along the road and begged for food at every house. The people opened their windows and looked out

at the Buddha as if he were a novel sight. They murmured, "Siddhattha is going on his round of begging." King Suddhodana, who received reports of this, was dumbstruck and saddened; clutching his robes, he went out into the streets, and standing before the World-Honored One he admonished him, "Why do you shame us? Why do you go around begging for food? Do you think you will not be able to receive at our house the amount of food gathered by a mendicant?" The Buddha said, "Great king, my ancestors also practiced begging." The king said, "What are you saying? We trace our lineage to the king Mahasammata; there is not one beggar in our family lineage." The Buddha said, "King, that royal lineage is your family lineage. I trace my lineage back to Dipankara Buddha and all subsequent Buddhas. All of these Buddhas practiced begging with a bowl, and they sustained their lives through begging." On the road, he expounded the teaching in verse:

> "Arise, free yourself from negligence and practice the Dharma. If you prac-
> tice the Dharma correctly, both this world and the next world will be blissful
> for you. Practice the Dharma, free yourself from evil, and if your mind is true,
> both this world and the next world will be blissful for you."

King Suddhodana, imbued with this teaching, awakened and rejoiced. Picking up the World-Honored One's bowl, he guided the World-Honored One and his disciples to the palace and served them a delicious meal. After the meal was finished, all the women of the palace, except for Yasodhara, came and bowed before the World-Honored One. The princess said, "If I possess even the slightest virtue, the World-Honored One will most likely come to my place; I shall bow down to him then," and she did not acquiesce to the urging of the people. The World-Honored One entrusted his bowl to the king and, accompanied by Sariputta and Moggallana, went to the rear palace. He said to them, "No matter what manner of worship she assumes, you must not utter a word." He then went to the seat that had been prepared for him. Princess Yasodhara nearly stumbled as she came forth, repeatedly rubbed her head against the feet of the World-Honored One, and bowed down to him to her heart's content. The king recounted the princess' fidelity to the World-Honored One: "World-Honored One, the princess, on hearing that you had donned the saffron robe, also clothed herself in a saffron robe. On hearing that you partook of only one meal a day, she also partook of only one meal a day. On hearing that you had forsaken large beds, she slept on straw mats. Hearing that you refrained from using incense and flowers, she also shunned their use. Although kings of related clans urged her to take another husband or attempted to win her in marriage, she paid them no heed and faithfully guarded herself for you. The princess embodies such virtues."

The World-Honored One said, "Great king, that is truly marvelous. The princess is guarded at this time by the great king; therefore with her matured wisdom she will no doubt guard herself. But years ago, unguarded by anyone, she walked through the deepest parts of the mountains, guarding herself with a wisdom that had yet to be perfected." Then the World-Honored One related the Jataka tale of the kinnara Canda:

(2) Long ago, when King Brahmadatta ruled Baranasi, there was a kinnara, a celestial musician, named Canda in the Himalayas; together with his wife, Moon Maiden, he dwelled atop Mount Silver Moon. At that time, the king of Baranasi entrusted the affairs of the state to the premier and clothed himself in two yellow robes. Arming himself with five weapons, he repeatedly traveled through the Himalayas.

One day, after his meal, the king wanted some water. He remembered that there was a small stream near where he was and started to climb up the hill. During the rainy season, it was the habit of the kinnaras to retreat into the mountains, while in the hot season, they came down from the mountains. At that time, Canda, accompanied by his wife, came down from the mountain. He rubbed incense on his body and garbed himself in a light robe made of flowers. He ate pollen and swung on vines. While singing in a soft voice, he came to that small stream and, together with his wife, went into the water. Scattering flowers and sprinkling water, he came out of the water. On the white silver-like sand, he laid out a bed of flowers and reclined on it. Taking up a flute of bamboo, he played on it and sang with a gentle voice. His wife accompanied him in song and dance. King Brahmadatta heard her voice and stealthily drew closer. With one look at Moon Maiden, he was made a prisoner of love. Deciding to slay the husband and to make her his wife, the king shot the kinnara. Writhing in agony the kinnara sang the following and crumpled onto the bed of flowers: "Death draws near, O Moon Maiden. Blood pours out, and my life is coming to an end. My breath dwindles down. My body feels itself failing, and my mind longs for you." With this, he drew his last breath. At first, Moon Maiden, dancing to the flowers and singing to the butterflies, was not aware of this shocking incident. She then came to herself and found what had happened. Unable to bear the shock and grief, she let out a loud cry. Soon she caught sight of the figure of the fearful king. Trembling in fear and rage, the Moon Maiden flew away, and standing atop the summit of the mountain, she sang, "Evil demon, my husband has fallen and lies on the ground. May the following grief be visited upon your wife: not being able to see her child and losing her husband, may she be seized by endless grief."

King Brahmadatta described in various ways the splendors of the royal palace in an attempt to entice her; however, he was unable to dispel Moon Maiden's grief or anger. Moon Maiden frantically embraced her husband's body and sang this lament: "The flowers of the trees are beautiful; the flowing streams are pure; the summits of the Himalayas glitter with golden colors. But without my husband, how am I to spend my days?"

Suddenly sensing a slight warmth around his breast, she then reproached the gods in a loud voice, "Are there no gods to guard the world? Are they out on a journey? Have they died? Why did they not guard my beloved husband?"

This expression of intense grief reached the gods, and Indra immediately inquired into it and discovered the reason for it. Changing himself into a brahmin, he appeared at the scene and poured water from a water jar onto the kinnara's body, whereupon the poison was destroyed. Then, completely healed, the kinnara stood up.

Indra said to him, "After this, you must not descend Mount Silver Moon or enter the world of men. You must dwell only in this place." He warned the kinnara with these words and returned to the celestial world. Moon Maiden sang, "Pleasant is the gentle breeze that rustles through the trees that stand on the river banks in the mountains, strewn with flowers. We now take leave and forever exchange whispers of love." She then departed with her husband.

The World-Honored One finished recounting this tale and concluded, "Great king, the princess was always faithful to me, not only now."

5. Nanda and Rahula

(1) The following day was a felicitous day on which were to take place the investiture and the marriage of Nanda, the World-Honored One's stepbrother. But the World-Honored One went to Nanda's house and spoke to Nanda, who came out to greet him. Then the Buddha bestowed upon him a begging bowl and departed. Nanda, with bowl in hand, followed the World-Honored One outside. His betrothed, the maiden Sundari, was at the time combing her hair. Noticing Nanda leaving, and with her hair in her hand, she asked intently, "Where are you going?" Ignoring Nanda's pleas to take back the begging bowl, the World-Honored One quickened his pace. Accompanied by Nanda, he went to Nigrodha Tree Park. He had the reluctant Nanda become a mendicant. This was on the third day of the World-Honored One's return to his city.

(2) On the seventh day, the World-Honored One entered the city to make his round of begging. Princess Yasodhara dressed Prince Rahula in splendid fashion and sent him to the World-Honored One. She said, "Look! That divine mendicant, surrounded by numerous mendicants, is your father. Your father possessed many treasures; after he became a mendicant, they have not been seen. Go to him and receive your just inheritance. You would do well to say, 'Father, I am your son. I am thinking of ascending the throne and becoming king. Please bestow your treasures on me.' "

As instructed, Rahula went to hear the World-Honored One; however, he naturally felt the love that flows between parent and child and said, "Mendicant, your shadow is delightful." He then stood to the side. When the World-Honored One finished his meal and stood up to leave, Rahula followed him and with outstretched hands said, "Please give me my inheritance; please give me my inheritance." The World-Honored One did not order Rahula to return to his home. Walking together, they entered a forest of nigrodha trees. The World-Honored One reflected, "This child seeks his inheritance from his father. That inheritance waxes and wanes and produces suffering. Rather, I shall bestow on him the spiritual treasure that I attained at the place of enlightenment. I shall make him the heir of a supernatural inheritance." He called for Sariputta and told him, "Have Rahula become a mendicant." Sariputta said, "How should I have Rahula become a mendicant?" The World-Honored One called his disciples together to explain this matter: "Disciples, young men are allowed to become mendicants in accordance with the Dharma of the Three Refuges. First, they shave off their beard and hair and put on saffron robes. They drape the upper part of the robes on one shoulder and bow down at the feet of the disciples. They then kneel with one knee touching the ground. They join their palms and repeat, 'I take refuge in the Buddha; I take refuge in the Dharma; I take refuge in the Sangha." Have them repeat the Three Refuges three times.' "

(3) Following these instructions, Sariputta had Rahula become a mendicant. Hearing reports of this, King Suddhodana was aggrieved; he hurried to the World-Honored One's place and said, "World-Honored One, I seek one blessing for myself." The World-Honored One said, "Great king, the Buddha is able to bestow any manner of blessing." The king said, "World-Honored One, the blessing that I seek is most fitting and is not tainted with greed. When the World-Honored One became a mendicant, it brought me profound suffering. It was the same when Nanda became a mendicant. Today Rahula became a mendicant. Thoughts of love for my grandchild rend my skin; they tear my flesh and pulverize my bones; they pierce my marrow and cause me pain. From now on, please prohibit the home-leaving of children who do not have their parents' consent." The World-Honored One acceded to this request, and thereafter he forbade the home-leaving of children who did not have the consent of their parents.

Around that time, among the many youthful disciples, there were some who were confused as to the number of precepts to which they would have to adhere. The World-Honored One learned of their confusion and established the ten precepts for youthful disciples: "Disciples, I prescribe ten precepts for youthful disciples. They must refrain from killing, refrain from stealing, refrain from licentious behavior, refrain from lying, refrain from drinking liquor, and refrain from partaking of meals except at the appointed times; they must refrain from drawing close to song, dance, music, and shows; refrain from putting on floral wreaths, smearing incense on the body, and using cosmetics; refrain from lying down on beds with adornments; and refrain from receiving money. These are the ten precepts for youthful disciples. Youthful disciples must observe these ten precepts."

(4) The World-Honored One had returned to his native home after a long absence. When the spiritual edification of his family and the people was finished, he headed once again for Rajagaha and travelled as far as the village of Anupiya of the Malla clan. At this place, many young and famous members of the Sakya clan became mendicants.

In the Sakya clan, there were two brothers named Mahanama and Anuruddha. Anuruddha was physically weak and was prone to seclude himself in his room. But his older brother Mahanama thought, "The eminent people of the Sakya clan, following the World-Honored One, have all become mendicants. One of us brothers must become a mendicant." He discussed this with Anuruddha. At first, because of his sickly condition, Anuruddha declined to become a mendicant. But he listened to his older brother, who said, "Life at home is also not easy. From plowing to harvesting, since the time of our distant ancestors, we have continued the same difficult work. Year after year, we have repeated this without end." Hearing this, Anuruddha resolved to become a mendicant. He then begged his mother for her permission. His mother repeatedly refused to grant his request.

In order to make Anuruddha abandon his aspiration to become a mendicant, his mother finally said, "If King Bhaddiya becomes a mendicant, I shall grant your request." Anuruddha immediately went to King Bhaddiya's palace and pressed him to remove the obstruction to his becoming a mendicant. Exhorting him, Anuruddha roused the king's mind. Taking Ananda, Bhagu, Kimbila, and Devadatta with him and accompanied by the barber Upali, Anuruddha left the city. After entering the neighboring country, they removed their bodily ornaments. They handed these over to Upali and had him return home. On his way back, Upali thought, "The Sakya clan is a fierce tribe; therefore if I take these treasures back now, they will think that I killed these young noblemen and robbed them. They may put me to death. The young noblemen became mendicants; there is no reason that I cannot become a mendicant." Upali hung the bundle on a tree with the idea that it was a gift for whomever found it. He then hurried after the young noblemen.

They suddenly caught sight of Upali's unexpected return and greatly rejoiced. They all went before the World-Honored One and asked to be allowed to become mendicants. They said, "World-Honored One, we are of the Sakya clan and are proud and arrogant. This Upali served us for a long time as a barber. So that we might crush our inborn pride and arrogance and revere Upali, we wish to have Upali become a mendicant first." Thereupon the World-Honored One had first Upali and then the young noblemen become mendicants.

(5) After the rainy season, Bhaddiya attained enlightenment. Sitting under a tree in the posture of meditation, he savored the bliss of a sage. Involuntarily, he cried out, "It is blissful; it is blissful!" The other disciples heard this and thinking that Bhaddiya was pursuing the pleasures of the floating world they relayed it to the World-Honored One. As a consequence, when Bhaddiya was summoned by the World-Honored One, he said, "World-Honored One, when I sat on the throne, at all places—inside and outside my room, in the city, in the country—I was protected by guards. Despite this, I always lived in fear. Now, although I am alone under a tree in the middle of a forest, my mind is as peaceful as a deer's. It was while thinking of this that I involuntarily cried out, "Oh, it is blissful; it is blissful!"

The World-Honored One replied in verse, "Whoever gets rid of anger within and transcends the suffering of both existence and nonexistence will be freed from fear and anxiety and attain boundless bliss. Even the gods do not know this frame of mind." The World-Honored One, at the head of these disciples, then returned to Rajagaha.

6. The Rich Man Anathapindika

(1) The rich man Anathapindika of the city of Savatthi was the brother-in-law of a prosperous merchant in Rajagaha. Once he came to Rajagaha and stayed at the merchant's house. The wealthy merchant had invited the World-Honored One and his disciples to his home on the following day; therefore, he was extremely busy ordering his servants to do this and that. Anathapindika thought, "Every time the master of this house sees me, he lets everything go and engages me in intimate conversation. Today, however, something is amiss. Is he preparing to

receive a bride? Is he preparing to make a large sacrifice? Or is he preparing to make a large sacrifice? Or is he preparing to receive the king of this country? Or its high-ranking ministers?"

After giving the servants their orders, the wealthy merchant for the first time approached Anathapindika and replied to his questions, "Tomorrow morning I am going to invite the Buddha and his disciples." Anathapindika said, "Did you just say 'Buddha'?" The merchant said, "Yes, I did say that." Anathapindika said, "In this world, it is difficult even to hear this word 'Buddha.' Can I now set out to see the Enlightened One revered by the world?" The merchant said, "Anathapindika, it is not the time to see the Buddha now; you would do well to set out early tomorrow morning."

(2) That night Anathapindika focused his thoughts on the Buddha; before daybreak, he woke up three times. When he left the city gates early in the morning and arrived at the outskirts of the city, suddenly the sun's light was concealed, and it became dark. Anathapindika became fearful and stopped in his tracks; he attempted to turn back. Then a voice was heard in the sky: "An offering of a hundred elephants, horses, or carriages, or of a maiden wearing earrings of precious gems, does not equal the merit of taking one step forward.

"Anathapindika, go forward; if you move forward, you will gain benefit; if you retreat, there will be no benefit."

And again sunlight showed itself. This phenomenon occurred three times. Anathapindika felt encouraged and advanced toward a desolate forest where he saw the World-Honored One, who happened to be walking along the road. The World-Honored One also caught sight of Anathapindika and, going to the seat prepared for him, called to him. He said, "Sudatta, come!" Anathapindika was elated, approached the Buddha, and bowed at his feet. He inquired, "World-Honored One, did you sleep peacefully last night?"

The Buddha replied, "Should you enter enlightenment and divorce yourself from desire, if you are not defiled and are pure, you will sleep blissfully. If you divorce yourself from all fetters and become free of suffering, if you enter quiescence of the mind, you will sleep blissfully."

The World-Honored One faced Anathapindika and expounded on the following: selfless giving, birth into the celestial world, and the benefits of freeing oneself from the misfortunes bound up with desire and its foul defilement. Gradually, he set forth the Dharma and brought the rich man's mind to fruition. Following this, he expounded the Four Noble Truths. Like white, unstained cloth that is easily dyed through with color, Anathapindika was dyed through with the Dharma and gave birth to the Dharma eye that perceived that all things that are born without fail are extinguished. And he was able to free himself from doubt and fear.

He said to the World-Honored One, "World-Honored One, this is most excellent. Showing the path to someone who was lost, you have opened the eye that perceives things. From now on, I take refuge in the World-Honored One, the Dharma, and the Sangha. Please accept me as a follower. Moreover, World-Honored One, tomorrow, together with your disciples, I beseech you to accept my offerings." The World-Honored One in silence accepted his offer. Anathapindika, having been given the World-Honored One's consent, left his seat, bowed to the World-Honored One, turned right, and departed.

(3) The wealthy merchant of Rajagaha heard that the following day Anathapindika was going to invite the World-Honored One and his disciples; he then said, "Please allow me to pay the expenses." But Anathapindika spurned this offer of help. At the home of the wealthy merchant, he prepared the meal and dispatched a messenger to notify the World-Honored One of the time. Before long, the World-Honored One was at the home of the wealthy merchant. Anathapindika personally made offerings to the World-Honored One and his disciples. After the World-Honored One had finished partaking of his meal, he said, "May the World-Honored One and his disciples spend this year's retreat at Rajagaha." He learned then that "Buddhas delight in empty houses." The World-Honored One expounded the Dharma to Anathapindika and returned to the Bamboo Grove.

(4) Anathapindika had numerous friends and acquaintances and was held in high esteem by them. On the road back from Rajagaha to Savatthi, he announced to his people, "Build a park for the monks, erect a monastery, prepare gifts; in response to my invitation, the Buddha who has appeared in this world will pass along this road." The people acceded to his words and prepared to greet the World-Honored One. Before long, Anathapindika returned to Savatthi; glancing in all directions, he said, "Is there not a suitable place, a place that is neither too far from nor too near to the village, a place convenient for both coming and going, a place accessible to all, a place that is free of crowds in the afternoon and of boisterous noise in the evening, a place that is free of people and suitable for secluded living?" And he looked here and there for such a place.

As a result, he discovered the park owned by Prince Jeta. He begged the prince for it and, by spreading gold coins throughout the park forest, purchased the park. He built a monastery that covered the entire forest. He constructed rooms, a storehouse, a guest house, a furnace room, a kitchen, separate toilets, a strolling area, wells, a hut for the wells, a bathhouse, a pond, and a shelter made of boughs and vines. Prince Jeta also built a two-tiered gate on the unoccupied grounds.

(5) From Rajagaha, the World-Honored One travelled toward Savatthi; on the way, he passed Vesali and stayed at the terraced hall in the large forest. The people of Vesali, however, urged on by Anathapindika, had already begun the construction; they treated the disciples who served as supervisors with warm hospitality. Watching the people constructing the monastery, a poor tailor, sensing the auspiciousness of this event, decided to build one building himself. He kneaded mud and built up a wall piece by piece. But he did not know the correct way to build a wall; it was crooked and eventually tumbled to the ground. This repeated itself two or three times. The tailor began to grumble, "The Sakya's followers oversee the construction of those who bring them generous offerings; however, they pay scant attention to the work of a poor man like me." The World-Honored One heard of this, and gathering his disciples after delivering a sermon, he ordered his disciples as follows: "Disciples, from now on, I allow the selection

of an overseer for new constructions. Those who have been selected to serve as overseers must discharge their duties diligently, making certain that construction proceeds without error. Whenever damage occurs, they must repair it."

(6) When the World-Honored One was on his way from Vesali to Savatthi, the disciples fought with each other over rooms at one monastery. As a result, Sariputta, who arrived a little later, was unable to find a room and slept under a tree that night. The World-Honored One awoke and left his room at daybreak. Seeing Sariputta, he asked why he was sleeping there. He then gathered the disciples and said, "Who is worthy of the first seat, the first water, and the first meal?" The disciples expressed their views; the Buddha then recounted the following:

Disciples, long ago, at the foothills of the Himalayas, there was a huge nigrodha tree. Near it lived a partridge, a monkey, and an elephant. The three did not respect, love, or live in harmony with each other. One day, they agreed to the following: "Let us find out who is the oldest one among us three; then let us venerate that elder and follow his teaching."

Thereupon, the partridge and the monkey asked the elephant, "Friend, how far back can you remember?" The elephant answered, "When I was a child, I straddled this nigrodha tree; I remember the topmost shoot brushing against my chest." The monkey said, "When I was a child, I remember sitting on the ground and biting the topmost shoot of this nigrodha tree." The partridge said, "Long ago, in this open land, there stood a huge nigrodha tree. I ate its fruit and expelled droppings on this place. This nigrodha tree grew from that spot. Therefore I am the oldest among the three of us." Thereupon, the monkey and the elephant said to the partridge, "Friend, among us three, you are the oldest. You are the one worthy of our veneration. We shall follow your teaching." Friends, they received the five precepts from the partridge and practiced them. They revered each other and lived in harmony; after death, they were born in the celestial world. These three are renowned for the purity of their acts. Take note, even animals revered, loved, and lived in harmony with each other. On the other hand, you left home and came into this good teaching; yet you are ignorant of such virtues. This will not help those who do not have faith to acquire faith nor help those who do have faith to deepen their faith. Rather, this will leave those without faith as they are and cause those with faith to regress in their faith. Disciples, toward the elders you must observe the rules of propriety, such as obeisance and kneeling in respect, placing one's palms together, and so forth; and you must offer the first seat, the first water, and the first food to the elders.

(7) The World-Honored One made his journey step by step, and when he reached Savatthi, Anathapindika organized a colorful procession and greeted the World-Honored One. He guided him to Anathapindika Monastery in Jeta Grove. The next day he invited the World-Honored One to his own home and made offerings to him. After the meal, he said to the World-Honored One, "World-Honored One, what do you think I should do with this Jeta Grove?" The Buddha said, "Elder, offer this Jeta Grove to the Sangha of the four directions, regardless of whether they come here or not." The rich man picked up a vase

made of gold, poured water on the hands of the World-Honored One, and did as he was instructed.

The World-Honored One expressed his gratitude in song:

> A multitude of Buddhas praise the offering to the Sangha of a tranquil monastery that protects against the heat and the cold, the wind and the rain.

> Therefore those possessed of wisdom should build monasteries and offer them to people of vast learning as dwelling places.

> With a mind of joy, they should offer food, water, robes, and rooms to those with upright minds.

> Listen to the Dharma that extinguishes suffering; then you will awaken and enter enlightenment.

Introduction

After delivering his First Sermon at the Deer Park near Benares when he was 35 years old, Gotama Buddha devoted the next 20 years, walking from place to place, from villages to urban areas, through forests and agricultural lands, in a supreme effort to spread his teachings to all levels of people, from members of the royal families and learned religious seekers to ordinary folks, whether merchants, farmers, or wandering entertainers. During the rainy (monsoon) season, from June to September, he stayed at the rest-houses (which eventually developed into large monasteries) established for the Buddha and his disciples by such wealthy merchants as Anathapindika at the Jetavana. After 20 years of wanderings, he settled permanently in Savatthi, staying alternately at the monastery in Jetavana or in Pubbarama, the Eastern Park.

Book Two contains a variety of discourses by the Buddha, who skillfully used metaphors, analogies, or similes to clarify his instructions to both his disciples and others who came to hear his teachings. For instance, when the farmers of the Sakya and the Koliya clans were preparing for war during a period of drought to gain control of the waters of the Rohini River for irrigation, the Buddha related animal stories to the people to illustrate the folly of destroying human lives over trivial matters and at the same time taught the importance of non-violence and peace. Also, at this time, because of Mahapajapati's (Buddha's aunt and foster mother) earnest pleading, women were permitted to enter the sangha, the community of Buddha's disciples.

He warned his disciples against demonstrating magical or superhuman powers as not leading to a proper understanding of life's truth. Yet, the ancient recorders of the Buddha's teaching describe how the Buddha used his supernatural ability to take a disciple to a heavenly place to emphasize a point. In this regard, the readers must remember that they should not become entangled with the words of such stories but must try to get at the inner meaning that the event is intended to convey.

For the disciples, the Buddha also promulgated monastic rules of conduct and observance of a regular schedule of meetings to recite the teachings and to reflect on correcting wrongful conduct. The latter practice was patterned after the traditional custom of non-Buddhist religious groups, which the Buddha recognized as having beneficial value for his disciples as well as to help maintain a unity of purpose.

Chapter 3 also introduces readers to the following profound, metaphysical concepts of the Mahayana (Large Vehicle) School of Buddhism, which is followed mainly in China, Korea, and Japan: sunyata (emptiness, or void), alaya-vijnana (store-consciousness), and Tathagata-garbha (womb of Tathagata, or Buddhahood). The concept of emptiness is found in early Pali scriptures, but it was not developed by the conservative followers of the Buddha-Dharma. The concept of alaya-vijnana is based on the early doctrine of the eight consciousnesses and anatman (no-self). The five consciousnesses arise separately from our five sense organs (eye, nose, ear, tongue, touch); the sixth is our mind that processes what is sensed by the other five into thoughts, feelings, and imagination; the seventh arises from the combination of the six consciousnesses which causes the individual to believe in the existence of a separate self within; and the eighth is the alaya-vijnana, that underlies the other seven consciousnesses, or where all cognitive knowledge is stored. Tathagata-garbha is, simply explained, a womb that contains the embryo of Buddhahood, implying that all beings have the potentiality to become a Buddha. Some Buddhists may believe that this pure and unchanging womb transcends all individual minds that falsely discriminate life's phenomena. However, a belief in a fundamental eternal mind, similar to a Creator Mind of some other religions, is in conflict with the Buddha's doctrine of anatman (no-self).

This question regarding an unchanging Tathagata-garbha was posed (in a passage in Chapter 3, Section 4) by a bodhisattva, a person who has vowed to save fellow beings and follows the Noble Middle Path toward enlightenment. The Buddha replies that those who have yet to attain a certain level of understanding may become fearful with the doctrine of anatman, and so the idea of an Eternal Self is a skillful means to stabilize them until they are ready to grasp the higher truth of sunyata. Book 3, chapter 1, section 4 presents a passage from another Mahayana scripture which discusses in detail the concept of Tathagata-garbha. To explain certain conflicts encountered in the ancient texts, Buddhists declare that there are 84,000 (many) paths to the summit of enlightenment, or that the Buddha taught the doctrine to suit the listeners' mental or spiritual level. Indeed, the readers will also discover that the concepts understood on the first day of reading will be seen in a different light as they advance in understanding the Buddha's teaching.

According to Mahayana philosophy, one cannot state that anything simply exists or does not exist, because, in truth, nothing is everlasting. Things exist according to certain causes and conditions that bring about a temporary existence. This concept applies also to the particular self, or ego, that one feels must exist within each one of us and will continue to exist after death. The Buddha taught his disciples that there is no intrinsic nature in any object we see in life; thus, it is said to be empty. Not that life is just dream-like but that all that we observe in life exists in relation to other things or conditions that cause it to come into being. It is because we believe things to be permanent and cling to them that suffering arises. Anything and everything is in a process of change. To clarify this point, the Buddha explains (in Chapter 4, Section 7) the principle of the Twelve Links of Dependent Origination. Death and decay arise because of birth; and desire and attachment develop through our five sensory perceptions, leading us, according to such cause and effect links, to a false understanding of existence.

The concepts that the readers will find in Chapter 3 are so profound in their implications that many articles and books have been written by scholars from the standpoint of their own interpretations or understanding, but readers should recognize that intellectual understanding alone is not sufficient to appreciate the teaching of the Buddha. The Buddha-Dharma must be lived and experienced. The emphasis is on direct experience rather than on mental speculation as to the meaning of these concepts. Dharma originally meant the natural condition of things or beings; therefore, it denotes the law of their existence. By reading through all of the selected passages in this book and by daily application of the teachings therein, readers may become increasingly aware of the Buddha's vision of the true nature of life.

Chapter 1

IN JETA GROVE

1. The Sermon at Anathapindika Monastery

(1) One day the World-Honored One, in Jeta Grove at Anathapindika Monastery, spoke to his disciples and instructed them as follows: "My disciples, I wish to see you become inheritors of the Dharma rather than merely inheritors of material things. I say this to you because I have deep concern for all of you. If you become mere inheritors of things, then people may say that the followers of Sakyamuni have renounced the world for the sake of acquiring things and not to inherit the Dharma. My disciples, assume that on some occasion I have not partaken of some of the food offered to me as alms. Assume that just at that moment two of my disciples arrive hungry and tired. Assume that I say to them that the food was being offered to them, to be eaten as they wished, and that if they did not wish to eat it, I should dispose of it where the growth of the grass would not be hampered or throw it into the water where there would be no possibility of harming living things.

"One of them would be sure to recall that at one time the World-Honored One had instructed them, 'I wish you to become inheritors of the Dharma rather than inheritors of things.' He remembers that this food is one of those things. Thus rather than eat the food, he prefers to bear his hunger and fatigue for an entire day, and he does exactly as his thought dictates. Another of the Buddha's disciples has this thought in mind, 'I shall partake of this food and satisfy my hunger, be relieved of my fatigue, and thus spend one whole day and night,' and let us assume that he carries this out. My disciples, I would not hesitate to praise the attitude of the first disciple, for he has, for a long time now, lessened desires and been satisfied with things as they are. He continues to remove the poisoned arrow of desires. It is because I have deep concern and care for all of you that I have instructed you to become inheritors of the Dharma and not of material things." Upon having given these instructions, the Buddha stood up from his seat and returned to his room.

(2) Immediately after the Buddha left the lecture hall, Sariputra addressed the disciples and said, "Friends, what does it mean for the Buddha's disciples not to reside in a state of tranquillity, and not to study it? Also, what does it mean

for them to study tranquillity?" The disciple asked, "Friend, was it not because of the wish to know more about this matter that we have come from afar to be near the Buddha? Please enlighten us on this matter, and we shall take your instructions to heart as we hear them."

Sariputta then said to the monks, "Not to study how to enter the state of tranquillity means that while failing to discard the material things that the master has instructed us to discard, one discards the mind that abides in a state of tranquillity and thus becomes arrogant, lazy, and degenerate. Studying tranquillity means to discard the material things that the master has instructed us to discard and, without becoming arrogant or lazy, to hasten to abide in a state of tranquillity.

"Friends, craving is evil; so are anger, hatred, and concealment. Blind passions, envy, avarice, flattery, self-indulgence, arrogance, and idleness are evil. Friends, in order to discard these evils, there is the Middle Path. The Middle Path means the way of the Eightfold Noble Path. By this Path, right wisdom can be cultivated and enlightenment attained."

(3) When the brahmin Janussoni of Savatthi started for the outskirts of town one day in a horse-driven cart covered with a white canopy, he met the travelling ascetic Pilotika. The brahmin asked the ascetic, "Where are you headed for this midday?" To this the ascetic replied that he had gone to seek guidance from Gotama the Buddha. The brahmin then inquired of the ascetic, "Is he truly the wise one?" To this the ascetic replied, "How can I ever fathom the knowledge and wisdom of Gotama the Buddha? Only those equal to Gotama will ever perceive the knowledge and wisdom of Gotama." To this the brahmin said that Pilotika was excessive in his praise of Gotama's virtues.

The latter replied, "How can I be excessive in my praise of Gotama's virtues? He is the greatest of all people and gods!" The brahmin retorted, "Well, then, what do you find in Gotama that is so exceptional?" To this Pilotika replied, "It is as when the keeper of an elephant forest enters the forest and sees the huge footprints of elephants. He knows by those prints that the elephants in the forest are large. Likewise, I have seen four of Gotama's footprints and have come to know that he is the Fully Awakened One, that the Dharma is exquisitely presented by him, and that his disciples practice the right way. By the four footprints, I mean the following four virtues. Some kshatriyas, wise and eloquent, tried to refute the teachings of Gotama. But every one of them, when confronted by Gotama and taught the Dharma, quickly became his followers. This is the first of the four footprints.

"Again, a wise brahmin tried to defeat Gotama in argument, but he became overjoyed when he heard Gotama's instructions, and he became his follower. This is the second footprint.

"Again, an eloquent and articulate householder tried to defeat Gotama in debate by employing various means. But upon meeting Gotama, he was profoundly struck by the teachings and became a follower. This is the third footprint.

"At yet another time an ascetic with a mind as sharp as a razor had fully prepared himself to refute the teaching of Gotama. However, in the end he, too, became Gotama's disciple. He remarked that formerly he had thought that he was an ascetic who had renounced all worldly things, but he now realized that he had become a true ascetic, and this only through the guidance of Gotama. This is the fourth footprint. It is by observing these four footprints that I have come to know that the World-Honored One is the truly Awakened One, that he teaches the Dharma exquisitely, and that his followers practice the right way."

(4) Then Janussoni came down from his carriage with its white canopy and, draping his robe on one shoulder, faced the direction where the Buddha resided, put his palms together, and uttered three times, "I seek refuge in the World-Honored One, the Awakened Buddha." Suddenly he exclaimed, "I shall go to meet the Holy One, Gotama, and listen to his teachings." He then headed for the place where Gotama Buddha was staying, and having paid his sincerest respects, he relayed to the Buddha what Pilotika had told him.

To this the Buddha answered, "O brahmin, the metaphor of the elephant's four footprints is not adequate. I shall now explain the metaphor for you. It is not true that an experienced elephant keeper would, upon entering the forest and seeing large footprints, immediately think that these were the footprints of a large elephant. This is because there are female elephants short in height and with large feet.

"Again, pursuing this further, even if there were large footprints and the branches overhead were broken, he would not think that these were left by a huge elephant. This is because there are elephants that are tall and leave large footprints. And again, even if there were large footprints and the branches overhead were broken and there were scars on the trunks of the trees made by elephants' tusks, still he would not think that these were left by a huge elephant. This is because there are large female elephants. Now, finally, if there were large footprints, with branches broken overhead and tree trunks bearing scars of elephants' tusks, and if in addition a large elephant were seen moving back and forth or lying on the ground, it is then that for the first time he would conclude that these were the footprints of a large elephant.

"O brahmin, as this example indicates, when the Buddha appears in this world and teaches the Dharma, the sons and daughters of good families become mendicants. Upon having faith and following pure practices, they turn away from all desires and learn true contentment just as birds take to wing. They keep the precepts, practice meditation, and cultivate wisdom. They therefore enter the first stage of meditation.

"O brahmin, these are known as the footprints of the Buddha and the scars of the elephants' tusks. Note, however, that it is not only on the strength of these observations that the disciples who receive these instructions arrive at the conclusion that the Buddha has attained the realm of the Awakened One, that the Buddha teaches the Dharma well, and that the disciples of the Buddha practice the right practice.

"O brahmin, those disciples will progress, step by step, in their pursuit of the way. And, advancing in various meditations, they will attain the power to know their previous lives and those of others, to know the minds of others, and to know the end of their defilements. O brahmin, these are also called the footprints and tusk scars of the Buddha. However, the disciples of the teaching will not say, 'The World-Honored One is the truly Awakened One' by observing only these signs. They will progress further, free themselves from defilements, and become aware that they have been released from defilements. O brahmin, these are called the footprints and tusk scars of the Buddha. And, at this point, for the first time, the disciples of the teaching will say, 'The World-Honored One is the truly Awakened One.' "

Janussoni was overjoyed, as though light were shed in darkness or something covered over had been uncovered. He left the place vowing that he would remain a follower of the Buddha for life.

(5) At one time, Janussoni came into the presence of the World-Honored One and said, "World-Honored One, is an offering made to a brahmin with the three knowledges a true offering?" The Buddha asked, "What is the nature of the three knowledges?" The brahmin answered, "O World-Honored One, the brahmin of the three knowledges is well versed in the three Vedas: the Rgveda, the Samaveda, and the Yajurveda. On both his father's and his mother's side for as far back as seven generations, there must not be a single case where the family lineage has been stained. He must never be the object of derision; his family name must be honorable and his livelihood pure. He must memorize the sacred books and incantations and be well versed in the terminology, rituals, liturgy, interpretations, stories, and accounts contained in the Vedas. He must be clear with regard to the origin of words and grammar. Then, after having learned the lokayata philosophy of materialism, and after having mastered knowledge of the marks of a great sage, this brahmin may well be called a brahmin of the three knowledges."

The Buddha then stated, "O brahmin, it is true that this is one version of the three knowledges, but it is not so when seen from the standpoint of the true teachings." To this the brahmin asked, "O World-Honored One, what then are the true three knowledges?" The Buddha then gave him the following teaching: "O brahmin, listen carefully to my teaching. When my disciple, pursuing the way to purity, first abandons desire and impurity, then there may still be remnants of the workings of the mind that questions and reasons, he enters the first level of concentration and experiences joy and happiness. At the second level of concentration, he enjoys the joy and happiness coming from meditation after abandoning questioning and reasoning. Advancing and leaving this joy and happiness, he resides in thoughts that are unbiased. Enjoying the happiness of right mind and right thought, he enters into the third level of concentration. Moving ahead, freed from thoughts of happiness and unhappiness, of joy and anxiety, he enters into the fourth concentration, which is the state of mind that is pure and undisturbed, transcending all suffering and pleasure.

"In this state the mind of my disciple is quiescent and clear, free of all wants and desires. His mind is not only clear but also freed of calculation; it is ready to function at all times and is firm and never to be upset by others. And when his mind is directed toward things of the past, then the happenings of the past, from one past life to a million past lives and beyond that can be brought to mind.

Matters such as his names and family lineages during past lives are remembered; moreover his professions, experiences, and life spans, even down to their minor characteristics, are clearly recollected. It is at this stage that he acquires the power of knowing his own and others' past lives, whereby ignorance is destroyed, darkness is dispelled, and light comes into being.

"Next, he will direct his mind toward knowing the births and deaths of other people. With divine eyes that transcend human sight, he is now able to discern that the noble and the base, the beautiful and the ugly, the happy and the unhappy, all appear and disappear according to their actions. Some commit evil with their bodies, mouths, and minds, slander the sages, and harbor impure thoughts. Because of these actions, they fall into the realms of hellish suffering. Others perform good acts with their bodies, mouths, and minds; they refrain from slandering the sages and have right attitudes and understanding. By virtue of their good actions, they are born in the realm of purity. This second wisdom is called knowing others' thoughts. In it ignorance is destroyed, darkness is dispelled, and light comes into being.

"At the next stage, he directs his mind toward the extinction of all defilements. He clearly perceives the reality of suffering, the cause of suffering, the removal of suffering, and the way to the removal of suffering.

"Likewise, he clearly perceives what is defilement, what is the cause of defilement, what is the extinction of defilement, and what is the way to the extinction of defilement. Now, upon having realized this, his mind is freed from the defilement arising from human desires, the defilement arising from existence itself, and the defilement arising from human blindness. Thus, he gains the awareness that he has been freed from these bondages. There arises in him the knowledge that the life of delusion has come to an end; that the pure practices have been completed; that what had to be accomplished has been accomplished; and that he will never again experience birth in delusion. This is the third wisdom, called the extinction of defilements, whereby ignorance is destroyed, darkness is dispelled, and light comes into being. O brahmin, by the expression 'brahmin of the three knowledges' we mean a person who possesses these three wisdoms."

To these instructions, the brahmin replied that, when comparing the three knowledges he had spoken of before with those of the Buddha, he realized that they were inferior, not even one-sixteenth as valuable. And he praised the superiority of the Buddha's teachings.

(6) One evening the World-Honored One, in the presence of the disciples at the lecture hall of the monastery, discoursed as follows: "Be like the moon, my disciples, when you beg alms be circumspect in both mind and demeanor; be humble like a novice. At a layman's house, it is important that you be as humble as a novice at all times. Be as cautious as when one peers into an old well, or looks down from the edge of a mountain cliff, or into an abyss. When approaching a layman's home, it is well to bear this in mind. Kassapa is like the moon when he begs alms, circumspect in both mind and demeanor and humble as a novice. My disciples, tell me what kind of monk should beg alms at a layman's house."

To this the disciples answered that since they all revered the World-Honored One as the source of the Dharma and the center of spiritual refuge, they would bear the Buddha's instructions in mind at all times. At that moment, the Buddha waved his hand in the air and gave the following instructions: "My disciples, just as my hand is unattached to space and is unbound, no matter which home you may call on, a monk must not be attached. He should always bear in mind the thought of enabling those who wish to acquire things to do so, and of enabling those who prefer spiritual virtues to attain them. Just as we feel satisfaction in acquiring things for ourselves, try to find joy and satisfaction in what others attain. It is with this attitude that you must approach the houses of lay people. My disciples, wherever Mahakassapa goes, he harbors no attachment to the house and is not bound in any way.

"My disciples, what do you think are the impure and pure sermons of the Buddha's disciples?"

The disciples simply asked for the Buddha's teachings. The Buddha then gave his instructions: "My disciples, I want you to listen carefully and ponder this. Assume that a disciple has the following thought in mind as he gives his instructions, 'I hope that people will listen to my sermon. I hope that upon having heard my sermon they will rejoice, and upon having rejoiced they will express their feeling of joy.' To deliver a sermon with this thought is delivering an impure sermon. Again, assume that there is another who teaches the Dharma with the thought, 'The Dharma has been presented well by the World-Honored One. Through this Dharma, in this world, one acquires instantaneous rewards. Moreover, this Dharma enables one to realize nirvana, and it can be duly conceived by anyone who is learned and wise. It is for this reason that I want people to listen to the Dharma as I teach it, to realize attainment, and to practice the teachings.' If he can have such thoughts and if his instructions are in accordance with the Dharma, and if he expounds the teachings with deep compassion, then his is called a pure sermon. My disciples, remember that Mahakassapa taught the Dharma in such a manner. I truly expect you to teach the Dharma in the manner of Mahakassapa."

(7) At one time the Buddha, with many disciples, left the Jeta Grove Monastery and entered the country of Kosala to teach the Dharma. Along the way, the Buddha saw roaring flames rising to the sky; avoiding the flames, he sat on the seat prepared for him and said to his disciples, "My disciples, can you all see those roaring flames?" The disciples answered that they could.

The Buddha then said, "My disciples, tell me which do you think is better, to embrace these roaring flames, or to embrace the soft arms and legs of a kshatriya maiden, a daughter of a brahmin, or the woman of a householder?" The disciples answered, "It would be far better to embrace the soft arms and legs of a young lady, since there is no telling how painful it would be to embrace the roaring flames." The Buddha said, "My disciples, I say to you that those who break the precepts, act against the Dharma, hide such actions from others, act like mendicants though they are not really mendicants, or like pure-seekers of the way though they are not such, and whose minds are corrupted and filled with impure thoughts, should embrace the roaring flames, because embracing fire is better than embracing the body of a maiden. The reason is that, in the former situation, the pain and agony may cause death or something near death, but it does not constitute the cause of falling into hell. The latter can become the cause of falling into hell, where there is endless pain and agony."

The Buddha continued, "My disciples, what do you think of a strong man who ties his legs at the shin bone with a strong rope and violently rubs his legs? In doing so his skin is torn, his muscles are damaged, his sinews are cut, his bones are broken. The damage reaches the bone marrow and finally stops there. Under these circumstances, there arises the question whether he prefers to undergo these pains or receive the hospitality of a wealthy kshatriya, a brahmin, or a lay devotee. My disciples, I say to you that for those who are inferior, who have discarded the precepts, and who have acted against the Dharma, it would be better to have both legs crushed. The reason for this is that in the former case, one's suffering is limited to dying or the excruciating pain that approximates the pain of dying; but it does not cause one to fall into hell. In the latter case, one's actions become the cause of falling into hell after death."

The Buddha continued, "My disciples, which do you think is better, to have one's sides slashed by a strong man with a sharpened sword or to be met veneration by a rich kshatriya, brahmin, or lay devotee? Or again, which is better, to have a flaming red-hot metal plate wrapped around one's body by a strong man or to receive food offerings from the heart of a rich kshatriya, brahmin, or lay devotee? Or, again, imagine that a strong man, with red-hot flaming metal tongs, drops a red-hot ball into one's open mouth. The ball burns the lips, mouth, and tongue; it will keep burning the throat, chest, and intestines and then burn right through the body and drop out from the underside. Or, in contrast to this, imagine receiving the food offering of a rich kshatriya, brahmin, or lay devotee coming from the heart. Which is preferable? Again, say that a strong man grabs hold of your head and makes you lie down on a bed of steel, glowing in flames, with a steel pillow. How does this compare with accepting an offering of bedding, made from the heart, from a rich kshatriya, brahmin, or lay devotee? Again, imagine that a strong man were to grasp you, holding you upside down by your feet; he then tosses you into an iron pot with flames blazing, leaving you bobbing up and down like a bubble in a boiling pot. Now, how would this compare to being offered a room by a wealthy kshatriya, brahmin, or lay devotee?

"My disciples, I wish to say to you that all these types of physical pain do not become causes of birth in hell; but those who violate the holy precepts, act in defiance of the Dharma, and then receive offerings of faith from the wealthy create the cause of lasting suffering. Therefore you must think, 'Those who practice offering are granted great benefits; and we shall receive clothing, food, mats, and medicine as offerings in such a manner that our becoming mendicants will not be in vain. In thinking about oneself, one is benefitted when one exerts oneself with diligence. The benefitting of others also results from such actions.' "

When the Buddha finished his instructions, sixty of his followers spat out warm blood. Another sixty disciples all declared in unison that the Buddha's path was extremely difficult and left it to return to lay life. Another sixty mendicants were freed from attachments and relieved of their cravings and desires.

2. Pasenadi

(1) Word that the World-Honored One was about to visit Savatthi for the purpose of spreading the Dharma also reached the royal palace. King Pasenadi had this thought in mind, "It is said that a prince of the Sakya clan has renounced worldly life and become a Buddha. It would be good to meet with him." In time the guidance given and influence exerted by the Buddha at Jeta Grove Monastery moved the king to call on the Buddha. After an exchange of salutations, the Buddha instructed him as follows: "O great king, there are four kinds of people. There are those who from darkness go further into darkness; then there are those who from darkness enter into light; again, there are those who enter into darkness from light; finally there are those who from light enter into light. The first type of people, who from darkness enter into darkness, are those who are born in poverty, who have no faith and are of lowly character, who never know how to share with others, who constantly harbor perverted views, and who have no respect for mendicants. These people may find themselves in hell after their deaths.

"The next type of people, who from darkness enter into light, may be poor in this life but have strong beliefs with noble ideas, are willing to share things with others with a serene mind, respect mendicants, and pursue acts of purity; they are reborn in a highly preferable place after their deaths. The third type of people, who from light enter into darkness, are those who are wealthy and prosperous in this world but have no faith. They are miserly and do not know how to give; they harbor perverted views and show no respect to mendicants. These people, upon meeting death, may fall into hell. The fourth type of people, who from light enter into light, are those who are rich and prosperous in this world, have faith and noble hearts, enjoy sharing things with others with a sincere mind, show deep respect to mendicants, and are born in a higher realm upon death. O great king, there are these four types of people in this world." King Pasenadi, overjoyed with these instructions, returned to his palace that day, and from then on he often visited the Buddha at Jeta Grove Monastery.

(2) One day the king visited the Buddha and bowed down reverently. The Buddha said, "O great king, at this noon hour, from where did you come?" The king answered, "World-Honored One, I am always occupied with my duties as a king. I was born into a kshatriya family; I was anointed with the sprinkling of the consecrated water and ascended the throne. Invested with the power of rule, I preserve the peace of this royal land; I do so in the midst of the world of the five desires. It is not a simple matter to govern a large territory." The Buddha said, "O great king, suppose a reliable person were to come here from the east and say to you, 'O great king, I have come from the east and have seen that a great mountain with its summit reaching up to the sky has started to move, crushing every form of life along the way. I think it is in order that proper measures be taken.' Along with this person, suppose that messengers arrive from the west, from the

south, and from the north bearing the same message, hoping for some appropriate measures to be taken. O great king, if and when such dreadful things did occur, we would be reminded that human birth is hard to come by. Now what would you propose to do about this predicament?"

The king then said to the Buddha, "When such dreadful things occur, I realize that it is rare to have human life. I believe that there is no other way for me than to do good in accordance with the Dharma and accumulate merit." The Buddha then asked the king, "O great king, both old age and death are falling upon you. In this situation what will you do?" To this the king answered, "In this situation, I believe that there is no other way for me than to do good in accordance with the Dharma and accumulate merit. O World-Honored One, despite the power a ruler may wield, old age and death are beyond his power. O World-Honored One, within the monarch's fold there is a group of magicians and sorcerers who can stop oncoming foes, but against old age and death there is nothing that one can do except to do that which is pure and in accordance with the Dharma, and to accumulate virtue against creeping old age and death." On this day, too, feeling appreciative of the Buddha's instructions, King Pasenadi returned to the palace glad.

(3) On yet another day the king paid a visit to the Buddha. On that occasion he asked whether the Enlightened One called himself an Awakened One. To this question the Buddha answered, "O great king, if there is anyone in this world who deserves to be called an Awakened One, that person is none other than myself. I am the Awakened One." The king then said that in the world there were many mendicants who, like the Buddha, had disciples, gave instructions, and were respected by the people. He said, "There are persons such as Purana Kassapa, Ajita Kesakambalin, Pakudha Kaccayana, Sanjaya Belatthiputta, Mahavira, and so forth. So far, I have had the opportunity to ask all of them the same question but none of them have called themselves an Awakened One. On the other hand, the World-Honored One is young and has become a mendicant just recently. I wonder how you can make such an assertion."

To this the World-Honored One said, "O great king, there are four things in this world that must not be taken lightly because of their youth. They are a royal prince, a serpent, fire, and a disciple of the Buddha. These things you should not disregard merely because of their age." This day, too, was a good one for the king, who was awestruck by the dignity of the Buddha; he returned in happiness to his castle.

(4) The consort of King Pasenadi, named Queen Mallika, was very wise. She was the daughter of the leader of the chaplet designers and was selected from among many to become the consort of the king. Long before, she had sought refuge in the Buddha and deeply appreciated the Dharma; she often gave spiritual guidance to the king.

There was a householder in Savatthi who lost his only son. This householder was in deep sorrow, unable to do any work, and not eating at all; he was always at the cemetery seeking to find out where his son had gone. Then one day he set out for Jeta Grove Monastery, and after worshipping the Buddha he sat down.

The World-Honored One, having heard the cause of the householder's sorrow, instructed him, "O householder, because of love there is uneasiness, sorrow, suffering, worry, and heartache." The householder, hearing this, was not happy at all. He then joined a company of gamblers and told them what had happened. He bitterly criticized the instructions of the Buddha, which made little sense to him. The gamblers, hearing this, agreed with the householder: it was because of love that happiness and pleasure arose, and there was no reason why such things as sadness or anxiety should arise; they joined in the criticism. This matter gradually spread to the palace and reached the ears of King Pasenadi. The king then mentioned this to the queen, who said to him that if something was said by the World-Honored One, it must be true. As the disciple follows the words of the master, the queen adhered to the words of the Buddha. But the king found himself unable to accept these words and showed displeasure.

Queen Mallika sent the brahmin Nalijangha to the Buddha to inquire as to the meaning of the Buddha's words. The Buddha then said to the brahmin, "O brahmin, there was once a young woman who lost her mother and was crazed over this loss, wandering from street to street, asking everyone wherever she went, 'Where is my mother?' There was also a woman who had lost her husband and who also pleaded to know where her husband had gone. There was a mother who had lost her child and wandered here and there seeking the infant. There was a loving couple who committed suicide when they knew they would be separated by force. Is it not because of love that there is anxiety, sorrow, suffering, uneasiness, and agony?" The brahmin told this to Queen Mallika, who later relayed this to the king and said, "O king, do you love our only daughter Princess Vajra?"

The king answered he did. The queen continued, "Tell me, O king, if some mishap should befall her, would you not be filled with anxiety and sorrow?" The king answered that he would. She asked, "O king, do you love me?" He answered that he did. The queen asked, "O king, if something were to happen to me, what would you do?" To this the king answered that if something were to happen to her, he would be in deep anxiety and sorrow. On hearing these words the queen remarked, "O king, this is the reason why the Buddha, the wisest of all men, has said that it is because of love that we have in our hearts anxiety, sorrow, suffering, worries, and anguish." The king then exclaimed, "Oh, what a great teaching! Mallika, my beloved queen, the World-Honored One has penetrating insight. Forgive my thoughtlessness!" The king then stood up from his throne and pulled his robe over one shoulder. Putting his hands together as he faced the direction where the Buddha resided, he exclaimed with joy three times, "O World-Honored One, I hereby seek refuge in the Buddha!"

3. Instructions to Nanda

(1) Nanda, who had previously become a mendicant under the guidance of the World-Honored One, was able to forget the power he once held as a worldly king. However, he was unable to erase the memory of Princess Sundari, who was known as the most beautiful maiden in the land. Although he donned the yellow robes of a monk, his mind wandered off toward the inner palace of Kapilavatthu; and he often spent his days in a trance. Forgetting that he was an ordained monk he wore ornaments on his body, put on soft clothing, and colored his eyelids. Bearing a beautiful bowl, he walked the streets to receive alms. To this there were voices raised in sharp criticism from within and without the Sangha, and the Buddha was deeply concerned.

One afternoon, the Buddha left the Jeta Grove and, taking Nanda by the hand, led him up the mountain called Exotic Fragrance. Just then strong gale winds shook the forest. The trees rubbed against each other and started burning. In no time black smoke filled the sky; the flames devoured all the trees and scorched the heavens. Hundreds of monkeys in the trees were enveloped in smoke and burned. They issued cries of agony and tried frantically to put out the flames that burned their bodies. Just at that moment, the Buddha pointed to a female monkey and said, "Nanda, compare the woman you crave and this monkey, and you will see that there is nothing that distinguishes them."

Nanda felt displeasure at the Buddha's words. The Buddha then led Nanda to the place of heavenly beings. Here, amid the rain of mandarava blossoms, Nanda could see the beautiful forms of heavenly maidens adorned with beautiful sleeved garments and dancing to the music of five instruments. Nanda was awestruck by the beauty of these celestial beings; and as he observed them he realized that when compared to their beauty, his betrothed, regarded as the most beautiful woman in the land, was no better than monkeys on the mountain. The Buddha, seeing this, told Nanda that if he wished for beauty on the level of heavenly beings, he must first pursue the way. Then, gradually directing Nanda's mind to the Dharma, the Buddha made him understand that for mendicants it was not appropriate to wear soft clothing, paint one's eyelids, or walk with a translucent bowl in hand; the appropriate thing to do was to live in the woods, receive alms, wear discarded clothing, and practice self-restraint by being freed of all wants and desires. Nanda was impressed by these instructions; entering the forest, he practiced self-restraint and gained peace of mind. Achieving deliverance from delusion, he sang the song of joy:

> My heart was perverse, concerned only about appearances.
>
> My mind wandered here and there, clouded by craving.
>
> Guided by the Buddha through his compassionate means,
>
> I now can do right, freed from all delusions and greed.

(2) The offering of Jeta Grove Monastery had greatly influenced many people. Around this time, Sirima and Sirivadda, two brothers, became the

Buddha's disciples. Sirivadda, the younger, was respected by the people as well as by the disciples of the same monastery. The other brother, Sirima, was said to be inferior to this brother and was scorned by others. Despite this, Sirima retreated to a quiet place and, concentrating his mind, attained enlightenment. The people, however, still praised the younger brother and disparaged the elder brother. Sirima realized that the praises of the people would only hamper his younger brother's pursuit of the way and composed the following verses as an encouragement to him:

> For the mind that does not reside at peace,
>
> Men's praises have no meaning.
>
> For the mind that resides in peace,
>
> Men's slanders have no meaning.

Sirivadda, hearing this, was greatly moved and, devoting himself to his Dharma practices, was able to realize an enlightenment equal to that of his brother.

4. Dialogue of the Bodhisattvas

(1) One night the Buddha instructed his disciples through the early hours of the morning. The voice of the Buddha resounded in the clear sky and, hearing the Buddha's voice, the bodhisattvas of the four directions gathered. At that time the following dialogue developed.

Manjusri said, "If the mind, which is the basis of actions, is one, why is it that there are so many varied results? Some are born in favorable places. Others are born in unfavorable places. Some are fair, while others are ugly. Regarding suffering and happiness, there are all kinds. Why is it that from one mind there arise so many varied results?" In answer to this the Bodhisattva Alokamukha instructed, "In regard to all that exists, there is no determined nature. Thus existing things do not know each other. But we cannot say that there is no connection between or among them. Observe swiftly flowing water, which keeps on flowing endlessly. The flowing water that is already downstream and the flowing water that is still upstream constitute two different rivers. Likewise, the burning flame keeps on burning endlessly, but the flame that burned a while back and the present flame are separate flames. Our five senses and minds work in the same manner. Through each of these senses all kinds of suffering are created; but in reality, each of these sufferings is brought about totally unknown to one another. Thus the basic nature of things does not of itself cause any suffering, but each action results in suffering."

The Bodhisattva Manjusri then posed the question, "We know that all beings are combinations of the four great elements and by nature are characterized by non-substantiality. Why then is it that these are the results of suffering, pleasure, good, and evil? Is it not true that in considering the basic nature of dharmas, there should never be good or bad, pure or impure?"

To this the Bodhisattva Ratnamukha gave the answer, "Whatever effect arises from one's actions, no other agent causes it to happen. This is similar to the case when a clear mirror reflects one's form as one stands before it. There is no object in the mirror or on the other side of the mirror that causes this to happen. The nature and effect of karmic forces is something like this. For instance, the soil and the seed sown are originally separate, but by the workings of nature they are brought closely together. A person suffering in agony does not suffer because something inflicts the suffering, but rather it is the result of his own action."

The Bodhisattva Manjusri then raised this question: "We all know that the Buddha was enlightened to one Dharma. So why is it that the Dharma he expounds is unlimited, that his voice resounds throughout the immeasurable worlds, and that his teachings awaken countless beings?"

To this Bodhisattva Gunamukha answered, "He is similar to the basic nature of fire, which is one and yet burns all kinds of things; to the water of the great ocean, which does not change in taste even though hundreds of thousands of rivers flow into it; and to the great earth, which also is one yet is able to grow all kinds of seedlings from itself."

(2) The Bodhisattva Manjusri then raised another question. "We have been told that once a person receives the Buddha's instructions, all of his anxieties should be eradicated. Why is it then that although a person hears the right Dharma, he is not able at once to eliminate all sufferings and anxieties?" The Bodhisattva Dharmamukha responded, "What you are describing is a person who listens well but does not practice. One cannot understand and accept the Buddha-Dharma by listening alone. Such a person is like someone who is floating on the surface of the water; he becomes unduly afraid of drowning and dies of thirst and dehydration. Fully to accept the Dharma, one must truly follow the way as instructed. Moreover, there are those who starve to death because they refuse to eat, although abundant food is given to them; there is the capable doctor who is well versed in medicine and yet cannot treat himself; there is the poor person who, day in and day out, counts the treasures belonging to another person but does not have even a penny of his own; there is the deaf person who plays beautiful music and brings joy to others but cannot hear a note himself; and again, there is the person who teaches the true Dharma to the many who come to hear him but who, in his inner self, has no true virtue. People who merely listen are exactly like these."

The Bodhisattva Manjusri then said, "Of the many gems in the Buddha-Dharma, wisdom is of the highest value. Despite this, the Buddha, in his instructions to others, highly praises the virtues of practicing charity, observing the precepts, forbearance, endeavor, and mental concentration, as well as compassion, blissfully acting, and gladly sharing with others. By adhering to only one of them, could one not attain liberation from one's attachment to the ego?"

To this the Bodhisattva Bodhimukha answered, "Not all the Buddhas throughout the three worlds have attained Buddhahood by adhering to only one Dharma. In fact, the Buddha is fully aware that all beings differ in their capacities. He teaches the Dharma in accordance with their basic natures. To those who do not share things with others, the Buddha praises the act of charity; to those who do not practice the precepts, the Buddha praises the observing of precepts; to those who are easily angered, forbearance is taught; to those who tend to slacken in their actions, the Buddha urges perseverance; to those whose minds tend to wander, the Buddha teaches mental concentration; to those who adhere to ignorance, the Buddha stresses wisdom; to the heartless the Buddha teaches compassion; to those whose intention is to harm others, the Buddha teaches great compassion; to those in agony, the Buddha bestows bliss and happiness; and to those who have strong feelings of hate and craving, the Buddha praises the virtues of equanimity and brotherhood. It is only by employing such means that those who aspire for the first time may gradually understand the truth of all Dharmas. To cite an analogy, just as we strengthen the foundation in building a house, the acts of charity and observance of precepts are the foundations of the practice of a bodhisattva. Likewise, just as a fortified castle withstands the onslaught of foes, forbearance and endeavor will protect the bodhisattva. Just as the powerful king governs his country with authority and virtue, mental concentration and wisdom are the means that enable the bodhisattva to achieve peace of mind. Again, as the universal monarch enjoys all the pleasures of this world, the virtues of practicing compassion and selfless giving bring pleasure to the bodhisattva."

(3) The Bodhisattva Manjusri posed the following question to the bodhisattvas; "Whereas all buddhas have crossed the ocean of samsara aboard the One Vehicle, why is it that sermons and other means of edification differ in each country? Does it mean that unless one acquires all of these ways of edification, it is impossible to attain enlightenment?" To this question the Bodhisattva Bhadramukha replied, "The Dharma of the universe is eternal; the highest Dharma is one Dharma. Those who are freed from all obstructions can be liberated from transmigration by this one Dharma. The body of all buddhas is the one Dharmakaya, one mind and one wisdom. All buddha lands are equally adorned; but because people all have different karma, they do not all see the same thing when they look at them. Thus the Buddha, the Buddha's doctrine, the Buddha's land, and the Buddha's discourses cannot be observed in their true light by the ordinary person. Only those who have pure minds and who have achieved their aspirations can see the true, ultimate reality. Such people have opened their clear eyes of wisdom. According to the aspiration of the person, along with his action and the results of that action, the Buddha enables him to see truth itself. This is possible because the power of the Buddha is totally free from all restrictions. In the land of the Buddha no one appears different from another; there is no one who harbors hatred or craving. If any difference appears to a person, then it is the result of his action."

(4) The Bodhisattva Bodhimukha then asked, "What must a bodhisattva do in order to realize pure action in regard to body, mouth, and mind, to acquire superior wisdom, to serve as a haven for persons in need, to become the cause of salvation for others, to become an island of refuge, and to become a master and guide of men?" To this the Bodhisattva Manjusri answered, "When a bodhisattva serves his parents, he hopes to secure peace for a long time by doing all in his power to protect them and provide for them. When he is with his wife and children, he hopes to be freed from the shackles of love and the bondage of family life. When he listens to music being played, he hopes to enjoy the bliss of the

Dharma. When he is in the seclusion of his room, he enters the realm of the wise and hopes to be released forever from any impurities. When he is about to practice charity, he wishes to offer all and be freed from the attachment to things. When he finds himself among his peers, he hopes that it will be a gathering of buddhas. When he meets with misfortune, he wishes to enjoy peace of mind, undisturbed by anything. When he seeks refuge in the Buddha, he hopes to arouse the aspiration for enlightenment by experiencing the great path with all beings. When he seeks refuge in the Dharma, he aspires to acquire wisdom as deep as the ocean by immersing himself in the sutras and teachings with all beings. And when he seeks refuge in the Sangha, he together with all beings aspires to be freed from all obstructions by bringing together and guiding all sentient beings.

"Again, when putting on his clothing he does not forget to regard the roots of good and deep self-reflection as his garments. As he excretes waste, he hopes to free himself of greed, anger, and ignorance. As he looks up to the way leading to a higher place, he aspires to free himself from bondage to the three realms by pursuing the way of the highest realm. As he looks at the way leading to a lower place, he aspires to enter deep into the realm of the Buddha's doctrine by becoming yielding and humble. Whenever he sees a bridge, he aspires to build a bridge of the Buddha's doctrine and at all times to help people reach the other shore. When he sees a person in deep anxiety and sorrow, he reminds himself to seek release from attachment to things that are constantly changing and crumbling.

"Whenever he sees people who indulge in the pleasures of the body, he should aspire to achieve the highest bliss and be freed from the ills of the body. Whenever he sees people in good health, he should hope to realize the diamond-like Dharmakaya, forever freed from aging and withering away. Wherever he sees a person stricken with sickness, he should realize the temporary nature of human existence and hope to be freed from all kinds of suffering. Again, when seeing a monk who has renounced all worldly ties, he should quiet and control his mind. When seeing a person engaging in arguments, he should employ his superior persuasive abilities and convince believers of other faiths. When observing a monarch, he must aspire to become a ruler in the Dharma and turn the Wheel of the Dharma with no obstructions. When partaking of delicious food, he must exercise temperance, limiting his wants and not being attached to the desires of the flesh. When given untempting food, he should push aside attachment. At extremely hot times, he should push away the heat of craving and desires and try to achieve cool and placid concentration; and when it is freezing cold, he should hope to achieve the cool quietude of deliverance. Again, when reading a sutra (scripture), he should adhere completely to the Dharma. When looking at the Buddha, upon having acquired the eyes of the truth of the Buddha, he should wish to see that which is superior to all that exists. When retiring at night, having the activities of the mind, speech, and body subdued, he must purify his mind and aspire to be freed from impurities. When waking in the morning, he must aspire to become aware of all things by realizing the highest truth. These are the ways by which the bodhisattva controls his actions of body, speech, and mind. This is the way by which all virtues may be attained."

(5) The Bodhisattva Manjusri then asked for a clarification of the virtue of aspiring for enlightenment:

(i) I have elaborated on the pure actions of a bodhisattva, but what is the great virtue of such actions and what are their profound implications?

To this the Bodhisattva Bhadramukha answered, "A bodhisattva, while in the realm of samsara, aspires to follow the way; and the virtues of even one thought are indeed vast and unlimited.

The Buddha nature is the cause; the teachings are the conditions. It is only by these causes and conditions that deep trust can be put in the Buddha. Not to seek pleasure or treasures or fame or easy ways, but to relieve people of their suffering—this must be your aspiration!

(ii) It is only upon putting one's faith in the Buddha's doctrine and in the ways of a bodhisattva that a bodhisattva can arouse the thought of enlightenment. Faith is truly the basis of the way and the mother of all virtues. By continuing to do good and eradicating all doubts, one can realize the highest way.

Faith drives away impurity. Upon clearing the mind, it eradicates arrogance and becomes the source of respect by others. Faith is placed in the Dharma store and is the first of all treasures. It becomes the pure hand that receives merits.

Faith is giving to all with no limitations; and the bliss of faith enables one to enter the realm of the Buddha's doctrine.

Faith enhances the virtues of wisdom and enables one to realize Buddhahood without fail.

Faith makes manifest all workings of the Buddha's doctrine; its strength is firm, never to be broken. It also eliminates the causes of anxieties and leads people to seek the Buddha's merits.

Faith sets no boundaries and spares one from calamities. It enables one to transcend the realms of the demons and realize the highest enlightenment.

Faith is the source of unbreakable virtues and is the seedling of the tree of wisdom. As it develops, it makes manifest the virtues of the Buddha.

Faith is excellent and not easily attainable, truly like the udumbara blossom.

When one has constant faith in the Dharma, one will never tire of listening to the Dharma. When one has trust in the Sangha at all times, that faith will never waver.

(iii) The deeds of a person of faith are pure; and this enables one to approach good people, to do good, and to acquire great power. One's wisdom keeps growing, and one is protected by the buddhas at all times. Therefore aspire for the way, follow the ways of the Buddha, be born in the house of the Buddha, and pursue the practices of wondrous skillful means. The mind that believes and rejoices is pure; this unexcelled mind grows, enables the person of faith to practice the six perfections, and makes one aspire all the more to follow the way of the Buddha. Thus a mind set on the Buddha, never unstable, enables one to see at all times the Buddha of unlimited virtues.

Having seen that the Buddha is eternal, having known that the Dharma will never crumble, and having acquired the power of speaking impressively, he now spreads the boundless Dharma, leading people while guided by sympathy. With a mind of great compassion, he enjoys the profound Dharma.

(iv) By his efforts the true Dharma will prevail in the world, never to crumble, and all the good, all the ways, and all the excellent treasures will appear in this world.

For those who do not know of the ways leading to spiritual release, and for those who tend to cling to samsara, a bodhisattva discards country and treasures and seeks the quietude of serenity, renouncing all worldly attachments.

Again, even if he chooses to stay in the world and give guidance to all beings, he is not polluted by worldly impurities, just as the lotus blossom remains pure. And when perverted views lead one to suffering, he employs skillful means to present the Dharma, leading people to enlightenment.

A bodhisattva makes the Buddha manifest and shows the way leading to the Dharma and the Sangha. Those who receive this light are able to realize the highest enlightenment by its unlimited virtues.

(v) The light of the Buddha leads one to awakening, makes one aspire for the way, and ferries one across the ocean of craving and desires.

The light leads one to awakening and with the water of deliverance removes the thirst of lust and desires.

The light leads one to awakening and enables one happily to enjoy and pursue the way of the Buddha.

The light leads one to awakening and enables one to realize that nothing really exists and that there is no true nonexistence, that everything is like the moon reflected in water, and that everything is an illusion.

The light leads one to awakening, and while enabling the Dharma to prevail, it leads one to respect the good and pure and protect the wise. It enables the unlimited virtues of the Dharma to flow.

The light leads one to awakening and enables one to think on the Buddha, observe the Buddha, and realize birth in the Buddha's land.

The light leads one to awakening, to hear the Dharma, to expound on it, to let others share the joy, to guard it, to transmit it, and to let the true Dharma prevail.

The light leads one to awakening and enables one to make all voices in the world sound as the voice of the Buddha.

(vi) One with eyesight can see the sun, but the blind cannot. Those who seek the way can see the light, but those of perverted views cannot. The jewel-bedecked castle, the treasure vehicle, sweet foods, and gems are all received naturally by the virtuous but never by the nonvirtuous. There are many inconceivable things in life, such as one's karmic forces, the skillful changes of form by dragons, and the powers of the gods, but there is nothing to match the power of the Buddha.

A warrior with a sword can be seen reflected on the limpid surface of water without showing any trace of hate or craving. The freedom of the Buddha's mind is exactly the same. Those who attain perfect freedom, who have the merit to save all beings with a voice sweet and mellow, have the power to suppress demons and to bring happiness to all without fail. I have now made known to you the merits of those who have entered the sea of the Dharma and have fathomed it. Those who are now exposed to the Dharma should accept it and spread it to others.

When the Bodhisattva Bhadramukha taught these words, the worlds in the ten directions shook strongly six times. The palaces of the demons ceased to glow, and all the ways of evil disappeared.

Chapter 2

RAJAGAHA

1. Uggasena and Talaputa

(1) It happened that the World-Honored One stayed for a time in the Jeta Grove, at Anathapindika Monastery of Savatthi, and then later returned to Rajagaha and spent the third rainy season at the Bamboo Grove Monastery. The master of acrobatics Uggasena was in town with his wife and his troupe of artists. Uggasena was the son of a rich merchant of this city. Formerly, when a group of entertainers came to the town and demonstrated their skills before the king, Uggasena fell in love with a maiden in the group and he left home and joined them.

In the beginning, when he was in training, his wife and other performers of the troupe laughed in derision and scorn at his lack of accomplishment, and he shed tears. But he persevered until he was able to become the head of the troupe and lead it from place to place for performances. He himself was to perform one day on a pole over sixty feet high, and people gathered eagerly to see him. The World-Honored One, with his disciples, was also present. The Buddha let Moggallana employ superhuman powers to reach the same height as Uggasena and teach the Dharma to him. The time must have been ripe for Uggasena, because he greatly appreciated the Dharma, and after sliding down the pole he threw himself before the Buddha and humbly requested that he become a disciple of the Buddha. The Buddha permitted this, and all the members of the group became disciples of the Buddha. Soon Uggasena achieved enlightenment and became one of the arhats.

(2) Talaputa was also a performer of Rajagaha. He led a troupe of five hundred girls, gave performances, and played at festivities in the towns and villages. At times, when invited, he also had his girls perform in the palace. After Uggasena became a monk, Talaputa was also inspired to join the Sangha and called on the Buddha at Jeta Grove Monastery. He said, "O World-Honored One, I have heard from my seniors that a performer amuses the audience by telling them something other than the truth. For this, upon his death, he is reborn in the realm of the heavens where all right thought is forgotten. What is your opinion on this matter?"

To this the Buddha answered that this was one question he should not ask of the Awakened One. Despite this, Talaputa asked the Buddha three times. Each time the Buddha did not give an answer. Finally, when the same question was asked a fourth time, the Buddha gave the following answer: "O Talaputa, a performer who arouses peoples' desires, causes confusion in the minds of the sincere by clowning, and causes others to lose sincerity is sure to fall into hell. What you have heard from your seniors is not the truth. Those who have distorted views will be born either in the realm of hell or in the realm of beasts."

When Talaputa heard this, he burst into tears. The Buddha then reminded him that he should not have asked such a question. To this Talaputa responded, "O World-Honored One, I shed tears not because you enlightened me about a dreadful future but because my seniors have deceived me into thinking that I would be born in heaven." Talaputa then listened intently to the teachings of the Buddha and then, having deep faith, became a mendicant, gradually worked through the practices, and became enlightened. He composed the following verses to express the many difficulties he encountered and the manner in which he controlled his mind:

(i) In time I shall live in a mountain cave, realizing the impermanence of all that exists.

In time I shall wear a tattered yellow robe, free of all attachments to things, free of greed, anger, and ignorance, and find peace in the forest.

In time I shall overcome death, old age, and sickness and reside in the forest with no anxieties.

In time I shall sever the vines of the thirst of desires; conquer devils with the sword of wisdom; never be at the mercy of laziness; never be bothered by the flames arising from sight, hearing, taste, and feeling; never despair when slandered; never feel elated when praised; reside in perfect peace in the Dharma; and look forward to the good day of fulfillment.

(ii) O mind of mine, how long has it been since you claimed to feel no need to stay a householder? Now after renunciation, why, oh! why do you not endeavor?

O mind of mine, how often did you entice me, saying that birds with beautiful feathers deep in the mountains and the thunder of Indra bring joy to one who resides in the forest!

Now having left household, friends, and worldly pleasures, you still, alas! know no happiness.

Seeing that all that exists changes, did you not pursue the way of impermanence? The Buddha has taught, 'The mind is like an unsettled monkey. Control over it can only come when it is freed from lust.'

To be deluded by beauty and to pursue life is the way to suffering. Even to be attracted to the mind leads to the suffering of hell.

(iii) Unaware that one is surrounded by leopards and tigers while in the forest where peacocks and waterfowl stay, one must now be freed from lust, losing no time. O mind of mine, have you not encouraged me? Pursue the way leading to release. Sever the roots of suffering and free yourself of needless calculations. Follow the way of the sages; teach to all everywhere while residing in the quietude of the forest. O mind of mine, was it not you that encouraged me? O mind, formless and always galloping off, I shall no longer need you, for in craving there is intense pain and great fear. I shall aspire for and pursue the way of deliverance. O mind of mine, wherever I found myself, I heeded your dictates.

For up to now this mind was disturbed and I followed its dictates; but now, having awakened, I shall be the pilot of my mind from today on.

(iv) O mind of mine, enable me to cross the sea of delusion, for I am no longer in my former state of delusion. I have no reason to be controlled by you, for I have accepted the way of the sages.

I am no longer one bound for extinction. The mountains, the rivers, and the oceans, too, in all six directions, all are impermanent and are causes for unhappiness. O mind of mine, where will you find happiness? In a herd of deer, in a flock of peacocks, or in the cool of a summer shower! Even lying asleep like a log on the floor of a cave in the mountains is like lying on cotton.

As the Buddha has taught, find contentment with what is provided. Avoid wrongful ways. Seek guidance from the sacred. Reside in the forest of beauty; enter the mountain of happiness. O mind of mine, attain the shore of enlightenment.

2. Pancasikha

(1) In this manner the World-Honored One spread the Dharma in and around Rajagaha, centering around the Bamboo Grove Monastery, at times going to the east and at times heading toward the west. At one time, when the Buddha was staying in the Indasala Cave on Mount Vediyaka located north of the brahmin village Ambasanda, east of Rajagaha, the god Indra wished to visit the Buddha. Accompanied by other gods, he went up to Mount Vediyaka.

Pancasikha, a son of a Gandhabba, taking along a lapis lazuli harp made of yellow wood, followed the god Indra.

Mount Vediyaka was enveloped by the glow of the gods. The people of the nearby villages were terribly frightened, thinking that there was a dreadful conflagration.

Indra, seeing the Buddha in meditation, instructed Pancasikha, "Pancasikha, the Buddha is in meditation, and it is difficult to approach him at this time. You must first entertain the Buddha with your music. I shall follow you."

Saying, "Yes," Pancasikha, with his lapis lazuli harp in his hand, approached the cave where the Buddha was staying, played the harp, and sang a song. In the song he praised the virtues of the Buddha, the Dharma, and the Sangha. Then he sang about his pure love:

(i) O beautiful princess Sunlight, who art like the rays of the sun, may thy father Cimpala enjoy prosperity, for he who is the light of the world is truly the source of my happiness.

Just as the gentle breeze brings great relief to those who labor in the burning sun, just as clear water gives pleasure to those with parched throats, O princess of the sun god, thou art the center of my affections.

Like the Dharma, the center of the sage's affections, like the medicine that brings relief to the sick, like food for the starving, thou hast stilled my heart as with pure water.

(ii) Just as the great elephant whose body rages with fever dips into the cool waters of the lake amid the pollen of lotus blossoms, I too find repose in thy bosom.

Like the great elephant, who, pierced by a spear, moves violently despite fences and poles, I, too, am dazzled by thy beauty and know not right from wrong.

My heart forever clings to thee, never to find release, like a fish with a hook imbedded within. Oh, what a great change! O princess, hold me in thine embrace and with loving eyes keep watch over me. This is my only wish.

(iii) At first my love was that of youth, but now, princess with wavy hair, it has broadened almost endlessly.

May virtue like the virtue of selfless giving to the Buddha be thine forever. Great is the virtue of my devotion; may thou receive it all. Just as the Buddha practiced perfect meditation, cultivated his mind with utmost sincerity and right concentration, and sought liberation, I say to Sunlight, 'I wish to have thee.'

Just as the Buddha rejoiced on achieving highest enlightenment, I, too, shall rejoice on becoming one with thee.

(iv) If Indra, lord of the Tavatimsa heaven, were to permit me one wish, I should choose thee. So great is my love.

My intelligent princess, I revere thy father as I do the forest of sala trees in full bloom, for he hath given thee the life I cherish.

(2) The World-Honored One, listening to the music of the lapis lazuli harp and the words of the song, made the following remark, "Pancasikha, your strings are in harmony with the words. Tell me where you learnt this song." To this Pancasikha responded, "O World-Honored One, it goes back to the time when you were under the nigrodha tree on the banks of the river Neranjara. At that time I was in love with Bhadda, also called Sunlight, the daughter of Tumburu, the king of Gandhabbas. However, the princess already had a lover, Sikhandhi, son of the chariot driver Matali. No matter how hard I thought about her, there was no way I could meet her. Then I took my harp and stood in front of the palace of Tumburu and played the harp and sang this song. Presently Sunlight Bhadda came from inside the house and said, 'I have not as yet been able to pay homage in person to the World-Honored One. The other day at the ball held in the Tavatimsa heaven, I was told about him. Today, in your song, you praised him most highly. This is why I have

chosen to meet with you today.' O World-Honored One, at a later date I was able to win her."

In this way was Indra able to get the World-Honored One to come out of his mental concentration so that he could meet him.

3. The Famine in Vesali

Just when the World-Honored One was at the Bamboo Grove Monastery and was spreading the teachings in four directions, the neighboring state of Vesali was struck by famine and epidemic. People died one after the other; and everyone was filled with fear, not knowing what to do.

The nobles in power had invited one of the six masters of the non-Buddhist teachings to drive away the demons. But because of the influence of another strong faction, messengers were sent to the World-Honored One. King Bimbisara, relaying the tragic situation, asked the World-Honored One to come and instruct them. The Buddha consented to this request, and the king repaired the road leading to the river Ganges and had his subjects escort the Buddha. The Buddha crossed the river Ganges and, having gone as far as 30 miles, set his feet on the land of Vesali. Immediately, the forces of the demons waned and the epidemic gradually subsided. The disciple Ananda chanted the Ratna Sutra and, circling the castle walls, sprinkled water about. The demons finally fled, and the epidemic was completely eradicated. The Buddha stayed at Vesali for two months to teach the Dharma and then returned to the Bamboo Grove Monastery.

4. Sariputta's Sermon

(1) Once again the World-Honored One left the Bamboo Grove Monastery, headed west toward Baranasi, and stayed at the Deer Park. One day the World-Honored One gave his disciples instructions on the Dharma: "My disciples, it was here at Baranasi that the Buddha set into motion the Wheel of the highest Dharma; this was never done by anyone else or at any other place in this world. By this the teaching of the Four Noble Truths was made clear and presented. 'What are the Four Noble Truths?' you may ask. They are the truths of suffering, the cause of suffering, the extinction of suffering, and the way leading to the extinction of suffering. My disciples, it was truly here that the Wheel of the highest Dharma was set into motion.

"O my disciples, you must revere Sariputta and Moggallana and accept them as your teachers. They are wise and are teachers of those who follow the ways of purity. O my disciples, Sariputta is like the mother who gave birth to you and Moggallana is like the mother who raised you. Sariputta guides those who have just entered the Sangha and Moggallana elevates them to reach enlightenment. Sariputta can instruct you on the Dharma through the Four Noble Truths." Having said this, the Buddha left the hall and went into his room.

(2) After the Buddha left the hall, Sariputta addressed those present: "Friends, the Buddha, here at Deer Park, taught the highest Dharma, which was never before spoken by anyone anywhere in this world. The Buddha elucidated the Four Noble Truths of suffering, the cause of suffering, the extinction of

suffering, and the way leading to the extinction of suffering. Friends, what is the truth of suffering? It means that birth is suffering, old age is suffering, death is suffering, and worry, sorrow, pain, anxiety, and agony are all suffering. Not having that which one wants is suffering. All in all, human existence is in itself suffering. What is birth? Every being is born into a specific species and inherits the conditions that are a part of that species. What are calamities and pain, and how does one suffer extreme mental anguish? What is sadness? When calamities strike and the pain is felt, one is bewildered and saddened, and in deep grief one cries out in agony. What is suffering? It is the pain that man feels with his body. What is affliction? It is the suffering that one experiences with one's mind. What is agony? It is the state in which one becomes heartbroken and hopeless as one encounters misfortune and suffering. What is the suffering resulting from not having what one wants? It is when a person wishes not to be born even when the conditions to be born are all present. Likewise, human life cannot escape old age, sickness, death, sorrow, or anguish, and yet a person prays that such misery not befall himself; this is all suffering. All in all, what does it mean that human existence itself is suffering? Basically, it means that existence is the result of impurities and thus cannot be characterized by anything else.

"What is the cause of suffering? It is the thirst of craving, or defilement, which brings forth a new future existence. There are three kinds of craving: the craving of lust, the craving for existence, and the craving for extinction.

"What is the extinction of suffering? It is the state in which the thirst of craving is made completely extinct and all traces of impurities are gone.

"What is the way leading to the extinction of suffering? It is the Eightfold Path that leads to the extinction of the cause of suffering. It is right view, right thought, right speech, right action, right livelihood, right endeavor, right mindfulness, and right meditation.

"Right view is to acquire clear insight regarding the teaching of the Four Noble Truths. Right thought is thought divorced from craving and devoid of anger and hatred. Right speech is speech free from falsehood, backbiting, and idle talk; it is speaking the truth at all times. Right action is to refrain from killing, stealing, and adultery, and to act with compassion. Right livelihood means never to indulge in actions unbecoming a monk. Right endeavor means to prevent evil that has not yet arisen and to discard that which has already arisen; to enhance good that has not yet arisen and to enlarge and perfect good that has already arisen; and to cultivate the mind by these efforts at all times. Right mindfulness is applying one's thinking at all times with a clear mind, observing the body, the senses, the mind, and the elements, and overcoming greed and that which arises from it. Right meditation is to free oneself from craving and evil and to reside in all levels of meditation. These, my friends, are the teachings on the Four Noble Truths imparted to us by the World-Honored One."

5. Dispute over Irrigation Water

(1) In the fourth year after the attainment of enlightenment, the World-Honored One stayed for a while in a large forest at Vesali. Then he headed north and came

to Savatthi and stayed at the Jeta Grove Monastery.

In the fifth month of that year there was a long dry spell, causing the rivers to slow to a trickle, which in turn created irrigation problems. The two cities of Kapilavatthu and Koliya saw struggles arising over the water of the River Rohini, which flowed between them. It happened to be the time when agriculture required water. The scarcity of water caused the farmers on one bank to speak ill of those on the opposite bank, until finally, armed with clubs and swords, they shed blood.

The World-Honored One heard of this strife at the Jeta Grove Monastery and hurried back to Kapilavatthu in time to position himself between the two opposing armies. From both armies came loud cries, "O World-Honored One, World-Honored One! Seeing you there makes it impossible to release our arrows!" Then those on both sides threw down their weapons. The World-Honored One, seeing this, summoned the leaders of both armies and asked them, "Why is it that you have congregated here? Why are you about to engage in battle?" To this both leaders answered that it was over water needed for irrigation. "Compared with human life, how valuable is water?" The leaders answered that compared with human life the value of water was almost nil.

"Why, then, is it that for water, which has so little value, you are all trying to destroy human lives, which is invaluable?" Saying this, the Buddha related the following story.

(2) "There was once a lion with black fur who always lay down at the root of the pandana tree and waited for other animals to come by. Once a dead branch, broken by the wind, fell on the lion's back. Suddenly frightened, the lion ran away. But as he looked behind, he could see that there was no one chasing after him. The lion then reasoned that the spirit of the tree hated him and was trying to keep him away from under the tree. Angered, the lion returned and, taking a firm bite on the trunk, remarked, 'I have not eaten even one of your leaves, nor have I broken even a branch. You allow other animals to rest under your branches but do not allow me to do so. What have I done to you? I shall have you uprooted and your branches cut.' Saying these unkind words, the lion went to look for someone to do this. Just then a carpenter who made carts came looking for a tree. The lion showed him where the pandana tree was and tried to get the carpenter to cut the tree down. As the carpenter started to cut, the tree spirit, terrified, appeared and told the carpenter what to do: 'You seem to want to cut this tree and make a cart. If you were to place the hide from the black lion's neck on the wheels, they will be greatly strengthened. You should kill the lion and take his hide.' The carpenter gladly followed the advice and killed the black lion. He then cut down the tree and returned to the village."

(3) The Buddha said, "As this story shows, it is common for beings to fight among themselves over trivial misunderstandings, hurting and even killing each other." He continued with another story. "Along the banks of the Western Sea there was a forest in which some horse chestnut trees grew. In that forest, in a hemp palm bush under a horse chestnut tree, there lived a rabbit. Suddenly the rabbit wondered what could be done if the world were to come to an end abruptly. At that very moment a horse chestnut fell on the leaves of the hemp palm bush

and made a sharp sound. The rabbit was frightened, thinking that now the world was falling apart. Without looking back, he ran off. The other rabbits, seeing him speeding away, sensed that something unusual had happened, followed him, and asked what was going on. The first rabbit answered that the world had started to fall apart and kept on running. The second rabbit, now alarmed, also started speeding away after the first. Then the third and fourth rabbits started running, until thousands of rabbits were running away. In this the deer joined and were followed by the boars, the water buffaloes, and along with them the rhinoceroses, tigers, lions, and elephants, as well as all the other animals, until the line of frightened animals extended for miles and miles.

"At that time there was a lion observing what was going on. Learning that the animals were afraid that the earth was falling apart, he felt that such a thing could not really happen and that the first rabbit must have heard a sharp noise and mistaken it for the earth's falling apart. Now, this lion thought that if he were to leave things to their course all the animals would be doomed. So the lion started running, passed the leaders of the herd, and waited for the herd at the foot of the mountain. As the animals came close, the lion gave a loud roar. Then the rabbit running ahead stopped, and the animals, tens of thousands in number, all stopped suddenly. The lion advanced to the middle of the herd and asked them why they were all running. The animals answered that it was because the earth was falling apart. When the lion asked if anyone had seen it, some animals said the elephant knew about it. When the elephant was asked if he had seen it or not, the elephant said that he did not know about it but had heard it from a lion. Then the animals started asking one another, the lion saying he heard it from the tiger, the tiger from the rhinoceros, and so on until it reached the first rabbit, who had seen it. The lion then asked the rabbit, 'Did you really see the world falling apart?' To this the rabbit answered that it was indeed true, and that he had seen the world fall apart. The lion asked again, 'Where were you at the time, and when did you see it happen?' The rabbit answered that he was under the horse chestnut tree by the Western Sea thinking that it would be a terrible thing if the world were to fall apart when he heard a sharp rattling sound and started running.

"The lion, now fully aware of the situation, had the animals remain there. With the rabbit at his back, he returned to the palm bush and told the rabbit to point to the exact place he had heard the sound. The rabbit was still frightened and would not approach the area. The lion made a careful study of the spot and, picking up the horse chestnut and confirming that there was nothing unusual, returned to the herd. Showing the animals the horse chestnut, he dispelled their fears." The Buddha continued, "If the lion had not taught them, countless animals would have kept on running until they had driven themselves into the sea and drowned. O leaders, one must have clear and sound understanding at all times. It must also be remembered that because of some small misunderstanding, tens of thousands can be agitated and in the end all can be led to their doom."

The people of the two cities rejoiced in the Buddha's instructions, and many from noble families entered the Buddha's Sangha. The Buddha had them follow him as he continued his instruction at the two palaces and stayed in the nigrodha forest outside Kapilavatthu.

(4) One day Mahapajapati, with two new robes in hand, called on the Buddha and said, "O Buddha, these two robes were made of thread that I made and were woven with my own hands. Please have pity on me by accepting them!"

To this the Buddha answered, "Mahapajapati, you should offer them to the Sangha and then I, too, will be receiving them." Mahapajapati asked the Buddha three times and the Buddha gave her the same answer each time, telling her to make the gift to the Sangha. Ananda, standing beside them and hearing the dialogue, now came forward, saying, "O World-Honored One, please accept the robes that Mahapajapati offers, for she has served you well. She is your aunt and she nurtured you; when you were an infant, after the passing of Queen Maya, she offered you her breast. The World-Honored One has also bestowed upon her great benefits. She sought refuge in the Three Treasures, and has abstained from taking life, has abstained from taking things not given to her, and has never engaged in sexual misconduct, lied, or taken liquor. Following the five precepts, she has put her unfaltering trust in the Three Treasures and has eradicated all doubts in the teaching of the Four Noble Truths. The Buddha has given her these great benefits. Please believe in the sincerity of her intentions." The Buddha accepted the charity of Mahapajapati as requested by Ananda, and he taught the virtues of the practice of charity.

6. Establishing the Nuns' Sangha

(1) The World-Honored One, along with many of the disciples, started toward the east and then later turned south and returned to Vesali. The retreat that year was held in a large forest on the outskirts of the palace.

Hearing that his father King Suddhodana was ill, the Buddha returned promptly to Kapilavatthu to visit him. Upon entering his father's sickroom, the rays that the Buddha gave off lit up the bed on which the king rested and greatly relieved the king of his pain. The Buddha, with his disciple Ananda, stood at the bedside and with words of comfort regarding the king's illness taught the Dharma. When the Buddha told him the truth of the impermanence of all that exists, the king, despite the pain, was able to realize enlightenment by virtue of the Buddha's instructions.

On the evening of the seventh day the king rose from his bed and, supported by the Buddha and Ananda, deeply repented of the past unkind actions that he had inflicted on his subjects; and then he offered comforting words to Mahapajapati. The king spoke on death, which cannot be overcome, and with the realization that he had done what had to be done in this world he breathed his last at the ripe old age of ninety-seven.

The Buddha then taught the Dharma to the disciples, to the nobles of the royal family, and to the royal servants. On the day of the funeral he placed the royal casket upon the funeral pyre and set it aflame. The sermon given by the Buddha on that day enabled many to be relieved of the suffering of this world.

(2) Now after the royal funeral rites for his father King Suddhodana, the Buddha stayed in the garden of nigrodha trees. It was at this time that Mahapajapati approached the Buddha and made a request: "O World-Honored One, I humbly request that I be given permission to be admitted into the Sangha." The Buddha did not give his permission. Mahapajapati asked three times, and each time the Buddha did not permit her to enter the Sangha. Greatly disappointed, she bowed to the Buddha and left his presence.

Later, the Buddha left Kapilavatthu, returned to Vesali, and stayed at the Kutagara lecture hall. Mahapajapati cut off her hair, put on a robe, and headed for Vesali, taking along the ladies of the nobles of the Sakya clan. When they reached Vesali, they stood at the entrance of the great forest lecture hall barefoot, covered with dust, and with tears flowing down their cheeks. Ananda, seeing this, was deeply impressed with their sincerity. He had the ladies wait outside, approached the Buddha, and made a request: "O World-Honored One, Mahapajapati and the other ladies have made a long journey; they are covered with dust and are in tears. They seek your guidance. They are now standing at the gateway of this lecture hall. Please, World-Honored One, permit them to join the Sangha."

To these words the Buddha answered that Ananda must not ask for permission to admit women to the Sangha. Ananda asked the Buddha a second time, and the Buddha refused again. Ananda then made his request once more: "O World-Honored One, if a woman were to become a mendicant according to the rules of the Buddha's doctrine, could she, by following the way of spiritual cultivation, reach enlightenment?"

To this question the Buddha answered that she could. "Ananda, women can achieve enlightenment if they become mendicants and devote themselves to the teaching." To these words of the Buddha, Ananda said, "O World-Honored One, if women are such, then it is appropriate for the Buddha to permit Mahapajapati, who is your aunt and has nurtured and raised you, and the other ladies of noble families, to enter the Buddha's Sangha."

The Buddha then said to Ananda that if the women would follow the eight observances, he would admit them, the eight being these:

1. Even if a nun has been a nun for over a hundred years, she must show respect to a monk by bowing in reverence to him even if he was ordained just that very day.

2. A nun must not conduct a retreat where there are no monks present.

3. A nun must confer with the monks' Sangha every half month on the date that the precepts are reviewed and must receive instructions on the precepts.

4. After the retreat, a nun must ask both the monks' Sangha and the nuns' Sangha to point out and present violations of the precepts.

5. A nun who has committed a serious offense must be separated from both Sanghas for a half-month.

6. After having been trained in the six basic abstentions as a novice for two years, a nun must request ordination rites by both Sanghas.

7. A nun must never shout at or criticize a monk at any time.

8. A nun must never point out violations by a monk. A monk may point out violations by a nun.

The Buddha said, "Ananda, if Mahapajapati is resolved to follow these eight observances, she may be permitted to enter the Sangha."

(3) Ananda immediately told the above to the ladies. Mahapajapati responded, "O venerable sir, just as a young woman who wishes to make herself beautiful washes her hair and carefully holds the beautiful flowers she has received high over her head, I shall respectfully receive these eight observances all my life and never violate them."

Ananda then reported to the Buddha, "O World-Honored One, Mahapajapati has accepted the eight observances and has been accepted into the Sangha." To this the Buddha said, "If women had not become mendicants, the teachings would have long remained. The Dharma would have remained pure and true for over one thousand years. Now that women have been admitted into the Sangha, the purity of the teachings may not continue for long, and the true Dharma will last for only five hundred years. Ananda, no matter whose home it is, if the women outnumber the men, it becomes easier for bandits to break in. Again, when a rice paddy is stricken with disease, the rice will not last long; likewise now that women have been admitted into the Sangha, the purity of the teachings will not be preserved for long. Embankments are built around a large lake to prevent the water from overflowing; thus have I laid down the eight observances for nuns."

At this time the princess Yasodhara and other ladies of the Sakya clan were admitted along with Mahapajapati.

7. The Buddha's Instructions in the Rear Garden

(1) That year the World-Honored One once again returned from Vesali and was staying at the Jeta Grove Monastery. One day Anathapindika visited the World-Honored One. At that time the Buddha gave the following instructions: "O Anathapindika, unless a person is able to guard his mind, it becomes impossible for him to guard the actions of his body, mouth, and mind. If he cannot do this, then the actions of his body, mouth, and mind will be polluted by desire. Once the three actions become impure, both the time of that person's death and the time thereafter will not be blissful. When the roof of a castle is not well laid, the ridgepoles, rafters, and walls are exposed to the rain and begin to rot. O Anathapindika, when the mind is guarded, the actions of the body, mouth, and mind are guarded. They are not polluted by desire, and therefore both the time of that person's death and the time thereafter are blissful. It is when the roofing of a castle is well laid that the ridgepoles, rafters, and walls are not exposed and do not rot."

(2) On another day, the World-Honored One instructed his disciples in the rear garden: "My disciples, there are three causes by which people generate their own karma. They are greed, anger, and ignorance. People create their own karma through these three types of actions, and they are reborn where karma directs them; they must reap the harvest of their karmic actions from this existence to the next. Just as the planted seed that receives rain at the appropriate time sprouts forth and grows, so people create their actions through these three causes, and when the karmic forces bear fruit, people must receive the results of their actions. O my disciples, there are three causes of realizing nirvana. They are non-greed, non-anger, and non-ignorance. If and when people are able to pursue their practice according to these three causes, they will not be born into delusion in the future and will enter nirvana. Like grass whose roots have been uprooted or like a palm tree whose buds have been nipped, these people will never again suffer birth in the realm of delusion."

The Buddha continued his teaching, saying the following: "My teachings are superior to other teachings for two reasons. One is that I teach that a person who commits an evil deed must look squarely at the evil being done. The other is that once a person commits an evil deed, I teach that person to dislike and abhor it and to detach himself from it. These are the two points that make my teachings superior."

(3) The Buddha also said, "O my disciples, there are two pure things that guard this world. They are inward shame, or repentance, and outward shame, or repentance. If these were to disappear from this world, the distinction between mother and aunt or between the master's wife and a friend's wife would be lost, and there would be total chaos, as seen in the realm of wild sheep, pigs, dogs, and foxes. It is because of these two aspects of shame that there is order in this world.

"O my disciples, ignorance precedes all that which is not pure and is followed by the two kinds of shamelessness. On the other hand, wisdom that is clear precedes all that which is pure, and man's repentance and remorse follow it."

(4) One evening the World-Honored One gathered the monks and said to them, "O my disciples, three heavenly messengers are sent to this world. I shall teach you about them. Once a certain person committed an evil act and fell into hell. A guard took hold of the person's hand in a violent manner and led him to King Yama and said that this person, while in human existence, was extremely disrespectful toward his parents, showed no respect to the monks, and held his master and elders in contempt. 'For these evil deeds he was reborn here. Please punish him accordingly.'

"O my disciples, King Yama first asked the man whether he had seen the first heavenly messenger, and the person suffering answered that he had not seen the first heavenly messenger. King Yama then asked him then whether he had not seen an old man, bent with age and with a walking stick, wobbling along. The man replied that he had seen such a man many times. Hearing this, King Yama asked, 'If you saw this old man, why did you not think that you, too, would become old and feeble, and that you ought to do good deeds immediately with body, mouth, and mind?' To this the person answered that he was not aware of such things since he was far too lax in his ways.

"King Yama said, 'Because of your indolence, you have neglected to do the things that had to be done even after you realized the situation clearly. For this reason you must be responsible for your indolence. These are not things that your parents did, nor your brothers or sisters, nor your friends or other people. They are things that you did, and thus you must accept the consequences.'

"Then King Yama asked him, 'Did you see the second heavenly messenger?' To this question, the person answered that he had not. King Yama said, 'But did you not happen to see a pathetic being who was ill and unable to get up by himself, and who lay in his own excrement?' The person answered, 'Great king, I did see such a scene.' The king said, 'As you gazed on that scene, did you not think to yourself that you, too, would someday become sick and that while healthy, you must purify your body, mouth, and mind?' The person said, 'Great king, I was too negligent to think in that manner.'

"King Yama then asked him, 'Now, did you see the third heavenly messenger?' To this the person answered that he had not seen the third heavenly messenger. The king then asked, 'Have you not seen a dead body two or three days after death, with the whole body swollen and pus oozing out?' The man said that he had seen that many times. Then King Yama said, 'After having seen all this, why is it that you were so negligent? You must now face the results of your negligence. These things are not the result of what your parents, brothers or sisters, or friends or relatives did to you, but they are the result of your own indolence. You must be prepared to face the consequences.' Having said this, King Yama sealed his lips. The attendant then led the person out by force and threw him into the burning flames of the inferno.

"My disciples, there are three heavenly messengers who are sent to this world. Those who are awakened by these heavenly messengers and who are in control are the fortunate ones, while those who fail to understand despite the signs given them must remain in sadness for a long time."

Chapter 3

THE EIGHT CONSCIOUSNESSES

1. Queen Khema

(1) The World-Honored One headed east from Savatthi and arrived at Rajagaha, staying at the Bamboo Grove Monastery. King Bimbisara's queen was called Khema. She was born in the city of Sagara in the country of Magadha and was selected to become the queen because of her natural beauty. She was always proud of this and did not cherish the idea of meeting with the World-Honored One.

The king, wishing that the queen would pay homage to the Buddha, had many persons speak highly of the World-Honored One in her presence until finally the queen was moved and stated that she desired to pay homage to the Buddha. The Buddha, seeing the queen coming his way, had a woman who resembled a heavenly maiden appear. She stood behind him with a banana leaf in her hand, waving it like a fan. The queen saw this and thought, "Oh, what a beautiful woman she is! The World-Honored One is served by such women! I am not fit to be in his presence. I was indeed wrong in my understanding of the World-Honored One!"

However, as the queen observed the woman, the features of that woman gradually changed, the youth in her complexion faded, old age crept in, her black hair turned gray, wrinkles appeared on her skin, and, while holding the banana leaf in her hand, she fell to the ground. The queen was frightened by what she saw and seemed deeply depressed. The World-Honored One then chanted a song:

> Those at the mercy of their greed
>
> Will be carried along the stream,
>
> Like a spider climbing down its web.
>
> The wise are aware of this.
>
> They are freed from craving.
>
> Leaving behind the pleasures of lust,
>
> They renounce worldly ties.

The queen, hearing this, awakened to true spiritual values and, blessed with the permission of the king, became a nun. She attained enlightenment quickly.

(2) Later, the World-Honored One, at the Jeta Grove Monastery, praised this nun by saying that of all the nuns in the Buddha's Sangha, Khema was the foremost as far as wisdom was concerned. However, the way of practice was far from easy for her. One day as she was seated in meditation under a shady tree, Mara appeared in the form of a young man and tried to seduce her with these words: "While you are young, if you are beautiful, your happiness is unsurpassed. Dance with the butterflies to the accompaniment of music in the garden where flowers bloom." However, the nun spurned these words with these verses: "The body that takes ill and wanes begins to rot. I destroy the foolishness of yearning after butterflies. Love is a spear; greed, a trident; if you draw near, they will cut you. How can they be called pleasurable? When one frees oneself from the pleasures of greed, the darkness is dispelled.

"O Mara, you have now been beaten. The unenlightened do not know the truth; they worship the stars and offer fire rituals in the woods, thinking that these are the ways of pleasure. When I worship the supreme Buddha, I am relieved of suffering and pursue the way."

The World-Honored One resided at Rajagaha for a short while. During that time he visited the towns and villages in Magadha, spreading the teachings wherever he went.

2. The Realm of Enlightenment

(1) The World-Honored One headed for the far south, through Central India, and by boat he went to the island of Lanka. The king Ravana invited the Buddha to his palace on Mount Malaya for instructions and praised him with the words, "Your mind is the store of the Dharma. Since you have realized egolessness, your views are purity itself. Please give us the highest wisdom of enlightenment, embraced by the true Dharma, at peace with the highest knowledge, freely exhibiting the wonders of the Dharma. O World-Honored One, please enter Lanka Palace. We single-mindedly wish to hear the Dharma."

When the Buddha agreed to give the teachings, all the people in the palace came out to the place where the Buddha was. The king said to the Bodhisattva Mahamati, "O Bodhisattva, please tell the Buddha on our behalf that we are sincerely eager to hear of the Buddha's enlightenment."

(2) The World-Honored One responded to Mahamati's question and taught, "All that exists is like a phantom." As the Buddha was expounding this, suddenly he disappeared into the sky, all the people and the forest instantly vanished, and King Ravana alone remained in the castle. The king reflected on what had happened. "What was it that was seen to appear? Who were those listening to the Buddha? Where have the Buddha, the castle, all of the treasures, and the forest gone? Is this happening in a dream? Is it real, or is it a mirage? Everything is so strange. It must be that in this way the Buddha is trying to show that all things are actually like a dream. All that appears is the result of one's own discrimination. People cannot perceive this. The truth is that the viewer and

that which is viewed, or the one who teaches and that which is taught, do not actually exist. Now, could not seeing the Buddha, or listening to the Dharma, be the result of such discrimination? Then the Buddha that I saw could have been a Buddha conceived by the mind. Now that I have been instructed by the Buddha and freed from discrimination, all that resulted from discrimination has completely disappeared. Truly, as long as discrimination exists, the true Buddha cannot be conceived, and to be free from discrimination is to see the Buddha truly."

Ravana perceived reality and became freed of impurity; he entered into a realm completely free of calculation and was able to see all things in their true light.

(3) At this time the World-Honored One, now seeing that the mind of the king was about to become enlightened, appeared before the king as before. Delighted, the king asked the World-Honored One the following questions: "O World-Honored One, you have constantly taught us that even dharmas [things] must be discarded. How much more so with adharmas [nonexistent things]. Why is it that these two kinds of dharmas must be discarded? What do the dharmas and adharmas mean?"

The Buddha answered saying, "O king, it is commonly accepted that a ceramic container will break. However, people tend to think that in the container there is an enduring essence that will not break. Such a notion of dharmas that assume an imagined enduring essence must be discarded. If one is able to see the basic nature of his mind-consciousness, there is no need for one to be attached to anything outside of it. To look at dharmas from a viewpoint that is based on the right view is what is meant by discarding the dharmas. Adharmas are like a hare's horns and a barren woman's child; they are far from the truth. These should not be adhered to, just as one should not be attached to a ceramic container; both should be discarded.

"O king, the Buddha's teachings are also totally separate from all human discriminations and meaningless arguments. They can only be known by true wisdom. The Buddha spreads the Dharma to lead people to spiritual peace, and he establishes wisdom freed from human discriminations. Thus, the Buddha is one with true wisdom and cannot be understood by those who try to understand him by wisdom based on discriminations.

"O king, sentient beings that have been painted on the wall have no sensations. In the same way, all people must be regarded as being phantoms. To view things in this way is called right thought, and to view things otherwise is called the view of discrimination. Because one discriminates, one becomes attached to the dharmas or to adharmas. O king, for example, a man sees his image on the water's surface, which serves as a mirror, or he sees his shadow, cast by a torch or by the moon. He creates discriminations and, becoming attached to them, he either rejoices or is beset with fears. Whether one speaks of dharmas or of adharmas, both are the products of discrimination. Because of this, one is not able to cast them off. Moreover, one adds to one's delusions and is unable to attain the extinction of defilements. Extinction refers to the mind that has freed itself from delusion. This extinction is the womb that gives birth to buddhas; it is called the Tathagata-garbha (Womb of the Buddhas)."

(4) At just that time the Bodhisattva Mahamati stood up and offered words of praise: "The Buddha with his compassion and wisdom, totally freed from the discrimination of birth and death, showed that this world is like a blossom floating in the sky. He taught that whether one discards or takes, all is unreal. The Dharmakaya is inconceivable, like things in a dream, and is beyond our words or praise.

"To realize that there is no definite nature in all that exists is to praise the wisdom of the Buddha. There is no form to see or to be seen in the Buddha. Not to see is really to see the true Buddha. Thus our own words of praise or slander make no difference to the Buddha.

"The Buddha with his compassion and wisdom has been freed from all discriminations and realizes that all that exists is like a delusion. Thus he regards both discarding and adhering as delusions.

"Having left the discriminations of knowing and known, and of existence and nonexistence, the Buddha does not dwell in enlightenment, and enlightenment is not the Buddha. If one observes the Buddha and enjoys serenity of mind, that will lead him to transcend birth and death. He will free himself from all discriminations in this life as well as in future lives."

3. The Eight Consciousnesses

(1) The World-Honored One said to the Bodhisattva Mahamati, "O Mahamati, the Buddha with eyes of wisdom looks at the original aspects of things, or the basic aspects common to all that exists. This view is not like the wrong views of non-Buddhist masters. They are not aware that the world is the result of their mind's discriminations but think that underlying all that exists there are two basic natures, existence and nonexistence. Mahamati, if they could see that the world is like a dream and is the result of one's own mind, then the suffering and blindness of the realm of delusion would be eradicated along with lust and its karmic forces."

(2) The Bodhisattva Mahamati then asked the Buddha, "O World-Honored One, please bestow upon me the teaching concerning heart, mind, consciousness and the nature and aspects of the five categories of name, form, delusion, right wisdom, and highest reality. I have been told that through this teaching all buddhas and bodhisattvas are able to become aware of the realms of their minds, are able to be freed from attachment to the aspects of their surroundings, and thus are able to be in full accord with the truth of the Dharma."

The Buddha then said, "In regard to eye-consciousness, the four agents, eye-organ, object, contact, and eye-consciousness, must come into play. However, in this instance one still does not know that objects and one's surroundings are the result of one's mind. This is not known because, from the beginningless past, man's delusion has clouded the mind, leading man to be attached to objects. Thus in the nature of consciousness there is the strong tendency to be attached to surroundings. The end result is that one wishes to find pleasure in the forms and shapes of all things around him.

"Mahamati, the alaya-vijnana [store or seed consciousness], which is the basic consciousness of man, also exists and works by virtue of these four agents. This is similar to the falling water of a waterfall causing waves to form; for when surroundings activate the human mind, the consciousness of eyesight, hearing, smell, taste, touch, the mind, and the seventh consciousness are activated. The seventh consciousness at times acts immediately, just as a mirror reflects an object, and at other times works gradually, just as the wind blows the waters of the sea. It is in this manner that the winds of stimulation from surroundings blow over the sea of the mind, and cause waves in the mind, and this sequence of activity continues. Mahamati, note that the fundamental eighth consciousness and the other seven consciousnesses are not actually one but at the same time are not actually different. All of the consciousnesses are interrelated and deeply bound together, but they cannot perceive the nature of things around them. From this basic misconception, the five sense consciousnesses of eyesight, hearing, smell, taste, and touch function in relation to the outside world.

"Mahamati, the function of the alaya-vijnana is indeed very fine and sensitive, and it is only those who sincerely devote themselves who will be able to know the realm of the mind by virtue of their knowledge and wisdom."

(3) At that time the Bodhisattva Mahamati asked, "If the alaya-vijnana is like the waves sweeping over the sea, why is it that people are not aware of this?" To this the World-Honored One answered, "The metaphor I used in saying that the alaya-vijnana is the ocean and the other consciousness are the waves was intended for the ignorant." To this the Bodhisattva Mahamati asked, "O World-Honored One, why is it that the World-Honored One does not reveal the truth to all those who are ignorant just as the sun shines on all equally?"

The Buddha responded, "Just as the waves of the sea, an image reflected in the mirror, or a dream are temporary appearances, the realm of the mind is no different. This is not to say that in the seven consciousnesses all phenomena are included, but through the eighth consciousness they all function in an orderly manner. The sixth consciousness enables one to discern, the seventh consciousness accepts the unenlightened mind as the center of one's ego, and the other five sense consciousness of sight, sound, smell, taste, and touch merely reflect the surroundings before one's eyes.

"To give an analogy, just as a skillful painter has the ability to represent all kinds of objects, what I have taught you will do the same for you. There is no design in color itself nor is there any in the brush or the canvas. However, by employing these, a painter creates beautiful images, bringing pleasure to man. It must be remembered that words and expressions change and that, alas! truth itself cannot be expressed in words. I have given these instructions for the sake of the bodhisattvas and will instruct those of lesser understanding on another occasion. If the instructions given do not match the listener's ability to accept them, it would be better not to have given them. Just as a good doctor prescribes medicine in accordance with the sickness, the Buddha teaches the Dharma in accordance with people's abilities."

(4) The Bodhisattva Mahamati then asked the Buddha this question, "O World-Honored One, whenever a person wishes to purify his mind by overcoming desires, is it purified in an instant or gradually?" To this the World-Honored One answered, "Mahamati, just as green fruit ripens, just as the potter creates his utensils, just as the earth enables plants to grow, just as man learns music, painting, and other skills, the Buddha purifies man's impurities gradually. Again, just as a mirror reflects an object, and just as the sun and moon shine on all objects at once, the Buddha purifies man's impurity instantaneously. In this way, the Buddha makes manifest all dharmas and shines on the world, thus enabling one to be freed from the ideas of existence and nonexistence."

(5) The Bodhisattva Mahamati asked the Buddha for instructions: "O World-Honored One, could this realm of the highest truth, which is beyond all ordinary human comprehension and everlasting and of which the Buddha now speaks, be the equivalent of the incomprehensible and everlasting creator of the other teachings?"

To this the Buddha responded, "Mahamati, the everlasting one that other teachings speak of is everlasting in the sense that it is the basic cause of all that is impermanent. This does not mean that it is in itself everlasting. In other words, it is in contrast to impermanence that they establish a state of everlasting existence. The Buddha teaches that all is impermanent.

"Mahamati, it is on the basis of such views that the other teachings understand something that is inconceivable and eternal. However, this has no real existence; it can be likened to the horns of a hare, which in reality do not exist. Such things are the result of calculations and are nothing but mere words. Why do I liken their idea to the horns of a hare? Because there is nothing in it that can serve as a cause of itself. Mahamati, the inconceivable and eternal that I speak of has to do with the attainment of enlightenment for oneself as the cause. One attains enlightenment and becomes eternal. In contrast to this, other teachings are ignorant of that which is truly inconceivable and place themselves outside of the realm of sagacious wisdom that attains enlightenment for itself. They are not in accord with the truth.

"Mahamati, the buddhas of the past, the present, and the future teach that all that exists does not come about of itself. The reason for this, according to the buddhas' view, is that there is no existence or nonexistence and there is no coming into being or becoming extinct. On the other hand, the unenlightened and ignorant tend to distinguish between existence and nonexistence and furthermore become attached to them. But the truth is that all that exists is basically characterized neither by existence nor by nonexistence, just as the hare has no horns. The outlook from the standpoint of the Buddha's wisdom is totally different from the way in which the ignorant tend to consider existence or nonexistence.

"Mahamati, the human body, the means of man's existence, and all things that exist are shadows of the alaya-vijnana. Both that which does the recognizing and the characteristics of that which is recognized appear from the alaya-vijnana. You should endeavor to learn about the meaning and reasoning regarding this matter.

(6) "Next, Mahamati, the bodhisattva must be aware of the three levels of the nature of things. The first is the character of pure imagination. This is the unenlightened view, based on attachment to things, which regards that which has come about by causes and multiple conditions as actually existing. The second is the idea that one thing's existence depends upon other things, that causes and conditions coming together bring things into temporary existence. The third is perfect wisdom set apart from all calculations. This is Thusness.

"Next, Mahamati, the bodhisattva must be aware of the two kinds of anatman [non-entity]. First is the anatman of personhood. This is to say that the aggregates that constitute this body, consciousness, and even surrounding conditions, are all free of 'I' consciousness and 'my' consciousness. It is the mind lacking wisdom that looks upon things as 'me' or 'mine' and adheres to them. This body and all its surroundings have come to be out of the alaya-vijnana, which keeps on changing, never still, not for a moment; it is like a river or an open flame constantly changing and at times flickering violently; it is like a restless monkey. All the doings of the body are similar to those of a puppet that can move only because of machinery. Those who can see the situation as such are said to know fully the anatman nature of a person.

"Second, there is the anatman of the dharmas. Based on this understanding, there must be no attachment to the body or to one's surroundings as being 'me' or 'mine.' In fact, it is by strong craving that all are bound together, one on top of the other. There is no first cause, no creator, nor is there any inherent nature like a soul in things themselves. To view them with one's subjective mind and then imagine various forms and shapes in one's mind is the doing of an ignorant person. To be able to see the world according to right view based on wisdom, and to know that there is nothing except that which is created in one's mind, is to know the anatman of dharmas."

4. Two Perverted Views

(1) At one time the Bodhisattva Mahamati asked the World-Honored One, "O World-Honored One, how can the two views of everlasting existence and complete extinction be shattered?" To this the Buddha answered, "A human being, his material possessions, and his surroundings are merely shadows of his mind. However, this truth cannot be understood by an ignorant person who thinks the thought that things exist everlastingly or that things become completely extinct. These two views originate in the mind, and nothing exists outside of this mind. Mahamati, for your sake I shall expound on sunyata, or emptiness, non-birth, and the absence of self-nature.

"The forms and aspects of all that exists, the individual and unique aspects of each existence, and the aspects possessed in common by all that exists are characterized by emptiness. These aspects are the results of every existence coming about by causes and conditions. Thus even if one were to analyze this relationship, one will not find a unique and independent essence along the way. The true aspect of all that exists is emptiness. Moreover, regarding all that exists, there is no birth or extinction from the standpoint of things themselves, nor can it be said that this is the birth aspect or this is the becoming extinct aspect. The ignorant try to grasp that which is ungraspable, and they try to establish that which cannot be established. They even say that all things have their own intrinsic natures from their limited understanding. But the truth is that their natures are empty.

"Mahamati, as you now know, regarding the basic nature of things, there is neither coming about nor extinction. It is because of this common nature of emptiness that I call it non-birth. All that exists can exist only in close inter-relationship with everything else and cannot exist standing completely alone. This is similar to the relationship between light and shadow, long and short, and white and black.

"In the same manner, nirvana does not exist apart from samsara [birth and death], and samsara does not exist apart from nirvana. These two do not stand in opposition to each other. In other words, things do not possess two different natures, and I teach that they are therefore devoid of the two natures.

"Mahamati, all buddhas expound the truths of emptiness, non-birth, absence of self-nature, and emptiness of the two natures. However, in actuality, their truths cannot be expressed in words. For example, a mirage deludes animals and makes them think that the mirage is actually water. The Buddha creates apparitions that cause joy to arise by expounding diverse teachings in accordance with the mental capacities of the people. However, the Dharma that has been realized by the wise cannot possibly be manifested in a direct manner. Therefore one must not be attached to words, but rather one must experience the words in accordance with their meaning."

(2) The Bodhisattva Mahamati asked the World-Honored One, "O World-Honored One, in regard to the Tathagata-garbha, you have taught us that its nature is purity itself, that it never becomes extinct or undergoes changes, and that it embodies all aspects of the Buddha and is inherent in all human beings, as well as in impure bodies and in all aspects of human defilement. You have taught that it is like a gem wrapped in a dirty cloth. If this is so, the Tathagata-garbha seems to be similar to what the believers of other teachings talk about, the atman, which they describe as the creator, free to do whatever it wishes, never to become extinct. Is this not in conflict with the teaching of anatman that you have taught us?"

To this the Buddha answered, "Mahamati, the Tathagata-garbha that I speak of is not the same as the atman of which the other masters speak. The Buddha explains that the Tathagata-garbha is the equivalent of emptiness, actual existence, nirvana, non-birth, no form, or wishlessness so that the ignorant may not be upset or afraid in hearing the teachings of anatman, and so that they can be freed from the delusions of discrimination and not be attached to the atman. Mahamati, just as a potter makes utensils from clay using water, stick, ring, and rope, the Buddha, using the skillful means of wisdom and other methods, speaks of the Tathagata-garbha or at other times of anatman. The names may differ, but they are the same. Mahamati, the reason I expounded on the Tathagata-garbha was to attract the masters of other teachings, who speak of and adhere to the atman; having freed them from their perverted views, I hope to lead them to enlightenment."

(3) The Bodhisattva Mahamati then requested the Buddha's instructions on the way to cultivate the path of the bodhisattva. The Buddha answered, "Mahamati, the bodhisattva cultivates the path by practicing the four ways. The first is to see that all that exists appears from the mind. The three realms of existence cannot exist independent of the mind. The realms originate from man's idea of 'I' and 'mine.' They are never in a state of going or coming, but because of enduring habits, which developed a long time ago, they appear as the three realms. Thus we must see that all things that exist, actions, words, bondage, the human body, treasures, or places of residence are all the results of man's discriminations.

"The second is to discard thoughts on arising, abiding, and perishing and to see that all is like a dream. This is because there is nothing that came into being by itself, nor is there anything created by another. Furthermore, nothing comes about through itself and others. Things are the creations of one's mind and they have no substance. Now, if there is no substance in external things, the discriminating mind cannot be aroused. Knowing that it is only by discrimination that the three realms exist, there is nothing, inwardly or outwardly, to grasp. All is like a dream, devoid of arising, abiding, and perishing. The bodhisattva, upon realizing this, is freed from the ideas of arising and perishing.

"The third is to contemplate on the absence of self-nature among external objects. One perceives all things to be like a mirage or a dream. One perceives that all things owe their existences to worthless arguments, a variety of attachments, and deluded habits, and that originally and in actuality, all things are without a substantive nature.

"The fourth is to view all that exists in this manner and to seek the highest wisdom."

(4) The Bodhisattva Mahamati then asked the World-Honored One about the nature of nirvana. To this the Buddha responded, "The state of nirvana is attained by overturning the delusive feeling that fills the self-nature of the unenlightened mind, the habitual forces of the alaya-vijnana, manas vijnana (the seventh ego-grasping consciousness), and one's mind. This realm is identical with that state in which a person realizes that the very nature of all that exists is characterized by emptiness and is also identical with the sacred wisdom free from the categories of cessation of existence, everlasting existence, existence, and nonexistence. Furthermore, there is no disintegration in nirvana, nor is there death. Suppose there were such a thing as death; then we must suppose that there is birth. If there is such a thing as disintegration, that means that things change. Nirvana is where there is no disintegration and no death; it is the realm where all who cultivate the path will arrive. Nirvana does not discard the dharmas in the mundane world; it is neither identical with the mundane dharmas nor different from them."

(5) The Bodhisattva Mahamati then asked the Buddha whether there could be names of things that did not exist. To this the Buddha replied, "Mahamati, even though things do not exist, there are words describing them. Actually, no one has ever seen a hair of a turtle, the horns of a hare, or a child born of a barren woman, and yet people use these expressions. Mahamati, it does not mean that these exist, and it cannot be said that they do not exist. They are actually names and expressions. Mahamati, if you adhere to the thesis that where there are words there are things that the words represent, then you are mistaken. Again, you should know that all Buddha lands do not necessarily have names or expressions. For instance, in a certain Buddha land the Dharma is revealed by merely setting one's eyes on a certain point, by moving the eyebrows or the eyes or by smiling or groaning, or by emitting coughs, while in places like the land of no blinking, or the world of wondrous incense, or the land of the Buddha Samantabhadra, the enlightenment of the bodhisattva is to be realized by looking on without blinking the eyes. Thus the existence of things is not dependent on the existence of words. In this world, is it not true that although the flies and ants do not have words, they manage to do what they must?"

(6) The Bodhisattva then asked the Buddha what the basis was of the World-Honored One's contention regarding the truth of permanence. To this the World-Honored One answered, "Mahamati, the realm of the everlasting Dharma can be explained by things in the realm of unenlightenment, which is ruled by the law of impermanence.

"Illusory dharmas also appear in the same way to the eyes of the sages, but the sages observe them in their true light. The unenlightened tend to view matters such as shimmering heat waves, fire rings, mirages, dreams, illusions, or reflections in a mirror in an inverted way; but the wise look at them correctly. These delusions are basically set apart from existence and nonexistence and thus are not impermanent. For instance, for the hungry devil, it would be impossible to say that there is water here because he does not see the river Ganges. On the other hand, because others can see the river, they cannot say there is no water here. Now in regard to all things that exist in the realm of delusion, originally there is neither existence nor nonexistence, and therefore they are said to exist eternally. Although there should be no distinctions among things, because of a person's perception distinctions are recognized; in truth, however, their essential nature is eternal existence. Mahamati, all that exists, though in the state of delusion, is true as it is. The sage does not consider things perverted although he may reside in the realm characterized by illusory existence. The illusory dharmas are, at the same time, real dharmas. If and when his subjective ego-conscious mind is activated in his observations, then he is no longer a sage."

(7) The Bodhisattva Mahamati then asked the Buddha whether all illusory existences were existing or nonexisting. The World-Honored One answered, "To adhere to either existence or nonexistence is an indication of attachment. Actually, all things that exist are originally set apart from such attachments and are therefore said to exist in a dream. If, however, all existences possess their own substance and do not undergo change, then these would be what the believers

of other teachings call atman. However, all things that exist come about because of countless conditions and therefore undergo change; for this reason I say that the existences in the world of delusions are existences in the process of undergoing change."

(8) The Bodhisattva Mahamati then asked the Buddha, "You say that the existences in the world of delusion are identical with illusions. If this is so, can they become the causes of other existences in the world of delusion?" To this the World-Honored One answered, "Mahamati, illusory existences cannot become the causes of other existences in the world of delusion. This is because illusory existences cannot become the causes of errors. In other words, illusory existences cannot exercise calculation and for this reason cannot bring about miscalculations. Through attachment to things the ignorant create illusion, but the sages free themselves from attachment and see the truth in temporary existences. If there were to be a truth besides transitory existence, then that truth would become also a part of temporary existence. Mahamati, by the nirvana that I speak of, I mean the annihilation of the sixth consciousness which is the mind that falsely discriminates phenomena in the plane of temporary existence."

(9) The Bodhisattva Mahamati asked the World-Honored One, "O World-Honored One, why is it that you speak of eight types of consciousness, and why is it that the sixth consciousness is to be overcome and the rest are not considered?" To this the Buddha answered, "Mahamati, it is because the sixth consciousness becomes either the basic cause or the supporting condition of the other seven. Whenever the sixth consciousness is activated through attachment to its surroundings, this causes a pattern of development, and this in turn feeds the alaya-vijnana. The seventh consciousness, because of its attachment to thoughts of 'I' and 'mine', keeps directing its thoughts toward the eighth consciousness. In this way, through being attached to the surroundings, which originally manifested themselves in one's own mind, all other consciousnesses arise, and each in turn works as the cause of the others. Mahamati, if I compare this to the waves of the ocean, it may be said that the wind blows on the surroundings and causes waves to appear and disappear. In accordance with this, when the sixth consciousness ceases to function the others also cease to function."

5. Not a Word Uttered

(1) The Bodhisattva Mahamati asked the Buddha to teach him the way of practice of the sages and those who follow the way of the One Vehicle. To this the Buddha responded, "Mahamati, the bodhisattva does not bring forth discriminations according to various teachings. The bodhisattva meditates on the Dharma while residing alone in quiet surroundings. He attains enlightenment alone without relying on anyone. He frees himself from all discriminations, advances onto higher spiritual planes, and enters the realm of Buddhahood. This way of practice is called the way of practice of the sages.

"Next, the way of the One Vehicle is for the pursuer to realize fully the truth. It means for one to dwell in complete freedom in the Dharma, being away from the duality of subject and object.

"If one becomes conscious of the vehicle, there is no vehicle. Once such consciousness subsides, the separation between the vehicle and the vehicle-rider disappears; and this state is truly the One Vehicle. Other vehicles are means to lead those who are of lower capacities. Greed and passion are the mother, basic human ignorance is the father, and it is by these two that the world comes into being. Those who realize this are to be called buddhas."

(2) The Bodhisattva Mahamati asked the Buddha, "O World-Honored One, you once taught that from the time of the Buddha's enlightenment to the final nirvana not a word will be uttered. Please enlighten us as to what was meant by this." To this the Buddha responded, "I taught you thus with two thoughts in mind. First, in relation to the Dharma that I have realized, I have realized the same goal of enlightenment that all the buddhas of the universe have realized. This enlightenment neither increases nor decreases. This wisdom transcends words, discriminations, and names.

"Second, in regard to the Dharma that underlies everything, just as pure gold is found in an ore, whether a buddha appears in this world or not, all that exists has, as its basic nature, the everlasting truth. If one continues one's way along in a wilderness and follows an old path, one may rediscover an old castle. Likewise, I have rediscovered the everlasting truth that the buddhas of the past had all realized, and I say to you that the nature of the Dharma is everlasting and unchanging. It is for this reason that I taught you that a buddha, from the time of realizing enlightenment up to the time of nirvana, will not utter even a word."

(3) The Bodhisattva Mahamati then asked the Buddha to teach him about not being concerned with words but taking the meaning seriously. To this the Buddha answered, "Mahamati, discrimination and the practice of discrimination are the causes of words. A great variety of sounds are produced by the throat, tongue, teeth, and lips, and these sounds are used by people to speak to each other. In contrast, there is a seeker of the way, who alone in a secluded place directs himself toward enlightenment. In doing so he employs three types of wisdom, that is, the wisdoms of listening, thinking, and practicing. He is fully aware of the world that he inhabits; he extinguishes the defilements within; and he practices the various practices on the path of spiritual training. Mahamati, those who practice the way to purity must see that words and their meanings are not one, nor are they entirely separate. If the meanings and the words were totally different, then the meanings could not be expressed by the words. To perceive the meanings through words is like revealing an object being by directing light at it, and it is through the light of words that the realm of enlightenment can be entered. This realm is beyond words.

"Mahamati, in regard to expressions such as non-birth, non-extinction, basic nature as emptiness, and nirvana, when we try to understand their meanings according to the words themselves, we fall into the problem of a permanent existence or extinction. It is similar to the situation where an illusion is thought to be a real thing, which is what the ignorant think. An ignorant person may say, 'The meaning and the words are not different. This is because the meaning has no permanent substance.' However, such a person is not aware of the basic nature of words and does not know that although words may fade and become extinct, the meaning of words does not. Mahamati, all words and expressions are limited to letters, but it is not so with the meaning. The meaning is free from existence and nonexistence. Since it does not have birth, it does not have substance either. The Buddha does not teach a Dharma that is limited by words. If there is anyone who teaches a Dharma limited by words, then he is not expounding the truth. This is because the self-nature of all that exists is set apart from words. It is for these reasons that I, together with all the buddhas, do not utter one word. As I have told you, all that exists is set apart from words and can only be talked about on the basis of their meaning.

"On the other hand, Mahamati, if no effort were made in teaching the Dharma, the teachings, they would cease to exist. If the buddha's doctrine ceased to exist, then the people who followed it and all the buddhas would cease to exist. If the Dharma and the buddhas, as well as the people, ceased to exist, who would continue to teach and to whom? Thus the Dharma should be taught by those who follow the way, who are not attached to words, and who employ effective means. I shall teach all in accordance with the defilements, understanding, and aspiration of each person; I shall make each realize that all that exists is the creation in one's mind, and that there are no real surroundings in actual existence. By enabling them to get away from discriminations regarding existence and nonexistence, I hope to transform their beclouded minds into clear and serene minds. This is not for the purpose of directly revealing enlightenment. Therefore the bodhisattva should adhere to the meaning and not be attached to words and expressions. Heavy reliance on words tends to lead people toward wrong views, making them unduly attached to that which they cherish, which in turn makes them unable to realize the true aspect of the Dharma and the meanings of the words and phrases of the teachings; this move then brings forth misfortune upon themselves as well as others.

"Mahamati, the true Dharma neither comes nor goes and does not undergo any change. All meaningless arguments will cease in its presence. Thus those who seek the path of purity, just as was pointed out with regard to words and expressions, must not be attached even with regard to meaning. This is because the Dharma is set apart from all words. If a person were to point to an object with his finger, a child would look at the finger and fail to see the object. Likewise, an ignorant person becomes unduly attached to the finger of words and clings on to the finger until his life ends, and never becomes aware of the highest truth.

"Mahamati, true meaning is always subtle; moreover, it is quiescent and is the cause of nirvana. Words and delusion are bound together; and together they wander about in the arena of birth and death. True meaning is apprehended through endless listening. Endless listening leads to the deepening of the meaning and not of words. Deepening of the meaning leads not only to the rejection of the evil thinking of false teachings but to efforts to have others do the same. This is described as 'endless listening based on meaning.' One ought to draw close to those who seek meaning, while keeping at a great distance those who are caught up in words."

(4) The Bodhisattva Mahamati asked the World-Honored One about the basic nature of the Enlightened One. To this the Buddha answered with the following verses:

> The Buddha transcends the limitations of the five senses and is neither result nor cause. The Buddha is set apart from the forms of all that exists.

> The forms and shapes of all that exists, the Buddha transcends them all; there being nothing to be seen, there can be no discrimination.

> Things are separate from one's perceptions; yet this does not mean that things have no existence. Of themselves, things exist as things.

> If one does not awaken to the truth of 'I' and 'mine' and is caught up with words, one drowns in the extremes of existence and nonexistence. Thereby one harms oneself and destroys the world.

> When one sees this Dharma, he then frees himself from false views.

(5) Mahamati, now inspired by the power of the World-Honored One, asked the Buddha for guidance. "O World-Honored One, are the ideas regarding the non-birth and non-extinction of things being proposed by the masters of other teachings and your teaching regarding this matter one and the same?" To this the World-Honored One answered, "Mahamati, the non-birth and non-extinction of all things that I speak of and that which is professed by other teachings are not the same. The reason for this is that the advocates of other teachings say that in all things that exist there is an intrinsic nature and form and that they are not born nor do they undergo change. I do not teach anything that would cause things to fall into the category of existence or nonexistence. What I teach is that the nature of things is neither of existence nor of nonexistence and is set apart from birth and decay. This nature is not of nonexistence, because all that exists is like a dream or a fantasy. Again, it is not of existence, because all that exists does not have a self-nature. I teach that all that exists does not have the nature of existence or nonexistence.

"If a person realizes that all that exists is a creation in his mind and frees himself from such delusions, then the problems of life are gone forever. To labor under delusions is what the unenlightened do and not the enlightened.

"Mahamati, the mind under delusions tends to create things that are not real. It is like a child who, looking at a mirage or a doll manipulated by a magician, thinks that they are real. For a person to consider this to be birth and death, or to be delusion or enlightenment, is similar to delusion. It is like saying 'this is birth and death' as one observes puppets appearing on the stage and making an exit. Mahamati, in a similar manner, unlike sages, people produce false views with regard to birth and death. 'False' means that people do not view the nature of things as they are but instead produce inverted views. They regard the basic nature of things to exist actually; they become attached to things and fail to perceive the nonexistent essential nature of things. They are therefore not able to divorce themselves from false perceptions.

"For this reason, Mahamati, to see that there is no enduring form or shape in things is excellent. To see that there is enduring form or shape in things and to be attached to it is the cause for rebirth in the realm of delusion. If one is able to free oneself from seeing such form or shape, then there will be no discrimination. Mahamati, by nirvana is meant the state in which the truth is conceived, the discriminating mind is discarded, and the highest Buddha wisdom is attained. This is nirvana."

(6) The Bodhisattva Mahamati then asked the Buddha what the World-Honored One meant when he said that the buddhas throughout the universe are as many as the grains of sand along the river Ganges. To this the World-Honored One answered, "Mahamati, you must not interpret this according to the letters of the words. This is because a buddha is perfection itself, transcending all worlds and realms, and cannot be explained through analogies. In fact, analogies bring out but one part of a buddha. It is true that one has a tendency to be attached to the world, which in turn enhances one's wrong views, causing one to repeat the cycle of birth and death. The Buddha, in order to make one abhor such a state and aspire for higher goals, has stated that one may easily attain Buddhahood and meet with a buddha, and that there are buddhas as many as the grains of sand along the river Ganges. However, if I were to meet with one who seeks guidance from a buddha then I would say that it is truly difficult to meet with a buddha, as difficult as seeing the udumbara flower in bloom.

"Mahamati, the true buddha cannot be described by the use of analogies, because he goes beyond the heart, mind, and consciousness of the unenlightened. However, there are times when metaphors are given, and there are reasons for this. Take the river Ganges, for instance. The river is stepped in by turtles, elephants, and horses; it is used as their habitat by fishes; despite this, it retains its purity. The highest wisdom of a buddha is like the great river; its ability to return to purity is like the countless sands. Although the believers of other teachings try to cause disturbances, the buddha produces not even one false perception but remains pure and clear. The buddha, motivated by his primal vow and the bliss of his meditation, pacifies people. He is similar to the sands of the river Ganges, which also are free of both love and hatred.

"Mahamati, just as the grains of sand along the Ganges are unlimited in number, the light of the buddha is unlimited. Because this light of a buddha brings peace of mind to all beings, it also shines on all gatherings of buddhas. Again, just as the sands along the Ganges do not decrease even when taken and do not increase when sands are strewn along the banks, when a buddha, employing the wisdom of skillful means, brings peace of mind to people, there is no increase or decrease in the virtues of a buddha. This is because the Dharmakaya of a buddha is not the worldly body. Moreover, even if the sands of the river Ganges were squeezed in order to produce oil, one would not obtain oil. In the same way, even though a buddha is pressed by the sufferings of the people, until they have all attained nirvana he will not produce thoughts of being weary or worn. The reason for this is that he cherishes a mind of Great Compassion that excludes no one.

"Again, Mahamati, just as the sands in the river Ganges are carried along with the flow, the many teachings of the Buddha must accord with the flow of nirvana. It was for these reasons that the Buddha has stated that the buddhas are like the sands along the river Ganges." The Buddha continued in verse:

(i)   Anyone hoping to see the truth must free himself from false perceptions and cultivate the right view; then one will certainly see the Buddha.

The world is like a dream; treasures too are fantasies. Once one knows this, one will be respected among men. The realms of delusion arise from the mind. With the realization that nothing exists apart from delusion, the way to purity is at hand.

(ii) The high and low that are painted on the canvas may be seen but never reached. All things are like this; they are like shimmering heat waves or dreams. One's discriminations are all unreal. Delusions are dreams or fantasies. Only by being freed from attachments can this be truly known.

(iii) There is no birth as such. It is all empty, devoid of self-nature. It exists by causes and conditions. The ignorant say there is birth and death. By words do things come about, though they lack self-nature. Without words nothing arises.

With a mind distorted by habitual defilement, the unenlightened are deluded by appearances, perceiving various forms and making discrimination where there is no distinction.

When one is freed from discrimination, the true nature of things appears. Thus emptiness is finally realized.

Chapter 4

THE GROWTH OF THE SANGHA

1. Relationship between Teacher and Disciples

(1) With the increase in the number of disciples, matters in the Sangha became more eventful. The new disciples who had no teacher to guide them became very disorderly. The World-Honored One, realizing that this situation would not be conducive to faith and trust in the Sangha, issued the following instructions: "My disciples, from this time on I shall allow you each to have your own teacher. A teacher must regard his disciple as his own son; a disciple must regard his teacher as a father. They must respect each other, and if they live together in happiness and sadness, they will progress in the teachings.

"My disciples, a disciple must serve his teacher in a proper manner. He must arise at a proper time, dress and put one end of his outer garment on one shoulder, offer the teacher a tooth cleaner and the water basin, and make a place for the teacher to sit. If there should be rice gruel in the morning, the disciple must wash the bowl and fill it with the gruel. After the teacher has finished eating his gruel, the disciple must give him water, receive his bowl, and carefully wash and put it back in its proper place. After the teacher has left his seat, the disciple must carefully fold the mat; if the place is unclean, he should clean it. When the teacher prepares to go out on his alms receiving round, the disciple should help him put on his robes and present his bowl to him. If the teacher needs an attendant, he must accompany the teacher. The disciple should not walk too far from the teacher, neither should he walk too close to the teacher.

"When the food that is offered to the teacher is too hot or too heavy, the disciple must hold the bowl for him; while the teacher is speaking, the disciple must not interrupt him with words of his own. When the teacher starts to utter words that are incorrect, the disciple must politely and respectfully put a stop to his words. In returning home, the disciple must return before the teacher and wait for him, have the mat ready for him, fetch water to wash his feet, and prepare the kindling wood to heat the water. When the teacher returns, he must receive the begging bowl and his robes. If the robes should be wet with perspiration, he should dry them and then fold them. In folding he should be careful not to produce creases, by folding the robes carefully over his four fingers; and he must place the belt carefully inside the folded robes. After washing, drying, and putting away the begging bowl, the disciple must chant the sutras under the orders of the teacher and must ask questions of the teacher. When the teacher feels sadness, the disciple should console him. When the teacher is regretful, the disciple should give him encouragement; when the teacher holds evil views, the disciple must return him to the right view. The disciple should do everything for the benefit of the teacher at all times. The disciple should not go out without the permission of his teacher. When the teacher becomes ill, the disciple must wish for his recovery and minister to him.

"Again, the teacher must have his disciple read the sutras, have him ask questions, cherish the teachings, and help him. If he possesses a begging bowl or robe or other article that he does not need and that his disciple does not possess, then he should give it to his disciple. When the disciple becomes ill, the teacher should nurse him with sincerity; when the disciple feels sadness, the teacher should console him; when the disciple is regretful, the teacher should encourage him; when the disciple harbors evil views, the teacher should have him return to the right view. The teacher should do everything for the benefit of the disciple at all times. My disciples, these are the duties of a teacher toward his disciple and the duties of a disciple toward his teacher.

"My disciples, if a disciple has no love, no faith, no feeling of shame, no respect, no compassion toward his teacher, it is right for the teacher to dismiss such a disciple."

(2) With the increase in the number of disciples, the Buddha found it impossible to conduct rites for the new converts who wished to enter the Sangha to learn the teachings. It was then that he allowed his disciples to officiate in the ordination rites in accordance with the formula of the Three Refuges.

Later there arose an occasion when a brahmin named Radha was refused entrance into the Sangha by a certain disciple, causing him such anguish that he became emaciated and weak. The World-Honored One asked the disciple for the reason and then said to his disciples: "Is there anyone among you who remembers having received aid from this brahmin?"

Sariputta answered, "World-Honored One, I remember having received aid from this brahmin. One time when I was walking around in the palace grounds of Rajagaha, I received a spoonful of food from him."

"Very good, very good, Sariputta. You have remembered well the debt of gratitude that you owe him. Will you have this brahmin receive the ordination rites?"

Sariputta asked, "World-Honored One, how shall the ordination rites be conducted?" The World-Honored One then uttered the following words to his disciples: "In the past I gave permission to have a person become my disciple by having him take refuge in the Three Treasures; but from now on, have him become my disciple by following the formula of the One Utterance and the Three Karmas. First, the disciples should all assemble in one place. Those who want to become disciples should come before the assemblage with their outer garments placed on one shoulder; then they should kneel on one knee and put the palms of their hands together and make the following request: 'Most virtuous ones, please allow me to become a disciple of the Buddha. Please help and guide me with compassion in your hearts.' This must be said three times. At this time a person with wisdom and high virtue will become the officiant of the rites, and making certain that the aspirant does not have any obstacles to becoming a disciple, he must address the assembled disciples as follows: 'Most virtuous ones, please listen to what I have to say. This person has expressed a wish to become a disciple of the Buddha with a certain elder as his master. He has no obstacles; he is prepared with his bowl and robes. If he meets with your approval, this person will become a disciple of the Buddha with the said elder as his master. This is my proposal.' This proposal is called the rite of the One Utterance.

"Then after making this proposal, he will continue and say, 'Most virtuous ones, I pray you listen to me. This person asks to become a disciple of the Buddha under the tutorship of a certain elder. He has no obstacles, and he is prepared with robe and bowl. Let the assemblage of disciples permit this person to become a disciple of the Buddha under a certain elder. If there is no objection among the virtuous ones, please remain silent. If there is any objection, please speak out.' He will say this three times. This is called the rite of the Three Karmas.

"If no one makes any comment, the officiant must continue with the following words: 'The members of the Sangha have approved the entrance of this disciple of the Buddha, who will serve under a certain elder. There were no words of opposition from the members of the Sangha, and I consider this silence to be a sign of assent.' My disciples, this will conclude the initiation ceremony.

"The disciple of the Buddha, as a part of the rules and regulations of a disciple, must be taught the four basics and the four grave prohibitions. The four basics are (1) the disciple of the Buddha must live by receiving alms; (2) the disciple of the Buddha must wear garments made of the coarsest materials; (3) the disciple of the Buddha must make the root of a tree his place of abode; (4) the disciple of the Buddha must use medicine made of urine. Exceptions to these basics can be made. The four grave prohibitions are prohibitions against unchaste conduct, stealing, killing, and pride in regard to the Dharma."

Sariputta then had the ordination of the brahmin Radha performed according to the order of the Buddha. Later Sariputta went on a pilgrimage and at that time saw the kind and gentle actions of Radha and uttered the following verse as words of encouragement: "If you commit a wrong and meet a man who will set you right, serve such a person as one who shows you the way to hidden treasures. Is it not good that you serve under such a man?"

2. Observance of Regular Meetings and Rainy Seasons

(1) According to the tradition of the brahmanic teachings, six days of each month were set apart to gather together and listen to the teachings: the eighth, fourteenth, fifteenth, twenty-third, twenty-ninth, and thirtieth. Because these occasions gave people opportunities to hear the teaching, these days were greatly looked forward to by those who practiced the brahmanic teachings, and the teachings flourished.

King Bimbisara thought to himself, "All the teachings with the exception of the teachings of the World-Honored One are gathering my people together; if the Sangha of the World-Honored One did the same thing, it would be good." The king expressed his opinion to the World-Honored One. The World-Honored One agreed and decided to set aside certain days in the month at which time the disciples would assemble, teach the Dharma, and discuss the Dharma together. The Buddha said, "My disciples, you will gather together on six occasions, the eighth, fourteenth, fifteenth, twenty-third, twenty-ninth, and thirtieth days of each month, and you will discuss the Dharma. At that time you should purify your transgressions of the past and try to avoid them in the days to come."

(2) Again, until then, as the retreat during the rainy season had not been instituted, the disciples, even in this period of the rainy season, would walk from place to place, stepping on the growing grass. The people, seeing this, criticized them, saying, "Even the birds that fly in the skies during the rainy season build nests in the tree tops and take a rest; even the people of the other teachings, which are looked down upon as false, gather in one place and rest during this season. Why do the followers of the Buddha walk around during the rainy season, treading on the grass and plants that are just beginning to sprout and killing the insects just born?"

These words of criticism came to the attention of the Buddha; from this time the World-Honored One established the practice of the rainy season retreat. He said, "My disciples, it is best that during the rainy season you gather and reside in one place, rest, and conduct a retreat.

"The retreat will be divided into two parts, the earlier retreat and the later retreat. The earlier retreat will start on the day after the full moon in June and terminate on the day before the full moon in September; the later retreat will start on the day after the full moon in July and terminate on the day before the full moon in October. My disciples, depending on the circumstances surrounding you, you may join either of these two retreats. You may also join the middle retreat, between the earlier retreat and the later retreat. Those who find it impossible through circumstances to join the earlier retreat on the designated day may join the retreat on any day preceding the start of the later retreat, terminating the retreat upon the completion of ninety days of practice.

"My disciples, during the period of the retreat, while you are residing together, you must not go to another place. However, if a disciple or a lay follower, wishing to build a temple or a garden for the sake of the Sangha or for the sake of a disciple of the Buddha, invites you to come to teach the Dharma to him, you may leave the retreat with the provision that you return within seven days. Further, if a disciple becomes ill, or suffers from despondency or from remorse, or holds evil views, or has committed a serious offense and must receive punishment from the Sangha, even though a messenger does not come to notify you, you are permitted to leave the retreat to give comfort and to relieve his sufferings. However, you must return to the retreat within seven days.

"My disciples, in the case of an illness of your mother, father, brother, sister, or relatives, you may leave the retreat for seven days. In the case of parents, you may leave even though a messenger does not come to call you. In the case of brothers, sisters, or relatives, you must wait for the messenger before you leave.

"My disciples, one more thing, if you have to leave the retreat for the sake of the Sangha, you may leave the retreat but not for more than seven days.

"My disciples, when you are in a retreat, if you are attacked by wild animals, or are harmed by brigands, or meet with the hazards of fire or flood, or cannot possibly obtain food or medicine, or find that the retreat location is not conducive to the practice of pure actions, if you meet with such obstacles, you may leave the retreat and move to another place."

3. Last Day of the Retreat

(1) Again, one year, the World-Honored One conducted a retreat at the Jeta Grove Monastery in the city of Savatthi. At that time seven or eight disciples who were close friends were in a retreat at a certain village in the country of Kosala. These disciples thought, "At this retreat what can we do together to make our stay here as easy as possible and make it easy to make the rounds in alms receiving?"

After pondering this for some time they decided to maintain silence among themselves. The first person who returned from the alms receiving practice would prepare a place to sit, water for washing feet, and water for drinking; the others who returned later would alternately wash the bowl and clean the dining room; and anything that needed to be done, would be done; if there was anything else to be done, hand signs would be used. No one was to speak a word. They decided to spend the rainy season in this manner.

When the retreat came to an end, it was the custom for the disciples to meet in the presence of the World-Honored One. This group of disciples, after terminating their three months' retreat and putting away their bedding and mats, went to the Jeta Grove to pay their respects to the World-Honored One. The World-Honored One addressed his disciples, saying, "My disciples, how is your health? During this retreat did you experience any deficiency or want? Were you able to pass the days in mutual harmony and peace? Did you feel any difficulties in your alms receiving?"

(2) At this time this group of disciples told the Buddha that they did not speak to each other all during the retreat. Then the World-Honored One addressed all the disciples and gave the following teachings: "My disciples, these disciples, while actually living uneasy lives, thought that they were living lives of tranquillity and peace. Living like animals, living like wild sheep, living like mutual enemies, they thought that they lived lives of tranquillity and peace. Why did these disciples follow this precept of being deaf and dumb, in imitation of those who follow other teachings? Such action as this is not befitting a disciple of the Buddha. When the disciples of the Buddha gather together, they should either maintain a noble silence or talk about the Dharma. There is no need to follow the example of deaf and dumb people.

"Again, when the retreat comes to an end, you must gather together and perform pavarana. By pavarana is meant the correction by one's colleagues of one's erroneous actions during the retreat.

"My disciples, this pavarana should be performed in the following manner. A disciple who is wise and capable must consult with his fellow disciples, saying, 'Most virtuous ones of the Sangha, please listen to me. Today is the pavarana, the day of self-reflection and confession. If the Sangha is ready, let us conduct this self-reflection and confession.'

"This pavarana should commence with the elders and gradually go down to the newest disciples. The disciple of the highest rank must maintain physical dignity; placing his right knee on the floor and the palms of his hands together, he should utter the following words: 'My friends, I shall ask the Sangha for pavarana. If any one of you has noticed any fault with my actions, if you have heard of anything I did wrong, or if there is any doubt in your mind as to my actions, with compassion in your heart, please let me know of this. I shall strive to correct my fault.' He must say this three times. The disciples of the highest rank thus finish and then the other disciples, down to the newest disciple, repeat the same request.

(3) "The pavarana will be conducted on two separate days. The first falls on the fifteenth day of the month in which the retreat is concluded; this is the day of the full moon. In the event that this is not possible, the pavarana will be performed the following month, on the day of the new moon.

"My disciples, on this day of pavarana, a person who knows that he has committed a transgression should not rely on another to point it out to him; so before pavarana, he must go to another disciple and confess his transgression and repent. If he has any doubts that he has committed a transgression, he must promise to correct his fault. Again, if a person recalls a transgression after the pavarana has commenced, he must turn to the person sitting next to him and say, 'Friend, I have just recalled a transgression. After leaving this seat I shall confess and ask forgiveness and will correct my fault.' So saying, he must continue the pavarana. Suppose an occasion arises when every one of those who are about to conduct the pavarana had committed transgressions, these disciples must choose a messenger from among themselves and send him to the nearest gathering of disciples, tell them of the transgressions committed and then later must go through the pavarana."

4. Powers

(1) Pindola was the son of the teacher of King Udena, ruler of the kingdom of Kosambi. He had studied the three Vedas and was giving instructions to brahmin children, but he soon lost interest in what he was doing. Coming to Rajagaha and seeing the high regard in which the Sangha of the World-Honored One was held, he unexpectedly thought of entering the Sangha, was ordained, and became a disciple of the Buddha. He was very greedy by nature; in the practice of the Dharma he underwent many difficulties because of this trait. However, eventually he was able to overcome his greed and he attained enlightenment. He often traveled together with Moggallana.

At this time Jotika, the son of Subhadda, a wealthy man of Rajagaha, obtained a piece of sandalwood and thought to himself, "I shall have this sandalwood made into a bowl and present it to the disciples of the Buddha, keeping the left-over shavings for myself." He had the beautiful bowl hung from a high pole and proclaimed that any mendicant who could bring this bowl down by supernatural powers would be given the bowl. Many famous mendicants of that time all gathered at this place. However, they just looked up at the bowl; no one attempted to bring it down through superhuman powers.

Just at this time Pindola, together with Moggallana, went to Rajagaha on an alms receiving round. Witnessing the scene before him, Pindola said to Moggallana, "Great teacher, you possess great powers. Why not exhibit these powers before all these people and obtain the bowl?" Moggallana refused this offer and suggested that Pindola get it instead. So Pindola, exhibiting his superhuman power, jumped high into the sky and amidst the cheers of the populace brought the bowl down. The rich man invited the two to his home, filled the bowl with delicacies, and as promised made offerings to them. The people gathered outside would not depart, so the two left the rich man's house to go to the Bamboo Grove Monastery with the people trailing behind them. The two monks arrived at the monastery with the accompanying crowd, breaking the quiet surrounding the monastery.

The World-Honored One, hearing the clamor outside, gathered his disciples together and asked Pindola for an explanation. Upon hearing the explanation, the World-Honored One said to Pindola, "Pindola, is this true?"

"World-Honored One, it is true."

"Pindola, this is an act not befitting a monk. Why did you exhibit supernatural powers for the sake of obtaining a lowly wooden bowl? You have exhibited your act for the purpose of gaining money. This is not the way to have people who do not have faith attain faith, neither is it the way by which those who have faith have their faith strengthened. My disciples, you should not exhibit your powers to the lay people. Destroy this wooden bowl and make powdered incense out of the broken pieces and mix this incense with powdered eye-medicine. From now on, you are prohibited from having such wooden bowls. This is to be the rule for the Sangha."

(2) As the fame of the World-Honored One spread, there were those who became disciples of the Buddha wishing to see the Buddha's performance of miracles. However, the true Dharma does not require supernatural elements. The World-Honored One taught the Four Noble Truths and prohibited his disciples from performing miracles. The followers of the other religions gleefully reviled him, saying that Sakyamuni did not have superhuman teachings and that his teachings were common and simple. Among his disciples there were some who left the Sangha, expressing their discontent; however, the World-Honored One adhered to his teaching.

5. The Lion's Roar

(1) The World-Honored One, while going north from Rajagaha, stopped in a grove west of the city of Vesali. At that time a person by the name of Sunakkhata, who was of the Licchavi clan and who had recently forsaken the teachings of the

World-Honored One, was telling the people of Vesali, "Gotama does not possess superhuman teachings. He does not have superior views and knowledge. He teaches things that he has thought up or things that come to his mind on the spur of the moment. According to those teachings, a person can attain the state where there is no suffering by just thinking about it without performing any difficult practices."

(2) Sariputta, while making his alms receiving rounds one early morning, heard about these remarks and reported them to the World-Honored One. The Buddha said, "Sariputta, Sunakkhata uttered those words in anger, but by attempting to revile me he has actually praised the Buddha. 'According to those teachings a person can attain the state where there is no suffering by just thinking about it.' These words are words in praise of the Buddha. Sariputta, this foolish person does not know that I possess ten epithets. They are Tathagata, Arhat, Rightly and Fully Awakened One, Endowed with Knowledge and Conduct, Well Gone, Knower of the World, Preeminent Leader of Those to be Trained, Teacher of Gods and Men, Buddha, and World-Honored One.

"Sariputta, the Buddha also has ten powers. With these ten powers the Buddha, knowing the states of all things, proclaims the Dharma to all people. These ten powers are that the Buddha knows what is possible and what is impossible; that the Buddha knows the effects of actions; that the Buddha knows the various propensities; that the Buddha knows the various realms; that the Buddha knows the supreme and non-supreme faculties; that the Buddha knows the path that goes everywhere; that the Buddha knows how to purify the defects in the many kinds of meditation; that the Buddha knows his former abodes; that the Buddha knows the life and death of beings with his divine eye; and that the Buddha knows the destruction of defilements. These are the ten powers of the Buddha.

"Sariputta, Sunakkhata, knowing this, says that Gotama does not possess superhuman teachings, and that he does not have any superior views or knowledge. He will descend into hell unless he recants his words and changes his ideas.

(3) "Sariputta, the Buddha possesses the four qualities of fearlessness or self-confidence. Someone in this world may criticize me, saying, 'You think that you have understood all dharmas, but you have not understood them; you think that you have extinguished all defilements, but you have not extinguished them; you think that you can explain what dharmas are obstacles to enlightenment, but you cannot explain them; you think that you can explain the path that leads to nirvana, but you cannot explain it.' But these words of revilement are not right. I do not accept the basis for such criticism. Because I do not accept the basis, my mind is at ease. I do not know any fear.

"Sariputta, I shall tell you this. I have gone many times to the meetings held by the kshatriyas. I have spoken with them on these occasions on a common basis of equality. I did not have any fear whatsoever. This is the same for any meeting I may attend.

"Sariputta, there are four kinds of birth. They are oviparous birth, viviparous birth, water birth, and metamorphic birth.

"Oviparous birth is birth from eggs, in which the egg breaks and birth takes place. Viviparous birth is birth from the womb, in which the womb is broken and birth takes place. Water birth is birth from decayed fish, from decayed meat, from spoiled rice gruel, or from stagnant water in a marsh or pond. Metamorphic birth is the birth that those in the heavens, those in hell, and some human beings undergo.

"Sariputta, I know all these. I know the paths that lead to these. Again, I know nirvana; I know the path that leads to nirvana. I know the actions by which one enters nirvana.

(4) "Sariputta, I know what will happen to certain persons. This person will undergo thus because he is walking the path in the manner that he is; I know that this person after death will fall into hell. After watching this person with my superhuman vision, I see that he has gone to hell and is undergoing acute suffering.

"Sariputta, this person who is reviling me says, 'Gotama does not possess superhuman teachings, neither does he possess superior knowledges and views; Gotama teaches anything that happens to come to his mind.' This person will descend into hell unless he discards these ideas."

(5) The World-Honored One then proceeded to the north and entered the town of Anupiya in Malla. One day he started to go out on his alms receiving rounds when he realized that it was still early, so he decided to visit a travelling teacher, Bhaggava-gotta, at his hermitage. Bhaggava-gotta said to the Buddha, "Most Virtuous One, the day before yesterday, Sunakkhata of the Licchavi clan came to my place. He was saying that he was no longer a disciple of the World-Honored One and has left your Sangha. Is this true?"

The World-Honored One answered, "Bhaggava-gotta, it is exactly as he said. Sunakkhata came to my presence several days ago saying, 'I am leaving you; I shall no longer stay with the World-Honored One because the World-Honored One does not teach me superhuman teachings and miracles.' To him I said, 'Sunakkhata, I never asked you to come and reside with me; I never promised you that I would teach you superhuman teachings and miracles. Then who has broken a commitment? Sunakkhata, my teachings are for those who wish to enter the state where there is no suffering. In this regard, what difference is there in the practice or nonpractice of miracles? Sunakkhata, you have praised the virtues of the Buddha, the Dharma, and the Sangha. If you leave this place of pure practices, people will say that you were not able to endure the practice of these pure activities.'

(6) "Bhaggava-gotta, this was my answer to him. I further counseled him as follows: 'Sunakkhata, when I was staying at the village of Uttaraka in Bhumu, I had you accompany me on an alms receiving round one early morning. At that time, a naked ascetic, Kora-khattiya, in accordance with the dog precepts, was crawling on the ground with his hands and feet and eating the food on the ground. Upon seeing this spectacle, you praised the actions of this ascetic who practiced

the dog precepts, saying, "Oh, what a good and wonderful thing this sage is doing!" I criticized this mistaken and shameful teaching and prophesied that this dog precept ascetic would die within seven days of stomach disorders. This happened just as I predicted. Sunakkhata, in spite of this, you are still attached to this type of teaching.

"'There was another similar incident while we were at the Kutagara Hall near Vesali, with a naked ascetic named Kandaramasuka. He performed such acts as not wearing clothes all his life; he would not permit women to come close to him; he would not drink alcohol or eat meat; he would not eat white rice or rice gruel; he would not even take a step outside the confines of Vesali. By performing these ascetic practices he had attained a high reputation. Sunakkhata, you, by becoming a slave to outward forms, thought that this ascetic had attained enlightenment. Again, just as I predicted, this ascetic gave up his ascetic practices and left for places unknown.

"'Again, a person named Patikaputta also gained acclaim from the people for his ascetic practices. He criticized me, claiming that his performance of miracles was far superior to mine. At that time, you believed what he said and you reported to me what he was saying. I said that Patikaputta would not recant or renounce his ideas and views; also I said that he would not come into my presence.

"'The next day, taking you with me, I went to Patikaputta's place of abode. People assembled, thinking that there was going to be a contest in the performance of miracles. Patikaputta secretly stole away to the hermitage of Tindukkhanu, a garden of wandering ascetics. The people followed him to this hermitage and pleaded with Patikaputta to have a contest with Gotama. Patikaputta, while saying, "I shall go, I shall go," would not come out from the hermitage. The people attempted to bring him out, but all attempts ended in failure. When all was said and done, Patikaputta would not come into my presence and did not recant his words or renounce his ideas and views.

"'Sunakkhata, even after having seen my superhuman teachings and powers, you still seek further superhuman teachings and abilities. Is not this a great mistake on your part?'

"Bhaggava-gotta, in this manner I tried to teach him, but he was so absorbed in outward forms that he could not see the inner meaning, so eventually he left my Sangha."

Bhaggava-gotta addressed the Buddha, saying, "Most virtuous one, I believe that those who revile the most virtuous one and his disciples are in the wrong. Most virtuous one, will you please teach me the path that will lead me to pure enlightenment?"

The World-Honored One said, "Bhaggava-gotta, it is difficult for a person like yourself who have different convictions and viewpoints to try to enter pure enlightenment. It will be well for you to maintain the faith that you have in me." And Bhaggava-gotta greatly rejoiced in these words of the World-Honored One; he vowed that he would maintain his faith in the World-Honored One.

(7) The World-Honored One travelled southward and entered the city of Rajagaha. There the non-Buddhists were uttering strange rumors, saying,

"In the teachings of the Buddha there is nothing superhuman. He has come to the end of his career. He does not possess any miraculous powers to show." The World-Honored One, realizing that the time had arrived when he could not avert a confrontation with the followers of other teachings, made the following proclamation: "Four months from this date, at a place east of Savatthi called Mango Grove, I shall show my miraculous powers." Then the World-Honored One left Rajagaha and took the road leading north and arrived at Savatthi.

South of Savatthi, and east of Jeta Grove, there is another grove. The World-Honored One, accompanied by his disciples, entered this grove. The people of Savatthi and the followers of other teachings followed the World-Honored One. The watchman of the grove presented the World-Honored One with a mango fruit. The World-Honored One ate the fruit, gave the seed to Ananda, and ordered him to plant it in the soil nearby. As soon as the seed was put into the soil, the World-Honored One washed his hands over the planted seed. Then to the astonishment of all, the earth suddenly opened up and a bud started growing out of the ground before the eyes of the spectators. Then leaves started to appear on the branches, and soon flowers started to bloom and fruit appeared. The people were all struck with awe, and all praised the greatness of the Buddha's power. The leader of the non-Buddhists started to make preparations to steal away.

While the people were in a state of amazement, suddenly there appeared a large road across the sky that ran from east to west. The World-Honored One quietly rose into the sky and stood astride the road. From the body of the Buddha issued two streams of fire and water. From each pore of his skin came similar kinds of wonders. It was a spectacle that could not possibly be expressed in words. Then the World-Honored One became two persons. The two forms of the World-Honored One stood, sat, and walked; while they were doing this, they conversed with each other. This dialogue consisted of discussions on the deep meaning of the Dharma. The people, looking upward, seeing this miraculous scene and hearing the deep meaning of the Dharma, all praised the virtues of the Buddha, and they came to understand the Four Noble Truths.

Thus did the World-Honored One exhibit his miraculous powers. Then, leaving the people, he ascended to the Tavatimsa heaven to the presence of his mother, Queen Maya. The multitudes, however, did not show any sign of departing.

6. Sermon in the Tavatimsa Heaven

(1) The palace at the Tavatimsa heaven was filled with the gods who had gathered from different places. At that time the light radiated by the World-Honored One illuminated all the worlds; it outshone the light of the sun, moon, and stars. Everyone in this heavenly world was enveloped in his radiant light. The radiance caused all the people in the heaven to quiver. At this time the Bodhisattva Manjusri was asked to go into the presence of Queen Maya. Manjusri recited a song in praise of the World-Honored One:

> The great sage of the Sakya clan possesses wisdom all encompassing.

> In the world he is like the god with a thousand eyes.

Constantly thinking of his mother,

He wished to meet her for a long time.

Seven days after giving me birth,

She came to this kingly palace;

She received the happiness of the world of the gods.

In order to repay the debt of gratitude

That I owe her from the past,

I have come here to teach the Dharma.

O, mother, please respect the Three Treasures and receive the true Dharma.

(2) When Queen Maya heard this song, milk started to stream forth from her breasts and she said, "If this is truly my son Siddhattha, the milk will enter his mouth." With these words, milk like white lotus blossoms entered the mouth of the World-Honored One. Queen Maya rejoiced at this and with a radiance on her face like the reflection of the sun on thousands of lotus petals, she said to the Bodhisattva Manjusri, "Ever since I became the mother of the Buddha, I have never met with such happiness and joy. I am like a person who, suffering the pangs of severe hunger, meets with delicious food." Thus together with the Bodhisattva Manjusri she went into the presence of the World-Honored One. Seeing his mother approaching from a distance, the World-Honored One's heart was filled with joy and reverence; seeing her coming closer and closer as if she had lifted herself and floated in the air, he said to his mother, "Until now your course has been a path of suffering and pleasure. From now on, please practice this path leading to enlightenment, and free yourself forever from the crossroads of suffering and pleasure."

Queen Maya, hearing these words, put her hands together in reverence, bowed her head, concentrated her thoughts, purified all her evil desires, and then uttered the following verses:

Throughout innumerable kalpas you partook of my milk;

You have gotten rid of all delusions

And attained the state of enlightenment.

If you wish to repay your debt of gratitude,

Cut off the roots of my three poisons.

I now place my trust and reliance on the Buddha,

The greatest of heroes

And the master of compassionate giving.

O king of the supreme teachings,

Possessor of the most fertile fields of happiness,

May you let the plants of virtue grow,

And with compassion in your heart

Lead me into enlightenment.

(3) Thus the merits of the queen mother ripened because of the power of the World-Honored One. Overcoming the bonds of transgression, she entered enlightenment; she attained the state of non-retrogression. Putting her palms together she said, "World-Honored One, I have escaped from the hell of birth and death and have attained enlightenment." Hearing these words, the people who had gathered raised their voices in joy.

The queen continued with these words: "Like one being burnt by touching iron heated by a fierce blaze, my mind and body were singed by heat and I was in a state of burning desire, like the leaves of a tree being fanned by a fierce wind." Reproaching her own mind, she continued, saying, "O my mind, why do you roam about within this futile realm and show no signs of calmness or composure; why are you so restless that you do not cease your motions? Why do you cause me to become confused and bedevil me to gather things? Such a life is like that of one trying to plow the fields with a plow that breaks into pieces before it even touches the ground. I have wandered aimlessly in the ocean of birth and death and have abandoned any number of lives; however, I have not been able to plow the fields of my mind. During this time, you had me rule as a great king or you had me wander here and there as a beggar, begging for food. On another occasion, you had me live in the palaces inhabited by gods and had me become weary of pleasures. Again, you sent me to hell and caused me to swallow molten copper and red hot iron pellets. Thus even though I went through various phases of life and death, you have not allowed me to escape from delusion. O foolish mind, you led me in so many different ways. I followed you all these lives and never disobeyed you. However, now I have heard the Dharma. Now do not cause me to suffer; do not become an obstacle in my path. Please strive to free yourself from various sufferings, immediately seek enlightenment, and preserve the quiescence within."

(4) Then she turned toward the World-Honored One and recited the following verses:

(i) May you let the rain of the Dharma fall and quench the thirst of those whose throats are parched; may you nourish the buds of the Dharma tree, and may they gently grow. Kindly favor us with the nectar and the fruit of wisdom. During the long night of wandering, we are bound in the darkness of prison; we have no means of seeking the path. May you show us the way to release, so that we may instantly enter the palace of joy.

(ii) Your wisdom is like the summit of the mountain; its peak soars, its valley is deep. Where the clear waters flow downward, there is the luxuriant growth of medicinal herbs. Truly you, O Buddha, are the king of physicians; you prescribe good medicine according to one's illness. If people have faith in you, their happiness knows no bounds. You, O Buddha, alone can take away all the suffering that has afflicted people from time immemorial and fulfill their wishes. O Buddha, now by your compassion for your mother who gave you birth, extend that compassion to all sentient beings; may you readily reveal the Dharma and let them receive it.

(5) The World-Honored One said to the queen mother, "Queen mother, the reasons why people cannot free themselves from illusion are their greed, anger, and ignorance. Because of these three poisons, they cannot even be reborn in the heavens. How much less when they attempt to leave the realm of birth and death!

"In this world they lose their reputations, they are shunned by their friends and relatives like clods of dirt, and at the time of death they are beset by fear. They lose control of their minds and leave only deep regrets because of these poisons. Wherefore, if one seeks the other shore of enlightenment, which is release from these bonds, one must cut the roots of suffering. Just as a wild horse is bound by ropes, a foolish mortal being is bound by evil desires and cannot move. So you should truly perceive the mind and body that make up yourself. Then you can be released from the sufferings of birth, old age, sickness, death, and sorrow. This is what is meant by cutting the roots of suffering. Thus you can free yourself from delusion, from attachment, and from hatred."

(6) At this time a god named Candradeva appeared from amidst the multitude and arranged his robes, paid respect to the World-Honored One, and praised his virtues by reciting the following verses:

(i)   Taking pity on people,
      You have sought enlightenment
      And spent immeasurable time
      Enduring many sufferings.
      You have benefitted many;
      Your mind is tranquil and peaceful;
      You are the source of incomparable happiness in the world;
      Your virtues are like the ocean.
      Since your mind is filled with compassion,
      You are far removed from fear;
      You love others just as you love yourself.

(ii) O great sage,
      Although you roam about in a million countries,
      You do not become attached to any country;
      Although you make offerings to millions of Buddhas,
      You do not become attached to any one Buddha.
      Evil is conquered, and the path is established;
      Darkness has disappeared forever.
      Thus the Dharma is founded;
      Heaven and earth tremble with joy.

(7) Ending his song of praise, the god asked the Buddha, "World-Honored One, for one who wishes to follow the path, how is it possible to attain the highest wisdom and practice and reach the shore of enlightenment?" The World-Honored One answered, saying, "O god, the bodhisattva knows that all things arise naturally, that all things are originally pure and without self, that

all things are not born, neither do they exist without change, nor do they come into existence. Therefore, when he talks about the teachings of the Buddha there is no thought of self, nor is there attachment to things.

"Again, O god, all things are like the sky. Because all things of the three worlds are products of the mind, if there is no attachment on the part of the mind, there should be neither matter nor form. Again, this mind is something we cannot see. It is neither matter nor form; it is like an apparition. If one tries to find things based on such a mind, none of those things will be attained. Further, if you seek the mind, there is no such mind; there will only be a temporary name without substance. In truth we know that there exists tranquillity free from the attachment to desire.

"Again, O god, a bodhisattva, in order to strengthen his vows, and to attain perfect wisdom, incessantly strives with diligence and without rest. Always with compassion for others, he endures all suffering and does not change his resolve.

"Next, the bodhisattva, without breaking with the path of the common people, prepares himself for the path of the Buddha. In other words, he does not slander the way of the common people; and he does not especially consider the benefits of the Buddha's way; neither does he try to praise the works of the Buddha. This is because he does not discriminate between the way of the common people as gross and vulgar and the way of the Buddha as noble and subtle. In truth, why should these two ways be differentiated? Actually they are not different; they only possess temporary names or labels. It is only discrimination that causes differences.

"Therefore, the Buddha's doctrine is none other than discerning things as they are with wisdom. If we see all things with this wisdom, there is only Emptiness. This does not mean that things do not exist. They exist, but they possess no determined substance that we can become attached to. Thus they are called Emptiness. The discriminatory forms of the common people's blind attachment arise because of ignorance.

"That is why, O god, things are different from what the common people see; they are not soiled by desire, are not discriminatory, and are absolutely equal. To see things with non-discrimination is the path of the Buddha.

"In fact, if one practices and follows the true teachings, not even one thing is separate from the Buddha's doctrine. Things become discriminated because of the habits of the common people; if those habits are discarded, things, which are freed from language and thinking, will absolutely have no definite forms. O god, although there may be no limit to the number of things, they are all part of the Buddha-Dharma. To know that all things in themselves are all Buddha-Dharma is the wisdom of the Buddha."

(8) Candradeva asked the Buddha, "World-Honored One, the bodhisattvas with their wisdom know the nature of birth and death, and they seek the path without any rest. How then do they regard the birth and destruction of things?" The World-Honored One answered, "O god, the bodhisattvas see that all things are like phantoms and that they manifest themselves as the six realms, but that in truth there is neither birth nor death." The god asked, "World-Honored One,

if your teachings are like this, then why did the World-Honored One come to this heaven and spend three months here for the sake of the mother who gave him birth? After all, the World-Honored One was born from Queen Maya, was he not?"

The World-Honored One said, "O god, the Buddha was not born from Queen Maya. The mother of the Buddha is the wisdom that enables one to reach the shore of enlightenment. In other words, she is the Perfection of Wisdom. The reason for this is that all the forms that are attributes of the Buddha, all the wisdom and power, were not due to Queen Maya; they were truly born because of the attainment of the Perfection of Wisdom." And Queen Maya and all the people received the teachings of the World-Honored One and rejoiced in their hearts.

7. The Twelve Links of Dependent Origination

(1) The World-Honored One then travelled to a country far to the west called Kuru. Accompanied by Ananda he entered the town of Kammassadhamma.

Now Ananda was still young; he still did not know the depth of the Buddha's teachings. One day he was sitting under a tree and thought on the teachings of the World-Honored One. As his mind became clearer, Ananda thought that he was able to comprehend the teaching of dependent origination that the World-Honored One had taught. In his elation he immediately went to the World-Honored One and said, "World-Honored One, the principle of dependent origination that you taught us is very deep, but today I have come to understand it."

The World-Honored One answered, "O Ananda, you should not speak thus. This principle of dependent origination is very difficult to understand. The reason people are in this world of suffering and affliction is that they cannot understand the principle of dependent origination, which is as difficult to unravel as a mass of tangled threads. O Ananda, decay and death arise because of birth; birth arises because of becoming; becoming arises because of attachment; attachment arises because of desire; desire arises because of sensation; sensation arises because of contact; contact arises because of the six organs of sense; the six organs of sense arise because of mind and body; mind and body arise because of consciousness; consciousness arises because of volition; volition arises because of ignorance.

"O Ananda, now I shall explain one of the twelve links of dependent origination: sensation is the condition for the arising of desire. If there is no sensation, desire does not arise. Sensation is the basis for the arising of desire. Because of desire the wish to seek arises; from this wish to seek the wish to obtain arises; upon obtaining, the choice of good and bad arises; because of this choice, attachment arises; because of attachment, jealousy arises; because of jealousy, greed is increased; because of greed we strive to protect our possessions. With canes and swords we quarrel and fight, slandering each other—all these evils arise.

(2) "O Ananda, next I shall talk about the ego. The concept that admits the existence of the ego cannot go beyond these four views: the ego is material and limited; the ego is material and unlimited; the ego is immaterial and limited; the ego is immaterial and unlimited. O Ananda, although there are these four ways of considering the ego, it is a mistake to consider the ego as having a definite

substance. Why? Because the ego only makes its appearance because of various conditions.

"O Ananda, there are people who say that the ego is identical with sensations; again, there are people who say that the ego is neither sensations nor perceptions. Again there are those who say that although the ego is neither sensations nor perceptions, it is the act of sensing and knowing.

"O Ananda, concerning the idea that the ego is identical with sensations, our sensations are those of suffering, pleasure, or neither suffering nor pleasure. If we have sensations of pleasure, for instance, those sensations of pleasure are not permanent; they are always in a state of change. So, when that pleasure disappears, we would have to say, 'My ego is no more.' Thus we cannot say that the ego is one with sensations.

"Again, there are people who say that the ego is neither sensations nor perceptions. But how can they say that the ego exists when there are no sensations nor perceptions? Since they cannot, it cannot be that the ego is neither sensations nor perceptions.

"Again, there are those who say that the ego is neither sensations nor perceptions but is the act of sensing and knowing itself; however, when all sensations and perceptions are completely extinguished, how can they say that the ego exists? Thus we must say that all these ideas of the existence of the ego are erroneous.

"O Ananda, disciples who have rid themselves of these mistaken concepts regarding the ego do not attach themselves to anything in this world, and thus without fear are able to get away from illusion and attain enlightenment."

Ananda greatly rejoiced in this teaching of the World-Honored One. He returned to the forest and continued his practice of meditation.

(3) In the town of Kammassadhamma there lived a brahmin named Magandiya. He had a daughter named Magandiya who was very beautiful. This brahmin was very proud of his daughter's beauty and wanted her to marry a fine young man. One day, by chance, he saw the World-Honored One walking by the roadside on his alms receiving mission. Impressed by the striking features of the World-Honored One, the brahmin thought that he was a most suitable husband for his daughter. He immediately returned to his home; bringing his wife and daughter with him, he followed the World-Honored One, but the World-Honored One had already left the town and entered the grove. The three members of the brahmin family took note of the footprints left by the World-Honored One. The wife said, "This person must have freed himself from all desires. Otherwise, he could not have left behind such orderly and gentle footprints. We must not say anything disrespectful to this venerable personality."

However, the brahmin did not heed her words of advice. Finding the World-Honored One sitting under a tree, he went toward the World-Honored One and said, "O mendicant, you have already attained your goal through your practices, so why do you not you return to your home? My daughter here is very beautiful, as you can see. If you will consent to take her as your wife, we shall consider it a great honor and it will make us very happy."

The World-Honored One answered, "O brahmin, I do not have anything to do even with a heavenly maiden, much less with a woman filled with foul smelling pus. What would I want with such a woman?" Then the World-Honored One expounded the precepts and other teachings. When he ended his discourse, the brahmin and his wife shed tears of joy, apologized for their discourteous behavior, and asked that they be allowed to join the Sangha as disciples.

However, the daughter was as conceited as a peacock and was too obstinate to be soaked through with the rain of the Dharma. She felt maligned when her beauteous appearance was called a polluted body filled with pus, and her wounded mind secretly vowed to take revenge. Soon afterward, the brahmin couple entered the Sangha; the daughter became the first queen consort of King Udena of Kosambi, who was struck by her beauty at first sight.

(4) People began to question the whereabouts of the World-Honored One. When they heard from Anuruddha that the World-Honored One would return three months after his ascending to the Tavatimsa heaven, they were eagerly looking forward to his return. The World-Honored One spent the year's retreat in the Tavatimsa heaven; then around the end of November he decided to descend to Samkassa. Indra ordered Vissakamma to make three jewelled stairways. That day the World-Honored One put his foot on the center golden stairway. Brahma, holding a white whisk on the Buddha's right side, stepped down on the silver steps; Indra, carrying a jewelled umbrella on the Buddha's left side, stepped down on the crystal steps. The gods followed flying in the air, scattering flower garlands and praising the virtues of the World-Honored One. The first one who knew of the descent of the World-Honored One was a nun by the name of Uppalavanna, who was considered the first in superhuman powers among the nuns. She immediately changed herself into the form of the great Wheel-Turning king and welcomed the Buddha. However, she was not the first person to welcome the World-Honored One.

At this time, Subhuti was sewing his robes in a cave on Vulture Peak outside of Rajagaha, which was several hundred miles east of the city of Samkassa. With the thought of welcoming the World-Honored One, Subhuti put to one side the robes that he had been sewing and started to stand up. As his right knee touched the ground, the following thoughts occurred in his mind: "Just what is the form of the Buddha whom I was about to welcome? This form of the Buddha is composed of matter. Is not my body also composed of matter? All these things are empty. There is no creator; there is nothing created.

"In paying homage to the Buddha, I pay homage to the impermanence and inconstancy of body and mind.

"In paying homage to the Buddha, I pay homage to the emptiness of all things.

"In paying homage to the Buddha, I pay homage to the lack of self in all things.

"I do not exist; there is no creator, nor is there anything created; everything is empty. I pay homage to the true Dharma." Returning to his seat, Subhuti commenced sewing his robes again.

When the World-Honored One returned to his disciples, he said to Uppalavanna, "O Uppalavanna, you were not the first to see me. Subhuti, seeing the true nature of things as empty, was the first to see me. He who sees my body is not the one who sees me; he who sees the Dharma is the one who sees me."

(5) At Samkassa, the disciple Sariputta became the leader and was teaching the disciples and the laymen. Now, when the World-Honored One stepped down the jewelled steps and was about to put his feet on the ground, Sariputta stepped forward and said, "World-Honored One, I welcome you. Today all the people are rejoicing at your return." The World-Honored One answered, "O Sariputta, you are very fortunate to rejoice for a person who has cut off all defilements and attained enlightenment and release." And many attained enlightenment by hearing this conversation between the World-Honored One and Sariputta.

8. Cinca

(1) Soon afterwards, the World-Honored One returned to Savatthi from Samkassa. The people's faith and trust in him grew at an increasing rate; offerings came into the Sangha like gushing water. The non-Buddhists were filled with envy and jealousy; they planned schemes and plots against him. There was a daughter of a brahmin, called Cinca. She was beautiful and was also a believer in a non-Buddhist religion. These nonbelievers planned to use Cinca for furthering their schemes.

One day, as was her wont, Cinca visited the grove where the nonbelievers lived. The head teacher of the nonbelievers did not greet her but remained silent and had a worried look on his face. Cinca feared that she might have been the cause of his displeasure. She asked him the reason. The nonbeliever said, "Because Gotama is teaching his doctrines, we are losing our adherents and offerings day by day. If you can damage Gotama's reputation through your power and cause people to cease respecting him, it will be a wonderful thing."

Cinca said, "Leave everything to me." Promising to undertake this task herself, she then departed.

From that time on, every day the figure of this woman was seen on the roadside between Savatthi and Jeta Grove. Around the time people were returning home from Jeta Grove, she would make her way toward the monastery. And when people began to go toward the monastery, she would make it appear that she was returning home. After some time had passed, she said that her lodging for the night was always the incense-scented room within the monastery.

After the passage of a few months' time, her abdomen began to swell, giving her the appearance of a woman in pregnancy, and people who did not know her started to have suspicions and began to worry.

One day the woman attended a discourse of the World-Honored One and, in the midst of the sermon, stood up and exclaimed, "O mendicant, you are teaching the great Dharma to the people. Then why do you not build a place for me to give birth to our child? You have many rich patrons who support you. You have taken your pleasure; why do you now fear the consequences?"

The World-Honored One answered, "Whether what you say is true or false, only you and I know."

At this time a rat appeared and approached Cinca and bit and cut her sash. Then a gust of wind suddenly arose and blew open her dress and a wooden bowl fell from her abdomen. Cinca's scheme was now revealed; amidst the angry clamor of people directed toward her, Cinca was able to escape from the monastery, but before she could get very far the ground opened up and swallowed her.

(2) A female wandering ascetic in a white robe, Sundari by name, was also renowned for her beauty and was also used by the nonbelievers. The nonbelievers, spreading rumors that there was some kind of relationship between her and the World-Honored One, later had someone kill her and throw her body into a junk pile near the Jeta Grove Monastery. However, this scheme was also exposed; all those who were implicated were severely punished by King Pasenadi. Thus the prestige of the World-Honored One fanned the flames of the nonbelievers' jealousy and caused the arising of persecutions; however, the light of the World-Honored One continued to spread over the four quarters.

(3) For some time the World-Honored One stayed at Jeta Grove Monastery and expounded the Dharma to his disciples: "O disciples, here are three wrong views. A wise man will discern these mistakes and attempt to have people discard them. If one persists in following these views, it will mean the denial of all human efforts in the world.

"What are these three wrong views? First, a certain mendicant declares that any kind of suffering, pleasure, or neither suffering nor pleasure that man experiences in this world is because of the karma of the past lives. Second, a certain mendicant says that everything is the result of creation by the god Mahissara. Third, a certain person declares that there is no cause and there are no conditions.

(4) "O disciples, thus I will go to the place of the mendicant who holds the view that all things are due to the karma of past lives and ask if he really holds to this view. If he says that he does, I shall tell him thus, 'O mendicant, the killing in this world, the stealing, the ignoble acts, words of evil, slander, flattery, greed, anger, and evil views must not be attributed to causes from our past lives. If they are decided by the karma of our past lives, there will be no hope for us and we shall make no effort to do this or not do that. Thus one will not know what one should do or should not do. One who, because of his delusion, cannot control his five senses cannot be called a true mendicant.' This is my fair criticism of those who hold this kind of view.

(5) "O disciples, to those mendicants who make Mahissara the cause of all things, I shall say, 'O mendicants, then the act of killing is caused by Mahissara. If you make Mahissara the cause of all things, people will have no hope nor make any effort to do this or not do that. They will truly be unable to know what to do or what not to do. Those who cannot control their five senses because of delusion cannot be called true mendicants.' This is my fair criticism of those who hold this kind of view.

(6) "O disciples, to those mendicants who maintain that there is neither cause nor condition, I shall tell them, 'Then, O mendicants, in the act of killing there is neither cause nor condition. If you say there is neither cause nor condition,

people will have no hope nor make any effort to do this or not to do that. Thus they truly will not know what to do or what not to do. Those who cannot control the five senses because of delusion cannot be called true mendicants.' O disciples, this is my fair criticism of those mendicants who hold these views. O disciples, in the final analysis, these are the three wrong views that deny all the efforts in this world; wise people will recognize these views as erroneous and strive to have people forsake these views.

(7) "O disciples, in opposition to these wrong views I teach the Four Noble Truths and the twelve links of dependent origination. This Dharma that I teach you, even in the slightest degree, cannot be slandered, defiled, or criticized by those who are thoughtful and considerate.

"O disciples, I say to you that all suffering and pleasure and neither suffering nor pleasure arise because of causes and conditions. How do they arise? I teach that because of ignorance and desire, decrepitude and death arise; worry, sadness, suffering, affliction, and troubles arise. In the Four Noble Truths these come under the Noble Truth of suffering and the Noble Truth of the cause of suffering. I teach that if ignorance and desire are extinguished, those things that arise from them, decrepitude, death, worry, sadness, suffering, affliction, and troubles, also are extinguished. Here we have the Noble Truth of the cessation of suffering and the Noble Truth of the way to the cessation of suffering in the Four Noble Truths.

"O disciples, this teaching of mine cannot even in the slightest degree be slandered, defiled, or criticized by those who are thoughtful and considerate."

(8) At one time the World-Honored One, accompanied by many followers, visited the country of Kosala and came to a brahmin village called Venagapura. The devotees at Venagapura heard about his coming; soon there spread beautiful praises of his high virtues, such as, "The World-Honored One is a Buddha who is worthy of receiving the offerings of the world; he is the great teacher of people and gods. He has attained enlightenment and he expounds the Dharma that is beautiful from beginning to end, in all the worlds; he sets an example of harmonious and pious practice. There is nothing exceeding the joy in seeing the Buddha."

Then the brahmin devotees of Venagapura went into the presence of the World-Honored One, and one by one they paid homage to him and sat to one side. At that time a brahmin named Vacchagotta addressed these words to the World-Honored One, "World-Honored One, how magnificent you are! Your figure is graceful, and your face shines forth in radiance. Just as the jujube fruit ripens to a pure gold color, your countenance shines forth like Jambunada gold. The ornamented seat is most befitting you. Is it not true that you may have a heavenly seat just by wishing for it?"

The World-Honored One said, "O brahmin, such a magnificent seat is difficult to obtain for a mendicant. Even though a mendicant might be able to obtain one, the use of such a seat is prohibited. O brahmin, now there are three seats that I can have immediately if my heart desires. They are the seat of heaven, the seat of Brahma, and the seat of a sage. These three magnificent seats I can have any time my heart wishes."

The brahmin asked, "World-Honored One, please explain these seats." The Buddha answered, "O brahmin, suppose that I reside near a village or town. Early in the morning I go out into the village or town to receive alms. After eating breakfast I return to the grove, gather some grass and leaves, and sit properly thinking right thoughts. Freeing myself from desire and evil, and practicing the various meditations, I am able to experience in my mind the purity that no longer brings suffering, pleasure, or neither suffering nor pleasure. Thus I feel the happiness of heaven even while I am walking, standing, sitting, or lying down. This is the seat of heaven that I can have any time I wish.

"Next, O brahmin, suppose that I reside near a village or town. I go into the village or town early in the morning for receiving alms; then after breakfast I return to the grove, gather some grass and leaves, and sit properly thinking right thoughts. In this way, I fill one direction with a mind full of compassion. With a mind of Great Compassion, everywhere, I fill, without spite or hatred, the myriad worlds that lie in two, three, or four directions of the compass, in the zenith, and in the nadir. I do so with a mind of pity, rejoicing, and equality. I experience pure happiness whether walking or standing still. This is the seat of Brahma that I can have any time I wish.

"Again, O brahmin, suppose that I reside near a village or town. Early in the morning I go into the village or town to receive alms. After breakfast I return to the grove, gather some grass and leaves, and sit properly and think right thoughts. Thereby I know that my thoughts of greed, anger, and ignorance will be uprooted and will not sprout new buds again. I know that I have attained the Dharma that ends my rebirths. Here I shall walk and rest, experiencing the boundless joy of the sages; I shall sit on the seat of the sage; I shall lie down on the couch of the sage. O brahmin, this is the seat of the sage that I can obtain any time I wish."

"World-Honored One, how marvellous these three magnificent seats are! How could anyone beside yourself obtain them any time they wished?"

(9) Again, at one time Ananda made the following remarks to the World-Honored One: "World-Honored One, there are three kinds of fragrance that float along with the wind and do not go against the wind. The three are the fragrance from the roots of trees, the fragrance from the centers of trees, and the fragrance from the flowers of trees. These three kinds of fragrance go with the wind and do not resist the wind. Are there fragrances that go both with and against the wind?" The Buddha answered, "O Ananda, such incenses do exist. Here let us suppose that there is a man or woman living in a village or town who pays homage to the Buddha, the Dharma, and the Sangha, parts with killing, stealing, impure sexual acts, and lying, does not become intoxicated with drink, does not lead a life of dissipation, follows the precepts, has a good nature, and always performs acts of giving with a mind that has parted with defiled greed. Such a person will be praised by the mendicants and the gods everywhere. Ananda, this is the fragrance that goes both with and against the wind.

"The fragrance of flowers does not go against the wind; the same with the fragrance of the sandalwood tree. However the fragrance of a righteous person goes against the wind and spreads the fragrance of a good person in the four directions."

9. Anuruddha

(1) The country of the Vacchas had not yet been favored by the teachings of the Buddha. Now, however, the time was gradually becoming ripe for the Buddha's teachings. In the capital city of Kosambi there were three rich people named Ghosita, Kukkuta, and Pavarika; the three were friends, and all three believed in a non-Buddhist religion. However, when the news spread throughout the country that the Buddha had appeared in the world, the teachers of the non-Buddhist religion travelled to Savatthi to meet the Buddha. Wishing to hear the teachings of the World-Honored One, the rich people followed them. The three became followers of the Buddha. Each of them promised that they would build a temple and invite the World-Honored One to the city. They returned and built the temples named after them: Ghosita Monastery, Kukkuta Monastery, and Pavarika Monastery. Then they sent emissaries to the World-Honored One, inviting him to their monasteries. Thus the World-Honored One went southward and crossed the river Ganges and went to Kosambi. On the way he entered the Deer Park in Bhesakala Grove in Sumsumara, and there he conducted a retreat.

The arrival of the World-Honored One immediately became widely known to the people; the people went together into the presence of the World-Honored One and listened to his discourses on the Dharma. Among these people there was a couple called Father of Nakula and Mother of Nakula. This couple from the first felt a strong attraction to the figure of the Buddha and vowed that they would continue to be firm believers for the rest of their lives. The next day they invited the World-Honored One to their home, and after the meal Father of Nakula said, "From the time I married my wife, whom I knew as a little child, I have never once doubted her loyalty, devotion, or chastity. Will you teach us the way by which we can live together in love and harmony in the future life in the same manner as in our present life?"

The World-Honored One answered, "Have the same faith; keep the same precepts; have the same feelings of charity; have the same wisdom. If you will do these, you will be able to be together in your future life." The World-Honored One later uttered words of praise, saying that this couple served as an example of a couple who trusted each other.

(2) Prior to this, Anuruddha had visited the World-Honored One and had said, "World-Honored One, with my divine eye I have witnessed many women who fell into hell after they died. Why do so many women fall into hell in this manner?"

The Buddha replied, "Anuruddha, women possess three traits that cause them to fall into hell. In the morning, their minds are seized by the defilement of regret, at noontime, by jealousy, and at evening, by sexual lust. Anuruddha, women who possess these three traits fall into hell after they die."

(3) At another time Anuruddha visited Sariputta and said to him, "My friend Sariputta, through my pure power of superhuman vision I am now able to extend my vision to a thousand worlds. My efforts know no end; my right concentration

is immovable. My body is calm and tranquil. My mind is not disturbed nor troubled. However, my mind is not free from attachment; my mind cannot get away from evil desires. Why is this?"

Sariputta answered with these words, "O Anuruddha, your words, 'through my power of superhuman vision I am able to extend my vision to a thousand worlds,' express arrogant pride. 'My efforts know no end; my right concentration is immovable' expresses overconfidence. 'However, my mind is not free from attachment; my mind cannot get away from evil desires' expresses regret. If you can get away from these things and lead your mind to the world of nirvana, this will be truly felicitous." Later, Anuruddha, freeing himself from these three things, directing his mind to the world of nirvana, and residing alone in a place of tranquillity, strove and constantly exerted himself.

(4) Now when the World-Honored One was residing in Bhesakala Grove, Anuruddha was residing at Pacinavamsa Grove in Ceti. One day in the afternoon while he was meditating, the following thought entered his mind: "This teaching is a teaching for those with small desires and not a teaching for those with avarice; it is a teaching that knows satisfaction and not a teaching that does not know satisfaction; it is a teaching to free oneself from a crowd of people and not a teaching to join crowds; it is a teaching of striving and not a teaching of laziness; it is a teaching of right thought and not a teaching of erroneous thought; it is a teaching of quietness and not a teaching of loudness; it is a teaching for the wise and not a teaching for the foolish."

At this time the World-Honored One, knowing the thoughts of Anuruddha, appeared before him at the grove of Pacinavamsa in the short time that it takes a strong man to extend his arm and said to Anuruddha, "Very good, very good, Anuruddha, you have just now been contemplating the seven enlightenments of a great man. Anuruddha, next contemplate the eighth enlightenment of a great man, namely, 'This teaching is a teaching that does not trifle with arguments.' If you can think on these eight teachings, you will free yourself from greed and evil teachings and enjoy the happiness that is attained by deliverance from evil desires, and you will be able to enter into the various meditations. Anuruddha, if you can enter freely into the various meditations, you will then be able to reach a state of satisfaction and happiness in donning the plain robes of a monk, in eating the food that you receive as alms, in sitting on a seat under a tree, in sleeping on a grass bed, and in taking medicine made from urine when you are ill. You will be just like a young girl who finds happiness and enjoyment when she finds her clothes container filled to the brim. O Anuruddha, for the coming retreat, reside here at the Pacinavamsa grove at Ceti."

Anuruddha answered the World-Honored One, "I shall do as you say." Thus Anuruddha had the retreat at this grove and practiced and studied alone and soon attained enlightenment.

10. The City of Kosambi

(1) Previous to this, Pindola had attained enlightenment under the teachings of the World-Honored One, and in order to spread the Dharma in his birthplace

of Kosambi, he had returned to reside there. Because of his efforts the seeds were sown in preparation for the spread of the Buddha's doctrine.

On the outskirts of the city of Kosambi there was a grove called Udaka, situated on the banks of the river Ganges; this grove was the property of the king. Rows of trees lined the banks extending as far as the eye could see, and the waves of the vast river Ganges sent forth cool breezes.

One day, Pindola, taking refuge from the heat of the mid-afternoon, was sitting in meditation under the luxuriantly growing trees of this grove. On this same day King Udena came to visit this grove accompanied by his ladies-in-waiting. Having disported himself with food and musical entertainment and feeling fatigued from the entertainment, he went off by himself to rest and nap. While the king was sleeping, his ladies-in-waiting wandered from one place to another; when suddenly they saw the meditating monk, they asked for a discourse and listened earnestly to his words.

After a while the king awakened from his sleep, and finding it strange that his ladies-in-waiting were not around, he started to search for them and found them clustered around the monk. Coarsened by lascivious living, the king lost all sense of judgment and ran toward the group with jealousy and anger in his heart, saying, "Is it not most unseemly for a monk to have women around him and to be engaged in idle talk with them?"

The monk, closing his eyes, remained silent. The king, crazed by anger, took out his sword and threatened to stab the monk in the throat, but the monk still did not utter a word. Then the king broke open an anthill and threw handfuls of red ants on the body of the monk, but the monk remained calm and did not move a muscle. The king then became ashamed of his violent actions, especially when he regained his composure; he realized that this monk Pindola was the son of one of the trusted teachers at his court. Feelings of remorse came over him, and with his ladies-in-waiting he asked for forgiveness for his actions. This incident caused one of the consorts, Samavati by name, to place great trust in the Buddha's teachings, and it became one of the causes of King Udena's reverence for the World-Honored One.

(2) After the passage of a few days the king visited Pindola at his abode in the grove and inquired with the following words, "O great teacher, here you are a young monk; you have cut off your black hair, abandoned the pleasures of the five desires, and will lead a pure life throughout your life. What power makes it possible for you to do this?"

"Great king, the Buddha, the Eye of the World, taught us and said, 'O disciples, regard an old woman as your mother, a middle-aged woman as your sister, and a young woman as your daughter.' That is why though we are young in body we can abandon the five passions and lead a pure life."

"Great teacher, a man's heart is full of craving. Even toward a woman as old as a mother, base feelings arise; even toward a woman the age of a sister, unclean thoughts may arise; even toward a woman as young as a daughter, licentious thought may arise. How can a young monk, with warm blood coursing through his body, refrain from the five desires and lead a life of purity?"

"Great king, the Buddha, the Light of the World, has taught us, saying, 'This human body from the tips of the toes to the top of the head is full of filth: hair, nails, teeth, saliva, blood, pus, phlegm, perspiration, tears, fat, urine, and excrement.' Knowing this is why young monks with young bodies are able to live pure lives."

"Great teacher, this may be easy for a monk who has undergone a long period of spiritual training and mind control, but I think it must be very difficult for an untrained monk. While attempting to meditate on the impure, before he realizes it, his mind will be filled with the thought that it is pure. While attempting to dwell on the ugly side of a thing, before he knows it, his mind will be drawn toward the beautiful side of a thing. Therefore there must be another way for young mendicants to guard themselves in a pure manner."

"Great king, the Buddha, who is all-knowing and all-seeing, taught us with the following words: 'Disciples, you must guard the gates of the five senses. When with the eyes you see a form, when with the ears you hear a sound, when with the nose you smell a fragrance, when with the tongue you taste a flavor, when with the body you feel a sensation of contact, do not become attached to the form, do not become attached to the objects. Guard the gates of the five senses. Thoughts of defilement will come in unless these gates are well guarded against their entrance.' This is how a young monk who is in the bloom of youth does not go to the five desires and lives a life of purity."

"Great teacher, the teachings of the Buddha are truly praiseworthy. This must be the reason a young monk with warm blood coursing through his body can lead a pure life throughout his life. Great teacher, I know from my own experience that if I enter the harem without guarding against the portals of the five organs and without guarding against the body, mouth, and mind, I immediately find myself becoming a slave to my base desires. On the other hand, if I guard against the actions of the body, mouth, and mind, I do not become a prisoner of evil desires. The teachings of the Buddha have clearly pointed this out to me."

(3) The World-Honored One, continuing his travel, came to Kosambi and entered the Ghosita Monastery built by the wealthy man Ghosita. Magandiya, who had now become the first queen of King Udena, was waiting for her chance for revenge. Hearing of the arrival of the World-Honored One, she bribed thugs in the city and had them denounce the Buddha. The disciples of the Buddha heard these slanderous attacks directed against their master and they were greatly troubled. Ananda went to the Buddha and said, "World-Honored One, it is my belief that we do not have to stay in such a place as this. I believe that it is better for us to move to another place."

"Ananda, if we move to another place and if such slanders should occur again, what will we do then?"

"World-Honored One, we should again move to another town."

"Ananda, in that case there will be no limit to this no matter where we go. I believe that it is better that I silently endure whatever slander I may receive and wait for it to cease. Then I can move to another place. Ananda, the Buddha is not moved by the eight things: gain, loss, fame, slander, praise, derision, suffering, and pleasure. These slanderous attacks will cease in seven days." The scheme of Magandiya completely failed; the number of persons who came to believe in the World-Honored One increased, and the slanders against the Buddha ceased.

At this time there was an adopted daughter of the rich man Ghosita, Samavati by name, who was the king's consort at the court. Her father was a good friend of the rich man Ghosita. In her childhood, the village in which she lived was beset by a severe famine, and when both of her parents died because of this famine, she was adopted by the rich man Ghosita. Then she became a queen at the palace of King Udena. Because of the deep faith that her adopted father Ghosita had had in the Buddha, Samavati secretly held a deep reverence for the Buddhist Sangha.

Among the ladies-in-waiting of the queen consort Samavati, there was a hunchback named Uttara. Her duty was to go out and buy flowers for the queen. One day as she went to buy flowers, the flower dealer told her, "Today, I am so busy that I have no time to tend to flowers. I must serve the World-Honored One. Will you join me in serving the Buddha?" So she went to serve the World-Honored One and heard his discourse. Since she had a good memory, she was able to recount word for word the Buddha's sermon to the queen consort. Subsequently, both of them took refuge in the Three Treasures. Uttara would go to the monastery, hear the discourses, and recount them to the queen.

Magandiya came to know about this and incessantly began to ply the king's ear with her slanderous words, saying, "Samavati is in love with Gotama. Uttara is being used as a messenger." With all her feminine wiles, she poisoned the mind of the king. The king became inflamed with anger and taking up a quiver of poisoned arrows went forth and summoned Samavati and all her retainers to appear before him. The queen, realizing the situation, quietly restrained her mind and prepared the others for their deaths and calmly stood before the king. Everyone was expecting to see the poisoned arrows leave the bow and blood being shed, but the arrows would not leave the hands of the king; they remained immovable in the king's hands. The surprised king's face soon oozed with oily perspiration; his body started to shake like straws in the wind; froth foamed from his mouth. Finally he was barely able to plead for help in a weak, veiled voice. Samavati told him to aim the arrow toward the ground. When the king did so, he was able to shoot the arrow. The king was startled at this miraculous circumstance; his heart was moved by the teachings of the Buddha. Thereafter he began to visit the monastery freely and allowed the disciples of the Buddha to be invited to the inner palace.

(4) The World-Honored One conducted a retreat at the Ghosita Monastery. During the three months of the rainy season Samavati made offerings at the monastery and invited a disciple each day to the inner palace and made offerings to him. Ananda tended to most of these offerings.

One day, at this monastery, Pindola made a disclosure regarding his enlightenment, saying, "My worldly life has ended; I have fulfilled all the pure practices. I have done all I had to do. Henceforth, for me there is no samsara that leads to illusion." The World-Honored One explained these words of Pindola to his disciples, saying, "Disciples, Pindola has made profession of his enlighten-ment by the three practices of right mindfulness, meditation, and wisdom while declaring, 'My worldly life has ended. I have fulfilled all the pure practices.'" Pindola expressed his happiness in the following song: "There is no life without the precepts. Because I know that my physical life is sustained by food, I go begging for food. But I have no attachment to food. The offerings of a well-to-do family are like dirt; they are like small arrows that cannot be pulled out. I know that the piety of evil persons, too, cannot be cast away."

(5) After the termination of the retreat, Samavati made an offering of five hundred pieces of cloth to Ananda, who divided the gift among the members of the Sangha. King Udena, hearing of this, was greatly surprised. He visited Ananda and reproached him, saying, "Is it not greedy for monks to accept such a large offering? And, great teacher, what are you going to do with all of these garments?"

"Great king, I shall divide them among the disciples whose garments are torn."

"What is going to happen to the torn garments?"

"The torn garments will be made into bed covers."

"What are you going to do with the old bed covers?"

"They will be made into pillow cases."

"What are you going to do with the old pillow cases?"

"They will be made into cushions."

"What are you going to do with the old cushions?"

"They will be made into wash cloths for wiping the feet."

"What are you going to do with the old washcloths?"

"They will be made into dry cloths."

"What are you going to do with the old dry cloths?"

"Great king, we shall rip the dry cloths into small pieces and mix them with dirt and clay and use them for plastering the walls of houses."

"Great teacher, how wonderful! The disciples of the Buddha truly know how to make use of material goods." The king left greatly impressed.

(6) Magandiya became more and more exasperated and irritable till she could not stand it any longer. All her schemes of slander had not borne any results; the king's heart was now turned toward the Buddha. Her determination now was directed toward Samavati. Contriving with her uncle, who was employed at the palace, and another evil person, Magandiya, during the time the king was away from the country, had them set fire to the residence of Samavati. Samavati, who had directed and encouraged her crying attendants who were trapped in the conflagration, remained calm and composed. Holding on to the Buddha's teachings in her heart, she gave up her life for the truth. Uttara, her hunchback servant, also perished in the flames. King Udena, who became livid with rage at this tragedy, had Magandiya and her accomplices burnt to death.

The World-Honored One mourned the death of those noble women and praised Samavati as the foremost in compassion among all the women and Uttara as the foremost in hearing the Dharma.

(7) One day the World-Honored One went into the suburbs of Kosambi and stood on the banks of the river Ganges. Seeing large logs floating down the river, he said to his disciples, "Disciples, do you see the large logs floating in the water and being washed away by the current? Disciples, if those logs do not come close to the banks, do not sink in the middle of the stream, do not get on the two banks, do not get taken by men, do not get taken by gods, do not get engulfed by whirlpools, and do not rot from within, then those logs will enter and remain in the ocean. Disciples, it is the same with you; you will enter nirvana and remain in nirvana. Why is this so? Because right views lead us to nirvana."

One disciple asked the World-Honored One, "World-Honored One, what is the meaning of the two banks? What is the meaning of sinking in the midstream, getting onto the bank, being taken by people, gods, or whirlpools, and rotting from within?"

"Disciples, this bank is the five organs; the other bank is the external objects. To sink in the midstream is to sink in the pleasures of desire. To get onto the banks is self-pride. To be taken by people is the monk's intermingling with lay people; they enjoy happiness and sadness together. When the lay people rejoice, the monk rejoices; when the lay people suffer, the monk suffers. They become companions in all things—this is what is meant by being taken by people. To be taken by gods is to make a vow to be born in the world of the gods and to practice toward that goal, hoping that by the practice of precepts, asceticism, and pure deeds, one can become a god. To be taken in by whirlpools means to be taken in by the five desires. To rot from within means that, although one is a disciple of the Buddha, one's nature is bad, one does not follow the precepts, one does evil and does not do good, and covers up one's deeds; one is not a monk, but puts on the appearance of a monk, and one is rotten inside."

(8) At this time a cowherd by the name of Nanda was standing at a place not too distant from the World-Honored One. Nanda addressed the Buddha, saying, "World-Honored One, I shall strive to free myself from all obstructions and strive to follow the path. World-Honored One, I should like to be with you and become your disciple."

"Nanda, then you had better go and return the cattle to your master."

"World-Honored One, these cows will return by themselves because of their love for their children."

"Nanda, it is better that you go and return the cattle to your master."

So the cowherd Nanda went to return the cattle to his master and, returning again to the Buddha, asked that he be allowed to become a disciple. This wish was granted, and Nanda, after undertaking practice, before long attained enlightenment.

(9) Again, one day the World-Honored One said thus while at the Ghosita Monastery, "Disciples, suppose there is a man who catches six different species of animals and ties them together with a strong rope. The animals caught are a snake, a crocodile, a bird, a dog, a fox, and a monkey. He ties each one of these animals with a strong rope and ties the ropes together and leaves the animals to their own devices. At this time each of the six species seeks to return to his

place of abode—the snake to a mound, the crocodile to water, the bird to the sky, the dog to a village, the fox to a cemetery, and the monkey to a grove. These six creatures will struggle against each other and become fatigued; each will finally be pulled in the direction of the strongest one and come under his control.

"Disciples, in the same way, if one does not contemplate the filth of the body and does not practice the three meditations on the defilements of the body, if one is remiss in these practices, the eye is attracted toward those forms that it likes and hates those that it does not like. It is the same with the ear, the nose, the tongue, the body, and the mind. They are attracted to things that are agreeable and are not attracted to things that are disagreeable. Disciples, this is called the absence of restraint.

"Disciples, what is meant by restraint? When one sees forms with his eyes, one does not become attached to those that are pleasant, neither does one become angry at those forms that are unpleasant. One resides in the meditation on the body and in the four boundless minds of compassion, mercy, joy, and nonattachment. One then truly knows the deliverance of the mind and the deliverance of wisdom; thus one gets away from all evil thoughts that may arise. It is the same with sound, fragrance, taste, and sensation—with the mind one comes to perceive all things, does not become attached to pleasant things, does not become angry at unpleasant things, and resides in the meditation on the body and the four boundless minds. Then one truly comes to know the deliverance of the mind and the deliverance of wisdom; thus one destroys all evil things that may arise.

"Disciples, creatures bound to a pole at first strive to return to their respective abodes, but eventually they become tired and stand or sit or lie down near the pole.

"Disciples, in the same way, if a person practices the meditation on the body, his eyes, ears, nose, tongue, body, and mind will not be influenced by the various states in which they may be. The meditation on the body is like a firm pole or tree. So you must practice meditation on the body." Thus the World-Honored One remained a long time at Kosambi; then he returned to Savatthi.

Introduction

This Book begins with the story of Ghatikara whose selfless generous acts earned him the complete trust of the Buddha. Next, by the use of parables the Buddha explains that simply learning the teaching without understanding its meaning leads to suffering rather than to happiness. For instance, by grasping a snake in the wrong way, one can die or suffer from its bite; therefore, one must learn proper control of mind and body with everything one undertakes.

The parable of the raft is about a man who builds a raft to cross a river but continues to carry it wherever he goes because it had been so useful in crossing the river. Buddha explains that like this man, people become attached to doctrine and teachings without properly understanding the nature of impermanence and changing conditions in life. One must throw away things that are no longer essential in order to avoid anxiety or suffering. Parable of the raft underscores the non-absolute nature of the doctrine.

The Buddha explains to Ananda that he must focus on the pure original mind, the basis of enlightenment, and not be moved by views that distract one from thinking of the true nature of things. The true mind is not affected by changing conditions and leads one to enlightenment. By not identifying this original mind with the phenomenal self, one is able to reach dharmadhatu, the imageless spiritual world that is not identical to the phenomenal world of finite particulars that we see and experience; yet, at the same time, there is mutual interpenetration between the two worlds. Of course, a question arises, as expressed by Purna (Chapter 1, Section 4:7), as to how this world of differences can arise from the pure mind. It is explained that the creations of the deluded mind do not truly exist but are manifested according to given conditions. The original pure mind, called Tathagata-garbha, is neither empty nor consists of materials or psychological elements; yet, it can manifest itself freely without obstruction. However, differentiated manifestations are like bubbles floating over the ocean; they have no substantial existence.

Finally, at the end of Book III, the reader finds the passages from the Avatamsaka Sutra, which D. T. Suzuki, the eminent Buddhist scholar, considered to be the consummation of Buddhist thought. This sutra is actually a collection of several sutras found in various versions and lengths of verses. The selection in Chapter 3, Section 7 represents a portion of the Gandavyuha, which narrates the wanderings of a youth called Sudhana, a son of a noble family, who travels all over India, seeking from one kalyanamitra (spiritual friend) after another, 53 teachers in all, the knowledge that would lead him to enlightenment.

This story of Sudhana's journey led to the establishment of the 53 stations along the Tokaido Highway from Tokyo to Kyoto, made famous by the set of woodcut prints produced by Hiroshige in 1832.

Chapter 1

THE IDEAL FOLLOWER

1. Ghatikara

(1) The World-Honored One, journeying to Savatthi with his many disciples, was passing through the country of Kosala when he stopped at a certain place off the side of the road. He stood there with a smile on his face. Ananda asked the Buddha the reason for his smile, and the World-Honored One answered him, "Ananda, in the far distant past this place was called Vehalinga. It was a wealthy and thriving town with many people residing in it; it was this town that the Buddha Kassapa favored as his place of abode. Ananda, this is the site where the Tathagata Kassapa sat and taught his disciples."

Hearing these words, Ananda took off his yellow robe and folded it in four and, laying it on the ground, said, "World-Honored One, please sit on this cushion. By so doing this place will become the site where two Buddhas have sat." The World-Honored One took his seat and told Ananda the story of Ghatikara and Jotipala.

(2) In this town of Vehalinga there lived a potter by the name of Ghatikara. He was a devoted follower of the Buddha Kassapa and was the leading donor among the followers. He had a good friend named Jotipala. One day Ghatikara turned to his friend Jotipala and said, "Let us go to visit and pay homage to the Buddha Kassapa. It is good to go and pay homage to the World-Honored One."

But Jotipala refused, saying, "What good does it do to go see a bald-headed monk?" Although he was asked two or three more times, he continued to refuse in the same manner. So Ghatikara led his friend to the river so that they could bathe together. While in the river, Ghatikara took hold of Jotipala's bracelet, rubbed it, and pleaded with him, saying, "Let us go to pay homage to the World-Honored One." Jotipala became annoyed and took off the bracelet from his wrist; becoming slightly angry, he refused again.

Thus the two started to wash their bodies, and when Jotipala bent down and started to wash his head, Ghatikara grabbed the hair of his friend's head and gently rubbing the hair said, "Let us go see the World-Honored One."

Then this thought rose in Jotipala's mind, "This is very strange. This Ghatikara in comparison to me is a person of low birth, so that he is prohibited from touching my head, yet he is grasping the hair on my head in order to get me to go see the Buddha. This is very strange and unusual." Jotipala pulled his head away from Ghatikara's hands and for the first time acceded to his friend's wish.

Thus these two went into the presence of the Buddha Kassapa, and Ghatikara pleaded with the Buddha, saying, "World-Honored One, this is my good and close friend. Will you please teach the Dharma to him?"

The Buddha Kassapa then taught the Dharma and made the two very happy. The two, rejoicing in hearing the doctrine, paid homage to the World-Honored One by walking around him to the right, and then they departed. Jotipala said, "You have just heard that wonderful discourse. Do not you want to become a monk?"

Ghatikara answered, "Jotipala, what are you saying? You are the one who knows best my family situation. I have to look after my aging parents, both of whom are blind."

Jotipala said, "Then, Ghatikara, I shall become a monk." Urged on by his friend, Jotipala met with the Buddha Kassapa, listened to the Dharma, and became a monk.

(3) It was approximately half a month after Jotipala became a monk that the Buddha Kassapa proceeded to Baranasi and resided at the Deer Park. The ruler of the country of Kasi, King Kiki, heard of this. Preparing his beautiful horse chariot, he went into the presence of the Buddha Kassapa, heard his discourse, and invited the Buddha for a meal on the next day. The Buddha went to the palace the morning of the following day and received an offering of food, but he declined the invitation to hold a retreat at the palace because of other commitments. The king pleaded with the Buddha many times to have the retreat at the palace, but he was met with the same refusal. Finally the king began to show his displeasure and said, "O World-Honored One, is there anyone besides myself who serves your Sangha so well?"

The Buddha answered, "O king, in the village of Vehalinga, there is a potter named Ghatikara. He is my foremost contributor. Even though he may be refused the invitation to the retreat, he never shows any signs of displeasure. O king, he has found refuge in the Buddha, the Dharma, and the Sangha; he follows the precept of non-killing; he does not engage in illicit sexual acts; he does not take things that do not belong to him; he does not utter false words; he does not indulge in intoxicants. He has a strong faith in the Buddha, the Dharma, and the Sangha. He follows the precepts followed by the sages; he has gotten away from doubts in regard to the Four Noble Truths. He follows the rule of one meal for one day; he does not accumulate wealth. He does not put the shovel into the ground with his own hands but uses the soil that has fallen from a bank or dug up by dogs or rats for his material in making pottery. He says, 'Take anything you want of the things I make, leaving any amount of rice, beans, or peas that you may have on hand.' He is supporting his two blind parents. He has gotten away from the five defilements, so he will not return to this world but will enter the world of nirvana.

(4) "O king, one morning when I was residing in the village of Vehalinga, I visited the home of Ghatikara. His parents were there. I asked, 'Is the master of the house at home?' 'No, World-Honored One, he has gone out on business, but

please partake of the rice that you find cooked in a pot and the soup that is in a pan.' O king, I did as they bade me do; then I left. Then Ghatikara came home and heard about the preceding events and exclaimed, 'Oh, what a fortunate person I am! I am thankful that the Buddha Kassapa trusts me this way.' Ghatikara was happy for half a month; his parents were happy for seven days' duration.

"O king, at another time, I found that my roof was leaking when it rained, so I called my disciples and told them to obtain some grass from Ghatikara's residence to cover my own roof. Then the disciples said to me, 'World-Honored One, there is no grass in Ghatikara's house; he has put new grass on his workshop.'

"'Then take the grass off the roof of his workshop and bring it here,' I ordered. My disciples went to the workshop as I ordered and removed the newly laid grass from the roof. Ghatikara's parents said, 'Who is this that is taking the grass from the roof?' Hearing that it was to repair the leak in the roof of the Buddha Kassapa's meditation room, the old couple said, 'Please take it, please take it.' These words were uttered with great joy.

"Ghatikara, on returning and hearing of this, said, 'What a fortunate person I am! I am happy to know that the Buddha Kassapa trusts me this way.' Just as in the incident mentioned before, he was engulfed in happiness and joy.

"O king, his workshop was left uncovered for three months, but fortunately there was not much rain. O king, Ghatikara is such a person as this."

King Kiki, hearing this, said, "Ghatikara is indeed a fortunate person; he has received the trust of such a person as the Buddha Kassapa. His happiness must be very great." The king had rice bushels on five hundred horse-drawn carts sent to Ghatikara, but Ghatikara refused this gift saying, "O king, you must have many expenditures to bear. I have enough."

All this the Buddha explained to Ananda, and he added, "Ananda, actually, at that time, I was Jotipala."

2. The Parable of the Snake and the Parable of the Raft

(1) The World-Honored One returned to the Jeta Grove Monastery. One day he said to his disciples, "My disciples, to know, to extinguish, and to free yourselves from greed, you must practice these three gates of liberation: first, the meditation of emptiness; second, the meditation of signlessness; and third, the meditation of desirelessness. Again, you must practice these three meditations in order to know, extinguish, and free yourselves from anger, ignorance, concealment, conceit, jealousy, stinginess, flattery, deceit, quarrelling, excessive pride, and neglect."

(2) At one time a certain brahmin said to the World-Honored One, "O Gotama, you say that your teaching has its effects in this present life, but how can you say that it has direct results in this present life? Again, are there persons who can know if your teachings lead persons to nirvana?" The Buddha answered, "O brahmin, a mind that is burnt, destroyed, and bound by thoughts of greed, anger, and ignorance brings harm to one who has these thoughts and brings thoughts that wish to harm others; in one's own mind one knows suffering and worries. If one frees himself from greed, anger, and ignorance, one does not

think of harming himself and does not know suffering or worries. O brahmin, this teaching is a teaching that has its effects in this present life; again, everyone knows that this teaching leads one to nirvana."

(3) Again, one day, there was a disciple named Arittha, who formerly hunted eagles and who held an evil view. He said, "The World-Honored One says that some acts are a hindrance to the practice of the path, but when you practice those things you find that they are not much of a hindrance."

Many of the disciples attempted to have him forsake this evil view, but no matter how much they tried to change his view by discussions and arguments, it was all in vain. The World-Honored One heard about this and called Arittha to him, and after reproaching him he instructed his disciples, "O disciples, if a snake-hunter finds a large snake and grasps it by the body or the tail, then the snake will turn his body around and bite the hands, wrists, or other parts of the man's body. Because of this, he will either die or suffer a deathlike agony. Why is this? It is because the manner in which he holds the snake is wrong. In the same way, foolish persons, learning the teachings of the Buddha, do not understand their meanings and therefore are not able to discern the truth. They study the teachings so that they can quote authoritative passages when they argue with others. These persons do not understand the meanings, although they study the teachings. They misunderstand the teachings and receive lasting suffering. This is because they misunderstand my teachings.

"O disciples, there are some children from good families; they learn these teachings and inquire into their meanings; they rightly understand the teachings and receive happiness for a long time. Why? Because they correctly understand the teachings. They act like a snake-hunter who takes a wooden fork and pins a snake to the ground by putting it on the snake's neck, and then grabs its neck. No matter how many times the snake may encircle its body around the hands, wrists, or any other part of his body, this person will not die or experience deathlike pain. Why? Because he has gotten firm control over the snake.

(4) "O disciples, so that you can get away from attachment, I shall tell you the parable of the raft. Here is a man who is making a long journey. When he sees a large ocean in front of him, he thinks thus: 'The shore on this side of the ocean seems dangerous, but the shore on the other side is safe. However, there is no boat, and there is no bridge. I shall get to the other shore by gathering straw, logs, and leaves together and building a raft.' Soon he completes the raft and is able to reach the other shore safely. As he gets safely on the bank, he thinks thus: 'This raft proved to be of great value to me. I was able to reach this shore safely because of this raft. I shall carry this raft on my head and shoulders and take it wherever I may want to go.' O disciples, what do you think of this? Do you think this person has done what he should have done regarding the raft?"

The disciples answered, "No, World-Honored One, he has not."

The Buddha continued, "O disciples, then what do you think the man should do with the raft? O disciples, this person, after reaching his destination, should either leave the raft on the beach of the other shore, or he should put the raft in the ocean and go wherever he wishes to go. O disciples, through this parable of the raft I am telling you that you should not become attached to the teachings. Even the teachings must be cast aside, as seen in this parable of the raft. How much more so in the case of false teachings!"

(5) The Buddha taught, "O disciples, there are four things from which evil views of 'I' and 'mine' arise; they are the body, the mind, perceptions like seeing and hearing, and the viewpoint of the mind. O disciples, one who does not study and practice, who does not associate with good people, and who is ignorant of the teachings of the sages and good people—such a person, regarding the four things, acknowledges and becomes attached to these things, thinking, 'These belong to me, this is 'I', this is my ego.'

"However, one who studies extensively, associates with good people, and is trained in the teachings of the sages and good people does not acknowledge and does not become attached to these four things. Thus even when those things cease to exist, he does not lose his right thoughts and is not threatened by fear."

At that time a certain disciple addressed the World-Honored One, saying, "World-Honored One, can one lose his right thoughts and be threatened with fear because of outside influences?" The World-Honored One answered, "Here is a person who thinks thus: 'Before, these belonged to me, but now they are no longer mine. Can I make these mine once more? Probably it will be impossible to make them mine a second time.' This person is saddened and cries, beating his chest in anguish. This is a case where a person, because of outside influences, loses his right thoughts and is threatened by fear. Again, even though thinking thus, if he is not saddened, knows no anguish, and does not cry, beating his chest in anguish, such a person does not lose his right thoughts and is not threatened by fear because of outside influences."

The disciple asked, "World-Honored One, is it possible that a person can lose his right thoughts and become threatened by fear because of inside influences?" The Buddha answered, "Here is a person who thinks that this world and his ego exist forever without change. When he hears the teaching of the Buddha regarding non-ego, he becomes saddened, cries, and beats his chest in anguish as he thinks, 'If I follow this teaching, what I call myself will be extinguished and will no longer exist.' This is a case where a person loses his right thoughts and is threatened by fear because of inside influences.

"If, hearing the Buddha's teaching of non-ego, a person does not become grieved or upset that he will be extinguished and will not exist, this is a case where a person does not lose his right thoughts and is not threatened with fear because of inside influences."

(6) The Buddha asked, "O disciples, have you ever possessed something that has continued to exist without any change whatsoever? Or have you ever seen anything that is permanent and unchanging?"

"O World-Honored One, no, we have never seen such a thing."

The Buddha continued, "O disciples, well said. I, too, have never seen such a thing. In this world there is nothing that exists permanently and eternally. If one becomes attached to the self, anxieties, troubles, and sufferings will arise. Disciples, if there is 'I', there arises 'mine'; if there is 'mine', there arises 'I'.

BUDDHA-DHARMA · BOOK THREE

However, because nowhere can we discover the existence of 'I' or 'mine', the idea that this world and 'I' exist and do not change for all eternity is most foolish."

The Buddha asked, "O disciples, is the body permanent or impermanent?" The disciples replied, "It is impermanent." "Is something impermanent suffering or happiness?" "It is suffering." "Regarding a thing that is impermanent, changing, and suffering, is it correct to say that it belongs to me or that it is 'I' or my ego?" "No, World-Honored One, it is not correct."

(7) The Buddha said, "O disciples, this does not apply to the body only; it applies to the mind as well. Therefore, we must know that, no matter what kind of body it may be, this body does not belong to me; it is not 'I'; it is not my ego. This applies also to the mind in the same manner.

"O disciples, these disciples see and hear of this teaching in this manner; they are repulsed by the body and the mind, get away from greed, and attain emancipation. Then wisdom that says, 'I have attained emancipation' arises, and they come to know that birth has ceased, that pure actions have been fulfilled, and that all things that needed to be achieved have been achieved; and for such a one there is no birth after the end of this life. Such a person is called a sage who has gotten away from all impediments and bondages and laid down his heavy burdens."

(8) "O disciples, some monks have criticized me without any basis, saying, 'Gotama teaches the destruction and the extinction of people.' O disciples, I do not say that. I have, in the past and at the present time, taught of the suffering of the present and of the extinction of suffering. Even though they may criticize, revile, and slander the Buddha, the Buddha does not become disturbed and does not become angry. Again, even though people may praise and revere the Buddha, and make offerings to him, the Buddha does not rejoice and does not experience pleasure or become proud. Again, when a person reveres and respects the Buddha and makes offerings to him, the Buddha thinks thus, 'The fact of their doing this for my sake—I knew about it from before.' Thus even though someone should criticize, revile, and slander you, you should not become disturbed or become angry. Again, you should not rejoice when another person praises you nor become proud and arrogant. You must think that you knew of this before in your past.

"O disciples, therefore, throw away all things that do not belong to you. If you throw them away, it will bring you many kalpas of happiness. What are the things that do not belong to you? Your body is something that does not belong to you; throw it away. Your mind also does not belong to you; throw your mind away. If you throw them away, you will receive benefits and contentment for many kalpas.

"O disciples, what do you think about the following? Suppose a person comes to this Jeta Grove, brings together grass, twigs, and leaves, and sets fire to them. At this time, would you think that this person had brought things that were yours and was burning them?"

The disciples answered, "O World-Honored One, we should not think in such a manner. The reason is that those things would not belong to us." The Buddha said, "O disciples, in this same manner, throw away all things that do not belong to you. If you throw them away, you will attain happiness for many kalpas."

3. Matangi

(1) One day the World-Honored One, upon the invitation of King Prasenajit, accompanied by many of his disciples, proceeded to the palace. Only Ananda among the disciples, having received a special invitation from another family, went alone and entered the city of Sravasti.

After he had received offerings from his host, Ananda set out on the way of return. While walking on the road, he became very thirsty. As he passed by the side of a large lake, he saw a young girl who was from the candalas, the untouchable caste, drawing water from a well. Ananda said to her, "O young sister, please give me some water."

The young girl hesitantly answered, "Venerable One, I am a person of low birth."

"Young sister, I am a monk. In my heart I do not make any distinctions between the high-born and the low-born."

The young girl, overjoyed by the repeated request, drew the pure water from the well and presented it to him. Ananda drank the water slowly and, having finished, he departed. But the noble features of Ananda and his gentle words made a deep impression on the young girl; she fell in love with Ananda. Returning home, she made a request to her mother, who was adept at magic, saying, "Please invite the sage Ananda to this house."

"Daughter, my magic cannot be applied to those who have gotten away from greed or to those who are dead. In particular, the master of this sage, Gautama, is a personage of high virtue. Because he is highly respected by King Prasenajit, if I have the sage brought here through my magic, all of us of the sudra caste may be killed." But the heart that was consumed by love could not be stopped. The young girl cried, saying, "There is only one path left; I shall die."

The mother, at her wits' end, finally decided to accede to her daughter's wish. In one room of the house she put some cow excrement on the dirt floor and piled some white congo grass on top; she lighted it and threw one hundred eight lotus petals into the raging flames; and at each throwing in of a lotus petal, she prayed to the gods of earth and of heaven, saying, "Have the sage Ananda brought to this house."

(2) At this time, strangely, Ananda, his mind confused, staggered into the house of the young girl. He was greeted with great joy by the mother and daughter, who were burning incense and scattering flowers. He sat on a beautiful cushion, but he became afraid, like one who is suddenly awakened from a dream, and he singlemindedly called on the power of the World-Honored One to help him escape this difficult situation.

At this time the World-Honored One, who had returned to the Jeta Grove from the palace of King Prasenajit, knew instantly of the danger that beset Ananda and recited a verse:

If the lake of precepts is pure, the defilements of people will be washed away.

Those with wisdom, entering this lake, will clear the darkness of ignorance forever.

This is uttered equally by the sages of the three worlds.

Please have my disciple return to me immediately.

Because of the power of the World-Honored One, Ananda was able to leave the house of the young girl and return to the Jeta Grove. "The sage has left," the young girl said, and so saying she spent the night crying.

(3) The next day Ananda was on an alms receiving mission at a certain place, when the young girl, wearing a new dress adorned with a corsage and a necklace, stood waiting for him. She followed Ananda wherever he went, like a moth that is attracted by a flame. If he stopped, she stopped; if he proceeded, she proceeded. They went outside the castle walls and returned to the Jeta Grove, and the young girl never let Ananda out of her sight. Ananda felt embarrassed and ashamed; he went immediately into the presence of the World-Honored One and pleaded for help.

The World-Honored One said, "Do not worry," comforting Ananda, and, turning to the young girl, uttered these words to her, "If you wish to become the wife of Ananda, go see your parents and obtain their permission."

The young girl greatly rejoiced, returned to her home, and soon came back into the World-Honored One's presence accompanied by her parents. The World-Honored One addressed the young girl, saying, "O maiden, in order to become the wife of Ananda you must become a nun and enter the Sangha." And the young girl with great reverence acceded to the Buddha's words.

The World-Honored One said, "It is well, it is well." He had her shave off her tresses and put on the robes of a nun. Seeing that the thoughts of the young girl had finally become calm, the World-Honored One said to her, "O maiden, passion and greed are the sources of suffering; their flavor is very short-lived, and their pitfalls are many. Like a moth that flies around a burning light, the foolish person throws his body into the burning flame of lust. A wise person is different; he gets away from greed and lust, and thoughts of passion do not arise."

Hearing these teachings of the Buddha, the young girl's mind became quiet and tranquil, and she was able to get away from all her bondages. She attained the state of enlightenment and was restored to a state of calm. She came to be called the Matangi nun.

4. The External Origin of Defilements

(1) From experiencing the seductive power of the candala maiden, Ananda learned how deficient his capacities were, and one day he carefully consulted with the World-Honored One, inquiring about the method of practicing the path. The World-Honored One then said, "O Ananda, when you decided for the first time to

enter the path of enlightenment, did you by observing its superior features forsake the world of desire?" Ananda replied, "O World-Honored One, when I encountered for the first time the superior marks of the World-Honored One's features, incomparable to anything of this world, I was convinced that the clear body of the World-Honored One, like that of a precious stone such as lapis lazuli, could never be born from worldly desires. For it is impossible for any man whose desire is coarse and whose mind is as murky as pus to emit such light. Because of this adoration, I decided to leave home and become a monk."

The World-Honored One said, "Well said, Ananda. If you really wish to realize the true enlightenment, answer my questions sincerely. Ananda, you have just said that, because of your sense of adoration for the features of the Tathagata, you decided to enter the path of the homeless. But through what sort of faculty did you see it and yearn for it?" Ananda replied, "O World-Honored One, I saw it through these eyes and yearned for it through this mind."

The World-Honored One said, "Ananda, there is no mistake in your answer, and yet you must also admit that it is these eyes and this mind that have let you transmigrate through the cycle of life and death till now. Therefore, Ananda, just as when the king of a country tries to subjugate bandits who infiltrate his territory, he must more than anything else know the area where they are; just so, in order to annihilate the dust of defilement, you must first find out where such eyes and mind are located. Where do you think your eyes and mind are located?"

Ananda replied, "My eyes are in my face and my mind within my body."

The World-Honored One said, "Now, what do your eyes see in this lecture hall?" Ananda replied, "They see the presence of the World-Honored One, then that of disciples, and then the forest outside the building."

The World-Honored One said, "As you said, since the windows are now open in the room, it is possible to see the distant forest. But among the disciples here, are there any who look outside only without paying attention to the Tathagata?" Ananda replied, "O World-Honored One, there is none such."

The World-Honored One said, "O Ananda, if the mind is located within your body, it naturally will see more than anything else the interior of the body. But people cannot know anything about the interior of their bodies. Then is it possible to say that the mind is located within the body?" Ananda replied, "O World-Honored One, because of your instruction, I now understand that the mind is not within the body but outside it. For instance, when a candle is placed within a room, it does not illumine only itself but also the interior of the room, and then it extends its illumination outside of it. By contrast, people do not see the interior of the body but only its exterior."

The World-Honored One said, "However, Ananda, if the mind is located outside the body, the body and the mind are separate. Then what the mind knows the body cannot sense; what the body senses the mind can never know. In actuality, however, what the mind knows the body also senses; what the body senses, the mind also recognizes. Therefore, Ananda, it cannot be said that the mind is outside the body."

(2) Thus instructed, Ananda, holding his palms together, addressed the World-Honored One, "If the mind is found neither within the body nor outside of it, where, may I ask, is the essence of the mind? May the World-Honored One, with his great compassion, clarify the truth as to where the mind is to be found and teach the essentials for those who practice the path."

The World-Honored One said, "O Ananda, all people are bound deeply by the fetters of karma from the immemorial past, because they do not realize two fundamental truths: first, they do not know that the ultimate root of life and death is the mind of delusion, believing that this mind is the essential nature of themselves; and second, they do not know that they are endowed with a pure mind, namely, the essence of enlightenment."

Having thus instructed him, the World-Honored One lifted his elbow, made a fist, and said, "Ananda, what do you see here?" Ananda replied, "The World-Honored One has now lifted his elbow and made a fist, to which the World-Honored One is calling our attention." "With what have you seen?" Ananda replied, "Together with the fellow disciples, I have seen with my eyes." "If it were with your eyes that you have seen, then you need not say that I have called your attention." Ananda said, "But what I have seen with my eyes, I have recognized as your fist with my mind." "Ananda, do you think that that which recognized it was your mind?" "Yes, I think so." The World-Honored One said, "Hush, Ananda, this is not your true mind."

Now at that moment Ananda was greatly surprised and said, "O World-Honored One, then what is my true mind?" The World-Honored One said, "Ananda, the mind of conceptualization is unreal and illusory, for it arises upon causes and conditions, changes upon changing causes and conditions, and hence is unreal, non-substantial, and empty. As you became convinced that such was your mind's substance, there has arisen your lasting delusion."

Next, the World-Honored One, once again making a fist and then opening it, asked Ananda, "O Ananda, how do you see this?" Ananda replied, "As I see it, the World-Honored One made a fist and then opened it." The World-Honored One said, "Did you see the opening and closing of my hand, or were the opening and closing in your own thinking?" Ananda replied, "It is the World-Honored One's hand in which I have seen the opening and closing. It is not my thinking that has determined them so." The World-Honored One said, "Then is it my hand that moves or your mind?" Ananda replied, "It is the World-Honored One's hand that moves." The World-Honored One further lifted his hand, moving it right and left, and thereby gave some hint to Ananda's mind. When Ananda, following the moves of the hand, moved his head right and left, the World-Honored One said, "O Ananda, when you move your head, do you think that your mind moves, or that your thinking moves?" Ananda replied, "O World-Honored One, it is my head that moves, but there is no movement in my thinking."

At that moment, the World-Honored One said to the entire group of his disciples, "O disciples, it is just like this: people in general have fallen into erroneous thought, because their pure original mind has been defiled by the desires objectively incurred. Those defilements that are induced by external causes and conditions are in constant movement and change. Like guests from outside, they stay on the original mind, and like dust, they externally stick on it and defile it. Nevertheless, the pure mind, the basis of enlightenment, is actually neither caused to move nor defiled by their presence. Though covered deeply under the dusts of defilement, the original nature of the mind is not lost. Consider Ananda's statement that his head moves and not his thinking, and that my hand moves and not his thinking. You should carefully examine the matter and should not regard the defilement caused by external dusts as your essential nature. By becoming aware of the original mind of enlightenment, you must know the nature of your true self. If you are caught by the defilements that externally move and change, you will be forever chased by an inverted view of the world and wander through the streets of delusion."

Having thus heard, Ananda and the remaining disciples were all delighted with this prompt opening up of their understanding, and they looked up at the World-Honored One's countenance, just as an infant, having missed his milk, does when once again held by his mother.

(3) At that moment, King Prasenajit stood up from his seat and reverentially said to the World-Honored One, "O World-Honored One, when I had not yet learned the teaching of the World-Honored One, I happened to meet Sanjayin Vairattiputra, and he taught me at that time that when one's body perishes after death, it is in the state of nirvana. That we shall perish totally after death is a lonesome prospect. Now, however, that the World-Honored One has just revealed that the original mind is imperishable. I feel a great consolation. May the World-Honored One further teach us on the path through which we can enter the state of this imperishable mind."

The World-Honored One said, "O great king, is your body as strong as a diamond, or is it perishable?" The king replied, "It is perishable, World-Honored One." The World-Honored One said, "While it is still not yet perished, how do you know that it is perishable?" The king replied, "This body is changing every moment, just like a fire gradually changing into ashes. O World-Honored One, when I was a child, even my skin was lovely, but now, because of aging, it is all wrinkled. Again, when I was young, my body was filled with youthful vigor; but now my spirit has declined and my mind has faltered. Though I am not clearly aware when and how far I have aged, looking back at the years of my life on a scale of decades I can clearly recognize the degrees of aging. And if I scrutinize the matter more closely, even by a yearly scale, or even by a monthly scale, I can detect the change. Indeed, this process goes on every moment incessantly. This is the impermanence of human life, and according to this rule I have not the slightest doubt that this body of mine also will perish before too long."

The World-Honored One addressed the king: "Your majesty has explained very well how the body will perish. Therefore I shall now explain what is imperishable within the perishable body. O great king, when did you see the Ganges for the first time?" The king replied, "It was when I was three years old and taken by the queen mother to visit a shrine of the gods that I saw the river for the first time." The World-Honored One asked, "Great king, has there been any difference in the water of the river between today and those days?" The king replied, "Although many years have passed, it is still flowing exactly in the same way as in those days." The World-Honored One said, "O great king, is there then any difference in the way of your observing the flow of the river water between those days and today when your hair is mixed with white and your face is showing some wrinkles?" The king replied, "There is no difference whatsoever." The World-Honored One said, "O great king, although your face shows some wrinkles, the way of your observation has not changed; though the changeable has changed, the unchangeable does not change. Whatever grows old changes, and whatever changes will perish. However, your majesty can see even within the perishable something that will not perish. O great king, therefore, contrary to the view of the non-Buddhist, we cannot say that when the body perishes, everything else also perishes."

Having thus listened to the World-Honored One's teaching, the king realized that even though one has to forsake the perishable body, there will remain something imperishable, assuring an everlasting life, and was extremely delighted along with other disciples.

(4) At that moment, Ananda stood up and addressed the World-Honored One, "O World-Honored One, if our way of seeing has neither beginning nor end, is not that contrary to the World-Honored One's teaching?" The World-Honored One replied, "Every phenomenon, Ananda, whether of things or of the mind, arises on the basis of causes and conditions, which are in turn also all originated from the mind. Till now, I have frequently explained this doctrine. Accordingly, you can comprehend that your body as well as your mind was originally manifested from the mind, which is, by nature, extremely subtle and clear. However, forgetting this subtle mind and experiencing delusion within the mind, whose essence is enlightenment, you believe that the resulting delusion is your essential nature, and that it is localized within the body. Thus you are not aware that hills and rivers, the great earth, and all things that exist in wide space have been manifested from that subtle original mind. Is it not, therefore, as foolish as, having caught the tiniest bubble, thinking that you have exhausted the great ocean?"

Ananda said, "By the words of the World-Honored One, I have become aware of the eternal nature of the mind. However, is it not true that my understanding of its presence is also accomplished by the discriminatory mind?" The World-Honored One replied, "Ananda, if you say it is the discriminatory mind through which you have understood my teaching, then the teaching that you understood will also be a thing discriminated and cannot be said to be the essential nature of the teaching. O Ananda, when a man points at the moon with his finger, if another man only sees the tip of the finger and believes that he has seen the moon, he not only fails to see the moon but also does not understand the meaning of the pointing finger. Moreover, since such a man mistakes the finger that has no light for the moon that does, it must be said that he does not know even the nature of light nor that of darkness. It is indeed not possible to know the true nature of things by means of the discriminatory faculty. O Ananda, you said that you understood my words through the mind of discrimination. If the discriminatory faculty is truly your own mind, this discriminatory mind must be existent at all times without changing; but the process of discrimination arises depending upon conditions, and when these conditions are gone, it is bound to change and even perish. Indeed, there is no nature of such a faculty apart from the presence of conditions. However, quite independent of these conditions, which come and go, there is the essential nature of the mind that neither moves nor perishes. Such is the essential nature of your mind, the master. O Ananda, I shall further explain it by a metaphor: In a country inn, there are the innkeeper and the guests. The guests represent the mind of discrimination, for they come and stay depending on conditions; while when these conditions are gone, they leave the inn. However, the innkeeper always stays there whether guests are coming or going. Even if all guests are gone, it cannot be said that the inn is gone. Likewise, even when the mind of discrimination is gone because of the absence of the necessary conditions, it cannot be said that man's self is gone. O Ananda, you must not take the mind of discrimination, which changes because of external conditions, as your essential nature; but by transcending this phenomenal mind, make the mind that neither moves nor changes your master."

(5) Ananda raised the question, "O World-Honored One, why does not the original mind that is not conditioned by external factors perish?" The World-Honored One replied, "Ananda, listen attentively. This lecture hall is now well-lighted because of the sun, but it will become dark when the sun sets. This light can be attributed to the day, the darkness to the night. The power of seeing, however, belongs to neither, for when brightness is present, it is not that the power to see darkness is lost; and when darkness is gone, it is not that there has arisen the capacity of seeing brightness. Whether brightness or darkness is coming or going, there remains the power of seeing brightness as well as darkness. Seeing the former is one moment of the mind, while seeing the latter is another. These phenomena do not represent the real nature of the mind; but that which is eternally existent, limited neither by brightness nor by darkness, is your true mind. Thus the true original mind must be known as affected neither by brightness nor by darkness; though being enveloped by various defilements, such as good and evil, love and hate, which come and go because of external causes and conditions, it is neither stained nor defiled; it is essentially subtle, pure, and imperishable.

"O Ananda, when water is poured into a round vessel, it takes on a round shape; when poured into a square one, it takes on a square shape. But there is neither a round nor a square form in the nature of the water. Just so, people perceive their lives, from the immemorial past, in varied ways, as when water is poured into large and small or round and square containers, and they experience good and evil, love and hate; and thereby they are caused to run after external things, subjecting themselves to various sufferings. This state of affairs is a form of delusion arisen from their erroneous conviction in identifying the original mind with the phenomenal self enchained by external conditions as exemplified by water vessels. Therefore when one gives the way of seeing himself bound by external conditions back to these conditions, and returns to his own true mind, which is not bound, he becomes identical with the Buddha, while his body and mind become perfect and clear. Unobstructed by anything, he is able to reach the Dharmadhatu of the ten directions directly through his own body.

"O Ananda, when you make fire by placing a lens between the sun and dry grass, do you think that the fire comes from the lens, or that it comes from the dry grass, or that it comes from the sun? The lens is held by the man, the ray comes from the sky, and the grass is from the ground. The sun and the grass are far apart and cannot come into contact, but there is no doubt that the fire in the sun manifests itself on the grass when the lens is an auxiliary condition. The true original mind of the Tathagata-garbha, from which the buddhas are born, is the root source of faith, like the fire in the metaphor, which is omnipresent throughout the Dharmadhatu. When this fire of faith once touches upon the grass of people with the Buddha's lens of insight as condition, there is no doubt that the flame of the fire that enlightens the Buddhahood within people will rise up with great intensity. Once the lens is directed toward a spot, there arises fire on that spot. Accordingly, when it is directed toward the totality of the Dharmadhatu, it is inevitable that the entire world will be filled with fire.

"O Ananda, it is on the basis of this principle that the Buddha directs his Dharma lens toward everyone and all."

(6) Because of the World-Honored One's teaching, Ananda as well as all the disciples at the gathering became aware of the original mind of enlightenment, understood that this physical body is like a tiny speck of dust floating in great space, and regretted how foolish they were to have been entrapped by the birth and death of their flesh and thereby to have been worried, saddened, caused to suffer, and afflicted. Thus they all at once saluted the World-Honored One and expressed their resolution by means of the verses:

> In possession of the wondrous Dharma as wide as the ocean, the immovable Buddha melts our delusion, which is as old as that of the immemorial past, and helps us at once to realize the Dharmakaya; his valor indeed has no limit.

> May we wish to become lords of the Dharma and save innumerable people. For endowed with this mind of profundity, to be in service in innumerable realms is the way to respond to the benefit of the doctrine.

> May the World-Honored One witness our resolution, that we shall enter the world that suffers from all evils, and that we shall not enter nirvana till the last one becomes a buddha.

> Even if the great sky should be exhausted, nothing will destroy this vow, which is as hard as diamond.

(7) At that moment, the venerable Purna, who was also in the assembly, stood up and with his palms together reverentially addressed the Buddha: "O World-Honored One, if this true original mind, which is enlightenment, and the mind of the Buddha are totally identified, having neither excess nor shortage, why is the world of differentiation born from such a Buddha mind?"

The World-Honored One replied, "O Purna, suppose a man enters a village but mistakes the direction of north and that of south. Does this mistake come from the mind of delusion or from the original mind of enlightenment?" Purna replied, "O World-Honored One, the mind of delusion arises depending upon external conditions and has no real essence; hence, it is, as it were, a root-less grass. Therefore there should be no budding out of delusion from the rootless mind of delusion. Moreover, since enlightenment itself does in no way produce delusion, it cannot be said to have been born from the mind of enlightenment, either." The World-Honored One said, "If, then, someone who knows the village well teaches that confused man the right directions, is he going to lose his direction again?" Purna answered, "There will be no more such mistakes." The World-Honored One said, "O Purna, it is the same with the Buddha. Once he comes to the right understanding that the nature of delusion is empty and rootless, he will have no more delusion. O Purna, a man of afflicted eyes will see flowers in the sky, but once the affliction is cured he will no longer see them. The flowers that appear in the delusions are not essentially existent; but since people are afflicted by the ignorance of their eyes of insight, they are caused to imagine the presence of the duality of delusion and enlightenment. Those buddhas whose eyes are free from affliction caused by ignorance have no more vision of sky-flowers; whatever they see is solely the world of right enlightenment. Therefore there is no world of differentiation at all in the minds of the buddhas. O Purna, pure gold once refined will not return to ore. Once wood becomes ashes, there is no way for it to return to the original state of wood. How could the world of differentiation arise within the minds of the buddhas who have severed the root of delusion? For it is merely a thought imagined from the deluded view.

"However, O Purna, the form of space is not determined; it is neither bright nor dark, neither moving nor still; and yet when the sun shines, brightness is manifest; when clouds spread, darkness is manifest; when winds blow, motion is manifest; when they die down, stillness is manifest. In short, since there is no determined form, space can manifest itself in whatever form it may take in accordance with given conditions. It is the same with the original mind of enlightenment, called the Tathagata-garbha. It is neither empty nor is it of any material factor such as earth, water, fire, or wind, nor is it any of the psychophysical elements, such as the seen, heard, smelled, tasted, or touched. Nor is it a world in which ignorance manifests itself, nor is it its cessation. Since it is none of these, when one pursues his path while attaching himself to material factors, earth, water, fire, or wind, it can manifest his path as consisting of these components. Again, for someone who holds the insight that these forms are configured depending upon causes and conditions and hence are without any own-being and empty, the Tathagata-garbha is able to manifest itself in emptiness. It is able to manifest itself freely as morally right or wrong, matter or mind, existent or nonexistent, without any obstruction. Moreover, people believe that, just as the moon reflected in water appears to move to the east along with a traveller proceeding eastward, or to the west along with another proceeding westward, the Tathagata-garbha is found wherever they intend to look for it.

"O Purna, people turn back from this originally endowed enlightenment and let their minds be bound by the forms of things, entrapped in the dusts of defilement and suffering bondage. However, the Buddha is one with the originally endowed enlightenment that permeates the entirety of the Dharmadhatu with no obstruction whatsoever. He can reveal one thing as innumerable things, innumerable things as one thing, small as large, and large as small, and he can identify one thing with innumerable things and vice versa, and small with large and vice versa, with no obstruction; while staying at the hall of practice, he can permeate himself in all of the ten directions, as well as absorb the innumerable worlds of the ten directions within his single body. He can show at the tip of a single hair the entire Dharmadhatu as precious as a gem and can demonstrate within a speck of dust the great turning of the Dharma Wheel in transforming delusion into enlightenment. Therefore to the eyes of the ordinary man the Buddha appears to be creating states of differentiation within the world of differentiation."

(8) Purna said, "O World-Honored One, if people are originally endowed with the true mind of enlightenment, why do they create illusions to obstruct its light and thereby place themselves in a position to be drowned in the cycles of life and death?" The World-Honored One replied, "O Purna, there was once a man called Yajnadatta in Sravasti. One morning, as he stood in front of a mirror, he was shocked because he found neither his face nor his head reflected in it. He was so convinced that he had become a specter that he lost his mind. Likewise, although there is no reason for which delusion should exist within enlightenment, people have for a long period of time imagined illusions because of the external dusts of defilement and thereby continued to live lives of insanity with delusion after delusion. Nevertheless, just as Yajnadatta, when he regained his mind, recognized his head still intact, so when people sweep their delusions away they will realize that each of them has the true mind of original enlightenment. Moreover, when Yajnadatta regained his mind, his head did not come from anywhere else, nor had it gone anywhere when he was in the state of insanity. Likewise, the mind of original enlightenment has neither a new origin because of man's enlightenment, nor is it lost while he is in delusion. Where erroneous thought ends, there enlightenment is. Hence delusion and enlightenment are essentially one.

"Purna, just as a foolish man, though possessing a fabulous gem, is unaware of his treasure and goes on wandering and begging for food, people who are unaware of possessing a mind of original enlightenment go on foolishly seeking it in others. When a foolish man is told by the wise of his fabulous gem, he is able to gain wealth at will. It is the same with people who, with the Buddha's instruction, must realize that they possess in themselves the true mind of original enlightenment." Because of this instruction given by the World-Honored One, those of the entire assembly were able to resolve their doubts and realize perfect insight.

5. The Circumstances Leading to Enlightenment

(1) Then the World-Honored One asked the great bodhisattvas who attended the assembly, "What among my teachings led you to realize enlightenment?" In response, the great bodhisattvas reverentially related their respective paths to enlightenment. The Bodhisattva Gandhavyuha said, "Once the World-

Honored One summoned us to meditate on the various aspects of phenomena, and I withdrew to a dark room and quietly engaged in meditation. At that time, I noted that some of the disciples were burning aloe incense, and a draft of air carried its fragrance into the room and it entered my nose. Then I thought, 'This fragrance is neither the original wood itself, nor air itself, nor smoke itself, nor fire itself; neither has it its determined direction in which to go, nor has it a definite passage from which to come; and yet, without the wood, air, smoke, or fire, and without the ways of its coming and going, I should not experience this fragrance.' Upon this reflection, I all at once understood the truth of ignorance. Thus through the clue of the world that fragrance embellishes, I realized enlightenment, having my body free from defilements and perfumed with wondrous fragrance."

(2) The Bodhisattva Pilindavatsa said, "One day, while I was mindful of the World-Honored One's remark that this world has little worth for enjoyment, I went to a town for alms begging. On the road, my foot was injured by a poisonous thorn, and I experienced a severe pain throughout my body. Then I thought, 'I feel this pain because I have a faculty of sensing it, and yet, while experiencing such a pain, as soon as I recollect the joy of the Dharma, I forget the pain of the wound. This being the case, there may not be a special faculty in my body to sense the pain, but, depending upon given conditions, the single mind may become pained or joyous. In short, this mind has no determined form, so that when confused it becomes defilement, whereas when controlled it becomes insight.' Thinking thus, I was in concentration for a while; and in the meantime, I totally forgot the pain, feeling both body and mind as empty, and I became no longer obstructed or bound by anything. Thus within twenty-one days I exhausted all of my defilements. Therefore my enlightenment was occasioned by mindfulness of the origin of sense perception."

(3) The Bodhisattva Ucchusma said, "Once upon a time, I recollect, my nature was filled with greed. But when Dharma-padma-srikusala-devata Buddha appeared in this world, he taught me that whoever has greed will become an aggregate of fires and therefore that I must meditate upon the presence of cool air as well as warm air within my body. While I was practicing this as instructed by the Buddha, there arose sacred rays from within my body, and the fuel of defilements of greed changed into the fire of insight and began to burn. O World-Honored One, in this way, I realized enlightenment by the power of the Fire-Emitting Meditation. Thus Buddhas call me Ucchusma (Fiery Head), while for my part, in order to respond to the benefit I received, I made a vow to appear as a protector for overcoming Maras whenever buddhas realize the supreme enlightenment."

(4) The Bodhisattva Dharanidhara said, "O World-Honored One, once upon a time, when the Buddha called Samantaprabha appeared in this world, I became his disciple and entered the life of a mendicant. For a long time, as my Dharma practice I took it upon myself to level the grounds and span bridges where there were dirty roads, estuaries, and fields that endangered the passage of carts and horses. I met many buddhas during this period of time. Again, whenever I found someone unable to handle his luggage within a crowd of people, I offered to help carry it without pay. In times of famine, I carried people on my back, not minding

the distance; when I happened to see an ox-drawn carriage stuck in the mud and having a hard time, I rendered help by pushing it from behind. While doing these practices, a buddha called Visvabhu appeared in this world, and on the way to the palace to accept a king's offering, he happened to pass the road that I had leveled for his passage. When the Buddha passed by, he patted my head and said to me, 'Make your mind-ground also even. When you accomplish this, the entire ground of the world will also be made level.' From this teaching, I realized that the world of differentiation had arisen originally over the Tathagata-garbha affected by the power of imagination. Not only the atomic particles that make up this body are manifested from illusory imagination but also those particles that build up the universe are equally manifested from the same source of illusory imagination. By understanding these two kinds of tiny particles as totally identical in their nature, my mind at once opened its horizon and perfected my insight."

(5) The Bodhisattva Vaiduryaprabha said, "O World-Honored One, an immeasurably long time ago, I happened to meet the appearance of Amitabha Buddha in this world and received from him various teachings: we are endowed with the true mind of original enlightenment; not only the world of differentiation but also the body of impermanence and suffering have all derived from our illusory imagination. Through practicing meditation on the subjects of the world, the body, and the mind, I eventually realized that those innumerable beings living in the ten directions are all illusory forms and are just like large numbers of mosquitoes, gadflies, and the like placed in a small bowl, busily flying around and crying aloud. Because of this understanding, soon after meeting the Buddha, I could enter the state in which my body and mind equally emitted light without any obstruction."

(6) Next, the Bodhisattva Mahasthamaprapta arose together with fifty-two other bodhisattvas and after saluting the World-Honored One at his feet said, "O World-Honored One, it was an uncountable number of years ago, comparable with the number of the grains of sand along the river Ganges, when a buddha called Amitabha appeared in this world, and following him twelve other buddhas successively appeared during the period of twelve kalpas. The last buddha of this series was called Vikramasurya-candra-prabha, who taught me about the practice of the concentration for recollecting the buddhas. O World-Honored One, this Buddha taught me that the buddhas of the ten worlds are compassionate toward people in the same way as a parent toward an only child. If people too recollect these buddhas in the depths of their hearts, just as a child looks for his mother, they will be able to see the buddhas before long either in this world or in the next. O World-Honored One, this practice, namely, the recollection of the buddhas, is called Embellishment with Fragrant Splendor. This means that, just as a man who is perfumed by incense always carries the fragrance with him, anyone who practices the concentration of recollecting the buddhas will always be embellished by the fragrance of the buddhas' wisdom. O World-Honored One, in this way I was able to understand the truth of emptiness that has neither birth nor death, during the period of my pursuit of the path, through the mind engaged in the recollection of the buddhas.

Therefore even today, as I have appeared in this world, I am trying to receive those people who practice the same discipline and to help them return to the Pure Land of Amitabha Buddha."

(7) At that moment, the World-Honored One emitted bright rays from his body and illuminated those innumerable buddhas and bodhisattvas who reside in the distant ten regions, while those buddhas and bodhisattvas returned the lights over the assembly. When trees, forests, ponds, and marshes were all illuminated, these objects all at once manifested the truth as it was inherent in themselves, each of them emitting its own rays in interaction with others and all together reflecting their splendors like a network of gems strung in innumerable meshes; the spaces of the ten directions were thereby transformed into a sublime cosmos consisting of seven kinds of precious jewels; not only the great earth but also mountains and rivers all extinguished their ugly features of differentiation, so that the entire cosmos totally melted into one single illumination. Songs in praise of the Buddha and the Dharma sprang up spontaneously.

At that time, summoned by the World-Honored One, the Bodhisattva Manjusri rose from his seat, saluted the World-Honored One at his feet, and sang,

> The ocean of enlightenment abides in clear perfection, for this is the very nature of it. Once it shines forth, the differentiation between the agent illumining and the object illumined disappears by itself.

> Deluded by the dusts of defilement, people look into the space wherein the world is manifested. They differentiate the non-sentient as the country and the sentient as the living beings in it.

> Because the original enlightenment of the true existence is vast, these differentiated manifestations in space resemble water bubbles floating over the ocean. Innumerable defiled lands are all equally born from this space.

> When these bubbles disappear, it is known that they are originally nonexistent. When dust particles are swept away, it is known that originally there is no space as well. Not only the land that appeared in the space perishes, but the beings too disappear like apparitions. Once these have disappeared, it is known that originally there is no differentiation but only varieties of skillful manifestations.

> Because the sublime nature of the absolutely real world is omnipresent, every aspect of this world, happiness and adversity, is known to be a skillful manifestation of the Buddha.

(8) Having listened to these accounts and songs by these bodhisattvas, Ananda and various other disciples experienced that their minds at once opened free, and they understood the true nature of the mind, the Tathagata-garbha, which constituted the true original world, just as a traveller can recollect his way back to his home though far away from it. Ananda, having fixed his robes and holding his palms together, reverentially addressed the World-Honored One: "O World-Honored One, I have now clearly seen the path through which we can become buddhas, and I have no more doubt about the practice of this path. I am only worried, however, for those in the distant future. Being more remote from the time of the World-Honored One, they may forever stray, under the influence of false

teachers. How can they keep their minds in control and not be disturbed by Maras, and courageously strive for the path of enlightenment?"

The World-Honored One replied, "O Ananda, your question will be of infinite benefit to the generations to come. Listen attentively to what I say to you. Ananda, I once taught on the subject of the three learnings, namely, precepts, concentration, and insight. It is through practicing the moral precepts that one keeps his mind in control; by way of the moral precepts, one develops the capacity in the discipline of meditation, and finally, by way of meditation, one opens the ultimate insight. As to how to keep the mind in control, my answer is that one must eliminate the mind of greed, for when one accomplishes this, one will no longer be subject to the cycle of life and death. As to the practice of meditation, it is basically to free oneself from defilements. Unless one eliminates greed, one cannot be free from defilement. Thus no matter how much one has practiced meditation and cultivated insight, unless one is free from greed he will be bound to fall into the path of Maras and disturb others also. One who has not realized enlightenment himself but speaks as if he had, and becomes a teacher who leads people to the hells of attachment, belongs to this ilk. Therefore in order to teach the practice of meditation, it is essential first to teach how to eliminate the mind of greed. All the buddhas taught this as the foremost important step. O Ananda, those who practice meditation without eradicating the mind of greed are, as it were, attempting to boil sand and gravel in order to obtain cooked rice. No matter how long, even one hundred thousand kalpas or more, they boil them, they will get nothing but heated sand and gravel; there is no other way for them but to fall into the three evil paths all through these kalpas.

"Moreover, Ananda, without parting from the mind of injuring others or eliminating that of stealing, no one can liberate himself from the dusts of defilement. No matter how long he practices meditation and sharpens his insight, unless he has parted from the mind of killing, he will fall into the path of devils; unless he eliminates the mind of stealing, he will fall into the path of evil spirits. O Ananda, moreover, even when he has parted from the mind of killing, stealing, and greed, if he speaks falsehood, he will lose the seed for becoming a buddha. He who claims that he has attained a certain state though he has actually not, or claims that he has realized enlightenment though he has not, or speaks of himself as if he were most superior and abuses people's offerings, is destroying good roots, making himself unable to return to the right understanding. It is like chopping up feces, making them look like sandalwood, and trying to seek in them the fragrance of the wood. Therefore a disciple of the Buddha must keep his mind in a state like that of a straight thread, so that he can enter the state of meditation, escape from the attempts of the Maras forever, and eventually realize the insight of bodhisattvas."

Chapter 2

DEFILEMENTS

1. The Three Poisons

(1) The World-Honored One continued his stay at the Jeta Grove Monastery and said to the disciples, "My disciples, assume that you are asked by itinerant monks of other religions about the three things greed, anger, and ignorance. Assume that they want to know about their meanings and their distinctions. Now, how would you explain these to them?"

To this the disciples answered, "The World-Honored One is the basis of all teachings. The Buddha is the final refuge. We wish to have instructions as they occur in the Buddha's mind. We shall maintain our thoughts in accordance with the Buddha's instructions." The Buddha then said, "Listen carefully, then. If you are asked about these things by the itinerants of other religions, you should answer in this way: 'In regard to greed, the negative impact of impurities is relatively small, but it will take a long time to get rid of it. On the other hand, the impact of anger is great, but it can be gotten rid of relatively quickly. Regarding ignorance, the impact of it is great, and the time required to get rid of it is long. My friends, remember that greed that has not risen in one's mind arises from thinking of pleasant things in a distorted way, and greed that has already arisen will intensify. Again, anger that has not risen in one's mind arises from looking at unpleasant things in a distorted way, and anger that has already arisen will intensify. Further, from wrong thoughts arises ignorance, and the ignorance that has already arisen will intensify. For this reason, it is good always to view properly with a compassionate mind both the pleasant and the unpleasant aspects of life. When this is done, neither greed nor anger will rise in one's mind, or if they do occur they will be overcome. Then, by virtue of this outlook, ignorance will no longer occur in one's mind; or if it does occur, it will be overcome.' My disciples, this is the way you should answer them."

(2) One day, the roaming ascetic Channa called on and addressed Ananda, "Venerable one, in your teachings, you say, 'Rid yourself of greed, overcome anger, and release yourself from ignorance.' We also say the same in our teachings. Now what misfortunes do you think are caused by greed, anger, and ignorance, which you are telling us to discard?" To this question Ananda answered, "Channa, those who flare up in greed are victims of their greed and at the mercy of their greed;

they harm themselves and others, rouse the feeling of harming themselves as well as others, and must face the agonies resulting from this. Those who free themselves from greed do not experience such agonies. Again, those whose minds are filled with greed will end in impure actions of the mind, speech, and body. Those who have freed themselves of greed will not engage in such actions.

"Again, those whose minds are filled with greed do not truly understand what self-benefit, benefitting others, and benefits for all are. Those who are freed of greed will realize the virtues of these as they are. My friend, note that greed makes one blind, causes one to lose wisdom, leads one to delusions, and obstructs one as he pursues the way to enlightenment. Both anger and ignorance make man do the same adverse things. Dear friend, we see these misfortunes in regard to greed, anger, and ignorance and teach our followers to rid themselves of greed, overcome anger, and free themselves from ignorance."

To this Channa asked, "O venerable sir, how can one be freed of greed, anger, and ignorance?" Ananda replied, "My friend, the way to be freed of these adversities is to follow the Eightfold Path. It contains the right view, the right thought, the right speech, the right action, the right livelihood, the right endeavor, the right mindfulness, and the right meditation." To this, Channa responded, "This way is excellent. This Eightfold Path should be practiced by all."

(3) One day, the World-Honored One, along with many disciples, left the Jeta Grove Monastery and headed for the country of Kosala and came to the town of Kesaputta where the people of the Kalama clan resided. The people, after saluting the Buddha, remarked, "O World-Honored One, when a group of monks visits our town, they praise their own teachings highly but ridicule and denounce other teachings. Then along comes another group of monks, and they do the same thing. Now we are confused and do not know which one of the groups is saying the truth and which is not."

To this the Buddha replied, "O people of Kalama, it is understandable that you have such doubts and are confused. O people of Kalama, you need not accept things that you have heard through hearsay. You need not accept legends as they are relayed, or even what is written in sutras, or speculations based on ideas such as 'it may well be,' or things that you feel are in line with your thinking, or words of a famous monk; all of these you need not accept as they are. O people of Kalama, you should maintain right views and avoid accepting anything that is not a good Dharma for you, anything that is polluted and impure, anything that is rejected by the wise, and anything that you know will bring about losses and agony if you become attached to it.

(4) "O people of Kalama, what is your opinion? Tell me, do you think that those who harbor greed or anger in their hearts will gain benefits or sustain losses?" To this, they answered that there could only be losses. The Buddha said, "O people of Kalama, a person who is greedy, quick to anger, and ignorant is the victim of his greed, anger, and ignorance; he is one whose mind is obsessed with things, who takes life, takes things not given, victimizes other persons' wives, tells lies, and also forces others to do these actions. Is it not true that such a person will suffer prolonged losses and agonies?

"O people of Kalama, are those actions good or bad? Moreover, are they impure and polluted, or are they not? Are they things that the wise would abhor or would they be welcomed by them? And, if one were to be attached to them, would they bring losses and agonies or not?"

To this, the people answered, "O World-Honored One, they are all evil and impure and could only bring untold losses and agonies."

(5) The Buddha said, "O people of Kalama, this is what I mean when I instruct you that you should not too readily accept hearsay, legends, contents of sutras, speculations, likes and dislikes, or things that are said even by those you respect. I mean that you should discard them if you have realized that the matter in question is not right according to your judgment, that it is impure, that it is something the truly wise look down on, and that it is something that will bring you losses and agonies. By the same token, once you are certain that the matter of concern is good, free of the defilements of evil, welcomed and liked by the wise, and sure to bring about benefits and happiness, then you should abide by it. O people of Kalama, do you think that to overcome craving, control anger, and not be at the mercy of one's ignorance is a blessing or is it a disadvantage?" The people answered, "It is an advantage for all persons." The Buddha said, "O people of Kalama, note that those who have freed themselves from greed, anger, and ignorance will not be the victims of their greed, anger, and ignorance. They will always be in full control of their minds, will not take life, will never take things not given, will not victimize other persons' wives, will not tell lies, and will not have others do such impure acts. This is, indeed, everlasting blessing and happiness for those persons.

"O people of Kalama, remember that if the people are able to be freed of greed, anger, and ignorance and lead their lives with right thoughts, with deep consideration, kindness, and sympathy, and with thoughts of goodwill and equality toward others, then they will not curse the world, and they will fill the entire world with wholesome thoughts. The disciples who receive such guidance will likewise be freed of greed and anger, and with pure minds freed from impure thoughts they will themselves achieve the four kinds of peace of mind, even in this world.

(6) "The first peace of mind is expressed in the following statement: 'If the next life exists and good and evil actions bring their effects, I will be born in better destination.' The second peace of mind is expressed in the following statement: 'Even if there is no next life and good and evil actions do not bring their effects, I will, in this life, reside in the happiness in which there is no greed, anger, or suffering.' The third peace of mind is expressed in the following statement: 'Even if a person who has committed evil actions receives the retributions for his actions, what kind of suffering could there be for a person like me who has never thought of any evil or committed any evil action?' The fourth peace of mind is expressed in the following statement: 'Even if evil retributions do not come to the person who has committed evil actions, I recognize myself as a pure person, since I have not committed any evil actions.'

"The disciples who abide by these instructions are in this way kind and imperturbable, are pure in body and mind, and enjoy in the present these four kinds of peace of mind."

To this the people of Kalama responded by saying, "O World-Honored One, it is exactly as you say. All of the Buddha's disciples are kind, tolerant, and freed of impurities; with pure minds they have all attained the four kinds of peace of mind. Please accept us as followers who will be seeking refuge in the Dharma for life."

2. Vulture Peak

(1) The World-Honored One continued, and passing through the country of Kosala he came to the village of Pankadha and remained there for some time. In the meantime, the Buddha gave detailed instructions on the rules, preparation, and determination of one pursuing the way. A disciple, Kassapa-gotta, was born in this village. Having joined the Sangha, he was angry because he thought that the Buddha was concerned too much with minor things.

In due time, the World-Honored One left Pankadha and reached Vulture Peak in Rajagaha. Soon after the World-Honored One left, Kassapa-gotta felt deep regret. He realized that he had lost a great blessing, for after having thought that the detailed repetition of the teaching by the Buddha on the ways of pursuing the Dharma was unbearable, he had become angry and thus suffered a great loss. He felt that he should go to the Buddha and ask forgiveness for his anger. He hurriedly went to Rajagaha, ascended the mountain, and addressed the Buddha, "O World-Honored One, the other day when you discoursed at Pankadha, I was dissatisfied and irritated. After the World-Honored One left, I could not help but deeply repent and have come here to make amends. O World-Honored One, it was my evil that had swayed my reasoning. Please forgive me my evil so that I may not become the victim of my emotions." Then the World-Honored One instructed Kassapa-gotta on many aspects of the Dharma, gave him encouragement, and forgave him for his unkind thought.

(2) The World-Honored One, on another day, instructed the disciples and stated, "My disciples, there are three learnings you must practice as a monk. They are precepts, meditation, and wisdom. To give an analogy, suppose that there is a donkey that does not have the color or looks of a cow, does not moo like a cow, and does not have a cow's legs, but that tags along with a herd of cows and claims that he is also a cow. This is ridiculous. Now, if certain kinds of disciples tag along with the other disciples of the Buddha and claim that they, too, are the Buddha's disciples, it is clear that they have not sought refuge in the three learnings that all disciples of the Buddha have, nor will they have the determination or wish to learn them. For this reason, my disciples, you are advised to have this determination: 'We must earnestly learn and practice precepts, meditation, and wisdom.'

(3) "My disciples, there are three things that a farmer must do before he can harvest his crops. First, he must till and level the soil. He must then sow his seeds at the right time. Then he must water the crops at the right time and let the water drain. Likewise, the Buddha's disciples must devote themselves to three

things before their enlightenment. These are the three learnings of precepts, meditation, and wisdom. For this reason, my disciples, you are advised to have this determination: 'We must earnestly learn and practice precepts, meditation, and wisdom.'

"My disciples, the farmer does not have the supernatural power to say, 'This day the plants shall bear seedlings, tomorrow they shall bear stalks and leaves, and the following day they shall bear grain.' The crop will require changes in the seasons, the seedlings must appear, the stalks must grow, and finally they will bear grain. In the same way, my disciples do not have the ability to be freed from attachments, to rid themselves of impurities, within the short period of today, tomorrow, or the day after. In fact, as they devote themselves to the three learnings of precepts, meditation, and wisdom, they will gradually be freed from attachments, and eventually they will be released from impurities. For this reason, you must have the strong determination earnestly to learn precepts, meditation, and wisdom.

(4) "First, my disciples, what is meant by the learning of precepts? It means that the Buddha's disciples observe precepts and regulate their minds and bodies according to the clauses of the precepts, they practice that which is pure, they keep full control of their five senses, and they have deep concern when committing even the smallest of violations or offenses; and they endeavor earnestly in their ways to purity. Second, what is meant by the learning of meditation? It is the process of gradually entering into the various states of meditation by my disciples who have overcome desires and have freed themselves from impure actions. Third, what is the learning of wisdom? It is to realize human existence as it is. Defilements exist; there is a cause of defilements; the cause can be overcome; and there is a way to the overcoming of the cause of defilements. After having overcome all defilements, one realizes enlightenment. These are the three learnings of precepts, meditation, and wisdom."

3. Instructions in the Kingdom of Vajji

(1) The World-Honored One then headed north; crossing the river Ganges, he entered the kingdom of Vajji and resided at Ukkala along the banks of the Ganges. One day, viewing the flow of the river, the Buddha remarked, "My disciples, there was once a stupid cowherd in the country of Magadha who had led his herd, without carefully studying the situation, toward the northern banks of the river Ganges where the flows were not shallow and when the river flow was high on the last month of the rainy season and the first day of autumn. At that time the herd of cattle was pulled into the main flow of the swirling river and was drowned in the swirling water. Likewise, to look at someone who does not have a good understanding of this world or other worlds, and does not know about the realms of the devils, as a person whose instructions you should listen to or believe in is to invite prolonged losses and unhappiness.

"My disciples, on the other hand, there was a wise cowherd who, at the same season, carefully studied the banks of the river Ganges and, selecting a shallow flow along the river, led his herd toward the northern bank. He first led the oxen into the river. Once the oxen were safely across, he led across the strong cows that were used to crossing the river. These cows were also able to get across safely. Next the cowherd led the stronger of the male and female calves into the river. They were also able to get across safely. Lastly, the weaker of the calves were led into the river, and they were all able to get across safely. My disciples, in the last group of calves there were newly born ones that were put in front of the mother cows, whimpering along the way. However, these were also able to get safely across the river to the other side. All this came about because the wise cowherd had studied all related conditions before he led the animals into the river.

(2) "My disciples, likewise, if you look up to one who is well versed in the matters of this world and other worlds and of the realm of Mara as the one whose words should be heeded and trusted, you will enjoy everlasting blessing and happiness. My disciples, just as the group of oxen leading the herd safely reached the other shore of the Ganges by crossing the river bed, the enlightened arhat who has completely extinguished defilements, achieved the pure practices, accomplished that which had to be accomplished, freed himself of his heavy burden, realized his goal, and realized perfect insight will cross the river of Mara and safely attain the other shore.

"Again, just as a strong and experienced cow will get across the river Ganges safely, a person who has completely extinguished the five defilements that bind him to this world, has attained birth in a heavenly realm, has reached enlightenment there, and will never return to this world will safely reach the other shore by crossing over the stream of Mara.

"Again, just as the strong calves cross the flow of the Ganges and reach the other shore, a person who extinguishes the three defilements, subdues greed, anger, and ignorance, and is released from suffering, having been reborn only once more in this world will be able to cross the flow of Mara and safely attain the other shore.

"Again, just as the weak calves cross the Ganges and get to the other shore safely, if a person extinguishes the three defilements, no longer falls into the evil realms, and is sure to reach enlightenment, he will cross over the flow of Mara and safely attain the other shore.

"Lastly, just as the newly born calf who snorts and whimpers in front of its mother safely crosses the flow of the Ganges and gets to the other side, the disciple who is at the elementary level in following the Dharma or in trusting others' words too will cross over the flow of Mara and safely get to the other shore.

"My disciples, I am well versed in the matters of this world, other worlds, and the realms of Mara. Therefore, those who think that the Buddha should be listened to and believed in will be blessed with everlasting happiness."

(3) The World-Honored One left the river bank; and heading north, he went to stay at a brick house in the village of Nadika. Just around that time, Anuruddha, Nandiya, and Kimbila were staying at Gosinga-sala Forest. One evening, emerging from meditation, the World-Honored One proceeded toward the Gosinga-sala Forest. Seeing this, the watchman of the forest said to the World-Honored

One, "Do not enter this forest; three mendicants are here trying to control their minds and keeping silence. Do not disturb them." Seeing this by chance, Anuruddha said to the watchman and told him not to deny entrance to the World-Honored One, since he was their master and the Buddha. Then Anuruddha went to the place where Nandiya and Kimbila were waiting and told them what had happened.

"My friends, the World-Honored One has come," he said. The three then proceeded to where the Buddha was. One of them received the Buddha's robe and bowl, another prepared the Buddha's seat, and the other prepared a bowl of water to wash the Buddha's feet. The Buddha then washed both feet and sat on the seat prepared for him. The disciples all bowed to the Buddha and took their mats beside the Buddha. The World-Honored One then addressed Anuruddha and asked, "O Anuruddha, are you all residing in peace of mind? Do you receive adequate offerings including food offerings?"

To this Anuruddha answered that they were in peace of mind, that offerings were adequate, and that they had no difficulty in obtaining food. The World-Honored One asked, "Anuruddha, are you all residing in a state of peace and harmony where there is friendliness without strife, and unity as milk and water would mix, with deep concern over each other's welfare?" To this question Anuruddha answered that they were.

The Buddha asked, "Anuruddha, tell me, how are you achieving this harmony amongst yourselves?" To this, Anuruddha answered by expressing his belief that he was indeed privileged to be able to live together with his fellow mendicants. He also stated that he was devoting himself to others through his kind actions known or not known to others. Anuruddha expressed his firm conviction by saying, "O World-Honored One, I hope to discard my personal intentions and become truly one with the hearts of all these people. O World-Honored One, although we are separate individuals, our hearts and minds are one."

Nandiya and Kimbila also joined in and stated, "O World-Honored One, this is our belief. It is indeed fortunate for us to be able to live with these fellow disciples. We shall endeavor to devote ourselves to others through our kind actions known or unknown to them. We shall discard attachment to our ego-consciousnesses and be in harmony with others." To these words the Buddha replied, "Well said. However, are you all residing at peace with earnestness, perseverance, and sincerity at heart?" They all answered and said that they were.

(4) The Buddha said, "Anuruddha, tell me how you are practicing these." To this Anuruddha replied, "O World-Honored One, of the monks residing here, the one who returns first from his morning alms begging prepares water for others, water to wash one's feet and water to drink; emptying the leftover food into a bowl, he prepares it. Those who return later and wish to eat it do so whenever there are leftovers. If they do not wish to eat it, they will either discard it in places where there is no grass growing or pour it into water in which there are no fish. Then the seats are cleared away, the drinking water is put away, the containers are stored, and the place of meals is cleaned. Other containers, such as for gargling water, drinking water, or water to wash one's hands, when empty, are filled

by anyone who notices them. If a certain monk cannot do the chores alone, he uses a hand signal to call for another to help him. We do the chores together. When doing chores we maintain silence and do not utter a word. O World-Honored One, every fifth day we gather to listen to the Dharma all night long. It is in this way that we reside here devoting ourselves with earnestness, diligence, and sincerity to the Dharma."

To this the Buddha said, "Well done, Anuruddha! However, even as you devote yourselves with eagerness, diligence, and sincerity, can you say that you reside in the realm that is beyond one's rules, pure and filled with peace and happiness?"

To this Anuruddha answered, "O World-Honored One, it could not possibly be otherwise; we can freely leave greed and impurities and enter various kinds of meditation filled with happiness and pleasure. This is the state that we have attained, which surpasses all human rules and laws, the realm unexcelled, freed from all defilements, pure, and filled with bliss and happiness. We do not know of any other realm higher or superior."

The Buddha said, "Well said, Anuruddha; it is true indeed that there is no other realm higher than this realm that you now enjoy."

Having delivered instructions to the three disciples, the World-Honored One was pleased; he stood up from his seat and left. The three disciples, seeing the World-Honored One off, returned to their place. Nandiya and Kimbila asked Anuruddha, "In the presence of the World-Honored One you referred to us as having been freed from all defilements. Have we ever told you that we had attained such a realm?"

To this Anuruddha answered, "It is true that you have not said that you have attained such states. However, knowing your minds intuitively with my mind, I stated to the Buddha what I stated."

(5) At this time, Digha resided in this forest. He approached the World-Honored One and said, "O World-Honored One, the people of Vajji are truly fortunate, for not only does the Buddha reside here, the three disciples, Anuruddha, Nandiya, and Kimbila also live here. They are truly fortunate!" These words of Digha were filled with so much power and truth that they moved the gods. The World-Honored One approvingly said, "O Digha, it is exactly as you say. Moreover, Digha, if the members of the families of these three disciples reflect upon these three disciples with minds of pure faith, they too will enjoy everlasting benefits and blessings. O Digha, if the people of the various groups, villages, towns, cities, and countries from which these three came maintain their thoughts on them with pure minds of faith, they too will enjoy everlasting blessings. Again, Digha, if the kshatriyas, brahmins, vaisyas, sudras, and all others, be they gods or monks, reflect upon these three sons of reputable families with pure minds of faith, they will all receive everlasting benefits and blessings. Digha, it would be well for you to consider how much benefit and blessings were received by so many by the actions of these three and to consider the state to which they have reached in their concern for benefitting people and gods."

(6) From this time on the World-Honored One resided for some time at the Pagoda Hall of the Great Forest just outside of Vesali. The venerable Ananda

was present in the Sangha of the Buddha. Abhaya of the Licchavi clan came to see Ananda with Pandita-kumaraka and said to Ananda, "The Jains profess that they have acquired the powers of knowing all and perceiving all. They bid us take up ascetic practices in order to eliminate karma. To eliminate the cause of suffering, they instruct us not to create other karma. They say, 'When karma is extinguished, suffering will cease. When suffering ceases, senses cease to exist. When senses cease to exist, all sufferings will cease. Thus by ascetic practices that are pure and free from the heat of defilements, all pain and suffering will be overcome.' How would the World-Honored One respond to this?"

Ananda said, "O Abhaya, note that the World-Honored One, a man of wisdom and insight, purifies sentient beings and, in order to overcome all agonies and sufferings, teaches three kinds of purity, which are free from the heat of defilements. Abhaya, these are, first, to observe precepts, regulating oneself according to the precepts, doing pure deeds, controlling the five senses, and fearing even the smallest of offenses as one pursues these ways with diligence; second, to reach the realm of meditation by observing the precepts; third, to realize enlightenment upon the extinguishing of defilements by observing precepts and entering meditation. Then there will be no further karma created; and while receiving only the retributions from previous karma, one overcomes agonies and sufferings by pursuing purity that is free from the heat of all impurities. O Abhaya, these are the three kinds of purity, freed of all impurities, that the World-Honored One, a man of wisdom and insight, has expounded."

At this time Pandita-kumaraka said to Abhaya, "O Abhaya, why is it that you show no sign of rejoicing at the wise words of Ananda upon listening to his sermon?" Abhaya answered, "My friend, how can it ever be that I would not rejoice in listening to the words of the venerable Ananda? If there be one who would not rejoice, that person's head would split in two."

(7) Again, at one time the World-Honored One instructed Ananda at the Pagoda Hall of the Great Forest: "Ananda, if you truly sympathize with your friends and relatives, you must teach and direct them to the three kinds of faith. They are, first, an unfaltering faith in the Buddha; second, an unfaltering faith in the Dharma; and third, an unfaltering faith in the Sangha. Regarding the Buddha, make them have faith in his enlightenment. Regarding the Dharma, make them realize the value of the Dharma. Regarding the Sangha, lead them to believe that it is the gathering of genuine practitioners, where the highest spiritual benefits may be attained.

"Ananda, bear in mind that even if all that exists in this world undergoes change, there will be no change concerning the disciples who have unfaltering faith in the Buddha, the Dharma, and the Sangha. In fact, if there is any change about them, it is that these persons who have deep faith in the Three Treasures will never be reborn in the evil realms. This is the great change. Ananda, if you are truly concerned about your friends and relatives, you must direct them to have faith in the Three Treasures."

(8) One day Ananda asked the World-Honored One regarding the matter of being or existence, which had been discussed by many, and he wanted to know

what being or existence meant. The Buddha asked, "Ananda, tell me, if there were no action that caused one to be reborn in the three worlds, then would the three worlds ever come into existence?"

To this question Ananda answered that there would not be such worlds. The Buddha continued, "Ananda, note that action is the soil. Consciousness is the seed. The thirst of craving is water. When a person who is covered by ignorance and is bound by the thirst of craving takes existence in the future, it is at the time of such a birth that the three worlds will appear. Thus, Ananda, this is what being or existence means."

(9) Again, at another time, the World-Honored One said to Ananda, "Ananda, can one say that all the observances of precepts, rituals and traditions, asceticism, religious practices, and convictions have good results?" To this Ananda answered, "It is not proper to give a general answer. If some observances of precepts, rituals and traditions, asceticism, religious practices, and convictions increase unwholesomeness and decrease wholesomeness, then such observances do not bring about favorable results. On the other hand, if some observances of precepts and so on increase wholesomeness and decrease unwholesomeness, then they bring about good results."

The World-Honored One accepted and endorsed these words by Ananda. Ananda rejoiced in knowing that his words were endorsed by the Buddha. He stood up, worshipped the Buddha, circumambulated him to the right, and left the hall. Upon seeing Ananda leave, the World-Honored One instructed his disciples, "My disciples, you should all note that although Ananda is still in the process of learning the way, it is truly difficult to find another who is equal to him in wisdom."

(10) At another time, the World-Honored One left the Great Forest and, with certain well-known leading disciples including Sariputta, Moggallana, Mahakassapa, Anuruddha, Revata, Ananda, and others, resided at the Gosinga-sala Forest near the village of Nadika.

One evening Moggallana arose from deep meditation and, calling on Mahakassapa, said, "Dear friend, let us go see Sariputta to listen to the Dharma." The disciple Anuruddha was also invited to go along, and the three headed for Sariputta's place of residence. Around this time, Ananda got to know about this and, approaching Revata, said, "O Revata, the three have gone to Sariputta's place to hear the Dharma. Shall we also join them?" With this the two headed toward Sariputta's place. Sariputta, seeing Ananda coming from the distance, called him and said, "Ananda, it is good that you have come. This Gosinga-sala Forest is indeed a delightful place. The night too is pleasant. The sala trees have borne fruit, and the flowers are in bloom, filling the air with a beautiful aroma. Ananda, tell me, what kind of Buddha's disciples can add further brilliance to this sala tree forest?" To this Ananda said, "Those who listen intently, remember things correctly and carefully, keep the Buddha's wonderful teachings in their minds, diligently strive for enlightenment, and teach their teaching to people correctly so that they too can be freed of their impurities will add brilliance to the Gosinga-sala Forest."

The disciple Sariputta said, "Revata, the venerable Ananda has given us his opinion. I should like to hear who you think would add brilliance to this Gosinga-sala Forest." Revata answered, "O Sariputta, I believe that those who like to be alone, strive to still their minds, and have insight are the ones who will add brilliance to the Gosinga-sala Forest."

(11) Sariputta then asked Anuruddha, Mahakassapa, and Moggallana each as follows, "Friend, Revata has given us his opinion. I wish to ask each one of you the same question. Who would add brilliance to the Gosinga-sala Forest?"

To this, Anuruddha answered, "Dear friend, they are persons who are able to see a thousand worlds with superhuman eyes that are much, much purer than those of humans, as when an ordinary person is able to see a thousand worlds when he ascends a high tower. Those who can see a thousand worlds with the superhuman power of sight are indeed those who will add brilliance to the Gosinga-sala Forest."

Mahakassapa answered, "Dear friend, the people who will add brilliance to the Gosinga-sala Forest are those who reside in a forest and praise the virtue of such a practice, those who beg for food and praise the virtue of such a practice, those who wear a robe made of discarded clothes and praise the virtue of such a practice, those who possess only three robes and praise the virtue of such a practice, those who have few desires and praise the virtue of such a practice, those who are appreciative of what they have and praise the virtue of such a practice, those who live by themselves and praise the virtue of such a practice, those who seek the Dharma diligently and undauntedly and praise the virtue of such a practice, those who avoid a crowd and praise the virtue of such a practice, those who observe the precepts and praise the virtue of such a practice, those who cultivate concentration and praise the virtue of such a practice, those who attain wisdom and praise the virtue of such a practice, those who experience liberation and praise the virtue of such a practice, and those who gain the wisdom of liberation and praise the virtue of such a practice."

The disciple Moggallana said, "O Sariputta, assume that there are two of the Buddha's disciples who, discussing the Dharma, would exchange a question and an answer in a manner that agrees with the Dharma. These persons will add brilliance to the Gosinga-sala Forest."

After all these answers were given, Moggallana then said to Sariputta, "O Sariputta, we have all expressed our own opinions. At this time we should like to ask you a question. Sariputta, this Gosinga-sala Forest is indeed a pleasant place, and the evening is truly pleasant. The sala trees are bearing fruit, flowers are blooming, and an air of holiness is everywhere. Now, Sariputta, tell us what kind of a disciple of the Buddha would add to the brilliance of the Gosinga-sala Forest?"

To this Sariputta answered, "Moggallana, assume that there is a disciple of the Buddha who is freely able to control his mind and is not controlled by his mind. As the king or the king's family member who has a boxful of clothing is freely able to change his or her clothes, morning, noon, and night, the person who can readily control his mind is the kind of person who will add to the brilliance of the Gosinga-sala Forest."

(12) After having given this answer, Sariputta said, "My friends, we have all voiced our opinions. Now let us go to the World-Honored One, tell him about our discussion, and hope to record in our memories the instructions of the Buddha on this matter." The disciples then went to the Buddha's dwelling. The Venerable Sariputta, representing those present, addressed the World-Honored One: "O World-Honored One, these friends came to see me this evening to discuss the Dharma. I asked my friends in the Dharma what kind of disciples would add brilliance to this Gosinga-sala Forest that we cherish dearly. After each one expressed his opinion, we decided to seek guidance from the Buddha. O World-Honored One, whose opinion should be considered superior to the rest?"

Then Sariputta recounted their respective opinions. Having listened to their words, the Buddha said, "O Sariputta, all of the opinions expressed are good. Such opinions can come only from you who have high levels of attainment. However, listen to the words of the Buddha in regard to those who will add brilliance to the Gosinga-sala Forest.

"O Sariputta, if among the Buddha's disciples there are those who, putting down their bowls after the meal and quietly sitting with bodies and minds in full control, can say with determination, 'I shall not leave this seat while my mind is not freed of attachment and released from defilements,' they are indeed those who will add brilliance to this forest."

4. The Pain of Craving

(1) In due time, the World-Honored One headed north and entered a nigrodha forest at the outskirts of the city of Kapilavatthu where the Sakya clan lived.

The king of the Sakya clan, Mahanama, approached the World-Honored One and addressed him as follows: "O World-Honored One, I have for a long time cherished the Buddha's teaching that greed, anger, and ignorance are defilements of the mind. May I state that despite my efforts, I feel at times that these impurities get hold of my mind. When this happens, I am inclined to think that there are still some remnants of things that I have not yet managed to discard from my mind."

To these words the World-Honored One said, "O Mahanama, it is exactly as you have stated. It is because greed, anger, and ignorance have not been discarded from your mind. If these are discarded from your mind, you will not choose to live a household life, nor will you pursue your cravings. Even if you know, through your wisdom, that no matter how much craving you may pursue, there is no end to it, that craving is filled with suffering, and that it makes you lose all your hopes and leads you to misfortunes, unless you attain true happiness free from craving you will be still bound by your cravings. If you attain both wisdom and true happiness free from craving, you will be able to get away from the chasing of cravings.

(2) "Mahanama, I shall tell you my own experience. Before I attained enlightenment, although I correctly understood that no matter how much craving I might

pursue, there would be no end to it, that it was filled with suffering, and that it made me lose all my hopes and led me to misfortunes, I was continuously haunted by craving, since I had not attained true happiness free from craving. Since I later attained not only wisdom but also true happiness free from craving, I was able to escape the persistent chasing of cravings.

"Mahanama, what are the so-called pleasures of man's desires? There are five desires. They are the desires for pleasing sights, sounds, smells, tastes, and touches. Pleasure and delight arise because of the five desires. These are the pleasures of the five desires.

"Mahanama, what are the misfortunes brought about by desires? All persons earn their living by their works; they have to bear heat and cold; they are constantly bothered by wind, rain, fleas, mosquitoes, and reptiles; and they suffer from hunger and thirst. Yet despite their backbreaking efforts, they cannot possess wealth. They become exhausted, agonize, and grieve; they strike their chests and moan, saying that their efforts were meaningless, and that their endeavors bore no fruit.

(3) "O Mahanama, assume that, as the result of their efforts and endeavors, they are able to amass wealth. Now in order to secure the wealth, they must endure all kinds of suffering. They now must think of how not to have this wealth confiscated by the ruler and how to protect it from thieves, from fires, from floods, and from relatives who would now try to take it away. All in all, it ends up being confiscated by the ruler, stolen by thieves, destroyed by floods or fire, or taken away by relatives. By this time, they are exhausted and in deep sorrow and agony, and striking their chests they cry out that what was theirs is no longer theirs. These are the misfortunes of indulging in desires. All sufferings in this world are based on desires and are the results of craving.

"O Mahanama, because of desires, kings battle with other kings, brahmins fight against brahmins, parents quarrel with their offspring, brothers fight with brothers, sisters contradict sisters, friends oppose friends. They always engage in fights, confrontations, and arguments and in the end resort to clubs and swords and kill each other. These are the misfortunes that desires bring.

"Moreover, Mahanama, because of desires, armies confront each other with shields and swords, and with bows and quivers tied in place they advance. The arrows fly, spears thrust, and swords flash; they pierce each other and cut each other's heads off. These are the misfortunes of man's desires.

(4) "Mahanama, again, it is because of greed that people invite physical destruction, conduct pilferages, commit highway robberies, and engage in immoral acts against women. Usually the king captures these people and punishes them. They are beaten with whips, with large sticks, or with clubs; their hands are cut off; their legs are severed; their ears are sliced off; their noses are slit off; their skulls are opened and heated iron bars are applied; their scalps are removed and their skulls rubbed with pebbles until they become as white as sea shells; their mouths are burned by fire and are torn open up to the ears; their bodies are wrapped in cloth soaked with oil and burned; their hands are burned; their skin is stripped off from the throat and chest to the ankle; the elbows and ankles are nailed on to

an iron pole with fire burning around it; the skin and blood vessels are torn with sharp pointed hooks; the bodies are chopped up like a checkerboard; the injured bodies are then washed in salt water; their bodies are stretched on the ground and iron bars are pushed through both ears and heads and the bodies are wound around it; the bodies are beaten and softened down like bunches of straw; the bodies are sprayed with boiling oil and fed to hungry dogs; the bodies are then pierced with broiling irons and the heads are cut off. These extreme types of suffering are brought about by desires.

"Again, Mahanama, it is because of desires that people keep on doing impure actions of body, speech, and mind, and because of these actions they must bear the various sufferings in hell after they die. These are the misfortunes arising from man's desires. The sufferings in the future life are also caused by desires and are dependent on desires.

(5) "At one time I was staying on Vulture Peak mountain in Rajagaha. Just at that time, on the Black Rock slope of Mount Isigiri there were many Jain ascetics who were practicing asceticism of prolonged upright standing and seemed to be in extreme pain. One evening I emerged from meditation and approached these ascetics and asked why they were doing the prolonged standing practice and enduring such extreme pain. To this the Jains answered that their master, Nigantha Nataputta, was the all-knowing and all-seeing one and possessed unlimited wisdom. According to them, his wisdom was awake at all times, and he instructed his disciples, 'You have done evil action in past lives. You must free yourselves from such evil karma by your ascetic practices. Now, if you control your actions, speech, and minds and eradicate the forces of your past karma and do not further create new karma, then in the future there will be no possibility of letting impure secretions of your desires leak out. Once this leaking is controlled, then karma will cease to be activated. Once karma ceases, then all suffering will cease. Once suffering ceases, then all human pain and agonies will be eliminated.' These, they said, were the instructions of their master, which they were eager to follow.

"O Mahanama, at that time I asked the ascetics if they knew whether they existed or did not exist in the past. They all answered that they did not know. Again, I asked them if they knew whether they had committed bad actions in the past or not. To this they answered that they did not know. I then asked them, 'Do you know what kind of bad actions you committed in the past?' To this they answered that they did not know. I then asked them whether they knew just how much of the suffering had been removed, or how much of it remained, or how much suffering had to be removed so that they might be freed from it completely. To this they answered that they did not know. I then instructed them: 'It is clear now that all of you are not aware of whether you existed or not in the past, or whether you committed evil actions in past lives or not, or the nature of the bad actions. Moreover, you do not know how much of the suffering has been removed or how much of it remains, or how much of it must be removed in order that all the sufferings may be eliminated forever. This amounts to saying that it is only people who have merciless blood stains on their hands who would become Jain ascetics.'"

(6) "The Jain ascetics then addressed me, 'O Gotama, true happiness is not derived from happiness. It is wrought out of suffering. If true happiness is to be had by happiness, King Bimbisara will have more happiness than you, simply because the king is at present enjoying more happiness than you.' To this I said that such statements should not be made without giving deep thought. I then asked whether the king was living more happily than I. The ascetics responded, 'O Gotama, true, we have made such remarks without giving deep thought. Pray, teach us. Which one of you is enjoying a truly happy life?' To this I, in turn, asked them a question, telling them that they should answer frankly. The question was whether or not King Bimbisara could live in perfect happiness without moving his body or uttering a word for seven days and seven nights. To this they answered the king could not. I asked whether without uttering a word for six days and six nights, or five days and five nights, or four days and four nights, or three days and three nights, or two days and two nights, or one day and one night, the king could be perfectly happy. To this the ascetics all answered that the king could not be happy.

"I continued my discourse, 'O ascetics of Jainism, I reside in perfect bliss without even moving the body or saying a word a whole day and night. I reside in perfect bliss for two days and two nights, three days and three nights, up to seven days and seven nights without moving the body or uttering a word. Now, observing the matter from this standpoint, which one of us enjoys perfect happiness, King Bimbisara or the Buddha?' To this the ascetics answered that it was obvious that Gotama resided in perfect bliss. Mahanama, this was the dialogue between the Jain ascetics and me." Mahanama rejoiced in listening to the Buddha and happily returned to his home.

(7) This also happened when the World-Honored One was staying at the nigrodha forest. Early one morning the Buddha went to Kapilavatthu to receive food offerings. Spending the noontime seated under a young bamboo tree, deep in the great forest, the Buddha avoided the heat of the day. Just then Dandapani of the Sakya clan entered the forest and, seeing the World-Honored One under the bamboo tree, paid his respects to the Buddha. Leaning on his walking stick, he stood at the side of the Buddha and inquired, "O venerable mendicant, what is your main teaching? What do you explain to others?"

To this the World-Honored One answered, "My friend, my main teaching is to live life without grasping any world. Remember that the true brahmin who has been released from desires, doubts, and delusion and freed from the thirst of lust concerning life and death will no longer be bothered by the thought of 'Is it this or is it that?' This is what I explain to others." Hearing these words of the Buddha, Dandapani nodded again and again; deeply impressed, he frowned; leaning heavily on his stick, he left.

(8) As the evening came, the World-Honored One emerged from meditation and returned to the nigrodha forest, sat in the Buddha's seat, and relayed to the

disciples all that had occurred that afternoon. Just then one of the disciples remarked that the words of the Buddha were not clearly understood by him and requested that the Buddha explain in further detail. Then the Buddha said, "My dear disciples, whenever there are inducing conditions then immediately sundry thoughts occur. If there are no conditions to be spoken of, to be delighted about, or to be attached to, then there is truly the end of the impurity of greed. This also spells the end of the impurity of anger, the impurity of wrong views, the impurity of doubts, the impurity of arrogance, the impurity of the craving for existence, and the impurity of ignorance. It also means the end of fights and confrontations with poles and swords; it means the end of arguments, mutual flattering, and lying. This is, indeed, where all impurities end."

With these words of wisdom, the World-Honored One stood up from his seat and retreated to his room. Seeing the Buddha retreat, the disciples remarked that since the Buddha had taught in brief and had now left, they would like to have the teachings explained in broader terms. They also thought that the leading disciple Maha-Kaccayana, who was always praised by the Buddha and respected by the Buddha's learned disciples, would be able to explain in detail the teachings of the Buddha. They decided to go to Maha-Kaccayana and ask him the meaning of the Buddha's words.

(9) Thus the disciples of the Buddha together went to see Maha-Kaccayana and asked him to enlighten them on the Buddha's sermon. Maha-Kaccayana answered and instructed them: "Friends, suppose there is a man who is seeking a red core in the trunk of a tree. He finds a large tree with a red core in the trunk, and he climbs up the tree and attempts to discover a red core in its branches and leaves. Just like that, you are leaving your own master and expecting me to tell you the meaning of his teaching. My friends, the Buddha is the all-knowing one of all peoples, the all-seeing one of all peoples, the teacher of the Dharma, the one who enlightens all to the true meaning, and the one residing in the Dharma. When the World-Honored One taught the Dharma, you should have inquired as to the true meaning of the Buddha's words; you should have retained this in your minds just as the Buddha had taught."

The disciples said, "O Maha-Kaccayana, it is exactly as you say. However, you are praised by the Buddha and respected by the learned ones of the Sangha and are able to elaborate on the words of the Buddha. Please understand our feelings and explain the meaning of the Buddha's instructions to us."

Maha-Kaccayana addressed the monks: "I shall now offer my understanding. I expect you to listen very intently. My friends, the brief instructions given to us by the World-Honored One, as I interpret them, have this meaning. Owing to the eyes and their object, eye-consciousness arises; owing to the eyes, object, and eye-consciousness coming into play, eye-sensation arises. Because of this eye-sensation perception arises. Once perception is received, conception arises. Based on conception, one thinks. Because one thinks, discrimination arises. Conditioned by discrimination, there arise sundry ideas. My friends, it is the same with hearing, smelling, tasting, bodily contact, and mental activity. Thus where there are no eyes, object, or eye-consciousness, there will be no eye-sensation. When there is no eye-sensation, there will be no perception. When there is no perception, there is no conception. When there is no conception, there is no thinking. Where there is no thinking, there is no discrimination. Where there is no discrimination, there are no sundry ideas. The same is the case with ears, nose, tongue, body, and mind. My friends, this is the way I interpret the brief instructions of the Buddha. If you have other personal thoughts, I encourage you to go to the World-Honored One, inquire as to the meaning of his thoughts, and retain to the letter the Buddha's instructions in your mind."

(10) The Buddha's disciples rejoiced in hearing Maha-Kaccayana's explanation and, leaving their seats, they approached the World-Honored One and exclaimed, "O World-Honored One, we disciples went to see Maha-Kaccayana and asked for his explanation of the brief sermon the Buddha had given us. Maha-Kaccayana explained it to us, using these words and expressions, and enlightened us."

The Buddha then said, "My disciples, Maha-Kaccayana is a learned one and a person of great wisdom. Even if you were to ask me to expound on my words, I should explain in the manner that Maha-Kaccayana did. This is because what you heard from Maha-Kaccayana is the true meaning. My disciples, retain these words in your minds."

At that time Ananda said to the Buddha, "O World-Honored One, assume that a person on the brink of death by hunger and fatigue is given tablets of honey. In this case, the more he tastes the stronger will the sweetness become. Likewise, the mindful and wise disciples of the Buddha, by following this teaching, by acquiring wisdom, and by pursuing the meaning of it, have gained still greater satisfaction and joy. O World-Honored One, what should this teaching be called?" The World-Honored One then said, "Ananda, let this teaching be known as the Sutra of the Analogy of the Honey Tablet."

Chapter 3

THE CONDUCT OF A BODHISATTVA

1. Sariputta's Discourse on the Dharma

(1) The World-Honored One, accompanied by many disciples, again returned to the Anathapindika Monastery. One day, the venerable Sariputta said to the other disciples, "Friends, there are four kinds of people in the world: those who possess defilements and yet do not know that they possess them; those who possess defilements and know that they possess them; those who do not possess defilements and yet do not know that they do not possess them; and those who do not possess defilements and know that they do not possess them. Of the first two kinds of people, those who do not know that they have defilements are inferior to those who know that they have them. The same thing can be said about the last two kinds of people. Whether the person is aware of his condition or not determines whether he is superior or inferior."

At that moment, the venerable Moggallana said to Sariputta, "Of these two persons with defilements, why do you say that the one is superior to the other?" Sariputta replied, "My friend, this is the reason. In the person who possesses defilements and yet does not know that he has them, there is no determination nor endeavor nor exertion to remove his defilements. Accordingly he will die with the defilements of greed, anger, and ignorance. He is like a dust-covered bronze bowl bought in a market. If one does not wash or clean it and throws it into a dusty corner of the house, it will become all the more dirty. Contrary to this, the person who knows that he has defilements will make up his mind to remove them with endeavor and exertion; and accordingly he will die without any defilement of greed, anger, or ignorance. He is like a dust-covered bronze bowl bought in a market and made clean when washed. Again, the person who does not possess defilements and yet does not know that he does not have them is attracted to the appearances of the things he likes, and he will be troubled by greed and entrapped by anger and ignorance; he will end his life with defilements. He is like a clean bronze bowl bought in a market and thrown into a dirty corner of the house without washing; it will become dirty. On the contrary, the person who does not have defilements and knows that he does not have them is not attracted to the appearances of things he likes. He is not troubled by greed nor entrapped by anger or ignorance; he will end his life without defilements. He is like a clean bronze bowl bought in a market and made all the more clean when washed. O venerable Moggallana, it is because of this that I say that the one is superior and that the other is inferior.

(2) "O friends, defilements mean unwholesome desires. For instance, when someone commits an offense, he wishes, 'May this not be known to others'; when it is known, he wishes, 'May I be reprimanded privately and not in front of the Sangha'; or again he wishes, 'May I be reprimanded by my close friend and not by others.' All these thoughts are defilements; and because of these defilements, when such wishes are not granted, he becomes angry, and his mind is irritated.

"Moreover, when someone attends a discourse by his teacher, he wishes, 'May the teacher give more attention toward me,' or 'May he choose me as his discussant,' or at the time of receiving offerings, he secretly wishes, 'May I receive the offering first.' All these thoughts are defilements. Because of these defilements, when such wishes are not gratified, he becomes angry, and his mind is irritated.

"O friends, no matter who he may be, unless he is free from these unwholesome desires, such defilements are naturally going to be known to other people. Then, even if he wears a humble robe, lives in a forest, and endeavors in the practice of freeing himself from greed for clothing, food, and dwelling, he will not gain others' respect. He is like a beautiful bronze bowl brought back from a market, in which the owner puts snakes, dogs, or human corpses, and places another bronze bowl as a lid on it, and returns it to the market. People will be attracted to the container, but when they open it to see its contents, they will surely be repelled by it.

"Again, if one is free from unwholesome desires, this will be, as a natural course, known to others; and even if he lives within a village, he will receive people's invitations; even if he wears lay clothing, people will pay their respects to him. He is like a bronze bowl brought back from a market and washed clean: the owner fills it with cooked white rice with meat sauce and places another bronze bowl on it as a lid and returns it to the market. Then people will be attracted to it, and when its content is examined, their appetite will be whetted."

(3) At that time, Moggallana addressed Sariputta, "O venerable Sariputta, once I was residing on a hill outside Rajagaha, and early one morning I went into the city for alms begging and saw an apprentice wheelwright working hard in cutting out the parts of a wheel. Now at that time there came a naked ascetic, Pandaputta, who had formerly been an apprentice wheelwright. He stood nearby, watching the work carefully. Pandaputta was thinking, "This apprentice is now carving out a wheel of a vehicle. He will shave away that felloe's crookedness, twists, and knots, so that the felloe will be without defect and everything will fit together perfectly." In the meantime, the apprentice, as expected, shaved away the crookedness, twists, and knots. Having seen this, Pandaputta let forth a cry of delight, 'He has carved out the wheel as if he knew my mind.' O my friend, just so, you have shaved off the vain, frivolous, and confused thoughts from some monks who became mendicants for livelihood as if you exactly knew their minds. Those disciples who came forth to the homeless life through their faith in the Dharma and are in possession of serious and quiet insight are as delighted with

your teaching as a thirsty and hungry man is delighted with water and food. Indeed, it is wonderful that you have roused the fellow disciples to rise up for what is wholesome and to free themselves from what is unwholesome." Thus the two venerable disciples rejoiced together for their well-spoken discourses.

(4) Sariputta said one day, "O friends, while people frequently speak of right view, in what way can the disciples of the Buddha be said to have the right understanding, to have an indestructible faith in the Dharma, and to reach the right Dharma? Friends, if the disciples of the Buddha know unwholesomeness and its roots and wholesomeness and its roots, they are said to have the right understanding, to have an indestructible faith in the Dharma, and to reach the right Dharma.

"But what are unwholesomeness and its roots? What are wholesomeness and its roots? Friends, the following ten acts are called unwholesome acts: killing, stealing, sensual indulgence, false talk, double talk, slander, flattery, greed, anger, and wrong view. The roots of unwholesomeness, the three poisons, are greed, anger, and ignorance. Also, refraining from the ten unwholesome acts is called wholesome conduct, and refraining from greed, refraining from anger, and refraining from ignorance are called the roots of wholesomeness. If one in this way understands unwholesomeness and its roots, and wholesomeness and its roots, and refrains from every desire and harmful thought, removes the defilement of the view of self, annihilates ignorance, and ends suffering in this present life, one is said to have found the right understanding, acquired an indestructible faith in the Dharma, and reached the right Dharma."

(5) Delighting in this discourse, other disciples asked Sariputta, "O friend, is there any other way through which the disciples of the Buddha can find the right understanding, acquire an indestructible faith in the Dharma, and reach the right Dharma?"

Sariputta replied, "Yes, there is, my friends. When the disciples of the Buddha know about the nature of sustenance, its cause, its cessation, and the way to reach its cessation, they are said to have the right understanding, to have an indestructible faith in the Dharma, and to reach the right Dharma. What is the nature of such sustenance and the way to reach its cessation? There are four kinds of such sustenance that support the bodies and minds of all beings and help to nourish those that are not yet born: material food, coarse or fine; sustenance for sense faculties; sustenance for thought and will; and sustenance for consciousness. Since the causal basis of such sustenance is the thirst of desire, when the thirst of desire is brought to its cessation, the cessation of sustenance is also accomplished. The way to accomplish this goal is the Eightfold Noble Path, namely right view, right thought, right speech, right action, right livelihood, right endeavor, right mindfulness, and right concentration. Therefore, when the disciples of the Buddha know about the nature of sustenance, its cause, its cessation, and the way to reach its cessation, and also have departed from every desire and harmful thought, removed the defilement of the view of self, annihilated ignorance, and ended suffering in this present life, they are said to have found the right understanding, acquired an indestructible faith in the

Dharma, and reached the right Dharma. The same can be said about suffering. Those who know the nature of suffering, its cause, its cessation, and the way to reach its cessation, are said to have found the right understanding, acquired an indestructible faith in the Dharma, and reached the right Dharma.

"Birth, old age, sickness, death, anxiety, sorrow, suffering, addiction, and agony are all the sources of suffering. In short, life is suffering, and the primary source of it is the intense craving called thirst, which leads to future delusion. Thus when this craving is extinguished without remainder, the cessation of suffering is by itself accomplished; and the Eightfold Noble Path is the way to do this." All those listening to Sariputta at that time were thoroughly delighted with his discourse.

2. The Parable of the Saw

(1) Around that time, the venerable Moliyaphagguna was too closely associated with certain nuns. If any disciple disparaged those nuns, he became very angry. In a similar manner, if disciples spoke to those nuns disparaging Moliyaphagguna, those nuns became angry.

When the World-Honored One heard of this, he called Moliyaphagguna to confirm the matter and asked him, "O Phagguna, did you become a mendicant because of your faith?" Phagguna replied, "Yes, World-Honored One." Then the World-Honored One told him, "O Phagguna, then it is not good for you to be closely associated with those nuns. Therefore, when someone speaks to you disparaging those nuns, you should have discarded such thoughts as are held by those who are bound to their families; you must discipline yourself and think, 'My mind never changes. I shall never utter rough words. I am determined to live with a mind of sympathy, commiseration, and love. I shall never hold anger even privately.' O Phagguna, moreover, if anyone hits those nuns in front of you with his fist, with dirt, or with a stick, or even with a sword, you must not hold such thoughts as are commonly held by householders who are bound to their families. You should behave the same way when someone disparages you or even hits you."

(2) Then the World-Honored One turned to the disciples and addressed them, "Disciples, on one occasion, I noted that the minds of my disciples were well controlled, and then I told them, 'Disciples, since I take one meal a day, I live a healthy and pleasant life. So I recommend that you also take one meal a day, so that you can live healthy and pleasant lives.' But, O disciples, there is no real need for this rule, and what is actually needed is that you live with right mindfulness. If an excellent coachman commands a team of well-trained horses to draw a carriage on a well-levelled road, he is able to drive it anywhere he wants even without the use of a whip. It is the same with the lives of disciples. Therefore you must discard evil and practice good; with this basic principle, you will make steady progress. Suppose there is a large forest of sala trees near a village or a town. Because the bark of these trees has become polluted, the growth of the trees has been halted. Then comes someone who loves the forest. When he crops off twisted branches and sickly sprouts, cleans up the entire forest by raking, and protects the good branches and healthy buds, the sala forest will soon grow and become

dense. It is the same with the lives of disciples. But, O disciples, you must keep in your minds one thing. Ordinarily quiet minds can be disturbed in times of emergency; you must train yourselves to be able to maintain composure even in times of emergency.

(3) "Once upon a time, disciples, there was a widow by the name of Vedehika in this very Savatthi. Her reputation was good. She was said to be gentle, meek, and quiet. Vedehika had a female woman named Kali who was a clever and diligent worker. One day, Kali thought, 'My mistress has a very good reputation, but might it not be that she is inwardly ill-tempered though she does not show it? Or is it because I have been doing my work with utmost effort that she has not shown it even if inwardly she was angry? Now suppose I test the mistress.' Then Kali stayed in bed late the next day and came out to work in mid-morning. Vedehika then said to Kali, 'Well now Kali, why did you get up so late today?' Kali replied, 'I think that it is no concern of yours.' 'Why not? You got up so late.' The widow became angry, showing her ill-temper on her forehead.

"Then Kali got up the next day even later than the day before to see her mistress' reaction. 'Well, Kali, why did you get up so late?' the mistress asked. Kali replied, 'Whether I get up early or late is no concern of yours.' 'Why not, you fool!' Vedehika was enraged and no longer controlled her ill-temper; she hit Kali on the head with a stick. Kali ran out of the house bloodstained and loudly reported to the neighbors, 'Look at me, look what the kind woman did to me! Look what the gentle and quiet woman did to me! She injured me just because I got up late!' O disciples, soon after this, the rumor spread that Vedehika was a terrible, violent woman.

(4) "Just so, O disciples, people in general are kind, modest, and tranquil as long as disagreeable words are not heard by them. When such words are directly heard, however, it will be tested whether or not he or she is truly gentle, modest, and calm.

"O disciples, I do not consider a monk a truly gentle disciple, who, just because he possesses robes, alms food, a sitting mat, and medicine, is gentle in speech and conduct. Why? It is because this monk is not gentle in speech and conduct unless he possesses robes, alms-food, sitting mat, and medicine. But whoever respects and reveres the Dharma and is gentle in speech and conduct, I call him a truly gentle disciple.

"O disciples, there are five pairs of opposites: opportune words and inopportune words, truthful words and untruthful words, gentle words and harsh words, beneficial words and non-beneficial words, and compassionate words and malicious words. When people speak to you in any of these ways, you must train yourselves as follows: 'I shall never change my mind, never utter evil words, abide in a mind of sympathy, commiseration, and love, never hold anger even privately, live with my mind full of love for others, and live in widening this mind, sheltering this world with the mind of wide, great, and infinite compassion, without hate or bitterness.'

(5) "My disciples, suppose a man tried to empty the ground soil by means of a spade and a bag to carry it. Shouting, 'May the ground soil disappear, may the

ground soil disappear,' he digs the ground and spreads the dirt. Do you think that this man could eventually empty the ground soil?" The disciples replied, "World-Honored One, he could not, because there is no limit to the depth of the earth."

"My disciples, it is the same with your speech. No matter how people speak to you, you must train yourselves to treat them with sympathy and commiseration in order to maintain your composure, and to fill the universe with the mind of love and compassion. My disciples, if someone tries to paint a picture in midair with paint, he cannot make the images of things in formless space. Again, if someone tries to heat up the river Ganges to dry its water by means of a small torch made of dry grass, he cannot succeed. Or again, if someone tries to create the sound of friction by rubbing well tanned cat's hides, he cannot succeed. It should be the same with your speech. No matter how people speak to you, you must, in order to keep your composure, train yourselves to maintain your mind as wide as the great earth, as unattached as the great sky, as deep as the Ganges, as gentle as a well-tanned hide; you must treat people with sympathy and commiseration and fill the universe with the mind of wide and great compassion.

(6) "My disciples, even if you encounter a situation where a thief grabs a man and is sawing off his limbs with a double-edged saw, if your mind becomes darkened you are not truly practicing my teaching. Even in such an extreme situation, you must train yourselves as follows: 'My mind will never be shaken. I shall never utter evil words; I shall treat the man with a mind of sympathy and commiseration and love, and never hold anger even privately. Then, widening this mind, I shall fill the universe with vast, great, and infinite compassion, without hate and bitterness.'

"My disciples, call to your mind frequently the Parable of the Saw. Do you see any error subtle or gross in the logic of my exhortation?"

The disciples replied, "No, World-Honored One, we do not see any error in it."

The World-Honored One said, "Then, my disciples, remind yourselves repeatedly of this exhortation, the Parable of the Saw. It will enhance your welfare and happiness for a long time."

3. Hatthaka, the Wealthy

(1) From there the World-Honored One travelled from Savatthi toward Kosambi and on the way entered a forest near Alavi, where the World-Honored One made his bed by piling leaves on the ground. The next morning, Hatthaka, a resident of Alavi, was strolling in the forest and happened to meet the World-Honored One.

He reverently inquired, "O World-Honored One, did you sleep well last night?" The World-Honored One replied, "Yes, I had a good rest, for I am one of those who sleep well in this world."

Then Hatthaka addressed the World-Honored One, "O World-Honored One, the wintry night is cold. During eight days, the last four days in the second month and the first four days in the third month, the ground becomes hardened as though

trampled down by cattle. A bed made of leaves is thin; the cold weather penetrates the yellow robes; and the withered leaves on the trees tremble in the cold
wind. With all this, why does the World-Honored One say that he slept well last
night and that he is one of those who sleep pleasantly at night?"

The World-Honored One replied, "O man of wealth, what would you think?
Suppose there is a palatial house of a wealthy man here. The walls of the room
are well plastered inside as well as outside, so that when the door is closed there
is no crevice through which the wind might blow into the room. There is a bed
with a thick, tufty covering on the floor, a beautiful mattress made of sheep fur,
a hanging canopy from above, a pillow with both its ends decorated with red
cloth, and lighting gently illuminating the room. Now, four women, his wives
and mistresses, are serving or consoling the master. O man of wealth, would you
think that this man would sleep well and happily?" Hatthaka replied, "Yes,
World-Honored One, he would."

The World-Honored One asked, "O man of wealth, think it over carefully
before you answer. A man feels a heat flush in his body and mind that has arisen
from his greed. Then would he not have difficulty in having a pleasant sleep?"
Hatthaka replied, "O World-Honored One, he would, as the World-Honored One
says." The World-Honored One said, "O man of wealth, it is greed, the cause of
this heat flush from which the man is suffering, that the Buddha has uprooted,
discarded, and thereby made unable to arise again. Because of this, I sleep well
in the night. Moreover, man of wealth, would not this householder feel in his
body and mind the same heat flush from anger and ignorance, and would he not
find it difficult to have good rest at night?" Then Hattaka replied, "Yes, World-
Honored One, it is as you say."

The World-Honored One said, "O man of wealth, it is anger and ignorance,
the causes of this heat flush from which the man is suffering, that the Buddha
has discarded, uprooted, and thereby made unable to arise again. Because of
this, I can pleasantly rest at night. Free from defilements of desire, with no anguish,
I sleep gently and pleasantly. Parting from all wishes, free from inner fears,
I sleep peacefully and pleasantly."

(2) The World-Honored One, accompanied by many disciples, entered the city
of Kosambi. While Ananda also stayed at the Ghosita Garden as he attended the
World-Honored One, he received one day a visit of a householder who was an
Ajivaka follower. The man asked, "O Venerable, whose teaching is supreme?
Who lives most uprightly in this world? Who is the happiest man?" Ananda
replied, "O dear householder, I shall now ask you a question. You may answer as
you think best. Dear householder, what would you think? If someone teaches the
Dharma for the sake of the renunciation of desire, anger, and ignorance, is not
his teaching most wisely taught?" The man replied, "O Venerable, that is so."

Ananda asked, "Dear householder, moreover, if someone lives his life for the
sake of renouncing desire, anger, and ignorance, is not his life the most virtuous?"
The man replied, "O Venerable, it is as you say."

Ananda asked, "Dear householder, then if someone has renounced desire,
anger, and ignorance, and made them no longer arise, like a palm tree whose

sprouts are eliminated, is not such a person the happiest man in this world?" The householder answered, "That also is true. O Venerable, you have expounded the Dharma truly well. You have explained it praising your own doctrine without disparaging others'; you have clarified the meaning of the Dharma without showing off your own virtues. O Venerable, you have taught for the sake of making others renounce desire, anger, and ignorance. Thus the Dharma is most wisely expounded by you. O Venerable, you have lived your life for the sake of renouncing desire, anger, and ignorance. Your life is most virtuously lived. O Venerable, you have renounced desire, anger, and ignorance without remainder. These causes of defilement have been totally uprooted, not to arise again, just like a palm tree whose sprouts have been eliminated. You are the happiest man in the world. O Venerable, your words are most excellent."

4. Homage to the Six Directions

(1) The World-Honored One then left Kosambi, travelled down along the river Ganges, and eventually entered Rajagaha and stayed at the Bamboo Grove Monastery. During that time, Singala, a son of a wealthy family in the city, got up early in the morning and left the city. Wetting his clothing and his hair and holding his palms together, he regularly paid homage toward the six directions, north, south, east, west, upward, and downward.

One morning, on the way to the city for alms begging, the World-Honored One saw his daily ritual and said to him, "O son of good family, for what reason do you get up so early, leave the city, wet your clothing and hair, and worship the six directions, north, south, east, west, upward, and downward?"

Singala replied, "O World-Honored One, when my father died, he instructed me to worship the six directions regularly, and in deference to his word I am keeping this daily ritual." The World-Honored One said to Singala. "O son of good family, in the true teaching, that is not the way to worship the six directions." Singala then asked, "O World-Honored One, may the World-Honored One instruct me on the true way of worshipping the six directions."

(2) "O son of good family, listen attentively. The disciples of the noble teaching are free from the four defiled actions, refrain from action in the four evil paths, are not associated with the six evil mouths that equally drain wealth, and accordingly keep themselves away from all these fourteen evils and take caution and protection against the six directions. Because of this, they win victory in this life as well as in the next, and upon death they will be born in the heavenly realm. The four defiled actions are killing, stealing, adultery, and lying; the four evil paths are greed, anger, ignorance, and fear." The World-Honored One explained to Singala in verse, "The honor of a person who commits offenses against the Dharma because of greed, hatred, fear, and ignorance diminishes every day like the waning moon. The honor of a person who commits no offense against the Dharma and is unaffected by greed, hate, fear, and ignorance increases every day like the waxing moon."

(3) The World-Honored One continued, "Keeping distance from the six evil mouths that inevitably drain wealth means to refrain from drinking intoxicants

and becoming self-indulgent, to refrain from wandering around in streets late at night, to refrain from playing around in the gaiety of song and dance or in festivities, to refrain from indulgence in gambling, to refrain from associating with evil friends, and to refrain from becoming indolent. All of these six are the evil mouths that drain wealth to nothing.

"O son of good family, drinking intoxicants and becoming self-indulgent are accompanied by the six misfortunes: drainage of wealth, quarrels and disputes, sickness, an unfavorable reputation, irritability and proneness to anger, and the decline of wisdom.

"Wandering around in streets late at night is accompanied by six kinds of misfortunes: no protection of one's own safety, no protection of his family, no protection of his properties, being threatened in evil localities, natural increase of deceptive words, and entanglement with a variety of sufferings.

"Playing around in the gaiety of song and dance or festivities is accompanied by the following six misfortunes: a tendency to look for dancing, singing, music, storytelling, a small drum, and a large drum.

"Indulgence in gambling also results in six misfortunes: anger against the winner, the distress of defeat, drainage of wealth, disdain from friends, having no defense in a court of law, having no willing partner for marriage, and having no sufficient support for one's family.

"Associating with evil friends is accompanied by six misfortunes: attracting only gamblers, drunkards, people of extreme greediness, hypocrites, swindlers, and cold-blooded people.

"Idle and indolent life is accompanied by six misfortunes: drainage of wealth by not working because of cold or heat, because it is early or because it is late, or because of an empty stomach or a full one.

(4) "O son of good family, there are four kinds of people who appear to be friends but cannot be true friends: a greedy person, a person of flowery words, a flatterer, and a wasteful person. The greedy person, because of his nature, gives little but demands a lot; he goes along reluctantly insofar as he is dictated by fear; but because his motivation is solely gain, he cannot become a true friend. A person of flowery speech speaks of some olden days to show intimacy, wheedling trifles to feign helpfulness; but at the time of real need, such a person runs away. He cannot become a true friend. The person of flattery does not remonstrate against wrong actions, nor does he promote good actions. Since he admires you to your face but speaks ill of you behind your back, he cannot be a true friend. The wasteful person goes along with other drunkards, wanders around in streets with them at late hours, plays around with them in the gaiety of song and dance or festivities, as well as in gambling. He cannot be a true friend.

"The truly good friend is a person who becomes a real help and support, shares joy and sorrow, does not hesitate to remonstrate, and has real sympathy. The person who is a real help and support prevents his friend from indulgence, helps him to protect his wealth, is a confidant or counsel in times of troubles, and does not hesitate to lend funds when necessary. The person who shares joy and sorrow does not betray his friend's secrets, does not leave him at times of misfortune, and risks his life for his friend. The person who does not hesitate to remonstrate prevents his friend from wrongdoing and promotes his good actions, tells him what he did not know, and shows the way to secure peace in the future. The person of sympathy is saddened at the time of separation and is delighted in meeting again, praises what is praiseworthy and remonstrates when it is appropriate. Therefore, these four kinds of people are regarded as true friends.

(5) "O son of good family, of the six directions, the east represents your father and mother, the south your teacher, the west your wife and children, the north your friends, the downward your servants and maids, and the upward the mendicants.

"A child should serve his parents in the east, keeping in mind the five practices: to provide food for his parents, to take the responsibility for the family livelihood, to keep intact the family lineage, to protect the inherited wealth, and after their deaths to make offerings on their behalf. Father and mother, being so served, will also love their child with the five practices: to have him refrain from wrong deeds, to promote good deeds, to educate him, to arrange an appropriate wife for him, and to transfer their property to him at an appropriate time. In this way, the eastern direction is properly observed and is in peace and without anxiety.

"Next, a disciple must serve his teacher in the south with the following five practices: to rise when his teacher comes in, to welcome and guide him to a seat, to serve him, to offer alms in a gentle manner, and to receive his teaching with reverence. The teacher, being so served, must love his disciple with the five practices: to have him control his body and mind in the same way he did, to let him realize what he himself realized, to make him learn all studies through correct instruction, to let his name be known to his colleagues, and to protect him in all areas. In this way, the southern direction is well observed in peace and without anxiety.

"Next, a husband will love his wife in the west with the following five practices: to respect her, to be polite toward her, to be faithful to her, to entrust family matters to her, and to give clothing and ornaments to her. The wife in the west, being so served, must love her husband with the following five practices: to work in good order, to learn how to deal with maids and servants, to be faithful, to protect property, and to be skillful and diligent in all kinds of work. In this way, the western direction is well observed in peace and without anxiety.

(6) "Next, a friend must serve his friends in the north with the following five practices: to maintain the four kinds of benevolent conduct, i.e., charity, loving words, beneficial deeds, and universal sharing, and to refrain from speaking poisonous words. The friends in the north, being so served, will serve him with the following five practices: to prevent him from any form of indulgence, to protect his property when he falls into indigence, to be his confidant or counsel when he is in trouble, not to leave him when he meets misfortune, and to return the favor of his friendship by helping his family to survive destitution. In this way, the northern direction is well observed in peace and without anxiety.

"Next, a householder must take care of his servants in the downward direction with the following five practices: to assign them work appropriate to their respective capacities, to provide them with food and pay, to attend to them in their sicknesses, to give them shares of rare things, and to let them take rest occasionally. Servants, being so treated, will serve their master with the following five practices: to get up earlier than their master, to go to bed later, to work honestly, to work with skill, and to let their master's good reputation be known. In this way, the downward direction is well observed in peace and without anxiety.

"Lastly, a person must serve mendicants in the upward direction with the following five practices: to keep his deeds, speech, and thought cordial toward them, not to close the door to them, and to offer food to them. The mendicants, being so served, will love him with the following six practices: to have him refrain from wrong actions, to encourage him to do good deeds, to love him with compassion, to teach him what he did not know before, to make him have clear understanding of what he heard, and to teach him the way of peace in the time to come. O son of good family, in this way the upward direction is well observed in peace and without anxiety.

"O Singala, as I have explained to you, the east represents your parents, the south your teacher, the west your wife and children, the north your friends, the downward your servants, and the upward the mendicants. Worship the six directions with the meanings shown to you; keep your conduct righteous, strengthen your wisdom, be humble and free from an obstinate mind, be diligent in your work, be undaunted by misfortune, and keep your deeds stainless. Associate with good friends and maintain the four kinds of benevolent conduct, charity, loving words, beneficial acts, and universal sharing. These deeds are indeed the norms of true filiality."

Singala was greatly delighted with these teachings just as if his eyes had opened for the first time. Thereafter, he became a devoted follower of the Three Treasures.

5. Punna and Sariputta

(1) That year, the World-Honored One spent the rainy season at the Squirrels' Feeding Place in the Bamboo Grove near Rajagaha. When the season was over, many disciples from various places where they had stayed during the rainy season came to the monastery to see the World-Honored One. Now, after saluting the World-Honored One, these disciples sat to one side. The World-Honored One said to them, "O disciples, is there anyone among you who while staying at the place of your retreat practiced little desiring, contentment, and diligence in a secluded abode, maintained moral precepts and practiced meditation, opened his insight and realized enlightenment, and enabled other disciples to accomplish the same, by being a remonstrant, an advisor, a guide, an inspirer, an encourager, and one who gave delight to his colleagues?"

Some disciples replied, speaking of Punna who was not present at the time, "O World-Honored One, Punna was such a person who, as the World-Honored One has said, practiced by himself little desiring, contentment, and diligence in a secluded abode, maintained moral precepts and practiced meditation, opened his insight and realized enlightenment, and also enabled other disciples to accomplish the same, by being a remonstrant, an advisor, a guide, an inspirer, an encourager, and one who gave delight to his colleagues."

At that moment, Sariputta, sitting somewhat closer to the World-Honored One and listening to this, thought to himself, "The Venerable Punna is fortunate, because his fellow disciples extol his virtues in front of the World-Honored One, and the venerable master was delighted. I wish to talk with Punna about something in the near future." Soon after, the World-Honored One together with Sariputta and others left Rajagaha for Savatthi, and after completing the travelling they entered the Anathapindika Monastery. Having heard of the arrival of the World-Honored One, Punna set out from his abode to visit the World-Honored One there; he heard a discourse that the Buddha gave there and was gladdened by it; and saluting him and keeping his right side toward him, he left for Blind Men's Grove to pass the day.

Seeing Punna leaving, Sariputta stood up and followed him, keeping him in sight. When Punna entered the forest and sat under a tree's shade, Sariputta also sat under another tree of the forest.

(2) Toward the evening, Sariputta stood up from the seat of meditation and approached Punna, asking, "Friend, are you practicing the way under the World-Honored One?" "Yes, Venerable, that is correct," replied Punna. Sariputta asked, "Are you engaged in practice in order to purify your moral precepts?" "No, Venerable," replied Punna. Sariputta asked, "Are you then engaged in practice in order to purify your mind?" "No, Venerable," replied Punna. Sariputta asked, "Are you then engaged in practice in order to make right your understanding?" "No, Venerable," replied Punna. Sariputta asked, "Are you then engaged in practice in order to be freed from doubt?" "No, Venerable," replied Punna. Sariputta asked, "Are you then engaged in practice in order to know the right way and what is not the way?" "No, Venerable," replied Punna. Sariputta asked, "Then are you engaged in practice in order to know the path of enlightenment?" "No, Venerable," replied Punna. Sariputta asked, "Are you then engaged in practice in order to realize insight?" "No, Venerable," replied Punna. Sariputta asked, "For what, then, are you engaged in practice?" "I am engaged in practice under the World-Honored One in order to realize perfect nirvana," replied Punna. Sariputta asked, "Is not purity of moral precepts perfect nirvana?" "No, Venerable," replied Punna. Sariputta asked, "Is not purity of mind perfect nirvana?" "No, Venerable," replied Punna. Sariputta asked, "Friend, is not purity of understanding nirvana?" "No, Venerable," replied Punna. Sariputta asked, "Friend, is not freedom from doubt perfect nirvana?" "No, Venerable," replied Punna. Sariputta asked, "Is not purity of knowledge about the right path and what is not the path perfect nirvana?" "No, Venerable," replied Punna. Sariputta asked, "Is not purity of knowledge about the path of enlightenment perfect nirvana?" "No, Venerable," replied Punna. Sariputta asked, "Is not purity of insight perfect nirvana?" "No, Venerable," replied Punna. Sariputta asked, "Is there any dharma other than these that is perfect nirvana?" "No, there is not, Venerable," replied Punna.

Sariputta then asked, "Friend, when you were asked if these dharmas I mentioned to you were perfect nirvana, you replied that they were not; and also when you were asked if these same dharmas were not perfect nirvana, you replied again negatively, meaning that they were. How should I understand the meaning of your contradictory answers?"

(3) Punna replied, "Friend, not only purity of moral conduct, mind, and understanding, but also purity of the insight of enlightenment, are all not the perfect state; they are yet to be perfected. They are not the state in which every bit of attachment is totally exhausted. And yet, if there is something called perfect nirvana other than these dharmas, ordinary people, too, will enter nirvana, because they do not possess these dharmas. Therefore I shall use an allegory to explain my point of view. Suppose that Pasenadi, the king of Kosala, has to make a hurried journey to Saketa upon some unexpected happening. He orders seven chariots to be readied at the seven places between Savatthi and Saketa and sets out from his castle by the first chariot. Upon reaching the second one, he abandons the first chariot and then travels by the second to reach the third one. Then, travelling by the third chariot, he reaches the fourth one; and in this way, he travels farther by riding different chariots successively. Finally, switching from the sixth to the seventh chariot, and riding this last one, he arrives at the castle in Saketa. Then, if someone asked the king, 'Have you reached Saketa by this chariot from Savatthi?' the king's right answer would be, 'No, I ordered seven chariots readied between Savatthi and Saketa, and I travelled by riding these chariots in succession to this city.'

"It is the same with practice under the World-Honored One. Purification of moral conduct is for the sake of purity of mind; purification of the mind is for the sake of right understanding; right understanding is for the sake of freedom from doubt; freedom from doubt is for the sake of purity of insight to distinguish what is the right path and what is not the right path; the latter is then for the sake of knowing the path of enlightenment; purification of knowledge of the path of enlightenment is for the sake of purity of the insight of enlightenment. Purification of the insight of enlightenment is for the sake of perfect nirvana in which all attachment is totally exhausted. It is for the sake of this perfect nirvana that I am engaged in practice under the World-Honored One."

(4) Sariputta said, "What is your name, Venerable?" "My name is Punna, and my fellow disciples call me son of Maitrayani," replied Punna. Sariputta said, "Friend, it is excellent that you, Venerable, are learned, understand the venerable master's teaching, and explain well the meaning of the profound Dharma. Those fellow disciples who see you and attend to you at your side are fortunate, and I am the same to have met you and sat together with you."

Punna also asked Sariputta his name. "My name is Upatissa, and my fellow disciples call me Sariputta," replied Sariputta. "Oh, you are the venerable disciple who is often compared even with the World-Honored One. While talking with you, I did not know who you were. If I had known who you were I would not have said so much. Friend, it is indeed excellent that as learned as you are, rightly understanding the Buddha's teaching, you asked me about the meaning of the profound Dharma variously and adequately. Those fellow disciples who can see you and attend to you at your side are indeed fortunate; and I am the same to have been able to meet you." Thus these two disciples discussed their understanding of the Dharma with each other and were equally delighted.

6. The World-Honored One and Various Gods

(1) In those days, the heavenly beings illuminated the Jeta Grove every evening, paid homage to the World-Honored One, and asked various questions. The following are the answers given by the World-Honored One in verses:

> (i) Craving is the cause of samsara. So deep is the sea of samsara, the cycle of life and death, that it is difficult to escape the state of suffering. Life based on greed is contrary to that of the path. While youth rapidly passes away day and night, people associate with women not knowing that women are temptations. Not only things in this life and those of the next, but also the lights shining in the sky, are equally the lures that Maras set forth to entrap people who have desires. Craving binds this world, wherein man is addicted, possessed by its force. Indeed, purity is the state of nirvana, emancipated from craving. The mind creates this world, addicts people, and subjugates all things.

> (ii) Faith is one's companion, insight his guide; may one escape from suffering, making nirvana his light. Faith is the supreme wealth, truth is the supreme taste, to accumulate merit is the supreme deed; may all realize peace and tranquillity. Faith is the provision for wayfaring, merit the abode of wealth, insight the light of this world, right mindfulness the safeguard of dark night. As life without defilement does not perish, he who overcomes desires alone becomes a man of freedom.

(2) Kamada, son of the gods, had once been a disciple of the Buddha in one of his previous lives and practiced the path. But because he had not realized enlightenment, he was born as a heavenly being. Kamada paid homage to the World-Honored One and lamented how difficult it was to realize enlightenment. The World-Honored One said in verse, "O Kamada, the Buddha has achieved what is difficult to achieve. Filled with peace and tranquillity is the heart of him who holds fast to moral precepts, calms the mind to quiescence, and has become a mendicant; but say not that the supreme delight is hard to realize. For the wise have realized what is hard to realize. Whoever enjoys the mind of tranquillity always disciplines his mind day and night. Say not that a tranquil mind is difficult to realize, for the wise have calmed what is difficult to calm. Whoever enjoys peace of body and mind has broken the mesh of Mara's net and strolls in the region of the wise. Say not that the path is difficult to go through, for the wise have gone through what is difficult to go through. When the mind is murky, the road is not level, and there is stumbling; whereas when the mind is pure, the road becomes level and even."

(3) The god Subrahma was one day playing with heavenly maidens in the Garden of Joy in the Tavatimsa heaven. While he was forgetting the time, climbing up on trees to shake flowers to scatter and enjoying songs and dances, he saw one of the maidens suddenly fall into hell because her good karma had been

exhausted. He was terrified and shaken and then came to the World-Honored One for instruction. He said, "In sorrow is this mind always. So is it in fear always. Not only with whatever has happened but also with whatever has not yet happened, this mind is in constant fear. May you teach me if there is a path that overcomes this fear."

The World-Honored One instructed him with the following verse: "Practice the path of enlightenment, refrain from desires, and renounce everything; there is no other way to realize peace and tranquillity."

(4) One day, the World-Honored One set out from Savatthi to Saketa and stayed in the forest of Anjana. That night, the god Kakudha illumined the forest with his glorious rays and descended to pay a visit to the World-Honored One. The god asked, "World-Honored One, are you in the state of delight?" The World-Honored One replied, "O Kakudha, do you think that I have anything with which I should be delighted?" The god asked, "If not, are you in the state of sorrow?" The World-Honored One replied, "O Kakudha, do you think that I have lost anything because of which I should be in sorrow?" Kakudha asked, "Then, World-Honored One, are you neither in delight nor in sorrow?" "That is so," replied the World-Honored One.

"O World-Honored One, you are neither in delight nor in sorrow. Is it not lonesome to be alone in the forest? Do you not feel something yet to be fulfilled?" The World-Honored One said, "Whenever there is sorrow, there is joy; whenever there is joy, there is sorrow. When both good and bad equally disappear, there is no more thought to be held on to." "Sublime is the World-Honored One. Freed equally from delight and sorrow, surpassing the world of attachment, let the man of enlightenment be with us for a long time."

(5) The World-Honored One returned to Savatthi and entered the Anathapindika Monastery. One day, the god Rohitassa asked the World-Honored One, "O World-Honored One, is there any place where there is neither birth, nor old age, nor death? Is it possible to reach on foot the place called the end of this world?"

The World-Honored One answered, "O Rohitassa, it is not possible to reach the end of this world on foot." Rohitassa said, "O World-Honored One, I was formerly Rohitassa, son of Bhoja, and I had the power to fly through the sky faster than an arrow. I could pass with one stride the distance from the edge of the eastern sea to the end of the western sea. At a certain time, I wanted to see the end of this world. I flew through the sky, abstaining from food and drink, with no sleep and no rest, but I could not accomplish my wish. I only ended my life. What the World-Honored One said is indeed excellent."

The World-Honored One said, "Rohitassa, you cannot annihilate suffering without reaching the end of this world, but you cannot reach it on foot. For not only this world, its origin as well as its end, but also the path to reach the end of this world, are equally found within one's body, and whoever knows this world is able to reach its limit. Keeping one's conduct pure and quieting any evil, thus knowing the limit of this world, one no longer has anything to seek in this world or in the next."

7. Sudhana

(1) At one time the Buddha was present at the Lecture Hall of the Jeta Grove Monastery together with an assembly of five hundred bodhisattvas. The assembly, presided over by the bodhisattvas Samantabhadra and Manjusri, all secretly wished for the World-Honored One to expound on the Buddha's discipline and the realm of wisdom.

The Buddha perceived the wishes of the assembly and compelled by his great compassion entered into the meditation called Simhavijrmbhita. Thereupon the Jeta Grove and the Lecture Hall were immediately transformed into a world without limit, filled with innumerable treasures that were brilliantly reflected in the clouds. The sky resonated with exquisite music praising the Buddha. The bodhisattvas of the ten directions together with countless of their kinsmen gathered like clouds. The assembly spontaneously raised their voices in praise of the Buddha:

(i) Enlightenment is without limit and yet not without limit. The noble Buddha is free from both of these. Like the sun that shatters the darkness and like the clear full moon, the noble Buddha is pure and undefiled. Like the tranquil ocean, the noble Buddha has completely quenched the thirst of desires. Like Mount Sumeru rising majestically from the ocean, the noble Buddha reigns serenely in the fathomless Dharma sea. Just as the flawless gem purifies defiled water, when we pay homage to the noble Buddha our bodies and minds are sanctified.

(ii) Just as the azure gemstone colors all things blue, all who venerate the Buddha will attain the Buddha's wisdom. The noble Buddha readily reveals himself in each dust mote to purify countless beings. A bodhisattva is divorced from ignorance. His thoughts are pure and he fully apprehends all dharmas. The bodhisattva's profound wisdom exhausts the ocean of the noble Buddha. The bodhisattva, replete with faith and wisdom, labors tirelessly and ceaselessly. And though the bodhisattva dwells in the world of illusion, his mind remains undefiled. Yes, the bodhisattva's discipline is difficult to fathom. There is no one in this world who comprehends it. The bodhisattva's discipline illuminates the world and saves all mankind.

(iii) Even though a man may live forever, only rarely can he hear the voice of the Buddha and only rarely does he meet him. How much more difficult is it to extinguish doubt! The noble Buddha is the lamp of the world who has penetrated all the dharmas. He is the fertile ground of peerless virtues through which man is purified. He is the torch of perfect virtue that appears in order to illuminate the world. He nurtures a being of immeasurable virtues. O Buddha, your appearance in the world is a blessing. The turning of the Dharma Wheel is due to your great compassion. You appear continuously in human form. The Buddha is profoundly involved with the world of the suffering, from where he expounds the Dharma."

(2) At that moment the Bodhisattva Manjusri quietly rose from his seat and proceeded southeast with his kinsmen in tow, to the great mansion in the Vicitra-saladhvaja-vyuha Forest, to the east of the city of Gaya. It was here that the buddhas of the past experienced their strict discipline. The populace, learning of the Bodhisattva's presence, rushed pell-mell to gather around him.

Intending to teach the Dharma, the Bodhisattva first surveyed the minds of his audience. He took notice of the pilgrim Sudhana. Having sown a store of good works in the past, Sudhana aspired to attain perfect enlightenment. The pilgrim was called Sudhana (Very Rich), because on the day of his birth jewels rained from the heavens to fill the treasure houses. The Bodhisattva said, "For your sake I shall teach the Buddha's doctrine." After teaching the Dharma, Manjusri once again proceeded southward.

Sudhana accompanied the Bodhisattva, aspiring for wisdom by learning the virtues of the Buddha. He recited the following verses:

(i) Illusion is a fortress, pride an obstruction; the sixfold world is a barrier, lust a moat. When we are overwhelmed by ignorance, defilement grows.

Considering the devil the master, the ignorant dwell within the fortress. When we are bound by greed, flattery deters action.

When doubt clouds the wisdom eye, ignorance compels us to transmigrate through the sixfold world.

Kindly witness that the sun of perfect compassion and pure wisdom exhaust the sea of defilement.

O great teacher who engenders the aspiration for wisdom, who increases merit, and who nurtures all things, please save me.

O great light with untainted power in this changing world, please show me the right path.

(ii) Like the sun that illuminates the world, all buddhas, following the dictates of the Dharma, go to enlightenment and return to the world. Please show me the path.

Please establish the pure Dharma world, and look at me with great compassion; grant me the unsurpassed vehicle graced with the flowers of virtue.

Reveal to me the path of the Dharma King who abides peacefully in pious practice and is attended in the morning by tranquil maidens playing the exquisite music of the Dharma.

The Bodhisattva Manjusri turned to Sudhana and said, "Son of good family, your mind is aspiring for supreme wisdom. Henceforth seek out good teachers and sincerely trust and honor them. It is best that you ask them how to master the path of enlightenment and how to fulfill the practice of enlightenment. Son of good family, there resides toward the south on Mount Sugriva in the country of Ramavaranta the monk Meghasri. It would be of value to hear what the monk has to say about the Buddha path."

(3) Taking heed of this, Sudhana ascended Mount Sugriva in the country of Ramavaranta. After seven days of searching, Sudhana finally found Meghasri quietly strolling at the very top of Mount Sugriva. Sudhana inquired about the path of supreme wisdom. The venerable master answered, "Sudhana, you have already quickened the aspiration to realize supreme wisdom. It is truly difficult

to aspire to seek the practice of enlightenment. Through the power of enlightenment my eye of faith has been purified, the brilliance of my wisdom illuminates throughout, and I perceive all worlds without the slightest obstruction. I am aware that the countless buddhas are freely revealing the Dharma by adapting their teachings to whomever they reach. Sudhana, this is the extent of my wisdom. I do not fully understand the perfect wisdom and the practice of the bodhisattva. It is best that you inquire further of the monk Sagaramegha who lives to the south in the country of Sagaramukha."

(4) Sudhana rejoiced in Meghasri's teaching and, as instructed, proceeded south to meet Sagaramegha. He said to him, "Holy one, though I seek to penetrate the ocean of perfect wisdom, I am unable. How can a bodhisattva free himself from samsara and be born in the house of the Buddha? How can he make a great vow to save all people?"

The holy Sagaramegha answered, "O Sudhana, unless one plants genuinely wholesome roots, one cannot quicken the passion for perfect enlightenment. Only one who lives near the good teacher, commits his body and his life, and aspires to the world of the Buddha can arouse the mind to enter the path. I have been living here in Sagaramukha for twelve years. The great ocean has been my lead for contemplation. The ocean is truly limitless; its depth is unfathomable. It possesses innumerable gems and is a reservoir of an unlimited amount of water. The great ocean manifests exquisite colors in a variety of ways; it is the home for many creatures. The ocean also reflects the large clouds. The great ocean never increases or decreases. One day while I was wondering whether there were anything greater, deeper, or more richly endowed than this great ocean, from its depths a great lotus ornamented with a multitude of jewels appeared spontaneously. Millions of gods and ocean deities paid homage to it. And on this lotus, surrounded by a great assembly, was a single Buddha whose power was beyond comprehension. This Buddha quietly extended his right hand and touched my head. Thereupon he began teaching the teaching of Samantabhadra. He revealed to me the world of the Buddha and made clear the practice of the bodhisattva. Though I received his instruction for twelve hundred years, this is the limit of my understanding. How can I claim to have mastered the bodhisattva practice? You must travel sixty yojanas south and ask the monk Supratisthita who lives in the country of Sagaratira."

(5) Sudhana, mindful of this instruction, journeyed to Sagaratira in search of this great teacher. He found Supratisthita strolling through the air, surrounded by a multitude who were scattering flowers and performing on musical instruments. Sudhana brought his palms together and honored the great teacher and asked, "O great sage, how must I implement the bodhisattva discipline?"

The venerable Supratisthita answered, "Sudhana, I know the non-obstruction of all things. I possess the light of illustrious wisdom with which I can perceive the minds of people without the slightest obstruction. In addition, through my superhuman powers I have complete recall of the teachings of all buddhas. Anyone who sees me will attain enlightenment. However, I comprehend only non-obstruction. Toward the south, in the town of Mantrausadhi in the country of Isanajarapad resides the good doctor Megha. Take your question to him."

(6) In accordance with this advice, Sudhana entered the southern city of Isanajarapad. Sudhana made obeisance at the feet of Megha who was teaching the Dharma to an assembly of ten thousand. He implored, "O great sage, I have already resolved to attain perfect enlightenment. How must I implement the bodhisattva discipline, and how can I live in the world of samsara without defiling my wisdom? Please instruct me."

Megha descended from his lion seat and prostrated himself on the ground before Sudhana. "Son of good family, you have admirably resolved to attain the highest wisdom. The realization of this wisdom sustains all buddhas, purifies all buddha lands, and is a beacon for all people. By virtue of this wisdom you will be protected by all buddhas and gods; and by the light of their pure wisdom you illuminate the bodhisattva path. O Sudhana, a bodhisattva is the father and mother of people and extinguishes their suffering. A bodhisattva nurtures good like the great earth; a bodhisattva possesses treasures like the great ocean; a bodhisattva is the radiance of the sun that destroys the darkness of ignorance in the world. A bodhisattva is the moon that refreshes people. A bodhisattva is the fire that burns attachments; a bodhisattva is the bridge by which people cross the ocean of transmigration. Though I am fluent in the language of every being in every world, all that I am certain of is this: the words of a bodhisattva are without falsehood. I am unable to expound on the practice of a bodhisattva. To the south in the country of Vanavasin lives the banker Vimuktika. It is best that you visit him and ask him."

(7) With this instruction, Sudhana realized profound faith and understood the right view based on the Dharma. He made obeisance at the feet of Megha and headed south. Sudhana's mind, now purified, was not attached to the notions of 'I' and 'mine', and he practiced sincerely and tirelessly. When he received the protection of the Buddha, his mind became equal to the Buddha's. With his profound aspiration, he received all realms within him.

Sudhana continued to travel to the south and after twelve years finally arrived in the country of Vanavasin. He paid homage to Vimuktika and thought, "It is difficult to meet good teachers. It is doubly difficult to approach them and follow their teachings." He said, "O great sage, I have resolved to attain the highest wisdom. I wish to fulfill the buddha vow and to acquire the buddha wisdom. I beg you to open the gate of the true Dharma, extract the thorn of doubt, and instruct me on how I may fulfill this practice."

The elder answered, "O son of good family, all things in themselves are endowed with the power of non-obstruction. When we apprehend the buddhas of the ten directions, we know that these buddhas do not come here nor do we go to them. And although neither do the buddhas arrive nor do we depart, through the power of non-obstruction we embrace the Buddha-Dharma, satisfactorily implement the bodhisattva discipline, and generate the great vow within us to instruct people. Through the light of wisdom you will be able to perceive your own mind and awaken a huge liberated mind equal to the Buddha's. However, this is all that

I know, because this is all that I have been pursuing. If you are intent on a full understanding of the non-obstructive wisdom of a bodhisattva and his discipline, then you should take your questions to the monk Saradhvaja who lives in the country of Jambudvipasirsa further south."

(8) Overjoyed, Sudhana praised the virtues of the elder. He gazed up at his face and wept with devotion. In gratitude, he made obeisance at the feet of the elder and turned southward.

The holy Saradhvaja was sitting in a quiet place. He entered into meditation and his inhalation and exhalation ceased. He barely moved. And although he was quite still, Saradhvaja's body exhibited energy. Light flowed from his body to destroy Maras and extract evil from people. This light expounded the Dharma, taught compassion, and revealed the true way to see reality as it really is.

Sudhana genuinely pondered this inscrutable meditation for a long while, but when the holy one eventually emerged from his meditation he placed his palms together and said, "O great sage, this is truly wonderful. This meditation is profound and expansive. It has the power of freedom. The light of wisdom illuminates all worlds, forever destroys the suffering in this world, and makes people happy. What is this meditation called?" Saradhvaja said, "O son of good family, this meditation is called the Meditation on the Realm of Wisdom That Is Filled with Pure Light. I proceeded to cultivate wisdom and mastered this meditation together with countless other meditative practices. However, I have only mastered meditation. All bodhisattvas have entered into the profound ocean of wisdom and have apprehended the pure Dharma realm. No capacity have I to fathom anything more. Toward the south in the country of Samudravetadin in the Samantavyuha Gardens is Asa, a devoted woman. Approach her and inquire into the bodhisattva path."

(9) By this instruction, Sudhana's already firm resolve became even firmer, and his brilliant wisdom became even more luminous. Filled with gladness, he proceeded south. Sudhana, always mindful of Saradhvaja, yearned for the sound of his voice, visualized his face, and recalled his kindness and meditation. He thought, "Because the good teacher reveals all the Buddha's teaching, I am able to see the Buddha through him. The good teacher is a truly shining lamp." When he finally arrived at the Samantavyuha Gardens, he found it surrounded by a seven-tiered wall; its trees rained fragrant flowers. The tranquil lakes filled with the waters of merits reflected countless golden towered mansions; herons, peacocks, and other birds sang from the palm trees. The devotee Asa was covered with countless jewels and was on her golden seat. She responded to Sudhana's question. "O Sudhana, I know only this. Those who see me have not shaken their resolve of seeking wisdom. The buddhas of the ten directions are always coming before me to teach the Dharma."

"When will you achieve enlightenment?" Sudhana asked her.

"O Sudhana, a bodhisattva knows the minds of all people and the rise and fall of all worlds. The bodhisattva has generated the desire to attain perfect enlightenment in order to destroy the defilements in people and fulfill their practices. Therefore, when I purify all worlds by cutting off the defilements of all people, my aspiration will be fulfilled. My knowledge is of quiescence, free of sorrow. Those who see me will attain peace. This is the limit of my wisdom. To the south in the country of Nalayus is the sage Bhismottaranirghosa. Take your question to him."

(10) Sudhana thanked Asa and departed. Mindful of the Buddha and apprehending the true nature of things, he travelled from place to place until he entered the country of Nalayus. There in a large forest Sudhana caught sight of Bhismottaranirghosa, dressed in tree bark, on a seat of straw. He was surrounded by a large retinue of hermits. Sudhana humbly inquired about the bodhisattva discipline. The sage answered, "I possess indestructible wisdom." He stretched his right hand and touched Sudhana's head and held his hands.

Sudhana observed his own body. He saw that he himself went to the abodes of countless buddhas of the ten directions. He also saw their auspicious marks, their retinues, and their radiances. Further, through the wisdom of non-obstruction he exhausted the Buddha's power and was able to pass a day and a night at the abode of one Buddha, seven days and seven nights at another, one month at another, one year at another, one hundred years at another, and eternity at another. And because he was bathed in this indestructible wisdom, Sudhana acquired knowledge of various meditations and wisdom.

When the sage withdrew his hand, Sudhana returned to his original state. The sage said, "Now, do you remember?"

"Through the power of the sage I am able to remember."

Then the sage answered, "O Sudhana, this is the extent of my wisdom. It is not within my power to know the discipline of a great bodhisattva. A bodhisattva can generate unlimited wisdom, he can realize the lamp of the Buddha's wisdom, he can know the three worlds in one thought, and he can manifest the wisdom body in all worlds. I am not capable of doing these things. O Sudhana, to the south is the country of Isana. There resides a brahmin by the name of Jayosmayatana. It is best that you consult with him."

8. A Brahmin in Ascetic Practice

(1) With immeasurable joy Sudhana respectfully paid homage to the sage and headed south. When he finally arrived at the country of Isana, the brahmin Jayosmayatana was undergoing the painful discipline of throwing himself from the treacherous Sword Mountain into a raging inferno. Jayosmayatana turned to Sudhana, who greeted him with great reverence. He responded to Sudhana's inquiry, saying, "O Sudhana, if you climb the Sword Mountain and throw yourself into this inferno, you will perfect the bodhisattva practice."

The youth pondered, "I was born a man; it is difficult to meet good teachers and to hear the true teaching. Is he a demon or is he a demon's messenger in the guise of a good teacher? He is asking me to give up my life. There is no mistake; his is not the Buddha's way."

But then from the heavens the gods encouraged Sudhana: "O Sudhana, your thinking is incorrect. This man is indeed a great sage. He possesses the torch of wisdom and works to drain the ocean of greed. When his body is consumed by the flames, it gives off a great light that illuminates the heavens and urges the gods to assemble at this place to teach the Dharma. This great light illuminates the Avici hell and causes those suffering to be born in the heavens."

Elated over this revelation, Sudhana realized that the brahmin was a genuine teacher. Regretting his error, Sudhana climbed the Sword Mountain and threw himself into the inferno below. Before he touched the flames, he entered into tranquil meditation. When he reached the flames, he achieved an even more quiescent and blissful meditation.

"O great sage," he said, "this is truly miraculous. When I came into contact with the Sword Mountain and the great fire, I, too, acquired genuine bliss."

"O Sudhana, I am familiar only with this one aspect of a bodhisattva's inexhaustible virtues. How can I talk about the great practice of a bodhisattva, which fulfills all aspirations and consumes the defilements of people? You must approach the good teacher Maitrayani, the virgin, who resides in the city of Simhavijrmbhita, and inquire into the bodhisattva path."

(2) Sudhana repeatedly thanked the brahmin before heading south. During his journey Sudhana quickened thoughts of reverence, realized an intimacy with the Buddha, and destroyed all illusions.

When he arrived and inquired about Maitrayani's residence, he was directed to the Simhaketu Castle. Sudhana entered the castle and met Maitrayani in a jewelled room. The room was embellished with thousands of golden bells suspended from the ceiling. Her skin sparkled of gold, and her eyes and hair were richer than indigo blue. She was teaching the Dharma to a multitude from the top of the Lion Seat. Sudhana approached her and respectfully inquired about the bodhisattva path. She said, "O Sudhana, observe the ornaments in this Dharma hall."

Sudhana, wide eyed, observed each lapis lazuli pillar, diamond wall, and jewelled mirror. Like the still water that mirrors the moon's image, the gold bells, jewelled trees, and streamers reflected the entire continuum of the possessors of enlightenment, from those who possessed the initial awakening of the Buddha mind to those who possessed final emancipation.

"Great sage, what is the Dharma that you possess?" he asked.

"Son of good family, it is the Dharma grounded in wisdom. This Dharma leads one to the shore of enlightenment. At one time I cultivated this Dharma under the direction of countless buddhas. Son of good family, when I penetrated this Dharma and quickened right thoughts and right thinking and the mind of equanimity, I committed to memory a hundred million verses relating to the Buddha, the Dharma, karma, good works, and the beginning of the universe. O son of good family, I know of this one Dharma. The mind of all the great bodhisattvas is like the sky. A bodhisattva has penetrated the profound Dharma and is filled with virtues. He embraces people with his skillful means. I lack full understanding of his virtues. To the south in the country of Trinayana is the monk Sudarsana. You should visit him and inquire about the path."

(3) Sudhana thanked Maitrayani and turned to the south. He reflected deeply on the instruction he received. Travelling steadily, he arrived at his destination. The holy one Sudarsana was quietly strolling in the forest. He had blue-black

hair, bronze skin, large eyes, and ruby lips. His wisdom was as vast as the ocean. Sudhana greeted him and respectfully inquired about the bodhisattva path. The holy one answered, "O Sudhana, I have cultivated the bodhisattva path under countless buddhas. I have made all kinds of vows, and I fulfilled every one of the bodhisattva disciplines. For this reason, while I am walking quietly like this, all worlds and buddhas appear before me in a single thought. All manner of skillful means to save people also appear before me. But, O Sudhana, I know only the wisdom of seeing things as they are. I do not possess the virtue of a bodhisattva, who is like a diamond lamp, the virtue of being born in the house of the Buddha, or the virtue of manifesting the eternal life that is unaffected by fire, poison, or swords. Nor do I have the virtues of overcoming demons and non-Buddhists, or of raining the sweet nectar of the Dharma everywhere. To the south in the country of Sramana-mandala is a child, Indriyesvara. You should ask him about the bodhisattva path."

(4) When Sudhana arrived at Sramana-mandala, he found Indriyesvara playing in the sand along the river bank with many children. Indriyesvara answered Sudhana's question,

"O Sudhana, the Bodhisattva Manjusri taught me the techniques of mole divination, mathematics, and mudra. I am a master of the occult. I am able to exorcise all anguish, poison, and demons in people. In addition, I have grasped the essence of mathematics; therefore I am able to calculate the number of grains of sand in the sand knolls created over countless miles. I also know the doings of all buddhas and bodhisattvas throughout all time. O Sudhana, I have mastered only these techniques. I know nothing of the virtue of the bodhisattva who grasps the profound principle of mathematics to count the dharmas. To the south in the city of Samudrapratisthana is the devotee Prabhuta. Ask her the secret of the bodhisattva path."

(5) Sudhana set out in high spirits. Like the great ocean that is constantly fed by countless rivers, Sudhana was ever mindful of his good teachers. He praised them, saying, "The sunshine of the good teacher with his illuminating wisdom makes the people's minds unfold like lotus petals. It nurtures a great tree whose trunk is wholesome roots and whose leaves and branches are virtues. The moonlight of the good teacher with his cooling teaching quenches the flames of defilements. His mind is like a treasure-filled ocean; his teaching is wondrous like the incredible feats of the Naga king in the sky."

Arriving in the city of Samudrapratisthana, Sudhana made his way to the inner chambers of the Prabhuta's castle. The chamber, with four open passageways, was decorated with jewelled railings. The beautiful and elegant Prabhuta was seated on her Lion Seat. She was exquisitely clothed; light flowed from her hair. She was attended by many goddess-like maidservants. Those who laid their eyes upon her were freed from desires; those who heard her voice were filled with joy. She addressed Sudhana, "O son of good family, I possess an inexhaustible store of virtue. With a single bowl of food I nourish and satisfy not only a hundred or a thousand but rather a countless number of people. My treasure house can also satisfy their needs for carriages, garments, and ornaments. Finally, all the bodhisattvas of the ten directions have received my gifts and have gained the highest wisdom. O son of good family, my ten thousand maidservants and the countless members of my retinue participate in the same discipline and hold the same vow. We save all beings with sincere great compassion."

Thereupon Prabhuta nourished the multitude that thronged through the four passageways leading to her Lion Seat. She continued, "O son of good family, I have realized only this inexhaustible store of virtue. I have yet to penetrate the vast ocean-like virtue of the great bodhisattvas. To the south in the city of Mahasambhava lives the elder Vidvat. Take your question to him."

(6) Sudhana made obeisance at Prabhuta's feet and turned southward. Sudhana had now realized the Dharma of inexhaustible virtue and had increased his discipline to benefit others. His mind, too, was enveloped by the Buddha's light. Arriving in the city, Sudhana eventually found the elder Vidvat seated in a seven-jewelled hall and surrounded by ten thousand people. Vidvat said to Sudhana, "O son of good family, I have taught the Dharma to these ten thousand people and quickened their birth in the house of the Buddha. O son of good family, I freely open my treasure house of virtue to give offerings to all people and fulfill their desires." Vidvat then directed Sudhana to the elder Ratnacuda who lived in the city of Simhapota.

(7) On the way Sudhana met Ratnacuda, who took his hand and led him to his home. Sudhana was instructed to observe the elder's residence. Observing the house and its environs, Sudhana saw that it was surrounded by a seven-jewelled hedge and luxuriant jewelled trees. Its pond overflowed with water of genuine virtue. The house itself was embellished with lapis lazuli, and its fluted pillars were covered by curtains embroidered with jewels. The elder's house had rooms piled ten stories high, and eight entrance ways. The first floor was filled with food and drink, the second floor with jewel-studded garments, the third with jewelled utensils, and the fourth sheltered righteous and moral maidens. Bodhisattvas of the fifth stage who were compiling the true Dharma occupied the fifth floor. On the sixth floor, bodhisattvas who realized the limits of wisdom were teaching on wisdom. Bodhisattvas who had realized the second and third stages were teaching on the wisdom of skillful means on the seventh floor. The eighth floor was the gathering place for those bodhisattvas who had acquired superhuman powers. On the ninth floor the bodhisattvas who had attained the highest stage prior to Buddhahood were assembled. All the buddhas were gathered on the tenth floor; and they were saving people.

Sudhana was astonished by this spectacle, and the elder said to him, "O son of good family, in the past I met with Amitabha the Dharmadhatu Buddha when he appeared in the world. I honored him with fragrant flowers. Thereupon I extinguished greed and perceived Buddhahood. I desired to hear the true Dharma, and thus I attained my present reward."

(8) After receiving the elder's instruction, Sudhana once again turned to the south, to the country of Vetramulaka, to meet with the elder Samantanetra, who lived in the castle of Samantamukha. The city, surrounded by numerous smaller

castles, soared majestically around them. The elder was present in the castle and seated on a perfumed throne. He responded to Sudhana's inquiry: "O son of good family, I know the illnesses of all people. Those with colds, chills, and fever who call on me are all cured. After ministering to their ailments, I expound on the various ways of the Dharma. For those who are filled with greed, I teach the meditation on impurity. To those consumed with hate, I teach the meditation on compassion; for the slow-witted I teach the meditation on the true aspects of the Dharma. Through my instruction all rejoice in the merit of the Dharma. In addition, O son of good family, I know how to combine the various ingredients for the manufacture of incense. When I honor the Buddha with this incense, I fulfill my desire to save people and glorify the Buddha realm. The flowing perfume of the incense reaches the buddhas of the ten directions. The scent becomes their palace, banisters, banners, and canopy.

"O son of good family, the only thing I can do is to arouse joy in people and perceive all the buddhas. The teachings of the great bodhisattva physicians are beyond my understanding."

(9) On instruction from the elder, Sudhana set off to the south to seek guidance from King Anala who resided in the city of Taladhvaja. Sudhana entered the king's palace and proceeded to the main hall. The king was observed administering his kingdom. When Sudhana entered the great hall, the king was on his diamond lion throne. The king bore a crown embellished with a half-moon made of Jambunada gold. His hair was blue-black and his earlobes were long. He wore a necklace made of jewels. Above the king were gold umbrellas studded with jewels. To his sides hung luminous banners that illuminated the eight directions. The ten thousand ministers to his left and right were administering the royal decrees. He was guarded by ten thousand generals with halberds.

The youth also perceived countless people who had violated the king's laws and who had been punished. Some had received the five admonishments, others had their hands and feet amputated, others were without ears and noses. He saw others with their eyes gouged out and those who had been scathed with boiling water. Sudhana took note of those who had been wrapped in wool cloth soaked with oil and burned. They were countless. Sudhana thought, "I have cultivated practices for the benefit of others. But this king is certainly extremely evil. He is the worst among evil beings."

At this time, however, the gods urged Sudhana to approach the king for instruction. The king took Sudhana's hand and led him through the palace, which accommodated five hundred goddess-like maidservants, and said, "O son of good family, I know the Dharma that all things are illusory. I also know that those who, among the people of my country, commit murder, steal, assault others' wives, or harbor perverted views cannot be persuaded to abandon their evil ways by simple instruction. There is no other recourse but to give them disciplinary punishments to make them accept the true way. By having them exposed to pains, I am trying to make them give up their evil ways. O son of good family, I do not have the heart to injure even a single ant, much less a person. People are the fertile field on which good deeds are nurtured."

(10) On the king's instruction, Sudhana continued south to the city of Suprabha. The majesty of the city was beyond words. The solemn dignity of the king Mahaprabha was like that of the sun. He emanated a grandeur comparable to the brilliance of the full moon that overwhelms the light of the stars. The king respectfully said to Sudhana, "O son of good family, I practice compassion. It is through compassion that I govern the country, teach my subjects, dispel the impurities in their minds, make gentle their entire being, let them reject the way of mundane pleasure, and lead them to seek the Dharma. When I am approached by the poor, I open my treasure house and tell them to take what they want. At the same time, I ask them to abstain from doing evil. O Sudhana, among my subjects there are some who perceive this city to be filthy and there are others who say that it is clean. While some perceive the city to be of woods and stones, still others perceive it to be made of precious gems. Those who cultivate good roots with a sincere and genuine mind perceive this city to be embellished with countless jewels."

When the king entered the meditation of great compassion, the city of Suprabha shook in six different ways. The jewelled ramparts, the palace, the turrets, the bells, and the lace-like embellishments that hung from the castle walls all praised the king with exquisite sounds. Subjects within and without the castle were overcome with joy and placed their palms together and paid homage to the king. The mountains and trees bowed to the king; the rivers and springs altered their courses and flowed toward the king. Even those evil demons who sucked blood and ate meat, and those evil beasts who lived on land or in the sea, embraced compassion and came to believe in rebirth. As a token of respect, all these demons and beasts offered obeisance before the king.

(11) Then the king emerged from this meditation and directed Sudhana to the devotee Acala in the city of Sthila. Sudhana, mindful of King Mahaprabha's teaching, attained a joyful mind, a mind free from desire, a humble mind, and a fearless mind. Further, when he was mindful of the virtues of good teachers, a voice from the sky spoke out, "O Sudhana, the Buddha rejoices when you follow the teachings of good teachers and thus grow closer to omniscience. Further, when you tirelessly seek the teachings of good teachers, all benefits will appear before you."

Sudhana gradually made his way toward the city of Sthila. When he arrived he entered the castle of the devotee Acala. The castle was enveloped by a golden glow that illuminated the four directions. When this glow touched Sudhana, his entire being became soft and flexible. And when Sudhana finally saw Acala, her beauty was without earthly peer. In praise, Sudhana sang to her:

> If you always observe the pure precepts,
>
> And if you cultivate patience diligently,
>
> You will be like the full moon
>
> Glowing among the stars in a cloudless sky.

Sudhana then respectfully inquired about the bodhisattva path. Acala said, "O Sudhana, when the Buddha appeared in the past world, I was the queen of this country. Late into the night when all music ceased, when my many maidservants drifted into sleep, and when alone on the turrets I gazed at the stars and saw the Buddha surrounded by gods and bodhisattvas, he hovered in the sky and glowed like a jewelled mountain. From his pores flowed fragrance that mellowed my body and mind. I immediately placed my hands together in reverence. I asked myself how he was able to possess the auspicious marks of such brilliance. The Buddha perceived my thoughts and responded, 'You must extinguish your defilements, accept the Buddha's teaching, and give rise to the light of wisdom.' O son of good family, from that moment I doubled my efforts in cultivating the path. Even in my sleep I have worshipped the Buddha. I have perceived all things with equanimity and am freely able to give rise to superhuman powers."

(12) According to Acala's instruction, Sudhana once again turned southward to the city of Tosala to meet Sarvagamin, a non-Buddhist master. Sudhana entered the city at dusk and searched in the night for Sarvagamin. A great mountain rising majestically to the north of the city glowed as if with the light of the dawn. Finally, at daybreak Sudhana left the city and climbed this mountain in search of Sarvagamin. He then came upon Sarvagamin, who was wandering about on the mountain. He responded to Sudhana's question, "O son of good family, I wander about in an attempt to save people. With the wisdom of equanimity I instruct beings on the various stages of the six realms in accordance with their capacity. But no one knows who I am."

(13) On Sarvagamin's advice Sudhana continued his journey south to inquire further on the bodhisattva discipline of the elder Utpalabhuti of Prthurastra. The elder said, "O Sudhana, I am familiar with the different varieties of incense. There are types of incense that give pleasure, types that increase defilement, and types that destroy defilement. Some types of incense support the meditation on the Buddha, others encourage you to follow the Dharma. O Sudhana, we have here an incense called Storehouse of the Great Assembly, which was produced as the result of many battles. If I burn a single grain of this, it creates a large luminous cloud that blankets the entire country. This cloud rains perfume for seven days and nights; and if this perfumed rain touches the body, it turns gold in color. All that touches it also turns gold in color. The scent gives great pleasure for seven days and nights and cures all diseases. The scent generates gracious and compassionate thoughts in all people. O Sudhana, I know of other wonderful types of incense. However, it is not within my power to penetrate the bodhisattva realm, which is endowed with the wonderful incense of wisdom."

(14) On advice from Utpalabhuti, Sudhana went southward to Kutagara to speak with the shipmaster Vaira. Sudhana arrived at Kutagara and saw Vaira at the harbor where ships gathered. He said, "O great sage, please instruct me on the bodhisattva discipline." Vaira answered, "O son of good family, through the discipline of great compassion I have endured many difficulties for the unfortunates of this city and fulfilled their desires. I have pleased them by teaching

the Dharma extensively to them. I want all people to perceive the Buddha Sea. O son of good family, I have knowledge of every shoal and treasure in the ocean. In addition, I know the location of every Naga palace and have eliminated disasters caused by dragons. I am also familiar with the palaces of demons and have eliminated disasters caused by demons. I have set sail with detailed knowledge of the currents, winds, waves, and movements of the sun, moon, and stars. I have expounded the Dharma to people in order that they might free themselves from the fear of samsara, enter the ocean of wisdom, and empty the ocean of desire. I have enabled them to realize the ocean of wisdom that is filled with light."

(15) Vaira's teachings caused Sudhana to shed tears of joy. Sudhana was advised to proceed south to the city of Nandihara and hear the elder Jayottama's views on bodhisattva discipline. "O son of good family, I eliminate discord among people, end warfare, and expel their anger and hate. I cut off their fetters to liberate them from prisons. In addition, I remove their perverted thoughts and all their evils. I also please them by sharing my skills and knowledge. I have guided the non-Buddhists so that they desire to seek the Buddha-Dharma. I have expounded the ways of the secular world so that they desire to abandon the secular world. I have revealed the bodhisattva path so that they may remove themselves from the evils of this transient world."

(16) The elder advised Sudhana to visit the nun Simhavijrmbhita, who lived in the country of Kalinga. When Sudhana arrived in that country, he found the nun seated on an infinitely large Lion Seat under a luminous tree in the Kalinga forest. The lion seat was covered with gold fabric and draped with a jewelled net. The nun was surrounded by innumerable clansmen. Through her superhuman powers she occupied every Lion Seat throughout the universe. Her posture was dignified and majestic; her mind was tranquil. She was awe-inspiring like a deep and still abyss. She responded quietly to Sudhana. "O son of good family, I have penetrated the depths of wisdom. To those who approach me I expound the means of obtaining wisdom. Yet I do not give rise to the thought that they are sentient beings. Though I have mastered every language there is to master, I am not caught up in words. Even though I perceive all buddhas, I am not attached to them because I have realized the profound essence of the Dharmakaya. Further, although I know all things in a single moment, I do not cling to them because I understand that all things are like illusions."

(17) Sudhana reverently thanked her, and on her advice he headed south to speak with Vasumitra, who lived in the city of Ratnavyuha in the country of Durgajanapada. The spacious city was enclosed by ten rows of walls and surrounded with palm trees. The ten moats that encircled the city flowed with crystal clear water; at the bottom of the moats gold sand sparkled. Blue, red, and white lotus blossoms sweetly perfumed the air. Enveloped in this exquisite fragrance, the jewelled castle and turrets were ornamented with bells that resembled falling snow. Swayed by breezes that scattered the blossoms, the bells resonated gently.

The beauty of Vasumitra's face was without compare. With a charming figure and an exquisite voice, she was skilled in arts and letters. She turned to Sudhana who respectfully inquired about the bodhisattva path. "O son of good family, I have mastered the realm without desire. Consequently, when I am seen by the gods I am ennobled and thought to be a goddess. When I am seen by people, I am seen as a woman of this world. This miraculous body of mine is unsurpassed both in the realm of the gods and in the realm of the people. When those who are bound by lust approach me, I teach them and they are liberated from their desires. Those who meet me realize pure joy. Those who hear my wonderful voice have their awareness of sound sharpened. Those who take my hand acquire the secret path to the Buddha's land. Those who dwell with me are touched by my light, which removes suffering. Those who embrace me attain the strength to save all people. Those who kiss me obtain a store of many virtues."

(18) Vasumitra instructed Sudhana to proceed south to Subhaparangama where he called on the lay elder Vesthila, who told him, "O son of good family, I understand that the buddhas never enter nirvana. When I opened a buddha stupa of sandalwood timbers, I mastered the meditation called the Eternity of Buddhahood. As I ascend to a higher stage in meditation, I realize an indescribable Dharma. O son of good family, I am familiar only with this teaching. The great bodhisattvas apprehend the three worlds in a single thought; they can enter all meditations in a single thought; their minds are bathed by the light of the Buddha's wisdom; they do not discriminate between all things. They know that they, the buddhas, and all other sentient beings are the same. But it is not for me to expound on their merits."

(19) With these words from the lay master, Sudhana proceeded south to Mount Potalaka, a peak that faced the southern sea and that was the home of the Bodhisattva Avalokitesvara. When Sudhana arrived at the mountain, he observed the Bodhisattva on the western face of the mountain, sitting on a Diamond Throne and teaching the Dharma of great compassion. His large audience was gathered between the streams that flowed weaving through soft grass and between full-bodied trees. Avalokitesvara immediately took notice of Sudhana who had single-mindedly come to inquire about the bodhisattva path. "O son of good family, it was good of you to have generated the desire to seek perfect enlightenment. I possess the Dharma of great compassion, the implementation of wisdom. When I guide people, I sometimes practice giving, I sometimes engage in the same activities as others, and I sometimes assume inconceivable forms. Further, at times I release light to extinguish the heat of evil passions. At other times I teach the Dharma with dignity and with a wonderful voice. I enable people to attain enlightenment through my superhuman skillful means. And at times I assume the same human form as theirs to save them. I have made a vow to save all people and have desired to let them remove themselves from the fearfulness of their grim path, the heat of passions, foolishness, fetters, killing, poverty, the fear of death and the future, and the fear of love and hate. Further, I have made a vow to free from all fears those who are mindful of me, recite my name, and perceive me. O son of good family, I am knowledgeable only with this one aspect of the Dharma. I am not familiar with the virtues of the great bodhisattvas who are filled with the great vow and the discipline of altruism."

9. Ratridevata

(1) Sudhana received many lessons during his journeys. Then he approached the god Ratridevata who lived in Lumbini Grove. "What must I do," inquired Sudhana, "to be born into the Buddha's house? And how can I become a lamp for the world?"

"O son of good family, a bodhisattva must first awaken the desire to honor all buddhas; he must teach people with great compassion and he must perceive the real marks of dharmas by exhausting the limits of his great wisdom. He must master all meditative practices and enter all buddha lands. He must nurture omniscience and be able freely to traverse all Dharmadhatus. Such a bodhisattva is the true disciple of the Buddha. O son of good family, the bodhisattva who masters these practices is born in the Buddha's house and becomes a lamp for the world."

(2) Ratridevata counseled Sudhana to proceed to Kapilavatthu and speak with Gopa, a gentlewoman of the Sakya clan. On his way to the Gandavyuha Lecture Hall, the deity Asokasridevata together with a host of other deities greeted Sudhana: "Welcome, youth of great wisdom. From your presence we know that you have steadfastly and courageously pursued the bodhisattva path; you have not lost your enthusiasm to enter the palace of the true Dharma; you have dignity, and your five organs are perfect. Indeed you will shortly acquire a buddha body, speech, and mind."

Suddhana responded, "It is as you have said. I have vowed to extinguish the anguish of people and deliver them to quiescence. Having committed many evil deeds, people have fallen into the three evil realms, and consequently their sufferings are without limit. The grief of a bodhisattva who observes their sufferings is akin to that of a parent who witnesses his child being hacked to death. A bodhisattva thus witnesses the sufferings of people and quickens his vows of great compassion with which he embraces all."

When Sudhana was about to enter the lecture hall, the gods sprinkled fragrant blossoms on him and raised their voices in song:

> The sun of virtue that is hard to see in countless kalpas has now come out to lighten the darkened world.

> You have quickened the sentiment of great compassion for all who are overshadowed by ignorance, and you have generously given of your body and life; you have single-mindedly approached teachers and searched for the Buddha's enlightenment.

> You have mastered the bodhisattva's discipline and are replete with virtues and wisdom.

> You have travelled freely throughout the world without leaving it, like the wind that has free rein in the sky.

> Your resolve for mastering the path is unending, like an inextinguishable flame.

(3) At this time, Gopa was present on the jewelled lotus Lion Seat. She was surrounded by eighty-four thousand princesses who loved each person as though he or she were her only child. She respectfully said to Sudhana, the noble seeker of truth, "O son of good family, I am ever mindful of a bodhisattva's profound meditation. I know the good and evil in people of this kingdom and all other kingdoms. I also know the resolve, discipline, and sermons of every buddha. I understand the minds of all people, the good roots they have acquired, and their natures. Finally, I know the teachings of non-obstruction by all seekers of the path and the buddhas. O great sage, has it been long since you resolved to attain enlightenment?

"O son of good family, once there was a prince, Abhiguna, who rode his jewelled chariot throughout Perfumed Tusk Mountain. The prince fell in love with Princess Ratiprabhasasri. Once he said before the princess and her mother who had come along with her, 'I should even sacrifice my wife and child for the sake of acquiring omniscience. Princess, if you do not obstruct my way, I shall welcome you as my consort.' The princess replied, 'Prince, if you desire me, I shall gladly experience the flames of hell for many kalpas.' Her mother said, 'It has been my lifelong wish to give my precious daughter, whose skin is as soft as divine fabric, to a prince who seeks the highest wisdom.'

"Later, led by the princess, the three approached the Tathagata by the name of Suryagatraprabha. This meeting prompted all three to realize the wisdom that does not regress from enlightenment. O son of good family, the prince was an incarnation of Sakyamuni, the World-Honored One, and the princess an incarnation of me. And although I was thus able to meet with countless buddhas and observe their Dharma disciplines, I have yet to apprehend the teachings of the Bodhisattva Samantabhadra whose teaching is like the limitless sky. O son of good family, for the longest time, I have worshipped the Bodhisattva Samantabhadra and have not grown tired of it. I see a limitless universe in each pore of the Bodhisattva; the number of the universes is equal to the number of the deluded thoughts that are generated by men and women who are passioately in love." Then Gopa, the queen, recited the following verses:

> The Bodhisattva saves all people who quicken feelings of respect after observing the Bodhisattva performing pure disciplines.

> The Bodhisattva sees that some worlds are pure and others defiled, but he does not choose only the pure or reject the defiled.

> The Bodhisattva apprehends all worlds, perceives the Buddhas who dwell in the realm of enlightenment, and releases in a single thought the light that illuminates all assemblies.

(4) By Gopa's instruction, Sudhana sought Queen Maya of Kapilavastu. During his journey, the rarefied body of Ratnanetra, the guardian deity of the city, appeared in the sky and said, "O son of good family, to escape from samsara you must guard the domain of the mind; to acquire the power of the Buddha, you must ornament the domain of the mind; to destroy the mind of greed and perversion, you must purify the domain of the mind; to continue to practice all

meditations and acquire the power of suchness, you must destroy the mind of burning passion; to illuminate the Buddha Ocean and others with the light of wisdom, you must illumine the domain of the mind; to acquire the greatness of the Buddha's virtues, you must extend the mind's domain; to save all people through boundless Great Compassion, you must open the gates to the city of the mind."

A second deity, Dharma-padma-srikusala-devata, sang in praise of Queen Maya with an exquisite voice. He released streams of light that illuminated every universe. The light, on its return, entered the nape of Sudhana's neck and filled his body. Sudhana then acquired a wisdom eye free from defilements. Freed from the darkness of ignorance, Sudhana apprehended the nature of man and perceived the Buddha's body. At this time Queen Maya was seated on the Lion Seat decorated with garlands of lotus flowers, which had emerged from the great earth. Many of her clansmen surrounded her exquisite presence. She said to Sudhana, the true seeker of the path: "O son of good family, I possess the great vow, wisdom, and superhuman powers. For this reason I have become the mother of all bodhisattvas. In this world, in Suddhodana's palace of Kapilavastu, I gave birth to the prince Siddhartha. O son of good family, while I resided in Suddhodana's castle, I met with a bodhisattva who descended from the Tusita heaven. The huge radiant light that emerged from his pores revealed in minute detail the life stories of uncountable bodhisattvas. After illuminating all the universe, his light returned and entered the nape of my neck. My body thus became the womb palace for Sakyamuni Buddha."

10. Bodhisattvas Maitreya and Samantabhadra

(1) Sudhana continued his southward journey to the city of Samanamukha. There he sought the children Srisambhava and Srimati. Both advised him to seek out the Bodhisattva Maitreya who lived in the Mahavyuha Forest in the kingdom of Samudrakaccha. Both children praised the virtues of the good teacher for Sudhana: "O son of good family, when you approach the good teacher, give rise to a mind that is knowledgeable of all things and is tireless like the great earth. And to complement this noble mind, you should generate a mind that is selfless and humble. Further, you should know that you are sick with passions and that the good teacher is an excellent physician. You must generate these thoughts, because only through sincerity of mind will you be able to recognize the good teacher. And it is through his teachings that your good roots will increase. The teachings are like the water that trickles down from the Himalayas to nourish the medicinal herbs. The purifying of the aspiration for enlightenment is akin to the heat treating of gold ore. The good teacher, like the lotus blooming in muddy water, remains undefiled in the world. The good teacher, like the sun that glows from afar, illuminates the Dharmadhatu. The good teacher does all this because he nurtures a bodhisattva like a mother who cares for her child. O son of good family, these virtues are based on the good teacher. Because of the good teacher, they arise, are born, and stay."

(2) Overjoyed with this message, Sudhana journeyed to Samudrakaccha. At length he arrived near Maitreya's mansion and prostrated himself before the tower. Standing at the gate, Sudhana observed the Bodhisattva Maitreya in the distance. He thought, "Herein reside all buddhas, bodhisattvas, and good teachers. Here, too, is the place of the Dharma treasure and of all the Dharmadhatu." Sudhana reflected further, "All things are like a dream and like an echo. All things arise through dependent origination. Things are neither existent nor nonexistent. Actions are the basis of our lives. We receive the results of actions. Further, when we achieve the highest wisdom through true faith, we are free of the ideas of 'I' and 'mine'. We understand the profound principle of causation and comprehend the real nature of things."

Thus Sudhana grasped the meaning of the Dharma. Before he made obeisance to Maitreya, he was filled with inconceivable good roots, and his body and mind became soft and flexible. He recited,

(i)   Profoundly compassionate Maitreya, replete with miraculous virtues, you show kindness to all people. Those who have expelled greed, anger, ignorance, and all illusions and desire a quiescent mind will rest in this Dharma hall.

Those who enter the ocean of illusion to conquer the dragons of defilement and receive the jewel of wisdom will be at peace in the Dharma hall.

Those who travel to the ends of the earth for all people and bear their sufferings will find quiescence in this Dharma hall.

(ii)   The disciples of the Buddha who are quiescent in this Dharma hall perceive all dharmas and understand that people, nations, and events are all without their own lasting nature. They know, too, that sentient beings and dharmas are identical; the Buddha and the vow are identical; this world and the three worlds are identical. I pay homage with all of the Buddha's disciples to the discipline of Maitreya, the Buddha's successor."

(3) Maitreya, who resided in the Buddha realm, filled with dignity, was encircled by countless gods and a multitude of people. Sudhana reverently brought his hands together and said, "O great sage, how can I be true to the original mind, not violate the Three Treasures, not slight gods and people, and practice the true Dharma where the bodhisattvas dwell?"

Addressing the great assembly, Maitreya pointed to Sudhana and said, "Do you not see that Sudhana's seeking perfect enlightenment is as urgent for him as extinguishing a fire that scorched his hair? He has tirelessly sought the teachings of Manjusri and many good teachers, and he has now come to me. Since he resolved to attain supreme enlightenment, Sudhana has saved all sentient beings and has transcended the difficulties and dangers of the evil paths and false views. He has lighted the torch of wisdom in the darkness of ignorance and has unlocked the prison of the three worlds. He has severed the bonds of perverted views with the sword of his wisdom. Nourished by the rains of the true Dharma, he labors tirelessly and courageously perfects every virtue. Sudhana has thus sought good teachers without sparing his body or life. Though he has accumulated the merits for enlightenment, he is not covetous of gain. He has not abandoned a bodhisattva's sincere mind; nor is he attached to his family's livelihood; nor is he impeded by the five desires. He has no attachment to his parents or relatives. It is very rare to meet someone who aspires single-mindedly to cultivate omniscience."

Turning to Sudhana, Maitreya said, "Sudhana, rejoice, for soon you will receive your great reward. Many bodhisattvas have cultivated their practices over many kalpas, but you have completed all the disciplines in a single lifetime. This has been possible because you have pursued the path with complete sincerity. Those who wish to attain the Dharma should follow Sudhana's example. O Sudhana, you should now approach the Bodhisattva Manjusri and ask him about many teachings, the realm of wisdom, and the practice of the Bodhisattva Samantabhadra."

After Maitreya's discourse, the Bodhisattva Manjusri extended his arms and solemnly presented a garland of flowers to Sudhana, who accepted it. Sudhana in turn joyfully offered it to the Bodhisattva Maitreya. Touching the nape of Sudhana's neck, the Bodhisattva Maitreya said, "O disciple of the Buddha, in a short while you will be my equal." Jubilant, Sudhana leaped ecstatically and said, "Thanks to the help of Manjusri, I am now befriended by many good teachers whom one can rarely meet even in millions of kalpas. O sage of great virtues, I shall be in your presence immediately."

(4) The Bodhisattva Maitreya said to Sudhana, "Son of good family, you are fortunate to have been born a human being and to have met the Buddha and Manjusri. Having become a receptacle for the Dharma, and full of good karmic roots, you have purified your defilements. You are embraced by good teachers and guarded by all buddhas, because you have made the resolution to attain supreme enlightenment. Resolution bears the Buddha's Dharma; therefore it is the seed of the Buddha. Resolution cultivates meritorious dharmas in people; therefore it is a fertile field of wisdom. Resolution cleanses the pains of defilement; therefore it is akin to pure water. Resolution recognizes the incorrect path; therefore it is a pure eye. Resolution leads to omniscience; therefore it is the great path. Resolution embraces all virtues; therefore it is the great sea. Resolution is the exquisite voice that resonates throughout the Dharmadhatu; therefore it is a musical instrument. Resolution reflects all facets of the Dharma; therefore it is a clear mirror.

"O Sudhana, just as no one can see a person who has the medicine to make himself invisible, one who possesses resolution cannot be seen by any devils. Again, just as a gem placed in muddy water purifies the water, resolution expels all defilements. Again, just as a buoy prevents one from drowning in a deep ocean, resolution prevents one from being swallowed by the sea of samsara. Just as a single candle is not exhausted when it is used to light a hundred thousand candles, resolution is not exhausted when it illuminates the buddhas of the three periods. Just as a single flame will destroy the darkness of an unlit room, resolution destroys the darkness of the mind and quickens wisdom. Just as the sinews of a lion used for stringing the zither break all other strings when the zither is played, resolution severs the five desires and other desires to seek inferior teachings. When milk from a lioness is poured into a vessel that holds a blend of milk from a cow, a mare, and a ewe, the milk in that vessel will take on the taste of the lioness's. In the same way the nourishment afforded by resolution completely overwhelms the aftertaste of karma and defilements that have accumulated through countless kalpas. O son of good family, resolution will perfect inexhaustible virtues. When a person quickens resolution, he will possess these virtues."

(5) At this time the Bodhisattva Maitreya snapped the fingers of his right hand, and the gates to the multistoried mansion opened by themselves. Sudhana entered, and the doors closed behind him by themselves. The interior of this mansion was as spacious as the heavens. There were innumerable crystalline lakes, countless windows, and banisters made from seven kinds of jewels. The interior was draped with silk banners and strands of jewels. The melody of the golden bells blended with the songs of the birds. Luminous flower petals rained unseasonably. This magnificent spectacle was similar in a hundred thousand multistoried mansions.

Observing this miraculous interpenetration and mutual adornment of these multistoried mansions, Sudhana was gladdened and his mind became pliant, dispelling illusionary thoughts and shattering the darkness of ignorance. When Sudhana respectfully bowed in awe, the Bodhisattva Maitreya revealed himself in each one of the mansions. Like the multitude of forms reflected in a mirror, Sudhana observed Maitreya revealing himself in innumerable forms to save gods and people. Just as one rejoices when one dreams of a beautiful mountain, lake, or palace, Sudhana too rejoiced when he was able to expel illusionary thoughts through the Bodhisattva's powers and perceive the dharmas of the three worlds. Just as a hundred years in the Dragon Palace seem to be only a moment, a hundred thousand kalpas seemed to be only a moment when Sudhana entered the Bodhisattva's abode.

Then Maitreya rescinded his powers. Snapping his fingers, he let Sudhana emerge from his meditation. He told Sudhana, "Indeed, this wisdom allows one to enter the three periods and store right thoughts."

(6) Sudhana respectfully thanked the Bodhisattva Maitreya and proceeded to seek out again the Bodhisattva Manjusri. Sudhana passed through one hundred eleven cities and approached the city of Samantamukha. His single-minded desire to meet Manjusri caused the Bodhisattva to appear. Manjusri touched the nape of his neck and said, "Very well, O son of good family. If faith is lost, the mind grievously degenerates, discipline is not practiced, conduct becomes disorderly, and effort is slackened. We are then content with small virtues and do not have the protection of good teachers; nor are we embraced in the thoughts of the buddhas. And we are unable to grasp the nature and essence of the Dharma and understand the Buddhist discipline."

This teaching filled Sudhana with the light of infinite wisdom. Manjusri then led Sudhana to Samantabhadra's meditation hall, placed him on his very own seat, and exited. There Sudhana communicated with good teachers whose number equalled that of the particles of dust in the trichiliocosm. He increased his knowledge and great compassion. Comfortable within the quiescent Dharma gates, Sudhana was mindful of all realms and practiced the bodhisattva discipline throughout all kalpas; he realized his great aspiration and apprehended the Bodhisattva Samantabhadra's name, discipline, vow, and virtues. Through Sudhana's sincere desire to meet the Bodhisattva Samantabhadra, he observed that through the power of the Buddha's great strength, the evil paths in every realm became extinct and that all people were practicing meditation on the Buddha with compassionate minds. Further, Sudhana became aware that every buddha residing in each particle of dust in the world was luminous and that every buddha was singing praises of the Bodhisattva Samantabhadra's practice and vow.

Sudhana reverently observed Samantabhadra ascending the lotus treasure Lion Seat, which was situated directly in front of the Buddha. Surrounded by the great assembly, Samantabhadra had a mind as vast as the heavens, free of all defilements. Dwelling in the sphere of omniscience, Samantabhadra guided people and observed the buddhas in the three periods.

Witnessing the inconceivable free powers of the Bodhisattva Samantabhadra, Sudhana was able to be present in all realms at each moment and meet with each of the Buddhas and listen to the true Dharma. He was also able to acquire the inconceivable free wisdom of the Buddha, the wisdom to know the defilements of all people, and the wisdom that Samantabhadra possessed. The virtues that Sudhana acquired by meeting an infinite number of good teachers did not equal even one billionth of the virtues that Samantabhadra possessed. But presently he, like the Buddha, will penetrate the universe; his realm, body, practice, enlightenment, power, propagation of the Dharma, and Great Compassion will equal the Buddha's.

(7) Samantabhadra then recited the following verses:

(i)   The light of perfect wisdom shatters the darkness of defilements and illuminates all the worlds to provide peace to people. A Buddha's appearance in the world after countless kalpas is akin to the blossoming of the udumbara flower. A Buddha undergoes many arduous disciplines over many kalpas for the sake of people; and though he wades through the defilements of the world, his mind is not stained.

(ii) The waxing and waning moonlight, which is reflected in all forms of water, overshadows the light from the tiny firefly. The waxing and waning moonlight of the Buddha's wisdom, which is reflected on the water of the honest mind, overshadows the teachings of small enlightenment.

Just as all beings appear in the deep and vast ocean in which countless gems are hidden, all kinds of images appear in the pure body of the Buddha—the deep sea of causes and conditions in which the gems of virtue are stored. Just as the dragon generates clouds, showers rain, and cools all beings, so the Buddha gives rise to the cloud of Great Compassion, sends down sweet rains, and extinguishes the fires of the three poisons.

(iii) The pure body of the Buddha is without peer in this world; it is neither existent nor nonexistent; nor is it dependent on anything. It does not leave its place but travels everywhere. Just like space, which is one, principles such as thusness, self-nature, nirvana, and unconditioned quiescence, which are taught by the Buddha, are all synonyms. Though we might be able to measure the number of human minds, the number of drops of water in the ocean, and the breadth of the empty sky, we cannot fully recount the virtues of the Buddha. He who rejoices in hearing the Dharma and has no doubt in his mind of faith will soon attain enlightenment and become the equal of all buddhas.

Introduction

The Buddha continues his travels, teaching the Dharma and engaging in dialogues with his disciples and with others, from all levels of life, who come to him to seek the path to enlightenment.

Book IV contains passages from three well-known scriptures. In Chapter 2, Section 2, is found the widely popular Diamond Sutra (Vajracchedika-prajna-paramita-sutra), which is a short text in the form of a dialogue between the Buddha and his disciple Subhuti. It aims to reveal the Buddha's Diamond Mind, or the Absolute Mind of supreme enlightenment.

The Buddha in this discourse tries to remove Subhuti's doubts regarding the true nature of the Buddha and the Dharma (Teaching), and whether a student is qualified to understand and practice this teaching. The Buddha explains that even if a being enters perfect nirvana, there would be, in truth, no one who entered nirvana, because a bodhisattva, who has vowed to attain full enlightenment, does not affirm the permanent existence of a self, or anything else in life. He does not become attached to the forms of things, so he does not seek Buddhahood with physical forms, because he considers all forms to be illusion.

Subhuti wonders if anyone would believe such words. Then, the Buddha asks Subhuti whether buddhas attained supreme enlightenment, or whether there is a Dharma that the Buddha ought to expound. Subhuti replies that there is no unchanging Dharma that might be labelled as supreme enlightenment, nor a fixed Dharma that a Buddha ought to expound since it cannot be grasped nor expounded.

Subhuti is further asked whether arhats regard enlightenment that they attained as 'something' they have attained. Subhuti acknowledges that arhats recognize that there is nothing that can be called enlightenment; otherwise, arhats would still be bound to self-attachment. Thus, it follows that Subhuti would not be an arhat if he were to entertain the idea that he has reached 'something.' In this principle of Emptiness, concepts like Dharma and enlightenment are to be used like a raft for the sake of crossing over this sea of suffering but are not to be grasped as absolute truths. In fact, all categories of Buddhist thought are unreal; they are simply names that one uses as a means to dispel one's delusions about life.

In Chapter 2, Section 3 is found the Heart Sutra (Prajna-paramita-sutra) which is another brief text that is probably the most widely chanted Buddhist scripture. In it, the speaker is Avalokitesvara who reveals the content of his transcendental spiritual contemplation that was experienced when he undertook the practice of profound wisdom that leads one to the Dharma's shore of enlightenment. He found that all things are empty. Feeling, perception, volition, and consciousness are also empty. The doctrinal categories established by conventional Buddhist teaching and practice are negated; and in the light of the concept of emptiness, the cessation of suffering and the path leading to the cessation do not exist in the absolute sense. There is actually nothing to attain. This concept leads to absolute altruism, because one performs compassionate acts for the welfare of others with no thought of gain. The wisdom that leads to the other shore is the Perfect Wisdom that is distilled in the dharani 'Gate Gate Paragate Parasamgate Bodhi Svaha,' the mantra that Buddhists, regardless of sect, recite in chanting the Heart Sutra to extinguish all suffering.

The third scripture, Vimalakirti Sutra, one of the oldest Mahayana scriptures, is found in Chapter 4, Section 3. It upholds the bodhisattva ideal and glorifies a layman, Vimalakirti, as exemplifying this highest virtue.

Vimalakirti is a wealthy householder living in Vaisali (P: Vesali). A bodhisattva uses skillful means to save sentient beings; thus, Vimalakirti uses his sickness as the occasion to preach the Dharma to the people who come to visit him at his sickbed.

Buddha asks Sariputra and the other disciples, 500 in all, to visit Vimalakirti, but each expresses a reason for being unworthy to visit him. Then, the Buddha asks all the bodhisattvas present, but even the bodhisattvas decline, explaining how in previous encounters with Vimalakirti, they had also engaged in a dialogue regarding the Dharma with this enlightened layman and did not feel qualified to compete with him.

Finally Manjusri agrees to visit Vimalakirti, who by his supernormal powers empties his room of everything except his bed to accomodate Manjusri and the hundreds of disciples and bodhisattvas who accompanied him. When Manjusri asks him about the nature of his illness, Vimalakirti responds that the sickness of a bodhisattva is caused by his great compassion for all beings, who are spiritually ill and who can become well by relying on his skillful means that would transfer to them the Perfect Wisdom that leads to enlightenment.

Sariputra worries about the lack of seats in the room, so Vimalakirti produces 32,000 'lion-thrones' while enlarging his room to accomodate them. At first, because of the height of the seats, only the advanced bodhisattvas were able to fit into them properly. The rest of the company were made to realize that they have not quite reached the necessary understanding of the Dharma.

Finally, Vimalakirti asks all the bodhisattvas to explain how a bodhisattva enters the Dharma Gate of Non-duality. Manjusri, who is the last to respond, declares that it is to have no word and no speech as well as no awareness about any dharmas and to keep away from questions and answers. When Vimalakirti is finally asked how he had entered the Dharma Gate of Non-duality, he remained silent. This is known as the "Thunderous Silence" of Vimalakirti.

Chapter 3, Section 4 introduces the reader to the concept of merit transference, which was developed to its highest degree in various schools of the Mahayana. A bodhisattva who has attained enlightenment vows to share the merits he has gained, through many kalpas (aeons) of supreme effort, with all sentient beings. After the bodhisattva becomes a Buddha and establishes his Buddha-land, all who are unable to attain understanding of the Dharma through their own feeble efforts can rely on the Buddha's all-encompassing Great Compassion to help them cross over to the shore of enlightenment.

Chapter 1

THE ESSENCE OF THE BUDDHA'S MIND

1. The Wisdom of the Buddha

(1) From there the World-Honored One traveled through Kosala and reached the city of Kapilavatthu. The king of the Sakya clan, Mahanama, learned of this and went to visit the World-Honored One.

The World-Honored One said, "Mahanama, I should like to have tonight's lodging arranged for me within the city." The king agreed to do so and searched for lodging within the city; however, he was unable to find suitable quarters. Thereupon, he went back and said to the World-Honored One, "World-Honored One, there is no suitable lodging within the city. Therefore, I should like to have you spend the night at the house of Bharandu Kalama, who in the past was your disciple." The Buddha said, "In that case, I should like to have you prepare my bed."

Mahanama prepared the bed, provided water for foot-washing, and led the World-Honored One to the house. At daybreak, he again visited the World-Honored One. The World-Honored One said, "Mahanama, in this world there are three types of teachers. The first type teaches the differentiation of desires, but he does not teach the differentiation between things and sensations. The second type teaches the differentiation between desires and things, but he does not teach the differentiations of sensations. The third type teaches the differentiations that exist among desires, things, and sensations. Mahanama, do these three teachers seek the same refuge, or do they seek different refuges?"

Kalama suggested, "Say that they seek the same refuge." The World-Honored One said, "Say that they seek different refuges." They repeated this three times. Kalama thought to himself, "Thrice the World-Honored One has shamed me in the presence of Mahanama; now is the time for me to leave Kapilavatthu." He then departed, never to return.

(2) The World-Honored One then dwelt for a while in a nigrodha forest. Mahanama visited the World-Honored One every day. One day, he asked, "World-Honored One, right now Kapilavatthu is flourishing; the congestion of people and horses is something to behold. After performing my services to the World-Honored One and his disciples, I return home in the evening; but on the way I am met by a congestion of elephants, horses, carriages, and people milling about.

Because of this, I am apt to forget any thoughts of the Buddha, the Dharma, and the Buddha's disciples. If I must die at a time like this, where shall I be born?"

The Buddha said, "Mahanama, there is nothing to fear. Your death will not be a misfortune. If you have cultivated your everyday mind through the precepts, listening, selfless giving, and wisdom, no matter when or where your body dies, your mind will go to an excellent place. Suppose you break jars filled with milk and oil in a pool of water. The jars' broken shards will sink to the bottom, but the milk and the oil will float to the top. You have cultivated your everyday mind with the precepts, listening, selfless giving, and wisdom; therefore your death will not be a misfortune. Mahanama, those who cherish an indestructible faith in the Buddha, the Dharma, and the Sangha and obey the precepts praised by the arhats will without fail enter nirvana. This is as certain as a tree leaning toward the east being cut down and falling eastward. No matter when death comes to you, it will in no way be a misfortune."

(3) One day Mahanama again visited the World-Honored One and asked, "World-Honored One, how do you determine who is a Buddhist devotee?" The Buddha said, "Mahanama, by merely taking refuge in the Buddha, the Dharma, and the Sangha, one is a devotee." Mahanama asked, "World-Honored One, what does it mean for a devotee to possess the precepts, faith, selfless giving, and wisdom?" The Buddha said, "Mahanama, the precepts of the devotee are those that prohibit him from taking life, stealing, lascivious acts, lying, and the imbibing of liquors. The faith of the devotee is to have faith in the Buddha's enlightenment. Selfless giving on the part of the devotee is to cast off the greedy and miserly mind and rejoice in acts of giving, while living in a house, as opposed to a monastery. The wisdom of the devotee is to know the truth that all things arise and perish; it is to know revulsion for the world of greed and to abandon it. It is to know the way that leads to the cessation of suffering."

(4) The World-Honored One spent three months at this retreat in the nigrodha forest. Putting his robe in order, he was about to set forth on another journey. Mahanama heard of this and, approaching the Buddha, said, "World-Honored One, you have put your robes in order and are about to depart. How should a devotee, whom you have just spoken about, visit and console another devotee who lies sick in bed? What should he do?"

The Buddha said, "Mahanama, a devotee should visit his sick friend and bolster his spirits with four consolations. He should console his sick friend with these words, 'Friend, you have cherished an indestructible faith in the Buddha, the Dharma, and the Sangha. You have obeyed the precepts that are praised by the arhats. These four are your consolations.' Then one should say, 'Do you have attachment to your parents?' If the sick friend replies that he does, then one should say, 'Whether you feel attachment or not, you must die; therefore you should cast off your attachment to your parents.' If he should say that he has no such attachment, then one should ask, 'Do you have attachment to your wife and child?' If he replies that he does, then one should exhort him with these words: 'You must die; therefore, you should abandon your attachment to your wife and child.' If he should say that he has abandoned his attachment to his wife and child, then one should ask, 'Does the attachment to the five desires of human beings linger on?' If he answers that it does, then one should teach him, 'The delights of the celestial world far exceed those of the five desires of the human world. Abandoning your attachment to the human world, let your mind find pleasure in the celestial realm.' Gradually strengthening his resolve, one should teach, 'The worlds of the gods are also transitory; thus you should direct your mind toward nirvana.' Should the sick devotee abandon the world of the gods, think of nirvana, and free himself from all defilements, there will then be no difference between him and a disciple who is a mendicant."

(5) The World-Honored One departed Kapilavatthu and proceeded to Kusinara where, in the forest of Baliharana, he stayed and taught his disciples: "Disciples, living near a village or town, you will be invited by lay people and receive sumptuous foods as offerings. If you delight in that, thinking, 'Please invite me over and over!,' you will be shackled by the food. You will be ignorant of the way that frees you from that evil. From this emanates feelings of greed, anger, and malice. Acts of giving performed for such a person bring no large reward, because he is negligent. On the other hand, should you be invited and offered sumptuous food and yet are not shackled by that food and are able to perceive the evil in it, you are freed from the feelings of greed, anger, and malice. Because of your diligence, acts of giving that are performed bring huge rewards.

"Disciples, it is unpleasant even to think of a place where people are constantly embroiled in fights, stabbing away at each other with rapier-like tongues. Much less do you feel like visiting there. Those people are crazed with the three thoughts of greed, anger, and malice. Compared with this, it is pleasant to think of a place where everyone is friendly to each other, blending like milk and water. It is all the more pleasant to go there. Those people have cast off all thoughts of greed, anger, and malice.

(6) "Disciples, there are three persons that are rarely seen in this world. The first is a buddha. The second is one who expounds and spreads the Dharma. The third is one who has awakened to his debt of gratitude and joy.

"Disciples, there are three types of people in the world. The first is a person whose nature is easily known. He is arrogant, careless, talkative, and always restless. The second is a person whose nature is difficult to grasp. He is quiet, humble, careful in all things, someone of few words; and he suppresses his greed. The third is a person whose nature cannot be known. He is a person who has completely extinguished all defilements.

"Disciples, in the world there are those who commit violations in three ways: in deeds, in livelihood, and in views. Those who commit violations in deeds kill living creatures, steal, commit lascivious acts, lie, slander, spew out words that disrupt the harmony of things, and prattle on endlessly. Those who commit violations in livelihood earn their livings in ways that are immoral. Those who commit violations in views harbor such wrong views as 'Neither selfless giving nor offering is necessary. There are neither good nor evil acts, nor are there any fruits that result from those acts. Neither this world nor other worlds exist. There is no need to perform acts of filial piety, to attain enlightenment, or to become a mendicant.'

"Disciples, you should always exert yourself to purify the three actions undertaken by body, mouth, and mind. To purify your bodily actions means not to kill living creatures, not to steal, and not to commit lascivious acts. To purify your verbal actions means not to spout lies, not to slander others, to abstain from using words that disrupt the harmony of things, and not to prattle on and on. To purify your mind's actions means not to crave things, not to get angry, and to cherish right views.

"Disciples, there are three types of groups: groups that have leaders, disorderly groups, and harmonious groups. In those groups that have leaders, the leader abstains from extravagance, is diligent in his studies, and exerts himself in his attempts to attain enlightenment. His followers emulate their leader and apply themselves with diligence. This is the nature of groups with leaders. As for disorderly groups, when conflicts arise in these groups, they harm each other with their rapier-like tongues. Harmonious groups are those in which everyone is friendly to each other, blending together like milk and water. A host of virtues are produced in the third group. The people in the third group lead the same life as that of a buddha. Their minds are filled with joy; and by virtue of this joy, they attain merits. Because of these merits, their bodies become relaxed. Because they are in harmony with each other, they gradually produce these virtues. Their minds experience joy, and avoiding disorders of the spirit they are able to become of one mind. This is like the heavy rain that pours down on mountain tops. The water flows down and gathers in pools, in small streams, and in large rivers, and in the end it fills up the great ocean.

(7) "Disciples, if a horse being kept by a king possesses the three traits of beauty, strength, and swiftness, that horse can become the king's personal steed. If a disciple of the Buddha possesses these three splendid traits, he will receive the world's offerings and become a field, unsurpassed in excellence, that produces merits. The beauty of the Buddha's disciple means that he obeys the precepts, performs good practices, restrains his desires, trembles at even a minor transgression, and exerts himself in the practice of the way. The strength of the Buddha's disciple means that he acquires the strength to exert himself on the way, abandons evil, and is earnest in his practice of the good. The swiftness of the Buddha's disciple means that he truly knows the teaching of the Four Noble Truths. Those who possess these three splendid traits are fields that produce merits; these fields are unsurpassed in this world in their excellence.

(8) "Disciples, if a soldier in the service of a king can shoot his arrows as quickly as lightning, if he can shoot far, and if he can hit a distant target, he can become a valued bodyguard of the king. In the same way, the Buddha's disciples who are able to perform these three actions can become worthy of receiving the world's offerings and become fields that produce merits unsurpassed in excellence.

"To shoot far, in the case of the Buddha's disciples, means that in all things they free themselves of attachments to the ideas of 'I' and 'mine' and cherish true wisdom. To shoot with the quickness of lightning means truly to know the teaching of the Four Noble Truths. Moreover, to hit a distant target means to shatter and destroy the darkness of ignorance. The Buddha's disciples who possess these three traits are fields that produce merits unsurpassed in this world.

(9) "Disciples, in order truly to know what greed is and to free oneself from it, one should practice the three Dharmas, emptiness, formlessness, and desirelessness. In order to know what anger, ignorance, and all other defilements are and to extinguish them, one should also practice the three Dharmas, emptiness, formlessness, and desirelessness.

"Disciples, among woven cloths, cloths made of hair are of the lowest grade; when it is cold, the cloth is chilly; when it is hot, it is hot. It is foul smelling, ugly, and unpleasant to the touch. Like haircloth, Makkhali Gosala is of the lowest grade. He spews out the evil view, 'Neither actions nor their rewards exist; there is no need to exert oneself.' However, disciples, both past and future buddhas expound both actions and their rewards; they also teach the necessity to exert oneself on the way. I, the Buddha of the present, teach in the same manner. Ignorant Makkhali, however, goes against the buddhas of the three worlds by asserting, 'Neither actions nor their rewards exist; there is no need to exert oneself.' He is like a net spread across the mouth of a river. For countless fishes, that net becomes the cause of injury, pain, and death. Like this net, Makkhali came into being in order to injure, to cause suffering to, and to kill countless human beings."

2. Dialogues with Non-Buddhist Teachers

(1) The World-Honored One departed from Kusinara and travelled to Vesali. There in the great forest he rested in the many-tiered lecture hall. At that time, numerous brahmins had been dispatched to that area on a mission by the two countries of Kosala and Magadha.

They heard that the World-Honored One was staying in the great forest and decided to visit him. They asked the Buddha's attendant Nagita, "Where is the World-Honored One now?" Nagita answered, "He has just entered his room; therefore, you are not allowed to see him now." The brahmins waited for the time to pass. Otthaddha of the Licchavi clan also came to visit the World-Honored One, bringing with him a large number of Licchavi people. He sat to the side and waited for a chance to meet the World-Honored One. At that time, Nagita's nephew Siha, a novice disciple, who was nearby, said to Nagita, "A large number of people have come to meet the World-Honored One; I would think it proper to convey this to him." Nagita said, "In that case, Siha, you ought to inform the World-Honored One." Siha said, "Very well, then," and he relayed the message to the World-Honored One.

(2) Following the World-Honored One's instructions, they prepared a seat in the shade in front of the monastery. The World-Honored One emerged from his room and sat down on the seat. The brahmins politely bowed in salutation and sat down nearby. Otthaddha said to the World-Honored One, "World-Honored One, two or three days ago Sunakkhatta of the Licchavi clan came to my place and said, 'Mahali, three years have passed since I came to live near

the World-Honored One. During that time, I have been able to witness delightful scenes where the gods fulfilled the aspirations of the people. However, I have yet to hear the voices of the gods.' World-Honored One, are there such things as the voices of the gods?" The World-Honored One said, "Mahali, naturally there are such things as the voices of the gods." Mahali said, "In that case, why is it that Sunakkhatta is unable to hear these voices?" The Buddha said, "Mahali, a disciple who wishes to see the splendid appearances of the gods enters meditation without losing his concentration; this disciple will surely gaze upon the beautiful appearances of the gods. And because he wishes to hear the delightful voices of the gods, he enters into meditation; he will surely hear the delightful voices of the gods." Mahali said, "World-Honored One, do the Buddha's disciples undergo pious practice under the guidance of the World-Honored One because they want to attain this meditation?" The Buddha said, "Mahali, they do not. They practice in order to realize a Dharma that is far more splendid and wondrous. Mahali, should you cut through the three fetters, you would enter the stage of a 'stream-winner', having entered the stream that leads to Buddhahood. You would never again enter an evil path, and you would finally attain enlightenment. Should you cut through the three fetters and diminish the defilements of greed, anger, and ignorance, you would enter the stage of the 'once-returner,' in which you would be reborn only once more into this world and attain the end of all suffering. Should you sever the five defilements that bind you to this world, you would be born in the celestial world and enter the stage of the 'nonreturner' in which you would never again return to this world and would enter nirvana. Should you perfectly extinguish the rampaging stream of the four defilements of desire, existence, ignorance, and deluded view, you would attain enlightenment in this world and become an arhat. Mahali, in order to attain this sublime state, the disciples practice the pure practices under my guidance and attain these four stages."

"World-Honored One, what is the way that leads to this sublime state?" The Buddha said, "Mahali, that way is the Eightfold Noble Path of right view, right thought, right speech, right action, right livelihood, right effort, right concentration, and right meditation.

(3) "Mahali, before, when I dwelt at the Ghosita Monastery at Kosambi, the wanderer Mandissa and the disciple of Darupattika, Jaliya, came to visit me, asking whether the soul and body were the same or different. At that time, I said, 'Jaliya, a buddha is born in this world and attains enlightenment himself, and he then teaches others. A certain person hears that teaching; rousing the mind of faith, he becomes a mendicant. Observing the precepts, he disciplines himself. He practices correctly and experiences joy. He stands in fear of even minor transgressions; guarding the entrances to the five sensory organs, he is endowed with true wisdom. He does not kill living creatures; he is filled with compassion. He does not steal; he purifies his mind. Freeing himself from lascivious acts, he does not spout lies or coarse language. He leads a spotless life; he frees himself from greed, eschews anger, and leaves drowsiness behind. His mind is free of restlessness, remorse, and doubt. He purifies his mind. Now when

that disciple practices in the manner described, he attains joy and bliss and enters meditations. Do you think that the question of whether the soul and the body are the same poses a problem for him?' Jaliya said, 'World-Honored One, that kind of problem would not arise.'

"I then said, 'Jaliya, I too perceive and view things in that way; therefore, I do not address myself to the problem of whether the soul and the body are the same or different. Jaliya, the same disciple gradually deepens his meditation, and finally his mind is filled with a feeling of purity and lucidity. His mind becomes impervious to all suffering. At that juncture, he contemplates his body; he perceives that his body is composed of physical elements and was born of his father and his mother. He perceives that he is being sustained by food, that he is not a permanent entity, and that he will eventually perish. Progressing still further, he faithfully perceives the truth of the Four Noble Truths. He is emancipated from the defilement of greed and awakens the insight that he has in fact achieved emancipation. Jaliya, that disciple perceives and sees in this manner. Do you think that he ponders over whether the soul and the body are the same or different?' Jaliya said, 'World-Honored One, he would not have that question.' I then said, 'Jaliya, I also perceive and see things in this manner; therefore, I never expound on the subject of whether the soul and body are the same or different.' Mahali, with such dialogues as these, Jaliya was satisfied with my teaching and returned home." Otthaddha and all the brahmins heard this discourse by the Buddha and rejoiced.

(4) The World-Honored One continued on with his travels, and after the year was over he entered Rajagaha and climbed the mountain called Vulture Peak. At that time, the wanderer Nigrodha and three thousand of his disciples were staying in a nearby grove that had been given to the Sangha by Queen Udumbarika. One day a lay disciple named Sandhana was on his way to visit the World-Honored One. While travelling, he thought, "The World-Honored One has withdrawn now and has entered meditation; his disciples have also followed his example. I should not visit him at this time. I think that I shall visit the wanderer Nigrodha who is at the Udumbarika Park." Sandhana then headed for that grove.

At that time, Nigrodha, surrounded by his disciples, was talking in a loud voice. They were all engaged in idle talk, exchanging stories of kings, bandits, palace ministers, armies, clothing and food, ghosts, and other random topics. Spying Sandhana in the distance as he came toward them, Nigrodha said, "Everyone, be quiet! Keep your voices down! A disciple of Gotama, Sandhana, comes toward us. Gotama's followers enjoy quiescence and praise those who are quiet. If we remain quiet, he may think that this is a quiet assembly." His disciples were quieted down by these words. Before long Sandhana arrived there and said, "Men of great virtue, it appears that you were boisterously engaged in idle talk. My teacher, the World-Honored One, sits deep in meditation in deserted and quiet forests conducive to inward contemplation."

Nigrodha said, "O lay disciple, do you know with whom Gotama talks and from whom he attains wisdom? Gotama lives in a deserted house and attains a whimsical wisdom. The wisdom that he has acquired is disjointed from tradition. Therefore he loiters forlornly in some corner. He is like a one-eyed cow wandering aimlessly along the edges of a pasture. If he were to make an appearance here, we would squelch him with one question. We would bowl him over as if he were an empty barrel."

(5) At that time, by chance, the World-Honored One was coming down from the Vulture Peak and was walking through the open spaces of the Peacock Garden, which was located near Lake Sumagadha. Nigrodha caught sight of him and quieted his cohorts and pondered over the questions that he should ask when the World-Honored One finally came to them. He prepared his mind and waited.

Finally, the World-Honored One came and sat down on the seat readied for him. He asked for what purpose they had gathered there. Nigrodha replied, "World-Honored One, I spied the World-Honored One strolling through the Peacock Garden and thought to myself that if he should come here, I should ask him about the Dharma with which he cultivates his disciples. Therefore, I have just now discontinued my own talk." The Buddha said, "Nigrodha, it would be difficult for someone like you, who differ from me in both teachings and views, to understand my teaching. Rather than this, you should clarify your own superb teaching of revulsion by asking, 'How can I perfect my ascetic practices and my revulsion toward greed?'"

(6) The wanderers who had been sitting in rows at the gathering exclaimed in a loud voice, "Gotama truly possesses great powers. Without stating his own assertions he causes his opponent to talk about his assertions." Nigrodha quieted that clamoring and said, "World-Honored One, we hold ascetic practices and revulsion toward the world to be our main doctrines. We base ourselves on these two doctrines. How can we perfect our ascetic practices and revulsion?"

The Buddha said, "Nigrodha, can it be said that you have perfected your ascetic practice and your revulsion toward the world by performing the following practices? You live naked, not following worldly conventions. Regarding foods, you refuse to go when invited to a meal even by someone practicing selfless giving. You do not heed requests to wait for food offerings. You refuse food brought to you for your sake. Fearing that you might damage the pots and pans, you refuse to accept food from the mouths of those pots and pans. You refuse to accept food especially prepared for your sake. You refuse food from a place where two people are dining. You refuse food from a pregnant woman. You refuse food from a woman who is breast-feeding. You refuse food from a place where men and women are engaged in play. You refuse food that has been gathered for your sake in time of famine. You refuse food prepared for you from a household that keeps dogs. You refuse food from a house swarming with flies. You refrain from eating fish and meat, and from imbibing any kind of liquor. You accept one mouthful of food from one household and return home. You accept two mouthfuls from two households and return home. You accept up to seven mouthfuls from up to seven households and return home. Pleased with this, you sustain yourselves with these foods. You eat one meal a day, or one meal every seven days. You observe fasts for two weeks. When you eat, you eat only wild parsley, soiled cereal husks, leftovers after the skins of animals have been stripped off, rice bran, the burnt portions left over in a pot, the dregs of rapeseed oil, cow dung, tree roots, and rotting fruits that have fallen to the ground. With regard to clothing, you wrap yourselves in hemp and other coarse cloths, in rags picked out of trash bins, in tree bark, animal hide, grass, or cloth woven with human hair or with tail feathers and ordinary feathers. You practice plucking out your beards and hair. You practice standing continuously for long periods. You practice continuous squatting. You practice lying on beds of thorns. You practice sleeping out on the great earth. You practice smearing your bodies with oil. You practice being covered over with dust and sleeping habitually on your side. You practice eating unclean things, not drinking water, and immersing yourself in water." Nigrodha said, "World-Honored One, I should think that I have attained perfection of these ascetic practices."

(7) The Buddha said, "I shall now point out the stains that come out of the ascetic practices and revulsion toward the world that you believe you have perfected. Let us say that an ascetic has accomplished ascetic practices. Because of this, he experiences joy and pride that he has accomplished ascetic practices. This is the first stain. Next, because he has faithfully fulfilled the ascetic practices, he elevates himself and disparages others. This is the second stain. Next, he becomes drunk with joy and pride at having undergone these ascetic practices. At the same time, he slides into negligence. This is the third stain. Next, by virtue of these ascetic practices, he receives fame, veneration, and profit, and he rejoices. This is the fourth stain. Next, because he has received fame, veneration, and profit, he elevates himself and disparages others. This is the fifth stain. Next, he becomes drunk with fame and profit and slides into negligence. This is the sixth stain. Next, he begins gradually to pick and choose his food; he rouses attachment to food and fails to see the evil in that. This is the seventh stain. Next, he gradually inflates his fame and profit, expecting everyone, kings and ministers included, to venerate him. This is the eighth stain. Next, he looks at other mendicants and rebukes them, saying that they are extravagant and allow themselves to eat any kind of food. This is the ninth stain. Next, he notices other mendicants receiving offerings and rouses feelings of jealousy, thinking, 'In this household, they make offerings to such extravagant people while failing to venerate a true ascetic like me.' This is the tenth stain. Next, he begins to practice in places that are watched by people. This is the eleventh stain. Next, he flaunts his virtues; visiting lay households, he boasts that these virtues are only one small part of his ascetic practices. This is the twelfth stain. Next, he begins to lie, claiming that he is able to bear that which in fact he is unable to bear. And he claims, on the other hand, that he is not able to bear that which is bearable. This is the thirteenth stain. Next, he disapproves of the Dharma taught by the Buddha and his disciples. This is the fourteenth stain. Next, he harbors anger and hatred and rouses the defilements of concealment, arrogance, jealousy, parsimony, deception, fraudulence, stupidity, pride, evil desires and so forth; he becomes shackled by this world. This is the fifteenth stain. Nigrodha, if the above is true, then ascetic practices and revulsion toward the world have stains that

befoul the disciple. Even if they do not have stains, these practices of asceticism and revulsion toward the world are not the ultimate stages of enlightenment.

"That ascetic continues on and refrains from killing, stealing, lying, and indulgence in the five desires. He keeps the precepts of the four restraints, withdraws to a secluded place, and sits in meditation. He frees himself from the five coverings that conceal enlightenment, desires, anger, drowsiness, agitation and remorse, and doubt. With the four boundless minds of affection, compassion, joy, and equanimity he fills all worlds. Next, recalling his past lives, he perceives his karmas; he perceives the differences that exist among people and acquires the power to read their minds. Nigrodha, having attained this stage, for the first time, asceticism and revulsion toward the world reach their ultimate stage. At the outset you asked me about the teaching with which I cultivate my disciples and by which my disciples are comforted. My teaching far exceeds the teachings of asceticism and revulsion toward the world."

When he expounded this Dharma, the wanderers who had been sitting in rows shouted out, "There is no teacher who surpasses this teacher; there is no one who is equal to him." They praised the Buddha from the bottom of their hearts.

(8) At that time, Sandhana said, "Venerable Nigrodha, in my presence you have disagreed with the World-Honored One in a number of different ways. So you ought to bowl over the World-Honored One like an empty barrel, as you said you would." Hearing this, Nigrodha hung his head and was not able to respond. The World-Honored One asked, "Nigrodha, is what Sandhana says true?" Nigrodha felt distressed and expressed contrition over his errors, saying, "World-Honored One, my mind was in disarray, so I did utter such things." The Buddha said, "Nigrodha, did you hear teachers say, 'Enlightened Ones of antiquity assembled a large number of disciples and in loud voices indulged themselves in idle talk over stories of kings, ministers, bandits, armies, and so forth?' Or did you hear them say, 'Enlightened Ones of antiquity sat in meditation in quiet and secluded forests suitable for contemplation?'" Nigrodha said, "World-Honored One, I heard them say the latter." The Buddha said, "Nigrodha, while you possess wisdom and right thought and are a mature man, why do you not say, 'The World-Honored One has attained enlightenment, and for the sake of enlightenment he expounds the path. Disciplining himself, he expounds the Dharma so that others may discipline themselves; putting an end to his defilements, he expounds the Dharma for the sake of putting an end to others' defilements. He has crossed over to the other shore of enlightenment and, for the sake of others' salvation, expounds the Dharma; he has entered nirvana, and to help others enter nirvana he expounds the Dharma.'" Nigrodha said, "World-Honored One, being ignorant and with my mind in disarray, I was overcome by transgressions. Please help me to refrain from repeating the same transgressions again by forgiving me my transgressions."

The Buddha said, "Nigrodha, without doubt, your mind was in disarray, and you were overcome by transgressions. So that you will, in the days ahead, discipline yourself, I shall forgive your transgressions. Nigrodha, I say this to you, 'Come forth, you who possess wisdom, you who neither deceive nor defraud others. You with an upright mind, I now expound the Dharma. Should you follow and practice this Dharma, you will accomplish the mendicant's goal in seven years, or in one year, or in seven days.' Nigrodha, you should not think, 'Gotama speaks in this manner because he wants to make me his disciple, because he wants to chase us out of this area, because he wants to deprive us of our livelihood, or because he wants to make us depart from the good and to go to the evil.' Regard your teacher as your teacher; regard your place as your place; regard your livelihood as your livelihood. I expound the Dharma so that you may cast off the ways that create the seeds that will lead you into a delusory cycle of births and deaths. If you train yourself in this way, your defiled ways will go away; your pure elements will increase; and you will be able to manifest perfect wisdom."

The throng of wanderers who had crowded around the Buddha remained silent and cast their eyes downward. Appearing restless, they sat there. The World-Honored One, with compassion, cast his eyes on these hollow men, who were entrapped by evil demons and who had no inclination to undertake practice for the sake of attaining nirvana, even for seven days. He looked upon them with pity and returned to the Vulture Peak.

3. The Universal Monarch

(1) Then the World-Honored One travelled throughout the country of Magadha and finally stopped at Matula. There he taught his disciples, "Disciples, be lamps unto yourselves; be refuges unto yourselves. Consider the Dharma your lamp and refuge. You should not take others to be your lamp or refuge. Exert yourselves with diligence, and adhere to right thought. Perceive that your bodies are impure, that everything that you undergo is suffering, that your minds are in flux, and that all things are devoid of a permanent self. Should you perceive these truths, free yourselves from worldly greed, and take leave of sorrow, you yourself and the Dharma will become lamps and refuges. Do not take others to be your lamp or refuge.

(2) "Disciples, when you travel, travel through the lands of your ancestors. Evil demons will not have an opportunity to take advantage of you, and your merits will multiply. Disciples, in the distant past, there was a universal monarch named Dalhanemi. First he ruled his own country justly. Then he subjugated the surrounding areas. He was endowed with these seven treasures: the wheel treasure, the elephant treasure, the horse treasure, the jewel treasure, the treasure of a woman of gemlike beauty, the treasure of a lay Buddhist counselor, and the treasure of a general. He also had one thousand children of extraordinary bravery who all possessed the strength to crush their enemies. In order to subjugate this world, which was bounded by oceans, he did not resort to the sword or to the bamboo cane. Instead, the king subjugated this world by the Dharma. Once Dalhanemi said to his officials in attendance, "If the wheel treasure moves from that spot, report it to me." After several thousand years had passed, the wheel treasure started to move away from that spot. Therefore the king's officials

reported it to the king. The king sent for his heir apparent and said, 'I have heard that should the wheel treasure move, my end would not be far off. As for the pleasures of this world, I have tasted them all to my heart's content. Now I seek those pleasures that are holy. I am going to become a mendicant and seek the way. You must be my successor.' The king then became a mendicant. Seven days later, the wheel treasure disappeared.

"The heir apparent learned of this and, grieving, went to his father's secluded retreat. He said, 'My father the king, the wheel treasure has disappeared.' The king said, 'Dear son, though the wheel treasure may have disappeared, it is not worth grieving over. That wheel treasure is not the legacy that I bequeath to you. Should you practice the true Dharma of a universal monarch, and climb up the many-tiered mansion and wash your head on the day of the fast on the fifteenth day of the month, you will be endowed with one thousand wheels and axles. You will witness the appearance of your wheel treasure adorned with perfect embellishments.' The son said, 'My father the king, what is the true Dharma of a universal monarch?' The king said, 'Rely on the Dharma. Venerate the Dharma; make the Dharma your banner; and find a guardian and a protector in the Dharma. Within your kingdom, make certain that there is no injustice. Return and bestow riches on those without riches; free yourself from pride and negligence. Practice both forbearance and gentleness. Discipline yourself. If there are mendicants who are advancing toward nirvana, go to them and listen to their discourses on the way. Free yourself from unwholesomeness and be joined with wholesomeness. Dear son, this is the true Dharma of a universal monarch.'

(3) "The heir apparent, who had now become the king, accepted the injunctions of his father. He practiced the Dharma of a universal monarch. On the fifteenth day of the month, on the day of the fast, he washed his head and climbed up the many-tiered mansion. There he witnessed the appearance of the wheel treasure and became a universal monarch. The king stood up from his seat; he draped his robes on one shoulder. In his left hand, he took up a gold jar; and with his right hand, he poured water onto the wheel treasure. While doing so, he shouted, 'Wheel treasure, turn! Wheel treasure, subjugate!' Immediately, the wheel treasure began to spin in an easterly direction. The king organized four armies and followed the wheel treasure. At the spot where the wheel treasure came to a halt, the king also stopped his carriage. The kings of the eastern quarters hurried over to the newly arrived king and greeted him joyfully, 'Great king, all is yours; we beseech you to impart your teachings to us.' The king said, 'You must not kill. You must not steal. You must free yourselves from lascivious acts. You must not spew out lies. You must refrain from imbibing liquors. You must restrain yourselves with regard to food.' He then subjugated all the countries in the east. The wheel treasure rolled into the ocean of the eastern quarter and once again came up onto land. It rolled southward, westward, and northward and showed the way for the king's subjugation of the people. It pacified the four oceans and returned to the royal palace. Like the embellishments of the king's inner palace, it halted at the most proper spot.

(4) "Disciples, the second universal monarch also pacified the four oceans in that manner. The third, fourth, fifth, sixth, and seventh universal monarchs also pacified the countries in that manner. When the seventh king became a mendicant, the heir apparent did not ask the universal monarch about the true Dharma, nor did he try to practice it. Because of this, there was a decrease in the population. The king's retainers became concerned over this and admonished the king. The king then listened to the Dharma of the universal monarch and also practiced it. However, he was remiss in the practice of returning riches to those who had been deprived of their wealth. Because of this neglect, the poor became poorer and also increased in number. People began to steal. Other people caught these thieves and brought them before the king. The king heard that these thieves had stolen only to survive, and he returned the riches to the thieves. He instructed the thieves to live just lives with the riches that now belonged to them. He instructed them to take good care of their parents, wives, and children, to perform good deeds, to give freely to mendicants, and to be born in the celestial realms. By leaps and bounds the number of thieves increased, and every one of them stole so that they might receive riches from the king. The king thought, 'As long as I give riches to those who steal, thieves will continue to increase in number. In order to stop and uproot such culprits, next time I will cut their heads off.' The king sent down this order to his men. When the next thief was caught, he was tied up. His head was shaved; he was dragged around the marketplace; and at the decapitation grounds on the outskirts of the town, his head was cut off.

"The townspeople learned of this, and in an attempt to uproot the thieves each readied himself with a sword. Because of this, raids on villages and towns multiplied. Because the king had failed to provide riches to the impoverished, the number of poor people grew larger. The number of thieves multiplied; swords came to be; and the taking of lives increased. Lies came to be; as a result, lives were shortened and people's statures became smaller. Informants appeared on the scene. Words that break up friendships proliferated. There were more and more people given to lascivious deeds; evil views began to appear. Greed and anger abounded; Dharmalessness and evil dharmas spread. People's life spans were gradually shortened.

(5) "As a consequence of Dharmalessness and evil dharmas growing rampant, in the end people's life spans will be merely ten years. Fresh butter, yogurt, sugar, and salt will all become depleted, and poppy will become a staple food. The ten virtues will disappear, and only the ten evils will exist. Because virtues will disappear, there will be no one who practices virtues. No one will practice filial piety toward his parents. No one will make offerings to mendicants. No one will serve the head of the household. As all human relations break down, there will be no such thing as mother, aunt, the teacher's wife or the elder's wife. Everywhere people will begin to act like dogs and foxes. Raging and murderous thoughts will arise toward each other. Mothers will turn on their children, children on their fathers, elder brothers on their younger brothers, and elder sisters on their younger sisters. Like the deer hunter who spots a deer,

they will harbor violent and murderous thoughts. In the end, for seven days, they will thrust their swords at each other while yelling, 'This is a deer! This is a deer!'

"Disciples, at that time, some of those people will be repelled by this mutual slaughter. For seven days, they will hide themselves in the underbrush and the thickets of the forest, or in mountain caves. After seven days have passed, they will emerge from their hiding places, and looking at and embracing each other they will congratulate each other, shouting, 'Look, we're alive! We're alive!' All of these people will understand that this tragic event came about because they were seized by evil. They will understand that they should, from now on, revert to virtue and begin to practice virtue. Because of their practice of virtue, their life spans will increase. Their bodies will grow larger, and they will gradually desist from Dharmalessness and evil dharmas. They will extinguish both greed and anger, free themselves from evil views, rid themselves of words that destroy friendships, and put a stop to lying. As a result, the life span, which had shrunk to ten years, will expand to eighty thousand years; a person's daughter will become a bride at five thousand years of age. Disciples, at this time, in the world of human beings, there will only be three types of illnesses: craving, not being able to eat, and old age. The world's population will grow like a forest of reeds or sala trees; the town of present-day Baranasi will become a metropolis called Ketumati. Its king, Sankha, as a king of the Dharma, will subjugate the surrounding areas. Endowed with the seven treasures, he will become a universal monarch.

(6) "Disciples, Maitreya will appear during the reign of this king and, like myself, he will realize enlightenment. Like myself, he will expound the Dharma and will lead several thousand disciples. King Sankha will ascend to the platform for celebrations built by King Mahapanada. There he will conduct a great gathering for selfless giving. He will become a mendicant, a disciple of Maitreya; and, exerting himself with great intensity, he will attain enlightenment, the goal of all mendicants.

"Disciples, be lamps unto yourselves; be refuges unto yourselves. Take the Dharma as your lamp and refuge. Do not take other people as your lamp or refuge. Disciples, when you travel, travel through the land of your ancestors. By virtue of so doing, you will heighten your life span, appearance, joy, treasures, and strength.

"Disciples, to heighten one's life span is to practice the four divine powers, namely, those of desire, exertion, mind, and thought, and to remain in this world as long as one wishes. To heighten one's appearance means to obey the precepts, to practice virtues, to fear even minor transgressions, and to be diligent in one's studies. To heighten one's joy means to enter a host of meditations and to experience the joy of meditation. To heighten one's treasures is to live while fulfilling the aspirations of all places with the four boundless minds of compassion, mercy, joy, and equanimity. To heighten one's strength is to exhaust the defilements and manifest enlightenment in this present world.

"Disciples, in this world there is nothing more difficult to conquer than the power of a demon. And yet, by preserving good dharmas, merits are heightened to the point that we are able to conquer the power of demons."

(7) From there, the World-Honored One went to Baranasi and stopped at the Deer Park. One morning, when he was making his rounds begging for food in the town of Baranasi, he spied under a fig tree a lone disciple whose mind had become deranged and who was not able to hold onto right thought. Thereupon, the Buddha said, "Disciple, you should not befoul yourself with impurities. Flies are swarming around your body, which is the nesting place for impurities." Hearing the words of the World-Honored One, the disciple became despondent and filled with anguish.

Before long, the World-Honored One returned to the Deer Park and said to his disciples, "Disciples, this morning, while making my rounds begging for food, I saw a disciple whose mind had become deranged and who was unable to hold onto right thought, and I said, 'Disciple, you should not befoul yourself with impurities. Flies are swarming around your body, which is the nesting place for impurities.' Disciples, by impurities, I mean greed. By the nesting place of impurities, I mean anger. By flies, I mean unvirtuous, evil thoughts. The flies of unvirtuous, evil thoughts will always swarm around those who befoul themselves with the impurity of greed and have become the nesting place of anger."

4. The Practice of Samantabhadra

(1) The World-Honored One once again returned to the mountain called Vulture Peak from the Deer Park, and there he was surrounded by a large number of his disciples. At that time, the Bodhisattva Samantabhadra addressed the large assembly and said, "Children of the Buddha, the bodhisattvas have perceived that all things have no names and no real substance; they are devoid of a self-nature; they neither come nor go and are devoid of a permanent entity. Therefore bodhisattvas are not held in bondage by either conventional truths or the absolute truth. Their minds are not held in bondage randomly by the forms of things; they do not become attached to the names of things; and they follow the quiescent nature of things. Moreover, they do not abandon all aspirations; in accordance with the absolute truth, they expound myriad dharmas with skillful means. They guide the people, and there is no end to their eloquence. From a wordless realm, they bring forth words. Furthermore, without destroying the nature of words, they apprehend all words and guide people. Eliminating doubts and in accordance with the season, they rain down the rain of the Dharma.

"Children of the Buddha, should bodhisattvas hear the true Dharma and, without being startled and without fear, hold onto their faith in the Dharma, joyfully follow it, cultivate it, and rest in it, they will attain the wisdom of sound, that is, the enlightenment of being in conformity with sound. Again, if, in conformity with quiescence, they perceive the equality of all dharmas, discern all things with a pure and true mind, and penetrate deeply into the nature of all things, they will attain the wisdom of being in accord, that is, the enlightenment of being in accord with the nature of all things. Again, advancing still further, they will no longer perceive the arising and perishing of things. Rather, they will perceive that things neither arise nor perish; that since there is no arising, there is no perishing; that since there is no perishing, things are never exhausted; that since they are never exhausted, they are free of the stain of defilements; that since they are free of this stain, they are never destroyed; and that since they are not destroyed, they are immovable. This is the realm in which defilements have become quiescent and extinguished. In this realm there is neither desire nor practice. This is the great vow. They live amidst the embellishments of the Buddha's country. This is the third wisdom called the wisdom of non-arising Dharma.

(2) "Children of the Buddha, a bodhisattva understands that the Buddha's voice does not come from the inside, the outside, or the inside and the outside together. He does not seek that voice within or without, or both together. The Buddha's voice, like an echo, arises from causes and conditions. A bodhisattva perceives that once the Buddha's voice manifests itself, it rains down the gift of the Dharma. In this way, he penetrates deep into the mystery of sound. He frees himself from the error of being held in bondage by voices, and he diligently studies all things.

(i)　All things are created by the mind; they are as empty as phantoms. Bodhisattvas awaken to the non-reality of everything and understand that all things are like myriad figures produced by an illusionist who enchants people. Although the Buddha views all things as being phantoms, he makes a great vow, he assumes the role of a guide, and, with Great Compassion of the greatest extent, he purifies people. Because all things are phantoms, purity manifests itself in this world, and it remains there because of the power of the phantoms.

(ii) Wisdom is as full as space and removes all obstructions. Since space is free of all forms, it has no impurities. The world is also like this, and so is wisdom. Space has no self-nature and cannot be destroyed. It has no beginning, no middle, no end, and no differentiated appearance. Wisdom also does not assume an illusory form. It is inexhaustible and boundless.

(iii) In each and every strand of hair, an infinite number of pure countries are contained. They are embellished with an infinite number of treasures. They have an infinite number of names and expound an infinite number of dharmas. Therefore the Buddha expounds those verses that are difficult to expound and that never cease. He expounds the truth that cannot be expounded. With each voice, he turns the Wheel of the Dharma that cannot be taught. And with each turn of the Wheel of the Dharma, he rains down the teaching that cannot be taught. It is difficult to expound the true nature of things. It is also difficult to worship the Buddha. It is equally difficult to know each and every skillful means. Only those who truly follow the Dharma enter the nature of a Buddha.

(3) "Children of the Buddha, the Buddha has Great Compassion within and never forsakes anyone. The Buddha's mind is free of the suffering of defilements. He gazes upon people and, seizing the moment, serenely harmonizes them. He destroys a host of evil demons and crushes a myriad of false paths. He enters all worlds and, guiding the people there, gladdens those who see him and bestows

benefits on them. If there are those who contemplate in the right way, the Buddha immediately appears before them and cultivates their roots of merit. Seizing the moment for teaching the Dharma, he, with the power of absolute freedom, constantly assumes different bodies and universally expounds the Dharma for the sake of people. Furthermore, the Buddha, with the eye's field of consciousness, performs the Buddha's work in the ear's field of consciousness; and with the ear's field of consciousness, he performs the Buddha's work in the eye's field of consciousness. The six sensory organs interfuse perfectly; in all fields of consciousness, the Buddha performs his work. The Buddha is a storehouse of inexhaustible merits. He causes people to rouse the mind of faith and gladdens their hearts. He causes those who have not roused the mind of the way to rouse the mind of the way. For those who have roused such a mind, he endows them with wisdom; he causes them to become enlightened without relying on others. Again, he teaches people to feel revulsion for the world and to conform to the Buddha's mind. He teaches the brevity of life and the absence of real pleasure in the world. He teaches that should one contemplate the Buddha with a pure mind, one will see the Buddha. He removes a large number of sufferings and causes people to rouse the pure way of the Buddha. He embraces all people and has them enter the profound realm of the buddhas. As for the negligent ones, he has them cherish the pure precepts.

"When those in hell are suffused by the Buddha's light and are about to be born in the Tusita heaven at the end of their lives, they hear wondrous, divine voices. These voices say to them, 'O children of the gods, you should go and worship the Buddha. When this world ends, even Mount Sumeru will be consumed and reduced to ashes by fire. Like this, even the mind of the five desires will be consumed and obliterated by fire if you contemplate the Buddha. You should know your debt of gratitude and venerate the Buddha. If you remain ignorant of your debt of gratitude, when your life draws to a close you must once again enter hell. Since you all dwelt in hell and have been benefitted by the light, you are about to be born in this celestial realm. Therefore, you should cultivate your roots of merit.'"

(4) At that time, the gods heard this, rejoiced, and asked, "How do bodhisattvas repent their errors?" The Bodhisattva Samantabhadra said, "Children of the gods, karmic obstructions do not enter from the outside to congregate in the mind; rather, they originate from inverted views. The action of greed, anger, and ignorance, in truth, has no real substance. Regardless of where you look, you will not be able to find its substance. Just as voices neither arise nor perish, all actions neither arise nor perish. But this does not mean that actions do not exist. People do receive their rewards in accordance with their actions. In a crystal mirror, an infinite number of figures are reflected; however, those figures neither come from outside the mirror nor do they go out of the mirror. Likewise, all actions lack a real substance; they neither come nor go. And yet they produce a myriad of karmic fruits. Should you perceive things in this manner, you are called one who is pure and true in his contrition over his errors.

"In the past, countless buddhas emitted great light and illuminated the countries of the ten directions. Receiving the illumination, bodhisattvas made vows, saying, 'I shall become a lamp unto this world. I shall adorn my body with merits and attain the wisdom of all the buddhas.

"'The people of this world burn with the fires of greed, anger, and ignorance. For their sake I shall extinguish the endless suffering of the evil path.'

"Having made this vow, they cultivated the bodhisattva practices resolutely, without retrogression, and attained a power that penetrates all things without any obstruction."

(5) At that time, from the white curl of hair between the Buddha's eyebrows, the Light That Illuminates the Buddha's Doctrine shot forth and shone universally on all worlds. It awakened the mind's eye of an infinite number of people; it destroyed the sufferings of all evil paths. Returning, it went around shining on a large assembly and entered the peak of a certain Bodhisattva's crown. That Bodhisattva said on behalf of the large assembly whose minds rejoiced, "Samantabhadra, we beseech you to manifest for us the expansive and infinite Dharma of the Origin of the Tathagata."

The Bodhisattva Samantabhadra answered, "Children of the Buddha, the Dharma of the Origin of the Tathagata cannot be conceived. That Dharma is ineffable because the Tathagata attained enlightenment by virtue of an infinitely large number of causes and conditions and then manifested himself in this world. That is, rousing infinite wisdom, he does not forsake all beings. For an infinitely long period of time, he practices the roots of merit with a true mind. With infinite compassion, he saves people. Pursuing infinite right practices without abandoning his great vow, he manifests the wisdom that employs an infinite number of skillful means with which he expounds the true meaning of the Dharma. He is like the clouds that pour down rain; no one is able to calculate the number of raindrops that fall.

"Children of the Buddha, raindrops are of one taste and yet, depending on where they happen to fall, there are differences in taste. The water of the Buddha's Great Compassion is also of one taste; however, since the Buddha manifests himself in accordance with the various potentials of all people, his manifestations are not uniformly the same. As for the Dharma of the Origin of the Buddha, it originates with the universal wisdom of all buddhas. Moreover, that wisdom that is of one taste produces infinite merits. People think that these merits are produced by the Buddha. But these merits are not products of the Buddha's efforts.

"Even a bodhisattva must implant roots of merit at the place of a Buddha; otherwise, he will not be able to attain even paltry wisdom. Because all buddhas, for the sake of all people, become good teachers, they attain great wisdom. There is ultimately nothing that is produced, and there is no one to produce these merits that come into being as the result of a coalescence of causes and conditions.

(6) "Children of the Buddha, Great Compassion becomes people's refuge, and Great Compassion saves people. Great Compassion is dependent on the

Buddha's wisdom of skillful means; the wisdom of skillful means is dependent on the Buddha. Furthermore, the Buddha does not depend on anything. Emitting the light of unobstructed wisdom, universally he shines upon the worlds of the ten directions.

"Children of the Buddha, as for the Dharma of the Origins of the Buddha, its practice is infinite; therefore its merit is infinite also. Since it neither comes nor goes, it fills the ten directions. Because it has no corporeal body, it is free of such bodies and consciousness. Because all things are equal for it, it is equal to the sky, which does not differentiate. Because it is inexhaustible, all people are freed of 'I' and 'mine'. Because it does not change, all countries never come to an end. Because it does not withdraw, future existence continues without a break. Because buddhas view all dharmas equally, their wisdom is unobstructed. Because they make the original vow and gladden all people at will, their enlightenment of equality benefits all people."

The Bodhisattva Samantabhadra then said in verse,

> Things do not change; they are empty and free of defilements. They are like space.

> Like all things, buddhas are also empty; they neither exist nor do not exist.

> The true Dharma transcends the way of words and is quiescent. The objects of cognition also transcend the way of words. They are quiescent like the sky that is devoid of birds' footprints.

> Amidst this quiescence, as a reward for his boundless vows, the pure body of the Buddha dwells; there, it manifests great inconceivableness.

> Therefore if you wish to perceive the profound Dharma of the Buddha, purify your heart until it is like space.

> Free yourself from delusory thoughts and evil views, and practice the way of purity; then you will attain a pure mind.

(7) "Children of the Buddha, the sun comes up and destroys the darkness. It nurtures all things and removes the cold. It shines in the sky and benefits the people. It shines upon lakes and causes the lotus flowers to bloom. It reveals the colors and forms of all things. It causes myriad worldly phenomena to be seen as they are. The reason for this is that the sun emits an infinite light. Like this, the Buddha also destroys evil and nurtures the good; the light of his wisdom removes the darkness of the people, and his Great Compassion benefits all beings and causes them to attain enlightenment."

The Bodhisattva Samantabhadra said in verse,

(i)   The sun comes up and first shines upon lofty peaks. It then turns to the other mountains. It shines upon hills and valleys and finally the world's great earth.

> The light of the Buddha's wisdom first shines upon those with superior minds and gradually turns to other people.

However, the light of wisdom is never conscious of such thoughts as, 'I am shining on the minds of the people.'

When the bright sun appears in the world, the blind man is unable to see it. However, the sun relaxes his body and he experiences pleasure.

Like the sun, the Buddha also emerges in this world and benefits even those who are blind to faith. These spiritually blind people, hearing the Buddha's voice and being touched by his light, will eventually attain wisdom.

(ii) The Buddha's voice naturally fills the Dharmadhatu, and nowhere is his voice not heard.

Should the people hear his voice, they will forever escape the ocean of delusion.

It is like an echo. If one shouts in a valley, the canyon resounds with an echo. Since this echo is produced because of manifold conditions, those who hear it hear it in manifold ways. But the echo itself does not think, 'I am creating different kinds of sound.'

The Buddha roars forth with an infinite sound in accordance with the needs of the people of the valleys and thereby saves them.

(8) "Children of the Buddha, how is the Buddha's mind to be perceived? The Buddha's mind is to be perceived only as infinite wisdom. The Buddha's wisdom is the basis of all other wisdoms; it itself has no other basis. Space is the basis of all things; however, space itself has no basis. The four great oceans water the lands of the four continents and the many islands. Therefore, if someone seeks water, he should be able to find water wherever he goes. However, the great ocean never rouses the thought, 'I bestow water on all things.' Likewise, the wisdom of the Buddha also waters people's minds. If these people, in accordance with the ways of their respective teachings, should practice the roots of merit, they will all attain the light of wisdom. But the Buddha never rouses the thought, 'I bestow wisdom on the people.'

"Children of the Buddha, there is nowhere that the wisdom of the Buddha does not reach. The reason for this is that there is no one who is not endowed with the Buddha's wisdom. It is merely that people think in an inverted manner and are ignorant of the Buddha's wisdom. Should they free themselves from inverted thoughts, they would rouse omniscience, the wisdom that perceives that all things are without form, the wisdom that is free from all obstructions. Those who are ignorant are merely covered over by inverted thoughts and remain oblivious to the Buddha's wisdom. They do not perceive it and fail to rouse the mind of faith. The Buddha perceives all people with the unobstructed celestial eye and says, 'Strange indeed! Strange indeed! Why is it that people, while possessing the Buddha's wisdom within themselves, remain ignorant of it? I shall teach them and awaken them to the Path of the Holy One. I shall free them forever from delusion and cause them to perceive that the Buddha's wisdom exists within themselves and that they are not different from the Buddha.'

(i) Thusness is never exhausted. It neither arises nor perishes. Since there is nothing to hold on to, there is no way to seek it. Likewise, the realm of the buddhas is immeasurable. It transcends the three periods, and its nature is Thusness.

(ii) When a bird flies through space, it is difficult to measure the space where it has flown and the space where it has not flown, even if one measures for a hundred thousand years. Should someone expound the Buddha's practice over an infinitely long period, it would be difficult to gauge what he had and had not expounded.

(iii) The golden bird Garuda, who has a wing span of thirty million miles, gazed down from space upon the palace of the dragon king. Spreading his wings, he burst apart the ocean waters and plucked out the dragon who was about to lose his life.

(iv) Likewise, the Buddha dwells in the practice of the buddhas, and with the wings of concentration and insight he bursts apart the ocean waters of desires. He plucks out of the ocean of defilements those whose roots of merit have come to fruition.

(v) Again, the sun and the moon travel through space and give pleasure to people. However, they are free from thoughts of doing so. The Buddha, who roams throughout the myriad Dharmadhatus and saves all beings, is also free from thoughts of saving others.

(9) "Children of the Buddha, the wisdom of the Buddha knows all principles; it destroys doubts. Freeing himself from the two extremes, the Buddha dwells in the middle path. He transcends all words and languages; he perceives the minds of all people, their actions, their defilements, and their conventions. In each moment of thought, he perceives all the dharmas of the three periods. All forms and images are reflected in the great ocean; because of this, the ocean is called Reflection. In the same way, in the ocean of enlightenment of the Buddha's wisdom, the thoughts and perceptions of all people are reflected. And yet there is nowhere for these images to be reflected. Therefore the Buddha is called Universal Wisdom.

"Children of the Buddha, when the Buddha attains enlightenment, by virtue of skillful means he attains a body that is equal to that of all people. He attains a body that is equal to all dharmas, to all countries, to all three periods, to all buddhas, to all languages, to all Dharmadhatus, and to the nirvana world. Moreover, both his mind and his voice are identical with his body. Regard all letters and words as expressions of the turning of the Wheel of the Dharma, for there is nowhere that the Buddha's voice does not reach. Again, know that the Wheel of the Dharma is like an echo, and that it neither comes nor goes, for the Wheel of the Dharma is none other than the true and real Dharma nature. Again, know that all sounds are of one voice, for with that one voice, the Buddha turns the Wheel of the Dharma.

"Children of the Buddha, the Buddha appeared in the world only to gladden people. He manifests nirvana so that people, seeing that the Buddha has passed away, may grieve and adore him ever increasingly. In truth, the Buddha neither appears in the world nor enters nirvana. The reason is that the Buddha, like the Dharma world, is eternal.

"Children of the Buddha, even though the sun shines on the world and casts its image on the water of a certain vessel, it does not think to itself, 'I cast my image in all waters that are pure.' Should the vessel break up, the sun's image no longer would appear there, but this would not be the sun's fault; rather, it would be due to the vessel having broken up. The sun of the Buddha's perfect wisdom manifests itself in one moment of thought. It shines upon all worlds and peoples and takes away their defilements and manifests itself in the vessel of the pure mind. Broken vessels and people with muddied minds never see the Dharmakaya of the Buddha. Therefore, when the people notice the Buddha's disappearance, they are especially startled and, for the first time, are saved, because they see beyond the body of the Buddha that appears and disappears and perceive the absolute Dharmakaya of the Buddha. It is for this reason that the Buddha manifests nirvana. But in truth, the Buddha neither arises nor perishes, nor does he conceal himself for a long time. If a great conflagration spreads throughout the world and burns away the grass and trees, and if that fire reaches an area in which there are no grass, trees, towns, or villages, that fire will of itself die out. This, however, does not mean that fire has disappeared from the world. Likewise, the Buddha burns with the fires of salvation throughout all the worlds; and at places where the grass of salvation is nowhere to be seen, he manifests nirvana. However, this does not mean that the Buddha has disappeared from the world.

(10) "Children of the Buddha, he who has taken on the Buddha's mind enters into the people's practices, spanning the three periods, past, present, and future. He enters into their practices both good and bad. He saves all people, and in order to bear suffering in place of all these people, he rouses the mind of Great Compassion. Again, so that he will let go of all his possessions, he regards selfless giving as being primary in importance. So that he will seek all Buddha dharmas, he regards meditations on universal wisdom as being primary in importance. He then contemplates, 'The mind is the basis of enlightenment. If the mind is pure, one becomes filled with all the roots of merit. Should the mind become free, one will attain supreme wisdom, accomplish great practices, fulfill all vows, and serve as a guide to all people.' This is called the practice of Samantabhadra.

"Children of the Buddha, he who has taken on the Buddha's mind acquires freedom in all realms. While dwelling in the realm of enlightenment, he appears in the realm of delusion. While dwelling in the realm in which defilements have been pacified, he does not abandon the human realm, which is in turmoil because of defilements. He rouses the vow of Great Compassion and Wisdom and is born in this muddied world in order to do works of compassion for the people. Once there, he becomes deeply involved in secular matters that arise from desires, and he maintains a householder's life with wife, children, and clansmen. He does so because he exclusively desires to teach and benefit people. He thinks, 'Even though I live amidst these defilements, I should not become deluded with regard to wisdom, emancipation, meditation, and so forth, because one who has taken on the Buddha's mind should attain freedom amidst all dharmas, attain tranquillity in wisdom, undergo practices, and reach the shore of enlightenment.'

"Moreover, his mind is endowed with all the wisdoms; it is firm and upright and is beautified with great adornment. Therefore, even in places that are not conducive to practicing the way or where there are evil people, he never loses the gem of universal wisdom. He is like the water gem known as Pure Light, which not only remains unchanged as to its nature even in muddied water but also thoroughly purifies that muddied water.

(11) "Children of the Buddha, that person has the power to burn. Because he successfully guides others, he is said to consume the human world in flames. Because he burns away impurity and purifies it, he is said to burn up the material world. Because he completes all the practices, he is said to burn up the Buddha. Because he accumulates a host of merits and virtuous forms, he is said to burn up the roots of merit. Because he destroys the sufferings of all people and has them dwell restfully in supreme pleasure, he is said to burn away Great Compassion. Because he clearly perceives all dharmas, he is said to burn away all dharmas.

"Children of the Buddha, he also has numerous arms. He believes wholeheartedly in the true Dharma of the Buddha; therefore, he has the arm of faith. He gladdens all those who seek; therefore, he has the arm that is not attached to treasures. Without end, he nurtures his merits and never tires of doing so; therefore, he has the arm of making offerings to all the buddhas. He destroys the doubts that people may harbor; therefore, he has the arm that attains enlightenment quickly and listens to the Dharma widely. He saves those who are cast adrift on the stream of defilement; therefore, he has the arm that dwells restfully in the enlightened realm. He destroys the darkness of defilement and manifests the light of the Dharma that is difficult to measure; therefore, he has the arm of the treasure of wisdom.

"Children of the Buddha, when that person seeks the Dharma, his mind is sincere; he frees himself from falsity and flattery. He exerts himself with diligence and is not neglectful; he is unsparing of both his body and his life. Moreover, he never seeks the means to maintain his livelihood, nor does he work for the sake of profit. He seeks the Dharma only to extirpate the defilements of the people and to benefit them; he seeks the Dharma so that he can enter deeply into wisdom, destroy all doubts, and fulfill the Buddha-Dharma.

(12) "Children of the Buddha, this person is assaulted by ten different kinds of demons: first, the demon of the body and mind that causes one to become attached to one's body and mind; second, the demon of defilement through which one becomes stained with defilements; third, the demon of karma that rouses obstructions; fourth, the demon of the mind that rouses the mind of arrogant pride; fifth, the demon of death that separates one from this world; sixth, the

demon of the heavens that causes the mind to become proud and negligent; seventh, the demon of losing the roots of merit that takes away the mind of contrition; eighth, the demon of deep meditation through which one becomes attached to meditation; ninth, the demon of the good teacher through which one becomes attached to one's spiritual guide; and tenth, the demon of the ignorance of the wisdom of the true Dharma through which one is unable to give birth to any vows. Children of the Buddha, with the use of skillful means, you should quickly distance yourself from such demons.

"Children of the Buddha, these demons are capable of creating numerous demonic acts in a person. After having lost his wisdom, the person continues to practice the roots of merit. With an evil mind, he offers things. With a mind filled with anger, he follows the precepts. He abandons and forsakes those who are evil and negligent. He scorns those who are ignorant and burdened with a deranged mind. He is begrudging of the true Dharma. He chastises those who are vessels of the Dharma. He expounds the Dharma publicly for the sake of his own profit. These are all demonic acts. To distance oneself from good teachers and to draw close to evil teachers, to malign the true Dharma and not listen to the teaching, to listen and not praise the teaching are all demonic acts. If there is a master of the Dharma who expounds the Dharma and yet is unable reverentially to humble his own mind, and who thinks, 'My doctrines are superb; his doctrines are worthless,' this also constitutes a demonic act. To expound the profound Dharma to those who pursue the study of worldly learning or who are not vessels for the Dharma is also a demonic act.

"Children of the Buddha, to this person appear the following ten different spheres of the Buddha: 1, the Buddha-sphere of non-attachment, where the person is attached neither to the world of nirvana nor to the world of transmigration and attains enlightenment while dwelling restfully in the world of illusion; 2, the Buddha-sphere of the vow, where the person is born in the Tusita heaven and attains the gateway that leads without fail to Buddhahood; 3, the Buddha-sphere of karmic rewards, where the person adorns his body with an infinite number of merits; 4, the Buddha-sphere of sustenance, where the person retains the power to sustain the Buddha's doctrine even after his death; 5, the Buddha-sphere of nirvana, where the person manifests nirvana in this world, rouses a sense of astonishment in people, and causes them to enter the Buddha's doctrine quickly; 6, the Buddha-sphere of the Dharmadhatu, where the person takes as his body the Dharmadhatu, which does not perish even after his corporeal body comes to an end; 7, the Buddha-sphere of the mind, where the person concentrates his mind on Great Compassion and causes people to know that the Buddha exists in compassion; 8, the Buddha-sphere of meditation, where the person remains unafflicted amidst the defilements of transmigration, focusing his mind on meditative concentration, and tastes the quiescence of nirvana; 9, the Buddha-sphere of nature, where the person is awakened to the truth of Buddhahood, which is originally possessed by all men and women; 10, the Buddha-sphere of free activities, where the person appears before the people at will and is able to teach, guide, and expound the Dharma.

(13) "Children of the Buddha, if he who has taken the Buddha's mind as his own rouses a mind that is negligent, abandons the Buddha's true Dharma, and lusts after things without getting tired of them, he is taken by a demon. Again, if he thinks of saving himself alone, desires the quiescence that is free of defilement, and departs from the real world, he is taken by a demon. If he abandons the mind that teaches and guides others, rouses doubts amidst the true Dharma, and maligns the Buddha's doctrine, he is taken by a demon. You should distance yourself quickly from such a being.

"Children of the Buddha, if one perceives that all things are impermanent and suffering, that all dharmas are without self, and that nirvana is a realm where defilements have been extinguished, he is taken by the Dharma. Again, if he perceives that myriads of delusions arise from evil thoughts and that delusions are destroyed when evil thoughts are destroyed, he is taken by the Dharma. If he perceives that all countries, dharmas, people, and worlds are the Buddha's field of consciousness and if he cuts off all thoughts, abandons all attachments, and accords with nirvana, he is taken by the Dharma.

(i)   The ocean of profound wisdom is full with the water of the true Dharma, which is of one taste. Although it is filled with the treasure of enlightenment, no one can fathom this ocean.

The upright mind is pure and expansive; it is the sea of universal wisdom. One can expound the ocean of a bodhisattva, but one cannot exhaust it. The bodhisattva is Mount Sumeru rising high above the world. The summit of divine power and meditative concentration is steadfast and immovable.

(ii) The profound mind is like a diamond; the faith in the three treasures is indestructible. It subdues all demons and destroys all defilements. It generates clouds of great compassion and lightning flashes of great piety. The thunder of the Dharma reverberates and saves the people.

With the pure Dharma as the castle, with wisdom as the wall, with contrition as the moat, it departs through the gate of emancipation of emptiness. In the three worlds, it plants an exquisite banner and destroys all the demons.

(iii) On a cool day, a bodhisattva roams the skies of ultimate emptiness. He showers down light on the three realms and reveals the mental dharmas of the people. In the land of boundless skillful means, he benefits people. With the water of pure compassion, he puts out the fires of defilement that burn furiously.

The raging fire of wisdom burns away the defilements and their lingering traces. Moving like the wind, it performs the work of a buddha in the ten directions.

The gem that grants all wishes dispels people's poverty; wisdom is like a diamond and crushes all evil views.

(iv) A bodhisattva is a river of merit. He flows with the stream of the true way, or he turns into bridges that span birth and death. He saves people without respite.

A bodhisattva is a ship of the true Dharma. He floats on the ocean of vows; his wisdom fulfills people and carries them over to the other shore.

A bodhisattva is an immaculate garden. The true Dharma is the flower of emancipation, and its fruit gladdens people. Moreover, a bodhisattva's wisdom is the garden's royal palace."

5. The Actions of the Body and of the Mind

(1) The World-Honored One departed Kapilavatthu, turned toward Nalanda, and entered the Mango Tree Grove of Pavarika. At that time Nigantha Nataputta, together with numerous disciples, dwelt in this area. After making his round of begging in the village, his disciple, Digha-tapassi, visited the World-Honored One at the Mango Tree Grove and sat near him.

The World-Honored One said, "Digha-tapassi, how many types of evil karmas does your teacher set forth?" Digha-tapassi said, "Gotama, my teacher does not use the term 'karma'; rather, he employs the term, 'retribution', as in physical retribution, verbal retribution, and mental retribution." The World-Honored One asked, "Digha-tapassi, of these three retributions, which one does he consider to be the most powerful?" Digha-tapassi said, "Physical retribution is thought to be the most powerful. And how many retributions do you, Gotama, expound?" The World-Honored One said, "Digha-tapassi, I do not use the term 'retribution'; I use the term 'karma'. I expound three separate karmas—physical karma, verbal karma, and mental karma—and I regard mental karma as being the most powerful."

Then Digha-tapassi left the World-Honored One, and returning to the place of his teacher he recounted what had happened between the two. Nataputta said, "Excellent! You have explained my teaching clearly to Gotama. In no way can feeble mental retribution be more powerful than powerful physical retribution. It is needless to say that physical retribution is more powerful." The well-known and prominent layman Upali happened to be present and said, "I think that I shall also visit Gotama. If he should start an argument with me, I shall hurl him like a powerful man who grabs a handful of the long hair of a sheep and hurls the sheep at someone." Emboldened, Upali would not be dissuaded even when he was told, "Gotama has knowledge of mysterious ruses; he is skillful in snatching away other people's disciples. You should give up your plan to visit Gotama." He set out on his journey, and upon meeting the World-Honored One, he engaged him in argument.

(2) The World-Honored One said, "Upali, if you will promise to base yourself on reason and not be carried away with emotions, I shall agree to enter into a debate with you. Now, let us say there is a follower of Nigantha, who falls sick and craves for cold water because of his illness. His teachings prohibit him from using cold water. He therefore receives warm water instead and dies without ever receiving cold water. Where do you think this man will be born?" Upali said, "He will be born in a place called the Heaven Where the Mind Is Attached. He goes there because he died with lingering attachment to cold water."

The World-Honored One said, "Upali, you should think carefully before you answer. From start to finish, you should not contradict yourself. Let us say, once again, that there is a follower of Nigantha. He observes the four injunctions, restrains himself night and day, and frees himself from all evils. On walking back and forth, let us say, he steps on and kills countless insects. According to Nataputta, what kind of retribution will there be?" Upali said, "If he did not do so willfully, Nataputta would say that it is not a great evil. If it were done willfully, then it would be a grave evil."

The World-Honored One said, "Upali, you should think carefully before you answer. From start to finish, you should not contradict yourself. Here is another example. Nalanda has prospered and has a large population. In this city, someone draws his sword and says that in one quick stroke he will turn the people of Nalanda into a pile of dead meat. Do you think that he will be able to accomplish this?" Upali said, "Of course he will not be able to do that. Even though ten, twenty, or fifty people might join in, they would not be able to accomplish such a feat."

The World-Honored One said, "On the other hand, a mendicant, who is endowed with magical powers and is able to manifest his mind and its wishes at will, appears. With anger in his mind, he attempts to turn this Nalanda into ashes. Do you think that he will be able to accomplish this?" Upali said, "Of course he will be able to do it. He will be able at will to turn ten, twenty, or even fifty Nalandas into ashes."

The World-Honored One said, "Upali, you should think carefully before you answer. From start to finish, you should not contradict yourself. Have you ever heard of a hermit-sage who turned countries into withered plains in a fit of anger?" Upali said, "World-Honored One, I have heard of such. World-Honored One, I should confess that I understood your point clearly with your first example." Thus was Upali convinced of the superior power of mental acts. "However, I wanted to have other questions answered and therefore remained silent. I take refuge in the Three Treasures. I beseech you to accept me as your follower from this day forward."

(3) The World-Honored One said, "After considering it carefully, do what you think you should. A man of renown such as yourself should do what he thinks is best." Upali said, "Just because you say this, I wish all the more to take refuge in the Three Treasures. Other teachers, when they take someone like myself as their disciple, are quick to spread the news throughout Nalanda. In contrast, the World-Honored One tells me to do what I think is right after deliberating on the matter. All the more do I prefer to take refuge in the Three Treasures."

The World-Honored One said, "Upali, up to now you have made offerings to the people of Nigantha. From now on also, you would do well to make offerings to them when they ask you." Upali said, "World-Honored One, after hearing these words, all the more do I feel like taking refuge in the Three Treasures. I had heard before from others that the World-Honored One said that offerings should be made only to the World-Honored One and his disciples and not to those of other teachings. However, the World-Honored One now instructs me to make offerings as before to the people of Nigantha. Hearing this, all the more do I feel like taking refuge in the Three Treasures."

Upali listened to the teaching of the World-Honored One and awakened to the truth that all things are impermanent. Feeling joy, he returned home, and to his gate-keeper he gave orders that henceforth when people from Nigantha came to his house, they should be given alms, but the gatekeeper should also say, "Upali has become a follower of Gotama; therefore, these gates are closed to the people of Nigantha and are opened only to the disciples of Gotama. If you desire food or alms, they will be brought to you here."

(4) The World-Honored One travelled eastward to the country of Anga and arrived at Campa, which was located downstream from Anga. At Campa, he lodged on the bank of the Gaggara lotus pond. In that area, there was a brahmin, Sonadanda. Having been granted a fief by King Bimbisara, he was a wealthy man and was respected by the people.

Having climbed up the many-tiered mansion, Sonadanda was napping in the afternoon. Just about that time, a great throng of people moved in the direction of Lake Gaggara. He was awakened by the noise of the crowd and discovered that they were all going to visit the World-Honored One. He also decided to visit the World-Honored One. Most of the brahmins who heard of this were dumbfounded and tried to dissuade him, saying, "That is not a wise thing to do. If you take the initiative and visit him, you will lower your reputation and no doubt elevate Gotama's reputation. You are someone of purity, born into a brahmin family that has been free of all impurities for seven generations. On top of that you are well versed in the three Vedas; you are a scholar of high morals. You have taught the scriptures to more than three hundred disciples; among brahmins you are regarded as a wise elder. You have gained the respect of the king of Magadha Bimbisara and of the brahmin Pokkharasati. You are of a status in which you have been granted a fief from the king. Therefore it is only proper that Gotama take the initiative to visit you."

Sonadanda said, "No, that is not so. It is proper for me to take the initiative to visit Gotama. Gotama was born into a noble lineage, and yet he cast aside that lineage and the family treasures and became a mendicant. His countenance is elegant and dignified. He abides by the precepts, believes in karma, is endowed with sublime marks, and has attained enlightenment. He has become a world teacher; he is kind toward people; therefore wherever he stays, there is no discord. He stands at the head of disciples, both mendicants and lay; he is the founder of a great teaching. Both King Bimbisara and the brahmin Pokkharasati, together with their whole families, have taken refuge in the Three Treasures, and revere him. At this moment, that Gotama is staying on the bank of the Gaggara lotus pond in Campa; therefore he is our guest. Guests should be honored; it is proper for me to take the initiative to visit him. Moreover, although I am able to count these many virtues of Gotama, his virtues are by no means limited to those that I have cited. Those who have faith should visit a teacher even if they must bear their provision on their backs, and they should not let distance be a hindrance."

(5) A large number of brahmins were persuaded by these words of Sonadanda, and together with him they set out for the Gaggara pond. On the way, while passing through a forest, Sonadanda thought to himself, "If I pose a question to Gotama and am told in return, 'Brahmin, you should not pose your question in that manner; you should pose it in this manner,' these people will start to look down on me. And because of that, this will lower my reputation; it may even affect my revenue. Or Gotama may ask me a question and if my answer does not satisfy him, he may say, 'You should not explain matters in that manner,' and the result would be the same. For all that, if I return home without meeting Gotama after setting out like this to see him, someone will see through my cowardice, and this will lower my reputation. This is truly a distressing problem. I shall carry on a dialogue on matters of scholarship pertaining to the three Vedas, which is my forte, and thus gain his approval."

After he had paid his respects to Gotama, he sat down near him. The World-Honored One noticed a certain wariness in Sonadanda's behavior; perceiving the state of his mind and wishing to reassure him, he said, "Brahmin, what qualifications should one possess in order to be called a true brahmin?"

This question gladdened Sonadanda's heart and also reassured him. He thought to himself, "I am glad, indeed, that Gotama has asked me this question. He no doubt will applaud my answer." Straightening his posture, he said, "World-Honored One, if one possesses five qualifications, one can be called a true brahmin. First, for seven generations one's bloodline must be pure, both on the father's side and on the mother's. Second, one must read the scriptures and be well-versed in the three Vedas. One must, in addition, be thoroughly conversant with the learning of the Lokayata school. One must know the Dharma that enables one to discern the marks of a great person. Third, one must be kind, elegant, and dignified in appearance. Fourth, one must be correct in one's disciplinary practices. Fifth, one must be wise and must be the foremost, or at least the second, in making offerings with the sacrificial ladle. If one possesses these five qualifications, one can be called a true brahmin."

The World-Honored One said, "Brahmin, of the five qualifications brought forth by you, can one be called a brahmin if one qualification were to be omitted?" Sonadanda said, "That is possible. Even if the third qualification regarding one's elegance of appearance were to be omitted, one can be called a brahmin." The World-Honored One said, "If still another qualification were to be omitted from the remaining four, can one still be called a brahmin?" Sonadanda said, "That is possible. The second can be omitted." The World-Honored One said, "Of the three remaining qualifications, can still another be omitted?" Sonadanda said, "That is possible. The first can be omitted."

(6) The other brahmins listened to this exchange and, feeling apprehensive, whispered to Sonadanda, "Venerable one, do not speak in that manner. You should not too readily agree with Gotama's ideas." The World-Honored One said, "All of you brahmins, if you think that Sonadanda is shallow in learning and inept with words and cannot bear to see him engage me in argument, you yourselves should come forth and speak out. On the other hand, if you think that

Sonadanda has studied widely and is capable of arguing with me, you should abstain."

Sonadanda said, "World-Honored One, please do not concern yourself over them. I shall speak directly to them: You people are under the impression that I belittle appearance and dharanis and disdain lineage. However, I neither belittle nor disdain these. I ask you to look at my nephew, Angaka; he is elegant in appearance and, excluding Gotama, there is no one to equal him. Moreover, he has studied the dharanis; he is well versed in the three Vedas. I took him in hand myself and instructed him. For seven generations, both on his father's side and on his mother's, his bloodline is pure. However, if this Angaka were to kill living beings, steal things, commit adultery with another man's wife, spew out lies, and imbibe liquors, ultimately what value would appearance, learning, and lineage have? For that reason, I affirmed that one who possesses wisdom and has the qualifications to be the foremost or the second in making offerings with the sacrificial ladle can be called a true brahmin."

The World-Honored One said, "Brahmin, of the last two, can one be omitted?" Sonadanda said, "World-Honored One, that would not be possible. Wisdom is made pure by disciplinary practices, and disciplinary practices are made pure by wisdom. Where there are disciplinary practices, there is wisdom, and where there is wisdom, there are disciplinary practices. Those who observe disciplinary practices possess wisdom, and those who possess wisdom observe the disciplinary practices. Disciplinary practices and wisdom are said to be the two most important virtues in the world. Like someone washing his hands with his hands or his feet with his feet, disciplinary practices and wisdom purify each other."

The World-Honored One said, "Brahmin, truly that is so. Disciplinary practices and wisdom do purify each other and are called the two most important virtues in this world. However, what do you mean by disciplinary practices and wisdom?" Sonadanda said, "O World-Honored One, this is all that I know; I beseech you to elaborate on what I have said."

(7) The World-Honored One said, "Brahmin, this is the meaning of disciplinary practice: a buddha appears in this world and expounds the Dharma. Lay people hear his teaching, rouse the mind of faith, and become mendicants. They observe the precepts, delight in true practices, regard even minor evils with alarm, and lead upright lives. They guard the gateways of the five sensory organs; they stop killing living creatures and are filled with compassion. They stop stealing, and forthrightly they purify their minds. They stop lascivious acts, free themselves from lying, stop using words that would destroy friendships, and refrain from coarse language. They stop idle talk and speak properly at the proper time. That is the meaning of precepts. Further, they free themselves from defilements and enter into a myriad of meditations. With minds that are quiescent, gentle, and steadfast, they perceive that all dharmas are impermanent and egoless. They perceive their own past lives as well as the past lives of others. They perceive the births and deaths of people. And they perceive the destruction of the defilements. That is the meaning of wisdom."

Sonadanda heard these words of the Buddha and rejoiced profoundly. He vowed to become a follower who seeks his refuge in the Three Treasures. He invited the Buddha to a meal the following day.

On the following day, after they had finished the meal, Sonadanda brought a low chair and sat down on it. He said to the World-Honored One, "World-Honored One, when I am amongst my peers, if I were to stand up and bow down to the World-Honored One, my peers would look down on me with disdain, and discord would arise. Therefore if I should extend my hands that are pressed together, I would have you understand that I have stood up from my seat. Again, if I should take my hat off, I would have you understand that I am bowing down to you. Again, when I meet you while driving my carriage, if I should point my staff downward and raise my hands to my head, I would have you understand that I have gotten off the carriage and have bowed to you." The World-Honored One agreed to interpret Sonadanda's actions in the manner prescribed by him. After the discussion on the Dharma, the World-Honored One returned to the bank of the Gaggara pond.

(8) Following this, the World-Honored One gradually made his way through the country of Anga. He remained for a time in the town of Assapura; at that place, he imparted the following teaching to the disciples: "Disciples, you are all known as mendicants. Moreover, when you are asked, you reply, 'I am a mendicant.' Therefore you should apply yourselves in the following manner: 'I shall follow the Dharma that should be practiced by the mendicant. Thereby shall I manifest the truth of a mendicant. I shall cause those who make offerings of robes, food, lodging, and medicine to me to acquire great happiness. I shall turn the life of a mendicant into something that is fruitful and not something that is useless.'

"Disciples, what is the Dharma that mendicants should practice? Mendicants should have inward and outward penitence. However, you should not believe that feeling penitent is sufficient. Beyond that you should purify your life and your actions with regard to your body, speech, and mind. You should be open and conceal nothing. You should not take pride in your actions and laud yourself nor malign others.

"Disciples, with these alone, you should not yet believe that you have fully achieved the goals of a mendicant. You should also guard the gateways to the five sensory organs. Gazing upon the outer realm, you should not become attached to it. With regard to food, you should know the proper amount; in partaking of food, you should not do so for the sake of pleasure. You should sustain and nurture the body, which is the vessel of the Dharma. You should nurture it as an aid in observing the pure practices. You should eat meals with correct reflection. Always you should remain fully awake. During the day, you should sit quietly in meditation, take contemplative strolls, and not commit acts that are prohibited. During the first watch of the night, you should sit quietly in meditation and take contemplative strolls. During the middle watch of the night, you should lie down on your right side, placing one leg on top of the other. With a right mind and right thought, you should think of the time for arising. And you should sleep like a lion. During the last watch of the night, you should awaken and sit quietly in meditation, take contemplative strolls, and purify your mind of the things that have been prohibited. And always, you should have a right mind, whether you are coming or going, looking far or near, putting on your robes, begging, eating, drinking water, moving, standing, sitting, or lying down. You should seek out a secluded retreat and sit in meditation underneath a tree in the forest, in a mountain cave, in a burial yard, or by a pile of straw. Holding both mind and body upright, you should purify your mind by freeing yourself from greed, anger, sloth, sleep, agitation, regret, and doubt. You should free yourself from these coverings of the mind. You should rejoice inwardly, relax your body, acquire concentration of your spirit, and enter into myriads of meditations. You should do so like someone suffering unbearable pain being cured of his illness, regaining his physical stamina, and experiencing great joy over his recovery; or like a slave who rejoices over being granted his freedom and being able to go wherever he wishes; or like a traveller who rejoices after carrying mounds of treasures on his back, moving through the wilderness and reaching his destination in good health.

"Disciples, beyond this, you will be cultivated by such meditations. With a mind that is prepared to function at any time, you should perceive your own past lives as well as the past lives of others. You should perceive the births and deaths of people and the destruction of defilements. Disciples, in this way for the first time you will be said to be a mendicant, a brahmin, a man of wisdom, a man of tranquillity, or an arhat. Disciples, these people, from the mendicant and brahmin to the arhat, are those who have pacified the source that gives rise to the foul dharmas of evil, gives rise to the fruits of suffering, and eventually leads to birth in the next world.

(9) "Disciples, if a mendicant does not abandon greed, if he does not free himself from anger, if he does not distance himself from wrath, hatred, concealment, self-pride, jealousy, deception, flattery, evil desire, and evil views, it will be like wrapping a double-edged sword into one's robe. As for myself, simply because someone is wearing robes, I do not call him a mendicant. Because someone is naked, I do not call him an ascetic. Moreover, an ascetic covered with ashes is merely someone who smears ashes on his body. An ascetic who immerses himself in water is merely someone who bathes himself thrice a day. None of these are mendicants. This includes those who live under trees, live in the wilderness, remain standing for long periods, indulge in fasting, or chant sutras.

"Disciples, you cannot free yourselves from anger and the other defilements merely by putting on the robes of a mendicant. If one could do that, parents would dress their infants in such robes. Ascetic practices are nothing but outward guises and are not the true way of the mendicant. What then is the true way of the mendicant? It is to free oneself from greed, anger, wrath, hatred, concealment, self-pride, jealousy, deception, flattery, evil desire, and evil views. When you free yourself from evil, you perceive that you are free and arouse joy; your body relaxes and your mind becomes harmonious. Accordingly you fill all worlds with a mind of compassion, a mind of mercy, a mind of joy, and a mind of equality. You do so without hatred or enmity.

"Disciples, suppose there is a lotus pond brimming over with limpid, cool waters and bordered by a bank spread over with pure sand. From the four directions, travellers drag their feet, tired from the heat, to this lotus pond. With its waters they quench their thirst and put an end to the misery stemming from the heat. In exactly the same way, kshatriyas, brahmins, sudras, and vaisyas, upon hearing the Dharma expounded by the Buddha, practice the four boundless minds of compassion, pity, joy, and detachment. They escape the misery that stems from the heat and attain coolness of the mind. When they do so, I call them people who have entered the path of the mendicant. In this way they pacify and destroy their defilements and become true mendicants."

Chapter 2

ABSOLUTE WISDOM

1. Emptiness

(1) At the beginning of the fourteenth year of his enlightenment, the World-Honored One travelled across the Ganges from Anga and entered the city of Vajji. Gradually he made his way to the great forest at Vesali and dwelt there for some time. One day he expounded thus to his disciples: "Disciples, what is meant by the uncreated state, devoid of the activity of birth and death? What is the way that leads to that state? That state in which greed, anger, and ignorance have been wholly extinguished and exhausted is the uncreated state. Meditation on emptiness, meditation on signlessness, and meditation on desirelessness comprise the way that leads to that state. Therefore, you should enter the forest or empty cottages where no one dwells and concentrate your minds on such meditations. Do not be negligent. Have no regrets. This is the teaching that I impart to you."

(2) One afternoon Ananda asked the World-Honored One, "World-Honored One, it is said that the world is empty. What is the meaning of such a statement?" The World-Honored One replied, "Ananda, there is neither the 'I' nor the 'mine'; therefore, the world is described as being empty. The emptiness of the 'I' and the 'mine' means that the eye is neither the 'I' nor the 'mine'. Forms or things that have shapes are neither the 'I' nor the 'mine'. The eye-consciousness is neither the 'I' nor the 'mine'. When the eye organ and its corresponding object and consciousness come together, an impression is produced; this impression is also neither the 'I' nor the 'mine'. The sensation that is produced from this impression is also neither the 'I' nor the 'mine'. In this way the impressions and sensations that are produced by the eye, ear, nose, tongue, skin, and mind, their corresponding objects of cognition, and their consciousnesses, and the coalescence of all these components, are also neither the 'I' nor the 'mine'. Both the 'I' and the 'mine' are absolutely empty; on the basis of this truth, the world is said to be empty."

(3) One evening, Sariputta stood up from his meditation and approached the World-Honored One, bowed, and sat down next to him. The World-Honored One said, "Sariputta, your appearance is pure and serene, and your complexion is glowing; what kind of meditation have you dwelt in today?" "World-Honored

One, today I entered the meditation on emptiness," answered Sariputta. The World-Honored One said, "Very well, Sariputta, today you have dwelt in the meditation of the buddhas. Emptiness is the meditation of the buddhas. If a disciple of the Buddha wishes to dwell in the meditation on Emptiness, he should contemplate in this manner: 'Today I went to the village to beg for food. During the course of my begging, there were shapes seen by my eyes, sounds heard by my ears, fragrances smelled by my nose, tastes savored by my tongue, tactile sensations felt by my body, and dharmas perceived by my mind. In all of these, were there obstructions of greed, anger, or ignorance present?' After contemplating in this manner, if one perceives that such obstructions were indeed present, then one must exert oneself to cast off such evils. If one perceives that they were not present, then with joy and bliss, night and day, one should persist in the practice of the good.

"Moreover, Sariputta, that same disciple should reflect in this manner, 'Have I cast off the five desires? Have I eradicated my defilements? Have I perceived the physical form and mind that make up this body? Have I practiced the multitude of ways that lead to enlightenment? Have I attained wisdom and enlightenment?' Sariputta, after having reflected on oneself in this manner, if one discovers that one has not freed oneself from defilement and has not attained enlightenment, one should exert oneself. If one has freed oneself from defilement and has attained enlightenment, then with joy and bliss, night and day, one should persist in the practice of the good.

"Sariputta, all mendicants who sanctify the food received through the act of selfless giving, whether they are of the remote past, the present, or the distant future, contemplate in the manner that I have described. Therefore, Sariputta, you should discipline yourself to sanctify the food that you have received through the act of selfless giving."

(4) Again one evening Ananda asked the World-Honored One, "World-Honored One, in the small village called Nangaraka that belongs to the Sakya clan, I recall that you said to me, 'Ananda, nowadays I almost always dwell in the meditation of Emptiness.' Is my memory correct?"

The World-Honored One said, "Ananda, your recollection is not faulty. Both in the past and now, I almost always dwell in the meditation of Emptiness. This many-tiered lecture hall that stands in this great forest is empty of elephants, cows, horses, and sheep; in this sense, it is empty. There is no gold or silver in this hall; in this sense, it is empty. The hall is not filled with a gathering of men and women; in this sense, it is empty. The only thing that it is not empty of is the Sangha. In like manner, a disciple restrains himself from arousing thoughts of his village, he does not rouse in himself thoughts of society, and he thinks only of those things that pertain to the forest. If he does this, his mind will rejoice at his thoughts of the forest; concerns related to the village and to society will vanish, and concerns related only to the forest will remain. Thoughts of his village and of society become empty, and only thoughts of the forest are not empty. In this way, when something is not present, it is called empty, and when it is present, it is said to exist.

"Advancing in his meditation, he casts off thoughts of the forest and rouses only thoughts of the earth. He views the great earth, which is filled with mountains, rivers, thickets, highlands, and lowlands, as flat land that is free of all wrinkles like a piece of cowhide stretched out as tight as a drum. His mind rejoices at this thought; concerns pertaining to the forest vanish, and only those concerns pertaining to the earth remain.

"In this way, step by step, he moves through a variety of meditations and advances to the meditation of no-thought. If he dwells in the meditation of no-thought, then his mind rejoices in the meditation of no-thought; the only thing that remains is the concern that pertains to his body. Entering the meditation of no-thought, he perceives that his meditation of no-thought is something that was created, something that was produced by thought. And because of this, he perceives that this meditation, too, is impermanent and will eventually perish. He then becomes enlightened with the realization that he is now free of the defilements of greed, existence, and ignorance, that what he had to accomplish has been achieved, and that henceforth he will never again be burdened with deluded birth. Entering this state, he is free of all concerns that arise from defilements. The only concerns that persist are those that arise from the body.

"In this way, all becomes empty; the only thing that is not empty is the body that continues to live on. In this way, when something is not there, it is perceived as being empty, and when something remains there, it is perceived as existing. If, in this way, one practices the meditation of Emptiness, one accords with the truth and is not entrapped by inverted thoughts. Ananda, exert yourself so that you will dwell in this pure and splendid meditation of Emptiness."

2. The Enlightenment of Non-Abiding

(1) One day the World-Honored One finished his round of begging at Sravasti and returned to the Jeta Grove Monastery. Putting away his robes and begging bowl, he washed his feet and sat down. Subhuti stood up from the large assembly, bowed to the World-Honored One, and said, "World-Honored One, the Buddha protects all those who seek the way; furthermore, the Buddha provides them with sublime counsel. I believe that this is a rare thing. World-Honored One, if people rouse the mind that seeks the supreme way, how should they restrain the mind?" The World-Honored One said, "Very good, Subhuti, bodhisattvas, in order to subjugate that mind, first of all, should have the myriad sentient beings enter perfect nirvana. And yet, even if they were to accomplish this, there would, in truth, be no one who entered nirvana. The reason is that any bodhisattva worthy of that name does not affirm the permanent existence of person, self, life, and so forth.

"Furthermore, Subhuti, a bodhisattva must not abide in the Dharma. That is, even in his practice of selfless giving, he should not dwell on the things that he has given. That is, he should not become attached to the forms of things. If he refrains from doing so, the merits and their benefits will be boundless; they will be as boundless as space, which is limitless and immeasurable, whether one turns to the east, the west, the south, or the north.

"Subhuti, you should not seek Buddhahood with physical forms. The reason is that the physical forms expounded by the buddhas are not actually physical forms. All forms are illusion. Therefore, if you perceive that all forms are not truly forms, then you have perceived Buddhahood. A verse says, 'If one sees me as a form or perceives me as a sound, then one walks a wrong path; one will not see the Buddha.'"

(2) Subhuti asked, "Do you think, World-Honored One, that people will believe such words?" The World-Honored One answered, "You should not speak in such a manner. Five hundred years after the Buddha enters nirvana, those who observe the precepts and practice the good will hear these words and will believe them to be the truth. These people, because they implanted merits at the place of three or four buddhas, will be able to rouse this pure faith in one moment of thought. In this way, they will attain boundless virtues; that is, they will do so because they affirm neither the form of 'I' nor the forms of people. Subhuti, have the buddhas attained supreme enlightenment? Are there dharmas that the buddhas ought to expound?"

Subhuti answered, "According to my understanding, I do not think that there is any immutable Dharma that might be labelled as supreme enlightenment. Again, I do not think that for the Buddha there exists a fixed dharma that he ought to expound. The reason is that the Dharma expounded by the Buddha can be neither grasped nor expounded. His teaching is neither Dharma nor non-Dharma, for all arhats are manifestations of the uncreated."

(3) The World-Honored One said, "Subhuti, do you think that all the arhats regard the enlightenment that they have attained as something that they have attained?" Subhuti said, "I do not believe that the arhats think in such a manner. The reason is that there is nothing in particular that can be called enlightenment. If the arhats should think, 'I have attained such and such enlightenment,' they would still be bound to self-attachment and could not be called arhats." The World-Honored One said, "Aeons ago, did the Buddha attain some kind of Dharma at the place of Dipankara Buddha?" Subhuti said, "I do not think that he attained anything." The World-Honored One said, "If there is a bodhisattva who claims to embellish a buddha's country, he does not speak the truth, because to embellish a country is not to embellish. To embellish and yet to be free of any thought of embellishing is really to embellish. Therefore, Subhuti, a bodhisattva should not settle his mind on whatever place or thing but should abide in the mind."

(4) Subhuti, upon hearing this profound teaching, shed tears of joy and said to the World-Honored One, "World-Honored One, up to now I have not heard such a teaching. If someone hears this teaching and rouses pure faith, he will no doubt gain insight into the true form of reality. This person will attain the world's most rare and foremost merit. I believe that you, World-Honored One, have described that which is originally undefinable as the true form of reality."

The World-Honored one said, "Even though one were selflessly to bestow boundless treasures on people, this would not compare with the merits that come from expounding this teaching to the people. How, then, does one expound this teaching for the sake of others? 'All things are dreams and illusions; they are like bubbles and shadows. View all things as dewdrops or as flashes of lightning.'" When the World-Honored One had finished speaking, Subhuti and the whole assembly immersed themselves in their joy over the Dharma, and their minds were joyful.

3. The Essence of Absolute Wisdom

The World-Honored One once again faced Sariputra and said, "The Bodhisattva Avalokitesvara undertook the practice of profound wisdom that leads to the shore of enlightenment. He contemplated that perceiving both the body and the mind as empty is the way to cross over all suffering. Therefore, Sariputra, form is simultaneously empty; Emptiness is simultaneously form. Emptiness is not separate from form, and form is not separate from emptiness. This is true also for the four other aggregates, feeling, perception, volition, and consciousness. Sariputra, all things are empty; they neither arise nor perish; they are neither defiled nor pure; they neither decrease nor increase. In Emptiness, the five aggregates such as form, the six sensory organs such as the eye, and the six objects of cognition such as form, do not exist. From the realm of eye-consciousness to the realm of manas [mind] consciousness, not one of these realms truly exists. There is neither ignorance nor the state in which ignorance has been extinguished. There is neither old age and death nor the state in which old age and death have been extinguished. Suffering, its cause, the cessation of suffering, and the way leading to that cessation do not exist. There is neither wisdom nor the attainment of wisdom. Because there is nothing to attain, a bodhisattva grounds himself in the wisdom that leads to the shore of enlightenment, and his mind is free of all obstructions. Because there are no obstructions, there are no fears for a bodhisattva. He frees himself from dreamlike inverted thoughts and attains ultimate nirvana. The buddhas of the three periods, by virtue of the wisdom that leads to the shore of enlightenment, awaken to the supreme enlightenment of equality. The wisdom that leads to the other shore, the Perfection of Wisdom, is a wondrous and incomparable dharani. This dharani is true and real; and it extinguishes all suffering. The dharani is 'Gate gate paragate parasamgate bodhi svaha'."

4. The Bodhisattva Sadaprarudita's Search for the Path

(1) In this way the World-Honored One expounded the Prajna-Paramita (or, Perfection of Wisdom); following this, he expounded on the seeking of the way by the Bodhisattva Sadaprarudita. "Subhuti, when seeking the Perfection of Wisdom, you should diligently seek it in the manner of the Bodhisattva Sadaprarudita." And he explained the following. When the Bodhisattva Sadaprarudita first sought the Perfection of Wisdom, he was willing to cast aside his life to do so. He secluded himself in the tranquil mountains, which were cut off from all human contact. He dismissed from his mind thoughts of fame and the floating world's notions. Single-mindedly he sought the way; just then, he suddenly heard a voice from the sky. "Proceed, good man, risking your life,

proceed from here in an easterly direction. Go forth with diligence, dismissing from your mind thoughts of fatigue, sleep, food, night and day, heat and cold, and so forth. Regarding your body and mind, refrain from generating discriminatory thoughts. The true nature of all things is Emptiness and is free of such discriminations. The mind of greed applies such distinctions and produces the seeds of anguish. Consequently, it destroys the true nature of all things. If one causes the mind of greed to burn with increasing fury, one wanders aimlessly forever in the world of suffering and is unable finally to attain the Perfection of Wisdom. Therefore you must never mar the true nature of all things."

(2) The Bodhisattva Sadaprarudita was filled with joy on receiving this teaching and said, "I shall certainly follow your teaching. For the sake of those who suffer in anguish amidst the vast darkness of misery, I aspire to become the bedazzling light of salvation. I shall ponder only on the aspiration to know all the Buddha's doctrine and to attain supreme enlightenment." At that moment, again, there was a roar from the sky.

"Very good, very good, son of good family! Seek the Perfection of Wisdom single-mindedly, rousing the mind of faith while being in the midst of the world, in which the Dharma is difficult to awaken to, and without rousing, even a little, a mind of attachment and discrimination. Part with evil friends and associate with good friends. Keep the company of those who expound this Dharma. Do not seek out teachers for the sake of worldly fame and profit; simply seek out those bodhisattvas who expound this Dharma out of a mind that cherishes and venerates the Dharma. Meanwhile, a host of demonic interferences may come to pass; however, no matter what the demons choose to do, do not become disheartened. Remember that a Buddha often saves people by skillful means; because of his desire to have people plant the roots of merit, he receives their offerings of the five worldly desires. He assumes the same physical form as people and lives as they do. Even though the demons may try to tell you that the teacher honors the five worldly desires, accept his actions as skillful means of the Buddha. If the actions of the demons are merciless, it is vital that you endure them with equanimity. If you seek the Dharma and your teacher in this manner, without fail you will attain the Perfection of Wisdom and be able to bring your great aspiration to fruition."

(3) The Bodhisattva Sadaprarudita, having listened to the teaching, immediately departed from that place. Strengthening his resolve, he set forth in an easterly direction in accordance with the Buddha's instructions. However, on the road, suddenly a whirlpool of anxiety swirled up in his heart. At the outset of his journey, he had forgotten to ask the voice in the sky questions such as, "Where am I to go? Is the place near or far? Under what teacher am I to listen to the Dharma?" And he lost his bearings. It is not that he was losing heart because of weariness, heat, or cold. He simply encountered a great obstruction that commonly blocks those who truly seek the Dharma. He stood on that spot and vowed that he would not depart from there until this darkness dissipated. Like a man who has lost his beloved only child and has suddenly begun to despair of this world, the suffering of having the jewel of faith, which he had cherished up to

now, snatched away was excruciating. After seven days he heard from the sky what sounded like the Buddha's voice.

"Good man, you should not agonize, even a little. Your suffering is by no means yours alone. All those who sought the way in the past have experienced the same suffering. Do not despair; exert yourself. Single-mindedly aspire to attain the Dharma. Proceed ever eastward; if you travel five thousand miles from here, you will arrive at a large castle called Fragrant; it is surrounded by seven concentric moats. It is a majestic castle in which the towers, parapets, and rows of trees are all embellished with seven kinds of gems. It is massive, and those who live there are great in number. It is filled with riches and pleasures, belonging to no one in particular. It is left up to everyone simply to take things and make them their own; therefore no one is burdened with thoughts of attachment or views things as belonging exclusively to himself. This is truly nothing less than the outward manifestation of the teaching of Emptiness. This is the reward of all those people living in this castle who sought absolute wisdom with fervor and who, with their bodies, practiced the way. In the middle of the town, there stands a lofty tower. There the Bodhisattva Dharmodgata expounds the Dharma. Both adults and children come to worship at this tower and make a variety of offerings to the Bodhisattva Dharmodgata. Some listen to him teaching on absolute wisdom; some commit the teaching to memory. Others read, write, and meditate in accordance with the teaching, or they practice with their bodies exactly as taught. Although their activities are diverse, their minds that venerate and rejoice in the absolute wisdom are one and the same. Now go there and listen to the Dharma. For your sake, the Bodhisattva Dharmodgata will without doubt serve as a good teacher. Do not be afraid; do not grow weary; forgetting both night and day and abandoning the mind that becomes an obstruction, go forth single-mindedly."

(4) Hearing this, the Bodhisattva Sadaprarudita's joy surged like the ocean tides. The mind of this Bodhisattva was like that of a man who has been shot by a poisoned arrow and quickly searches for a skilled physician. He desired to see the teacher soon and have his mind's darkness illuminated by him. Contemplating only the thought of the good teacher, and suffused by light, he roused within himself a firm and unyielding resolve. He brought forth an immovable wisdom that could not be obstructed by any demon. Thoughts that were free and devoid of obstructions regarding all things manifested themselves within him. At that time, buddhas in the sky said to him, "Good man, the way that fulfills your aspirations has now been realized. Formerly when we, too, were practicing the way, just like yourself now, the mind of meditation manifested itself, and we realized the Perfection of Wisdom. The power to save people was aroused, and we ascended to the state from which there is no regression. Therefore now is the time that you should cherish and venerate the Buddha's doctrine; toward your good teacher you should cherish the same thoughts as you have toward the Buddha."

"Who is my good teacher?" asked the Bodhisattva Sadaprarudita. The voice replied, "Your good teacher is none other than the Bodhisattva Dharmodgata.

From the distant past, this Bodhisattva has devoted his energy to guiding you. When you reflect on this, you will see that even if you offered him all the treasures of this world for the long duration of one hundred thousand years, it would not be sufficient to repay even a small portion of your debt of gratitude."

(5) The Bodhisattva Sadaprarudita's mind immediately rushed toward his teacher, the Bodhisattva Dharmodgata, and he thought to himself, "In aeons past, having practiced the Perfection of Wisdom, the Bodhisattva Dharmodgata attained enlightenment. I must seek out this teacher immediately." The more he thought of this teacher, the more the Bodhisattva mulled over what offering he should make to his teacher. He thought, "When I go to the teacher's place, I must make an offering, but I do not own even one piece of clothing, not to speak of riches such as gold and silver. If I appear before him as I am, without an offering, my teacher may forgive me, but I shall be unable to manifest my true heart." The Bodhisattva again thought, "Since I have nothing to offer, I shall simply sacrifice my body and make it my offering. Because of greed, I have passed through endless rounds of birth and death, always turning back to the flames of hell. I have not thrown my life away even once for the sake of the Dharma or out of gratitude. Now is the time to offer up my life for the sake of the noble way." With this resolve, he moved forward in an easterly direction and soon reached a large town. Making up his mind to sell his body in this town, he walked through its streets in search of a buyer, calling out, "Is there anyone in need of a man? Is there anyone in need of a man?" At this time, the Devil thought, "If I allow this Bodhisattva to acquire the funds for his offering, he will no doubt attain enlightenment. If that happens, our world will be destroyed. In whatever manner, I must block his efforts and prevent him from finding a buyer." The Devil then proceeded to plug up the ears of everyone in the city. The Bodhisattva Sadaprarudita, who was unaware of all this, felt dejected, because no matter how far he walked or how loudly he called out, not one person stopped him or responded to his offer. He thought, "With what evil am I burdened that I am unable to find even one buyer in this large city?" Standing on a street corner, he burst into tears.

(6) At this time, Indra, king of the gods, the guardian deity of the Buddha's doctrine, became aware of this event. Making up his mind to provide the Bodhisattva, after testing the Bodhisattva's resolve, with a guardian, he assumed the form of a young man and appeared before the Bodhisattva. He then asked, "Why are you weeping?"

The Bodhisattva answered, "Single-mindedly seeking the Dharma, I arrived at this place. I have drawn close to the place of the Bodhisattva Dharmodgata. Therefore, I thought that I would sell myself and thus acquire the funds for an offering. However, perhaps because my merits are feeble, I have been unable to find even one buyer. This is why I am reproaching myself."

Indra as the young man peered into the Bodhisattva's face as he said, "That is unfortunate. I myself have no need of a man. But my father wishes to offer a human sacrifice and thus requires a man's heart, his blood, and the marrow of his bones. If you give me these, I shall pay you for them." The Bodhisattva thought, "After all I have easily found a buyer," and he said in great joy, "I shall sell you this body, since you have a use for it." The brahmin asked, "What price do you ask?" The Bodhisattva said, "I shall leave the price up to you." And Sadaprarudita took up a sharp sword and severed his left elbow so that the blood gushed out. Then he cut away at the right thigh; its bones were broken and he hacked it into pieces so that the marrow was about to ooze out.

(7) At this time, there lived a merchant's daughter who alone, because of her past karma, had escaped the Devil's obstruction of people's hearing. From the second floor she had been gazing down on this bloody scene; overcome by its excessive brutality, she came down into the street without any regard for her own safety. And she asked him how this came to be.

The Bodhisattva said, "Single-mindedly seeking the Dharma, I arrived at this place. And in order to raise funds for an offering to the Bodhisattva Dharmodgata, I sold my body." The maiden said, "You threw your life away for the sake of an offering to someone. What kind of person is he who is of greater value than your own life?" The Bodhisattva said, "This is one who, endowed with the Perfection of Wisdom, for my sake will reveal the bodhisattva practice. Through his guidance, I shall attain supreme enlightenment and become a refuge for all people. And I shall be able to save all people at will."

This reply was truly a noble teaching that rarely appears in this world. The maiden broke into tears of joy as soon as she heard the Bodhisattva's words. She said, "I believe you are right. If the teaching is as noble as that, even if one were to throw away one's body as many times as there are sand grains on the beach, it would still be a paltry offering. If it is offerings that you seek, I shall offer anything you want. Please accept it in good grace. And I beseech you to take me along with you."

At that time Indra shed his form as a young man and reassumed his appearance as a god. He said, "Very good, very good, son of good family; I have been deeply moved by your resolve to seek the way. In truth, I am Indra. I was simply testing your resolve and in no way was it my true intention to abuse you." After saying this, he suddenly vanished; simultaneously, the Bodhisattva's body reverted to its original condition, free from any trace of any wound.

The maiden had the Bodhisattva wait in front of the gate, and she rushed to her parents and explained everything in great detail to them; and she begged them to give her the funds for a offering to the Bodhisattva together with five hundred carts and her five hundred servant girls. The parents said, "Just as you say, there is no doubt that he is a noble man. As you wish, we shall offer him anything that he desires. Truly you have awakened to something of great value. From this day onward, together with that person, you should walk the path of making offerings."

(8) All the preparations were made. Five hundred carts made of the seven types of gems were piled high with rare flowers that grow on water and on land, expensive garments, fragrant incenses, necklaces, and a variety of provisions. The Bodhisattva Sadaprarudita was at the center, surrounded by the maiden and her five hundred servant girls. They all set out in an easterly direction toward

the castle of Fragrant; they were met by a scene that was of greater beauty than any painting. There were embellishments made up of the seven different kinds of gems, a wall of the seven gems, moats of the seven gems that encircled the castle seven times, and rows of trees of the seven gems that went around the castle in seven rows. In due time, they entered the city and were able to bow reverently to the Bodhisattva Dharmodgata, who atop a lofty tower was surrounded by a great multitude. The Bodhisattva Sadaprarudita's joy soared to the highest summit. They all climbed off the carts quietly and approached the Bodhisattva Dharmodgata. There was a dais of the seven gems, adorned with fragrant sandalwood trees. From above hung down nets made of pearls. In the four corners, many gems glittered, and in the incense burner exquisite incense was kept burning. In the center of the dais, there was a large cushion of seven gems. On top was a small square cushion. There the Prajna-paramita Sutra, written in golden letters, was enshrined. Above it there were myriad adornments and a canopy over the cushion. Indra led his retinue of gods over these adornments; there, the gods scattered divine mandarava flowers and exquisite incenses, and they played divine music. The Bodhisattva Sadaprarudita was stunned by this scene, the like of which he had never seen, and turning to Indra, he asked, "O god, why do you afford us the pleasure of this dais?" Indra replied, "Verily, the reason is that this dais is the place where the Perfection of Wisdom, the mother of all buddhas and bodhisattvas, is enshrined."

The Bodhisattva Sadaprarudita was filled with joy when he heard that this was the place where the Perfection of Wisdom was enshrined. He said, "This is the very thing that I sought even at the expense of my life. I assume that it dwells amidst a host of buddhas. Please let me see it." Indra replied, "I cannot allow that. The Bodhisattva Dharmodgata has impressed upon it a seal made of the seven gems, and I am not allowed to break that seal."

The Bodhisattva Sadaprarudita, together with the young maiden and the five hundred servant girls, divided the mounds of articles that they had brought as offerings into two groups. The first group they offered to the Perfection of Wisdom, and the second they offered to the Bodhisattva Dharmodgata. Wondrously the flowers, incenses, and clothing hung suspended in space and turned into a dais of flowers. The powdered sandalwood incense and the golden and silver flowers turned into jewelled curtains that covered the dais, and they turned into jewelled canopies and jewelled streamers that adorned the dais. All this was brought about by the divine power of the Bodhisattva Dharmodgata. The joy of the merchant's daughter and the servant girls was boundless, and they roused the mind of the way. They roused the aspiration that they, too, like the Bodhisattva Dharmodgata, might someday be endowed with marvellous powers and expound the Perfection of Wisdom.

(9) At that time, the Bodhisattva Sadaprarudita, together with the merchant's daughter and the servant girls, approached the Bodhisattva Dharmodgata, and reverently bowing down to him he placed his palms together and recounted his past life up to that day. He then said, "From where have come the buddhas of the ten directions, who have guided me to the place of the Honored One, and

to where have they departed? I never want to leave the buddhas' side. That I am unable to remain continually before the buddhas is my greatest sorrow."

The Bodhisattva Dharmodgata explained, "Good man, one cannot say from where the buddhas have come nor to where they have gone, for the true form of all things is emptiness. They neither arise nor perish, though they appear to when viewed through the eyes of attachment. Furthermore, they do not, yielding to minds of attachment, manifest themselves as good or bad, ugly or pure, hateful or lovable. They are not stained, even a little, by the mind of attachment. Although they remain in the midst of raging defilements, their stillness is not affected at all. Transformations such as birth and extinction and good and evil appear because of the viewer's attachment. The buddhas teach us to abandon that mind of attachment and see the truth of Emptiness, which is serene and immovable. The buddhas are beings who have been enlightened to the true nature, which is Emptiness, of all things; therefore, for buddhas, there are no such things as coming or going. The truth of all things and the body of all buddhas are one and the same; in no respect are they different. Good man, if you decide to differentiate, this world will divide itself up in a myriad of ways; the truth, however, is not bound by such differentiations. If someone in search of water chases after shimmering heat waves that rise upward at noon on a spring day, do you consider this to be a wise act?"

The Bodhisattva Sadaprarudita said, "Great teacher, water cannot be found in shimmering heat waves."

(10) The Bodhisattva Dharmodgata said, "That is correct. It is indeed foolish for someone suffering from heat and thirst to rejoice while mistaking shimmering heat waves for water. Seizing upon buddhas and pondering where they come from and where they go to is equally foolish. The bodies of the buddhas become manifest for the sake of the people; they do so for brief periods as skillful means. Therefore, with this body alone, one cannot perceive the true Buddha. The true Buddha and real truth are one and the same. The Buddha in the form of a body is a vessel; because this vessel is filled to the brim with enlightenment, even the vessel, that is, the body, is called a Buddha. For true enlightenment, there is no such thing as coming or going; therefore this is also true for buddhas. Good man, after seeing all sorts of things in a dream, it would be foolish to think that they existed even after awakening. The buddhas have always taught that all things are like these dreams. It would be foolish to seize upon buddhas who manifest, as in dreams, their fleeting forms in this human world. Ignorant of the real truth of their enlightenment, it would be the height of foolishness to pursue buddhas because of attachment to their names or bodies. Good man, you should therefore perceive all things' true nature, which is serene, immovable, and free of birth and extinction, of coming and going. One must cast off one's attachment to all things. If you are unable to bestow merits on others, you should not accept the gifts offered to you by the people. On the other hand, upon receiving gifts, if you are able to cause the people to plant merits, then you should gladly receive those gifts and become a merit-producing field. Casting off attachment, one does not do things for one's own sake;

if it is for the sake of others, then one receives both gifts and offerings. Thus one can create the way of skillful means. This man is called a true disciple of the Buddha.

"Good man, the great ocean is filled with a myriad of treasures. However, these treasures neither rained down from the heavens nor did they come springing up from the earth. They were all born of causes and conditions. Therefore, when these causes and conditions come to an end, these treasures will also disappear. In like manner, the lute, which produces melodious sounds, is not a product solely of the body, the neck, the skin, the strings, or the pegs. Its sound is not produced by human hands alone. The proper causes and conditions coalesce, and then for the first time melodious sounds are produced. The birth and extinction, coming and going of buddhas do not come about due to one single cause, one single condition, or one single merit. All the causes and conditions must come to fruition in unison, and when the proper moment for the salvation of people has arrived, the buddhas appear in this world. When those causes and conditions come to an end, the buddhas will withdraw from this world. Birth and extinction and coming and going only exist because of causes and conditions. Even though birth and extinction and coming and going exist temporarily, their true nature is serene and immutable. Should you awaken to this truth, there will be no need to be awed or feel sorrowful with regard to the birth, extinction, coming, and going of the buddhas. In the end, you will attain supreme enlightenment and be able to practice skillful means and wisdom."

(11) When this speech had ended, Indra bestowed divine mandarava flowers on the Bodhisattva Sadaprarudita and said, "Good man, offer these flowers to the Bodhisattva Dharmodgata. I shall guard you. For an immeasurably long duration, you have undergone hardships so that you would be able to save people. Such a virtuous person as you will not easily arise again. Your seeking enlightenment with such fervor will without doubt bring benefits to a great multitude and bestow supreme enlightenment upon them."

The Bodhisattva Sadaprarudita rejoiced at these words of Indra. Having received the flowers from Indra, he scattered them over the head of Dharmodgata and said, "O great teacher, from today I give myself to you as a present, and I shall serve you with the totality of my being." Then the merchant's daughter and the five hundred servant girls said to the Bodhisattva Sadaprarudita, "We, too, for our part give ourselves to you as presents and shall serve you with the totality of our being from today. We shall together with you give offerings to all buddhas in all ages. Do with us as you will."

The Bodhisattva Sadaprarudita then offered to Dharmodgata the merchant's daughter and the five hundred servant girls and the myriad of treasures in the five hundred carts, that had been brought there. He said, "Great teacher, please allow these five hundred servant girls to remain by your side to serve you night and day. And please also make use of these treasures from five hundred carts for your daily needs." Hearing this, Indra said, "This is truly a superb event. You perceive that the true nature of all things is Emptiness. Without becoming attached to any virtuous thing or merit, you selflessly give them to others for the sake of attaining enlightenment. This is truly noble; all bodhisattvas should be like this. All the buddhas of the past practiced in this way, attained the Perfection of Wisdom, and became endowed with the power of skillful means. This Bodhisattva will also, without fail, become like this." With these words, Indra praised the Bodhisattva Sadaprarudita.

So that they might plant the roots of merit, the Bodhisattva Dharmodgata gladly accepted their offerings. But then he returned them to the Bodhisattva Sadaprarudita. Then when evening came, he stood up and went into the palace.

At that time, the Bodhisattva Sadaprarudita thought, "I came to seek the Dharma; I did not come to this world lusting for dreamlike pleasures. Therefore I shall not lie down or sit down until the Dharma master emerges and expounds the Dharma again."

(12) In the palace, the Bodhisattva Dharmodgata entered meditation, and for seven years he undertook the meditation on the Perfection of Wisdom. However, the Bodhisattva Sadaprarudita did not grow weary waiting; he did not rouse the defilements of greed, anger, or ignorance, nor did he become addicted to enlightenment itself. He only continued to stand and walk, waiting intently for the moment that the teacher would once again expound the Dharma. After seven years a voice from the sky told the Bodhisattva Sadaprarudita that in seven days the teacher would emerge from his meditation, and the Bodhisattva Sadaprarudita together with the merchant's daughter and the five hundred servant girls constructed a dais made of seven gems. On the dais, they each spread out his or her upper garment and prayed that the teacher would expound the Dharma while sitting on these garments. Wishing to sprinkle water to settle the dust, lest any dust fall on the body of the teacher, Sadaprarudita sought water but was unable to find any because the Devil had hidden all the water, and Sadaprarudita became extremely disconsolate. But he then took up a sword and repeatedly pierced his body and used the blood from his own body to sprinkle on the ground to settle the dust, and the maidens did the same. Holding to the thought that from beginningless time he had suffered numerous injuries to the body and that this was the first time that he had suffered such an injury for such a purpose, the Bodhisattva Sadaprarudita was filled with joy, and in spite of the pain neither he nor any of the maidens had a change of heart. Indra was deeply moved and sang his praises, "This is truly a noble act. Because he sought enlightenment with this kind of effort, his mind remains immovable. Truly, all the buddhas of the past were exactly like this." And Indra changed all the blood into heavenly sandalwood-scented water.

(13) Thus after the seven years had passed the Bodhisattva Dharmodgata, surrounded by a huge multitude of people, advanced toward the dais that had been prepared for him. The Bodhisattva Sadaprarudita reverently worshipped the teacher, and his heart was filled with joy. Then the Bodhisattva Dharmodgata expounded the Dharma: "Good man, listen well; retain this in the heart of your mind. I shall for your sake expound the Perfection of Wisdom. Good man, all dharmas are equal, and the absolute differentiations that ignorant people believe in do not exist. To perceive this is the Perfection of Wisdom; therefore,

the Perfection of Wisdom is also equal. All dharmas are equal; therefore, there are no differentiations such as love and hate or good and bad as believed by a mind filled with desire. Accordingly, all dharmas are detached from people's attachments; the Perfection of Wisdom, which brings about this detachment, is also detached from the realm of attachment. Good man, all dharmas in this way are equal; they are detached from attachment. Therefore to think, after viewing things with the eye of attachment, that birth and extinction and coming and going exist is erroneous. That is, the fundamental nature of dharmas is free of all movement. Furthermore, the dharmas do not manifest forms of love and hate because of their thoughts; therefore, it should be said that dharmas have no thoughts. Because they are free of thoughts, dharmas are never beset by fearful enemies. Dharmas are, therefore, called fearless dharmas, and because they are imbued with the same worth, they are called dharmas of one taste. The Perfection of Wisdom, which is one with the dharmas, is also immovable, thoughtless, fearless, and of one taste. Good man, because all dharmas are without bounds, the Perfection of Wisdom is also boundless. Because all dharmas neither arise nor perish, the Perfection of Wisdom is also birthless and deathless. Good man, space and the great ocean have no bounds; the Perfection of Wisdom also possesses the great embellishment of boundlessness, much like the embellishments of Mount Sumeru in their utmost beauty. At times, space produces unexpected calamities; however, space does not do so as a result of thinking; in the same way, the Perfection of Wisdom is also free of differentiations, which are the result of thinking. The true nature of all dharmas is like a diamond; therefore the Perfection of Wisdom is also like a diamond. In this way all dharmas and the Perfection of Wisdom are absolutely one and the same. They both do not differentiate; their true natures are difficult to grasp; they are free of attachment; their actions are not performed willfully; they are inconceivable and cannot be fathomed by thought; they are the dharmas that are without differentiation, ungraspable, without karmic accumulations, without actions, and inconceivable."

When hearing this teaching, the Bodhisattva Sadaprarudita at that very moment was able to dwell serenely in the Dharma and was able to attain all the meditations and see all the buddhas of the three periods and the ten directions, as innumerable as the sands of the Ganges, expounding the Perfection of Wisdom to their crowds of disciples.

(14) Thus did the World-Honored One expound this history of the Bodhisattva Sadaprarudita's search for the Dharma; and to Subhuti he said, "Subhuti, I now, surrounded by innumerable disciples, expound the Perfection of Wisdom in this world. In the manner of which I spoke in the history of the Bodhisattva Sadaprarudita, buddhas of the three periods and the ten directions, as innumerable as the sands of the Ganges, are expounding the Perfection of Wisdom. The Perfection of Wisdom is truly a noble teaching shared by all the buddhas. Subhuti, the Bodhisattva Sadaprarudita thereafter listened well and retained the teaching, like the great ocean that takes in all the waters and loses not a drop. He always remained next to a buddha, appearing in country after country where buddhas reside. He now has the power to be born at the place of

any buddha, in accordance with his aspirations. He is able to do so by virtue of his practice of the Perfection of Wisdom. You should know that it is only after applying oneself in this way that one is able to attain all merits and universal wisdom."

(15) The World-Honored One, having finished expounding the Dharma, asked Ananda, "Ananda, do you believe, from the bottom of your heart, that I am your teacher and that you are my disciple?" Ananda replied, "I rejoice that the World-Honored One is my teacher and that I am a disciple of the World-Honored One."

The World-Honored One said, "Very well, Ananda, I am your teacher and you are my unswerving disciple. To this day, you have continuously carried out your duties as a disciple. Ananda, everything you have thought, said, and done has been in accordance with my wishes. The manner in which you are serving me is truly splendid; after my demise, you must serve the Perfection of Wisdom with the same feeling with which you have served me. Do not forget to do this; do not let go of this; as the bearer of this teaching, I ask you to fulfill your duty. Ananda, you should think that wherever a seeker of the way exists, there will be the Perfection of Wisdom, and wherever the Perfection of Wisdom appears, the Buddha will also be there, expounding the Dharma." When the World-Honored One had finished expounding the Dharma, the minds of the people were filled with joy.

Chapter 3

THE TRANSFERENCE OF MERIT

1. The Three Kinds of Teachers

(1) The World-Honored One now headed north and entered Savatthi. He then journeyed through the country of Kosala and stayed at a village called Salavatika. This village was given to the brahmin Lohicca by King Pasenadi. With a large amount of grazing land and many rice paddies, the villagers prospered and were well off. The leader Lohicca had this thought in mind, "It may be that a monk may achieve the good to which he aspires, but he should not teach others about it. This is because it would be hard for him to conceive what another person would be able to do. Teaching would be like cutting away an old fetter and creating a new one. It is after all, a kind of self-indulgence."

Hearing that the World-Honored One had come to the village, Lohicca called the hairdresser Bhesika to convey his respects to the World-Honored One and to invite the Buddha to dinner the next day. Bhesika, having relayed the wishes of Lohicca, accompanied the Buddha. Along the way he mentioned to the Buddha the thoughts that the master Lohicca had had in his mind and pleaded with the Buddha to employ his power in driving away the wrong thoughts within Lohicca.

(2) Having offered food to the Buddha, Lohicca took his seat in a lower position in the presence of the Buddha. The World-Honored One, referring to the thoughts that he had been told that Lohicca had had in his mind, asked him whether he had had such thoughts. Lohicca said that he had. The Buddha then asked Lohicca, "Lohicca, you are presently the lord of this village of Salavatika. There could be a person who might say that you, the brahmin, should keep all of the harvest and produce to yourself and should not share them with others. Now, could such a person become a threat to keeping peace and harmony in this village?"

To this question, Lohicca answered that he would surely be such a threat. The World-Honored One continued and said, "Such a person becomes a threat because he is not sympathetic and has animosity in his heart. Does not a person have wrong views if he has animosity in his heart? It is well understood that a person of wrong views will be reborn in hell. Now, in extending the situation I mentioned to you, it will apply in the case of King Pasenadi. The king rules over the countries of Kasi and Kosala; however, if there are some who argue that the harvest and fruits of these two countries ought to be given only to the king and not to other people, such people pose a threat to the inhabitants of these two countries. They lack compassion, are filled with enmity, live perverted lives, and must fall into hell. O Lohicca, those who say, 'The mendicant should not speak to other people of the good that he has realized', erect barriers for those who have entered the Buddha's teaching and are nurturing the seeds of enlightenment. They lack compassion, are filled with enmity, reside in evil, and therefore must fall into hell.

(3) "Lohicca, there are three kinds of masters who should be admonished. The first are those who, having become mendicants, have failed to achieve their goals and yet instruct their disciples, saying, 'These teachings are good for you and will bring you happiness,' and whose disciples do not listen to what these monks tell them and eventually leave them. This type of teacher should be admonished as follows: 'Although you have been ordained a monk, you have not reached your goal as yet. Now, because you try to teach your disciples, the disciples choose not to listen to your teachings but look to other masters for guidance. Your teachings are disliked, just as a man who becomes infatuated with a woman who dislikes him and tries to hold onto her is disliked. This is a kind of undue attachment.' Such an admonition is justified.

"The second kind are those who have become mendicants but have failed to achieve their goal and yet instruct their disciples, saying, 'These teachings are good for you and will bring you happiness,' and whose disciples listen intently to the masters' instructions and follow their path in earnest. These masters should also be admonished as follows: 'You have forgotten about your own field and are weeding somebody else's field. This is also a kind of undue attachment.' Such an admonition is justified.

"The third kind are those who have achieved the purpose of their renunciation and are teaching their disciples, but whose disciples do not listen to the masters' teachings and are drifting away from the masters. These masters, too, should be admonished as follows: 'What you are doing is like cutting yourself free from old bonds and at the same time tying new ones, which is a form of bad attachment. How can one impose his wishes on another?' Such an admonition is justified."

(4) Lohicca asked the Buddha whether there were any teachers in the world who should not be criticized. To this the World-Honored One answered, "Lohicca, say, for instance, that from the time of the appearance of the Buddha in this world, the Dharma has been taught. Laymen, hearing this, have put their trust in the Dharma and become monks. They continue their lives according to the precepts and find happiness through right actions, are fearful of committing even a minor offense, are ever cautious of the five senses, attain meditation by overcoming desires with minds cultivated through concentration, and realize the power to know past events and others' thoughts and to overcome defilements. Thus having realized complete release, they are fully aware of this realization. Now, Lohicca, any master whose disciples have attained such

levels of emancipation under his guidance will never deserve criticism. Criticizing him is not only uncalled for but is equal to committing a transgression."

Lohicca, hearing these instructions from the Buddha, greatly rejoiced, saying, "Like a man who was about to fall down a cliff but was saved by another who grasped him by the collar, I, who was destined to fall into hell, was saved by the Buddha." Lohicca took refuge in the Buddha and became his disciple.

(5) The World-Honored One continued his travels and arrived at Manasakata village, which was ruled by a brahmin leader. He rested in a forest along the river Aciravati. Just at that time the well-known brahmins Tarukkha and Pokkharasati had matters to attend to and were staying at the village. The leading follower of the latter master, Vasettha, and that of the former master, Bharadvaja, were discussing matters regarding the true and false nature of the way as they quietly strolled along the sandy bank after taking their evening showers. According to Vasettha, the teaching that he received from the master Pokkharasati was so authentic that as long as one faithfully followed this way, he would without fail find birth in the realm of gods. But according to Bharadvaja, the teaching of the brahmin Tarukkha was rather the true teaching. Thus the two were unable to defeat each other in argument. They finally agreed to approach the famous Gotama and seek his decision.

(6) The Buddha asked them a question: "Vasettha says that the way taught him by his master is the way leading one to birth in the realm of gods, and Bharadvaja also claims that his master teaches the right way. What is the difference of opinion, the cause of controversy?"

To this question by the Buddha they answered, "We are arguing about the true or the false nature of the path. There are many brahmin masters who are teaching the path. Perhaps all the teachings being taught by the teachers and masters will enable us to realize birth in the realm of gods. Is this not similar to the convergence of many roads near towns and villages, when they become one road?" To this the Buddha answered, "Vasettha, do you mean to say that the teachings of those brahmins will lead their followers to their goals without fail?" To this he answered, "Yes."

The Buddha asked, "Vasettha, of all the brahmins who study the main Vedic texts, do you know of any who have actually seen a god?" To this he answered, "No." The Buddha then asked, "Vasettha, of all the teachers of the brahmins, or further, the teachers of the teachers of the masters, has there been even one who has seen a god?" To this he answered that none had seen a god. The Buddha asked, "Vasettha, has there been one master amongst the ancestors up to seven generations back who has seen a god?" To this he answered, "No." "Vasettha, among those sages of the past who formulated the prayers of the brahmins, is there even one who proclaimed where a god was to be found or how a god came into being or that a god clearly perceives and observes someone?" To this Vasettha answered, "No."

(7) The Buddha then said to Vasettha, "From this it is clear that from olden times, among the sages and brahmins who are well versed in the three Vedic texts, there has not been even one who has seen a god. They claim, 'We teach

a path that leads to a place that we have neither known nor seen. This path is straight, and if you follow it faithfully, you will reach a place that we have neither known nor seen.'" The Buddha continued, "Suppose there is a group of blind people who are linked together. Neither the blind man in front, nor the one at the back, nor the one in the middle would be able to see a thing. Likewise, the brahmins in this case, too, are unable to see, even though they are prone to make such claims. Such words are nothing but meaningless talk."

The Buddha continued, "Vasettha, suppose that a person who speaks of his love were to say that he is in love with the most beautiful woman in the kingdom. Another person then asks whether the object of his affection is the queen or the daughter of a brahmin, or the daughter of a merchant or a servant. To this the person answers that he does not know. Other questions are asked, such as her first name and family name, or whether she is tall or short, or whether she is fair or dark, or where she lives, and to these he answers that he does not know. He is asked, 'You say you are in love, but is it not true that you do not know this woman nor have you ever met her?' To this question he answers that this is exactly so. Vasettha, the teaching of the brahmins, which says one can be born in the realm of gods, is exactly like this."

The Buddha continued, "Vasettha, assume that after a heavy rain the river Aciravati nearly overflows its banks. A person who has some business to tend to on the other shore shouts, 'Other shore, come here!' Would the other shore come over to his side in answer to such a prayer? He is like a brahmin who has discarded what a brahmin should do and is concerned with matters most inappropriate for a brahmin, invoking the power of the gods.

"Moreover, Vasettha, at the time of the overflowing of the river Aciravati, if someone, wishing to get across to the other shore, were to have his hands tied behind him with a chain, would it be possible for this man to get across? The brahmins have discarded the way they should follow and, while by intention on the way of the sages, are bound by the chains of five desires.

"Again, Vasettha, there is someone sleeping on the banks of the flooded Aciravati River. His whole body, even his head, is covered over with a blanket. Would it be possible for him to cross the river and reach the other shore? The brahmins, too, have discarded the way that they should be practicing and are covered over with impurities that are hindrances to the way of the sages. Will these brahmins then be able to cross to the other shore?

"Vasettha, according to what the elders of your brahmins say, the gods do not have families nor material wealth. In their minds there is no anger, no hatred, no impurity, only purity itself. How do the brahmins who are active today appear to you?"

To this question by the World-Honored One, Vasettha answered that on the contrary the brahmins had families and wealth and their minds were filled with anger, hatred, and impurity. The Buddha said, "Vasettha, it is clear now that there is nothing in common between the gods and the brahmins. Without a common ground, the brahmins cannot possibly enter into the ranks of gods. Actually, while sitting in meditation, the brahmins will sink into the abyss of hell. They will sink while thinking that they are ascending to heaven. Thus the teachings of the three Vedas are like a desert without water and a bamboo grove with no road passing through it; they are nothing but destruction itself."

(8) Vasettha then asked the Buddha whether the way leading to birth in the realm of the gods was known to him. To this the Buddha replied, "Vasettha, is the hamlet Manasakata near or far from here?" To this Vasettha replied that it was not far away. "Vasettha, will a person who was born in Manasakata and raised there be at a loss for an answer when asked the way to the village? Vasettha, even if he is, I shall never be perplexed if asked whether I know about the realm of gods or the way leading to it. This is because I am as well aware of it as the gods themselves."

Vasettha asked of the World-Honored One, "World-Honored One, I have been told that you are fully aware of that. Please teach me the way so that I, a brahmin, can be saved."

To this the World-Honored One replied, "Vasettha, you would do well to listen carefully to what I say. With the appearance of the Buddha in this world, the Dharma was set forth. The lay followers, hearing the teachings, awaken to faith and lead their everyday lives in accordance with the precepts. They pursue honorable professions, ever cautious not to commit the smallest transgression, careful of the gates of the five senses. They are freed from all defilements. Their bodies are relaxed, and their minds are serene and calm, with their thoughts concentrated on one point. They also share thoughts of deep understanding, of compassion, of happiness, and of true equanimity. Just as the bugler is able to reach people's ears easily throughout the four directions, with boundless minds they do so with no thoughts of hatred or anger. Vasettha, this is the way to realize birth in the realm of gods. The disciples of the Buddha, whose hearts overflow with these four boundless minds, have no family ties and no material possessions, and their minds are free of anger, hatred, and impurity. These followers are, as it were, the equals of the gods; they may be said to be in the ranks of the gods." Vasettha and Bharadvaja deeply rejoiced in having heard this teaching by the Buddha and vowed to become the Buddha's disciples.

(9) The World-Honored One then taught throughout the villages of Kosala and, returning to Savatthi, entered the Jeta Grove Monastery. One day, summoning the disciples, the World-Honored One gave the following instructions: "My disciples, I shall now teach you the way by which all defilements can be overcome. I trust that you will heed my words with the utmost care. My disciples, I direct my words to those who know what should be known and see what should be seen. By what should be known and seen, I mean right thought and wrong thought. In right thought, the defilements that have not yet arisen will not arise, while the defilements that have already arisen will go out of existence. In wrong thought, the defilements that have not yet arisen will arise, while the defilements that have arisen will increase. Disciples, defilements can be pacified through the correct view, restraint, correct use, forbearance, avoidance, rejection, and discipline.

"What do I mean when I say defilements can be pacified through the correct view? My disciples, suppose there is one who has never seen a sage, has never known the way of the sages, has never learned the way of the sages, has never seen a good person, has never known the way of the good person, and has never learned the way of the good person. This person is not aware of the things he should or should not dwell upon; he thinks of the things that he should not think of and neglects to think of the things that he should think of. He has thoughts such as 'Did I or did I not exist in the past? If I existed, what was I and what was I doing? Why did I became such a being? Will I exist or not exist in the future? If I am going to exist in the future, what shall I become? What shall I be doing? Why shall I become such a being? Do I exist in the present or not? If I do exist now, what am I and what am I doing? Where have I come from and where am I going? What is to become of me?'

"These thoughts in turn lead to other thoughts such as 'the self is mine,' 'the self is not mine,' 'I see the self with my self,' 'I see the non-self with my self,' 'I see the self with my non-self.' They lead to the thought, 'The self that I know and feel experiences the effect of good and evil action in this life or in the next. This self is everlasting and will forever remain unchanged.' My disciples, these thoughts are perverted views. Perverted views are a kind of attachment and bondage. Because of this bondage people cannot be released from birth, old age, death, anxiety, sorrow, suffering, worry, and agony.

(10) "My disciples, on the other hand, the person who has seen a sage, has known the way of the sages, has learned the way of the sages, has seen a good person, has known the way of the good person, and has the willingness to learn the way of the good person can discern what he should think from what he should not think. He thinks of the things that he should; he does not think of the things that he should not. He thinks correctly, 'This is suffering. This is the cause of suffering. This is the extinction of suffering. This is the way to the extinction of suffering.' By virtue of this right thought, he can be freed from mistaken views concerning his body, ideas, and actions. This explains how defilements can be purified through correct view.

"That defilements can be pacified through restraint means that someone who holds right thoughts can control his six sense organs, the eyes, ears, nose, tongue, body, and mind. Thus the defilements, which are the basis of his delusion and suffering, cannot arise through them.

"That defilements can be pacified through correct use means that someone who holds right thoughts thinks that he will use his clothing and food not for pleasure but for protecting himself from heat and cold, for hiding his body, and for nurturing his body, so that it can perform the pure practices. By virtue of this thought, the defilements, which are the basis of his delusion and suffering, cannot arise when he uses all kinds of things.

"That defilements can be pacified through forbearance means that someone who holds right thoughts endures cold, heat, hunger, thirst, slander, ridicule, and suffering that threatens his life. By virtue of this forbearance, the defilements, which are the basis of his delusion and suffering, cannot arise.

"That defilements can be pacified through avoidance means that someone who holds right thoughts avoids ferocious elephants, horses, cattle, dogs, places that are improper for sitting, forbidden places, and friends who are bad influences.

Because of this avoidance, the defilements, which are the basis of his delusion and suffering, cannot arise.

"That defilements can be pacified through rejection means that someone who holds right thoughts rejects, smashes, and annihilates greed, anger, hatred, and any other evil ideas in his mind. Because of this rejection, the defilements, which are the basis of his delusion and suffering, cannot arise.

"That defilements can be pacified through discipline means that someone who holds right thoughts lives alone, is free from desire, strengthens his idea of eliminating the impurities in his mind, and cultivates the way of enlightenment. Because of this discipline, the defilements, which are the basis of his delusion and suffering, cannot arise.

"Disciples, if you put an end to defilements through correct view, restraint, correct use, forbearance, avoidance, rejection, and discipline, all defilements will be pacified, the thirst of craving will be nullified, bonds will be severed, and the elimination of suffering will be achieved."

2. Four Dangers

(1) The World-Honored One left the city of Savatthi and, arriving at the country of the Sakya clan, stayed in the Amalaki-grove, which belonged to the Catuma village. At that time, Sariputta and Moggallana had just arrived at the village with five hundred disciples to pay homage to the Buddha. There was some commotion as the visiting disciples and the resident disciples were exchanging greetings, while some were arranging their seating mats and others were putting away their robes and alms bowls. The World-Honored One summoned Ananda and asked the reason for the loud exchange of words, which sounded like the clamor of fishermen fighting over the same catch. Having heard the reason for the commotion from Ananda, the Buddha had the disciples summoned and said to them, "My disciples, I ask you to leave at once. I shall not permit you to stay near me!"

The disciples responded by saying that they understood the Buddha's instructions, and standing up from their seats they bowed to the Buddha; then turning to the right they took their robes and bowls and left the place.

At that time, the people of the Sakya clan of Catuma village were gathered in the village hall for a meeting. They saw the Buddha's disciples coming from a distance and asked the reason. They asked the disciples to wait awhile, and approaching the World-Honored One they asked forgiveness for them, saying, "O World-Honored One, please forgive the commotion caused by the disciples. Please protect the Sangha just as you have done in the past. In this Sangha there are those who have newly sought refuge in the teachings. If they are not able to see the Buddha now, some may change their minds and regress to lower levels. Just as the seedling withers away if it lacks water and as the calf tends to weaken if it does not see its mother, they too may regress to lower levels. For this reason, O World-Honored One, please forgive the disciples and give the Sangha your protection."

(2) Because of this sincere request, the disciples were pardoned. Moggallana then once again encouraged people to sit close to the Buddha. Upon bowing to the World-Honored One, they sat near the Buddha. The World-Honored One then asked Sariputta, "O Sariputta, what did you think when I admonished the disciples?"

To this Sariputta answered that at that time he had reasoned that the World-Honored One preferred to let matters stand as they were and to enter into the bliss of meditation instead of pursuing the matter, and that they, too, should prefer not to pursue the matter but engage in the meditation of mind concentration. To these words of Sariputta, the Buddha said, "Wait, Sariputta. I suggest that you not harbor such thoughts again."

The World-Honored One turned to Moggallana and asked, "O Moggallana, what did you think about the matter?" To this Moggallana answered, "O World-Honored One, this is what I thought and felt. The World-Honored One, now having admonished the noisy disciples, preferred not to pursue the matter but to enter into the bliss of meditation; therefore, I, together with Sariputta, shall, on behalf of the World-Honored One, lead the disciples." To this the World-Honored One answered, "Well said, Moggallana. Those who lead the disciples are the Buddha, Sariputta, or Moggallana."

(3) The Buddha addressed the disciples, "My disciples, those who venture out to sea should expect four kinds of dangers. They are the dangers of waves, crocodiles, whirlpools, and susuka fish. Those who have renounced the household life and have sought refuge in the teachings should also be prepared for four dangers.

"My disciples, what do you think is the danger of waves? Say, for instance, that a son of a noble family has faith in the Dharma and vows his renunciation with these thoughts: 'I am deeply immersed in birth, old age, sickness, death, anxiety, sorrow, pain, worry, and agony and am at a loss because of pain. I should find a way to be released from these sufferings.'

"To these thoughts his colleagues say in wishing to help him: 'You should proceed in this way. You should return in this way. You should be able to oversee in this manner. You should observe in this manner. You should stretch and fold your arm in this manner. You should put on your robe this way.'

"At this point he has this thought in mind: 'I, too, when I was a householder, gave guidance to others. However, now I must receive instructions from young men who are like my sons and grandsons. It is indeed a shameful thing!' He is enraged and, discarding the teachings, returns to the layman's status. My disciples, by the danger of waves I mean such anger and despair.

"My disciples, by the danger of crocodiles, I mean a situation in which a person vows renunciation and becomes a monk. His fellow monks tell him, 'You should eat this. You should not eat that. You should drink this. You should not drink that.' Having been told these things, the person may think in this manner: 'When I was still a layman, I ate what I wanted, and I drank what I wanted. There were never problems about foods being appropriate for me or the time for eating being correct. Supposing some devout lay followers were to offer delicious food right now. If it were not an appropriate time to partake of food, my mouth would be sealed because of this frustrating precept.' Thus abandoning the teaching, he might return to the laity. My disciples, this is the danger of crocodiles, which is to be bothered by food and rules concerning it.

"My disciples, what do you think is the danger of whirlpools? Assume that a person enters monkhood. At daybreak he puts on his robe but does not control his bodily actions, speech, or thought, nor does he hold right thoughts or control his five senses. He starts off to the towns and villages to receive food offerings. Along the way, he observes laymen enjoying themselves by indulging in the five senses and thinks, 'When I too was a lay person, I indulged in such pleasures. Because I had wealth, I was able to accumulate virtues joyfully.' With these thoughts, and now disliking the teachings, he returns to the layman's status. This is the danger of whirlpools, which is to indulge in the pleasures of the five senses.

"My disciples, what do you think is the danger of the susuka fish? Assume that a person becomes a mendicant. Now, having made his renunciation and being on his way to receive offerings of food, he comes across a woman who wears her gown in an extremely disorderly fashion. Experiencing a feeling of lust toward her and then discarding the teachings, he returns to lay life. My disciples, this is the danger of the susuka fish, which is the temptation of women. My disciples, those who have made renunciation to pursue the Dharma should be prepared to meet with these four dangers."

(4) The World-Honored One now journeyed toward the east. Then, after a considerable time, he headed south, and upon reaching Vesali he once again resided in a large forest. At that time, Saccaka, a Nigantha follower, was also staying at Vesali. Because of his superior oratory, people praised Saccaka. He was proud of this and boasted to others about it: "There is no mendicant who could debate me without breaking out in a cold sweat. If a wooden pillar were able to engage in a debate with me, even it would surely tremble in fear."

One day, as Assaji, a disciple of the Buddha, walked through the town of Vesali to receive food offerings, Saccaka happened to be going for a stroll in the forest. Seeing Assaji, he approached him and asked, "O Venerable Sir, tell me how Gotama teaches his disciples and what teachings are widely practiced by his disciples."

To this Assaji replied, "Saccaka, the World-Honored One teaches that the body is temporary; the mind is also temporary; all that is put together is temporary and is devoid of a self. This is the teaching that is being practiced among the disciples."

To this Saccaka replied, "Venerable Sir, to tell us such teachings is to pollute our ears. Be it at any time or any place, I should like to meet with Gotama to relieve him of such views."

Saying this, Saccaka immediately left for the town hall. There were about five hundred noblemen of the Licchavi clan assembled there for a meeting. Here he made an announcement, "Noblemen, I wish to have a debate with Gotama today. Now, if the teachings of Gotama are as one of the disciples, Assaji, says they are, I shall take up the words of Gotama and swing them around just as a strong man would grab hold of the long fleece of a sheep and swing it around time and time again!" Hearing these words, some thought that Saccaka would win the debate and others thought that the World-Honored One would emerge the winner.

(5) As Saccaka, surrounded by many, headed toward the multistoried pagoda hall, many of the Buddha's disciples were also slowly approaching. They all headed toward the Buddha and took their seats. At that time Saccaka asked, "If the venerable one, Gotama, will permit it, there is one thing that I would like to ask him." To this the Buddha stated, "Saccaka, do not hesitate to ask me anything that comes to your mind."

Saccaka then asked, "O Gotama, how does the World-Honored One teach his disciples the Dharma and what are the teachings being widely practiced by them?"

To this the Buddha answered, "Saccaka, this is the way I teach them, 'My disciples, nothing, whether it is the body or the mind, remains constant; there is no permanent entity. All that is brought into experience has no permanence and is no permanent entity.' This is the teaching that is being practiced by my disciples."

Saccaka spoke of his impressions: "O World-Honored One, here is an analogy that occurs to me. No matter what the plant may be, or what its seed may be, it relies on the good earth, and it has its root in the earth, which sustains it. Those who labor, too, rely on the earth. They, too, are sustained by the earth. O venerable one, I believe that likewise the body is the atman; based on this body it does pure and impure acts; the mind is the atman, and standing on this mind it engages in pure and impure acts." Then the Buddha said, "O Saccaka, is it correct that what you are really saying is that your body is the atman and your mind is the atman?" To this, Saccaka answered that this was his opinion and that many people there, too, had the same opinion. To this the World-Honored One said, "O Saccaka, why is it necessary to talk about these many people? Should you not express only those thoughts that occur in your own mind?" Saccaka answered that he would still adhere to his statement that the body was the atman and that the mind was also the atman.

(6) The World-Honored One then asked of Saccaka, "O Saccaka, I wish to ask you a question, the answer to which I hope will come directly from your mind. Now, do you believe that kings, such as King Pasenadi of Kosala, King Bimbisara of Magadha, or any other kings, are able to kill those who should be killed, take what should be taken, ostracize those who should be ostracized, and do as they wish in those lands that they have conquered?" To this Saccaka answered that such things can be done because the ruler of the land has the authority and power to do them.

The Buddha asked, "O Saccaka, you stated that your body was your atman. Can you actually do everything that you wish with your body, ordering it to be or not to be a certain way?" To this question posed by the World-Honored One, Saccaka kept his silence. He did not attempt to answer the Buddha's question even when he was asked a second time. When the Buddha urged Saccaka to answer the question, Saccaka finally answered that his body could not be freely controlled.

(7) The World-Honored One said to Saccaka, "You should answer my question after thinking well. You should not be inconsistent. To ask the same question about the mind, which you also say is the atman, is it possible freely to control it, ordering it to be or not to be such and such?" Saccaka answered, "No, it is not possible." The Buddha then asked, "Saccaka, it would be well for you to consider carefully so that there is no inconsistency in your answer to the following question. Is the human body eternal or temporary?" Saccaka answered, "It is not eternal."

The Buddha continued his questioning, "Then Saccaka, is that which is not eternal suffering or bliss?" Saccaka answered, "It is suffering." The Buddha continued, "Then, Saccaka, is it correct to say that that which is impermanent, suffering, and transient is mine, me, or my atman?" To this Saccaka answered, "No, it is not correct."

The Buddha said, "O Saccaka, the same may be said of the mind, for it is undue attachment to the mind that causes one's suffering, that makes one attached to suffering, and that makes one think that suffering is his, that suffering is himself, that suffering is his atman. Can we say that such a person has realized the nature of suffering and has found release from suffering?" To this, Saccaka answered, "No, we cannot."

"O Saccaka, suppose a person enters a forest with an ax, seeking the core of a tree. He comes across a coconut palm tree and cuts it down. Try as he might, he will find only layer after layer of bark and will never find any hard part of the tree. What you have been doing is similar to this, for in response to my questions you have only brought to light that your views are meaningless, wrong, and impure. Tell me, Saccaka, why did you boast to these people of Vesali that if anyone were to debate with you, he would break out in a cold sweat? Are you not right now perspiring and is your clothing not drenched with sweat?"

(8) As Saccaka stood there, someone called Dummuka of the Licchavi clan exclaimed, "O World-Honored One, right now I have this parable in my mind: Once, in a pond, there lived a huge crab that tried to cut off the limbs of little children. One day the crab was caught by the children, who threw it on the ground and hit it with stones and pebbles. Injured, it could not even flee into the water. Saccaka is like this crab."

Saccaka then said, "Dummuka, we were not speaking to you, so please keep quiet. O Gotama, I truly realize the uselessness of engaging in arguments. Sir, how do your disciples practice the teachings, overcome doubts, not turn their minds to other things, and rely entirely on your teachings?"

To this the World-Honored One answered, "Saccaka, my disciples truthfully understand that their bodies and minds are not theirs, not their selves, not their atmans. Thus by following the teachings, by freeing themselves from doubts, and by not turning their minds to others, they rely solely on the teachings of the master."

(9) On another day, the World-Honored One was about to leave the pagoda hall when Saccaka came strolling toward the large forest. Ananda saw him and informed the World-Honored One, "O World-Honored One, here comes Saccaka, who still speaks ill of the Three Treasures. Please have pity on him. Please be seated here for a while."

Saccaka then approached where the World-Honored One was seated and said, "Venerable one, there is a mendicant who has disciplined his body but not his mind. He suffers from bodily pain, his thighs are benumbed, his heart is torn, and he bleeds from his mouth. His mind is disturbed and he becomes insane. Now, in this case, his mind is completely under the influence of his body because his mind is not disciplined. There are others who have disciplined their minds but not their bodies. When they experience mental pain, their thighs become numbed, their hearts are broken, and they bleed through their mouths. They become mentally disturbed and then insane. In this case, the body is completely under the control of the mind. All this is due to the body not being disciplined. When I think about your disciples, I feel they have disciplined their minds but have not disciplined their bodies."

To these words the Buddha replied, "Saccaka, what do you mean by disciplining the body?" Saccaka answered that there were right then people like Nanda Vaccha, Kisa Sankicca, and Makkhali Gosala who were enduring difficult practices regarding food, clothing, and mats and enduring bodily discipline. To this the World-Honored One asked, "Saccaka, are those people maintaining their bodies by engaging in difficult practices involving food?"

To this Saccaka answered that they did not and that at times they ate nutritious food and nourished their bodies. The Buddha asked, "Saccaka, from what I have gathered, it seems as if you are merely picking up what you have once discarded, putting on weight and losing it. Now what do you mean by disciplining your mind?"

(10) As Saccaka stood there, unable to answer the Buddha's question, the Buddha continued and said, "Saccaka, the way to discipline your mind that you indicated is not the correct way. Truly, since you do not even know the way to discipline your body, there is no way you can know the way to discipline your mind. Saccaka, assume that a person experiences an enjoyable sensation. In this case, he becomes attached to this sensation. Thus when the sensation is gone, there is the uneasy feeling of having lost it, and he laments and cries over it. This is because there is no discipline of body or mind. On the other hand, if both mind and body are disciplined, even if there is the sensation of pleasure, there will be no attachments. So even if the sensation of pleasure is gone and the feeling of displeasure is activated, there will be no sadness nor lamentation."

Saccaka then said to the World-Honored One that if he were the one who had disciplined the body and mind, then he would strongly believe that the Buddha was the one who had full control of mind and body. To this the World-Honored One remarked, "Saccaka, are you saying such things to ridicule me? If so, I hereby tell you that ever since my renunciation, whether sensations were pleasant or unpleasant, there has never been a time when my mind has become attached."

To this Saccaka inquired, "O World-Honored One, is it not the case that of the many sensations you have experienced, a sensation of real intensity has fortunately never occurred?"

To this the World-Honored One replied, "Saccaka, you should know that I performed all types of ascetic practices. Indeed, I am confident in saying that in the past and in the future there has never been, and never will be, anyone who has endured what I have endured. As far as I am concerned, such ways were simply found not to be the true way and were discarded. I was never attached to any of the painful sensations that the practices offered. Once set upon the right path to enlightenment, the body was nurtured and the mind was directed to meditation. Even when the pleasant sensation of deep meditation was aroused, my mind was not attached to it. Even when the pleasure of having been released from human agony was experienced, my mind was not in any way attached to it."

Saccaka then asked the World-Honored One whether the Buddha, too, had ever taken a nap during the day. To this the Buddha admitted, "Saccaka, it was around the end of summer that right after a meal, I folded my robe into four and, resting on my side, took a nap." To this answer by the Buddha, Saccaka remarked that another ascetic had called this residing in a state of indulgence.

"Saccaka, taking a nap during the day cannot be called either indulgence or non-indulgence. This is because anyone who has not yet freed himself from the thirst of lust and other impurities, which are the causes of future birth for all indulgent ones, is not free from indulgence. Only those who have completely severed themselves from the bondage of the thirst of lust and other impurities are free from indulgence, just as a tree is killed only when the core of its trunk is cut." To these words of the Buddha, Saccaka replied, "O venerable one, your instructions are truly marvellous. While resolving immediate problems in an orderly way, you retain the pure color of your skin at all times, and your whole being is calm. Other masters evade the issues in question; they become irritated and confused. O venerable one, please excuse me, for I have many things I have to attend to." Saccaka, who was pleased with the Buddha's instructions, then left the forest.

3. The Path of a Sovereign

(1) In due time, Saccaka, although a follower of Jainism, began to appreciate the teachings of the World-Honored One more and more, and finally he sought refuge in the Buddha and later obtained many disciples.

At one time, as Saccaka was headed toward the city of Ujjeni with many disciples, King Pajjota gladly received him as a famous teacher. The king asked for Saccaka's instructions on the way of a king. Saccaka said, "O great king, the first duty of a king is to protect his subjects. The reason why the ruler is called the king is that he is the father and mother of the people. He is called the king because he protects his people in accordance with the law and brings peace to their hearts. O great king, the ruler should raise his subjects just as parents raise their own children. Parents need not be told when it is time to change diapers. In this manner, a king should at all times bring happiness to his subjects while removing their suffering and showing tender care and love in their upbringing. The ruler always considers his subjects national treasures. If the people do not enjoy peace of mind, then the rule of the sovereign is not a successful one.

"O great king, for this reason, a king should be concerned about his subjects at all times. He should be concerned about the happiness and suffering of his subjects and enhance their prosperity. To do this, the king should be fully knowledgeable about water, droughts, winds, rains, good or bad crops, and the worries and happiness of his subjects. Regarding the crimes of his people, he should carefully observe whether crimes are being committed or not and whether they are minor or serious. The king should be aware of the good and bad deeds of his people and reward or punish them. In this manner the king should know the mind of his people, protecting them with his authority and power. That which should be given to them should be given to them at the proper time. That which has to be collected should be collected with due consideration. The king must refrain from depriving his subjects of their happiness by imposing merciless taxes. Good kings like this are always concerned about their subjects, offer them protection, and are thus worthy of being called kings.

"O great king, the king of kings is called a cakkavatti or universal monarch. The lineage of this king is unblemished. His person is honorable. He governs the four quarters and emerges as the Dharma king who protects the virtuous teaching. Wherever this king goes, there are neither swords nor hatred. Basing himself on the Dharma, he spreads virtues. He brings peace to the people and subjugates evil and wrongdoing.

"O great king, a universal monarch practices the ten virtues: he refrains from killing, stealing, adultery, lying, malicious gossip, being fork-tongued, flattery, greed, anger, and foolishness. By doing so, he enables the people also to part with the ten evils. He governs with the teachings; therefore, throughout the world, he is able to rule freely. There are no cases of people attacking each other. The people are harmonious, and the countries are at peace. He is able to bring pleasure to everyone's lives. For these reasons is he called a Dharma king.

"O great king, a universal monarch is the king among kings. All the kings rejoice in his virtues. Following his example, they govern their countries while remaining faithful to his teaching. A universal monarch enables all the kings to be at peace in their respective countries and enables them to fulfill their duties as kings, relying on the true Dharma."

At this time King Pajjota inquired, "I can fully understand that a king should protect his people by ruling his country with compassion according to the teachings of the Dharma. But how should this king execute his duties when there are those who violate the laws of the land?"

To this, Saccaka answered, "O great king, even in such cases, a king should rule with compassion. With the clear eyes of wisdom, a king should observe every situation and take appropriate measures according to the five standards. By the five standards I mean the following: First, abide by the truth and discard the untruthful; after studying the facts, take measures based on the facts. Second, act at the right time and avoid inappropriate times. When a king has power, it is the right time. When he does not have power, it is an inappropriate time. When a king has power, his efforts to punish will prove effective, whereas when he does not have power, his attempts to punish can only lead to chaos. The king should wait for the right moment. Third, apply reason in rendering judgments and avoid that which is unreasonable. Always consider the mind of the criminal, discerning whether he intended to commit a crime or not. If there is no ill intention behind the action, that action should be forgiven. Fourth, speak kindly and avoid unkind words. Evaluate the crime in the light of statutory provisions, contain the effects of the crime, clarify the nature of the offense in kind words, and make the criminal aware of the crime he has committed. Fifth, always be compassionate and never be misled by anger. The crime should be abhorred, not the criminal. Be understanding and make every effort to have the criminal repent the evil he has committed."

To these words of Saccaka, the king now said, "O teacher, if there are ministers of the state who have no concern about the policies of the state but are only concerned about personal gain, who accept bribes, distort state policies, and rouse corruption in the minds of the people, people become distrustful of one another. Moreover, the strong pressure the weak, the high in rank slight the low, and the rich deceive the poor. Since the dishonest defeat the honest, misfortunes go unchecked. As a result, the sincere and loyal leave their posts, while the scheming and two-faced take over the reins of government. The concerned no longer voice their opinions, fearing harm, while grafters abuse their authority for personal gain and completely disregard the needs of the poor. The government is not able to function effectively, and corruption in politics takes place primarily because officials lack sincere minds. How should such officials be looked upon?"

To this Saccaka replied, "O king, such corrupt officials are thieves who rob the people of their happiness and should be considered the state's worst enemies. This is because they deceive the rulers as well as the people and cause disorder and chaos in the country. A ruler should punish these people severely.

"O king, in a kingdom where the matters of the state are conducted according to the Dharma, one of the most serious offenses is that people do not gratefully recall what they owe to their parents for their upbringing; they steal from their parents or do not follow the teachings of their parents. What a child owes his parents is great. Even if he were to devote his whole life to taking care of them, he would never be able to repay them. Truly, those who are not loyal to their ruler and those who do not devote themselves to their parents are to be considered the worst criminals and should be punished accordingly.

"Again, O king, in a kingdom ruled according to the Dharma, those who do not believe in the Three Treasures but destroy temples and burn sutras, those who capture monks and employ them for their own purposes, and those who abuse the Dharma are guilty of the most grievous offenses. They undermine the trust and belief of the people, which is the basis of good acts. Such people have burnt to cinders the roots of good actions and are digging their own graves.

"O king, these three crimes are the most serious and should be judged and punished accordingly. The rest, although heavy, should be considered light by comparison."

The king now said to Saccaka, "O teacher, if a rebellion arises against a king who follows the Dharma, or if there is an attack by another country, it is usual to mobilize the army and prepare for it. In such instances, how should a king understand the situation?"

To this Saccaka answered, "O king, in this case, a king who follows the Dharma should have three thoughts in his mind, first, 'Since the rebels or foreign invaders think only to kill my people and to torture them, I as ruler shall prevent my people from suffering by the use of military force'; second, 'If I can find any means other than resorting to force, I shall employ them in overcoming the rebels or foreign invaders'; third, 'I shall make every effort to capture my enemies alive and not kill them, thus eliminating their attacking forces.' O king, a ruler should have these thoughts in his mind first; then, assigning leaders to their posts with specific orders, he should lead them into battle. Once these ways are followed, the soldiers on the battle line will free themselves of cowardice in response to the authority and dignity of the ruler. They will realize the authority of the ruler, appreciate the benevolence of the king's rule, and understand the nature of the battle. Now giving full support to the wishes of the king, they will rejoice in the thought that their king's benevolence will erase the afflictions of later years, and they will respond to the debt of gratitude they owe to the king by exerting themselves in battle. With these thoughts, wars are won. In this sense, even battles can become virtues."

4. The Transference of Merit

(1) The World-Honored One continued his travels to various places in the country of Magadha, once again returned to Rajagriha, and stayed atop Vulture Peak. One evening, many gods and bodhisattvas gathered around the Buddha. The Buddha appeared to be shining brightly, just as the moon outshines the stars around it. At just that moment, the Bodhisattva Vajraketu stood up and, having received power from the Buddha, instructed the bodhisattvas: "Fellow disciples of the Buddha, I wish to emphasize to you that a bodhisattva shares wholesome roots of merit with all, regardless of whether they are near or not. This is because a bodhisattva regards all that exists as equal, harboring no discriminating thoughts and looking at people through the eyes of great compassion. Even if people harbor hatred based on impure thoughts toward a bodhisattva, he becomes a good teacher to them all and teaches the profound Dharma. He is like the great ocean in that it is impossible to pollute it no matter what kind of poison is used. Likewise, although people do not repay the benevolence they receive because of their ignorance, and although they are unaware of the true teachings because of their anger and arrogance, they are not able to disturb the minds of those who pursue the ways of a bodhisattva.

"Moreover, a bodhisattva has this thought, 'To arouse the aspiration for enlightenment is entirely the working of the power of the Buddha. The one who has this aspiration is magnanimous, composed, and untiring in his learning. No matter how long it may take, he is determined to realize it. This aspiration is identical with the essence of all buddhas.'

(2) "As we have seen, a bodhisattva is always conscious of wholesome roots. He cultivates his compassionate mind with pure convictions and shares wholesome roots with others. This is done not only by his speech but also by his mind, which is joyous, flexible, compassionate, loving, all-embracing, nurturing, peaceful, and superior. A bodhisattva has these thoughts, 'All people commit evil acts. Because of these evil acts, they suffer unendingly and are unable to see the Buddha. They are unable to listen to the true Dharma and to know a good teacher who can guide them on the way. Since they have committed countless transgressions, they have to suffer endlessly. Therefore, in the midst of hell I shall in their stead take all their suffering upon myself. Thus with my body I shall save all the people on evil paths and release them from suffering.

"'By the power of the wholesome roots that I share with them, I shall make them see the Buddha. I shall make them arouse in themselves indestructible trust in the Buddha. I shall enable them to listen to the Dharma and have no doubts. I shall make them practice in accordance with the teaching, attain gentle and flexible minds, and perform pure verbal and bodily actions.

"'I shall become a great torch for the people, and by showing them the land of peace I shall enable them to free themselves from hindrances and to understand all of the teachings. I shall also become a ship of omniscience that will ferry people across the sea of transmigration and show them the shore of enlightenment.

"'In this world of ours, there is only one sun that shines upon all living beings. The people do not do their daily work thinking that night and day exist because of their own light. They are able to engage in their work because of the sun. Likewise, people do not themselves have the light of wisdom that shines upon them. They are not able to give light to others. Thus I shall attempt to know all people, lead them into the profound Dharma, remove all their doubts, and guide them to joy.'

(3) "O disciples of the Buddha, a bodhisattva makes every effort to enable all persons to see the Buddha. He listens to the Dharma and approaches good people with sincere and deep respect. He also leads people to think wholeheartedly of the Three Treasures and to respect them.

"Although a bodhisattva may stay at home with his wife and children, his mind never goes astray from the Dharma. He is always concerned about wisdom. He works for his own salvation, leads others to salvation, and with a sincere and clear mind provides skillful means for his family and relatives. Although he lives a householder's life, his life is not in conflict with the way of a bodhisattva, because of his compassion. In his everyday activities, putting on his clothes, eating and drinking, sitting or lying down, he maintains the purity of his mind, body, and speech. He has his senses in control and shows no loss of dignity.

"O disciples of the Buddha, those who forget their own selves will eventually possess all. Because they seek no reward, all their wholesome roots remain with them. Because they offer themselves, they gain the basic enlightenment of all buddhas. Because they cut off hindrances, they gain access to everything. Because they realize the pure root of equality, they have in them the virtues of all bodhisattvas. Because they have realized the vows, they gain the virtues of the practices of the bodhisattvas. Because they purify all human defilements, they embrace everyone. And because they protect and abide by all of the Buddha's doctrine, they inherit the wondrous nature of all the buddhas.

"O disciples of the Buddha, know that the bodhisattvas, upon having transferred these roots of purity, purify all Buddha lands, purify all persons, and enable all buddhas to permeate all Dharma worlds.

(4) "O disciples of the Buddha, if a bodhisattva becomes a king, he rules a great country and overcomes all enemies. He rules his kingdom according to the right laws; the kingdom flourishes and enjoys peace; morality prevails in the land; and all other countries choose to draw closer and do not turn against each other. Because force is not employed, peace and harmony prevail.

"The features of a bodhisattva are beauty itself. Freed from all evils and obstructions, a bodhisattva practices the act of selfless giving with pleasure. Whenever he sees another suffering in prison, a bodhisattva will enter that prison in order to ease that suffering. For those being sent to their deaths, a bodhisattva will offer his life to save the condemned. When he sees sentient beings victimized, a bodhisattva will attempt to save them out of great compassion and will enable all people to hear the name of the Buddha.

"Again, a bodhisattva will construct temples, build residences for monks, and devote himself to serving the Buddha, trying to purify the minds of people. His actions of selfless giving are most sincere, with no attachment and no sense of expecting a reward.

(5) "O disciples of the Buddha, when a bodhisattva offers a lamp, this thought occurs in his mind, 'By this merit may I benefit all people and make them gain the light that will eliminate their ignorance. May I enable them to realize the empty nature of this world and to illuminate an uncountable number of Buddha lands.'

"When a bodhisattva gives medicine to others, these are the thoughts in his mind, 'May these roots of purity enable people to leave their sick bodies and acquire the pure Dharma body of the Buddha; may these roots remove the sickness of evil and pluck out the thorns of defilements. May they cause people to approach the sacred ones and attain the light of wisdom, come to know the way of treatment, and cure the many sicknesses that afflict people.'

"A bodhisattva, when imparting the teachings to other bodhisattvas and good teachers, performs the transference of merit in this manner: 'By this merit, may all understand the benevolence of good teachers and respond with gratitude to their benevolence; may they approach all good teachers, respect them, and make offerings to them with honest hearts; for the sake of good teachers, may they not reflect on their own well-being but abide by the teachings; and having heard the true Dharma, may they encourage all to follow it.'

"A bodhisattva enables all people to hear the Buddha's doctrine. He makes certain that the merits of listening to the Dharma are not lost. He causes them to attain enlightenment. He has them for their part expound the Dharma to which they listened. These people will always seek the true Dharma of the Buddha and will work to remove the evil views of non-Buddhists.

"O disciples of the Buddha, a bodhisattva gives away a variety of flags and banners and thinks to himself, 'By these wholesome roots, may I enable all people to make flags and banners of wholesome roots and virtues that will make them attain freedom in all things. May I enable them to protect the true Dharma, light the torch of wisdom, illuminate all people, and overcome all evil ones.'

(6) "O disciples of the Buddha, suppose that when a bodhisattva pursues the Dharma, someone says, 'If you throw yourself into a pit of fire seven fathoms wide, I shall reveal the Dharma to you.' In this case, a bodhisattva should say, 'If it is for the sake of the Dharma, I shall gladly bear the sufferings of hell. It would be a trifling thing, then, to throw my body into a burning pit if by doing so I can listen to the Dharma. Please reveal the way to me. I shall go into the burning pit.'

"Again, if a bodhisattva is able to experience the appearance of a buddha, he will let others know that a buddha has appeared in the world. The people in turn will hearken to the voice of the Buddha and freeing themselves from arrogance and indolence will peacefully reside in the meditation of the recollection of the Buddha and tirelessly pursue the goal of reaching the Buddha's realm. Innumerable people will be purified and made to reside in peace by the power of the Buddha.

"Again, when a bodhisattva offers himself to serve the Buddha, he frees himself from pride and serves with a mind of humility. He holds a mind that bows, a mind as all-embracing as the great earth, a mind that bears all pain, a mind that untiringly serves all, a mind that never slackens, a mind that gives wholesome roots to the poor and wretched, a mind that respects the noble, the rich, the children, and the stupid, a mind that cultivates wholesome roots because of having found peace in the wonderful teachings. This is the mental attitude of a bodhisattva.

"Again, a bodhisattva serves all buddhas, rouses in his mind a sense of gratitude to all buddhas, rouses in all a sense of gratitude toward their parents, cultivates pure and deep thoughts, abides by the rules of the way, accepts the Buddha's doctrine and discards worldly things, is born in the house of the Buddha, follows all buddhas and protects the true Dharma, avoids the realms of the devil, learns the sphere of the Buddha, and perfects himself as a vessel for the Buddha's doctrine.

(7) "A bodhisattva also enables people to attain the level of a Dharma king. He overcomes the enemy of defilements; he sets into motion the highest Dharma wheel at will; and, by bringing about skillful means, he guards the Buddha's doctrine and keeps it everlastingly.

"Further, a bodhisattva has this thought in mind, 'I aspire to bring unlimited happiness to all people. I aspire to open the gates of the pure Dharma and enable them to transcend the world of delusions. I shall lead them to fulfill all their aspirations, giving them enlightenment. I shall become the father of all sentient beings and observe all worlds with eyes of wisdom. I shall also become a compassionate mother, producing wholesome roots and fulfilling their aspirations.'

"A bodhisattva considers each person as if he or she were his only child. When someone seeks his guidance, a bodhisattva rejoices in the thought that he considers him his true teacher in the Dharma. In this manner, a bodhisattva cultivates a greatly compassionate mind, a heart that rejoices, a mind that never fails, and a spirit of giving.

"When a bodhisattva transfers his wholesome roots, he has no attachment to his body or to things; he has no attachment to anything that exists. For this reason, he holds to no fixed views of things. This is because, in reality, things neither arise nor perish and possess no fixed self-nature. O disciples of the Buddha, a bodhisattva transfers all wholesome roots to the all-knowing wisdom, and while roaming throughout the ten directions he gives guidance to people.

(8) "O disciples of the Buddha, in the act of transferring his merits, a bodhisattva purifies all worlds; therefore, he makes all Buddha lands equal. Because he expounds the Dharma that is indestructible, he makes all worlds equal. Because he rouses aspirations that originate in universal wisdom, he makes all bodhisattvas equal. Moreover, he refrains from destroying the self-nature of things and views all things as equal. Not attached to the world, he performs good acts that are free of worldly attachments; therefore, all karmic rewards are equal. He manifests the workings of the Buddha in accordance with worldly needs; therefore, his freedom of action is equal to that of all the buddhas." And he said in verse,

(i) A bodhisattva resides in peace, has a right mind,
     And is freed from ignorance.
     Because he practices forbearance,
     He has no anxieties and accumulates unlimited virtue.
     There is no hatred in his mind;
     It is untainted and pure.
     His actions adorn this world,
     And his wisdom shines on all activities.
     His thoughts are unfathomable,
     And he constantly nurtures all people.
     He lives and acts according to the laws of the world
     And brings joy to people.
     He exercises discretion,
     Is fully aware of the Dharma and its significance,
     Resides in the realm of harmonious restraint,
     And brings blessings to all.

(ii) Just as all things appear as thusness,
     Arising and perishing are also thusness.

Just as the nature of thusness is true,
All actions of a bodhisattva are also true.
Just as thusness cannot be measured,
His actions too cannot be conceived.
If there is no bondage, there is no release;
All of his actions are without defilement.
True disciples of the Buddha
Are at peace and are never disturbed.
Now, with all the power of wisdom,
They enter into the store of skillful means.
The Dharma king, seeing the Dharma,
Is no longer bound or conditioned.
With no obstructions, the mind is clear;
There is no element of disharmony.

(iii) Inconceivability may be pondered on
But never exhausted.
When one enters into inconceivability,
Both thinking and non-thinking perish.
Thinking of the Dharma,
Discerning all actions,
The one who annihilates impurity
Is the king of virtues.
Mind is neither in nor out of the self.
Therefore, it does not exist.
If one is attached, things exist.
If one is unattached, they are extinguished and quiescent.
All things are empty, devoid of self-nature.
Know that things are devoid of self-nature.
The Buddha's disciples, like the Buddha, are awakened
To the truth of non-self.

(9) "A bodhisattva respects all wholesome roots. He thinks it important to detach himself from the world, to accumulate wholesome roots, to regret his own mistakes, and to strive toward wholesome roots. He never thinks lightly of paying homage to the Buddha by putting his palms together in reverence or worshipping temples and shrines. He always cherishes wholesome roots, nurtures them, finds peace of mind in them, ponders over them, and, following the wholesome roots in the realm of the Buddha, sees the Buddha's power of freedom.

"A bodhisattva does not have others undertake any practice unless he has practiced it himself. It is utterly inconceivable that others should enjoy the practices and find peace in performing them if he himself did not do them. A bodhisattva acts according to his own words, speaks the truth, and puts the truth into practice. He is forbearing and stills his mind. He encourages others to still their minds and leads them to forbearance. Freeing himself from doubts, he has a joyous mind. He enables others to free themselves from doubt, leading them to unshakable faith in the Dharma.

"A bodhisattva transfers his merits in this manner, 'It is my sincere wish that, because of these wholesome roots, all people will be able to see the Buddha at all times, will be able to devote themselves to the Buddha, and will with pure minds enjoy true happiness. Moreover, may they always see the Buddha, bring forth the unlimited powers of a bodhisattva, and never forget the Dharma.'

"Again, by transferring merit, a bodhisattva strives to enlighten people so that they see that there is nothing that is a permanent entity or has a self-nature, that all is suchness, that there is no fixed foundation, that there is no falsity in all that exists, that true reality is devoid of all forms, that the truth is tranquillity itself, and that in the realm of the Dharma there is no going away or coming together.

"Again, a bodhisattva tries to transfer wholesome roots in the following manner, he wishes to make all persons great Dharma masters and enable them to be in the embrace of the buddhas. Making them Dharma masters who support the Dharma, he wants them to teach the Dharma fluently, not letting even one bit of its taste be lost. Again, making all persons Dharma masters who are adorned with light, just like the sun, whose light is undimmed, he wishes that they might radiate the light of the Buddha's wisdom to all sentient beings. He also wants them to become Dharma masters who are aware of the workings of Mara and destroy his forces."

5. The Five Virtues of the Buddha

(1) The World-Honored One once again left Vulture Peak and at the Bamboo Grove Monastery went into the sixteenth summer retreat. One day, one of the Buddha's disciples, Gulissani, who had some business to attend to, was present at the gathering of monks. He was always greedy and never well disciplined. Because he was not able to control his mind, he appeared quite unseemly. The disciple Sariputta instructed the disciples about Gulissani: "Fellow disciples, I wish to remind you that those who live in the forest and who have renounced worldly ties must show respect for their colleagues and should have someone among the elders whom they can truly respect. If this is not done, someone may say, 'What good is it for these persons to live alone in the forest?'

"Again, those who reside in the forest and who wish to seat themselves where the monks are gathered must make every effort not to be in the way of the elders and not to inconvenience the novices. They must not enter villages at unexpected times or fail to leave at the usual times. They must not meet householders immediately before or after meals. They must not have unsettled minds and must not act carelessly.

"They must not speak in agitated tones but should use good language. They should associate with good friends, control their desires, and be well aware of the proper amount of food to take. They should also practice at night. They must still their minds at all times. With their wisdom, they must be clearly conscious of the Dharma and the precepts. They should dedicate themselves to the way leading to the cessation of suffering and pursue the way that surpasses all human and worldly things. If these guidelines are not followed, someone may say that these people are not aware of the purpose of becoming a mendicant."

At just that time, the disciple Moggallana asked, "Sariputta, are these instructions to be followed only by those who reside in the forest, or should they be followed also by those who reside near the forest?" To this question, Sariputta answered, "My friend, since those who reside in the forest should observe them, how much more should those near the forest follow them!"

(2) Around this time, many famous ascetics, such as Anugara, Varadhara, and Sakuludayin, were staying in the Peacock Park. One day the World-Honored One left the Bamboo Grove Monastery and headed toward the Peacock Park, because it was too early to make his rounds for food.

At that time, Sakuludayin, along with many other practicers of the way, was engaged in conversation in a loud voice. Seeing the World-Honored One approaching, he signaled the others to keep quiet and then quietly greeted the World-Honored One. The World-Honored One, assuming the seat provided, gave instructions, "Udayin, what were you discussing with the others gathered here?"

"O World-Honored One, I hope to explain this matter to you later. Actually, the other day when the monks of various schools gathered at the discussion hall, someone said, 'The people of Anga and Magadha are indeed fortunate because famous masters, such as Purana Kassapa, Ajita Kesakambalin, Nigantha Nataputta, and Gotama, along with their followers, are here in Rajagaha. Which of these masters is the most highly respected by the people and by their followers?' At this time a person said that Purana Kassapa was not respected by his disciples, while another said that Ajita Kesakambalin was not respected either, giving actual examples. Just then, a person said, 'Gotama is respected by all persons as well as by his followers. Once when Gotama Buddha was giving discourse to hundreds of followers, there was one among the quiet listeners who coughed. The follower seated beside him signaled by poking his knee to remind him that the World-Honored One was expounding the teachings. From then on no one made a noise or coughed. Just as people gather on a street corner to watch breathlessly as honey is being extracted from a wonderful honeycomb, people listening to the Buddha are extremely attentive, not wishing to miss even one word. Even if a follower of Gotama leaves the Sangha and returns to a layman's status, he praises the virtues of the master, the Dharma, and the Sangha; he laments that, because of faults of his own, he was not able to practice the pure practices of the teachings. Others become lay followers, while others become temple custodians and observe the five precepts. These are the ways in which the followers of Gotama respect the World-Honored One.'"

(3) The Buddha asked Udayin, "Udayin, for how many reasons do you think my disciples respect me?" To this Udayin replied, "O World-Honored One, I believe that there are five reasons for which they revere you. First, the World-Honored One partakes of little food and also praises this practice. Second, the World-Honored One appreciates whatever robe is offered regardless of its quality and praises this practice. Third, the World-Honored One is satisfied with any food that is offered and praises this practice. Fourth, the World-Honored One is satisfied with any bedding that is offered and praises this practice. Fifth, the World-Honored One leaves the secular world and praises those who seek seclusion."

To these words the World-Honored One instructed, "O Udayin, if to eat little and to praise that practice is one of my virtues, then consider that among my disciples there is one who eats as little as one half of a bilva nut. Consider that I partake of a bowl of food and occasionally eat more than a bowl. Again, if to be satisfied with whatever robe I receive and to praise that practice is one of my virtues, then there is one follower in the Sangha who salvages rags from rubbish heaps and graves, sews them together, and wears them. At times I wear the beautiful and impressive clothing given by my lay followers. Again, if being satisfied with the food that is offered and praising that practice is one of my virtues, then in the Buddha's Sangha there are those who beg door to door receiving alms, those who pick up the fallen grain in the fields and eat it, and those who do not partake of food even when they are invited into homes. I am at times invited into homes and partake of the carefully selected white rice that is offered. Again, if being satisfied with any bedding that is offered and praising this practice is one of my virtues, then consider that there are those in the Buddha's Sangha who sleep under trees or on the bare ground and do not seek shelter under a roof for eight months at a time. I, however, on occasion, sleep in a two-storied mansion, in houses that shield the World-Honored One from the wind, and where the windows and doors are securely closed. Again, if to seek seclusion and to praise this practice is a virtue of the Buddha, then there are those in the Buddha's Sangha who enter the forest, reside away from villages, and only gather to recite the precepts once every two weeks. I oftentimes reside with my disciples, my followers, kings, ministers of kings, and the masters and followers of other religions.

"It is not simply for the five reasons you indicated that disciples respect me. Actually, there are five other reasons. These five are that the Buddha has laid down five wonderful basic moral precepts, that the Buddha has excellent power to perceive the truth, that the Buddha has unexcelled wisdom, that the Four Noble Truths have been clearly explained by him and have given people the inspiration to follow them, and that the various ways leading to enlightenment have been laid down, inspiring the disciples to follow them according to the letter and thus realize enlightenment. It is, indeed, because of these five wonderful ways that I am respected and revered by the followers."

(4) Some time before this, there lived in Rajagaha a lay instructor and leader called Visakha. His house prospered, and taking Dhammadinna as his wife, he enjoyed a happy family. Many years back, he had received the Buddha's teachings, and while in layman's status he had attained enlightenment. Dhammadinna was able to accept the teachings of the Buddha with the guidance of her husband. Her wish to leave the secular life was strong, and finally, her husband agreed to let her cut her hair and become a nun. From that day on, she devoted herself to the practice of the path.

It so happened that the Sangha of nuns, accompanying the World-Honored One, was staying at the Bamboo Grove of Rajagaha. Visakha called on Dhammadinna and had the following dialogue: "O Dhammadinna, it is customary for people to say 'I'. How does the World-Honored One explain this

'I'?" To this the nun answered, "O Visakha, the World-Honored One has taught us that the 'I' is an aggregate of the bodily and mental elements."

Then Visakha asked, "Pray, tell me, what is the basis of that 'I'?" To this she answered, "The World-Honored One has taught that the basis of the 'I' is the thirst of human craving."

"Then, venerable nun, what is it that disintegrates the 'I'?"

"The World-Honored One taught us that when the thirst of craving is completely subdued, that is when the 'I' is annihilated."

"Then, venerable nun, pray tell me the way leading to the annihilation of the 'I'."

"It is the Eightfold Path: the right view, the right thought, the right speech, the right conduct, the right livelihood, the right endeavor, the right mindfulness, and the right meditation. This Eightfold Path is the path that leads to the annihilation of the 'I'."

(5) "Then, venerable nun, how is it that the illusionary 'I' occurs in one's mind, and how can one be freed of such illusionary consciousness?"

"Those who do not see the sages, those who do not know the way of the sages, and those who do not practice the way of the sages consider that the body and the mind are the 'I' and that the 'I' possesses the body and the mind; that the body and the mind exist in the 'I'; and that the 'I' exists in the body and the mind. Thus they entertain wrong notions about the 'I'. Those who see the sages, those who know the Dharma of the sages, and those who practice the way of the sages can be relieved from harboring such wrong views."

(6) Visakha greatly appreciated this discourse and went to call on the World-Honored One, to whom he relayed the whole dialogue. The World-Honored One said, "Visakha, know that Dhammadinna is a person of wisdom. If you were to ask the reason for the existence of the 'I', there would be nothing I could say beyond what was said by her. This is because she has spoken the truth." The World-Honored One later praised the nun Dhammadinna as being the first of those who were proficient in expounding the Dharma.

Chapter 4

THE DEGREES OF ENLIGHTENMENT

1. Rahula

(1) The World-Honored One was staying at the Bamboo Grove, and Rahula was staying at the neighboring Ambalatthika. One evening, the Buddha went to see Rahula. Rahula welcomed the Buddha and prepared the seating mat and some water to wash his feet. After washing his feet, the Buddha left some water in the jar and said to Rahula, "Rahula, do you see this small amount of water remaining?" "Yes, World-Honored One, I see a small amount of water." The Buddha said, "Rahula, the merit of a mendicant is as small as this when he consciously lies and does not know shame."

Then the Buddha threw away the remaining water in the jar and said, "Rahula, did you see the remaining water being thrown away?" "I did see it," said Rahula. The Buddha said, "Rahula, the respect for the mendicant who consciously lies and does not know shame will be thrown away in the same manner." The Buddha then overturned the jar and said, "Rahula, did you see the jar overturned?" Rahula answered, "World-Honored One, I did see the jar overturned." The Buddha said, "Rahula, the worth of the mendicant will be overturned in the same manner who consciously lies and does not know shame." Then the Buddha again set the jar into upright position and said, "Rahula, do you see that the jar has no water at all?" Rahula said, "Yes, I see it."

The Buddha then said, "Rahula, the worth of the mendicant who consciously lies and does not know shame is nil. As long as the furious elephant, with long tusks, guards its trunk on the battlefield, using its fore and hind legs, its ears, its tusks, its tail, and every part of its body, the elephant driver will have no doubt that the elephant is safe; but when the elephant starts using its trunk, the driver knows that it is going to die in battle. Likewise, one who consciously lies and does not know shame, I say, will commit every evil act. Rahula, therefore, even in jest, you should not lie."

(2) "For what purpose do you use a mirror?" asked the Buddha. Rahula replied, "It is to see oneself reflected." The Buddha said, "Rahula, as you reflect yourself in the mirror, only after repeated deliberations should you act. Deeds that you do with your mind, mouth, and body should be done likewise. Rahula, when you are about to perform a bodily, verbal, or mental act, you should stop to think

whether the deed might harm yourself, or others, or both yourself and others; whether it is an evil deed; and whether it is such as might become the cause of suffering. If so, you should not do such a deed. If, after giving due consideration, you arrive at the conclusion that it is not, then you should do it.

"Again, while in the midst of an act or even after it is done, you should reflect in this manner. If it is harmful to yourself or others, you should refrain from doing it and repent in front of your teacher and friends. If, after giving due consideration, you decide that it is not harmful to yourself or others but is a good act that brings happiness to others, you should do it. Furthermore, you should continue to do so and be gratified that you are able to do such good deeds.

"Rahula, the monks of the past cleansed themselves in this way; those in the future will cleanse themselves in this way; and those at present are cleansing themselves in this way. You, too, should think deeply and learn to purify the three actions of body, mouth, and mind."

2. The Ten Stages

(1) One day the Buddha was in the company of many Mahasattvas. At that time, the Bodhisattva Vajragarbha, thanks to the guidance of the Buddha, entered the Meditation of the Light of Great Wisdom, attained undefiled wisdom and unhindered power in discourse, and said to the multitude assembled, "Offspring of the buddhas, the aspiration of one who pursues the Dharma is unshakable, is indestructible, and is equal to the Dharmadhatu in its greatness. It is guarded by all the buddhas. This is because those bodhisattvas attain the rank of Buddha wisdom, advancing through ten progressive stages. They are the stage of joy, the stage of purity, the stage of the light of wisdom, the stage of glowing wisdom, the stage of overcoming extreme difficulties, the stage of the appearance of great wisdom, the stage of going far, the stage of the unmoving, the stage of good wisdom, and the stage of the Dharma clouds.

"At the first stage, the stage of joy, a bodhisattva attains joy and faith. He is pure and gentle and is able to persevere. He does not quarrel with others nor cause others to suffer. His thought is constantly on the Buddha, the Dharma, and the Sangha, which yield joy. He is freed from all fears—fears concerning livelihood, ill-repute, death, falling into hell, and facing a crowd. This is because a bodhisattva at this stage is free from the notion of self; thus he is not covetous. Since he is not covetous of possessions, he is free from fear about his livelihood. Since he does not desire to be respected by others, he has no fear of ill-repute. Since he is free from the notion of self, death is not a fearful event. Since he has the thought of seeing the Buddha in the next birth, he has no fear of falling into hell. Since he is confident that there is nothing equal or superior to that which he desires, he has no fear in facing the multitude.

"Again, a bodhisattva has great compassion and has no dislike for others; with a sincere and pure mind, he willingly practices the good. He has faith; he has shame for both mental and bodily evil deeds; he is gentle and patient. He has respect for the teachings and good teachers. He never becomes weary of listening to the Dharma and retains correctly the Dharma that he has heard.

He does not ask for honors, neither does he seek profits. He acts true to his word and never uses flattery. His mind is as immovable as a mountain because of his wisdom concerning all things. He tirelessly gathers the teachings that will be helpful in attaining the Dharma and always seeks the supreme way among the superior ways. He reveres all buddhas and vows to practice all of their Dharmas. His vow is as great as the Dharmadhatu and extends everywhere like the sky. Thus he practices the Dharma with unremitting zeal.

"Further, he makes the following vows: 'Let all who walk the same path with the same intention and the same practices accumulate good deeds, freeing themselves from hatred and jealousy. With minds of non-discrimination, let them live in harmony in the same spiritual sphere; and when conditions ripen, let them reveal the Buddha's bodies. Perceiving the Buddha's realms and his divine powers, let them travel to all countries, appear at all gatherings, and practice the way of bodhisattvas.'

"Again, he thinks in this manner: 'The Buddha's teaching is deep and vast, but people have fallen into the pit of wrong views. Their wisdom eyes are covered by ignorance; their minds are imbued with arrogance and the thirst of craving; they harbor thoughts of flattery, parsimony, jealousy, greed, and anger while fanning the flames of hatred. Even if, by chance, they happen to give something in charity, they reverse the merit by inverted views. Thus they delude themselves all the more. I shall now save these suffering people and lead them to the joy of following the way of the Buddha.'

(i) One who hears the treasure of the Dharma will receive the Buddha's protection, and attaining enlightenment, he will finally attain the Buddha's way. One who is not remiss in listening will hear the teachings even at the bottom of the ocean or in a burning fire. But one who is foolish and doubts the teachings will eventually fail to hear them.

One who, sowing the seeds of good deeds, draws nearer to the Buddha and faithfully submits to his compassionate heart will attain immeasurable wisdom. The compassionate heart has wisdom as its master and is accompanied by skillful means. His honest mind is pure and its strength is immeasurable.

(ii) Should the Buddha's child arouse this noble mind, he will leave the stage of the ordinary person and enter the life of the Buddha and be born in the house of the Buddha.

His mind will attain the stage of joy.
It will be as immovable as a mountain.
Great joy will be born.
His mind will be pure,
And he will be able to attain ultimate wisdom.
Disliking conflicts, harboring no hatred,
Knowing shame and also respect,
He will nurture the sincere mind.
All buddhas' countries are filled with the buddhas' children.
They are of the same mind.
Whatever they do is not in vain.

(2) "In the second stage, the stage of purity, a bodhisattva keeps away from killing, discards swords and whips, refrains from adultery, and has no thought of wanting other women besides his wife. A bodhisattva thinks, 'People, because of their wrong views, discriminate between self and others; they fight, always covet wealth, are continuously covered over by ignorance, and go through endless sufferings. How pitiful it is! I shall lead them to the right path first; then they, extinguishing the fires of defilement, will gain the eyes of wisdom. All severe sufferings, and the body that is being burnt in hell, are the result of an evil mind. I shall now be free from evil and proceed to the true path. All joys of this and the coming worlds are born of the ten good deeds.'

"Many of the Buddha's children living in the stage of purity will become Wheel-Turning Kings, leading all people to the ten good deeds.

(3) "Living in the third stage, the stage of the light of wisdom, a bodhisattva sees all dharmas as they are; that is to say, he sees that all things are impermanent, full of pain, and impure, and that there is no abiding self. The true aspect of things is that they do not arise because of their own causes and conditions."

> All things in this world are like diseases and carbuncles.
> People are encumbered with lust and suffer from sorrow and anxieties.
> The raging flames of the three poisons have not ceased since the infinite
>   past.
> The wisdom of the buddhas alone is pure and painless, deep, and
>   boundless.

"A bodhisattva thinks, 'People are poor and without good fortune. Sunk in the sea of defilements and blinded, they have lost sight of the Dharma. They have fear when there is nothing to fear. I shall do all within my power to save them.'"

> Wisdom alone can deliver people from suffering.
> Hear and learn; there is no other way.
> Hearing the Dharma is the basis of the Buddha's doctrine.

(4) "In the fourth stage, the stage of glowing wisdom, a bodhisattva draws close to all buddhas. He gives offerings with reverence. His heart is pure; his faith in the Three Treasures is all the more firm; his wholesome roots are well nurtured.

(5) "In the fifth stage, the stage of overcoming extreme difficulties, a bodhisattva with great compassion vows, 'The good that I do is to remove others' suffering and lead them to enlightenment and fulfill their aspirations.'

(6) "In the sixth stage, the stage of the appearance of great wisdom, a bodhisattva discerns clearly the truth of the twelve links of the chain of causation.

(i) He who comes to know the true nature of the dharma will not be disturbed by the two views of existence and nonexistence. With a compassionate heart, he will save others. He is called a Buddha's child. Although his mind is pure, he keeps the precepts. No longer harboring the thought of harming, he also prevents other people's persecution. Although he has already awakened to the dharma nature, he makes efforts in learning. Although he has already destroyed defilements, he practices meditation. Although he knows the emptiness of all things, he clearly distinguishes all things. Although he dwells in the wisdom of nirvana, he benefits the world, destroying evil. He is called a Mahasattva.

(ii) The three worlds arise from the mind of greed; the twelve links of causation also exist in the mind. Thus samsara arises only from the mind; when the worldly mind is overcome, samsara is exhausted.

From ignorance arise actions; from actions suffering is born.
If ignorance exists, the mundane world arises.
If ignorance is eliminated, the mundane world perishes.
Knowing this causal relation, the wise sees emptiness.
Since things perish and do not have continued existence,
He enters the practice of formlessness.
Knowing the falsity of the dualistic view, his mind arrives at
    desirelessness.
He is only concerned with saving all.

(iii) Making offerings to innumerable buddhas, he is praised by the Buddha.
    Entering the storehouse of the Buddha's doctrine, his wholesome roots
        increase.
    They are like pure gold polished with lapis lazuli, which becomes even
        more brilliant,
    Or like the moon travelling through the sky, shedding its refreshing cool-
        ness on all;
    Storms from all directions cannot obstruct its passage.
    The wisdom light of a bodhisattva extinguishes the fire of defilement;
    Even the four evil ones cannot destroy him.

(7) "At the seventh stage, the stage of going far, a bodhisattva leads people with his countless skillful means to practice the Six Perfections. Again, although a bodhisattva deeply appreciates nirvana, he does not forsake the world. Although living ostensibly in the world of delusion, he is uncontaminated by the world. Although his mind is quiescent, it is fervently burning with compassion because of the power of his skillful means. Although he outwardly manifests the activities of Mara, he is not outside the Buddha's wisdom. Although he manifests false acts, he does not deviate from the Buddha's doctrine.

"Although a bodhisattva sees emptiness with his wisdom, he tirelessly cultivates the virtues. Although he dwells in the three worlds, he delights in being free of them. Although his mind is calm, he bestirs himself to destroy evil. Although living the life of the void, he does not lose the heart of compassion. Although he knows that buddhas have no form, he sees the thirty-two marks of a buddha. Although he knows that the voice cannot convey the truth, he praises the voice of the Buddha and thereby gladdens the hearts of all. Although he is aware that all buddhas attain enlightenment in one moment of thought, he guides people in specific times and places according to their capacities.

(8) "When a bodhisattva enters the eighth stage, the stage of the unmoving, he is described as a bodhisattva who practices deeply. At this stage, a bodhisattva frees himself from all thoughts, all greed, all means of endeavor, and all deeds

of body, mouth, and mind. He is like someone in a dream who ponders over the means to cross a deep river. When he awakens from the dream before he has crossed the river, what he thought was the means of crossing the river is discarded as now unnecessary.

"Just then, the Buddha states: 'My good man, you have attained deep quiescence and are living in accordance with the Buddha's doctrine; but you have not yet attained all the Buddha's virtues. Ordinary people of the world are estranged from the quiescence that you have attained and are being harmed by their own defilements. You should have pity on all of these people. My good man, remind yourself therefore of your original vow to be kind to them and aspire to attain that inconceivable wisdom. The nature and form of all things do not change whether or not a buddha appears. All buddhas are called buddhas by virtue of knowing this truth. My good man, think of the indescribably pure body, the infinite wisdom, the boundless country, the immeasurable skillful means, and the light and voice of a buddha. You have now attained the wisdom of the Quietude of the Dharma. But buddhas have infinite wisdom dharmas. You should attain these dharmas by all means.'

"My disciples, if the Buddha did not give this exhortation, a bodhisattva would abandon the aspirations to attain nirvana and to save others. By being given this counsel, he gains wisdom incomparably superior to the one he hitherto possessed. It is as if one walked with much effort to a shore and boarded a boat to cross the ocean. Once one is on the boat, the distance covered in a day is much greater than that covered by walking on land. My disciples, once you attain the eighth state, there will arise from the wisdom of great skillful means a mind that will function naturally, that will enable you to envisage the power of a buddha's wisdom while still in the rank of a bodhisattva, and that will be able to discern clearly the causal relations of life and death. Further, like the sun or the moon showing its reflection on all waters, you will be able to manifest yourself in an infinite number of forms in accordance with the capacities of people. You will attain power that may be used at will for any occasion.

(9) "At the ninth stage, the stage of good wisdom, a bodhisattva will be able to enter the secret storehouse of the Dharma. He will be able to know the differences among all things and among all minds. He will know the lives of all beings. Action is the soil, as it were; desire is the water; ignorance is the covering; consciousness is the seed; body is the bud. Body and mind grow together and become inseparable. Foolishness and lust arise one after the other followed by the thoughts of living, doing, and lusting, but never the aspiration for nirvana. Thus a bodhisattva will see as they are the Three Worlds, the Desire World, the Form World, and the Formless World arising in succession.

(10) "As one enters the tenth and final stage, the stage of the Dharma clouds, and approaches Buddhahood with its infinite wisdom, he will be able to attain all superior meditations. Together with these meditations, there emerges a large jewelled lotus. The circumference of the flower is a hundred thousand times that of the world; it is bedecked with all kinds of gems. When a bodhisattva ascends onto the lotus, all the worlds tremble, a light shines throughout, and all evil

worlds come to a standstill at once. A bodhisattva, enabled by his power of enlightenment, goes to all buddhas in an instant and receives the unlimited Dharma. He is like a great ocean accepting the rain no matter how torrential it may be.

"My disciples, the ocean has these ten characteristics: first, it becomes deeper gradually; second, it washes ashore dead bodies and does not accept them; third, all the rivers flowing into it lose their original names; fourth, the water becomes of one taste; fifth, it contains many treasures; sixth, it is deep and difficult to fathom; seventh, it is boundless; eighth, it allows a large number of living beings to inhabit it; ninth, it never fails to keep the right time for tides; and tenth, it never overflows however heavy the rain may be. Nothing can destroy these characteristics. To one seeking the path, there exist the causal relations of the ten stages, which no one can destroy.

"At the stage of joy, a bodhisattva resolves firmly to follow his aspiration; at the stage of purity, he breaks off from those who violate the precepts; at the stage of the light of wisdom, he discards names with no substances; at the stage of glowing wisdom, he in revering the Buddha attains a unitary mind that is indestructibly pure; at the stage of overcoming extreme difficulties, he works for the world by generating various skillful means and superhuman powers; at the stage of appearance of great wisdom, he discerns the law of causal relations; at the stage of going far, he with a magnanimous heart sees all things; at the stage of the unmoving, he realizes the great adornment; at the stage of good wisdom, he attains superior freedom and is clearly aware of all secular things; and at the stage of the Dharma clouds, a bodhisattva receives the rain of the great teachings of all buddhas."

3. Vimalakirti

(1) The World-Honored One left Rajagriha and crossed the Ganges to enter Vaisali. He sojourned in the Amrapali Woods together with many bodhisattvas and disciples. Ratnakara, a wealthy man accompanied by his five hundred children, came to the park to offer a canopy made of gems. Ratnakara approached the Buddha and praised his virtues in verses:

(i) Your limpid eyes are like lotuses; your mind is quietly in concentration.
    For long you have lived a clean life; you lead people to quietude.
    Giving the treasure of the Dharma, you make clear what the Dharma is.
    You have taught us clearly
    That all things arise out of causal relations.
    There is neither I nor God,
    And there is none that is created by God.
    Good and evil karmas go on continually.

(ii) O great king of medicine, who save us from old age, sickness, and death,
     Your virtues are as vast as the ocean.
     Like a mountain, you are unmoved by praise and blame.
     To the good and to the evil, with a mind unbiased as empty space,
     You give your grace equally.
     By your gracious power, we have seen all worlds.

> Aware of the great unhindered power of the Dharma king,
> We have now given rise to pure faith.

(iii) Although the Buddha uses the same words to all,
  Each understands in his own way:
  All think they mean the same.
  With the same words of the World-Honored One,
  Some were gladdened and some become afraid,
  Some become weary of worldly life,
  Some see an end to their doubts.
  O master of incomparable might,
  O greatest teacher of the world,
  Severing passions, you attained enlightenment,
  And save all, forsaking none.
  We prostrate to you in deep reverence.

(2) Ratnakara said to the World-Honored One, "World-Honored One, all these young people are aspiring to become buddhas. I beg you to expound on the undefiled buddhas' worlds and the way to establish such worlds." The World-Honored One said, "Very well, Ratnakara. I shall now make it clear to you. Listen well and think thoroughly. Ratnakara, to one who is seeking the way, every place where he exists is a buddha's world.

"By nature a buddha establishes his world in order to help people. To do this, a buddha world will be built on the minds of people as houses are built on the ground. Ratnakara, what builds a buddha world is a sincere mind. This mind is at the same time a deep mind, a mind seeking the way, a mind that keeps precepts, a mind of giving, a patient mind, an endeavoring mind, a controlled mind, a mind that begets wisdom and compassion. Such a mind enables people to attain the Dharma by all skillful means. Therefore, Ratnakara, if you wish to be in a buddha's pure world, you should first purify your mind. When the mind is pure, the world is pure also."

Sariputra then thought to himself, "If the world is pure only when the mind is pure, did the World-Honored One have an impure mind when he sought the way? Why is this world so contaminated?"

The Buddha immediately perceived Sariputra's thought and said, "Blind people are not able to see the sun or the moon. But they cannot say that there is no sun or moon. That they cannot see them cannot be blamed on the sun or the moon; it is because of their delusion that people cannot see the purity of buddhas' worlds. This world is pure, but its purity is not visible to you."

A brahmin who was in the assembly at the time said, "Venerable Sariputra, this world is not contaminated. It is as limpid as the celestial palaces." To this Sariputra replied, "I do not see it in that way. This world is full of hills, mountains, gravel, holes, and ugly, unclean things." To this, the brahmin said, "That is because you look with your discriminative mind instead of with the Buddha's wisdom. Since a bodhisattva has a pure mind of equality, the world appears pure to him."

Just then the World-Honored One lifted his foot and pointed toward the ground, and in an instant, the world underwent a complete change. It emitted light widely; all the people, to their astonishment, found themselves on lotus seats inlaid with jewels. The World-Honored One asked, "Sariputra, how do you see this world?" Sariputra replied, "World-Honored One, I have never seen such a wonderfully beautiful world."

The Buddha then said, "My world is always as beautiful as this. However, to the inferior mind, it will seem only as a world full of evil and pollution. Therefore, Sariputra, if you look at this world with a purified mind, as all these people did, with a mind purified by my discourses, you will be able to see a brilliantly shining world all the time." When the World-Honored One withdrew his superhuman power, the world returned to its former appearance. Ratnakara and many young people rejoiced in gaining the eyes to see the true aspect of things.

(3) Around that time, there lived in Vaisali a wealthy man by the name of Vimalakirti. He had done many good actions in his previous lives, and he knew the truth that things neither arise nor perish. Mastering all the teachings, he was able to refute wrong views. He praised the vow to save others, knew their minds, and led them to the truly noble teaching. He had completely satisfied the Buddha's mind and was highly regarded by all. He gave generously to the poor from his great wealth, observed the precepts, was persevering, always suppressed his anger, was constantly endeavoring, and disciplined his mind to have concentration; his brilliant wisdom enlightened the darkened minds of the unwise. Even though he lived a secular life, he was not attached to mundane things; though he had a wife and children, he was never drawn to human affection; though he was served by many, he did not lose the state of solitary quietude; though he wore fine clothes befitting his status, he never lost his natural personality; and no matter what kinds of foods he consumed, his mind was deeply appreciative of the savor of the Dharma.

In his association with others, he visited the places of pleasure, but he led people in them to the right teachings; he listened to non-Buddhist teachings, yet he did not lose his true faith; he read secular books, but he enjoyed the true Dharma. At times, he involved himself in the administration of the state to give peace to the people. When he entered schools, he taught young people the right Dharma. When he visited the pleasure quarters or entered taverns, he used such an opportunity to teach the evil of lust and the importance of having firm resolution. In mingling with wealthy people and merchants, he taught that the Dharma and good deeds were more precious than wealth. He stressed the importance of perseverance to kings who relied on their power, and the importance of discarding arrogance to priests and monks who were apt to be proud; to people in general, he stressed the importance of having true happiness rather than pursuing immediately lucrative ways. Vimalakirti, highly respected as the teacher of the age, was then lying in bed sick. From all walks of life people came to visit him.

Vimalakirti took advantage of their visits to teach them the Dharma. He said, "You who are listening, realize that your bodies are constantly changing. They will lose their vigor no matter how healthy they may be. Indeed, the body is where various diseases swarm, and the man of wisdom does not rely on it. It is as elusive as a spray of water, quickly disappearing like bubbles; born from the thirst of desire like the shimmering heat, the body is as weak as a plantain and arises from various causes and conditions, like phantoms or shadows or sounds. It is as changeable as the floating clouds, instantly vanishing like lightning.

"Again, this body has no abiding self or entity. Like the earth that has no owner, like the fire that has no body, like the winds that pass away instantly, there is no abiding life. Like the water that changes its shape depending on the container, there is no unchanging personality. Although many elements gather to form the body, there is no core.

"Again, this body is impure. Although it bathes and consumes food, sooner or later it will be caught up by old age and will be led to death. Thus those who know this should not be attached to the physical body but should aspire to attain the Buddha body. The body of the Buddha is the body of the Dharma. It is born of all goodness, wisdom, and truth. You, therefore, should aspire to attain the way to true enlightenment." Thus did Vimalakirti lead many people to the true way while lying in his sickbed.

(4) At one point the thought occurred in his mind, "Now I am sick in bed. Should the World-Honored One have pity on me, he probably would send someone to visit me." The World-Honored One knew Vimalakirti's wish and said to Sariputra, "Go visit Vimalakirti and see how he is."

Sariputra answered, "World-Honored One, I am not worthy of visiting the householder Vimalakirti. Some time ago, while I was sitting in meditation, Vimalakirti came and said, 'Sariputra, sitting is not necessarily true meditation. When one is totally free from the notion of body and mind, this is true meditation. True meditation is the state in which the mind is quiet and unmoving while being engaged in various activities. True meditation is following the way of the sages while living a common ordinary life. Listening to various non-Buddhist doctrines yet not being confused and practicing the way to enlightenment is true meditation. Attaining nirvana without severing defilement is true meditation. This is the kind of meditation that the World-Honored One acknowledges.' World-Honored One, I could not offer any answer to this and remained silent. Because of this I am not qualified to visit him."

So the World-Honored One appointed Maudgalyayana to go, but Maudgalyayana said, "World-Honored One, I, too, am not worthy of visiting Vimalakirti. Once while I was expounding on the Dharma to a large number of followers in Vaisali, Vimalakirti came and said, 'When you talk about the Dharma, you should explain the Dharma as it is. The truth of Suchness is non-discriminatory. Therefore, there should be no discriminating thought like "I have taught" on the part of the teacher, and no discriminating thought like "I have heard" on the part of the hearer. It should be like the puppeteer talking to his puppet. While teaching, you should know that there are some whose capacities are superior and some whose capacities are inferior. Knowing this, with a heart of great compassion you should teach the Dharma of no hindrance, always keeping in mind the thought of repaying the Buddha's mercy and of the continuing growth of the Three Treasures.' World-Honored One, when Vimalakirti said this, the eight hundred people who gathered there resolved to seek the path. Since I have no such ability, I cannot visit him.'"

(5) The World-Honored One next called on Mahakasyapa, who replied, "World-Honored One, neither am I qualified to visit Vimalakirti. Some time ago, when I was alms begging in a poor hamlet, he came to me and said, 'Mahakasyapa, although you have a heart of compassion, you are unable to extend it to all equally. Now you have forsaken the wealthy and are begging for food in an impoverished village. You should go begging impartially from house to house for food. Upon entering a village, think of the village as Emptiness; do not become possessed by things; think of the voice that you hear as mere sounds; think of fragrances you smell as winds; do not think of taste when you eat; and whomever you come into contact with, think of the person as contributing to your attaining the wisdom of enlightenment. In this way, whenever you receive food, give the donor the mind to follow the path; and the food should be offered to all the buddhas and sages before you eat. In doing so, you should not have any attachment to worldly life nor any thought of avoiding the world of delusion by entering nirvana. Kasyapa, do not look for any difference in the merits of gifts received, neither should you think of loss or profit. Alms begging in this spirit will make the giving not futile.' World-Honored One, when I heard these words, I was overjoyed and began to have deep respect for all path-seekers. I am not in a position to visit and comfort such a great layman."

The World-Honored One then chose Subhuti, but he also asked to be excused. "Once, when I went to Vimalakirti's house to beg for food, he took my bowl, filled it with rice, and said to me, 'Subhuti, if you know that all things are equal, you may accept this food. You may accept this food if you are not bothered by defilements and do not sever them; if you attain the wisdom to be free from love and lust even though being clung to by love and lust; and if you do not cling to discrimination although living in it. Subhuti, if I offer this to you, while you still retain the mind of discrimination, you will not gain benefit but rather fall into the three evil destinations.' World-Honored One, when I heard these words, I was at a loss and did not know how to answer. As I was about to leave, Vimalakirti said, 'Subhuti, take this food. Do not be afraid. Should the Buddha have someone appear magically and criticize you in such a way, would you be afraid?' I said that that I should not. He said, 'All things are illusory. There is nothing to be afraid of. Wise people do not cling to words. You need not fear. That is because words are not the true nature of things. Spiritual liberation exists where there are no words.' World-Honored One, I cannot possibly visit and comfort him in his sickness."

(6) The World-Honored One then appointed Purna. But Purna answered, "I cannot visit Vimalakirti at his sickbed. I was once expounding the Dharma to new disciples who had recently left their homes. Vimalakirti came and said, 'Purna, first you should be in meditation, perceiving the people's minds, and then teach the Dharma. Polluted food should not fill a bowl made of gems. That you

are trying to teach the Dharma with shallow understanding will injure the uninjured. It would be like putting the great ocean in a cow's footprint, or identifying the light of a firefly with that of the sun. Purna, these disciples once resolved to practice the Mahayana Dharma but later lost sight of it. How is it possible to lead these people with a shallow wisdom like the sight of a blind person?' Then he himself went into meditation and let those disciples recover their original minds of seeking the Mahayana Dharma. The disciples paid reverence at his feet, listened to his teaching, and attained the stage of non-retrogression from enlightenment. I became convinced then that without knowing the capacities of the listeners, it was impossible to teach the Dharma. This is the reason I am not able to visit Vimalakirti."

The World-Honored One then appointed Maha-Katyayana, who also declined, saying, "World-Honored One, I, too, cannot visit Vimalakirti. Once, when the World-Honored One expounded on the essentials of the Dharma, I further elaborated on the teaching on impermanence, suffering, Emptiness, non-self, and nirvana. Then Vimalakirti came and said, 'Katyayana, you should not talk about the Dharma of reality with a transient mind. All things do not come into existence, nor do they cease to exist. This is what impermanence means. Various sensations arise. They are really nonexistent; therefore there is neither suffering nor joy. This is the gist of what suffering is. To know that all things are ultimately not one's own is to know Emptiness; to know that self and non-self are not two different things is to know non-self. To know that all things do not come into existence and do not cease to exist is the meaning of nirvana.' When Vimalakirti explained things in this manner, the disciples were freed from the bondage of the mind. This is the reason why I am not in a position to visit him."

The World-Honored One then appointed Aniruddha, but he replied, "World-Honored One, I cannot assume that responsibility. Some time ago, when I was taking a walk, a god came to me and asked me about the superhuman power of the heavenly eye. I pointed to the mango I had in my hand and told him, 'I can see the three thousand great worlds as clearly as I see this fruit.' Vimalakirti appeared then and said, 'Aniruddha, does the heavenly eye possess the function to see or does it not? If it does, then it is no different from the so-called divine power of the non-Buddhists; if it does not, then for it there is no such thing as seeing.' I could not say anything to these words and remained silent. The gods were amazed, paid homage to him, and asked, 'Who possesses the true heavenly eye?' Vimalakirti answered, 'It is only the World-Honored One. He is continuously in the state of concentration and perceives all Buddha worlds but never has any thought of discrimination between self and others, or between existence and nonexistence.' Hearing this, the gods resolved to seek the Buddha's way, paid homage to Vimalakirti at his feet, and departed. This is the reason why I cannot visit Vimalakirti."

(7) The World-Honored One then told Upali to make the visit. Upali said, "World-Honored One, I am not able to fulfill this command. Once there were two disciples who, because of a breach of discipline, were ashamed to be in the presence of the World-Honored One. They came to me and asked how they could

resolve their doubts and remorse and be forgiven their offenses against the disciplinary rules. I instructed them to confess before twenty disciples in accordance with the rules of the Sangha. Vimalakirti came then and said, 'Upali, do not aggravate their transgressions by saying those things. You should immediately relieve them of their offenses and not disturb their minds. Upali, when the mind is liberated, is the defilement still remaining?' When I said, 'No, there will be no defilements remaining,' Vimalakirti said, 'Upali, the delusion, inverted views, and attachment to self are all defilements, but when you free yourself from them, you are pure. All things come into existence and go out of existence. They are constantly changing and do not cease to be so; they are like illusions and lightning. It is wrong to view them as really existing. Like dreams, flames, or the moon on the surface of the water and the forms in the mirror, all things are figures reflected in the erroneous mind. Knowing this is to abide by the disciplinary rules.' The two disciples were freed from the thoughts of doubt and remorse; they even wished to obtain the power of eloquence and persuasion that Vimalakirti possessed. This is the reason that I cannot make the visit."

The World-Honored One then appointed Rahula, who said, "I am like the others; I am not able to go to him. Once, the sons of the wealthy people of Vaisali came to me and asked me, 'Why have you, who were destined to become a king, renounced the throne and left home for the sake of the way? What benefits do you find in being a mendicant?' I explained to them the merits and benefits of being a mendicant as I had been taught them by the World-Honored One. Then came Vimalakirti and said, 'Rahula, you should not explain the merits and benefits of the mendicant. The reason is that merits and benefits can be talked about in regard only to relative things and cannot be talked about in regard to things absolute. Mendicants possess immeasurable value and therefore do not have merits or benefits.' Further, Vimalakirti told the sons of the wealthy, 'I advise you to leave home to follow the way of the right Dharma. It is rare that one is born in an age when a buddha exists.' Then the sons of the wealthy said, 'We hear that the World-Honored One does not allow us to leave home unless we obtain permission from our parents.' Vimalakirti answered, 'You need only to seek the true path, because that is leaving home.' The sons of the wealthy then resolved to seek the true path. This is my reason for not being able to make the visit."

Then the World-Honored One ordered Ananda to do the task. Ananda replied, "I am not able to assume the responsibility. Some time ago, when the World-Honored One suffered a slight illness, I wanted to offer him some milk. As I was standing by the huge gate of a brahmin's house with an alms bowl in my hands, Vimalakirti came and asked me the reason for my doing so. When I told him the reason, he said, 'Stop, Ananda, the World-Honored One has the body of a diamond. In one who has severed all evils and gathered all virtues, what disease or what vexation could there be? If those of other teachings hear about this, they will surely say, "How could he who cannot even cure his own disease cure those of others? Such a person is not worthy of being our teacher." You should leave here immediately so that no one will hear this.' World-Honored One, when

I heard this, I felt deeply ashamed and thought, 'I have always been close to the World-Honored One, but perhaps I have misunderstood the teaching.' Then a voice was heard from above, saying, 'It is indeed as Vimalakirti says. However, the World-Honored One, having come to this world, which is contaminated by the five pollutions, has made the appearance of being ill to save people. You need not consider it a shame to give milk to him.' World-Honored One, such was the wisdom and the persuasive power of Vimalakirti. I am not worthy of making the visit or of comforting him." And each of the five hundred other great disciples expressed his own reason for declining the role.

(8) Then the World-Honored One ordered the Bodhisattva Maitreya to make the visit and inquire about his illness. But the Bodhisattva, too, declined, saying, "World-Honored One, I, like the others, cannot go there. Here is the reason. Once when I was with the gods of the Tusita heaven, discoursing on the practice that leads to the stage where one will not retrogress to evil realms, Vimalakirti came and said, 'Maitreya, I am told that the World-Honored One has given you a prediction that you will attain true wisdom in your next life. Now, what does life mean? If it means the past life, it is already gone; if it means the future life, it is not here yet; if it means the present life, it is constantly changing and never the same for a moment. Moreover, if it means the life of enlightenment where there is neither arising nor perishing, it already is by itself the state of enlightenment that needs no prediction of attainment. Since all beings cannot exist outside of suchness, if Maitreya is able to receive the prediction of attainment, all others should also receive it. If Maitreya is able to extinguish the defilements, all should be able to do so. Maitreya, therefore, you should not lead the gods with your teaching.' World-Honored One, as Vimalakirti gave this discourse, all the gods gained the eye of the Dharma. It is not possible for me to visit him."

The World-Honored One then ordered a youth by the name of Prabhavyuha to go, but he, too, declined, saying, "World-Honored One, at one time when I was about to leave the city of Vaisali, he happened to be there. I asked him where he came from, and he said that he came from the place for learning the Dharma. When I asked him where the place for learning the Dharma was, he said, 'The straight mind is the place for learning the Dharma, because there is no falsity in it. Resolving to practice is the place for learning the Dharma, because it accomplishes one's endeavor. The deep mind is the place for learning the Dharma, because it increases virtues. The mind to seek the way is the place for learning the Dharma, because there is no error. The Six Perfections of giving without expecting any reward, observing the precepts with aspiration, patience with no barrier toward anyone, endeavoring without any laziness, concentration that controls the mind, and wisdom that enables one to see all things, are all the places for learning the Dharma. The four immeasurable minds of loving-kindness that loves all equally, compassion that alleviates others' sufferings, joy in the Dharma and in the happiness of others, and non-discrimination between love and hate, are the learning place for the Dharma. Hearing about the skillful means by which one can lead others to enlightenment is the place for learning the Dharma. Defilements are the place for learning the Dharma, because by them true reality can be known. People are the place for learning the Dharma, because by them selflessness can be known. All things are the place for learning the Dharma, because by them the emptiness of all things is known. The three worlds are the place for learning the Dharma, because there is nowhere else to go. The lion's roar that knows no fear is the place for learning the Dharma. To know all things in one thought through omniscience is the place for learning the Dharma. If a bodhisattva in this way cultivates the path and guides others, then all his actions, even an action like raising or lowering his leg, will become the place for learning the Dharma.' When Vimalakirti ended this discourse, five hundred gods resolved to pursue the way. This is why I am not able to visit him."

(9) When the World-Honored One appointed the Bodhisattva Jagatimdhara, he, too, declined, saying, "Once while I was sitting in a quiet room, a demon impersonating the guardian god Indra accompanied by twelve thousand goddesses, singing in tune with harps and drums, descended. After paying respect at my feet, he stood to one side. At that time, I thought that he was Indra and said to him, 'Indra, no matter how much pleasure is at your command, do not enjoy it. Realize how fleeting desire is. Seek the source of the good. Instead of clinging onto your body, life, and treasures, practice the Dharma, which is inexhaustible.'

"To this he replied, 'Bodhisattva, please accept these heavenly maidens and use them as your servants to cleanse your place.' I said, 'They are of no use to a mendicant.' Just then, Vimalakirti came and told me, 'This is not Indra. He is a demon, who is trying to entice you.' Then he said to the demon, 'You should give these women to me.' When the demon disappeared in fright, Vimalakirti said to the heavenly maidens, 'Now that the demon has given all of you to me, you should resolve to seek the way.' He led them to aspiration, each according to her capacity, and said, 'Now that you have resolved to follow the way, take delight in the Dharma. You should not enjoy the pleasure of desires.' One of the maidens asked, 'What is joy in the Dharma?' Vimalakirti said, 'Joy in the Dharma means having faith in the Buddha, wishing to listen to the Dharma, and having respect for and being charitable to others. Furthermore, it means freeing yourselves from desire and regarding your bodies as your enemies. Living in accordance with the Dharma, severing defilements, having no fear by listening to the Dharma, guarding yourselves against evil friends, having closer relations with good friends, keeping your minds pure, and practicing the boundless Dharma. These are the ways to take delight in the Dharma.'

"The heavenly maidens were overjoyed by the teaching of Vimalakirti and relinquished the desire for pleasure and were permitted to return to the demon's palace. But one maiden asked, 'How should we conduct ourselves at the demon's palace?' Vimalakirti said, 'Sisters, learn the way of the perpetual lamp. A hundred thousand lamps can be lighted from a single lamp. Then what formerly was dark becomes illuminated. Similarly, a bodhisattva teaches a hundred thousand persons and leads them to the resolve to seek the Buddha's path. The minds once resolved to follow the way will not change. If you live in the demon's palace, you should lead countless demons to the resolve to seek the path in accordance with the teaching of the perpetual lamp and thereby return the Buddha's mercy.'

"The maidens reverently paid homage to Vimalakirti and returned to the demon's palace. World-Honored One, Vimalakirti possesses so great a superhuman power, wisdom, and power of persuasion that I cannot possibly visit him."

The World-Honored One then appointed the Bodhisattva Sudatta who was the son of a wealthy man. Sudatta, too, declined and said, "World-Honored One, I do not qualify to be the messenger. Some years ago, I organized a Dharma gathering for charitable giving, and for days I offered gifts to the monks and to the poor. Vimalakirti came and said, 'Son of a wealthy man, instead of having a gathering for giving treasures, you should sponsor a gathering for the giving of the Dharma.' I asked him what was meant by the giving of the Dharma, and he replied, 'A Dharma gift is given at one time to all. That is to say, seeking the Buddha's way, have great compassion to save others; have the mind of joy to let the Dharma prevail; have the mind of non-discrimination to attain the true wisdom; give in charity to suppress greed; observe the discipline to guide those who violate the precepts; be patient and make efforts; attain wisdom by concentration; know the truth of emptiness while teaching others; know that all things are a temporary coalescence of elements and that there is no abiding self-nature; resolve to restrain evil passions by being close to the sages; avoid attachment to the world with a mind focused on the Buddha; listen intently and live according to the teaching; stay in quietude and live the Dharma that knows no strife; practice meditation to approach a Buddha's wisdom; release others from their fetters and lead them to virtuous lives; cut off defilements and make the land pure and gain all sorts of wisdom. This is called the assembly of giving the Dharma. A bodhisattva in this gathering is called the master giver and the soil of happiness.'

"World-Honored One, when Vimalakirti taught this Dharma, two hundred brahmins resolved to seek the Buddha's way. My mind was purged. I paid homage at his feet and offered my necklace to him. He accepted it and split it in two. He gave one of the halves to the most lowly beggar in the gathering and offered the other half to Sudurjana Buddha. Vimalakirti said, 'If the giver with a mind of equality does not discriminate when giving to the most lowly or making offerings to the Buddha and at the same time does not expect any favorable results from it, it is called the perfect Dharma gift.' From then on the lowly beggar resolved to seek the Dharma. For this reason, I am not able to go to him."

Thus did all these bodhisattvas decline to accept the mission of visiting the ailing Vimalakirti.

(10) The World-Honored One then appointed the Bodhisattva Manjusri. Manjusri replied, "World-Honored One, Vimalakirti has mastered the Dharma thoroughly. He has unobstructed wisdom and knows how he should expound and practice the Dharma. He has conquered all demons and uses superhuman power

at will. I am not qualified to compete with him, but since it is the wish of the World-Honored One, I shall go and visit him."

Many, including bodhisattvas and disciples, accompanied Manjusri to Vaisali. Vimalakirti foresaw his coming. With his superhuman power, he removed all his possessions and attendants and made the room empty except for the bed on which he lay and waited for Manjusri. "It was kind of you to come. Manjusri, you came without coming and in invisible form." Manjusri said, "It is as you say. Once I am here, I shall not come again, and once gone, I shall not go again, because for the one who comes, there is no place to come to, and for one who goes, there is no place to go to. Be that as it may, how is your sickness, Vimalakirti? What is the cause of your illness and how long will it last?"

Vimalakirti replied, "From ignorance arises attachment. My illness started from there. I am ill because all are ill. If they become no longer ill, my illness will be no more. For a bodhisattva comes into this world of delusion for the sake of the people. Parents become sick when their child is sick; they become well when the child becomes well."

Manjusri asked, "What is the cause of your illness?" Vimalakirti answered, "The illness of a bodhisattva is caused by great compassion." Manjusri, "Why is this room empty and without any attendants?" Vimalakirti answered, "This room is empty because all the worlds are empty. You say that there are no attendants, but all the demons and adherents to wrong teachings are my attendants. The reason is that demons wish people to have delusion while a bodhisattva saves people from delusion. Again, the adherents of wrong teachings wish for wrong views, but the bodhisattvas are not influenced by these views."

Manjusri asked, "Is it your mind or your body that is ill?" Vimalakirti answered, "I am not one with the body; therefore, my body is not ill. I know that the mind is like an illusion; therefore, the mind is not ill. Only because people are ill, I, too, am ill." Manjusri asked, "How should a bodhisattva comfort those who are ill?" Vimalakirti replied, "Let them know that the body is impermanent, but do not tell them to dislike the body. Tell them that the body is suffering, but do not tell them to remain in nirvana. Tell them that the body has no self, but that this does not mean to forsake people. A bodhisattva should not forget to teach them well. It is important that they have regrets for their past wrongs, but do not let them suffer because of their past wrongs. Through one's own experience, a bodhisattva should have sympathy with the sick person. Let them know of the pains they suffered from the infinite past, but encourage them by advising them to endeavor to become buddhas, the great kings of medicine, and cure the illnesses of all people."

Manjusri then asked, "How should sick people control their minds?" Vimalakirti answered, "Sick people should think in this way: 'This disease was caused by the poison of defilement, and it does not have any substantial entity. Moreover, this body is a mere temporary aggregation, and there is neither a master nor a self. Where then can diseases be received?'

"Again, a sick person should think that there is no real sickness either in him or in others. A bodhisattva should discard the sympathy that arises from attachment. Rather he should rouse compassion after discarding countless delusions; for the sympathy arising from attachment at times becomes weary. When attachment is discarded, there will be no more bondage. One who is in bondage cannot free others in bondage. What, then, is it to be in bondage and what is it to be liberated? To indulge in the ecstasy of meditation is to be in bondage, and to have rebirth as a skillful means is to be liberated. Wisdom without skillful means is bondage; wisdom with skillful means is liberation. Skillful means without wisdom is bondage, and skillful means with wisdom is liberation. To see that the body is impermanent and filled with pain and that there is no abiding substance is wisdom. Though the body may be in the world of delusion and diseased, if one gives abundantly and tirelessly, that is called skillful means. The body cannot be separated from disease, and disease cannot be separated from the body; if the disease and the body are seen as neither new or old, that is called wisdom. Though the body may be diseased, if one does not forsake this world and does not intend to enter nirvana, that is called skillful means.

"Furthermore, a sick person should not adhere too closely to the thought of controlling the mind. But this does not mean that the control of the mind is not necessary. Too much stress on control is putting too much importance on the virtues, but to neglect control is being foolish. The bodhisattva way is free from the two extremes; it is the Middle Path. The practice of bodhisattvas is neither the way of foolish ordinary people nor the way of the sage. It is neither the defiled way nor the pure way. Going along with the demon's way and yet destroying the demon's way is the bodhisattva practice. Again, though one wishes to leave the world of delusion, one has no intention of extinguishing his body and mind: this is the bodhisattva practice. Though a bodhisattva knows that all things are neither born nor cease to exist, he still endeavors to make this world beautiful: this is the bodhisattva practice. A bodhisattva knows that a buddha's country is eternally quiet and void, yet he sees various pure buddha countries; attaining the Buddha path, teaching the Buddha-Dharma, or even entering nirvana, he does not neglect the bodhisattva way of giving abundantly to others: this is the bodhisattva practice."

(11) At that time, Sariputra noticed that there were no seats in the room. He thought to himself, "Where do these bodhisattvas and disciples sit?" Vimalakirti immediately knew what was in Sariputra's mind and asked, "Did you come here to seek the Dharma or to sit?" To this Sariputra answered, "To seek the Dharma." Vimalakirti said, "Sariputra, one who is truly seeking the Dharma has no greed in regard to his body or his mind. To one who truly seeks the Dharma, there is nothing that he seeks in all the worlds, not even the Three Treasures, the Buddha, Dharma, and Sangha. Therefore, even if he sees suffering, he does not think of severing defilement, which is its cause. Neither does he think of practicing the way for his enlightenment. These would be needless thought-constructions arising from the idea that defilement and nirvana are different.

"Sariputra, all things are quiescent. Clinging to the thought of birth and extinction is not seeking the Dharma. All things are free from the grasping and discriminative mind. Being attached to this is not the way to seek the Dharma. The Dharma exists everywhere. It has no abiding place or shape. Therefore, if one sees the Dharma at any one location or perceives its form, one is not seeking the Dharma. The Dharma neither remains at one place nor is it the object of seeing, hearing, or knowing. Thus it is impossible to attain the Dharma through perception or thinking. Also, since the Dharma cannot be created, it is called uncreated. If one clings to the created, one is not seeking the Dharma. Therefore, Sariputra, one who seeks the Dharma should not be attached to anything." Then Vimalakirti turned to Manjusri and said, "You have travelled to many countries. In what country is the supreme Lion's Seat found?" Manjusri replied, "After one passes through innumerable countries to the east, one finds one called Sumerudhvaja. In that country there is a buddha by the name of Sumerupradiparaja. He is on the high and wide Lion's Seat even now. That seat is the supreme seat." Upon hearing this, Vimalakirti, with the consent of Sumerupradiparaja Buddha, had thirty two thousand Lion's Seats brought into the room by his superhuman power. But the room was large enough to accommodate all these. The city and the country were not obstructed by the large number of huge seats.

Vimalakirti then invited all those in the room to the adorned seats. Those bodhisattvas who had superhuman power changed their forms and took the seats, but the bodhisattvas in the early stages and those disciples who were satisfied with inferior teachings were not able to get onto the large seats. To them Vimalakirti said that if they meditated on Sumerupradiparaja Buddha they would be able to get onto the seats. After they were all seated, Vimalakirti said to Sariputra, who was still in a state of bewilderment, "Sariputra, all buddhas and bodhisattvas have attained inconceivable liberation. All who have reached this state are able to insert the towering Mount Sumeru into a tiny poppy seed or put the four great seas into a pore of the skin; yet the mountain still retains its original size and shape while the fishes, Nagas, and Asuras are not even conscious of what has taken place. Again, depending on the wish of each person, seven days of life can be felt to be as long as one kalpa, or a period of one kalpa can be felt to be as short as seven days. Or, one can inhale all the winds of the worlds in the ten directions and still not injure one's health or that of the trees. Further, Sariputra, one can appear in a buddha's body, or in the body of a sage or a god, change all the voices in the world to those of buddhas, and let all people hear the Dharma, for instance, on impermanence, suffering, Emptiness, and non-self. Sariputra, I have given merely a cursory description of inconceivable liberation. If I were to describe it in detail, I should not be able to do so even in a period of a kalpa."

(12) Manjusri asked, "How does a bodhisattva look at people?" Vimalakirti answered, "He looks at people as illusions that a magician produces, or a moon reflected on the water's surface, or the figure in a mirror, or shimmering heat

waves, or floating clouds in the sky, or bubbles in water, or flashes of lightning, or the traces of flying birds, or children of barren women, or dreams after awakening." Manjusri asked, "If a bodhisattva looks at people in such wise, how is it possible to have compassion for them?" Vimalakirti replied, "A bodhisattva, after discovering people thus, has true compassion. With serenity, free from defilement, and compassion as boundless as the vast sky, pure and calm, he leads people to attain peace of mind." Manjusri asked further, "What are benevolence and joy?" Vimalakirti answered, "To share the merits achieved with all beings is benevolence and to find gladness in giving is joy."

Manjusri then asked, "What should those bodhisattvas who are fearful of birth and death rely on?" Vimalakirti's reply was, "They should rely on the meritorious power of the Buddha." Manjusri asked, "What should one do to rely on the meritorious power of the Buddha?" Vimalakirti answered, "One should help all beings to attain deliverance." Manjusri asked, "In order to save others, what should be eliminated?" Vimalakirti answered, "Let them rid themselves of their defilements." Manjusri asked, "What should they do to rid themselves of defilements?" Vimalakirti answered, "Let them dwell in right mindfulness."

Manjusri asked, "How should one lead them to right mindfulness?" Vimalakirti answered, "Let them understand that all things are not born and do not perish." Manjusri asked, "What is that which is not born and does not perish?" Vimalakirti answered, "Evil is not born and good does not perish." Manjusri asked, "What is the root of good and evil?" Vimalakirti answered, "The body." Manjusri asked, "What is the root of the body?" Vimalakirti answered, "Greed." Manjusri asked, "What is the root of greed?" Vimalakirti answered, "Discrimination." Manjusri asked, "What is the root of discrimination?" Vimalakirti answered, "The inverted view." Manjusri asked, "What is the root of the inverted view?" Vimalakirti answered, "It comes from that which does not have a fixed nature." Manjusri asked, "Where does that which does not have a fixed nature come from?" Vimalakirti answered, "Since that which does not have a fixed nature does not stay at one place, it is called baselessness. Baselessness does not have a root. All things arise from baselessness."

(13) Just then a heavenly maiden appeared and scattered heavenly flowers over the people. All the flowers that fell on the bodhisattvas fell off, but those that fell on the disciples clung to their bodies and did not come off. The disciples tried to brush them off but to no avail. The heavenly maiden asked Sariputra, "Why are you trying to brush the flowers off?" Sariputra said, "Flowers are not becoming to mendicants." The heavenly maiden said, "Why should flowers be unbecoming to monks? The flowers do not have any discriminating thoughts. Discriminating thoughts are in you, Venerable One. It is not becoming for one who left home in order to practice the Buddha's path to have a discriminating mind. When there is no discrimination, things will be in accordance with the Dharma, or naturalness. That those flowers do not cling to the bodhisattvas is because they have freed themselves from all discriminatory thoughts. When one has fear, one is liable to be possessed by an evil spirit. Likewise, you venerable ones still have some fears about birth and death; that is why attachment sneaks

into your being. Since some habitual forces of defilements remain in you, they make you cling to the thought of the flowers."

Sariputra asked, "Have you been in this room long?" The heavenly maiden replied. "My being in this room is like the venerable ones' deliverance from delusions." Sariputra again asked, "Have you been here long?" The heavenly maiden asked, "How long has it been since the venerable ones have attained deliverance?" Sariputra remained silent and did not answer. The heavenly maiden said, "Venerable One of great wisdom, why do you keep your lips tight?" "Deliverance is an experience that cannot be expressed in words," replied Sariputra.

The heavenly maiden said, "Words and letters are both manifestations of deliverance. Deliverance cannot fall outside the pale of words and letters because all things are the manifestations of deliverance." To this Sariputra retorted, "But is freedom from greed, anger, and ignorance not deliverance?" The heavenly maiden said, "The World-Honored One taught so as a skillful means to those who were arrogant. To those without arrogance, he taught that greed, anger, and ignorance are, as they are, deliverance." Sariputra, said, "Heavenly maiden, what you are saying is most excellent. On what basis of attainment and realization are you discoursing in this manner?" The heavenly maiden replied, "Because I have nothing to attain and nothing to realize I am able to talk in this manner. If I had something to attain and something to realize, it would cause me to become arrogant over the Dharma."

Then Sariputra asked, "Heavenly maiden, there is more than one way to seek the way. What way did you follow?" The heavenly maiden said, "I do not necessarily seek a fixed path. It is like entering a campaka forest; one smells only the fragrance of campaka flowers and does not smell other things. Once one enters this room, one need not wish to smell the fragrance of any saint other than the supreme fragrance of the Buddha. Indeed, the golden light is shining day and night in this room so that no sunlight or moonlight is needed. No impurities to plague us are found in this room. Instead, gods and bodhisattvas gather here and always teach the way that will benefit oneself as well as others. Beautiful heavenly music sounds endlessly the strains of the Dharma. Abundant Dharma treasures save the poor. Sakyamuni Buddha and Amitabha Buddha as well as other buddhas appear here in response to the wishes of those here and teach the essence of the Dharma. Also in this room are seen the beautiful palaces of the gods and the pure, taintless buddha countries. Venerable One, as this room is filled with supreme virtues, there is no one who raises discriminatory thoughts."

Sariputra then asked, "Why do you not change your feminine form?" The heavenly maiden answered, "I pondered on it for a long time, but I still cannot think that I am a woman. Why, then, is there a necessity for a change? Suppose a magician conjures up an illusory woman, and someone comes and asks, 'Why do you not change that woman?' Would that be a proper question?" Sariputra answered, "In magic, there is no definite form to follow; therefore, it is not necessary to change." The heavenly maiden said, "All things are like that. There is no definite unchangeable form. It is not necessary to ask about changing a woman's body."

Just then, the heavenly maiden used her superhuman power and transformed Sariputra to a heavenly maiden and herself to Sariputra, saying, "Why do you not change your woman's form?" Sariputra who had turned into a woman said to himself, "How strange! I became a woman without my intending it." Then the heavenly maiden said, "If the Venerable One can change his feminine form, probably all women, too, will change. As the Venerable One, though not a woman, appears in feminine form, all women are not so-called women. Therefore, the World-Honored One has said, 'There is no such being as man or woman.'"

When the heavenly maiden withdrew her superhuman power, both Sariputra and the heavenly maiden returned to their original forms. The heavenly maiden asked, "Where did the feminine form go to?" "It exists and at the same time does not exist," replied Sariputra. The heavenly maiden then said, "All phenomenal things are as though existing and at the same time not existing. This is what the World-Honored One teaches us." Sariputra asked, "After your death, where will you be born?" The heavenly maiden said, "My birth will be like the provisional birth of living beings that are created by the Buddha." Sariputra asked, "What the Buddha makes is phenomenal life and not real life." The heavenly maiden said, "People, too, are the same way. There is no real birth or death." Sariputra asked, "When will you attain the Buddha's enlightenment?" The heavenly maiden answered, "When you, the Venerable One, return to being a common mortal again, I shall attain the Buddha's enlightenment." Sariputra said, "I shall never return to being a common mortal." The heavenly maiden said, "I, too, shall never attain the Buddha's enlightenment. That is because there is no place of abode in enlightenment; thus there is no one that attains it."

Sariputra said, "Nevertheless, all the buddhas have attained the supreme truth. Those who have attained it and those who will attain it in the future are said to be as numerous as the sands on the banks of the Ganges." To this the heavenly maiden said, "It was in the conventional worldly sense that the three periods of past, present, and future were spoken of. In true enlightenment, there are no distinctions such as past, present, and future. Venerable One, have you attained the state of the sages?" Sariputra answered, "I have understood that there is no state to be attained." The heavenly maiden said, "All buddhas and bodhisattvas have attained the understanding that there is no state to be attained."

Just then Vimalakirti told Sariputra that this heavenly maiden had practiced the way for a long time and had reached the rank in which one realizes the truth that there is no birth or extinction and was teaching others at will.

(14) Manjusri then asked Vimalakirti, "How does a bodhisattva reach the Buddha's way?" Vimalakirti answered, "It is by doing things that deviate from the way that he reaches it. Even falling into hell by committing atrocious deeds, he does not have any agony. In entering the realm of animals, he does not have any ignorance. In falling into the realm of hungry devils, merits are accumulated. Even if it appears as though he has greed, he is free from attachment. Even showing anger, he controls his mind. Even showing parsimony, he discards everything, including his own life. Appearing as though violating the precepts,

he is cautious not to commit even the slightest of evils. Even though appearing to flatter, he is using skillful means to accord with the Dharma. Though appearing arrogant, he is really humble. Though appearing to enter evil ways, he is living in harmony with the Buddha's wisdom. Though living in abundance, he recognizes impermanence, not falling into indulgence. Though having a wife, he is free from lust. Though entering an evil life, he is leading others to a good life. While showing an entry into nirvana, he is not extricating himself from the state of birth and death. Manjusri, by doing these things that are against the way, he will reach the Buddha's way."

Manjusri posed the question, "What is the seed that enables one to become a buddha?" To this query Vimalakirti answered, "All wrong views of other teachings and all defilements are the seeds of a buddha; those who believe that nirvana is independent of defilements cannot attain the Buddha's path. The lotus does not grow on high plains but blooms in muddy water. Likewise, one generates the Buddha-Dharma living in the mud of defilements. Moreover, seeds will not grow when planted in the sky; planted in dirt and manure, they sprout forth vigorously. In the same way, those who completely immerse themselves in the uncreated nirvana cannot produce the Dharma. Rather, those who come forth with an ego as large as a mountain are the very ones who rouse the mind that aspires to the way and are able to produce the Dharma. That is to say, all defilements are seeds to attain Buddhahood. Unless one goes down deep to the bottom of the sea, one will not be able to obtain the priceless gems. Likewise, without going into the ocean of defilements, one cannot attain the gem of omniscience."

At this juncture, the Bodhisattva Sarvarupasam-darsana asked Vimalakirti, "Householder, who are your parents, wife and children, relatives, teachers, and friends? And where are your servants, domestic animals and carriages?" To this, Vimalakirti answered in verse:

(i)   Wisdom is my mother, and skillful means my father;
      Bodhisattvas leading the multitude are born of these parents.
      The joy of the Dharma is my wife,
      And compassion is my daughter.
      Sincerity is my son,
      And the calm Emptiness is my house.
      Defilements are my disciples,
      Who follow the dictates of my mind
      Virtues are my good friends:
      My enlightenment depends on all these.

(ii) Charities are my courtesans,
      Who sing the songs of the Dharma.
      In the garden of the Dharma, flowers of enlightenment bloom;
      And the trees bear the fruits of wisdom.
      The elephants and horses of godly powers,
      Drawing carriages loaded with the supreme teaching,
      And driven by singleness of mind,
      Run over the roads of the Eightfold Path.
      Penitence is my garment;

And a deep mind is my garland;
Giving faith and discipline,
They practice great kindness.

(iii) Listening extensively and deepening his wisdom,
Savoring the nectar of the Dharma,
Courageously conquering the demons of defilements,
The bodhisattva raises high the victory banner in the place of learning.
Travelling to all countries,
Making suffering and wars the occasions for teaching,
Using opportune means to teach the Dharma,
He saves people from their sufferings.
Like lotuses emerging from a fire,
He practices meditation in the middle of desires.
Or, assuming the form of a courtesan,
He guides licentious people to the Buddha's wisdom
By using the hook of lust.
With fathomless wisdom, and practicing countless ways,
He saves innumerable beings,
And his merit is beyond praise.

(15) Vimalakirti then asked all the bodhisattvas, "How can one enter the Dharma gate of non-duality? Let each of you tell me his own thoughts on this."

The Bodhisattva Dharmavikurvana was the first to answer. "I gained entrance into the gate of non-duality by knowing that there is no difference between the birth and death of all things. Since there is no birth, there is no death."

The Bodhisattva Srigandha said, "There is the notion of 'mine' because of the notion of 'I'; where there is no notion of 'I', there will be no 'mine'. I entered the gate of non-duality by knowing that there is no difference between 'I' and 'mine'."

The Bodhisattva Srikuta said, "With regard to purity and impurity, originally there is neither purity nor impurity in the Dharma. The thoughts of purity and impurity arise from discriminatory thinking. By realizing this, I entered the gate of non-duality."

The Bodhisattva Sunetra said, "I entered the gate of non-duality by contemplating form and non-form. All things in this universe are originally one and there should not be differences. Therefore, there is no definite form. Therefore, there is nothing that can be held on to. Viewing the non-difference of all things, I entered the gate of non-duality."

Next, the Bodhisattva Tisya said, "I entered the gate by considering good and evil. If one does not cling to the thought of good and evil and attains the state of non-attachment, he will be able to reach non-duality."

Then the Bodhisattva Simha said, "I attained non-duality by thinking about transgression and happiness. As I view these two with true wisdom, I see that transgression, as it is, is happiness. Thus there is no longer bondage nor liberation. This was my entry into the gate of non-duality."

The Bodhisattva Suddhadhimukti said, "I entered the gate of non-duality by knowing the created and the uncreated. If one is freed from all thoughts of discrimination, the mind will be like the empty sky, and there will be nothing that hinders the pure wisdom. Thus is one able to know that the created, as it is, is the uncreated. This is the gate of non-duality."

Next, the Bodhisattva Dantamati said, "I entered the gate by seeing the nature of samsara and nirvana. When the true nature of samsara is known, there is neither birth nor death. There is neither bondage nor liberation and neither burning nor extinction. This is the entry into the gate of non-duality."

The Bodhisattva Vidyuddeva said, "I entered by contemplating wisdom and ignorance. The true nature of ignorance is wisdom. But wisdom itself should not be clung to. It was by discerning that everything is equal and that there is no duality that I entered the gate of non-duality."

Then the Bodhisattva Santendriya said, "It was the identity of the Three Treasures, the Buddha, Dharma, and Sangha, that led me to the gate of non-duality. The Buddha is none other than the Dharma, and the Dharma is none other than the Sangha. These three are uncreated and are like space."

The Bodhisattva Manikutaraja said, "I entered the gate by contemplating the right path and the wrong path. Those who are on the right path do not discriminate between the right and wrong paths. The path that is free from the two is the gate of non-duality."

The Bodhisattva Satyarata said, "I entered by thinking on truth and untruth. One who really sees truth does not even have the thought of seeing truth. This is because not to have any discrimination between truth and untruth is the state of truly seeing truth. It is not the physical eye but the wisdom eye that is able to see. Furthermore, the wisdom eye does not discriminate between seeing and not seeing. By knowing this, I entered the gate of non-duality."

After these bodhisattvas had expressed themselves, Manjusri was asked for his thoughts on the subject. Manjusri said, "In my view, regarding all things, there can be no word, no concept, and no knowing. That is to say, the Dharma gate of non-duality is beyond all words and thoughts." Lastly, Manjusri asked Vimalakirti for his understanding of non-duality, but Vimalakirti was silent and uttered not a word. Manjusri praised him, saying, "Good. When letters and words no longer exist, this is the entrance to the Dharma gate of non-duality." Thus did all the bodhisattvas enter the gate and come to a firm conviction that there was no birth or death.

(16) Vimalakirti now said to Manjusri, "Let us now go together to see the World-Honored One and listen to his wonderful Dharma." Manjusri was very much pleased and he and all the assembly went up to where the World-Honored One was. They all put their palms together, reverently paid homage at his feet, and sat to one side. The World-Honored One said to Vimalakirti, "I understand that you wish to see the Buddha. But what does it mean to see the Buddha?" Vimalakirti answered, "To see the Buddha means to see oneself as one really is. The Buddha's body did not come from the past nor does it go away in the future. Neither is it in the present. It is not a physical body, nor does it possess the characteristics of a physical body. Therefore, it is beyond being seen by the eyes, being touched by the body, and being thought by the mind. It is free from greed, anger, and ignorance; it is neither one nor many; it does not differentiate between self

and other, being and non-being. The Buddha is neither on this shore of delusion nor on the other shore of enlightenment; neither is he anywhere in between. Yet he teaches people. He appears to be quiescent but is not in an eternal extinction. He is free from all discriminations, and although he has no permanent abode, he does not leave his abode. He is neither charitable nor parsimonious; he does not observe the precepts, and at the same time he does not violate the precepts. He is neither patient nor irritable; he is not diligent, yet is not indolent; he is neither calm nor disturbed. He is neither wise nor ignorant; he is not truthful, but he is not deceiving. He does not come or go; he does not exit, neither does he enter. Completely beyond words and thoughts is the Buddha. World-Honored One, thus the body of the Buddha cannot be shown by any means. To see him in this wise, I believe, is right and to see him in other ways is wrong." Then Indra said to the World-Honored One, "World-Honored One, in the past I heard many teachings, but I have not yet heard any teaching that is as uniquely true as this. If one believes and holds on to this teaching, he will surely attain the Dharma. Further, he will close the gate of evil paths and open the gate of all wholesomeness; he will be guarded by the buddhas and will convince the followers of other teachings. He will attain the right enlightenment and will follow in the Buddha's footsteps. World-Honored One, I, together with all my kinfolk, shall make offerings to serve those who practice this Dharma." The World-Honored One said, "Good, Indra, it is just as you say. I shall help you to enhance your happiness."

Introduction

The Buddha continues his travels from Rajagaha (Skt: Rajagriha) in the east to the Ghosita Monastery at Kosambi in the west. On the way, he stops near Baranasi (Benares) in the country of Kasi and advises his disciples to eat only one meal a day. When two disciples refused to follow this rule, the Buddha patiently explains that he does not lay down a rule without first testing it himself. He reminds them that a disciple must faithfully follow his teacher, carefully reflecting on the teachings, and practice the Dharma. Otherwise, the disciple would go astray.

Later, the Buddha toured the country of Kosala where he teaches that cultivating wisdom and upholding the precepts have nothing to do with family lineage. These passages in Chapter 1, Section 3, reveal the Buddha's belief in social equality. He points out that regardless of whether a disciple is from a higher or lower caste, each must discard the notion of class distinctions; and concentrating on proper mind control, cultivate wisdom and uphold the rules of the sangha.

Chapter 2, Section 1, contains the ten major and 48 minor precepts laid down for the bodhisattvas, who have vowed to achieve highest enlightenment for the welfare of all beings. Specific rules for every aspect of their life as monks are delineated, including the conditions that constitute transgressions of the moral code.

The following Section 2 relates the disgraceful discord in the Buddhist sangha that became widely known not only to contemporary followers of the Buddha but to later Buddhists as an example of disharmony that must be avoided. When the Buddha was staying at the Ghosita Monastery in Kosambi, a learned disciple committed a minor offence. The other disciples argued vigorously whether it was a violation or not. Finally, they decided to expel the disciple from the sangha. Even after the Buddha repeatedly talked to the angry disputing monks in an attempt to restore harmony, they split into two factions and continued their bitter disputes. Some monks asked the Buddha to wait, because they wanted to take the responsibility to settle the quarrel. Then the Buddha realized that these monks were caught in formality, forgetting the true spirit of compassion; therefore, he left to get away from this disturbing situation and to find peace in a quiet place. Even the people of Kosambi were upset with the quarreling disciples and stopped giving them food. The physically weakened disciples finally recognized the error of their ways and together went to seek the Buddha, who by then had gone to the Jeta Grove in Savatthi (Skt: Sravasti). Since the Buddha had already admonished them several times before, he calmly counseled them to have compassion in their hearts and follow the precepts for the single purpose of discarding delusion that hold the mind captive. The disciple who had committed the offence also softened, and harmony was restored to the sangha.

Chapter 3, Section 3 contains the frightening story of Angulimala, which means Finger Necklace. His real name was Ahimsaka, the main disciple of a brahmin priest who discovered that his wife had tried to seduce his disciple. Thus, the master, taking revenge, instructed Ahimsaka to take the lives of 100 people and cut off a finger from each and make a necklace. The disciple believed that he must obey his teacher regardless how distasteful the instruction. When he had killed 99 people, the Buddha was informed by his disciples of this cruel act. The Buddha approached Ahimsaka, who found that he could not kill the Buddha. At the Jeta Grove, after the Buddha explained the Dharma to Ahimsaka, he awakened as if from a dreadful nightmare and immediately attained enlightenment.

These passages regarding the Buddha's advice of eating one meal a day, disharmony in the sangha, and the story of Ahimsaka point not only to the importance of faithfully following one's teacher but also the need to understand that a faithful adherence to the rules must be tempered by proper respect and compassion, and that one's action must be adjusted appropriately and wisely to the situation.

Chapter 3 Section 6 relates how Ananda, the Buddha's cousin, became the Buddha's attendant. Ananda followed and served the Buddha faithfully for many years until the final parting at the Buddha's death in Kusinara, when the Buddha consoled the weeping Ananda and thanked him for having been such a devoted friend and assistant.

Book Five ends with the Buddha's instructions regarding how a bodhisattva with compassion and wisdom must endeavor diligently to master deep meditation and attain a true and unchanging understanding of the Buddha's teaching for the sake of saving all beings and leading them to enlightenment. These passages again attempt to explain the concept of 'emptiness' that the "world is already empty; the Buddha and the Dharma, too, are empty. The nature of these three are without substance." The Buddha teaches that as long as we cling to things as if they have a substantial, unchanging nature, we would not waken to the reality of life.

Chapter 1

EDUCATION

1. The Right Teacher and the Wrong Teacher

(1) The Buddha left the Bamboo Grove Monastery and headed west and entered the Deer Park. From there, on his way to Kosambi, he toured the country of Kasi. On the road he said to his disciples, "My disciples, I have stopped eating in the afternoon. As a result, I suffer no sickness, am in good health, and feel a sense of peace. I advise you to do the same and eat only once a day." Thereafter the Buddha entered the village of Kitagiri in Kasi and stayed there for a while.

(2) At that time two disciples of the Buddha, named Assaji and Punabbasuka, lived in Kitagiri. When they heard what the Buddha had said, they remarked, "We eat three meals, morning, noon, and evening, and yet we have not become sick but are in good health. There is no reason that we should abandon this good practice and follow another way that has not been proven to be better." They would not listen to the Buddha's advice given to the disciples and showed a strong reluctance to follow it.

When the disciples spoke about this to the Buddha, he summoned the two monks to ascertain the facts and asked them, "Do you think that evil teachings will decrease and good teachings will increase regardless of how you feel about suffering, pleasure, non-suffering or non-pleasure?"

"World-Honored One, we do not think so."

"My disciples, then do you think that some pleasant feelings will increase evil teachings and decrease good teachings and that other pleasant feelings will increase good teachings and decrease evil teachings? And do you think that the same applies to the feelings of suffering and non-suffering or non-pleasure?"

"World-Honored One, that is exactly what we believe."

"My disciples, if I were to teach this code of conduct without testing it and experiencing it myself, it would not be proper. However, I have actually tested and experienced it in my life. My disciples, I do not warn disciples not to neglect the teachings, because those who have already attained deliverance will never neglect the teachings. But if those who advance toward the unsurpassed peace discipline their minds according to the teachings, they will realize their goals now. Therefore it is unnecessary to warn those monks not to neglect the teachings.

"My disciples, you cannot attain enlightenment readily. You can attain the unsurpassed true enlightenment only after you awaken faith and serve under a master, listen to the Dharma and accept it in your mind, think about its meaning and understand it, and single-mindedly practice the Dharma. You do not have faith and do not serve your master; you listen to the teachings but do not retain them in your minds; you do not think about their meanings and do not understand them; you do not practice the Dharma single-mindedly. You miss the true way and enter the wrong way, and you stray far from the teaching.

(3) "My disciples, even in the master-disciple relationship of the secular world you will not find people who treat it like a business transaction, in which one receives something in exchange for some service or article. In our relationship especially, the World-Honored One is the master and you are his disciples. The disciple who has faith receives the teachings and vows not to leave his seat until he attains his goal. Only those disciples who have such strong faith can attain enlightenment."

(4) The World-Honored One, in the accompaniment of many disciples, passed through the country of Kasi and entered Kosambi and stayed in the Ghosita Monastery. At that time the itinerant mendicant Sandaka was staying in the Fig Tree Cave with five hundred disciples.

One afternoon Ananda finished his meditation and, with several fellow monks, went to see a huge hole made during a recent storm. Sandaka saw Ananda coming from afar. He told his followers to stop their idle chatter, and they quietly waited for Ananda to approach. After they exchanged greetings, Ananda asked Sandaka why there was such a crowd and what they were talking about. Sandaka did not answer this and said that they wanted the venerable Ananda to give a discourse on his master's teaching. Ananda then addressed the group: "The World-Honored One knows and sees the truth. He advises all that there are four kinds of shameful wrong practices and four kinds of ineffective religious practices; he teaches people not to rush into these unproductive and injurious practices.

"Sandaka, there are people who insist that there is no merit in giving or offering, no result from good or evil action, no afterlife, no mother or father, and no teacher to lead the people; that all human beings return to their original elements and the five senses disappear into nothingness; that death is just four people singing songs as they carry the casket to the funeral grounds where the body is cremated and turned into bleached bones and the funeral offerings reduced to ashes. They say that one who teaches selfless giving is an ignorant person, and furthermore, they say that it is foolish and nonsensical to say that giving has merit. They say that both fools and sages simply disappear when they die.

"Then there are some who say, 'It is not evil to kill people, to make people suffer, to steal, to plunder, to commit adultery, or to lie. Also, it is not evil to drag a wagon with razor-sharp swords attached to the wheels and, lumping all living things together, to mow them down in one sweep. Even if one kills on the southern bank of the Ganges and practices giving on the northern bank, there is no evil and no merit. Even if one practices giving, restrains himself, and teaches the truth, there is absolutely no merit.'

"Again, there are some who say, 'Whether a person rises or falls is not dependent on causes and conditions; he rises or falls for no reason at all; there is no such thing as a person's own power or devotion or right effort, because all joys and sorrows are determined by fate.'

"Then there are others who state, 'Earth, water, fire, wind, suffering, joy, and life, the seven elements, are neither created nor uncreated; they give birth to nothing; they are steadfast like a mountain or a pillar, unmoved and unchanging. Neither do they harm each other nor do they influence each other's joys and sufferings. Therefore, there is neither one that kills nor one that is killed, neither one that hears nor one that is heard; neither one that knows nor one that is known. Even if one cuts off another's head with a sharp sword, no one has taken another's life. The sword has simply acted as an agent and entered amidst the seven elements.'

(5) "Sandaka, thoughtful people will think about these four kinds of assertions, saying, 'If what these people say is true, then I have done things that I have not done and have practiced those disciplines that I have not practiced. There will be no difference between the masters who have endured all kinds of difficult disciplines and I, who have a wife and children and live a life of materialistic pursuits; I shall be able to attain the same enlightenment as these masters and go to the same world in the next life. Then what need is there to perform those pure practices?' But thoughtful people will realize that this is not a pure teaching and will discard it. Sandaka, these are the four kinds of shameful practices that my master teaches all thoughtful people to avoid.

"Again, Sandaka, some masters maintain that they have attained omniscience and the power to see all and that these powers are apparent in their daily lives. Nonetheless, they enter vacant houses and do not receive food; they are bitten by dogs; they are driven away by dogs and cows; they ask the names of women, men, and villages, and they ask directions. Thus their contention that they know and see all is contradicted. Yet when their assertions are questioned, they evade the inquiry and say that those things were what they had to do under the circumstances. Some masters teach things transmitted to them through the ages, some of which are incorrectly transmitted, so that what they teach is sometimes correct and sometimes incorrect. Some masters teach ideas and concepts that they thought out by themselves; therefore, some are good and some are not. Some masters are not only unwise but are also out of their minds, so that whatever questions they are asked, their answers are full of confusions. Sensible persons will see through all these and will leave these masters, understanding that to practice under their tutorship is useless. These, Sandaka, are the four kinds of teachers that the World-Honored One advises you not to rely upon, since you will not obtain benefit from them."

"Venerable Ananda, it is as you state. Venerable One, what is the true teaching, then, that all thinking people must rely on to receive real benefits?"

(6) "Sandaka, those who hear that the Buddha appears in this world will awaken faith, become monks, and follow the discipline. They will be afraid of even the slightest evil, and leaving all blind passions behind, will enter meditation. They will cultivate their minds and attain the highest wisdom. Thus they will know that they have no more birth, that they have mastered the pure discipline, and that they have done all that needed to be done. Never again will they return to the life of delusion. Disciples who study earnestly under this master attain this supreme state, and all thinking people receive the true benefits."

"Venerable Ananda, will the disciples of the master, who have destroyed their blind passions and have attained deliverance through true wisdom, still indulge in worldly desires?"

"Sandaka, those disciples who have become holy men will not knowingly kill sentient beings, not take things not given, not have sexual relationships with women, nor intentionally tell lies. Unlike lay persons they will not become engrossed in pursuing their greed and hoarding things."

"Venerable Ananda, will these holy men always be conscious of their knowledge that all earthly desires have vanished?"

"Sandaka, I shall give you an analogy. Here is a man whose arm has been amputated. He is thus without an arm, but only when he becomes conscious of this does he realize that he is without it. It is the same with these holy men. They are without evil passions at all times, but only when they become conscious of this do they realize that they are without evil passions."

Sandaka addressed his disciples thus, "I advise you to practice under Gotama, the World-Honored One. If you become like me, it is difficult to abandon the notion of profit and loss. Therefore I advise you to seek the path under the guidance of the World-Honored One."

2. The Demons in the Wild Plains

(1) The World-Honored One retraced his journey somewhat and entered Alavi. At this time a man-eating demon known as Alavaka who was inflicting suffering on the people dwelt here. Once, when the king of Alavi went on a hunt alone and lost his way in a pathless forest, he became tired and, while resting in the shade of a giant nigrodha tree, he was captured by the demon.

Only after he had promised to sacrifice a human being each day was he released and his life spared. First, robbers who were sentenced to death were used as human sacrifices. When the number of robbers was exhausted, infants were sacrificed, but soon the infants were no more. Finally the demon demanded that the king sacrifice his own child. The people of the city trembled in constant fear.

The World-Honored One saw what was happening and in order to save the inhabitants of the castle entered the demon's dwelling place. At this time Alavaka was attending a gathering of demons in the Himalayas and was absent. The World-Honored One asked Garava, one of the demons guarding the gate, to give him a night's lodging. Garava told him of his master's terrible disposition and refused. But upon the World-Honored One's insistence, Garava said he would go and see his master and departed for the Himalayas. The World honored One entered the demon's palace and, while waiting for Garava's return, taught the Dharma to the ladies-in-waiting.

Satagira, another of the demons, was a follower of the Buddha. He was on his way to the Himalayas and was flying over the palace when he suddenly came under the influence of the Buddha and could not fly any more. He wondered what was happening to him, but when he saw the Buddha, he understood and listened to his sermon. Then he resumed his journey through the sky and came to the Himalayan meeting. He sat next to Alavaka and congratulated him. "This is your lucky day. The World-Honored One is staying at your palace."

(2) The demon Alavaka possessed a violent temper and had no respect for anyone. He became very angry when he learned that the Buddha had entered his home without his permission and was even teaching the women. When he heard Satagira praising the Buddha's virtues, he was enraged. He shouted, "I am Alavaka. Today I shall truly show my power." He quickly returned home and caused the wind to blow and the rain to fall. He swung his sword, shot his arrows, hurled his spears, and attacked the Buddha with a firestorm. But as soon as these weapons approached the Buddha's body, all turned into flower petals and fell quietly around the place where the Buddha was seated.

When Alavaka saw what was happening he was surprised, but he was not so easily defeated. He resorted to his ultimate weapon, a giant magical cloth, and tried to spread it over the Buddha. It was said that when this cloth was spread, the rain would stop, the earth would dry up, the waters of the ocean would decrease, and the mountains would crumble. But his cloth was powerless before the Buddha, and it dropped beside him like a rag to wipe his feet.

The demon was frustrated by his powerlessness. His most fearful weapon was ineffective because he could not conquer the Buddha's compassion. He thought that if he were to irritate the Buddha, perhaps he might be able to defeat him. He changed his approach and said to the Buddha, "Leave this place at once." The Buddha wanted to pacify Alavaka's mind so that he could teach him, and he did as he was told. The Buddha yielded so easily that the demon's heart was somewhat softened. But he wanted to test the Buddha further, and this time he said, "You must now enter." When the Buddha returned to his seat, the demon said, "You must leave." Again the Buddha obeyed. But when the demon ordered him a fourth time, the Buddha said, "I have obeyed your orders three times, but this time I will not do what you say. You may do what you want."

The demon said, "Then I shall ask you a question. If you cannot answer my question, I will tear out your heart and take your legs and throw them to the other side of the river Ganges." The Buddha replied, "In this world I have never known anyone who could tear out my heart or my legs and throw them away. But you may ask me any question you wish."

(3) Alavaka had received a set of questions from his parents. Hoping that someday someone would provide the answers to these questions, he had engraved them in indelible red ink on a bronze plate and put the tablet in storage. He now

remembered these questions and presented them to the Buddha. The questions were:

> What is the greatest wealth in this world?
> What gives ultimate peace?
> What is the taste that surpasses all tastes?
> How shall I live to achieve the superior life?

The Buddha replied:

> Faith is the greatest wealth.
> Right practice is the way to peace.
> The taste of truth surpasses all tastes.
> The life of wisdom is the superior life.

Then the demon asked:

> How can I cross over the current of life and death?
> How can I transcend evil?
> How can I leave behind suffering?
> How can I attain the realm of purity?

The Buddha replied:

> By faith one crosses the current of life and death.
> By diligence one transcends evil.
> By right effort one leaves suffering behind.
> By wisdom one attains the realm of purity.

The demon asked:

> What is the way to attain wisdom?
> What is the way to accumulate wealth?
> What is the way to gain honor?
> What must one do so that he will not part from friends
> What must one do to achieve the state of no sorrow
> After one leaves this world for the next?

The Buddha replied, "If one has faith in the holy men, listens to the teaching of enlightenment, and is not self-indulgent but is understanding, one will attain wisdom. If one pursues right action, endures the heavy burdens of life, and deliberately cultivates patience, he will gain wealth. If one is truthful in speech, he will receive honor. If one is not miserly but gives freely, his friends will not leave him. If one has faith and embraces the four virtues of sincerity, truthfulness, diligence, and a spirit of giving, even a lay person will be free of sorrow after this life."

(4) When Alavaka heard the clear answers to his questions, his heart was filled with happiness. He was ashamed of his violent temperament and vowed before the Buddha that he would become a follower of his teaching. This took place exactly at the break of day.

In the meantime, the people of the palace tearfully brought the young prince as a sacrifice to the demon. When they saw the fearful demon on bended knees before the Buddha, his hands with palms together and his head lowered in an attitude of reverence, they were both astonished and overjoyed at the miraculous transformation that had taken place. Since they had made a promise, they asked the demon to take the young prince.

The demon accepted the prince with extended arms and presented him to the Buddha who, in turn, gave him back to the people. The Buddha said, "Please bring him up as a healthy child and when he has grown to adulthood bring him to me." Because the prince was passed from hand to hand, he was called Hatthaka, literally 'of the hand.' After Hatthaka grew up he learned that his life was saved by the Buddha and he became the Buddha's faithful disciple.

3. Family Lineage

(1) The Buddha entered Saketa and then proceeded north to tour the country of Kosala. Here he came upon the brahmin village of Icchanankala and entered its forest. At this time there lived a famous brahmin, Pokkharasati, who had received a grant from King Pasenadi and lived in a wealthy village known as Ukkattha.

Pokkharasati had previously heard rumors of a Sakya prince who had renounced his home and had become a Buddha. Now that the Buddha was staying nearby, the brahmin summoned his disciple Ambattha and said to him, "Ambattha, Gotama is staying in the forest of Icchanankala. As you have heard, the name Gotama is more widely known than the names of the gods. Therefore go to Gotama's place and ascertain if he is really a Buddha."

"Master, how could I ascertain such a thing?"

"Ambattha, our scriptures classify thirty-two bodily features of the great person. Any person possessing these characteristics, if he stays in the world, will become a king who rules the four seas, but if he renounces the world, he will become a Buddha and dispel the darkness of the world. You have already heard me speak of this."

Ambattha said, "I understand." He took a horse cart and drove to the Icchanankala Forest. He saw a large number of monks strolling in the forest and asked them, "Where is Gotama? I wish to meet him."

Since Ambattha was born to a famous family and was now a disciple of the eminent brahmin Pokkharasati, the disciples felt that it would be good for the Buddha to meet him. They said to Ambattha, "Beyond that closed door is Gotama's room. Go quietly to the entrance, clear your throat, and knock on the crossbar securing the door."

Ambattha did as he was told and knocked on the crossbar. The Buddha opened the door and welcomed Ambattha into the room. Ambattha entered and, while still standing and walking around, extended a lengthy greeting to the Buddha, who was seated.

(2) The Buddha asked him, "Ambattha, I am seated but you are standing and walking around while greeting me. Is this a way a disciple greets an elder brahmin?"

Ambattha answered, "No, this is not the way. It is proper to walk when greeting a walking brahmin, to stand when greeting a standing brahmin, and to sit when greeting a sitting brahmin. But while greeting a lowly homeless monk with his head shaved, I think that this way is sufficient."

"Ambattha, you came here for some reason. Think of that purpose. It seems that you are very proud of your training, but unless you have received very bad training, how can you do what you are doing now?"

Ambattha became angry at the Buddha's words and used abusive language. "Gotama, people of the Sakya clan are truly cruel, easily angered, and violent, and they do not know that they must respect brahmins and give offerings to them. This is not proper. They are also vulgar. Once I went to the castle of Kapilavatthu on an errand for my master. The Sakyas were assembled in the public hall and were poking each other and playing and paid no attention to me. Not one offered me a seat, and I am sure that they were ridiculing me. They did not know that they must respect a brahmin and make offerings to him. That is how vulgar they are."

"Ambattha, small quails can sing in their nests to their hearts' content. Like them the Sakyas were only enjoying themselves freely in their castle. You must not be angry over such a trivial thing."

"Gotama, in the caste system there exist four distinct classes, brahmin, kshatriya, vaisya, and sudra. In this system those of the three lower classes must serve the brahmins. Although the Sakyas belong to a lower caste, they neither respect the brahmins nor hold them in high esteem, nor do they make offerings to them. This is not good."

(3) At that time the Buddha thought to himself, "This young man mischievously relegates the Sakya clan to a lowly status. I wonder how he would feel if I told him about his family lineage?"

"Ambattha, what is your family lineage?"

"I belong to the Kanhayana family line."

"Ambattha, if you retraced your family tree, you would discover that you are a descendant of a family that served the Sakyas as their masters. According to tradition, in the ancestral line of the Sakya clan there was a king, Okkaka, who wanted to give the throne to a child born from one of his favorite queens. He therefore expelled four of the older princes from the country. The expelled princes established their kingdoms by the lotus lake in the foothills of the Himalayas. The Sakyas are descended from these people. King Okkaka also had a maid who bore someone a child called Kanha. Soon after his birth, the boy asked his mother, 'Please wash me. Mother, please cleanse my impurity, it will be to your benefit.' This is a well-known story. People said that a Kanha, a dark fellow, an evil demon, had been born. He is your ancestor, the beginning of the Kanhayana family line."

The young people who were there said to the Buddha, "Please do not speak too harshly to Ambattha. He has a good family line and is descended from distinguished ancestors. He has a good education and is a great orator. Please do not belittle him for being descended from a lowly maid."

"Young people," the Buddha answered them, "If you think that Ambattha is not educated enough to debate me, then you must set him aside and you yourselves should ask me questions. If you think that he is educated, let him debate freely." The Buddha continued, "I should like to ask you a logical question, Ambattha, and you should answer without considering whether it will be good or bad for you. If you try to evade the question with a muddled reply, your head will split into seven pieces. Ambattha, have you ever heard from the elder brahmins how they would explain the origin of the family line of Kanhayana?"

(4) Ambattha remained silent. The World-Honored One said, "Ambattha, this is not the time for silence. When the Buddha asks a question a third time and you still remain silent, your head will split in seven ways."

At that moment Ambattha saw in the sky the demon Vajrapani, poised and ready to attack him with a huge, burning red halberd. Ambattha shook with fear and approached the Buddha to seek protection from this fearful figure. He asked, "Will you please repeat what you said?" When he again heard the Buddha's words, he said, "Sire, it is as you say." When the young people heard Ambattha's confession, they scorned him and hurled insults at him, saying that he was descended from a lowly maid. But the World-Honored One came to his rescue and said that Kanha was a great man.

The Buddha continued, "Young people, that Kanha mastered the difficult practices and became a great holy man, who studied advanced dharanis in the Deccan region. One day he came before King Okkaka and asked for the hand of Princess Khuddarupi in marriage. Because he was a king who took great pride in his family line, King Okkaka became very angry at such a request. He immediately picked up his bow and arrow and was about to shoot him. But by some mysterious power, the king's hand was glued to the bow and the arrow would not leave the string. The king was helpless. The king's ministers were astonished and begged Kanha to forgive the king. Kanha said, 'Your Highness, if you shoot your arrows into the ground, the earth will split into places throughout your country; and if you shoot your arrows into the sky, rain will not fall on your land for seven years. But you can shoot your arrows at your prince and you will not harm a single strand of his hair.' Thus the king did as Kanha bade him and the prince was not harmed. King Okkaka, awed by Kanha's great powers, gave him the princess in marriage."

The World-Honored One explained to Ambattha the differences in the rank of the brahmin and kshatriya classes and taught him the foolishness of having pride in family lineage and birthright. He told him that cultivating wisdom and upholding the precepts were considered the most superior way of life among human beings and gods.

Ambattha asked, "Gotama, what do you mean by cultivating wisdom and upholding the precepts?"

"Ambattha, the cultivation of wisdom and the upholding of the precepts have nothing to do with family lineage or birthright. To say that someone is a suitable or unsuitable partner is important only in marital relationships. In spiritual training one can neither cultivate wisdom nor uphold the precepts if one is attached to one's birthright, one's family lineage, or class distinctions."

(5) Thus the World-Honored One taught the meaning of wisdom and religious discipline and went on to explain the control of mind through meditation.

Then he said, "Ambattha, even if one tries to realize the way of wisdom and discipline, there are four conditions that will forever prevent one from achieving his goal.

"First, here is a monk who says that he will support himself only on nuts that have fallen and goes into the forest with an assortment of bags to collect the nuts. The second monk thinks that he cannot support himself just by feeding on fallen nuts, so he takes a shovel to dig up roots for food and a basket to collect them. The third monk thinks that he cannot support himself only on nuts and roots, so he builds a temple dedicated to fire near a city or a village and worships the fire. People offer him gifts, which enable him to support himself. He tries to gain merit by tending the fire. The fourth monk thinks that he must build a hut with a door on each of the four sides, at a busy intersection in the city. He will live in it and offer help and gifts as much as possible to travelling monks.

"Ambattha, all these monks are attached only to the formalities of the religious life and will never gain wisdom nor be able to live the religiously disciplined life. The closest that any of them can come to the religious life is to become a servant to a holy man. Ambattha, you once received from a master instructions on the way of wisdom and discipline. Have you ever followed his instructions?"

"Gotama, I have not. I have strayed far from the way of wisdom and discipline."

"Ambattha, although you are a disciple of the way, you have not been able to realize the way of wisdom and discipline, nor have you tried to realize the way. Moreover, your master Pokkharasati is uttering slanderous words by saying that the mendicants with shaven heads are dark men of low class, born from the heels of the gods and audaciously hoping to talk with brahmins. This is one of the sins of your master. You further state that King Pasenadi supports Pokkharasati by giving him a grant, but the king does not ask for his advice. Whenever there is a conversation between the two, they are separated by a curtain. Ambattha, what do you think? Suppose a servant overheard the conversation between the king and his minister and he recalls that the king said this and the minister said that. Do you think that this servant has become the king or the minister just because he repeated their conversation? Similarly, just because you recite dharanis that were written by the holy men of the past, can you say that you are a holy man or have attained the rank of a holy man? Ambattha, what do you think? Did those ancient holy men that are praised by our elders behave like you, taking great care of your hair and beard, rubbing perfume on your body, carrying garlands of flowers, wearing bracelets and white robes, and enjoying the pleasures of the five senses?"

"Gotama, I do not think so."

"And did those holy men cook their rice by taking out all the black impurities and eat white rice seasoned with all kinds of herbs and spices? Were they attended by women wearing ornaments? Did they ride around on chariots drawn by horses with braided tails? Did they live in castles, surrounded by moats and fortified by guards with their long swords?"

"Gotama, I do not think so."

"Ambattha, if so, you are neither a holy man nor a person who has attained the rank of a holy man. If you have any doubts about me, you are free to ask questions."

(6) The World-Honored One left his seat and went out of his room for a walk. Ambattha followed the Buddha and examined him for the thirty-two features of a great person. By the power of the Buddha he was able to see all the thirty-two features. He then took his leave and went home.

At that time Pokkharasati had left the village of Ukkattha and leading a large number of brahmins had entered a forest to wait for Ambattha. Ambattha came before his master and bowed in reverence and told him about the Buddha possessing the thirty-two features of a great person. When he related in detail the conversation that took place, Pokkharasati became very angry, saying, "What an impertinent fellow you are! You think you know everything. You have committed an evil act that will condemn you to hell. You criticize such a holy person as the Buddha. I am humbled and embarrassed!"

He wanted to go to meet the Buddha, but because it was too late in the day, he was detained by his disciples. He therefore went home and had the offering meal prepared. Early the next morning, with his disciples carrying torches to light the predawn darkness, he called on the Buddha. He first apologized for the evil that Ambattha had committed. Then he saw the thirty-two features of a great person. He invited the Buddha to a meal and joyfully received his teaching. The World-Honored One taught him about selfless giving, the precepts, and birth in the heavenly realms. He pointed out the danger and the defilement of desires as well as the benefits one receives when freed from desires. Gradually the message of the Dharma softened the brahmin's heart, and the Buddha taught him the Four Noble Truths. Like a pure white cloth that can be dyed any color, Pokkharasati's heart was dyed the color of the Dharma, and he became a lifelong follower of the Buddha.

4. The Question of Self

(1) The World-Honored One entered the Jeta Grove Monastery at Savatthi. At that time the itinerant mendicant Potthapada was living with many mendicants in the great hall built by Queen Mallika. While on his begging rounds early one morning the Buddha visited Potthapada. Potthapada told the mendicants to stop their idle talk and welcome the Buddha.

After they had exchanged greetings Potthapada asked the Buddha, "Venerable one, we have often assembled in the great hall and discussed with many people of various schools the subject of the destruction of concepts. There are some who say that the destruction of concepts does not depend on conditions; such thoughts appear when it is time for them to appear and disappear when it is time to disappear. Others say that thoughts represent a person's ego and that when a person is aware of his ego, thoughts appear, and that when the awareness of this ego disappears, the thoughts also disappear. Still others maintain that those who have cultivated miraculous powers can either inject or extract thoughts to or from another person. At such times I wished the World-Honored One had been here. That is because you are so knowledgeable on this subject. O World-Honored One, how are concepts destroyed?"

(2) "Potthapada, it is a mistake to say that there is no cause or condition for the destruction of concepts. Thoughts arise or disappear depending on the person's religious discipline. Potthapada, what is religious discipline? Suppose that here is a person who believes in the Buddha, becomes a monk following his teachings, controls his five senses, is afraid of committing even the slightest evil, has removed the scab of blind passions, and enters the first meditation. Such a person, having destroyed his thoughts of greed, realizes joy and happiness because he is thus free from greed. This freedom produces thoughts that are true and splendid, bringing him happiness and joy. This is what is meant by religious discipline producing or destroying certain thoughts. The monk progresses from the second to the third and fourth meditations, and when he reaches the fourth meditation, he destroys all coarse thoughts. He is free from pain and pleasure and his thoughts are noble and true. This is what is meant by the producing or destroying of certain thoughts by religious discipline.

"Potthapada, when one reaches the meditation called Limitless Space one destroys all matters, hindrances, discriminations, and thoughts. Then there arises in him a thought that space alone is limitless. In the meditation called Limitless Consciousness, the thought that space alone is limitless disappears and there arises the thought that consciousness alone is limitless. In the meditation called Nonexistence, the thought that consciousness alone is limitless disappears and the thought that nothing exists arises. This is what is meant by the producing or destroying of thoughts by religious discipline.

"Potthapada, my disciple, in this way, progresses from one form of meditation to another and arrives at the highest thought. When he has reached this point, he thinks even further this way: 'Thinking is an inferior action and not thinking is better. When I keep on thinking or pondering, some thoughts created in thinking will perish, but other coarse thoughts will arise. Therefore, I will stop thinking and pondering.' Thus this disciple ends his thinking and pondering, and he destroys thoughts. No other thoughts arise, and the arising of thoughts completely ceases."

(3) "World-Honored One, which arises first, thought or knowledge?"

"Potthapada, thought arises first and knowledge follows."

"World-Honored One, is the thought process the self or is it something completely different?"

"Potthapada, do you believe in the self?"

"World-Honored One, I believe in the physical self that is created from material things and sustained by food."

"Potthapada, even if the self were something like what you say it is, because thought is always appearing and disappearing, we know that thoughts and the self are different."

"World-Honored One, I believe that the self is not made of material things but of thoughts."

"Potthapada, as I stated before, thoughts and the self are completely different. Potthapada, for a person like you, who has a different opinion, follows a different teaching, and proceeds toward a different goal, it is extremely difficult to understand my teaching."

"World-Honored One, then is the world eternal?"

"Potthapada, I do not teach that."

"Then is the world always changing?"

"I do not teach that, either."

"Then is the world bounded or unbounded?"

"Potthapada, that, too, I do not teach."

"Is life one with the body, or is it separate?"

"That, too, I do not teach."

"Does a person exist after death, or does he not exist after death? Or, after death, is it that he both exists and does not exist; or is it that he neither exists nor does not exist?"

"Potthapada, that, too, is something I do not teach."

"World-Honored One, why do you not teach these things?"

"Potthapada, these things do not have any meaning, they are not according to the Dharma, and they have no relation to the practice of the Dharma. These things do not free us from attachment and desires, nor do they make us realize true wisdom. Nor do they lead us to nirvana."

"Then what does the World-Honored One teach?"

"Potthapada, I explain suffering, the cause of suffering, the destruction of suffering, and the way to the destruction of suffering."

"Why does the World-Honored One teach this?"

"Potthapada, I teach this because it is meaningful and according to the Dharma and the practice of the Dharma. It frees us from attachment and desires. It makes us realize true wisdom and leads us to nirvana."

(4) The World-Honored One rose from his seat and departed. As soon as he disappeared from sight the itinerant mendicants derided Potthapada from all sides. "Potthapada, you agreed with everything Gotama said. However, Gotama said nothing certain, whether the world was eternal or changing, or whether the world was bounded or unbounded."

Potthapada said, "It is true that Gotama did not explain whether or not the world was eternal. However, he showed us the truth that is founded on the Dharma and accords with the Dharma. How can I possibly turn my back on such an excellent teaching?"

Two or three days later Potthapada visited the Buddha with Citta, the son of an elephant driver, and told the Buddha that he was being derided by the mendicants. The Buddha said that they were like blind men making mock of one who could see. The Buddha then dispelled the notion that the self departs from the body after death and attains a state of complete happiness where there is no sickness. One who believed such a thing was like someone who talked of love without ever meeting the loved one, or like someone who makes a ladder without knowing where he is trying to reach with the ladder.

"Potthapada, there are three classes of people who believe in the existence of the self: first, those who believe that the self is made up of material things; second, those who believe that the self is made of a mind that is equipped with the four limbs; and third, those who believe in a self made up of consciousness that have no physical substance. I teach a Dharma that does not recognize any of these three views. If you follow the Dharma and practice the way, you will be freed from defilements and thus be purified. You will realize fulfillment and spiritual progress in wisdom in the present life.

"Potthapada, in that state you might still think that there would be suffering, but instead there will be only joy, happiness, and peace. You will thus live with your mind at perfect peace.

"Potthapada, if someone should ask me what is the self that one must discard, I should answer that it is that very self that you see before you. Potthapada, do you think that my teaching has no foundation?"

"World-Honored One, your teaching indeed has a foundation. It is like building a ladder and being able to show where one is trying to reach." Potthapada was deeply moved by the Buddha's teaching and became a lifelong follower of the Three Treasures. Citta, the son of the elephant driver, was ordained by the Buddha and became his disciple.

(5) One day the Buddha, while making his rounds begging for food, visited the Peacock Garden where some itinerant mendicants were engaging in idle conversation. When they saw the World-Honored One, they stopped talking and welcomed him. Sakuludayin said, "Before I arrived, these people were engaged in idle talk, but when I came they wanted to ask me questions. Now that you are here, they want to ask you questions."

"Udayin, they may ask any questions that are on their minds."

"World-Honored One, a long time ago when I met a person claiming all-knowing and all-seeing powers, I asked that person about my past lives. That person changed the subject and, without any reason, became angry eventually. At that time I thought of you and how knowledgeable you were on this subject."

"Udayin, who was that person?"

"It was Nigantha."

"Udayin, since I have the ability to know the past, I am familiar with past lives. And since I possess superhuman foresight, I can also see into the future. However, let us not deal with past and future lives. I teach the Dharma. Because this exists, that exists. Because this arises, that arises. Because this does not exist, that does not exist. Because this perishes, that perishes. This is the Dharma of dependent origination."

"World-Honored One, I cannot even remember what I have experienced in this life. How can I possibly remember what happened in my past life? Furthermore, I cannot see a spirit in this life. How can I see the afterworld? You say that because this exists, that exists; because this does not exist, that does not exist.

I really cannot understand your teaching. Therefore by answering your questions, I should like to explain to you the teaching that I heard from my master."

(6) "Udayin, what does your master teach?"

"My master teaches that there is a light with the most wonderful colors."

"What is this light with the most wonderful colors?"

"It is the most wonderful light that has no comparison."

"What is this most wonderful light that has no comparison?"

"It is a superior light with most wonderful colors without any comparison."

"Udayin, you repeat the same thing over and over again. It is like a person's saying that he loves the most beautiful woman in the world, but when asked about her, he is unable to tell you where she was born, where she lives, whether she is fair or dark, or whether she is tall or short. You tell me that there is a light with the most wonderful colors but you cannot tell me what it is."

"World-Honored one, when the self dies it shines like this light with the most wonderful colors. The self will have no sickness nor suffering. It will sparkle like a pure emerald of the highest quality, cut into an octagonal shape and finely polished and placed on a light yellow wool cloth."

"Udayin, which is brighter, the sparkling emerald or the light of the firefly on a dark night?"

"The light of the firefly on a dark night."

"Now, compare the light of the firefly to a lamplight, the lamplight to a huge torchlight, the torchlight to a starlight in a cloudless sky, the starlight to the moonlight in the middle of the night, and the moonlight to the sunlight in the summer sky. Which light is the brighter?"

"Undoubtedly, the lamplight is brighter than the light of the firefly and the light of the sun is brighter than the light of the moon."

"Udayin, there are countless gods whose light surpasses the light of the sun and moon. Since I know this for a fact, I do not say that there are no lights superior to this light. Yet you say that a light that is weaker than the light of a firefly is superior and full of exquisite colors."

"World-Honored One, I shall not pursue this subject further. I can no longer claim that there is a superior light with the most wonderful colors."

(7) "Udayin, is there a world where only pleasure exists? Or is there a way to realize such a world?"

"The way to realize such a world is to refrain from killing, stealing, committing adultery, lying, and being intoxicated, and to practice asceticism."

"And Udayin, when you refrain from killing, stealing, committing adultery, lying, and being intoxicated, and when you practice asceticism, will you realize only pleasure, or pleasure mixed with suffering?"

"Pleasure mixed with suffering."

"Udayin, in the process of realizing the world of pleasure only, is the pleasure mixed with suffering?"

"World-Honored One, let us not pursue this subject any longer. When I talk with you, my words become meaningless. Is there really a world of pleasure only and is there a way to realize that world?"

"Udayin, renounce greed and evil and enter the first meditation; then proceed to the second and third meditation; this is the way."

"World-Honored One, then this is not just the way to the world of pleasure; the world of pleasure has already been realized."

"Udayin, that is not so. The world of pleasure has not been realized yet. It is only the way to the world of pleasure."

At that time the itinerant mendicants heard the conversation and shouted in a loud voice. "Oh, then our master has nothing higher to teach. We have not been taught anything more." They had been taught that the third meditation was the world of pleasure only, and they tried to discipline themselves in the five precepts. That is why they were greatly perturbed. Sakuludayin calmed the men and put further questions to the Buddha.

(8) "World-Honored One, what more must we do to realize the world of pleasure only?"

"Udayin, you must renounce entirely the states of suffering, pleasure, joy, and grief and enter the right mental state that is not attached to any state. Only when you enter the pure fourth meditation can you consort with the gods and realize the state where there is only pleasure."

"World-Honored One, are your disciples practicing under you the pure discipline to realize this state of only pleasure?"

"Udayin, they are not. There is a higher goal. To realize this higher goal the disciples practice the pure discipline. The Buddha appeared in this world to teach laypersons to have faith in the Dharma, then to become ordained as monks, to renounce all worldly desires, to enter the first meditation, and from there gradually to proceed to the fourth meditation. In this meditation the disciple's mind becomes peaceful and trained, and he will gain the wisdom to know past lives, to know other people's minds, and to eliminate defilements. He will then realize that his life of illusion has ended, that he has finally completed the pure discipline, and that he will never again return to the life of illusion. This is the highest teaching of deliverance that the disciples must study, practicing the pure discipline under my guidance."

"World-Honored One, what you have said is truly wonderful. It is as if you brought light into the darkness or gave the right directions to a person who was lost. I shall take refuge in the Three Treasures and become your disciple."

When Udayin said he wanted to become a disciple, the itinerant mendicants were astonished and remonstrated against him.

"Venerable Udayin, do not simply become a disciple of the Buddha. You can be both a pot of water and a ladle at the same time, performing two functions, acting as both a storage device and a carrier for the water. In other words, you can be both a master and a disciple at the same time." Sakuludayin thus listened to their words and did not formally become a disciple of the Buddha; but deep in his heart he took refuge in the Buddha.

(9) One day Janussoni the brahmin came to the Jeta Grove and asked the Buddha, "World-Honored One, are there any laypersons who place their faith in you, become mendicants, accept you as their master, and follow your teaching?"

"Yes, there are."

"World-Honored One, it must be difficult to live in the forest far removed from human habitation; it must be difficult to lead a life of seclusion. Especially for a person who has not attained meditation, the forest is a lonely place."

"Brahmin, you are right. Before I attained enlightenment, I thought that the forest was a lonely place for a person who had not attained meditation, but then, brahmin, I thought again. Even for a monk the forest is a fearful place if the three actions of his body, speech, and mind, as well as his life, are not pure. But for me, because all my three actions and my life are pure, I have no fear of the forest. Therefore my life in the forest gave me the joy of tranquillity.

"Brahmin, then I also think thus. If a monk has carnal desires, uncontrollable greed, anger, and evil thoughts, is prone to negligence and sleepiness, is superficial in his views and has a doubting mind, praises himself but criticizes others, is attached to his own profits and fame, is always idle and never diligently practices, has neither a right mind nor right thoughts, has his mind in a state of disarray, and has no wisdom, this monk, who lives in the forest far from human habitation, will find it a frightful place. But for me it is not so. Brahmin, I therefore found the joy of peace in the forest.

"Brahmin, I have thought to myself, 'I shall enter a cemetery in the forest on the night of the new or full moon, or on special nights such as six days before or eight days after the full moon; I may then experience such fright as would make my hair stand on end.'

"Brahmin, I entered the cemetery on such a night. Animals approached me in the middle of the night. Birds dropped branches on me, and the wind scattered leaves over me. I gradually started to grow frightened. But then I thought, 'It is foolish to wait for fear to come to me. If it comes, I will conquer it.'

"Brahmin, therefore, if fear stalks me when I am walking, I conquer it as I walk. When it comes to me when I am sitting, I conquer it as I sit. When it comes to me when I am standing still, I conquer it just as I am. I do not change my position just to conquer fear.

"Brahmin, once there was a monk who purposely thought of night as the same as day and day as the same as night, in order to overcome his fear. For me such thinking is illusory. I think of day as day and night as night.

"Brahmin, if the statement that someone's appearance in this world was for the sake of giving benefits and happiness to beings is true of anyone, then it can be said of me. With great effort I became courageous and developed right thought, so that nothing would bother me. I have maintained a sense of composure by mental concentration. I have renounced self-love and all evil paths and have entered meditation with gentle, peaceful, alert, and organized thoughts. I know that I have extinguished evil passions. Thus ignorance has been dispelled and knowledge has been born. Darkness has departed and light has appeared.

"Brahmin, you may think thus, 'Even now Gotama has not escaped from his greed, anger, and ignorance. Therefore in order to escape these blind passions, he lives in the forest far from human habitation.' However, you should not think so. I have two reasons for living in the forest. First, I find peace in my present mode of living; second, out of love for future generations, I am setting an example." The brahmin Janussoni was overjoyed by the Buddha's teaching and grateful for his compassion extended even to the people of future generations, and he departed from the place.

(10) Once when the Buddha taught his disciples to take one meal a day, Bhaddali disobeyed him and said, "World-Honored One, I cannot take just one meal a day. With such meager food I doubt if I can endure a lifetime of practice."

"Then, Bhaddali, when you are invited to someone's home, just eat a part of the food and take the rest home to eat. You will be able to nourish your body."

"World-Honored One, no, I cannot do that, either."

Although all the other disciples followed the rules set down by the Buddha, Bhaddali disobeyed them. He insisted that he was unable to follow them. He felt ashamed and did not appear before the Buddha during the three-month retreat.

When the three-month rainy season ended and the robes had been repaired, the Buddha was ready to start on his teaching tour. Urged on by his fellow monks, Bhaddali appeared before the Buddha and said, "I foolishly lost my mind and committed evil deeds by not following your rules. Please forgive me."

The World-Honored One said, "Bhaddali, it is as you say. Did you know that for the past three months my disciples and followers and even those who follow other teachings have ignored you? Bhaddali, if I told my disciples to roll in the mud, do you think that they would disobey?"

"World-Honored One, I do not think so."

"Bhaddali, no one should order anyone to roll in the mud. Furthermore, it is not right for anyone to answer 'no' so rudely. Yet, you, lacking any virtue, disobey valid orders by rudely replying 'no.' Bhaddali, how can a person who does not follow his master's discipline, even if he enters the forest to attain enlightenment and lives in a hut, who despises not only his master and brother disciples but also himself, possibly attain enlightenment? Obviously, he cannot, because it is unnatural for anyone who does not follow the discipline. Bhaddali, only he who follows the discipline, who, entering the forest and living in a vacant hut, does not despise his master nor his brother disciples nor himself, can attain enlightenment."

(11) "World-Honored One, why is it that the members of the Sangha reproach only some monks for their evil conduct and advise them to mend their ways, while they do nothing about other monks' evil ways?"

"Bhaddali, the members of the Sangha will not associate with those who, when reproached, make contradictory excuses, show unspeakable anger and malicious intent, and do nothing to contribute to the happiness of the Sangha. Also it is better not to reproach those whose faith and devotion are shallow; it is better to leave them alone lest they lose what faith and devotion they have. Friends care for and help someone who is blind in one eye. The members of the Sangha reproach only those who are gentle and do not quickly become angry nor show malice but can be guided to change their evil ways."

"World-Honored One, why did more monks attain enlightenment when the rules of discipline were fewer than they are now and fewer monks attain enlightenment when there are more rules to follow?"

"Bhaddali, when people do not faithfully follow the true teaching, their moral life declines. As a result, the rules of discipline have to be increased. This is a time when there is a marked decrease in the number of people attaining enlightenment. I would not have to make rules if members of the Sangha were not led astray by their blind passions. However, when the Sangha has become big and its possessions have increased with time, there is a greater possibility of people being moved by blind passions. In order to avoid this possibility, I have to make more rules.

"Bhaddali, do you remember that when there was only a small number of monks I told you the story of the good horse?"

"World-Honored One, I do not remember. For a long time I did not follow the rules of discipline."

"Bhaddali, for a long time I have understood your mind. I knew you were not earnest with my teaching and did not listen eagerly to the Dharma. I shall now tell you the story of the good horse. Bhaddali, here is an expert horseman who puts a bridle on a good horse. Since the horse has never before been bridled, it jumps and causes a commotion. But gradually it becomes used to the bridle and becomes quiet. Next the horseman puts a helmet and a shin guard on the horse. After training, with one crack of the whip the horse raises its legs and breaks into a gallop. The horseman can make the animal run in a circle so that the rider can pick up a weapon from the ground. The horse can be made to trot or gallop and be unafraid of any noise. The horse becomes used to its master's goodness and becomes a suitable riding horse. With the application of the whip the horse can be made to obey its master's orders. Thus with proper training the untamed horse becomes an excellent horse suitable for a king to ride.

"Bhaddali, when the disciples have mastered the tenfold path they will be respected by all men and be worthy of their gifts and will become sources of happiness. The tenfold path of the sage is right view, right thought, right speech, right action, right livelihood, right effort, right concentration, right meditation, right wisdom, and right emancipation."

5. The Prince with Five Weapons

(1) The World-Honored One left Alavi with a large following of disciples and, after passing through Saketa, entered Savatthi where he stayed in the Jeta Grove in the Anathapindika Monastery. One of the disciples in the monastery told the Buddha that, although he assiduously practiced the way, he could not see the light. He therefore became lazy, and he retrogressed. The Buddha admonished this disciple and told him the following story.

In the distant past there was a king in Baranasi whose name was Brahmadatta. His son, called Five Weapons, was studying in Takkasila. When he had completed his studies and was about to depart for home, the prince's master gave him five weapons and advised him with great kindness to be particularly care-ful of his mind and its activity.

The prince hurried on his way home. He was about to enter a forest on his way to Baranasi when people stopped him and warned him, "In this forest there is a demon called Oily Hairs. No one has ever passed through this forest safely. Do not enter it." But the prince, who had confidence in himself, went deep into the forest without heeding the warning of these people. When he reached the middle of the forest the demon appeared. He was as tall as a palm tree, and his eyes, which were as big and round as trays, were burning like fire. He had sharp fangs and a beak like that of a wild eagle. His protruding belly was purplish in color; the palms of his hands and the heels of his feet were gleaming with bluish black light. He was an ugly monster with his entire body covered with oily hairs. He shouted in a thunderous voice, "Where are you going? Stop! You will become my prey!"

The prince replied quietly, "When I entered the forest, I knew that I should meet you. It was your bad fate to have met me, for in my hand are poisoned arrows." The prince released an arrow, but it stuck to the demon's hair and did not hurt his body. The prince repeatedly shot his arrows but they only stuck to his hair. The demon pulled out the arrows and crushed them with his feet and approached the prince. The prince then attacked the demon with his sword, but the sword also stuck to the demon's hair. When the prince fought with his hal-berd, it, too, was immediately sucked up by the hair. Another weapon, a pole, also had no effect on the demon; it, too, was sucked up by the demon's oily hair.

Then the prince said, "Demon, have you not heard that my name was Five Weapons? In entering this forest I rely not only on my arrows, sword, halberd, and pole but also on my own prowess. You will now taste my iron fist." When he struck the monster with his right fist it stuck to his hair. His left fist and even his feet became entangled in his hair, rendering them completely useless. Then the prince butted against the demon's chest, but his head got stuck in the demon's hair, and the prince's body became suspended in the air. But the prince showed no sign of fear and did not admit defeat.

It was the first time the demon had ever met such a brave person in this for-est. He wondered why this small human being never feared death, and he asked, "You are now completely at my mercy. Why are you not afraid?"

The prince replied, "Demon, why should I be afraid? All men have to die once. Furthermore, I have one more weapon, a weapon that is as durable as a diamond and is in the depth of my being. Even if you devour me, you will not be able to digest this weapon. If this weapon enters your stomach, it will cut you up into small pieces from the inside, and your death will be inevitable. That is why I am not afraid."

The demon was astonished and thought, "This young man is telling the truth. Indeed, I shall never be able to digest even one morsel of his flesh. I shall let him go." The demon said to the prince, "Just as the moon separates itself from the hands of Rahu, god of lunar eclipses, so you must separate yourself from me. Hurry home and make your parents happy."

The prince said, "Then I shall go home. You became a man-eating demon because of your past evil karma. If you continue in your evil ways, you will only sink deeper into darkness. Our encounter was fortuitous. From this day forward, do not commit any more evil."

Taking advantage of this opportune moment the prince taught him the five evil actions and the five good deeds. Thereupon the demon gladly took the five precepts. The prince then carried his five weapons and happily returned to Baranasi where he succeeded his father and ruled his country by establishing a good government.

The Buddha said, "My disciples, I want you to understand the deep significance of this story. If you never relax your efforts in whatever you do and are not overcome by hardships, you will surely attain your goal."

(2) Now the Buddha's teaching spread even into the inner court of the king, and the queen and the courtiers, too, accepted the teachings with great joy. They realized how difficult it was to be born as human beings and to have the opportunity to meet the Buddha in person. They knew that it was a rare opportunity to be able to visit his monastery so frequently and to be able to hear the teaching from his very lips. They thus came to the king to ask for his permission to invite the Sangha of monks to the castle in order to hear the Dharma. The king was overjoyed and immediately granted permission.

One day the king was preparing to visit his garden when his gardener came and said that the Buddha was sitting under a tree in the garden. "I understand," the king said. Rising from his couch, he ordered a horse-drawn carriage to take him to visit the Buddha.

The king saw the Buddha sitting under a tree, seemingly teaching someone who was squatting at his feet. The king hesitated because he did not want to disturb them. He thought that the man who was listening so intently to the Buddha must be virtuous. The king felt at ease. He paid his respects to the Buddha and sat down beside him. The man receiving instruction was Chattapani, who had deep faith in the Buddha. Chattapani felt that to rise and pay his respects to a worldly ruler at this time would be disrespectful to the World-Honored One, so he did not move. The king was not happy with this and became angry. The World-Honored One understood how the king felt, and in order to pacify his anger he told him that the man was a virtuous person who had gained wisdom and had attained enlightenment. The king felt that if the man was regarded so highly by the Buddha, he was not just an ordinary person. Therefore the king said to him, "If you desire anything, please tell me."

Chattapani only replied, "Thank you." That day also the king was gladdened by the Buddha's teaching and forgot about what the court ladies had asked for and went home. A few days later, when the king was on his way to the Anathapindika Monastery in the Jeta Grove, he met Chattapani. He summoned him to his side and asked, "I heard from the Buddha that you were a very knowledgeable person. The women in my court are very eager to hear the Dharma. Will you teach them the Dharma?" Chattapani replied, "I believe that it is not proper for a layperson to teach the Dharma, let alone to go into the inner court to do so. Teaching the Dharma is the work of the monk." Because Chattapani refused, the Buddha acquiesced to King Pasenadi and sent Ananda to teach the Dharma to the courtiers.

One day Ananda went to the castle and sensed a dark, gloomy cloud over the entire assembly, which he could not dispel even with his talk on the joy of the Dharma. It happened that someone had stolen a valuable jewel from the king's crown, and all the courtiers were under harsh investigation. They all feared the king's wrath that threatened their lives. Ananda told them not to worry and went to see the king. He advised the king, "I have a plan to recover your lost gem without inflicting suffering on many people. Make some balls out of mud and give them to people whom you suspect. Tell them to leave the balls at a designated place by tomorrow morning. Then go and examine them in the morning. If you cannot obtain results the first day, keep trying this plan for a few days. If you follow this plan, your gem will return without causing so much suffering on all the people."

The king followed this plan but it did not work. When Ananda heard that the plan was unsuccessful, he had another idea. He told the king to fill a huge tub with water and leave it in a secret room, then order each one to take off his clothes and wash his hands in the tub and then leave the room. The king followed his directions. The thief thought to himself, "Ananda is trying very hard, and I know he will persist until the gem is found. I think it is better to return the gem." The thief took the gem with him into the tub and left it at the bottom of the tub. After everyone had followed the king's order, the water was emptied. Thus the gem was found at the bottom of the tub without making anyone suffer. The gem was returned to the king and the matter was resolved.

(3) The story of this incident gradually spread among the monks in the Anathapindika Monastery. One evening, as the monks were praising Ananda's wisdom, the Buddha happened to visit them. The monks gave a detailed account of the incident to the Buddha. The Buddha then related the following story. "Disciples, in the distant past there was a similar incident. The king of Baranasi and his numerous consorts were playing in the flower garden. After they had enjoyed themselves, the women took off their robes and their necklaces and went swimming in the pure waters of the lake. The queen, too, took off her pearl necklace, wrapped it in her clothes, and placed it in a box. After ordering her maid in attendance to watch the box, she entered the water. Now nearby in the shade of a tree there was a female monkey who had been watching the scene for some time. As soon as the maidservant relaxed her watch and began to nap, the monkey darted out from her hiding place as swiftly as a running rabbit and snatched the necklace from the box. She immediately climbed the nearby tree and hid the necklace in a hole in the trunk so that other monkeys would not see it. Feigning innocence, she sat on a branch to watch her loot. When the maidservant awoke, she found the contents of the box scattered about and the necklace missing. She screamed in astonishment and the guards immediately appeared at her side. The maidservant did not want to admit she was sleeping so she said that a man appeared and ran away with the necklace. The

guards ran in all directions to locate the thief. A farmer who was working in the fields nearby heard the commotion, became afraid, and started to run. He was soon captured and questioned by the guards.

"Afraid of being put to torture, the man confessed to a crime he did not commit. He was led before the king and asked where he had hidden the necklace. The farmer replied, 'Your Majesty, I am a poor farmer and possess nothing of value. I have no use for such a valuable necklace. A rich man ordered me to steal it. I have already given it to him.' When the rich man was summoned before the king, he said, 'I gave it to my assistant.' When the assistant was asked, he said, 'I gave it to a musician.' When the musician was questioned, he said, 'I gave it to a harlot.' And the harlot said, 'I don't know anything about it.'

"As the evening approached all the suspects were confined in a jail. That night one of the king's ministers went home and thought to himself, 'This is a very strange case. The necklace disappeared within the flower garden compound where the gates are tightly secured. Therefore an outsider could not possibly have stolen it, and an insider could not have escaped from the garden. This poor farmer who says he gave it to the rich man is lying. The rich man pointed to his assistant to save himself. The assistant involved the musician so that, if he were to be confined for any length of time, at least he would be able to enjoy some music. And the musician accused the harlot so that there would be one pretty face among the prisoners. The thief is not among this group. There are some monkeys in the garden, so some monkey must have taken it.' The minister then ordered a servant to look in on the prisoners. The servant found the five suspects in heated argument, accusing one another. When the minister saw the innocence of the five suspects, he ordered the capture of some monkeys. On each monkey he placed a necklace made of imitation jewels, and he then released them all into the garden. Happy with their ornaments, the monkeys strutted around in the garden with their necklaces clattering around their necks. The monkey who was the real thief thought to herself, 'What good is a necklace made of imitation jewels?' In order to show the other monkeys that she had real jewels, she recovered the necklace from its hiding place and, placing it around her neck, proudly showed it off to the others. The guards who were carefully watching the monkeys immediately snatched the necklace and brought it before the minister. The minister returned the necklace to the king and told him about the innocence of the five suspects. The king was very happy and composed the following poem:

> When there is a battle, a brave soldier,
> When there is a conference, a thinking person,
> When there is someone you love, sweets,
> When a problem arises, a wise person—
> These are what we need.

"My disciples, this took place a long time ago. Ananda is indeed the wise person needed when a problem arises."

(4) Once there was a very faithful youth in Savatthi. After the death of his father he supported his mother with great care. Because he knew that his aged mother's days were numbered, he tried to make his mother's life as peaceful as

possible and made sure that she would not be lacking anything. Although the mother was very grateful to her son, she was worried because, despite her urging to take a wife, he remained single. Therefore she herself picked a young woman for his wife.

The young man was most appreciative of his mother's kindness, and peace and happiness filled the home. Occasionally he would go to the monastery to listen to the Buddha's message. But suddenly the bride's mind changed and she began to hate her mother-in-law. She urged her husband to have her mother-in-law removed to another house. Now there was no longer peace in the home. Shouts and quarrels arose constantly and a corrupt air of self-interest raged through the house. However, the young man had great patience, and with the help of the Buddha's power he endured his difficulties. The wife finally realized her selfishness; and peace and joy once again returned to the household. One day, when the young man called on the Buddha, the World-Honored One asked him if he was treating his mother with tender care. The young man related what had happened. Then the Buddha encouraged him with the story about the caring son who was filled with filial piety.

(5) "Young man, once there was a son like you who lost his father and took care of his mother with deep devotion. The mother chose for him a bride who came from a similar family background. At first a harmonious relationship existed between the mother and the daughter-in-law, but in time they started to exert their selfish ways. The bride soon disregarded her mother-in-law and planned to oust her from the house. Even the devoted son was influenced by his wife and decided to send his mother away. The mother tearfully left her home and sought refuge in a relative's house. She barely eked out a living doing menial jobs. Shortly thereafter, the bride became pregnant and in due time gave birth to a child. The new mother told her husband and neighbors, 'While my mother-in-law lived here, I could not have a child and I was lonely. Now that she is not here, this beautiful child was born. You can see how bad she was for us.' When the mother-in-law heard rumors of what was being said about her, she sadly said, 'Right living is dead in the world. If a daughter-in-law can claim that after expelling her mother-in-law, the home became happier and she was able to give birth to a child, right living is dead. I must have a funeral for right living.' The enraged mother-in-law, taking a ladle, a pan, and rice, went to the cemetery. She went into a river wearing a white gown, her hair in disarray, and began to wash the rice. Just at that time Indra was surveying the world of human beings and felt sorry for the woman. Taking the form of Brahma, he appeared before the mother-in-law. 'Before you continue with this ritual, it would be better for you to think about what you are doing. Who told you right living is dead? I, who possess these powerful thousand eyes of the truth, am not dead.'

"The woman replied, 'No, indeed, right living is dead. I have proof. I have seen it with my own eyes. Someone who commits evil deeds is successful. A daughter-in-law who could not conceive gives birth to a child after expelling me from my own house. She manipulates her husband and lives happily.'

"Indra as Brahma replied, 'Woman, I truly live in the Dharma. Since I came into this world for your benefit, with my fire I shall burn up your bad daughter-in-law and your grandchild.'

"The woman was shocked. She could not have her grandchild burned up. She pleaded, 'Oh, please help me to live harmoniously with my daughter-in-law and grandchild.'

"The Brahma said, 'Woman, even if suffering is inflicted upon you, if you do not abandon the right way, you can live peacefully with your daughter-in-law and your loving grandchild. Do not fear. Your son and daughter have realized that they have done something wrong and are now on their way to welcome you home. You must put forth all your effort to perform good deeds.' After he had uttered these words the Brahma disappeared and returned to heaven.

"The son and the daughter-in-law came to the cemetery with their child and repented their evil ways. They all welcomed their mother home. The family lived in peace thereafter. Young man, for him who never abandons the Dharma, it never dies. You must take care of your mother and live in peace."

6. Ratthapala

(1) The Buddha taught the Dharma to the Kuru people and proceeded to the Simsapa Grove located north of the village of Thullakotthita. When people heard of the Buddha, they came from all directions to listen to the Dharma with the deepest joy. Among the people of this village there was a young man called Ratthapala, the son of a wealthy man. The Buddha spoke to a group, and after all the others had departed, Ratthapala came before the Buddha, payed his respects, and said, "World-Honored One, if I stay in a lay household, I shall be troubled by worldly things and shall not be able to practice the way. Please grant me permission to become a monk."

The World-Honored One said, "You may enter my Sangha only if you receive permission from your parents." Therefore Ratthapala had no choice but to return to his home and ask for his parents' permission. His parents were surprised by their son's wish and said, "You are our only son. Day and night we showered affection on you. Even if you died, we could not abandon you. How can we possibly bear the loss of a living son?"

Although his parents continued to plead with him, Ratthapala was determined to become a monk. He lay on the ground and fasted for seven days. His parents came to his side and entreated him, "Son, you are delicate in health. Whether you were sitting or sleeping, you always had a soft cushion for a bed. It is not an easy life for a monk to pursue the Dharma. Why do you not remain a lay householder and find happiness by giving selflessly and supporting the Sangha?"

Ratthapala closed his lips and did not reply. Many relatives and friends, who were asked to come by his parents, tried to discourage him from going into the hard life of a monk. But, like the ground that becomes harder with each rainfall, the more people urged him to change his mind, the more resolute he became. The relatives found their words falling on deaf ears, and finally they said to

Ratthapala's parents, "Grant your son his wish. If he finds happiness in the life of a monk, you will be able to meet him again in this life. If he does not find satisfaction, he will return to your home anyway. If his wish is not granted, he will surely die."

His parents listened to this reasoning and said to themselves, "If he follows the teachings of the Buddha, he will surely care about us." And they granted their son his wish to become a monk. Ratthapala's heart leaped with joy. Straightway he went to the Simsapa Grove where the Buddha was staying and received permission to become a monk and a disciple.

Ratthapala then went to the Anathapindika Monastery in the Jeta Grove. He settled in a quiet place, exerted himself in the practice of the way, and attained enlightenment.

When ten years had passed, Ratthapala wanted to visit his parents in his native village, and he asked for the Buddha's permission. The Buddha said, "Even if you return to your native village, there is now no danger of your abandoning the precepts and falling back into the life of desires. Go, therefore, and save those who are not saved and enlighten those who are not enlightened."

(2) He respectfully received the Buddha's instruction and returned to his room to put his bedding in order. He then donned his robes, took up his begging bowl, and started on his journey as a wandering mendicant. At last he reached the Simsapa Grove, situated north of the village of Thullakotthita, and spent the night there. Next morning he entered the village and started begging for food from house to house. When he came to his father's house, his father was combing his hair in the garden. When he saw the figure of a young monk, he scornfully said, "It was on account of an evil shaven-headed monk like you that I lost my only son, on whom I had showered my love. Now I have no one to succeed me, and this house will perish. I shall not offer any food to such a person." Ratthapala heard these words and promptly departed. At the gate he met a maidservant who had come to dispose of some foul-smelling spoiled food in the dump. He stopped her and begged her to put the food in his bowl. The maid recognized Ratthapala and swiftly went to her master to tell him that his son was here. The father was astonished and at the same time overjoyed. Gathering up his clothes in his left hand and straightening his hair with his right hand, he asked the maid where his son was. He found his son facing the wall and eating the foul-smelling food. He was dumbfounded and said, "O Ratthapala, why have you fallen so low as not to come straight home when you entered this village?" He quietly replied, "O householder, I entered my father's house, but I received no offering. In fact I was only scorned, so I left immediately."

The father heard the reason for his son's quick departure and asked for his forgiveness. With deep respect and compassion he invited his son to his house and explained everything to his wife. The monk's mother was overjoyed at her son's homecoming and immediately set about to prepare his food; she ordered the servants to pile money and treasures as high as the mountains, and then went before Ratthapala. She said, "My son, these are my treasures, but your father's wealth is unlimited. We shall give you all these treasures. Please leave the life of a monk and return to our house. You can give away these treasures and thereby gain merit."

The son said softly to his mother, "Dear mother, if it is for my sake, please put all these treasures in a large bag, take them in a cart to the river Ganges, and sink all of them into the deepest part of the river. I ask you to do this because people have experienced sorrow and suffering on account of their worldly treasures and have never been able to experience true happiness."

Thus his mother found that worldly goods would not change her son's mind. She then brought pretty young maidens dressed in their finest to wait on him. They gently approached him and asked, "Why do you reject us young girls and take up the cold way of the Dharma?" He replied, "My young sisters, I did not become a monk for the purpose of pursuing women. I have now mastered the way of the Dharma, and my mind seeks nothing. I have no use for you, pretty sisters." The young girls realized they were being addressed as "young sisters" and could do nothing. They broke down and wept.

Ratthapala said to his parents, "Why do you trouble me in this way? If you wish to offer me food, please do so at once." Thereupon, his parents stood up and personally served him water and gave him many kinds of delicious food to satisfy him. Then they prepared for him a place to sit and approached him. He began to teach them the Dharma, and his parents received it with great joy. After he finished, he stood up and recited the following poem:

> Beautiful hair ornaments, precious necklaces, deep blue eyebrow paint,
> And painted moon-shaped eyebrows have no meaning for the enlightened.
> Covering the bad odor of the body with pretty patterned silk
> And rubbing it with fragrant incense are only falsehood and illusion.
> Like the deer that has escaped from captivity by ripping the net that
>   covered him,
> I have now cast aside the bait and shall depart.
> Who shall really enjoy the bonds of worldly entanglement?

(3) As soon as he had recited this verse, he left Thullakotthita and sat under a tree. At that time King Koravya had left the castle to divert himself in the forest. When he heard from his servant that Ratthapala was nearby, he got off his chariot, approached the monk, and took a place beside him. Then the king asked, "If you became a monk because your family declined, I shall give you treasures. Why do you not abandon this life and return to your home to give offerings?"

Ratthapala replied, "O king, by saying so you are not according me true hospitality. If you were to tell me, 'This nation is under good government; the people are enjoying peace and a bountiful harvest of rice, wheat, chestnut, millet, and bean crops; there is no fear or conflict; and food is easily obtained. If you live in my country, I shall follow the Dharma,' then you would truly show me your hospitality."

The king answered by saying all this sincerely and then asked, "I have heard that there are four types of persons who become monks: first, a person who has been sick for a long time and is unable to fulfill his desires; second, a person who is old and unable to move freely and has no place to go to enjoy himself; third, a person who has lost his wealth and is unable to provide for his own food and lodging; fourth, a person who has lost his family through death and is weary of the world. But in your case you are young and healthy, and your family is rich and encountering no difficulty. Why did you abandon all worldly pleasures and become a monk?"

Ratthapala replied, "O king, I became a monk by following the four important things that the Buddha teaches. These deal with the inescapable suffering that all human beings encounter. When you compare your strength and martial arts both now and during your youth, do you think that your energies have not declined? And when you are ill and in painful suffering, do you think that you can change places with your servants? Furthermore, you may be enjoying great wealth and prosperity, but can you escape death? When death comes, you will pass away, leaving all material things behind. There is nothing in this world upon which you can absolutely rely. Moreover, all human beings have insatiable desires. Your country is wealthy, but suppose someone tells you that there is a country to the east that is even wealthier than yours; would you not attack that country with your armies to capture its wealth? If there were such countries to the south, west, or north, you would relentlessly attack these countries and conquer them. Truly, in this life there is no end to the satisfaction of one's selfish pursuits. This desire is not motivated by material things but by one's attachment to the self. Your Majesty, I have understood these four points of the Buddha's teaching and have chosen the way of the monk.

"Because of their ignorance, wealthy people do not practice giving. When they obtain wealth, they desire more and become miserly and acquire more things. Even if one rules a country, one desires one country after another, and before his greed is gratified, his life comes to an end. His wife and children weep while his body burns on the funeral pyre. His wife and children do not follow him in death. He may be rich but in death there is no difference between the rich and the poor. Foolish people commit evil and thus bind themselves, and thus, like ripe fruit that falls, they always fall into the darkness of delusion. The mind desires a poison that appears beautiful, and because of this desire it commits a grave error. Your Majesty, I have become enlightened to life's suffering and have entered the way of the Buddha."

The king accepted this teaching with faith and joy and said, "Respected teacher, you have truly abandoned delusion. I take refuge in you." Ratthapala said, "You should not take refuge in me. It will be better for you to take refuge in the Buddha, the Dharma, and the Sangha." The king took his advice and became a faithful follower.

Chapter 2

ORGANIZATION OF THE ORDER

1. The Ten Major and Forty-Eight Minor Bodhisattva Precepts

(1) The World-Honored One was once with an assembly of innumerable gods and bodhisattvas. He expounded Vairocana's song on bodhisattvas' aspiration for enlightenment.

I, Vairocana, while seated on a lotus, upon the thousand petals of the flowers around me, made appear a thousand Sakyamunis.

Within each flower were a billion worlds; within each world was a Sakyamuni sitting under a Bodhi tree,

And all realized true enlightenment together.

These myriad Sakyamunis, accompanied by innumerable people, came to my abode and listened to me recite the precepts of the buddhas.

Truly did the immortal gate open. Each returned to his world and recited the precepts he received from me. They are the ten major and forty-eight minor precepts. The precepts shone brightly like the sun and moon, resembling jewels strung together; innumerable bodhisattvas, depending on them, have realized true enlightenment.

You new bodhisattvas should take up these precepts and pass them on to others.

Listen carefully and take them to heart. You are truly to become buddhas. I have already become a Buddha.

If you continually believe thus, you will have embodied the precepts. A person who has accepted the precepts has already entered the stage of a buddha. Because the stage is synonymous with great enlightenment, that person is truly a child of the Buddha.

(2) The World-Honored One thus finished this explanation and then said to the huge gathering, "One who will not accept the ten major and forty-eight minor precepts cannot be called a bodhisattva and cannot become a buddha-child. For your sake, I shall now briefly explain the precepts of a bodhisattva.

1. Precept against taking life. If a buddha-child kills with his own hand, causes a person to be killed, helps to kill, praises killing, derives joy from killing, or kills with a curse, these are the causes, conditions, ways, and acts of killing. In no case should one take the life of a sentient being. Bodhisattvas should always have compassionate hearts and save and protect all sentient beings. If one kills intentionally, he commits a transgression punishable by expulsion from the Sangha.

2. Precept against stealing. If a buddha-child steals, causes another to steal, helps to steal, or praises stealing, these are causes and acts of stealing. A bodhisattva must not take a single needle or a single blade of grass that belongs to someone else. He must continually awaken his desire to be in accord with the Buddha's heart, awaken a compassionate heart, and help all people to attain joy and happiness. If a bodhisattva steals another's possessions, it is a transgression punishable by expulsion from the Sangha.

3. Precept against licentiousness. If a buddha-child behaves licentiously or causes another so to behave, that is a cause and an act of licentiousness. He must not violate any woman. He should not engage in any immoral sexual acts. A bodhisattva should continually awaken a dutiful mind and help people and give them a way of purity. If a bodhisattva engages in immoral sexual acts, this is a transgression punishable by expulsion from the Sangha.

4. Precept against lying. If a buddha-child tells lies or causes another to do so or lies as a means, these are causes and acts of lying. A bodhisattva should always use right words and awaken right views and exhort all others to use right words and to see correctly. If a bodhisattva causes others to use evil words or to have wrong views, this is a transgression punishable by expulsion from the Sangha.

5. Precept against dealing with intoxicants. If a buddha-child deals with intoxicants or causes another to do so, these are causes and acts of dealing with intoxicants. Intoxicants are causes and conditions for wicked behavior. A bodhisattva should cause others to bring forth a bright wisdom. If a bodhisattva causes people's minds to become deluded, this is a transgression punishable by expulsion from the Sangha.

6. Precept against talking about other people's faults. If a buddha-child talks of the errors of a person who, as a monk or a householder, practices the Buddha's way, or causes another to do so, that is a cause and an act of error. A bodhisattva, even when evil persons of other paths say that the Buddha's way is not the true way, must always feel compassion and teach and lead them to awaken faith in the Mahayana. To talk of the errors of the practicers of the Buddha's way is, for a bodhisattva, a transgression punishable by expulsion from the Sangha.

7. Precept against praising oneself and dispraising others. If a buddha-child praises himself and dispraises others or causes another to do so, that is a cause and an act of dispraising another. A bodhisattva should take upon himself the dispraise and shame meant for all others, turn the bad toward himself, and give the good to others. If one displays one's own virtues and hides the good qualities

of another or causes another to be dispraised, this, for a bodhisattva, is a transgression punishable by expulsion from the Sangha.

8. Precept against being miserly. If a buddha-child is miserly or causes another to be so, that is a cause and an act of stinginess. If a bodhisattva is asked for something by a poor person, he must give whatever is asked. If a bodhisattva, with malicious intent, gives neither a material offering nor a teaching and rebukes the person, this is a transgression punishable by expulsion from the Sangha.

9. Precept against anger. If a buddha-child becomes angry or causes another to become so, this is a cause and an act of anger. A bodhisattva, while among people, must give rise to the root of good and continually awaken a heart of compassion. If a bodhisattva rebukes beings or punishes them with swords or rods, or is unable, even though they repent their errors and apologize for their misconduct, to dissolve his anger, this is a transgression punishable by expulsion from the Sangha.

10. Precept against slandering the Three Treasures. If a buddha-child slanders the Three Treasures or causes another to do so, that is a cause and an act of slandering. If a bodhisattva hears a non-buddhist or an evil person slander the Buddha, he should feel as though his breast were pierced by three hundred halberds all at one time. If he himself slanders the Three Treasures and loses his faith in them or causes another to do so, this is a transgression punishable by expulsion from the Sangha.

(3) "O children of the Buddha, these are the ten major precepts of a bodhisattva. You must not break these precepts even slightly. If you do break them, you will lose the will to seek the way and destroy whatever merit you have accumulated. I shall now explain the forty-eight minor precepts.

1. Precept against slighting one's teachers and friends. If a buddha-child is to receive the rank of a king or of that of any government official, he must take upon himself the precepts of a bodhisattva. If he does, all the gods will protect him and the buddhas will rejoice. If he has accepted the precepts, he must respect the elder monks, his master, those as learned as he, and those practicing the same way. If he does not, he is committing a minor offence.

2. Precept against drinking intoxicants. If a buddha-child deliberately drinks an intoxicant or personally hands a cup of an intoxicant to another and causes him to drink it, he will lose his hand for five hundred generations, for there is no limit to the mistakes caused by intoxicants. Therefore to indulge deliberately is to commit a minor offence.

3. Precept against eating meat. If a buddha-child deliberately eats meat, he will destroy the seed of the great compassionate Buddhahood. Therefore a bodhisattva must not eat the meat of any living being. If one deliberately eats meat, one commits a minor offence.

4. Precept against eating the five pungent herbs. A buddha-child must not eat the five pungent herbs. If he deliberately eats one of the five pungent herbs, namely, sand leek, garlic, or the three kinds of onions, he commits a minor offence.

5. Precept against not teaching or advising. If a buddha-child sees people breaking rules intentionally, he must teach them and reason with them so that they will repent. If he shares their profits and dwells among them, he commits a minor offence.

6. Precept against not asking for the teachings. When a master of the Mahayana or one of similar understanding comes from afar, a buddha-child must respectfully give offerings to him and ask for explications of the teachings to remove the pain in his heart, without being neglectful even for a moment. If he does not do so, he commits a minor offence.

7. Precept against being neglectful in listening to the teachings. Wherever the doctrine or precepts are being explicated, a novice bodhisattva must listen and ask questions. If he does not do so, he commits a minor offence.

8. Precept against violating the Mahayana precepts. If a buddha-child goes against the Mahayana sutras and the Vinaya, says they were not taught by the Buddha, and follows inferior precepts, he commits a minor offence.

9. Precept against not taking care of the sick. If a buddha-child sees a sick person, he must act toward him as though giving an offering to the Buddha. Among all good-producing acts, nursing the sick is supreme. If he does not do so, he commits a minor offence.

10. Precept against stocking weapons. A buddha-child must not stock swords, bows, or other weapons. A bodhisattva will not seek revenge even on someone who kills his father or mother. One who deliberately stocks weapons commits a minor offence.

11. Precept against becoming a government offcial. A buddha-child must not become a government official because of an evil desire for personal gain, become an envoy to a battleground, or wage war. Even less should he become a rebel. If he does, he commits a minor offence.

12. Precept against selling and dealing. A buddha-child must not deliberately sell or deal in servants, domestic animals, or materials for coffins, or cause another to do so. If he does so, he commits a minor offence.

13. Precept against slandering. If a buddha-child with evil intent deliberately slanders a good person, a teacher of the Dharma, a king, a person of the nobility, or one of his six close relatives, father, mother, older or younger brother, or older or younger sister, and forces such a one into a situation wherein they are unable to do as they wish, he commits a minor offence.

14. Precept against arson. If a buddha-child with evil intent deliberately sets fire to a forest, a house, a temple, or the like, he commits a minor offence.

15. Precept against perverse teachings. A buddha-child must cause non-buddhists and even evil persons to hold the Mahayana sutras and the Vinaya and to understand their meanings. If he with evil intent expounds the perverse teachings of non-buddhists, he commits a minor offence.

16. Precept against expounding the Sutras and the Vinaya wrongfully. A buddha-child must first study the Mahayana sutras and the Vinaya and broadly understand their meaning. When novice bodhisattvas come from afar, even if he must sacrifice himself, he must make offerings to them. Then he must

gradually teach them the right Dharma and have them open their hearts and minds and awaken to it. If a buddha-child for his own gain should wrongfully teach the Sutras and the Vinaya and slander the Three Treasures, he commits a minor offence.

17. Precept against relying on power to seek wealth. If a buddha-child, for the sake of fame or fortune, should become friendly with a king or his ministers and rely on their power to seek riches, he commits a minor offence.

18. Precept against becoming a teacher when one does not understand the Dharma. A buddha-child must maintain throughout the six periods of the day and night the precepts of a bodhisattva and awaken to their meaning and to the nature of Buddhahood. However, he who, without understanding the whys and wherefores of maintaining the Vinaya, acts as though he does, commits a minor offence.

19. Precept against speaking with a double tongue. A buddha-child who stands among people practicing the practices of bodhisattvas and deliberately causes them to argue by pointing out their errors and slandering right persons commits a minor offence.

20. Precept against not practicing the release of animals. A buddha-child must practice, with a compassionate heart, freeing living beings. All living beings have been our parents in our former lives. Therefore on the memorial days of family members, he must invite a Dharma teacher and listen to the teachings, save the lives of animals, relieve their suffering, and give them the conditions ultimately to become buddhas. If he does not do so, he commits a minor offence.

21. Precept against taking revenge. A buddha-child must not answer anger with anger. Even if someone were to kill one of his six close relatives or his king, he must not take revenge. Taking a life in revenge for a life is not in accord with the way of piety. He who deliberately takes revenge commits a minor offence.

22. Precept against being prideful. If a buddha-child who has newly entered the Sangha and still has not gained any insight into the teaching relies on his own intelligence or relies on his social class, seniority, or wealth, or will not ask a Dharma-master about the Sutras or the Vinaya, he commits a minor offence.

23. Precept on receiving the precepts. When a buddha-child, after the death of the Buddha, desires to receive the precepts of a bodhisattva, if there is no master within a thousand miles who is capable of administering them, he should administer them to himself by vowing before symbols of the Buddha and bodhisattvas to follow the precepts. Then for seven days he should be repentant. If he does not see marvellous signs during this time, he cannot be said to have received the precepts. If he receives them before a Dharma teacher who has received the bodhisattva precepts, he need not see any marvelous signs. Furthermore, if a Dharma teacher who has some insight into the Mahayana Sutras and Vinaya wishes to mingle with kings and government officials, and therefore out of arrogance does not explain to novice bodhisattvas the meaning of the Sutras and the Vinaya, he commits a minor offence.

24. Precept against not studying the Buddha's Sutras and the Vinaya. If a buddha-child does not study the Buddha's right Sutras and the Vinaya and instead studies non-buddhist or worldly texts, he creates the causes and conditions that hinder the way and destroy his Buddhahood. He commits a minor offence.

25. Precept against not being in harmony with the masses. After the Buddha's death, if a buddha-child is to become a master teacher of the Dharma, a master of meditation, or a wandering master of conversion, he must have a compassionate heart and must reconcile arguments and protect the properties of the Three Treasures. If he causes dissension among the masses and uses the properties of the Three Treasures any way he wants, he commits a minor offence.

26. Precept against receiving nourishment alone. A buddha-child who is living in a monastery must, when a travelling monk comes there for the summer retreat, courteously meet him and give him food, drink, a room, and the like. If a donor invites all the monks, give the travelling monk a share. If the resident monk accepts the invitation only for himself, his sin is without bounds and he is not different from an animal. He commits a minor offence.

27. Precept against accepting an individual invitation. A buddha-child must not accept an individual invitation. Because this benefit belongs to the monks of the ten directions, to accept an individual invitation is to make what belongs to monks of the ten directions one's own. He would be using for himself what belongs to all buddhas, to the saints, to each teacher of monks in all fields of virtue, and to parents and the sick. Therefore he commits a minor offence.

28. Precept against inviting a monk separately. If a buddha-child wishes to invite a monk, he should speak with a monastery's director of affairs and invite one according to the rules. Thereby he will gain the wise, saintly monks of the ten directions. Even if he were to invite separately five hundred saints, the merit he would gain thereby would not equal even that of inviting a single common monk according to the rules. To invite separately is the way of non-buddhists. It is a violation, a minor offence.

29. Precept against a wicked livelihood. If for profit a buddha-child deals in male or female prostitutes, fortune-telling, magical spells, mixing poisons or the like, not because of a compassionate or dutiful mind, he is committing a minor offence.

30. Precept against not honoring the fast days. If a buddha-child, with evil intent, lies and falsely comes close to the Three Treasures, talking about emptiness while his actions are rooted in existence, acting as go-between for the sexual behavior of men and women for the sake of householders, thereby awakening their attachments, or, during the six fast days, takes life, steals, or breaks the precepts, he commits a minor offence.

31. Precept against not redeeming what must be redeemed. If a buddha-child, after the Buddha's death, sees non-buddhists or various evil persons selling symbols of buddhas or bodhisattvas, or selling Sutras, or making slaves of monks, nuns, or novice bodhisattvas, he should use skillful means and save

them with a compassionate heart, redeeming them all. If he does not do so, he commits a minor offence.

32. Precept against harming sentient beings. If a buddha-child deals in the sale of weapons, such as swords, bows, or the like, or of balances or measures; or takes people's belongings through the use of official powers; or nullifies other people's merits; or raises cats or dogs that kill other living beings, he commits a minor offence.

33. Precept against watching perverse acts. If a buddha-child, with evil intent, watches a battle or a ransacking band of thieves; or if he indulges in enjoying such trivialities as the harp, the flute, singing, dancing, or masked drama; or in playing such games as cards, go, chess, or football; or in telling fortunes by manipulating such things as fingertips, grass stalks, willow twigs, bowls, or skulls as means of divination; or if he becomes an errand-runner for thieves, he commits a minor offence.

34. Precept against thinking about inferior precepts. A buddha-child must hold adamantly to the precepts of the Mahayana without forgetting them day or night, thinking of them as though they were a float taking him across a huge ocean. He must continually awaken in himself Mahayana faith. Knowing that he has not yet become a buddha, while the buddhas have already become buddhas, if he gives even one thought to non-Buddhist ways, he commits a minor offence.

35. Precept against not awakening resolves. A buddha-child should awaken all resolves, attending to his parents and his master monk, learning the Mahayana sutras and the Vinaya from his fellow monks, and resolving rather to give up his life than not to hold to the Buddha's precepts. If he does not awaken these resolves, he commits a minor offence.

36. Precept against not making the vows. A buddha-child must make the following vows: 'Even if my body is thrown into a hole blazing with fire, I shall not do anything impure with a female. Again, even if my body is wrapped in a net of hot metal, I shall not, if I have physically violated the precepts, accept robes from a faithful donor. Again, even if I am forced to drink molten metal, I shall not, if I have orally violated the precepts, eat or drink food or drink of a hundred flavors offered by a faithful donor. Furthermore, even if I am forced to lie on a bed of hot metal, I shall not accept a bed of fine grass; even if I am pierced by three hundred spears, I shall not accept medicine; if I have physically violated the precepts, I shall not sleep in a nice room, accept the reverence of a donor, accept pleasing colors, listen to pleasing voices, or smell pleasing scents.' If he does not make these vows, he commits a minor offence.

37. Precepts for dhutaguna discipline and retreats. A buddha-child should observe the twelve dhutagunas during two periods in a year [January 15 to March 15 and August 15 to October 15] and go into retreat in the summer and winter. He should carry with him the eighteen things: willow twigs for tooth cleaning, soap, the three garments, a water bottle, a begging bowl, a mat, a staff, a censer, a filter, a wash cloth, a knife, a flint to start a fire, scissors, a hammock, Sutras, the Vinaya, a buddha image, and a bodhisattva image and

wander throughout the land. The novice bodhisattvas should fast every half-month and chant the ten major and forty-eight minor precepts in front of the images of the Buddha and the Bodhisattva. One person should sit on a high seat and chant, while the others should be seated lower and listen. All should be wearing a nine, seven, or five panelled monk's robe. When he observes the dhutagunas, he must not enter a land of travail, or a land with an evil king, or a forest with wild animals or poisonous snakes. If he does, he commits a minor offence.

38. Precept against a wrong seating order. The order of the seating of disciples should be determined according to the time of their receiving the precepts; that is, it should not be determined according to whether they are older or younger, male or female, of the nobility or royalty or servants. If this is not practiced, a minor offence is committed.

39. Precept against not practicing virtues that give happiness. A buddha-child should teach, lead people, and build monasteries and buddha-stupas. For the sake of people suffering from illness or national calamity, of people observing memorials for relatives or teachers, of people suffering the aftermath of flood or fire or the recompense of all their offences, and especially for the sake of those heavily afflicted with greed, anger, or ignorance, a bodhisattva should explicate the Mahayana sutras and the Vinaya. If a novice bodhisattva does not do so, he commits a minor offence.

40. Precept against being discriminatory when people are to receive the precepts. When a buddha-child has people receive the precepts, he should not discriminate even a little whether someone is a king, a government official, a monk, a nun, a man or woman of faith, a licentious man or woman, or a person without all five senses. However, those who have committed any of the seven rebellious transgressions—shedding a buddha's blood, killing one's father or mother, killing a precept-giver or teacher, destroying the harmony of the Sangha, or killing an arhat—are excluded.

One who has left home and become a monk does not pay homage to a king or to his parents, does not show respect to his six kinds of relatives, and does not bow to gods. But if with bad intent he does not give the precepts to a person who has come from afar seeking the Dharma, he commits a minor offence.

41. Precept against becoming a teacher for one's own gain. If a buddha-child sees a person who receives the precepts, he should have him follow two teachers—a personal precept-giver and a master. The two teachers will face him and ask whether or not he has committed any of the seven rebellious transgressions. If he has not committed any of these transgressions, he can receive the precepts. If there is someone who has violated one of the ten major precepts, he can remove the transgression by asking for forgiveness before an image of a buddha or a bodhisattva for a period of seven days up to one year.

Again, one who has violated one of the forty-eight minor precepts can remove the transgressions by asking for forgiveness when he has violated it. A teacher of the teachings must discern these several characteristics and further know the many natural dispositions of the people who practice the way. If a buddha-child covetously treats disciples for the sake of fame or fortune and lies and says he understands all of the Sutras and the Vinaya, he commits a minor offence.

42. Precept against expounding the precepts to evil persons. A buddha-child must not expound these superior precepts before those who will not accept the bodhisattva precepts, non-buddhists, or evil persons. Other than to a king, he must not expound them before anyone with perverted views. Because these evil persons will not follow the Buddha's precepts, they are equal to animals. Furthermore, just as trees and rocks are without minds, so too are they. Therefore if he intentionally expounds these superior precepts in front of them, he commits a minor offence.

43. Precept against receiving offerings without shame. If a buddha-child with a mind of faith leaves home and receives the Buddha's correct precepts and intentionally breaks them, he may not accept offerings from any donor. Nor may he cross a king's land nor drink his water. The people of the world will rebuke him as a thief within the Buddha's doctrine. Therefore if he intentionally violates the right precepts, he commits a minor offence.

44. Precept against disrespecting the Sutras. A buddha-child must single-mindedly receive and retain the Mahayana sutras and the Vinaya. He must copy the Buddha's precepts even if he has to use his own skin for paper, his own blood for ink, his own marrow for water, and his own bones for pens, and all the more so when using tree bark, rice paper, or bamboo paper. He should always pile the Sutras and the Vinaya on bags and boxes inlaid with the seven treasures containing incense and flowers of the seven precious things. If he does not do so, he commits a minor offence.

45. Precept against not teaching sentient beings. A buddha-child must always have a mind of great compassion; wherever he sees any sentient beings, he must say 'You should all take refuge in the Three Treasures and receive the ten precepts.' When he sees beasts such as cows, horses, and sheep, he should think in his mind and say with his mouth, 'You should all awaken the intent to realize enlightenment.' A bodhisattva who does not awaken such thoughts commits a minor offence.

46. Precept against expounding the teachings not in accord with the norm. A buddha-child must always teach with a mind of great compassion. No matter how highly ranked the person may be in whose home he is, when he expounds the teachings, he must sit in the highest position. Whenever the teachings are expounded, the teacher of the Dharma is to be in the highest position and the listeners must respectfully occupy the lower positions. If he does not expound in such a manner, he commits a minor offence.

47. Precept against making restrictions with wrong rules. There may be kings or government officials who rely on their noble rank and violate the rules of the Buddha's doctrine, making rules clearly meant to restrict both lay and disciples, not allowing people to leave home to become monks, not allowing the making of buddha-images, of buddha-stupas, or of Sutras or Vinayas, setting up governing officials to restrict monks, or, further, daring to cause monks to stand on the earth while home dwellers occupy the high positions. Bodhisattvas

are deserving of everyone's offerings; how can they be forced to be used by governments? Whether they be kings or government officials, those who have accepted the Buddhist precepts must not commit the evil act of destroying the Three Treasures. If they intentionally violate the Dharma, they commit a minor offence.

48. Precept against violating the teachings. If a buddha-child has, with good intentions, become a monk, yet for the sake of fame and fortune expounds the Buddhist precepts before kings or government officials, he is actually violating the Buddha's teachings. One who has received the Buddhist precepts must protect those precepts as he might think of an only child or be dedicated to his parents. If he intentionally falls into this error, he commits a minor offence."

2. Disharmony in the Order

(1) The World-Honored One next went to the south, crossed the river Ganges, and wandered throughout the country of Vamsa. He then entered Kosambi and stayed for a while in the Ghosita Monastery.

At that time, a disciple committed a trifling offence. At first, he thought that he had committed an offence, while the other disciples did not think that he had. After a time, he came to think that indeed he had not committed a violation, while the other disciples came to think that he had. The disciples said to him, "Friend, you have committed an offence. You should admit it." "I have not committed an offence." Because he would not admit it, the disciples, in accordance with the rules of the Sangha, expelled him from their order.

Because he was very learned, clear in the teachings, knowledgeable in the rules, intelligent, and endowed with the desire to practice the way, he did not follow the rules of this Sangha. He said to his fellows, "Friends, this is not a violation. It is not right that I should be expelled. I wish that you would, relying on the teachings and the rules, become my defenders." Furthermore, he sent messengers to his friends who had moved to other places and asked them, too, to be his defenders, and he won their agreement.

In this way, the disciples who expelled him and those who defended him began to quarrel. The breach between them gradually became deeper. A disciple told the World-Honored One about the expulsion. The World-Honored One said, "The harmony of the disciples has been destroyed." He went to the disciples who had expelled their fellow monk and said, "O disciples, it is a mistake for you to say that it is your duty, whatever the case, to expel a disciple. O disciples, suppose that we have a disciple who has committed an offence. That disciple does not think that it is an offence, but the other disciples think that it is. Suppose that the disciple is deep in learning, clear in the teachings, knowledgeable in the rules, and has the desire to practice the way. If you expel that disciple and refuse to have anything to do with him, there will arise disharmony in the Sangha and fighting. Therefore you must give more importance to the harmony of the Sangha and not expel that monk."

The World-Honored One then went to the disciples who defended the disciple and said, "O disciples, when you have committed an offence, you must not think that you have not done so and therefore have no need to correct the transgression. Suppose that a disciple has committed an offence but thinks that he did not. Other disciples think that he did. Suppose that that disciple recognizes that the opposing disciples are deep in learning, clear in the teachings, knowledgeable in the rules, intelligent, determined to practice the way, and free from greed, anger, stupidity, and fear. That disciple then realizes that if he does not admit his offence, the opposing disciples will be put in the position of having to expel him and thereby causing disharmony and strife within the Sangha. He should admit his transgression for the sake of the harmony and the faith of his fellow disciples." The World-Honored One in this way taught and enlightened the disciples on both sides and returned to his quarters.

(2) However, even with the World-Honored One's admonitions, the disciples who had split into two factions practiced separate fasts and performed the ceremonies of the Sangha separately. They increased the vehemence of their arguments, and gradually their three kinds of actions, physical, verbal, mental, became very unseemly for disciples of the Buddha. The World-Honored One again gathered them together and said, "O disciples, when the Sangha is not in harmony, each member's actions must be even more respectful. When actions are not in accord with the rules or are unkind, you must resolve not to do anything unseemly and stay in your place. When actions are in accord with the rules and are kind, you must sit together in one place. O disciples, stop fighting. You must not continue in disharmony." A disciple said, "World-Honored One, please wait a little longer. Please savor the deep meditation of a World-Honored One. We shall take responsibility for this fighting and disharmony and resolve it."

The World-Honored One repeated his words, "O disciples, stop fighting. You must not continue in disharmony." The disciple again faced the World-Honored One and repeated the same thing, rejecting the World-Honored One's admonition. At that point, the World-Honored One said to the disciples, "O disciples, long ago in the city of Baranasi there was a king, Brahmadatta, of the kingdom of Kasi. Prosperous and flourishing, he had a strong army and many wheeled vehicles and was followed by many kingdoms. At that time, there was in the kingdom of Kosala a king named Dighiti. He was poor, having only a small army and a small kingdom. Indeed, he was no threat to King Brahmadatta. He heard that Brahmadatta had prepared four armies and was coming to defeat him in battle. He thought, 'My kingdom is small and defenseless. Because it would be difficult to face Brahmadatta and engage him in even one battle, it might be best to leave the castle and flee.' Thereupon, without fighting, he left his kingdom to Brahmadatta. Taking his queen, he secretly escaped to a town in the vicinity of Baranasi, took on the guise of a wanderer, and hid in the home of a potter. After some time, the queen became pregnant and, as is wont to happen during pregnancy, she began to have a strange craving: she wanted to drink the water used to wash the swords of soldiers who had lined up on a levelled training field as the sun was rising. 'O queen, we are now a defeated people. How can I do something like that?' 'O great king, if this wish cannot be fulfilled, I shall die.'

"Now King Dighiti had a friend, a brahmin, who was an adviser to the house of King Brahmadatta. King Dighiti, having no choice but to try to fulfill the queen's wish, went to the brahmin's home to get his advice. The brahmin said that he would like to meet the queen, so King Dighiti brought her to see the brahmin. Upon seeing the queen, the brahmin rose from his seat, draped his robe over one shoulder, and faced her. He put his palms together in respectful greeting and three times sang a song of joy, 'Oh, truly has the king of Kosala come to stay in her womb.' Then he said, 'O queen, do not lose hope. Your wish will surely be fulfilled.'

"The brahmin, being the king's adviser, immediately went to see King Brahmadatta and said, 'Great king, an auspicious sign has manifested itself. Tomorrow, with the rising of the sun, have your four armies line up on the training field. They must wash their swords.' The king immediately gave the order to do what the brahmin said.

"In this way the queen's wish was fulfilled, and when her pregnancy reached full term, she gave birth to a prince, who was given the name Dighavu. When the prince reached the age of discretion, King Dighiti thought, 'Brahmadatta hopes for our disadvantage. If the three of us are found at the same time, we shall surely all be killed. It would be better for Dighavu to be raised elsewhere.' So he and his wife continued to live in the same town, and Dighavu was taken outside the town for his upbringing.

(3) "At that time, a barber who had formerly lived in the palace at Kosala was now living in Brahmadatta's palace. One day, he saw his former lord King Dighiti and his queen dressed as wanderers and learned that they lived in a town near Baranasi. He reported this to the king. King Dighiti and his wife were immediately captured, had their hands tied behind them, and were dragged from crossroads to crossroads to the execution grounds.

"Just at that time, Prince Dighavu entered the town and, by chance and for the first time in a long while, saw his pitiful father and mother. Surprised, he was about to rush to their sides, when King Dighiti's voice made him stop in his tracks, 'Dighavu, you must not look too long. You must not look too short. The reason is that hatred is not allayed by hatred. Hatred is allayed by the absence of hatred.' Because people did not know who Dighavu was, they could not understand the meaning of these words. They thought that King Dighiti had gone insane and was blathering meaningless words. King Dighiti went on, 'I am not insane. What I am saying is not nonsense. Those with heart will understand the meaning. Dighavu, do not look too long. Do not look too short. The reason is that hatred is not allayed by hatred. Hatred is allayed by the absence of hatred.' He repeated these words three times.

"Before Dighavu could do anything, his father and mother were drawn and quartered, and their remains were discarded. A corps of soldiers was left to stand guard. Dighavu went to the town and bought wine. He gave it to the guards and got them completely drunk. He then gathered up firewood and cremated the remains of his father and mother. He put his hands together and bowed in reverence. It was the only thing he could do under the circumstances to console himself. The king of Kasi, Brahmadatta, saw the fire from an upper floor of his palace and thought that it was probably the work of someone related to the Kosala royal family. Why was no one coming to inform him? He felt both displeasure and fear.

"Prince Dighavu went into the forest and fasted, passing many days in tears and waiting for his heart to find some peace. The day finally came and he made up his mind to leave the forest. He went to the palace grounds and asked the elephant trainer to take him on as an apprentice. The elephant trainer gladly accepted him.

"Dighavu spent the night in the elephant stable, and upon waking at dawn he went outside and began playing his flute and singing. By chance the king was also enjoying the refreshing dawn breezes. He was moved by the beautiful singing and the sound of the flute. When he heard that the voice belonged to the apprentice elephant trainer, he gave him a position as an attendant. Dighavu obeyed the king's commands and did all he could to win his favor. The king was overjoyed, trusted him, and elevated him to a higher rank.

(4) "One day the king took Dighavu hunting. Dighavu drove the king's chariot, intentionally outdistanced his soldiers, and went out into the fields. The king said, 'Young man, stop the chariot. I am tired and want to take a nap.' Dighavu stopped the chariot and sat on the ground. The king used his lap for a pillow and soon fell into a light sleep.

"Then Dighavu thought, 'This king of Kasi is the enemy of my deceased father and mother. Because of him they lost their kingdom and their lives. Now is the time to take revenge.' Joyfully and bravely, he took his sword out of its scabbard and pointed it. Just then unexpectedly his father's last words came floating into his heart. When he remembered these words, he returned the sword to the scabbard. Twice and three times Dighavu thought, 'Now there is a good opportunity, I must take revenge.' He would aim his sword, but each time his father's words would dissuade him and he would sheath his sword.

"After a while, King Brahmadatta opened his eyes with a start, woke up filled with fear, and looked around. Dighavu asked, 'Great king, what are you afraid of that you wake with such a start?' 'Young man, just now I dreamed that Dighavu, prince of the kingdom of Kosala, was bearing down on me with sword in hand. That is why I awoke with such a fright.' At that, Dighavu, forcing down the king's head with his left hand and unsheathing his sword with his right hand, said, 'Great king, I am Dighavu, son of Dighiti of Kosala. You brought misery to my kingdom. You killed my father and mother. I shall never have a better chance to cleanse myself of hatred.' The king placed his head on Dighavu's feet and said, 'Dear Dighavu, please spare my life.' At that Dighavu remembered his father's last words and then begged the king's pardon. The king was both amazed and joyful and said, 'Good, you will spare my life, and I shall spare your life!' The two spared each other's lives and, clasping each other's hands, promised to help each other from then on, each vowing never to harm the other.

(5) "The two men left the hunt and returned to the castle. The king gathered his councillors together and said to them, 'If you were to find Dighavu, prince of Kosala, here, what would you do to him?' 'I should cut off his hands.' 'I should cut off his feet.' 'I should cut off both his hands and his feet.' 'I should slice off his ears.' There were various answers. The king said, 'That kind of action is no longer necessary. I was spared my life by Prince Dighavu, and I, too, have spared his life.'

"The king then faced Dighavu and said, 'Dear Dighavu, what is the meaning of your father's last words?' 'Great king, of my father's last words, "Do not look long" means not to hold a grudge long. "Do not look short" means not to break friendships quickly. "Hatred is not allayed by hatred; hatred is allayed by the absence of hatred" means that if, because my father and mother were killed by the great king, I should take the great king's life, those who support the great king would take my life. If that were to happen, then my followers would kill them. In this way, hatred would never be allayed by hatred. If the king now spares my life, then I shall also spare his life. In this way, hatred is allayed by the absence of hatred. That is why my father taught me those things just before he died.'

"O disciples, at that, Brahmadatta king of Kasi praised the prince Dighavu for his wisdom and returned his kingdom to him. He further gave him his daughter as a bride and vowed eternal peace.

"O disciples, this is the forbearance and gentle love of a king who carries weapons and swords in his hands. You are monks who left your homes to enter this well-taught teaching and discipline, are you not? You, too, must glow with forbearance and gentle love. O disciples, you must not fight. You must not continue to be in disharmony."

(6) In spite of this kindly admonition by the World-Honored One, the erring disciples would not accept his words, and they said, "World-Honored One, please wait a little longer. The World-Honored One should enter the deep meditation of a World-Honored One. We shall take responsibility and settle this quarrel."

At that, the World-Honored One thought, "These ignorant ones are caught up in formality and have lost sight of the spirit, so it is not easy to reason with them." He rose from his seat and left. Thus the World-Honored One went to the village of Balaka, to the bamboo grove of Parileyyaka, and finally stopped to dwell in the Rakkhita Park, away from those who would quarrel and far from the turmoil. He took pleasure in the silence of dwelling alone. Just as an elephant king will leave his herd of female, male, and baby elephants from time to time in order to enjoy peace and quiet, so did he dwell in peace and quiet. Soon after, the World-Honored One entered Savatthi and dwelled in the Jeta Grove.

After the World-Honored One left, the people of Kosambi became angry with the disharmonious disciples. "These disciples are the reason the World-Honored One left. These disciples will be disadvantageous to us. Let us stop revering them and giving to them. Then these disciples will leave the Sangha and return to householder status. That will bring peace to the World-Honored One's heart." They did just as they thought and stopped giving food to the monks. These disciples no longer received food and became weak from hunger; then they decided to cease their quarreling in the presence of the World-Honored One. Putting away their cushions, they took their robes and offering bowls and left Kosambi for Savatthi.

In Savatthi, Sariputta and a host of other disciples, having asked the World-Honored One how they should treat these disciples from Kosambi, were told to differentiate the correct from the incorrect and to treat correct as well as possible. Many faithful followers, including the elder Anathapindika, also asked how they should treat them and were taught to give them food equally.

When the Kosambi disciples entered the Jeta Grove, the disciple who committed the violations began to understand those violations. In this way the hearts of the disciples gradually softened and they came together and were able to revive a peaceful, harmonious Sangha in the presence of the World-Honored One.

(7) The World-Honored One called the disciples together and taught them, "O disciples, there are six laws that you should hold, love, and honor in your hearts. By doing them you will gain harmony, togetherness, and the absence of quarrels.

"O disciples, a disciple should, with regard to fellow followers, practice compassionate acts within and without. This is the first law. Next, with regard to fellow followers, he should speak compassionate words within and without. This is the second law. Next, with regard to fellow followers, he should think compassionate thoughts within and without. This is the third law. Next, when the disciple, according to the rules, goes out to receive offerings and food, he should share it equally with his fellow followers who hold to the precepts. This is the fourth law. Next, the disciple should dwell, together with people of like mind, in the precepts that are praised by knowledgeable people who are pure and without fault. This is the fifth law. Next, the disciple should dwell, together with those of like mind, in the view that is saintly and does away with suffering. This is the sixth law.

"O disciples, among these six laws, the major one is the view that is saintly and does away with suffering. This view includes the other five. O disciples, this is the meaning of that. Suppose a disciple goes into a forest, or under a tree, or into an empty dwelling and thinks, 'Is there still within my mind something that holds it captive, some delusion that will not allow me to see things correctly, as they are?'

"O disciples, if that disciple is subject to desire, anger, carelessness, sleepiness, lamentation, bad habits, or doubt, then his mind is captive. If he thinks only about matters of this world or of the world after death, his mind is captive. Again, if he continually causes disharmony and fights or attacks others, his mind is captive. If the disciple searches his own mind and discovers, 'There is no delusion left in my mind; my mind is well prepared to see the true principle,' he has reached the first wisdom that is saintly and surpasses the world.

"O disciples, if the disciple further looks within and asks, 'Have I practiced well this right view and reached tranquillity?' and knows that he has reached tranquillity, he has reached the second wisdom that is saintly and surpasses the world.

"O disciples, if the disciple, again, considers whether there are monks who have reached this right view other than through these teachings and sees that there are none, he has reached the third wisdom.

(8) "O disciples, if the disciple further considers whether he has achieved the practice achieved by one equipped with the right view and knows that he has, he has achieved the fourth wisdom. What is that practice? The person with this right view will, as a child who has touched hot coal with hand or foot will immediately withdraw it, if he has committed a violation to which he should confess, confess immediately to it and refrain from committing the violation again.

"O disciples, if the disciple further considers whether he has achieved other practices achieved by people with the right view and knows that he has, he has reached the fifth wisdom. What is that practice? As a mother cow with a calf will not let it stray even if she has to break the tethering pole, the person with this right view works diligently on matters affecting his fellow monks and diligently strives for the three learnings: precepts, meditation, and wisdom.

"O disciples, again, if a disciple knows that he has the kind of power that someone equipped with the right view has, he has reached the sixth wisdom. That power is the power to listen with complete concentration of mind when the Buddha explicates the teachings or the precepts.

"O disciples, again, if a disciple knows he has the power that someone with the right view has, he has reached the seventh wisdom. That power is the power to understand the Dharma and obtain joy when the Buddha explicates the teachings or the precepts."

"O disciples, the disciple who is equipped with these seven wisdoms is one who is in the stream of the saintly path." All the disciples rejoiced in the teaching of the World-Honored One and harmony was restored.

(9) The World-Honored One again wandered from place to place and reached Kapilavatthu. He stayed outside the town in a grove of banyan trees. Early one morning he entered the castle town to receive offerings. After his meal, in order to pass the afternoon heat, he went to the home of Kala-khemaka. There were many cushions prepared in the home. At that time, Ananda, together with many disciples, was sewing robes at the home of Gataya of the Sakya clan. That evening the World-Honored One went to Gataya's home, sat on the prepared cushion, and said to Ananda. "Ananda, there were many cushions prepared at the home of Kalakhemaka. Are there many disciples living there?" "World-Honored One, just as you say, there are many disciples living there. The reason is that it is now the time for us to make our robes."

"Ananda, a disciple who rejoices and finds pleasure in gathering with many others is not wise. It is not the way for him to gain easily the joys of leaving the world of suffering, of retiring from it, of experiencing silence, or of attaining true enlightenment. Neither is it the way for him to realize freedom. Ananda, there is nothing that does not decline and perish among those things that we love and enjoy or that does not give rise to grief, sadness, and turmoil.

"Ananda, think not of outward forms; the dwelling place of the buddhas is the thought of the emptiness of the self within. A buddha enters and dwells in this inner emptiness. Even though people approach, he takes joy in leaving and in distancing; he expounds the teachings in order to exhort them to free their minds from all passions. Ananda, if a disciple wishes to enter and dwell in inner emptiness, he should direct his mind inward, focus all his attention on one point, and calm his mind.

"Ananda, to say that the disciple should direct his mind inward, focus all his attention on one point, and calm his mind means that he should free himself from desire and non-good and enter and dwell in deep meditation.

"If a disciple observes inner emptiness and his mind does not become calm, he must become aware that it is not calm and observe the emptiness of all things outside of himself or the emptiness of everything within and without himself. If observing the emptiness within and without himself does not calm his mind, he must observe the immovable mind. If observing the immovable mind does not calm his mind, he must focus his mind on the form of the previously practiced deep meditation and calm it. In this way, he observes inner emptiness and takes joy in it, becomes free, and becomes aware of it. Observing outer emptiness, observing inner and outer emptiness, and observing the immovable mind, he will know joy and become free, and he will become aware of being emancipated.

(10) "Ananda, in this way a disciple should dwell in the deep meditation on emptiness. If his mind thinks of doing walking meditation, he should do it. If his mind thinks of standing motionless, he should do it; if of sitting or lying down, he should do it. Walking, standing, sitting, or lying down, he should be aware that the evils of greed and lamentation do not arise. Even when he talks, he should not talk of trivial or vulgar matters; instead he should talk of matters that will be of benefit in destroying the passions, in freeing the mind, or in leading to nirvana. Again, in thinking of things, he should not think trivial, vulgar thoughts that arise from the three evil mental states, greed, anger, and harm. Instead, he should think of world-renunciation, compassion, and love. He should, finally, be clearly aware of these.

"Ananda, he should reflect many times on the five desires awakened by the five senses. If he sees his mind moved by any of the five desires, he will know that his strong desires have not yet ceased. If his mind is not moved by any of them, he will know with clear awareness that he is free of strong desires.

"Ananda, what needs to be seen before it can be said that a disciple is suitable for following and serving his teacher? It is not the memorizing of the words of Sutras. One needs to hear words that enable one to know that a minimum of desire leads to freedom and nirvana, one needs to hear about the knowledge that makes one aware of freedom, and one needs to make these real; thus one makes himself suitable to serve his teacher.

"Ananda, here is the distress of a teacher and of a disciple. Whether a teacher or a disciple, his task is to leave the world of suffering, making his dwelling under a tree in a grove, in a cave in the mountains, or in a cemetery. Although dwelling in surroundings where other people will not come, his mind weakens and his desire for home will arise. While following after the Buddha and fixing his practice-dwelling away from other people, his resolve weakens and his desire for home arises. This is the distress of the practicing monk. From this increase the evil things that result in suffering and birth in the future. Ananda, therefore, for the sake of your eternal benefit and happiness, with respect to me, you should follow me as a friend, not as an enemy. What is meant by behaving like an enemy is that, although your teacher compassionately explains the Dharma, you do not turn your ears toward him nor listen carefully. Instead you turn your mind toward another teacher and leave the teachings of your teacher. To direct your ears and listen carefully and not turn your mind to another teacher nor leave your master's teachings is to follow behaving as a friend. Ananda, I do not treat disciples delicately as a potter treats soft clay. I attack and teach them. Only those with a wick in their spirit will remain."

3. Lessons on the Journey

(1) The World-Honored One travelled on toward the southeast and, along the way, taught the disciples and said, "Disciples, discard one thing. If you discard that thing, you will never again return to the world of illusion. That one thing is the mind pervaded by greed, anger, and stupidity; it is the mind that covers and hides; it is the mind of arrogance.

"Disciples, being unaware of arrogance, the mind does not detest and discard it and suffers endlessly. It is the same with greed, anger, and stupidity. Only when the mind knows and understands them completely and detests and discards them does suffering come to an end.

"Disciples, I do not see anyone revolving for so long a time in the cycle of birth and death as the people blinded by the absence of light. Nor do I see anyone revolving for so long a time in the cycle of birth and death as those bound by the ties of attachment. Bound by these two, people continue for a long time in the cycle of birth and death.

"Disciples, for those hoping for unsurpassed peace and endeavoring to reach it, we say, speaking in terms of something within, that there is nothing that will aid one more than right thinking. Right thinking will naturally cause you to discard non-good and practice good. Speaking in terms of something outside oneself, nothing is seen that will aid one more than a good friend. If you become close to a good friend, you will naturally discard non-good and practice good.

(2) "Disciples, there is one problem that, if it arises, will be not beneficial and will bring unhappiness and suffering to many people. That one problem is the destroying of the Sangha's harmony. If the harmony of the Sangha is destroyed, there will be fighting and slandering; barriers will be built, and the Sangha will be split asunder. Because of that, those without faith will remain without faith, and some with faith will lose it.

"Disciples, if one thing arises, many people will be benefitted and become happy. That one thing is the harmony of the Sangha. If the Sangha is in harmony, people will not fight nor build barriers nor split asunder. Because of that, those without faith will gain faith, and those with faith will grow even deeper in faith.

"Disciples, with my mind I know through and through some people whose minds are defiled. These people will, when their lives end, certainly fall into hell. The reason is that their minds are defiled. Because their minds are defiled, these people will enter the hell of suffering when their lives end.

"Disciples, with my mind I know thoroughly people with minds of sincere, joyful faith in the Dharma. I know that these people will, when their lives end, when they lay their burdens down, certainly be born in the world of gods. The reason is that they have minds of faith and are filled with joy. Because of their minds of sincere desire, these people will be born in the heavens when their lives end.

(3) "Disciples, practice one way and repeat it often and you will gain something for both the present and the future. By one way I mean that you should not be self-indulgent with respect to the good.

"Disciples, if you piled up the bones you have left behind during your round of births and deaths from the infinite past, the pile would be as large as Mount Vepula. It would not be an easy thing to get rid of. Disciples, I say without doubt that people who have transgressed in one way are not immune from doing something bad. By one way I mean knowingly to lie.

"Disciples, if someone were to know as well as I the fruits of giving, his mind would not be defiled by covetousness. He would not eat even the smallest left-over piece of food without sharing it. Disciples, whatever acts of merit there are in the world, compared to the mind of compassion, they are not worth even one-sixteenth part. The brightness of the light of the heart of compassion surpasses them as the brightness of the moon outshines the light of all the stars, which does not come to even one-sixteenth part of the moon's." And he said in verse,

> With right thought, those who practice immeasurable compassion
> Will untie the bonds of passions
> And transcend the world of delusions.
> It is a good thing to face another living being
> Not with anger but with compassion.
> To be compassionate toward all living things
> Is to gain unlimited merit.
> Even the merit of the wandering saints,
> Who have conquered the land on which crowds of people live
> And who gave the five offerings of unguents, rosaries,
> Incense, food, and lamps or candles,
> Is only one-sixteenth the worth of the well-practiced compassionate mind.
> Not killing, not causing others to kill,
> Not injuring, not causing others to injure,
> If you have compassion toward all living beings,
> You have no resentment whatsoever.

(4) "Disciples, when you have two habits, you should expect in this world to suffer, to worry, and to be anxious; and in the future, you should expect an evil path. These habits are to neglect to guard the openings of the five senses and to eat without knowing limits. Again, when you have two habits, you can expect

that there will be no suffering, no worry, and no anxiety; you will spend your days happily; and in the future, you can expect a good path. They are to guard the doors of the five senses and to know limits when eating.

> Eyes, ears, nose, tongue, body, and mind:
> Not guarding these doors,
> Eating without knowing limits,
> And being without control,
> You obtain suffering of both body and mind.
>
> Burning within and without,
> You will suffer both night and day.
> Guard these openings well,
> Know limits, and control your eating,
> And your body and mind will be at peace
> And night and day you will be happy.

"Disciples, I suffer in two ways: when people do not do good deeds and do not protect those in fear, and when people do evil deeds and commit cruel acts. However, I take joy in two ways: when people do good deeds and protect the fearful, and when no one commits cruel acts.

"Disciples, there are two things which, if you have them, will, as surely as a burden is lowered to the ground, bring you into hell: they are evil precepts and evil views. Again, there are two things which, if you have them, will, as surely as a burden is lowered to the ground, gain you birth in a heavenly realm: they are good precepts and good views.

(5) "Disciples, if you are not earnest and do not have a sense of shame, you will not be able to realize true enlightenment, enter nirvana, or attain unsurpassed tranquillity. "Disciples, dwelling in pure actions is not for the sake of deceiving people, or saying useless things, or gaining respect, fame, or personal gain. Rather, it is for the sake of controlling oneself, discarding all evil, and knowing completely.

"Disciples, having two things, you gain in this world much happiness and joy, and you begin to destroy the passions rightly. They are to be alarmed where one should be alarmed and, being alarmed, to practice correctly.

> Those who are intelligent, practice diligently, and think deeply,
> Depend on their wisdom, compare, and are alarmed.
> Calmly, without getting excited,
> Diligently practicing the practices of concentration and contemplation,
> They will reach the end of suffering.

(6) "Disciples, two thoughts frequently arise in a buddha. They are the thought of tranquillity and the thought of distancing. A buddha is happy and joyful when there is no injuring, but in a buddha this thought frequently arises, 'Walking, standing, sitting, or lying down, I shall not cause injury to either animals or plants.' Again, a buddha is happy and joyful in quietude, away from disturbances; in a buddha this thought frequently arises, 'I have discarded all things not good.' You, too, should dwell in the happiness and joy of non-injury. Further, you should dwell in the happiness and joy of quietude, away from disturbances.

"Disciples, those who lack pure wisdom are woeful. They will suffer, be distressed and troubled in this world, and must expect an evil path in the coming world. Those who have pure wisdom are fortunate. They will be tranquil in this world and can expect a good path in the world to come.

(7) "Disciples, there are two kinds of nirvana: nirvana with remainder and nirvana without remainder. Nirvana with remainder is that experienced by the sage who has destroyed the passions and accomplished the pure practices, who has done what had to be done and set down his heavy burden, who has achieved his goal and completely destroyed the passions that invite the next life, and who has through true wisdom become free. However, he still has the five senses and tastes the sufferings and joys arising from things to be loved and not to be loved. This is nirvana with remainder. Nirvana without remainder is experienced by the sage who does not savor sensations and who does not feel the heat of passions but remains cool.

"Disciples, take pleasure and joy in a secluded retreat, endeavor to quiet your inner mind, do not hinder silent contemplation, clearly examine things, and endeavor to live in an empty dwelling. Disciples, hold to the benefits of the three learnings, precepts, meditation, and wisdom; furnish yourselves with the surpassing wisdom; and live under the governance of a good mind.

"Disciples, be not careless; be single-minded; with a tranquil, happy, and joyful mind, live always seeing the good. If you practice these ways, you will either realize the enlightenment of the sages in the present life or attain the enlightenment that makes it possible never to return to the realm of delusion; you can expect one of these two results. Disciples, there are two kinds of people who will not discard evil and who will fall into hell: those who vow to undertake the pious practice and yet do defiled practice, and those who hinder people who are undertaking perfectly pure practice.

"Disciples, people who are captives of biased views either cling to existence or hate existence. However, those with eyes simply see things as they are. Disciples, how does one cling to existence? Some people take joy in existence and like existence. Even though they hear that existing things are subject to destruction, their minds do not turn to that fact and do not like hearing about it. Again, how does one hate existence? Some people hate existence and mourn it; they dislike existence and find joy in nonexistence. They are joyful that they will completely disappear after death. Again, how does a person with eyes see? He sees existence as existence and, in dislike of it, frees himself from existence; he frees himself from craving for it and endeavors to make it cease.

(8) "Disciples, there are three perceptions in the world; the perception of suffering, the perception of pleasure, and the perception of neither suffering nor pleasure. The perception of pleasure must be seen as suffering. The perception of suffering must be seen as a poisoned arrow. The perception of neither suffering nor pleasure must be seen as impermanence. When you see these in these ways, correctly seeing them, you will destroy insatiable craving, loose the bonds, and depending on the right mind's understanding you will become a sage who has ended suffering.

"Disciples, there are three kinds of insatiable craving: sexual craving, craving for existence, and craving for nonexistence.

> Bound by the yoke of craving,
> Those who rejoice in existence or nonexistence
> Are prisoners of evil spirits and find no peace.
> Pitiful, indeed, are the paths of aging, death, and returning to the cycle.
> Only when free from desire
> And having exhausted the mind's defilements,
> Can you reach the other shore in this life.

"Disciples, when you are equipped with three things, you can leave the land of evil spirits and you will shine like the sun. The three things are the sage's precepts, meditation, and wisdom.

"Disciples, there are three things of the sage: the silence of body, thought, and word. Disciples, whoever you may be, if you do not discard greed, anger, and ignorance, you will be caught in the Devil's trap, and you will have to move according to his orders. Only when you discard greed, anger, and ignorance will you be able to leave the realm of evil spirits. Disciples, if you do not free yourselves from these three, you will be in the ocean. Therein large and small waves will overwhelm you, whirlpools will pull you down, and there is the fear of sharks and human-flesh-eating demons. Only when you discard the three can it be said that you leave this ocean, cross to that ideal shore, and stand on the ground of purity.

"Disciples, there are three things that cause people to fall back during their undertaking: wanting things to happen, indulging in useless talk, and lusting for sleep. Disciples, hoping for fame, hoping for the increase of wealth, and desiring to be born in a good place in the future are common human wishes. If you hope for these three pleasures, you must adhere to good precepts.

(9) "Disciples, people are ruined by fame and infamy and after death fall into evil paths. You must stand outside criticism and praise. Disciples, examine yourselves for impurities. Do not lose right mindfulness between exhalation and inhalation. Examine the impermanence of all things. If you examine the impurities of this body, the craving that arises from mistakenly thinking that this body is pure will disappear. If you preserve right mindfulness between exhalation and inhalation, the hindrance of being a prisoner to things outside will disappear. If you see the impermanence of all things, ignorance ceases and becomes wisdom.

"Disciples, there are three kinds of fire: the fire of greed, the fire of anger, and the fire of ignorance. The fire of greed burns those whose minds have grown weak with desire. The fire of anger burns those who become angry and injure living beings. The fire of ignorance burns those whose minds are deluded and do not know the holy teachings. Those totally without the brilliance of wisdom and who know love only for themselves are burned by these three fires. Disciples, practice the examination of impurity to extinguish the fire of desire. Extinguish the fire of anger with a compassionate mind. Extinguish the fire of ignorance with the wisdom that leads to nirvana. Those who, with deep mindfulness, endeavor wholeheartedly day and night will extinguish these three fires and reach the end of suffering.

"Disciples, there are three things that constitute the filth within, the adversary within, and the enemy within. They are greed, anger, and ignorance.

(10) "Disciples, the most humble way of living is that of the beggar who, with begging bowl in hand, begs for food at every door. Suppose a householder's son comes to this base way of life of his own volition. He does not come to it brought by the king; he does not come to it frightened by thieves; he does not come to it because of debts or fear; and he does not come to it because he has no means of livelihood. He comes to it simply because, having been born into this world and being overwhelmed by birth, old age, death, grief, sadness, suffering, distress, and agony, he thinks, 'Here, indeed, shall I learn to put an end to suffering and distress.' Disciples, the mind of the householder's son who has left home, if he cannot free himself from greed, is constantly in anger; his mindfulness is defiled, he has no control over his senses, and his mind is flighty; this person, though he be free from the pleasures of the householders, cannot accomplish his goal as one who has left home.

"Disciples, here are four things trivial, easy to get, and not a crime to get. The four things are the monk's garment of castaway rags, food that has been begged for, a dwelling under a tree, and medicine made of fermented urine. If a buddha disciple is satisfied with these worthless, easily gotten things, I call him a Buddha's disciple.

"Disciples, I say that by knowing and seeing, the passions cease; but by knowing and seeing what do the passions cease? Disciples, it is suffering. Knowing and seeing suffering, the passions cease. Knowing and seeing the cause of suffering, passions cease. Knowing and seeing the cessation of suffering, the passions cease. Knowing and seeing the way to the cessation of suffering, the passions cease.

"Disciples, a mendicant, no matter who, cannot be called a true mendicant unless he really knows what is suffering, what is the cause of suffering, what is the cessation of suffering, and what is the way to the cessation of suffering. One can be said to be a true monk only when one knows as they really are the Four Noble Truths.

(11) "Disciples, householders who give to you as offerings robes, food, dwelling places, and medicines are your great helpers. You, too, are helpers to those to whom you expound the pure teaching that is beautiful in the beginning and in the end. Mendicants and householders who in this way rely on each other and help each other cross over the wild river of the passions and put an end to suffering.

"Disciples, observe the precepts and, relying on these precepts, live in control of your bodies. Behave correctly and beware of even a small violation; study and practice diligently. Even when you are standing still, part from greed; part from anger; part from idleness and drowsiness; part from the restlessness and regrets of the heart; part from doubt, and endeavor without bending or relaxing; thinking correctly, quietly concentrate your mind on one point. When you are sitting, when you are standing, or when you are lying down, do likewise. Disciples, if you do so, whether walking, standing, sitting, or lying down, with single-mindedness you will know shame, and you will deserve to be called one who exerts himself endlessly and sincerely."

4. The White Hair

(1) The World-Honored One presently entered the country of Mithila and sojourned at a mango grove called Mahadeva.

One day at a certain place in that grove, seeing the World-Honored One smile, Ananda thought, "The World-Honored One does not smile without reason. There must be a reason." He asked the World-Honored One for that reason.

The World-Honored One answered, "Ananda, long, long ago, there used to be a good king called Mahadeva here in Mithila. He relied on the Dharma to govern the country, and six times a month he practiced fasting. Ananda, after the king enjoyed his kingly status for several thousand years, one day he called his barber and said, 'When you find a white hair on my head, tell me.' After a few thousand years, the barber found a single white hair on the king's head and told him. 'Great king, a messenger from the gods has appeared; a white hair has grown.' He pulled it out with a hair puller and placed it on the king's palm. Seeing it, the king gave the barber a reward. He had the prince called and gave him his final advice. 'Prince, a messenger from the gods has appeared to me. Because I have experienced the pleasures of the human world, now is the time for me to seek the pleasures of the divine world. I am about to leave home. Prince, when you, too, see a white hair on your head, you should pass on the kingly rank to your eldest son and leave home. Now, since I am about to set this good tradition, you should inherit it without letting it die. Do not be the last one to inherit this tradition.'

"Ananda, in this manner King Mahadeva left everything behind and dwelled in this mango grove called Mahadeva. He practiced the four immeasurable minds—compassion, mercy, joy, and equanimity—and when his life in this world was over, he was born in the realm of Brahmadeva. Afterwards, his descendants one after the other left home, practiced the four immeasurable minds, and were born in the divine world. The last king, called Nimi, governed the country according to the way and, six times a month, practiced fasting; he was a good king.

(2) "Ananda, one day in the Tavatimsa heavens, in the Hall of the Good Dharma of the thirty-three gods, there was an assembly of the gods. There the following talk occurred. 'The people of Mahadeva are truly happy, because King Nimi is a good king.' Indra, lord of the heavens, said, 'Gods, do you want to see King Nimi?' At that time, King Nimi was in the midst of the full moon fast, his hair washed, fasting, and sitting atop a high tower. Indra immediately appeared before King Nimi and said, 'Great king, you are truly fortunate. The gods of the thirty-three heavens are assembled and are praising you and wish to see you. Great king, I shall send a chariot pulled by a thousand horses, so get on and ride up to the world of the gods.' King Nimi agreed to Indra's invitation, and Indra immediately returned to the heavens.

"In the heavens, Indra called for the charioteer Matali and commanded him immediately to go to King Nimi. Matali obeyed and went to King Nimi. Because the king requested it, Matali took, on the journey up to heaven, both the path by those receiving the evil effects of their evil actions and the path by those receiving the good effects of their good actions and then led him into the Hall of the Good Dharma of the thirty-three gods. Seeing King Nimi arrive, the gods greeted him, praised his virtues, and urged him to savor the pleasures of the heavenly world. However, the king declined their favors, returned to Mithila, preserved the practice of fasting, and governed the country according to the way. Seeing a white hair, he turned over the reign of the country to his eldest son. He gave his son his final advice and left home. He practiced the four immeasurable minds and became one born into the world of Brahmadeva. The king's eldest son was called Kalarajanaka. He broke the tradition set by his ancestors and did not leave home. He became the last of the line.

"Ananda, do not think of King Mahadeva as someone else. I was that king. However, the good tradition that I set at that time was not such as to make the evil passions nonexistent, to lead one to tranquillity, or to cause one to enter nirvana. It simply led to birth in the world of Brahmadeva. Ananda, the good tradition I set now is such as to make the evil passions nonexistent, to lead one to tranquillity, and to cause one to enter nirvana. What is that good tradition? It is the Eightfold Noble Path—right view, right thought, right speech, right action, right livelihood, right endeavor, right mindfulness and right concentration. Ananda, you must continue this good tradition and not let it cease. You must not be the last of the line."

(3) The World-Honored One, together with many disciples, wandered again throughout the country of Kosala and finally came to a brahmin village called Sala. The people of the village heard of the arrival of the World-Honored One and together they visited him. They asked him, "O World-Honored One, why do some die and fall into hell while others are born in the heavenly world?"

"People, because some people do things not in accord with the Path, because of their incorrect deeds, they fall into hell. Again, because others' deeds depend on the Path and are correct, they are born in the heavenly world."

"O World-Honored One, we cannot understand these succinct words. Please explain in detail."

"O people, listen well, then. There are three actions against the Path in the body. There are four actions against the Path in speech. There are three actions against the Path in thought. These actions of the body are as follows: taking life, savage in mind, desiring blood, having no compassion for living beings; stealing, taking what is not given; and indulging in licentiousness. These are the three actions of the body that are against the Path.

"The four verbal actions are as follows: because of fear or for one's own gain, one knowingly lies; one speaks words to rend asunder people's relationships; one indiscriminately and harshly slanders other people; and one amuses oneself with needless idle talk. These are the four verbal actions against the Path.

"The three mental actions are as follows: awakening the thought out of avarice to take the gains of others; becoming angry and embracing the perverse thought of deriving pleasure in seeing others' suffering; embracing perverse views and saying that charity and offerings of nourishment are useless, that there are no recompenses for one's good actions, that there is no virtue in piety or fidelity, or that there is no enlightenment. These are the three mental actions against the Path. Through the causes of these actions of the body, mouth, and mind, which are against the Path, some people enter hell after they die.

"In contrast to this, because others do not do the three bodily actions against the Path, nor the four verbal actions against the Path, nor the three mental actions against the Path, they are born in the heavenly world. Those who avoid doing the ten bodily, verbal, and mental actions against the Path are able to be born at will in any god's world. Furthermore, if they want, they can extinguish all the passions and awaken enlightenment in the present."

The villagers of Sala rejoiced at the World-Honored One's words, and each asked to be counted as a lifelong disciple of his teachings.

Chapter 3

WISDOM AND IGNORANCE

1. Nanda and Rahula

(1) It had been some time since Nanda had received the World-Honored One's teachings and been enabled to free himself from a life of desire. One day Nanda was alone in the forest and thought, "Meeting with a buddha is not an easy matter. As rare as it is for an udumbara flower to bloom, so rare is it for a buddha to appear in this world. Now that I have had the joy of meeting a buddha, I have endeavored to practice and have realized the bliss of nirvana." However, even into the heart of such a sage person, evil spirits continued to try and enter. Knowing Nanda's heart, they appeared in the inner palace of Kapilavatthu Castle and enticed Princess Sundarinanda.

> Be joyful, princess.
> Bedeck your body,
> Play music, and enjoy yourself.
> Your beloved one is coming home
> And will rush into your arms.

Princess Sundarinanda heard these words and was joyful. She adorned her body and the room, played music, and waited for her husband to return to the castle. King Pasenadi of Savatthi also heard this rumor and was greatly surprised. He hurried to the forest in which Nanda dwelled. Nanda asked, "Great king, why have you come here in such great haste? You look rather unwell." "I heard a rumor that you had quit the life of a monk and had returned home or were returning home. That troubled me, so I came to see you."

Hearing this, Nanda smiled and said, "Great king, when you were with the World-Honored One, did you not hear about me? The bonds of my delusion have been severed, and I shall never again be born into delusion." "I had not heard that. Today the rumor is that you are returning to the lay state, returning to the castle and your former princess. The princess is said to have bedecked herself to her former beauty, to have decorated your old room with flowers, and to be waiting your return to the castle."

"Great king, for one who has left home to become a monk, there are the joys of tranquillity, of nirvana. Desire is fearful, like a pit of fire or a knife covered with honey. Why should one resting in this tranquil forest and drinking the cool, nectar-like water of the Dharma ever again enter a thicket of swords or use an injurious drug? I have learned the source of the fire of desire and have crossed over the rivers of desire, of recurring life, and of non-enlightenment. I have done the things that I had to do." "Hearing that, I have not the slightest doubt. I shall return with my mind at rest." But the evil spirits even more tenaciously tried to tempt Nanda.

> Her form smells lovely as a flower;
> Her face is pure as the moon.
> On this spring night adorned by voices and lutes,
> Why do you not return to your wife's side?

Nanda rejected these voices and sang,

> Long ago I had such a mind.
> Surrounded by inexhaustible desire,
> I was headed toward old age and death.
> However, I have now crossed the chasm of sexual desire.
> Without impurities, and impervious to stains,
> I do not miss at all the rank of king.
> The true Dharma is trustworthy.
> Evil spirits, leave! Disappear!

The disciples heard about this and told the World-Honored One. The World-Honored One praised him, saying "Nanda has great strength. He is very handsome. His desire is strong, but he has controlled it well and protected the five senses. He knows moderation in eating. At night he does not lie down but instead strives to practice. He has perfected both wisdom and practice."

(2) One morning the World-Honored One put on his robe, and took up his alms bowl, and started for Savatthi to make the rounds for alms; and Rahula, too, put on his robe, took up his alms bowl, and went with him. The World-Honored One turned to him and said, "Rahula, nothing in the three periods, past, present, or future, is 'mine'; neither is anything 'I', nor is anything 'self'. Relying on true wisdom, you should know things as they are."

"Does the World-Honored One say this only with regard to things?" "Rahula, as it is with things, so it is with the mind." At that time, Rahula thought, "Today, the World-Honored One personally gave me a teaching. I shall not go on the alms-round." Turning back and going to the foot of a tree, he sat with his body straight and his mind correct. Seeing him, Sariputta approached and said, "Rahula, control your breathing. If you practice mindful breathing often, you will benefit greatly."

In the evening, Rahula finished his meditation practice, went to the World-Honored One, and asked, "O World-Honored One, how should one master mindful breathing, and what great benefit is there?" The World-Honored One answered as follows.

(3) "Rahula, go to a grove or under a tree or to a house wherein no one lives, and sit with your body straight and your mind correct. Whether exhaling or inhaling, be single-minded; when taking a long breath, be aware that you are taking a long breath. When taking a short breath, be aware that you are taking

a short breath. When exhaling long, be aware that you are doing so. When exhaling short, be aware that you are doing so. You will be aware of your whole body when you inhale and exhale. You will be calm in body as you inhale and exhale. You will feel joy as you inhale and exhale. You will train yourself to calm your mind as you inhale and exhale. Your mind will be free of attachments as you inhale and exhale. You will contemplate impermanence and freedom as you inhale and exhale. If you are mindful in this way of your breathing, and you practice this over and over, there will be great benefit; your final breath will disappear not in the midst of unconsciousness but in the midst of consciousness. Rahula, this, then, is the way in which you should master mindful breathing.

(4) "Rahula, furthermore, you should master the practice called Equal Earth. If you master this practice, your mind will not cling to the emotions of liking and disliking that arise. Whether you place something pure or impure on the great earth, it does not hate or dislike it. Furthermore, you should master the practice called Equal Water. If you master this practice, your mind will not cling to the emotions of liking and disliking that will arise. Whether you put something pure or impure into water, it does not hate or dislike it; let your mind be so also.

"Rahula, further master the practices of compassion, mercy, joy, and equanimity. If you master the practice of compassion, you can avoid anger. If you master the practice of mercy, you can avoid anguish. If you master the practice of joy, you can avoid frustration. If you master the practice of equanimity, you can avoid the will to injure.

"Rahula, further master the meditation on impure objects and the meditation on impermanence. If you master the meditation on impurity, greed will disappear. If you master the meditation on impermanence, self-pride will disappear. Rahula, these are the great benefits you will gain by mastering mindful breathing." Rahula was joyful over the World-Honored One's teachings.

2. The Ignorant and the Wise

(1) One night the World-Honored One spoke to his disciples in the front garden in the Jeta Grove. "O disciples, homes where children honor and respect their parents are homes in which live gods and buddhas. Gods and buddhas are the names of parents. Disciples, parents are the gods who give birth to children and nurture them. Parents are the buddhas who teach children the good and bad of this world.

(2) "Disciples, on the eighth day of every half-month, the messengers of the gods move throughout this world to see how many people in this world of humans are accumulating merit by serving their parents and monks, by following their elders, and by following the eight precepts on the fast days, and to see who are reverential on the days before and after. Disciples, again, on the fourteenth day of each half-month, the princes of the gods also move throughout this world in this manner. Furthermore, on the fifteenth day of each half-month, the gods themselves move throughout the world in the same way.

"Disciples, in this way the gods look throughout the human world. When there are only a few people accumulating merit, the gods assemble in the Lecture Hall of the Good Dharma and lament, 'There are few in the human world accumulating merit by attending to their parents and monks, by respecting their elders, by observing the eight precepts on fast days, or by being reverential on the days before and after. Oh, the number of gods diminishes while that of the demons increases.' When there are many people accumulating merit, they rejoice, saying, 'Oh, the gods increase while the demons diminish.'

(3) "Disciples, long, long ago, the lord of the gods, Indra, assembled the gods of the thirty-three heavens and sang to them,

> If you hope to be my equal,
> Every half-month,
> On the eighth, fourteenth, and fifteenth days,
> And on the days before and after,
> Observe the eight precepts.

"Disciples, it cannot be said that it is very appropriate for Indra to sing this song. The reason is that he is saying, 'If you want to be my equal,' even though he himself is not free from greed, anger, and ignorance, nor from birth, aging, death, grief, sadness, suffering, anguish, or agony.

"Disciples, only when one has exhausted the passions, mastered the pure practices, completed what had to be done, put down the heavy burden of offences, and become a sage who is truly liberated, is one qualified to sing this song. The reason is that such a sage indeed is liberated from greed, anger, ignorance, and from birth, aging, death, grief, sadness, suffering, anguish, and agony.

(4) "Disciples, those with a mind of trust give birth to many virtues if they have three things: the first is a mind of faith, the second is the ability to give, and the third is someone worthy to whom they can give.

"Disciples, a householder who has a mind of trust can be known by these three qualities: first, he has a desire to see a person who correctly holds to the precepts; second, he has a desire to listen to the true Dharma; third, he is free from the defilement of greed and with pure hands gives extensively to many and derives joy from giving to those who constantly follow him and ask him. If these three qualities are in one person, he is someone with a mind of trust."

(5) Again, on another night, he said, "O disciples, there are three situations that the people call parent-abandoning and child-abandoning situations. First is when a huge fire breaks out, and the strength of the fire is such that a mother cannot save her child nor can a child save his mother. Second is when there is a tremendous storm of wind and rain and there is great flooding; when people are swept away by the strength of the water, a mother cannot save her child nor a child his mother. Third is when a band of thieves living in the woods begins robbing and the villagers run away, and a mother cannot save her child nor a child his mother. Nevertheless, disciples, in these three situations there are times when mother and child can save each other. But there are three other situations when mother and child truly become separated and truly must abandon each other. It is when old age, illness, and death come upon them.

"Seeing her child growing old, a mother cannot say, 'I shall grow old in my child's stead.' Seeing his mother growing old, a child cannot say, 'I shall grow old in my mother's stead.' Again, seeing her child ill, a mother cannot say, 'I shall be ill in my child's stead.' Seeing his mother ill, a child cannot say, 'I shall be ill in my mother's stead.' Again, a mother, seeing her child dead, cannot revive him, saying, 'I shall die in my child's stead, if he can live again.' A child cannot save his dead mother by saying, 'I shall take her place, if she is saved.' These are the true abandoning of a parent and abandoning of a child. However, there is a way to transcend and free oneself from these six situations—the former and latter three. The way is the Eightfold Noble Path.

(6) "Disciples, all fears arise from ignorance. All sufferings also arise from ignorance. Whatever unhappiness there is also arises from ignorance. Whether a house has a rush roof or a grass roof, or whether it is a hut that stops the wind with plastered walls or a stately mansion with its doors and windows tightly shut, every house will burn. In like manner, whatever fears, sufferings, or unhappinesses there are, they all arise from ignorance.

"Disciples, they are the possessions of ignorant persons; they are not the possessions of wise ones. That is why you should free yourself from the three paths of the ignorant and work to attain the three paths of the wise. Disciples, the ignorant and the wise are known by their actions. Wisdom shines depending on action. The three paths of the ignorant are the evil acts of body, mouth, and mind. The three paths of the wise are the good acts of body, mouth, and mind. The three evil acts of body, mouth, and mind are the form of an ignorant person. The three good acts are the form of a wise person.

"O disciples, there are three further ways of ignorant and wise persons. The three ways of an ignorant person are the following: not to know an immoral act as immoral; even though knowing an immoral act to be such, not trying to change in accordance with the Path; and, being shown one's immoral act by another, not accepting it as such in accordance with the Path. The three ways of a wise person are to know an immoral act as immoral; to change in accordance with the Path; when shown one's immoral act by another, to accept it as such and correct it in accordance with the Path. Disciples, the ignorant and evil person by these three ways uproots his own merit. He is censured and ridiculed by sensible persons and gathers many demerits to himself. The wise and good man who possesses the three good ways does not uproot his own merit, is not censured nor ridiculed by sensible persons, and gathers many merits to himself."

3. Angulimala, the Transgressor

(1) In the country of Anga, in the town of Bhaddiya, lived Visakha, granddaughter of the elder Mendaka. When the World-Honored One travelled through Bhaddiya, she accompanied her grandfather to hear the Dharma of the World-Honored One and became a disciple of the Buddha. She later moved with her father Dhananjaya to Saketa in Kosala. She became the wife of Punnavaddhana, son of the wealthy man Migara of Savatthi. Migara's family originally followed the teachings of Nigantha, but after Visakha married into the family, she

gradually led them to listen to the teachings of the World-Honored One. Migara showed his joy by calling Visakha not his daughter but his mother. She came to be called Mother Visakha.

In this way Visakha led her husband's entire clan to become faithful followers of the World-Honored One. She herself went daily to the Jeta Grove to listen to the teachings and give offerings. In time she began to cherish the wish to build a temple herself.

She asked for advice from Queen Mallika, the consort of King Pasenadi of Kosala, in choosing the land. She then bought from the king a forest situated outside the castle, southwest of the city and northeast of the Jeta Grove. In the newly purchased forest, Visakha immediately ordered the construction of a two-story building with four hundred rooms on each floor. Moggallana took charge of the construction. It was completed only after spending a vast sum and over a period of nine months. The World-Honored One immediately moved in and used it for a four-month retreat. It was named the Eastern Monastery of Migara's Mother.

(2) One day the World-Honored One went to the home of the elder Anathapindika. For some reason or other, it was noisy in the house and loud voices were heard. The World-Honored One sat down and asked the elder the reason for the commotion. The elder answered, "My eldest son's wife, Sujata, prideful of her own family's wealth and power, does not respect her parents-in-law, nor will she do her husband's bidding. Neither does she revere the World-Honored One. That is why we sometimes have this commotion."

The World-Honored One had Sujata called and said to her, "Sujata, there are seven types of wives in the world: first, a wife like a killer; second, a wife like a thief; third, a wife like a lord; fourth, a wife like a mother; fifth, a wife like a younger sister; sixth, a wife like a friend; and seventh, a wife like a servant. Sugata, which of these seven types of wives are you?" "World-Honored One, I cannot understand the intent of your brief words. I should be fortunate were you to speak to me in more detail."

"All right, Sujata, listen well. A wife who has a defiled heart, has no love for her husband, gives her heart to another man, takes her husband lightly, and hires someone to kill her husband is a killer-wife. A wife who does not under-stand her husband's work and steals his wealth is a wife resembling a thief. A wife who does not want to work, is lazy, runs after only the desires of her mouth and stomach, uses rough language, and tyrannizes over her husband is a wife like a lord. A wife who always loves her husband, who protects her husband as a mother her child, and who protects the wealth gained by her husband is a mother-like wife. A wife who serves her husband with complete sincerity, has a sisterly heart and the sympathy of a blood relation, and serves her husband with a mind of shyness is a wife like a younger sister. A wife who greets her husband joyfully as if meeting a friend not seen in a long time, and who modestly corrects her behavior and respects her husband, is a friend-like wife. Finally, a wife who, although scolded and beaten by her husband, endures it without a defiled mind, does not feel anger, and serves her husband is a wife like a servant.

The wife like a killer, a thief, or a lord acts evilly, uses rough language, and respects no one; how can she expect good recompense after she dies? The wife like a mother, a younger sister, a friend, or a servant, because of her beautiful acts and her bodily control, will gain good recompense after she dies. Sujata, which of these seven types are you?" Because of this teaching, Sujata's prideful feelings were broken and she repented. Thereafter, until the end of her life, she vowed before the Buddha that she would be a servant-like wife.

(3) The following happened around that time. In the castle-town of Savatthi there was a learned brahmin who was respected by many and who had five hundred disciples. His main disciple was named Ahimsaka.

Ahimsaka was physically strong and very intelligent, and he had a gentle disposition. Furthermore, he was especially handsome and was loved by everyone. One day the learned brahmin's wife, while her husband was away, saw a chance to visit Ahimsaka, whom she secretly loved. She confessed her long-hidden desire and tried to seduce him. Ahimsaka was alarmed and fell to his knees, saying, "The master is like a father, and you are like a mother. Such improprieties would be extremely painful to me." The wife said, "Why is it immoral to give food to a starving person or water to a thirsty one?" Ahimsaka answered, "To become intimate with my master's beloved wife would be no different from wrapping a poisonous snake around my body and drinking its poison." The wife had nothing to say to that, so she returned to her room. In order to dispel the bitterness of her shame, she tore her dress, made herself appear pale, threw herself on the bed, and waited for her husband's return.

Upon his return, she lied to him. "Because of your admired, sagacious disciple, I have been subjected to a terrifying shame." When the master heard this, jealousy burned his heart. But his disciple was too strong to punish physically, so he schemed to give him a perverted instruction to make him commit murder. Ahimsaka would then be executed in this life and fall into hell in the next. The master called Ahimsaka to him and said, "Your wisdom has penetrated to the depths. But there is one last thing you must do." He solemnly gave him a sword and commanded, "Take this and stand at the crossroads. In one day take the lives of a hundred people. Cut off one finger from each person, and make a necklace by stringing together the hundred fingers. Thereby will you accomplish the true path."

(4) Ahimsaka took the sword. He was overwhelmed with dread and deeply distressed. If he followed his master's command, he would lose his principles. If he disobeyed his master's command, he would not be considered a good disciple. He had been told that to endeavor in pure actions—being pious toward one's father and mother, doing good for the sake of others, discarding the perverse and aiming at the right, and being tender and compassionate—was the way of a brahmin. He could not understand why his master would give him such an inhuman instruction. Having withdrawn from his master's presence, caught in an inescapable contradiction, he struggled with the agony as though it were death.

He arrived at the crossroads without knowing how and by then had lost his usual composure. His agony turned into fiery anger: blood ran in his eyes, and

his hair stood on end. Breathing fiercely and swinging the sword as if he were
an evil and malicious demon, he began killing the passersby on the road so that
a mist of blood formed. The busy crossroads soon became a mountain of corpses.
Cries of terror were heard throughout the city. Voices of rebuke and bitterness
streamed from street to street. Soon, someone ran to tell the palace authorities.
Heedlessly, the disciple gathered up the fingers of the people he had slaughtered
and made a necklace with them. He became known as Angulimala or Finger
Necklace.

The World-Honored One's disciples heard about this in the course of their
morning begging rounds, and when they returned to the Jeta Grove they told
the Buddha. The Buddha said, "Disciples, I shall go now and save him" and immediately set out. On the road, some men with a cart loaded with feed-grass saw
the World-Honored One and said, "World-Honored One, you must not take this
road. A terrible killer is barring the way." The World-Honored One answered,
"There would be no need for fear even if the whole world came at me, much less
a single killer."

Meanwhile, Ahimsaka's mother grew tired of waiting for her son's return;
so she prepared some food and went to meet him. Ahimsaka had already killed
ninety-nine people and had strung together ninety-nine fingers into a necklace.
He was looking around the deserted neighborhood for his final victim when he
saw his mother. He was about to ambush her when the World-Honored One quietly moved in and blocked him. Ahimsaka thought this was good fortune and
nodded. Brandishing his sword, Ahimsaka tried to move in against the Buddha;
but, strangely, he could not move even one foot. Without thinking he yelled,
"Monk, stop." The World-Honored One answered, "I am right here. You are the
one who is moving around." "What is happening?" Ahimsaka cried. The World-
Honored One said, "Because of ignorance, you are taking people's lives. Because
I have unlimited wisdom, my mind is tranquil even here. Out of pity for you,
I have come here."

The World-Honored One's voice was like water pouring over Ahimsaka's
burning heart. As though waking from a nightmare, he returned to himself.
He threw away the sword and prostrated himself. "World-Honored One, please
take pity on me for my delusions! I tried to attain the way by collecting fingers.
Please save me and count me among your disciples!" Thus he accompanied the
World-Honored One to the Jeta Grove, where he received the teachings and
immediately attained enlightenment. He was able to cut the bonds of birth-and-
death forever.

(5) At this time, King Pasenadi, together with his soldiers, was looking for
the killer. He went to the Jeta Grove and met the World-Honored One, who said,
"Angulimala, whom you seek, has shaved his head and beard and become a good
monk. He has reformed from his previous evil, and his heart is now filled
with compassion." The king was momentarily astonished but finally went to
Angulimala and paid his respects to him as a monk, saying, "I shall give offerings
to you, Honorable One, until the day that you die." He then said to the World-
Honored One, "You have compassion always for evil-doers, and you overcome

them and have them join the brotherhood of the Dharma. Please do as much for my people and guide us." Saying this, the king left the grove and returned to his palace.

The next day Angulimala took his alms bowl and walked the streets asking for food. But the news of his coming again struck fear in the townspeople. In one house, a pregnant woman became so frightened that she suddenly felt the baby coming and became anguished. Hearing the voices of rebuke, Angulimala felt pity. He returned to the grove, told the World-Honored One what had happened, and asked for some means to help her. The World-Honored One said, "Angulimala, go at once and say to the woman, 'I have never since birth killed anyone. If this is true, you will give birth safely.' "Angulimala was astonished and said, "World-Honored One, I have killed ninety-nine people. Would that not be double-tongued of me?" "The time you entered the way is your previous life. 'Since birth' means the time after you attained enlightenment. Therefore it will not by any means be a lie."

Angulimala immediately went to the woman's side and spoke to her, and she was able to give birth safely. However, on his return to the Jeta Grove, people who felt enmity toward him threw rocks and shards at him and injured him grievously with sticks and swords. His whole body was red with blood, and he was barely able to return to the grove. He bowed at the feet of the World-Honored One and with joy in his heart said, "O World-Honored One, when I had the name Ahimsaka, because I was ignorant I took many lives. I collected fingers whose blood could not be washed clean and gained the name Angulimala. Now I have taken refuge in the Three Treasures and have attained enlightenment. To train horses and cows, a staff is used; to train elephants, an iron hook is used. But the World-Honored One used neither sword nor staff to train this inhuman heart of mine. It is as though the moon were obscured by clouds, and after the clouds cleared away, its light shone. I have now received just recompense. Listening to the right Dharma, I have gained the eye of the pure Dharma. I am mastering the mind of forbearance, and I shall never again fight. World-Honored One, I do not desire to live; neither do I hope to die. I am simply waiting for the time to enter nirvana."

The World-Honored One heard this and praised Angulimala. "Disciples, among my disciples, the one who has the wisdom enabling him to listen to the way and quickly understand is Angulimala."

(6) Many of the disciples were astonished at Angulimala's exceedingly rapid change and asked to be told of his previous life. The World-Honored One told them the following. "In the very distant past, after the passing of Kassapa Buddha, this world was governed by a king named Mahaphala. He had a prince born to him after he grew old; he named the prince Mahabala. Even as he approached thirty years of age, Mahabala would not accept a princess; so the people called him Prince Pure. The king worried that the prince would remain a bachelor and not produce an heir-successor. Finally, he had a bell rung and the following announcement made throughout the country. 'I shall give a thousand pieces of gold to the one who is able to entice the prince to savor the joy of

sexual desire.' At this time, a woman skilled in the sixty-four ways of pleasing a man answered this call.

"Late one night, she stood at the palace gate, and like a soft spring shower she cried with bitterly sad sobs. The prince was alarmed and had a servant ask the cause of her tears. She said, 'I have been deserted by my heartless husband, and I am without anyone to rely on.' The prince felt pity for her and let her stay in the elephant stables. But she did not stop crying. He again had someone ask the cause, and she answered, 'Because of the loneliness of a person alone.' The prince finally had the woman brought to his bed. Wordlessly lying face to face, her unbearably charming figure easily tempted his masculine heart. Enraptured, the prince took her hand.

"After that, the prince gave himself up to carnal pleasure. Finally, the prince gave the command throughout the kingdom that all new brides were to be attendants in his bedchamber on their first night. One day, Suban, daughter of an elder, walked naked among a crowd. People scolded her, calling her a shameless woman. Suban answered, 'Everyone in this kingdom is a woman. What is wrong with a woman walking naked among women? Only the prince is a man, so I shall wear clothing just in his presence.' Shamed by this stinging censure, people took up weapons and advanced on the palace. Telling the king of the prince's outrageous acts, they declared, 'We want either your life or the prince's life.' The king heard this and said,

> For the sake of a family, one person is sacrificed;
> For the sake of a village, a family is sacrificed;
> For the sake of a kingdom, a village is sacrificed;
> For the sake of my true self, I shall forsake the world.

"He then turned over the prince to the people. They tied his arms up and took him outside the castle. They all got shards and rocks and beat the prince to death. As the prince was dying, he despised the king and cursed the people, saying, 'Someday I shall get my revenge.' He also said, 'I shall meet a true person and attain enlightenment.' "

Thus spoke the World-Honored One, and he said, "O disciples, that King Mahaphala is Angulimala's former teacher; the woman who seduced the prince is the master's wife; the prince is Angulimala; and the people who killed the prince then are the people killed now by Angulimala. That is, the promise made by the prince just before he died came to fruition now. He avenged himself and then attained enlightenment."

4. The Origin of Society

(1) Around that time two men, Vasettha and Bharadvaja, who wanted to become disciples of the Buddha, had been living for four months in the Eastern Monastery of Migara's Mother in Savatthi. One evening the World-Honored One stood up from his meditation, left the Lecture Hall, and was walking in the open area in back, when Vasettha, with his sharp eyes, saw him and got the attention of Bharadvaja. "Friend, let us go quickly to the World-Honored One to receive the teachings directly from his mouth." The two went up to the World-Honored One

and, after paying their respects, walked along behind him.

The World-Honored One regarded them and said, "Vasettha and Bharadvaja, you are from brahmin families. Do the brahmins ever rebuke you for becoming monks?" "O World-Honored One, they rebuke us to an extreme." "How do they rebuke you?" "World-Honored One, they say that the brahmin is an excellent caste and that others are inferior; that brahmins are born from the mouths of gods and are their inheritors. They say that we were born into this excellent caste and yet have run to the place of bald-headed monks who were born into inferior castes from the feet of the gods. This is not a good thing, they say. This is how they rebuke us."

"Vasettha, the brahmins say such things because they do not remember the past. Do not brahmin women, like women of other castes, have monthly menstruation, and become pregnant, and breast-feed their babies? They, too, are born from their mothers' wombs and not from the mouths of gods. They call themselves inheritors of the gods and superior to others, but that is simply vain contempt. Their words are untruths that give rise to defilements.

(2) "Vasettha, concerning the four castes of kshatriyas, brahmins, vaisyas, and sudras, if it is immoral for kshatriyas to kill, steal, rape, lie, slander, indulge in idle talk or fabrication, fall victim to greed or anger, or embrace a perverse view, then it must also be immoral for brahmins, vaisyas, and sudras to do so.

"Furthermore, if for kshatriyas it is a good thing not to do these immoral acts, it must be likewise so for brahmins, vaisyas, and sudras. Furthermore, even though a brahmin may be prideful of the excellence of his caste, there is not the slightest reason to be so. Knowledgeable people do not recognize any such reason. If a person of whatever caste leaves home to become a monk and masters the way, destroying the defilements and mastering the pious practice and gaining enlightenment, people call him the highest among people. The Dharma is superior to birth both in the present world and in future worlds.

"Vasettha, King Pasenadi of Kosala knows that I am one who left home from the Sakya clan, which lives within his boundaries. The people of the Sakya clan truly are subordinate to King Pasenadi and respect him as their ruler. But King Pasenadi himself follows the Buddha, serves the Buddha, and prostrates himself in reverence before the Buddha. He states that Gotama comes from a good lineage and is powerful and just, while he himself is from an evil lineage and is powerless and ignoble. He honors and serves the Dharma. The Dharma truly excels birth, in the present and in the future.

"Vasettha and others, you disciples have left homes of various castes, but if you are asked, 'Who are you?' you should answer, 'I am one of the Sakya-sons who have become monks.' Those who believe in and follow the Buddha and whose minds are sure and not vacillating, whether they be mendicants, brahmins, gods, demons, or whatever, are qualified to say, 'I am a child of the World-Honored One. I was born from his mouth. Nurtured by the Dharma, I am an inheritor of the Dharma.' The Buddha is the embodiment of the Dharma, the embodiment of the gods, the life within the Dharma, and the life within the way of the gods.

(3) "Vasettha, over a long, long span of time has this world become and ceased. When this world ceased, many people were born in the heaven of light and sound, wherein their bodies were made of mind and their food was joy; they shone from within and were flying in the air. When this world came into existence, those people came down from the heaven of light and sound into this world. But they still had their bodies made of mind, and they still fed on joy, shone from within, and flew through the air. At that time, this world was simply water and darkness. The moon shone not, nor the sun, nor the stars; there was no night, no day; there was no day, month, or year; and there was no distinction between man and woman. However, with the passing of time a land of ambrosia appeared on the surface of the water. It was like the skin formed by boiled cow's milk; with a beautiful scent, it had the color of condensed milk or butter and the sweet taste of honey.

"Among the people of that world, those who were very greedy by nature tasted this ambrosial earth with their fingers and awakened attachments. Following them, others also tasted the flavor of the earth. Finally, they scooped it up with their hands, made it into pills, and ate it. Then the light from their bodies disappeared; the moon, sun, and stars appeared; nights and days, months and years were fixed. In this way, this world came to be. Those people lived in that manner for a long time, but as they continued to eat the earth their bodies became heavy, and their appearances manifested changes. The distinction between beauty and ugliness was made: the beautiful became arrogant toward the ugly. When pride appeared in this world, the ambrosial earth disappeared. The people gathered together and lamented its disappearance.

"Vasettha, when the ambrosial land disappeared, a landskin just like a snake-skin appeared; but it disappeared, and reeds appeared. The reeds disappeared, and nonglutinous rice appeared.

"Gradually, desire began to control people's minds. If nonglutinous rice was picked in the evening, by morning there was more; if it was harvested in the morning, there was more by evening. People ate this, and gradually their bodies became heavier. The distinction between beauty and ugliness became conspicuous. As differences between man and woman became manifest, sexual desire arose. In the beginning, when man and woman touched each other, they disliked the impure feeling. But gradually, such immoralities became today's mores, and the relationship between husband and wife appeared; thus the relationship called a family came into existence.

(4) "There came to be people too lazy to harvest the rice in the morning and evening. They harvested both the evening and morning crops together in the morning; and finally they began harvesting two and three days' crops at one time. Because of that, the fields became desolate, and only a little rice remained. People lamented this situation, fixed boundaries, divided the rice, and finally fixed ownership. Moreover, people who were lazy and greedy now began stealing other people's crops and harvesting them. Thus appeared stealing, rebukes, and lying; and beating with staves began. People lamented this, and they chose one strong, just person and gave him the power to punish people who stole or

lied. The one they chose punished whomever should be punished, scolded whomever should be scolded, and banished whomever should be banished. People paid him with a share of rice. Because people were glad they chose him, they called him Mahasammata, or Great Justice; because he protected their fields, he was called a kshatriya; because he ruled according to the way, he was called a ruler or king. This was the origin of the kshatriyas.

"Vasettha, some people lamented the gradual appearance of evil and wished to remove it. They built huts of leaves in the forests, disdained fire, did not store food, and quietly spent their time in deep meditation. Others did not enter leaf huts in the forest but lived near towns and villages and produced writings. Thus it was that those who would remove evil, that is, priests, meditators, and poets, originated. This was the origin of the brahmins. Again, some men and women built homes and worked at various businesses. This was the origin of the vaisyas, the traders. Finally, some people worked at cruel, coarse work that most abhorred. This was the origin of the sudras or serfs. In this manner, the four castes originated naturally. Vasettha, from among these kshatriyas, brahmins, vaisyas, and sudras came those who abhorred these ways of life and left home to become monks. These were the people known as mendicants. They came from these four castes.

(5) "Vasettha, whether you are a kshatriya, a brahmin, a vaisya, or a sudra, if you do evil with your body, mouth, or mind, or embrace a perverse view, at death you will fall into hell like anyone else. Whatever your caste, if you do good with your body, mouth, and mind and embrace right views, you will be born in a heavenly realm after death. Whether you are a kshatriya, a brahmin, a vaisya, or a sudra, if you quell the evil in your body, mouth, and mind and master the teachings leading to enlightenment, you will certainly enter enlightenment. That is why, Vasettha, if you have left home from one of the four castes to become a disciple of the Buddha, destroyed the defilements, accomplished the pure practices, laid down the heavy burden of offences, and awakened enlightenment and became a saint, you will be called the highest among people. This is in accordance with the Dharma and not contrary to the Dharma. The reason is that the Dharma is superior to birth both in the present world and in future worlds." Vasettha and Bharadvaja were joyful over the World-Honored One's teaching.

5. The Two Wheels of a Cart

(1) The World-Honored One again returned to Kapilavatthu and gave a sermon at the Banyan Grove outside the castle grounds. "O disciples, well-known disciples of the Buddha do not make people unhappy in three ways. The three ways are to encourage people to do things with their body, mouth, and mind that are not in accord with the Dharma. Disciples, well-known disciples of the Buddha benefit people and make them happy in three ways: they encourage others to behave with body, mouth, and mind in accord with the Dharma.

"Disciples, a kshatriya who has been consecrated king by the sprinkling of water on his head at his accession should remember three places during his lifetime: the place where he was born, the place where he was consecrated king, and the place where he stood at the head of his army and won a battle. In the same way, a buddha or his disciple, too, should remember three places: the place where he shaved off his beard and hair and donned the saffron robe, leaving home and becoming a monk, the place where he learned as reality the Four Noble Truths, and the place where he destroyed all defilements and where he became enlightened in this world to the realm of freedom where there are no defilements. These are the places a buddha's disciple should remember throughout his life.

"Disciples, there are three kinds of people in the world: those without hope, those with hope, and those who have transcended hope. People without hope are those born into lowly families, such as slaves, hunters, basket-makers, cart-makers, and street-sweepers. They are poor and without food or dwelling, and they live in miserable conditions. Moreover, they are ugly and sickly. They are crippled and cannot walk. If they hear that so-and-so has been consecrated as king, they do not even think about the possibility that one of them could be consecrated as king. These are the people without hope. Those with hope are the princes of the kshatriyas who, when they reach sixteen, the age of consecration, think, 'When will I be consecrated?' when they hear that so-and-so, a kshatriya, has been consecrated and has become king. These are people with hope. And those who have transcended hope are the rulers of the kshatriyas who are already consecrated. If they hear of another's consecration, they do not raise hope anew. These are people who have transcended hope.

"O disciples, likewise, there are three kinds of Buddha's disciples: those without hope, those with hope, and those who have transcended hope. Those Buddha's disciples without hope are those who do not keep the precepts and are of bad character, who are not pure, whose behavior cannot be trusted, who conceal what they have done, and whose minds have rotted and became lustful. Even if they hear that a Buddha's disciple has destroyed the defilements and awakened to enlightenment, they do not think, 'When will I destroy the defilements and attain enlightenment?' These are the hopeless Buddha's disciples. Buddha's disciples with hope are those who hold to the precepts, have good character, and who, when they hear that a Buddha's disciple has destroyed the defilements and awakened to enlightenment, think, 'When will I be like that?' These are the Buddha's disciples with hope. Buddha's disciples who have transcended hope are those who have destroyed the defilements and awakened to enlightenment. Even when they hear that someone has attained enlightenment, they do not think, 'When will I attain enlightenment?' The reason is that they have already accomplished that hope. Disciples, these are the three kinds of Buddha's disciples.

(2) "O disciples, even a just emperor who follows the path cannot govern unless he depends on the path. The just emperor who follows the path depends on the path, respects the path, esteems and honors the path, and considers the path his lord. He provides protection, defense, and support according to the path to all his family, his people, and even to the birds and animals. Because he governs in accord with the path, the wheel of his governance cannot be overthrown.

"Disciples, likewise, the Buddha, who follows the Dharma and is the king of the right Dharma, depends on the Dharma, respects it, esteems and honors it, and considers it his lord. He provides protection, defense, and support depending on the Dharma, saying, 'You must not do these things with body, mouth, or mind. You must do these physical, oral, and mental acts.' Because he turns the supreme Dharma Wheel depending on the Dharma, no one is able to topple the Dharma Wheel.

"Disciples, this happened a very long time ago: there was a king named Pacetana. One day he called in a cart-maker and said, 'Cart-maker, six months from now we must go into battle. Can you make a two-wheeled cart by then?' The cart-maker said he could and began making the wheels. Six days before the six months were up, he finally finished one wheel. The king called in the cart-maker and said, 'There are only six days left before the six months are up. Have you finished the cart?' 'I have finished only one wheel.' 'Can you finish the other wheel in the remaining six days?' 'Of course I can.'

"The cart-maker finished the other wheel within the six days and brought it to the king. The king compared the two wheels, but he could not discern which was the one that took months to make and which only six days. The cart-maker said that he would show the king the difference and first rolled the wheel he had made in six days. The wheel continued to roll as long as it had momentum, but when the momentum was exhausted it fell over. The second wheel rolled as long as it had momentum, and, when the momentum was exhausted it stopped upright as though it had an axle through it.

"The cart-maker said, 'Great king, on the wheel I finished in six days, the rim, spokes, and hub have distortions; the wheel has knots, warps, and flaws. That is why it falls over when it has lost momentum. On the other wheel, the rim, spokes, and hub have no distortions; the wheel has no knots, warps, or flaws. That is why it remains standing even when it has lost momentum.'

"Disciples, just as the cart-maker is skilled in correcting distortions, knots, warps, and flaws in wood, a buddha is skilled in correcting the distortions, knots, warps, and flaws of physical, oral, and mental actions. Those whose physical, oral, or mental actions are distorted or warped, like the wheel made in six days, will topple because of their disregard for the teachings and rules. Those without distortions or warps, like the other wheel, will stand on the teachings and rules. Therefore, you must endeavor to rid yourselves of any distortions, knots, warps, or flaws in your physical, oral, and mental actions.

(3) "Disciples, if you are asked by a follower of another teaching whether you follow Gotama and do the pure practices in order to be born in a heaven, would you detest this question?" "World-Honored One, we would." "Disciples, if you detest the question whether you are following and practicing the path in order to have a god's life, a god's face, a god's happiness, or a god's prosperity, you should detest even more your evil physical, oral, and mental deeds. Disciples, merchants with three characteristics cannot gain wealth they do not already have nor increase what wealth they have. The three characteristics are not being enthusiastic for work in the morning, afternoon, and evening. In like manner, if a Buddha's disciple does not practice whole-heartedly in the morning, afternoon, and evening, he will not be able to gain merit nor add to what merit he may already have.

(4) "Disciples, if a merchant has eyes to see, works enthusiastically, and gains a backer, he will realize great wealth in the blink of an eye. By 'eyes to see,' I mean that a merchant must know his merchandise and how to buy it and how to sell it. 'To work enthusiastically' means to be skilled in marketing: buying goods where there is plenty and selling them where they are scarce. 'Gain a backer' means to find a wealthy person who is able to see that this merchant has eyes, works enthusiastically, is able to support his wife and children, and has the ability to repay interest; and who will lend the merchant money.

"Disciples, in like manner, if a Buddha's disciple has eyes to see, is enthusiastic in his work, and gains a backer, he will realize a great advance on the path. 'To have eyes' means to know as reality what is suffering, what is the origin of suffering, what is the cessation of suffering, and what is the way to the cessation of suffering. 'To be enthusiastic in work' means to discard evil ways and endeavor enthusiastically to create good. 'To gain a backer' means to ask an elder monk who has studied much, is knowledgeable in the Sutras, and is clear in the precepts to reveal the concealed, to illuminate the dark, and to remove doubt. If a Buddha's disciple gains these three things, in a very short time he will realize great advances on the way."

6. The Thicket of Human Nature

(1) The World-Honored One returned to Rajagaha and held that year's retreat at the Bamboo Grove. At the time, the World-Honored One was fifty-five years of age, twenty years since his completion of the path. At this retreat, the World-Honored One called his disciples together and said, "Disciples, I am approaching old age. From now on, I wish to have an attendant at all times. I should like to have you suggest someone from amongst you."

Because of these words from the World-Honored One, Sariputta, Moggallana, Anuruddha, and Kaccayana all volunteered and asked that they be allowed to serve as his attendant, but the World-Honored One refused them. Moggallana knew that the World-Honored One was well disposed toward Ananda; so he consulted with the other disciples and then went to Ananda to encourage him to volunteer. However, Ananda refused, saying it was too great a responsibility. Moggallana pressed him several times until finally he said that he would be his attendant under three conditions: that he could refuse offerings of robes and food given to the World-Honored One even if given to him; that he would not necessarily accompany the World-Honored One to the home of a lay person; and that he could have an audience with the World-Honored One at any time. The World-Honored One granted the three requests. From then on Ananda served the World-Honored One as his attendant, following him as a shadow its form.

(2) The World-Honored One went to Vesali and then east to Campa, where he stayed with many disciples on the bank of Lake Gaggara, at the outskirts of the city. One day the young elephant trainer Pessa and the wandering ascetic Kandaraka visited the World-Honored One at the lakeshore. Kandaraka was surprised when he saw the disciples in silent attendance around the World-Honored One. Amazed, he said, "It is amazing that the World-Honored One has

so properly trained his many disciples! Did the buddhas of old train their disciples as you have? And will the buddhas of the future do as you have done?"

"Kandaraka, it is just as you say. Among these disciples are many who have already destroyed the defilements, accomplished what must be done, and realized the enlightenment of the saints liberated by true wisdom. Furthermore, there are many who are in the midst of practice, whose mastery of the precepts is beautiful, whose wisdom is quick, and whose minds are always in the four stages of mindfulness. The four stages of mindfulness refer to examining single-mindedly and ardently the impurity of the body, perception as suffering, the impermanence of the mind, and the insubstantiality of things. By doing so, one conquers the greed and despair of the world."

Pessa, the young elephant trainer, upon hearing this, said, "O World-Honored One, it is truly an excellent teaching! These four stages of mindfulness are for the sake of purifying people, of transcending suffering, sadness, and affliction, and of awakening wisdom and realizing nirvana. O World-Honored One, although I am a householder, I shall always practice the four stages of mindfulness and conquer worldly greed and despair. That the World-Honored One, in this thicket of human nature, in the midst of man's evil and deceit, knows what is of benefit and what is not, is truly laudable. Man's nature, like a thicket, is very difficult to untangle. In comparison, the natures of animals are easily known. The reason I am saying this is that I am reminded of handling elephants. Between the stables and the castle gates of Campa, elephants show all their characteristics: the perverse, the wicked, the deceitful, and the sly. On the other hand, the menials, servants, and helpers we employ all differ in thought, speech, and action and are truly difficult to know. In this thicket of human characteristics, in the midst of man's evil and deceit, to know what is beneficial to man and what is not is truly laudable."

(3) "Pessa, it is just as you say. Man's characteristics are like a thicket, while the characteristics of animals are easily known. In this world there are four types of people: those who bring suffering upon themselves, those who cause others to suffer, those who bring suffering upon both themselves and others, and those who do not cause suffering either to themselves or to others, and who, in this world, free themselves from desire and experience tranquillity, cool peace, and joy. Pessa, among these four types of people, which would bring you joy?" "World-Honored One, those who cause suffering to themselves, to others, or to both themselves and others would not bring joy to my heart. Those who do not cause suffering either to themselves or to others, and who, in this world, free themselves from desire and experience tranquillity, cool peace, and joy, would bring joy to my heart." Pessa rejoiced at the World-Honored One's teaching. He stood and paid obeisance, circled him to the right, and returned home.

(4) After Pessa left, the World-Honored One looked around at his disciples and said, "Disciples, the young elephant trainer Pessa is an intelligent person. Had he stayed a little longer while I explained the four types of people in more detail, he would have gained great benefit. However, even with what I have said up to now, he has gone home with great benefit.

"Disciples, those who cause their own suffering are those who, having received an erroneous teaching, cause pain to their own bodies, fast and wear rough clothing, and follow austere practices. Those who cause suffering to others are slaughterers of sheep and pigs, fishermen, hunters, thieves, jailers, and all others who do cruel things. Those who cause suffering to themselves and to others are those in power like kings who follow erroneous teachings and imitate monks who leave home, covering themselves with deerskin, smearing their bodies with butter and oil, scarring their bodies with deer antlers, moving to a new palace with their queens and assistants, sleeping on bare ground, drinking milk meant for calves and giving some to their queens and assistants, sacrificing cows, goats, and sheep to the gods, and having trees and grass cut; and their servants, slaves, and stewards all do the work in fear of being executed. These are the people who cause suffering to themselves and others.

"Disciples, those who cause suffering neither to themselves nor to others, and who, in this world, free themselves from desire and experience tranquillity, cool peace, and joy, are those who listen to the Buddha's right teaching, leave their homes and become disciples of the Buddha, do not kill, have compassion, do not steal, do pure practices, do not tell lies, do not take the lives of grass or trees, lessen their desires and know sufficiency, and prepare themselves with the right ways and receive the pleasure of knowing that they are without transgressions. Even though they see things with their eyes, hear sounds with their ears, smell fragrances with their noses, taste flavors with their tongues, and feel and touch things with their bodies, their minds do not cling, and they perceive joy in controlling the five senses. Whether they are moving, standing, sitting, or lying down, they do so consciously. They enter quietude, and with pure minds they enjoy seats far separated from desire. They attain the wisdom to know that they have transcended this birth and that there will be no further births of delusion for them. In this manner, they experience tranquillity, cool peace, and joy, and they live the excellent life."

Chapter 4

THE FOUR NOBLE TRUTHS

1. Becoming Free of the Defilements

(1) The World-Honored One again returned to Savatthi and dwelled in the Jeta Grove. One day at dusk, Cunda arose from deep meditation, went to the World-Honored One, and said, "World-Honored One, there are many views concerning the self and the world. What should be the thought of a Buddha's disciple so that he can discard these views?"

"Cunda, there are many views concerning the self and the world, partisans of each trying to influence the others. But if one correctly sees things as they are—this is not 'mine', this is not 'I' this is not my 'self'—one can discard those views.

"Cunda, someone may enter into all kinds of meditations and think that he is then dwelling in a condition free of the defilements. However, in this teaching, it would not be said that this is a condition free of the defilements. It is called dwelling in the joy of the present or, sometimes, dwelling in tranquillity.

"Cunda, to free oneself of the defilements, one must think: 'People injure others. They kill, steal, commit perverted sexual acts, tell lies, are double-tongued, are foul-mouthed, indulge in useless talk, are greedy, harbor angry minds, have perverse views, do various evils, and harbor evil minds. I shall never do these things.' Cunda, to free yourself of the defilements, this is what you must think.

"Cunda, simply to raise a good mind has great benefit. To manifest that mind in bodily or oral actions has even greater benefit. Metaphorically, as there might be a flat road next to one that has high and low spots, or a smooth wharf next to a bumpy one, if, in the vicinity of a person who injures or kills others, there is a way that teaches that one should not take life, one is given a chance to enter the path with this good teaching.

"Furthermore, all evil actions drag one down lower and lower; good actions raise one higher and higher. For the one who injures or kills others, the person who does not injure or kill becomes the way to rise up. Cunda, if you yourself are stuck in the mud, you cannot pull someone else out of it. If you have not yourself gained control over your five senses and have not destroyed your defilements, you cannot teach someone else to control his five senses and destroy his defilements. In this same way, for someone who injures and kills others, one who does not injure or kill becomes the cause to have him enter the state without defilements.

"Cunda, I have taught you how to destroy the defilements, how to raise a good mind, how to replace a bad way with a good way, how to elevate oneself, and how to enter the state free of defilements. Cunda, with these I have done what a loving, compassionate teacher must do."

(2) One day, an old brahmin bent with age came to the World-Honored One and said, "World-Honored One, I am old and shall soon die. However, I have not done all that needs to be done. I have not rid myself of fear. Please give me a teaching that will benefit me for all eternity."

"O brahmin, it is truly just as you say. In this world where you are carried away by old age, sickness, and death, controlling the body, mouth, and mind is your protection as you go toward death; it is your foundation, your lamp, and your support.

> Life is short, and time runs on.
> There is no shelter for one carried off by old age.
> If you see the fear of death ahead,
> Practice that which has merit
> And you will have your shelter.

(3) On another day, a brahmin came to the World-Honored One and said, "World-Honored One, it is said that your teaching bears fruit in this life. In what way does it bear fruit in the present? What does it mean to say that it has a direct effect, that one can say, 'Come and see,' and that it is a teaching worth holding in one's mind?"

"Brahmin, if your mind is burning with greed, you hurt both yourself and others. Thinking that you are hurting both yourself and others, your mind knows suffering and torment. If you rid yourself of greed, you no longer have these sufferings. Brahmin, it is the same with the mind crazed by anger or the mind deluded by ignorance. If you rid yourself of anger and free yourself from ignorance, thoughts of injury will disappear. These are the fruits of the present. This is the direct effect. This is why you can say, 'Come and see.' This is why it is the teaching worth holding in your mind."

(4) Again on another day, a brahmin named Sangarava visited the World-Honored One and said, "O Venerable One, Gotama, because I am a brahmin, I offer sacrifices and have others offer sacrifices. By offering these sacrifices and having sacrifices offered, because these sacrifices have been prepared, we are able to enter the path of the virtues that come out of the bodies of the sacrificed animals. It is truly a great virtue that both self and others receive. To the contrary, those who leave their families and become mendicants control only their own bodies, make tranquil only themselves, and destroy only their own desires. Therefore they enter a path of virtue only for themselves alone."

"If that is the case, brahmin, answer my questions as you will. What do you think? A Buddha appears in this world and teaches the following: 'Come. This is the path. I shall show you the supreme nirvana to which I myself have awakened. If you also master the path, you will be awakened to that supreme nirvana.' If many people follow this Buddha's teaching, and hundreds, thousands, even hundreds of thousands practice this path, brahmin, would you still say the virtue of a monk is only his alone?" "World-Honored One, Gotama, if that is the case, the virtue of a monk extends to many people."

At that point, Ananda, who had been standing there, said, "Brahmin, which of these two ways do you think is better? Which do you think is less difficult, has greater effect, and is more beneficial?" The brahmin evaded this question by saying, "Persons like the venerable Gotama and the venerable Ananda are worthy of my offerings and my praise." Ananda said, "Brahmin, I am not asking to whom you should give offerings or praise. I am asking which of these two ways is the better." He asked the question two and three times, but the brahmin gave the same answer and tried to evade his question.

(5) The World-Honored One watched this exchange and decided to save the brahmin from his predicament. He asked, "Brahmin, what did the people talk about today when they gathered at the palace?" "Gotama, today at the palace they were saying that in the past the monks were fewer than they are now, while people with divine powers were more numerous than they are now."

"Brahmin, there are three kinds of divine powers of which you speak: the superhuman divine powers, the divine power to read the minds of others, and the divine power to teach. The superhuman divine powers refer to those superhuman feats such as becoming many although only one and vice versa, appearing and disappearing, being able to go through hedges and walls, being able to go through mountains as though they were air, being able to go in and out of the ground as though it were water, being able to walk on water as though it were earth, being able to touch with the hands the sun and moon that possess great augustness and power, and being able with this physical body to go to the worlds of the gods. These are the superhuman divine powers.

"The divine mind-reading power is the power to know what another person is thinking by observing signs. Also, without depending on any sign, one is able to know what is being thought by a person, a god, or an animal by listening to the sounds that they make. One can say what is being thought without depending on anything. This is what is known as the divine mind-reading power.

"The divine teaching power enables one to make another think in one way and not in another, to discard that and to concentrate on this. This is the divine teaching power. Brahmin, which of these three divine powers do you think is the best?"

"Gotama, the superhuman divine powers and the divine mind-reading power affect only the person using them. Only he has them, so they are like illusions. On the other hand, the divine teaching power affects both self and others, and both self and others have it. Therefore among the three divine powers, it is supreme. Gotama, I have received a truly excellent teaching. I believe that you possess these three kinds of divine powers. Are there others who possess these powers?" "Brahmin, of course there are. Disciples who possess these three kinds of divine powers number more than one hundred, two hundred, and even five hundred. There are many more." "Gotama, where are these disciples of yours now?" "Brahmin, they are right here in this gathering." Sangarava rejoiced in this teaching and vowed that he would be a faithful devotee for the rest of his life.

2. Maha-Kaccayana

(1) Around that time, Maha-Kaccayana was staying on the shores of Lake Kaddama, near the city of Varana. One day the brahmin Alamandanda came to Maha-Kaccayana and after greeting him asked, "Venerable One, why does a warrior argue with a warrior, a brahmin with a brahmin, or a merchant with a merchant?" "Brahmin, it is because they are bound by greed, they are drowning in it, and they are stabbed and beaten by it."

"Venerable One, is there in this world anyone who is free from greed?" "Brahmin, at this time, to the east in Savatthi, lives the World-Honored One of this world, who is a Buddha. He is free from greed."

Upon hearing this, the brahmin got up from his seat, put his robe on one shoulder, put his right knee to the ground, put his palms together, faced the direction of the World-Honored One, and three times paid homage, saying, "I take refuge in the Buddha, the World-Honored One." He praised him, saying, "Oh, the World-Honored One has freed himself from greed." He rejoiced at Maha-Kaccayana's teaching and vowed to be a faithful devotee for the rest of his life.

(2) Again, at another time, Maha-Kaccayana was staying in the Gunda Grove near the Madhura. One day, the brahmin Kandarayana visited him and said, "Venerable one, I have heard that you do not bow to elder brahmins, that you do not rise from your seat to greet them, and that you do not even offer them a seat. If this is true, is it proper conduct?"

"Brahmin, the Buddha, the World-Honored One, taught an interpretation regarding the old and young. According to this, even if a brahmin is eighty or ninety, if he is addicted to desire, burning in its flames, seeking it insatiably, he is immature. Again, even if the brahmin is young in age, if he does not indulge in desire or does not seek it, he must be said to be mature and wise." Hearing this, Kandarayana stood up from his seat, put his robe over one shoulder, touched his head to the feet of the young disciples of the Buddha who had been standing there, and said, "You are truly elders. I am nothing but a youngster." He vowed to become a faithful devotee for the rest of his life.

(3) The World-Honored One was staying in the Jeta Grove. One day, Savittha and Maha-Kotthita went to Sariputta to discuss the Dharma. Sariputta said, "There are three kinds of people in the world: those who experience enlightenment with their whole bodies; those who realize enlightenment through wisdom; and those who realize freedom through faith. Which do you think is supreme?"

Savittha answered, "I think that among these three the person of faith is supreme, because faith is supreme."

Maha-Kotthita answered, "I think that the person who bodily experiences enlightenment is supreme, because his deep meditation is supreme. However, Sariputta, who do you think is supreme among these three kinds of people?"

Sariputta said, "I think that the seer is supreme, because wisdom is supreme. But, friends, we have each given his opinion; let us go to the World-Honored One and ask him. We should remember the World-Honored One's answer." They went together to the World-Honored One and told him about their discussion.

"Sariputta, it is difficult to say definitely who among these three kinds of people is supreme, because of the following situations. The person of faith may become a saint, while the bodily enlightened and the seer may not. On the other hand, the bodily enlightened person may become a saint, while the seer and the person of faith may not. Or the seer may become a saint, while the others may not. Therefore it is difficult to compare the three and say definitely which is supreme."

(4) The World-Honored One one day said to his disciples, "Disciples, it is possible to distinguish three kinds of sick persons: the sick person who cannot get well even if he gets nutritious food, proper medicine, and an appropriate nurse; the sick person who will get well even if he does not get nutritious food, proper medicine, or an appropriate nurse; and the sick person who will get well if he gets nutritious food, proper medicine, and an appropriate nurse, but otherwise will not. Disciples, because there is this third type of sick person, the first and second types are also given a sick person's diet, medicine, and nursing.

"In the same way, there are three kinds of people with respect to the teachings: those who, even if they meet a Buddha and receive his teachings, cannot advance to the good way; those who can advance to the good way, even if they do not meet a Buddha or receive his teachings; and those who will advance to the good way if they meet a Buddha and receive his teachings but who will not advance to the way if they do not meet a Buddha and receive his teachings. Disciples, because there is this third type of person, the Dharma is taught as well to the first and second types.

(5) "Disciples, there are people with three kinds of minds: those whose minds are like wounds, those whose minds are like lightning, and those whose minds are like adamant.

"Those whose minds resemble wounds are those who are quick to anger and quick to despair, who are impatient, and who are just like wounds that when touched by a stick or a broken piece of pottery exude pus. Those whose minds resemble lightning are those who know truly what is suffering, what is its cause, what is its cessation, and what is the way to the cessation of suffering. When lightning flashes, its light enables one to see clearly the form of a thing. Those whose minds resemble adamant are those who have destroyed the defilements and attained enlightenment. They are like adamant, which is able to cut gemstones, rock, or any other thing. In this world there are these three kinds of people."

(6) Once, when Ananda went to the World-Honored One, the World-Honored One said, "Ananda, I am one who rigorously condemns any evil actions of the body, mouth, or mind." Ananda asked, "World-Honored One, if one breaks the prohibitions and does an evil act of the three, what retribution will there be?"

"Ananda, if one does an evil act of the three, one will torture himself, be censured by thoughtful people, get a bad name, have an agitated mind as one dies, and will enter the hells after death. This is his retribution. Ananda, I am one who strongly urges the three good actions of the body, mouth, and mind."

"World-Honored One, if one does the three good actions, what is the recompense?"

"Ananda, one will not torture himself, will be praised by thoughtful people, will gain honor, will not have an agitated mind as he dies, and will be born into the heavens after death. This is the good recompense."

(7) The World-Honored One went on, "Disciples, here are two excellent paths: stopping and examining. If you master stopping, your mind will be prepared to free itself from defilement. If you master examining, you will increase wisdom and be able to free yourself from ignorance. If your mind is defiled by desire, your mind cannot be calmed; if it is defiled by ignorance, wisdom cannot be increased. Freeing oneself from ignorance depends on increasing wisdom.

(8) "Disciples, let me explain to you the grounds on which evil persons and good persons stand. On what ground do evil people stand? Evil people do not know indebtedness or gratitude. Not knowing indebtedness or gratitude is bad. On what grounds do good people stand? Good people know indebtedness and gratitude. Knowing indebtedness and gratitude is good.

"Disciples, no matter how much you try there are two people to whom you can never repay your indebtedness. The two people are your father and your mother. Even if you were to live for a hundred years, and during those hundred years you carried your mother on your right shoulder and your father on your left shoulder, and rubbed their bodies with perfume, bathed them, massaged them, and attended to their impurities, you would still not be able to repay your indebtedness to them. Even if you were able to get them raised to the ranks of royalty, it would not be enough. The reason is that your father and mother brought you into this world, have nourished and brought you up, and have given you much assistance. However, if you make them aware of their unbelief and lead them to faith, make them discard bad ways and stand on right ways, and make them free themselves from greed and lead them into the way of giving, you will be able to repay your indebtedness to your father and mother. Furthermore, you will be able to go beyond mere repayment.

(9) "Disciples, in this world there are two people of endeavor that are superior and honorable: a householder offering to monks robes, food, cushions, and medicine; and a monk himself destroying the defilements. You must endeavor to destroy the defilements.

(10) "Disciples, you must hold to the determination not to become less diligent in reaching your goal. Even if your blood and body dry up, as long as you have skin, muscle, and bone, you must use all your manly strength and effort. Through this determination, you will, in the not too distant future, realize the goal for which you left home and became monks. You will realize pure actions in this world.

(11) "Disciples, here are two views: the view of attachment with respect to the way of binding; the view of loathing with respect to the way of binding.

Through the view of attachment, one cannot rid oneself of greed, anger, and ignorance; therefore one cannot become free of birth, old age, death, grief, sadness, suffering, affliction, and torment. One must continually cry in suffering. Through the view of loathing, one rids oneself of greed, anger, and ignorance; thereby one becomes free of birth, old age, death, grief, sadness, suffering, addiction, and torment. One becomes able to raise a joyous voice in true pleasure.

"Disciples, here are two types of ways: the black way and white way. The white way protects the world and the black way destroys it. The two kinds of black way are shamelessness toward oneself and shamelessness toward others. The two kinds of white way are to know shame toward oneself and toward others.

"Disciples, here are two types of power: the power of mindfulness and the power of practice. The power of mindfulness refers to keeping in mind that evil actions of the body, mouth, and mind have their evil effects in the present and in the future, and becoming free from the three evil actions. The power of practice refers to mastering the practices that free one from greed, anger, and ignorance; mastering the way to enlightenment and deep meditation; and freeing oneself from evil and adhering to good."

3. The Seat of the Four Noble Truths

(1) The World-Honored One left Savatthi going south and stayed in a simsapa grove, in the country of Alavi, making the grass his bed. From time to time, he taught his disciples and said, "Disciples, if you lay down the beards of rice or wheat, and place your hand or foot on them, you cannot hurt yourself even if you try. This is because the beards are not standing. In like manner, if you try to destroy ignorance and realize wisdom without correcting your mind, you will not be able to do it. The reason is that the mind is not properly set. Disciples, if, on the other hand, you stand the rice and wheat beards and try to hurt yourself, you can. In like manner, if your mind is correct, you can destroy ignorance and realize wisdom.

(2) "Disciples, if you stand on the bank of a muddy lake, you cannot see the pearl oysters or small rocks on the bottom, or the schools of fish, or anything else in the turbid water; similarly, one cannot know what is beneficial to oneself, to others, or to both oneself and others, and cannot really manifest a pure knowledge, if one's mind is beclouded.

(3) "Disciples, among trees, none is so pliant and useful in making things as teak. In like manner, there is nothing as well ordered as the flexible mind that has been cultivated and trained.

"Disciples, there is nothing as easily turned as the mind. The mind is originally pure. It is defiled by defilements that come from outside. Therefore it is possible for the mind to free itself from the defilements. People who are without wisdom do not know that the mind is originally pure and is defiled by defilements that come from outside. That is why people without wisdom do not train their minds. Disciples of this teaching truly know this as reality, so they train and prepare their minds.

(4) "Disciples, those who, for even a short time, practice compassion, increase it, and are mindful of it dwell in the deep meditation that is not meaningless, follow the master's teachings, and are worthy of all offerings. Even more so are those who practice often.

"Disciples, whether the way be good or bad, the mind is the guide. The mind is the guide for these ways, and these ways follow it.

(5) "Disciples, negligence, indolence, desire, insatiability, incorrect thinking, bad friends, all of these bring forth bad things that are not yet born. They destroy good things that are already born. Effort, exertion, having few desires, knowing what is enough, right thinking, and good friends, all these bring forth good things that are not yet born, and they destroy bad things that are already born.

"Disciples, the increase in the number of clansmen, in treasure, or in fame is not worth talking about. But the awakening of knowledge is excellent. You must strive to increase it.

"Disciples, he who has perverted views will fall into hell after he dies; if he has right views, he will go to the heavenly realm. Because a person with perverse views acts in accordance with those views, everything—his physical, oral, and mental actions, his hopes and desires, and all the workings of his mind—invites the sad effect of suffering. If one sows nimba seeds in the ground, whatever the flavor of the soil or the water, all will taste bitter because the seeds are bad. But for the person with right views, everything—his physical, oral, and mental actions, his hopes and aspirations, and all the workings of his mind—invites beautiful and joyous effects. If one sows sugar cane seeds in the ground, whatever the flavor of the soil or the water, all will taste and smell sweet, because the seeds are good.

(6) "Disciples, in this world, pleasurable flower gardens, beautiful forests, and clear lakes are few; while hills, ridges, precipitous places, tree stumps, and bramble fences are many. Likewise, sentient beings born on land are few, while those born in water are many. Those born into the human realm are few, while those born into the four evil realms are many. Again, those born in the middle land are few, while those born in the hinterlands and in barbarian lands are many.

"Disciples, in the same way, those who are intelligent and have wisdom and who have the power to discriminate between good and evil are few. Those who know little and are ignorant, those born deaf or mute, and those who do not have the power to discriminate between good and evil are many. Those who have the eye of holy wisdom are few, while those who are enveloped by darkness and enter delusion are many. Disciples, in the same way, those who see a buddha are few, while those who do not see a buddha are many. Among those able to see a buddha, only a few are able to listen to him explain the Dharma; many are unable to listen. Further, among those who hear the Dharma, only a few receive it; many do not receive it.

"Disciples, again, even if they receive the Dharma, those who are able to understand the meaning are few; many cannot understand. Even if they receive the Dharma and are able to understand the meaning, few practice in accordance with the Dharma; many do not practice. Likewise, those who are alarmed when they should be alarmed are few; many are those who are not alarmed. Few are they who endeavor correctly in order to alleviate sadness; many do not. Few are they who, in order to enter nirvana, concentrate their minds on a single point and attain a tranquil mind; many do not. Again, few are they who come to appreciate the principle of the Dharma and of freedom; many do not. Disciples, you must endeavor to know and appreciate these things.

(7) "Disciples, there is virtue in taking refuge in the Three Treasures, the Buddha, the Dharma, and the Sangha. The Buddha is supreme among all people; there is no one who can match him. He is like ghee, refined from cow's milk, the best among all dairy products. Because one takes refuge in this supreme Buddha, one gains supreme virtue and is born in the human realm and receives its happiness. The Dharma is disclosed and manifested by the Buddha and surpasses all other teachings. It, too, is like ghee, the best of all dairy products. Because one takes refuge in the best Dharma, one gains supreme virtue and is born in the human realm and receives its happiness. The Sangha is the harmonious brotherhood of the Buddha's disciples. It is superior to all other groups. This, too, is like ghee, which surpasses all other dairy products. Because one takes refuge in this supreme Sangha, one gains supreme virtue and is born in the human realm and receives its happiness."

4. Indebtedness to One's Parents

(1) A man of Vesali, Sabbakama, wearied of life in the floating world, left his wife, and went to the World-Honored One and became a monk. He was given a problem that would force him to practice deep concentration and insight, and he returned to a quiet place, corrected his actions, disciplined his mind, and refined his wisdom. Living as a wanderer, he went from place to place. After some time, he returned to his birthplace and visited his own home. His wife had lost her former looks and had grown thin and haggard, and her long-suffering figure had become pitiful. She greeted him with tearful eyes and sat off to the side. Deeply affected by her condition, he was overcome by a feeling of pity. He almost lost control of his mind and returned to lay life; but as a good horse will start running at the mere shadow of the whip, he became alarmed and left. Using this as an opportunity, he exerted himself in practice and finally awakened to enlightenment.

His parents-in-law, rejoicing that Sabbakama had come to the neighborhood, wanted him to return home so that they might again see their daughter with a cheerful face. They took their beautifully dressed daughter to the temple and entreated Sabbakama to return to lay life. Sabbakama refused their request in verse:

> This two-legged body embraced by men is impure and has a loathsome smell; various defilements imbue it and ooze out from here and there.

> As a deer is caught by a trap, a fish by a hook, or a monkey by a lime, a worldling is enthralled by her form.

A pleasing complexion, voice, taste, scent, and touch, stirring the five desires, are all inherent in woman's form.

His mind enthralled by the form, a worldling grows intimate with it and widens his own fearful grave, thus amassing the seeds of delusion.

As one might kick the head of a snake with one's foot, righteous people who would repulse these things avoid the world's poisons with right mindfulness.

Seeing the misery of desire and the tranquillity of freedom, I discard desire and free myself from the defilements of the mind.

Ananda met Sabbakama's parents-in-law and their daughter. Worrying about Sabbakama, Ananda asked if they had met. They answered, "We met him, but we might as well not have." Ananda asked if they had spoken with him. They answered, "We spoke with him, but we might as well not have." Ananda sang the following song and returned to the temple. "As one who seeks water in fire, fire in water, or things in space is foolish, so is one foolish who asks a person without desire to have desire."

Sabbakama met Ananda and told him about his enlightenment. Ananda sang in praise of Sabbakama's enlightenment, "One who well protects pure practices, masters the path, and destroys delusion is a true disciple of the Buddha."

(2) The World-Honored One crossed over the Ganges, onto the southern bank, followed the river to Baranasi, and stayed in the Deer Park. One day the World-Honored One taught his disciples the following. "Disciples, there are three kinds of people in the world: those who are like words engraved on stone, those who are like words written on sand, and those who are like words written on water. Those who are like words engraved on stone are people who often get angry and harbor grudges for a long time. Their anger is like words engraved on stone that do not disappear, even though rained and blown upon, and last for a long time. Those who are like words written on sand are people who get angry often, but their anger is like words written on sand—they disappear quickly. Those who are like words written on water are people who get angry, but their anger is like words written on water that disappear immediately without trace; they do not hold traces in their minds and are filled with feelings of harmony.

(3) "Disciples, cloth from the fibers of Makaci, whether new, used, or old, is ugly, rough to the touch, and cheap. Old rags from this cloth are good only for wiping jars or throwing away in the trash. Likewise, a buddha's disciple, whether he is a novice, someone well into his career, or an elder, who does not hold to the precepts and has a bad character I call ugly. If you associate with him and assume his views, you will be forever disadvantaged and unhappy, because he is what I call rough to the touch. If he receives robes, food, cushions, or medicine from a faithful lay person, that faithful one's offering cannot gain a large recompense, because he is what I call cheap. Further, if this kind of elder disciple disparages another within the Sangha or leads him astray, other disciples will say, 'What use is it for you to disparage another? Do you not think that you are the one who should be disparaged?' Hearing this, he will become angry and spew out very

rough words, and finally he will be expelled from the Sangha. This is what I call being thrown into the trash.

"Disciples, the silk cloth of Kasi, whether new, used, or old, is beautiful, smooth to the touch, and expensive. An old piece of silk is used to wrap jewelry or put inside a box of incense. Likewise, whether he is a novice, someone well into his career, or an elder, if a disciple holds to the precepts and is of good character, I call him beautiful. If you associate with him and assume his views, you will be benefitted and happy forever, because he is what I call smooth to the touch. Further, if he is given robes, food, cushions, or medicine from a faithful follower, the donor, through that, will earn a great recompense, because he is what I call valuable. Disciples, if this kind of elder says something within the Sangha, the disciples will say, 'Be quiet everyone, the elder is giving us the teaching and precepts.' Disciples, therefore, you must learn not to become like Makaci cloth but to become like Kasi silk.

(4) "Disciples, some say, 'One receives recompense strictly according to what he himself does,' but if that were true there would be no need for pure actions, nor would there be an opportunity to destroy suffering. Disciples, there are some who commit a seemingly insignificant immoral act and fall into hell. Again, there are some who commit the same immoral act but receive full recompense in this life. In the next life they receive not even the least suffering, let alone extreme suffering. The former occurs when a person does not master his body, the precepts, his mind, or wisdom; when he has little virtue and is small-minded, he writhes in agony at the smallest thing. This kind of person will fall into hell for even a minor immoral act. In contrast to this, the person who masters his body, the precepts, his mind, and wisdom, the person who has much virtue and is broad-minded and filled with immeasurable good, even if he commits a minor transgression, will receive full recompense in this life. In the next life, he will receive no extreme suffering or even the least suffering.

"Disciples, if you put a small amount of salt into a small bowl of water, the water will taste salty; if you put it into the waters of the Ganges, it will not taste salty. Again, some will have to go to prison over a very small amount of money, while others will not have to go to prison over the same amount of money.

"Disciples, therefore, a person may fall into hell for even a minor transgression, while another may receive full recompense in this life and not receive a painful effect in the next life. Therefore it is not that one receives recompense in correspondence with his actions but that one does something and receives the recompense that he must receive. Only in this way is there a necessity for doing pure acts; and only in this way does an opportunity to end suffering become manifest.

(5) "Disciples, gold is beautiful, but its ore, mixed with earth, sand, and gravel, is dirty. This dirty ore is put into a basin and washed many times. The still dirty ore is washed many more times until it becomes clean. In this way, the impurities gradually are got rid of until only the gold dust remains. The goldsmith puts this gold dust into a heated crucible and melts it with a bellows. At first it is hard to melt; the impurities do not come off and will not soften. It does not shine; it is

brittle and cannot be worked. Repeated application of the bellows will finally melt it and eliminate the impurities. Its sheen appears and it will become pliable enough to be worked. The goldsmith now uses this at will to stretch into gold wires or to make earrings, bracelets, or gold chains.

"Likewise, disciples, one who is to master deep meditation is in the beginning very impure because of the evils of his body, mouth, and mind. The intelligent one gradually rids himself of impurities, destroying them and making them nonexistent. However, he still has the mental impurities of desire, anger, and harmfulness. He rids himself of these, too. Even then, he still has the thought not to be made lightly of by his relatives, by his country, or by others. He rids himself of this impurity but still is conscious of things. Because of this, his meditation does not become pure, and his mind does not concentrate on one point. His meditation is still not proper. Disciples, the mindful and intelligent one gradually destroys these impurities and attains right meditation, divine powers, and wisdom; he destroys the passions and attains enlightenment. He is able to effect his goals as he wishes.

"Disciples, he who would master deep meditation should become absorbed, should endeavor, and should discard the thought of discrimination. If he is to be mindful about being absorbed, because there is fear of becoming lazy, he must be mindful to endeavor. If he is to be mindful about endeavoring, because there is the fear of becoming agitated, he must be mindful of discarding the thought of discrimination. Further, if he attempts to discard the thought of discrimination, there is the fear that he will not move toward destroying the passions. Therefore if he always keeps these three characteristics in mind, his mind will become flexible and useful for his work and take on brilliance and become healthy. This is as when a goldsmith puts gold ore into a crucible, heats it with fire, wets it with water, and tests it from time to time. If he just heats it with fire, the gold will become ash. If he just wets it with water, it will just get cold. If he just keeps testing it, it will be of no use. Only when he heats it with fire, wets it with water, and tests it from time to time will the gold eventually glitter and become flexible and be useful for work. Only then will the goldsmith be able to craft it as he wishes. Disciples, one who would master deep meditation must keep in mind these three characteristics. If he keeps the three characteristics in mind in this way and practices, he will be able to attain various divine powers and wisdom."

5. The Mind and the World

(1) Once many bodhisattvas gathered like clouds from the ten directions, and they praised the Buddha's virtues:

  (i)   For a limitless time have we seen the Buddha, but we have not gained the truth of the right Dharma. As our net of doubt widens, we are bound in the prison of death and birth. We are blind and do not see the Buddha.

  (ii) The Buddha's wisdom is deep and hard to fathom. If we do not know the true Dharma, all the world seems deluded. Those without wisdom, since they see all things falsely, do not see the Buddha. As one cannot see treasures in the dark without light, even the wise cannot understand the teachings without someone to explain them to him. If one's eyes are not clear, one cannot see even exquisite colors; an impure mind cannot understand the Buddha's teachings.

(iii) Although all things are empty, the ignorant think that they have substance. They go around and around in the cycle of death and birth. If they think that something bad is superior to the Dharma and do not know the right way, how can they know their own minds? From perverse thoughts pile up increasing evils. Having no view is the true view. Look closely at the true Dharma. In one who sees the truth in the Dharma, there is no view.

(iv) In one who hears the excellent teachings, the light of pure wisdom is born. Because this light shines throughout the world, one sees all buddhas. If one calculates that there is a person, his mind treads a dangerous path. There is no true master in things; it is simply a provisional word. He who is deluded does not know himself; he acts as though he really exists. Because the Buddha is free from being and non-being, the deluded cannot see the Buddha. The defilements of the mind hinder the eye of wisdom, and they are unable to see people of enlightenment.

For an immeasurably long time, one has been going around and around in the ocean of death and birth. Transmigrating is death and birth. Not transmigrating is nirvana. Death and birth and nirvana are not two things. He who chases temporary names sees these two as different; confused in the path of the sages, he cannot know the unsurpassed way.

(v) Even if a person says, 'Buddha,' if he has perverse thoughts, he does not see the Buddha. If a person comes to know that tranquil form as the real Dharma, he sees an enlightened person and transcends the way of words. Even though words are used to explain the Dharma, the real form is not manifest. Only the thought of oneness allows one to see the Buddha and the Dharma.

The past, future, and present have always been tranquil. If one knows this, he is called a Buddha.

(vi) Even should you experience immeasurable suffering, listen well to the Buddha's voice. If you do not hear his name, you will not experience any joy.

Indeed, the reason one goes around and around in the ocean of suffering from time immemorial is that one does not hear the name of the Buddha. Not seeing things from a deluded perspective, awakening to things as they really are, he who becomes free from characteristics born of conditions is called an enlightened one.

In the past, present, and future, all things are without characteristics. Being without characteristics is indeed the substance of the Buddha. If one sees in this way the deep principle of all things, one will see the unfathomable true characteristics of the Buddha.

Should one become enlightened, if there is nothing to be enlightened about, this is indeed the Buddha's true Dharma. In things we cannot find anything on which we can depend; all arise from the coming together of causes and conditions. There is no maker, nothing made; things are born simply from the thought of karma. Therefore there is no thing that is grasped; this is truly the Buddha's ground. In things we cannot find anything on which we can depend. Enlightened people are without attachment.

(vii) Great is the Buddha's light; brave is the unsurpassed hero; to benefit deluded people did he appear in this world.

The Buddha, looking compassionately at this world, sees the suffering people on evil paths; without the Buddha, there is no one to save them. Were the Buddha not in this world, people would not have true joy. The Buddha came into the world and blessed us with joy.

Those who see the Buddha gain great merit. Those who rejoice at the Buddha's name tower like stupas in this world.

(2) Then a bodhisattva rose from his seat and explained the Dharma: "All you Buddha's children, he who seeks the way must first meet the difficult-to-meet Buddha and listen to the Dharma. Further, upon seeing suffering people, he must rouse the mind to seek the way, get close to good friends, and work hard to hear as much as possible. He must not seek in another the Dharma that he hears but should understand it with respect to himself. He should free himself from desire and master deep meditation, attain the deep principle of the right Dharma, and see that all things are impermanent, suffering, empty, and without self, and that they are without joy.

"Furthermore, he should trust the Buddha, see into the Dharma, and, with his mind in tranquil deep meditation, contemplate people, the Buddha's land, this world, karmic recompense, or transmigration and nirvana. He should be mindful, when practicing, that the good root that is gained is for the sake of saving all people and leading them to enter nirvana.

"O Buddha's children, a bodhisattva dwells with a right mind on the thought of determination. Whether he hears someone praise or castigate the Buddha, he is unmoved, for his mind is fixed on the Buddha's doctrine. Whether someone praises or slanders one who seeks the way or his practice, he is unmoved, for his mind is fixed on the Buddha's doctrine. Again, in relation to people, if he hears that they are capable or not, or that they are with or without defilement, he is unmoved, for his mind is fixed on the Buddha's doctrine. Again, with respect to the Dharmadhatu, if he hears that it is measurable or not, or that it is complete or destroyed, or whether he hears a positive or a negative way of teaching, he is unmoved, for his mind is fixed on the Buddha's doctrine. He will know the circumstances under which people receive births, the many passions, and the many habits. He will gain the wisdom of the means to distinguish the immeasurable things, and he will know how to teach both worldly truths and the Absolute Truth.

"Buddha's children, a bodhisattva will here gain the great power of wisdom. He will shake and move the world, illuminate the world, sustain it, and completely adorn it; he will know people's minds and actions, and through various skillful means he will discipline them well and liberate them.

(3) "Buddha's children, in seeing all things, a bodhisattva sees no discriminated characteristics; he sees them as being equal to space, because he knows that all things are without self-nature. Again, a bodhisattva contemplates the limitless power of the Buddha and thereby is furnished with the Buddha's great compassionate mind and nourishes it. He thinks about people and does not reject them; he practices good actions and does not seek recompense.

"Buddha's children, if a bodhisattva sees matters in this way, with just a little skillful means, he will gain all the merit of the Buddha. He will know the true nature of all things and be endowed with wisdom. He will become enlightened to all of these, relying on himself as a lamp and not depending on others.

(i) Through the Buddha's ultimate power, he will gain the non-retrogressive stage, illuminate the world with the light of compassion, and become the people's refuge. Because the Buddha safeguards him, his merit is immeasurable. Because he always contemplates the realm of the Buddha, the Buddha sprinkles him with the nectar of wisdom. His faith is like adamant, and he knows his debt to the Buddha. Equipped with all skillful means, he moves through all worlds; he is indeed a true Buddha's child.

With a dispassionate mind, he removes the thirst of desire; with great compassion, he thinks of people unhinderingly. He leads people to attain fearlessness. As he acts in accord with the truth, he is equal to the Buddha.

(ii) Since he is possessed of wisdom and strength from faith, and since his mind is just and pure, he is certain to understand the truth. In order to have all future worlds prosper, he will even suffer the tortures of hell many times. Because of compassion, he will accord with the world and explain the teaching of the unfathomable Dharma.

(iii) His body will fill the Dharmadhatu, and though he is in accord with a person's mind he will be free from the discrimination of subject and object; he will have no discrimination between the defiled and the pure. He will forget the distinction between being bound and being free. He will simply aspire to be joyful together with other people. All people of the world think of power. He is not afraid, because he enters with wisdom. Although space can be measured, the greatness of the mind of enlightenment is difficult to know. This is because great compassion is immeasurable and fills the ten directions.

(iv) The buddhas of all lands praise the awakening of the minds of the bodhisattvas, who consider immeasurable merit as their adornment and whose nature, when they reach the pure shore, is not different from that of the buddhas.

All the joys experienced by the buddhas of all worlds and by the people are born from the thought of enlightenment.

This thought adorns the land of a buddha; this thought gives people the supreme wisdom.

(4) "Buddha's children, a bodhisattva who has gained the merit of awakening the mind to seek enlightenment must free himself from an ignorant mind and endeavor to destroy the negligent mind. That is, he must practice in accordance with the teachings, discard trifling and negligent actions, seek the Dharma without tiring of it, and have a true and real view of the Dharma that he hears. He must give rise to supreme wisdom, enter the Buddha's realm of freedom, and make his mind tranquil and not distracted or agitated. Whether he hears something good or evil, like the great earth, he will not raise a thought of joy or grief.

Whatever kind of person he meets, he will not be a hindrance. Further, he will revere and make offerings to his teachers, good friends, and Dharma masters.

"Buddha's children, a bodhisattva will further master the following kinds of practices and bring joy to the Buddha. He will endeavor with all his might and not retrogress. He will not begrudge his life nor seek material gain. In knowing all things, he will be unhindered, like the sky. Using skillful means, he will see into all things, and he will enter all Dharmadhatus everywhere. He will be unbiased in knowing things; and he will always have a great vow. He will gain the pure wisdom to be forbearing, and he will know the gains and losses associated with all things.

"Buddha's children, if bodhisattvas master the way in this manner, the Three Treasures will long flourish. The reason is that when bodhisattvas teach people to awaken their minds to seek the way, the Buddha Treasure will not be exhausted. Further, when they show various wonderful Dharmas, the Dharma Treasure will not be exhausted. When they keep the dignity and the teachings, the Sangha Treasure will not be exhausted. Again, because they praise all great vows, the Buddha Treasure will not be exhausted. Because they teach the principle of causes and conditions, the Dharma Treasure will not be exhausted. Because they love each other with mutual respect and preserve all the precepts, the Sangha Treasure will not be exhausted. Again, because they sow the seed of Buddhahood in the fields of people's minds and make the bud of enlightenment appear, the Buddha Treasure will not be exhausted. Because they protect the right Dharma without regard to their lives, the Dharma Treasure will not be exhausted. Because they govern the masses tirelessly, the Sangha Treasure will not be exhausted. In this way, because bodhisattvas master the way without deviating from the teachings of the buddhas of the three periods, they cause the Three Treasures to flourish."

(5) Just then, even more bodhisattvas gathered like clouds from the ten directions, and each offerred these verses.

(i) Because pure light illuminates the ten directions, all people are able to see the Buddha.
    The Buddha is now in the palace of Yama. Such an event rarely occurs in this world. In this world and in the palace of Yama, people see the Buddha. His merit is deep and unfathomable. One body is innumerable bodies; the innumerable bodies are one. Depending on people's needs, he moves unhindered throughout the ten directions.

(ii) Though an immeasurable time passes, difficult it is to meet with a teacher of peoples and gods. The light of wisdom removes the darkness of the world. The wonderful Dharma benefits people. Over and over through immeasurable time, he mastered the practices and attained enlightenment and saves people widely. People who see the teacher of peoples and gods escape the suffering of the evil ways.

(iii) The light from a summer moon in a cloudless sky illumines immeasurably. Even people with eyes do not know how far, much less the sightless. The Buddha's light is likewise. Coming from nowhere and going nowhere, it is not born, nor does it die. It is empty and silent, and it is without substance. As with the light, all things too are likewise. Things from the beginning have never had a self-nature. If one realizes this true nature, one's mind is finally without delusion.

(iv) The body of the Buddha fills the Dharma realm. Without leaving his seat, he reaches everywhere. He who trusts this teaching will be forever free of the suffering of the three evil paths. The person who hears of the unhindered power of the Buddha and single-mindedly trusts it attains enlightenment and expounds the Dharma. Even throughout immeasurable time, this Dharma is hard to meet with. If one does hear it, it is because of the Buddha's vow.

(v) Among all things there is no distinction; only the Buddha knows. Just as there is no distinction between the nature of gold and its color, there is no difference between the Dharma and non-Dharma, nor between sentient and nonsentient beings. Just as past forms do not exist in the future, there is no distinction among all things. Metaphorically, although numbers extend from one to infinity, they are all numbers and there is no discrimination. Depending simply on the consciousness of discrimination, it is as though there is a distinction of numbers. Again, although there is no difference in the space of the ten directions, people create a distinction. If one clings in that manner, one will never see the Buddha.

(vi) The three periods of sentient beings—past, present, and future—are subsumed in the five aggregates. The five aggregates originate because of karma. That karma originates because of the mind. Because that mind is like an illusion, sentient beings are no different from illusions. The world does not create itself, nor is it created by another. As long as one does not know the nature of true reality, one will be caught in the rut of birth and death. The turning of the world is the turning of suffering. As long as people do not know this, the wheel of birth and death will forever turn. Both the world and the non-world are not real. People are without wisdom and are ignorant; they cling to the forms of all things indiscriminately. The five aggregates of the three periods are called the world, but it exists only because of delusion. If one destroys the world, one leaves the world. One does not know the deteriorating five aggregates and thinks them permanent without reason, but the five aggregates are empty and temporary and are not truly real. The reality of things is tranquil and does not change. It is free of discrimination in the end.

　　The world is already empty; the Buddha and the Dharma, too, are empty. The nature of these three is without substance. Those who are rid of perverse views and see the true reality clearly see the Buddha always appearing before them.

(vii) The nature of all forms and actions, though one thinks and looks hard, cannot be known. It is likewise with the nature of consciousness and with the Buddha's body. Although the immeasurable, wonderful body appears in all countries, the body is not the Buddha. The Buddha is not the body. Only the Dharma is the body. It pervades all things. If one sees the pure Buddha body, one will have no doubt about the Buddha's doctrine. If one sees that the nature of true reality is equal to nirvana, one sees the Buddha and is always peaceful. He is called a son of the Dharma king.

(viii) A skillful painter uses colors to make any form, and the form is not different from the color. But the form is not one with the colors, and the colors are not one with the form. One can know this because the form apart from its outline is without color. The mind is not the color of the picture; the color of the picture is not the mind. However, apart from the mind there is no picture; apart from the picture there is no mind. That mind is not permanent. Because it is measureless, it cannot be measured. It manifests all colors, but the colors are ignorant of each other.

Exactly as even a skillful painter does not know the mind of a painting, so it is with the nature of the Dharma. The mind is like a skillful painter; it draws the five aggregates variously. Within all worlds, there is nothing it does not create. As the mind, so the Buddha; as the Buddha, so sentient beings. These three—mind, the Buddha, and sentient beings—are without distinction. All buddhas correctly know that all things evolve from the mind. People who understand this see the true Buddha.

The mind is not the body; the body is not the mind. However, they practice all Buddha deeds, and their freedom from encumbrances has no comparison. If you wish to know the Buddha of the three periods, see that the mind creates all buddhas.

(ix) The taken, the seen, the heard, the thought—all are unattainable. Whether measurable or not, the limits are difficult to ascertain. These two are without anything to grasp. He who teaches what cannot be taught deludes himself. What is not one's own cannot please people. Although the sky is pure and without color, it manifests all colors; yet its nature is unseen. In like manner, the person of great wisdom shows unlimited forms yet is not known to the consciousness. There is nothing to be seen. In hearing the Buddha's voice, although the sound of the voice is not the Buddha, he cannot be known apart from the voice. This principle is very deep. If one is able to discern it well, the path is certain to be his.

Introduction

The Buddha continues his effort to spread the Dharma throughout India, travelling over 300 miles southeast from Savatthi in Kosala to Rajagaha in Magadha. He also travels over 200 miles from Savatthi to Kosambi in the southwest. As was the usual method of travel in those days, he walked these long distances, resting at the small villages along the way or in the forest, teaching the Dharma to whomever came to listen. Savatthi is also the location of Rajakarama, a convent for nuns, built by the Kosala king Pasenadi (Skt: Prasenajit) within the city as a protection for the female disciples of the Buddha. Also located at Savatthi is the Pubbarama, the Eastern Garden, established for the Sangha by Visakha outside the city near the east city gate. Anathapindika's Monastery in the Jeta Grove also lay outside the city but near the south city gate.

Chapter 1 Section 5 contains the 423 verses of the Pali Dhammapada. It is an anthology of verses on Buddhist ethical thoughts and precepts. There are three versions of this widely known collection: Pali, Sanskrit, and Prakrit (popular dialect). The Pali version has been translated into many languages. Because of the simplicity of expressions and the poetic beauty of the verses, the Dhammapada is highly valued. In ordinary terms, 'dhamma' means discipline, or virtuous living, and 'pada' means the path; thus, the Dhammapada is the Path of Virtuous Living.

In Chapter 2 the reader will encounter passages from the Sukhavati-vyuha Sutra, a Mahayana (Larger Vehicle) teaching of simple faith in the saving power of Amitayus Buddha's Primal Vow. This sutra presents the bodhisattva idea of attaining supreme enlightenment not for one's sake alone but for the benefit and welfare of all sentient beings. In contrast, arhatship is the highest spiritual goal of monks and nuns, and is the individual's liberation from attachment to conditioned existence.

In this Mahayana sutra, Ananda asks the Buddha the reason for his glowing countenance. In reply, the Buddha relates the story of Dharmakara, a king who lived many eons ago who became a monk and vowed before the Buddha Lokesvararaja that he would become a Buddha and establish a Buddha-land where all beings who aspire to attain enlightenment can be born and also become buddhas.

Dharmakara makes 48 vows, only 15 of which are included in Chapter 2, Section 4 (shortened in the Japanese text), but these 15 vows represent the most significant of Dharmakara's declarations. The 8th of the listed vows corresponds to the 18th vow, called the primal (fundamental) vow, because the 48 vows can be distilled into this one essential vow that promises anyone who would single-mindedly rely on him as the Amitayus (Eternal Life) Buddha would be born in his Land of Peace and Happiness (Sukhavati) where conditions would be conducive for the proper practice that leads to enlightenment. Since no impurities can exist in the Buddha-land, it is also called the Pure Land.

The readers who encounter the Pure Land doctrine for the first time, may undoubtedly be puzzled with the idea of relying on the power of a Buddha, which seems to contradict the doctrine of following the path of right living and mental concentration that leads to enlightenment as exhorted by the historical Buddha. However difficult it may be to understand this concept, the truth is that it is founded on the original teachings and principles of Gotama Buddha, whose goal was, indeed, to rescue all sentient beings from the life of suffering. The Pure Land doctrine is generally considered to be an "easy path" for ordinary beings, who are unable to follow the difficult "path of the sages" followed by the early disciples during the time of the Buddha.

The Four Noble Truths do include the Eightfold Path as the way that leads to the cessation of suffering. However, the followers of the Mahayana doctrine realized that they needed to grasp the essential spirit and not simply conform to the letter of the Buddha's teaching. That spiritual essence, they believe, is the universal compassion and wisdom underlying the Dharma. Thus, they embodied this compassionate spirit into the story of Dharmakara, who symbolizes the Buddha's search and effort that led to his full awakening to the true nature of reality, and who became Amitayus Buddha, a symbol of limitless compassion and wisdom. After eons of great discipline, he had accumulated incalculable merits that can be transferred to all beings for their salvation. This mythological story can be understood in the context of the interrelated oneness of life, in which the Buddha's supreme vitality and insight can flow into all other beings who, by letting go of their self-centered desires, can open their receptive minds to receive the benefits of the Buddha's enlightenment.

Seen from the modern perspective, it is clear that if we are not in harmony with the flow and rhythms of the universe, we sense a disturbing dysfunction. Whether we recognize it or not, the rhythms in our brains are primarily caused by planetary movements, such as the rotation of the earth on its axis, its revolution around the sun, and the movement of the moon in relation to the earth. Living organisms, including human beings, have adapted to these rhythms by evolving their own biological rhythms. If there is a disruption in these rhythms, for example when we change our work hours from day to nighttime, we experience physical and psychological effects. Jet lag is a modern form of biological disruption. We are a combination of cycles piled one on top of another; thus, the restoration of the proper functioning of the nervous system leads to emotional health. We need to maintain harmony with the universal rhythms of life as well as maintain the ecological balance in life for the health of the earth itself. The ancients seem to have been aware, from their own primitive but wise perspective regarding the interrelatedness of life, that it was imperative for all beings to become one with the dynamic flow and rhythms of the universe. We can do this only by letting go of our attachment to selfish needs and desires that cause stress and unhappiness not only for ourselves but also pain and even violence to all other beings that exist in the world.

The oft-repeated allegory of the arrow is found in Chapter 4, Section 4. The Buddha was often asked such questions as whether the world was eternal or not, whether the body and spirit are one or not, whether one exists after death or not, and so forth. The Buddha refused to answer these questions, because he felt that discussions of such matters were not conducive to the practice that leads to enlightenment. He gives the example of a man pierced by a poisoned arrow. If this person should insist that the doctor must not pull out the arrow and treat him until he knows all about the archer and the kind of arrow that was used, and so forth, the man would surely die. A person must first take the essential step and avoid pointless speculation.

The Buddha explains in Chapter 4, Section 6 that in order to remove one's passions and awaken the supreme wisdom that leads to enlightenment, one needs to understand the Four Noble Truths: 1. There is suffering in life, such as old age, illness, death, parting with loved ones, being with a person one dislikes, failing to get what one desires, etc.; 2. There is the cause of suffering, which is the craving for pleasures and for the continued existence of the objects of our desires; 3. Cessation of suffering can be achieved by the total elimination of craving and liberation from attachments to things that are impermanent; 4. There is the Eightfold Path that leads to the true awareness of life: right view, right thought, right speech, right action, right livelihood, right effort, right mindfulness, and right meditation. This Middle Path that avoids the two extremes of religious effort is first encountered in Book 1, Chapter 3, Section 1:4.

Chapter 1

KNOWING THE DHARMA

1. Karma

(1) After travelling around the country of Kosala, the World-Honored One returned to Savatthi. One day he said to his disciples, "Disciples, people all wish that there will be no unpleasant things and hope for pleasant things to increase, but in actuality the reverse happens. Why is this so?" They replied, "World-Honored One, you are fully enlightened to the essence of the Dharma; may we ask you to explain it to us? We have complete faith in your teaching."

"My disciples, you would do well, then, to listen attentively. Suppose there is a man who has seen neither a sage nor a good person, or who has known neither the holy teaching nor the path that ought to be practiced. Since he does not know what he should and should not do, he will not do what he should and will do what he should not. Because of this, unpleasant things will increase for him and pleasant things will not come to be. But since my disciples see the sages and know the path, unpleasant things decrease for them and pleasant things increase.

(2) "My disciples, there are four paths: the path that leads to suffering in this present life and also in future lives; the path that leads to suffering in this life but to happiness in future lives; the path that leads to happiness in the present life but to suffering in future lives; and the path that leads to happiness in both the present life and future lives. Those whose minds are covered over with ignorance are unable to see, as they really are, the path that leads to suffering both in this life and in future lives or the path that leads to pleasure in this life but to suffering in future lives. Thus they do not endeavor to avoid these, and as a result, unhoped for things increase and hoped for things diminish. These are the natural states of the unwise. Again, since they know as it is neither the path that leads to suffering in the present life but to happiness in future lives nor the path that leads to happiness in both this life and future lives, they do not make an effort to follow the path, a failing that leads to the increase of unhoped for things and the decrease of hoped for things. These, too, are the natural states of the unwise.

"My disciples, in contrast to this, men of wisdom see these four paths as they are. They do not do what they should not do and do what they should do. As a result, hoped for things increase for them and the unhoped for things diminish. These are the natural states for those possessed of wisdom.

"My disciples, what is the path that leads to unhappiness in both the present and future lives? Here is a man who takes life, steals, and commits adultery and other evil deeds; these deeds will lead to his own suffering. Because of these deeds, he suffers in the present life and will fall into evil realms in future lives. The path that leads to pleasure in the present but to suffering in the future is that path on which, while committing evil acts such as killing, stealing, adultery, and the like, one thinks that they will not cause suffering but will bring pleasure and joy. The truth is, even if they do bring pleasure in the present, they will surely cause birth in evil realms in lives to come. The path that leads to suffering in the present life but to happiness in future lives is that path on which one discards the evil deeds mentioned above, abandons greed and anger, and cherishes right views. The life thus lived may cause suffering in the present but will bear good results in future lives. The path that leads to pleasure and joy both in the present life and in future lives is that path on which, by living it, one experiences joy in this life and good results in lives to come.

(3) "My disciples, by way of analogy, a person shows a gourd that contains poison to another person, who holds his life dear, saying, 'Here is a gourd that contains poison. You may drink it if you wish, but it has a bad taste and a foul smell. And you will die if you drink it.' The one who practices the path that leads to suffering both in the present life and in future lives is like the man who drinks out of this gourd.

"Again, there is poison in food that appears beautiful and is delicious. A person who holds his life dear and dislikes suffering comes and eats it even though he was told that the food contained poison. He is like one who practices the path that leads to pleasure in the present life but to suffering in future lives.

"Suppose there is some dirty water in which are mixed various medicines. Upon being urged, a person suffering from jaundice drinks this. Both the taste and the smell are unbearably unpleasant, but the pains from the disease are greatly alleviated. He is like the person who practices the path that leads to suffering in the present life but to joy in future lives.

"Finally, a person suffering from dysentery, upon being urged, takes a medicine made of butter, molasses, sugar, and ghee. The medicine is excellent both in taste and in smell, and when taken it cures the disease. He is like the person who practices the path that leads to pleasure and joy both in the present and in future lives.

"My disciples, like the sun shining brightly in the cloudless autumn sky and enlightening the universe, the Dharma that gives joy to the present life and future lives alike will dispel the arguments of the false mendicants."

(4) Again, one day the World-Honored One beckoned his disciples and said, "O disciples, even though a dyer takes a piece of stained cloth and dyes it yellow, red, or blue, the cloth cannot be dyed in a beautiful manner. The reason for this is that the cloth was originally stained. In a similar manner, the outcome of a stained mind will also, without fail, be bad. O disciples, if you wash the cloth clean and then dye it yellow, red, or blue, the cloth will be dyed in

a beautiful manner. The reason is that original cloth was washed clean. In a similar manner, the outcome of a clean mind will also, without fail, be good.

· "My disciples, greed, anger, a concealing mind, self-deceit, jealousy, flattery, deception, stubbornness, retaliatory intention, arrogance, sloth, boasting, and negligence are the dirt and dust of the mind. He who identifies this dust and dirt of the mind and cleanses it will attain a firm conviction in the Buddha, the Dharma, and the Sangha. He will destroy the selfish mind, open and gladden his mind, and feel his body relax, and his mind will achieve concentration and calmness. He will not be harmed even if he eats a large and delicious meal made of green vegetables, curry, and refined rice. For him, all dust and dirt will be cleansed. He is like a dirty cloth that becomes clean when it is rinsed in clear water, or gold that becomes increasingly pure when processed in a furnace. He will practice the four immeasurable virtues, compassion, mercy, joy, and equanimity, will come to know that there is a liberation beyond thought, and will extinguish defilements and attain enlightenment."

(5) The brahmin Sundarika Bharadvaja, who was listening nearby, asked the World-Honored One, "World-Honored One, do you go to the river Bahuka?" "Brahmin, what is there at the river Bahuka?" "World-Honored One, the river Bahuka is said to refine coarse acts, give merits, and wash away evil karma."

The World-Honored One said, "There are nonsensical legends that have grown around the Rivers Bahuka, Sundarika, and Gaya; but what causal relations do they have with the evil acts of man? If, by bathing in my teaching, all attain peace of mind, do not kill living beings, do not tell lies, do not take things not given, do not have greed, and do have faith, this is true bathing. This has nothing to do with the rivers."

The brahmin rejoiced upon hearing the teaching and asked for permission to be a disciple. He attained enlightenment not long after.

(6) One day the Buddha told his disciples, "My disciples, one cannot make progress along my path as long as he does not discard the five fetters of the mind and loosen the five bondages of the mind. The five fetters of the mind are first, having doubts about one's teacher and not having faith in him; second, being unsure about the teaching and not having faith in it; third, having doubts about the Sangha and not having faith in it; fourth, having doubts about learning and not having faith in it; and fifth, being irritated by friends and becoming depressed. Unless these five are discarded, one does not have zeal, lacks patience, and does not exert effort.

"The five bondages of the mind are first, not being free from greed that begets thirst for earthly things; second, not being free from greed in regard to one's body; third, being bound to greed for material goods; fourth, indulging in naps after filling one's stomach with food; and fifth, being bound to the desire to be born in a heavenly realm by doing pure deeds. Unless these five are loosened, one will not have any zeal, patience, or incentive to exert effort.

"My disciples, if one severs the five fetters of the mind and loosens the five bondages of the mind and, in their stead, relentlessly cultivates the five powers of aspiration, effort, mindfulness, concentration, and wisdom, eventually one will reach the peace of enlightenment, like a chick cracking the shell from the inside just at the moment that the hen warming the egg is hoping for it to do so. With the addition of effort, if one fulfills these fifteen paths, one will be able to destroy defilements, attain enlightenment, and arrive at unsurpassable peace."

(7) One day, the brahmin Janussoni came to the Jeta Grove to the Buddha and said, "World-Honored One, I am destined to die, and there is no one that does not fear death." The Buddha said, "Brahmin, among those who must die, there are those who fear and those who do not fear death. Those who fear death are the ones who do not discard greed in regard to the five desires and cannot free themselves from attachment. When they become seriously ill, they suffer, agonize, grieve, and cry, beating their chests, thinking that they have to leave all those things that they hold dear. Also, those who cannot discard the greed for and attachment to their physical bodies, when they are down with a serious illness, suffer, thinking that they will have to leave their bodies. Also, those who have done only evil deeds, not doing any good actions and not taking refuge in the Dharma, grieve and agonize when they face death. Those who have doubts about the right Dharma, too, will fear death. However, brahmin, those who are free from the greed of the five senses and from attachments, who do not commit evil deeds but seek refuge in doing good deeds, and who have no doubts about the right Dharma do not have fears even if they fall seriously ill."

(8) At one time a disciple asked, "World-Honored One, by what is this world guided, pulled, or controlled?" The Buddha said, "Your query is very good. This world is guided, pulled, and controlled by the mind." The disciple asked further, "World-Honored One, we are frequently told to listen well and practice the Dharma. What does the phrase mean?" The Buddha again praised the disciple: "Your query is very good. I have given you many teachings in the forms of sutras, verses, songs, predictions of attainment of enlightenment, odes of joy, accounts of previous lives, Jatakas, rare accounts, and elaborations. However, one can be said to have listened well and practiced the Dharma by knowing the meaning of and following the teaching in accordance with a four-line verse." "World-Honored One, I am also frequently told to learn the teaching and acquire wisdom to penetrate into its meaning. What does this mean?" The Buddha said, "Your question is very good. If a disciple hears, 'This is suffering, this is the cause of suffering, this is the annihilation of suffering, and this is the way to the annihilation of suffering' and penetrates into the true meaning of these truths with his own wisdom, then he is said to have the wisdom to learn and to penetrate to the essence of the teaching." The disciple asked, "World-Honored One, what does it mean to be a person of sagacity and great wisdom?" The World-Honored One again praised the disciple, saying, "Your query is very good. One who does not harm himself, does not harm others, does not harm both himself and others, but benefits both himself and others and thinks of the well-being of the community is a person of sagacity and great wisdom."

(9) While he was staying at the Jeta Grove Monastery, the World-Honored One often went to the lecture hall in the house of Migara's mother in Savatthi.

At one uposatha he was sitting in the hall surrounded by his disciples. He looked at the quiet assembly and said, "My disciples, there is no one talking in this assembly. This is noble and good. This is an assembly that you do not see in ordinary gatherings. This assembly is worthy of receiving offerings and homage; it is a field of good fortune unequalled by any in the world. This is an assembly worth attending, travelling miles with provisions on one's back. In this assembly there are those who have attained the rank of the gods, of Brahma, of the immovable stage, and of the sages.

"The ones who have attained the rank of the gods are those who have been freed from evil ways and have entered the first, second, third, or fourth stage of meditation. Those who have reached the rank of Brahma are the ones who have acquired the four immeasurable minds of compassion, mercy, joy, and impartiality. The ones who have entered the immovable stage are the ones who have attained the four formless contemplations of infinite perception, infinite space, nothingness, and neither thinking nor non-thinking. Ones who have entered the rank of sages are the ones who have already understood the truths of suffering, the cause of suffering, the annihilation of suffering, and the way to the annihilation of suffering."

(10) At one time, Ananda, with the permission of the Buddha, stayed alone at the town of the Koliya tribe called Saputha, where he imparted the teachings to those who gathered. He told them, "My dear Koliyans, four pure disciplines have been taught by the Buddha, in order to cleanse the body, eliminate sorrows, free one from sufferings, and attain enlightenment. The discipline of the precepts is to adhere faithfully to the precepts. The discipline of the mind is to free oneself from desire and the unvirtuous and to enter various meditative states. The discipline of perception is to view things as they are, that is, to the cause of suffering, the cessation of suffering, and the path that leads to the cessation of suffering. The discipline of emancipation is to embody these pure disciplines of the precepts, mind, and perception and to liberate the mind from defilement. These four pure disciplines purify people, eliminate sorrow, take leave of suffering, and lead to the attainment of enlightenment. For this reason were they taught by the Buddha."

2. The Brahmin Called Deer Head

(1) The World-Honored One, after making tours of the country, returned to Rajagaha and entered the Bamboo Grove. About that time, there was a brahmin called Deer Head in the country of Kosala. He was skilled in the art of divination by examining skulls. He would recite an incantation, strike the skull, and guess where the person was reborn. Even three years after a person's death he could tell the realm of the person's rebirth. He disliked being encumbered with family life and joined a group of mendicants. He had a large following because of his skill in divination and was travelling from country to country. When he heard that the World-Honored One was staying at the Vulture Peak in Rajagaha, he went to pay a visit and prepared to try his skill against the Buddha.

The World-Honored One then descended from the peak, and, accompanied by Deer Head, went to a burial mound. He picked up a skull and said to Deer Head, "I am told that you are adept in the art of divination by examining skulls. Are you able to tell whether this skull belonged to a man or a woman?" Deer Head, after reciting a mantra and striking the skull, said, "This was a man." "From what disease did he die?" "He died of various diseases but he could have been saved if he had taken myrobalan fruit mixed with honey." "In what realm is he reborn?" "He has sunk down into the three evil realms."

The World-Honored One picked up another skull and asked, "Was this a man or woman?" "It was a woman." "Of what illness did she die?" "She died of a difficult delivery." "Where is she living now?" "In the realm of beasts." Several skulls were shown to him, and Deer Head was able to tell whether they were male or female, the causes of their deaths, and where they were reborn. Then the World-Honored One picked up another skull and showed it to him. It was the skull of a disciple of his who had attained nirvana. Deer Head, with his mind concentrated, recited the mantra, tapped the head with his fingers, and struggled to discern to whom the skull belonged, but to no avail. He finally asked the Buddha. The World-Honored One said, "This belonged to a disciple of mine who attained nirvana." The brahmin Deer Head thought that the Buddha had some mystic power and wished to learn it from him. The World-Honored One agreed to teach him on the condition that he become a monk; and so Deer Head became a yellow-robed disciple. He faithfully followed the Buddha's instruction and finally attained enlightenment. Then he did not need to know to whom skulls belonged. He expressed his state of enlightenment in verses:

> Following the path taught by the Buddha,
> I freed myself from defilements.
> Now I have transcended the world of desire.
> Being guarded by the Buddha,
> My mind became free.
> With all fetters severed,
> My enlightenment will not waver.

(2) During the time the World-Honored One was staying at the Vulture Peak, there were a number of famous wandering monks gathered in a grove by the shore of Sapphia Lake. One day the World-Honored One visited the place. At the time these monks were discussing the question, "What is the truth in this world?" They mentioned this to the World-Honored One, who gave the following discourse: "Dear wandering monks, I have attained by myself four truths and am now expounding them. They are that all living beings are born from ignorance; that all objects of the five desires are impermanent, pain-causing, and changing; that all existences are impermanent, pain-causing, and changing; and that there is no 'I' or 'mine'. These four are true and are not false. I was awakened to these brahminic truths and expound them to others."

(3) On another day, the World-Honored One said to his disciples, "My disciples, there are two persons that appear in this world for the sake of the benefit

and happiness of all: they are the Buddha and the universal monarch. These two descend to this world as teachers of mankind. Their deaths are mourned by many. They are worthy of stupas built in their honor.

(4) "My disciples, there are two types of people who slander the Buddha. One secretly harbors ill will, and the other harbors wrong belief. There are, again, two types of people. One maintains that the Buddha has taught something that in reality he has not. The other maintains that the Buddha has not taught something that in reality he has.

(5) "In this world there are two who are not afraid of thunder. One is the disciple of the Buddha who has extinguished defilement, and the other is the lion who rules over beasts. Again, there are two types of exceptional people. One is the person who bestows blessings on others, and the other is the person who knows and responds to blessings.

(6) "My disciples, there are two other people that are rare: one who rejoices and one who makes others rejoice together with him.

(7) "My disciples, there are two who are never satisfied, one who hoards everything that he gets, and one who throws away everything. In this world, there are two who are easy to satisfy, one who does not hoard but uses things to advantage, and one who does not throw things away but uses them.

(8) "O disciples, there are two causes that lead to the arising of greed. One is a thing that satisfies desire, and the other is erroneous thought. There are two causes that lead to the arising of anger. One is a thing that does not satisfy desire, and the other is erroneous thought. There are two causes that lead to the arising of wrong views. One is listening to teachers of misguided teachings, and the other is erroneous thought. There are two causes that lead to the arising of right views. One is listening to teachers of the right path, and the other is right thought."

(9) One day Princess Cudi, accompanied by five hundred maidens, came into the presence of the World-Honored One and said, "World-Honored One, my brother Cunda tells me that, whether man or woman, if one takes refuge in the Buddha, the Dharma, and the Sangha and does not kill, does not take anything not given, does not commit adultery, does not lie, and does not drink intoxicants, one will not fall into an evil realm. Now I wish to ask the World-Honored One this question. How am I to take refuge in the Buddha, the Dharma, and the Sangha; and how am I to abide by the precepts so that I shall be born in a good realm in my next life?" To this the World-Honored One answered, "Cudi, the Buddha is the master of all living beings; therefore faith in the Buddha is the supreme faith, and its fruit is supreme.

"Among all teachings, the teaching of nirvana, which is free of attachment, destroys arrogance, quenches thirst, extinguishes defilements, stops the cycle of samsara, and destroys the thirst of lust, is supreme. The faith in the nirvana of non-attachment, therefore, is the supreme faith, and the fruit of that faith is supreme.

"Among many precepts, these precepts are indestructible and pure, and all the saints and wise people praise them as supreme. Thus to abide by these precepts is to fulfill and guard the supreme teaching, and their fruit is also supreme."

(10) The World-Honored One embarked on another journey and arrived at the Jatiya Grove of Bhaddiya. Ugga, grandson of Mendaka, invited the Buddha to his house, and after the offering of a meal he said, "All these daughters of ours are about to be married. World-Honored One, may I beseech you to impart some teachings to them?" The Buddha said, "Maidens, you should think in this way: 'I shall be thankful to my husband's parents, who are concerned about our well-being and love us with compassion. I shall arise early in the morning and retire late and be ever ready to be able to serve them. I shall comfort them with kind words. I shall respect and give offerings to our parents and to the mendicants whom my husband holds in high regard. I shall have understanding of the kind of work my husband is doing and I shall adapt myself to it and work hard to be of help to him. As to the servants and others who work for the family, I shall find out their natures and abilities and even their likes and dislikes and look out after them. I shall take good care of my husband's earnings and shall not waste them.' Maidens, keep these ideas in mind."

(11) The World-Honored One went to Vesali and stayed in the two-storied hall. General Simha of Vesali came to the Buddha and asked, "World-Honored One, it is said that giving is a good deed. Will you please tell me what effects giving will have in the present world?" The World-Honored One said, "General, he who gives will be loved by people. This is one of the effects in the present life. Good people will follow and serve the one who gives; this is the second effect in this present life. The one who gives will be honored highly; this is the third effect in this life. The one who gives has no fear but has confidence in going to gatherings of kings, scholars, rich people, and mendicants; this is the fourth effect of giving in this present life. And the one who gives will, because of his merits, be born in a heavenly world; this is the fruit that one receives in the next life." The general said, "World-Honored One, among the five effects of giving that you have explained, I know the first four. But as to the fruit in the next life, it is beyond me to know. I shall single-mindedly have faith in your words."

(12) Ugga, a wealthy man, lived in Vesali. One day the Buddha entered his house by invitation. Ugga said, "World-Honored One, I heard you saying that one who gives good things will receive good things. These dumplings taste good. Please kindly accept this offering." The World-Honored One nodded and accepted them. Ugga then offered pork with dates and rice from which all black grains were picked out, and soup and side dishes. Observing that the World-Honored One accepted them, he said, "World-Honored One, to offer drapes with long tassels, sheepskin rugs with coverings, and chairs with red pillows at both ends perhaps is good, but I do not think that they are befitting the World-Honored One. Therefore I should like to offer this sandalwood chair. Please have pity on me and accept this." The World-Honored One nodded and accepted it. Then he recited verses of thanks:

> For those who act correctly, there is love. Those who bestow merits receive merits.

> Those who realize that the enlightened are fields of merit and who give to them that which is difficult to give—robes, food, bedding, medicines, and so forth—will receive good rewards.

Not long after, Ugga fell ill and departed from the world and was reborn as a god in the heavenly world. One evening, lighting up Jeta Grove, Ugga came to the World-Honored One and sat by him. The World-Honored One asked, "Have you had your wish fulfilled?" Ugga thanked the World-Honored One and sang:

> Bestowing merits, I received merits.
> Bestowing that which was excellent,
> I received that which was excellent.
> Now, bestowing merits and that which is excellent,
> My life will be long and my honor lofty.

3. Discarding Greed, Anger, and Ignorance

(1) Ananda accompanied the World-Honored One down to Kosambi and stayed at the Ghosita Monastery. One day a householder who was the follower of a non-Buddhist who practiced a form of naked asceticism came to Ananda and said, "Venerable One, who can give us the best teaching? And who is living the best life and is the happiest?" To this Ananda answered, "Sir, the one who exhorts us to discard greed, anger, and ignorance imparts the best teaching; and those who have discarded greed, anger, and ignorance are the ones who are living the best lives and are the most fortunate." "Venerable one, this is most excellent. I vow that from today on until my life ends, I shall take refuge in the Buddha, the Dharma, and the Sangha and will be a firm believer."

(2) The World-Honored One expounded the Dharma and said, "My disciples, there are the five powers of faith, outward shame, inward shame, effort, and wisdom, with which the disciples practice the path. You must remind yourself to strive to attain these five powers.

(3) "My disciples, there are five things which, if one has them, will cause one to suffer in this world and cause one in the next to go into the evil world. The five are faithlessness, lack of inward shame, lack of outward shame, idleness, and ignorance.

(4) "My disciples, when a mendicant discards his robes and returns to lay life, he will face five reproaches: 'You did not have faith in the good Dharma, you did not have inward shame, you did not have outward shame, you did not exert effort, and you did not have wisdom.' My disciples, even if one suffers, agonizes, and is in tears, if one's deeds are clean and the practices complete, there will be five praises: 'You had faith in the good Dharma, you had inward shame, you had outward shame, you exerted effort, and you had wisdom.'

(5) "My disciples, I became a Buddha by becoming awakened to the Four Noble Truths, which had not hitherto been known. Faith, inward shame, outward shame, endeavor, and wisdom are the five powers of the Buddha. By virtue of having these, a Buddha becomes the king of bulls; and he expounds the Dharma roaring like a lion.

(6) "My disciples, among these five powers, faith, inward and outward shame, endeavor, and wisdom, the power of wisdom is the most important. The other

four powers are inherent in this. It is like the spire, which is the most important part of a tower; all other parts are centered around this spire.

(7) "My disciples, there are five powers other than the ones mentioned. They are faith, endeavor, right thought, concentration, and wisdom. Among these five powers, again wisdom is central and all others are concentrated in it and tied to it.

(8) "My disciples, he who observes the precepts and induces others to observe them, who lives in concentration and induces others to live in concentration, who attains wisdom and induces others to attain wisdom, who attains liberation and induces others to attain liberation, and who possesses insight and induces others to possess insight is the one who has the capacity to benefit both himself and others."

(9) The World-Honored One then went to Kapilavatthu and stayed at a nigrodha forest not far from the city. There he had a slight illness from which he soon recovered.

One day, a certain Mahanama of the Sakya clan came to the Buddha and, after paying homage to him, sat down by him and said, "World-Honored One, I remember that long ago you said that the one whose mind is calm has wisdom and that the one whose mind is not calm does not possess wisdom. Then is meditation prior to wisdom or is wisdom prior to meditation?" Ananda heard this and thought, "The World-Honored One has just recovered from his illness. Mahanama is now asking a deep question and this will bother the World-Honored One. I shall take him elsewhere and explain things to him." Ananda took Mahanama by the hand and took him to another place and said, "Mahanama, in regard to the precepts, meditation, and wisdom, the World-Honored One spoke about them in relation to the one who is still in the midst of practice, and he spoke about them in another way for the one who has completed his practice. Precepts for the one who is still in the midst of practice are to control the body by doing good deeds, to restrain the five senses, to fear even a slight violation, and to keep oneself upright and learn with diligence. Concentration for him is to enter and dwell in the calmness of his mind. Wisdom for him is to know the meaning of the Four Noble Truths as they are. The three learnings of precepts, concentration, and wisdom for the one who is already awakened are those which only the Enlightened Ones practice. Mahanama, this is how the World-Honored One has explained matters."

(10) After he had completely recovered, the World-Honored One went to the Great Forest Lecture Hall of Vesali by way of Kusinara; and Ananda accompanied him. One day he asked, "World-Honored One, to what extent can you talk of existence?" The World-Honored One replied with the question, "Ananda, if there were no action that brought about the world of darkness, would there be the existence of the delusory world?" Ananda answered, "No, there would be no existence of the delusory world." The Buddha said, "Thus karma is the cause, mind is the seed, and the thirst of desire is the water. Being covered by delusion and bound by the thirst of lust, the mind remains in the lower realms, causing the cycle of rebirths."

(11) On another day, the World-Honored One said to Ananda, "Will all practice and faith bear good fruit?" Ananda replied, "World-Honored One, that

cannot be stated categorically. If practice and faith beget more evil and less good, then they do not bear good fruit. If practice and faith beget less evil and more good, then they do bear good fruit." The World-Honored One was pleased with Ananda's reply. After Ananda left, the World-Honored One said to the other disciples, "Ananda is still on his way to attainment; but it is not easy to find his equal in wisdom."

4. Endeavor and Its Incentive

(1) Soon the World-Honored One moved to Rajagaha and stayed at the Bamboo Grove, where he continued to teach his disciples and said, "My disciples, the disciple who dwells in the forest may have five fears. He may talk about them as follows: 'I am now living alone. I might be bitten by a snake or a scorpion and die; I might become ill and even die from food poisoning, cold, or consumption; I might be killed by a lion, a tiger, a leopard, or a bear; seeing that I am alone, some young ruffians might come, accuse me of things that I have done or have not done, and kill me in a rage; or I might be killed by some devil or demon that makes this forest its habitat. These five fears are the obstacles that always lie before me.' My disciples, when you are dwelling alone in the forest, and think of these five fears, think, 'I must reach what I have not yet reached and must be awakened to what I have not yet been awakened and be determined to exert more zeal and effort.

(2) "My disciples, as in the case of the five fears just mentioned, when you are confronted with the following five fears, you should take the same attitude. 'First, I am now full of vigor, but this body will be old before long, and then I shall not be able to think about the teaching of the Buddha, to practice alone in the forest, or to appreciate living in the Dharma. I must exert more zeal and effort to reach what I have not yet reached and to be awakened to what I have not yet been awakened to before old age approaches. With a true understanding of the Dharma, I shall be able to live with peace of mind even in old age.

"Second, although I am now enjoying good health and have no sign of infirmity, I am bound to become ill sooner or later. Then I shall not be able to think about the Dharma, to practice alone in the forest, or to appreciate living in the Dharma. Therefore, before being attacked by illness, I must exert more zeal and effort to reach what I have not yet reached and to be awakened to what I have not yet been awakened. With a true understanding of the Dharma, I shall be able to live with peace of mind even in my sickbed.

"Third, there is now an abundance of grains, and I find no difficulty in alms begging. It is easy to subsist even by picking gleanings. But the time may come when there is a famine and food is not available. At such a time, people will migrate to wherever there is an abundance of food. We, too, will have to join the horde and live with the multitude. But in the bustling crowd, it will be difficult to contemplate the Buddha's teaching, to meditate in solitude, and to live the life of the Dharma. Before this happens, I must exert more zeal and effort to reach what I have not yet reached and be awakened to what I have not yet been awakened. With a true understanding of the Dharma, I shall be able to live in peace of mind even in time of famine.

"Fourth, people are now living in harmony and being kind to each other. But once they are attacked by bandits from the mountains, or are visited by an earthquake, they will all escape to some safer place. We, too, shall have to live among the crowd. In the hustle and bustle, it will become difficult to contemplate the Buddha's teaching, to meditate in solitude, and to live the life of the Dharma. Before this happens, I must exert more effort to reach what I have not yet reached and to be awakened to what I have not yet been awakened. With a true understanding of the Dharma, I shall be able to live with peace of mind even in such cases.

"Fifth, although the Sangha to which I belong is in harmony, and all are living peacefully in one teaching, the time may come when the Sangha will be in disharmony and will become disorganized. In a group in discord, it will be difficult to contemplate the Buddha's teaching, to meditate in solitude, and to live the life of the Dharma. Before that happens, I must exert more effort to reach what I have not yet reached and to be awakened to what I have not yet been awakened. With a true understanding of the Dharma, I shall be able to live with peace of mind even in a Sangha that has lost its harmony.

"My disciples, thinking of these five possible situations, you must constantly exert zeal and effort to reach what you have not yet reached and to become awakened to what you have not yet been awakened."

(3) One day a disciple went to his tutor and said, "My body is so weakened today that I feel that I am completely befuddled and that I can no longer think with reason; nor am I able to see the Dharma. I am depressed, have become unwilling to practice the pure Dharma, and have even begun to harbor doubts about the Dharma." The tutor took the disciple along with him to the World-Honored One and explained the situation. The Buddha said, "You have not been careful with the five senses; you have eaten without knowing the proper limits, indulged in idle slumber, and have not sought the good Dharma. Unless you are arduously striving to practice day and night the Buddha's path, you will necessarily be in such a plight. Always bear in mind, therefore, 'I shall guard my five senses, refrain from indulging in slumber, seek the good Dharma, and practice day and night and strive to follow the Buddha's path.' "

The disciple, after receiving this admonition, went into the forest alone and vigorously applied himself in the practice. Later, he was able to attain enlightenment, and he returned to his tutor and said, "Great Virtuous One, today I feel as though I have become completely sober. My mind is clear and I am able to see the Dharma distinctly. I do not fall into indolence, and doubts in regard to the Dharma have been dispelled." The tutor again took his disciple to the Buddha and explained what took place. The World-Honored One said, "That must be so. If you follow thoroughly my instructions, good results necessarily will appear. Always be mindful of this."

(4) The World-Honored One gathered his disciples and said, "My disciples, whether man or woman, householder or mendicant, there are five things that one should always keep in mind: 'I am aging and I cannot avoid old age; I am bound to be ill and I cannot avoid illness; I am destined to die and I cannot avoid

death; persons I love and the things I like to possess are all impermanent; I am the inheritor of my actions, and I must inherit the karma that I have accumulated.'

"My disciples, in youth, people invariably have pride in their youth, and intoxicated by pride they do evil deeds with body, mouth, and mind. It is when one realizes that one cannot transcend old age that one realizes that one must either destroy his pride or lessen it. Again, in health, people have pride in their health, and intoxicated by pride they do evil deeds with body, mouth, and mind. But when one realizes that one cannot overcome illness, one can destroy or weaken that pride. Finally, people, as long as they are living, think that they will live forever and have pride in their life. Intoxicated by this pride, they do evil deeds with body, mouth, and mind. But when one reflects and sees that one must die, then one can destroy the pride or diminish it. For the objects of love and pleasure, everyone rouses desire and does wrong deeds with body, mouth, and mind. But when one realizes that all things are impermanent and constantly changing, one can either destroy or weaken the greed. Everyone does evils with body, mouth and mind; it is only when one realizes that one is the inheritor of his evil action that one will either destroy or lessen them.

"My disciples, as long as there is samsara, people cannot transcend old age, illness, and death. All are the inheritors of their actions. If one reflects on this constantly, one will be able to discover the path, and if one repeatedly practices the path, one can liberate oneself from the fetters and annihilate the defilements."

(5) When the World-Honored One was on the Vulture Peak just outside of the city, a disciple named Vakkali was staying at the house of a potter and was suffering from severe illness. One day he called his attending monk and said, "Friend, please go to the World-Honored One and pay homage at his feet in my name and say, 'World-Honored One, Vakkali is now suffering from grave illness. I bow at your feet and beg you to have pity on him and visit him.'" The attending monk complied; he went to the World-Honored One, payed homage at his feet, sat down to one side, and conveyed Vakkali's request. The World-Honored One nodded and granted his wish. Putting on his robe and taking his bowl, he went to see Vakkali. When he caught sight of the World-Honored One coming, Vakkali arose from his bed. The World-Honored One said, "You need not arise from your bed. I see a seat prepared for me, so I shall sit here." Seating himself, the World-Honored One asked, "How do you feel? Can you hear? Are you eating well? Are you well supplied? Do you feel that the pains have subsided somewhat and that you are on your way to recovery?"

Vakkali replied, "No, World-Honored One; I have no desire to eat. The pains are becoming more severe and the condition is getting more serious." The Buddha then said, "Vakkali, do you have any regrets or discontents?" "World-Honored One, I have more than a few regrets." "Are you reproaching yourself in regard to the precepts?" "No, World-Honored One." "Then what are you regretful about, and what is on your mind?" "World-Honored One, for a long time I wished to pay a visit to you but I had no strength to do so." "Vakkali, what good is there in seeing this decaying body? He who sees the Dharma sees me. He who truly sees me sees the Dharma. Seeing the Dharma, one sees me; and seeing me, one sees the Dharma. Vakkali, is your body permanently existent or is it impermanent?" "World-Honored One, the body is impermanent." "Vakkali, is your mind permanent or impermanent?" "World-Honored One, the mind is impermanent." "Vakkali, impermanence gives rise to pains. Painful things are without a substantial self. Concerning things impermanent, it is not possible to say, 'This is mine' or 'This is I.' Thus you should know things as they really are. Seeing in this way, the disciples of this teaching free themselves from body and mind; liberating themselves from desire, they become aware of their liberation. With this awareness, they know that their lives of fetters have ended, that all that had to be done has been done, and that there will be no more life in delusion."

(6) After thus instructing Vakkali, the World-Honored One rose from his seat and returned to the Vulture Peak. Soon after the World-Honored One left, Vakkali said to his attendant, "My friend, please put me on a bed and take me to Black Rock on the side of Mount Isigiri. A person like me should not die in a house." The attending monk, in deference to his wish, carried him to Black Rock by Mount Isigiri.

The World-Honored One spent the afternoon and night on the Vulture Peak. That night, the World-Honored One thought about Vakkali and was certain that he would attain liberation. The following morning, the World-Honored One called his disciples and said, "O disciples, go visit Vakkali and tell him that the Buddha has thought about him; tell him that he will certainly attain liberation, and say, 'Vakkali, have no fear. Your death will not be a misfortune.'" The disciples, in accordance with the order, went to Vakkali and said, "Friend Vakkali, listen to the words of the World-Honored One." Upon hearing no more than this, Vakkali said to his attendant, "My friend, lower me from this bed. How can a person like me, sitting on a high bed, listen to the Buddha's instruction?" When the attendant did what he asked, the disciples conveyed the Buddha's message. Vakkali said, "Please say this as my reply to the World-Honored One, after paying homage at his feet, 'World-Honored One, I, Vakkali, am in pain because of severe illness. After paying homage at your feet, I have this to say. I have absolutely no doubt that body and mind are impermanent or that the impermanent is painful. Also, it is certain that I do not arouse desire, greed, or lust over what is impermanent, painful, and constantly changing.'"

The disciples agreed to do this and went back to the World-Honored One. A while after the disciples left, Vakkali took hold of a sword to kill himself.

(7) At that moment, the World-Honored One said, "My disciples, let us go. Vakkali has just held up a sword." Thus the World-Honored One, with his disciples following, set out, but on the way he saw from afar Vakkali rolling on his bed with his body and shoulders moving. The World-Honored One looked back at his disciples and said, "My disciples, do not wonder where Vakkali's life went. He has just attained nirvana."

5. Dhammapada

Twin Verses

1. Everything is led by the mind; the mind is the leader; everything is made up of the mind. If one speaks or acts with an evil mind, suffering follows him like the wheel that follows the foot of the ox that draws it.

2. Everything is led by the mind; the mind is the leader; everything is made up of the mind. If one speaks or acts with a pure mind, happiness follows him like the shadow that never leaves him.

3. "He abused me; he beat me; he defeated me; he robbed me." The hatred in him who harbors such thoughts is never pacified.

4. "He abused me; he beat me; he defeated me; he robbed me." The mind of one who has no such thoughts is always at peace.

5. Indeed, hatred is never pacified by hatred; it is pacified by the absence of hatred. This is the law from antiquity.

6. The unwise do not know that they, too, will come to an end. He who realizes this has his struggles brought to an end.

7. He who thinks that his body is without defilement, who does not control his senses, who does not know moderation in food, who is indolent, and who does not exert effort will be overcome by demons like a weak tree downed by the wind.

8. He who thinks that his body is full of defilements, who restrains his senses, who knows moderation in food, who has faith, and who exerts effort will never be overcome by demons. He will be like a mountain of rock that is never moved by the wind.

9. He who is defiled and is without self-control is not worthy of wearing a yellow robe.

10. He who has discarded all defilements, is well disciplined, and has self-control is indeed worthy of wearing a yellow robe.

11. He who thinks of the unreal as the real and the real as the unreal will never reach the real but will merely hold onto wrong views.

12. He who sees the true as the true and the false as the false will reach the true and dwell in right thought.

13. As rain leaks into a poorly thatched house, greed enters into an undisciplined mind.

14. As rain does not leak into a well thatched house, greed does not penetrate into a disciplined mind.

15. The evildoer grieves both in this world and in the hereafter. Seeing his own evil deeds, he grieves.

16. The one who has accumulated merits rejoices both in this world and in the hereafter. Seeing the purity of his actions, he rejoices.

17. Suffering here and suffering in the hereafter, in both worlds does the evildoer suffer. Thinking, "I have done evil," he suffers all the more in the evil realm.

18. Being happy both in this world and in the next, the one who has accumulated merits is happy. Thinking, "I have done good deeds," he rejoices all the more in the good realm.

19. Though he may commit to memory large portions of the teaching, if he neglects to practice the teaching, he is like a cowherd who keeps tabs on the cows belonging to another. He is not worthy of being a mendicant.

20. Though he may commit only a small portion of the teaching to memory, if he should practice in accordance with the Dharma, detach himself from greed, anger, and ignorance, attain wisdom and emancipation, and be unattached to this world and the next, he is worthy of being a mendicant.

Diligence

21. Diligence is the path of deathlessness; negligence is the path of death. He who is negligent is like a dead person. He who is not negligent does not die.

22. Understanding this clearly, the wise are not negligent, and they delight in diligence and rejoice in the way of the sages.

23. The courageous one who practices concentration, steadfastly persevering and striving at all times, will enter the peace of nirvana.

24. The honor of one who is full of energy, is rightly mindful, is pure in deed, is considerate, is self-controlled, lives the life of the Dharma, and is diligent will ascend ever higher.

25. By bracing himself up through diligence, discipline, and self-control, the wise person will make for himself an island not overwhelmed by the flood of defilements.

26. The ignorant and unwise person is indolent; the wise person guards diligence as the most precious treasure.

27. Do not give way to indolence or to the pleasure of lust; one who is diligent and meditative will attain great peace.

28. The wise person destroys negligence with diligence and ascends to the tower of wisdom. Freed from all worries, he looks upon the ignorant like a person who climbs to the top of a mountain and gazes down on those standing on level ground.

29. A person of wisdom who is diligent among the negligent and awake among the sleeping will outrun the ignorant like a fleet steed that outruns the hacks.

30. Indra rose to become the king of the gods by diligence; the diligent are praised, while the indolent are disparaged.

31. One who delights in diligence and is fearful of self-indulgence burns away like fire the bonds of defilements, big or small.

32. He who delights in diligence and is fearful of negligence will not fall back; he is close to nirvana.

The Mind

33. Like a fletcher who straightens the arrow, the wise person straightens this trembling mind, which is difficult to guard and difficult to restrain.

34. Like a fish taken from its watery abode and thrown upon the ground, this mind struggles to escape the dominion of Mara.

35. It is good to control this mind, which is difficult to control, is frivolous, and runs about as it wishes; the controlled mind alone brings peace.

36. The wise person restrains this mind, which is so subtle that it is difficult to perceive, and which runs about at will. This guarded mind alone brings peace.

37. Travelling afar, alone, formless, and hiding in the cave of the heart is the mind. One who controls this mind will free himself from the bondages of Mara.

38. He whose mind is weak, who does not know the right Dharma, and whose faith wavers does not attain the fulfillment of wisdom.

39. There is no fear in the mind of one who is awake, has not been dampened by greed, has not been hindered by anger, and is detached from the thought of good and evil.

40. Knowing that the body is like a jar, fortify the mind as if it were a castle. With wisdom as the weapon, battle against the Maras. If you keep watch over the defeated Maras, you will be freed from the house of defilements.

41. This body, before long, will fall to the ground; its consciousness will depart, and it will become like a worthless log.

42. A misguided mind will do even greater wrongs than does a foe to a foe or the hater to the hated.

43. More than father or mother or relatives, a well-guided mind will do good to others.

Flowers

44. Who is it that conquers the world of Yama and of human and celestial beings? Who is it that gathers the words of the Dharma like a skillful garland-maker who gathers flowers?

45. Only the one who practices the Dharma will conquer the world of Yama and the worlds of human and celestial beings. Only the one who practices the Dharma alone, like a skillful garland-maker who gathers flowers, collects the well-taught Dharma words.

46. Only the one who knows this body to be like bubbles and understands its illusory nature will break the devil's flower-tipped arrows and reach beyond the realm of King Mara.

47. Like the flood sweeping away the village steeped in lazy slumber, death will carry away those who gather flowers of lust and are steeped in greed.

48. Death will make captives of those who gather flowers of lust and are steeped in greed even before they are satiated.

49. Like a bee that gathers only the honey without harming the flower, its color, or its scent, the sage wanders from village to village.

50. Rather than watching the evils of others or what they have done or left undone, reflect on what you yourself have done or left undone.

51. Like a flower with a beautiful color but without scent, fruitless are the fine words of one who does not practice them.

52. Like a flower that is beautiful and fragrant, fruitful are the fine words of one who practices them.

53. From a pile of flowers many garlands are made; likewise many good acts must be performed when one is born as a human being.

54. The fragrance of flowers does not float against the wind, nor does that of sandalwood, tagara, or jasmine; but the beautiful fragrance of a good person floats against the wind.

55. Among the fragrances of sandalwood and tagara, lotus and vassiki, most excellent is the fragrance of the precepts.

56. The fragrances of tagara and sandalwood are weak, but the fragrance of one practicing the precepts has no equal and reaches even to the gods.

57. The path of the one who observes the precepts, is diligent, and is liberated through the right wisdom is never detected by Mara.

58–59. Like the fragrant lotus growing out of a heap of rubbish thrown alongside a road, the disciples of the Buddha shine with wisdom among those who wander about in the dark.

The Ignorant

60. Long is the night to one who is awake, and long is the way to one who is weary; long is samsara to the ignorant, who do not know the true Dharma.

61. On walking the path, if you are not able to accompany someone who is superior or equal to you, go on by yourself. There is no merit in having an ignorant man as your friend.

62. "I have children," "I have wealth." With these thoughts, the ignorant person is tormented. Even he himself is not his, so how can he possess children and wealth?

63. The ignorant person who knows that he is ignorant is still wise; the ignorant one who thinks that he is wise is indeed a fool.

64. Even though associating with the wise person throughout his life, the ignorant man does not know the Dharma, as a spoon does not know taste.

65. Even though serving the wise for only a short while, the wise will soon understand the Dharma, just as the tongue knows taste.

66. The ignorant person treats himself as his own foe, because he does evil, which bears evil fruit.

67. Evil is the deed if, after it is done, one suffers and receives its fruits with tears in one's eyes.

68. Good is the deed if, after it is done, one does not suffer and receives its fruits with delight.

69. The ignorant person thinks that an evil deed is like honey, until it ripens; then he suffers, when the evil fruits manifest themselves.

70. The merit of the ignorant person who, month after month, eats as little an amount of food as that which collects on the tip of a blade of grass and who undergoes ascetic practices is not comparable to one-sixteenth of the merit of one who practices the right Dharma.

71. As fresh milk does not curdle immediately, an evil deed does not immediately bear fruit; it follows the unwise like a fire covered with ashes, that smoulders although unseen.

72. The ignorant person seeks wealth and fame, which turn out to be his woe; they destroy his virtue and even crush his head.

73. The ignorant person seeks empty fame; among monks, he seeks out the seat of eminence. In the monastery, he seeks positions of authority. In other houses, he seeks offerings (from the laity).

74. "Let the monks and householders know what I have done; let what should be done and what should not be done be decided by my will." Thinking thus, the unwise person increases his greed and arrogance.

75. "This path leads to worldly gain, and that to nirvana." Knowing thus, the disciples of the Buddha should not delight in worldly fame but should take to a life of solitude.

76. If one meets a person who points out his faults and scolds him, he should associate with such a wise person as though he were the revealer of great treasure; there will be much weal and no woe in serving such a person.

The Wise

77. Guide others. Teach others. Avoid evil. Those who do so, while not loved by the evil, are loved by the virtuous.

78. Do not associate with evil friends; do not become a friend to an inferior person; associate with good friends, and associate with noble persons.

79. One who rejoices in the Dharma lives in happiness with a pure mind and sleeps well; the wise always enjoys the Dharma taught by the sage.

80. The irrigator makes the water flow; the fletcher sharpens the arrow; the carpenter straightens the wood; the wise person controls himself.

81. Hard rock is not shaken by wind; likewise the wise are not disturbed by praise or blame.

82. Like a deep and clear pond, the mind of the wise one is clear after hearing the Dharma.

83. The virtuous person gives up greed and does not complain out of greed; the wise person does not change his attitude whether he meets with happiness or misfortune.

84. Whether for oneself or for another's sake, one does not wish for descendants. One hopes neither for land nor for wealth. One does not seek one's success by unjust means. Such is the person who observes the precepts, possesses wisdom, and is just.

85. There are very few who reach the other shore; most remain on this shore and wander about.

86. Those who practice the teaching of the Dharma will pass over the impassable world of evil and reach the shore of enlightenment.

87–88. The wise should abandon the wrong path and practice the right path, abandon home and become a mendicant, seek delight in solitude and detachment, and rid himself of the impurities of the mind.

89. He who, going on the path of enlightenment, purifies his mind, discards attachment, delights in non-attachment, eliminates evil passions, and emanates light will attain nirvana in this world.

The Arhat

90. For one who has completed the journey, for one who is free from sorrow, for one who is free from all fetters, there are no anxieties.

91. Those who have right mindfulness exert themselves. They are not desirous of staying home, and they leave their homes like swans that leave their ponds.

92. The path of those who do not hoard possessions, who know moderation in eating, and who thoroughly see the void and are liberated cannot be traced, as that of birds in the sky cannot.

93. The path of those who have conquered defilements, who are not attached to food, who thoroughly discern the void and the formless, and who have been spiritually emancipated, cannot be traced, as that of birds in the sky cannot.

94. Those who have subdued their senses like well-trained horses, who have eliminated arrogance, and who have freed themselves from defilements are envied even by the gods.

95. Those who observe well the disciplines are free from vexations, like the great earth, or the great pillar; they are like clear lakes without mud; there will be no more transmigration for them to go through.

96. The mind, speech, and deeds of those who are delivered by right wisdom and have attained peace are calm.

97. One who has abandoned wrong faith, who understands the uncreated, who has cut the chains of samsara, who has severed the remnants of good and evil, and who has rejected all desires is indeed the most noble.

98. Be it a village, a forest, a valley, or a hill, where sages live is delightful.

99. In the forest that should give delight, an ordinary person does not find pleasure; but one who has discarded greed and does not seek lust will find happiness in it.

Thousands

100. Better than a talk made up of a thousand words is a single meaningful word that calms the mind of the hearer.

101. Better than a thousand meaningless verses is one single verse if, by hearing it, one's mind is calmed.

102. Better than a hundred verses is one single Dharma statement that gives the hearer calmness of mind.

103. Better than conquering a thousand in battle is to conquer oneself, which is the greatest victory.

104–105. Self-conquest is indeed far greater than the conquest of all others; neither a god, nor a heavenly being, nor a gandhabba, nor the king of maras, nor a brahmin can overthrow him.

106. Superior to monthly offerings of a thousand pieces of gold for a hundred years is the offering even of one moment to the one who controls himself.

107. Superior to living in the forest and sacrificing to Agni for a hundred years is the offering of one moment to the one who has won over himself.

108. Better is paying homage to a true follower of the path than making sacrifices and offerings for a year with the thought of gaining merits; the latter is not worth even a quarter of the former.

109. For a person who always honors and respects elders, four things increase: life span, beauty, happiness, and strength.

110. It is indeed better to live one single day well disciplined and calmed than to live a hundred years doing evil and with the mind uncontrolled.

111. Better than to live a hundred years without wisdom and calmness of mind is to live one single day with wisdom and the mind quiescent.

112. It is indeed better to live a single day making intense effort than to live a hundred years in idleness.

113. Better than to live a hundred years without knowing the arising and perishing of things is to live a single day knowing the arising and perishing of things.

114. It is better to live a single day knowing the way of deathlessness than to live a hundred years without knowing the deathless way.

115. Better than to live a hundred years not knowing the supreme Dharma is to live a single day seeing the supreme Dharma.

Evil Conduct

116. Make haste in doing good; guard your mind from evil; if one is slow in doing virtuous deeds, it is because his mind delights in evil.

117. If a person does evil, he should not do it again and again; he should not think of doing evil; the accumulation of evil is indeed painful.

118. If a person does good, he should do it again and again; he should find delight in doing good; the accumulation of good is indeed blissful.

119. An evildoer sees happiness as long as his evil deeds do not bear fruits; but when they bear fruits, he sees unhappiness.

120. A good person may see evil so long as good does not bear fruit, but when it bears fruit, then he sees happiness.

121. Do not belittle evil, saying, "It will not come to me." Dripping water can fill a vat; so does a fool, piling evil little by little, fill himself with evil.

122. Do not belittle good, saying, "It will not come to me." Dripping water can fill a vat; so does a wise person, gathering good little by little, fill himself with good.

123. Like a merchant, who, with a small number of attendants but with great wealth, avoids a risky path, and like one who values life and avoids poison, one should avoid evil.

124. If there is no wound on the hand, one may touch poison with it; poison does not affect one who has no wound; there is no evil for a person who does no evil.

125. To a fool who dishonors a clean, faultless, and pure person, evil comes back, as the dust thrown against the wind comes back to the thrower.

126. Some are born as human beings; evildoers are born in hell; good persons are born in the heavenly world; the undefiled go to nirvana.

127. Nowhere can a person escape from his evil actions, be it in the sky, in the ocean, or in the mountain cave.

128. In the sky, in the ocean, or in a mountain cave, there is no place that death does not occupy.

Punishment

129. All beings fear death; all fear sword and cane. Put yourself in another's position, and do not kill nor harm.

130. All beings fear sword and cane; all beings love their lives. Put yourself in another's position, and do not kill nor harm.

131. All living beings seek happiness. In the pursuit of happiness, if one harms another with sword or cane, one will not gain happiness after his death.

132. All beings seek happiness; a happiness-seeker will gain happiness hereafter if he does not harm others with sword or cane.

133. Do not speak harshly; those thus spoken to will thus retort. Words spoken in anger give pain; they will return to you in retaliation.

134. Like a cracked gong, if you remain quiet, you will arrive in nirvana; there will be no anger in you.

135. Like a herdsman driving cows to pasture with a cane, old age and death drive out the lives of beings.

136. A fool does wrong deeds without experiencing enlightenment; as if he were being burnt by fire, the fool is burnt by the fire of his deeds.

137–140. If a person with a cane harms the harmless and sinless, soon he will receive one of the ten results: acute pain, death, bodily injury, serious illness, loss of mind, punishment by the king, harsh false accusation, loss of relatives, loss of wealth, or a fire caused by thunder that burns his house. Upon death, this unwise person will be born in hell.

141. Practicing naked asceticism, worshipping fire, wearing matted hair, fasting, lying on the ground, lying in dust, squatting on one's heels, the practitioner will never purify himself if he is not free from doubt.

142. Even though he is adorned, if he lives in peace, acts correctly, is quiescent, is pure, does not use the cane on any living being, he is indeed a brahmin, a renunciant, a disciple of the Buddha.

143. How rare is the person who knows shame without being censured, like a thoroughbred that need not be spurred! With intense will, practice the path like a good horse that has been whipped.

144. By faith, precepts, effort, concentration, judgment, knowledge, conduct, and being fully mindful, rid yourself of this painful suffering.

145. Ditchdiggers guide water; fletchers shape arrows; carpenters straighten wood; prudent people mold their own personalities.

Old Age

146. How can you laugh, how can you enjoy, when the world is ever burning? Being covered with darkness, why do you not seek the light?

147. Look at this painted and decorated clod of flesh, barely held together, a mass of sores with a calculating mind. There is nothing firm and constant about this.

148. This body is to age and rot; it is, indeed, the vessel for diseases. The decaying body is breaking up; life finally ends in death.

149. Like gourds thrown away in autumn are these bleached bones. What pleasure is there in looking at them?

150. In this castle of a body composed of bones and plastered with flesh and blood is stored old age, death, arrogance, and conceit.

151. A beautifully decorated king's chariot, too, will decay; so will this body age. But the good Dharma will never age; thus teach the good to each other.

152. One who learns little grows old like the cow; his flesh fattens but his wisdom does not grow.

153. I wandered in transmigration through many lives, seeking in vain the builder of this house.

154. Now, however, you, the builder of the house, have been seen. You shall not build the house again. All your rafters are broken; your ridgepole is destroyed. My mind has been freed from the thirst of craving and has entered nirvana.

155. Those who, while young, did not lead a life of purity and did not gain wealth will fade away like old herons on a pond without fish.

156. Those who have not led a life of purity while they were young and have failed to acquire wealth will deplore their past and like spent arrows lie down to rot.

The Self

157. He who loves himself dearly should conduct himself well; during any of the three stages of life, adolescence, middle age, and old age, the wise should become awakened at least once.

158. First, you yourself live properly, and then lead others. Then you will never become weary nor tired.

159. As you teach others, you yourself must practice; fully taming yourself, tame others, for oneself is most difficult to tame.

160. Truly, one is the master of oneself. What other master could there be? Only after controlling oneself is one able to gain a valuable and worthy master.

161. Evil is done by oneself alone; it is self-born; it is self-caused; evil crushes the unwise like the diamond that crushes gems.

162. He who is corrupted, like a creeper strangling a sala tree, does to himself what an enemy would wish to do to him.

163. Things that are bad and not beneficial to oneself are easy to do; but things that are beneficial and good are indeed very difficult to do.

164. He who, because of his perverted views, foolishly vilifies the noble teaching of the Arhats, living in the noble Dharma, will, like the kastakha seeds, destroy himself.

165. Evil is done by oneself; one is defiled by oneself; evil is discarded by oneself; one is purified only by oneself. Purity or impurity depends on oneself. No one purifies another.

166. Do not forget your own well-being because of others' well-being; you must concentrate on your own well-being.

The World

167. Do not follow an inferior view; do not live in self-indulgence; do not harbor perverted views; do not aggravate worldly matters.

168. Do not live in self-indulgence. Practice the right way; he who observes the way of the Dharma can sleep pleasantly both in this world and the next.

169. Practice the right path; do not follow the wrong path; he who follows the path of the Dharma will sleep pleasantly both in this world and the next.

170. You should look at this world as a bubble or a mirage. Then Yama, the ruler of the dead, will not see you.

171. Look at this world; it is like a beautifully decorated royal carriage; the unwise agonize in it, but the wise have no attachment to it.

172. One who was in self-indulgence but later has left it will brighten this world like the moon freed from clouds.

173. One who undoes the past evil by doing good deeds brightens this world like the moon freed from clouds.

174. This world is dark; there are few who clearly see; those who go to the heavenly realm are few, like birds that escape the net.

175. Swans fly along the path of the sun; those with superhuman power go through the air; having conquered the evil king and his army, the sages leave this world forever.

176. He who transgresses the Dharma, lies, and is not concerned about the world to come will do any evil.

177. The miser does not go to a heavenly realm; the unwise do not enjoy giving; the wise rejoice in giving and will be happy and peaceful in the world to come.

178. Better than becoming king over the whole world, better than going to a heavenly realm, better than becoming king of all the gods is to enter the tradition of the Dharma.

The Buddha

179. There is no one who can defeat the Buddha. There is no one in this world who has reached the victorious realm as he has. The wisdom of the Buddha is boundless. By what path can you lead the Buddha, who has no trace of greed, anger, or ignorance?

180. Boundless is the wisdom of the Buddha, who is completely free of greed, which is like a snare or a poison. By what path can you lead the Buddha, who has no trace of greed, anger, or ignorance?

181. Even the gods envy sages absorbed in the quiet contemplation of nirvana and the enlightened who are rightly mindful.

182. Hard it is to be born as a human being, hard it is to live the life of a human being, hard it is to hear the teaching of the true Dharma, and rare is the appearance of the Buddha.

183. Do not do evil, do good, cleanse your mind—this is the teaching of all buddhas.

184. Patience is the highest austere practice, and nirvana is supreme, so have said all the buddhas. The World-Honored One never afflicts nor harms others.

185. Do not slander and do not harm, but guard yourself with the precepts. Know moderation in food, live in solitude, and practice meditation—this is the teaching of all the buddhas.

186. Greed is never satiated even by a shower of gold pieces. In greed there is little happiness but much pain. One who knows this is called a wise person.

187. Seeing no happiness even in heavenly pleasures, the disciples of the Buddha delight in the elimination of defilement.

188. Many who are stricken with fears take refuge in the gods of the hills, woods, gardens, trees, and graves;

189. But there is no peace of mind in these refuges; no such refuges are supreme; no one can be freed from suffering by taking refuge in these.

190. Only one who takes refuge in the Buddha, the Dharma, and the Sangha with true wisdom sees the Four Noble Truths.

191. The Four Noble Truths are sorrow, the cause of sorrow, the cessation of the cause of sorrow, and the Eightfold Noble Path that leads to the cessation of sorrow.

192. This is indeed the secure refuge; this is indeed the supreme refuge. By taking refuge in these, one is freed from all sufferings.

193. It is hard to find a superior person like this; he is not born just anywhere; the family where such a person is born prospers in peace and happiness.

194. Happiness is the appearance of the Buddha; happiness is to hear the right Dharma; happiness is harmony in the Sangha; happiness is practice and cultivation within the Sangha.

195. He who is free from illusions, grief, and lamentations reveres those worthy of reverence, whether buddhas or disciples;

196. The virtue of persons who revere such peaceful and fearless ones cannot be measured.

Happiness

197. Oh, let us live happily without hate among the hating; among hating persons, let us live without hate.

198. Oh, let us live without anxieties among the anxious; among the anxious, let us live without anxieties.

199. Oh, let us live without craving among craving people; among craving people, let us live without craving.

200. Oh, let us live happily without having attachment to a single thing; let us live like the gods of the Radiant Realm who subsist on joy.

201. Victory gives birth to hatred; the defeated live in pain. Giving up victory and defeat, one should live in the peace of serenity.

202. There is no fire equal to greed, no harm equal to anger; there is no pain equal to having this body, no bliss higher than serenity.

203. Hunger is the greatest disease; having this body is the greatest pain; by knowing this as it is, one attains nirvana, the highest happiness.

204. Health is the highest gain; contentment is the greatest wealth; trust is the best kinsman, and nirvana is the highest bliss.

205. Having tasted the flavor of renunciation, serenity, and the joy of the Dharma, one has no fear and no evil.

206. Seeing the sages is good; to live with them is joyful; not seeing fools is a lasting happiness.

207. Travelling in the company of a fool, one grieves that the road is long; living with a fool is just like living with an enemy. Living with the wise is like meeting with kinsfolk.

208. Like the moon following the course of the stars, accompany and serve, therefore, the wise and the good who are intelligent, sagacious, learned, and patient and who adhere to their principles.

Pleasure

209. He who does what is improper and does not do what is proper, who discards the truly valuable, and who is attached to what he likes will eventually come to envy the one who does what is proper.

210. Be not attached to either the pleasant or the unpleasant. For not seeing the pleasant is painful, and to see the unpleasant is also painful.

211. So, empty the mind of likes and dislikes, for unhappy it is to part with the likes. Unattached, the mind is free.

212. From likes arise sorrows, from likes arise fears. Freed from likes, one has no sorrow. How could he have fear?

213. From pleasure arises grief and fear; freed from pleasure, one has no more grief. How could he have fear?

214. Grief springs from enjoyment; so does fear; for one freed from enjoyment, there is no grief, much less fear.

215. Grief springs from craving, so does fear; for one freed from craving, there is no grief, much less fear.

216. Grief springs from love; so does fear. No sorrow is there for one who is freed from love, much less fear.

217. If one practices pure precepts, has the right view, is well established in the Dharma, speaks the truth, and does what he should do, he is held dear by all.

218. He who aspires for nirvana, that which cannot be described, with a greedless and fulfilled mind, is said to be going upstream.

219. Returning from afar after being away for long, one will be received warmly by one's kinsfolk and friends;

220. So will one with a store of merits be received by his merits in the next world.

Anger

221. Discard anger, abandon pride, and leave fetters. Suffering does not follow him who is not attached to his body or possessions.

222. He who controls his rising temper as a rolling chariot is controlled I call a true charioteer. Others are charioteers in name only, merely holding the reins.

223. Overcome anger by having no anger; overcome evil by good; overcome miserliness by giving; overcome lies by truth.

224. Speak truth; be not angry; when asked, give even if you have only a little. By these three you will be born in heavenly realms.

225. The sage who does not harm other lives and restrains his body will go to the deathless realm, where there is no sorrow.

226. He who is always intent on nirvana, well awake and training himself day and night, will attain the destruction of defilements.

227. This, Atula, is an old saying, and there is nothing new about it: "They blame those who sit in silence, they blame those who speak much, and they blame even those who speak moderately. In this world, there is no one not blamed."

228. There is no one who is always blamed or always praised. This was true in the past, is true now, and will be true in the future.

229. A person whom intelligent ones, after observing him day after day, praise by saying, "He is perfect in behavior, intelligent and wise, well disciplined, and calm,"

230. Is like refined Jambu River gold. Could there be anyone to blame him? Even gods and brahmins will praise him.

231. Guard against anger caused by the body, and restrain the body; refrain from evil bodily acts, and do good bodily acts.

232. Guard against anger caused by speech, and restrain speech; giving up evil speech, speak good words.

233. Guard against anger caused by the mind, and restrain the mind; give up evil thoughts, and have good thoughts.

234. The wise restrains his deeds; he restrains his speech as well as his mind; he is, indeed, well restrained.

Impurity

235. You are now a withered leaf; the messenger of death attends you. You are about to start your journey to death but without provisions for the journey.

236. Make an island of refuge for yourself; without delay strive to become wise; freed from defilements, you will be born in a heavenly realm.

237. You are now on the verge of death, are at your life's end; and there is no place to take shelter on the journey, for you have made no provisions for it.

238. Make an island for yourself; without delay strive to become wise; freed from defilements, you will not receive birth and old age again.

239. Like a smith refining silver, the wise person gradually, from moment to moment, will remove his impurities.

240. As rust issuing from iron eats it away, deeds violating the precepts lead one to an evil realm.

241. Not being recited is a taint to a sutra; not being repaired is a taint to a house; idleness is a taint to the body; being careless is a taint to the watchful.

242. Misconduct is a taint of a woman; stinginess is a taint of a giver; an evil dharma, indeed, is a taint in this and the next world.

243. But an even worse taint is that of ignorance. Disciples, discard this taint and become taintless.

244. Easy is the life of the defiled one who knows no shame, brazenly slanders people like a crow, and whose conduct is rude and arrogant.

245. Hard is the life of the person of wisdom who knows shame, always seeks purity, is without attachment, and lives an upright and serene life.

246. He who destroys life, tells lies, takes what is not given, goes to others' wives,

247. And is addicted to intoxicating drinks, digs up his own roots even in this life.

248. Know that intemperance is an evil path; do not drag yourself into long suffering by your greed and evil deeds.

249. People give with faith and joy; he who is displeased with the food and drink given will never enter quiet meditation, either day or night.

250. He who has completely severed and uprooted such thoughts will enter quiet meditation.

251. There is no fire equal to greed, no crocodile equal to anger, no meshes equal to ignorance, and no river equal to lust.

252. Others' faults are easily seen, but one's own are difficult to see; one airs others' faults like blowing chaff but hides one's own faults as a crooked gambler hides his dice.

253. For him who is irritated on seeing others' faults, defilements increase and never diminish.

254. There is no track in the sky; there is no true mendicant in wrong teachings. People delight in evil; in buddhas there is no evil.

255. There is no track in the sky; there is no true mendicant in the wrong teachings. Everything worldly changes; there is no instability in buddhas.

Person of Dharma

256. A person of the Dharma does not do things violently; a person of the Dharma knows what is proper from what is improper.

257. One who is not violent, relies on the Dharma, and leads others equitably honors the Dharma and is wise.

258. One is not wise because he talks much; one who is serene, is without hate, and is fearless is called wise.

259. One is not a person of the Dharma because one talks much; one who practices the Dharma and does not neglect the Dharma is a person of the Dharma even if one hears little.

260. One is not an elder just because one has gray hair; he who is merely aged is called a dotard.

261. One who is sincere, is just, does not harm living beings, knows moderation, is controlled, and has discarded impurities of mind, indeed, is called an elder.

262. One who is possessed of jealousy, stinginess, and arrogance cannot be called a beautiful person by cajolement and flattery.

263. One who is totally freed from these and has uprooted them and thrown away the hatred in one's mind is called a beautiful person.

264. One is not a mendicant just because one has a shaven head; how could one be called a mendicant when one does not follow the precepts, tells lies, and is greedy?

265. One who subdues evil, small or great, is called a mendicant, for having renounced evils.

266. Because one receives food from others does not mean that he is a mendicant. One is not a mendicant as long as he follows impure ways.

267. One who discards both virtue and vice and practices the pure acts and lives with wisdom, indeed, is called a mendicant.

268. Even though one keeps silence, if one is foolish and has no wisdom, one is not a sage.

269. One is a sage if one chooses the good and discards the evil after weighing both. A sage has the capacity to weigh the good and evil of the world.

270. If one harms living beings, one is not a holy person; because of harmlessness toward all living beings is one called a sage.

271. Not only by observing precepts, learning much, attaining meditation, and living in solitude

272. have I arrived at the bliss that no ordinary person experiences. Disciples, do not rest content so long as you have not attained the extinction of defilements.

The Path

273. Supreme is the Eightfold Noble path among paths, the Four Noble Truths among truths, the teaching to free oneself from greed among teachings, and the Buddha among people.

274. This is the only way; there is no other way for purifying one's view. Follow this path. This is the way to discomfit the demons.

275. By practicing this path, you will have an end to suffering; this is the path that I taught when I removed the poisoned arrow with wisdom.

276. You yourself have to make the effort; the Buddha is only the teacher. One who enters the path and practices concentration will surely be delivered from the bonds of devils.

277. "All things are transient." When one sees this with wisdom, one becomes weary of suffering. This is the path to purity.

278. "All things are suffering." When one sees this with wisdom, one becomes weary of suffering. This is the path to purity.

279. "All things have no self." When one sees this with wisdom, one becomes weary of suffering. This is the path to purity.

280. One who does not bestir oneself when one should, who, when young and strong, is indolent and weak-willed, will never know the path of wisdom.

281. Control your words, control your mind, and do no evil with your body. Purifying these three actions, you enter the ways of sages.

282. Meditation gives birth to wisdom; without meditation, wisdom is no more. Knowing this twofold path of gain and loss, let one conduct oneself so that wisdom many grow.

283. Cut down the forest of defilements, not just a tree. Dangers grow in the forest. Cutting down both forest and brushwood, deliver yourself from defilements.

284. As long as the lust of man toward woman, however slight it may be, is not cut off, one's mind will not be freed from bondage, as a calf clinging to its mother is not.

285. Cut off your affection for yourself as you do an autumn lotus with your hand; cultivate only the path of serenity, the nirvana taught by the Buddha.

286. "I shall live here in the rainy season, in autumn, and in summer." Thinking thus, the fool does not realize the approach of imminent death.

287. Like the great flood washing away a sleeping village, death seizes people with their minds set on their children and herds.

288. To one who is caught by death, sons and daughters cannot be relied upon. Father and mother cannot be depended upon, neither can one take refuge among his kinsfolk.

289. Knowing this, the virtuous and wise quickly purify the path to nirvana.

Miscellaneous Verses

290. One who discards a small pleasure gains a larger happiness. The wise, seeing this large happiness, should throw away the smaller pleasure.

291. One who wants to attain one's happiness by causing others to suffer will be caught in hatred and will never free oneself from hatred.

292. For one who leaves undone what should be done, does what should be left undone, and who is arrogant and negligent, only defilements increase.

293. For one who is always aware of the defilement of the body, does not do what should not be done, does what should be done, and is mindful and reflective, defilements will come to an end.

294. Having killed the father of conceit, the mother of craving, and the two kings of the wrong views of existence and nonexistence, and having destroyed the country and people of greed, the true brahmin has no misery.

295. Having killed the father of conceit, the mother of craving, and the two kings of the wrong views of existence and nonexistence, and having killed the enemy of doubt, the true brahmin has no anxieties.

296. Always awake, the disciples of the Buddha day and night contemplate the Buddha.

297. Always awake, the disciples of the Buddha day and night contemplate the Dharma.

298. Always awake, the disciples of the Buddha day and night contemplate the Sangha.

299. Always awake, the disciples of the Buddha day and night contemplate the body.

300. Always awake, the disciples of the Buddha day and night delight in being harmless.

301. Always awake, the disciples of the Buddha day and night delight in the practice of the path.

302. To leave home is difficult, to delight in the practice of a mendicant is difficult, to live in the monk's quarters is difficult, and being a householder is suffering. For a noble to live with the lowly is difficult. To travel far in the cycle of life and death is suffering. Therefore do not travel far and suffering will not follow you.

303. One who has faith, observes discipline, and has honor and wealth is highly respected wherever he may be.

304. A good person is known from afar, like the Himalayas, but the evil one is not seen, like an arrow shot in the dark.

305. One who sits in one place, sleeps in one place, walks alone unremittingly, and restrains and controls himself will be delighted in the extinction of desires.

Downward Course

306. One who lies goes to hell; so does one who, though one has done evil, says one has not done evil. These two will equally become vulgar human beings in the next life.

307. Though wearing a yellow robe, an evil one who has many evil thoughts and does not restrain nor control oneself, because of one's evil, will go into hell.

308. If one does not observe precepts and control his body, one might as well swallow a red-hot iron ball breathing flame as receive an offering of food.

309. One who is negligent and commits adultery with another's wife will receive four results; being unvirtuous, not sleeping peacefully, being censured by others, and falling into hell.

310. The pleasure of a fearful man with a fearful woman is brief. The king imposes a severe punishment, and they themselves will fall into hell. Therefore never go to another man's wife.

311. Wrongly grasped blades of grass cut the hand. Likewise, the practices of the mendicant, if wrongly done, will drag one into hell.

312. There is no great merit in pure deeds done with doubt and hesitation, or in clean practices done with indolence.

313. Do whatever should be done with vigor; an indolent mendicant scatters the dust all the more.

314. Do not do evil deeds, for one will regret them thereafter; do good deeds, and there will be no regret thereafter.

315. Like a castle well guarded within and without, guard yourself well. Do not pass time in vain; if you let even a moment pass in a meaningless way, you will fall into hell and suffer.

316. One who is ashamed of what is not shameful and not ashamed of what is shameful harbors an evil view and will fall into hell.

317. One who has fear of what is not to be feared and has no fear of the fearsome embraces an evil view and falls into hell.

318. One who sees wrong where there is no wrong and sees no wrong where there is wrong embraces an evil view and will fall into hell.

319. One who knows evil as evil and not evil as not evil embraces the right view and will be born in a good realm.

Elephant

320. As an elephant on the battlefield endures the arrows shot at it, I, too, will bear the slanders directed at me, since most people are unvirtuous.

321. People lead well-trained elephants to the battlefield. The king mounts the well-trained elephant. One who controls oneself and bears slanders is supreme among people.

322. Mules are good if well-trained, and so are the horses of the Indus and the elephants with big tusks; but one who controls oneself is far superior.

323. That is because even with those riding animals, one cannot go to untrodden places, but one who restrains oneself, with one's self-control, can go anywhere.

324. The elephant called Treasure Guardian is difficult to control while he is in rut; he does not eat but longs for the forest where he once dwelt.

325. The foolish one, lethargic, gluttonous, and dozing day and night like a big cloyed hog, will go through the cycle of rebirth again and again.

326. Formerly, this mind of mine went wandering wherever it desired, as it pleased and listed; now I am able rightly to restrain it like an elephant trainer controlling a raging elephant.

327. Learn to delight in diligence; guard your mind and pull yourself out of the evil way like an elephant rising from the mud into which it had fallen.

328. One who is fortunate enough to have a friend who is wise, lives the right life, and has forethought should, with right mindfulness, go along with him, finding joy in overcoming dangers.

329. One who has not found a friend who is wise, lives the right life, and has forethought should go alone, like a king who abandons the country he has conquered or like an elephant king in the forest.

330. An evil one is not worthy of being a friend; it is better to go alone, like a lone elephant king in the forest, and do no evil.

331. When needs arise, to have friends is happiness; to know contentment in anything and everything is happiness; virtuous merits are happiness when life comes to an end; to cast away all sufferings is pleasant.

332. It is happiness that there are fathers in this world; it is happiness that there are mothers; it is happiness that there are mendicants, and it is happiness that there are sages in this world.

333. Abiding by the precepts until old age is happiness; to have faith firmly rooted is happiness; the attainment of wisdom is happiness; not doing evil deeds is happiness.

Craving

334. To self-indulgent ones, craving grows like a creeper; they wander from life to life, like monkeys in search of fruits.

335. The sorrows of the one who is overcome by this base and poisonous lust will grow like birana grass.

336. The sorrows of the one who overcomes this base and hard-to-sever craving will leave him like the water drop slipping from the leaf.

337. Therefore, I say these good words to all of you who are assembled here: "Uproot your craving as one who seeks a fragrant root digs up the birana weeds. Let not King Mara conquer you again and again like a stream breaking the reeds and sweeping them away."

338. A tree, even though cut down, will grow again if its roots are strong and firm. Likewise, unless the defilements of lust are removed, suffering will arise again.

339. As thirty-six unclean rushing streams flow through the plain of lust, the current of craving will sweep away those men of wrong view.

340. The streams of craving flow everywhere; the creepers of greed sprout constantly. When you see the creeper sprouting, uproot it with your wisdom.

341. Pleasure constantly wanders about and clings to sense-objects. They who attach themselves to pleasure will go through the samsara of life and death.

342. One whose mind is caught by craving, like a hare caught in a snare, runs around. Caught in the fetters of defilement, one will suffer for a long time, again and again.

343. One whose mind is caught by craving runs around like a hare caught in a trap; one should, therefore, discard greed and rid oneself of the thirst of lust.

344. One who frees oneself from defilement again enters another forest of defilement; after freeing oneself from this, one runs into still another forest. Look at this person who goes into bondage after being freed, again and again.

345. The wise say that bonds made of iron, wood, or grass are not strong; attachments to rings made of precious stones and to wife and children are strong.

346. "Those bonds are coarse and loose, but they are difficult to escape," says the wise person. He has cut these ties; with no one to have affection for, he discards greed and pleasure and becomes a mendicant.

347. One who indulges in greed flows down the stream of one's own making like a spider following the web of its own spinning. The wise severs this greed and, freeing oneself from attachments and all sufferings, leaves one's home.

348. Let go the past, let go the future, let go the present; this is reaching the other shore. With a mind released from everything, one does not go back to birth and old age.

349. One who is led astray by discriminative thoughts is of strong passions and sees only the pleasurable; as craving steadily grows, one makes the bondage strong.

350. One who delights in subduing discriminative thoughts, meditates on impurity, and is always rightly mindful will sever the bondage of Mara.

351. One who has reached the goal is fearless, is without craving or defilement, and has plucked out the arrow of existence; this is one's final bodily existence.

352. One who is without craving and attachment, is knowledgeable of the sacred words, and knows the meaning of the words in their contexts is called a person of profound wisdom, the bearer of one's final body.

353. I have overcome all; I know all; I am detached from all; I have renounced all; I have extirpated craving; and I have delivered myself with my wisdom. Whom shall I call my teacher?

354. The gift of the Dharma excels all gifts; the taste of the Dharma excels all tastes; the happiness of the Dharma excels all happiness; one who has eliminated craving overcomes all suffering.

355. If one does not seek the other shore, wealth ruins the foolish one; by craving for wealth, the foolish one ruins oneself.

356. Weeds destroy the field; craving destroys people; hence offerings to the person who has no craving bring great reward.

357. Weeds destroy the field; anger destroys people; hence offerings to the person who has no anger bring great reward.

358. Weeds destroy the field; ignorance destroys people; hence offerings to the person who has no ignorance bring great reward.

359. Weeds destroy the field; desire destroys people; hence offerings to the person who has no greed bring great reward.

The Buddha's Disciples

360. Restraining the eye is good, restraining the ear is good, restraining the nose is good, and restraining the tongue is good.

361. Restraining bodily action is good, restraining speech is good, restraining the mind is good, restraining everything is good. The disciples of the Buddha restrain all and are free from all sufferings.

362. One whose hands, feet, and mouth are controlled in the highest degree has inner joy. One who delights in meditation and is alone and contented is called a disciple of the Buddha.

363. The disciple who is controlled in tongue, speaks wisely, and is not disquieted sets forth the Dharma well. His speech is indeed good.

364. The disciple who lives in the Dharma, who well remembers the Dharma, who meditates on the Dharma, and who delights in the Dharma does not fall back from the Dharma.

365. Do not belittle what you have received nor envy what others have received. The disciple who envies what others have attained does not attain a peaceful mind.

366. Even if what the disciple has received is small, if he does not slight what he has received and is pure in livelihood and not idle, even the gods praise him.

367. One who has no thought of "mine" toward anything, one who does not grieve for what he does not have, is indeed called a disciple.

368. The disciple who lives in loving-kindness and delights in the Buddha's teaching attains that state of peace and happiness.

369. Disciples, scoop the water out of the boat, and it will sail swiftly. Severing greed and anger, you will attain nirvana.

370. Sever the five defilements, give up the five illusions, and cultivate the five virtues. The disciple who has gone beyond the five defilements is called one who has crossed the stream.

371. Disciples, meditate quietly. Do not be negligent. Do not direct your mind toward the pleasures of the five senses. Do not be negligent and do not in hell swallow hot iron balls. Do not be burnt by the fire to cry out, "This is painful!"

372. There is no concentration of mind to one who lacks wisdom; and there is no wisdom to one who lacks concentration. One who has both is, indeed, close to enlightenment.

373. The disciple who goes into solitude and calms his mind clearly perceives the Dharma and experiences a joy transcending this world.

374. The right knowledge of the birth and death of body and mind becomes a nectar to the knower. He will gain joy and happiness.

375. These are what the mendicants should do: Control the five senses, know contentment, restrain themselves with discipline, live a clean life, associate with good friends who make a constant effort,

376. And have warm friendships. If they form the habit of conducting themselves well, they will find much joy and will make an end of suffering.

377. Like the jasmine that lets its withered flowers fall, disciples, you should cast off greed and anger.

378. The disciple who is calm in body, calm in speech, and calm in mind and who is free from worldly pleasures is called a person of quietude.

379. Censuring oneself by oneself, examining oneself by oneself, the disciple retains his right mindfulness and lives happily.

380. Oneself is the master of oneself, oneself is one's own refuge; therefore control your own self as a travelling merchant controls his horse.

381. The disciple who greatly rejoices in and believes in the Buddha's teaching will attain the quiet and peaceful state where the sorrows of the world cease.

382. The disciple who devotes himself to the Buddha's teaching even when young illumines this world like the moon emerging from the clouds.

The Brahmin

383. Courageously cut off the stream of defilements and eliminate all desires. Dear brahmin, if you know that all things are calm, then you know nirvana.

384. Dear brahmin, if you know self-control and quiet meditation, then all your fetters are cut off.

385. The one for whom there is neither this shore nor that, the one who is fearless and free from bondage, I call a brahmin.

386. The one who is meditative, is undefiled, sits unwaveringly, has done what he should do, is free from defilement, and has attained the highest goal I call a brahmin.

387. The sun heats up the day; the moon lights up the night; the warrior is resplendent when armored; the brahmin is bright as he meditates in calmness; but the Buddha shines with his awe-inspiring majesty both day and night.

388. Because one is free of evil deeds, he is called a brahmin; because he discards stains, he is called mendicant.

389. Do not strike a brahmin; a brahmin when struck should not become angered. One who strikes a brahmin will be execrated; a brahmin struck and angered will be execrated even more.

390. It is good for a brahmin to stand aloof from what pleases him; when the intent to harm is resisted, suffering ends.

391. One who, with no evil in body, mouth, or mind, controls these three, I call a brahmin.

392. Whoever conveys to you the teaching of the Buddha, revere him like a brahmin worshipping the fire.

393. Not because of matted hair, nor because of family lineage or birth, is one a brahmin; with truth and righteousness is one a true brahmin.

394. Oh, you foolish one, what is there to having matted hair and wearing animal skin? You are just feigning purity but are really full of defilements within.

395. Wearing a robe of cast-off rags, gaunt with veins showing, if one sits in solitary meditation deep in the forest, I call him a brahmin.

396. Not because of his birth nor because of his mother do I call a man a brahmin. One who is arrogant and possesses things is not a brahmin. One who is without possessions or attachments is called a brahmin.

397. One who has cut off all fetters, is fearless, has freed himself from attachments, and is unbound, I call a brahmin.

398. One who has cut off the cord, strap, rope, and other articles that go along with them, all of which are carried by brahmins, and who has cast away the crossbar of fetters and is awakened, I call a brahmin.

399. One who is without evil, endures reproach, whips, and fetters, and has a strong power of patience, I call a brahmin.

400. One who is without anger and greed, is self-controlled, observes the precepts, conducts himself properly, and is freed from the birth of delusion is called a brahmin.

401. One who, like a drop of water on a lotus leaf, like a grain of poppy seed on the point of a needle, does not attach himself to sensual lust, I call a brahmin.

402. One who, while in this world, realizes the annihilation of suffering, has laid his burden aside, and is free from fetters, I call a brahmin.

403. One who has deep wisdom, is intelligent, discerns right from wrong, and has fulfilled the highest goal, I call a brahmin.

404. One who keeps aloof from both householders and mendicants, who wanders without abode, and who is without desire, I call a brahmin.

405. One who does not harm living beings nor cause others to harm them, I call a brahmin.

406. One who has no conflict among the hostile, is peaceful among the violent, and has no attachment though being among those who have, I call a brahmin.

407. One from whom greed, anger, pride, and detraction have fallen away, like a poppy seed dropping off from the point of a needle, I call a brahmin.

408. One who speaks no harsh words but rather true words that contain the teaching, and who gives no offense to anyone, I call a brahmin.

409. One who, while in this world, takes nothing that is not given, be it small or great, pure or impure, I call a brahmin.

410. One who has no craving, either in this world or in the next, and is freed from fetters, I call a brahmin.

411. One who no longer has attachment, is freed from doubts by wisdom, and has reached the state wholly free from death, I call a brahmin.

412. One who is free from the attachment to both merit and demerit, is without anguish or defilement, and is pure, I call a brahmin.

413. One who is free from the desire for life, like the clear moon serene in the cloudless sky, I call a brahmin.

414. One who has passed beyond the path of the mire, of evilness, of the life-death cycle, and of ignorance, and who has reached the other shore and is now calmly meditating, without greed, doubt, or attachment, and who dwells in peace, I call a brahmin.

415. One who, while in this world, has freed himself from greed, who has become homeless, who leads a wandering life, and who has given up lust, I call a brahmin.

416. One who, while in this world, has freed himself from craving, who has become homeless, who leads a wandering life, and who has given up lust, I call a brahmin.

417. One who has transcended the bonds of human and heavenly realms and has severed all fetters, I call a brahmin.

418. One who has cast away the discrimination of pleasant and unpleasant, is cooled and freed from the source of delusion, and is the most courageous in all the worlds, I call a brahmin.

419. One who knows the births and deaths of all beings, has the joy of being freed from attachment, and is awakened, I call a brahmin.

420. One whose path is not known even to the gods, who has eliminated defilements, and who has attained enlightenment, I call a brahmin.

421. One who in the past, present, or future has nothing to cling to, who possesses nothing and is without attachment, I call a brahmin.

422. One who is fearless, noble, heroic, greatly sagacious, victorious, desireless, and thoroughly learned, I call a brahmin.

423. The sage who knows his former lives, knows heaven and hell, has reached the end of births, has perfect wisdom, and has attained perfection in all things, I call a brahmin.

Chapter 2

AMITAYUS BUDDHA'S PRIMAL VOW AND SALVATION

1. Bodhisattva Dharmakara

(1) The Buddha was on the mountain called Vulture Peak. One day, when many disciples were sitting around the Buddha, Ananda rose from his seat, arranged his upper garment over one shoulder, and placed his right knee on the ground; then, putting his hands together, he addressed the Buddha, "World-Honored One, today your appearance is pure, and your countenance is limpid. I have never seen you look so sublime as you do now. The question occurs to me: Is not the World-Honored One today at peace, dwelling in the state of a Buddha's enlightenment, in the practice of a Great Leader, and in contemplation of all the buddhas of the three periods, and are they not in turn contemplating the World-Honored One?"

The Buddha said to Ananda, "Excellent, Ananda! Did the gods suggest that you ask this question, or was it through your own thought?" Ananda said to the Buddha, "The gods did not suggest this question to me. It was through my own thought that it occurred to me."

The World-Honored One said to Ananda, "Well said, Ananda; your question is very good. When you asked this question, you manifested deep understanding and showed compassion toward sentient beings. The reason that the Buddha with his infinite compassion toward all appeared in this world was to spread the Dharma, to save all sentient beings, and to bestow true benefit upon them. Even in all the innumerable kalpas it is hard to meet with the appearance of a Buddha; the appearance of a Buddha is an occurrence as rare as the blossoming of the udumbara tree. Your question will benefit all beings. Ananda, the Buddha's wisdom of enlightenment is beyond comprehension, and nothing can hinder the wisdom of enlightenment. The Buddha can live for hundreds of thousands of millions of kalpas on a single meal; his appearance with its bright lights will never change. Why is this? Because the Buddha's wisdom has no limit and he is able to use his omnipotence at will. Indeed, Ananda, your question about the appearance of the Buddha in this world has been made possible by the power of the Buddha. Listen well with all your heart. I shall speak for your sake now.

(2) "In the infinitely remote past, Dipankara Buddha appeared in this world. He taught the Dharma to a countless number of beings, leading them to enlightenment. Then fifty-three buddhas appeared successively in this world, and in the end the Buddha Lokesvararaja appeared in this world. At that time there was a king who heard the teaching of this Buddha, felt a great joy, and aspired to seek the true path. He abandoned his country and throne, became a mendicant, and called himself Dharmakara. His brilliance and wisdom, as well as his diligence, had no equal in the world. He called on Lokesvararaja Buddha and praised the Buddha's virtue in verse.

(i)   Your graceful countenance, immeasurable dignity, and light so brilliant have no equal in the world. No other light can shine in your presence. Even the sun and moon and jewels seem like a heap of char before you. Your great voice echoes and reaches the ten directions. The virtues of your disciplines, listening, efforts, meditation, and wisdom are incomparable. Your deep wisdom meditates on the ocean of the Buddha's Dharma, whose depth and breadth you fully understand.

(ii)   Ignorance, greed, and anger the World-Honored One has long been without. The merits of the world's courageous Buddha are innumerable. Your wisdom is deep; your virtuous light illuminates the worlds. Upon attaining Buddhahood and becoming equal to the masters of the Dharma, I shall deliver all people from the suffering of birth and death. Practicing giving, precepts, mind control, forbearance, effort, meditation, and wisdom, I aspire to become a savior for people who are full of fears.

(iii) There are many buddhas; their number is as great as that of the sands of the Ganges. But rather than paying homage to these buddhas, I choose to seek the path and not to regress. I shall illumine the countless Buddha worlds that are as many as the sands of the Ganges. There will be no limit to my efforts and powers. Upon my becoming a Buddha, my land will be supreme; those who dwell there will be most wonderful; the place of teaching will be most excellent. My land will be as joyous as nirvana and will be without comparison. With abiding compassion I shall save all people.

(iv)   All people coming from the ten directions will be with pure and joyous hearts; they will know happiness and peace unsurpassable. I beg you, O Buddha, to teach me the truth, and I shall strive in accordance with my vows. The buddhas in the ten directions have unimpeded wisdom; let them know my mind all the time. Whatever suffering I may undergo, I shall make the utmost effort and never change my vows.

(3) "The monk Dharmakara, having thus praised Lokesvararaja Buddha, said to him, 'World-Honored One, I vow to attain true enlightenment. Please instruct me about all the ways of truth. I shall practice them to realize a pure Buddha country. I wish to save all people who are suffering in the world of birth and death.' Then Lokesvararaja Buddha said, 'You must yourself know already how to establish a Buddha land.' The monk Dharmakara said, 'This is so wide and deep a matter that it is beyond my comprehension. Please teach me the practices that all the buddhas have engaged in to construct their countries.'

"Then Lokesvararaja Buddha, seeing the deep, wide, and noble aspiration of the monk Dharmakara, said to him, 'It is as when a person tries to dry up a great ocean. If one continues to scoop tirelessly for countless kalpas, one will reach the bottom and will be able to get the treasures. Similarly he who single-mindedly continues to pursue the path surely will fulfill his aspiration.'

"The Buddha made manifest before the Bodhisattva twenty-one billion buddha countries and explained to him all the unique features of each country. After observing these pure countries, the Bodhisattva Dharmakara made a great vow unsurpassed in the world. For five long kalpas, the Bodhisattva contemplated on the ways to establish and to adorn the ideal land with virtues. The Bodhisattva again came to the presence of Lokesvararaja Buddha and said,

(4) "'World-Honored One, I shall disclose now my special vows. Upon my attainment of Buddhahood, my country will be adorned with these virtues difficult even to conceive of:

(i) Upon my attainment of Buddhahood, if there should be a hell, a world of hungry ghosts, or a world of beasts, may I not achieve enlightenment.

(ii) If, upon my attainment of Buddhahood, people in my country fall back into those three evil realms, may I not achieve enlightenment.

(iii) If, upon my attainment of Buddhahood, the people born in my country give rise to the thought of a self or what is possessed by a self, may I not achieve enlightenment.

(iv) If, upon my attainment of Buddhahood, people in my country cannot attain the rank of the truly assured and reach nirvana without fail, may I not achieve enlightenment.

(v) If, upon my attainment of Buddhahood, my light is limited and does not illumine ten billion nayutas of Buddha lands, may I not achieve enlightenment.

(vi) If, upon my attainment of Buddhahood, my life span is limited and does not exceed at least ten billion nayutas of kalpas, may I not achieve enlightenment.

(vii) If, upon my attainment of Buddhahood, all the innumerable buddhas in the ten directions should not praise my name, may I not achieve enlightenment.

(viii)If, upon my attainment of Buddhahood, all beings in the ten directions, with sincerity of heart, have faith and joy and, aspiring to be born in my country, repeat my name perhaps even ten times, yet are not born there, may I not achieve enlightenment. Those who have committed the five grave offences and those who have slandered the true Dharma, however, are excluded.

(ix) If, upon my attainment of Buddhahood, beings in the ten directions arouse the intention of seeking the path, practice virtuous deeds, and single-mindedly aspire to be born in my country, and I do not, at the time of their deaths, appear before them surrounded by a great assembly, may I not achieve enlightenment.

(x) If, upon my attainment of Buddhahood, beings in the ten directions who hear my name, keep their thoughts on my country, foster various good roots of merit, and single-mindedly aspire to be born in my country cannot attain it, may I not achieve enlightenment.

(xi) Upon my attainment of Buddhahood, the bodhisattvas of other buddha countries born in my country should attain the rank of being assured of becoming buddhas in the next life. Moreover, those bodhisattvas who wish to save others at will should wear the armor of vows, wander in all countries, lead as many people as the number of sands of the Ganges to the right path to enlightenment, and accumulate the merits of great compassion. If this is unattainable, may I not achieve enlightenment.

(xii) If, upon my attainment of Buddhahood, my country is not pure and limpid and does not reflect like a clear mirror a countless number of buddha countries in the ten directions, may I not achieve enlightenment.

(xiii) If, upon my attainment of Buddhahood, in my country from the great earth up to the empty sky, all the palaces, towers, lakes, streams, and flower gardens are not adorned with countless gems and fragrances, may I not achieve enlightenment.

(xiv)If, upon my attainment of Buddhahood, all beings in countless countries in the ten directions, when touched by my light, do not become gentle in both body and mind and do not have joy superior to that of beings and gods, may I not achieve enlightenment.

(xv) If, upon my attainment of Buddhahood, all beings in my country do not have the same joy as that of the sages who have freed themselves of defilements, may I not achieve enlightenment.

(5) "At this, the Bodhisattva Dharmakara, having made these vows, said in verse:

(i) I establish the vows unexcelled to reach enlightenment. If these vows are unfulfilled, may I never attain enlightenment. I would be the great provider throughout innumerable kalpas. If I fail to save all who are poor and suffering, may I never attain enlightenment. Upon my attaining Buddhahood, if my name is not heard throughout the ten directions, may I never attain enlightenment.

(ii) Freed from greed and steeped in right thought, with wisdom pure, I shall practice the noble way. Seeking the highest path, I shall be the teacher of all beings and gods.

Becoming the master of the great light, brightening the countless countries throughout and removing the darkness of greed, anger, and ignorance, I shall deliver all from suffering in darkness.

Opening the eyes of wisdom, I shall end this darkness of ignorance. Blocking all the paths to evil realms, I shall open the gate to the good realms.

Having virtues fulfilled, my awe-inspiring light will illumine the ten directions. The sun and the moon being outshone, the gods' light will remain hidden.

(iii) Opening the storehouse of the Dharma, I shall bestow the treasures of my virtues to all. Constantly going among the masses, I shall teach the

Dharma with a lion's roar. Paying homage to all the buddhas, I shall be endowed with all virtues. Vows and wisdom completely fulfilled, I shall be the master of the three worlds.

The Buddha's unimpeded wisdom reaches everything; so my powers of virtue and wisdom will be equal to those of the Buddha. If my vows are to be fulfilled, may this whole universe quake, and may the gods in heaven rain beautiful blossoms from above.

(6) The Buddha said to Ananda, "When the Bodhisattva Dharmakara recited these verses, the earth trembled in the six directions. Beautiful flowers rained from above, and heavenly music was heard from nowhere, praising the Bodhisattva in this wise: 'He will certainly attain enlightenment.' The Bodhisattva Dharmakara proclaimed the vows at every assembly and put forth the effort to establish a Buddha land that would never decline. For innumerable long kalpas he accumulated immeasurable virtues; he never generated thoughts of greed, of anger, or of harming others; he never had a sense of attachment under any circumstances; he was easily contented with very few wants; he was always serene in meditation; he was unhindered in his wisdom; he cultivated patience; he had no thought of falsity nor flattery; he spoke tenderly and with a kind countenance; he strove tirelessly, ever seeking the pure Dharma; he led all others to accumulate virtues. As he lived in the truth of emptiness, formlessness, and desirelessness, he refrained from using harsh words that would harm both himself and others; he learned to use good words. Once he was born a king, he abandoned the throne, avoided wealth and lust, and practiced the Six Perfections and also taught others to practice them. Ananda, the Bodhisattva Dharmakara accumulated virtues and merits and led a countless number of people to enlightenment. It is impossible to mention all his great virtues."

2. Buddha of Infinite Life

(1) Ananda asked the Buddha, "Has the Bodhisattva Dharmakara already attained enlightenment and entered nirvana? Or has he not yet attained enlightenment?"

The Buddha said to Ananda, "The Bodhisattva Dharmakara has already become the Buddha Amitayus (Infinite Life) ten kalpas ago and is now living and teaching the Dharma in the western quarter ten billion countries away from here. His Buddha land is called Land of Peace and Happiness. The ground of that Buddha land is made of gold, silver, lapis lazuli, and other jewels. The land is wide and extensive; it has no bounds. The lights shine brightly. In that land there are no mountains, seas, or valleys, but because of the great power of the Buddha one can see these the moment one wishes to see them. There are no three evil realms and there are no such seasons as spring or autumn. It is neither cold nor hot but always mildly warm. The light that emanates from the Buddha is august, and none of the lights of any other Buddha is comparable. Because of this, the Buddha Infinite Life is also called the Buddha Infinite Light, the Buddha Boundless Light, the Buddha Unimpeded Light, the Buddha Incomparable Light, the Buddha Flame King, the Buddha Pure Light, the Buddha

Joyous Light, the Buddha Wisdom Light, the Buddha Incessant Light, the Buddha Inconceivable Light, the Buddha Inexpressible Light, and the Buddha Light That Surpasses the Sun and the Moon.

"He who sees this light will free himself from the defilements of greed, anger, and ignorance. His body and mind will become gentle. His heart will rejoice, and good will spring up in his mind. He who comes across this light in the painful and sorrowful evil realms of hell, hungry spirits, and beasts will have respite from suffering; and when life ends he will attain liberation. The light of the Buddha Amitayus is bright and shines over the lands of the ten directions; and there is no country it does not reach. It is not I alone who praise his light; all the buddhas and bodhisattvas praise it.

(2) "And in the land of highest bliss, there are various scents from different kinds of aromatic trees where beautiful birds are singing. When soft breezes come, the branches of the trees touch each other, sending the voice of the excellent Dharma to every single land; those who hear the sound of the Dharma arouse deep faith in their minds and reach the state of non-retrogression to the evil path. Indeed, the single sound of the treasure trees surpasses billions of times over the music of the worlds of the gods. And the lecture halls, monks' quarters, palaces, and towers are all adorned with gems; and here and there lie great ponds full of clear water. Each pond, with golden sands, jewelled banks, and agate and coral sands, is made of gems where red and blue lotus flowers bloom with beautiful scents.

"Bodhisattvas who go into the pond can have any depth of water that they wish; the water will wash their bodies as they wish. The warmth of the water is pleasantly suited to their bodies; it will open their hearts and wash away impurities.

"Pure, clear, and clean is the water, looking as if nonexistent; it reflects on the golden sands and makes small ripples that flow down, making wonderfully beautiful sounds. The sounds become the voices of the Buddha, the Dharma, and the Sangha, or those of emptiness, non-self, and great compassion. The land of the Buddha is pure and peaceful; the joy in the land is the blissful joy of enlightenment free from suffering. Those who dwell in the land acquire high wisdom and unsurpassable powers. All are endowed with beautiful features, with the bodies of the world of nirvana, and with infinite life spans. And the clothing, the meals, the flowers, the incense, the strings of gems, the mansions, the palaces, and the towers come out as one pleases and as one thinks about them. The four corners of the towers are decorated with jewelled screens with inlaid pearls and bells of gems. As the pleasant breezes gently start blowing on the jewelled screens and pass through the trees of gems, wonderfully beautiful sounds of the Dharma flow in the four directions together with various fragrances. As one listens to the sounds of these, illusion and suffering disappear, and one attains the joy of sages who are free from defilements.

(3) "The breezes scatter the flowers widely on the ground. The flowers are so configured that there is no mixture or confusion of colors. The scents float strongly and the flowers are softly bright and softly fragrant. As one steps on them, they sink four inches, but as one raises one's foot, they return to the former level.

When the flowers start to wilt, the earth opens, and they disappear one after another. But the winds scatter down new flowers six times in one day and night. Varieties of lotuses bloom throughout the land. Each flower of gems possesses hundreds of thousands of millions of petals, and the innumerable lights of the petals possess various colors.

"The blue lotuses emit blue light and the white, white. Similarly dark red, yellow, vermillion, and purple lotuses emit each its own color. Their brightness outshines the lights of the sun and the moon. Each flower sends forth thirty-six hundred thousand million rays, and from each ray come out thirty-six hundred thousand million buddhas. The color of the bodies is purple gold, and their marks and characteristics are wonderful. Each Buddha sends forth again hundreds and thousands of rays and gives the beings of the ten directions the Dharma wonderful and marvelous. Each Buddha enlightens countless beings, enabling each to find peace in the right path."

3. Awakening of Faith

(1) The Buddha said to Ananda, "All the beings who are born in the land of Amitayus Buddha are destined to reach the perfect state, for in that Buddha land no beings can be born who are destined for evil births, or whose destinies are not yet determined. All the buddhas of the ten directions praise the inconceivably wonderful and unsurpassable virtues of Amitayus Buddha. All who hear the name of this Buddha, joyfully trust in him, and, at that moment of thought, transfer their merit to being born in the Buddha's land will immediately be born there and unfailingly attain the stage of non-retrogression in their progress toward full enlightenment. Excluded, however, are those who have committed the five grave offences and those who have slandered the True Teaching."

The Buddha said to Ananda, "There are three kinds of people in the world who sincerely wish to be born in the Buddha's land. Those of the first kind are those who leave their homes aspiring to attain enlightenment, directing their thought exclusively toward Amitayus Buddha, and desiring to be born in his Buddha land by practicing all virtues. As they are about to depart from this life, Amitayus Buddha, with a great assemblage, will appear before them. Assisted by the Buddha, they will be born in flowers made of seven gems in his land, attain the state of great wisdom, and gain the free exercise of superhuman powers. Therefore, Ananda, he who wishes to see Amitayus Buddha in this world should aspire to seek the way, should practice virtue, and should desire to be born in the Buddha land.

"Those of the second kind are those who do not renounce home and are unable to practice virtues exclusively but aspire to attain enlightenment and direct their thought exclusively toward Amitayus Buddha. They desire to be born in that land by practicing virtues to some extent, following precepts, erecting stupas, making offerings to mendicants, and offering light and flowers and incense to the Buddha. As they are about to depart from this life, they will be met by Amitayus Buddha manifesting himself in a transformed body; and they will be born in the Buddha land. Their virtue and wisdom will be equal to those of the first kind of beings.

"Those of the third kind are those who aspire to attain enlightenment while not being able to practice the virtues; they direct their thought single-heartedly and exclusively, one to ten times during a lifetime, toward Amitayus Buddha, and they aspire to be born in the Buddha land. They hear the profound Dharma, joyously believe in it without having any doubts, produce even just one thought and direct it toward that Buddha, and with the sincerest heart aspire to be born in his Buddha land. As they are about to depart from this life, they will see the Buddha in a dream and be born in his land. Their virtue and wisdom will be equal to those of the second kind of beings."

(2) The Buddha said to Ananda, "There is no limit to the majesty of Amitayus Buddha. All the innumerable bodhisattvas of the buddha lands in the east, who are as innumerable as the sands of the river Ganges, pay homage to Amitayus Buddha, listen to his teachings, and in turn teach others. Those of the south, the west, the north, the four intermediate directions, the zenith, and the nadir do likewise." Then the Buddha said in verse:

(i) All the children of the Buddha bring with them marvellous flowers, incenses, and robes and offer them to Amitayus Buddha.

They all play blissful tunes, singing and praising the virtues of the Buddha, and they give offerings to Amitayus Buddha and say,

'Fully attaining supernatural power and wisdom, the Buddha has attained the profound knowledge of the Dharma and acquired a treasury of virtues. His wondrous wisdom is without equal.

His wisdom shines upon the world as does the sun and disperses all the clouds of delusions.'

(ii) The bodhisattvas circumambulate Amitayus Buddha three times, paying homage to him in praise: The solemn and excellent land of the Buddha is indeed beyond measure; awakening our hearts and minds toward enlightenment, we too shall aspire to attain the land of such excellent and majestic holiness. At this, the Buddha smiles, and numberless lights come out of his mouth; they brighten the lands in the ten directions. The lights go around him three times and then withdraw to his head, and those who observe this sight are overjoyed.

(iii) Then the Bodhisattva Avalokitesvara kneels down with his robe properly arranged and, prostrating himself on the ground, asks, 'Why is it that you smile? Please tell me what was in your thought.'

And the Buddha says in a voice as clear as thunder, in the eight reverberating tones, 'I shall predict to those who are assembled here the day that you will attain enlightenment. Listen to me carefully and well.

Bodhisattvas who have come from the ten directions, I know well your vows to seek the land of purity. You will become buddhas.

Though all phenomena are like dreams, like phantoms, and like echoes, if you perfect your vows, then you will certainly realize such a land. Though

everything is like mere lightning or shadows, if you practice the path of
a bodhisattva and cultivate all the virtues, then you will certainly become
a buddha. Though everything is impermanent and impersonal, if you single-
heartedly seek the land of purity, you will unfailingly gain such a land.'

(iv) And all the buddhas spoke to the bodhisattvas and made them see Amitayus Buddha and said, 'Listen to the teaching and practice the path with
joy, and be reborn at once in the land of purity.

Arriving in the Buddha land, you will attain unsurpassable power and
hear the prophecy of your day of enlightenment; you will arrive at the
stage of non-retrogression in your progress toward full enlightenment.

Thanks to the vow that the Buddha has made, all those who have heard
his name and aspired to be born in his land will be sure to be born there
and arrive at the stage of non-retrogression in their progress toward full
enlightenment.

O Bodhisattvas, make vows that your lands will be the same as that of
Amitayus Buddha; aspire to save all sentient beings and let the name be
heard in all lands.

Serve the countless buddhas and visit all their lands. Humbly serve them,
rejoice in them, and take leave of them and return to the Buddha land.'

(v) Those who do not sow the seed of virtues cannot hear this sutra. Those
who observe the pure disciplines can hear this teaching.

Those who in their past lives saw the Buddha can believe in this teaching.
If they hear the Dharma with a humble heart, they will be elated and
immersed in great joy.

It is difficult for arrogant, secretive, and lazy minds to believe in the teaching. They cannot see the heart of the Buddha. The great ocean of wisdom
of the Buddha is deep, broad, and unfathomable. Those who are still in the
causal state cannot fathom it; the Buddha alone can know it.

(vi) Hard it is to be blessed with human life, hard it is to be in a Buddha land,
and hard it is to be blessed with faith. Listen to the teaching with utmost
effort. If you listen to the teaching and do not forget it, and rejoice greatly
in it, you are then my best friends. Therefore awaken and seek the way.
Even if the whole world is on fire, go at all costs to listen to the teaching,
and then you will surely attain enlightenment, become buddhas, and save
sentient beings, who are suffering in transmigration.

(3) The Buddha said to Ananda, "Those who are born in the Buddha land
are destined to become buddhas. Aspiring to save all beings with the armor of
the main vow, they are diligently working for their salvation. They always teach
the right teaching and are led by wisdom. Toward all things in the land, they
have no attachment, and no thought of possession or clinging binds them. They
do not think in terms of 'mine.' They come and go, move or stop, and nothing
binds them. They are free in will. They have no distinctions, no likes or dislikes.
For them there is no discrimination of 'he' and 'I': there is no competition;
neither is there complaint. They have compassionate hearts, hearts to benefit

all beings. Their minds are supple and harmonious, and no anger or enmity binds them. Illusion and indolence are gone, and their minds are completely pure.

"With minds of non-discrimination, minds superior, deep, and settled, minds that love and feel joy in the teaching, these bodhisattvas discard all defilements. Cultivating all the practices of bodhisattvas, they accumulate innumerable virtues. Being accomplished in deep meditation, they gain wisdom. Their physical eyes are keen, and there is nothing that they do not see in the world. Their divine eyes see everything in all the worlds of the ten directions. Their Dharma eyes observe the hidden phenomena in the world. Their wisdom eyes see the truth and lead them to nirvana. Thus they possess the eyes of the Buddha and awaken to the nature of all things. With unobstructed wisdom they teach all beings that the world is empty and impermanent, and they teach them the way to destroy their passions. Having come out of the realm of the truth, they comprehend the Thusness of all things. They dislike taking part in idle talk, and they prefer good discussions. They practice, seek, and revere the way of the Buddha. Listening to the profound teaching of the buddhas, they have no doubts or fears. They always show extensive compassion, covering all beings like the sky and sustaining all like the earth. They master completely the teaching of the One Vehicle and reach the Other Shore. Their minds are saturated with the wisdom that cuts the net of doubt.

(4) "They have complete knowledge of all the buddhas' teachings; their wisdom is like a great ocean, and their meditation is like a high mountain. They are like the Himalayas, because they shine upon all virtues equally, and they are pure.

"They are like the great earth, because their minds do not discriminate between purity and impurity, love and hatred. They are like pure water, because they wash away all passions and impurities. They are like conflagrations, because they burn away all illusions. They are like violent windstorms, because they can pass through all the worlds unhindered. They are like the air, because they do not cling to anything. They are like lotuses, because they are not contaminated by worldly impurities. They are like large vehicles, because they carry all beings out of the world of illusion. They are like great clouds, because they roll the great thunder of the teaching and awaken the unawakened. They are like great rains, because they pour down the sweet rain of the Dharma, quenching the thirst of all beings. They are like the diamond mountains, because no other teaching can shake them. They are like garudas, because they subdue all wrong views. They are like elephant kings, because they restrain themselves well. They are like lion kings, because they fear nothing. They are like the sky, because their compassion is equal to all. They are freed from jealousy, because they do not dislike those who excel. They single-mindedly and tirelessly seek the Dharma. They always teach extensively and do not become weary. They beat the drum of the Dharma, hoist the banner of the Dharma, let shine the sun of wisdom, and dispel the darkness of ignorance. They are vigorous in spreading the Dharma, thereby becoming the sources of light and happiness in the world. They are the leaders who have neither hatred nor partial love; they happily walk the right path and endow people with peace of mind. They possess all superhuman powers and are praised by all buddhas. I give a brief account of their virtues; if I were to give a full description, it would not be complete even if I spent a hundred thousand million kalpas on it."

4. Reality of Life and the Teaching

(1) Further, the Buddha said to the Bodhisattva Maitreya, "It is not possible to go into the full details of the virtues and wisdom of the people in the land of Amitayus Buddha. The land is wonderfully delightful and pure as described. Why do the people of the world here below not make efforts to do good, think of the natural way, and attain the boundless state in which there is no distinction between high and low? They should strive for it, each by himself. Then without doubt they will be born in the land of peace and happiness; and there they will avoid an evil destiny by the power of the Buddha and attain enlightenment.

"The gate to that land is always open, and there is nothing to obstruct the entrance. It is easy to go there, yet there are hardly any who gain entrance to it. If they abandon the mundane life and make an effort to seek the way, they will gain eternal life and will have endless happiness.

(2) "However, people are thoughtless and struggle for immediate but unimportant matters. Living in the great evil and suffering of this world, they concern themselves with worldly affairs, keeping themselves barely alive. High or low, poor or rich, young or old, men or women, all worry about money. The haves and the have-nots worry equally. They are bogged down by mounting sorrows, pains, and worries. Driven by these, they have no peace of mind. If they have fields, they worry about the fields. If they have houses, they worry about the houses. Similarly, they worry about cows, horses, servants, money and wealth, food and clothing, and household things. Moreover, when these possessions are swept away by floods, burned up in fires, stolen by thieves, destroyed by enemies, or confiscated by creditors, poisonous worries press upon them and there is no detoxication. Anger clots into worry, and the mind becomes hardened and does not function well. When misfortune and death come, one must go alone, with none to follow. The high and the wealthy, too, cannot escape these. There is no end to worries and fears and there is not even a pause. Living through cold and heat, they are immersed in pain.

(3) "The poor and lowly live lives of deprivation. Having neither fields nor houses, they worry and are anxious to possess them. Having no cows, horses, money or wealth, food or clothing, or household things, they are anxious to possess them. If by chance they happen to have something, there is always something else that is lacking. If they are able to possess one thing, there are other things that are lacking. While hoping to possess all, they let things slip away. Thus they are plagued, feel pain, and seek to possess, but they are not able to possess; while they are weighed down with anxieties, both body and mind get weary. Every day is a day of uneasiness. Worries follow one after another. They live through cold and heat and are immersed in pain. Living thus, death sometimes comes prematurely. Not having performed good deeds or practiced

the path or accumulated virtues, at life's end they must travel afar all alone. Moreover, none knows the destiny they attain as a result of their deeds.

"You who are parents, children, brothers, sisters, husbands, wives, other family members, and relatives, should respect and love each other. Do not hate each other nor be jealous of each other. One who has should give to one who has not. Refrain from covetousness. Do not begrudge in giving. Always be gentle in speech and manner and do not offend each other. Even the most insignificant anger experienced in the present life will grow in intensity in the lives to come. Harming each other may not bring its results immediately, but poisonous hatred will accumulate and live in the mind. It will gradually strengthen in the mind. It will become the cause of continuous hatred for many lives to come. In this world of desire, a person is born alone and dies alone. Whether one lives a life of pain or a life of ease, one must experience it by oneself, and nobody else can take one's place. Good and evil vary in results. It is certain that good and evil actions will be followed by happiness and unhappiness in accordance with the strict law of causality. Each goes to his own destiny and is born in different realms; since the destinies are different, there will be no meeting with others.

(4) "Therefore, you must abandon all earthly things; while still young and healthy, try to cultivate the good, and seek to attain eternal life. If you are not seeking the path, what can you rely on with which to find happiness? The people in this world do not believe that good comes out of good, or that the path comes out of aspiring to the path. They do not believe that to die is to be born or that joy comes out of giving. They do not believe in the causal relations between phenomena, and they say that things do not occur in that way; so people reason. Forefathers teach descendants the same. The forefathers did not practice the good; ignorant and blind, their minds were closed, and they could not see where birth and death led and did not know the ways of good and evil. Fortunes and misfortunes alternately occur, yet none raises the question why they do so. The cycle of birth and death continues indefinitely. Sometimes parents mourn their children, and sometimes children mourn their parents. Brother, sister, husband, wife, each wails for the other. Frequently, things happen in reverse order. This is because of the impermanence of all things. The flux of birth and death never stops, and nothing remains. Few believe in the teachings; therefore there is no end to the stream of birth and death. Since these people are ignorant and their minds are in turmoil, they never believe in the teaching of the Buddha.

"Their minds do not think of the distant future; all seek instant pleasure. Their minds are lost in a life of lust. They do not arrive at the right path. They are absorbed in anger. Like wolves, they crave for wealth and sexual pleasure. They remain in the painful world of an unhappy destiny, and there is no end to transmigration. Indeed, this is most sorrowful.

(5) "At times, among the family members, parents and children, brothers and sisters, men and wives, one dies and another is born. Bound by human affection, worry, and pity, they think of each other. Days pass, and years go by, and no alleviation or end comes. Even if the teaching is taught, the mind will

not accept it. Clinging to affections and lust, their minds are enclosed in darkness; they cannot contemplate things deeply; nor can they practice the right way and make correct decisions even on worldly matters. They live in anxiety while the end approaches. Life's end close at hand, they still grope for the way. While greedily seeking pleasure, most people lose the way, and only a few find it. All worldly things pass quickly; nothing is there upon which one can rely. Highborn or lowborn, rich or poor, all are painfully engaged in mundane affairs and harbor harmful thoughts in their minds. Evil intents arise just like smoke and cause chaos. They act against the way of nature and live in discord with human nature, engendering evil deeds that lead them to their inevitable end. Because of this they meet untimely death and sink into evil destinies. For many lives continuously during millions of kalpas, they will continuously suffer with no hope of relief. This is most pitiful and lamentable."

(6) The Buddha said to the Bodhisattva Maitreya, "I have now depicted for you what people's lives are. Because of their conditions, they cannot attain the path. Think well and keep away from evils, seek the good, and practice it. Pleasure and prosperity never last long. In due course you must part with them. There is nothing to be enjoyed. If you are fortunate enough to be in the world when a Buddha appears, you must aspire with a sincere mind to be born in the land of Amitayus Buddha. You will attain a state of clear wisdom and supreme virtue. Do not act against the teachings by following your desires. If you have doubts, ask me about them."

(7) The Bodhisattva Maitreya knelt down and said, "Your virtues are noble and your words are most pleasant. As I listen to your words and ponder over them, I realize that this world is, indeed, as you have depicted it. Now the World-Honored One compassionately has shown us the great way. With what we have heard and seen, we have been delivered eternally from delusions. We are not the only ones gladdened by the World-Honored One's teaching. From the gods in the heavens down to the lowly worms, all live in your compassion and are thereby freed from suffering. Deep and excellent is the teaching of the Buddha. Wisdom's light reaches the ten directions and illumines the three worlds of past, future, and present, and there is no place that is not reached by it. Owing to the austere discipline that you subjected yourself to while you were seeking the way, we are now delivered from delusion. Your compassion extends to all corners and your virtues are as lofty as the mountains. Your light reaches the deep recesses, shows us emptiness, and opens the gateway to enlightenment. Using every efficient means, you teach us as well as reprimand us and inspire us. The Buddha is the king of truth, the most holy, who stands far above all saintly sages. If people wish, the Buddha shows the way to all beings who seek it. We have now met you and have heard the name of Amitayus Buddha. Our minds are full of joy and our minds' eyes are open and bright."

(8) The Buddha said to the Bodhisattva Maitreya, "You speak rightly. There is nothing more meritorious than paying reverence to a buddha. The appearance of a buddha in this world is, indeed, rare. I attained Buddhahood while in this world; I am expounding the teaching, cutting away all the nets of

doubts, extracting the roots of desire, and obstructing all sources of evil. I travel in the three worlds, and nothing hinders my way. Wisdom is the most important thing in religious practices. It clearly illuminates the reality of the world of delusions more brightly than fire, and it leads those who are not saved to the way of enlightenment. Maitreya, you have in infinitely distant past lives cultivated the bodhisattva practice, aspiring to save all beings. Countless numbers of people have reached the shore of enlightenment following your teaching. However, you and all sentient beings also passed through the worlds of delusion during innumerable past lives and floundered in sufferings; it is, indeed, beyond description. And even up to the present, there was no cessation of delusion. But now you have met the Buddha, heard the name of Amitayus Buddha, and sincerely believe in the Buddha. This is excellent!

"I have now helped you and made you happy. You, too, now should avoid the pains of birth, death, old age, and illness. This world is full of evil and impurity; there is nothing in it that can make us happy. You should be determined to remain upright in your conduct, to discipline your body and action, and to do good. Wash off the defilements of the mind. Be right and sincere in speech and action, so that there is consistency in them, and let there be no double-dealing. First seek your own salvation and then help others to be saved, and build the foundation of good with a clear aspiration. However strenuously you may have to work in this life, it will be but for a short while. Birth in the land of Amitayus Buddha follows, where you will have endless happiness. You will then eternally be one with the law of nature and will uproot the source of delusion. There will be no more sufferings arising from greed, anger, or ignorance. You may extend or shorten the span of your life at will. Everything is in accordance with the law of nature. It is a state almost the equal of enlightenment itself. You should each make an effort and realize your aspirations. Have no doubts!"

Maitreya said to the Buddha, "After listening to your kind counsel, I shall strive hard to practice what you have taught me. I shall never have any mistrust."

The Buddha said to Maitreya, "There will be no one in all the worlds in the ten directions who can have virtues equal to those of one who can abstain from evil deeds by keeping his mind upright in this world. That is because the people in such lands will spontaneously do good deeds and refrain from doing wrong things. Therefore they can be easily taught to perform good deeds. Now I have attained Buddhahood in this world, where people are living in the midst of the sufferings of the five evils, which are five pains and five burnings. I shall teach those people to discard these sufferings and subdue their wills and enable them thereby to attain happiness, eternal life, and salvation.

(9) "The first evil is done by all sentient beings from human beings down to the ilk of worms. The strong suppress the weak. They kill, harm, and swallow each other. Doing good is something foreign to them. They go against the right way with wicked minds; they will meet misfortune as the result of the natural law of cause and effect. Thus there are in the world the poor, the lowly, the beggars, the deaf, the blind, the dumb, those with low intellect, the mad. And there

are those born in noble families, the wealthy, the highly talented, and the clever. They are all so born because of their having in lives past been merciful and practiced good and cultivated virtues. In this world there are prisons established by the law of the state in which those who deliberately commit crimes are confined. They cannot flee from the prisons as they would wish. This is a fact that we can see with our own eyes. In just the same way, in the life after death, the effect of what people have done is deep and violent; they sink into worlds of darkness, receiving different forms of life. Just as if they received punishment according to the laws of the state, they are born in hell, become hungry ghosts, or become animals and sink into unfathomable depths of suffering. Their lives may be long or short. Following a natural course, they will go to their respective destinies. There those who used to hate each other encounter each other, and each repays the other's hatred. Floundering in suffering, there is no hope of their being released from this state. Their pain is beyond words. There is the natural law of causality in the universe: the results of good and evil deeds sometimes may not occur immediately, but certainly they will occur. All this is called the first evil, the first pain, and the first burning. The pain is like being burnt in a great fire. If, while living in this state, one controls one's mind, rectifies oneself, acts rightly, does good deeds only, and abstains from all evil deeds, one will attain deliverance and find happiness, eternal life, and salvation. This is the first great good."

(10) "The second evil is that people, whether parents or children, brothers or sisters, husbands or wives, or relatives among relatives, have no sense of duty or propriety. They are arrogant, lustful, and indulgent in luxury. All seek pleasure to their hearts' content while deceiving each other. What they say and what they think are different; they lack sincerity. With honeyed tongues, they flatter each other obsequiously. With faithless minds, they harbor jealousy toward the wise, speak ill of good persons, and falsely incriminate them. The king lacks wisdom and keeps as vassals those who want only to contrive intrigues. If there happen to be vassals who are wise, act rightly, are conversant with the world's affairs, and take measures appropriate to situations, the king who is neither wise nor right finds himself beguiled and will thoughtlessly misuse loyal vassals; thus he goes against the right path. Vassals delude their king. Brothers and sisters, men and wives, friends intimate or not intimate, all deceive each other. All harbor greed, anger, and ignorance. They care but for their own interest and desire more possessions. Of noble or mean birth, high or low, all are of the same mind. They cause discord in their homes and ruin themselves. They do not think of the consequences. Relatives and others become entangled and are brought to ruin.

"At times, those who are in different circumstances become involved with each other. They quarrel on account of their own gains and become angry and resentful. The rich become miserly and do not share their wealth. They torment both mind and body because of their greed for wealth. Thus the end comes, but there is nothing for them to rely upon. One comes alone and goes alone, and none follows. Good and evil deeds, after life ends, lead them to fortune and misfortune respectively. A happy life or a painful one comes accordingly. What good will repenting afterward do? The people of the world are ignorant and of little wisdom. As they see others doing good, rather than having respect and wanting to befriend them, they loathe and vilify them. All they are concerned about is doing evil. They act without prudence. A thieving mind is always with them; they are envious of what others gain. Occasionally, when they acquire wealth, they waste it. Seeking to get it back, they harbor devious thoughts and fear the unknown and anxiously examine the facial expressions of others. Nothing is planned beforehand, and as things turn out in failure, they become remorseful. In this world they receive punishments in prisons according to the crimes they have committed. Because these people did not believe in the right path and did evil deeds in their previous lives, they now again do wrongs. They will enter an evil destiny and will sink into interminable pains. There is no possibility of being delivered from this plight for many lives and kalpas to come. It is the most pitiable life. This is the second evil, the second pain, and the second burning. It is like one's own body being burnt by fire. If, while living in this state, one restrains one's mind and acts rightly, one will attain happiness, eternal life, and salvation. This is the second great good."

(11) The Buddha said, "The third evil is as follows: The people of the world depend upon each other and together maintain life in this world. Their life span is not long. As for the higher class, there are the wise, the leaders, those of noble families, and the wealthy; as for the lower, there are the poor, the lowly, the feebleminded, and the ignorant. Among them, there are the unvirtuous. They always harbor vile thoughts and rankle their minds with desire. Thoughts of love and desire disturb their minds. There is no calmness in their demeanor. They do not give to others what they have; they seek more possessions. They make eyes at beautiful women and give rise to evil desire. They dislike their own wives; they secretly make continual visits to other women's places, wasting the family wealth. Whatever they do is always unlawful. Some, by banding together in factions, commit such atrocities as taking up arms, harming, attacking, slaying, and plundering each other. Some direct their evil thoughts toward others. They are not diligent in their business. They may steal and gain little, but their greed drives them to further thefts. They perpetrate crimes at first with fear and apprehension, but later they threaten others and thus they support their wives and children. They indulge in bodily pleasures. Among their relatives, they fail to distinguish between those who deserve respect and those who do not. Family and friends worry and suffer because of this. And persons of this ilk are not hesitant in breaking the law of the state. Such evil deeds will become known to everybody. The sun and the moon will see them. In accord with the law of nature they will fall into evil destinies and will suffer interminable pains. There is no hope of being released from such a destiny for lives and kalpas to come. This is the third evil, the third pain, and the third burning. The pains are as severe as being burnt in fire. If, while living in this state, one restrains the mind and acts rightly, one will be able to attain happiness, eternal life, and salvation. This is the third great good."

(12) The Buddha said, "The fourth evil is that people of the world do not intend to do good deeds. They inveigle each other and commit evil deeds. With

falsehoods, abusive words, lies, and flattery, they fight and hurt each other. They hate good people; they secretly take pleasure in slandering the wise. They do not respect their parents. They hold their teachers in light esteem. They lack sincerity toward their friends. Truthfulness is hardly to be expected of them. They are arrogant; they hold themselves to be great. They say that what they do agrees well with the path. They unreasonably oppress others with their power, and they do not reflect on themselves. They commit evil but do not feel ashamed. Because of the power they possess, they expect respect from others. As they have no reverence for the way of nature nor for the sun or the moon, they do not try to do good. Indeed, they are hard to exhort. They are slow to perform good deeds. They do not show any shame. They know no fear and are always arrogant. The gods will remember all such evil deeds. The ten good deeds done a little in previous lives will bolster them for a while. But because of the evil deeds done in the present life, their merits will soon be exhausted, as they do evil deeds now. They stand alone and have nothing to rely on. At the end of life, all their great evil has its results in accordance with the way of nature and leads them to their appropriate destinies. Evil draws them and they cannot resist. The evil effects of their transgressions will cling to them and will not leave. The burning cauldron awaits them, and their bodies and minds will become torn and broken and suffer pains. Of what use is repentance at this hour? Without fail the way of nature works, and they will sink into interminable pains in the evil realms. There is no possibility of being delivered from this plight for lives and for kalpas to come. This is the fourth evil, the fourth pain, and the fourth burning. The pains are as severe as being burnt by a fire. If, living in this state, one restrains the mind and acts rightly, one will attain happiness, eternal life, and salvation. This is the fourth great good."

(13) The Buddha said, "The fifth evil is that the people of the world are indolent and do not try to do good, to discipline themselves, or to work for their livelihood. Their families and relatives suffer from hunger and cold. When their parents admonish them, they contradict their parents with angry eyes and harsh words. The house becomes a place where bitter enemies live together. When things come to this pass, it would have been better not to have had a child. People practice slovenliness in matters pertaining to money, which all people resent. They are ungrateful to those who have shown kindness. They have no sense of duty. They have no thought of returning favors. Pressed by poverty, they have no means of gaining anything. Eventually, they become selfish and commit robberies, and then they waste their gains in lavish ways. They indulge themselves in wine and luxurious food; in food they do not know a limit. They lead willful lives. Thereby they offend others. Because they are coldhearted, they desire to suppress others by force.

"If others do good, they become jealous and resentful. They know no justice or courtesy. Since they have no capacity for self-reflection, there can be no way to admonish them. They do not care whether their families have enough to support themselves. They do not think about what they owe their parents. Neither do they think of their obligations to their teachers and friends. Their minds always have evil thoughts, their mouths always use evil words, and their bodies always do evil deeds. Not once have they done good deeds. They do not believe in the teachings of the sages or that of the Buddha. They do not believe that by practicing the path they can free themselves from delusions. They do not believe that good acts bring good results and evil acts bring evil results. Thus they even kill arhats and cause disharmony among the monks. They will try to harm parents, brothers, sisters, and relatives. Even their families will hate them and wish them dead. The minds of such people are foolish and dark. They do not know where life comes from or where it goes. They have no kind hearts and they act against the way of heaven and earth. They just look for strokes of luck and hope for long lives. But they will meet their inevitable deaths. It is useless for compassionate and sympathetic persons to offer counsel so as to turn them to good deeds and to make them know that the end of birth and death and good and evil will surely come someday. Their minds are closed and they do not listen to advice.

"As the end of life approaches, regrets and fears one after the other occur in their minds. But at this late moment, what good is there in repentance? The five destinies are all clear and well regulated between heaven and earth, and they are extensively clear and deep. Good and evil deeds bring forth the results of fortune and misfortune. Each one must accept the results as they come, and no one else can take his place. This is the way of nature. Depending on what one has done, evils follow one's life and never leave him. Good people do good deeds and move from happiness to happiness and from bright state to bright state. Bad people do evil deeds and move from pain to pain and from darkness to darkness. No one is aware of this truth. Only the Buddha knows, and he teaches the truth, but few believe. There is no end to evil deeds. Thus there comes, as a matter of course, the endless sufferings of the evil path. Wallowing in these realms, there is no hope of getting out of the cycle of transmigrations for kalpas to come. This is the fifth evil, the fifth pain, and the fifth burning. It is like a great fire burning one's own body. If, living in this state, one controls the mind, is sincere in his words and deeds, and acts rightly, such a one will attain happiness, eternal life, and salvation. This is the fifth great good."

(14) The Buddha continued, "I have now made clear to you how this world really is. People are born in suffering, doing evil deeds without practicing the roots of good. Because of this, in accord with the way of nature, they will sink into the various evil destinies. At times, while in the present life, one suffers from illness. Even if one seeks death, it will not come. Even if one wishes for life, it will not come. All these are caused by one's own misconduct; this will serve as a lesson to others. As life ends, one will go to an evil destiny commensurate with his deeds, where the suffering will be unending, and where one's own fire will burn himself. After much suffering, one will be born into the human world, but then he will become bitter with others. Some small evil deeds will gradually grow to be greater evil. All this comes from coveting wealth and pleasure and not knowing the merit of sharing one's good fortune. Instigated by greed and covetousness, bound by all sorts of passions, one will have no release. One thinks

only of his own well-being and argues merely for his own gains. One does not know that one should reflect on himself. Attaining high rank, one may enjoy worldly honor for a while. But since one cannot restrain his ever-increasing desire to reach higher, one does not do good deeds. His power will soon wane, but the suffering will become aggravated. The law of nature pervades everything and will leave no evil unpunished, whether high or low. Alone and full of fear, one gets caught therein. There is no difference between the past and present, and this is most to be pitied."

(15) The Buddha said to Maitreya, "This is the world as it is. The Buddha pities all this. With his divine power, the Buddha crushes all evils and makes all people turn toward the good. If one learns the teaching and lives in accordance with it, one will finally attain enlightenment and be delivered from the world of transmigration.

"If you are in the present world or the world to come, and hear the words of the Buddha, then think well and restrain your mind, and rectify your acts. Those who are high ought to do good and lead the lower. Instructions should be passed from one to another. Each should revere and respect the sages and good people. Be compassionate and love all. Do not act against the teaching of the Buddha. Thus leave the world of delusion and uproot evil. Thus you will part with all the fears and pains of the evil destinies. Praise the name of the Buddha that is the source of all virtue. Be loving and compassionate. Do not transgress the Dharma. Forbear well, make effort strenuously, and with one and the same mind and wisdom teach one another. If you with effort improve your mind, control your thoughts, and keep your conduct clean and pure for a full day and night, this will be superior to practicing good for a hundred years in the land of Amitayus Buddha. This is because the people in that Buddha land can effortlessly and spontaneously perform good deeds, and there is not even a minimal evil to be seen there. Good deeds done in this world for ten days and ten nights will be superior to doing good in other buddha lands for a thousand years. This is because in the lands of those buddhas, there are many who do good and few who do evil deeds. There virtuous deeds are spontaneously performed, and no evil deeds are ever performed. Only this world is full of evil deeds and deprived of natural goodness. On account of greed, people suffer pain, and they deceive each other. Their minds are weary; their bodies feel pain; they drink pain and eat poison. They are restless and lack equanimity.

(16) "I have pity for you all, and I shall show you the way of performing good. I shall use every means to lead you to salvation in accordance with your capacity. I shall let you attain enlightenment as you wish. Wherever the Buddha visits, town, village, or hamlet, there will be no one who does not receive his teaching. The various countries will become peaceful. The sun and the moon will shine clear and pure. The wind and rain will come seasonally. No misfortune will befall the land. The country will be rich and the people will be peaceful. There will be no need for warriors or arms. Virtue will be held high and benevolence will prevail. Propriety will be observed by all beings there.

"My pity for you is deeper than parents' love of their children. I now have become the Buddha in this world. I shall annihilate the five evils, the five pains, and the five burnings. With good I shall attack evil, uproot the cause of suffering, and let people reach the city of nirvana. When I am gone from this world, the light of the teaching will gradually be dimmed. People will do evil deeds and gradually worsen. You should think of this well, advise and caution each other, and never disregard the teaching of the Buddha."

The Bodhisattva Maitreya, folding his hands, said, "As the Buddha tells us, this world is extremely painful. Only the Buddha pities all the people in the world of suffering with compassion and saves them all. I shall preserve the Buddha's teaching and never deviate from it."

5. Seeing Amitayus Buddha

(1) The Buddha said to Ananda, "Adjust your robe, fold your hands, and piously pay reverence to Amitayus Buddha. All the buddhas always praise that Buddha."

Hearing this, Ananda, facing toward the west and reverently putting his palms together, prostrated himself on the ground and worshipped Amitayus Buddha, saying, "World-Honored One, I sincerely wish to see the land of that Buddha and also all the sages in that land." No sooner than he said this, Amitayus Buddha emitted a great light, shining over all the lands of all the buddhas. Everything became resplendent with color; it was like a great flood covering all lands, submerging everything under the waters of the ocean. The lights gleaming from the sages were hidden, and only the light of the Buddha shone out. When Ananda looked up at Amitayus Buddha, he looked as awe-inspiring as Mount Sumeru standing above all other mountains. All the people in the assemblage saw at once the land of the Buddha, and people in his land, too, saw this assemblage on Vulture Peak.

(2) Then the Bodhisattva Maitreya said to the World-Honored One, "I observe that in the Pure Land, there are those of viviparous birth who are enjoying pleasant lives in the palace, while those of metamorphic birth seem to be living different kinds of lives. What are the reasons for the difference?"

The Buddha said to Maitreya, "People who have not awakened to the wonderful wisdom of the Buddha because they harbor doubts in their minds, but who desire to be born in that land, if they shun evil and practice virtuous deeds for happiness, will be born in a heavenly palace where for five hundred years they will not see the Buddha or hear his sermons or see the sages in the land. This is viviparous birth. It is as if a prince of a universal monarch were punished by the king and fettered with golden chains in his palace. There is enough pleasure for him, but he always wishes to be freed from the palace. Those who harbor doubt about the wisdom of the Buddha will face a chastisement similar to that of that prince. If, however, people sincerely believe in the Buddha's wisdom, they will be born in flowers of the seven gems, and they will be adorned by the light of wisdom and virtues equal to those of all bodhisattvas. That is metamorphic birth."

The Buddha said to Maitreya, "If those who take viviparous birth come to know the cause of evil, deeply repent, and wish to be delivered from there, they may be able to meet Amitayus Buddha and worship him. Maitreya, by doubting the wisdom of the Buddha, people may lose great benefit. You should believe in the supreme wisdom of the Buddha. Anyone who hears the name of Amitayus Buddha and feels joy, even for the one moment, will gain a great benefit. He will attain the highest virtues. Therefore, Maitreya, even if one has to go through the great fire that fills the three thousand great thousand worlds, one must hear this teaching, believe in it, and rejoice in it. And then one will never regress from the path of enlightenment."

(3) The Buddha said to Maitreya, "In later ages, even after the day comes for the teaching to decline, I shall let this sutra remain another hundred years, so that anyone who is fortunate enough to come across this sutra will attain enlightenment as he aspires to do. It is hard to meet with a Buddha; it is hard to meet good teacher-friends and hear the teaching and practice the way; it is the hardest of the hard to believe in it. Thus I have composed my teaching, have preached my teaching, and have taught my teaching. You should believe in and practice what I have taught."

Then, as the World-Honored One gave this discourse, innumerable beings aspired to the path, destroyed passions, and attained the state of non-retrogression. The three thousand great thousand worlds trembled with joy, and a great light shone over all the worlds. Heavenly music spontaneously filled the air; the sky showered beautiful flowers; and all those who were assembled there felt great joy.

Chapter 3

THE SIGNIFICANCE OF TATHAGATA

1. A Life of Reverence

(1) Once the World-Honored One crossed the river Ganges and entered Vesali. Stopping in the great forest, he began his discourse to his disciples: "O disciples, immediately after I attained enlightenment, as I was staying on the bank of the river Neranjara in the forest near Uruvela, this thought came to me from the quietness of my heart, 'A life without reverence and obedience is a painful one. Whom can I honor and revere?' Next, I thought, 'If I had a precept unfulfilled, then in order to fulfill it, I should pass the day attending the teacher. Moreover, if I had an aspect of meditation, wisdom, or emancipation that was unfulfilled, then in order to fulfill it, I would pass the day attending the teacher. However, in regard to the fulfilling of precepts, meditation, wisdom, and emancipation, there is no one greater than I. For this reason, I honor and revere the Dharma to which I myself have awoken.'

"O disciples, the god Brahma appeared when I thought this. With his robe draped over one shoulder, he put his hands together and bowed, saying to me, 'World-Honored One, it is indeed a marvelous thing. Past buddhas revered the Dharma, and future buddhas, too, will do the same. Please, World-Honored One, Buddha of the present, pass your days revering the Dharma.' Then, the god Brahma sang the following, 'The buddhas of the past, those who will become the buddhas in the future, and the buddhas of the present who are helping all sentient beings to go beyond their suffering live their lives honoring the true Dharma. This is the fixed custom of all the buddhas. If you wish to attain well-being and greatness, think of the Buddha-Dharma, and honor the true Dharma.'

"O disciples, the god Brahma, having recited this verse, bowed to me. Then he turned to the right and disappeared. Having learnt the mind of Brahma, I decided to spend the day revering the Dharma to which I had awoken.

(2) "O disciples, the Tathagata, awakening to suffering, was freed from the defilements of this world; awakening to the cause of this world's suffering, he has cast aside the cause; awakening to the cessation of this suffering, he has realized the cessation of suffering; awakening to the path to the cessation of suffering, he has practiced the path of the cessation of suffering. O disciples, all things in this world that should be seen, heard, recalled, and known are all realized by the

Tathagata. This is why he is called the Tathagata. The Tathagata, from the dawn of his enlightenment to the evening of his full emancipation, has spoken no falsehood. This is why he is called the Tathagata.

"O disciples, the Tathagata acts according to what he teaches, and he teaches exactly the way he acts. This is why he is called the Tathagata. O disciples, the Tathagata is the supremely victorious, and nobody can conquer him. He is the one who sees things correctly. This is why he is called the Tathagata."

(3) The World-Honored One continued his journey and again entered the Jeta Grove outside the city of Savatthi. One day Ananda, accompanied by Vangisa, entered the town in order to beg alms. On one street, they came across a beautiful maiden, and Vangisa's mind was distracted and he was unable to restrain his mind. He asked for Ananda's aid. "I am burning with thoughts of desire; my heart is aflame. Out of compassion, teach me the truth that will extinguish this fire."

Ananda answered with a verse. "With wrong views of reality, you give rise to desire that burns your heart. Destroy attachment to impure objects. Realize that all things are impermanent, suffering, and without substance. If you do not desire to be aflame time and time again, extinguish desire. Meditate, and quietly concentrate on the impurity of objects. Make your thoughts truthful, concentrate on the body, and realize its distastefulness. Realize that appearances are not true, and remove the passion of pride. Controlling the heart of pride, act with a quiet heart."

(4) Vangisa was now able to extinguish the flame of his heart as with pure water. The maiden smiled invitingly, but Vangisa's heart was unmoved. Concentrating on the impure, he escaped from danger. He had finally found the source of desire and realized that thought was this source.

Vangisa, returning to the Buddha, recounted his experience of the day in the following verse: "Desire, your source is thought. Without thought you are no more. Form is like foam, feeling is like a floating bubble, perception is like the ephemeral dayfly, volition is like the banana leaf, consciousness is like a dream. Analyzing phenomena according to the Buddha's teachings, I realized that all is empty, quiet, and transient, and that there is nothing real. That which is perceived as beautiful is in fact impure; that which is perceived as long-lasting is weak. My body itself will fall apart; there is nothing real."

The World-Honored One, rejoicing at Vangisa's words, taught that, indeed, the body is not permanent and easily falls apart, and he encouraged all to think on this.

2. Indra

(1) At one time the World-Honored One was residing in the Eastern Monastery in the house of Migara's mother. The god Indra sought him out and said the following: "World-Honored One, please tell me simply how your disciples, extinguishing the thirst of desire, attain release, reach quietude, and engage in pious practice, thus becoming the greatest in this world."

"Indra, my disciples have learned that their various views were not valid. By listening to my teaching, they come to know phenomena thoroughly, thus seeing all phenomena as impermanent no matter what notions arise. Merely by renouncing wrong views about the world, my disciples overcome suffering. They enter the quietude of nirvana of their own accord and know that the cycle of birth and death for them has ended; that their religious practice has been accomplished; that what was to be completed has been completed; and that for them there is no other life after this. O Indra, simply stated, this is how my disciples, extinguishing the thirst of desire, attain emancipation, become perfect, and become the greatest in this world."

Indra rejoiced at the teaching of the World-Honored One and, bowing toward him, turned to the right and returned to the heavens.

(2) At that time, Moggallana, who was near the World-Honored One and heard this exchange, thought the following: "I wonder, indeed, whether Indra truly understood and rejoiced at the Buddha's teachings. Let me test him." At once he disappeared from the temple garden and manifested himself in the heavens. At that time, Indra was being entertained by five hundred musicians and was seated in a garden where lotuses were blooming. Seeing Moggallana coming in the distance, he stood up. "O Honored One, welcome; please sit down."

Moggallana said, "Indra, I should be grateful indeed to hear the teaching that you heard from the World-Honored One regarding the extinguishing of the thirst of desire and the attainment of emancipation."

"Honored One, we are very busy, having a lot to do for ourselves and for the heavens. However, I have listened intently, understood, and memorized well the teachings of the World-Honored One that were briefly expounded to me, and I shall not ever forget them.

"Honored One, long ago the gods and titans fought. At that time, the gods defeated the titans, and upon my return I built as a memento of the victory a palace called the Castle of Victory. This palace has ten thousand pillars, each with one hundred seven-storied towers. In each of the towers there are forty-nine heavenly princesses, each with forty-nine hand-maidens. O Honored One, do you wish to see this Castle of Victory?"

Nodding in agreement, Moggallana followed Indra's wishes. Accompanied by Vissavana, Indra led Moggallana and went toward the palace. The princesses and maidens, seeing Moggallana, a holy one who had left home and cast aside desire, blushed like brides and fled to their rooms.

(3) Indra, accompanied by Vissavana, pointed out things here and there in the palace to Moggallana and said the following: "Honored One, look at this. The adornments in this Tavatimsa heaven are so splendid because of the merit that I gained in my past lives. This is why when people on earth see something beautiful, they use the expression 'as beautiful as Tavatimsa heaven.' This, indeed, is all dependent on the merit of my former lives."

Moggallana thought, "Just as I had supposed, this god is drunk with his own glory and is swept along by excesses of delights. Let me frighten him." Thinking thus, he placed a toe on one corner of the palace building; the palace shook and seemed about to fall. All the gods, even Indra himself, were taken aback and terrified. "What awesome divine power! Just touching it with a toe caused this great quake; how truly frightening!" Saying this, all but Indra ran off quite dumbfounded.

Moggallana looked at the trembling Indra with his hair standing on end and quietly asked the same question again. "Indra, I would be grateful indeed to hear the teaching that you have heard from the World-Honored One regarding the extinguishing of the thirst of desire and the attainment of emancipation."

Now Indra reluctantly told Moggallana what he had asked the Buddha and what the World-Honored One had answered. Upon hearing these words Moggallana returned to earth. The heavenly princesses surrounding Indra rose up with frightened voices, saying, "O Lord, was the person with you the World-Honored One?" "No, he was not the master. He is my fellow student called Moggallana." "O Lord, you are most fortunate to have a fellow student endowed with such great divine power. If a disciple has such power, how great indeed must be that of his master, the World-Honored One."

And Moggallana returned to the Eastern Monastery, narrated this episode, and listened to the teaching of the World-Honored One with delight.

3. The Hunter's Bait

(1) The World-Honored One taught his disciples and said, "O disciples, when a hunter sets out bait, it is not so that the deer may enjoy long, healthy lives. He does so to lure them, thereby causing them to grow careless and to fall into his hands. There are four types of deer reacting to the bait.

"The first are those who, immediately fooled by the bait, grow careless and thus fall into the hunter's hands. The second are those who, seeing the first group, stay away from this fearful bait, and hide in the depths of the forest. However, in the heat of summer their food vanishes; because of weakening resolve, they return to the bait, grow careless, and are caught by the hunter. The third are those who, having observed the deer before, are cautious. They return to the bait but avoid growing careless. Building shelters near the bait, they eat the bait, avoid growing careless, and do not fall into the hunter's trap. But the hunter builds a trap around the area of the bait, and finally they fall into it and into the hands of the hunter. The fourth are those who, having observed the deer before, build refuges beyond the hunter's grasp. These refrain from relying on others, avoid falling into carelessness or into traps, eat the hunter's bait, and then return to their refuges. The hunter can do nothing but give up and let these deer have their freedom. These deer, in short, are beyond the power of the hunter.

"O disciples, the bait is the five desires, the hunter is Mara the tempter, and the deer are the students of the path. The students of the path who become drunk with the five desires are the prisoners of Mara. Those who hide in the depths of the forest are those who are recluses separating themselves from people and living on poor food. However, in the summer, food vanishes and their resolve weakens; thus they give up the way and fall into the five desires, falling into the hands of Mara. To build a shelter near the bait is not to fall into the five desires and to avoid growing careless. However, even here, those who do this can fall into useless discourses on, and attachment to, whether the world is eternal or not, or whether it has a limit or not, thereby falling into the hands of Mara. To build a refuge out of the reach of the hunter is to separate oneself from desire and impurity and to enter into the quietude of meditation, thus controlling one's heart and strengthening one's resolve. This is the leaving behind of the entanglements of Mara by blinding Mara by destroying his eyes.

(2) "O disciples, follow the precepts and refrain from transgression. Conduct yourselves properly, see the danger of even the slightest transgression, and tirelessly practice the path. All of you, if you wish to be loved and respected by your fellow students, completely uphold the precepts, engage in meditation, and live in a quiet place. If you wish that the benefit should be great for those who offer you clothes, food, housing, and medicine, then uphold the precepts perfectly, engage in meditation, and live in a quiet place. If you love relatives who have already passed away, then observe the precepts perfectly, engage in meditation, and live in a quiet place. Moreover, if you are burdened by thoughts of dissatisfaction and fear and you do not wish to be so burdened, observe the precepts perfectly, engage in meditation, and live in a quiet place. If you wish to advance in the practice of meditation, then uphold the precepts perfectly, engage in meditation, and live in a quiet place. If you wish to become a buddha who has gradually destroyed the passions of desire, anger, and ignorance in his heart and who has done what had to be done, then uphold the precepts perfectly, engage in meditation, and live in a quiet place."

4. Queen Srimala

(1) King Pasenadi and Queen Mallika gradually came to rejoice in the World-Honored One's teachings. Thinking of their daughter, Queen Srimala of Ayodhya, they said the following: "Our daughter, being wise, has the quality of quickly awakening to the truth; therefore if she came to the Buddha, she would certainly awaken to the Dharma. Let us send a messenger so that the aspiration to seek the way may be awakened in her."

A letter briefly praising the merit of the Buddha was sent by a palace official and given to Queen Srimala. The queen gladly received the letter, and upon reading it she rejoiced and said to the messenger, "Previously I had heard that the words of the Buddha were supreme. If what is written in this letter is true, I shall receive his instructions."

Looking toward the sky above Sravasti, she called out, "World-Honored One, you came into this world for the sake of all people. Please take pity on me and allow me to bow before you."

Leading his disciples, the World-Honored One soon appeared at Ayodhya. The queen greeted the World-Honored One and praised him in verse:

> O Buddha, your wondrous form and wisdom are incomparable; you have
> realized Buddhahood, which will never perish. This is why I take refuge in you.

You have overcome all faults of body, speech, and mind, and you have
thereby entered into Buddhahood. This is why I bow to you, O king of the
Dharma.

You know all things knowable, and your wisdom is free from delusion.
This is why I respectfully bow to you who are incomparable and whose merit is
unfathomable.

With compassion protect me and make my faith deepen ever more. May
the Buddha accept me as a follower in this and in all future lives.

The World-Honored One said, "Long ago have I pacified your mind, and in
that previous life I enlightened you. Now again I take you in, and in the future
I shall do so yet again." The queen said, "If this be so, I gained merit in my past
lives, and so in this and in future lives I must again accumulate virtues. Please
allow me to become your follower."

The World-Honored One said, "You are now filled with the real virtue and
merit of the Buddha, and with this merit you will have perfect freedom in your
future life. You will be able to see me anywhere and at any time. Later you will
become a buddha yourself, and your land will be free from even the names of
evils. Neither will there be old age, sickness, decrepitude, or suffering. The lives
and bodies of beings there will be filled with joy, and people who have awakened
to the path and practice the good will gather there."

(2) Queen Srimala, hearing of this future day of enlightenment, respectfully
arose and made ten vows. "World-Honored One, from now until I realize enlightenment I vow to do the following:

1. I shall never break any precept.

2. I shall never hold my teachers in contempt.

3. I shall never rise in anger against anyone.

4. I shall never have envy toward another's appearance or possessions.

5. I shall never be parsimonious about anything spiritual or material.

6. I shall never accumulate wealth for myself; I shall give all that I receive
to the poor and make them happy.

7. By giving, pleasant speech, and beneficial deeds, I shall convert people
just for their own sake, not for my sake. I shall convert all people tirelessly, with
a heart free from impurity and impediments.

8. If I see people who are deranged, imprisoned, or suffering illness or other
pains, then I shall immediately, for the purpose of comforting them, teach them
the Dharma and save from their suffering.

9. If I see hunters capturing and hurting animals or those who violate the
precepts, then as long as my strength endures I shall punish those who must be
punished and admonish those who must be admonished and thereby put an end
to their evil actions. With such punishment and admonition, the Dharma shall
be made to last forever. Thus making joy overflow and pain decrease, I shall
make the Buddha's teaching spread ever more.

10. I shall never forget the true Dharma. Those who forget the true Dharma
cannot cross over to the shore of enlightenment. When people forget the true

Dharma they leave everything up to their impulses and are incapable of going beyond this world of suffering. Seeing such misfortune, and seeing also the limitless benefit that comes to those who try to seek the true Dharma in this world, I make these vows.

"O World-Honored One, king of the Dharma, please be my witness. Even though these vows are made in your presence, some people, because of the lack of the roots of goodness, will not be able to fulfill these ten vows. Or, giving rise to doubts, they will fall into the enjoyment of the evil destinies and may never attain true bliss. To assure these people, I make these vows, and I intend to carry them out. If there is nothing false about these vows, then let the gods rain down flowers from the sky and let wondrous music be heard."

And at that moment, flowers rained from the heavens and a wondrous voice called out, "Everything you have said is true." For all those who saw and heard this, their doubtful minds vanished, and their minds were filled with boundless joy. They all made the vow: "We shall always be together with Queen Srimala." The World-Honored One confirmed that the vows of all the people in the assembly were identical with hers.

5. The Three Great Vows

(1) The queen also made three more great vows before the World-Honored One:

    (i)   By the virtue of this true and real vow, and by the roots of goodness that I have accumulated, may I gain the wisdom of the true Dharma regardless of what kind of birth I may undergo.

    (ii) After attaining the wisdom of the true Dharma, may I tirelessly teach others.

    (iii) And casting aside all regard for my life or material gain, may I master the true Dharma.

And at that moment, the World-Honored One served as witness to the three great vows of the queen. "As everything material is embraced by space, the countless vows of the bodhisattvas are included in these three great vows. These vows are true, real, and great."

The queen said to the World-Honored One again, "I wish to receive the power of eloquence of the World-Honored One now, so that I may teach about the truth of the great vow. All the vows of bodhisattvas are contained in one great vow, the vow of mastering the true Dharma."

The World-Honored One praised the queen, saying, "Very good, indeed, O queen! Your deep wisdom and skillful means are quite superior. You have until now cultivated a variety of roots of goodness. People in the future, who, like you, practice the good for a long time, will speak as you do. Indeed, the buddhas of the three times, past, present, and future, all teach as you have taught just now on the mastering of the true Dharma. I, too, upon attaining enlightenment, have always taught that Dharma. The merit and benefit of this mastering of the true Dharma have no limit; and the one who masters it, the Buddha, has no limit to his wisdom or his method of teaching."

(2) The queen then said, "Having received the strength of the World-Honored One, the thought of teaching the truth of mastering the true Dharma arises within me again. The greatness of the power of mastering the true Dharma cannot be measured. First of all, it is the acquiring of all the Buddha-Dharma, which encompasses eighty-four thousand teachings. It is said that when a world is first created, a great cloud appears from which fall rains of a variety of colors and a variety of jewels. In the same way, when the true Dharma is mastered, rains of unlimited happiness and goodness fall.

"World-Honored One, moreover, when the world was first created, from amidst the waters, the world's continents and islands were created. In the same way, to master the true Dharma means that the variety of teachings in which all living things believe, the spiritual power of all the sages, the happiness and peace of this world, and the true joy of the world beyond were created. When this world was created, those things difficult to attain even for gods and humans emerged from amidst the Dharma. Again, as the great earth supports four things, oceans, mountains, trees and grass, and animals, those who master the true Dharma become like the earth itself and bear four types of great burdens. The first is to teach the good how to instruct those who, not having good teachers, do not hear the Dharma and thus do not master the Dharma. The second is to give an appropriate teaching to those who, earnestly listening to the teachings, seek to attain enlightenment on their own. The third is to give the appropriate teaching to those who, contemplating the reality of the cosmos, try to attain enlightenment on their own. The fourth is to give the appropriate teaching to those who, searching for the way for themselves and others, try to attain the great enlightenment. World-Honored One, the person who masters the Dharma in this way bears four heavy burdens. For the sake of all people, he becomes the mother of the Dharma who, without being asked, becomes a friend who teaches and comforts and loves.

(3) "World-Honored One, the true Dharma mastered and to master the true Dharma are not separate things. The true Dharma is to master the true Dharma.

"World-Honored One, moreover, to reach the shore of enlightenment and to master the true Dharma are not separate things. In other words, to master the true Dharma is to reach the shore of enlightenment. The reason is that whether the person who tries to master the true Dharma is male or female, that person first of all relies on giving. That is, even if the body were mutilated, he upholds the aspiration and performs the act of giving. These people master the true Dharma and act accordingly. This is the meaning of 'Through giving, enlightenment is reached.' Second, through the disciplines, the five senses are restrained, and the actions of body, mouth, and mind are purified. Third, through patience, no matter how abused or shamed one is, one has no fear or anger, the power of patience is strengthened, and the heart of benefitting others is made stronger. Even the color of one's face does not change. Fourth, by means of zealous practice, one avoids any slackening of effort and laziness of mind, and right conduct is always maintained. Fifth, through meditation a disturbed mind and a distracted mind are settled, and right thinking is accomplished. Sixth, wisdom is perfected, and thereby all truth, learning, and methods are perfected. In this way, through each activity the true Dharma is mastered. Thereby the shore of enlightenment is reached."

(4) Receiving permission from the World-Honored One again and receiving the Buddha's power of eloquence, she expounded on the great meaning of mastering the Dharma. "World-Honored One, to say that the true Dharma that is correctly mastered and the mastering of the Dharma are not different is to say that people who master the true Dharma are themselves the realization of the true Dharma. The reason for this is that the person who masters the true Dharma casts aside three things for that purpose. These three things are body, life, and material wealth. First, if the body is cast away, one is freed in this world and the next from old age, sickness, and death, and one attains the body of the imperishable Dharma. Second, if life is cast aside, timeless virtue is gained, and one reaches the very depths of the Buddha-Dharma. Third, if material wealth is cast aside, inexhaustible virtue unattainable by the ignorant is gained, and one gains the respect of all people. World-Honored One, in this way people who cast aside these three things, having grasped the essence of the true Dharma, receive the verification and the approval of the Buddha and everyone's respect.

"World-Honored One, moreover, when the Dharma is about to perish, and the men and women of the Sangha will form factions to slander each other, wreck the teaching, and destroy the harmony of the group, those people who master the true Dharma, loving the Dharma without hearts of flattery, deceit, or lies, and holding on to the true Dharma, will lead these people into that Sangha that holds to the true Dharma.

"World-Honored One, in this way I saw within the mastering of the true Dharma a great power. From the beginning, the Buddha has dwelt in the true spiritual eye, true wisdom, and the true nature of the Dharma. Having realized the Dharma, he is the foundation of the true Dharma. I believe, therefore, that he is cognizant of all things."

(5) The World-Honored One was pleased by the teaching of the queen about the greatness of the power of the mastering of the true Dharma. "O Queen, it is as you say. The power of the mastering of the true Dharma is indeed great. As a strong man even lightly touching the body of a person causes pain, so just partially mastering the true Dharma pains Mara. Any good that can cause pain to Mara is incomparable to even the slightest power of mastering the true Dharma. Just as the form of the powerful bull king is superior to that of all cattle, the mastering of the true Dharma is superior to both steadfastly following the teaching of one's teacher and cultivating one's own thoughts. Mount Sumeru soars majestically above other mountain summits. Like Mount Sumeru, to uphold the true Dharma by casting off one's body, life, and wealth for the sake of the Dharma is an enormous sacrifice that towers high above all other good deeds. Therefore, O Queen, lead others by teaching them of the mastering of the true Dharma. Show them that to live by the true Dharma is good. Even if I were to teach endlessly on its merits and benefits, I should never be able to exhaust this teaching."

(6) The queen said, "World-Honored One, to master the true Dharma is to point to the heart of the Mahayana. Why is this so? As all seeds come to life and grow from the soil, all the world's good dharmas arise from and grow from the heart of the Mahayana. Therefore, World-Honored One, grounding oneself in the heart of the Mahayana and holding to it is tantamount to embodying all other good teachings. World-Honored One, there are two types of passion. One is the fundamental passion in which there is the distortion of views as a result of being confused about the truth. The second is the distortion of thought as a result of being confused about phenomenal things. The two are the fundamental passions, but what arises from time to time in accord with such a mind that has them is called the arisen passion. The distortions of view and of thought are the bases of all other passions; if their basis is sought out, it is ignorance. Ignorance is more powerful than the defilements of distorted views and thoughts, like the powerful King Mara, who holds sway and does as he wills in the highest realm of desire. Ignorance gives birth to the defilements of distorted views and thoughts and works to maintain their continuity.

"World-Honored One, the person who sincerely and ardently follows the master's teachings, desires to gain awakening, and who desires for himself to gain enlightenment quickly by his own power cuts off the two passions of view and thought. However, as long as he cannot cut off ignorance, the passions arising from this passion of ignorance hinder him, and he is unable to know the Dharma completely. Since he is unable to know the Dharma, he is unable to cut off that which must be cut off. Therefore his enlightenment cannot be called real enlightenment. He has just gained a semblance of nirvana, nothing more. However, if he becomes aware of all suffering and cuts off that fundamental cause that is the basis of all passions, if he awakens to all facts that need to be destroyed, and if he practices the right way, then in this transient and painful world he will gain the timeless enlightenment. In this unreliable world, he becomes the source of ultimate reliance. In a world without safeguards, he becomes the protector. Why is this so? The basis of all passions, ignorance, is completely cut off; therefore, the world that opens up is completely without differentiation. There are no superior or inferior dharmas, there is undifferentiated wisdom, emancipation, and purity; and in short, the nirvana that is of one taste. Thus the person who attains all of the Buddha-Dharma has no hindrances and gains all-knowing wisdom and virtue. Becoming a king of the Dharma, who is to become a buddha, he possesses the power to act freely; he is able to expound the Dharma with the power of a lion who terrifies all other animals with his roar.

(7) "World-Honored One, let us consider those who wish to gain their emancipation quickly by cutting off the passions of distorted views and thoughts, thereby attaining a certain degree of quietude in the belief that they will not retrogress to the painful state of delusion. This is only an inferior enlightenment. But in the end, even they will attain undifferentiated, absolute, and true enlightenment, if they, upon reflecting on the Dharma that they have so far gained, realize that they must further pursue the path. Why is this so? Those who have not yet attained the complete teachings strive to attain them. The complete

teaching is the Mahayana, and it is the vehicle by which one becomes a buddha. In this sense, all teachings are, just as they are, the One Buddha Vehicle or Ekayana. Those who gain this vehicle gain the path of the supreme and real enlightenment, nirvana, the Dharmakaya of the Buddha. In other words, the One Buddha Vehicle is the depth of all the teachings, the state toward which all things finally proceed, the home of all things, the home of the teachings. Moreover, it is the Dharmakaya, the fundamental body of all things. In other words, it is the timeless Buddha. Thus, World-Honored One, the Buddha is timeless and boundless, and with boundless compassion he sorrows for and comforts all people. The Buddha is truly like this. Moreover, the inexhaustible, timeless Dharma is that upon which all people rely.

"World-Honored One, the Buddha is he in whom all beings take refuge forever, and his Dharma is the way of the One Buddha Vehicle. If the Sangha, which practices the path, does not acquire the real path, then that path cannot be called the timeless place in which to take refuge. Therefore, if there is a person who is disciplined by the Buddha, who relies on the Buddha, who awakens a mind of faith according to the teachings, and who relies on the Dharma and the Sangha, then that is a person who takes refuge in the Buddha. Why is this so? That person is one who relies on the ultimate reality, namely, the Buddha. To rely on the Buddha is to rely on the Dharma and the Sangha.

"Thus, World-Honored One, the core of what the Buddha teaches is the One Buddha Vehicle. Those teachings in accord with time and place, those accommodated teachings, all enter into the Mahayana, and are the Mahayana, just as they are the teaching of the One Vehicle, the ultimate vehicle."

Chapter 4

TO REALIZE THE PATH OF EMANCIPATION

1. Moggallana and Punna

(1) At one time, Moggallana was staying by himself in the Bhesakala Grove in the Deer Park near Sumsumaragiri in the country of Bhagga. As Moggallana was walking quietly in the fields, a Mara entered his stomach and hid himself there. Moggallana felt a lumplike heaviness in his stomach, stopped his stroll, entered a room, reflected on this, realized that it was a Mara, and said, "Mara, get out. You should not disturb the Buddha or a disciple of the Buddha, because it will mean endless woe for you." The Mara thought, "This monk, without even seeing me, tells me to get out. Even his master should be unable to notice me so quickly; how is a mere disciple able to accomplish this?"

Moggallana said, "Mara, I noticed you and I know what you are thinking." The Mara, surprised, leaped out of Moggallana's mouth and stood atop the frame of the door. "Mara," Moggallana said, "you must not think that I do not see you. You are standing on top of the door frame. Long ago, I was a Mara called Dusin, and you were the child of my sister Kali. At that time, Kakusandha Buddha appeared in this world, and he had two great disciples, Vidhura and Sanjiva. Vidhura's wisdom was superior and he was most skillful at teaching. Sanjiva was most skillful at meditation. Once when he entered into meditation and extinguished all thoughts and perceptions, the villagers, thinking him dead, conducted a funeral for him. At dawn, emerging from meditation, he extinguished the flames of the funeral pyre, and taking his alms bowl he went out begging. It was only then that they realized that he was still alive.

"One day, the Mara Dusin thought, 'I do not know from where these disciples who rightly uphold the precepts come, nor do I know where they go. I shall take this opportunity to enter into the hearts and minds of the villagers; and by slandering and making trouble for these disciples, I shall unsettle the disciples' hearts and minds.' The villagers abused the disciples. However, those who spoke ill of the disciples—'O dirty, bald monks, parasitic men of leisure, you are like owls on the branch of a tree longingly looking at a mouse below, men of leisure endlessly looking below for something to grasp'—fell into hell upon their deaths.

"The Buddha taught his disciples, 'All this slander and abuse is because of Mara Dusin. Disciples, cultivate hearts and minds of compassion, mercy, joy, and

484 BUDDHA-DHARMA · BOOK SIX

equanimity.' Receiving this teaching, the disciples' hearts and minds were not moved by the slander, and they entered into the forest and practiced the four immeasurable minds.

(2) "Thus Mara Dusin was unable to use this opportunity for unsettling their minds by the device of abuse and slander. He therefore let the villagers honor and support the disciples. Those who honored and supported the disciples were born in the heavenly realms after their deaths. The Buddha taught his disciples, 'This honor and support are also the workings of Mara Dusin. Take care and do not let your hearts and minds be moved so as to give him a chance. Realize that your bodies are impure and that life is suffering and impermanent, and live accordingly.' The disciples were not moved by the honor and support and practiced the path toward realizing the teachings of suffering, emptiness, impermanence, and selflessness.

"Because these two schemes had no effect, Mara Dusin, one day when the Buddha and Vidhura were begging in the village, entered into a child's heart and taking a broken piece of pottery flung it at the head of Vidhura. Vidhura, without even looking back, followed the Buddha, letting the blood flow from the wound on his head. The Buddha, looking at his head, said, 'Mara Dusin does not know any limits of misbehavior.' Dusin, being sucked up by the great earth, fell into hell. From that moment on, Dusin endlessly experienced the mounting pains of hell.

"O Mara, you should not trouble the disciples of the Buddha. That will be the cause of your endless ill fortune. To think that one's evil will not in turn hurt oneself is a mistake. You have gathered the evil of many long nights. You had better not come near the Buddha, and you had better not confuse his disciples."

The Mara, noticed by Moggallana, lost heart and disappeared.

(3) One evening Punna came out of meditation, approached the World-Honored One, and said, "World-Honored One, I wish to hear a succinct teaching. Hearing that teaching, I should like to live quietly and alone. I should like to concentrate on ridding myself of negligence and exert myself with diligence."

"Punna, if that is so, listen carefully. The form that the eyes see, the sound that the ears hear, the odor that the nose smells, the flavor that the tongue tastes, and the sensation that the body feels are things that are delightful and pleasing to the senses, causing desire to arise. If you delight in them, want them, and become attached to them, then delight will arise. Punna, as I have said, the cause of delight is the cause of suffering. Moreover, I have also said that if you do not delight in them, do not want them, and do not become attached to them, then delight will not arise. Punna, delight not arising is suffering not arising. Punna, upon receiving this succinct teaching of mine, tell me where you plan to live."

"World-Honored One, receiving the teachings, I am planning to live in Sunaparanta." "Punna, those people of Sunaparanta are fierce and violent; if they ridicule and shame you, what will you do?" "World-Honored One, at that time, I shall think that since the people of Sunaparanta are good in nature, they will not strike me with their fists." "Punna, if the people do strike you with their fists, what will you do?" "World-Honored One, at that time, I shall think that since the people of Sunaparanta are good in nature, they will not throw clods of dirt at me or hit me with staves." "Punna, if those people do throw clods of dirt at you and hit you with staves, what will you do?" "World-Honored One, at that time, I shall think that since the people of Sunaparanta are good in nature, they will not cut me with swords." "Punna, if those people do cut you with swords, what will you do?" "World-Honored One, at that time, I shall think that since the people of Sunaparanta are good in nature, they will not take my life." "Punna, if those people attempt to take your life, what will you do?" "World-Honored One, at that time, I shall think that the disciples of the Buddha, hating this impure body and life, hope for death; and I shall think that I have been able to achieve the death that is difficult to accomplish." "Very good indeed, Punna, you have attained self-discipline and quietude, and so you may live in Sunaparanta. Punna, go as you wish."

Punna rejoiced at the World-Honored One's teaching and put away the seating mat; taking his robe and begging bowl, he journeyed to Sunaparanta. Presently, he arrived there and taught the Buddha's teaching. Within the year, he gathered a following of five hundred men and women, and he himself was able to attain enlightenment. Before long, Punna passed away into the clouds of nirvana.

At one time, a number of disciples came to the World-Honored One and asked about Punna's death. The World-Honored One said, "Disciples, Punna was indeed a holy man. He followed the teaching, and he was not difficult to teach the teaching. Punna has truly entered into nirvana."

2. Potaliya

(1) The World-Honored One, leaving Savatthi, journeyed and entered a nigrodha grove outside of Kapilavatthu. The people of Kapilavatthu, having just built a new assembly hall, asked the World-Honored One to attend the dedication ceremonies. The World-Honored One consented and went toward the assembly hall; having washed his feet, he entered the hall. Leaning on the central pillar, he faced east and took his seat. The disciples, lining up near the west wall, faced east and sat down; and the people of Kapilavatthu, lining up near the east wall, faced west and sat down. The oil light flickering, the World-Honored One discoursed deep into the night. Later, looking back at Ananda, he said "Ananda, teach these people of the Sakya clan the path of the seeker. Because my back aches, I think I shall lie down awhile." The World-Honored One, folding his garment into four, laid it down and lying on his right side rested for a while. Ananda began his discourse.

(2) "O Mahanama, the disciples of the Buddha uphold the precepts, protect the five senses, know the correct amount to eat, try not to sleep on the night watch, possess the seven mental attitudes, and live endowed with the joy of meditation in this world.

"Upholding the precepts means that one holds to the precepts that the Buddha has established, observes the rules, acts correctly, sees the danger of even a small offense, and perseveres in earnest study. To guard the five senses means to guide and lead the mind to control the five senses so that there will be no attachment to objects seen by the eyes, heard by the ears, smelled by the nose, tasted by the tongue, touched by the skin, or thought by the mind.

"Knowing the correct amount to eat means taking food with correct thought, not paying attention to its appearance or taste, and taking food only for the sake of keeping the body fit for the practice of the path without giving rise to undue suffering. Trying not to sleep on the night watch means that one should stay awake in the afternoon when one either sits or walks, preventing his mind from desiring prohibited things. In the first part of the night also, one should stay awake when one either sits or walks, preventing his mind from desiring prohibited things. In the middle part of the night, one should put his feet together and sleep on his right side with a correct mind, thinking of the time to awaken. In the last part of the night, one should awaken and stay awake when one either sits or walks, preventing his mind from desiring prohibited things.

"Possessing the seven mental attitudes means possessing faith, humbleness, modesty, diligence, effort, intelligence, and the wisdom that clearly knows the causes and effects of phenomena. Living with the joy of meditation in this world means separating oneself from desire and evil deeds and entering into a variety of meditations.

"Mahanama, since the disciples of the Buddha act in this way, they, like the mother hen warming the egg and waiting for the chick to appear, ridding themselves of passions, attain enlightenment and reach an unsurpassed peace. Mahanama, disciples like this are said to be completely possessed of wisdom and practices, and they are able to attain in this world the emancipation of the mind." At that moment, the World-Honored One arose and rejoiced at Ananda's discourse. Then the people of the Sakya clan rejoiced and left.

(3) The World-Honored One, crossing the river Ganges, entered Anguttarapa and stayed near the town of Apana. One day he entered the town, and after begging alms he entered a grove to pass the afternoon hours. At that time the householder Potaliya, holding an umbrella and wearing shoes, strolled through the grove and approached the place where the World-Honored One rested. Greeting the World-Honored One, he stood nearby.

The World-Honored One turned to look at Potaliya and said, "Householder, there is a seat, so sit." Being called a householder, Potaliya was angered and remained silent. The World-Honored One repeated the invitation two or three times; then Potaliya spoke. "Gotama, it is not proper to call me a householder." "Householder, is your appearance not like that of a householder?" "Gotama, I have stopped working and retired from the mundane life." "Householder, how did you stop work and retire from the world?" "Gotama, I gave all my wealth to my children, I stopped all unneeded chatter and meddling, and I gradually reduced my need for food and clothes and became a retired person. This is how I stopped working and took leave of the world." "Your taking leave of the world and taking leave of the world in the Dharma are different." "Gotama, please tell me about taking leave of the world in the Dharma."

"Householder, in regard to this teaching, there are eight ways to free oneself from the mundane life. The first is not to kill. The second is not to steal.

The third is not to lie. The fourth is not to speak words that will cause disharmony. The fifth is to rid oneself of desire. The sixth is to rid oneself of anger. The seventh is to rid oneself of envy. The eighth is to rid oneself of pride. It is through these eight that one takes leave of the world. Yet, this is not the most decisive way to free oneself from the mundane life. There is another way that allows one to free oneself completely from the world." "World-Honored One, please teach it to me."

(4) "Householder, would giving a hungry dog a meatless bone stained with blood satisfy its hunger or would it only make the dog more frustrated and miserable? Householder, with their wisdom my disciples discern things as they really are and the pleasures of the senses and come to know that the pleasures of the senses cause more pain and woe. They thus practice by destroying attachment to the five desires.

"Again, an eagle, a hawk, or some other bird picks up a piece of meat. Just then, another ferocious bird swoops down and tries to steal that bit of meat. If the first bird does not let go that piece of the desired meat, it will receive a wound that is fatal or close to fatal. Moreover, if one takes up a burning grass torch and heads off into the wind, unless that torch is dropped, one's hand or foot will burn and even death is possible. Again, if hot coals are tossed into a hole as deep as a man's height and if two strong men attempt to throw a man into that hole, that man will no doubt struggle desperately and attempt to pull back. However, in the end he will most likely fall in and die. If one comes upon a terrifying poisonous snake, no one will let it bite him. If one borrows another's money, one's possessions will finally be carried off by the lender. If a person seeing ripened fruit climbs up a tree to eat it, and at the same time another person comes along with an ax and cuts the tree down, then unless that person on the tree immediately climbs down, his arm or leg will surely break and he may even die.

"Householder, all these are analogies for the pleasures of the senses. The disciples of this teaching thus meditate on the pleasures of the senses, and with the wisdom that truly sees things as they are they know that the pleasures of the senses cause pain and make afflictions grow greater. They cultivate the thought of detachment whereby they cast aside and destroy attachment to mundane desires. Householder, my disciples by the pure power of equanimity attain the highest wisdom and the mind of emancipation. Through this teaching, one completely frees oneself from the mundane life. Householder, have you taken leave of the world in such a way?"

"World-Honored One, how could I be capable of doing such a thing? Previously, being confused by different teachings, I thought that I knew what I did not know, and I did not know what I knew. Now I know that I do not know what I do not know, and I know what I do know. World-Honored One, you have truly taught me to love, have faith in, and respect the mendicant. From this day forward, as long as I am alive, I vow to remain a follower of the Teaching of the World-Honored One."

(5) The Jatila ascetic Keniya also heard that the World-Honored One was at Anguttarapa, and he visited the Buddha and rejoiced in his teachings. He

invited the World-Honored One and the disciples to his house. The Buddha said, "Keniya, my disciples number twelve hundred fifty, and besides, are you not a follower of the brahminical teaching?"

"World-Honored One, even though I follow the brahminical teaching, and even though your disciples number twelve hundred fifty, please come and accept my offering tomorrow."

The World-Honored One, nodding his head, consented. Keniya quickly went home and, gathering his relatives, friends, and servants together, prepared the food for the next day. One person dug a pit for a fire, another cut firewood, another washed the utensils, another laid out the water jars, another prepared the seats, and Keniya himself prepared a small round hut. At that time, the deeply faithful brahmin Sela with five hundred disciples came walking by and asked Keniya if all this bustling was because of a spectacular wedding, a great sacrifice, or the visit of King Bimbisara of Magadha. "Sela," Keniya said, "it is for none of those reasons. It is for a great offering. Gotama of the Sakya clan, who left home and became a Buddha, and his disciples are invited tomorrow." "Keniya, did you say a Buddha?" "Sela, that is correct. I said a Buddha."

Sela was surprised at the word Buddha. "It is difficult even to hear the word Buddha. In our books, it is written that the one who possesses the thirty-two signs of the great person will become either a universal monarch if he stays home or a Buddha if he leaves home. He will either bring peace to the world without a sword across the four oceans or rid himself of the obstacles of the world. Keniya, where is this Buddha now?" Keniya pointed to the yonder green grove with his right hand. Sela with his five hundred disciples left and went to the World-Honored One. Rejoicing at the wondrous and perfect form of the World-Honored One, he soon took refuge in the teaching and became the disciple of the World-Honored One. The next day, he together with the others received Keniya's offering. Earnestly practicing, he attained enlightenment in seven days.

3. To Realize the Path of Emancipation

(1) The World-Honored One returned to Rajagaha and stopped in a bamboo grove outside of the city. One day he called his disciples and said, "Disciples, one who has taken leave of his relatives and of his home and who knows his mind and realizes the way is called a mendicant. The mendicant casts aside worldly wealth and by begging comes to know what is enough, eats once a day, rests at the foot of a tree, and is careful never again to commit a violation. Disciples, what makes one unwise is desire.

(2) "Disciples, even when there are people who slander us, we guard them with compassion. Even when they harm us, we still treat them with kindness. The element of benefit is with us; the element of harm is with the others. An evil person harming a holy person is like one spitting in the air. The spit does not pollute the sky but returns and pollutes oneself. Moreover, it is like turning into the wind and throwing trash trying to dirty another. The trash does not dirty the other but rather dirties oneself. You cannot defeat a wise person. Misfortune

will certainly fall on those who try to harm a holy person. If you give widely for the sake of the path, it will not automatically become a great giving. But if you should uphold the original intention and respect the way, then the goodness will be great.

(3) "To others practice the virtue of giving, to aid their efforts, and to rejoice in them results in the attainment of the reward of happiness. For example, hundreds of thousands of people light their torches from one torch, and yet that torch remains the same. Like this torch, the happiness of giving is never extinguished.

"In the world there are twenty difficult things. Being poor, it is difficult to give. Being rich, it is difficult to study the path. It is difficult to throw away one's life and search for the path. It is difficult to get a chance to hear a Buddha's teachings. It is even more difficult to get a chance to meet a Buddha. It is difficult to suppress desire and free oneself from desire. When one sees something that one likes, it is difficult not to seek after it. Possessing power, it is difficult not to confront another with power. Being put to shame, it is difficult to hold one's temper. When something unpleasant happens, it is difficult not to be disturbed by it. It is difficult to study the way widely and deeply. It is difficult not to take a beginner lightly. It is difficult to rid oneself of pride. It is difficult to meet a true friend. It is difficult to see one's nature and to study the way. It is difficult not to be disturbed by one's surroundings. It is difficult to save people according to their capacities. It is difficult to hold one's mind steady. It is difficult not to criticize. It is difficult to exercise skillful means.

(4) "One who practices the way is like one who enters a dark room with a torch. The darkness immediately disappears and the room is filled with light. After studying the path, when you see the path with clarity, then the darkness of ignorance disappears, and the light of wisdom is attained.

"All of you, what do I hold in my mind when I reflect on the path? What do I practice when I cultivate the path? What do I teach when I expound the path? I merely reflect on, practice, and teach the Four Noble Truths. Seeing the sky and the earth, I am aware of their impermanence. Seeing the mountains and rivers, I am aware of their impermanence. Seeing any thing that flourish, I am aware of their impermanence. If you should hold your minds in this manner, you will attain enlightenment quickly. For one day, practice the path without a break. Should you attain the roots of faith by practicing the path, the bliss resulting therefrom will be infinite.

(5) "People boldly pursue fame with the flame of desire burning in them, which flame is like a burning stick of incense: as the incense gives off fragrance, it burns itself up. The unwise are eager for vain compliments and do not guard the truth of the path, thereby gaining glorious fame but endangering themselves. Regret will without doubt pain the heart later.

"To seek wealth and sensual pleasure is like licking a blade coated with honey. For an amount of sweet taste less than just one lick, the tongue will be cut and a wound will remain. Worries over home, wife, and child are greater than being bound in a prison with the hands and feet shackled. In prison, there are moments when the shackles are loosened; but though affection for wife and children is as woeful as being held in the mouth of a tiger, there is no moment when the fetters are untied.

"People who seek sensual pleasure are like those who take up a torch and hold it against the wind. They will burn their hands and they will suffer the pain of burnt flesh; the poisons of greed, anger, and ignorance are in the body. If one does not hurry and rid oneself of those poisons by means of the path, then pain and woe will surely come to one. This leather bag, the body, with all its impurities packed inside may deceive these people of this world, but the person who has attained enlightenment is indifferent to it. 'I have no need for her' was my answer to an evil one who tried to test me by offering a jewelled lady to me. Do not ever trust your mind, for your mind is not to be trusted. On no account indulge in sexual pleasure. If you do, misfortune will arise.

(6) "Those who hope to reach the path should extinguish the fire of desire. Those wearing dry grass garments, upon seeing a prairie fire coming, would get out of its way; in a similar manner, those who practice the path, seeing the fire of desire, should get as far away as possible.

"There was a person who, in turmoil because he was unable to control his sexual passions, tried to castrate himself with a blade. I said to him, 'Instead of cutting that off, it would be better to cut off your mind. The mind is the master. If the master stops, then all of the followers will stop too. If you cannot stop the erring mind, what good is it to castrate yourself?'

"Indeed, it is painful to attain the path, but it is even more painful not to attain it. Being born into the world, one will age, grow sick, and die. Suffering and pain have no limit. If one is suffering and committing offenses, then birth and death will not stop. The suffering and pain experienced by beings cannot be fully described in words.

"To reach the path one must pull out the root of passion. If one pulls out the beads of a bead screen one by one, the time will come when all the beads will be exhausted. Likewise, when all the passions are extinguished, the path will be attained.

"One should practice the path like an ox with a heavy load trodding along a deeply muddy road, looking neither to the right nor to the left even when tired; after going past the mud it will rest. The mud of passion is deeper and fiercer, but by perfecting the mind and focusing on the path one can overcome all of one's suffering."

4. The Allegory of the Arrow

(1) At that time, Sariputta, Maha-Cunda, and Channa were staying near each other on the Vulture Peak. Channa was extremely ill. One evening after he came out of meditation, Sariputta said to Maha-Cunda that they should go and attend to Channa, and they did so. They asked him, "Channa, how is your illness? has the pain lessened?" "Friends, my illness is quite grave, and the pain only increases. I want to die immediately. I have thought of killing myself with a knife."

"Channa, that will not do. We are hoping that you will get over this illness and live a longer life. If there is something you wish to eat or some medicine you do not have, we shall search for it. We shall look after you, so please get better and go on living."

"Friends, I am not lacking in food or medicine, and there is no lack of people taking care of me. Moreover, I have with delight served the World-Honored One for a long time, and as a disciple I have done what was expected of me. Please know that I, Channa, will not again be born into the realm of delusion, and that I killed myself of my own accord."

"Channa, we have some questions that we want you to answer. If it pleases you, please answer them."

"I shall answer any question. Please feel free to ask."

"Channa, can the eye, seeing, and the object of the eye be viewed as being mine, or as the 'I', or as possessed by the 'I'? In the same way, are the ear, hearing, and what is heard, the nose, smelling and what is smelled, the tongue, tasting, and what is tasted, the body, touching, and what is touched, and the mind, thinking, and what is thought mine, the 'I', or possessed by the 'I'?"

"Friends, I see that all these sense organs, the consciousnesses, and the objects of consciousness are not mine, not the 'I', nor the self."

"Channa, what do you observe and realize?"

"Friends, I observe the cessation of the six sense organs, the consciousnesses, and the objects of consciousness, and I realize the cessation of them."

Then Maha-Cunda said, "Channa, that is why we must always think on this teaching of the World-Honored One. If one has attachment, then there is disconcertment. If one has no attachment, then there is no disconcertment. If there is no disconcertment, then there is peace of mind. If there is peace of mind, then there is no desire, and because of no desire there is no rebirth. If there is no rebirth, there is no life and death. If there is no life and death, there is neither this world nor the next. This is the end of suffering."

Speaking in this way, Sariputta and Maha-Cunda left. Immediately after they left, Channa took a knife and killed himself.

Sariputta talked to the World-Honored One about this. The World-Honored One responded, "Did not Channa with his own lips say that he would not be born in this realm of delusion again? Channa, becoming one who never again will receive another body, discarded this physical body and died. Channa has attained nirvana."

(2) The World-Honored One then continued his journey; he went north, crossed the river Ganges, and returned to the Jeta Grove and Anathapindika Monastery. One day, the disciple Malunkyaputta, retiring to a quiet spot, thought, "Is the world eternal or not? Is the world finite or not? Is the body one with or different from the spirit? Do people exist after death or not? The World-Honored One ignores these questions and does not discuss them. I simply cannot bear this. Going to the World-Honored One, I shall ask these questions. If the World-Honored One discusses these questions, then I shall continue to practice under him. If there is no discussion, then I shall cease my practice." Immediately, then, he went to the World-Honored One and asked these

questions. "World-Honored One, please discuss them as you know things. If you do not discuss them, then I shall leave you and return home."

The World-Honored One said, "Malunkyaputta, when you came to me to practice under me, did I promise you that I should discuss these questions, whether the world was eternal, whether it was finite, whether the body and spirit were one, or whether people existed after their deaths?" "World-Honored One, you did not do so." "Moreover, did you promise me that you would practice under me only if I discussed these questions?" "World-Honored One, I did not do so." "Malunkyaputta, if that is so, I did not promise and you did not promise. What promise am I supposedly evading?

"Malunkyaputta, if there is a person who says that he will refrain from practice until I discuss these questions, then that person will die in the meantime. Consider a person pierced with a poisoned arrow. Relatives and friends gather and bring a doctor to pull out the arrow. Then that person says he that will not allow the arrow to be removed until he knows the sex of the archer, the caste, the countenance, and the place he is from. Moreover, until he knows whether the bow was a big bow or a small bow, whether the bowstring was a wisteria vine, a string, or a tendon, whether the shaft was made of cane or bulrush, whether the feathers were from an eagle, a heron, a hawk, or a peacock, whether the shaft was bound with cow sinew, water buffalo muscle, deer sinew, or grass, and whether the arrowhead was horseshoe shaped, spear shaped, a tooth of a calf, or the feather of a bird, he will not allow the arrow to be taken out. Malunkyaputta, if he keeps on saying such things, he will die in the meantime.

(3) "Malunkyaputta, it is not proper for you to think that holding the view that the world is eternal is necessarily conducive to the holy life. Moreover, it is not proper to think that holding the view that the world is not eternal is necessarily conducive to the holy life. Even holding the view that the world is both eternal and not eternal, one cannot overcome rebirth, old age, death, anxiety, sorrow, and suffering. My teaching aims at removing all these now.

"It is wrong to assume that one is able to attain the holy life by holding any view regarding whether the world is finite, or whether a person exists after death. Whether one holds the view that the world is finite and likewise whether one believes that a person exists after death, one cannot overcome rebirth, old age, death, anxiety, sorrow, and suffering. My teaching aims at removing all these now.

"Malunkyaputta, it is best to think that I teach what needs to be taught and do not teach what does not need to be taught. Such questions as these do not need to be answered. Why? Because discussion of these questions is neither conducive to the goal nor fundamental to the holy life. Neither does it help people to destroy passions, awaken to the supreme wisdom, or attain enlightenment and enter nirvana. The things that need to be taught are the Four Noble Truths. Why? Because knowing them is conducive to the goal, is fundamental to the holy life, and helps people to destroy passion, awaken to the supreme wisdom, attain enlightenment, and enter nirvana."

Malunkyaputta rejoiced from the depths of his heart at this teaching of the World-Honored One.

5. Rajakarama—The Temple of the King

(1) In Savatthi, there was a convent called the Rajakarama that King Pasenadi built especially for Buddhist nuns. It would have been appropriate for the nuns as ascetics to live outside the town; but there might be many dangers for nuns living outside the town, so the king, receiving the World-Honored One's permission, built the convent inside the city. There were many nuns living there, and in the afternoons it was always the custom of many to go into the dark forest outside the town to meditate. Maras very often attacked the nuns and tried to seduce them. Without flinching, the nuns fought back and repelled all attacks.

Sela, the princess of Alavi, was called the Alavi nun. One day she went alone into the dark forest and quietly meditated. A Mara, thinking of frightening her, appeared and said the following:

> In this changing world devoid of enlightenment,
> It is useless to renounce this world;
> Indulge in the pleasures of the five desires.
> It is best to live a life without regret.

Knowing the intent of the Mara, the nun answered back.

> Because this is a changing world, there is enlightenment.
> With wisdom have I attained that state.
> Mara, you negligent fellow,
> You do not know the path;
> The five desires are like a sword and a spear:
> They cut the body.
> What you call bliss is what I call misery.

(2) Also a nun called Soma, after begging for alms in Savatthi, went to the dark forest and sat in meditation. A Mara said, "It is difficult indeed to enter the rank of the holy. With a sewing needle of wisdom do you expect that a woman will attain this?" Soma responded, "For one who quiets the mind, awakens wisdom, and sees the true Dharma, there is no difference between a man and a woman. One who has the thought of male and female and sees such a distinction, Mara, is not entitled to speak out."

(3) Kisa Gotami was one of the nuns who lived in that convent. This woman was from a poor family of Savatthi, and because she was so thin people called her Kisa Gotami, skinny Gotami. But through the good deeds of past lives she was a woman blessed with merit and virtue. At one time, before she became a nun, there was a well-known rich man living in Savatthi, who was known for being miserly. On a certain occasion Kisa Gotami was discovered by the rich man and was asked to become his son's wife. It happened this way. The rich man, looking upon the gold bars that he kept in his vault, discovered that they had suddenly turned into charcoal. Surprised, he thought, "This is clearly a sign that my luck is nil. If one with much luck saw this charcoal, perhaps it would be transformed back to the original gold." So even while trying to resign himself to his misfortune, he could not get rid of his attachment to the gold, so he packed the charcoal in boxes and took them to the nearby market town to leave them out for passersby to see. One day Kisa Gotami passed by those boxes and saw them

filled to overflowing with gold at an open-front store; she was surprised and cried out without thinking, "My, what a lot of gold there is!" Hearing this, the rich man, who had hidden himself, became happy; looking into the boxes, he saw that the charcoal had changed back into the original gold and was glittering there. The rich man became attracted to her good fortune. Thus he ardently sought her and finally won her as his oldest son's bride.

Thus by such strange circumstances, this woman came overnight into the home of the rich man. She was truly loved by her husband, and a truly happy and loving home was created by them. In time a child was born, and this added even more happiness to the home. Yet even in this home of happiness the breeze of good fortune did not always blow. The precious only child, at about the time it was crawling around and was about to stand, was suddenly taken by illness and left on the journey from which there is no return. Her sorrow was great. Holding the cold body, she cried and lamented. Finally, unnoticed by people of the household, she took her baby's body and ran out of the compound; at every door and stopping every passerby, she asked for a way to help her child. She had indeed lost her sanity. Everyone showed pity, but since there was no means by which to resurrect one who had breathed one's last, nobody could do anything but offer tears of sympathy. For many days, the figure of this woman gone crazy with grief, wandering from one village to another, brought tears to the eyes of the people.

One day an ardent follower of the Buddha, unable to look upon this any longer, called to her and spoke to her. "Sister, your child's sickness is indeed grave. It is a thing beyond the skill of the world's doctors. There is only one person who can cure this sickness, and fortunately he is now at the Jeta Grove, at the Anathapindika Monastery. He is the Buddha."

Upon hearing this her heart leapt with joy as if she had been already helped. She immediately hurried to the Jeta Grove, to the Anathapindika Monastery, and asked to see the World-Honored One. She implored him to save her beloved child from his sickness. The World-Honored One listened quietly to what she had to say and gently responded, "It will be easy to cure the child's illness, but five or six poppy seeds are needed. Hurry to town and get some." It was such an easy request that Gotami quickly stood up and was about to leave for the town. But the World-Honored One stopped her and said, "Those seeds, however, must come from a home that has never had a funeral, that has not seen a death." Hearing this, as she was worried about her beloved child, she did not really think deeply on its meaning. Receiving the Buddha's words, she quickly went to town and asked for poppy seeds at every door. However, though there was not one house that did not offer to give her the poppy seeds, she could not find one home within the entire town from end to end that had not experienced the death of someone. At first, she thought it strange, but as she continued asking, she began to understand. Among human beings, there are none who, having been born, do not die. A house that has not been visited by the sorrow of the parting of death is nonexistent. Whether it is for the loss of a beloved wife, an adorable child, irreplaceable parents, or a dependable husband, the grief of people in this world is endless, for impermanence is inherent in the body. The woman felt a chill. She lost the energy, and the ignorance, to continue asking for the poppy seeds. Without waiting for the Buddha's words, the eye of the Dharma had already opened up in her heart. Thus after a number of days of holding dearly to her beloved child's body, she buried it and hurriedly returned to the Jeta grove and went to the World-Honored One. The World-Honored One quietly looked at her and asked, "How is your child? Have you found the poppy seeds?" She spoke of the joy of awakening from her dreamlike existence by the skillful means of compassion that the World-Honored One had employed and asked to be one of his disciples. Joining their ranks, she practiced and gradually approached the day of her enlightenment. However, one day a Mara, thinking to tempt her, appeared before her and said,

> You who were separated from a beloved child,
> Sitting alone here crying,
> Should come into the forest
> To seek out a good companion.

The nun answered,

> Separated from a beloved child,
> Past is the day I was a mother.
> A good partner is nonexistent.
> I am not sad. I am not crying.
> Nor do I fear you.
> The empty joys of all the worlds are extinguished.
> Darkness is broken; the battle with Mara is won,
> Pain is gone; I meditate quietly.

(4) A Mara tried to tempt the young and beautiful nun Vijaya:

> Youthful days will not last forever; come, princess,
> Let us make music together and be filled with joy.

Answering the attempt to entice her, she responded,

> The ignoble five desires, though pleasing and enjoyable,
> Are needless and useless. I leave them to you, Mara.
> This easily decaying, impure body is only a source of shame.
> I have abandoned desires for the pleasure
> Of this world, the other world, and the heavenly world;
> I have forsaken all the darkness of such thoughts of desire.

(5) Cala, Upacala and Sisupacala were all sisters of Sariputta. Together they all put their faith in the teachings of the Buddha and practiced the holy life. A Mara appeared at the place of meditation of Cala and asked, "Why do you not enjoy anything and sit like this here alone?" Cala answered,

> I cannot find joy in life.
> With life there is death;
> With birth one comes to know pain.
> Bonds, torments, and other pains,
> Are relieved by the Buddha's teaching.
> He teaches us the way to rid ourselves of these pains.

> The pleasures of the divine realm are great indeed,
> But if one does not know the Dharma,
> The pleasure will change into misery.

(6) The Mara sought to turn Upacala toward the pleasures of the heavenly realms, to which Upacala replied,

> The pleasures of the heavenly realms are stained with impurity,
> They will cause one to fall into the hands of Mara.
> Even heavens are worlds of bondage.
> All the world is burning, smoking, crackling with flames, and shaking.
> My heart and mind rest in a place immovable and unshaking,
> In a place where the ignorant cannot go,
> In a place that is out of reach of Mara.

(7) Appearing before Sisupacala, Mara asked in what path she found pleasure. She answered that she found pleasure in no path.

> Other than the way that the Buddha taught,
> I find no pleasure in the paths of different views.
> He who has enlightenment true and matchless,
> Who has swept away Mara and conquered all things,
> He who is the Buddha, who sees everything,
> The World-Honored One, is my master, in whose teachings I rejoice.

(8) One day, Maha-Pajapati, accompanied by five hundred nuns, came to the World-Honored One and asked that someone give teaching to them on the following day. In those days, it was customary for the disciples of the World-Honored One to take turns expounding the teachings to the nuns. It was Nandaka's turn for the next day; however, he did not wish to speak. The World-Honored One, asking Ananda whose turn it was, found out that Nandaka did not wish to speak. The World-Honored One called Nandaka and ordered him to teach the nuns.

The following morning Nandaka, obeying the order, went to Savatthi with one other disciple. After begging and then eating, Nandaka went to Rajakarama. Seeing Nandaka coming, the nuns prepared a seat and water to wash his feet. Nandaka, washing his feet and sitting on the prepared seat, spoke to the nuns. "Sisters, let us engage in some questions and answers. When asked, say what you know and say what you do not know. Moreover, if you have a question or doubt, ask, 'What is this?' or 'Why is this so?'" Hearing this, the nuns rejoiced at the opportunity for the free exchange of questions and answers with Nandaka.

He asked them, "Sisters, is the eye everlasting or impermanent?" "It is impermanent." "Is an impermanent thing painful or pleasurable?" "It is painful." "Can one see whether this fragile thing that is impermanent and painful is mine, me, or the self?" "Great sage, this cannot be done. It cannot be done either with the ear, nose, tongue, body, or mind. Why? Because already with true wisdom we have seen how things really are; we have seen the six sense organs to be impermanent."

(9) Nandaka went on and asked the same question about the six objects of sense, form, sounds, smells, tastes, tangibles, and thoughts and about the six

consciousness, those of the eye, ear, nose, tongue, body, and mind; and he received the same answers. He then said to the nuns, "Very good, indeed, sisters, this is the true wisdom by which the disciples of the teachings see things as they really are. Sisters, it is like a burning oil lantern; the oil is impermanent and changing, and so are the wick, flame, and light. Now if there were a person who said that the oil, wick, and flame were impermanent, but that the light was permanent and did not change, would this be correct?" "It would be incorrect. If the oil, wick, and flame are impermanent, the light would, of course, be impermanent."

"Sisters, if this is so, then would it be correct to say that the feelings of pain, pleasure, and neither pain nor pleasure coming from the impermanent six sense organs are permanent?" "Great sage, it would be incorrect. Why? Because one thing is conditioned by another, so that if the cause becomes nonexistent, then the result, too, naturally becomes nonexistent."

"Very good indeed, sisters, truly it is as you say. Next, for example, would it be correct to say that while the branches and leaves of a tree are impermanent, the shadow of the tree is permanent?" "Great sage, it would be incorrect. Since the roots, trunk, branches, and leaves are impermanent, the shadow would of course also be impermanent."

"Very good indeed, sisters, truly it is as you say. Now, for example, after a skilled butcher has killed a cow and then with a sharp butcher knife separated the hide and the inner flesh without any damage and did the same with the inner membranes, muscles, and tendons, and then wrapped the hide that was so carefully separated around the inner flesh, would it then be correct to say that the cow is as it was and that the hide is not separated?" "Great sage, it would be incorrect. The hide and the cow are separated."

"Sisters, I gave you this metaphor to teach you the meaning of the teachings. The inner flesh is the inner six sense organs. The outer hide is the outer six sense obejcts. The inner membranes, muscles, and tendons are the passions. The sharp butcher knife is the wisdom that cuts off the passions within the mind. Sisters, if you practice the seven limbs of enlightenment, memory, truth, effort, joy, quietude, meditation, and indifference, the passions will be extinguished and you will attain emancipation from passions and ignorance in this present life." After instructing the nuns in this manner, Nandaka exhorted them, saying, "Sisters, go on practicing the path now."

(10) Rejoicing at the teachings of Nandaka, they arose from their seats and went to the Buddha and respectfully bowed to him. After the nuns left, the Buddha instructed his disciples and said, "Disciples, on the fourteenth, the eve of Uposatha, there is no one who is confused about whether the moon is full or not when, indeed, it is not full. In the same way, though the nuns rejoicingly received Nandaka's teaching, their thinking is not yet perfect." The World-Honored One ordered Nandaka to speak again to the nuns the next day.

Nandaka again, after begging at Savatthi, went to Rajakarama the next day and, as on the day before, spoke through questions. The nuns, as on the day before, went to the World-Honored One and paid their respects. After the nuns left, the World-Honored One spoke to his disciples and said, "Disciples, on the the fifteenth, the night of the Uposatha, there is no one who is confused about whether the moon is full or not when, indeed, it is full. In the same way, receiving the teachings of Nandaka, the nuns rejoiced, and their thinking became perfect. Even the last of these five hundred nuns will enter the non-retrogressive stage, characterized by a settled faith that leads with certainty to the attainment of enlightenment."

6. Leaves in the Hand

(1) The World-Honored One again moved south and entered a simsapa grove in Kosambi. Taking some leaves of a tree in his hand, he said, "Disciples, which do you think are more, the leaves in this grove or the leaves in my hand?" "World-Honored One, the leaves in the grove are much more." "Disciples, in the same way, the things I know but do not teach are as numerous as the leaves in the grove. The things I do teach are as few as the leaves in my hand. The reason I do not teach certain things is that they are of no benefit, and they have nothing to do with the holy life, with removing one's passions, awakening the supreme wisdom, realizing enlightenment, or attaining nirvana. I teach the Four Noble Truths, suffering, the cause of suffering, the cessation of suffering, and the path to the cessation of suffering; these are beneficial and conducive to the holy life and aid one in destroying passions, attaining the supreme wisdom, realizing enlightenment, and entering nirvana. This is why, disciples, knowing these Four Noble Truths, you must practice with diligence."

(2) "Disciples, pleasure appears pleasurable, but in reality it is something that will kill the body. It is similar to the fruit of a vine that, during autumn, once fell upon the roots of a sala tree around which it was wound. The spirit living in that sala tree, becoming startled and frightened, shook within the tree. His fellow spirits gathered there to comfort the spirit of the tree. 'Friend, it is unnecessary to be afraid. That seed of the vine will be swallowed by a bird, eaten by a sheep, burnt by a brush fire, munched by a lumberjack, or carried off by an ant. That seed will hardly be able to sprout.'

"However, the seed was not swallowed by a bird, eaten by a sheep, burnt by a brushfire, munched by a lumberjack, or carried off by an ant. With spring it sprouted, and with the rainy season, the vine suddenly grew and became lush. With young, tender curls the vine wrapped itself around the sala tree. The spirit of the sala tree, feeling pleasant from the soft touch, thought, 'Previously my friends came to comfort me from the fear of the vines. But look, with the pleasantness of this gentle feeling of these vine curls, it was foolish of me to shake with fear waiting for a danger that did not come.'

"The vine gradually wrapped itself more and more around the sala tree, appearing to fatten the tree, and even covered the top of the tree. The vines extended out onto the limbs and flourished, making a dark shadow and finally withering the branches. The spirit of the sala tree for the first time realized the great pain and remembered the words of comfort from his friends. 'Disciples, pleasure is enjoyable and causes you to feel good; however, it destroys one'."

(3) The World-Honored One again went north and, returning to Savatthi, entered the Jeta Grove. One day, King Pasenadi was outside the town on official business, riding a chariot. The king's grandmother was still alive even though his mother had already died. She was quite old, being one hundred twenty years of age. Feeble and senile as she was, the king was a person of deep devotion and enjoyed serving her. However, on this day the old grandmother, in spite of her attendant's care, suddenly died like an old, withered tree toppling over. The state minister of the king thought, "The king, hearing of the sudden death of his beloved grandmother, will suffer great grief. There must be some way to lessen the grief the king will feel." So thinking, he prepared numerous elephants, horses, and chariots, gathered numberless jewels and dancing girls, set up banners and let music sound, and covered the casket; he took all these outside the town, placing them where the returning king would see them. The king, seeing them, questioned the then approaching state minister. "Whose offering is this?" "Sire, it is for the mother of one of the town's elders who has died." "What are these elephants, horses, and chariots for?" "There are five hundred each of the elephants, horses, and chariots. They are to be sent to Yama so that the mother's life can be bought." "What stupidity!" the king said. "Life can be neither preserved nor bought. Should you fall into the jaws of a crocodile, you will surely lose your life. In the same way, should you fall into the clutches of Yama, there is no way to escape." "There are five hundred dancing girls and they are to be traded to buy her life." "The girls and the jewels are of no use." "Then he would like to buy her life with the magic of a brahmin or the power of a monk with matchless merit."

Upon hearing this, Pasenadi laughed and said, "This is the thinking of a fool. Once in the jaws of a crocodile, there is no way out. Is not the teaching of the Buddha true, according to which every living being is certain to die?" At that moment the state minister kneeled before the king and said, "Sire, it is as you say, all living beings will die. Please do not grieve too much. Sire, your grandmother passed away today." Upon hearing this, King Pasenadi cried and sorrowed, and though sobbing, he said, "Very good, indeed, my minister, with skillful means you kept my mind and heart from shattering. You are truly knowledgeable with regard to the use of skillful means."

Returning to the town, he took incense, flowers, and candles and offered them to his grandmother. Though it was the middle of the day, he went immediately to the World-Honored One in his hut and questioned him.

(4) The World-Honored One said to King Pasenadi, "Sire, where do you come from at this hour in the middle of the day?" "World-Honored One, my grandmother died today. She was elderly and feeble and aged one hundred twenty years. I loved my grandmother and would have happily given up my royal family if it could have bought her life. I would have happily given up priceless horses, carriages, jewels, the castle, and even the country of Kasi if I could buy her life. However, truly, as you have always taught, all living things die and will certainly perish. There is nothing that can be done." "Great king, as you say, all living things die and will certainly perish. They are just like pots, unglazed or

glazed, which will certainly break one day." Saying this, the World-Honored One recited the following verse:

> All living beings die. That is, all things end in death.
> According to one's actions, one will receive the fruit of virtue or evil.
> Having done evil, one goes to a hell; having accumulated merit, one goes to a heaven.
> Thus, doing good, one prepares for the next world.
> Truly merit is the boat for people to cross over into the next world.

Introduction

As Book Seven opens, the Buddha is travelling southeast toward Rajagaha (Skt: Rajagriha), passing through Vesali (Skt: Vaisali) to stay at the Vulture Peak.

One day when the Buddha was meditating at the Peak, a marvelous thing happened. Flowers from heaven scattered over the Buddha and the assembled disciples; the earth trembled; and a brilliant light issued forth from the tuft of white hair between the Buddha's brows and illuminated the entire universe. On behalf of all who were greatly puzzled, Bodhisattva Maitreya asks Manjusri for an explanation and receives the reply that perhaps the time has come for the Buddha to expound the ultimate truth.

Such is the dramatic opening of the famous Lotus Sutra. Chapter 1 of Book Seven presents selected passages from this sutra, highly revered by all followers of the Mahayana. The Lotus Sutra was written down in stages. The older versions were in verse form, using a common dialect to reach a greater audience; and the later versions were in both verse and prose, using Sanskrit to impart some dignity to this precious work. The words of the Buddha were elaborated upon with supernatural touches to impress the readers regarding the importance of this sacred teaching.

The profound doctrine can be explained in very simple terms. There are three types of seekers of the Dharma: 1. sravakas, who listen to the Buddha's teaching and exert themselves to practice it in good faith; 2. pratyekabuddhas, who aim to be liberated by their own efforts without teachers; 3. bodhisattvas, who aim not only to liberate themselves but to save all other sentient beings. The Lotus Sutra teaches by means of various parables that the ultimate goal must be buddhahood and that there are not three ways to attain it but only one way, or one vehicle (ekayana) that applies to all who seek the true awakening. The one vehicle concept was first encountered in Book Six, Section 7, in the story of Queen Srimala.

Sariputra asks the Buddha three times for an explanation of this teaching, and the Buddha refuses three times. Before he begins his discourse, 5,000 disciples leave, assuming that they had already attained enlightenment and did not need to listen to it. The Buddha remarks that those disciples were arrogant for believing in their limited attainment, but now that the "useless twigs and leaves" have departed, he was ready to expound the wonderful teaching.

The Buddha explains the One Vehicle doctrine by relating the parable of the burning house. A wealthy old man with many children has a large house which is terribly dilapidated and has only one narrow door. One day a fire spreads throughout the house, but the children are unaware of the danger. In order to entice the children to leave the house, the old man offers three kinds of playthings, a goat-drawn carriage, a deer-drawn carriage, and an ox-drawn carriage. The children finally rush out, but when they ask for the carriages, the old man gives each a magnificent carriage drawn by a large white ox.

The goat-drawn carriage represents the sravaka; the deer-drawn carriage represents the pratyekabuddha; and the ox-drawn carriage represents the bodhisattva. The carriage drawn by the large white ox represents the One Vehicle that is available to all beings. The Buddha explains that he had used skillful means of the various vehicles to accommodate the various needs, capacities, and natures of the seekers. Other parables reveal other aspects the Buddha wished to convey, such as the parable of the herbs in which it is shown that the rain falls equally on all plants and herbs, just as the compassion of the Buddha shines on all beings; and the parable of the physician's children, in Chapter 1, Section 5, which relates the story of the physician who leaves medicine for his children when he goes on a journey. He sends a messenger back to the children to tell them that the father had died. Becoming ill with sadness, the children remember the words of the father and take the medicine to get well. The Buddha explains that he also uses skillful means to announce his imminent death, so that people will earnestly listen to his teaching before his demise. However, the Buddha declares that he exists beyond time and space, and can teach the doctrine any time at any place if anyone wished to hear his doctrine. The implication here is that the Dharma itself is eternally available to all beings anywhere in the universe.

Chapter 2 relates the pitiful story of Prince Ajatasatru, son of King Bimbisara. The Buddha's cousin Devadatta wanted to start a new order in opposition to the Buddha by laying down stricter rules. When the Buddha explained that such restrictive rules were not necessary, Devadatta decides that he would gain the support of Ajatasatru to establish his new group of followers. The Prince first attempts to usurp the throne by killing his father as suggested by Devadatta, but since he was unable to do so, the King is imprisoned. Despite Queen Vaidehi's attempt to sustain his health secretly, the King finally dies. The Queen is also confined in a private room for disobeying orders. At her request, the Buddha appears in her presence to teach her about Amitayus Buddha and how by contemplating his compassion and simply reciting "namo Amitayus Buddha," she would be born in his Land of Happiness (Sukhavati). After various failed attempts to kill the Buddha, Devadatta is swallowed up by the earth and burns to death. Ajatasatru, on the other hand, becomes gravely ill due to deep remorse for his cruel efforts to kill his father. Jivaka, the physician, unable to cure him, advises him to seek spiritual help from the Buddha, who eventually cures him by his compassionate teaching.

These passages (Chapter 2, Section 3) are from the Amitayur-dhyana-sutra (Contemplation Sutra), one of the three main scriptures of the Pure Land sects, of which the Jodo Shin Sect (True Pure Land Sect) is the largest Buddhist group in Japan. The other two scriptures are the Larger Sukhavati-vyuha-sutra, passages of which the reader encountered in Book VI, Chapter 2, and the Smaller Sukhavati-vyuha-sutra, select passages of which are found in Chapter 4, Section 6, of this Book VII. The latter describes the Land of Happiness, or Pure Land, where conditions are conducive for attaining enlightenment. However, the founder of the Jodo Shin Sect, Shinran, presented an interpretation of the 'birth in Pure Land' to signify a letting go of our self-efforts and with single-mindedness being embraced by the Infinite Compassion of the Amitayus-Amitabha Buddha, who can transfer his merits and awaken us to full enlightenment. This view is related to the teaching of the One Vehicle in the Lotus Sutra, in which the Buddha warns his disciples not to become so arrogant as to believe that, in an age of degeneracy, they would be able to become liberated by their own efforts.

In Chapter 4, Section 4, Pasenadi, King of Kosala, is facing his final years so he pays his last respects to the Buddha, remarking that they are now both eighty years old. Shortly after, due to Prince Vidudabha's feelings of revenge caused by the Sakya clan's wily deception regarding King Pasenadi's request before he was born, the Kosalan army attacked and conquered Kapilavatthu, the Buddha's native place.

Chapter 1

THE WONDROUS DHARMA IS REVEALED

1. The One Vehicle Teaching

(1) The World-Honored One now headed south, passed Vaisali, and returned to Rajagriha, where he stayed at the Vulture Peak. One day, when many disciples and bodhisattvas were present, the World-Honored One taught a doctrine called Great Principles. As the World-Honored One entered the meditation called the Abode of Boundless Principle, the gods scattered flowers and the earth shook in six different ways. All those present were delighted to witness the unusual happenings, and with their hands together they gazed attentively at the Buddha.

At just that instant a ray of light flashed from the white curl between the Buddha's eyebrows and illuminated all the eighteen thousand worlds in the eastern region; from the lowest hell of Avici to the highest heaven of Akanistha, all sentient beings were illuminated brightly, together with the buddhas expounding the Dharma, the buddhas entering nirvana, the people who were practicing the way, and the structures enshrining the Buddhas' relics. Bodhisattva Maitreya, sensing the minds of the people, asked Bodhisattva Manjusri a question in a set of verses:

> (i) Why does the Buddha emit this great ray?
> Flowers rain from the sky, and
> The fragrance of sandalwood is everywhere.
> The earth shakes in purity,
> And people rejoice in gratitude.
> Wherever the ray shines,
> The eighteen thousand worlds in the east,
> The births and deaths of living beings,
> As well as their good and bad deeds, are clearly illuminated.

> (ii) In each country dwell countless Buddhas,
> Who employ skillful means
> To expound the profound Dharma and
> To give guidance to countless beings.
> In this world of suffering,
> To those who seek liberation,
> They teach the path to nirvana
> To help overcome the root of suffering.
> To those blessed by good deeds of the past,

And who seek the Dharma,
The path of the Pratyekabuddha is taught along with other paths.
While seeking the highest truth,
They encourage others to seek the Buddha's doctrine.

(iii) There are also countless bodhisattvas,
All of them pursuing the path.
They make joyful offerings of
Treasures and foods,
That they may inherit the true teachings
As they devote themselves to the truth.
There are those who give away their
Wives and children and even their own limbs to the needy
That they may inherit the wisdom of the Buddha.
Some leave families and countries
And, completely shaven,
Approach masters and
Seek the truth in order to reach spiritual peace.
Some reside in the forests, or in the fields, and
Drive away demons by seeking the path
And beating the drum of the Dharma.
When they are revered by gods
Humbly they accept their goodwill,
Refraining from showing delight.

(iv) There indeed were times when by the arrogant
The bodhisattvas were reviled, but even then
They pursued their ways to purity.
Having left those who seek vain pleasures,
And seeking the guidance of teachers of the path,
And preferring seclusion and meditation,
They found the way to eternal peace.
All these are illuminated by the light of the Buddha.
We ask of you, Manjusri,
Give guidance that beings may free
Themselves from doubts and ignorance.

(2) At that time, Bodhisattva Manjusri said to Maitreya and the other bodhisattvas present at the assembly, "The World-Honored One wishes to reveal to us the great Dharma, to bestow upon us the rains of the Dharma, and to teach to us the meaning of the Dharma. Immediately before the buddhas of the past promulgated the Dharma, they emitted the rays of a Buddha's wisdom. The World-Honored One, too, has presented an unusual happening in order to teach people the Dharma that is truly inconceivable to them.

"In the immeasurable past there resided the Buddha Candrasuryapradipa—Light of the Moon and the Sun—by name, who taught the true Dharma. This instruction was profound in meaning; his language was most appropriate, and he enabled everyone in his own way to find the path. Following this Buddha there appeared over twenty thousand buddhas of the same name. The last of these buddhas, before becoming a monk, was a king who had eight princes, all of whom were of noble character and ruled the land in the four directions. Then when the king attained enlightenment and his sons heard about this, they all renounced their crowns and became monks and, serving under many buddhas, established their foundations of merits.

"At that time, the last Buddha in the line, Candrasuryapradipa, taught the teachings of the Dharma just as the World-Honored One is now about to teach and, entering into the meditation of Boundless Principle, emitted light from his eyebrows that shone on all the countries exactly as it does now.

"Bodhisattvas who had gathered, two billion in all, wanted to know the meaning of this wonderful light. The Buddha, having emerged from his meditation, directed his instruction at Bodhisattva Varaprabha—Wonderful Light—and expounded the teaching of the Saddharmapundarika—The Lotus of the Wondrous Dharma. The Buddha continued the sermon for a long time, and the audience listened intently, their bodies and minds immovable. Though the discourse was almost infinitely long, it seemed indeed to last only one mealtime, and no one showed any sign of fatigue.

"The Buddha entered nirvana after having predicted that the Bodhisattva Srigarbha (Store of Virtues) would attain Buddhahood, and that the Bodhisattva Varaprabha would maintain the Saddharmapundarika and expound its teachings indefinitely.

"The eight princes of Candrasuryapradipa Buddha all attained the path by the guidance of this Buddha. The last prince to attain Buddhahood was Dipamkara Buddha (Burning Torch Buddha). A disciple of this Buddha, whose name was Yasaskama—Fame Seeker—was strongly attached to worldly gains and, although he read the sutras, he could not understand them and quickly forgot the words. Despite these things, on account of having accumulated roots of goodness, he was able to meet with many buddhas to whom he made offerings and whom he revered and praised. O Maitreya, that Bodhisattva Varaprabha at that time was none other than I, and the Bodhisattva Yasaskama at that time was actually you. Now in observing these unusual happenings, what happened then and what is happening now are one and the same. It is now time for the Buddha to reveal to all the teaching of the Saddharmapundarika, the Lotus of the Wondrous Dharma."

(3) A little later, the Buddha quietly emerged from meditation and said to Sariputra, "The wisdom of a Buddha is profound and immeasurable; the teaching is difficult to comprehend and hard to practice. The teachings of the Wondrous Dharma will never be understood by those who prefer to adhere only to the instructions of their masters or those who seek their own enlightenment and forget others. This is because the Buddha has sought guidance from and associated with countless buddhas, has performed all the practices, has endeavored to live the teachings with courage, has a name heard everywhere, has realized a depth of the Dharma heretofore unknown, and now teaches it to meet everybody's needs, which make it most difficult to comprehend.

"O Sariputra, since the attainment of enlightenment the Buddha has employed various parables, metaphors, and stories of the Buddha's previous lives to relay the teachings, has used skillful means to guide sentient beings, and was thus able to lead them away from attachments. This is because the buddhas have both the skillful means and the wisdom to lead others to the enlightenment of the Buddha. O Sariputra, since the Dharma is hard to comprehend and difficult to explain, it is indeed the buddhas alone who can completely know the true nature of all that exists. The true pertains to the aspects of the Dharma, the nature of the Dharma, the essence of the Dharma, the potential of the Dharma, the functions of the Dharma, the causes of the Dharma, the conditions of the Dharma, the result of the Dharma, the effects of the Dharma, and the essential unity of the Dharma."

The numerous disciples and believers present thought, "Upon having heard the teaching of the World-Honored One on emancipation, we were able to arrive at the shores of release. But now, what is it that the World-Honored One is trying to teach us?"

Sariputra then on behalf of those present asked the Buddha to elaborate on the Wondrous Dharma. The World-Honored One remarked, "Sariputra, you should abandon such an idea, because if the Buddha were to reveal this wonderful teaching, people would be not only surprised but doubtful as well." But Sariputra besought him again. "There are many present here who have clear wisdom and will reverently believe the Dharma if the World-Honored One expounds it. Please teach us the Wondrous Dharma." The World-Honored One once again discouraged Sariputra and said, "Sariputra, you should not have such a thought, because the Wondrous Dharma is hard to perceive. Especially those who are arrogant may never be able to accept it." Sariputra then for the third time asked earnestly that the Buddha expound the teachings. Thus finally the Buddha said, "Very well; the Buddha will now reveal this teaching." And with this the Buddha commenced the discourse on the teaching.

(4) Just at that time, a group of the Buddha's disciples and believers, five thousand in number, arose from their seats, bowed to the Buddha with reverence, and left. They left because the roots of error among them had been deeply planted; they were arrogant and thought that they had attained what they had not attained. This was why they could not bear to be in the Buddha's presence. The Buddha remained quiet and made no attempt to stop those who wished to leave; then he said to Sariputra, "My assembly here is now free of useless twigs and leaves; only the pure essence remains. O Sariputra, it is good that the arrogant have left us. The Buddha will now expound the Dharma."

The Buddha said, "O Sariputra, a doctrine such as this is seldom taught even by the buddhas. This is indeed as rare as the blossoming of the udumbara tree. Sariputra, you and others should accept and believe the words of the Buddha. The meaning of the Buddha's instructions given for specific occasions is hard to comprehend. This is because the Buddha has employed unlimited skillful means and examples in relaying the Dharma, which is indeed hard for people to understand and can be fully understood only by buddhas. Moreover, the appearance of the Buddha in this world is solely for one purpose. O Sariputra, the Buddha appears in this world to show all beings the wisdom of the Buddha and to lead them to the realization of the wisdom and insight of the Buddha.

"O Sariputra, what the Buddha achieves is always one thing. It is to enable all beings to attain the wisdom of the Buddha and to let them achieve it. The Buddha teaches for this purpose one teaching, the One Vehicle Teaching. There is no second or third teaching. O Sariputra, all the buddhas of the ten directions of the universe also teach this teaching.

"Sariputra, you should know that the Buddha appears in this world when there are the five signs of degeneracy. The duration of life decreases; living beings are degenerate; their offences and passions increase; they hold wrong views; and the great cosmic age itself nears its end. Sariputra, when there is the sign of degeneracy of the great cosmic age, degeneracy of living beings becomes heavier, and the passions of avarice, greed, and jealousy intensify and become the causes of all bad deeds. It is for this reason that the Buddha has provided skillful means by teaching the single Buddha Vehicle as the Three Vehicles. Therefore, Sariputra, if among my disciples some think they have attained enlightenment and have no intention of pursuing the highest right attainment, they harbor ever-growing arrogance in their hearts. Thus, Sariputra, the Buddha encourages all to believe and accept this teaching single-mindedly and maintain it at all times. The Buddha speaks the truth; therefore be convinced that beside the One Vehicle teaching there really is no other teaching."

(5) The Buddha continued in verse:

(i) The Buddha will now employ the skillful means
To enable you to enter into the realm of the wisdom of a Buddha.
These teachings were not presented heretofore
Because the time to do so had not come.
The disciples of the Buddha have now,
Under the guidance of countless buddhas,
Pursued profound and wondrous paths.
Their minds are pure and ready,
And now the Buddha will teach the Wonderful Dharma.
My disciples, even if it be one verse of the Dharma,
There is no cause to doubt it,
For it will enable you all to realize enlightenment.

(ii) In all the Buddha countries,
There is only the One Vehicle teaching.
There is the One Vehicle, not two or three Vehicles,
For these are skillful means.
The Buddha has appeared under the name of Sakyamuni
Merely to guide sentient beings and reveal the truth.
The One Vehicle is the truth; the other two are not.
The Buddha will not employ lesser Vehicles
In guiding sentient beings.
Supreme indeed is the highest teaching.
The Buddha, too, has endeavored along the right path
And arrived at the truth of nondiscrimination.
If the Buddha were to guide another by a lesser Vehicle,
The Buddha would fall into the ranks of the miserly,
And the Buddha is far from being miserly.
The Buddha guides all to overcome evil;

The Buddha fears none in the ten directions.
Those who seek refuge in the Buddha are never forsaken.

(iii) In utmost majesty and solemnity,
The Buddha emits light in the ten directions.
Revered and cherished by all,
The Buddha expounds the truth of ultimate reality,
Enabling all to become one with him.
This is what the Buddha aspired to do;
And this aspiration is now fulfilled,
And the Buddha leads all to the way of enlightenment.
Whosoever comes in contact with the Buddha
Will be admitted into the teachings.
The obsessed, with their distracted minds,
Will never see the truth.
There are those who strive not,
And on account of their ignorance and blindness
They enter into the forest of wrong views and adhere to ways untrue
With ever growing conceit.
Their minds are twisted and lack sincerity;
Even if they were to take endless time,
They might never hear the truth.
Difficult indeed it is to save them.

(iv) O Sariputra, the Buddha,
By employing skillful means, taught the path,
The path leading to the perfect nirvana.
Nirvana will not crumble, for
All the ways in the Dharma
Lead all beings to serene peace.
Those following the path of the Buddha
Will realize enlightenment in future births;
The Three Vehicle teachings are indeed
Skillful means of the Buddha.
But all buddhas indeed teach the teaching of the One Vehicle.

(v) All you who seek the path,
Free yourselves from delusions,
For the Buddha teaches only the teaching of the One Vehicle
And teaches no other way.
Buddhas of the past
Have employed many skillful means;
They taught only the One Vehicle,
Guiding all beings to the right path.
The followers of the Buddha
Have reached mental concentration and wisdom.
Some hear the Dharma, making offerings to it;
Some observe the precepts.
There are those who erect stupas of gold and jewels
In which the buddhas' relics are enshrined;
Some erect earthen mounds as buddhas' mausoleums,
While children, too, play in joy
As they build mounds of sand and make their offerings;

While painters paint pictures or carve images of the Buddha.
The people in pure joy play musical instruments
And sincerely praise the virtues of the Buddha,
While others, disturbed by worldly matters,
Enter the stupas and seek refuge in the Buddha.
All these devoted people, by virtue of these good conditions,
Have already achieved their ends.

(vi) Buddhas of the universe,
By employing skillful means unlimited in number,
Have led many beings to the attainment of a Buddha's wisdom,
And those who are taught the Dharma
All attain the realm of Buddhahood.
Why do all buddhas make their vows?
It is because of their wish to see
All sentient beings follow the path
To reach the shores of attainment.
All the countless buddhas of the universe,
Who teach the teaching of emancipation,
Will teach this one teaching,
The teaching of the One Buddha Vehicle.
All buddhas of the universe teach
That all things are in truth selfless.
The attainment of a buddha's wisdom
Is the interplay of conditions.
This is based on the One Vehicle teaching.
The teaching that,
At the level of the Dharma,
All that exists is eternal
Is the teaching of the masters as skillful means.
The Buddha employs the power of wisdom,
Knowing human nature and desires.
The Dharma taught through skillful means will
Enable all to rejoice in the attainment of enlightenment.

(vii) In the Buddha's eyes,
Sentient beings flounder in the six destinies.
They lack benevolence and wisdom.
They are deeply sunk in greed
Like the ox pursuing its own tail.
They are blinded by passions
And fail to seek the Buddha-Dharma,
Transmigrating from one unhappy destiny to another.
The Buddha for these people
Arouses great compassion.
At the time of realizing enlightenment, the Buddha pondered:
"If the Buddha Vehicle is emphasized,
Sentient beings will not accept it.
They may even slander the Dharma
And invite suffering for a period unknown.
But should the Buddha enter the final nirvana
Without teaching this teaching?"
Then the buddhas of the past,

Who employed skillful means, came to his mind:
"Should not this teaching of the Three Vehicles
Also be revealed to humanity?"

(viii) So with determination the Dharma was taught.
Now that the seekers of the path
Keep increasing in number,
It is the right time to teach the Dharma.
To the brilliant and to the arrogant
This teaching may not appeal;
But now that there is no impediment for
The bodhisattvas in expounding the teachings,
All skillful means will be discarded.
The ultimate Dharma itself will be relayed.
This wonderful Dharma, no matter how many ages pass,
Is difficult to encounter.
Rejoice in hearing this teaching,
For even if there be only a word of praise,
It will become one's offering to all buddhas.
Rare indeed are such people,
As rare as the udumbara flower.
Doubt not, my disciples,
For the Buddha is the king of the Dharma.

(ix) To all, the Buddha proclaims,
"Those who pursue the One Vehicle teaching
Will be the receivers of the Buddha's guidance.
Those who seek lesser Vehicles
Are not the disciples of the Buddha.
Hearken, O Sariputra, and disciples,
This Saddharmapundarika is indeed
The essence of the Buddha's teaching.
Those who seek the pleasures of the flesh
Will never become aware of the Dharma.
The countless evil ones coming hereafter,
Perplexed in mind, will not accept it, and by slander
And abuse of the Dharma they will pursue eternal suffering.
Those with pure minds and repentance,
Those who choose to seek the Dharma,
Those who are fully aware of the Buddha's wondrous skillful means,
Are now joyfully freed of all doubts.
The Buddha assures your future Buddhahood."

2. The Parable of the Burning House

(1) Having heard the Buddha's discourse, Sariputra was moved to joy; placing his palms together and looking reverently at the Buddha's august countenance, he said, "World-Honored One, now that I have heard such a sermon as this, my mind is incomparably joyous. The reason is this: formerly when I heard this Dharma, I witnessed the bodhisattvas receive a prophecy that they would one day become buddhas; however, I was not a part of that prophecy. I felt aggrieved that I had been deprived of a Buddha's wisdom and insight. World-Honored One,

I have always dwelt alone in the mountains and forests and at the feet of trees. And whether sitting or walking, I thought to myself in this manner, 'We have all realized the true nature of the Dharma equally. Why then does the World-Honored One try to save us with the teaching of an inferior Vehicle?' However, this is our fault and not that of the World-Honored One. If we had brought to fruition the seeds that led to Buddhahood and had waited for the Buddha to expound on supreme enlightenment, without fail he would have saved us with the teaching of the Great Vehicle. However, without realizing that this teaching was a skillful means that molded itself to what was fitting, when we first heard the Dharma, immediately we believed it, reflected on it, and attained enlightenment. World-Honored One, until today, all day and all night I have chastised myself; but now that I have heard the incomparable Dharma from the World-Honored One, I have cut off my doubts, and both my mind and my body are at ease. Now for the first time I know that I am truly a son of the Buddha, born of the Buddha's mouth, incarnated from the Dharma, and that I have inherited partially the Buddha-Dharma."

(i) Formerly we, as children of the Buddha,
     Together possessed the undefiled Dharma;
     However, we found it difficult to pursue
     The supreme path to future worlds.
     Now the World-Honored One, in a large assembly,
     Predicts that I shall become a Buddha.
     I hear his words and my doubts are dispelled.
     When I first heard the words of the World-Honored One,
     My mind was given over to alarm and suspicion.
     "Surely a Mara has taken
     The form of a Buddha and is confusing my mind."
     The World-Honored One brings forth
     Myriads of reasons, parables, and stories of his previous lives;
     His mind is like a calm sea.
     When I listen to him, the net of doubt is cut away.

(ii) Truly, as the World-Honored One teaches,
     Countless buddhas of the past, present, and future,
     At ease amid skillful means, all expound this Dharma.
     The World-Honored One also, like all others,
     Expounds the Dharma, resorting to skillful means.
     The World-Honored One knows the true path; no Mara has any of this.
     Having fallen into the net of doubt,
     I suspected that this was the work of Mara.
     The exquisite voice of the World-Honored One
     Gladdens the very bottom of my heart.
     It dispels my doubts and puts me at ease amid true wisdom.
     Without fail, I shall become a Buddha.
     Revered by gods and people,
     I shall turn the supreme Wheel of the Dharma and guide bodhisattvas.

(2) At that time, the World-Honored One said to Sariputra, "Sariputra, from long, long ago, I taught and guided you so that you might attain the path of the

Buddha. You also, for a long time, followed me and studied the path. Due to my skillful means, you have now been born into my Dharma. You had completely forgotten this and thought that you had attained nirvana on your own. In order to stir your memory of your original vow and of the path that you practiced, I expounded this exquisite Dharma. Sariputra, you, in a later age, after having passed through an infinite number of kalpas, after having made offerings to an infinite number of buddhas, after having upheld the Dharma, and after being endowed with the path of the bodhisattva, will become a Buddha called Padmaprabha—Lotus Light. Your Buddha land will be immaculate and peaceful; and its earth will be level. Its people will prosper. And for a long time, bodhisattvas who have implanted the seeds of merit will gather there like clouds and will practice the path."

Those who gathered there heard the Buddha's prophecy that foretold the day that Sariputra would become a Buddha, and with joyful hearts they recited this verse.

> Long ago, in Varanasi, you turned
> The Wheel of the Dharma of the Four Noble Truths.
> Now, for our sakes, you expound the supremely great Dharma.
> This Dharma is truly profound and exquisite,
> And few are those who believe in it.
> We have heard the teaching often
> And yet we have not heard such an exquisite Dharma.
> Like Sariputra, who is possessed of great wisdom,
> We shall one day attain the path of the Buddha.
> Oh, the path of the Buddha is difficult to grasp.
> Only the Buddha, by resorting to
> Skillful means, expounds this Dharma.
> All the meritorious deeds that we possess
> And the merits that we have gained by meeting
> The Buddha in this and later ages,
> We give over to the path of the Buddha.

(3) Then Sariputra said to the World-Honored One, "World-Honored One, we now no longer have any doubts. However, these twelve hundred disciples, hearing the World-Honored One say, 'Our Dharma frees one from birth, old age, illness, and death and leads one to nirvana,' believed that they were free from wrong views about the self, existence, and nonexistence and declared that they had attained nirvana. Now, in the presence of the World-Honored One, having heard a teaching that they had not heard before, they have all fallen into doubt. We beseech you, World-Honored One, for the sake of men and women who are monks or nuns or lay people, to explain the causes and conditions and to free them from doubt."

The World-Honored One said to Sariputra, "Did I not say before that when myriad buddhas expound the Dharma by resorting to diverse stories of the Buddha's previous lives, and by resorting to reasoning, parables, and skillful means, it was all for the sake of a Buddha's enlightenment? They are all for the purpose of teaching and guiding bodhisattvas.

"Sariputra, I shall now clarify the Dharma's meaning by resorting to a parable. In a certain town, there was a wealthy man, well advanced in years.
He possessed endless riches and numerous fields and servants. His house was
large, and many people lived there; however, there was only one doorway.
The hall and mansion were decaying and rotting. Sections of the wall had
crumbled and fallen to the ground; the wall itself leaned over and looked precarious. One day suddenly a fire broke out all around the house. The wealthy
man, in great alarm, left through the doorway and thought to himself, 'I was
able safely to leave the house through this doorway; however, the children
are lost in play in this burning house. They are unaware of the dangers of
the flames that burn and press toward them. They have no mind at all to be
frightened or to escape. I am strong, and therefore I can take them out of the
house. However, there is only one doorway and it is narrow. On top of that,
the children are still young and are lost in their playing. They may fall down
and be burnt by the fire. First of all, I must warn them of the fearful thing that
presses in toward them.'

"The wealthy man, therefore, called to his children, shouting, 'Come out
quickly!' However, the children who were playing, oblivious to everything, did
not listen to their father's words. Romping around playfully, they merely glanced
over at their father and had no mind at all to leave. He then thought that by
employing skillful means, he might cause them to escape this disastrous fire. He
said to them, 'There are some rare playthings outside; if you do not take them
now, you will regret it. Outside the doorway, right now, there are goat-drawn
carriages, deer-drawn carriages, and ox-drawn carriages. All of you children,
come out from this burning house! I shall give all of these to you according to
your hearts' desires, so that you may play with these things.'

"Hearing that there were rare playthings, they pranced around with delight
since those things were exactly what they wanted. Shoving each other aside,
they dashed out in a mad scramble and left the burning house. The wealthy
father, seeing his children safely outside, was relieved and joyful. The children
then appealed to their father, 'Please give us the goat-drawn carriages, deer-
drawn carriages, and ox-drawn carriages that you promised us!'

"Sariputra, at that time, the wealthy man gave to each child one large
carriage. Each carriage was high, wide, and decorated with many kinds of
jewels. A railing went around the carriage, and on all four sides little bells hung
down. On top was spread out a curtain that covered the carriage. Moreover,
it was adorned with jewels; carpets were laid out and vermillion-colored
pillows were placed about. Each was drawn by a large white ox, which was
attended to by numerous servants. The wealthy man thought to himself,
'I possess an abundance of wealth. I must not give them inferior carriages.
These are all my children. I love them all, without any bias. I own countless great
carriages such as this, adorned with the seven jewels; I shall give them equally
to the children.'

(4) "At this time, each of the children climbed onto one of the large carriages
and experienced a joy that exceeded their fondest hopes and would not ever be

repeated again. Sariputra, when this wealthy man promised these children three kinds of jewelled carriages, did he deceive them?"

Sariputra said, "No, World-Honored One, he did not deceive them. The wealthy man had but made up his mind to bring the children out of the burning house by the use of skillful means."

The World-Honored One said, "Well said, Sariputra, it is exactly as you say. The Buddha is the father to all the world's people. Aeons past, he exhausted the darkness of myriad fears, sufferings, anguishes, and ignorances; endowed with boundless wisdom and power, he benefits all with his great compassion. He was born into these decaying and rotting worlds of suffering out of his wish to save the people from the suffering of birth, old age, illness, and death and from the fires of the three poisons; he was born here out of his wish to have all people attain the enlightenment of the buddhas. People of this world are marked by grief and suffering. They despair in their poverty; they wail when parting with loved ones, or they are, at times, made to suffer because of their own hatred. However, immersing themselves in their suffering, they caper about in glee. Incapable of perceiving the suffering of their world, they are unable to feel revulsion toward it or free themselves from it. Therefore, like the wealthy man who saved the children by the use of skillful means, the Buddha spoke to the people and said, 'All of you, you must not dwell in the burning house of the three worlds. If you are lustfully attached to this house, you will surely be burned. Quickly leave and obtain the Three Vehicles.'

"Sariputra, there are people who follow the Buddha, listen to his teaching, place their trust in it, exert themselves with diligence, and seek their nirvana. These are called those who ride the Sravaka Vehicle; that is, they are the people who follow the path of hearing the Dharma to become enlightened. They are like the wealthy man's children who left the burning house in search of goat-drawn carriage. Again, there are people who follow the Buddha, listen to his teaching, place their trust in it, exert themselves with diligence, seek wisdom for themselves, desire the quiescence of solitude, and perceive the causes and conditions of all phenomena. These are called those who ride the Pratyekabuddha Vehicle; that is, they are the people who follow the teaching according to which one attains enlightenment for oneself alone. They are like the wealthy man's children who left the burning house in search of deer-drawn carriages. Yet again, there are those who follow the Buddha, hear the teaching, place their trust in it, exert themselves with diligence, seek the omniscience and the power of the buddhas, and feel compassion for boundless people. These are called ones who ride on the supreme Vehicle of the Bodhisattva, that is, they are those who follow the teaching of the Bodhisattva. They are like the wealthy man's children who left the burning house in search of ox-drawn carriages.

(5) "Sariputra, when that wealthy man saw the children who had emerged from the burning house, he thought of the boundless wealth that was in his possession and presented them equally with large carriages. Like him, the Buddha, seeing innumerable people freeing themselves from the suffering of the three worlds and attaining the bliss of nirvana, thought of the treasury that he had

in his possession, which was filled with the Dharma of boundless wisdom and power. He then bestowed on them the meditation and emancipation of the buddhas. He did so with this thought: 'All these people are my children; I shall equally bestow on each a superb vehicle. I must not allow them to fall into a debased form of extinction that is concerned with one's own welfare only; I shall guide them to the expansive nirvana of the buddhas. They are all one and the same; this nirvana, praised by the arhats, gives birth to a bliss that is pure, wondrous, and foremost.'

"Sariputra, that wealthy man at first enticed his children with words about the Three Vehicles, but later he gave them only superb carriages; but he was not guilty of falsehood. In the same manner, the Buddha expounds the Three Vehicles and guides the people, and later he saves them with a single superb Vehicle. He is, however, not at all guilty of falsehood. The Buddha possesses a treasury filled with the Dharma of boundless wisdom and power, and he first bestows a single superb Vehicle on the people. However, the people do not yet have the capacity of understanding it. Therefore the Buddha, using skillful means, divides the Buddha's One Vehicle into the Three Vehicles and thus expounds the Dharma in three ways."

(6) (i) Sariputra, I am like this, too. I am the most venerated among arhats.
I am the father of the world; all people are my children.
They are strongly attached to worldly pleasures.
They are devoid of all traces of wisdom.
The three worlds are unsafe; they are like a house on fire.
Their world is filled with suffering. It is fearful.
The fires of old age, illness, and death burn furiously without end.
The Buddha leaves the burning house of the three worlds
And dwells in a tranquil forest.
Now these three worlds are my possessions
And all the people who dwell there are my children.
I alone am able to save them from the unending miseries of these worlds.

(ii) Although I teach and exhort them,
They fail to believe me,
For they have been stained through and through with greed.
Therefore I expound the Vehicles to them;
I reveal the sufferings of these worlds
To all people and set forth the path
That leads out of these worlds.
Now the minds of the people should quiet down;
With this example I shall expound the One Buddha Vehicle.
If they believe in my words,
They shall all attain the path of the buddhas.
This Vehicle is wondrous; buddhas rejoice over it.
All people worship it.
It is endowed with boundless power, wisdom, and meditation.
Bestowing this Vehicle on them,
I enable the children to enjoy themselves in play for aeons.
All those who follow the path board this jewelled Vehicle

And will immediately arrive at the place of practicing the path.
Although one may search in all the ten directions,
Not a single vehicle can be found aside from this Vehicle.

(iii) I previously spoke of nirvana;
However, that was merely the cessation of birth and death.
Because this is true extinction, what one must achieve now is
None other than the wisdom of the Buddha.
If there are those who would arouse the great mind,
They should, without fail, listen single-mindedly to the Dharma.
Though the buddhas make use of skillful means,
Those who receive the teaching are all bodhisattvas.
To those of meager wisdom who drown in lustful desires,
The Buddha expounds the nature of suffering.
To those who do not know the cause of suffering,
The Buddha expounds that desire is the very cause.
Should one extinguish greed,
There is nowhere on which suffering can come to rest;
And then suffering is destroyed.
In order to attain this state, one practices the path.

(iv) To free oneself from the fetters of suffering is called deliverance.
However, such a person merely frees himself from falsehood.
He has yet to attain complete deliverance.
Therefore, the Buddha does not set this forth as being the true nirvana.
I am truly the king of the Dharma.
With regard to the Dharma, I am free.
In order to put people at ease, I appeared in this world.
Sariputra, this Dharma was expounded for the benefit of this world.
You should neither expound it nor propagate it without good reason.
If there is someone who hears the Dharma and rejoices,
That person dwells in the stage from which there is no retrogression.
Those who believe in this Dharma have already seen a buddha in the
distant past.

(v) Those who believe what you expound see me;
They are those who see myriad bodhisattvas.
One enters this teaching by virtue of faith.
One believes in the Buddha's words and follows this teaching.
It has nothing to do with one's own wisdom.
Therefore, do not expound this teaching to those who are ignorant.
Teach this to those who are lucid in their wisdom,
Who have listened widely to the Buddha's teachings,
Who diligently practice the mind of compassion,
And who begrudge neither their bodies nor their lives.

3. The Mind of Faith

(1) At that time, Subhuti, Maha-Kasyapa and Maudgalyayana, hearing that the
Buddha had spoken of a prophecy foretelling the attainment of Buddhahood by
Sariputra, were struck with joy and arose from their seats. Bowing to the World-
Honored One, they said, "For a long time, we stood at the head of the Sangha;
we aged ones believed that we had already attained nirvana and did not actively

attempt to seek the enlightenment of the buddhas. We found no joy at all in establishing a Buddha's country or in perfecting the minds of the people. However, now having heard this peerless teaching, we have attained a great benefit. It is as if we had gained boundless treasures, spontaneously and without even seeking them out. World-Honored One, by resorting to a parable, we shall try to explain what we mean.

(2) "In his childhood, a man abandoned his father and went to another country. Reaching the age of fifty, he suffered more and more from poverty. He roamed through the four quarters in search of food and clothing, and by chance he continued his journey in the direction of the country where he was born. This man's father, who was in search of his son, came to dwell at a certain town. The father's house was truly wealthy and prosperous; boundless treasures such as gold, silver, lapis lazuli, coral, and so forth filled his numerous treasuries. He also had a large number of servants and owned livestock such as elephants, horses, cows, and goats. He conducted trade with other countries, and a host of merchants and buyers always assembled at his house. The impoverished son wandered here and there, and finally he came to the town in which his father dwelt. During the fifty years that they had been separated, there was no time that the father had failed to remember his son. Although he did not openly mention it to others, in his heart there was not a moment when he was free from the pain of separation. He thought to himself, 'I am a man of great wealth; however, I have grown old and have no son to succeed to my fortune. Should my life come to an end, all of this wealth will be scattered and lost. If I had a son to whom I could leave my wealth, I would have no distress. How delightful it would be!' With such thoughts, he always remembered his lost son.

"On the other hand, his son went around the town, being hired here and there for menial tasks. During that time, one day, he accidentally arrived at his father's house without knowing that the owner was his father. For a while, he stood toward the side of the gate. When he peered inside, his father, though the son did not recognize him, was seated on a lion throne. He was draped in priceless necklaces; on his left and right sides, he was surrounded by servants holding white whisks in their hands. The ceiling was covered with a jewelled canopy; the walls were adorned with floral streamers.

"The impoverished son who caught sight of this, gazing upon the sight of this overwhelmingly majestic man, suddenly grew fearful and regretful that he had come to this place. He thought to himself, 'This man is either a king or someone who is the equal of a king. This is not a place for me to seek work. It would be much easier to find food and clothing in an impoverished village. If I linger on at a place like this, I do not know what kind of grief I shall come to.' And he ran off. The venerable father saw this in the distance and realizing that it was his son, his heart leapt with joy. He thought to himself, 'My beloved son, whom I was unable to forget even for a moment, has returned; my prayers have been answered. Now life is worth living even for this aged man.' At once he dispatched an attendant to bring his son back. However, his son was frightened and fearful. He said, 'I did not do anything wrong against you; why do you pounce on me?' The messenger gripped the son in a tight grasp and took him off back to the father's house. The poor son thought, 'To be blameless and to be seized like this must mean that I am surely going to be killed.' Overwhelmed with fear, he fainted and fell to the ground. The father witnessed this in the distance and said to his servant, 'You must not restrain him with such force. Sprinkle cold water on his face and revive him. Beyond that, you must not say anything to him.' The father perceived that this son's aspirations were lowly and that his son, noticing the father's nobility, was filled with fear. The father purposely employed skillful means and did not mention that he was his son. Set free by the servant, the son was so relieved that he thought it must be a dream. The son picked himself off the ground, and in order to seek food and clothing he headed toward an impoverished village.

(3) "Later, the wealthy father, in order to entice his son, deliberately dispatched two shabbily dressed servants to speak to his son. He had them say, 'We have a job for you. The job is to sweep away dust. They will pay you twice what you are making now. Why not take this job together with us?' Hearing this, the son was overjoyed; he took the job and swept away dust with them for the wages agreed upon. The father felt pity for his son and gazed on him from a distance. His son was emaciated and exhausted; covered with dust, he was doing his work. The wealthy man purposely put on shabby clothing and, covering himself with dust, took hold of a dustpan in his right hand and spoke to the hired hands from a distance. 'All of you, work hard! Do not be lazy!' By such skillful means, the father drew closer to the son. He said to him, 'You should always work here; you should not go elsewhere. I shall increase your wages. If you want bowls, rice, salt and so forth, I shall give them to you. There are aged servants that you can make use of. Put your mind at ease and think of me as your father. There is no need to feel uneasy. Truly, I have many years behind me while you are in your prime. In your work, it seems that there is no sham as in the cases of other workers. From now on, I am going to think of you as my natural son.'

(4) "Since then, the wealthy man called him, 'my son,' but the son, although happy about this turn of events, was still imbued with the thought that he was only a poor, lowly stranger in town; and for twenty more years he continued to sweep the dust. He was now allowed to go in and out of the rich man's house at will, but his own dwelling was still but a little shack. The wealthy father became ill in the meantime and, realizing that he was not going to live much longer, said to his son, 'My treasuries are full of gold, silver, and other valuables. You should know how much there is and what to choose for yourself. Do understand what I have in my mind. This I ask you to do because you and I are not two unrelated persons. Be mindful and do not lose them.' When told of this, the son became aware of the great storage of treasures in the warehouses but still had no idea that they were his. He remained in the dilapidated shack and could not discard the thought that he was a lowly poor man.

"After a while, the wealthy father noticed that his son was becoming more secure about himself. Then he called together his relatives, the king, and the state ministers and said, 'To all of you who are gathered here, I wish to announce that this man is my son. He left me when he was still a youth, and for fifty years he suffered a destitute and lowly life. I know his name; I am his father. I looked for him in the town where I used to reside, but it was here in this town that I was able to find him. All the treasures that I possess are now his. He is in charge of them.'

(5) "World-Honored One, the son was overjoyed upon hearing these words and said, 'All these treasuries filled with treasures became mine without my even asking for them.'

"World-Honored One, the wealthy father in this story is you, the World-Honored One. And the poor son is each of us. We are suffering lives in samsara and, because of our stupidity, we have been misled by, and were holding fast to, an inferior teaching. World-Honored One, owing to your skillful means, we are at long last discerning the right thought and are discarding the dust of the useless arguments of the inverted views. Being gratified with our small progress toward quietude, we were not exerting ourselves to seek the superior path. The World-Honored One, knowing our weaker resolution and using his skillful means, let us realize that we have been seeking an inferior Dharma and set our minds toward the great wisdom. This is similar to the way the wealthy man, knowing the inferior desire of his son, prepared his mind first and only then gave him all the treasures in store. Our gaining great wisdom is similar to the destitute son inheriting a great store of treasures. World-Honored One, we have observed the precepts for a long time and now have received the supreme Dharma and become true disciples of yours. We have now become worthy of receiving offerings of alms. This is because the World-Honored One has, with a compassion rarely found in this world, taught and led us to the greater path. Even in an infinite length of time, could anyone hope to be able to return such a great gift?"

(6) At that time, the World-Honored One addressed Maha-Kasyapa and the other disciples, "Very good, Kasyapa! you have skillfully expounded the true merits of the Tathagata. But even if you expound them for innumerable kalpas, you would not be able to describe them all. Kasyapa, the Tathagata is the king of all the dharmas. The words that he pronounces are devoid of falsehood. With his wisdom and his skillful means, he expounds and teaches all the dharmas; and all of these dharmas lead to the attainment of the stage of omniscience. The Buddha unobstructedly perceives the underlying mental dispositions of all sentient beings. He masters all the dharmas and manifests wisdom for the sake of all sentient beings.

"Kasyapa, suppose a heavy rain pours down on the grasses, shrubs, medicinal herbs, and trees that grow in the mountains, streams, and valleys. The roots, stems, branches, and leaves of these grasses and trees grow in keeping with the natures of their respective species. Each of them bears a different kind of flower or fruit. They grow from the same earth, and the same rain waters them; and yet the grasses and the trees retain their distinctive traits. Kasyapa, the Tathagata is like this; his appearance in this world is like the great cloud that spreads over the whole world. His great voice is heard throughout the world. That voice proclaims, 'I am the Tathagata that shall save the world. I shall enlighten those who have not attained enlightenment; I shall put at ease those who are not yet at ease; I shall enable those who have not yet attained nirvana to attain nirvana. I am enlightened to the path of omniscience; I am one who expounds and opens up the path. All of you should come here in order to listen to the Dharma.'

At this time, countless people come to the Buddha to listen to the teaching; the Tathagata perceives the differences in their capacities, in their astuteness or dullness. He expounds the Dharma in accordance with the abilities of each person; he enables them all to gain joy and benefits. While in this world, they live at ease; in the future, they will be born into good destinies. By virtue of the path, they attain peace of mind and are able to hear the Dharma, and they free themselves from obstructions. Dwelling in the midst of myriad dharmas, they entrust themselves to their abilities and gradually enter the path. They are like the grasses and the trees that are watered by the rain and grow in keeping with the natures of their respective species. The Dharma expounded by the Tathagata possesses one mark and one taste, that is to say, the mark of deliverance, of freedom from passion, of extinction, which ultimately leads to a single taste of omniscience. Even if a person hears the Tathagata's Dharma and practices it, he will not be able to perceive the merits that he will have acquired. He is like the grasses, the trees, and the medicinal herbs, which are ignorant of the different gradations that exist in their natures. Only the Tathagata is able to perceive the characters, dispositions, and abilities of sentient beings. He is fully aware of what dharmas they should contemplate and practice, and what dharmas they will eventually attain. The Tathagata is truly of one mark and one taste; he is enlightened to the Dharma that leads sentient beings to the eternal tranquillity that leads to emptiness. However, carefully considering the people's understanding, the Buddha refrains from expounding omniscience itself, which might discourage, perplex, or frighten people by its profundity. Kasyapa, all of you have heard the Tathagata's Dharma that has been set forth in keeping with that which is appropriate; you have believed in and accepted it well; this is an extremely rare thing."

> The Dharma expounded by the Tathagata
> Waters the flowers with the rain of one taste,
> And it freely causes them, each in its own way, to bear fruit.
> Making use of various explanations and illustrations,
> I open up the path; these are my skillful means.
> Now, to you all, I make known the truth.
> There is no Sravaka who attains nirvana.
> The path that you have been practicing is the path of a bodhisattva.
> If you cultivate the path step by step,
> You will all attain Buddhahood.

(7) The World-Honored One addressed his disciples, "In the immeasurably distant past, a Buddha called Mahabhijnajnanabhibhu (Victorious through Great Penetrating Knowledge) Tathagata appeared in this world. For the sake of an infinitely great number of sentient beings, he expounded the Dharma and enabled them all to attain deliverance. However, prior to his renunciation of

the household life, he had had sixteen sons, all of whom had eventually become disciples of the Buddha.

"These sixteen princes all attained the enlightenment of the buddhas and taught and guided an immeasurably large number of sentient beings. I, too, as one of these sixteen princes, became a Buddha in this world and showed the way to an incalculably great number of sentient beings. All disciples, beginning with you and those disciples of later generations, received teaching at that time. Because one seeks the path from the distant past, one is able finally to enter the path of the buddhas. The reason that it takes so long is that the wisdom of the Buddha is difficult both to believe in and to attain. After I have crossed over to nirvana, there will be those who, having failed to hear the Dharma of the One Vehicle, will end their lives in this world in the belief that what they will have attained on their own is nirvana. But because of what they heard from me in their previous lives, they will once again seek the wisdom of the buddhas. Entrance into nirvana is gained only through the Buddha Vehicle and not through the other Vehicles. Disciples, the Buddha sees deep into the nature of sentient beings. Knowing that sentient beings seek inferior dharmas and are deeply attached to the five desires, he brought forth the teaching of nirvana.

"Suppose that five hundred yojanas away in the distance there is a treasure. The road that leads there is precarious and fraught with all sorts of dangers. Yet there is one guide who knows its condition and guides countless people over this precarious road. In the middle of their journey, the people moan, 'We are exhausted and are unable to press on. Our destination is still a long way off. Let us turn back.' The guide, resorting to skillful means, magically creates a large city a few yojanas ahead. He says, 'All of you, there is no need to turn back in fear. You ought to go on to that city and rest as you please. Then you will feel more at ease. If you press on and reach the place with the treasure, you will be able to make that treasure your own and return home.' In this way the guide gives hope to their weary minds. They enter the city and rest for a time. Then the guide shows them that the treasure is near. He says, 'All of you, the cache of treasures is now close by. When I made the city here, it was to put you at ease. This city is not real. I made it up as skillful means.'

"Disciples, the Buddha is exactly like this guide. He becomes your guide and enables you to pass over the long, sorrowful road of birth and death. The Buddha perceived that the minds of the people were faint and inferior, and that if he expounded the Great Vehicle that leads to Buddhahood, people would not be able readily to listen to the Buddha, nor would they draw closer to the Buddha. For this reason, the Buddha expounded the teachings of Sravakas and Pratyekabuddhas. As soon as these disciples entered into these two states, the Buddha taught, 'All of you have not yet accomplished what you must accomplish. You dwell in a state that is close to the wisdom of the Buddha. But you must contemplate further; what you have attained is not nirvana. What you have attained are the Three Vehicles, which, as skillful means, are distinguished by the Buddha from the One Vehicle of the Buddha.' "

(8) The World-Honored One addressed Purna and the host of disciples who had assembled there and foretold the day that they would become buddhas. The disciples' hearts were joyous, and, arising from their seats, they bowed down to the Buddha and said, "We thought that we had already attained nirvana; for the first time, we discover that this was utter foolishness. Despite our ability to attain the wisdom of the Buddha, we were satisfied with our attainment of paltry wisdom. World-Honored One, we were like a man who goes to the house of a friend. Drunk with liquor, he lies down. His friend is about to leave the house on official duty; but before he leaves, he sews a priceless gem within the folds of the drunken man's garment. Not knowing this, the man awakens from his drunken stupor and travels to another country. He works and struggles for his food and clothing; if he earns even a paltry amount, he is satisfied. Later when he mentions his travels to his friend upon meeting him again, the friend says, 'Why are you struggling so for food and clothing? Hoping to make you secure, I sewed a priceless gem in the folds of your garment. Now, unaware that this gem is here, you are struggling to eke out a livelihood. How foolish indeed! You ought to exchange that gem for gold, and then you will be able to enjoy yourself to your heart's content.'

"We were just like this ignorant man. Aeons ago when the World-Honored One was a bodhisattva, the World-Honored One taught and guided us and enabled us to arouse the aspiration for omniscience. Then, having forgotten this, we remained satisfied with having attained a shallow enlightenment. We were like the man in the parable who worked for his livelihood and remained satisfied with what little he had earned. However, this did not mean that we had truly abandoned our aspiration for omniscience. Now the World-Honored One awakens us, saying, 'Disciples, what you have attained is not ultimate enlightenment. For aeons, I had you cultivate the roots of merit. However, I was simply showing you an aspect of nirvana through the use of skillful means, and you mistook this for true enlightenment.' World-Honored One, at long last, we now realize that we are bodhisattvas who seek the path of the Buddha. At this time, you have spoken of a prophecy regarding the day that we shall attain the enlightenment of the Buddha, and we are overcome with joy."

(9) Under the pretext of speaking to the Bodhisattva Bhaisajyaraja (Medicine King), the World-Honored One addressed the eighty thousand bodhisattvas, "Bhaisajyaraja, after I enter the final nirvana, if a person repeats even one phrase of the Saddharmapundarika for the sake of just one person, that person is a bearer of the Buddha's message; he is dispatched by the Buddha and performs the work of the Buddha. Should he expound the teaching in the midst of the great masses of sentient beings, he is more so a messenger of the Buddha. Bhaisajyaraja, if an evil person with a vicious mind maligns the Buddha for one long kalpa, that offence is not grave. However, if a person maligns those who expound this teaching, this offence is grave. Those who expound this teaching are adorned with the Buddha adornments and will carry the Tathagata on their shoulders.

"Bhaisajyaraja, I have expounded innumerable teachings; however, this teaching is the most difficult to believe and to awaken to. This is the treasury of the secret essence of the Buddha-Dharma. You must not randomly pass it on to people. Heretofore it has been safeguarded by the buddhas and has never been openly expounded. Even when the Buddha is still present in this world, this teaching has countless enemies; after the Tathagata enters into the final nirvana, there will be an even larger number of enemies. Therefore after the Tathagata has entered into the final nirvana, those who uphold this teaching and expound it for the sake of sentient beings will be enrobed in the Buddha's garments, and a host of buddhas will bless them. They will be endowed with the powers of great faith, of aspiration, and of myriad roots of merit and will dwell together with the Buddha. Moreover, those who hear this teaching are ones who tread the path of the bodhisattvas. Those who hear this teaching, believe in it, and uphold it will draw closer to supreme enlightenment. A man who is parched seeks water on a high plain. He digs down and sees dry earth. Knowing that water is still far down, he digs without cease until he sees moist earth. Soon he begins to see mud, and he knows that water must not be far off. Truly this teaching opens up the gates of skillful means and reveals the mark of truth and reality. It is so profound and distant that it is difficult to reach it. The Buddha therefore now teaches and guides the bodhisattvas, perfects their minds, and reveals this teaching to them. Bhaisajyaraja, should a bodhisattva upon hearing this teaching feel alarmed or fearful, he is a novice bodhisattva who has entered the path for the first time. Should there be a disciple who has heard the Buddha's voice who upon hearing this teaching becomes alarmed, doubtful, or fearful, he is one who is filled with overweening pride.

"Bhaisajyaraja, after the Tathagata enters the final nirvana, should a man contemplate expounding this teaching for the sake of sentient beings, he ought to don the robes of a buddha, sit on the seat of a buddha, enter the room of a buddha, and then extensively expound the teaching. The Buddha's robes symbolize gentleness and forbearance. The Buddha's seat symbolizes the realization that all existence is emptiness. The Buddha's room denotes great compassion toward all sentient beings. Dwelling restfully in this teaching, and with a mind of diligence, you would do well to expound this teaching for the sake of sentient beings."

(10) At that time, a seven-jewelled stupa came welling up from the earth and came to a stop in midair. Its height was five hundred yojanas; its length and width were two hundred fifty yojanas. It was adorned with five thousand banisters, ten thousand rooms, innumerable streamers, innumerable strings of jewels, and a trillion jewelled bells. From the four quarters, the fragrance of sandalwood wafted everywhere and permeated to the end of the world. Moreover, the canopy adorned with seven jewels soared high in space, and the gods rained down flowers. An infinite number of people brought offerings of flowers, incense, necklaces, and music to the stupa and worshipfully sang its praises.

Then from inside the stupa, a large voice boomed forth, saying, "Excellent indeed! Sakyamuni, the World-Honored One, has taught the teaching of wisdom that is attainable by every sentient being. It is the teaching of the bodhisattva. He has expounded the teaching of the Saddharmapundarika that has been safeguarded by all the buddhas. That which is expounded by the World-Honored One is the true reality."

Those who had assembled there witnessed this auspicious sign and were struck with awe. They stood up from their seats and, placing their palms together, they praised the World-Honored One and then sat down quietly to one side. The Bodhisattva Mahapratibhana, for the sake of sentient beings, asked the World-Honored One about the causes and conditions that produced this auspicious sign. The World-Honored One said, "Inside of this stupa the remains of a buddha are preserved. The voice that you heard was emitted by that Buddha. In the eastern quarter, on the other side of countless lands, there exists a land called Ratnavisuddha (Purified by Jewels). Dwelling there was a buddha named Prabhutaratna (Abundant Jewels). When this Buddha undertook the path of a bodhisattva, he made a great vow, saying, 'After my final nirvana a huge stupa that contains the whole of my remains will be built. And wherever the teaching of the Saddharmapundarika is expounded, in whatever land it may be, this stupa will well up and serve as a light.' Mahapratibhana, this stupa welled up from the earth for this reason."

Mahapratibhana said, "I beseech you, please manifest to us, with the power of World-Honored One, the body of this Buddha." The World-Honored One said, "This Buddha has vowed that should anyone wish him to reveal his body to sentient beings, they must gather together in one place all the manifested bodies of the Buddha who expounds the Wonderful Dharma; then he will manifest his body. Therefore, I shall bring together all my manifested bodies that I left behind in past worlds in the lands of the ten directions."

At that time, the World-Honored One emitted light from the curl of white hair in the middle of his forehead. In the eastern quarter, in an infinite number of wondrous lands, a scene in which an infinity of buddhas expounded the Dharma to an infinity of bodhisattvas manifested itself. The same occurred in lands to the south, the west, the north, the four intermediate directions, and the upper and lower regions wherever this light penetrated. These buddhas of the ten directions addressed each of the bodhisattvas, "Good child, we shall now go to the place of Sakyamuni Buddha who dwells in Saha, the world in which one has to bear suffering, and bow down to the stupa of the Buddha Prabhutaratna." At that time, this Saha world suddenly changed into something pure. The earth became as bright as lapis lazuli. Trees glittered with jewels. Mountains, rivers, great oceans, forests, cities, and villages all withdrew from view. Flowers blanketed the earth; every place was redolent with fragrances. All the buddhas, accompanied by their bodhisattvas, infinite in number, assembled there. This was repeated twice, and soon all the manifested bodies of the Buddha had assembled there and had seated themselves on the Lion Thrones. Thereupon the World-Honored One Sakyamuni arose from his seat and ascended into space. Sentient beings placed their palms together and gazed intently upward at the Buddha. With his right finger, the Buddha opened the doors to the stupa;

the loud sound was like that of a bar being shoved to the side in order to open up the gates of a walled city. Those who had gathered there worshipped the remains of Prabhutaratna Buddha, and they heard a voice say, "Excellent indeed! The World-Honored One Sakyamuni opens the teaching of the Saddharmapundarika. I came here in order to listen to that teaching."

Thereupon Prabhutaratna Buddha gave up half of his seat to the World-Honored One; the World-Honored One, with his divine powers, pulled all sentient beings up into space. The World-Honored One then addressed those in the assembly, "Among those assembled here in this land, who will expound the teaching of the Saddharmapundarika? Now is truly the time to expound this Dharma. Before long, I shall enter nirvana. I wish to entrust this Dharma to you to retain for aeons in this world."

4. The Attainment of Buddhahood by the Daughter of the Naga King

(1) The World-Honored One again addressed the bodhisattvas and the disciples, both monks and lay. He said, "In the past, through innumerable kalpas, I sought the Saddharmapundarika with unflagging diligence. Throughout many kalpas in which I was always born as a king, I took a vow, sought supreme enlightenment, and fulfilled the Six Perfections. In order to accomplish this, I gave away lands, treasures, my family, and my body, without begrudging them at all. Finally, for the sake of the Dharma, I relinquished my title and entrusted the government to my heir. Beating a drum, I addressed the four quarters, 'Is there someone, who, for my sake, will expound the Great Vehicle teaching called the Saddharmapundarika?' At that time, a sage appeared and said, 'I have the Great Vehicle teaching called the Saddharmapundarika; if you will agree to be my servant, I shall expound that Dharma to you.' Hearing this I was filled with joy, and from that moment I waited upon the sage as his servant. I harvested fruit, drew water, gathered firewood, prepared food, and at times even used my own body as a bed for the sage. I did so with unflagging diligence. In this way, with unswerving diligence, I served the sage for the sake of the Dharma for a span of ten thousand years. Disciples, the king at that time was none other than myself, and the sage was none other than the man who is now known as Devadatta. Truly, I attained enlightenment through my good friend, Devadatta; and because of him I was able to save all people everywhere. Therefore, I now say to you that Devadatta, after passing through innumerable kalpas, will become a Buddha called Devaraja."

(2) At that time, the Bodhisattva Prajnakuta, who was accompanying Prabhutaratna Buddha, said to the latter, "Allow me to return to my native land." The World-Honored One said to the Bodhisattva Prajnakuta, "O son of a virtuous family, wait for a while. You should return to your native land only after you first meet with Manjusri and discuss the Dharma with him."

At that time, Manjusri sat atop a lotus with one thousand leaves; he was accompanied by a large number of bodhisattvas. Welling up spontaneously from the palace of the Naga king Sagara at the bottom of the ocean, he ascended into space. Going to the Vulture Peak, he descended from the lotus. After bowing down to the World-Honored One, he went to the place of the Bodhisattva Prajnakuta, and after exchanging salutations with him he sat down.

The Bodhisattva Prajnakuta asked, "At the Naga palace, how many people did you teach and guide?" Manjusri replied, "A countless number of people; in a moment, I shall offer you proof of my accomplishments." Before he had finished speaking, an infinite number of bodhisattvas, each seated on a jewelled lotus, welled up from the ocean floor. They went to the Vulture Peak, and in midair they expounded the teaching of the Great Vehicle. The Bodhisattva Prajnakuta sang Manjusri's praise with this verse:

> His vast wisdom is filled with vigor.
> He saves an infinite number of sentient beings.
> He sets forth the meaning of real existence.
> He opens up the teaching of the One Vehicle
> And guides all sentient beings everywhere.
> He enables them to attain enlightenment instantaneously.

Manjusri said, "In the ocean I constantly expounded the teaching of the Saddharmapundarika." The Bodhisattva Prajnakuta said, "This teaching is wondrous and profound; it is a jewel among all teachings. Will there be one who exerts himself with diligence, practices this teaching, and instantaneously attains Buddhahood?"

Manjusri said, "The eight-year-old daughter of the Naga king Sagara possesses subtle wisdom, and in an instant she has produced the thought of enlightenment. She has gained entrance into the stage of non-regression. Endowed with innumerable merits, she feels compassion for all sentient beings as if they were her children. She is able to attain supreme enlightenment." The Bodhisattva Prajnakuta said, "When I contemplate the career of the World-Honored One Sakyamuni, I see that over an infinite number of kalpas he has practiced difficult disciplines, accumulating merits and virtues. He sought enlightenment without resting even for a moment. For the sake of sentient beings, in his past lives he cast away his body and his life. There was no place in this world, not even of the size of a mustard seed, where he did not do so. After all this, he was finally able to attain enlightenment. It is unbelievable then that this young girl, in a brief instant, could attain enlightenment."

(3) Before he was through speaking, the daughter of the Naga king suddenly manifested her body; she bowed down to the World-Honored One and sang his praise with this verse:

> Having profoundly perceived the forms of transgression and merit,
> He shines universally upon the four quarters.
> There is no one in this world
> Who does not worship his wondrous and pure image.

"I have heard that only buddhas know who hears and attains enlightenment. I hear the superb Dharma and save those who are in suffering."

Sariputra said to the daughter of the Naga king, "You believe that you will attain supreme enlightenment within a brief span of time. That is difficult to credit. The reason is that a woman's body is befouled and is not a vessel for the Dharma. How can you attain supreme enlightenment?"

At that time, the daughter of the Naga king made an offering of a priceless jewel to the World-Honored One, and the World-Honored One accepted it. The daughter of the Naga king said to the Bodhisattva Prajnakuta and to Sariputra, "Quicker than the time that it took the World-Honored One to accept the jewel that I offered, I shall become a buddha."

Then everyone assembled there saw the daughter of the Naga king instantly transform herself into a man, perfect the practice of a bodhisattva, and travel southward to the Vimala world. Seated on a jewelled lotus, he attained enlightenment. To myriad people, he expounded the Dharma; sentient beings witnessed this and rejoiced, and each roused the mind that seeks the path.

(4) At that time, before the World-Honored One, a large number of bodhisattvas took a vow that they would accept and spread this teaching. Raising their voices in unison, they sang this verse:

(i)   We beseech the World-Honored One not to be distressed
      After he has entered the final nirvana,
      For everywhere in this fearful and evil world
      We shall expound and spread the teaching.
      Even though foolish people may malign us viciously
      And strike us with knives and staves,
      We shall endure this with forbearance.
      There are those who egoistically seek their own practice;
      They disparage others and expound the Dharma out of their greed for profit.
      They are revered by sentient beings who have been deceived,
      And they take delight in holding up our faults for display.
      They malign us with such words as these:
      "Out of their greed for fame and profit,
      These disciples expound teachings that belong to false ways,
      And they lead sentient beings astray."

(ii) In order to slander us among sentient beings,
      They turn to them and accuse us of harboring erroneous views.
      However, because we revere the Buddha,
      We shall bear such evils.
      Those who have been muddied by passions become possessed by Maras;
      They malign and humiliate us.
      However, we shall place our trust in the Buddha and don the armor of forbearance.
      In order to expound this teaching, we shall bear these tribulations.
      We are attached neither to our bodies nor to our lives;
      We only revere the supreme path.

(iii) For aeons, in the ages to come,
      We shall safeguard that which has been entrusted to us by the Buddha.
      Disciples who dwell in this muddied world are ignorant of the Dharma of skillful means;
      They viciously slander us, drive us off repeatedly,
      And in the end expel us from the monasteries.

Although they commit such offences against us,
We shall patiently endure them all, holding fast to the words of the
Buddha.
Wherever there is someone who seeks the Dharma,
We shall go there and expound the Dharma entrusted to us by the
Buddha.
We are the messengers of the World-Honored One, and we fear no one.
We shall skillfully expound and spread this Dharma.
World-Honored One, we beseech you to remain at peace.
We come before the World-Honored One
And before the buddhas of the four quarters; we vow this.
We pray that this may be made known.

(5) The Bodhisattva Manjusri said to the World-Honored One, "World-Honored One, these bodhisattvas, out of their veneration for you, vow to expound this teaching. In the troubled world to come, in what manner should these bodhisattvas expound this Saddharmapundarika?"

The World-Honored One said, "In the future troubled world, those who aspire to expound this teaching must follow four kinds of practice. First, they must endure with forbearance, be gentle and free of violence, and act fearlessly. They must not become attached to things and must perceive all phenomena as they are, without discriminative thought.

"The second concerns with whom they become close. That is, they must not draw close to those who follow different paths, those who are involved in fine literature, those who indulge themselves in various forms of entertainment, and those who earn their livelihood by taking the lives of living beings. Should such people approach them, they must limit themselves solely to expounding the Dharma and must not harbor any expectations toward them. Furthermore, they must not keep close to those who seek base teachings. With regard to women, they must not expound the Dharma with any thought of desire to see a woman. Again, they must not, in their desire to gaze upon women, enter the home of a maiden or a widow or engage them in intimate conversation. If they enter such homes alone, they must, in their minds, single-mindedly focus on the Buddha. In case they expound the Dharma to women, they must not smile and show their teeth. They must not reveal their chests. Even for the sake of the Dharma, they must not become intimate with women; therefore, it is more true in other cases. Again, they must not harbor the desire to nurture a young disciple. Always dwelling in a quiet place, they must control their minds. This is called the first place with which they must become familiar.

"Bodhisattvas should practice the way of nondiscrimination. But they should recognize the distinction between men and women. They should view all existences as being emptiness. They must aspire to realize that all things exist only through dependency, as arising from inversions. This is the second place with which they must become familiar.

(6) "Again, Manjusri, in the third place, after the Buddha has gone to the final nirvana, those who aspire to expound this teaching must be at peace in their minds. When they expound the Dharma, they should not disparage the

masters of other schools. They should not point out others' faults, bad characteristics, or shortcomings. Even for those who practice the Sravaka path they should feel compassion for that shortcoming. They must neither laud nor loathe them. In this way they should maintain a mind that is at peace; those who listen to such bodhisattvas will also refrain from becoming recalcitrant. Therefore there will be no one who slanders others, drives others away, or assaults others with knives or staves. The reason for this is that their minds are endowed with forbearance. When someone poses a question, they should not respond with the Sravaka teachings but rather they should expound and clarify the superior Dharma, and in doing so they should enable him to attain omniscience.

"Again, Manjusri, those who uphold this teaching should not harbor thoughts of envy or flattery. Moreover, they should not make light of those who study a variety of Buddha paths. They should neither cause distress nor engender doubt by saying to them, 'All of you have strayed far from the path. The reason for this is that you have been negligent in your practice of the path.' And they should not contend with each other resorting to disputations. That is, they must rouse thought of great compassion toward all people. They must regard the myriad buddhas as being their compassionate fathers. They must view the myriad bodhisattvas as being their teachers. In this way, they must destroy their proud minds; and they must expound the Dharma in the same manner to all sentient beings. Even to those who follow and love the Dharma, they should not expound the Dharma in a biased way. Manjusri, there is no one who is able to cause distress and disorder in those who expound the Dharma, after having completed the third form of peaceful practice.

"Again, Manjusri, in the fourth place, those who uphold this teaching should produce the mind of great compassion toward those who are unable to seek the path of a bodhisattva. They must think, 'These people do not hear, know, attain, ask about, or believe in the skillful means of the Buddha-Dharma, which conforms to that which is appropriate. They have lost that Dharma completely; however, when I attain the enlightenment of a buddha, wherever it may be, with wisdom and power I shall draw them into this Dharma.' Manjusri, those who perfect this fourth are venerated and praised by all people. And they are always guarded by a host of gods and buddhas. A universal monarch bestows on warriors who have distinguished themselves in battle rewards such as elephants, horses, carriages, garments, property and so forth and thus gladdens their hearts. However, to the bravest of his warriors, who has accomplished that which is most difficult to accomplish, he unfastens the pearl hidden in his topknot and bestows it on him. The Buddha is also like this. The Buddha is truly the king of the Dharma. He is endowed with great forbearance; he is a treasury of wisdom. The Buddha sees people seeking deliverance from suffering and battling with a host of Maras. For their sake, he expounds innumerable Dharmas, and when he perceives that these people have attained greater power, finally, he expounds this Saddharmapundarika. He is like the universal monarch unfastening the pearl from his topknot and bestowing it on his bravest warrior. Truly, this teaching is the supreme and the deepest teaching of the Buddha. Now it is truly the time to expound this teaching; therefore I expound it for your benefit. If you wish to expound this teaching calmly, draw close to these four practices."

(7) At that time, the countless bodhisattvas who had arrived there from the lands of all the different directions arose from their seats and addressed the World-Honored One, "World-Honored One, if you allow us, after you enter the final nirvana, in this Saha world we shall exert ourselves with diligence to uphold this sutra, and we shall expound it everywhere." The World-Honored One said, "Good disciples, you need not uphold this teaching. In our Saha world, there exist countless bodhisattvas; after I enter the final nirvana, they will expound this teaching."

When the World-Honored One spoke in this manner, the earth shook and split apart. From its bowels, an infinite number of bodhisattvas welled up, went up to Prabhutaratna Buddha and Sakyamuni Buddha, bowed down to them, and paid homage to them. Among these bodhisattvas there were four leaders. The first was called Visistacaritra (Superior Practice); the second, Anantacaritra (Boundless Practice); the third, Visuddhacaritra (Pure Practice); and the fourth, Supratisthitacaritra (Standing Firm Practice). These four bodhisattvas came to the World-Honored One and earnestly asked, "Are you at ease?"

(8) The Bodhisattva Maitreya, knowing what countless bodhisattvas were thinking, asked the World-Honored One, "World-Honored One, I have not met even one of these countless great bodhisattvas who suddenly welled up from the earth. From where did they come, and through what causes and conditions did they assemble here? I beseech you to explain the causal process of this event." And the World-Honored One, for Maitreya's sake, set forth this verse:

(i)   You should exert yourself with diligence and be single-minded.
      I shall now expound on this matter.
      Do not harbor doubts; the Buddha's wisdom is boundless.
      Now, bring forth the power of your faith, and dwell in forbearance.
      You will be able to hear the Dharma that you have not heard before.
      I now console you; do not harbor any doubts.
      The Buddha does not mouth falsehoods.
      His wisdom is difficult to fathom.
      The primary teaching that I have attained is profound and difficult to comprehend.
      I now expound that teaching.
      Single-mindedly listen to my words.

(ii) Maitreya, understand clearly that all of these great bodhisattvas,
      From the immeasurable past, have been practicing the wisdom of the Buddha.
      Through my guidance, they have roused the mind of the great path.
      They are all my children.
      Dwelling in the Saha world, they always stay in tranquil places.
      There they practice the path; night and day, they exert themselves.
      Underneath the Bodhi Tree in the forest of Gaya,
      I attained enlightenment.
      I set in motion the wheel of the supreme Dharma
      And enabled them to rouse the mind of the path.

Now, all of these bodhisattvas dwell in a stage from which there is no
retrogression;
They will all attain Buddhahood.
I expound nothing but true words; single-mindedly believe in them.
From the infinitely distant past, I have been teaching these people.

The Bodhisattva Maitreya said to the World-Honored One, "World-Honored
One, since the World-Honored One attained enlightenment, only a mere forty
years have gone by. During such a short time span how were you able to guide
such an immeasurably large number of bodhisattvas, enabling them to attain
enlightenment? These bodhisattvas, moreover, from the infinite past, have been
cultivating the roots of merit in the presence of countless buddhas. Always they
practiced the paths of benefitting themselves and of benefitting others. Therefore this claim of having guided these bodhisattvas to enlightenment is difficult
to believe. It is as if a person twenty-five years old, of beautiful complexion and
black hair, should point to a person who is one hundred years old and claim that
he is his son. We beseech you to explain this matter to us and, for our sake and
for the sake of beings of the later ages, remove all of our doubts."

5. The Life Span of the Buddha

(1) The World-Honored One said to the bodhisattvas and all present, "You should
believe what the Buddha expounds." He repeated these words three times. The
assembly said, "World-Honored One, we beg you to teach us. We certainly have
faith in your teaching." They requested this three times. Seeing that they
earnestly wanted to hear, the World-Honored One said, "My disciples, listen
well and understand what an extraordinary power the Buddha has. People
believe that Sakyamuni Buddha left Kapilavastu and attained the supreme
enlightenment at Gaya. The truth is that countless kalpas have passed since
I became a Buddha. During these kalpas, I have always been in this world of
suffering to lead and teach people in this and in countless other worlds.
What I have related about my making a resolution in the presence of Dipamkara
Buddha, or about my nearing death, were all my skillful means. My disciples,
I have been causing joy to the multitudes by seeing their capacities individu-
ally and by using various means such as different names and epithets, showing
different life spans, or even by entering nirvana. To those with few virtues and
many defilements and aspiring for the Sravaka teaching, I said, 'I left home
when I was young and attained Buddhahood.' But the truth is that it was in
the remote past that my awakening took place. It was only as a device that
I taught in that manner. The purpose of giving a sutra is to lead people away
from delusion. Although various ways have been employed to teach the Dharma,
they are all true, and there is not one falsehood in them.

"The Buddha sees the world as it is. Therefore for the Buddha there is no
delusion of transmigration; neither is there being in this world nor being in the
world beyond; nothing can be called true nor can anything be called false; and
nothing can be said that it is as it is or otherwise. The Buddha's view of this
world is entirely different from that of the deluded. The Buddha sees all things
with the right view and never with erroneous views. People have different natures;

each has his own peculiar desires, deeds, thoughts, and reasons. The Buddha uses varying means such as stories of the Buddha's previous lives and parables to teach the Dharma. My life is endless, but to let people who are full of greed arouse reverence and affection for the Buddha, I tell them as skillful means that as the Buddha appears in this world only on rare occasions, it is difficult for them to see the Buddha.

"Suppose that there is a physician with many children. He goes on a journey. In his absence, the children unknowingly take poison and are in agony because of it. The physician returns home and gives an antidote. Among the children, those who have not lost their minds take the medicine and get well. But those who lost their minds do not take the medicine. Therefore the doctor uses skillful means and says to the children, 'Now I am old and my death is near. I shall leave some medicines here for you to take.' He leaves on another journey. Away from home, he sends a messenger and has him tell the children that their father has died. Hearing this, the children become deeply saddened and lament, 'If he were alive, he would love us dearly. Now that he has died in a country far away, we have become orphans with no one to depend upon.' Then they remember the last words of their father and take the medicine and become well again. And the father returns home. The Buddha uses skillful means in like manner.

"My disciples, will anyone blame the physician for what he has done? It has been long since my attaining Buddhahood. Now I am using my skillful means to save people by telling them that I will be leaving this world."

(2):

(i) Billions of kalpas have passed since my attainment of Buddhahood;
All the while I taught the Dharma, leading countless people to the path.
For a countless number of kalpas, to save sentient beings,
I feigned death, but I did not enter nirvana.
Always here on Vulture Peak, I have taught the Dharma.
Though I remain here revealing the divine power, the blind, not knowing this,
Thought I really died and venerating my remains they longed for me.

(ii) To him who, with focused mind and sincerity of heart, even risking his life,
Wishes to see me, I with a host of my disciples shall appear on Vulture Peak and speak.
Being here eternally, I shall never cease to be; only as skillful means
Do I show extinction and nonextinction.
Even for those in many other worlds, if only they have faith and reverence,
I shall appear before them and teach the supreme Dharma.
You who do not know this believe that I really died.
But being in the world of suffering, it is only that you see not my Dharma body.
If you, with adoration, sincerely wish to see me,
I shall immediately appear before you and teach.

(iii) In timeless time, always shall I be on Vulture Peak and other
abodes;
At the end of many ages, even when all people will be burnt,
My land will forever be in peace.

There the gods ever gather, gardens and palaces are studded with
gems

And trees of gems, full of blossoms and fruits, where people play in
joy;

The gods tap on hand drums and shower flowers over the Buddha
and the people.

(iv) The pure realm of mine never ceases to be;
People with their burning desires think it full of sufferings.
The suffering beings, due to their own evil deeds,
Will not hear the names of the Three Treasures even in innumerable
kalpas.
But those who do virtuous deeds and have kindly natures and
sincere minds
Will see that I am always here, always teaching the Dharma.

(v) For them, at times, I say my life is eternal, but to those who seldom
see me,
I say that the Buddha is hard to see.
My power of wisdom is such that there is no place
Where the light of my wisdom does not reach,
And there is no end to my power of wisdom.
All these powers are due to merits acquired through the ages.
You who are men of wisdom, do not
Have any doubts about this, for there
Is no falsehood in the Buddha's words.

(3) Just then the Bodhisattva Maitreya arose and, paying homage to the
World-Honored One, said in verse,

(i) The Buddha now expounds on a rare Dharma never heard before.
The World-Honored One has a great power and life that lasts forever.
Countless people in all the worlds, which themselves are numberless,
Hearing of the Buddha's infinite life, all roused their minds
To aspire to become buddhas themselves.
The Buddha taught this supreme Dharma;
The vastness of his compassion is like the sky that has no bounds.

(ii) Showering flowers, gods descend; like the birds they come flying
Scattering sandalwood perfume, they pay homage to the Buddha.
Heavenly drums are heard in the sky; robes of heavenly beings come
falling;
And songs are sung in praise of the Buddha.

(iii) This from earliest times never happened before.
Having heard that the Buddha has an infinite life,
Gladdened, they all are filled with joy.
His name resounds in all ten directions, and he showers compassion
far and wide.

He lets them become replete with the roots of good
And produce the aspiration to enlightenment.

(4) The World-Honored One said to the Bodhisattva Maitreya, "If one, upon hearing the teaching on the infinite life of the Buddha, produces one thought of faith, he will gain immeasurable merits. For the merit contained in one single thought of faith is thousands of times greater than that gained by practicing giving, discipline, patience, zeal, and meditation.

"Therefore, Maitreya, he who is endowed with such great merit can never regress from the enlightenment of a Buddha. Maitreya, he who hears the teaching on my eternal life and understands it will gain immeasurable merits and will attain the supreme wisdom of a Buddha. Moreover, Maitreya, he who hears the teaching on my eternal life and has faith deep in his mind will see the Buddha surrounded by the multitudes on Vulture Peak and expounding the Dharma. And he will also see that this world is in reality a pure land glittering with gems and gold. He will see also innumerable sentient beings seeking the Buddha's enlightenment.

"After the Buddha enters the final nirvana, if one upon hearing the teaching does not vilify it but awakens a mind of joy, that is deep belief in the teaching. He who preserves this sutra is one who honors the Buddha. Maitreya, he does not need to accumulate merit by building stupas or monasteries or erecting chambers for the monks. For one who preserves and recites this sutra has already attained such merits."

(5) The World-Honored One then said to the Bodhisattva Satatasamitabhiyukta, "Those sons or daughters of good families who preserve this sutra and share it with others will attain superior merits; and they will gain the virtuous power whereby their eyes will be able to see all the sentient beings in the world; and their ears, endowed with virtuous merits, will be able to hear all the voices in the world. Their noses, tongues, bodies, and minds also will be endowed with similar merits. What they say will be in accordance with reason, and what they do will be in accordance with the Dharma."

(6) The World-Honored One said to the Bodhisattva Mahasthamaprapta, "In the distant past, there appeared the Buddha Bhismagarjitasvararaja who led multitudes to enlightenment. But after he had entered the final nirvana, following a period of the true Dharma, and entering upon the period of the counterfeit Dharma, excessively proud and overbearing monks gained power. At that time there was a Bodhisattva by the name of Sadaparibhuta, who, whenever he saw a disciple, a householder, or a mendicant, would say, 'I revere you highly. I shall never think lightly of you. The reason is that you will in time unfailingly become a Buddha.' Thus he was named Sadaparibhuta (Always Not Despising). This Bodhisattva did not read sutras but devoted his life solely to the practice of reverence. There were some who felt uncomfortable and annoyed by this and spoke ill of him, saying, 'Where did this monk come from falsely to predict our enlightenments?' He was never angered by such remarks and kept on saying, 'You will eventually attain enlightenment.' When people, angered by what he said, tried to strike him with sticks and rocks, he would avoid them by

running away from them and still kept on repeating the same words. At the end of his life, he heard countless verses of the Saddharmapundarika resounding in the sky, preserved all of them in his mind, and expounded the Dharma to multitudes. Mahasthamaprapta, that Bodhisattva Sadaparibhuta of that time was in fact myself. It was by virtue of my practicing and expounding the teaching that I was able to attain the supreme enlightenment quickly."

(7) At that time, a multitude of bodhisattvas welled up from the great earth. They single-mindedly pressed their palms together and promised the Buddha, "O World-Honored One, we shall appear in those realms where the World-Honored One has been and widely teach this sutra. We shall do this because we aspire to preserve, recite, explain, copy, and make offerings to the great Dharma after your entering the final nirvana."

Upon hearing these words, the World-Honored One, for the benefit of the assembly, revealed his transcendent powers. Every Buddha who was present also revealed his miraculous powers. Overjoyed, those assembled drew their palms together and praised this magnificent spectacle in humble reverence. The World-Honored One said to the multitude of bodhisattvas, "Sons of virtuous families, the powers of the Buddha are limitless, universal, vast, and indescribable. Even though the Buddha's power has been praised through innumerable kalpas, these praises are insufficient. However, this sutra profoundly contains all those teachings and tells of the powers and key mysteries possessed by all the buddhas. All these virtues are illuminated herein. It is for this reason that all of you should, after my final nirvana, single-mindedly hold, recite, explain, copy, transmit, and continue to practice the Dharma according to my teaching. O sons of virtuous families, a stupa to which offerings can be made should be erected wherever this sutra is, be it in a garden, in a forest, in a monk's dwelling, in the home of a layman, or wherever appropriate. For what reason? Because any place where the sutra is kept should be regarded as the august place for the practice of the Dharma. You should regard the stupa site as the place where all buddhas attain enlightenment, teach the Dharma, and attain the final nirvana."

(8) At that time, through his transcendent powers, the World-Honored One touched with his right hand the crown of each of the innumerable bodhisattvas present and proclaimed, "I have indeed acquired the difficult-to-attain Dharma. At this time I entrust this Dharma to all of you. Hold fast to this Dharma and widely recite it for all to hear. The Buddha is a being of great compassion. There is not even the slightest need for fear. I give to all sentient beings the Buddha's wisdom, which is omniscience. The Buddha is the great benefactor of all sentient beings. Accordingly, you should not quicken a mind of greed. In the future, if people believe in the Buddha's wisdom, they can truly receive the blessings of the Buddha." All the bodhisattvas understood, and their bodies and minds trembled with joy.

(9) In response to the Bodhisattva Naksatraraja-samkusumitabhijna's question, the World-Honored One spoke of the Bodhisattva Bhaisajyaraja's past. "In dim antiquity there was a bodhisattva called Sarvasattvapriyadarsana who earnestly sought enlightenment under the guidance of the Buddha known as

Candrasurya-vimalapratibhasri. After twelve thousand long kalpas of practice the Bodhisattva achieved the meditation that enabled him to manifest all kinds of forms. This Bodhisattva was able to realize this glorious goal because he earnestly listened to the Saddharmapundarika. After attaining this goal, straight way he thought to honor the Buddha and entered into deep meditation. Immediately sandalwood perfume rained from the heavens. For the next twelve thousand years the Bodhisattva ate fragrant substances and drank fragrant oils and applied various scents over his body. Finally at the end of this period he clothed himself in garments sprinkled with sweet perfumes and presented himself to the Buddha Candrasurya-vimalapratibhasri. Then he burned his own body as an offering to the Buddha and to the Saddharmapundarika sutra, and the flames lit up countless worlds, and countless buddhas exclaimed, 'Well done, son of virtuous family! This is the true worship of the Tathagata!' And the body blazed for twelve thousand years, after which the Bodhisattva was reborn in the same world. Immediately after his birth he approached the Buddha and praised his virtues in the following verse.

> Your countenance is wonderful;
> Your light illuminates the ten directions.
> I performed obeisance at your feet in the ancient past.
> I am once again in your presence.

"At that time the Buddha Candrasurya-vimalapratibhasri entrusted the entire Dharma to this Bodhisattva, and that night he peacefully entered the final nirvana. The Bodhisattva was moved with profound grief and erected eighty-four thousand stupas to honor the Buddha. Still dissatisfied, the Bodhisattva burnt his virtue-endowed forearm in front of every stupa. He continued this offering for seventy-two thousand kalpas.

"O Naksatraraja-samkusumitabhijna, the Bodhisattva Sarvasattva-priyadarsana is none other than the Bodhisattva Bhaisajyaraja who offered his body over countless kalpas. Therefore those who seek the wisdom of the Buddha should honor the stupa of the Buddha by offering their fingers and toes, because this offering surpasses all giving. Again, even if I honor the buddhas and sages by covering three billion worlds with the seven kinds of jewels, this gift would not exceed the virtue of one who possesses four lines from the Saddharmapundarika. O Naksatraraja-samkusumitabhijna, just as the ocean is greater than all the streams and rivers, so this teaching is the most profound and universal. Just as the pure water of the lake quenches the thirst of the thirsty and fire warms the cold, this teaching successfully frees all from suffering and delusion. Again, just as the naked seek clothing and darkness searches for light, this teaching enables beings to distance themselves from their sufferings and delusion.

"Further, O Naksatraraja-samkusumitabhijna, if there is a man who hears of the deeds of the Bodhisattva Bhaisajyaraja and if he conducts himself in accord with this teaching, after his demise he will reach the dwelling of Amitayus Buddha in the Sukhavati world and will be born there on a jewelled lotus seat.

And he will never again be tormented by greed, anger, ignorance, pride, or envy. He will gain the powers and the wisdom-eye of a bodhisattva."

(10) At that time, the Bodhisattva Aksayamati stood up from his seat, paid his homage to the World-Honored One, and asked, "Why was the Bodhisattva Avalokitesvara named so?" The World-Honored One replied, "When countless sentient beings, having great pains and suffering, hear the name of this Bodhisattva and sincerely recite his name, the Bodhisattva Avalokitesvara will immediately perceive their voices and will free them from their suffering. He who thinks of his name will not, thanks to the Bodhisattva's divine power, be burnt in fire or drown in water.

"Again, the Bodhisattva Avalokitesvara will appear in this Saha world in the form of a Buddha to those who are to become buddhas. For the kings, wealthy men, masters of non-Buddhist teachings, disciples of monks, lay followers, or even Nagas and devils, he will assume their own forms to save them and teach the Dharma to them."

(11) The Bodhisattva Aksayamati inquired of the World-Honored One in verse:

(i) O World-Honored One, you who are replete with auspicious marks,
Once more I ask, why is this Bodhisattva named Avalokitesvara?

The World-Honored One responded,

Listen and I shall speak of the deeds of the Bodhisattva
Avalokitesvara.
His vows are ever present in all places and they are,
Like the deep ocean, formless and timeless.
He has served countless buddhas, and his vows are great and pure.
I shall now speak briefly of his exploits.

(ii) By hearing the name of Avalokitesvara
And by seeing his body and being mindful of him,
If done not in vain, all our sufferings can be extinguished.
If someone with a malicious intent shoves you into a great pit of fire,
Your continual mindfulness of Avalokitesvara's virtue
Will transform the pit of fire into a lake.
Or, if you are afloat in the vast ocean and meet with Nagas, fish, and
Maras,
Your continual mindfulness of Avalokitesvara's virtue
Will not allow the waves to drown you.
Or if you are pushed off a mountain precipice,
By means of continual mindfulness of Avalokitesvara's virtue,
You will be suspended in space and will not fall.

(iii) Or should you be pursued by an evil person from a high mountain
peak,
Due to your continual mindfulness of Avalokitesvara's virtues,
Not even a single hair will be lost.
Or should you be surrounded by enemies
Who cause you harm with the swords they carry,
Your continual mindfulness of Avalokitesvara's virtues
Will quicken a mind of compassion in all your adversaries.
Or should you be met with imperial decrees and face the death
penalty,

Your continual mindfulness of Avalokitesvara's virtue
Will immediately shatter the executioner's sword.
Or should you be shackled and chained, or be stocked hand and foot,
Your continual mindfulness of Avalokitesvara's virtues
Will instantly free you.

(iv) When you are threatened by spells, curses, and poisons,
Your continual mindfulness of Avalokitesvara's virtues
Will turn these evils back to their instigators.
When you encounter demons, poisonous Nagas, and beasts,
Through your continual mindfulness of Avalokitesvara's virtues,
These creatures will immediately flee.
Although the thundercloud and lightning bolt may dispatch hail and
heavy rains,
Your continual mindfulness of Avalokitesvara's virtues
Will quickly dissipate and dry up the hail and rain.
When misfortune happens and causes suffering,
Your continual mindfulness of Avalokitesvara's virtues
Will quickly diminish it.

(v) Avalokitesvara possesses unusual powers;
Blessed with the wisdom of skillful means,
There is no place in the ten directions of the universe
Where he does not reveal himself.
His appearance extinguishes all traces of the three unhappy
destinies,
Hell and the realms of hungry ghosts and animals,
As well as the sufferings of birth, old age, sickness, and death.
Avalokitesvara's gaze is true and pure; it is the gaze of wisdom and
compassion.
We forever yearn for and praise Avalokitesvara's spotless light of
wisdom,
Which shatters every darkness, stills the fires and winds of
misfortune,
And blesses the world with its radiance.

(vi) Avalokitesvara's compassionate body thunders forth our rules
of conduct.
His compassion is like a great cloud
That rains the sweet nectar of the Dharma
To extinguish the flames of passions.
When we are terrified by a court of law or the arena of battle,
Our continued mindfulness of Avalokitesvara's virtues will dispel all
fears.
Avalokitesvara's voice surpasses all the subtle voices of the world;
His voice is a voice of one who observes the world,
A voice like the tide or the voices of the gods.
Therefore we should be ever mindful of Avalokitesvara.

(vii) Always be mindful and at no moment harbor any doubts of the
virtue of Avalokitesvara.
He is our strength in suffering, danger, and death.
Avalokitesvara is replete with all virtues;
He perceives mankind with the eye of compassion;

He is the limitless ocean of happiness.
For this reason let us revere him.

Then all the bodhisattvas and disciples rejoiced in the World-Honored One's instruction.

6. Thinking

(1) The World-Honored One once more entered the city of Savatthi and rested at the Jeta Grove Monastery. One day during this interval, Sariputra said to his fellow disciples, "Noble friends, when we are ridiculed and slandered, we say to ourselves, 'My ears hear it. But the sensation of hearing is impermanent; so are the feelings of pain and pleasure; so are the perception, the volition, and the consciousness arising from it. All elements that compose my mind and body are impermanent.' Thinking in this manner, your mind will not be depressed but will become calm and settled.

"Sons of good family, if we are tyrannized by those who hit us with their fists, beset by mud thrown at us, and struck by their staves and swords, we should channel our thoughts by thinking, 'This body is meant to experience abuse.' The World-Honored One once related the parable of the saw. He said, 'Even if a thief should cut your body with a two-edged saw, those who feel wretched have not yet made my teaching their own.' We should say, 'I am resolved and unflinching; I shall not let my true will be shattered. My body will be relaxed and my mind focused. Though my body may be struck by a flurry of fists, staves, and swords, these abuses are for the sake of my fulfilling the teaching of the Buddha.' During these times, if one is mindful of the Buddha, the Dharma, and the Sangha and still fails to achieve a mind of equanimity, the mind, like the heart of the new bride who sees her father-in-law for the first time, will become unsettled. If one is mindful of the Buddha, the Dharma, and the Sangha and achieves a mind of equanimity, then he will attain great joy and gain much.

"O friends, just as we say that a hut is made of logs, vines, grass, and mud, so do we say that our body consists of bones, muscle, flesh, and skin. Within the body, organs of sense, objects of sense, and consciousness give rise to the activities of seeing and hearing. O friends, the World-Honored One has stated, 'He who sees dependent origination (paticca-samuppada) sees the Dharma. He who sees the Dharma sees dependent origination.' Indeed this body and mind are established through dependent origination. The desires that arise through the mutuality of body and mind are the causes of suffering. Removing wants and desires destroys suffering. The extinction of suffering, O friends, is your final goal."

(2) On another occasion, Sariputra was happily returning home after serving the World-Honored One and hearing his teaching, when he met with Purutika, a wandering ascetic and a nonbeliever who inquired, "Where have you come from?" "I am returning home now, after hearing the teaching of the World-Honored One." Purutika asked Sariputta, "Are you still suckling milk? I left my teacher ages ago and am now seeking the truth by myself. Are you still listening to the teachings of your master?" Sariputta replied, "I am not yet

weaned from my master's milk. I still rejoice when I hear my master's teaching. I am of the opinion that your master has yet to arrive at the true realization and that his teaching is not the true Dharma. Just as a calf quickly leaves his mother's milk if it is bad or insufficient, you have cut your ties with your master. My master possesses the true enlightenment, and his teaching is the true teaching. Consequently, just as a calf does not separate from his mother's milk if it is good and nourishing, I have not left my master. I rejoice in his teaching."

(3) While the World-Honored One was still in the city of Savatthi he addressed his disciples, "O my disciples, before I had attained enlightenment and while I was still a bodhisattva, I entertained two kinds of thoughts. On the one hand, I possessed thoughts of greed, anger, and maliciousness. On the other, I possessed the thoughts of non-greed, non-anger, and non-maliciousness.

"Aware that I possessed this duality of thought, on those occasions when I gave rise to thoughts of greed, I would think, 'I have given rise to thoughts of greed; this kind of thinking is injurious to me, to others, to both myself and others. Further, this kind of thinking is detrimental to wisdom and leads to disaster.' Conscious of this danger, I eradicated thoughts of greed. I eliminated thoughts of anger and malice in the same manner. When these three types of evil thoughts arose, I immediately destroyed and removed them from my mind.

"O disciples, a person's mind has the tendency to drift and harden. If you give rise to covetous thoughts, then your greed becomes stronger and stronger. If you give rise to angry thoughts, then your anger is inflamed. If you give rise to malicious thoughts, your mind drifts toward evil. After the rainy season, during the fall harvest, the herdsman leads his herd into a barn. The cattle are then bound and slaughtered because he is fearful that the herd might damage the harvest. O my disciples, in the same way, when I observed evil, I fixed my mind, destroyed the evil, and expelled it. The thought to expel greed, anger, and malice arose in me. I knew that these thoughts were injurious to me, to others, to both myself and others. I realized that these thoughts were contrived, and therefore even though these thoughts were strengthened, they contained a danger that I did not perceive. But I knew that if I continued to entertain the same thoughts for any length of time, my body would tire, my mind would become cloudy, and I would lose my concentration. Consequently I stilled my mind and focused it.

"O my disciples, the mind has a tendency to drift and harden on what one thinks; therefore when you think of expelling greed, anger, and malice, the mind locks in on its objects, and thoughts of greed, anger, and malice are nullified. During the last month of summer, when the wheat is threshed at the edge of the village, the herdsman watches over the wandering of his herd. Are they beneath the trees or are they in the pasture? He knows exactly where his herd is. I am the same. I carefully observe the wanderings of my mind. I know what kind of thoughts I quicken. O my disciples, with courage, vigor, and fearlessness, I always possessed right thought, my body was relaxed, and my mind was focused.

"O my disciples, in this way I entered the many meditations. My mind was still, pure, and penetrating; it was without greed and without passions; it was gentle and always vigorous. I proceeded on the path with a firm resolve that could not be influenced by others. Finally I was able to destroy passions and give rise to wisdom.

(4) "O my disciples, a herd of deer lives in a great forest highland. Nearby lies a low-lying swamp. Scheming to disrupt the idyllic and peaceful life in the forest, a man blocks the trail that leads to the forest and forces the deer to remain in the swamp. Living in this damp and wet land, the deer meet with hardship and misfortunes, and their numbers are greatly reduced. In contrast, a man who is mindful of the well-being of the deer blocks the path that leads to the swamp and clears the path that leads to the highland forest. As a consequence, the number of deer is greatly increased.

"O my disciples, I offer this parable in order that you may come to understand my teaching. The large low-lying swamp represents the pasture of pleasure and desire; the herds of deer represent sentient beings; the trail that leads to the lowland symbolizes the eight wrong paths; grazing on the damp earth represents the search for relief; the swamp is ignorance. He who is mindful of the well-being of the deer is the Buddha, and the path that he clears leading to the highland is the Eightfold Noble path. O my disciples, in this manner it is through my teachings that the path to peace and happiness is made available, and the way to the damp lowland swamp is blocked.

"O my disciples, because of my sympathy and compassion I have done what was necessary for your sake. Here beneath this tree we have shade and an empty hut. Think on this. Do not neglect things lest you be filled with regret later. This is my advice."

(5) Again on another occasion the World-Honored One said, "O my disciples, to master meditation you must consider the following five methods. When you perceive objects and give rise to passions of greed, anger, and ignorance, immediately turn your passions away from those objects. You must then think on another object that will give rise to good thoughts. If you focus your mind on another object, then your greed, anger, and ignorance will decrease. Your mind will then be settled, quiet, and focused. This is similar to that of a skillful carpenter who dislodges a large nail by hitting it with a smaller one.

"O my disciples, when your mind is unfocused and the evil passion that accompanies greed, anger, and ignorance is not extinguished, you must say, 'This mind is defiled and evil and will give rise to suffering.' You must examine the danger of entertaining such thoughts. If you inquire in this manner, these evil passions will disappear, and the mind will settle, become quiet, and be focused. Evil passions should be disdained in the way a beautiful girl or a handsome young man would disdain festering flesh that had been wrapped around her or his head.

"O my disciples, if evil passions cannot be extinguished in the manner that I have just suggested, then you must not give rise to such thoughts. These evil passions will not arise, and the mind will settle and become quiet and focused, just as one cannot perceive what is directly before him if he closes his eyes or if he looks in another direction.

"O my disciples, if, having tried what I have just instructed, evil passions still persist, you must examine the causes and bases for these passions. Then the evil passions will not arise, and the mind will settle and become quiet and focused. This method of examination is like a man who is running and says to himself, 'Why am I in such a hurry? How would it be if I just walked?' When he is leisurely walking he asks himself, 'Why am I walking? How would it be if I just stood?' When he is standing he asks, 'Why am I standing? How would it be if I just sat?' When he sits he continues his inquiry.

"O my disciples, if you seek the causes and bases and still are unable to overcome evil passions, you should grit your teeth, press your tongue on the upper palate, and determinedly resolve to suppress and quiet evil passions. This method is similar to a strong man who grasps and squeezes the neck of a frail man. In this way evil passions should subside, and the mind will settle and become quiet and focused.

"O my disciples, these five methods of suppressing evil passions—five ways of directing one's mind in dealing with evil passions—have been well tested. Through these methods you can distance yourself from all evil passions, destroy the roots of evil deeds, and completely eradicate the cause of suffering."

Chapter 2

THE TRAGEDY AT RAJAGRIHA

1. The Defection of Devadatta

(1) Once again the World-Honored One travelled back to Rajagriha. There he stayed at the Bamboo Grove Monastery, which was located outside the city. At that time, for a long period there was no rain. The rice plants withered away, and the Buddha's disciples suffered as they made their rounds begging for food. Devadatta especially brooded over his own inability to control the weather because of his lack of divine powers. One day he appeared before the World-Honored One and begged to be instructed into the way of acquiring divine powers. The World-Honored One said, "Devadatta, rather than seeking to acquire divine powers, reflect on the truths of impermanence, of suffering, of emptiness, and of selflessness." With these words, the Buddha rejected Devadatta's plea. However, instead of delighting in this teaching imparted to him, Devadatta's mind was deeply scarred by discontent.

That summer the World-Honored One, accompanied by his disciples, travelled to Kausambi where he held a retreat. It was customary for such disciples as Sariputra, Maudgalyayana, Aniruddha, Ananda and others to engage, in an amicable manner, in discussions on the Buddha-Dharma. To Devadatta's mind, however, these discussions had the appearance of treating him as an outcast; he therefore abandoned the order and headed for Rajagriha.

At Rajagriha, Devadatta plotted to gain the devotion of Prince Ajatasatru, sixteen years of age, who was the beloved son of King Bimbisara. One day he sought out the prince and, resorting to all manner of ruses, he was able to gain control of the prince's pious following, and in the neighborhood of Rajagriha he built a temple. Gradually, he began to receive offerings of robes and food, brought to him on numerous carts.

(2) In this way Devadatta gained numerous young supporters, and daily his power increased. Even among the disciples of the World-Honored One, there were some who turned toward Devadatta. The World-Honored One, hearing that Devadatta was receiving offerings from Prince Ajatasatru for the sake of profit, addressed his disciples, "Fools regard profit as the most important thing, and they do more and more evil deeds. However, like a sharp sword that in the blink of an eye severs arms and legs, their thoughts sever the life of pure merits. There

are those who attempt to attract followers and seek to stand as their leader, claiming that they are masters of the Dharma. While undertaking this for the sake of profit, they seek to gain nirvana. In such people, due to their thoughts of profit, the mind that seeks nirvana turns into an evil mind. Moreover, they injure themselves; they injure others; and for aeons they must suffer in their unhappy destinies. You must never feel envious of Devadatta." And he said in verse,

> Bearing fruit, the banana plant withers.
> The reed that is abloom with flowers also withers.
> The filly becomes pregnant and dies.
> Human beings are destroyed as a result of desire.

(3) One day the World-Honored One made his rounds of begging in Rajagriha; Devadatta was also making his rounds in the same city. The World-Honored One saw Devadatta from afar and attempted to take leave of that locale. At that moment, Ananda asked, "Why do you take leave of this place?" The World-Honored One said, "Devadatta is in this city and I shall avoid him." Ananda said, "Do you fear Devadatta?" The World-Honored One replied, "No, I do not fear him. I leave because evil men ought to be avoided." Ananda said, "Why do you not make Devadatta take leave of the city?" The World-Honored One said, "There is no need to make him leave; allow him to conduct himself as he will. Ananda, you must avoid foolish people; you must not cast your lot with foolish people. You must not engage in fruitless arguments. Foolish people, of their own free will, perform evil deeds, they violate the precepts, and with each passing day they breed more wrong views. Devadatta has gained some profit, and his mind swells with arrogance. Confronting Devadatta is like taking a whip to an ill-tempered dog. The more you flog that dog, the more violent it becomes." Having spoken these words, the World-Honored One travelled to another city in order to beg for food, taking Ananda along with him.

On the other hand, Devadatta aggressively plotted to seize control over the order in place of the World-Honored One. At this time, Maudgalyayana found himself in the country of Cedi; however, when he heard of Devadatta's treacherous mind, he became alarmed and headed for the Bamboo Grove Monastery. When he informed the World-Honored One of Devadatta's motives, the World-Honored One replied, "I have known this for some time."

Unaware, Devadatta hastily made his way to the Bamboo Grove Monastery, accompanied by his close disciples such as Kokalika, Khandadeviyaputra, Katamodrakatisyaka, Samudradatta and others. The World-Honored One observed their arrival and said, "Those ignorant men will no doubt address me by lavishing words of praise on themselves and by revealing their plot to usurp my authority." Maudgalyayana once again returned to the country of Cedi. Devadatta's party appeared before the World-Honored One; he bowed and then said, "The World-Honored One is now old in years. Your strength has waned. The training of your disciples must be unbearably burdensome. From this day, in your place, I shall expound the Dharma for the sake of the disciples. The World-Honored One should simply enjoy his meditation."

The World-Honored One said, "Devadatta, I have refrained from entrusting the training of this large assembly of disciples even to such arhats as Sariputra and Maudgalyayana, whose wisdom is clear and whose practice is perfect. How, then, can I entrust this large assembly to someone like you, who swallow other men's spittle for the sake of gaining profit?" Devadatta was unable to utter one word in response to these harsh words of the World-Honored One. Dejected, he backed away from the Buddha and departed. In his heart, however, he harbored a deep hatred, thinking to himself, "In front of the large assembly of disciples, the World-Honored One praised Sariputra and Maudgalyayana, and he humiliated me. Someday this insult must be avenged."

(4) One day, on the pretext that the observance of the order's precepts had become lax, Devadatta expressed the desire to formulate five new precepts; he expressed his wishes before the World-Honored One. Devadatta proposed the following five new precepts.

1. Disciples must live in the forest and must not live on the outskirts of villages.
2. Disciples must beg from door to door and must not accept invitations.
3. Disciples must wear robes made of patches of discarded cloth throughout their lives.
4. Disciples must live underneath trees and must not sleep in houses.
5. Disciples must not partake of meat.

The World-Honored One, however, had always stressed the eradicating of defilements of the mind; he refrained from creating needlessly severe precepts that would constrict the actions of the disciples. He therefore rejected this proposal brought forth by Devadatta. Immediately the Buddha called for Sariputra and said, "Go forth now to where Devadatta's followers are gathered and convey to them that should they accept Devadatta's five precepts, they will have departed from the true teaching." Sariputra said, "World-Honored One, in days past, there were times when I praised Devadatta. I cannot bear to censure him now." The World-Honored One said, "To praise someone is a sincere act; to censure someone is also a sincere act. One must correct someone who is in error." Sariputra acceded to the Buddha's instructions. He travelled to the place where Devadatta's group of followers had gathered, and he recounted to them the gist of the Buddha's words. Since they were all followers of Devadatta, they said to each other, "Oh, the disciples of the World-Honored One have seen the generous offerings received by the honored Devadatta and are beset with feelings of envy." Sariputra once again returned to Rajagriha and conveyed the same message to the disciples faithful to the Buddha.

Devadatta, however, was firm in his resolve to proceed with establishing the new precepts. He made plans, together with Samudradatta, who was the cleverest amongst his disciples, and on the day of the uposadha he proclaimed his new precepts and sought the support of sentient beings. At that time, five hundred men from Vaisali who had just become monks were present at the gathering. Because they were not aware of the precepts of the Buddha, they accepted these new precepts. At that time, great disciples such as Sariputra and Maudgalyayana were not present; however, Ananda, who was there, put on his upper garment and rose from his seat. He then said, "These newly formulated precepts are not those that were established by the World-Honored One. Elders, if you agree with what I say, wearing your upper garments, rise from your seats." Sixty elders responded to these words spoken by Ananda. Devadatta, however, had collected five hundred new disciples, and he ordered these elders to leave the order. Accompanied by his disciples, Devadatta travelled to Mount Gayasirsa, which was located approximately twenty-five miles southwest of Rajagriha. It was his plan to undertake the training of his disciples at this site.

The departure of the disciples, five hundred in number, who were led away by Devadatta, shook the minds of those disciples who remained within the Buddha's order. Sariputra and Maudgalyayana, having received the Buddha's consent, headed for Mount Gayasirsa for the purpose of freeing those disciples who had been seized by Devadatta. Among the Buddha's disciples, some lamented, "Oh, most likely those two are also going to become Devadatta's disciples." The World-Honored One said to his disciples, "You need not be concerned; without fail, those two will manifest at that place the august powers of the Dharma."

(5) When Sariputra and Maudgalyayana finally reached Mount Gayasirsa, Devadatta was busily expounding his dharma. Devadatta, however, caught sight of their arrival and greeted them joyfully, "Previously you did not accept my new precepts; by now you have clearly understood my intentions and have come here to join us." Moments later, he said to Sariputra, "I am beginning to feel fatigued now; would you, therefore, expound the teaching in my place?" Imitating the Buddha's practice, he then folded his robes in four, and he lay down on his right side. At that time, Maudgalyayana manifested divine powers, and Sariputra followed by expounding the Dharma. The five hundred disciples, as if waking from a dream, repented their errors. Immediately they were led away by Sariputra and Maudgalyayana and left the mountain. Samudradatta roused the slumbering Devadatta, shouting to him that Sariputra and Maudgalyayana had departed with the five hundred disciples. Startled, Devadatta woke up and screamed, "You evil men have stolen my disciples from me!" He then stamped the great earth and went into a frenzy of rage, and hot blood spurted out from his nose.

The fact that Sariputra and Maudgalyayana had brought back five hundred disciples with them astonished the disciples of the Buddha's order. So great was their shock that the Buddha, for their sake, recounted a tale of one of the Buddha's previous lives. He said, "Disciples, in years past, there was a master archer named Kovali; he had a disciple named Sanna who, for a period of six years, practiced the art of holding the bow and notching the arrow to the bowstring. And yet not once did he shoot an arrow. One day to test his prowess, he shot at a large tree; the arrow dazzled everyone by piercing the tree and plunging deep into the ground. The master was delighted and said, 'You have mastered the art of archery. From now on, go forth to subdue those bandits that plague those who travel on our roads.' The master then gave his disciple one bow, five hundred golden arrows, a beautiful maiden, and a carriage. Obeying his master's orders, the disciple, together with the maiden, boarded the carriage and set out in search of the bandits.

"Accompanied by five hundred of his underlings, the bandit leader waited for travellers to come his way. Just then Sanna's carriage arrived. The bandit leader restrained his underlings and stopped them from attacking Sanna. Soon the beautiful maiden lowered herself from the carriage and holding a gold bowl in her hands sought food from the bandits. Seeing the beautiful maiden and the golden bowl, the bandits could not stifle their lustful minds. Still the bandit leader was able to restrain his hot-blooded underlings, and into the maiden's golden bowl he heaped mounds of tasty morsels. The maiden repeatedly asked that her share of the food be given to her. Unable to restrain themselves any longer, the bandits rushed toward Sanna who was in the carriage. Zigzagging right and left, he drove the carriage while felling one bandit with one arrow. Felling four hundred ninety-nine bandits, he was left with one arrow in the end. However, the bandit leader was nowhere in sight; thereupon, Sanna had the beautiful maiden take off her clothes and walk around underneath the tree, parading her naked body. Then the bandit leader was tempted and came out of hiding. In the end, struck by Sanna's arrow, he was killed. Disciples, Sanna at that time is none other than Sariputra; the beautiful maiden is Maudgalyayana; the five hundred bandits are none other than the five hundred new disciples. The bandit leader is Devadatta, and the master archer is myself."

(6) Not long after Devadatta left the order, the World-Honored One said to his disciples, "Disciples, I once used the example of a tree and its essence. We enter the way of the mendicant in order to extinguish our sufferings of birth, old age, death, anxiety, sorrow, pain, and misery. There are some people who, having acquired offerings, veneration, and renown, become full of pride, and they seek praise for themselves and abuse for others. They are wrongly pursuing the pious practice, just as one grasps a branch of a tree and believes that he has attained the essence of the tree. They, due to negligence, plunge into suffering.

"We observe precepts. There are, however, some who seek praise for themselves and abuse for others. They are wrongly pursuing the pious practice, just as one grasps the bark of the tree and believes that he has attained the essence of the tree. They, due to negligence, plunge into suffering.

"We engage in steadfast meditation. There are some people who seek praise for themselves and abuse for others. They are wrongly pursuing the pious practice, just as one takes hold of the inner covering of the bark and believes he has attained the essence of the tree. They, due to negligence, plunge into suffering.

"We develop wisdom. Some, however, are ignorant and their minds become filled with pride. They seek praise for themselves and abuse for others. They are wrongly pursuing the pious practice, just as one cuts out a piece of the tree's flesh and believes that he has attained the essence of the tree. They, due to negligence, plunge into suffering.

"Not losing one's composure over the offerings, veneration, and fame that may come to oneself; not being intoxicated by precepts that one observes; not being deluded by one's steadfast meditation; not feeling proud over one's wisdom; not becoming negligent; attaining emancipation by pursuing the pious practice: this is what is meant by seeking after the essence of the tree. There is no falling back from this emancipation. Disciples, offerings, veneration, and renown are not the goals of pure practices. Observing precepts is also not the goal of pure practices; steadfast meditation is not the aim of pure practices; wisdom is not the aim of pure practices. Emancipation is the aim of pure practices. This is the essence and the end of pure practices."

(7) Around this time, the son of King Bimbisara, prince Abhayarajakumara, once visited Nigantha, who urged him, "Prince, defeat Gotama in argument; your renown will spread and reverberate throughout the land." The prince said, "Venerable One, how can someone such as I defeat Gotama in argument? He possesses awesome powers."

Nigantha said, "Prince, go to the place where Gotama dwells and ask, 'Does the Buddha address others with disagreeable words?' Should he acknowledge that he does, you would do well to attack him with the argument, 'In that case what difference is there between the Buddha and the ordinary man?' On the other hand, if the Buddha maintains that he does not use disagreeable words, then chastise him with the questions, 'Why did the Buddha speak words that angered Devadatta? Why did the Buddha say that Devadatta would sink into hell for aeons and that he was beyond salvation?' Prince, Gotama will be caught between these two prongs and will not be able to move."

The prince listened to Nigantha and went to the place of the World-Honored One. Planning for the most favorable moment, the prince perceived that it would be better to delay the meeting one day. Thereupon, he invited the World-Honored One and three of his disciples to a meal at his house for the following day. The next day the World-Honored One went to the prince's house. After the meal was over, the prince, taking a lower seat for himself, faced the World-Honored One. He asked, "Does the World-Honored One address others with disagreeable words?" The Buddha answered, "Prince, I cannot give you an unqualified answer." The prince said, "World-Honored One, with that answer, Nigantha has been defeated." The Buddha said, "Prince, why is that so?" The prince said, "World-Honored One, my question was in truth suggested to me by Nigantha Nataputta. The question was posed for the sake of defeating the World-Honored One in argument." The prince then confessed in detail the plot that was formed the day before.

(8) As he was talking, the prince Abhayarajakumara carried his infant child on his lap. The World-Honored One said, "Prince, if, due to your laxness or the wet nurse's carelessness, this infant put a splinter of wood or a shard of broken pottery into its mouth, what would you do?" The prince answered, "Naturally

I should take it out. If I did not succeed the first time, I should hold its head down with the left hand while bending the finger of the right hand and inserting it into its mouth. Even though the mouth might bleed, I should remove it. I should do so because this child is dear to me."

The Buddha said, "Prince, that is so. I do not address others with words that are disagreeable, untrue, and unbeneficial. Even though what I might say be true, if it does not benefit others, I do not speak disagreeable words. If something is true and is of benefit, a Buddha looks for a propitious moment and may address someone with disagreeable words. I do so because I cherish and have compassion for all people."

The prince said, "World-Honored One, wise men of all classes—kshatriyas, brahmins, laymen, monks and so forth—prepare their questions beforehand and bring them to you. Does the World-Honored One anticipate questions and prepare his answers beforehand, or does he answer all questions spontaneously, on the spur of the moment?"

The Buddha said, "Prince, I believe you have thorough knowledge of the details regarding carriages. When you are asked about some matter regarding carriages, do you have an answer readied beforehand?" The prince replied, "World-Honored One, I have thorough knowledge of matters regarding carriages; therefore, no matter what the question, I am able to respond immediately, without any preparation." The Buddha said, "Prince, that is so. The Buddha has thorough knowledge of the Dharma world and therefore no matter what question it is I am able to answer immediately, without preparation."

Prince Abhayarajakumara was gladdened by the teaching of the World-Honored One and he vowed to become the Buddha's follower for the remainder of his life.

2. Ajatasatru's Usurpation of the Throne

(1) Devadatta's order suffered the loss of five hundred disciples; he was dealt a blow from which they could scarcely recover. His only hope lay in Prince Ajatasatru. One day Devadatta visited the prince and said, "Prince, your father the king gives every appearance of forever remaining on the throne. While he is alive, you cannot ascend the throne. Even though you do ascend the throne after your father the king passes on, your enjoyment of the throne will be brief. Therefore at the earliest possible moment you must replace your father and succeed to the throne. I shall on my part destroy Gotama and assume the role of the King of the Dharma. Would it not be delightful for the newly crowned king and the new Buddha to stand side by side reigning over the country of Magadha?"

The prince replied, "The debt of gratitude that I owe to my father and mother is greater than the moon and the sun. I shall never be able to repay their long years of rearing me to adulthood. Why then do you provoke me to commit such a treacherous deed?" Devadatta, however, skillfully wove his words and seduced the prince's mind; and in the end Ajatasatru agreed do to Devadatta's bidding.

The manner of Ajatasatru's birth was this. When King Bimbisara was already past his middle years, his consort Vaidehi found herself with child. She was addicted with a strange malady that made her thirst for blood from the king's shoulders, though she did not act on her desire at first. But each day she became increasingly emaciated. The king asked her why this was occurring, and upon learning the cause he squeezed blood from his shoulder and had her drink it. A seer prophesied, "The child that is born will regard his father the king as his enemy." Because of this dark prophecy, she attempted to abort the fetus a number of times. But the king succeeded in restraining her, and finally she gave birth to a son. Because the sage predicted even before the child's birth that the child would become his father's enemy, he was named Ajatasatru, which meant Unborn Enemy. Devadatta recounted this in detail and succeeded in leading Ajatasatru astray.

One day, with great stealth, the prince with a sharp sword strapped to his side moved toward the gate of the king's palace. However, the treacherous intention that he harbored within caused his whole body to shudder, and unexpectedly he collapsed on the ground. The sentries who guarded the gates noticed the prince's shattered and abnormal appearance and asked the prince why he was in such straits. The prince confessed, "Provoked by Devadatta, I planned to kill my father the king." The officials became alarmed and reported this to the great king and waited for his instructions. The king could not bear to put the prince his sole heir to death. Acceding to the prince's wishes, the king abdicated his throne in favor of the prince. The prince, however, provoked once again by Devadatta, seized his father the king, imprisoned him in the royal palace, and denied him food.

(2) The king's consort Vaidehi bathed and purified her body. She mixed honey with the flour of roasted barley and smeared it on her body. When she entered the room in which the great king had been imprisoned, she noticed that his face was haggard and his flesh had wasted away. He had become emaciated in a most pitiful way. His consort shed tears and said, "Truly, as expounded by the World-Honored One, prosperity is an ephemeral thing; the fruits of our evil deeds assault us now." The great king said, "I have been denied food, and the long starvation is excruciatingly painful, as if several hundred insects were churning in my stomach. Most of my blood and flesh have wasted away, and I am about to die." The king nearly lost consciousness and he sobbed. When his consort offered him the mixture of honey and flour of roasted barley that she had smeared on her body, the king devoured it.

After he finished, with tears in his eyes, he turned toward the place where the Buddha dwelt and prostrating himself said, "As the World-Honored One has proclaimed, the glories of this world are ephemeral and are difficult to preserve; they are like dreams and phantoms." He then turned toward his consort and said, "When I sat on the throne, the country was vast, clothing and food were plentiful, and there was not one thing that was lacking. Now confined in jail, I am about to die of starvation. My son has been misled by an evil teacher and he turns his back on the teaching of the World-Honored One. I do not fear death; I only regret not being able to receive the Buddha's teaching and not being able to discuss the path with such disciples as Sariputra, Maudgalyayana,

Maha-Kasyapa and others. Truly, as the World-Honored One teaches, the love of human beings is as flighty as a flock of birds that nest overnight on treetops and then go their separate ways to receive their karmically fixed fortune or misfortune.

"The honored Maudgalyayana has destroyed the defilements of the mind and attained supernatural powers, and yet he was struck once by a brahmin who had grown envious of him. It is all the more fitting, then, that I, with my mind filled with defilements, should suffer such grief as this. Misfortune chases after people as closely as a shadow hunting for its body, or like an echo answering its voice. It is hard to meet the Buddha, and it is hard to hear his teaching. Again, it is hard to spread compassion and to govern sentient beings according to the teaching. I shall now end my life and travel to some faraway place. Among those who believe in the teaching of the World-Honored One, there are none who fail to serve it. You, too, my consort, must with reverence guard the teaching; you, too, must put up a barricade against the misfortunes that are sure to come." The consort listened to the king's exhortation and burst into tears.

(3) The king put his palms together and reverentially turned toward the Vulture Peak and bowed to the Buddha. He then said, "Honored Maudgalyayana, my good friend, with compassion please show me the way that must be taken by a layman."

Then Maudgalyayana sped toward the king like a falcon on the wing, and every day he expounded the path of the layman. Moreover, the World-Honored One dispatched Purna and had him expound the Dharma for the king's sake. In this way, the king, for a period of twenty-one days, ate the mixture of roasted barley flour and honey and was able to hear the Dharma. His countenance, therefore, was serene and his complexion was flushed with joy.

3. Vaidehi

(1) Ajatasatru asked the sentries guarding the gates, "Is my father the king still alive?" They said, "The king's consort smears honey mixed with roasted barley flour on her body. She then fills her jewelled crown with juices and offers it to the king. The Buddha's disciples such as Maudgalyayana and Purna and others come swooping down from the sky to expound the Dharma for the sake of the king. We have not been able to prevent this."

Ajatasatru heard this account and was angry. He said, "Even though she is my mother, if she consorts with those who violate the laws of the country, she must also be considered an enemy of the state. Moreover, how dare these evil monks with their magical powers keep this evil king alive!" Then he drew his sword and attempted to kill Vaidehi the consort of the king. At that moment the minister Candraprabha together with the physician Jivaka bowed down to the king and said, "From the Vedas we learn that since the creation of heaven and earth, there have been eighteen thousand evil kings who slew their fathers in order to usurp the throne. But there is none so vicious that he slew his own mother. If you commit this foul deed you will bring disgrace upon the kshatriya caste. We cannot bear such a deed, for anyone who performs such an act is an outcaste. We cannot stay here any longer." The two men, with their hands on the hilts of their swords, spoke these words as they slowly inched their way backwards. Ajatasatru was stunned and terrified; he said to Jivaka, "Are you not going to help me?" Jivaka said, "Do not kill your mother." The king repented his erroneous ways and sought their help; he threw away his sword and ordered the palace officials to confine his mother to the private palace.

(2) Vaidehi, the consort of the king, imprisoned by her own son and wasting away with grief, bowed down in the direction of the World-Honored One, who remained afar on Vulture Peak. She said, "The World-Honored One once before dispatched the Venerable Maudgalyayana and the Venerable Sariputra in order to comfort me. Right now I am drowning in sorrow. The World-Honored One is of great stature and I am unworthy of meeting with you. Please let me instead meet with the two venerable ones Maudgalyayana and Ananda."

Her tears poured down like rain, and Vaidehi bowed low to the World-Honored One, who was far away. But the World-Honored One perceived Vaidehi's mind; striding across the sky, he descended to the royal palace. When the king's consort raised her head and saw him, the World-Honored One's body shone with a golden glow. On his left side, Maudgalyayana served as his attendant, while on his right side, Ananda performed the same duty. The gods hovered in the sky and sprinkled heavenly flowers. The king's consort, of her own accord, tore away her necklace and threw herself onto the great earth. Bursting into tears, she said to the World-Honored One, "World-Honored One, what evil deeds did I commit that I must bear the fruit of giving birth to such an evil child as this, and by what conditions did the World-Honored One become a relative of Devadatta? World-Honored One, for my sake, please show me the path that is free of sorrow; I have grown weary of this wretched, evil world. This world is an assembly of unhappy beings such as hell beings, hungry ghosts, and animals. From now on, I do not wish to hear unhappy voices nor see unhappy beings. I now face the World-Honored One and prostrate myself on the great earth. I beg for your pity as I drown in tears of contrition. I beg of you, World-Honored One who dwell amidst the world's light, please let me gaze upon a pure land."

(3) At that moment, the World-Honored One emitted light from the center of his forehead. That light was of a golden color; it shone upon the innumerable lands of the ten directions. The light then returned to the top of his head and there it glittered as a golden tower. Myriad pure lands of the buddhas manifested themselves in that tower. One was built of seven different gems. Another was resplendent with lotuses. Still another glittered brilliantly like a mirror made of crystal. After the king's consort had gazed upon this sight, she said to the World-Honored One, "World-Honored One, all of these worlds are filled with pure light; however, what I aspire for is to be born at the place of Amitayus Buddha who dwells in the land of Sukhavati. I beseech you to show me how to meditate. I beseech you to show me how to receive the teaching properly."

At that time, the World-Honored One smiled, and a light of five different hues shot forth; that light shone on the head of King Bimbisara. Although the king was imprisoned, his mind's eye saw the World-Honored One at a distance, and nothing blocked his view. He reverently bowed; the bonds of delusion of themselves came loose, and the king attained enlightenment.

The World-Honored One said to Vaidehi, the king's consort, "Are you not aware that Amitayus Buddha does not dwell far from this place? You ought to think upon Amitayus Buddha's land of Sukhavati, which was created by virtuous deeds. If you wish to be born in his country, you must perform three kinds of virtuous deeds. First, you must dutifully attend your parents, serve your teacher faithfully, and be compassionate and refrain from committing the ten grave offences of murder, theft, sexual misconduct, false speech, slander, harsh speech, frivolous talk, covetousness, ill-will, and false views. Second, you must take refuge in the Buddha, the Dharma, and the Sangha, observe all the precepts, and uphold your dignity. Third, you must aspire to seek enlightenment, profoundly believe in the principle of cause and effect, read the sutras, and expound their teachings to others. Vaidehi, these three are the virtuous deeds that lead to birth in the Pure Land. The buddhas of the past, present, and future all attained enlightenment on account of these three deeds that functioned as the true cause of their attainment."

(4) The World-Honored One said to Ananda and to Vaidehi, "You will do well to listen carefully and contemplate profoundly. For the sake of those who have been harmed by passions, both in this world and in the worlds to come, I shall expound the pious practice. It is truly marvelous that the king's consort has brought forth questions on this matter. Ananda, you must commit the Buddha's words to memory and expound them for the sake of all sentient beings everywhere. To the king's consort and to all sentient beings of later worlds, I shall now reveal the world of Sukhavati in the western quarter. With a Buddha's power, I shall show that Pure Land as clearly as one's face shows in a bright mirror. When they gaze upon the wondrous bliss of that land, they will rejoice and immediately acquire the insight into the non-origination of all existence."

The World-Honored One said to Vaidehi, "Your mind is both feeble and defective. Because you have not yet acquired the divine eye, you are unable to see afar. However, the Buddha possesses wondrous skillful means; therefore, now I shall enable you to see afar."

Vaidehi said, "World-Honored One, by the power of the Buddha, I gaze upon yon Amitayus' land called Sukhavati. However, in the worlds to come, in which the Buddha's light will have been lost, in which all will have been muddied by evil, in which people will suffer over old age and illness, fear death, and grieve over separation from loved ones, how will sentient beings be able to see the buddhas' lands?"

The World-Honored One said, "Listen carefully and contemplate well; for your sake, I shall now expound the Dharma that puts an end to suffering. You should uphold this Dharma and teach it to all sentient beings." At that time, Amitayus Buddha appeared in the sky; the two Bodhisattvas Avalokitesvara and Mahasthamaprapta stood on his right and left sides. The brilliance of his light far exceeded the light of gold. The king's consort said, "World-Honored One, by the Buddha's power, I am now able to behold Amitayus Buddha and his two attendant Bodhisattvas. How will sentient beings living in the worlds to come be able to do the same?"

(5) The World-Honored One said, "First of all, contemplate the physical form of Amitayus Buddha. That body shines forth with the brilliance of an immeasurable amount of gold. The height of his body is as many yojanas as all the sands of the river Ganges. His eyes are clear; even the waters of the great ocean cannot match them. His body possesses eighty-four thousand marvellous features. Each marvellous feature possesses eighty-four thousand lights. Each light shines everywhere upon every land of the ten directions. The Buddha sees those who contemplate him; and he takes them in and never forsakes them.

"By seeing the body of this Buddha, one sees the mind of the Buddha. The mind of the Buddha is none other than his great compassion. By virtue of myriad conditions, he saves all sentient beings. Therefore contemplate the Buddha; the Buddha's light fills the whole universe, and therefore it also fills the minds of all sentient beings. Therefore when one contemplates the Buddha, one's mind is a Buddha endowed with the marvellous features of perfection. One's mind becomes a Buddha; one's mind is, as it is, the Buddha. The ocean of true wisdom that spreads to all corners is born of the mind. Therefore, people, make your minds one with the Buddha, and with clarity contemplate Amitayus Buddha.

"Moreover, Amitayus Buddha possesses innumerable manifested bodies. Together with the two Bodhisattvas Avalokitesvara and Mahasthamaprapta, he appears before those who contemplate the Buddha. The essence of Amitayus Buddha's body fills the universe and is boundless. The ordinary person is unable to conceive of such a body. However, there are those who, by virtue of the Bodhisattva's original vow, are able to contemplate his body; they, without fail, are able to bow down to his body. Even the contemplation of his manifested bodies results in countless blessings; this is even more true when one contemplates the essence of the Buddha in full possession of all of his wondrous features. Furthermore, using his divine power, the Buddha at one time fills the vast skies with his expansive body; at another time, he manifests himself in the form of a diminished body, twenty feet tall. In the lands of the ten directions, he manifests at will incomprehensible power."

(6) The World-Honored One said to Ananda and to Vaidehi, "Among those who are born in Amitayus Buddha's land, there are nine grades of people. If those who belong to the highest grade within the highest grade rouse the three minds, they will immediately be born in the Buddha's land. The three minds are as follows: first, a sincere mind; second, a mind of deep faith; third, a mind that aspires to birth in the Buddha's land. Those who are endowed with these three minds will be born, without fail, in that land. Again, those who have the following three characteristics will also be born there: first, with deep compassion, one does not take the life of other beings, and one observes the precepts; second, one reads the sutras expounded by the Buddha; third, one contemplates the Buddha, the Dharma, and the Sangha. One contemplates the precepts, selfless giving, and the supreme reward. Endowed with these merits, if one undertakes

these practices, without fail one is able to be born in Amitayus' land. Such a person exerts himself with great energy, and therefore Amitayus Buddha, together with Avalokitesvara and Mahasthamaprapta and numerous attendants, sends forth a great light and shines upon this person's body. The Buddha extends his hand and welcomes him. Innumerable bodhisattvas sing his praise and uphold his mind. This man is uplifted with joy, and immediately he is born in that land and gazes upon the Buddha. He hears the Dharma that spontaneously comes forth from a forest of glittering gems and is enlightened to the reality of things. For a period, he travels to the buddhas of the ten directions in order to serve them. He listens to how one is enlightened, and upon returning home, he becomes the master of an infinite variety of teachings.

"Those who are of the middle grade within the highest grade have not necessarily gained mastery of the sutras; however, they have grasped the essence. Even when they face profound principles of absolute truth, their minds are not bewildered. They believe profoundly in the principle of cause and effect, and they never malign the Buddha's teaching. Should they transfer these merits and aspire to be born in the Sukhavati of Amitayus Buddha, when their lives draw to a close, Amitayus Buddha, accompanied by the two Bodhisattvas Avalokitesvara and Mahasthamaprapta and numerous other attendants, will manifest himself. The Buddha will have these attendants sit on a dais of gold and copper alloy and, in the instant of one moment of thought he will have the people attain birth in his land. Those who are born there will listen to the voices of all things as being the sound of the principle of absolute truth. After seven days have passed, they will attain the status of beings who never regress from a Buddha's enlightenment. Immediately, they go from buddha to buddha in order to serve them. They concentrate their thoughts on the places where the buddhas dwell, and awakening to truth they receive the prediction of the day in which they will attain enlightenment.

"Those who belong to the lowest grade of the highest grade understand the principle of cause and effect. They do not malign the Buddha's teaching, and they earnestly aspire to attain enlightenment. Should they turn their merits over and aspire to be born in that land, when their life draws to a close, Amitayus Buddha, accompanied by the two Bodhisattvas Avalokitesvara and Mahasthamaprapta and numerous other attendants, will come forth to greet them. The Buddha will have them sit on golden lotuses and cause them to be born in his land. After seven days, they will see the Buddha vaguely. After three seven-day periods, they will see the Buddha with clarity. They will be allowed to hear the expounding of all teachings by every conceivable voice. Moreover, they will go to the buddhas of the ten directions in order to serve them and hear all the teachings. They will rejoice at the inexhaustibility of the teachings.

(7) "Next, those of the highest grade within the middle grade observe the five precepts that forbid murder, theft, sexual misconduct, false speech, and the use of intoxicating drinks. Should they not commit the five grave offences or other sundry offences, and should they turn over their merits and aspire to be born in his land, when their lives draw to a close, Amitayus Buddha, together

with a host of attendants, will emit a light of golden color and come forth to greet them. When Amitayus Buddha expounds that the world is suffering and empty, that it is transient and egoless, their minds will be filled with joy and enveloped in glittering lotuses; they will be born in his land. When those flowers unfold, all voices will expound the Dharma of the Four Noble Truths. Immediately they will enter the enlightenment of the Self-enlightened and will be transformed into beings who freely manifest divine powers.

"Those of the middle grade within the middle grade observe a diversity of precepts, but only over a period of one day and one night. They, however, uphold their dignity; and should they, by virtue of their merits, aspire to be born in his land, their bodies will be redolent with the fragrance of the precepts. When their lives draw to a close, Amitayus Buddha, together with a host of attendants, will emit a light of golden color; he will come forth to greet them. Enveloped in jewelled lotuses, they will be immediately born in his land. When those flowers unfold after a period of seven days, they will place their hands together and praise the Buddha. They will hear the Dharma and be filled with joy; and in the end, they will attain enlightenment.

"Those of the lowest grade within the middle grade devote themselves to acts of filial piety; they offer compassion to all sentient beings. When their lives draw to a close, with the help of good friends, they will hear of the bliss of Amitayus Buddha's land and of the essence of the Buddha's original vow. Immediately, they will be born in his land; after seven days, they will be met by the two Bodhisattvas Avalokitesvara and Mahasthamaprapta; they will hear the Dharma and rejoice; and in the end, they will attain enlightenment.

(8) "Those of the highest grade of the lowest grade do not malign the Buddha's teaching; but because they are ignorant, they commit a host of evil deeds, and yet they are never contrite. When their lives draw to a close, with the help of good friends, they utter the names of sutras of the Great Vehicle and thereby destroy grave offences. Furthermore, because of the teaching imparted to them by those good friends, they place their hands together and utter 'Namo Amitayus Buddha.' By uttering the name of the Buddha, they destroy the evil deeds that bind them to transmigration. They are greeted by the buddhas and bodhisattvas in manifested bodies that have been dispatched by Amitayus Buddha. They gaze upon the light that abounds brilliantly in the room, and their minds rejoice. After their lives draw to an end, they are born in his land. After seven periods of seven days pass by, they hear the teachings of the two Bodhisattvas Avalokitesvara and Mahasthamaprapta and arouse the mind of faith. In the end, they become masters of the Dharma and enter the stage of abundant joy.

"Those of the middle grade of the lowest grade, because of their ignorance, violate a diversity of precepts. They steal such objects as articles and offerings that belong to the Sangha. They expound the Dharma for their own profit and fame and are never contrite. When their lives draw to an end, they tremble before the raging fires of hell that presses upon them from eight different directions. At this moment, if they, on account of the compassion of their good friends, hear the praises of Amitayus Buddha's great power, merit, and light, and if they believe in them, the grave evils that bind them to endless transmigration are destroyed. The raging fires are transformed into cool breezes; greeted by buddhas and bodhisattvas in manifested bodies, in one moment of thought they are born in his land, and after a long period of time they hear the Dharma and arouse a mind conducive to enlightenment.

"Those of the lowest grade within the lowest grade, because of their ignorance, commit a multitude of evils such as the five grave offences and the ten evil deeds. Dragged along by their evil acts, they are bound to endure inexhaustible sufferings in unhappy destinies. When their lives draw to an end, good friends appear and with kindness say, 'If you are burdened by suffering and are unable to contemplate the Buddha, simply utter 'Namo Amitayus Buddha.' These people encourage them to utter the name; with each utterance, evils that lead them into endless transmigration are destroyed. In one moment of thought, they are born into the land of Sukhavati; after several aeons, they hear the teaching and arouse the mind conducive to enlightenment."

When the World-Honored One had finished expounding this, the consort Vaidehi and a host of ladies-in-waiting all saw the world of Sukhavati, Amitayus Buddha, and his two attendant Bodhisattvas. Their minds overflowed with joy; great enlightenment unfolded spontaneously; and they were able to see the world as it was. The World-Honored One then predicted the day on which they would attain enlightenment.

(9) The World-Honored One said, "If a person hears the name of Amitayus Buddha, evils that lead to endless transmigration are destroyed. Should they contemplate his name, all the more so will this be true. Truly, those who contemplate the Buddha are lotuses among evil people. The two Bodhisattvas Avalokitesvara and Mahasthamaprapta become their friends; they never deviate from the path, and in the end they will be born in Sukhavati." He then said to Ananda, "Uphold these words. To uphold these words means to uphold the name of Amitayus Buddha."

After expounding the Dharma, the World-Honored One returned to the Vulture Peak; Ananda, for the sake of sentient beings, travelled everywhere expounding this teaching. Because of his efforts, those who heard this teaching placed their trust in the Dharma and rejoiced.

4. The Agony of Ajatasatru

(1) Meanwhile, Devadatta asked King Ajatasatru for some soldiers. First, Devadatta dispatched two soldiers; he ordered them to kill the World-Honored One and return using an alternate route. Then he dispatched four men to lie in ambush along the return route used by these two men in order to kill them. Next he dispatched eight men to kill the four men who had gone forth before them. He continued to double the number of men until he dispatched sixty-four men to kill the thirty-two men who had gone before them. In this way Devadatta schemed to hide from the world the number of men involved in the killing of the World-Honored One out of hatred.

At this time, the World-Honored One emerged from a cave on Vulture Peak and was strolling along the mountain paths. The two soldiers put on armor, took out their swords, and attempted to draw closer to the World-Honored One. However, they were awe-struck by his spiritual power and were unable to move forward. When, startled, they gazed up at the face of the World-Honored One, the serenity of his visage appeared to be like that of a huge tame elephant; and his mind appeared to be like limpid water. Unexpectedly, the two men were struck by feelings of veneration. Casting aside their swords, they came before the Buddha, and having heard him expound various teachings, they opened their Dharma eyes. In contrast to their former selves, they sought refuge in the Three Treasures. Before long, taking an alternate route, they travelled to where Devadatta was staying. They conveyed to him the spiritual power of the World-Honored One and said that they could not harm the Buddha. In this way Devadatta's plot was all for naught.

In a rage, Devadatta climbed up to the Vulture peak, and picking up a huge rock he hurled it down from the mountain top, aiming it at the World-Honored One who was strolling near the cave. A piece from that rock grazed the World-Honored One's feet; it tore his skin and flesh and his blood spilled onto the ground. The World-Honored One, however, slowly went back into the cave, folded his robes into four, lay on his side atop his robes and bore the pain with single-minded patience. For the sake of a multitude of disciples who were in an uproar, the Buddha emerged from the cave and said, "Monks must not shout like fishermen. You must each return to your places, and concentrating your minds you must practice the path. The myriad buddhas have all been victorious over every form of hatred. Regardless of the enemy, any universal monarch is never injured; in the same way, no matter who the enemy is, the Buddha is never injured." As time passed, the Buddha's wound did not easily heal; therefore the physician Jivaka lanced the wound and drew out the infected blood.

(2) Then Devadatta asked King Ajatasatru for an elephant; he plotted to set the huge elephant loose on the World-Honored One in order to kill him. He said to the elephant driver, "Tomorrow, on the road on which Gautama will travel to come here, intoxicate the elephant and set him loose. Gautama has a proud mind, so it is unlikely that he will shy away. In which case he will, without fail, be trampled to death." The next morning the World-Honored One put on his robes, and taking up his begging bowl he entered the city and made his rounds, begging for food. The elephant driver spied this from a distance and set loose the drunken elephant. Sentient beings begged the World-Honored One to travel by an alternate route, but he continued slowly along that same road.

The drunken elephant saw the World-Honored One in the distance and flapping his ears and making trumpeting sounds with his trunk he charged. However, the World-Honored One immersed his mind in compassion and sang this verse:

> Do not harm the great Naga.
> It is difficult for the great Naga to appear in the world.
> Should you harm the great Naga, in the worlds to come,
> You will plunge into the unhappy destinies.

Awe-struck by the power of the Buddha's Great Compassion, the elephant dropped to his knees, took hold of the World-Honored One's legs, withdrew, and departed. All those who saw this sang the praise of the World-Honored One.

(3) Ever since his consort was imprisoned, King Bimbisara was denied all food. Peering through his window, he gazed upon the verdant green Vulture Peak; this provided some consolation for his mind. However, when Ajatasatru heard of this, he blocked up the window and slashed the soles of the king's feet, so that the king could not stand. Around that time, Ajatasatru's child Udaya was suffering from a boil on the tip of his finger. Therefore Ajatasatru, while hugging his child to his bosom, sucked away the pus. Vaidehi, the king's consort, who was sitting nearby, observed this and said, "King, when you were small, you suffered from an identical boil. Your father, the great king, just as you did, sucked away its pus." When Ajatasatru heard this, his anger toward his father the king suddenly changed into thoughts of love. He said to his ministers, "If there is someone who will report that my father the king is alive, I shall grant him half of this country." People rushed to the place where his father the king was being held. But the king, hearing the clamorous footsteps, became terrified and thought, "They are going to inflict severe punishment on me." In agony, he collapsed onto the bed and breathed his last breath.

(4) Blinded by worldly pleasures, Ajatasatru, who thus caused the death of his innocent father the king, was now beset with contrition. His body suffered from high temperature; his whole body was covered with boils. The boils oozed with pus and were so foul smelling that it was hard to come near him. He pondered, "Now, in this world, I receive something like the fruits of hell. Before long, I shall receive the fruits of the actual hell." His mother Vaidehi was struck with grief and smeared various medicines on his body, but the boils would not heal. King Ajatasatru said to his mother, "These boils grow out of the mind and not from the body. They cannot be healed by human power."

Hearing of Ajatasatru's illness, his ministers one by one visited his sickbed. The minister Candraprabha said, "Why does the great king appear so drawn? Are you steeped in grief? Are you in physical pain? Or do you suffer from mental anguish?" The king replied, "How can my body and mind, which despicably caused the death of my innocent father the king, escape without suffering? I heard once from a wise man that those who commit in this world the five grave offences of killing one's parents and so forth cannot escape hell. Now I bear the weight of infinite evils. In this world, there are no physicians who possess the skill to heal my body and mind." The minister said, "There is a verse that says,

> If you suffer from grief, the grief becomes more intense.
> When sleep deepens, when one lusts for things, when one relishes liquors,
> It is the same; anxiety only increases one's anxiety and is of no use.

"Great king, you say that if you commit the five grave offences you will plunge into hell. However, who actually saw hell to make such a claim? Generally, hell means this world. You say that in this world there are no skilled physicians. However, there is a man named Purnakasyapa. That man is known for his superior wisdom and meditation; he disciplines himself in the holy life and he expounds the path of enlightenment to countless people. He teaches that in this world there is no such thing as an evil deed or the fruit of an evil deed, that there is no such thing as a good deed or the fruit of a good deed. He also affirms that there is neither a good nor an evil deed. Great king, this teacher now resides in Rajagriha. I beg of you, under this teacher's care, heal the pain of your body and mind." The king said, "If he is able to heal my suffering as you say, I shall entrust myself to that man."

(5) Furthermore, the minister Gunagarbha visited him and said, "Great king, why have your cheeks become so sunken and hollow, your lips so parched, and your voice so hoarse? Why is your complexion so wretched, like that of a man who is afraid of the world or like that of a man who has been attacked by his enemies?" The king said, "How could I now not suffer in both mind and body? In ignorance, I caused the death of the legitimate king. Once I heard, 'If one with an unvirtuous mind commits evil deeds against father or mother, or the Buddha or his disciples, one will not be able to escape the Avici hell.' My mind trembles in fear of hell."

The ministers said, "Great king, your fear is unworthy. In this world there are two dharmas—the dharma of monks and the dharma of kings. Speaking from the view of the king's dharma, killing one's father and becoming king is not an evil deed. An embryo tears open its mother's stomach and is born; however, this is the dharma of nature and is not an evil deed. The dharma of ruling lands is like this; killing your father or older brother cannot be regarded as an evil deed. When speaking of the dharma of a mendicant, even taking the life of a mosquito or an ant becomes an evil deed. But for you it is not worth grieving over. There is a teacher called Maskarin Gosaliputra; he is endowed with omniscience and pities all people as if they were his own children. He skill-fully uproots the causes of the sufferings in people's minds. According to the teachings of this teacher, a man's body is divided into the seven elements of earth, water, fire, wind, suffering, pleasure, and life. These seven do not change or evolve. There is no creation in the world. Like reeds, they cannot be destroyed, and like Mount Sumeru, they are immovable. Like milk, they cannot be got rid of. The seven elements are never at war with each other. Neither pain nor pleasure, neither good nor evil, nor the power of the sword, can harm these seven elements. The reason is that these seven, like the sky, are free of all obstructions. One's life also cannot be harmed. The reason for this is that both the one who harms and the one who is harmed, both the creator and the created, both the one who expounds and the one who hears, both the one who meditates and the one who upholds the teaching are nonexistent. Great king, that teacher consistently expounds his dharma in this manner and destroys a host of grave offences borne by sentient beings. If the great king should go to the place of this teacher, all evils of themselves will fade and disappear." The king answered, "If he is able to heal my suffering as you say, I shall entrust myself to that teacher."

(6) Another minister, Satyaguna, said, "Great king, why do you take off your crown and shake your tresses and, like a flowering tree blown about by winds, tremble with anxiety and fear?" The king replied as before. The minister said,

"Great king, if your father the king, were a mendicant, then harming him would be a grave offence. However, because you caused his death for the sake of ruling the country, it is not an evil deed. Great king, I beg you to quiet your mind and listen. People receive the fruits of birth and death because of excessive deeds. The previous king was slain because of his own excessive deeds; therefore, no misfortune at all will befall the great king. Right now, a teacher named Sanjaya Vairattiputra, with ocean-like wisdom, is cutting off the doubts held by people. According to what this teacher expounds, among myriad sentient beings, a king of the people is allowed to do whatever he wishes. No matter what wrong he commits, it does not become a grave offence. Just like the fire that consumes both pure and foul things without discrimination, or like the great earth that harbors neither joy nor anger toward pure and foul things, so are the deeds of a king among people. Furthermore, if a tree that has been cut down in the fall sprouts forth buds when spring arrives, the cutting of the tree cannot be regarded as a grave offence. A human being's life is like that of a tree. One is born here and reborn there. How can there be evil in the form of killing in relation to someone who is reborn? A man's fortune and misfortune do not depend on his actions in this world. He simply receives in the present the fruits of past actions. In the present there is no cause, and in the future there is no fruit that is effect. Great king, it is my fervent wish that you should go to the place of this teacher and be healed of your illness in both mind and body." The king replied to the minister, "If the teacher is able to heal my suffering as you say, I shall entrust myself to that teacher."

(7) Another minister, Sarvasthanu, came and said, "Great king, why have you become such a wretched figure? Is it due to the suffering of the body or the mind?" When the king answered as before, the minister said, "Great king, let go of your grief. Long ago the king Rama killed his father and usurped the throne; again, the great king Bhadrika, the king Virudhaka, and a multitude of other kings killed their fathers and succeeded to the throne. And yet not one fell into hell. The king Virudhaka, the king Udaya and others also killed their fathers and ascended to the throne but not one agonized over the deed. Although people speak of hell, celestial worlds and so forth, no one has actually seen these places. There are only two destinies, the destiny of human beings and the destiny of animals. These two were not created from causes and conditions. If there are no causes and conditions, then there is no need to have such notions as good and evil. Now there is a teacher named Ajita Kesakambala. Endowed with the highest wisdom, he views gold and dirt as being equal; he bestows the same friendly mind on both the man who cuts off his right elbow and the man who rubs sandalwood on his left elbow. This teacher is indeed the world's most skilled physician. Whether standing or lying down, he is steeped in meditation. He tells his disciples that whether you act on your own accord or cause others to act, there is no evil in these deeds. It does not matter whether you perform great deeds of selfless giving south of the Ganges or take the lives of people north of the Ganges. You shall neither be rewarded with good fortune nor invite evil fruits. This teacher now resides in Rajagriha. I beg you to go to this teacher and

receive his teaching." The king replied to the minister, "If this teacher is able to heal my suffering as you say, I shall entrust myself to him."

(8) The minister Sriguna said, "Great king, why does your face lack luster and why are you like a ruler who has lost his country? Right now along all four borders of this country there is no fear of enemies. Why are you immersed in grief? Most princes ponder when they will be able to ascend the throne and wield their powers freely. And yet for you that aspiration has been already fulfilled. You reign over this large country of Magadha, and moreover the treasures left by the former king fill the treasury. You ought to immerse yourself freely in pleasures. Why do you choose to suffer within?" After listening to the king's reply, he continued, "Who spoke of hell and deceived the great king? Water is wet; rock is hard. Wind moves; fire is hot. All things of themselves are born and of themselves they perish. It is no one's doing. 'Hell' is a word made up by wise men. It connotes both earth and destruction; that is, if you were to destroy hell, there would be no such things as the fruits of offence. Again, hell connotes both man and god. It means that one harms living beings and reaches the celestial world. Therefore the hermit Vasu killed sheep and gained the pleasures of the gods. Hell connotes both life and longevity. It means that if one takes the lives of living beings, one gains longevity. Therefore in actuality there is no such thing as hell. Great king, from the seed of wheat one gains wheat. From the seed of rice, one gains rice. If you kill hell, you will gain hell; if you kill human beings, you will gain human beings. Great king, I shall now validate the act of killing. If a human being possesses a self, since the self never changes, one cannot kill it. The self is indestructible and cannot be held in bondage. It feels neither anger nor joy, like the sky. How then can there be such a thing as killing? If the self does not exist, this would mean that all things are impermanent and that with each moment of thought they are extinguished. Therefore both the slayer and the slain are free of bearing the burden of the offence of killing. Neither the hatchet that cuts down the tree, nor the sickle that cuts the grass, nor the sword that kills human beings bears any offence. How is it possible then for man alone to have offences? Great king, now in Rajagriha there is a teacher named Kakuda Katyayana. Gazing upon the three worlds with omniscience, he purifies the sins of all people like the waters of the Ganges. According to the teaching of this master, even if a person kills someone, if there is no contrition over the act, he will not fall into hell, as the sky does not accept muddy water. However, if there is contrition, one plunges into hell, as water seeping into the great earth. All living creatures are the creation of Isvara. When Isvara fumes, they all suffer. Both offences and merits are created by Isvara; how then can people themselves be charged with offences and merits? For example, an artisan fashions a puppet; whether that puppet walks or stays still, sits or lies down, it is unable to speak even one word. Living creatures are like these puppets. Which of these creations is going to burden itself with offences? Great king, I beg you to receive the teaching of this teacher." The king replied to the minister, "If this teacher is able to heal my suffering as you say, I shall entrust myself to him."

(9) Minister Visarada said, "Great king, there was once an ignorant man; during the course of a day, one hundred times he would rejoice and grieve, sleep and awake, become startled and weep. A wise man does not act in such a way. Great king, why are you so distressed, like a traveller who has lost his companions, or like a lost soul who has no one to guide him? Great king, I beg you not to produce the poison of grief. In the first place, as a king, when you take someone's life for the sake of the country and for sentient beings, in no way is it an offence. The former king venerated monks, but he never served brahmins. Such a mind lacks equity; one who has lost its sense of equality cannot be called a king. Now, great king, even though you have killed the former king, it is an offering to the brahmins, so how can there be any offence attached to this? Again, great king, in this world there is no such thing as killing. The original meaning of killing is to harm life. Life is like wind; one cannot harm wind. Therefore one cannot kill life. How then can killing be an offence? Now in Rajagriha, there is a teacher named Nirgrantha Jnatiputra. He skillfully perceives the fundamental nature of people and has mastered a multitude of skillful means; he is never distressed by worldly fluctuations. Undertaking pure practices, he teaches his disciples in the following manner: In this world, there is neither selfless giving nor virtue, neither in this world nor in the afterworld; neither parents nor sages; neither ways nor the practicing of ways. After eighty thousand kalpas have passed by, birth and death of themselves come to a stop and people, both the offender and those that are free of offence, of themselves and in an equal manner are able to attain emancipation. The four great rivers of themselves pour into the great ocean and become the same ocean water. When people enter the state of emancipation, they also lose all distinctions. Great king, I beg you to receive the teaching of this teacher." The king replied to the minister, "If this teacher is able to heal my suffering as you say, I shall entrust myself to him."

(10) At that time, there was a great physician named Jivaka. This man also visited the king's sickbed and said, "Great king, are you able to sleep soundly?" The king said, "Jivaka, I have been suffering from a grave illness. I inflicted vicious and grievous injury on my father the king, who followed the true Dharma. The grave illness that resulted from that act cannot be healed, no matter how great the physician, the incantation, or the care. The reason is that the former king ruled the country well, in accordance with the Dharma. Although he was not guilty of any offence, I inflicted on him vicious and grievous injury. It was as if I had pulled a fish out of the water and thrown it onto land. I once heard from a sage that those whose three actions of body, mouth, and mind are not pure will without fail plunge into hell. I am an example of that; how can I sleep in peace? There are no physicians who, expounding the medicine of the Dharma, can heal me of this illness and its suffering."

Jivaka said in response to this, "Now, now. Although you have committed offences, now you are experiencing profound remorse and contrition. Great king, the Buddha always teaches that there are two minds that save one. The first is the mind that strives not to commit offences. The second is the mind that strives not to cause others to commit offences. Or, the first is the mind that looks within and repents, and the second is the mind that is contrite toward others. Or, the first is to feel remorse before other people, and the second is to feel remorse before the gods. These are the meanings of contrition. He who lacks this mind of contrition is not a human being but rather an animal. Because we possess this mind of contrition, the mind that venerates parents and teachers also comes into being, and harmony between brothers and sisters is established. I am truly joyful that you have experienced this contrition. Great king, you just said that there is no physician who is able to heal you of your grave illness; that is exactly so. However, great king, please consider this well. The great Arhat, the World-Honored One, is the person most worthy of the world's veneration. He possesses a diamond-like wisdom that destroys all obstructions with ease; he destroys all offences. The Buddha, the World-Honored One, will heal you of your grave illness."

(11) At that time, from the sky, a voice spoke out, "Great king, if you commit one grave offence, you will receive a corresponding retribution. If you commit three grave offences, this increases threefold. If you commit five grave offences, this increases fivefold. Because of the offences you have committed up to now, you cannot escape falling into hell. Therefore go immediately to the place of the World-Honored One; aside from the World-Honored One, there is no one who can save you."

Hearing this voice from the sky, Ajatasatru was beset with great fear. Like the leaf of a banana plant, he trembled in fear. Looking upward at the sky, he said, "Who might you be?" From the sky, without revealing its form, as before, only the voice was heard. "I am your father, Bimbisara. Deferring to Jivaka's advice, go quickly to the place of the World-Honored One; under no circumstances must you be misled by the words of the six ministers who teach erroneous views."

Hearing his father, Ajatasatru collapsed and fell onto the great earth. The boils that covered his whole body spontaneously spread; their foul smell was worse than before. His aides smeared ointment on them and attempted to treat the boils, but they opened up like flowering buds and threw off a toxic fever. This continued without letup.

(12) The World-Honored One watched this from afar and said to Kasyapa, who happened to be by his side, "Son of good family, for Ajatasatru's sake I shall prolong my life and refrain from entering the final nirvana. Kasyapa, you most likely do not understand the hidden meanings of my words. For example, when I say 'for Ajatasatru's sake' I mean 'for the sake of all sentient beings.' I merely brought Ajatasatru forth as an example to take the place of all those who had committed the five grave offences. I do not remain in this world for the sake of those who have attained enlightenment. Ajatasatru represents ignorant beings who have manifold and diverse defilements. Moreover, 'for Ajatasatru's sake' means 'for the sake of those who have not yet been able to perceive their Buddha nature.' I do not remain in this world for the sake of those who have perceived their Buddha nature. The reason is that those who have perceived their Buddha nature are no longer deluded people. Ajatasatru represents all those who have yet to arouse the mind of the supreme enlightenment. Again, 'ajata' means Buddha nature that has not been manifested. 'Ajatasatru' means

enemy of the Buddha nature. Because he does not sprout the bud of the Buddha nature, in the course of one day he develops defilement that is the enemy of the Buddha nature. Because the defilement rises up, he is unable to see his Buddha nature. If he did not develop such defilements, he would be able to see his original Buddha nature and would dwell in the enlightenment of great nirvana. Because Ajatasatru has not attained such a state so far, he has defilements that are the enemy of the Buddha nature; this is the reason he is called Ajatasatru. Son of good family, 'Ajata' means 'not yet born.' 'Not yet born' denotes nirvana, which is neither born nor extinguished. 'Satru' denotes the eight characteristics of this world: profit, decline, slander, fame, and so forth. Furthermore, 'Ajatasatru' means nirvana in this world, that is, something undefiled. Without being defiled by the eight characteristics of the world such as praise and slander, one refrains from entering nirvana for an endless eternity. Therefore for the sake of Ajatasatru, I remain in this world for an infinitely long time. Son of good family, one cannot apprehend the hidden meaning of the Buddha's words. The three treasures, the Buddha, the Dharma, and the Sangha, are also inconceivable."

(13) In this way, the World-Honored One for the sake of Ajatasatru entered into the Moon-Loving Meditation and emitted a great light; this light was pure and soothing. It shone upon Ajatasatru's body from afar. The boils that covered his whole body spontaneously healed without a trace.

King Ajatasatru said, "Jivaka, the World-Honored One is the highest god among gods. Why did he send forth this light?" Jivaka replied, "Great king, this auspicious sign in the form of a light was sent forth for your sake. As you said before, there was no physician who could cure your illness, and therefore the World-Honored One emitted this light and healed the illness of your body. Next he will heal the illness of your mind." The king said, "Jivaka, will the World-Honored One wish to see me again?" Jivaka said, "Yes. Suppose one has seven children; they are all equally precious. However, if one amongst them becomes ill, the parent's mind is especially drawn to the sick child. In the same way, although the Buddha equally loves all his children, as a mother loves an only child, he especially worries over those who have committed grave offences. The Buddha is especially compassionate toward those who are negligent of the path. Toward those who are able to practice the path diligently, the Buddha, to the contrary, relaxes his mind. 'Those who diligently' refers to bodhisattvas in the upper stages. Great king, no Buddha ponders over sentient beings' lineages or family names; they do not ponder over distinctions of poverty and wealth, the month or day of one's birth, one's astrological sign, or one's skill in the arts. They seek only those with virtuous minds, and on them they bestow compassionate thoughts. Great king, the World-Honored One emits such auspicious signs after entering the Moon-Loving Meditation." The king asked, "What is this Moon-Loving Meditation?" Jivaka answered, "Moonlight has the power to make all blue lotuses bloom beautifully. In the same way, this meditation has the power to rouse people's virtuous minds; this is why it is called the Moon-Loving Meditation. Again, as moonlight gladdens all travellers, the Moon-Loving Meditation also gladdens those who trudge along the path to nirvana. This is why it is called the Moon-Loving Meditation. Among virtues, this meditation is the king; it has the taste of nectar. All people joyfully wish for this meditation; this is why it is called the Moon-Loving Meditation."

(14) At that time, the World-Honored One addressed a large assembly. "When people seek enlightenment, the most important factor is a good friend. For example, if King Ajatasatru had not followed Jivaka's counsel, he would never have been saved. Therefore I say that in attaining enlightenment, the good friend is the most important factor." On his way to the place of the World-Honored One, Jivaka told Ajatasatru of the monk Kokalika, who, after the great earth split open, plunged into the Avici hell while he was still alive. He also told him of Sunaksatra who amassed myriad evil deeds and yet rushed to the World-Honored One; all of his offences thereupon were extinguished. Hearing these stories, Ajatasatru said to Jivaka, "I have now heard these two accounts; however, I am still at a loss. Jivaka, I plan to ride with you on the same elephant. In that case, even if I am about to fall into the Avici hell, you will catch hold of me and will not let me fall. The reason is that I have heard before that an arhat who has attained nirvana never falls into hell."

On the night of the full moon, several hundred elephant carriages with torches at their heads quietly made their way toward the forest. When at last they entered the forest, King Ajatasatru was suddenly beset with fear; trembling, he said to Jivaka, "Jivaka, you are not planning to betray and hand me over to the enemy, are you? What an eerie silence! They say there are over one thousand disciples, and yet not one sneeze or cough can be heard. I cannot help but think that there is some kind of plot afoot." Jivaka said, "Great king, advance without fear. There is a light burning in that forest retreat. The World-Honored One resides there."

The king was bolstered by Jivaka's words, and lowering himself from the elephant he went into the forest. Approaching the World-Honored One, he bowed and begged to be taught by the Buddha.

5. Expounding of the Dharma by the World-Honored One

(1) The World-Honored One bestowed a diversity of teachings on Ajatasatru. He said, "Great king, for those with a mind of contrition, offences are no longer offences. Those without a mind of contrition will be chastised forever by their offences. You are a man of contrition; your offences will be purified; there is no need to be afraid."

(2) Having received the teaching, Ajatasatru said to the World-Honored One, "As I survey the world, I observe that from the seed of the toxic tree called the castor oil tree, a castor oil tree grows. I have yet to see a sandalwood tree grow from the seed of a castor oil tree. However, now for the first time, I have witnessed a sandalwood tree grow from the fruit of a castor oil tree. I am talking about myself. The sandalwood tree refers to the rootless faith that has sprouted forth in my mind. So far I have yet to serve the Buddha with reverence or seek refuge in the Dharma or the Sangha. Nevertheless, faith has suddenly sprouted in me; therefore I call this faith rootless faith. World-Honored One, if I had been unable to meet the Buddha, I should have fallen into hell for an infinite number

of kalpas and addicted with endless suffering. Now I bow to the Buddha; with all of the merits that I can accumulate, my fervent wish for the future is to destroy other people's defilements."

The World-Honored One said, "Very good, very good, great king! I have foreseen that you will destroy people's defilements with your merits, expunging the defilements in their minds." Ajatasatru said, "World-Honored One, if I am able to destroy people's evil intentions, even though I should experience enormous suffering for an infinite number of kalpas in the Avici hell, I shall not think of this as suffering."

Hearing these words of Ajatasatru, a large number of Magadhans spontaneously aroused the aspiration for enlightenment. Because of this, Ajatasatru was able to mitigate his grave offences.

(3) At that time, Ajatasatru said to Jivaka, "I was faced with imminent death, and yet I have escaped that fate and have become king. Escaping an early death, I have attained long life. Moreover, I helped a large number of people to arouse the aspiration for enlightenment. This person is a divine being, a being of long life; this is a disciple of all the buddhas." Thus with a variety of jewelled streamers he made an offering to the Buddha; and with the following verses he sang the praise of the World-Honored One.

> For the sake of all people, the Buddha becomes a compassionate father and a merciful mother.

> Therefore, everyone is a child of the Buddha.

> The Buddha, with great compassion, for the sake of all sentient beings of this world, undergoes spiritual disciplines. He does so as if in a frenzy, like a man possessed by some mountain spirit.

> I now perceive the Buddha and offer up the virtuous merits that I have accumulated to his highest enlightenment.

> I make offerings to the Three Treasures. By virtue of the roots of merit that I have accumulated, I pray that the Three Treasures may exist for ever in this world.

> By virtue of the merits that I will have accumulated for the sake of sentient beings, may all Maras be destroyed.

(4) At that time, the World-Honored One praised Ajatasatru and said, "Since just one person arouses the aspiration for enlightenment, this person embellishes the large gathering that has gathered at the Buddha assembly. Great king, from this day forward, you must always strive not to lose this aspiration for enlightenment. The reason is that with this aspiration for enlightenment, you will be able to extinguish innumerable evil deeds." Hearing this, Ajatasatru and the people of Magadha each rose from their seats and thrice circumambulated the World-Honored One and bowed reverently to the Buddha and departed that assembly.

(5) Ajatasatru then said to the ministers, "From this day forward, I seek my refuge in the World-Honored One and his disciples. From now on, we must invite

the World-Honored One and his disciples to my palace, but we must not allow Devadatta and his cohorts to enter the palace."

Unaware of this, one day Devadatta arrived at the palace gates. The sentries who guarded the gates repeated what the king had said and blocked Devadatta's path. Seething inside with anger, he stood outside the gate. Just then the nun Utpalavarna, who had finished her round of begging, came walking out of the gate. When he spied the nun, instantaneously he exploded with anger. "What hatred do you harbor toward me that prompts you to bar me from passing through this gate?" Using abusive language, he clenched his fist and struck the nun's head. The nun endured the pain and told him that this was unreasonable, but in the end Devadatta broke her head. The nun endured the pain and returned to her nunnery. She said to the nuns who were horror-struck and grieving, "Sisters, one's life span cannot be calculated; all things are impermanent. A quiescent place free of defilements is nirvana. All of you, exert yourselves with diligence and cultivate the virtuous path." After speaking these words, she entered nirvana.

(6) Finally Devadatta smeared poison onto the nails of his ten fingers and plotted to draw near the World-Honored One, who was staying at the Jeta Grove Monastery. The disciples spied Devadatta's figure, and because they were concerned about the safety of the World-Honored One, they felt great fear. However, the World-Honored One said, "There is no need to be afraid. Today, Devadatta will not be able to see me." Meanwhile, Devadatta approached the monastery and went to the shore of the lake where the disciples washed their feet. There for some time he rested under the shade of a tree. Repeating what he had said before, the World-Honored One pacified his fearful disciples. At this moment, the great earth on which Devadatta stood of itself sank down and burst into flames. It soon buried his knees, then it reached up to his navel and finally his shoulders. Burned by the fire, Devadatta repented his grave offences and sank down. Two gold levers squeezed Devadatta from the front and the back, pulled him downward into the great earth, which was consumed in flames, and dragged him down into the Avici hell.

Chapter 3

DEVOTION TO THE PATH

1. To Give Oneself to the Path

(1) The World-Honored One, wandering from place to place, returned to Sravasti and entered the Anathapindada Monastery in the Jeta Grove. Anathapindada of Sravasti was a famous and wealthy man. He had countless treasuries filled with gold, silver, and other valuables and numerous male and female servants. About that time, there was in Ugga a rich man called Ugrasresthin whose wealth was comparable in size to a mountain. From his youth he was a friend of Anathapindada. The two were close, and it was a relationship that they could not forget. It was a common practice for Anathapindada to sell merchandise in Ugga and for Ugrasresthin to do business in Sravasti; and thus the two were always coming and going between each other's homes.

One day, Ugrasresthin came to Sravasti on business and stayed at Anathapindada's house. Anathapindada's daughter Sumati had a natural charm like that of the peach blossom and was indeed a beauty most rare. Hearing that there was a guest, she quietly entered the room and bowing respectfully to her parents greeted the guest and then returned to her room. Knowing that she was his host's daughter, Ugrasresthin said, "I have a son who has not chosen a wife. I would therefore like to welcome her as his bride." "I am sorry, but I must refuse," Anathapindada said. "Why is that? Is his family or caste different or is it that his wealth cannot be compared to yours?" "There is nothing about family, caste, or wealth that is a problem; however, in regard to that essential aspect of religion, there is a difference. My daughter is a disciple of the World-Honored One and your son believes in another teaching."

"Is that all?" Ugrasresthin said. "There is nothing drastic about a difference in religion. There is no problem as long as each worships in his or her own way. Please be flexible and honor us by bestowing your daughter on my son."

Anathapindada struggled for words of refusal and thought to refuse by mentioning monetary matters. He requested a large sum as a dowry, but Ugrasresthin readily agreed to the terms. Anathapindada could do nothing now; therefore he asked for some time so that he could consult with the World-Honored One himself. He immediately went to the World-Honored one and told him of the situation. The World-Honored One responded, saying, "Sir, if your daughter, Sumati, goes to Ugga, she will save numerous people. There is nothing greater than this."

Hearing these words, Anathapindada made up his mind and went home. He again treated Ugrasresthin to a grand meal. He consented to the proposal, and the engagement was announced.

(2) In anticipation of the happy event, they hurried and immediately began preparation for the marriage ceremony. On the appointed day, Ugrasresthin put his son in an ornate carriage and sent him out to welcome the bride. On that day Anathapindada also dressed Sumati brightly, and putting her on a seven-jewel inlaid carriage of great beauty, he arranged that she should meet them part way. Thus on the road they had a wondrous meeting, and they all returned to Ugga for a glorious wedding.

In those days, there was a certain law in Ugga that prohibited marriage with a person of another kingdom. If that law was broken, the punishment was to invite one thousand brahmin ascetics to a lavish banquet. However, for the wealthy Ugrasresthin, this was no problem, and he soon invited numerous ascetics to a banquet.

When the day arrived, one after another the ascetics gathered at Ugrasresthin's house. They were all naked. The wealthy Ugrasresthin greeted them and offered them a seat. After treating them with a feast, he called Sumati and said, "Dress and prepare yourself, and come into the banquet room to pay respect to our masters." Sumati, trying to avoid this, said; "I cannot worship a naked person. I simply cannot worship as masters people who do not know shame." Ugrasresthin said, "It is not on account of lack of shame that these people are naked, for they are wearing the clothes of the Dharma on their bodies." "To be naked cannot be being clothed in the clothes of the Dharma. My teacher, the World-Honored One, has taught that there are two things that are most sacred in this world. They are shame and modesty, and if these are lacking, the difference between mother and father, elder and younger brother, elder and younger sister, and among relatives will also be lacking. There would be no difference between oneself and a chicken or dog. These people here are without shame and modesty and are naked; therefore there is no way of seeing a difference between them and chickens and dogs. How can I go and pay respect to them?" Her husband repeatedly tried to persuade her to go out and greet them, but she said that she would not fall into such a false doctrine even if they were to tear her limb from limb; and thus she refused.

Learning about the situation, the ascetics became angry and shouted to Ugrasresthin, "Stop it, stop it at once. What is the meaning of this vile woman spreading such abusive words? We have come at your invitation, so would it not be appropriate to bring the offering now?" Ugrasresthin could do nothing else and so stopped trying to persuade Sumati. Delicious food was brought out and offered to the ascetics. They enjoyed the offerings, and having finished eating, they left the house.

(3) Ugrasresthin was not happy, and he climbed atop the tower to be by himself. "Oh, what a bride we have let into the house! Surely, harmony will not come

to this house, but rather it will be torn apart. This house has not experienced such humiliation as it did on this occasion," he lamented. At that time there was a practitioner called Good Wisdom in Ugga. He had attained the five divine powers and numerous forms of meditation. He had asked to visit with the elder since he had not seen him for some time; but upon hearing that he was alone atop the tower with something heavily weighing on his mind, he quickly went to Ugrasresthin and asked him the reason for his worry. "Why are you so worried? Have the authorities asked you to bring something unreasonable? Or has a calamity in the form of a burglar or a fire or a flood visited you? Or has something sad come into your house? Please unburden yourself and tell me the reason for your worry."

"Thank you very much for your kindness. But it is not that I have received injury from the authorities or a thief, nor is it that I have had a calamity visit me in the form of a fire or a flood. It is only that something quite sad has occurred in my home. My son has taken a bride recently, and because a law of the kingdom was broken, as punishment for the crime I had to invite some brahmin masters to a feast. The bride refused to obey my orders and did not pay respect to these masters." "Whose daughter is this girl?" "She is the daughter of Anathapindada of Sravasti." Hearing this, Good Wisdom was quite surprised and, covering his ears with his hands, said, "Did she not, upon hearing those orders, climb the tower and attempt to throw herself off and die? The teacher of this bride is truly a person who observes the highest and most pious practice. He is indeed a great and spiritually powerful person."

"Is it not strange that you praise Gautama who is of another faith?" "Far from it! The spiritual power of Gautama is even beyond our imagination. Let me just tell you about what I saw. It was just a short time ago. I was to the north of the Himalaya Mountains, and after begging I came to the vicinity of Lake Anuttara where a number of deities appeared. Putting a knife to me, they said, 'Good Wisdom, you cannot stop in the vicinity of this lake and dirty the waters. If you do not listen to us we shall kill you.' Being frightened by these words, I left there. Then appeared Cunda, the youngest disciple of the World-Honored One, holding an extra robe picked up from a filthy trash pile. Then these same deities who threatened me came out to meet him respectfully and extended every courtesy and sign of esteem to him. There was a golden platform in the lake. Cunda put the soiled robe in the water, left it there to soak, and after eating and washing his bowl he entered into meditation on the platform. After a while, he came out of meditation and took out the robe to wash. At that moment, some of the deities washed the robe, some rinsed it, and finally after finishing the washing they took the robe and flew off with it to their home. As I was watching this, I could not make myself get any closer. Ugrasresthin, even the youngest disciple of your daughter's teacher has such extraordinary power. The divine power of the enlightened World-Honored One must be truly beyond our comprehension. Since your daughter was forcefully requested to pay respect to those monks of a different faith, you should rejoice that she did not throw herself from the tower and die."

"Can I pay respect to the teacher of my daughter, I wonder?" asked Ugrasresthin. "Instead of asking me, you should ask your daughter."

(4) Thereupon, Ugrasresthin, calling Sumati, asked if he could invite her teacher here, since he wanted to pay respect to him. Sumati was overjoyed, and she related the request of the elder, singing, with censer in hand, on the top of the tower, holding her hands together, "World-Honored One, you know everything and you must know that now I am in a difficult situation, so please appear before me out of compassion. Overseeing the whole world, you conquered Maras, counseled Hariti, saved the mother-killing Angulimala, and calmed a crazed elephant in Rajagriha. I am now deep in suffering; I beg of you, kindly come and save me."

When she sang this verse, suddenly a fragrance floated out like a cloud and filled the Jeta Grove; the deities rejoiced and rained down flowers while praising the wish of Sumati. The Buddha, seeing this, let a smile escape. Ananda, seeing the cloud of elegant fragrance fill the grove, and thinking it to be something special, went to the World-Honored One and asked him the reason for it. Then he learned of Sumati's invitation for the following day. The World-Honored One said, "Of the sages who have destroyed their passions and attained enlightenment, we are going to choose by drawing lots tomorrow those who will go to Ugga." Ananda, receiving the instructions, gathered the disciples and conveyed to them the words of the World-Honored One.

Among the assembled disciples was one called Kutadanta who thought to himself, "It has been a long time since I left home and became a monk; nevertheless I have been unable to destroy my passions and attain enlightenment. Cunda, even though he is the youngest among the assembly, has destroyed his passions and attained enlightenment. In order to be able to go with the World-Honored One to Ugga tomorrow, I must certainly practice sincerely today and attain nirvana." Sure enough, he attained his wish for enlightenment. That day, when lots were drawn, he was chosen first. The World-Honored One said that among his disciples the first chosen by lot was Kutadanta.

(5) The next day, following the World-Honored One's instructions, Maudgalyayana, Mahakasyapa, Aniruddha, Revata, Subhuti, Uruvilvakasyapa, Rahula, Ksullapanthaka, Cunda and others having the divine power to go anywhere at will headed toward Ugga by their divine power. A temple boy named Gandha also of his own accord carried a large cauldron and proceeded first toward the town. Ugrasresthin, standing in the tower and seeing many people approaching from afar, bowed, thinking that the World-Honored One was nearing. Upon seeing Gandha, he asked Sumati, "Is that person wearing a white robe with long hair, carrying a large cauldron and coming here like a tornado, your teacher?" "No, he is not. He is Gandha, a temple boy; however, he has attained enlightenment."

Cunda came surrounded by five hundred stemmed flowers of various colors that he made. "My, how many flowers!" Ugrasresthin said. "The sky is flooded with them. Is he your teacher?" "No, he is not. He is Cunda whom the sage Good Wisdom talked about. He is Sariputta's disciple."

Ksullapanthaka with five hundred blue cattle came, sitting in meditation on top of one of them. "Is that person coming here, with the blue cattle and sitting in meditation, your teacher?" "No, he is not. He is Ksullapanthaka." Rahula came leading five hundred peacocks; Mahakalpina came leading five hundred kimnaras; Uruvilvakasyapa came leading five hundred great Nagas; Mahakalyayana came leading five hundred geese; Revata came leading five hundred tigers; Aniruddha came leading five hundred lions; Mahakasyapa came leading five hundred white horses; and Maudgalyayana came leading five hundred white elephants. Each of the white elephants had six tusks adorned with gold and silver that produced a brilliant light. In the air there was music and on the ground was a multitude of flowers. It was truly a beautiful sight. In response to Ugrasresthin's questions, Sumati taught him the names and merits of each of the disciples.

(6) Soon, the World-Honored One came flying, with Ajnatakaundinya on his right, Sariputta on his left, and Ananda following behind holding a whisk and with a group of deities surrounding him. Pancasikha came, playing his jewelled harp and praising the Buddha. Flowers rained down on the Buddha; and King Prasenajit of Sravasti and Anathapindada and others with immeasurable joy each offered wondrous incense. Anathapindada sang the following hymn:

> The power of the Buddha is immeasurable,
> And he loves all sentient beings as though they were his children.
> It is most joyful that my child Sumati
> Received the teachings of the Buddha.
> Plucking the strings of a jewelled harp,
> Pancasikha sang from the sky.
> The passions of ignorance have long ago been exhausted,
> The mind is not confused,
> And the impure obstacles are removed
> In the Buddha who now approaches us.
> His heart is pure,
> And he has abandoned wrong thoughts.
> He is an ocean of merit
> With features wondrous and divine;
> And passions have long not arisen in him.
> With compassion he does not stop at himself.
> The Buddha now is approaching;
> The Buddha now is approaching.
> Crossing over the river of desire,
> Freed from birth and death,
> Cutting off the root of illusion,
> The Buddha now is approaching.

Ugrasresthin was dazzled as if hit by a light as great as Mount Sumeru and was stunned. "Are these the rays of the sun? I have never seen anything like them in my whole life. Countless rays of light are shining, I cannot even look at them." "They are not the rays of the sun. However, excluding the sun, how can one describe the light? The countless rays of light are all for each of us. He, indeed, is the teacher. The Buddha is here, and what you hear are the voices praising the merits of the Buddha. Please give offerings to him and gain a great reward."

(7) Ugrasresthin, kneeling with his right knee on the ground and placing hands together, took refuge in the World-Honored One.

> I place my faith in the Buddha.
> In the serene glow of gold
> Whom the gods praise
> I now place my faith.
> The Buddha, like the light of the sun,
> And like the light of the moon among the stars,
> Grants salvation to all.
> I now place my faith in him.
> His form is like that of Indra, the king of the gods,
> His compassion is like that of Brahma,
> Enlightening himself and others.
> I now place my faith in him.
> In this man among men,
> And god among gods,
> Who crushes the wayward doctrines,
> I now place my faith.

Sumati also knelt, and putting her hands together she sang:

> Putting oneself in order and putting others in order,
> Making oneself right and making others right,
> Awakening to enlightenment in oneself and making others awaken to
> enlightenment,
> Ridding oneself of the impurities of the mind
> And making others rid themselves of the impurities of the mind,
> Shining forth and making others shine forth,
> He saves all, forsaking none.
> Stopping wars,
> Ridding the world of battles,
> Calming thought and purifying it,
> The great Buddha, having an unshakable heart,
> Has true concern for and loves this world.
> I again place my faith in him.

Ugrasresthin and Sumati both, giving their hearts and bodies, placed their faith in the Buddha, the world's most honored one. Then the monks of the various other faiths, having their powers and skills nullified and losing the trust of sentient beings, left the town. Indeed, it was as if a lion, the king of beasts, came into a valley, looked in the four directions, and roared three times, making the birds and beasts and even the powerful elephants all run off and hide themselves. At this moment, the World-Honored One came down from the sky and entered Ugga in the eternal way of the Dharma. As he stepped on the threshold of the town gate, the earth shook and beautiful flowers fluttered down like rain and carpeted the ground. Seeing the World-Honored One's brilliantly clear and noble bearing, the people sang,

> The Buddha is the most honored of beings;
> The masters of other faiths cannot be compared to him.
> Our eyes were darkened,
> And we erred about whom to serve.

(8) The World-Honored One entered Ugrasresthin's house; and the people, all wanting to see the one who had overcome the self, entered, too, so many that the house was about to be torn apart. The World-Honored One, knowing the thoughts of sentient beings, immediately transformed the house into a crystal hall through which every nook and corner could be seen. Unable to contain herself because of her joy and sadness, Sumati said,

> I place my faith in the Buddha,
> Possessed of all wisdom, freed from illusion, and casting aside all passions.
> Poor I, separated from a home of the true Dharma,
> Came as a bride to a house of another teaching
> And must mix with people of incorrect views.
> What I hope for is the Buddha's mercy.
> What a marriage!
> Coming to a house of another faith as a bride,
> I am like a bird in a fog.
> My only wish is for the Buddha's compassion.

With a verse the World-Honored One comforted her:

> Brighten your thoughts,
> And lighten your heart.
> It is not because of past misdeeds that you came as a bride to this house.
> All this is fulfilling your prime wish.
> Long ago you were related to these people.
> Now your hopes will be answered.

Sumati upon hearing this hymn greatly rejoiced. Soon, Ugrasresthin with family and servants gave offerings first to the World-Honored One and then to the disciples. After eating, he sat before the World-Honored One on a lower seat. Then the World-Honored One gave a talk as thanksgiving. He taught of the merit of giving and the impurity of the desires of this world, and one by one he tamed the minds of those who were listening; and in the end he taught the wondrous Four Noble Truths. Ugrasresthin and Sumati first of all, and many others of the listeners, were freed from impurities of the mind and gained the eye of the Dharma; cutting the pangs of doubt, they put their faith in the Three Treasures. And Sumati sang this verse of joy:

> The ears of the Buddha
> Are pure and clear.
> Hearing our wishes,
> He kindly visited us,
> Making his carriage detour.
> He spread the teaching
> And made many people
> Gain the eye of the Dharma.

(9) At this time, the disciples said to the World-Honored One, "What were the karmic conditions for Sumati to be born in the house of a rich man like Anathapindada; why did she go in marriage to a house of the wrong views of a different doctrine; and how later was she able to attain enlightenment for herself and for so many other people?" The World-Honored One answered,

"Disciples, in the age of Kasyapa Buddha, there was a king in Varanasi called Karunayamana. The queen was named Sumana. She placed her faith in Kasyapa Buddha and always upheld the pious practice; she practiced the four means of conversion, giving, speaking lovingly, benefitting others, and sharing the joys and sorrows of others; and she sat in the tower reading sutras. She always took this vow, 'Even though my practicing of the four means of conversion and the reading of the sutras are scant, if there are merits attained, by them may I not have an unhappy birth in the future. Meeting the Buddha and without transforming my womanly body, may I attain the pure eye of the Dharma.'

"The townspeople, hearing of the queen's vow, gathered around the tower and hoped for the same virtue as the queen's if her vow was fulfilled. The queen, knowing of this, vowed that they would attain the same enlightenment, thus spreading the merit equally to all. Disciples, that Karunayamana is now Anathapindada and Sumana is Sumati. By the vow in her past life, Sumati met me, and today she and those people who were around the tower at that time have all gained the eye of the Dharma. Disciples, the four means of conversion are the most superior sources of virtue. As Buddha's disciples, if you become familiar with these four means of conversion, you will awaken to the verity of the Four Noble Truths. Therefore, disciples, do not forget to perfect the four means of conversion." The World-Honored One, leading his disciples, arose from his seat and returned to the Jeta Grove.

2. Prince Bodhi

(1) With his disciples, the World-Honored One entered Bhagga. At that time the new residence of Prince Bodhi, Kokanada, had just been finished, though the dedication ceremony had yet to be held. Hearing that the World-Honored One had arrived at Bhagga, Prince Bodhi greatly rejoiced, and through Sanjikaputta as messenger he addressed the World-Honored One. "World-Honored One, Prince Bodhi bows at your feet and inquires after your health. He asks you whether you with your disciples will accept an offering tomorrow." The World-Honored One nodded, signifying consent.

Prince Bodhi passed the night preparing the meal. When the World-Honored One was told it was ready, holding the bowl in his hands he with his disciples went toward Kokanada. On the stairs of the mansion fragrant with new wood, a white cotton cloth was laid. The World-Honored One stopped before it. Prince Bodhi said, "World-Honored One, please walk on this white cloth for the sake of my timeless benefit and happiness." The World-Honored One looked back at Ananda. Ananda, facing Prince Bodhi, said, "Prince, please remove the white cloth. The World-Honored One has compassion for sentient beings of the future; setting an example, he does not walk on a cloth." The prince then removed the white cloth. The World-Honored One walked up the stairs and came to the seat in the mansion. The prince prepared many rare dishes and served them to the World-Honored One. When he had finished eating, the prince went to a lower seat and sat near the World-Honored One. He said to the Buddha, "World-Honored One, I cannot attain bliss through pleasure. I think that through pain I may be able to gain bliss." The World-Honored One related the stories of his long life of searching for the way before and after his leaving home. When he was a prince, he, too, thought that bliss could not be bought by pleasure, and that bliss could be gained through pain. However, in reality, true bliss can be gained by a blissful path, he told the prince.

(2) Prince Bodhi said, "World-Honored One, with you, the Buddha, as my teacher, how many years after leaving home would it take for me to be able to reach my goal?" "Prince, in response to my questions, answer me freely. Can you skillfully handle an elephant?" "I can handle one rather well." "Prince, suppose a person were to learn the art of handling an elephant from you, and that person was unreliable, weak of body, a teller of lies, lazy, and had no wisdom at all. Would that person be able to learn the art of handling an elephant at your side?" "Even with one of the characteristics cited, he would be unable to learn the art, how much more so with the five. From the start, he is just no good." "Prince, suppose another person were to learn the art of handling an elephant from you and he was reliable, without sickness, not a teller of lies, hardworking, and wise, would this person be able to learn the art of handling an elephant at your side?" "World-Honored One, with one of those characteristics, he would be able to learn the art, how much more so with the five. From the beginning he would surely be able to do it."

"Prince, it is just like that. If a disciple of the Buddha, having the five qualities of being reliable, without sickness, not a teller of lies, hardworking, and wise and has the Buddha as his teacher, then in seven years or one year or even in one month or one day, he will attain enlightenment. No, not even one day; hearing in the morning, then in the evening, or hearing in the evening, then in the morning, enlightenment will be attained."

After hearing this, the prince said in praise, "Ah, Buddha, ah, Dharma, hearing in the morning, then in the evening, hearing in the evening, then in the morning, enlightenment is awakened: what an aptly stated Dharma!"

(3) Sanjikaputta said, "Prince, you in praise say, 'Ah, ah,' but would it not be best to say that you put your faith in the Buddha, the Dharma, and the Sangha?" "Sanjikaputta, do not say that, do not say that. I said these with my mother. Long ago, the World-Honored One came to Kosambi and when he was staying at the Ghosita Monastery, my mother, in whose womb I was at the time, visited the Buddha and said, 'World-Honored One, whether the child in my womb is a girl or a boy, I shall have it take refuge in the Three Treasures. World-Honored One, please accept it as a follower who will have lifelong faith.' Moreover, Sanjikaputta, before, when the World-Honored One came to Bhagga, my wet nurse, taking me to the World-Honored One, said for me the same words of taking refuge in the Three Treasures. Therefore, Sanjikaputta, this is the third time I take refuge in the Three Treasures. World-Honored One, I take refuge in the Three Treasures. Please accept me as a follower throughout my life."

3. The Wealthy Citta

(1) Citta of Macchikasanda frequently invited to his house the disciples who were staying at the Mango Grove. Inviting the disciples one day, he asked the elders a question. "Elders, there are many wrong views in the world. For example, there are the various views that the world is permanent or impermanent, with a limit or without a limit, that people exist after death, or do not exist, or both exist and do not exist, or neither exist nor do not exist, that the spirit is one with the body or separate. The World-Honored One indicated all sixty-two types of wrong views in the Brahmajalasutta. My question is why these wrong views arise. What is the basis of these views?"

To these questions, the elder disciples remained silent. Asked a second and a third time, they still remained silent. Then the youngest among those disciples, Isidatta, came forward and asked the elders for permission to answer. "Citta, they arise because of belief in individuality. If there were no such wrong view, then they would not arise."

"Venerable, what is this belief in individuality?" "Citta, it is regarding the mind and body as consisting of an 'I' or a 'self'. It is the thought that arises in the minds of those ordinary persons who are ignorant of the Dharma. Those who have learned the Buddha's teachings and refined their minds through it do not see a self in the mind or body."

"Venerable, where are you from?" "I am from Avanti."

"Venerable, there is a friend by the name of Isidatta, whom I have not seen yet, who left the world. Do you know him?" "Citta, I know him." "Where is that Venerable One now?" Asked this, Isidatta remained silent and did not answer.

"Venerable, are you the one called Isidatta?" "Yes." "Venerable, please stay here at Macchikasanda a long time. While I cannot fully do it, I will provide you with robes, food, seats, bedding, comforts, and medicine." "Citta, I am grateful for your words."

Citta rejoiced from his heart at the words of Isidatta, and he gave the disciples the offerings. After returning to the grove, the disciples thanked him for his efforts. Putting things in order and taking his bowl, he left to an unknown destination, never to return to Macchikasanda.

(2) Before this, Citta once heard that Kassapa, a naked Ajivaka ascetic and an old family friend, had come to Macchikasanda, Citta visited him and after greeting him asked him how long it had been since he left the world. "It has been thirty years already."

"Venerable, in those thirty years, what superior Dharma have you attained, what superior wisdom have you attained, and what quietude of mind have you attained?" "Citta, though thirty years have passed, I am only naked, bald, and skillful at debate. Other than that nothing has changed at all."

"Venerable, if after thirty years you are only naked, bald, and skillful at debate, it means that the Dharma that you, venerable, attained is indeed rare." "Householder, how many years has it been since you became a follower of the Buddha?" "It has been thirty years." "In those thirty years, did you attain a superhuman Dharma, open up a superior wisdom, and attain a quietude of mind?" "Venerable, if I had not, what could I do? I can freely enter into meditation; moreover, if I die earlier than the World-Honored One, he will no doubt say that I have rid myself of the passions that would make me return again to this world." "Householder, if a householder is able to attain such a superior state, it means that this is the most superior Dharma. Would it be possible for me to be a disciple of that teaching?" And Citta, taking Kassapa, went to the Buddha's disciples and made it possible for him to hear the teachings.

(3) At this time, the World-Honored One was in Ujunna and staying at Kannakathala Deer Park. Kassapa, the naked ascetic, questioned the World-Honored One. "Venerable, I have heard that you dislike all ascetic practices and slander ascetics. Is this true?" "Kassapa, I do not; this is an incorrect account of my thoughts. Kassapa, I have divine eyes, and I see that among the ascetics, upon death some fall into hell, and some are born into heaven; and I see that among those who engage in ascetic practices, some fall into hell and some enter heaven. I see the effect of ascetic practices in this way, so how can I dislike ascetic practices and slander asceticism?"

Kassapa said, "Venerable, it is believed that ascetic practices like staying naked, not receiving offerings of food, fasting every half month, eating the dung of cows, wearing the bark of trees or the hides of beasts, upholding the practice of constant standing, or taking a cold water bath three times a night are appropriate for the samana, for the brahmin."

"Kassapa, even if one did these ascetic practices, without the realization of the precepts, meditation, and wisdom, one is quite far from being a true mendicant and a brahmin. If one is without anger and malice, practices compassion, destroys the passions, and attains enlightenment, then he should be called a true samana and a brahmin."

"Venerable, how difficult it is to be a true samana and a brahmin." "Kassapa, that difficulty does not lie in the practice of asceticism. As for the ascetic practices, as even a servant girl is able to move a water jar with the power of her hips, they are not impossible to do. It is truly difficult to rid oneself of anger and malice, practice compassion, destroy the passions, and attain enlightenment.

"Venerable, thus it is difficult to know whether someone is a true samana or a brahmin." "Kassapa, it would not be so difficult to know whether someone were a samana or a brahmin, if it were a matter of ascetic practices. As for ascetic practices, as even a servant girl is able to move a water jar with the power of her hips, they are not impossible to do. It is difficult to know a samana or a brahmin, since it is a matter of being without anger or malice, practicing compassion, destroying passions, and attaining enlightenment in the present."

(4) "Venerable, what then is this realization of the precepts, meditation, and wisdom?" "Kassapa, to realize the precepts means this. The Buddha appearing in this world attains enlightenment for himself and teaches others. A person leaving home upon hearing the teachings with a newly awakened faith follows the precepts; thus maintaining the body, acting correctly; thus becoming blissful, seeing the danger of the smallest transgression and controlling the five sense

organs; thus possessing the true wisdom, stopping stealing; thus purifying the mind, avoiding confusion and telling lies, not saying coarse words, and leading a good life.

"To realize meditation means this. Even when one sees objects with the eye, the five sense organs are controlled, and there is no attachment to the external form of an object. Whether going or coming, standing or lying down, the eye of the mind is opened clearly and the mind and thought are made right. As a bird flies with only wings attached to its body, one rejoices in having only the clothes on one's back and food that will fill one's stomach. Choosing the solitude at the foot of a tree or in a cave, a forest, a plain, or a graveyard, one sits quietly. One frees himself from desire, anger, sloth, regret, and doubt and becomes a vigorous, free, and peaceful person. Thus gaining joy and bliss, one enters into meditation.

"To realize wisdom is to become purely transparent through this meditation; one's mind is not attached to objects; one knows that his body is impermanent and without a self-substance; one gains the five supernatural powers; one completely understands the Four Noble Truths; one destroys the passions, one attains enlightenment, and one becomes aware of having attained emancipation.

"Kassapa, there is no greater way of practice. There are samanas and brahmins who are proud of their precepts, ascetic practices, distaste of the world, wisdom, and emancipation. However, there are none who are possessed of purer and better precepts, ascetic practices, distaste of the world, wisdom, or emancipation than I. It is I who have reached the most perfect fulfillment of these.

"Kassapa, one may criticize what I say in the following way. 'Gotama may roar where there is no one, but he does not have conviction in what he says. Even if he did, people would not question him. If questioned, he would be unable to answer. Even if he answered, he could not make people rejoice or believe.' Kassapa, you should not think in this way. I stress the true Dharma in front of crowds of people and I proclaim the way with conviction. I answer people's questions and make them rejoice and have faith. Kassapa, once on the Vulture Peak at Rajagriha, an ascetic like yourself called Nigrodha asked me the best way of abandoning the impure life. Hearing my explanation, he experienced the highest joy."

(5) "World-Honored One, is there anyone who does not rejoice at hearing your teaching? I have now experienced this matchless joy. I want now to put my faith in the Three Treasures and become your disciple. Please permit me to do so." "Kassapa, anyone who previously belonged to another teaching and who intends to join the Sangha by becoming a disciple of my teaching is required to live apart for four months before he is allowed to join the Sangha. Of course there may be special cases, but that has become the rule."

"World-Honored One, if four months living apart is the rule, then I shall live four months apart. Let me join the Sangha." Kassapa thus became a disciple and was welcomed into the Sangha. In a short time, through great and intent effort, he awakened to enlightenment.

(6) One day a disciple of the Buddha, Kamabhu, invited by Citta, came to his house and spoke to the wealthy man. "Citta, do you understand the meaning of this verse?

> Pure, white-canopied, one-spoked, the carriage moves on.
> Look at that moving on, cutting the stream, without bonds, and without passions.

"Venerable, is that a verse by the World-Honored One?" "Yes." "Then please wait and let me think." Citta thought for a while and then spoke. "Venerable, 'pure' refers to the precepts. 'White-canopied' is emancipation. 'One-spoked' is this body. 'Cutting the stream' is overcoming desire and being without passions. 'Without bonds' refers to freeing oneself from the bonds of lust, anger, and ignorance. 'Without passions' is to rid oneself of passions. 'Moving on' means fulfilling of one's goal that is enlightenment." "Very good, indeed, Citta, your eyes of wisdom of have completely awakened to the words of the Buddha."

When Citta was on his deathbed, the spirit of the trees of the forest appeared. "Citta, pray that you may become a universal monarch in the next life." "This, too, would be an impermanent and transient state. I must avoid it." The relatives and friends nearby hearing this said, "Rich man, please get hold of yourself." "All of you, do not treat me as if I were crazy. The spirit of the trees of the forest appeared and encouraged me to become a universal monarch in the next life. I said that this, too, would be an impermanent and transient state and that I must avoid it. All of you, keep steadfast faith in the Buddha, Dharma, and Sangha. Observe the precepts and offer charity with a mind of nondiscrimination." Citta in this way gave those people teaching on cultivating the hearts and minds of giving and of faith in the Three Treasures; and then he died.

4. Parables

(1) While the World-Honored One was staying at Rajagriha, he sometimes told various tales to his disciples. "Disciples, long ago there was a country that cast out its elderly people. When people of the country saw an elderly person, then they had to chase that person away to a faraway place. There was one government minister who, according to the law of the land, had to cast away his elderly father. However, his parental regard was deep, and he just could not bear to abandon him. He therefore dug deeply into the earth and built a house in it where he hid his father and took care of him.

"At that time, a deity appeared and taking two snakes and holding them over the king of the country said to him, 'If you cannot distinguish between the male and female of these snakes, then after seven days the whole country, with you the king first, will be destroyed.' Being distressed by this, he called his ministers together and related the details to them. No one had a solution to the problem. It was proclaimed throughout the country that the person who could solve the problem would receive a grand reward.

"Returning home, the minister discussed the problem with his father. The father said, 'That is easy to solve. Place the snakes on a soft surface, and the one that is restless is the male and the one that does not move is the female.' Upon doing that, the king and the minister were able to distinguish the two snakes.

"The deity again posed a riddle. 'Who is meant when one says that he is awake in relation to a sleeping person and that he is asleep in relation to someone who is awake?' The ministers again could not solve the riddle. The father said to his son the minister, 'The person who practices the way is indicated. In comparison to ordinary people, he is awake, yet in comparison to the Venerable One who has attained enlightenment, he is asleep.'

"The deity again posed a problem. 'How can you know the weight of a large elephant?' The father of the minister said, 'Put the elephant in a boat and mark the boat at the water line. Next, put rocks in the boat and when the boat is at the same water line, weigh the rocks.'

"The deity posed yet another problem. 'What is described when it is said that one handful of water is greater than the great ocean?' The minister's father said, 'If one offers a handful of water with pious faith to the Three Treasures, to one's mother and father, or to a sick person, the merit of that deed will be the acquiring of timeless happiness. Though the waters of the ocean are great, they could not last over one kalpa.'

"At that time the deity made appear a hungry person with his bones showing and made him say, 'Is there one more hungry and suffering than I in this world?' The minister's father said, 'If a person is miserly and jealous, does not believe in the Three Treasures, and does not pay respect through offerings to his parents and teachers, then in the next life he will fall into the realm of hungry ghosts. During hundreds of thousands of years, even the names of water and food will not be heard. The body will be like mountains, the stomach will be like a valley, the throat will be thinner than a needle, and the hair, like wire, will coil around the legs and body. If one moves his body, the joints will be aflame. It is not known how many times greater the suffering of this person is in comparison with that of this hungry person.'

"The deity then made appear a person whose hands and feet were shackled, whose neck and stomach were fastened by chains, and from whose body a fire belched, scorching and festering him. He said, 'Is there one suffering more than I in this world?' The minister's father said, 'If there is a person who does not honor his parents, harms his teacher, rebels against his king, and slanders the Three Treasures, then in the next world he will fall into hell. He will experience limitless pain from things like a mountain of blades, a forest of swords, a carriage of fire, a flaming oven, and a river of boiling urine. He will suffer hundreds of thousands of times more than this present person.'

"The deity again made appear an incomparably beautiful girl who said, 'Is there one more beautiful than I in this world?' The minister's father said, 'If a person honors his parents, believes in and respects the Three Treasures, likes to give, observes the precepts, endures well, and works with great effort, then in the next world, he will be born in the heavenly realm. That person would have a hundred thousand times more beauty than the present girl.'

"The deity then brought forth a perfectly square cedar beam and said, 'Which is the top and which is the root?' The minister's father said, 'Put the wood in water and the root side will sink.'

"As a last problem the deity made two identical white horses appear and asked which was the mare and which was the foal. The minister's father again taught how to distinguish one from another. 'Give the horses some fodder and the mare will without doubt push the grass to the foal.'

"In this way the teachings of the minister's father completely solved the problems, and the deity greatly rejoiced and gave the king many treasures. He pledged, 'From now on, I shall protect this country and never let any foreign enemies invade the country.' The king was filled with joy and praised the cleverness of the minister. The minister said in response, 'Your Majesty, this was not my wisdom. If Your Majesty permits me, I shall tell fully of the circumstances.' The king said, 'Even if there is a capital offence, I shall ask no questions.' The minister said, 'According to the law of the land, I could not take care of my elderly father; however, I could not bear to cast out my father, so I secretly broke the law and in a cellar I cared for him. The answers to these problems were all through the wisdom of my father. Your Majesty, please from this day forth allow us to care for the elderly.'

"The king rejoiced from his heart and honored the father and looked up to him as the national teacher. Throughout the land it was forbidden to cast out the elderly, and one had to do one's utmost to honor and care for them. It was proclaimed that there would be a heavy penalty for making light of one's parents and not honoring one's teacher.

(2) "Again, long ago in Varanasi, there was a householder called Maitreya. His father had died young and left no money, and so every day Maitreya sold wood and made two coins, supporting his mother therewith. Day after day his income increased, four coins, eight coins, sixteen coins, and so he could generously take care of his mother. People seeing his high character and his being endowed with good fortune encouraged him by saying, 'Your father used to go to sea to collect pearls; why do you not follow in his footsteps?' Hearing this, Maitreya returned home and asked permission from his mother to go to sea. His mother thought him to be too considerate of her to be able to go to sea and leave her alone and in jest gave her permission saying, 'You may go to sea.'

"Receiving his mother's permission, he gathered friends and made various preparations. He then came to say goodbye to his mother. This time his mother was frightened and lamented, 'How can I be separated from my only child? Please wait until I die.' 'Mother, you granted my wish previously. I cannot change my mind now.' Seeing that it would be difficult to change his mind, she wrapped her arms around his legs crying, 'Stop!' However, Maitreya had made up his mind, and pushing his mother aside he went to sea. At that time, he cut ten strands of his mother's hair. He and his friends went to the seacoast and gathered many pearls. Deciding to come back on land, they quickly returned.

"At that time, there was a law of the land that said that in a robbery, as long as the victim was not captured by the thief, the thief had to return the treasure to the victim. However, if the victim was caught by the thief, then the treasure would be considered the property of the thief. Because of this, every night Maitreya separated from his friends and stayed alone at different places. At dawn, they would hurriedly come after him and continue on their journey. One night, there was a storm, and his friends awoke suddenly and forgot to go after him.

"Separated from his friends, he did not know the way to go. Having no other recourse, he climbed a mountain and saw an emerald blue castle. Being hungry and thirsty, he entered it, and four beautiful maidens welcomed him in rejoicing, each holding a magic jewel. He spent forty thousand years there in the pleasure of heavenly music. However, he eventually became bored with the pleasure, but when he bade them farewell, they stopped him and made him stay another forty thousand years there. Finally he left there and entered a crystal castle where he spent eighty thousand years of pleasure with eight beautiful maidens. Again, he left there and went toward a silver castle where he spent one hundred sixty thousand years of pleasure with sixteen beautiful girls. Again, he went to a golden castle and spent three hundred thousand years of pleasure there with thirty-two beautiful maidens. Finally, he became tired of that place and was about to leave when the maidens stopped him saying, 'Until now you have spent your time in good places, but from now they will not be good. You may stay here as long as you wish.' However, he thought, 'These girls love me and therefore they say such things.' Thus he was off again in a hurry.

"In the distance, there was an austere iron castle that soared up into the sky. Entering it he saw a man with a wreath of fire around his head who, upon seeing Maitreya, placed the wreath on his head and left. Maitreya was frightened and asked the devilish guard, 'When can I take off this fearsome wreath?' He answered, 'Until someone who has done the same thing that you have done comes here.' He asked the reason for it. He answered, 'When you were in the world you cared for your mother with two coins a day, so in the emerald blue castle you received the pleasure of four wish-granting jewels and four beautiful maidens for forty thousand years. The four coins every day became eighty thousand years of pleasure in the crystal castle, the eight coins became one hundred eighty thousand years of pleasure in the silver castle, and the sixteen coins became three hundred twenty thousand years of pleasure in the golden castle. But now the result of evil deeds has caught up with you, and because you cut off strands of your mother's hair, you must wear the fire wreath in the iron castle.'

"Again, he asked whether there were others who received the same torment and the guard answered, 'There are unlimited numbers.' Maitreya at this point thought in the depths of his heart, 'Well, I cannot get out of this. All right, I alone shall take upon myself the torments of all the others.' Then the fearsome wreath of fire fell to the ground. Facing the guard he asked, 'Why did this wreath of fire fall, even though it was not supposed to fall?' The guard was angered, and with the staff held in his hand he killed Maitreya with one blow. But Maitreya was reborn immediately in heaven.

"Disciples, it was I who was Maitreya. The good and evil resulting in serving one's parents is like this," said the World-Honored One.

(3) A girl was born in the house of a rich man in Sravasti. Immediately upon birth she said, "Shun evil and shameless and ungrateful deeds for grace." With such virtue, she was named Wisdom. As she became older she held the Dharma in high regard, and with this as her incentive she renounced world and became a nun. Practicing diligently she attained enlightenment. When she realized that she had not been at the World-Honored One's side for a while, she immediately went to him. "Please receive my confession of repentance." The World-Honored One, saying that he had also previously received her confession of repentance, told the following story.

"Long ago there was a six-tusked white elephant with two wives named Wisdom and Good Wisdom. While leading a group of elephants in the forest, he came upon a lotus flower. He thought of giving it to Wisdom. However, Good Wisdom took it instead. Having the flower taken from her, Wisdom became jealous and began to think that her husband really loved Good Wisdom more than herself. Going to the Buddha stupa in the mountains where she always had made flower offerings, she made this wish. 'Upon being born a woman, may I know the past and pull out the tusks of the white elephant.' Jumping off the mountain top, she died and was born as the daughter of King Videha, and when she grew older she became the queen of King Brahmadatta. Then she remembered her previous life and said to the king, 'O great king, please have constructed for me a bed from elephant tusks. If you do not, my life is meaningless.'

"The king, listening to her fervent wish, announced to hunters that the one to bring in the most elephant tusks would get one hundred pieces of gold. A hunter who knew of a six-tusked white elephant put on a monk's robe, took a poisoned arrow, and went off toward the forest where it lived. The white elephant heard from his wife Good Wisdom the warning that a hunter was coming near, but when he saw the man in a monk's robe he relaxed his caution, saying, 'Since he is wearing a robe, he will do no evil deeds.' Thus the hunter without any difficulty approached and shot deep into the elephant with the poisoned arrow. Good Wisdom cried, 'Nothing bad was supposed to happen since he was wearing a robe. What is this?' The elephant, trying to comfort her, said, 'It was not the fault of the robe but the fault of the heart's passions.' The white elephant stopped her from killing the hunter, and when five hundred elephants came charging, he feared that they would kill the hunter who had angered them and hid him between his legs. After they left, he asked, 'Why did you shoot me with your arrow?' 'Because the king is after the tusks.' Hearing this reason, he said, 'Hurry, then, and pull out the tusks.' The hunter was struck by the compassion of the elephant. Seeing that he could not lift his arms so high, the elephant pulled out his own tusks and gave them to the hunter. He then made the vow. 'I shall in the next world pull out the tusks of the three poisons of all people.'

"Thus the queen got her tusks, but when she heard the circumstances she began to have regrets. 'How could I take the tusks of one who upheld such superior precepts?' From then on, she practiced to attain virtue and made the vow, 'In the next world, may I learn the path under him and gain enlightenment.'

"Wisdom, that white elephant was I, the hunter was Devadatta, the elephant Wisdom was you, and Good Wisdom was Yasodhara.'

(4) "Disciples, in a past life there were many birds and beasts playing as they gathered in a bamboo grove at the base of the Himalaya Mountains. Among the birds, there was a parrot. At one time, a storm suddenly arose, and bamboos rubbed each other, thereby causing a fire that set the bamboo grove ablaze. The birds and beasts were frightened and tried to flee. They were running here and there among the rising flames. The parrot, being moved by deep compassion, felt the pain of his fellow animals. He soaked his wings in water and flew up into the sky sprinkling water over the raging flames. With unlimited concern, he repeated this without cease. This shook the heavenly abode of Indra, and the deity came forth and said to the parrot, 'This great fire in the bamboo grove extends over many miles; how do you expect to extinguish it by dripping water from your wings?' The parrot answered, 'I have a great heart, and if I work hard and am not slack in my efforts, then I am sure to be able to extinguish this great fire. If I cannot accomplish it in this life, I will be able to finish it in the next.' Indra was moved by the parrot's aspiration and let fall a great rain that extinguished the fire.

"Disciples, that parrot was I. As I am trying to extinguish the flames of the three poisons of all people now, so did I in my previous life have the same concern for all beings.

(5) "Long ago, there were two brothers who both rejoiced in the teachings of the Buddha. They left home and practiced the path. The elder brother practiced the good diligently, concentrated his thought in the forest, and attained enlightenment. The younger brother, being naturally wise, read a large range of sutras. Receiving a commission from a government minister, he built a temple. Soon he also constructed living quarters for monks, a lecture hall, and a pagoda. The skill of the design impressed the minister.

"The younger brother told the minister about his elder brother and said that he would like to call him to the newly built temple. The minister agreed and sent some people to give a warm welcome to this holy elder brother, who then came to the new temple; and the minister generously supported him. Now once the minister gave the elder brother a wool rug valued at one thousand pieces of gold. The elder brother had no choice but to accept it, and thinking that something of such value might be useful to his younger brother, he immediately gave it to him. At the same time, the minister gave a cheap wool rug to the younger brother, and this angered him deeply. Later, the minister again gave the elder brother a valuable wool rug, and again he for his part gave it to his younger brother. The younger brother no longer could contain his jealousy and spoke to the minister's daughter, who was engaged to him. 'Your father was very warm to me, but since my brother's arrival, his heart has been deceived and is warm only to my brother and quite cold to me. With this rug, make a dress and tell your father that my elder brother sent it to you.'

"The daughter said that she could not speak badly of someone her father believed in and thought highly of; but the younger brother said, 'If you do not do as I ask, our engagement will be broken forever.' She therefore did as the younger brother requested. The minister listened to what his daughter said and angrily asked, 'What kind of monk is it that would try to seduce my daughter with the precious gift I gave him?' From then on, when the elder brother came to visit, he did not rise as was his custom, and he showed signs of anger. The elder brother concluded that someone had slandered him, and so he directly flew up into the sky and manifested his supernatural powers. Seeing this, the minister deeply regretted his actions and immediately banished the younger brother and his daughter.

"Disciples, that younger brother was I. Through slandering another, I have suffered much pain over endless kalpas. That is why I have now been slandered by Sundari."

(6) The disciples said to the World-Honored One, "World-Honored One, Devadatta is your cousin, so why does he harbor hatred for you and want to harm you?" The World-Honored One replied, "Long ago, there was a jivamjivaka bird in the Himalaya Mountains. This bird had one body but two heads. One was always eating sweet fruit and sought to comfort the body. The other head, being envious, said that it had never even once tasted such sweet fruit and so ate a poisonous fruit and both heads lost their lives.

"Disciples, the one who ate the sweet fruit was I and the one that ate the poisonous fruit was Devadatta. Long ago, we both had the same body and now we both have the same blood. In this way, he tried to harm me."

(7) In Rajagriha there was a wealthy man who went to the World-Honored One and listened to his teachings every day. His wife, thinking that he had a mistress, was suspicious and asked her husband, "Since you go to the World-Honored One day after day, can you tell me in what way he is so great?" The husband described the World-Honored One's various virtues, and the wife was overjoyed. She immediately went to the World-Honored One by carriage; but since it was crowded with kings and officials and many other people, she could not get near him. She only bowed to him and went home. She later died and was born in the heavenly realm. Remembering the blessings of her past life, she came down and, coming before the Buddha, she heard the Dharma and attained enlightenment.

(8) "Long ago, there was an artist called Kenika in the country of Gandhara. For three years he was someone's guest away from home; upon making thirty pieces of gold he was about to return home when he saw another person call a Dharma gathering for the monks. He thought, 'I have yet to sow the seeds of merit. I now have the opportunity to work the field of merit; how can I let it pass?' He found out from the person in charge of the Dharma gathering the cost of such a gathering and later asked, 'Please beat the drum and gather the monks. I want to have a gathering to offer something.' He gave him the thirty pieces of gold.

"The gathering was held and the artist went home filled with joy. His wife asked him, 'In the three years, how much did you make?' 'The money earned is put aside in a treasury.' 'Where is that treasury?' 'It is in the midst of the honorable monks.' His wife was disgusted at this, and she called her relatives together and had him bound up. She then lodged a complaint with the authorities. 'My children and I are suffering in poverty; we have no clothes and no food. And my husband recklessly spent the money he earned.' People hearing the complaint asked the husband the reason for his spending the money. 'My life is like a flash of lightning; it cannot last long. Moreover, it is like the morning dew; it must evaporate in a short while. In my previous life I did not sow the seeds of merit, and that is why I am so poor now. Thinking deeply on the pain of being without clothes or food and seeing the pious Dharma gathering held in the city of Pukala, I rejoiced. I was filled with faith and I gave the thirty pieces of gold I had earned in three years and thereby provided food for one day to the community of monks.'

"Upon hearing this the people hearing the complaint deeply rejoiced and gave him the many jewels they were wearing; and moreover, they gave him one village. His reward was thus truly great.

(9) "Long ago there was a poor man named Kelayi. One day, he saw a group of wealthy people go to a temple to hold a large Dharma gathering. He went home and thought intently, 'Those wealthy people sowed the seeds of merit in their previous lives, so they became wealthy, but my merit was rather slight, so I have to struggle now in the pain of this hard poverty.' In spite of himself, he started to shed tears. His wife, wondering what happened, asked him about it, and he told her his thoughts. His wife said, 'Crying will do nothing. Sell me as a maid and with that money sow some merit.' 'If I sell you, how can I go on living?' 'In that case, let us both sell ourselves.' They both went to a rich man's house. 'Please lend us ten pieces of gold. If we are not able to return it in seven days, we shall become your servants .' With that promise, they borrowed ten pieces of gold and went immediately to the temple and arranged to have a Dharma gathering in seven days. The two working together pounded rice day and night. If they were unable to return the money by the appointed time, they would have to give themselves to that rich man. They therefore worked with all their might.

"On the sixth day, the king came to the temple and said that he would like to have a Dharma gathering for the next day. The monks told him that they had promised to accept the hospitality of the poor couple on that day and therefore refused the king. The king immediately called Kelayi and asked him to change his Dharma gathering to another day. He told the king, 'If we miss that day, we shall not have another chance, for it is certain that we shall spend the rest of our lives as servants,' and he explained the circumstances. Hearing this, the king was deeply touched. 'This is indeed a most rare thing. You are truly ones who have understood true poverty. You changed a slack body into an upright one, no treasure into real treasure, and a slack life into an upright one.' The king first and then the queen both took off their garments and jewelry and gave them to the two. Moreover they gave them ten villages also."

(10) Kaniska, the king of Kusana, was friendly with three wise men. One of them was the Bodhisattva Asvaghosa. He said to the king, "Sire, if you take heed of my words, your mind will always be in quietude, and in the next life you will be one with goodness, and you will not be born in unhappy destinies for a long time." Next the minister Mathala spoke to the king. "Sire, if you take heed of my mystic teachings and do not divulge them, Your Highness will be

able to govern all the world." The third was the physician Caraka, who said to the king, "Sire, if you take heed of what I say, you will suffer from no illness your whole life long, and you will be able to enjoy a myriad of fine tasting foods." The king followed Caraka's words and had not even the slightest illness.

The king also followed the words of Mathala and sent forth armies across the four seas; and he conquered the countries in three directions. When only the east remained to be conquered, he prepared his forces for the conquest. With a procession led by the defeated peoples and by white elephants, the king went forth following behind. They came to the Asian Pamirs and were about to go over a sharp cliff when his horse suddenly stopped. The king was surprised and said to the horse, "You have up till now carried me to conquest many a time; now the three directions are settled and only the east is left, so why do you not proceed?" At that moment, the minister Mathala said, "I made you promise not to reveal what I said, yet now you have revealed it. I think that you do not have long to live." The king also felt that, as the minister said, his death was approaching. Thinking about the many people he had killed through his many conquests, he deeply regretted his heavy sins, and upon returning to his own country he built a temple and gave offerings to the monks. He immersed himself in the thought of repentance and upheld the precepts.

The king's ministers said among themselves, "The king has killed so many people that at this late date, even by practicing so much good, how can he rid himself of his offences?" The king heard this and in order to answer their doubts called them and filled a big cauldron with water and boiled it for seven days and nights. The king himself then threw a ring into the cauldron and ordered them to get it. But no one could follow the order. Then the king said, "Then think of some method to get it out." One of them said, "Stop the fire and put cold water into the cauldron. You can then put your hand in it without getting burned." The king again spoke to them. "The evil things I did before are like the boiling cauldron. Now, the good I do by the arising of the thought of repentance is like stopping the fire and pouring in cold water. This is how I can avoid the pain of the unhappy destinies and gain the happy destinies." Hearing this they rejoiced and praised the virtue of the king who now followed the words of the wisest one, the Bodhisattva Asvaghosa.

(11) There was a brahmin in the land of Kausambi who acted as prime minister. He was by nature quite violent, and he was apt to act in a most improper way. His wife, too, was violent and acted in the same way as her husband. At one time, the husband ordered his wife, "Gotama has now come to this country. If he comes here, close the gates and do not let him in." However, one day the World-Honored One by chance came to visit their home. The wife gave no greeting and was silent. The World-Honored One said, "You are ignorant and hold wrong views. You do not believe in the Three Treasures." Hearing this, she was angry, and she tore off her jewelry, put on dirty clothes, and sat on the ground. When her husband came home, he saw this and asked the reason; she said that she had been insulted by Gotama. When the gate was opened the next day, the World-Honored One entered the house. Seeing this the brahmin grabbed a sword and

was about to use it when the World-Honored One suddenly went up into the sky. Seeing this act of great supernatural power, the man was filled with regret and threw himself on the ground, crying, "World-Honored One, please return to earth and accept my repentance." Hearing this plea, the World-Honored One taught the Dharma to the husband and wife and let them enter the path.

The disciples thought it strange that the World-Honored One would come down to earth for such evil people, so he told them of the past circumstances that caused this event.

"Long ago," he told them, "there was a king called Acceptor of Evil in the country of Kasi. He did all kinds of improper things and made sentient beings suffer. He confiscated as taxes all the rare things that the merchants had gathered from the four quarters of the earth; he took them all. Therefore all the country's treasures were in the hands of the king. The talk of the infamy of this king spread from person to person.

"At that time, there was a parrot that, hearing travellers through the forest talk of the evils of the king, thought to admonish him and so flew off and entered the king's garden and alighted on a tree limb. Seeing the queen enter the garden, he flapped his wings and said, 'The king is now doing most improper things and oppressing sentient beings, and the poison from it is even felt among the birds and beasts. Indeed, the land is filled with cries of resentment and anger. You, too, are as guilty as the king in your cruelty. Is this what the mother and father of sentient beings should do?'

"The queen was greatly angered and got people to catch the bird. The bird was not at all frightened and fearlessly let itself be caught. It was immediately brought before the king. The king asked why he was slandering him, and the parrot enumerated the king's seven transgressions. 'Wallowing in sexual indulgence, indulging in liquor, gambling, liking to kill living beings, indulgently saying evil words, harshly taxing people, and taking peoples' possessions in devious ways: these seven transgressions put a king in danger. Moreover, there are three things that will ruin the country: a king's being intimate with insincere flatterers and not heeding the curing words of a sage; his invading another country because he wants it; and his forgetting to care for sentient beings. If the king does not stop doing these three evil deeds, then in no time the country will be ruined. The true king is, in the first place, the one the whole country looks up to; he is the bridge by which all people cross; to all people close to him and distant, he, like a scale, is fair. He does not violate the way walked by earlier holy men; like the sun he shines on all the world; like the moon he gives coolness to all; and like parents, he gives to all. He is like the heavens that cover all, like the earth that supports all, and like the water that wets down the fires of evil. The great kings of the past all upheld these ten virtues and taught and guided sentient beings.'

"Hearing this, the king was deeply ashamed of his actions, and having received the parrot's teachings he spread them throughout the land; and good people gathered round. Sentient beings were truly overjoyed. Disciples, that parrot was I, the king was the brahmin prime minister, and the queen was the wife."

(12) If one uses various means when seeking after a thing that should be sought, one will gain it. However, forcibly trying to obtain a thing that should not be sought, one will not gain it. It is like squeezing sand looking for oil or rubbing pieces of ice together looking for milk.

Long ago, there was a king called Brahmadatta in Varanasi. One night, he heard a voice from a faraway graveyard calling, "Sire, sire." This occurred three times in one night. The king was quite frightened, and he gathered brahmins and soothsayers, asking, "What should I do?" They answered, "This is without doubt the doings of the graveyard spirit. You should choose a brave person and have him investigate the voice." The king proclaimed throughout the land, "The one who will investigate the graveyard voice will be given five hundred pieces of gold." At that time, there was a poor single man of courage who answered the call. He put on armor and helmet and took up a sword, and he went to the graveyard at night and asked the voice, "Who are you?" The voice answered, "I am a treasure hidden in the earth. Every night I call the king, but he is afraid and does not answer. If the king had come here, I would have led him to the treasure house. You, however, are quite brave. I shall give the treasure to you. I have seven helpers and tomorrow morning I shall with them become a monk and go to your house." The man asked, "How should I greet you?" He answered, "Just purify the room, adorn it, and fill eight bowls with grape juice or milk curd and let us be able to partake of it. After eating, bring a pillow and hit the head of the monk who is on the main seat. Take him to the corner room and in so doing you will gain the treasure."

The man went home, and the next day he went to the palace early and said, "The voice was that of a spirit." He received the five hundred pieces of gold. Returning home, he called a barber and made himself presentable, purified the room, and prepared the food. Presently, he greeted the eight monks and, after eating, he carried off the monk on the main seat and entered the corner room. The monk turned into a golden turtle. He repeated this with the seven other monks and they all became golden turtles. The barber, seeing this, thought that he might get treasures in the same way. He followed the same preparations and, inviting eight monks, offered them food. He closed the gate and hit the monk on the main seat, but his head split open and blood flowed out. He presently pushed him into the corner room and in his excitement soiled himself. The other seven monks, one after another, were struck by the barber and writhed on the floor. Finally one of them broke down the door and escaped, shouting out, "Murder, murder!" Soon the barber was arrested by the authorities and told everything to the king. The king immediately sent men to get the golden turtles from the other man and bring them back to the palace. However, the turtles became poisonous snakes right before the officials' eyes.

Hearing this, the king said to the man, "All that treasure was given to you. No one can take treasures not given. In the same way, a person upholding the precepts and practicing the path earnestly will gain a good reward, but an ignorant one seeing only the reward and upholding the precepts outwardly, but inwardly with no faith, falsely seeking peace and bliss, will not be able to gain it."

(13) The sly person seems righteous on the outside, but in his heart he harbors evil thoughts. Long ago, there was an elderly brahmin who took a young second wife. She disliked her husband and hoping to take her pleasure with other men suggested that they hold a gathering for young brahmins. The husband suspected her and, making excuses, postponed the gathering. On one occasion, his son by a former wife accidentally fell into a fire; the wife did nothing to save him. When questioned about it, she said, "I do not grab another woman's child." The elder brahmin was moved by this and held the postponed gathering of young brahmins. The young wife used this occasion to take her pleasure as she desired. The husband came to know about this and was pained. Finally he took his valuables and left the house alone. On the road he met another brahmin, and the two of them travelled together and lodged together. The next day they left their lodgings, and after quite a distance the other brahmin thought of something and said, "Until now I have not even taken the smallest thing from another; however, last night a piece of grass stuck to my garment. I must return it to the innkeeper. Please wait; I shall soon return." He took the path by which they came. Hearing this, the elderly brahmin was greatly impressed. He thought that this person above all others should be respected and honored. However, the brahmin entered a ditch near the road and lay on his stomach resting; after a while, he returned to the elderly brahmin. At that time, in order to wash something dirty, the elderly brahmin handed over his valuables to the other brahmin without any fear or doubt. In this way, the elderly brahmin lost his valuables.

The elderly brahmin was pained with grief and walked aimlessly like a man without a spirit. He came to a tree and rested. There, a stork, holding grass in its bill, spoke to the other numerous birds, "Let us help each other out and live in one place." Those birds all believed him and gathered there. As soon as he saw the birds fly off, the stork looked at each nest and pecked at the eggs and ate up many a chick. When the birds returned, he put on an innocent face as before, pulling at the grass.

Somewhat later, there quietly came a lone ascetic wearing torn robes who was saying, "Worms, take care." The elderly brahmin wondered what he was doing and asked him about it. He answered, "I feel sorry for living beings. Thinking I may kill these worms by stepping on them, I walk in this manner." The elderly brahmin felt deep respect for this humble person and following after him stopped at the ascetic's house as night fell. While lying down in the hut, he rejoiced in meeting a truly religious person. In the middle of the night, the dreams of the traveller's sleep were suddenly interrupted by the sounds of singing and music. He went to see what this was all about. The austere practitioner of the afternoon was enjoying himself with a young maiden. When the girl danced, the man played the harp. When the man danced, the girl sang. The heart of the elderly brahmin chilled like ice. "I can believe nothing in this world."

There was a rich man in a country who one night had his valuables stolen and reported it to the king. "There was no one suspicious nearby. Only a brahmin came in and out. He was wearing leaves and was leading a pious life." Hearing this, the king immediately arrested the brahmin and thoroughly questioned him. Finally he confessed.

(14) When the World-Honored One was staying in the Jeta Grove, there was a man called At Will in Sravasti. He was a thief, a murderer, and a wanton. Finally the authorities arrested him, and after dragging him around the town they took him to the place of execution. This man facing death unexpectedly met the World-Honored One and told him thoroughly of his sins. "World-Honored One, my life is ending; please let your compassion reach me and ask the king if I may become your disciple. If that happens, then even if I immediately die there will be nothing to be bitter about." The World-Honored One heeded his request and asked Ananda to talk to King Prasenajit and ask him if this criminal could become a disciple. Permission was immediately granted, and he became a disciple of the World-Honored One. Practicing hard he attained enlightenment.

(15) A merchant called Floating Sea of Rajagriha went to sea with many people to search for treasure. He had a young and beautiful wife who thought of him day and night. In the end, she went to a small shrine of a deity and made a wish. "Lord, if you fulfill my wish and allow my husband to return safely, I shall give you jewelry of gold and silver. If you do not listen to my wish, I shall dirty this shrine with some foul thing."

After some time, her husband returned home safely. The wife rejoiced, and she gathered up her gold and silver jewelry and left with a maid. Before reaching the shrine, she met the World-Honored One, who with many disciples had entered the town. His noble bearing put the sun to shame. She paid her respects to this noble spirit and without thinking gave the jewelry in her hands to him. The jewelry became a jewelled canopy that hung in the air and moved following the steps of the World-Honored One. Seeing this wondrous thing, the woman was deeply impressed, and throwing herself on the ground she asked, "Please, because of what has happened, please make me as noble as you are, World-Honored One." Seeing this, the World-Honored One smiled because he knew that she would attain enlightenment eventually.

(16) At one time, the World-Honored One with a number of disciples was travelling through Magadha. Reaching the embankment of the river Ganges, he spoke to a captain who was tying up a ferryboat on the riverbank. "Please ferry us over to the other side." The captain said, "No problem, if you pay the ferry fee." "Captain, I am a captain of a ferry too. I take many people across this world's ocean of illusion. Is it not pleasant that we both ferry people across? Without taking any fee, I have ferried people like Angulimala who had harmed so many people and like Mantoda who haughtily looked down on people on account of pride. Please see fit to ferry us over without taking a fee." The captain, however, did not answer. Another ferry captain downstream heard the World-Honored One's words and welcomed the World-Honored One's party. Among the disciples some showed their supernatural power by going across to the other

shore by walking on the water. Seeing this, the first ferry captain regretted his actions greatly and threw himself on the ground and placed his faith in the World-Honored One and his disciples. Receiving permission, he invited the World-Honored One and his party to his home and offered them food and received the teaching. He rejoiced in the Dharma.

(17) In Rajagriha, there was a maid to a rich man who was by nature sincere and believed in the Buddha's teachings. From time to time, the girl, at the request of her master, ground sandalwood incense. At one time, after grinding the incense, she stepped outside and saw the World-Honored One in town begging for food. Her heart was filled with joy and without thinking she went back inside to get a bit of the sandalwood incense to rub on the World-Honored One's feet. The World-Honored One approved of the girl's heart of faith and with his supernatural powers changed the incense into clouds of incense that trailed and covered Rajagriha. Seeing this wondrous act, she had even deeper faith and vowed, "I wish to have the same enlightenment as the World-Honored One." The World-Honored One smiled because he knew that she would eventually attain enlightenment.

(18) The rich people of Sravasti one day put on their fine clothes and, carrying incense and flowers in their hands and playing music to enjoy themselves, went on an outing at the outskirts of the town. At the gate they met the World-Honored One with many disciples coming into town to beg for food. Paying their respects to the glowing figure of the World-Honored One, they were overjoyed and without thinking bowed at his feet. Playing music, they comforted the party and tossed the many flowers in their hands into the air over the World-Honored One. With his supernatural powers, the World-Honored One made a beautiful flower canopy that he enlarged to cover all of Sravasti. Seeing this auspicious omen, all of them made the same vow, "I wish to have the same enlightenment as the World-Honored One." The World-Honored One smiled because he knew that they would all eventually attain enlightenment.

(19) Long ago, a king called Surupa ruled Varanasi, and the people prospered. The king's wisdom was pure, and he earnestly sought the path. He left the treasures in the city, and he announced that he would give valuables to anyone who would teach an excellent teaching. This sincere heart and mind of the king was felt all the way to the heavenly abode of the deities and shook it to its foundations. Indra, wanting to test the king's sincerity, appeared in the form of a devil and came to the gate of the palace. He said, "I am in possession of a most wondrous teaching." As the king greeted him happily, the devil, grinding his fearsome sword-like tusks, said, "I am starved now and cannot teach the Dharma." When the king gave him various kinds of food, the devil said, "My hunger will not be satisfied unless I have warm human blood and fresh human flesh."

At that time, the prince Sundara came forward and spoke to his father. "I understand that attaining the Dharma is most difficult. I want to give myself to the devil." Knowing the great will of the prince who did not cling to his life, the king thought to himself, 'From long past, I have been bound by clinging love, and I could not stop the cycle of rebirths. It is now time for me to give up my beloved son for the sake of the Dharma.' He decided to grant his son's wish.

The prince went courageously to the devil. The devil tore the prince apart on the floor in front of the king, and he drank his blood and ate his flesh. But his hunger was not yet satisfied. The queen, being encouraged by the bravery of the prince in giving up his life for the Dharma, received the king's permission to give herself as food to the devil. The devil, still not filled, sought the king himself. The king quietly said, "I do not cling to my life; however, if this body of mine dies, I shall be unable to listen to the Dharma. If you teach me the Dharma first, I shall give my body to you." Realizing the sincerity of the king, the devil recited this verse of the Dharma for him:

> Grief and fear arise from clinging.
> Those who free themselves from clinging love
> Will cut forever the root of fear.

Reciting this verse the devil immediately changed into Indra, and the prince and queen also resumed their original forms. The king was filled with joy.

After saying this, the World-Honored One explained, "The king was I, the prince was Ananda, and the queen was Yasodhara. I, too, long ago cast aside clinging love and sought the path."

(20) One morning, the World-Honored One with many disciples entered Sravasti, and as they were begging for food they came across a brahmin in the street. The brahmin pointed to the earth with his finger and told them, "You must pay me five hundred pieces of gold. If you do not, I shall not let you pass." The World-Honored One merely stood there silently. This startled many people, and King Prasenajit heard of it and quickly sent someone to give the money. However, the brahmin would not accept it. Then Sudatta the rich man came carrying five hundred coins and gave it to the brahmin, who then let the World-Honored One pass. Knowing that the disciples thought this strange, the World-Honored One explained the situation.

"Long ago, there was a prince called Sujati in Varanasi. One day, he was playing with a close friend and he saw the son of the prime minister lose five hundred pieces of gold gambling with a gambler in the streets. He said to the gambler, 'If the son of the prime minister cannot pay, I shall pay.' But relying on his father's power, the prince did not pay off the debt. Thus the debt has been carried over endless lives until today. That prince was I, the son of the prime minister was Sudatta, and the gambler was the present brahmin. Thus, disciples, you must pay off all debts. If you do not, then even if you gain enlightenment, you will not be able to escape that difficulty."

(21) When the World-Honored One was in the Jeta Grove there was a thief called Rudra in Sravasti. With a sharp sword and with bow and arrow, he hid by the roadway and robbed the passersby. One day, close to starvation, seeing in the distance a monk under a tree holding a begging bowl, he thought, "There is surely food in that begging bowl. I shall take it and eat it. If he has already eaten, then I shall kill him and cut his stomach open and eat." He quietly approached the monk and stopped close by. The monk had read his mind and

thought, "If I do not give him food, he will surely kill me. If that happens he will have committed a most serious crime." He therefore immediately spoke to him and gave him the food. When his hunger was satisfied and he rejoiced, the monk taught the Dharma in a variety of ways. Faith immediately arose in his heart and he became a monk and awakened to enlightenment.

(22) When the World-Honored One was in a bamboo grove near Rajagriha, the rich men of the city held a festival and took pleasure in music and singing. Among the women was a dance teacher from the south who brought along her lovely daughter Utpala. She was not only beautiful but did not lack even one of the sixty-four arts of a woman. The gracefulness of her dancing had no equal. She herself said, "Is there one in this city who can match my dancing or my knowledge of the scriptures?" People told her that the World-Honored One was in the bamboo grove, so she went dancing and singing into the grove with many people. Immodestly laughing, she did not even bow to the World-Honored One. Seeing this, the World-Honored One with his supernatural powers changed her into a one-hundred-year-old woman. Her hair white, her face wrinkled, her teeth gone, her back bent, she had to walk doubled over. She was surprised and saddened by the decline of her body; and thinking about the power of the World-Honored One, she greatly regretted her actions. She prostrated herself before him, and repenting her pride and her previous errors, she sincerely asked for his forgiveness.

Knowing her heart, the World-Honored One again with his supernatural powers changed her back to her original state. The crowd of people vividly saw the uncertainty of age and youth, and there were many who attained the eye of wisdom. The girl and her parents, receiving his permission, became disciples and attained enlightenment.

5. The Anthill

(1) The World-Honored One returned to Savatthi and entered the Jeta Grove. At that time Kumara-Kassapa dwelt in the Dark Grove. One night, a deity with a brilliance that lit up the whole grove came near him and said, "Kassapa, a person said to a brahmin, 'This anthill smokes at night and burns during the day.' The brahmin said to him, 'If that is the case, get a sword and dig deeply.' The person dug and a bar came out. The brahmin said, 'Take the bar out and dig deeper.' This time he saw some water bubbles. 'Take the bubbles out and dig deeper.' This time he saw a pitchfork. 'Take the pitchfork out and dig deeper.' This time he saw a box. 'Take the box out and dig deeper.' This time he saw a turtle. 'Take the turtle out and dig deeper.' This time he saw a butcher's knife. 'Take that out and dig deeper.' This time he saw a slice of flesh. 'Take that flesh out and dig some more.' This time he saw a Naga. At this, the brahmin said, 'Wise one, leave the Naga just like that; do not disturb it. Pay your respects to the Naga. Go to the World-Honored One and relate this enigma to him. It would be best to remember his explanations. There is no one among the world's many people except for the World-Honored One, his disciples, and those who have heard his teachings who can explain this riddle." Saying this, the deity disappeared.

(2) Kumara-Kassapa passed the rest of the night and went to the World-Honored One, told him about what happened, and asked for an explanation of each item of the story. The World-Honored One answered him, "Kassapa, the anthill is this physical body. Thinking at night about the things that one has done during the day is what is meant by 'smokes at night.' Acting by body and speaking by mouth during the day the things one thinks about at night is the meaning of 'burns during the day.' The brahmin is the Buddha. The person is a samana who is searching on the path. The sword is wisdom, and to dig deeply is effort. The bar is ignorance, and to take the bar out is to rid oneself of ignorance. Kassapa, to dig deeply with the knife means that with holy wisdom one exerts his utmost and one gets rid of ignorance.

"Next, the water bubbles are anger and pain, the pitchfork means doubt and uneasiness, the box is the five hindrances of the mind—desire, anger, sloth, restlessness, and doubt—the turtle is the body and mind, the butcher's knife that slaughters cattle is the five desires, and the one slice of flesh is the thirst for pleasure. In short, the story describes ridding oneself of these things.

"Kassapa, the Naga is the exhaustion of the passions. To leave the Naga as it is means not to disturb it; and to pay reverence to it means that if passions are extinguished, just leave things as they are and pay your respects to one who has extinguished all passions." Hearing this explanation, Kumara-Kassapa greatly rejoiced.

(3) The World-Honored One returned to Rajagaha and entered the Hot Spring Monastery on the southwest. Near daybreak, when it was still dark, Samiddhi bathed in the hot spring. While he was drying his body, a deity came, illuminating the whole grove with his light. "Disciple of the Buddha, do you know the verse of the One Good Night?" "Friend, I do not. Do you?" "I do not know it either. To know that verse and its meaning is of great benefit, so it would be good to know it."

After the deity left and night was about to end, Samiddhi went to the World-Honored One and talked to him about what happened. He asked the Buddha to teach him the verse of the One Good Night. The World-Honored One taught him the verse:

> Do not follow the past nor wait for the future.
> The past has passed by and the future is yet to come.
> Solely look to the present.
> Knowing again and again that it cannot be ousted nor can it be moved,
> Try hard today.
> Tomorrow, who knows the course of life?
> The army of death does not wait.
> Thus working hard without relief day and night is One Good Night.
> This, a holy sage proclaimed.

Samiddhi and the other disciples heard this verse. Before anyone could ask the meaning of it, the World-Honored One stood up from his seat and entered his room. So they went to Maha-Kaccana and asked him to explain the verse. Kaccana said, "Friends, ask the World-Honored One to explain the verse.

Coming to me is like entering a grove to search for the core of a tree, overlooking the root and trunk and believing that one finds the core in the branches and leaves. It will be best to remember what he says."

"Kaccana," they replied, "it is as you say. But he has entered his room, and you are praised by the Buddha and honored by your fellow monks. You have the ability to explain the meaning of the verse, so please do so."

"All right," he said, "I shall explain it. Listen carefully. 'Do not follow the past' means not to pursue and cling to things that have already gone. 'Do not wait for the future' means not to hope for something that is yet to come. 'Look to the present' means to direct your mind to what you see now in front of you and take in well the teachings of the Buddha. Friends, this is my explanation of the verse." And all the disciples, hearing this explanation by Kaccana, rejoiced greatly.

Chapter 4

THE STUPA

1. The Death of Nigantha Nataputta

(1) One day in his later years, King Pasenadi came to the Jeta Grove to hear the teachings of the Buddha and suddenly learned that Queen Mallika had passed away. Remembering the past, he fell into despair over this parting, and he sat silently with shoulders stooped and head down. The World-Honored One comforted the despairing king.

"Sire, in the world there are five things that one cannot avoid. They are old age, illness, death, exhaustion, and extinction. There is no way to escape from these five.

"Sire, ignorant people with slight wisdom uselessly cry and lament and fall into confusion when beings that must age age, when beings that must become ill become ill, when beings that must die die, when beings that must be exhausted are exhausted, and when beings that must become extinct become extinct. The disciples of the Buddha, rich in wisdom, at such a moment think in the following way. 'Old age, sickness, death, and the others, do not happen only to me. If I were to cry and lament, fall into confusion, not eat, let my body decline, and be unable to work, then the enemy Mara would rejoice, and my allies would be saddened.' Thinking in this way, they do not cry and lament. The ignorant thus shoot themselves with a poisonous arrow and make themselves suffer, while the disciples of the Buddha, avoiding the poisonous arrow, do not lament but of their own accord enter a realm of undefiled quietude."

(2) From there, the World-Honored One journeyed to the land of the Sakyas and stayed at a town called Vedhanna. At that time, Cunda was having the rainy season retreat in Pava. Cunda saw Nigantha's disciples split into two factions and fight with each other upon Nigantha's death. Finishing his retreat, he went to Ananda who was staying at Samagama and told him of what he had witnessed. Ananda immediately went to the World-Honored One, taking Cunda along with him.

"World-Honored One, Cunda has just spent his retreat at Pava, and he tells me that Nigantha has recently passed away there. After that, his disciples split into two factions and accused each other of not understanding the teachings and precepts, and of proclaiming the other party as maintaining a mistaken doctrine.

Because of this, both monks and householder followers began to hate the teachings, and their morale has declined precipitously."

The World-Honored One said in response, "Cunda, the teachings taught by those who have not gained true enlightenment do not lead to nirvana but always end like this. Cunda, if the teacher is not possessed of true enlightenment, and if therefore the teachings are false, it is a good thing that the disciples do not practice the path according to the teachings and discard those teachings. You should criticize such a teacher and teachings and praise such disciples. However, those who tell these disciples to keep to the teacher's teachings and those disciples who adhere to the wrong teachings will sink into vice.

"Cunda, if the teacher is not possessed of true enlightenment, and if therefore the teachings are false, when the disciples practice the way according to the teachings and hold fast to the teachings and follow them, then one must make efforts to have the disciples discard the teachings. If one praises adherence to such teachings, then the one who praises and the ones who are praised are both in the wrong. Cunda, if the teacher is possessed of true enlightenment, and therefore the Dharma is true, then the disciples must hold fast to the teaching and practice the path according to it.

"Cunda, suppose a teacher possessed of true enlightenment appears and teaches; if the teacher dies before his disciples master his teachings and before his teachings become established, this is most unfortunate for the disciples. If the teacher dies after the disciples master the teachings and practice according to them, and his teachings become established, that is fortunate for the disciples.

"Cunda, if the teaching has all the following points, it must be called perfect. The teacher has been a monk for a long time and is an elder of the world of faiths. The disciples, both monks and householders, are wise and diligent in training their minds to reach the state of peace and quietude. The disciples pass on the teachings correctly and have the strength to resolve all doctrinal disputes among the followers. The teachings spread and become known throughout the world. The teaching is beneficial and renowned in this world. If a teaching is lacking even one of these qualities, it is not perfect.

(3) "Cunda, I have appeared as one who has awakened to enlightenment and as a teacher of the world. I proclaim the Dharma that guides one to the peace and quietude of nirvana. My disciples realize the true Dharma and perfectly engage in the pious practice. Moreover, a long time ago I cast aside the world and became an elder in the world of faiths. My disciples, both householders and monks, are wise and diligent in training their minds to reach peace and quietude. The Dharma is proclaimed correctly, and so the doctrinal disputes arising among the followers can be resolved. My teachings have spread and they are well known throughout the world. Moreover, in the world there is no teacher and no assembly of disciples that has received more offerings or honors. If there is one who wants to name correctly a perfect teaching, he would have to indicate my teachings.

"Cunda, Uddaka Ramaputta often uses the phrase 'seeing but not seeing.' He uses it in reference to seeing the flat of a sharp razor but not seeing the blade. It is most petty. However, if the phrase is correctly used, it refers to hearing the perfect teaching and looking to make it clearer and nearer to perfection, yet finding nothing to add to it.

"It is on account of this, Cunda, that when you assemble to recite to each other the Dharma proclaimed by me, you should not argue. For the sake of the benefit and happiness of mankind, transmit this Dharma forever and clarify the passages and meanings of the passages.

"Cunda, when you assemble, if you think that the one who proclaims the Dharma has made a mistake reciting a passage or an error in explanation, do not immediately criticize it. Quietly face the person and ask, 'Does the passage correspond to that explanation and does that explanation agree with the passage?' Even if he says that they conform to each other, do not immediately criticize him. Rather, considerately try to teach him about that passage and that explanation.

"The true meaning should be taught to the one who proclaims a correct passage but a wrong explanation, and to the one who proclaims a correct explanation but a wrong passage. If one proclaims both the passage and the explanation correctly then just say, 'Very good indeed, very good indeed,' and follow him."

(4) "Cunda, I do not proclaim the Dharma in order to extinguish only these present passions nor in order to extinguish only future passions. I proclaim the Dharma in order to extinguish both future and present passions. Cunda, this is why your garments, which I have authorized, are to protect you from heat, cold, mosquitoes, and flies and cover the body enough for the sake of decency. Your food is enough to support this container of the Dharma and help you engage in religious practices. Your abode is also just enough to protect you from heat, cold, mosquitoes, and flies, and it lets you enjoy quiet solitude. Medicine also is used just enough to rid you of the pain of illness and let you gain good health. Cunda, those of other faiths may say that the disciples of the World-Honored One are addicted to pleasure. In this case it is good to ask those people of other faiths, 'When you say we are addicted to pleasure, what type of pleasure are you indicating, since there are so many types?'

"Cunda, there are four kinds of wrong pleasures. The first is the pleasure of taking the lives of living beings. The second is the pleasure of stealing others' possessions. The third is the pleasure of lying. The fourth is the pleasure of wallowing in the five desires. These four are what we are avoiding. If there is a person who criticizes us with one of these, it is baseless and false criticism.

"Cunda, besides these, there is also the pleasure that leads people to nirvana. It is simply the pleasure of meditation by freeing oneself from desires and evil deeds. Those who become absorbed in this pleasure will enjoy the benefit of gaining enlightenment.

(5) "Cunda, those of other faiths may say that with your wisdom you speak a lot about the past but very little about the future. Cunda, the Buddha speaks about the past to the heart's content with the wisdom of right mindfulness. With

regard to the future, he only says, with the wisdom born from his enlightenment, that this will be his last life of delusion.

"Cunda, when the Buddha speaks of the past, his teaching is truthful and to one's benefit. He talks at an appropriate time and does not tell lies. Moreover, even though a teaching be true, unless it will be of benefit he will not talk of it. With regard to the future, the same is true, and with regard to the present the same is true.

"Cunda, the Buddha is the one who has awakened to reality. Moreover, from the dawn of enlightenment to the evening of final nirvana, all of what he says is true and real. He acts as he speaks and speaks as he acts. In all the world there is nothing that can defeat him; he is the victor, the omniscient, the ruler. Cunda, the Buddha does not say anything that is not conducive to the attainment of enlightenment. He only teaches the Four Truths: suffering, the cause of suffering, the extinction of suffering, and the path to the extinction of suffering. Why? Because they alone are conducive to enlightenment. Cunda, the Buddha does not discuss whether the world is permanent or impermanent, limited or unlimited, or other matters that are not conducive to attaining enlightenment. He declares the sundering of all wrong views in regard to the past and future; he propounds the meditations on the body, on sensation, on the heart and mind, and on all things; and he proclaims the victory over worldly desires and suffering."

Then Upavana, who was standing behind the World-Honored One fanning him, said, "World-Honored One, this is the most joy-producing teaching. What should it be called?" "Upavana, it should be called the Teaching of Rejoicing."

2. Vassakara

(1) The World-Honored One returned again to Rajagaha and stayed at the Bamboo Grove Monastery. One day, Vassakara, the minister of Magadha, visited and spoke to the World-Honored One. "World-Honored One, we say that wise ones possess four qualities, and we call them great persons. The first is wide knowledge, with which one understands the meaning of what one hears; one knows that these words' meaning is this, and that those words' meaning is that. The second is a good and accurate memory, whereby one remembers events that happened ages ago and keeps in mind the things said today. The third is the skill with which one goes about one's business and does what one must without any hint of laziness. The fourth is cleverness at thinking of various methods and means to accomplish things. I say that the person who possesses these four qualities is a person of great wisdom and I call him a great person. What is your thought on this?"

"Vassakara, I will neither agree with what you said nor disagree. I also say that a person who possesses four qualities is a person of great wisdom, and I call him a great person. The four qualities I speak of are these: first, concern about the benefit and happiness of other people, whereby a person makes it possible for others to pursue the holy path; second, thinking what should be thought and not thinking what should not be thought; third, with regard to the way of thinking, controlling one's mind and heart; fourth, entering meditation with no difficulty, extinguishing the passions, and attaining emancipation. The person possessing these four qualities is a person of great wisdom and is called a great person."

"World-Honored One, that was a marvellous statement. I see you, World-Honored One, as the one who possesses the cited four qualities." "Vassakara, it seems as though you are making fun of me. Nevertheless, I shall say that I do have concern for the benefit and happiness of many people, and I make it possible for them to pursue the holy path. I think what should be thought and do not think what should not be thought. As for the way of thought, I am one who can control my mind and heart. Entering meditation without difficulty, and extinguishing passions, I attain emancipation."

(2) One day, Vassakara came to visit the World-Honored One at the Bamboo Grove. "World-Honored One, there is no transgression to say, on whatever matter, that I have seen what I have seen, that I have heard what I have heard, that I have thought what I have thought, or that I have known what I have known."

"Vassakara, I do not say that one must relate all that one sees, nor do I say one must not relate all that one sees. The same is true with what one hears, thinks, and knows. Vassakara, I say that one must not talk about something that encourages evil and discourages good deeds even if one sees it. On the contrary, one should talk about that which discourages evil and encourages good. The same is true for things heard, thought, and known. One should not talk of things that encourage evil and discourage good but rather talk of that which discourages evil and encourages good." Vassakara, rejoicing at what he heard the World-Honored One teach, then went home.

(3) One day Vassakara again visited the World-Honored One and asked, "World-Honored One, does an evil person know an evil person?" "Vassakara, there is no way that an evil person can know an evil person." "World-Honored One, does an evil person know a good person?" "Vassakara, there is no way that an evil person can know a good person." "World-Honored One, does a good person know an evil person?" "Vassakara, a good person can know an evil person." "World-Honored One, does a good person know a good person?" "Vassakara, a good person can know a good person." "World-Honored One, this is indeed good. As you say, evil persons do not know evil persons or good persons, but good persons can know evil persons and good persons. At one time, disciples of the brahmin Todeyya spoke ill of others. They said it was stupid for King Eleyya to honor and bow to the monk Ramaputta and stupid that those close to the king, Yamaka, Moggallana, Ugga, and others numbering six also had faith in, honored, and bowed to Ramaputta.

"At that time the brahmin Todeyya said to these people, 'What do you think? Do King Eleyya's deeds and words mark him as a wise person?' 'It is so; the king is a wise person.' 'The monk Ramaputta's acts and speech mark him as wiser and as a person of wisdom that knows the nature of things; and so the king honors him and pays respects to him and bows to him. Moreover, those close to him, Yamaka, Moggallana, and others, numbering six, all have faith in him.' World-Honored One, in this way, from Todeyya's own good, he praised the king Eleyya, those close to the king, and the monk Ramaputta. It is as you say; evil ones cannot know evil or good ones, but good ones can know good and evil ones." Vassakara rejoiced at the teachings of the World-Honored One that day and, on account of government matters, he took his leave and returned home.

3. Bhaddiya

(1) At that time there was in Rajagaha a wealthy man by the name of Bhaddiya. He had great wealth, unlimited amounts of gold, silver, and jewels, and treasures and treasuries filled with grain. Nevertheless, he was quite a greedy fellow who knew nothing of charity or accumulating virtues and wrapped himself in erroneous views: "There is no charity in the world, no virtues, no karma or its result, no parents to respect, and no enlightenment to awaken to." He built sevenfold gates to keep beggars out of his house and put up a wire net to stop birds from pecking fruit in the garden. He had an elder sister called Nanda who also held to such views.

One day, Moggallana, Maha-Kassapa, Anuruddha, and Pindola-Bharadvaja gathered and talked among themselves of leading and guiding into faith one who did not have faith in the Three Treasures. They chose Bhaddiya. The rich man was in his room eating rice cakes so that no one would know it, when Anuruddha appeared with a bowl as if falling from the sky or rising from the earth and asked for food. Surprised by this unexpected appearance, he was unable to refuse the request. Without thinking, he gave him a portion of rice cake. Receiving it, Anuruddha went home. The rich man called his guards and demanded an explanation for the intrusion of the monk, but the guards said that the gate was secured and a monk could not have entered.

(2) Next, as the rich man was enjoying a dish of cooked fish, Maha-Kassapa suddenly appeared before him. With no other recourse, the rich man gave him a portion of the fish. After Maha-Kassapa left, he called the guards and demanded an explanation, but as before no place of entrance could be found. He became more angry and shouted that the monks used magical powers to deceive people. The wife of the rich man was the younger sister of Citta, a disciple of the Buddha, and was from the village of Macchikasanda. When she heard the rich man speaking ill of monks, she stopped him and said, "It is improper to speak ill of others. Do you know who these two persons are? The first person is the son of King Dona of Kapilavatthu, Anuruddha. When he was born the earth shook and great wealth came bubbling forth and blessed his house." "I see; I do recall the name Anuruddha now." "That person became a monk and awakened to enlightenment and is the foremost of those possessing divine eyes. The next person is called Maha-Kassapa and is the only son of the wealthy family of Kapila. He married a beautiful bride of good family, but they both renounced the world and attained enlightenment. He freed himself from desire; and by the World-Honored One he was praisingly called the foremost of those who practice strict observance. Now these two honorable ones have used their supernatural powers to come to this house. It is indeed a most joyful thing. Do not disparage them by calling it magical power."

(3) At that time, Moggallana came out of the heavens and tore the wire net. Folding his legs, he sat in the air not too far off the ground. The rich man was startled and filled with fear. He asked whether he was a deity, a demon, or a being that ate people. He identified himself, saying, "I am not a deity, a demon, or a being that eats people. I am Moggallana, a disciple of the Buddha." He said that he had appeared for the sake of expounding the Dharma. Hearing that he was a monk, the rich man immediately thought of a beggar seeking charity. He thought he would refuse him, telling him that even though charity was sought, he had nothing to give.

"The Buddha talks about two kinds of charity, giving the Dharma and giving material things. Now, awaken the intention of wanting to hear proclaimed the charity of the Dharma, and listen."

The rich man first of all rejoiced at hearing about the charity of the Dharma and aroused the aspiration to listen to the Dharma for the first time. Moggallana said, "O man of wealth, I shall now teach you the charity of the Dharma, one of the two charities, giving the Dharma and giving material things. The Buddha teaches that there are five great acts of charity in the charity of the Dharma. The first is not killing. This great charity must be maintained one's whole life. The second is not stealing. The third is not living wantonly. The fourth is not lying. The fifth is not drinking liquor. Rich man, you must uphold these great acts of charity all your life."

The rich man first of all rejoiced that upholding the five acts of charity of the Dharma did not require any expenditure. Not killing was for him a most easy thing to do. Not stealing, for one as rich as he, was no problem; and moreover, that another should not steal his wealth was something to be grateful about. Not living wantonly and not lying were both important, and not drinking liquor was a key to not spending his fortune. He rejoiced in the Buddha's teachings and vowed to uphold these five precepts. He invited Moggallana and for the first time gave food of his own accord. After eating, he thought he would give away some cloth and entered his treasury searching for some woolen material. He thought to choose something that he did not particularly like, but his hand moved to a piece of good white woolen material, and he was perplexed whether to take it up or not. At that time, Moggallana's voice rang out.

> A wise one does not fight with a mind intent on giving.
> Do not fight the act of giving; just act as your mind and heart tell you.

Hearing this verse, the rich man knew that his heart had been read and he took up the white woolen cloth and gave it to Moggallana. Moggallana accepted it and again taught the Dharma. He spoke of charity, upholding precepts, being born in the heavenly realm, and the nature of this world and the path to release from it. On and on, he guided the heart and mind of the rich man. He opened the eye of the rich man's mind there and then. The rich man rejoiced greatly, vowed to uphold the five precepts all his life, and became a follower of the Buddha.

(4) Pindola-Bharadvaja faced the task of teaching and guiding the rich man's sister Nanda. Nanda, too, was led by Pindola-Bharadvaja to the World-Honored

One. Through the teaching, she opened the eye of her heart like a white woolen cloth easily dyed. She exhausted her inner greed and awoke to the Dharma. She placed her faith in the Three Treasures and became a lay follower.

The rich man's younger brother Upakani, like his elder brother and sister, rejoiced in his heart and mind and placed his faith in the teachings of the Buddha. He went to King Ajatasattu and told him of this and told of the happiness in their house. Ajatasattu also rejoiced greatly and praised the virtue of the Buddha, saying that the fellowship of the Dharma had grown.

4. The Last Years of King Pasenadi

(1) One day the World-Honored One spent the hot afternoon hours meditating in the Eastern Monastery in the palace of Migara's mother. Toward the evening he came out of meditation, took a bath, and sat down to dry off. Ananda, rubbing his body with his hands, said, "World-Honored One, the luster of your beautiful skin has faded, and there are wrinkles in your body; your back is bent, and your eyes and ears have changed."

"Ananda, it is as you say. Youth is overcome by old age, health is replaced by sickness, and life is replaced by death. I am already eighty years of age. The luster of my skin has faded, wrinkles have appeared, and my eyes and ears have changed."

> Old age bites; old age damages beauty.
> It tramples on that which looks beautiful.
> Even with a life of one hundred years, death cannot be avoided.
> It excludes nothing and tramples on all.

(2) King Pasenadi came to the place of the teaching in his beautiful carriage, beautifully dressed, and approached the Buddha saying, "World-Honored One, is there anyone among the living who escapes aging and death?"

"Sire, there is no living being that escapes aging and death. Sire, even for a brahmin or a kshatriya who has riches and power, there is no life separated from aging and death. Even the body of a Venerable, who has exhausted the passions, who has lifted off the burden of offences, and who has accomplished the pure end, cannot escape this decay and will eventually be cast off." And looking at the beautiful carriage that the king came in, he spoke the following.

> This beautiful carriage will break apart,
> And so will the body age.
> Only the true Dharma will not age;
> This is what the buddhas have always taught.

King Pasenadi rejoiced at the words of the World-Honored One and paying kind respects went home. Calling his disciples, the World-Honored One taught them, "Disciples, people of this world rejoice in four things and hate four things. The four things that they rejoice in are youth, health, life, and living with people they love. The four things they hate are youth turning to old age, health turning to illness, life turning to death, and parting with loved ones. Moreover, disciples, there are another four that when realized will enable one to separate from the above pairs of four. Without the four, one will be forever unable to separate from them. The four are holy precepts, holy meditation, holy wisdom, and holy emancipation. Disciples, in seeking to reach the realm of nirvana, which is separated from birth, age, illness, and death, it is best to think of the impermanence of the world when parting with loved ones."

(3) Before this, King Pasenadi had a general called Bandhula. He was strong and honest and had the respect of people. However, when the king became old and lost the one person who comforted and advised him, his wife Mallika, he mistreated the general, believing some slanderous lies about him; and he killed the general and his children. Later the king felt great remorse and made the general's nephew Digha-Karayana a general; thus he tried to comfort himself.

This took place when the World-Honored One was in the Sakya clan village of Medalumpa. King Pasenadi had some business and came to Nagaraka. He called Digha-Karayana and ordered, "Make a carriage ready. I want to go to a garden and look at some beautiful scenery." He left town and with a grand parade entered a garden accompanied by many retainers.

As the king was strolling through the grove of the garden, he saw a quiet secluded spot that was ideal for solitary living underneath a beautiful tree. He thought of the World-Honored One and thought that this would be a good place to pledge his devotion to the World-Honored One. "Digha-Karayana, I was thinking of pledging my devotion to the World-Honored One here beneath this beautiful tree. Where is the World-Honored One now?" "Sire, the World-Honored One is now in the village of Medalumpa in the land of the Sakyas." "How far is it from here to there?" "Sire, it is not too far. Because it is about seven miles, it can be reached by sunset." "If that is the case, make a carriage ready and let us go to visit the World-Honored One."

Thus the king left the city in a beautiful carriage and reached Medalumpa by sunset. They continued on to the monastery, and he, getting off the carriage, entered on foot. At that time there were a number of disciples walking on the path. Coming near them, he said he wanted to meet with the World-Honored One and asked where he was now. "Sire, the World-Honored One is in the room behind this closed door. Quietly approach it, clear your throat lightly, and shake the door bolt. The World-Honored One will open the door."

The king took off his sword, his crown, and the other five symbols of his royalty and went forth and gave them to Digha-Karayana and proceeded as he had been taught. He knocked on the bolt of the room in which the World-Honored One was, and the World-Honored One opened it.

(4) The king entered the room and lifted up the World-Honored One's feet to his head and kissed them and rubbed them with his hands. And thus did he identify himself: "World-Honored One, I am Pasenadi, the king of Kosala." "Sire, why have you so ceremoniously greeted me?"

"World-Honored One, I have true faith in you. The World-Honored One is the truly Enlightened One; the Dharma is well expounded by you; and the Sangha is a gathering of people of good practice. World-Honored One, while I have engaged in pious practice in this world for ten, twenty, thirty, and forty years, I have seen ascetics and brahmins who rub on oils after taking a bath and who shave and cut their hair and wallow in the five desires. I have also seen the disciples of the Buddha who, to the end of their lives, engage in the perfectly pure practices. World-Honored One, I have seen no one outside this assembly who has engaged in such pure and perfect practice. World-Honored One, this is one reason I have true faith in you, the Buddha, and in the Dharma and the Sangha.

"World-Honored One, I see that in this world of king fighting with king, kshatriya with kshatriya, brahmin with brahmin, householder with householder, mother with child, child with father, brothers and sisters among themselves, and friends among themselves, only the disciples in this assembly have mutual harmony; as with water and milk mixing together, there is no fighting among them; with eyes of compassion do they look upon things. I have not been able to see a group with such peace and harmony as in this assembly. This, too, is a reason for my true faith in you.

"World-Honored One, moreover, when I was strolling through the garden grove, I saw monks of other faiths who were emaciated, whose facial color was ashen, whose blood vessels popped out, and who looked at others with shifty eyes. I thought then that either these persons did not enjoy engaging in pious practice, or that on account of some evil deeds they became emaciated to hide these deeds and so looked at people with shifty eyes. I, therefore, went to these persons' abodes and asked them the reason. They said they were sick. But here, World-Honored One, I see all enjoying their pracitce and living in humbleness and respect like deer, with kind hearts. Seeing this, I thought that these truly spiritual ones must see something superior in the teachings of the World-Honored One to live like this. This, too, is another reason I have true faith in you.

(5) "World-Honored One, I am an anointed king of the kshatriya caste, and so I am able, if I so wish, to kill, to let live, or to banish. However, I cannot stop people from interrupting me during a council meeting. Even if I say, 'Wait until I finish,' there are those who talk while I talk. Here, however, in your assemblies that amount to hundreds, when the World-Honored One is expounding the Dharma there is not one who allows himself a sneeze or a cough.

"Further, once you were giving a discourse on the Dharma to an assembly of several hundred; one disciple coughed, and another poked him with his knee and told him to be quiet, since the master was teaching. I think that it is marvellous that without sword or staff decorum can be achieved in the assembly. World-Honored One, I have been unable to see any assembly other than this that can keep order so well. This, too, is a reason I have true faith in you.

"World-Honored One, moreover, I have seen some kshatriyas, clever and skilled at splitting hairs, who travel around successfully tearing each others' arguments apart. Hearing that the World-Honored One has stopped somewhere, they once decided to confront you and go to where you were and argue with you. They laid their plans to ask you questions and counter your answers. However, as they were nearing the place where you were, the World-Honored One proclaimed the Dharma, and they were inspired and rejoiced. Because of the power of the Dharma, they did not ask questions or argue but professed that they would certainly become disciples of the World-Honored One. This, too, is a reason why I have true faith in you.

(6) "World-Honored One, in the same way other quite clever people go to the World-Honored One, receive his teachings, and greatly rejoice and ask permission to become disciples. They retire from this world and earnestly engage in practices, and awakening to an incomparable enlightenment they say that they have lost nothing from being holy ones. This is also a reason I have true faith in you.

"World-Honored One, the two commanders Isidatta and Purana receive my allowance and have gained from me recognition, but they do not honor me in the way they honor you. I checked on the two; they were living in a crowded house. They engaged in a discussion of the Dharma until dark, and then they asked where the World-Honored One was and lay down with their heads in that direction and their feet in my direction. This I thought quite remarkable. These two live off my allowance and do not honor me as they honor the World-Honored One. They have seen something in the teachings of the World-Honored One that is particularly superior. This is also a reason I have faith in you.

"World-Honored One, both you and I are kshatriyas from Kosala, and we both are eighty. World-Honored One, therefore, I pay you the highest respects from the bottom of my heart. World-Honored One, I shall now take my leave." Turning to the right, he left.

Immediately after the king left, the World-Honored One called his disciples. "Disciples, Kosala's King Pasenadi has built a stupa of the Dharma. Disciples, protect this stupa of the Dharma and study the teaching again and again and transmit it. Disciples, there are benefits in this stupa of the Dharma. It is the true beginning of practice."

While King Pasenadi was proclaiming his true faith in the World-Honored One, Digha-Karayana took the five symbols of royalty and went back to Savatthi and established Prince Vidudabha as king. King Pasenadi after leaving the World-Honored One learned of this and immediately realized that it was dangerous to return to Savatthi. With a few soldiers to protect him, he went south, thinking to take refuge with his son-in-law, King Ajatasattu. But the old king was unable to fulfill his wish, for he became ill on the way and left this world.

5. The Fall of Kapilavatthu

(1) Before this, soon after the World-Honored One travelled to Savatthi, King Pasenadi, when he was not close to the disciples of the World-Honored One, thought that he could gain their trust by marrying a princess of the Sakya clan. He therefore ordered a messenger to go to Kapilavatthu to find a bride. He also thought that it would be good to be related to a family that then enjoyed prestige.

His messenger conveyed this wish to people in Kapilavatthu, and the Sakyas gathered to discuss the proposal. However, even though he was king of a large country, they could not allow one of their own clan to marry one of such low status. Yet if they did not listen to his wish, the king with a large force might try to enforce his will. They therefore sent him, instead of an authentic princess, a girl of mixed blood, the daughter of the rich man Mahanama and a servant. On

King Pasenadi's orders, the messenger made sure that the woman and her father Mahanama enjoyed dinner together, and he went home reassured.

Before long, the queen gave birth to a prince who was named Vidudabha. The king raised him with love; and when he was eight, he was sent to Kapilavatthu to learn the art of archery. He stayed at the house of his grandfather, Mahanama. At that time, a new hall of the Sakya clan was built, and the site was decorated with banners and adornments and made beautiful for the dedicatory offering to the World-Honored One whom they awaited. The prince with some friends entered the hall and played there. People of the Sakya clan were angered and they dragged him out by his arm. They scolded him, saying, "How dare the child of a maid go inside such a holy place." Shamed unbearably, his young body burned with anger, and he vowed that when he became king he would come to Kapilavatthu and kill all its people. The prince returned to Savatthi and he made one brahmin chant this vow to him thrice each day. With his anger renewed again and again, he bided his time. Moreover, the general Digha-Karayana, knowing about this, awaited the day of revenge.

(2) Upon usurping the throne, Vidudabha knew that the time had come, gathered his followers, and asked them, "Who is now your leader?" "Of course, it is the great king." "If that is the case, gather four divisions of troops. We are marching off to Kapilavatthu now." As ordered, four divisions were gathered, and with the king following, they advanced to Kapilavatthu. Upon hearing this, the disciples were aghast and went to tell the World-Honored One. The World-Honored One stood up from his seat and went to a dead tree with no branches or leaves standing on the road to Kapilavatthu, and he sat down under it and waited for King Vidudabha. Seeing the World-Honored One in the wake of his advancing troops, the king got off his carriage and approached him. "World-Honored One, the trees in the nigrodha grove are lush with limbs and leaves and are quite plentiful; why do you sit under such a dead tree?" "Sire, the shade of one's relations is most cool."

Vidudabha, understanding the World-Honored One's intent, turned back the army and returned to the town. But the brahmin who had been ordered to chant the hymn of vengeance again resumed his chant thrice a day, which renewed the anger in the king's heart. The king again assembled troops and advanced toward Kapilavatthu. The World-Honored One again sat under the dead tree. The king, seeing this, again returned home with his troops. The same thing happened yet a third time. But on the fourth advance of the troops, the World-Honored One, knowing the impossibility of undoing the past karma of the Sakya clan, stayed in the temple and quietly contemplated the Dharma. The king advanced with his troops and attacked Kapilavatthu.

(3) The people of Kapilavatthu were skillful in archery, and they faced the advancing army of Vidudabha with drawn bows. But they made the arrows graze the enemy's ears or hit their top knots, bows, or bow strings. This frustrated the advancing troops and lessened their military power, but not one life was taken. Even the courageous young King Vidudabha was frightened by the skill of the archers and pulled back his troops. But later the hymn of the brahmin again

aroused his intent, and further, another brahmin gave encouragement and said, "The Sakya clan all uphold the precepts, and since they will not kill even a worm, if you advance, you will surely win. If you miss this opportunity, the Sakya clan will never be destroyed." Hearing this, he ordered an attack. The Sakya forces retreated behind the town walls and securely barred the gates. The king shouted from outside the walls, threatening to kill all if the gates were not opened.

There was a youth called Sama of the Sakyas who, hearing that Vidudabha was just outside the town wall, put on armor and took up a sword and went outside alone and challenged the king to fight. Like an angry demon king, he advanced and killed some soldiers and approached the king. Being opposed by such a fierce youth, the king turned and ran. A rich man of the Sakya clan hearing of this shouted, "How dare a mere youth shame the clan. The Sakyas all act in goodness and do not take the life of even a worm. It would be most easy to throw back Vidudabha's forces, but it would mean the deaths of many people. Our Buddha has taught us not to kill. Has he not taught that the result of killing would be to fall into hell or, even if one be reborn as a human being, a life of very short duration? You have broken the clan's law so go, leave here!" Unable to go back home, Sama left.

(4) Vidudabha once again came forward to the town gate and told them to open it. He assured them that if they opened the gate, he would not fight. However, if they did not, he would break the walls and open the gate and kill the entire clan. The Sakyas had no intention of opening the gate; however, a Mara appearing as one of the clan pressed for opening the gate and finally Vidudabha was permitted to enter. Upon entering, Vidudabha gathered up the Sakya clan members and killed and tortured a great number of them. He buried some alive in a pit and had a great elephant walk over them. He took five hundred beautiful maidens and enslaved them. He then planned to kill the rest without discriminating between male and female or young and old.

The grandfather of King Vidudabha, Mahanama, was a follower of the World-Honored One. He went to the king and said, "Please listen to my one request." "What is the request?" "Please allow people in the town to escape during the short time it will take me to rise to the surface of the river after I enter it. After I break the surface, you can go ahead and kill them." Thinking that allowing them to escape for such a short time was all right, he permitted this. Mahanama greatly rejoiced and swam to the bottom of the water. Tying his hair to a tree root, he met a noble death. During this time, the Sakyas escaped from the gates in the four directions. However, being already prepared for death, they just escaped for a short time and soon returned to the town. Those leaving by the north gate returned by the south gate. Those leaving by the east gate returned by the west gate.

Mahanama was under the water such a long time that the king investigated and discovered the death of his grandfather. He regretted his actions and allowed the remaining people to live. He then planned to return with the five hundred maidens. Forced to separate from their parents and husbands, the Sakya women decided that they would at least protect themselves from this tyrant, and so they refused to follow his orders. Becoming angry, the king threw the women into a ravine, and with one division he entered his town. On nearing the castle, he heard some wondrous music. The brother of the king, Jeta, having been separated from his father and now hearing that his brother was off to battle, fell into despair. He thought that he would console himself with some music. He entered into the recesses of the castle and stayed there. The king approached his brother's room, killed the guard posted outside, and entered it. "Why were you here with this girl enjoying music and not helping in our battle?" "I dislike taking another's life." The king was angered and struck out at his brother the prince and killed him. People sang out the praises of the virtues of the gentle Prince Jeta and mourned his death.

> On earth, being the child of a king,
> In heaven, being the child of a god,
> This all is the result of good deeds.
> We honor the virtue of Prince Jeta.
> This world's grief and that world's grief:
> When one does evil, there are evil results.
> This world's happiness and that world's happiness:
> When one does good, there are good results.
> On earth, being the child of a king,
> In heaven, being the child of a god,
> This all is the result of good deeds.
> We honor the virtue of Prince Jeta.

(5) Five hundred women of the Sakya clan had their hands and feet bound and were thrown into a pit; with one mind, they thought of the Buddha. "Since the World-Honored One left our clan, he has showered down upon all under the heavens the rain of the Dharma. We are now suffering. Please extend your compassion and save us." The World-honored One, accompanied by his disciples, appeared at the harrowing scene. The five hundred women saw the World-Honored One and were filled with joy and with shame because of their nakedness. The World-Honored One's follower, the god Indra, gave them all robes; the god Vessavana gave them food and assuaged their hunger. The World-Honored One quietly expounded the principle that that which is thriving will certainly become enfeebled, and that the living will certainly die. Because we have this body, we have the five desires; because we have the five desires, attachment arises. Knowing this, he taught, we must transcend the fear of birth, aging, sickness, and death. Because of this teaching, the women were able to free themselves of impurity and gain the eye of the Dharma; they went to their deaths joyfully, and all were born in the divine realm.

The World-Honored One called his disciples together, faced the east gate, looked at the huge fire roaring within the castle, and said,

> There is no permanency in anything:
> Things are destined to appear and disappear.
> When one is freed from birth and death,
> There is a joy in permanence.

Again, the World-Honored One entered the nigrodha grove, which once was the dwelling place for him and his Sangha, looked at the changes that took place in time, taught his disciples, and returned to Savatthi. At that time, from nowhere, the rumor circulated that the king and his army would die within seven days and fall into hell. The king went to his priests for advice; for six days he was careful and nothing happened. However, on the seventh day, he went to the river Aciravati for amusement. That night he stayed on the river bank. In the middle of the night a violent rainstorm came up, and, along with his armies, the king's life was taken. His palace, too, was hit by lightning and burned to the ground.

(6) The World-Honored One again taught his disciples about this.

> When one does evil with body, mouth, and mind,
> One has a short life and suffers in this world,
> And one suffers in that world.
> At home one is burned by fire;
> On the water, one is drowned in water.
> When one's life ends, one is burned by the fires of hell.

The World-Honored One further told the following story. "Disciples, long ago there was a famine in Rajagaha. People took the fish from the large lake outside the castle to sustain their lives. Among the fish of that lake were two named Capturing Chain and Double Tongue, who said, 'We are without offences, and we committed no wrong to people of this city, yet they take our lives and devour us. Let us put our minds together and dispel this bitterness.' At that time there was a child barely eight years old in that city. He did not himself take the lives of any fish, but when people caught the fishes and threw them on the shore, he found it amusing to watch them writhing and leaping about to their deaths. Disciples, the law of dependent origination operates with an almost frightening certainty. King Vidudabha was Capturing Chain and was seduced by the double-tongued brahmin to dispel his bitterness through the people of Kapilavatthu. In this manner, bitterness piles upon bitterness and digs the rut of the wheel of birth and death ever deeper. Right now my head hurts as though it were being smashed by a heavy rock. This, too, is a bitterness that cannot be erased."

6. The Land of Sukhavati

(1) The World-Honored One stayed on in the Jeta Grove in the Anathapindada Monastery. One day he said to Sariputra, "Sariputra, far to the west of here, there is a land called Sukhavati (Blissful). A Buddha named Amitayus is there and is presently expounding the Dharma. Sentient beings of that land do not know suffering and pass each day in bliss; therefore, the land is named Sukhavati (Blissful).

"Sariputra, in that land there is a lake made up of seven gems, and it is filled with pure water. Its bottom is covered with gold sand, and there are lotuses as huge as chariot wheels blooming therein. The blue flowers have a blue glow; the yellow, a yellow glow; the red, a red glow; and the white, a white glow. A pure and wonderful fragrance permeates the surrounding air. Further, in the four directions of that lake, there are stairs made of gold, silver, lapis lazuli, and crystal. There are stately mansions decorated with many kinds of gems. Heavenly musical instruments are constantly played. The ground is of golden color. Six times during the night and day, divine flowers shining with light rain down. Early in the morning, sentient beings of that land fill flower bowls with flowers, offer them to all the buddhas in other buddha lands, and return before breakfast. Further, such birds as geese, peacocks, parrots, mynas, kalavinkas, and jivamjivakas are always singing elegant songs of virtue, strength, and the teaching. People hear these songs and remember the Buddha, the Dharma, and the Sangha. Sariputra, these birds have not been born as results of sinful deeds. In that land, even the words 'three unhappy destinies' do not exist. Those birds all transmit the sound of the Dharma; they are created magically by the Buddha as skillful means.

"A gentle breeze blows across the bejewelled trees, and the wonderful sounds it creates as it touches the shining beaded nets are like the playing of a hundred thousand instruments at once. Those who hear the sounds again naturally remember the Buddha, the Dharma, and the Sangha. Sariputra, that Buddha land is furnished with arrays of excellent qualities such as these.

(2) "Sariputra, the length of the life of that Tathagata and of those people in that land is immeasurable; whence that Tathagata is called Amitayus (Immeasurable Life). Since he became a Buddha, ten kalpas have passed.

"Sariputra, that Buddha light has no hindrance shining over all Buddha lands; whence that Tathagata is called Amitabha (Immeasurable Light). Further, Sariputra, the number of his disciples and bodhisattvas is exceedingly great; it cannot be counted by worldly count.

"Furthermore, sentient beings born in his land are all at a stage of non-retrogression in their progress toward full enlightenment. They are bound only to one birth before enlightenment. Their number too is difficult to count. Sariputra, people who hear this should desire to be born in that land, for there they can be together with all these holy ones. However, Sariputra, one cannot be born in that land with minor mundane virtue. If one holds to the name of Amitayus Buddha for one, two, or as much as seven days, single-mindedly and without being distracted or becoming confused, then, when one's life ends, Amitayus Buddha, together with many holy ones, will appear before him. His mind will not shrink away, and he will be able to be born in that land immediately. Sariputra, because I see this benefit, I declare that all who hear this should raise the aspiration to be born in that land.

(3) "Sariputra, just as I am praising the incomprehensible virtues of Amitayus Buddha, buddhas as numerous as the sands of the river Ganges, in the ten directions, each in his land, praise his virtues with the voices of truth and says, 'You should trust in this Dharma called the Favor of All Buddhas, that all buddhas protect.'

"Sariputra, if a person trusts in the name and the teaching expounded by Amitayus Buddha, he will receive the protection of all buddhas, and he will not regress on the way to the highest enlightenment. Therefore, Sariputra, you should trust my words and those of other buddhas. If a person aspires to be born in that land, in the past, the present, or the future, he enters the stage of non-retrogression in his progress toward the highest enlightenment.

"Sariputra, just as I am praising the incomprehensible virtues of Amitayus Buddha, those Buddhas also praise my virtues. 'In a murky world overgrown with perverted views, rampant with passions, defiled people, and short life spans, Sakyamuni Buddha has well realized right enlightenment and expounded the Dharma, so difficult to believe, to all the world's people. Truly does he do what is difficult to do!' Sariputra, indeed have I accomplished what is difficult to accomplish in this murky world and realized enlightenment. I have expounded the Dharma that all people find difficult to believe. I have expounded an extremely difficult Dharma."

As the World-Honored One finished expounding this teaching, all the disciples, beginning with Sariputra, and all sentient beings gathered there, rejoiced and trusted this teaching that they heard; and they all gave thanks.

(4) Again, on another occasion, the World-Honored One assembled his disciples and taught them of the dominant features of the disciples who had followed him up to now. "Disciples, among my disciples, Anna Kondanna is the eldest; Sariputta excels in wisdom; Moggallana in supernatural powers; Maha-Kassapa in observing strict precepts; and Anuruddha in divine insight.

"Highest in nobility is Bhaddiya, son of Kaligodha; with the most beautiful voice is Lakuntaka-Bhaddiya; best in debate is Pindola-Bharadvaja; best in expounding the Dharma is Punna, son of Matani; best in explaining something that was only briefly dealt with is Maha-Kaccana. Best at skillfully disguising himself is Culla-Panthaka; best at skillfully freeing his mind is also Culla-Panthaka. Best at freeing his thought is Maha-Panthaka; best at living without strife, Subhuti; most worthy of offerings is also Subhuti. Most able to live in a forest is Revata Khadiravaniya; best in meditation is Kankha-Revata; best in endeavor is Sona Kolivisa; best with beautiful words is Sona Kutikanna; with the most gained is Sivali; and with the strongest faith is Vakkali.

"Disciples, the one with the most desire to study is Rahula; the first to become a mendicant because of his faith was Ratthapala; most fortunate in winning raffle-drawings is Kundadhana; first in poetic skill is Vangisa; most welcomed by all people is Upasena, the son of Vanganta; most skilled in the management of seating mats is Dabba Malla-putta; most loved and revered by the gods is Pilindavaccha; quickest to grasp the essence of any matter is Bahiya-Daruciriya; expounding the Dharma most beautifully is Kumara-Kassapa; and most intelligent is Mahakotthita.

"Disciples, he who has heard the most is Ananda; he with the best memory is also Ananda; with the most understanding wisdom, also Ananda; most endeavoring, also Ananda; and most serving, also Ananda. Best in controlling large crowds is Uruvela-Kassapa; best in making families happy is Kal-Udayin; least ill of all is Bakkula; with the best memory of past lives is Sobhita; strictest in observing precepts is Upali; best in counseling nuns is Nandaka;

best in controlling the five senses is Nanda; best in counseling the disciples is Maha-Kappina; most skillful in entering the fire meditation is Sagata; best in asking the Buddha to expound the Dharma is Radha; and most completely satisfied with coarse robes is Mogharaja.

(5) "Disciples, among nuns, the eldest in Dharma order is Maha-Pajapati Gotami; highest in wisdom is Khema; highest in supernatural powers is Uppala-vanna; best in remembering and observing precepts is Patacara; best in expounding the Dharma is Dhammadinna; best in meditation is Nanda; most effortful is Sona; the foremost of those possessed of divine eyes is Sakula; the foremost of those possessed of the quickest wisdom is Bhadda Kundalakesa; with the best memory of past lives is Bhadda-Kapilani; most completely satisfied with coarse robes is Kisa Gotami; and having the strongest faith is Singalakamata.

"Disciples, among my male lay followers, the first to take refuge were Tapussa and Bhallika; he who has given away the most is Sudatta, the elder Anathapindika; most skilled in expounding the Dharma is Citta, the elder of Macchikasanda; excelling in the four kinds of benevolent conduct is Hatthaka, the elder of Alavi; best in offering delicious food is Mahanama of the Sakya clan; best in offering food one is desiring is Ugga, the elder of Vesali; best serving the Sangha is Uggata; most joyous in a strong mind of faith is Sura-Ambattha; most welcomed by people is the physician Jivaka; and most sincere is father of Nakula.

"Disciples, among my female lay followers, the first to take refuge was Sujata, daughter of Senani; she who gives most is Visakha, mother of Migara; she who heard the most is Uttara, the hunchback; offering the most delicious food is Suppavasa, daughter of Koliyan; best in nursing is Suppiya; strongest in faith is Katiyani; most sincere is Nakula's mother; first in awakening faith by listening to the virtues of the Three Treasures is Kali of Kurara-ghara."

Introduction

The Buddha is now eighty years old and has made his final journey to Rajagriha. The selected passages for Chapter 1 provide a final view of how the Buddha dealt with a variety of people who came to him for guidance. First, King Ajatasatru sends Varsakara, his prime minister, to ask his advice regarding the planned attack on the Vrjis (P: Vajjis). Instead of immediately condemning the King's intent, the Buddha patiently explains how the Vrjis are well prepared for any emergency, how they respect their laws, and how they try to maintain harmony among their people. Thus, by instructing Varsakara not only on the seven principles of prosperity for a country but also on the seven principles of well-being for all peoples, the Buddha had convinced the prime minister that it would be useless for the King to engage in a war with the Vrjis.

Next, the Buddha visits Pataliputra (Patna) with his disciples, and resting in a bamboo grove, he reminds the disciples of the Four Noble Truths. Then, after addressing the people of Pataliputra regarding the Dharma, he gave instructions to various people at villages where he rested along the way to the city of Vaisali, where a courtesan named Amrapali requested a discourse on the Buddha's teaching. At that time, he also instructed the Licchavis, whose headquarters were at Vaisali and who were a powerful part of the Vrjian Confederacy.

North of a village near Vaisali, the Buddha expounded the Dharma to a brahmin who came to see him. At that time, the village was suffering from crop failure, so the Buddha advised his disciples to return to Vaisali so that they would be able to find food and shelter during the rainy season. This provides a glimpse into the difficulties the Buddha and the disciples must have experienced as mendicants as well as the compassionate care and understanding the Buddha demonstrated for all alike under varying conditions and circumstances.

Chapter 1, Section 4 describes the final meeting of Sariputra, a leading disciple, with the Buddha. Sariputra returns to his birthplace in Nalanda (which later became the site of the world famous center for Buddhist studies) and dies in his mother's house. The Buddha erected a stupa in his honor. A short time later, Maudgalyayana (P: Moggallana), another of the Buddha's great disciples, was attacked by jealous opponents of the Buddha and died of injuries. The

Buddha again had a stupa erected and declared to his disciples that the deaths of these two noble leaders were a great loss to the sangha.

Chapter 2 introduces the Mahayana concept of the three bodies of the Buddha: Body of Transformation (Nirmanakaya), Body of Enjoyment (Sambhogakaya), and Body of the Dharma (Dharmakaya). At the early stage of Buddhism, Gotama Buddha was simply considered a superior human being who attained perfect wisdom in his lifetime, but later the idea of a supermundane and transcendent Buddha developed. Thus, the Buddha is seen as a Body of Transformation, which allows him to manifest himself as a human being, as Sakyamuni, who passed away at age eighty after spreading his doctrine. The Body of Enjoyment is also called the Body of Recompense, or Reward Body, because it is a reward for fulfilling the vows and practices that led to the establishment of a buddha-land, such as the Pure Land of Amitayus-Amitabha Buddha (Amitayus signifying immeasurable life, and Amitabha signifying boundless light, or wisdom). The Body of the Dharma is the highest, or the fundamental, being which comprises all others. It is the essence of wisdom and compassion, the ultimate reality, the buddha-nature that is beyond time and space.

The Mahayana is also encrusted with the varying traditional beliefs and practices that developed in various parts of the religious world. Thus, Amitayus and Amitabha, for instance, are not considered as an identical entity in Tibet and Nepal but as separate buddhas or bodhisattvas with separate functions, or attributes. In China and Japan, the belief in Amitayus and Amitabha is based on the Sukhavativyuha Sutra, the passages of which the readers encountered in Book VI, describing the story of Bodhisattva Dharmakara who established a buddha-land for all beings aspiring to full enlightenment.

When readers become confused or overwhelmed with these metaphysical concepts of the Mahayana, they should firmly keep in mind the Four Noble Truths and the Middle Path doctrine first expressed by the Buddha in the Deer Park to his first five disciples. This teaching has been reiterated many times in this book of selected passages, but it appears first in Book I, Chapter 3, Section 1. The Buddha teaches the impermanence of everything in life, including the self; and we suffer because we desire and become attached to things and conditions that change. The Eightfold Noble Path of moral conduct keeps us focused on this truth. Regardless of how the different schools and sects of Buddhism express their view of the Buddha-Dharma, all are based on the Four Noble Truths.

In Book VIII, Chapter 3, Kasyapa asks the Buddha why he returns to the Four Noble Truths (in Section 4) after having discoursed through the years on a variety of virtues and practices. The Buddha explains that the path is one, but he had expounded the Dharma differently in accordance with the capacities of the listeners, or with the circumstances or conditions at the time of his discourse.

Chapter 4 delves into the profound concept of buddha nature. It is expressed in many ways: as the great loving-kindness and great compassion inherent in all beings; as the mind of great faith, as the state of great joy and emancipation, as the Buddha itself. Since all beings possess buddha nature, they will all attain enlightenment by discarding the defilements that cloud their buddha nature. It means simply to gain insight into the true nature of reality.

Ananda, who has served the Buddha for over 20 years, feels profound sorrow over the knowledge that this greatest of teachers is about to enter parinirvana as he lies between two sala trees in a grove near Kusinara. The Buddha praises Ananda and patiently consoles him saying that the Dharma he has taught Ananda and the others will guide him after he is gone and that he must diligently practice the precepts to help others to cultivate the teachings as well.

Before the Buddha passes away at age 80, a very old mendicant named Subhadra (P: Subhadda) becomes the Buddha's last disciple, because he believes that the appearance of a buddha is as rare as the blooming of the udumbara tree. In ancient India, it was believed that the flower of the udumbara (ficus racemosa) blooms only once in 3000 years, but in truth, the fruit of this plant, like the fig, contains the flower within so that it cannot be seen. Thus, it is no wonder that no one claims to have seen its flower bloom.

In the last several thousand years, there has never lived another spiritual teacher as fully awakened, with such charismatic magnetism, that caused people from all social and intellectual levels to seek guidance from him. Of the world's great religious leaders, only the Buddha has systematically based his teaching on a rational analysis of life's problem and led his contemporary thinkers and followers away from superstitious notions and practices, or from a singular belief in a divine power that can intervene in the life and affairs of the world. Not only was he an intellectual genius of the highest sort, he was supremely compassionate and sympathetic. The Jataka tales, which purport to relate the Buddha's former lives, indicate the highest esteem in which the Buddha was held by his followers, for the stories invariably describe his utmost concerns for all who suffer and his extreme sacrifices to relieve them of their painful or helpless situations. We may never encounter such a brilliant spiritual teacher, but we possess his teaching which was passed down orally by his immediate disciples and finally written down long after his demise.

Chapter 1

THE PROPHECY OF THE BUDDHA'S GREAT DEMISE

1. The Seven Principles of Well-being

(1) Having now reached the age of eighty years, the Buddha returned to Rajagriha and dwelt on the Vulture Peak. At that time, Ajatasatru, the king of Magadha, was desirous of conquering the Vrji Republic, and thus he said to his minister Varsakara. "O Varsakara, the World-Honored One is staying not far from here. Pay a visit to him at once and request his instruction on my behalf. Listen carefully to whatever the World-Honored One may teach you and repeat it to me. The Buddha speaks nothing untrue."

Following the king's words, Varsakara boarded a carriage and went to Vulture Peak to see the Buddha. Upon arriving, he said, "On behalf of the king of Magadha, Ajatasatru, I bow in adoration at your feet and inquire how the World-Honored One fares and whether he is free from illness and enjoys daily food and drink." The Buddha replied, "I am very well, O Varsakara," and in return asked him, "Are your king and the people in peace? Are the prices of things fair?" Varsakara replied, "Owing to the World-Honored One's compassion, there is good fortune for both king and people, so that life is harmonious, wind and rain are in proper order, and the entire country is prosperous and flourishing."

After this exchange of civility, Varsakara said to the World-Honored One, "O World-Honored One, Ajatasatru, the king of Magadha, has always been eager to attack the Vrji Republic. What would you think of such a campaign? May I request, on behalf of my king, your advice?" The Buddha then addressed Varsakara and said, "O Varsakara, when I was once staying at the Capala Shrine in Vaisali, the elders of that country visited me and told me that since the king of Magadha had been wanting to invade their country, they were vigilant among themselves, guarding against his invasion. I taught the Vrji elders, I recollect, that so long as they maintained seven principles steadfastly in governing their republic, they need be in no fear. Their country would never be destroyed by Ajatasatru. So long as they are steadfast with these principles today, it would not be possible for anyone to destroy their country." "World-Honored One, please kindly elaborate on the seven principles," begged Varsakara.

(2) Now at that moment, Ananda was standing behind the Buddha, fanning him. The Buddha, looking back, said to him, "Have you heard, O Ananda, that the Vrjis are holding full and frequent public assemblies to discuss the affairs of state and are always well prepared for any emergency?" "So I have heard, O World-Honored One," replied Ananda. Then the Buddha, in like manner, continued to ask Ananda, "Have you heard, then, Ananda, that the Vrjis, whether high or low, meet together in concord and discuss in concord matters of the state; that they respect ancient laws, abrogate nothing unduly, and abide with propriety and respect; that they recognize the natural distinctions between male and female and the clear order between the young and the old; that they honor and serve their parents and are obedient to their teachers; that they revere their ancestral shrines and allow no discarding of the rites; that they esteem and respect moral principles and virtues and provide arhats who enter the country from afar with clothing, food and drink, mats, medicine, and various things, and serve them well? Now, have you heard, O Ananda, that they fully maintain all these principles and neglect nothing?" "World-Honored One, so I have heard," replied Ananda in like manner.

The World-Honored One then addressed Varsakara and said, "As the Vrjis fully maintain all these principles and neglect nothing, we cannot expect them to decline. If the ruler of any country esteems and maintains these principles steadfastly, even the entire armies of the world, assaulting at once, will not be able to destroy that country."

Having heard this, Varsakara said, "O World-Honored One, the Vrjis cannot be overcome by the king of Magadha when they are practicing any one of these principles of prosperity; how much less so when they are practicing all seven!" With due reverence and delight in his heart, Varsakara went to report to his king what he had learned, and he persuaded him to abandon the idea of the war.

(3) Now soon after Varsakara had gone, the World-Honored summoned Ananda to assemble in the lecture hall all the disciples who were sojourning in the neighborhood of Rajagriha. Sitting before all the disciples gathered in the hall, the World-Honored One said, "My disciples, I shall teach you seven principles of well-being. Listen attentively and keep them fast in your mind. O disciples, meet together frequently in assemblies to discuss the Dharma, and the Dharma will not decline but thrive for a long time. Disciples, meet together, young and old, in concord, respect each other and refrain from disputes, revere the Dharma and obey the precepts, abrogating nothing unduly. O disciples, whether young or old, whether elder or novice, be courteous to each other with propriety and respect in your hearts; purify your conduct; abiding in solitude, let others be first and let yourself go after them in matters of order; be compassionate and have great generosity toward those who come for help, and tend with care those who are sick, and the Dharma will not decline but prosper for a long time.

"O disciples, there are also another seven principles of well-being, which enable the Dharma not to decline but to flourish. Maintain purity of heart and do not be involved in worldly matters; maintain yourselves free from avarice and do not become greedy; practice the virtue of patience and become involved in no disputes; uphold silence and do not take part in idle talk; abide by the rules and be not arrogant; concentrate on one thing and do not divide your attention among other things; be frugal and refrain from immoderation in food and clothing; and the Dharma will not decline.

(4) "O disciples, be compassionate to all living beings. Upon meeting with a dying man, have pity on him, for neither he who is facing death nor others who mourn know anything as to where death leads. It is only he who understands the Buddha's teaching who knows, and it is for the sake of this goal that the Buddha teaches his Dharma. O disciples, you have the Dharma to learn and the path to practice. There are many paths in this world, and the path of the king is great, and yet the path of the Buddha is even greater.

"O disciples, in the practice of the Buddha path, when you see some companions who have realized it, you should feel no grief about your wayfaring, on account of your not having accomplished the path. While many people learn archery, some of them learn to shoot at the target quickly, whereas others can only do so later. Though the time required for their successful learning may be longer, if a person continues to practice shooting, he should be able to hit the target sooner or later. Again, just as the water flowing through a narrow ravine will soon enter into a wider valley, then into a large river, and finally into the great ocean, anyone who continues to practice with diligence should eventually be able to attain enlightenment." Having listened to the Buddha, his disciples were greatly delighted with his teaching.

2. The Mirror of Truth

(1) Now the World-Honored One became aware of the approaching time of his demise; he called Ananda and said, "Come, Ananda, let us go to Pataliputra." Gathering his robes and alms bowl, Ananda followed him together with other disciples and left Rajagriha for Pataliputra to the north.

When they passed the village of Venuyastika, the Buddha took rest in a bamboo grove and said to his disciples, "O disciples, anyone who wishes to practice the path must know the Four Noble Truths. Because people do not understand this doctrine, they stray into the realms of delusion and wander on this weary path without ending. O disciples, the Four Noble Truths are the truth of suffering, that of the cause of suffering, that of the cessation of suffering, and that of the path to the cessation of suffering. Suffering is birth, old age, disease, and death, and also separation from the beloved, contact with the hated, and failing to get what is wanted. Suffering is induced by mental defilements; they are its cause. The annihilation of this causal composite is cessation, and the way that leads to this cessation is the path. O disciples, if you understand suffering and annihilate its causal basis, you are a person who has acquired insight. You are freed from delusion and are no longer liable to be in the state of suffering. O disciples, therefore, set your minds to understand this doctrine. Stay away from avarice, do not dispute with the world, and become committed to not killing, not stealing, and not committing adultery. Neither deceive nor slander, and refrain from flattering and superficial praising, from hate and abuse, from jealousy and anger, and from foolishness and doubt. Always keep in mind that the body is impermanent and unclean and is bound eventually to return to dust. All the buddhas of the past perceived and expounded this truth; all the buddhas of the future will also perceive and expound this truth.

"O disciples, those who enjoy family life, seek for love and emotion, and crave worldly fame will not be able to realize the path of enlightenment. For no one finds delight in this path with a mind that finds delight in worldly affairs. The path of enlightenment arises from the mind, and when one's mind becomes pure, one will, as a matter of course, realize the path. Now the Tathagata has freed himself from delusion and opened the right path for the benefit of the world. If you wish to avoid evil destinies, you must concentrate upon upholding the Dharma and the precepts steadfastly. When you practice the moral precepts, you will be able to proceed to mental concentration; when you practice mental concentration, you will be able to proceed to insight. When you deepen this insight, your mind will realize absolute purity. O disciples, be firmly mindful of this teaching."

(2) When the World-Honored One stayed overnight in this village, Sariputra came to the place where he stayed, and after respectfully saluting him he said, "O World-Honored One, I firmly believe that there never has been, nor will be, nor is there now any person who is greater or has deeper insight into the truth than you." The World-Honored One said, "How do you know that this is so?" "O World-Honored One," replied Sariputra, "Although I could not know in detail the three worlds of the past, future, and present, I have been able to know the Dharma with your guidance. O World-Honored One, you know, with your immeasurable insight, the worlds of the present, past, and future. The World-Honored One is the highest, totally freed from every passion and is endowed with every excellent virtue."

Now the Buddha proceeded on his way from the village of Venuyastika to Nalanda where he was received by the villagers with greetings. The Buddha taught for them and stayed for a while in that village.

(3) The Buddha, accompanied by Ananda and his disciples, now left Nalanda and proceeded toward Pataliputra. Upon his arrival, the Buddha sat under a tree outside the gate of Pataliputra. The town was located by the river Ganges at the edge of Magadhan territory, facing the neighboring country across the river.

Now the people of Pataliputra heard of his arrival and came to the place where he was resting under the tree. Recognizing the Buddha's august figure from afar, they quickly approached him with joy, and after saluting him by bowing at his feet, they took their seats at one side. The Buddha then expounded the Dharma for them. After listening to the Dharma, the townsmen said to him, "We shall humbly take refuge in the Three Treasures, the Buddha, the Dharma, and the Sangha. Please, out of compassion, accept us as your followers. From now on we shall refrain from killing, stealing, indulging in sensual pleasure, lying, and intoxication." The Buddha signified his consent by silence.

The townsmen wished to make offerings to the Buddha and his disciples; and with his consent they emptied the public hall, washed it with water, scented it with incense, and placed mats on the floor. The Buddha and his disciples arrived the next day, and after washing their hands and feet they entered the hall. The Buddha sat by the central pillar facing eastward, the disciples seated behind him, while the townsmen took their seats facing the Buddha. The Buddha addressed the townsmen and said, "Fivefold is the loss resulting from the pursuit of greed and an unrestrained mind. In the first place, a greedy man loses his wealth every day; second, he is not respected; third, he is regretful at the time of death; fourth, his ill repute gets around everywhere abroad; and finally, even after death, he will be reborn into some unhappy realm of suffering. If, however, a man restrains his mind so that it cannot run wild, fivefold is his gain. In the first place, his wealth increases every day; second, he will be respected everywhere; third, he has no regret at his death; fourth, his good repute is spread abroad; and last, upon his death he will be reborn in some happy realm."

When the Buddha completed his teaching, it was far into the night. "It is time for you to do what you deem most fit," he said, dismissing the townsmen; and the Buddha returned to the grove with his disciples.

The Buddha now asked Ananda, "Who is it, Ananda, that built the fortress at Pataliputra?" "O World-Honored One, it was the minister of Magadha, Varsakara, together with another minister, Sunidha, who built the fortress under Ajatasatru's command in order to keep back a Vrjian invasion," replied Ananda. The Buddha then said, "Indeed, wise is Varsakara. This city will become the most flourishing center for people of wisdom as well as for those engaged in trade and commerce of all kinds in later days. But three dangers will hang over Pataliputra in some remote future, namely, the danger of fire, that of flood, and that of rebellion within the city walls, resulting in its destruction."

(4) Now Varsakara heard of the arrival of the Buddha and his disciples, so he came to the Buddha with his retainers, and after saluting him he respectfully took his seat on one side. The Buddha then taught for him, and after it was over, Varsakara, delighted with the teaching, said, "May the World-Honored One do us the honor of taking his meal together with the company of disciples at my house tomorrow." The Buddha signified his consent. Varsakara returned home and cleaned the house through the night, prepared the meals, and after waiting for the morning informed the Buddha, "The hour for the meal has come, O World-Honored One; all is ready." The Buddha then entered the house with a company of his disciples. After the meal, the Buddha taught, "Let the prudent man revere whomsoever is worthy of reverence; let him support whomsoever is worthy of support; let him give alms widely and love others; let him always wish to listen to the Dharma. O Varsakara, let those in governing positions not have greed or anger. They should not be oppressive or self-indulgent. If you act avoiding these wrongdoings, you will have no regret, and after death you will be free from suffering. O Varsakara, practice these." Thus Varsakara respectfully followed his instruction.

The Buddha left Varsakara's house and proceeded toward the river Ganges by way of the eastern gate of the town wall. But the river was swollen and overflowing. Travellers were fighting each other to board the ferry. Then, as quickly as a strong man might stretch forth his arm from its drawn back position, the Buddha vanished from this side of the river and stood on the opposite bank with the company of his disciples. Then said the Buddha, "The buddhas are sailors who cross the ocean of suffering on board the Dharma and now help people cross to the yonder shore of enlightenment." Varsakara saw the Buddha's departure and named the gate from which he left Gautama's Gate, and the site on the riverbank where he crossed Gautama's Ferry.

(5) The Buddha then proceeded to Kutigramaka. Entering this village, he stopped in a grove and told his disciples, "O disciples, observe strictly the noble precepts, mental concentration, and insight, and thereby realize emancipation. This Dharma is extremely subtle and difficult to understand. Because people do not know this, they go on living in an endless cycle of delusion and suffering. O disciples, exert yourselves in the practice of the noble precepts, and purify the mind by knowing its nature. Without disputing with the world, be concerned about your spiritual well-being and reflect upon your inner being. In so doing, your mind will become clear and will eliminate the three defilements of greed, hatred, and ignorance, and as a natural course it will realize the path; the mind will no longer run wild, nor will it need any restraining. O disciples, just as the king is the master of his people, the mind is the master of all things; of this you should always be aware."

(6) The Buddha, now leaving Kutigramaka, entered the village of Nadakantha and rested under a tree by the bank. At that time, an epidemic was spreading in the area, and many people died. A disciple Salhri, a nun Nanda, the laymen Kalinga, Bhadra, Subhadra, and others, and a laywoman Sujata were among the dead, and their relatives visited to ask Ananda as to what destinies these dead had gone to, and Ananda conveyed these questions to the Buddha.

The Buddha replied, "O Ananda, Salhri became an arhat while in this world. Those fifty lay followers, Nanda, Kalinga, Bhadra, Subhadra, and others have been reborn in heaven and attained enlightenment. Sudatta and ninety other followers will be reborn once more in this world to exhaust the karmic cause of suffering. Sujata, along with another five hundred, will completely destroy the three defilements within seven rebirths and will be freed from all their passions and will attain enlightenment. O Ananda, it is natural that whenever there is birth there follows death. However, it is wearisome to the Buddha that whenever a death occurs, people ask him about the dead person's destiny. Therefore, I shall show you by the Mirror of Truth the realms in which my disciples will be born. O Ananda, if any one of my disciples is in firm possession of faith in the Buddha, in the Dharma, and in the Sangha, he will be able to free himself from evil passions. Even if he moves back and forth between heavenly and human worlds, he will, before repeating seven rebirths, overcome the state of suffering. Thus, people are in delusion because of their ignorance, whereas the wise, on account of their being firm on the path, will not return to delusion. O disciples, be mindful of the Buddha, the Dharma, and the Sangha, and also of the precepts, so as to be free from grief and sorrow forever."

3. Amrapali the Courtesan

(1) The Buddha then proceeded with Ananda to Vaisali and stayed at a grove outside the city wall. The grove belonged to Amrapali, a courtesan of Vaisali. Now, Amrapali heard that the Buddha had arrived at Vaisali and was staying at her grove. Arranging a number of vehicles to be made ready, she dressed neatly and got into one of the vehicles accompanied by a company of five hundred courtesans and proceeded toward her garden. The Buddha, having perceived the approaching company from afar, said to his disciples, "O disciples, set your mind upon the right path. No matter whether you are thrown into a tiger's mouth, or placed under an insane man's sword, or whether both your eyes are gouged out by a heated spear, be not deluded by desires, and prevent those desires that have not yet arisen from arising; promote good thoughts that have already arisen, and encourage those good thoughts that are still latent to appear. Regulate your mind in this manner and restrain it at the very beginning, for it will be difficult to restrain it later. Therefore, be firm in your mind control and never relax it. Take the bow of right effort and the spear of right insight, wear the armor of right mindfulness, and be ready to fight the five kinds of desires. Since I began to seek for the path, I have experienced innumerable occasions of fighting my own desires. Throughout my career, I did not follow the evil course of the mind but have steadfastly striven for and finally realized my enlightenment. O my disciples, set the mind right, for the mind has been in defilement for a long time. It is the time now for you to free yourselves and escape from suffering. For those who remain within birth and death, everything appears to be suffering whether they look within or without."

(2) Now Amrapali, seeing the Buddha, alighted from the carriage and proceeded on foot respectfully toward the Buddha, and after paying him due reverence she took her seat at one side. The Buddha then addressed Amrapali and said, "Why have you come here?"Amrapali replied, "I have frequently heard that the World-Honored One is far superior to the gods, and therefore I wish to listen to your teaching and try to follow your instruction day and night, so that I may prevent myself from falling into the evil destinies." The Buddha then asked, "Are you delighted in having been born as a woman?" Amrapali replied, "The gods made me born as woman, and I have no particular delight in it." The Buddha asked, "If you are not particularly delighted in being a woman, who has made you keep five hundred courtesans?" "It is my own foolish action," was the reply. "Very well, O Amrapali, fivefold is the hindrance to those whose actions are disordered; namely, they are defamed, hated, feared, and suspected, and finally they fall into hell after death or receive beasts' forms; all of these derive from lust. Again, fivefold is the benefit for those whose action is pure; namely, their names are praised, they have no fear of the rulers, they feel easy, and after death, they will be reborn in heaven and finally attain the path of

enlightenment. Therefore, be concerned about yourself and practice the teaching and precepts so that you can realize the path of purity."

As the Buddha taught Amrapali about the Dharma, her mind was filled with delight. The Buddha said to her, "Your mind is already purified; but it is extremely difficult for a woman to follow my teaching, especially for someone like you who are young, wealthy, and beautiful. O Amrapali, wealth and physical beauty are not everlasting treasures; the path alone is precious. A strong body is defeated by sickness, while youth is transformed into old age; life is tormented by the shadow of death, by separation from the beloved, by proximity to the hated, and by not obtaining desired objects. The Dharma alone gives freedom. If you follow it, there is nothing that can obstruct its freedom."

After expressing her gratitude for his teaching, Amrapali respectfully knelt down and said to the Buddha, "May the World-Honored One do me the honor of taking his meal together with the disciples at my house tomorrow." Receiving the Buddha's consent, she was delighted and rose from her seat, bowed down before him, and departed.

(3) Now the Licchavis, the residents of Vaisali, heard that the Buddha had arrived at Vaisali and was staying at Amrapali's grove. Intending to pay their respects to the Buddha, the Licchavis, as many as five hundred kinsmen, mounted their carriages and proceeded outside the city wall. They happened to meet Amrapali and her company on the way. The carriages passed each other with their wheels and axles chafing each other, and this resulted in damage to the canopies of the carriages on which the Licchavis were riding. "How is it, Amrapali, that you drove up against us and caused this damage?"asked the Licchavis. She replied, "My lords, I have just invited the World-Honored One and his disciples for tomorrow's meal, and because of this, I was hurrying home." Surprised by her answer, the Licchavis said, "Have you already received the World-Honored One's consent? O Amrapali, give up this meal to us for a hundred thousand gold pieces." "My lords, the date has already been set. I cannot comply with your request," replied Amrapali. "Then we shall increase the price sixteen times. Give up this meal to us." Despite this, Amrapali refused. The Licchavis, throwing up their hands, exclaimed, "We are outdone by this woman," and rearranging themselves they went on to Amrapali's grove.

(4) When the Buddha saw the Licchavis approaching in the distance, he said to the disciples, "O disciples, let those of you who want to see the glory of the gods in the Trayastrimsa heaven behold this company of the Licchavis; their dignity is like that of the gods. My disciples, keep your minds restrained and your miens proper. Be diligent in meditation on the body as impure, perception as resulting in suffering, the mind as impermanent, and all things as having no self. Go when it is proper to go, stop when it is proper to stop; even in holding your robes or bowls and in using medicine, follow propriety. Control the mind whether sitting, lying, talking, or keeping silence."

Then the Licchavis alighted from the carriages and proceeded toward the Buddha, taking their seats in due order; those who were in the front knelt down, those in the middle bowed their heads, and those in the rear held both palms together. The Buddha addressed them and said, "O Licchavis, why have you come here?" "Having heard of your arrival here, we came to honor the World-Honored One," replied the Licchavis. The Buddha then said to them, "O sons of good family, by being negligent, you will not attain wealth or fame. Neither will you enjoy alms giving, nor will you wish to see others practicing the path; you will only enjoy worldly matters and talking, slumbering, and useless arguments; you will associate only with evil characters desiring an idle life. Thus you will be slighted by others, forget whatever you hear, prefer to live in an inappropriate locality, be unable to control the mind, never be satisfied with food, and dislike quietude. Hence whatever view you entertain will be wrong. O sons of good family, by not being negligent you can proceed on the worldly path as well as the path to emancipation. If you want to proceed on the path, you must practice non-negligence. Anyone who is negligent, even if he is physically near the Buddha and his disciples, is far from attaining enlightenment." The Licchavis replied, "We know ourselves that we are negligent. We think that the World-Honored One also is negligent. Otherwise, the World-Honored One would have come to our country before."

(5) At that time, there was one, Pingiya by name, among the listeners, and he said to the Licchavis, "King Bimbisara of Magadha earned great good fortune, and the World-Honored One's presence in his country was comparable to a wondrous lotus blooming in a pond. You are called negligent because you have indulged in the five desires and thereby do not know how to come nearer to the Buddha. It is wrong to say that the Buddha is negligent because he did not come to your country, though he appeared in Magadha many times. For the Buddha's appearance in Magadha was not simply for the sake of one person or two, but, like the sun and the moon, for the sake of many and all." Pingiya then arose and approached the Buddha and directly stared at his countenance. The Buddha said to him, "What are you looking at?" Pingiya replied, "O World-Honored One, your virtue is comparable to a towering great mountain; there is nothing equal to you in this world. Now, adoring the World-Honored One, I am determined to follow your teaching, and my mind is no longer disturbed." The Buddha then said to him, "Look at me as you please, and you will acquire good fortune." "O World-Honored One, grant me my wish and allow me to speak my thoughts," said Pingiya. Upon the Buddha's consent, Pingiya sang,

> The king of Anga wore armor made of precious stones.
> The king of Magadha became enormously rich.
> Now the World-Honored One has appeared in this world,
> And his excellent virtue has shaken the world.
> The name of the World-Honored One is distinguished,
> Like that of the Himalaya, and the excellence
> Of his virtue is like the scent of the lotus flower.
> The brightness of his presence is like that
> Of the rising sun and the moon traversing the sky.
> The World-Honored One illumines this world with that brilliance
> And bestows on everyone the eyes of insight
> And dispels all doubts from the minds of people.
> His supreme insight is lofty and subtle

And also clear and without dust, like a garden torch
Perceived through the darkness of night.
May I undertake the observance of the precepts of purity,
And take my refuge in the Three Treasures?

The five hundred Licchavis, deeply moved by Pingiya's song, said, "O Pingiya, great is your virtue. Sing that song for us again, if you will." Thus Pingiya sang it again and a third time. The Licchavis took off their beautiful garments and each made gifts to him. Pingiya then offered all of them to the Buddha.

(6) The Buddha accepted them, as he understood Pingiya's intent, and addressed the people present, "O Licchavis, discard your pride and accept the light of the Dharma. Treasures, beauty, scents, flowers, none of these can be compared with the precepts as ornaments. The way to great prosperity in life and greater security for your people lies solely in how you control your minds. If you can add to this a delight in the practice of the path, then your virtue will be all the more enhanced. If you succeed in gathering many wise people to your country, regenerate your virtue, increase the welfare of the people, and guide them toward a higher moral standard, there will be no end to such virtue through many generations to come.

"Precious gems come out of the ground, and precepts are the source from which all good actions come. Those who hold insight make their way through the plains of delusion by practicing the noble precepts. Depart from the view of self. Pride destroys the sense of shame, destroys many good deeds, and annihilates merits. External looks and social status are all impermanent. These are bound to change and eventually come to nothing. How can anyone be proud of them?

"Moreover, greed causes great misfortune. Like an enemy, it courts one and secretly strikes him from the rear. Like fire, greed arises within and burns the whole body. No matter how intense it may be, fire can be extinguished by water, but not the fire of greed. Fire fiercely burns the field but does not prevent the quick regrowth of grass from its roots. It is, however, difficult for the mind that is burnt once by the fire of greed to regrow the mind of aspiration to the Dharma. Greed leads to worldly pleasures, which in turn increase inner defilements, and these defilements misguide us further toward evil destinies. Verily, there is no stronger enemy than greed. Moreover, greed creates attachment, which in turn causes greed. Since greed give rises to many sufferings, there is no evil more powerful than greed.

"O Licchavi people, do not yield to anger. It destroys one's good countenance and obstructs right vision, harms friendship, and induces social scorn. Therefore discard anger. If you cannot control your anger, the fire of regret and anxiety will follow to consume yourself first and then others. You feel greed when something is agreeable to your mind and experience anger when it is not. If you control both feelings, agreeableness and disagreeableness, you will be able to remove both greed and anger.

"O Licchavis, the Buddha who appeared in this world is extraordinary. Those who expound the Dharma that the Buddha taught are extraordinary. Those who listen to and believe in the Dharma are extraordinary. Those who accomplish the goal of the Dharma are extraordinary. Those who know how to be grateful when they are saved are extraordinary. O Licchavis, be obedient to your teachers, act respectfully toward them, praise them in their absence, and after they die, always remember them."

Having listened to the Buddha's instruction, the Licchavis arose from their seats and thanked him. "O World-Honored One, will you do us the honor of taking your meal together with the disciples at our house tomorrow?" "O Licchavis, I have accepted the invitation of the courtesan Amrapali for tomorrow," the Buddha replied. Then the Licchavis threw up their hands, exclaiming, "We are outdone by that woman." Nevertheless, they realized that the Buddha was equally concerned with all beings, and after paying homage to him at his feet and circumambulating him thrice, they left.

(7) Amrapali prepared food through the night and prepared her mansion with decorations and newly spread carpet, and she came to the Buddha at dawn to announce the time. The Buddha took his bowl and walked with his disciples and entered the city. The townsmen welcomed the procession and commented on it by comparing the Buddha with the bright moon and his disciples with the bright morning star. The Buddha now entered Amrapali's mansion and took the seat prepared for him. Amrapali herself waited upon him till he completed the meal. After the meal was over, she brought in a pitcher made of gold, and pouring water for the Buddha to wash his hands, Amrapali said to him, "O World-Honored One, among the groves that the people of this city have, my grove is the most beautiful. May I offer this grove to the World-Honored One? May you be compassionate enough to accept my offering!" The Buddha accepted it and said, "O Amrapali, construct a stupa and residences for monks, lay a cool garden, build bridges and ferries for people, irrigate the fields, plant grasses, and set up rest houses for the travellers. O Amrapali, there will be no enemy nor fear for one who leads a pious life. The name of such is praised, and the residence of such is safe. Noble precepts are honored and valued highly in the world. Wherever one may go, the person of precepts will be respected and favored. Desires are troublesome and ignoble, and one should endeavor to discard them as quickly as possible." The Buddha, observing that Amrapali's mind was becoming more receptive to the teaching, taught her the essentials of the Four Noble Truths. As her mind became pure, she, like a white carpet ready for any coloring, at once understood the Dharma and entered the state of fearlessness.

Amrapali then addressed the Buddha and said, "O World-Honored One, I shall resort to the Buddha, the Dharma, and the Sangha for my refuge. Please include me among your followers. From now on, I shall refrain from murder, theft, sexual misconduct, false speech, and the use of intoxicating drinks." The Buddha granted her wish and thus Amrapali discarded her evil habits and was purified of her past defilements.

(8) The village called Venuvagrama was located at the foot of a hill not too far from Vaisali. Arriving at the village, the Buddha sojourned in a forest north of the village. There was a brahmin, Vaisadya by name, who hearing of the Buddha's arrival thought, "The fame of Gautama is spread throughout the world;

he is known to be endowed with noble virtues, and whatever he teaches is said to be true, be it in the beginning, in the middle, or in the end. I should at once visit the World-Honored One to welcome him." Then Vaisadya came to the place where the Buddha was, and the Buddha expounded the teaching to him. Delighted, Vaisadya invited the Buddha and his disciples to have a meal at his house the following day. Next morning, the Buddha visited the house, and after the meal he taught Vaisadya the following, "If you support those who observe the precepts by giving them clothing, food, or seat mats, you will receive a great reward. The virtue of your charity will follow everywhere you go as a true companion, like your shadow. Therefore plant good seeds for the sake of a future harvest. Anyone who acquires such virtues will be at peace." Then the Buddha left the house with his disciples.

During that time, it was a year of crop failure for the village, and grain was expensive; so as long as they stayed in this small village it would be difficult for all of the Buddha's party to receive food. Therefore the Buddha assembled his disciples and said, "Go, disciples, to Vaisali in Vrji to seek friends and acquaintances where you may take up your abode for the rainy season so that you may receive sufficient alms. I shall remain here with Ananda." When his disciples were all ready to depart, the Buddha instructed them, "O disciples, you must control yourselves. Do not indulge in good food nor be displeased with food of lower quality. Be not greedy over food, which is meant only to support the body. If you become greedy about food, you can never free yourselves from delusion. Only those who learn to restrain themselves and gain victory over themselves will be able to realize the goal of quiescence." The disciples, all delighted in their hearts, left for their neighboring towns.

(9) The Buddha now went to the forty-fifth rainy season retreat in Venuvagrama with Ananda. During that period, the Buddha was stricken with a fearful illness and severe pains came upon him. The Buddha thought to himself, "The disciples are not here; they are all concerned with my health; and it would not be right for me to enter final nirvana without addressing them. Besides, this is not a suitable place for my entering nirvana. Let me now, by a strong effort of will, keep my hold on life." Thus the Buddha managed to have a little lull in his illness, and he came out of the room and sat in the cool shade of a tree. At that time, Ananda was also in the shade of the tree. He hurriedly approached the Buddha and said, "O World-Honored One, how do you feel? As I have seen you suffering, I have been so worried that I could hardly breathe, thinking that the World-Honored One might pass away. Now, I have some little comfort. O World-Honored One, why is it that you do not leave some instructions to us now?"

The Buddha then said, "O Ananda, what do the disciples expect of me? If someone thinks, 'It is I who lead my disciples,' or 'They are dependent upon me,' then he should give instructions to them. But I have never said so, and hence I am not bound to make final instructions as such. I have hidden nothing. I have no such thing as the closed fist of a teacher who keeps some things back. I have taught whatever was to be taught. My disciples should keep my teaching in their minds and put them into practice. In this way, I should be in their minds at all times.

"O Ananda, my body is old and decaying; and my journey is drawing to its close. I am turning eighty years of age. Just like a worn-out cart, my body is neither sturdy nor strong. Have I not taught you before that for birth and for death there is a time, and that there is no one who once born is not bound to death? Born in this world, I have discovered the path to nirvana and severed the root of delusion. Therefore after I am gone be not negligent about this Dharma.

"O Ananda, let yourself be your light and your refuge; seek no other refuge. Let the Dharma be your light and your refuge; seek no other refuge. O Ananda, be mindful of the impure nature of the body, and be not trapped by greed. Be mindful of the painful nature of feelings, and do not indulge in them. Be mindful of the transitory nature of the mind, and do not be attached to it. Be mindful of the nonsubstantial nature of all phenomena, and do not be deluded about them. Through these practices, suffering of all kinds will eventually disappear. After I am gone, he who practices the path in this manner, O Ananda, is my real disciple and my offspring. He will reach the very height of enlightenment. I left my kingly rank to become a mendicant because I was concerned with the state of sentient beings in all worlds. I have become a Tathagata and have been helping them overcome their fate. Be concerned with your own selves, and hurriedly sever the roots of all evils." And the Buddha, while passing the rainy season in Venuvagrama, repaired his own robes.

4. The Demise of Sariputra and Maudgalyayana

(1) One day, coming out of meditation, Sariputra thought, "The buddhas of olden days each had their great disciples who, as a rule, entered nirvana prior to their masters. I, too, shall also, within the following seven days, leave this world before the World-Honored One. Since, however, my aged mother has not taken refuge in the Buddha or the Dharma, I shall visit her to encourage her to pursue the path. Then I shall enter nirvana in the room where I was born. I must first obtain permission of the World-Honored One." After tidying up his room, Sariputra arose and solemnly glanced at the room, saying to himself, "This is the last time I shall see this room, to which I shall return no more." Then, coming to the Buddha, Sariputra said, "O World-Honored One, I say farewell to you, since I shall soon be entering nirvana." The Buddha was silent and did not reply. After this was repeated three times, the Buddha said, "Why, O Sariputra, do you not stay here?" Sariputra replied, "O World-Honored One, I was told by gods that although Sakyamuni Buddha has lived in this world for some time, he has now reached his eightieth year and will enter nirvana before long. O World-Honored One, I cannot bear seeing your demise. Moreover, as you once told us, before the Tathagatas enter nirvana, their best disciples as a rule make their way preceding their masters. Just so am I going to take my leave before the World-Honored One."

The Buddha asked, "Where then will you pass away?" "I shall die at the village of Nalanda in Magadha where I was born," replied Sariputra. "O Sariputra, you know the time very well. It is very hard to find an able man like you as my disciple. Will you once more expound on the Dharma to the disciples?" Upon this request, Sariputra respectfully saluted the Buddha, took his seat in front of the disciples, and taught the Dharma.

After he had finished his teaching, Sariputra said to the Buddha, "For a long time I have earnestly wished to meet with the buddhas, and now in this life, I have fulfilled my wish by becoming your disciple and adoring you. O World-Honored One, my life is approaching its end. I shall be freed within seven days as a person who has completed his task. This is my last occasion to offer my reverence to the World-Honored One." This said, Sariputra held his palms together, respectfully kneeled down, and withdrew from the room.

(2) Now many disciples followed Sariputra with flowers and incense in hand. Sariputra asked, "Where are you intending to go?" "O Sariputra, we are coming to make offerings at your passing away," they replied. Sariputra then said to them, "Leave me. You have already made offerings to me. I have a novice monk who can help me from now on. Return therefore to the World-Honored One and be concerned with your own path. It is difficult to meet with a buddha, whose appearance in this world is very rare; nor is it easy for people to attain a firm belief in the path and renounce family life to master the Dharma. Everything is impermanent, suffering, and without self; it is only nirvana that is quiescent forever. Be mindful of this Dharma." The disciples all became tearful.

It was just at dusk when Sariputra reached the edge of the village of Nalanda. While he sat under a tree for a rest, there came a young man who stopped and greeted him. This man happened to be his nephew Upalivata. Sariputra asked, "Is your grandmother at home?" "Yes, she is at home, sir," he answered. "Will you then go and tell her that Sariputra will be home very soon?" Upalivata hurriedly returned home to convey the message to his grandmother Sari. Sari secretly thought, "My son became a wandering mendicant in his youth. I wonder if, having aged, he is giving up his mendicant life." She tidied up the room and waited for his return.

In the evening, Sariputra reached the house. As soon as he entered the house, his condition became suddenly acute, and he vomited a large quantity of blood. Startled, his mother withdrew to her room. Gods came down to attend respectfully on Sariputra. The mother felt strange about all this and asked the attending novice Cunda, who was Sariputra's younger brother, "What is happening?" Cunda answered, "This is because the venerable Sariputra has supreme virtues." Astonished by Cunda's remark, Sariputra's mother said to herself, "Even my own son is so revered, how much more so must the World-Honored One be!"

(3) Knowing that the time was right, Sariputra said to his mother, "O my dear mother, it is said that the great earth trembled in six different ways when my venerable master was born, when he was enlightened, and when he gave his first discourse. There is no one superior to my master in virtue and insight." Sariputra then proceeded to teach the Dharma, and his mother responded in delight, "My dear son, why did you not teach me such a noble Dharma earlier?"

"Dear mother," said Sariputra, "For the first time now have I returned my indebtedness to you. Please leave the room and let me be alone." And Sariputra called Cunda, asking the hour of the day. "It is close to dawn, sir," replied Cunda. Sariputra then sat up, and facing his disciples who gathered around him he said, "O disciples, for forty-four years you have been with me. During all these years, if I unintentionally happened to hurt your feelings or hindered you in your pursuit of the Dharma, I beg your forgiveness." They unanimously replied, "Master, we have accompanied you like a shadow that follows an object. There has never been a moment that we felt harmed or ill at ease. We rather beg for your generous forgiveness." Sariputra then taught them the verse

> Fall not to laxity; strive for enlightenment.
> This is my teaching.
> I am about to enter nirvana.
> I have been emancipated from all.

(4) It was on a beautiful full moon night that Sariputra had entered the room where he was born. During that night he suffered from acute pains, but toward the dawn he spread the floor mat, lay on his right side, and quietly entered nirvana. Sari, his mother, wept by his side. "O my son, you speak no more. It was much too late that I came to realize your supreme virtue. Had I known it earlier, I should have invited many sages to my house for meals and offered them sets of three robes." When the morning came, Sari brought out a chest and opened her treasure to prepare for the funeral. Many neighbors came to help her, and Sariputra's nurse Revati offered three flowers made of gold; but falling ill in the bustling crowd, she passed away. She is said to have been born in heaven because of her virtuous deed.

For seven days, manifold offerings were made in honor of the venerable Sariputra, and this was followed by the cremation rites. Anuruddha extinguished the fire by scented water, and Cunda respectfully gathered the ashes and Sariputra's robes and bowl.

(5) Cunda first went to tell Ananda that Sariputra had passed away and then presented to him Sariputra's ashes, robes, and bowl. Ananda wept and grieved, saying, "This day is dark everywhere in all directions," and he came to the Buddha to report and said, "Upon losing the venerable Sariputra, we have lost our composure." The Buddha said to Ananda, "O Ananda, do not grieve about his death. It is not in accord with nature to wish that a mortal being should live forever. O Ananda, thus did even all the buddhas of the past pass away. Everything is impermanent; every living being will necessarily die. One must not grieve about this but yearn for the realm of nirvana, where one is neither born nor perishes, the realization of which is of the highest value. O Ananda, give me the remains of Sariputra." Upon receiving the ashes in his right hand, the Buddha called the disciples together and told them this: "O disciples, these are the ashes that belonged to the person who spoke to you on the Dharma several days ago. He devoted himself for many years to the practice of virtues and realized perfection. He taught the Dharma like the buddhas, and many people followed him to learn his teachings; his insight was broad and filled with delight; his mind

was alert and clear; he had little desire and enjoyed quietude, refrained from evil, avoided dispute, did not like senseless talk, and held a determination as firm as the earth for the spread of the teaching. O disciples, pay respect to the ashes of this wise man of the Dharma." The Buddha then erected a stupa in honor of Sariputra near the gate of Vaisali and once again proceeded back toward Rajagriha.

(6) Entering Rajagriha, the Buddha stayed at the Bamboo Grove Monastery. A short time later, the venerable Maudgalyayana also died. His death occurred in the following manner. A group of naked ascetics who resided at the edge of Rajagriha had been jealous of the Buddha, and they were convinced that one of the reasons that the Buddha and his disciples were honored by people was the superior magical powers of Maudgalyayana. Maudgalyayana had been attacked already twice when he was residing in the cave of the Rsigiri Hill, but fortunately he had escaped their assault on both occasions. One day, however, when he entered the city of Rajagriha to receive alms, those pseudo-ascetics hastened to surround him for the third time, seized him, and finally struck him with tiles and stones and, leaving him for dead, threw him into the bushes by the roadside and went away. Maudgalyayana's bones were broken, and his flesh was torn; in unbearable pain he finally passed away. When this was heard by King Ajatasatru, the king rounded up the members of the naked ascetics' group and executed them.

The Buddha again ordered a stupa to be built at the entrance of the Bamboo Grove Monastery, this time in honor of Maudgalyayana. He called his disciples together and said to them, "O disciples, when Sariputra and Maudgalyayana were still alive in this world, wherever they visited for the teaching of the Dharma, people were all benefitted and given happiness, for they possessed the capacity to overcome false views. They are no longer among you. This Sangha has suffered a great loss."

5. The Buddha's Admonition Prior to His Demise

(1) The Buddha left Rajagriha once again for Vaisali accompanied by Ananda, and at the bank of the Ganges he thought about the deaths of Sariputra and Maudgalyayana and honored them. Crossing the Ganges and arriving at Vaisali, the Buddha went for alms begging in the morning, and on the way back he passed by the Capala Shrine, where he decided to take a rest. "O Ananda, how pleasant Vaisali is; how pleasant Vrji is; the sixteen countries and their various cities are all pleasant. The river Hiranyavati produces much gold; the land of Jambudvipa is as beautiful as a painting. O Ananda, those who acquire superhuman power can remain in this world if they so wish." The Buddha carefully repeated these words three times. But Ananda could not fathom the meaning intended and remained silent. The Buddha told him to think on them in solitude, and he himself sat alone in the tree shade by the bank of a brook.

(2) At that time, Mara, the evil one, appeared before the Buddha and said to him, "O World-Honored One, pass away without hesitation. Your teaching mission has been completed. Now is the time for the World-Honored One to pass

away from this world!" The Buddha replied, "Go, Mara! To me is the time clearly known. It is not the time yet. I shall not die until all of my monks and lay disciples become ready and are able to receive the path." Mara said, "O World-Honored One, when you stayed near the river Nairanjana immediately after your enlightenment, I came before you at the seat where you were in meditation and urged you to enter nirvana immediately. At that time, too, you said, 'Go, Mara! I know the time very well; it is not the time yet. I shall not die until, with my disciples gathered around me, the heavenly gods and people equally have witnessed the supernatural powers of the Tathagata.' O World-Honored One, have not your disciples gathered, and have not gods and people equally witnessed your supernatural powers? Now, O World-Honored One, is the suitable moment for you to pass away. Why do you not pass away without hesitation?" The Buddha then replied, "Go away, Mara! The Tathagata knows the appropriate time. Three months from now, at the village of Kusinagara, with which one of my past lives had some association, under the sala trees, I shall die." Mara, hearing this, jumped for joy, because the Buddha, who never lies, would certainly pass away soon; and he quickly disappeared.

(3) The Buddha adjusted the floor mat and again entered meditation. Quietly reflecting on his entering final nirvana, the Buddha said to himself, "To escape from three kinds of delusion is as easy as for a chick to break out from the egg. Now, my mind is peaceful, like that of a military general returning from the battlefield after a victory over his enemy." Just at that moment, the earth trembled severely.

Ananda was awakened in surprise and came to the Buddha asking, "O World-Honored One, why has the earth trembled? I have just dreamed that while I was in the forest a large verdantly foliaged tree was suddenly crushed by a storm so that no trace remained. Can it be that the World-Honored One will pass away?" The Buddha then said, "O Ananda, in three months I shall enter nirvana." Ananda was shocked and grieved. "O World-Honored One, may I beseech you, with your compassion for us, to remain in life for a kalpa, or even for half a kalpa, for the benefit of gods and people." He said this three times; but the Buddha replied, "O Ananda, it is no longer the time to say it. I have already told Mara that I shall pass away three months from now. During all the years you have served me, have you ever heard me be deceitful?" Ananda answered, "O World-Honored One, I have never heard you be deceitful. But from your own mouth I have received this saying, 'Whosoever has realized superhuman power can extend his life span should he so wish.' " The Buddha replied, "It is true that I have said that to you. At that time, however, you did not answer my words, nor did you ask the Tathagata to prolong his life. The words of the Tathagata that once come out from his mouth cannot change. The unwise say one thing and mean another, but I do not do this."

Ananda was anguished, distressed, could not bear it, and said to the Buddha, weeping, "How swift is the passing away of the Tathagata! Why should it be so soon that the Eye of the World should perish?" The Buddha felt pity for Ananda and said, "O Ananda, be not grieved. Whatever is subject to causality is like this. When one person meets another, they can never remain together but without exception will be separated." "However, O World-Honored One," said Ananda, "The people will lose their benevolent father, for this is comparable to a calf just born being abandoned by its mother."

"O Ananda, be not grieved; even if I could remain for the duration of another kalpa, beings that come together will sooner or later be separated. Such is the way everything is. Be not distressed about my passing away. Even though this physical body perishes, the body of the Dharma that I taught remains forever. O Ananda, bring me my floor mat. Let us go back to the rest house." Ananda took the floor mat, followed the Buddha, and entered the rest house in the sala grove.

(4) That evening, the Buddha told Ananda, "O Ananda, go and gather the disciples who come around in the neighborhood of this grove in the lecture hall." Ananda conveyed this message to them, and all the disciples in the neighborhood gathered together in the hall. The Buddha came out from his room and entered the hall, and the disciples all stood up and saluted him. The Buddha sat down on the seat and told them this: "O disciples, of all the teachings that I have taught you up to this moment you should always be mindful; keep them in memory, and always practice them; do not discard them. If all the people in the world rectify their minds by themselves, the gods will be delighted, and the human world will be benefitted. O disciples, you should restrain your desires and gain control over yourselves. You should right your physical, mental, and verbal actions. Discard anger, avoid evil, throw away avarice, and keep your thoughts on death; even when the mind is inclined to wickedness, you should never follow it. When the mind happens to think of sensual things, never let it get out of control. When it wishes to have a luxurious life, do not allow it. The mind must follow the person, not the person the mind. The mind becomes a god, a human, an animal, or another being, creating six worlds; and yet it becomes enlightened to become a sublime Buddha.

(5) "O disciples, therefore, you must set your minds right and practice the path. Only those who practice the path are able to realize the state of peace in this life. In this way the noble path that I have taught will perpetuate itself in the world, save beings in this world, guide the gods, and let all people rest in peace.

"O disciples, be mindful of the impure nature of the body, and do not let greed rise on its account. Be mindful of pleasant feelings. They lead to suffering, so do not indulge in them. Be mindful of the transitory nature of the mind, and be not trapped in it. Also, be mindful of the insubstantial nature of all things, and be not attached to them. These are the four fields of mindfulness. O disciples, prevent evils from arising. If they have already arisen, annihilate their causal roots. If good elements have already arisen, try to strengthen them. If good elements have not yet arisen, encourage them to arise. These are the four right exertions. O disciples, aspire to attain goodness, and always keep the mind in concentration and be mindful of the Dharma; always exert yourselves without laxity, and always be thoughtful and control the mind. These are the four steps toward supernatural power.

"O disciples, keep faith in the path, proceed in it for the practice of the path, be mindful of the path, keep your concentration on the path, and cultivate the wisdom of the Four Noble Truths. In these ways, you may nourish and strengthen the roots of merit. These are the five spiritual faculties. O disciples, believe firmly in the path and discard doubt and affliction, endeavor to proceed on the path to remove negligence, be mindful of the path, set the mind right and repudiate confused thoughts, understand the Four Noble Truths, and be free from wrong views. In these ways, you may gain the power of cultivating the roots of merit. These are the five spiritual powers.

"O disciples, be mindful of the Dharma, differentiate between true and false when choosing teachings, always endeavor, always be delighted, let the mind be faithful, have remembrance, keep the mind in concentration to prevent false views from arising, and put the mind in a state of equanimity to avoid the extreme views of eternalism and nihilism. These are the seven limbs of enlightenment, the path to realize true insight. O disciples, right view, right thought, right speech, right conduct, right livelihood, right endeavor, right mindfulness, and right meditation are the Eightfold Noble Path.

(6) "O disciples, this is the noble path that truly saves the world. For the happiness and benefit of all people, you must practice this path and spread it throughout the world. O disciples, these thirty-seven wings of enlightenment are the basis of all good. With these paths, discipline your minds and free yourselves from greed, from dispute, from lies, from pursuing amusements, from jealousy, and from pride. Through the eyes of insight, compassion, and reverence, you will see the Body of the Dharma that is far superior to mine. Only those who rightly perceive the Body of the Dharma will become aware that I shall remain in this world as before and never leave their sides.

"I now wish for you that the trees of suffering may be transformed so that they bear fruits that produce nectar. Maintain mutual reverence in the Dharma and refrain from disputes, for all of you were converted to the Dharma by one and the same teacher; hence be harmonious and mutually respectful like water and milk; incur no strife like water and oil. Uphold the Dharma that I taught all of you together, and share the fruit of prosperity and happiness. Do not waste your lives in troubling your minds with trifles, but feed yourselves with the nectar of the flower of enlightenment so that you can produce many fruits of the path, and strive to nourish the world with them. O disciples, I have realized this Dharma myself and taught it to others. This Dharma will enable you to reach the final goal of emancipation. Keep the Dharma constantly and apply it to your lives in every context. I shall be passing into nirvana after three months."

(7) Having heard this, the disciples were dismayed and saddened, tossing themselves to the ground and exclaiming, "Why is the Tathagata passing away so soon? Why is the Eye of the World so quickly perishing? O World-Honored One, we beseech you to remain in this world longer and not to pass away so soon. All beings are still in the state of delusion and groping in the darkness of ignorance. We beseech you to stay in this world and illumine the world as its lamp.

People are still being tossed around on the rough sea of ignorance. We beseech you to remain as a raft for them. Otherwise all these people will stray forever from the path that they should follow."

The Buddha, in exhorting the disciples, said, "O disciples, stop your wailing and grief. The world is impermanent, and there is nothing that is strong and unchanging forever; the physical body is as evanescent as lightning. Even the gods in the heavens will die, and no king on earth can avoid death. Whether poor or rich, high or low, irrespective of these differences, no one, once born, can escape death. Nor is it possible to prevent change in whatever is subject to change. Stay in purity, strive for emancipation, and never become negligent. Now my life has completed itself. The end of my life has come. You will remain in this world, while I, as I wish, go to the abode of peace and rest. Guard your minds with restraint and caution.

"The Dharma that I have taught you through the years is the teacher that you must follow. Uphold it fast as you have followed me in devotion. If you advance on this path unfalteringly, it will mean that you will have upheld the true Dharma. Therefore keep the Dharma constantly, even after I am gone, just as you are now doing while I am still here. In this way alone, I assure you, will you be able to realize your emancipation and thereby benefit all other people." It had already become dark, and the Buddha returned to his room accompanied by Ananda.

Chapter 2

THE GOLDEN LIGHT

1. The Three Bodies of the Buddha

(1) Having heard the Buddha prophesy that he would be passing away after three months, the Bodhisattva Ruciraketu, a native of Rajagriha, was astonished and hurriedly came to the Buddha and said to him, "O World-Honored One, why are you going to shorten your life span to eighty years? Once you taught us that there are two ways for anyone to enjoy longevity: one is not to kill living beings, and the other is to sustain others' lives by charity. O World-Honored One, you have not harmed any living being since the infinitely distant past and have always done good for others, such as feeding the hungry. You sometimes even provided them with your own flesh and blood. Why then is your life going to be so short?" Taking this opportunity for teaching, the Buddha gave the discourse on the bodies of the Buddha, a recondite truth not known to ordinary people. "O sons of good family, listen carefully and ponder. Every Buddha is endowed with three kinds of body. It is only when these are fully attained that one is said to have realized the supreme enlightenment. If one becomes capable of understanding why this is so, one will be able to transcend delusion.

"O sons of good family, the three bodies of the Tathagata are the Body of Transformation, the Body of Enjoyment, and the Body of the Dharma. The Body of Transformation is the earthly, manifested body of the Buddha, born in this world for the sake of human salvation, engaged in the pursuit of various paths and in the realization of enlightenment. The Buddha with the Body of Transformation strove in the career of teaching, in acquiring the power of knowing people's individual capacities as well as fitting times and environments, and in revealing his physical body before them. The Tathagata whom you have known through your eyes is this Body of Transformation, which may have been varied according to each individual's perceptions.

"Next, the Body of Enjoyment is the body of skillful means, which is intended to avoid a direct teaching of the absolute truth. It is also intended to eliminate the sense of pleasure or dread from the mind that man incurs because of his attachment to the body of flesh. This body came into being as the result of the original vow and the insight of the Buddha.

"Lastly, the Body of the Dharma is the Dharma itself, the body in its essential nature and hence the ultimate ground of the Bodies of the Buddha, in which the absolute truth and the insight into the truth are not yet differentiated into two. The first two Bodies, namely those of Transformation and Enjoyment, are temporary manifestations derived from this Dharmakaya (Body of the Dharma). Therefore, the entire Buddhist doctrine is to be included in or attributed to the Body of the Dharma.

(2) "Moreover, O sons of good family, the Buddha knows the truth by the power of the original vow. Hence this transcendental knowledge implies no empirical purposive thought as such and yet conducts manifold activities spontaneously. The sun and the moon have no particular purpose, and their rays and a mirror are equally non-purposive, yet the three together spontaneously produce the images of things as they really are, as reflected in the mirror. Here the truth of things is likened to the sun or the moon, the insight intuiting this truth is its light, and the power of the vow is the mirror. The Dharmakaya, though with no purposive thought, spontaneously creates as images the Bodies of Enjoyment and of Transformation for the sake of people.

"O sons of good family, just as the mirror, though there is nothing in it, creates various images by reflecting light, the disciples are guided, upon receiving the teachings, by the image of the Buddha produced within the Dharmakaya, which however has no form whatsoever. While the Bodies of Enjoyment and Transformation manifest themselves in varied forms due to the power of the vow, the Dharmakaya totally transcends these changes; there is no change in the transcendental state. Nevertheless, it is said that the Tathagata is impermanent, and that he does not remain in nirvana. Why so? The first two bodies are provisional and frequently appear in this world, but they do not remain with any permanent form, and hence they naturally enter the state of nirvana. On the other hand, it cannot be said that the Dharmakaya remains in nirvana forever, because this third cannot be said to comprise the two features, namely, the two bodies that appear in history and the one that transcends it. In a word, the Dharmakaya is threefold and yet one, one and yet threefold; it manifests itself in change and yet is unchanged, is unchanged and yet manifests itself in change.

"O sons of good family, ordinary people who do not know the three forms of existence cannot see the three Bodies of the Buddha. The three are the form of imagined existence, the form of dependent existence, and the form of perfected existence. The imagined nature of things refers to the reality that the ordinary person's consciousness is always trapped by its own inclinations, just as a man imagines a snake looking at a rope and is frightened by it. The dependent nature of things refers to the reality taught by the Buddha that everything arises out of multiple causes and conditions and hence is a temporary configuration, just useful for understanding that the rope is a temporary form of the substance of hemp. The perfected nature of things points to the truth that although things are of the transient and imaginary nature, their true form and causal basis must be known as inseparable from their empirical form of manifestation, and hence that the absolute truth is intuited in the transient world. The Body of Transformation is a skillful means to edify ordinary people who are entrapped in the imagined forms. The Body of Enjoyment is the Buddha seen by those who intuit the dependent nature of things. The Dharmakaya is the Buddha only known by the person of enlightenment who thoroughly delves into the true nature of the Dharma and intuits the absolute within the temporary forms of the world. Thus the two contingent Bodies of Enjoyment and Transformation are necessarily bound to be transient, but ordinary people are incapable of understanding the threefold aspect of the Buddha Body and accordingly they are frightened and grieved when the Buddha appears to be gone forever beyond the clouds into nirvana.

"O sons of good family, there are three types of human consciousness, on account of which it is difficult for an ordinary person to see the three Bodies of the Buddha. First is the consciousness that responds to external events and consists of six forms of consciousness, which are seeing, hearing, smelling, tasting, touching, and thinking; it perceives external things and is attracted by them, thus resulting in delusion. Second is the 'I' consciousness that depends upon the third consciousness and underlies all passions. Third is the consciousness that constitutes the ultimate ground underlying the foregoing conceptual operation. Accordingly, when a person realizes reality as it is and thereby annihilates all delusions, he should be able to see the Body of Transformation. Moreover, when he annihilates the source of passions, he should be able to see the Body of Enjoyment. And finally, when he practices the highest path and thereby annihilates the fundamental agent of the consciousness, he should be able to see the Dharmakaya.

(3) "O sons of good family, all buddhas share the same activities in the Body of Transformation, share the same intention in the Body of Enjoyment, and share the same essence in the Dharmakaya. The Body of Transformation is manifested in varied forms in accordance with man's various inclinations and is therefore defined as manifold; the Body of Enjoyment manifests itself in one singular form in response to the singular intention of the disciples and is therefore defined as one; and the Dharmakaya embodies the state that transcends all forms and cannot be grasped by means of forms and is therefore defined as neither one nor two.

"O sons of good family, the Body of Transformation arises on the basis of the Body of Enjoyment, and the latter arises on the basis of the Dharmakaya, and this Dharmakaya is the absolute existence, which requires no basis and depends on nothing.

"O sons of good family, these three Bodies of the Buddha are regarded, in accordance with their intended meanings, as both permanent and impermanent. The Body of Transformation always teaches the teaching of the truth and never exhausts its skillful means appropriate to various conditions; therefore it is defined as permanent. However, this is not the fundamental body, nor does it manifest a greater function; hence it is defined as impermanent. Next, the Body of Enjoyment from the immemorial past has never ceased to teach the Dharma that is accessible only to the buddhas, nor will it exhaust its function as long as mankind continues to exist; hence it is defined as permanent. However, this body is neither the ultimate body nor does it manifest on all things; hence it is defined as impermanent. The Dharmakaya is, of course, not transient, nor does it have form, rather it is the ultimate, fundamental body comparable to space; therefore, it is defined solely as permanent.

"O sons of good family, there is no perfect insight separated from the insight of a particular object. There is no universal object separated from particular objects. The phenomena, their natures, and the insight into them are neither one nor different. And the Dharmakaya consists of pure insight free from passions and of pure quiescence; hence it is pure and free from passions.

(4) "Moreover, O sons of good family, the Dharmakaya cannot be described as either existent or nonexistent, as either one or not one, as either measurable or immeasurable, as either light or dark. It is totally beyond the understanding of ordinary people; and the insight into suchness, or the truth as it is, is totally beyond the ordinary knowledge deduced from human experience. Therefore the Dharmakaya is beyond human cognition; its casual basis, objective sphere, cognitive faculty, and function are beyond human knowledge. If you understand the meaning of all this, you should be able to reach the state of non-retrogression on the path to enlightenment and then proceed to the rank of a person destined to become a buddha and attain the mind of diamond, the mind of the buddhas, the true Dharma.

"Moreover, the Dharmakaya is called permanent, or having self, from the absolute point of view; it is called bliss with regard to the meditational states; and it is called pure with regard to insight. Thus the Dharmakaya is immutable, independent, peaceful, and pure. From the meditation on the Dharmakaya arise varieties of meditations, supernatural powers, and compassion. From the insight into the Dharmakaya spring all powers, such as persuasive powers, and immeasurable and wondrous doctrines, just as all kinds of precious stones are produced from the magical cintamani, the wish-granting gem. O sons of good family, in this way meditation and insight attributed to the Dharmakaya transcend all forms and are not entrapped by any form and thus bear no particular purposive thought for whatever is to be done. Since it cannot be determined as either permanent or impermanent, it is called the Middle path and transcends the cycle of birth and death. It is the abode that cannot be reached by ordinary people; it is indeed the abode of buddhas and bodhisattvas.

(5) "O sons of good family, the abode of the buddhas is the sphere where defilement, suffering, and form are all purified and is called the absolute. It is like well-refined gold that has no stain in it; this is due to the nature of gold itself having no stain. Gold is already pure while it is contained in the ore. It is not created anew by the refining processes, nor is its purity lost when it is in the ore. The Dharmakaya is like this, for it is essentially pure. Even when it appears in defilements and manifests itself in the Bodies of Enjoyment and Transformation, the Dharmakaya cannot be said to have lost its essential purity. This is why the states of all buddhas are said to be pure. Take another analogy: someone dreamed that he was swimming in a huge river, crossing it by moving his arms and legs, and thus finally reaching the yonder shore; but when he was

awakened from the dream, he found neither the river nor its bank. Just so, when one has destroyed passion, one no longer finds the flowing of birth and death nor the banks of enlightenment and delusion. Nevertheless, the awakening from the dream does not empty the presence of the mind, nor does the exhaustion of delusion mean the emptying of enlightenment either. The purity of the mind, like that of empty space, remains after everything is emptied and is itself enlightenment. This is why the abode of the buddhas is said to be pure.

"O sons of good family, the Dharmakaya overcomes the hindrances created by passions, thereby manifesting the Body of Enjoyment, and it also overcomes the hindrances created by actions, thereby manifesting the Body of Transformation. Moreover, it overcomes the hindrances that obstruct insight, thereby manifesting the Dharmakaya itself. This is comparable to the sky that displays lightning, and the lightning that creates illumination. Moreover, the Dharmakaya manifests itself in its essentially pure form; the Body of Enjoyment manifests itself when the insight is purified; and the Body of Transformation manifests itself when the concentration is purified. The three Bodies of the Buddha are equally pure on account of reality as it is. The reality of phenomena is to be found in one universal taste; it is free from the attachment caused by all passions, and it is the absolute foundation of all phenomena. Accordingly, the three Bodies of the Buddha, which are identical with that absolute foundation, are said to be one and not different.

(6) "O sons of good family, if a layman or a laywoman holds the firm belief that the Buddha is his or her great teacher, he or she will thoroughly understand that there are no essential differences among the three Bodies of the Buddha. Thus any wrong thoughts liable to rise in regard to phenomena will be totally eliminated. He or she will understand that there is neither duality of form nor any differentiation in reality, and as a result he or she will not be affected by passions and will be able genuinely to practice the path. Thus the truth of things as they really are and the insight into that truth are equally pure, resulting in the removal of hindrances as well as in the spontaneous reception of all reality as it really is. This is called the supreme insight into suchness, or the form of supreme reality; this is also called the correct way of seeing things or the true way of seeing the Buddha."

Hearing these teachings, the audience marveled at the wondrous bodies of the Buddha, and the thought arose in their minds to yearn for the Dharmakaya that is eternal; and thereby they overcame their grief and doubt about the Buddha's passing away.

2. The Land of the True Dharma

(1) At that time, all the gods present at the scene said in unison, "O World-Honored One, this is a wondrously superior doctrine that we have never heard before. By our words, we shall protect and let prosper the kings who firmly hold to this teaching and spread it."

Then the World-Honored One said to the Kings of the Four Quarters, "O Kings of the Four Quarters, it is truly excellent that you have promised to protect this teaching. During a period of many thousands of kalpas, I have carried out many difficult practices and finally realized enlightenment, and I am now teaching the Dharma. If any ruler of people firmly holds this doctrine, honors it, and makes offerings to it, all his enemies will retreat and run away; and as a result, all the cities and villages of his country will become peaceful and prosperous. O Kings of the Four Quarters, if any rulers firmly hold to this doctrine, they will enjoy life as they wish, they will have less and less desire, their treasures will abundantly increase, and they will eventually discard bows and arrows, as they will be no longer covetous of other countries. The people of such a country will certainly enjoy well-being and treat each other well, maintaining the harmony between high and low just as between water and milk. They will also find delight in mutual love and respect, become compassionate and humble, and thereby promote all good things. Thus the people will prosper, the land will be fertile, the cold and heat will be moderate, and the seasons will change in due order; the sun, moon, and stars will keep to their regular courses, wind and rain will follow seasonal order, and all disasters will disappear."

Then the Kings of the Four Quarters, holding their palms together in salute, said to the Buddha, "O World-Honored One, if any ruler of people does not wish to listen to this teaching, or neither honors it nor makes offerings to it, we King of the Four Quarters and all of our retainers will not protect his country. In that country, then, the true Dharma will lose its brilliance, evil will prevail, the people will stray into wrong ways and act against the path of enlightenment, and multiple disasters will fall upon the country. The people will lose their good nature, will be angry, and will engage in disputes; backbiting each other and making false charges, they will see epidemics spread, shooting stars fall, the earth shake, wells dry up, storms and hurricanes rage frequently, the suffering of famine increase, and all kinds of detestable enemies attack from all directions. O World-Honored One, therefore, if any ruler of people wishes his country to prosper, his subjects to enjoy peace, and the true Dharma to spread in his land, he must uphold this teaching and honor it. Then we, as well as innumerable gods, will thrive upon the nectar of this teaching and protect the king by our supernatural powers, eliminate disasters, and thereby make his realm peaceful."

(2) At that time, Drdha, the earth goddess, arose from her seat and respectfully bowed to the Buddha and said, "O World-Honored One, if any ruler of people does not maintain the true Dharma, he will not be able to govern his country nor maintain peace for his people, and hence he will not be able to stay on the throne for long. O World-Honored One, please instruct me in the true Dharma and the essentials of ruling the country, so that I may cause every human ruler to listen to the Dharma, act in accordance with the Dharma, govern his country righteously, and keep his throne for a long time; thereby, I may help his people throughout the country enjoy the benefits therefrom."

The Buddha then addressed Drdha and told her, "There was a king who when he was still the crown prince was instructed by his father the king on the subject of the true Dharma of the ruler. Later, on the ceremonial occasion when he himself installed his own son as crown prince, he instructed his own son in verse on the subject he had once been taught:

(i) As a result of good deeds, one is born as a god and becomes the chief of gods, or one is born as a human and becomes the ruler of people. Though one is born in the human world, if one is of lofty and noble nature and protected by gods, he is called the Son of Heaven. When the ruler forbids people to do wrong, this injunction must be in accord with proper reasoning. Apply it in accordance with the Dharma. Indeed, one is called the king only when he devotes himself to the Dharma. If he neglects to practice it, the king will harm his countrymen like an elephant trampling on a lotus pond.

(ii) Hurricanes and deluges of rain attack, strange stars and evil spirits appear, the sun and moon equally lose their brilliance, crops fail, and the people suffer famine; all these result from the ruler's negligence in the true Dharma. If he spreads an evil Dharma throughout his country, the land will be filled with disputes and deceptions and lose the protection of the gods; his minister, the pillar of the country, will die by violence, and the king, too, will be harmed bodily, and outside enemies will all descend upon the country. Thus, as battles spread here and there, many people will die unjustly, ministers and councillors will be corrupted, honoring wrongdoers and punishing the righteous, and finally, the true Dharma will be eclipsed, resulting in the eventual destruction of the country.

(iii) Therefore, even faced with the danger of losing his throne or his life, the king should never practice injustice. The worst harm a king can experience is to lose the country, and this may occur due to flatterers. If the king associates with sycophants as friends, he will lose his throne and his corrupt statecraft like an elephant rushing into a flower garden. Therefore, one should treat one's kin and others equally, and stay away from factions; then the name of the Dharma king will spread throughout the world. Thus, every ruler of people must forget his own interest and spread the true Dharma and have the people practice the tenfold merits in honor of the Dharma-treasure; in this way he will bring prosperity and peace to his country.

3. Giving His Flesh to the Starving Tigress

(1) Immediately after the foregoing discourse, the Buddha responded to the question raised by Kuladevata, the goddess of the Bodhi Tree. He explained the past lives of those gods to as many as ten thousand who gathered at this Dharma assembly.

"O goddess Kuladevata, there was once a rich man called Jatindhara in the immemorial past who was well versed in medicine and cured many varieties of illness. The son of this man, Jalavahana by name, had noble features and was endowed with an intelligent mind, as he excelled in various branches of learning. At one time, an epidemic spread in the country, and innumerable people were suffering in their sickbeds. As he was compassionate, Jalavahana thought, 'Although my father excels in medicine, he is now aged and barely able to walk with the help of a cane. I am going to learn the secrets of medicine from him, so that I can save those who are suffering.' Setting his mind thus, Jalavahana came to his father and told his idea to him. His father was delighted and taught him all the details of medicine, each depending on the nature of each illness and its cause.

" 'O Jalavahana, when you know the causes of illnesses in this manner, you can prescribe medicines according to the needs of each illness. Even if the condition appears to be very severe, the first thing to do is to treat the root cause and eliminate it. If there is no sign of dying in a given patient, he may be able to survive it. The shadow of death can be recognized in that the left eye turns white, the tongue becomes dark, the nose bridge becomes unusually raised, the earlobe looks different from before, or the lower lip hangs down. The shadow of death can also be observed in the abnormal conditions of eyes, nose, and ears, in an arrogant attitude toward a person or a doctor who is to be respected, or in the kind of speech that creates indignation in close friends.' Then his father told Jalavahana the kinds of medicines in detail, and finally he completed his teaching with the following instructions. 'A doctor must have a sense of compassion toward patients and never think of making wealth. Now these are the essentials of the medical art, and you may go to help those who are suffering from illnesses. In doing so, you will be able to receive an incalculable reward.'

"Thus Jalavahana, son of the rich man, realized that by applying skillfully what he had learnt from his father, he could treat and cure illness; and he himself travelled around widely in cities, towns, and villages, attending to the sick and consoling them, telling them, 'I am a doctor, and am going to cure your illness.' Those who were suffering from sickness were deeply gladdened, and many people were cured of their illnesses.

(2) "Thus Jalavahana was praised by the people throughout the country as a compassionate bodhisattva. One day, as he went around the country, taking along his two children, and passing by a marshy area in an isolated region, he saw wolves, foxes, hawks, eagles, and other flesh-eating birds and beasts, all hurrying in the same direction like a stream. Thinking it strange, he followed them and came to a large pond almost dry and found in it a multitude of fish struggling to survive. At that moment, a tree god, manifesting half of his body, said to Jalavahana, 'O son of good family, just as your name means, be compassionate to these fishes. As your name has two meanings, flowing of water and making effort in giving, please practice what is befitting your name.'

"Informed that the number of the fishes was as many as several thousand, and seeing them directly exposed to the sun's rays and splashing in the shallow water, Jalavahana had a deep commiseration for them, while the fishes, too, as if showing their minds, appeared to be staring at him. Forgetting all other things, he wanted now to rescue them. Running all over the area to look for water, he could not find any water, so he broke tree branches and leaves to make shades for them. Next, he looked for the source of the pond's water. There was a large river but it was all dried up, because fishermen had diverted the water flow by damming the upper stream in order to catch fish; as a result, the pond's water had not been replenished but was steadily drying up. In order to repair the destroyed portion in the upper stream, it would take more than three months with a work force of several hundred people. Thus, he returned to the city and borrowed from the king twenty large elephants and also many large leather bags from a brewery to transport water from the river. Within a short time, he filled the pond with water as it had been before. Moreover, he had his people transport much food from his house and fed the fishes with it until they were all satiated.

"Jalavahana thought, 'Now that I have rescued these fishes by feeding them, I shall provide them with the food of the Dharma, so that they will be saved in their next lives without exception.' He entered the pond and let the fishes hear the name of the Buddha and further taught them the two different paths leading to delusion and enlightenment.

"In a later period, these fishes attained rebirth in heaven by the merit of their listening to Jalavahana's teaching of the Dharma. Wishing to repay him for the gift that they received in their previous lives, the fishes visited him while he was asleep in a palatial room and offered him many ornaments made of pearls; they filled his room with brightly colored flowers so deep as to reach to his knees."

(3) Having completed the story, the Buddha told Kuladevata, "Jalavahana in this story was myself, and the ten thousand fishes were the gods who have congregated here. In this way, I have continued for a long period of repeated births and deaths to benefit an incalculable number of beings and have helped them gradually to reach enlightenment. You also must seek for yourself emancipation from the state of delusion, exerting yourself always without falling back into negligence."

The audience understood the meaning of the teaching and were delighted in the resolution that they, too, would strive to help all others with great compassion, diligently practice the path, and realize supreme enlightenment.

(4) Then the Buddha led the assemblage and arrived at a certain grove in the country of Pancala. Here the ground was even and covered with no thorny bush but with beautiful flowers and soft grass throughout the area. Asking Ananda to make a seat, the Buddha sat in the lotus posture. Straightening his body and mind, he asked the audience, "Would you like to see the ashes of a buddha who once practiced the difficult way of a bodhisattva?" They unanimously answered that they would. The Buddha then pointed to the ground. Suddenly, the earth trembled in six different ways and opened its surface, from which sprang a stupa decorated with the seven kinds of precious stones. The Buddha stood up, bowed to it, circled it once on the right, and returned to sit on his seat. He ordered Ananda to open the door of the stupa. There appeared a treasure chest decorated with the seven precious stones, in which was a pile of ashes like white snow and fragrant like a white lotus. The Buddha gently lifted the ashes and spoke to his assembly, "These truly are the ashes of a bodhisattva who had completed his training," and he recited the following verse

> A bodhisattva has excellent virtues and wisdom.,
> His courageous endeavors to perfect of the Six Practices
> Is solely for the realization of enlightenment.
> With unswerving equanimity, he practices the path.

"O my disciples, pay your tribute to these remains of the Bodhisattva, which bear an incalculably great practice of moral discipline, mental concentration, and perfect insight. He is the source of supreme blessing, with which it is extremely difficult to meet." As suggested by the Buddha, all the listeners paid their reverence to the ashes. The Buddha then told them the following story about the remains.

(5) "O Ananda, once upon a time there was a king, Maharatha by name, whose country was rich and flourishing and whose army was valiant; and the king governed his subjects in accord with the true Dharma. He had three sons by his queen: Mahabala, the oldest; Mahadeva, the middle; and Mahasattva, the youngest. One day these princes made an excursion to the forest and happened to find a tigress. The tigress had just given birth to seven cubs and she was extremely lean and bony, almost starved to death, and was about to devour her own cubs. The older princes were deeply moved and told the youngest, 'Like leopards and lions, tigers feed only on the blood and flesh of animals, so no other feed can save this tigress from starvation.' While they left the scene, the third prince thought to himself, 'One loves one's own body but does not know how to benefit others; it is the superior man alone who forgets himself to rescue others because of his great compassion. The hundreds or even thousands of lives I have gone through have been mere meaningless repetitions, lives ending with rotting and festering bodies. Now I am going to throw away my body so that this tigress can be saved. Indeed, this body of mine is transitory. No matter how I desire to keep my body, I cannot preserve it. I shall now throw away this body for the sake of enlightenment.' Without hesitation he took off his clothing and hung it over a bamboo stalk nearby, and he sang,

> Now I wish to realize enlightenment
> For the sake of all beings in the world of the Dharma.
> With an unwavering mind of great compassion,
> I am determined to throw off the body, which people cling to.
> There is no suffering for those who attain enlightenment;
> It is the state every person of wisdom wishes to realize.
> May I rescue those who are sunk in the sea of suffering
> And thereby lead them to the state of final peace.

"Thus the prince laid his body down in front of the starved tigress. Struck by the Bodhisattva's power of compassion, the tigress did not try to devour him. Noting this, the prince now threw his body from a cliff, pierced his neck with a dried bamboo stalk, and approached the tigress with gushing blood. At that moment, the earth and the mountains shook and trembled, while the ocean swirled in astonishment. The tigress glanced at the gushing blood, immediately jumped on the prince, and devoured him, leaving only chips of bone behind.

(6) "The two older princes, noting the sudden change of the heavens and the earth, and worrying about their youngest brother, returned to the spot where they had left him. Finding only his clothes hanging on a bamboo stalk and blood-stained bone chips scattered on the ground, they were shocked with grief to the point of fainting.

"At that moment, the queen, lying in a palatial room, dreamed that her two breasts broke open, two of her teeth fell out, and one of her three dove chicks was snatched away by a hawk. She immediately awakened and found that the heavens and the earth were darkened. Her breasts were still trembling and her heart was pained as if shot by an arrow. Just at that moment, her maid came to report that the three princes were missing. With dread, she went along with the king and many people and entered the village to look for the princes. Though they found the two elder princes, they could not find the youngest anywhere. In grief, the king exclaimed,

> At the beginning, when my son was born, my joy was not extremely great;
> Later, now that I have lost him, my grief is extremely great.
> There will be no regret even if I lose this body of mine for the sake of his life.

"Gradually, the king and queen came to know what and how things had happened; they rushed to the spot where the prince had sacrificed his body, threw their bodies to the ground like trees blown down by winds, and bewailed him from the depths of their hearts.

"Thus, the remains of the Bodhisattva were placed in a tower embellished with the seven kinds of precious stones and enshrined with due ceremony amid tears. Now this tower, having sunk to the ground through incalculable ages, has once again sprung out from it for the sake of people. O Ananda, the third prince in this story was, indeed, myself, and the father was Suddhodana and the mother Maya."

Having listened to this story, the people resolved each in himself to seek the path. Then, when the Buddha withdrew his superhuman power, the treasure tower sank into the ground of itself.

When the Buddha completed his teaching, an uncountable number of bodhisattvas all came to this Dharma assembly from the ten directions, paid homage to him with their palms together, and praised his supreme virtue with their voices in unison,

> With his sublime features and light bright as that of a golden mountain,
> The Buddha illumines all the worlds of the ten directions;
> By using every possible means,
> He saves people wherever they may be.
> Free from defilement and attachment,
> And burning the lamp of the Dharma incessantly,
> The Buddha extends his compassion to all people,
> Giving them the life of happiness in this world and the next.
> With his great virtue, with his deep insight,
> And with his skillful means of compassion,
> The Buddha is busily engaged in the task of saving people.
> We praise even a single drop of his merit as vast as the ocean.
> May this merit be transferred to others so that they may swiftly realize enlightenment.

4. The Mind of Enlightenment, Great Compassion, and Skillful Means

(1) One day the World-Honored One manifested himself as Mahavairocana Buddha, embellished with immeasurable ornaments and sitting among many bodhisattvas headed by Samantabhadra and many Vajrapanis led by Guhyakadhipati.

Guhyakadhipati asked the Buddha, "O World-Honored One, the buddhas have realized omniscience and are now propagating this insight for all sentient beings according to their individual capacities. They manifest themselves in varied human forms, using varied languages of respective worlds. And yet, the path that all the buddhas teach is the same and is of a single universal taste. It is totally free from all differentiation like empty space and is the ground of all things like the great earth. And like fire it burns away the firewood of ignorance; and like the wind it eliminates the taints of passion. But what is this omniscience grounded on? What root does this omniscience have? And what ultimate goal does this omniscience have?"

(2) Mahavairocana Buddha said to Guhyakadhipati, "Well said, Guhyakadhipati. Now I shall answer these questions for you. O Guhyakadhipati, this omniscience has its ground in the mind that seeks enlightenment, has its root in the Great Compassion, and has its ultimate goal in skillful means. Enlightenment, like empty space, has no determined form. It cannot be recognized by the senses or explained. O Guhyakadhipati, there is no definite form as such in every and all things; everything is like empty space."

Guhyakadhipati asked, "O World-Honored One, then who is he who seeks omniscience and realizes supreme enlightenment?" The Buddha said, "O Guhyakadhipati, one's own mind is the seeker, and that itself is enlightenment. Again, it is omniscience. Why? It is because the essence of the mind is pure and totally free from defilement. Now the mind is neither within nor without nor in between; it transcends totally every and all form and color; hence it cannot be recognized by the six senses. Why? It is because the mind is free from conceptual discrimination and is identical with empty space. The nature of enlightenment is also identical with empty space because the latter is identical with the mind. Accordingly, the mind, empty space, and enlightenment, though being three, are one. These three have the Great Compassion as their root and are perfectly endowed with skillful means. O Guhyakadhipati, the reason that I teach is to let people know that their own minds are themselves the pure minds of enlightenment. If anyone wishes to attain this enlightenment, he should understand it as I have said. Then how does one know his own mind? This mind cannot be sought in any objective sphere, nor can it be sought in one's body or mind, or even in one's self or in things regarded as one's own, and so on. Guhyakadhipati, he who sees things in this way, this bodhisattva, can attain the first path for understanding the Dharma. If he thus practices the path, he will be able to eliminate all hindrances of the mind before long, and thereby he will understand innumerable words just as the buddhas do. Thus, he will be able to know the minds and actions of people, and under the Buddha's protection he will not be stained while he stays in the state of delusion. He will never become weary of serving others; and, staying with right views, he will be able to acquire innumerable virtues."

(3) Guhyakadhipati asked, "O World-Honored One, how is enlightenment born from this mind? And in what way is it known that the mind of enlightenment has arisen? Again, by what steps will the mind proceed toward the path?" The Buddha replied, "O Guhyakadhipati, the ordinary man who has been sunk in the state of delusion from the immemorial past is entrapped by passion attached to his self and to the things regarded as his. This is because he does not yet see what his own essential nature is. As a result, he holds wrong views on human existence and regards himself as being transcendent, beyond space and time, or he believes in a god and his power of creation, or else he maintains the objective reality of the external world, or he claims that there is a soul internally and that it is really the agent of knowing, seeing, and existing.

"O Guhyakadhipati, the foolish ordinary man is like a sheep indulging in greed. Now initially he observes a single day of abstinence and repeats this simple virtue frequently with joy. This step is comparable to the initial growth of a good seed. Next, on the six monthly days of abstinence, he practices charity for his relatives. This is the second step, comparable to the coming out of a sprout. When he extends this practice of charity toward others beyond his own kin, this is the third step, comparable to the seed swollen as it roots down. Now he practices charity for mendicants, and this is the fourth step, comparable to the growth of leaves; further, he practices charity for musicians and singers as well as for elderly people, and this is the fifth step, comparable to the blooming of flowers. Also, if he practices his charity with the sense of affection, this is the sixth step, comparable to the bearing of fruits. Next, then, rebirth in the heavenly world is the seventh step, comparable to the seed grain to be used for the next year's planting. Now he is reborn in this world, and though his mind is deluded, he earnestly worships the gods under the influence of his good friends. This so-called infantile naive mind that has no fear about this world is the eighth step. Finally, there is the superior practice in accordance with the principles of impermanence, suffering, and emptiness, which gives the insight through which he seeks for his emancipation. This practice is intended to make him understand the meaning of the emptiness of all things, because otherwise he cannot know the meaning of nirvana. Thus by understanding emptiness he has to free himself from both erroneous extreme views, eternalist and nihilist."

(4) Guhyakadhipati asked, "O World-Honored One, will you explain the mind for us?" The World-Honored One answered, "The modes of the mind are many, namely, the mind of greed, of non-greed, of anger, of affection, of ignorance, of insight, of confidence, of doubt, of darkness, of brightness, of dispute, of reflection, of a god, of a Mara, of a Naga, of a man, of a woman, of a merchant, of a farmer, of a river, of a pond, of a well, of protection, of stinginess, of a dog, of a badger, of a mouse, of singing, of dancing, of drumming, of a lion, of an owl, of a crow, of wind, of water, of fire, of delusion, of trapping, of fetters, of clouds, of rice fields,

of salt, of a razor, also the mind equivalent to Mount Sumeru, to the ocean, to a hole in the ground, also the mind receiving rebirth and so on.

"O Guhyakadhipati, the mind of greed means the mind that indulges in passion, while that of non-greed is the mind that does not indulge in passion. The mind of anger is the mind that follows the way of anger, while that of compassion is the mind that follows the way of compassion. In a similar manner, the mind of ignorance has no idea of practicing the path, whereas that of insight proceeds in practicing the superior Dharma. The mind of confidence is to practice the noble teaching exactly as it is taught, whereas that of doubt is to have thoughts of indetermination. The mind of darkness is to hesitate upon things on which there is no need for hesitation, whereas that of brightness is to practice the path with no hesitation. The mind of dispute is to argue with others as to right and wrong, while that of reflection is to judge oneself as to right and wrong. The mind of a god is to realize whatever it wishes, while that of a Mara is to be delighted in delusion. The mind of a Naga is to think of a multitude of treasures; the mind of a man is to think of benefitting others; the mind of a woman is to be faithful to one's feelings; the mind of a merchant is to gather at the beginning and to divide later; the mind of a farmer is to listen widely in the beginning and later to follow the Dharma one aspires for. The mind of a river is to follow the Dharmas that are inclined toward two extremes; that of a pond is to follow unquenchable thirst; that of a well is to think deeply; the mind of protection is to believe that one's own mind is true and that all others are false; the mind of stinginess is to think of oneself only and not to practice charity; that of a dog is to be delighted with a little portion given; that of a badger is to proceed without haste; that of a mouse is to try to cut bonds; those of singing, dancing, and drumming are to manifest varied superhuman powers by advancing the practice of the Dharma and beating the drum of the Dharma. The mind of a lion is to be fearless; the mind of an owl is to think of darkness; that of a crow is to be frightened by all things; that of wind is to be ever-changing; that of water is to wash away every evil thing; that of fire is to aspire for something with passion. The mind of delusion is to create discrepancy between one's intention and reality. The mind of trapping is to entrap oneself everywhere; that of fetters is to have both feet fettered. The mind of clouds is to have always the thought of inducing rain; that of a rice field is to be always in service of oneself; that of salt is to increase one's thought all the more; that of a razor is to shave everything off. The mind equal to Mount Sumeru is to be always arrogant; that equal to the ocean is to be satisfied with whatever one has done; that equal to a hole in the ground is to decide one thing earlier and change it later; the mind that receives rebirth is to be born in various states because of various karmas.

(5) "O Guhyakadhipati, next, by discarding the three kinds of attachment, one attains the transcendental mind. This mind understands that there is no abiding entity in either body or mind; it is engaged in the practice of the path by renouncing the feelings of suffering and enjoyment; and it escapes from the twelve-linked chain of dependent origination that arises from karma, thirst, and ignorance. O Guhyakadhipati, this quiescence of the mind cannot be realized

through false doctrines. O Guhyakadhipati, if there is the mind that aspires to renounce this world, there arises insight. This means that if, by discarding the attachment to body and mind, one sees that these are like water bubbles, plantain leaves, illusions, or mirages, then one can be emancipated. This emancipation means being free from all the attachment to self and others and thereby to experience the state of absolute quiescence. This mind is called the transcendental mind completely freed from all the passions. In order to realize this release from the snare of thirst, the continuity of consciousness, karma, one must practice for a long period of time that exceeds a kalpa.

"Also, O Guhyakadhipati, next there is the practice of the Mahayana, according to which all things are known to have no reality that exists forever; hence they are like illusions, mirages, shadows, and echoes. When thus one is rid of the mind of self, this mind becomes the agent of freedom and will realize the truth that one's own mind is essentially neither born nor perishing and hence has no origination. The reason for this is that there is no mind in the past, neither is there one in the future, where nothing has yet occurred. Neither can it be grasped in the immediate moment of the present, because it is instantaneously passing away. To know the nature of the mind itself requires the practice of a long period of time that exceeds two kalpas. Next, O Guhyakadhipati, he who practices the path of bodhisattva in accordance with the esoteric doctrine will be endowed with incalculable merit, insight, and skillful means and will become the refuge for gods and human beings. To explain this differently, all the Buddha-Dharma is like empty space, which is totally free from sense faculties and objects, is successively born on account of its empty nature, and begets the mind that is totally free from any determination, namely the mind without a self-nature. O Guhyakadhipati, such an initially resolved mind is called the cause for becoming a buddha. Moreover, though it is free from karma, passion, and attachment, it becomes the basis of karma and passion.

(6) "O Guhyakadhipati, one must observe the three minds, namely, the mind of enlightenment, the mind of great compassion, and the mind of skillful means, in the stages of the aspirations. These principles enable a bodhisattva to proceed from the initial stage up to the tenth stage; and by means of the insight that leads to the supreme enlightenment, one is endowed with the Four Means of Conversion. Indeed, this state is incomparable and inconceivable. Whatever I teach can be acquired in this state. Therefore, the wise must be mindful of omniscience and the stage of aspiration. This state is to be realized after another period of a kalpa and is attained through the last skillful means, namely, the resulting state of buddhahood."

Guhyakadhipati said to the Buddha, "O World-Honored One, how many states of self-confidence does a bodhisattva attain?" The Buddha replied, "O Guhyakadhipati, if an ordinary man practices good conduct and eliminates evil actions, he will attain the self-confidence in doing good. If one knows himself as he really is, he attains self-confidence. Again, if one sees his body by renouncing the idea of his own body, he attains the conviction of non-self; if he abides within the interdependence of phenomena, while forgetting his body and mind, then he attains the conviction of the Dharma. Moreover, forgetting this law, if he abides in no dependence, he attains the conviction of non-substantiality. Finally, if one thinks of the emptiness of phenomena and realizes that they have no essence, he attains the conviction of the principle that the essences of phenomena are totally identical.

(7) "O Guhyakadhipati, those who practice the norms of a bodhisattva through mantra will reach enlightenment by observing the ten clue conditions. They are the phenomena of apparition, the simmering of heated air, a dream, the figure reflected in a mirror, a mirage, an echo, the moon reflected in water, bubbles, a sky-flower, and a fiery circle.

"Illusory objects are created in visions by magic or drugs, and their forms appear and move, but they are actually neither coming nor going. It is the same with the esoteric view that through visual illusion it is possible to create everything. Next, the nature of images created by a shimmering of heat is empty, because they arise only from people's delusive thoughts. It is the same with the esoteric view that they are temporary and mere names. In a dream one perceives the sun's light, various forms, or suffering and pleasure, but when one is awakened, one finds nothing remaining. It is the same with the esoteric view of events. Just as someone's face can be shown in a mirror, it is possible also to realize the goal of the doctrine by means of a metaphor of such reflected images. In like manner, it is possible to use the metaphor of the mirage of the city of the Gandharvas to understand the true nature of whatever object of appearance. Again, by means of the analogy that echoes are created by man's voice, it is possible to understand the doctrine as to their true origin. Also, as to the moon reflected in clear water, it is possible to indicate the abode of enlightenment, the true source of illumination. Further, just as the rain falling from the sky creates bubbles on the surface of water, it is possible to know the goal realized by the doctrine in multifarious manifestations. Although nothing can be created in empty space, people see flowers in the sky due to the delusions of their minds. Likewise people create all kinds of wrong views. Again, as a fiery circle can be created in the air by spinning a torch, it is possible to understand the scriptural statements of the Mahayana teaching in regard to illusory views. If anyone understands the esoteric doctrine in these terms, he may be able to acquire the treasure of the Dharma, produce in himself the great insight capable of all skillful means, and widely know all the facets of the mind."

Chapter 3

THE TATHAGATA-GARBHA

1. Farewell

(1) The next morning the World-Honored One accompanied by Ananda entered the city of Vesali for alms begging and then proceeded to the village of Bhanda with a company of his disciples. Upon leaving Vesali, the World-Honored One looked back toward the city with a faint smile. "This is the last occasion of my seeing this city," he said. "I shall not be returning here again." It was raining at that time though there were no clouds in the sky.

Having heard these words, the disciples were saddened once again, each falling to the ground and mourning. When the news spread among the Licchavi clansmen, they were dismayed and striking their chests exclaimed, "It is sad indeed. Upon whose teaching can we rely from now on? Let us go to see the World-Honored One and ask him to remain in this world longer." They rushed out of the city on carriages. Finding the World-Honored One's company in the distance, and seeing Ananda and other disciples equally distressed, and becoming all the more sorrowful, they saluted the World-Honored One at his feet and said, "O World-Honored One, if the World-Honored One passes away now, all of us will lose the eye of wisdom and will surely go astray once again in the darkness of ignorance. When that happens, how will we be able to recognize the right path that the World-Honored One has taught us? We beseech you to remain in this world even for the duration of a single kalpa." In this way the Licchavis thrice implored him.

(2) In reply, the World-Honored One said to them, "O Licchavis, whatever is created is impermanent without exception. Even if I remain here for another kalpa, I am yet bound to die eventually. O Licchavis, no matter how lofty Mount Sumeru may be, it will eventually crumble down; and no matter how deep the great ocean may be, there will be a time when it dries up. The sun and the moon, though brightly shining, will set in the west before long. Though the ground appears to be firm in supporting everything today, it is bound to perish when the doomsday fire breaks out at the end of the present kalpa. Meeting is necessarily followed by eventual parting; no one can escape the fate of separation. All the buddhas of the past have physically passed away as well. How then can I alone survive death against the law that whoever is born dies? O Licchavis, be

not so grieved or distressed about my death. For now I shall give you my final instruction." Subduing their sorrow, the Licchavis said, "May the World-Honored One teach us, and we shall surely be in accord with your teaching in conducting ourselves."

The World-Honored one then said to them, "O Licchavis, be happy and be in harmony, create no discord among yourselves, advise each other, think of good things, uphold moral precepts, maintain propriety, respect parents and elders, and keep harmony among your relatives and defer to each other. Conduct rites at the ancestral shrines and the stupas of the sages. Have firm faith in the Dharma and deep reverence toward the Buddha's disciples, and praise those who hold the noble faith and protect them. Govern the country according to the Dharma, and refrain from the injustice of oppressing countrymen. Learn the principles of causality, believe in the path the Buddha taught, and know that even after physical death the Buddha continues to live in the Dharma and thus never perishes. He who possesses these qualities is indeed a man of conscience, whom the Buddha will always protect. Such a man surely will realize the path before long. Thus your country will prosper and the people live in abundance. You should follow these teachings as long as you live, even unto death." The Licchavis responded, "O World-Honored One, as long as we live we shall follow these instructions."

(3) Immediately after this discourse, the World-Honored One turned to his disciples and said, "O disciples, you, too, should live in joy and keep harmony among yourselves, like milk and water, creating no discord; assemble frequently to share with others the study of the path; and be steadfast in observing the moral precepts and allow no thought of breaking them to arise. Respect your teachers and elders and choose associates who are diligent in the practice of the path in solitude. Again, persuade others to attend the Dharma gatherings, and follow the Dharma of the buddhas. O disciples, do not engage in any work of livelihood like ordinary householders. Do not indulge in idle talk, nor in lethargy, nor in worthless disputes. Stay away from wrong characters, but associate with good friends, thereby guarding yourselves against evil thoughts. If you note progress in the practice of the Dharma, exert yourselves for further advance toward a higher level of achievement."

(4) Then the wives of the Licchavi clansmen, who also heard of the World-Honored One's approaching demise, rushed to the place where the World-Honored One was; and having made various offerings, they said to him in tears, "O World-Honored One, may we earnestly ask that the World-Honored One remain in this world and guide us? If the World-Honored One passes away, blind as we are without the eye of wisdom, we shall never be able to find the true path. We were born as women, and hindered by various daily chores, we have not been able to see the World-Honored One as frequently as we wished. If the World-Honored One passes away, whatever we think to be good will diminish in its influence every day."

The World-Honored One replied, "O Licchavi women, be not in grief to no purpose, but as long as you live, exert yourselves to uphold the precepts, keep your minds gentle, refrain from flattery and jealousy, and you will be able to see me at all times."

Overcome with sorrow, the Licchavi women withdrew to the side and seated themselves. Then the World-Honored One addressed everyone gathered there and said, "From now on keep the precepts and refrain from breaking them. For whoever breaks the precepts will be disliked by the gods, and others also will find no delight in seeing him. Such a person will be fear-stricken at the time of death and will suffer in unhappy destinies for a long time. On the other hand, whoever upholds the precepts will be respected not only by the gods but also by the people, who will be delighted to see him. He will be in firm possession of right thought at the time of death and born into the world of purity." Upon listening to this teaching, sixty disciples realized the path and innumerable people and gods overcame their defilements.

(5) The World-Honored One reached the village of Bhanda, and after entering the grove north of the village he rested under a tree. Then the World-Honored One told his disciples, "O disciples, you must be steadfast with the precepts, practice meditation, and seek wisdom; thereby realize your emancipation. He who keeps the precepts will not follow evils; he who practices meditation will have an undisturbed mind; he who seeks wisdom will be freed from desires and will be able to act at will. In this way his virtues will become loftier and his honor more heightened, and he will eventually enter the path of purity. I, too, since I did not learn this teaching for a long time, could not realize enlightenment earlier. May you, therefore, be diligent in practicing these three teachings."

The World-Honored One proceeded to a village called Ambagama, and upon entering the village he seated himself in a grove. Once again he said to his disciples, "O disciples, whoever practices precepts, meditation, and wisdom will be able to cross the ocean of delusion. Once he has accomplished the practice of the precepts, he is able to accomplish the practice of meditation. Once he has accomplished the practice of meditation, he is able to attain wisdom. A cloth when clean can be beautifully dyed; if one has these three disciplines, he will have no difficulty in realizing the path. Exert yourselves, therefore, in the practice of these disciplines. Just as one can see every color of the sand at the bottom of a mountain brook when its water is clear, so when one has realized the path he will be able to see all things as they are by virtue of the purity of his mind. Therefore whoever seeks the path must purify his mind. Once he has accomplished this, he will be able to realize the path spontaneously."

The World-Honored One moved from Ambagama to a village called Jambugama and extended his visits to the neighboring villages. The World-Honored One taught during this sojourn about passion. "There are three passions of the mind. They are greed, anger, and ignorance. The precepts destroy the passion of greed. Meditation removes the passion of anger. Wisdom annihilates the passion of ignorance. Indeed, these disciplines constitute the way to rescue people; with them the disciples, too, can sever the roots of suffering."

(6) The World-Honored One summoned Ananda to take up the robes and bowls and said to him, "Let us go to the city called Bhoganagara." Accompanying the World-Honored One, Ananda and other disciples entered Bhoganagara and settled in the forest of simsapa trees located at the north of the city wall.

It was approaching twilight. Ananda sat under a tree, wondering why the earth was trembling. After a while he went to the World-Honored One and asked him. "Why does the earth tremble?" "O Ananda," replied the World-Honored One, "The earth is supported by a layer of water, while the water is in turn supported by a layer of wind. Thus when the wind moves, it causes the movement of the water, and this in turn causes the earth to tremble. This is one of the reasons for the earth's trembling. Next, when someone has accomplished the path, he causes the earth to tremble to express his experience of joy. This is the second reason. Again, the Buddha may cause the earth to tremble through his great supernatural power, which is the third reason. O Ananda, the great power of the Buddha is not confined to causing the earth to tremble; it can cause also the heavens to tremble. All this power originates in the righteous mind. O Ananda, from the immemorial past, I continuously accumulated merits and virtues, through which I have acquired this wondrous supernatural power. I see everything, I know everything, and there is none whom I cannot edify. In remote antiquity, motivated by compassion, I travelled widely to many countries, where, following their respective customs and speaking their languages, I taught ascetics, scholars, kings, and the people time after time. I made them feel at ease and at peace; I comforted them and made them walk steadfastly toward their goals; then I left their countries. Yet none of them knew who I really was. In this way also I visited the heavens and taught the gods, teaching the holy Dharma to those who desired it, encouraging those who had attained purity to teach others diligently, and guiding everyone through various skillful means; then I left there. Yet none of them knew who I really was. O Ananda, my power is wide and great, and there is nothing it cannot do. O Ananda, there is no place I have not seen. However, I regard nirvana as the most delightful place of all.

(7) "Now you must also realize this path and endeavor to teach others. To see a Buddha's appearance in this world is extremely rare, like the blooming of the udumbara tree. It is equally difficult to hear a Buddha's discourses on the Dharma. Hence once you have learned them, you must preserve them and reveal them and never conceal or hide them.

"O disciples, after my passing away, if someone claims that he directly heard such and such teachings from the Buddha or from the elder disciples, you must judge him by referring to the Sutras and the Vinaya as to whether his teaching is true or false, and decide whether it is consistent or inconsistent. If what he teaches does not come from the Sutras, or the Vinaya, it is Mara's doctrine. You must reprimand him by the authority of the words of the Buddha; let him learn the Sutras and the Vinaya. If he does not follow the Sutras or the Vinaya, you must reject him, because unless the weeds are eliminated good seedlings will be thwarted in their growth. If there is someone who clearly understands

the teaching, whether he is an elder or a novice, you should visit him and ask
for instruction. Lay devotees, too, should visit him, offering robes, food, mats,
and medicine. Since you all share the same path, there is no reason why you
cannot be in harmony with each other. If any of you fall into evil destinies, it
will be because you are not harmonious with each other. You must refrain from
claiming that you know the path more than others, or that others do not know
the path. For irrespective of the amount of knowledge, if you do not actually
practice it yourselves, it is useless. If what is said in words is in accordance with
the teachings, you should practice it; if not, discard it. O disciples, you must
depend on the Dharma. Indeed, the Dharma is the noblest and highest authority to rely on. If you forget the Dharma, your mind will be easily disturbed. You
must not forget that in taking up a sword, unless you rely on the way of the
sword, you can injure your own hand." While sojourning at Bhoganagara,
the World-Honored One also taught the Four Noble Truths, and many disciples
realized enlightenment.

(8) The World-Honored One now moved from Bhoganagara to the village of
Kumba. There was in that village a brahmin called Bavan, who, having heard
of the World-Honored One's arrival, rushed to the place where he stayed together
with many of the other brahmins and wealthy people. He asked, "O World-
Honored One, why have you extended your visit to this village?" The World-
Honored One answered, "I shall be passing away after three months. Hence
after leaving Vesali I have made extended visits to neighboring towns and
villages, and now I arrive at this village." Having heard this, surprised
and grieved, they threw themselves onto the ground and lamented. The World-
Honored One then said to them, "There is no need of such distress. For this is
exactly the nature of whatever has come into being. Discard your grief and
listen quietly to what I shall say to you as my last instructions. You must respect
your fathers and mothers, honor them, guide your wives and children with good
teaching, be sympathetic to servants and know their wishes, associate with good
characters, and stay away from bad ones. In this way, you will be respected in
this world, and in the lives after death you will always be born in the happy
destinies. O Bavan, it is pleasant to be at home and to depend upon no one, and
not to know any disgrace. It is also a pleasure not to spend money on oneself,
nor on anyone else, and thereby to accumulate wealth. Again, it is also a pleasure to become greatly prosperous, to spend on oneself as well as on parents and
relatives, and to make offerings to sages and scholars. Moreover, it is also a
pleasure to refrain from evil deeds in body, speech, and thought and to be
delighted in listening and understanding many teachings with good insight.
Out of these four, however, the former two are a lower kind of pleasure, whereas
the third is mediocre and the last a superior kind of pleasure. Therefore, from
now on, young or old, you should lead each other to practice the third and the
highest kinds of good."

(9) Bavan then replied to the World-Honored One, "O World-Honored One,
we shall follow your instructions to guide each other." Then all together they
came forward to express their sincere intentions; and they took refuge in him

and took the five precepts. Then Bavan requested, "May the World-Honored One, together with his disciples, accept my humble offerings in the morning." And his wish was granted.

At the meal the following morning, one of the disciples displayed bad manners, and the people there showed displeasure in observing it. Having noticed this, the World-Honored One said to them, "The Buddha-Dharma is deep and wide, like the ocean. Just as various kinds of creatures live in the ocean, in the ocean of the Buddha-Dharma some disciples have accomplished the path, while some have not. Let this not be a hindrance in your effort to follow the Dharma. Whether some disciple knows manners or not, the merit of offering to the Buddha and the Sangha will be returned to the donor as his merit and happiness, just as all different rivers equally return to the same ocean."

After this initial instruction, the World-Honored One expounded the Dharma in detail, and the people all together joined in the path. The World-Honored One then departed for the town of Pava, while the people, in tears, stayed for a long time in seeing him off.

(10) Having arrived at the town of Pava, the World-Honored One stayed in the grove outside the city wall. It was the fourteenth day of the second month. The grove belonged to Cunda, who was a son of the smith of the town and had heard the Buddha's teaching and became a follower. It was indeed a place of tranquillity.

The townsmen all came out to greet the World-Honored One, and the World-Honored One said to them, "The wise one curtails his expenditure at home, but spares one portion for his parents, his wife, and his children, a second portion for guests and servants, a third portion for relatives and friends, and a fourth portion for the ruler and the mendicants, whereby he realizes happiness. In this way, one may enjoy long life, secure his family's well-being, and acquire power, health, wealth, honor, and happiness after death." All were delighted with this instruction and went home.

Now Cunda was also much delighted to know that the World-Honored One had settled in his grove with a company of his disciples. After attiring himself properly, he hurried to the place where the World-Honored One was staying. Greeting him at his feet, he asked, "For what reason has the World-Honored One come here? Is there any special purpose for your being here?" "O Cunda," replied the World-Honored One, "I shall be passing away before long, and I wanted to see you for the last time."

Cunda became astonished and anguished and falling to the ground exclaimed, "O World-Honored One, is it that you no longer have compassion for us? Why would you think of passing away? I pray that you may remain in this world for the duration of a kalpa. For when the Eye of the World is gone, how can we be freed from the state of delusion?" "O Cunda," said the World-Honored One, "do not grieve. Everything is subject to change. Once people meet, they cannot escape from eventual separation." Cunda replied, "O World-Honored One, I, too, know that. Nevertheless, now that the supreme and noblest one is about to pass away, how can I help not being anguished about it? O World-Honored One, it is very difficult to be born as a human being in this world, and it is even more difficult to have an opportunity to hear a buddha's teaching; it is as difficult as throwing a needle at a poppy seed, or as a blind turtle encountering a drifting log in the great ocean. I beseech you, O World-Honored One, with your compassion for us, not to pass away!" Then the World-Honored One said, "O Cunda, you must not say so. The world is impermanent, and in it there is always sorrow. The body is where all kinds of sufferings come together. It is by transcending the body that I have realized the truth and overcome various sufferings. For me there is neither old age nor sickness nor death, nor is there an end to life. O Cunda, it is because of my compassion for you and all people that I am about to pass away. For the Dharma of all the buddhas is always like this. O Cunda, just as geese flock on Lake Anavatapta when spring comes, so do all the buddhas similarly enter nirvana."

Having listened to the World-Honored One's speech, Cunda was delighted, and standing up from his seat, he requested the World-Honored One to accept his offering the following day. When this was granted, he left for home at once and prepared the morrow's meal throughout the night with care.

2. The Buddha Nature

(1) After Cunda left, the World-Honored One said to his disciples, "O disciples, if you have doubts, you should ask me about them while I am still here. In accordance with your wishes, I shall dispel your doubts, after which I shall die. O disciples, the appearance of a buddha in this world is indeed very rare; it is also rare to be born a human being. It is even more difficult to follow the Buddha, to cherish the faith, to bear what is difficult to bear, to keep the precepts steadfastly without breaking them, and to attain the state of the sage. It is comparable to looking for one golden grain of sand in a desert or for an udumbara flower. O disciples, now that you have met me in this life, you must not pass the time in vain. For I have attained this supreme power through various practices. For an immeasurably long time, I have continued to practice for your sake, even giving up my limbs and the very marrow of my bones. You must not be negligent. O disciples, at the castle of the Dharma there are stored the treasures of virtues; they are protected by the walls and moats of the precepts, meditation, and wisdom. Since you have now entered this castle of the treasures, you must not be misled into picking up false teachings like merchants who, having entered a castle of treasures, pick up the tiles and gravel instead of the genuine precious stones.

"You should not be easily satisfied with an inferior teaching. You have renounced your lives and left your homes, but you have not yet resolved to follow the Mahayana. Though wearing the robes, your minds are not yet fully dyed in the pure color of the Dharma. Though engaged in alms begging here and there, you are not yet practicing the alms begging of the Mahayana. Though you have shaved your heads and beards, you have not yet eliminated various defilements for the sake of the true Dharma. I tell you that the Dharma taught by the Buddha is true and not false. You should exert yourselves to control your minds and zealously destroy the various defilements. If the sun of wisdom sinks in the west, you will be shrouded in the darkness of ignorance.

"O disciples, just as various herbs benefit people, my Dharma will give the nectar that will rescue the people from the sickness of defilements. I, too, shall now let all of my disciples, monastic and lay, who are my children, rest in peace in the secret treasury. I, too, shall rest in this treasury where I shall enter nirvana. What is this secret treasury then? It is indeed the Dharmakaya, wisdom, and emancipation of the Buddha. O disciples, the Dharmakaya of the Buddha is eternal; nirvana is happiness; the Buddha is the self. The true Dharma of the Buddha is pure, while what is created is impure. Self refers to the Buddha, eternity to the Dharma, happiness to nirvana, and purity to the true Dharma.

"People regard what is suffering as happiness, and what is real happiness as suffering; they regard what is impermanent as permanent, and what is really permanent as impermanent; they also regard what is non-self as having self, and what is real self as not being it; and again they regard what is impure as pure, and what is pure as impure. All these are distorted views, from which all of you must free yourselves."

(2) Now the disciples said to the World-Honored One, "O World-Honored One, as you have been free from these four kinds of distorted views for a long time, why can you not extend your life in this world for another kalpa to give us further guidance? If the Buddha is gone forever, how can we practice the disciplines with our defiled bodies?" The World-Honored One replied, "O disciples, you should not speak so. The Dharma taught by me will continue forever. Just as the Buddha makes you feel at peace, the Dharma, which remains after his passing away, will make you feel at ease, too. Wherever you are, therefore, you must exert yourselves and be mindful of the teaching of permanence, happiness, self, and purity as the nature of the Dharma."

The disciples then asked, "O World-Honored One, previously you taught us that there is no self in all things, and that we must discard the idea of self by learning the truth of non-self. Once we managed to be free from it, we should be able to enter nirvana. Now, how are we to understand the meaning of the teaching you have just taught us?"

(3) The World-Honored One said to the disciples, "You have asked the essential matter of the doctrine. I shall explain it by way of a story. Once upon a time, there was a king with little intelligence. He had an official doctor who was also stubborn and unwise. This doctor knew only one medicine, made of cow's milk, but even his knowledge about this was not certain, because when anyone became ill, he indiscriminately applied it without regard to the nature of the illness. The king himself was not suspicious about it. Now a travelling doctor, who possessed a thorough knowledge of illnesses and medicines, happened to come to this country. The official doctor, looking down upon the travelling doctor, did not try to learn from him. Thus, the travelling doctor asked the official doctor, 'Will you allow me to serve you?' The latter said, 'If you promise to serve me for forty-eight years, I shall surely teach you medicine.' The travelling doctor agreed. One day, the official doctor, accompanied by the travelling doctor,

met the king. The travelling doctor explained various medicines to the king, who now began to realize that his official doctor was a fool. He dismissed the old doctor and deeply respected the new one. Thinking that it was time, the new doctor explained to the king, 'O my king, please issue a decree to prohibit the use of milk as medicine, because often it is more harmful to people than helpful.' Thus, the king prohibited the use of milk and punished anyone who violated his order. In the meantime, the new official doctor prepared varieties of medicines and healed many people who suffered from various sickness. After some time, however, the king became ill and summoned the doctor, saying, 'I am seriously ill and feel pain as if I were dying. How can this be cured?' The doctor replied then that there was no other way than by taking milk as medicine. Upon hearing this, the king became enraged and said, 'Are you insane, or are you deceiving me? Previously you said that milk as medicine was poisonous, and now you say it is the only medicine to cure my illness. This is ridiculous!' The doctor said, 'O my king, a worm may gnaw on a leaf in the form of a letter, but it does not know whether it is a word or not, nor do we say that it knows letters. O my king, the former doctor gave milk as medicine to all cases without discriminating between different kinds of illness and did not even know at all whether it was actually working or not.' 'What do you mean,' asked the king, 'by saying that he did not know whether the medicine was working or not?' The doctor answered, 'O my king, milk as medicine can become a poison as well as a nectar. If a cow is fed properly, given clean water, but not brewers' grains, and if the pasture is neither in a high ground nor in a low wet area, and also if the cows are kept away from bulls and if their calves are gentle, then the milk produced from them will be effective for a variety of illnesses. This is what I call nectar; all other products are mostly harmful.' Now, the king exclaimed, 'Alas, I finally came to know today which kind of milk medicine is good and which is not good.' After taking the prescribed milk medicine, the king recovered from his illness and issued a decree throughout the country permitting the use of that medicine. His countrymen were all enraged and approached the king, saying, 'O king, have you been fooled by a Mara?' The king explained to them in detail what he had learned, and together with them he ever more deeply respected the doctor.

(4) "O disciples, it is the same with the Buddha. Appearing in this world as a great medicine king, he taught the doctrine that there was no self for the sake of rectifying false doctrines and freeing people from them. For the idea of a self in the false doctrines has no real meaning, just like the letter that a worm makes on a leaf by chance. I know the right times to teach things; I previously taught that there was no self, and now, because there is a good reason, I have introduced the opposite view that there is a self. This is comparable to the prescription given by the doctor who knows when milk is a good medicine and when it is not. Some fools claim that the self resembles the thumb; others say that it is like a poppy seed or a dust particle. The Buddha, however, does not talk of a self as an entity. Therefore he states that there is no self as such. But this does not necessarily mean the total nonexistence of anything that might be called a self.

"Then what is it that can be called self? I call a self anything true, eternal, unconditioned, and hence unchanging. Just like that good doctor who knew medicine well, the Buddha teaches that there is a self in all things. You must understand this doctrine very thoroughly."

(5) There was a young man called Kasyapa in the gathering. He was a member of a brahmin family in the village of Uttara. Holding his palms together reverently, he said to the World-Honored One. "O World-Honored One, in what way can I attain a firm faith like a diamond that never breaks, and also in what way can I acquire a steadfast power?" The World-Honored One answered, "You can acquire them like this: if a prince is imprisoned for a crime, his father, the king, out of love, may visit him at the prison by directing his carriage there. It is the same with the sramana; because he extends to all people the love that he feels toward his own children, he will help them realize nirvana and free them from all fears. Thus will you attain the life of eternity and realize the highest insight."

Kasyapa asked, "But how can one extend kind thoughts, as if toward one's children, even to those who break the precepts and speak against the Dharma?" "There is no difference," replied the World-Honored One, "between my feeling for my son Rahula and my feeling for all other people."

Then Kasyapa said, "Once on the night of the posadha gathering, there was a child whose conduct was not proper. Then Vajrapani receiving supernatural power from the Buddha, crushed the boy into dust with the diamond pestle. How could you say that the Buddha sees everyone just as he sees his son Rahula?" The World-Honored One replied, "You cannot bring up such an example, because this child and Vajrapani were equally illusory beings manifested by the skillful power of the Buddha. Both were not real beings. O Kasyapa, even if someone slanders the true Dharma, destroys the roots of merit, murders people, falls into wrong views, and deliberately breaks the precepts, I have equal compassion for him, and there is no difference between my feeling toward him and the feeling I have toward Rahula. In order to show that there is a definite moral retribution to all wrongdoers, I contrived an aggressive way of subduing evil. If one of my disciples should witness someone transgressing the precepts and does not censure him nor excommunicate him nor bring him in for punishment, that disciple will become an offender against the Buddha despite his being in accordance with the Dharma. If, however, the disciple censures the offender, excommunicates him, or brings punishment on him, he must be said to be my true disciple. O Kasyapa, this is comparable to the deed of a king who sends his son to serve a stern teacher in order to straighten his character. There is no fault on the part of the king, because it is done out of his love for his son. It is the same with the Buddha, because there is no difference between my viewing an offender of the Dharma and my viewing my own son's offence. I shall now hand down this true Dharma to kings, ministers, prime ministers, ascetics, and lay disciples. All of you must encourage the practitioners to augment their merits in precepts, meditation, and wisdom. If they become negligent, transgress the precepts, or slander the Dharma, you must censure them and rectify their actions."

(6) Kasyapa asked, "O World-Honored One, if the buddhas can have long lives, why is the World-Honored One's life span going to be so short, less than a hundred years?" "O Kasyapa," answered the World-Honored One, "why do you make such a thoughtless statement? The longevity of the Buddha is superior to all those of other beings, and the truth he realizes is superior to all others' realizations. O Kasyapa, there are eight large rivers in this country, and there are also innumerable small rivers, but each and every river goes into the same ocean. It is the same with the rivers of the lives of all people, because they all return to the great life of the Buddha. Therefore the life of the Buddha is immeasurable. Also, O Kasyapa, just as Lake Anavatapta is the source of four great rivers, the Buddha is also the source from which all lives are originated. Again, just as ghee is the best among all medicines, the Buddha is the best of all human lives. For it must be known that the Buddha is eternal. For the sake of saving mankind, however, he manifests himself in a human body with defilements and thereby demonstrates his entering into nirvana. O Kasyapa, exert yourself to learn this most important principle and let it be known widely for the sake of people. If you do so, you will follow where I go, and you will be able to reach where I reach. O Kasyapa, you must be aware that the Buddha, the Dharma, and the Sangha endure forever. Just as there is a shadow when there is a tree, so, because the Dharma is eternal, you can rely on it as your refuge. Had the Buddha's physical body been eternal, it would not have been the refuge for people's salvation."

(7) Kasyapa said, "O World-Honored One, from now on, I shall help my parents to understand this teaching and also help all the parents of seven generations to believe in this Dharma. This is marvellous! O World-Honored One, I shall study the teaching myself and shall teach it to other people."

The World-Honored One said, "O Kasyapa, the Dharmakaya of the buddhas abides forever, and it never perishes. It is the body of diamond, not the body sustained by food. It is not the body of a human being encumbered by fear but the Dharmakaya. Suffering illness is shown now solely to help people understand the truth of the Dharmakaya."

Kasyapa said, "O World-Honored One, how can we attain this Dharmakaya?" The World-Honored One replied, "O Kasyapa, I have attained this Dharmakaya because I exerted myself to sustain this true Dharma, and likewise, whether one is a mendicant or a householder, one has to exert himself to uphold this Dharma. If there is anyone who teaches the Dharma, guard him even by taking sword or stick. I have now entrusted this supreme secret treasury to you. O Kasyapa, when beings believe that the Buddha abides forever and is immutable, then the Buddha is within their bodies. O Kasyapa, it is the Dharma that the buddhas have as their teacher. Since the Dharma is eternal, the buddhas are eternal. O Kasyapa, just as ashes remain when wood burns out, when defilements are destroyed, there is manifested nirvana. Iron is cool, but it can also be heated, but not the Buddha. For since all his defilements were destroyed, he is forever cool and there will be no more flaring up of defilement. You must know that people are like iron, and that I shall burn the iron of the defilements of all people by the fire of wisdom. O Kasyapa, when a king enjoys a garden party at his palace grove, even if he is not found among the court ladies, it cannot be said that he is dead. It is the same with the Buddha, for even when he is not found or not visible in this world, he cannot be said to have perished. The Buddha has destroyed countless defilements and has entered the eternal and sublime nirvana, and he enjoys his garden party amid the blossoms of enlightenment.

(8) "O Kasyapa, I have been in nirvana for some time and have revealed various superhuman powers in this world. At Lumbini I have shown my birth from my mother Maya, at which people marvelled and were delighted, seeing me as an infant. However, from ancient times till now, I have throughout all lives transcended the confinement of human existence. Nevertheless, I have shown my birth in accord with the way of the world. The body of the Buddha is the Dharma, and hence it does not consist of flesh, blood, tendons, veins, or bones. Seven days after my birth, the people shaved my head and took me to the ancestral shrine of yaksas. Moreover, upon reaching youth, I was educated and then married. Yet from ancient times I have long since transcended these human ways. After renouncing family life and beginning to practice the path, people said that Prince Siddhartha had abandoned his family for the first time, and when I meditated under the Bodhi Tree and defeated the Maras, they said that I defeated the tempters for the first time. The truth is, however, that I had long before left the state of a worldly ruler and become the ruler of the Dharma, and long before did I defeat the Maras. All these have been done again recently only to let people become aware of their own intense defilements; so I followed the way of people. And until now I have shown from time to time my passing away, and people again thought that the Buddha really departed forever. However, the Buddha himself never perishes. You should know that this is the eternal Dharma. O Kasyapa, nirvana is the ultimate realm of the Buddha.

"O Kasyapa, sometimes I have appeared in this world assuming the form of a man of little faith or that of a Mara, or showing a female body, or assuming a godly figure, and sometimes I entered a house of courtesans, visited a place of gambling, or appeared as the king of a country, or as a scholar. Whenever epidemics spread, I appeared as a doctor dispensing medicines and then taught the Dharma; when wars broke out, I taught the Dharma in order to help the people to escape from the disasters. For those attached to eternalism, I taught that everything is impermanent; for those attached to this world on account of its being pleasant, I taught suffering; for those entrapped by the idea of a self, I taught that there is no self; for those bound by the idea that this world is pure, I taught that it is not pure; for those who are greedy about this world, I taught that the supreme Dharma alone is happiness; in order to help people to annihilate defilements, I taught the most subtle Dharma; in order to save many non-Buddhists, I taught the true Dharma. In this way, I appeared in this world and became the teacher of people, but I have no thought in myself that I am the teacher. Even when I live among the lower classes to teach the Dharma, it is entirely for the sake of helping them and is not caused by any evil karmic force. As I have been explaining, the Buddha's enlightenment thus abides in peaceful and limitless nirvana. Hence it is eternal and unchanging. This is called the great nirvana. If a sramana resides in nirvana, he will be ready to show his super-human power without any fear.

"O Kasyapa, you must not consider the Buddha passing away as perishing into nonexistence as when a lamp goes out. For the light burns as long as oil remains in the dish, but as soon as the oil is destroyed, the light also is extinguished. Though the flame burns out, the oil dish remains; and it is the same with the Buddha, for while defilements are all destroyed, there remains the unchanging Dharmakaya."

(9) Kasyapa asked, "Is the Dharmakaya also impermanent in the way the oil dish of a lamp is?" "You must not think so," said the World-Honored One. "The Buddha is the vehicle of the highest Dharma. Of all things, nirvana alone is eternal; and because the Buddha makes nirvana his body, he is eternal."

Kasyapa said, "The World-Honored One has said that the Buddha has a secret treasury, but that may not be so. Why? I surmise that it is because the Buddha enables everyone to see and to know everything as it is." The World-Honored One said, "Very good; it is precisely as you say. There is no secret treasury for the Buddha. The word of the Buddha is as pure and faultless as the autumnal moon in the clear sky. Because the foolish do not understand this, they call it a secret treasury. O Kasyapa, if a wealthy man has an only child and loves him very much, he certainly will show his child all the treasures he has. It is the same with the Buddha, for he regards all people in the way he regards a child of his own, and therefore he keeps no secret from anyone."

(10) Kasyapa asked, "O World-honored One, what then is nirvana?" The World-Honored One replied, "O Kasyapa, nirvana means emancipation." "May you explain the meaning of emancipation," Kasyapa requested. Thus, the World-Honored One gave a long discourse on the subject. "Very well, O Kasyapa, the true emancipation is called transcending because it means absolute removal from the bonds of love and desire. It is also called non-birth because emancipation is not born out of parents; it is also called non-illness because it is not harmed by any or all illnesses; it is also called non-fighting because it has no thought of greedy competition; it is also called peaceful rest because it accompanies no worry or fear; it is also called stainless because there is no dust or mist that obstructs the light of insight; it is also called debtless because it has no debts, like a wealthy man who does not owe anything to anyone; it is also called non-constraint because it is properly controlled like nectar; it is also called non-moving because it cannot be moved; it is also called uncommon, because it is as rare as the growth of a lotus in fire; it is also called immeasurable, because it is beyond measuring, like an ocean; it is also called unsurpassed, because like the vacuous sky there is nothing to reveal in it. Emancipation does not decay, because it is firm; it is filled fully within, not empty inside like a bamboo or a reed. It has a singular taste like milk and is universally equitable to all like parents to their children. It makes one know contentment, letting no one rush for anything as the starved rush for ambrosia. Unlike a spreading flood it is tranquil. It is a state where all people can abide together with ease, and unlike a narrow passage where two cannot go together. It embodies the transcendental love of

the Dharma, as it is compassionate toward people, but it is forever free from the greedy lust of a hungry ghost. When one relies on it, one no longer needs to look to anything else to rely on, just as when retainers rely upon their king, they do not need anybody else to rely on. Like an open field, through which it is safe to return home, it poses no danger. O Kasyapa, in these ways, emancipation saves everyone from every fear, removes various causes and conditions, controls self-conceit, rectifies negligence, and throws away delusion through the annihilation of ignorance. All this can be compared to water, which can irrigate all trees and grasses and moisten all living beings. O Kasyapa, the true emancipation is the Buddha; the Buddha is nirvana. Nirvana is the inexhaustible, the inexhaustible is the nature of the Buddha, the nature of the Buddha is unconditionally determined, and this absolute determinedness is the supreme right path."

(11) Kasyapa said, "O World-Honored One, I have now realized for the first time that the Buddha has reached the inexhaustible state, and that since the state is inexhaustible, the age of the Buddha is also inexhaustible." The World-Honored One said, "Well said, O Kasyapa! You now have attained the true Dharma. If one wants to destroy defilements, one must maintain the true Dharma in this way. O Kasyapa, wherever this teaching spreads, it will be as valuable as diamonds, and people therein also will become exalted like precious stones. If anyone learns this Dharma, he will not stumble on obstacles and will be able to realize whatever he wishes to accomplish."

Now Kasyapa asked, "O World-Honored One, will a disciple who holds fast to the precepts ever transgress them?" The World-Honored One answered, "Suppose the Dharma declined, the sages no longer appeared in this world, and the disciples could no longer distinguish between true disciplines and false ones. In order to rectify them, a man of wisdom may associate himself with them, and he may indulge in the same defilements with them, but he will be unspoiled by the dusts of those defilements; he simply reduces the brightness of the light of his insight. Of such a man, even though he is seemingly transgressing along with others, you cannot say that he has broken the precepts. On the other hand, if someone tries to hide his transgression because of his self-conceit and with no remorse, such a man must be called a transgressor."

Kasyapa said, "O World-Honored One, there are people of the truth among people, and yet there are also those who are not. It is very difficult to differentiate between these two kinds of people; it is almost as difficult as distinguishing the ripe mango from the unripe. How can we distinguish them?" The World-Honored One answered, "You must rely on the Sutras. Relying on the Sutras, you will be able to sharpen the eye of the mind, by which you should be able to distinguish them."

(12) Kasyapa said, "What the Buddha has said is true, and I believe in it. As the World-Honored One has explained to us, we disciples shall rely on the Dharma and not on the man, on the meaning and not on the words, on intuition and not on inference, and on the perfectly explained Sutras and not on any imperfectly explained Sutras."

The World-Honored One said, "The Dharma means the essence of the teaching. The man means the man who expounds the teachings. The Buddha expounds the teaching and undergoes life and death. The Dharma is eternal, while the world of life and death is transient. At times you may hear that the Buddha is also impermanent, but you should never believe it.

"The meaning refers to the truth of things in which the Buddha abides forever, while the words refer to various sophistries and affected words. Because the Buddha is eternal, the true Dharma is eternal. Various words admit greed and falsity, even to the extent that the Buddha permitted the disciples to store things. One must, therefore, rely on the meaning and not on the words.

"Intuition means the wisdom pertaining to the Buddha. People of inferior teachings cannot know fully the virtue of the Buddha. Therefore, one must not rely on such inferior knowledge. On the other hand, knowing that the Buddha is the Dharmakaya is the true insight upon which one must rely.

"O Kasyapa, as I have been explaining to you, you must have quietude; various false teachers will gradually appear in the form of monks and laity to obstruct the true Dharma. O Kasyapa, if someone teaches that every man has buddha nature, but that it is concealed by his defilements, so that he neither knows it nor sees it, and that, therefore, he must exert himself to terminate his defilement, then this teacher does not transgress. On the other hand, if he claims that he has realized the path because of his buddha nature, unless he practices the path, it will not manifest itself, and if it is not manifested, the person has not realized it. O Kasyapa, people contend that they all have their own selves but do not know that they have buddha nature. They are imputing the idea of self where there is none as such, and hence it is a wrong view. On the other hand, when I say that there is the self in the Buddha-Dharma, this refers to the existence of buddha nature. People insist on saying that there is no idea of self in the Buddha's teaching, but in this way they are denying the reality of buddha nature as well. This is another form of a wrong view.

(13) "O Kasyapa, suppose there was a poor woman who did not know that there was a box of gold in her own house. Then someone came to ask her to help him to weed his field. The woman agreed then to do so, but only if he could show her where the box of gold was. When the man agreed to do this, she wondered and said to him, 'None of my family members know about it; how on earth do you know of it?' Simply answering that he knows it well, the man dug up the box within the house. The woman marvelled and was delighted and deeply respected him. O Kasyapa, it is the same with me, for I am trying to make everyone see for himself that he has buddha nature.

"Also, Kasyapa, suppose there was a woman who had a baby that became ill and asked a doctor to see the child. The doctor examined him and prescribed medicine for him but instructed her that she should not feed him with her milk for a while until the medicine was fully digested. Thus the woman coated a bitter element over her breasts and told the child that since her milk was poisonous, he could not drink it. The child wanted to have the milk because of his hunger, but he did not try to drink her milk. Now after a while, when the medicine was completely digested in the child, the mother washed her breasts and called him to have her milk. However, because of his fear of the bitter taste, he did not come near. Thus she told him that a while ago she had coated a bitter element over her breasts so that he could digest the medicine that he had taken, and that now, since it was all digested, she had washed her breasts so that he might drink from them safely. O Kasyapa, it is the same with the Buddha, for he tries to remove all the wrong views of the world first by teaching that there is no self. Having taught this, he now teaches the doctrine of the Tathagatagarbha. Therefore no one should be afraid. Just like that child who listened to his mother's call and drank her milk, one must understand the secret treasury of the Buddha."

(14) Kasyapa said, "O World-Honored One, if there is a self, when a baby is born, why does he not have this insight? Why is he destined to die once he has been born? If there is the eternal buddha nature, why are there differences of kinds, such as noble and base, poor and rich, and so on? Why are there evils, such as murder, old age, drunkenness, failure of memory, and so on? Moreover, where is the buddha nature, the real self, to be found?"

The World-Honored One replied, "O Kasyapa, suppose there were a wrestler at the palace of a king, who kept a diamond on his forehead. Then he wrestled with another wrestler, and his forehead hit the opponent's head hard, and the diamond sank into his skin, and a scab formed over his forehead. Then the wrestler called for a doctor to treat it. The doctor realized that the scab was created because of the diamond sunk beneath the skin and asked the wrestler whether he knew where it had gone. The wrestler was surprised and lamented as if the precious gem were lost. The doctor told him not to worry because it was beneath the skin. The wrestler became angry and asked him, 'Are you lying to me? because if it is beneath the skin, why is there not any pus or blood? Or if it is behind a sinew, how can you see it?' Then the doctor treated the injury and then held a mirror in front of the wrestler's face, and the diamond was clearly reflected in it. The wrestler marvelled at this. O Kasyapa, it is the same with all people; because they are not associated with people of insight, they are unable to realize that there is buddha nature. Among my disciples also, because they do not approach people of insight, they learn only that there is no self but do not know why that is so. When they do not understand this truth, how can they know the true nature of things, that there is a self? O Kasyapa, just as the wrestler could see the diamond in the bright mirror, people should be able to experience buddha nature clearly.

"Again, O Kasyapa, in the Himalayas, there was a medicinal mineral that had a singular taste of sweetness. Since the area surrounding it was all covered by bushes, people could not see it directly, and only by following its scent could they guess the area of its presence. Then there was a saintly king who built wooden troughs and finally found the mineral medicine, which flowed out and sank into the bottom of the troughs. After the death of this king, however, the mineral medicine became sour, salty, pungent, or bitter tasting depending on where it flowed out. The original taste remained in the mountain. People worked hard to build mines to get it out, but in vain. In a later age, another saintly king appeared and finally found the medicine with the original taste. O Kasyapa, it is the same with the secret treasury of the Buddha, for buddha nature was concealed by the bushes of defilements, and because of their ignorance people could not see it. The original taste can be compared to buddha nature. Although buddha nature is singular in its taste, on account of defilements people are born into different worlds.

"O Kasyapa, no one can destroy buddha nature, because it is strong, nor can anyone damage it. Yet no one can see it directly. Only when you realize enlightenment will you be able to experience it."

(15) Kasyapa asked, "O World-Honored One, if someone does not kill, does this mean that there is no evil act in him?" The World-Honored One replied, "O Kasyapa, indeed there are occasions when the buddha nature of a particular person is destroyed. The buddha nature abides in the bodies and minds of people. So if someone harms a person's body and mind, the latter's buddha nature may be spared, but whosoever kills another person is destined to fall into the unhappy destinies. People try to conceive arbitrarily the form of a self, but all of their thoughts are based on illusory imagination. Since whatever is imagined is not a real thing, buddha nature is entirely different from any form conceived by worldly imagination. This is the highest form of human thought. O Kasyapa, gravel can be crushed, but not diamonds. Maras and people can destroy the body and mind but never the buddha nature. O Kasyapa, the buddha nature is inconceivable.

"O Kasyapa, the Mahayana is the nectar of the Dharma, through which anyone can reach nirvana. When people know this doctrine, they will be able to transcend life as well as death. O Kasyapa, you should understand that you ought to be steadfast, with faith in the Three Treasures. The nature of people who rely upon these treasures is the nature of the self. He who clearly sees the nature of the self as identical with buddha nature will be able to see the unmanifest Buddha. O Kasyapa, whosoever relies upon the Buddha does not rely on gods. Such a man is truly a man of faith. Whosoever takes his refuge in the Dharma does not seek false paths, and thereby he becomes fearless.

(16) "O Kasyapa, for your sake, I shall explain the Tathagatagarbha. If a person totally remains with the attachment to the self, he cannot depart from suffering at all. If he is totally cut off from the belief in the existence of self, for him there is no use in practicing the path. If one holds that there is absolutely no self, this is a wrong view. If one holds that the self is permanent, this also is a wrong view. If it is held one-sidedly that everything changes, this is a wrong view, while its opposite, that nothing changes, is also a wrong view. If one speaks only of the suffering of life, this again is a wrong view, while speaking only of the pleasure is another wrong view. Therefore, the Middle path of the Buddha departs from both of the two extremes in order to express the ultimate truth. The Buddha is like a good doctor who knows the cause of illness and cures it by treating its cause. In the same way, the Buddha annihilates human defilements by knowing their natures, characteristics, and differences, and thus he reveals the pure buddha nature that has been concealed in people. Ordinary people,

however, do not understand this. Thus when they hear about the suffering of life, they do not think of the presence of happiness. When they hear that everything changes, they do not think of buddha nature that is immutable. When they hear about the nonexistence of the self, they think that all the Dharma of the Buddha has no self either. When they hear that though buddha nature is concealed by defilements, it is totally free from the defilements and quiescent, they cherish the idea of nihilism. However, the wise know that the Buddha is eternal and immutable. If it is said that emancipation is like an illusion, ordinary people think that it will perish, but the wise know that though the Buddha appears in a human body and undergoes birth and death, his body of the Dharma is eternal and immutable. When it is said that ignorance is the cause of all phenomenal bondage, common people think that enlightenment and ignorance are two different things, whereas the wise know that they are in reality not two things. For this non-dual nature is the true nature. If it is said that there is no self in all things, ordinary people think that there are two positions, that there is a self and that there is no self. But the wise know that there are not two. When there is no differentiation of the two, there is the real nature. O Kasyapa, when cows eat sweet grasses, their milk becomes sweet; when they eat bitter grasses, their milk becomes bitter. People conceive of two forms, enlightenment and ignorance, because of their ignorance. However, just as ignorance becomes enlightenment when it changes, it is the same with all dharmas good or evil. O Kasyapa, there are varieties of grasses in the Himalaya, some of which are poisonous and some of which are healing. When cows feed on the latter, their milk is said to become ghee. It is the same with the body of an ordinary person, which, though regarded as an impermanent and poisonous thing, is also an excellent vessel of buddha nature. Only because ordinary people are obstructed by their defilements do they not see it. He who sees it will realize the supreme enlightenment. This person responds well to the compassion of the Buddha. He is the real son of the Buddha."

(17) Kasyapa asked, "O World-Honored One, how can we see this buddha nature?" The World-Honored one answered, "Believe in the Sutras, and you will know how. O Kasyapa, in the days of high summer, when the water surface rises, mandarin ducks choose a higher hill to place their chicks on and then fly around at will without worries. In the same way, the Buddha appears in this world, teaches innumerable people, helps their minds concentrate on the true Dharma, and then enters nirvana. O Kasyapa, every change is suffering, while nirvana is happiness. It is the highest and the subtlest, and it transcends all changes. It is the state of nectar thoroughly prudent and with no negligence whatsoever. Being negligent and imprudent leads to death. Negligence is delusion, and delusion is suffering, whereas non-negligence is nirvana, the highest happiness. If one chooses the direction of changes, one will meet death and endure unbearable sufferings. Therefore, there is death for ordinary people, whereas there is neither old age nor death for the sages. For they enter nirvana, which is the highest and eternal happiness.

"O Kasyapa, when the moon is set, people think that the moon has sunk. When it appears in the opposite direction, they think that it has risen. Nevertheless, there is no change on the part of the moon, which has neither appearing nor disappearing in its nature. It is the same with the Buddha, for buddha nature neither appears nor disappears in itself; it is only for the sake of teaching people that the Buddha undergoes birth and death. O Kasyapa, people say that at the beginning of each month the moon waxes and toward the end of it it wanes; but there is no change in its own nature; there is neither increase nor decrease. It is the same with the Buddha, for though people see him differently, he is the same at all times.

(18) "O Kasyapa, the moon appears over all things, over cities, villages, mountains, marshes, even over wells and ponds, and even in vats and in cauldrons everywhere. Whether one travels for a distance of one hundred miles or one thousand miles, the moon always accompanies him. People say that the moon is like the mouth of a cauldron or like a wheel, but the nature of the moon is the same, of which there is no varied form. It is the same with the Buddha, for he manifests himself in manifold ways in accordance with different causes and conditions, while his nature is eternally unchanged.

"O Kasyapa, the Buddha throws away his physical body like a snake casting away its old skin. He is comparable to a metalworker who obtains well-refined metal and creates varieties of vessels at will. It is the same with the Buddha, for he manifests himself in varieties of forms in this world. All this is for the sake of rescuing people from delusion.

"O Kasyapa, there is the manly form that is the nature of the Buddha. If someone does not know buddha nature, then such a man has no manly form. Even if he is biologically male, he may be called a woman. On the other hand, even if one is biologically female, if she knows that there is buddha nature in herself, she is endowed with manly form and is called a man."

Kasyapa said to the World-Honored One, "O World-Honored One, I have now manly form, for I have become capable of understanding the teaching about the way to see buddha nature." The World-Honored One replied, "Well said, Kasyapa! It is difficult to know the supreme Dharma, as it is profound, but you have accomplished it just as the bees collect honey."

(19) Kasyapa said to the World-Honored One, "O World-Honored One, you have taught us that with regard to buddha nature there is no difference between buddhas and those who receive their teachings. May you further explain this point for the sake of us all!" The World-Honored One said, "O Kasyapa, suppose the son of a wealthy man was keeping many milk cows with varied hide colors. One day, he milked the cows in preparation for a certain festival, but all the cows produced the same white milk. He thought, 'Cows are varied in color, so why is the milk that comes from them all alike, white?' After thinking it over for a while, he realized that the reason was the common retribution of the cows' past karma.

"O Kasyapa, it is the same with the truth that buddha nature is one in all people, for they are equally free from the leaking of defilements. O Kasyapa, when gold ore is melted, refined, and transformed into a lump of gold, its value becomes much higher. It is the same with the one buddha nature, which everyone can realize. For just as removing the scum of the ore purifies metals by eliminating defilements, people can let buddha nature, which all people equally possess, manifest itself.

"O Kasyapa, if a being does not know the eternal nature of the Buddha, he is born blind, but when he realizes it, then he becomes a man of extraordinary vision. For, even if one potentially possesses such a faculty, unless one is aware of it one is no different from having an ordinary earthly eye of flesh, because one does not know, as it were, one's own hands and feet, nor can one let others know their own.

"O Kasyapa, the Buddha is always the parent of all people. When he teaches in one language, each person can understand it. Thus, all of them praise his remarkable capacity, each thinking that the World-Honored One spoke only for himself. O Kasyapa, when a baby is born, for sixteen months the parents speak infant's language and then gradually they teach him how to speak properly. It is the same with the Buddha, for he teaches people according to their language and manifests himself variously in accordance with their power of vision. All this is for the sake of helping them abide with the true Dharma easily."

3. The Offering of Cunda

(1) The next morning the World-Honored One, accompanied by his disciples, entered Cunda's house and received his offering of food. Cunda personally served the food to the World-Honored One and his disciples and separately served cooked mushrooms to the World-Honored One. During the meal, one of the disciples picked up a vessel to drink water from and accidentally broke it.

After the meal was over, Cunda placed a small table in front of the World-Honored One and asked, "O World-Honored One, how many groups of mendicants are there in this world?" The World-Honored One replied, "There is one group of mendicants that consists of those who have crossed the ocean of suffering through diligent practice of the path and entered nirvana, transcending the human and heavenly worlds. The next group of mendicants consists of those who teach the meaning of the Dharma well, without marring it, and compassionately and clearly solve whatever doubts the listeners may have. The third group of mendicants consists of those who yearn for the state of purity and indefatigably strive for and nourish themselves with the Dharma they have received. The last group of mendicants consists of those who look externally holy but are unholy internally; because they are insincere they act disgracefully. O Cunda, just because of a single unworthy disciple, you must not accuse the rest. Since there are good things as well as bad things in this world, pure and impure all mingled, you must not make a judgment categorically. Therefore, you must not hastily become close to anyone because of his appearance, because good appearance does not necessarily mean goodness; the one whose thinking is pure is good."

Cunda asked, "Once the World-Honored One taught us that it is praiseworthy to offer whatever one possesses to others. What, may I ask, does this mean?"

The World-Honored One replied, "You may exclude one group of people from among the recipients of your charity." "Who are those people?" asked Cunda. "They are the ones who break the precepts. Those who violate the precepts are ones who destroy the roots of merits." "What kind of people are they?" Cunda asked. The World-Honored One replied, "They are those who slander the true Dharma in vulgar language and do not change this attitude for a long time nor repent it at all. Those who break the four grave prohibitions and commit the five grave offences, having neither fear nor shame nor thought of guarding the true Dharma, but on the contrary slight it and slander it with offensive language, all equally cut the roots of merit. Again, those who do not believe in the Buddha, the Dharma, or the Sangha also cut the roots of merit. All charity that is practiced, excluding these people as recipients, is praiseworthy."

(2) Cunda asked, "Can these grave offenders be saved?" The World-Honored One replied, "They can be saved if proper causal conditions are met. If they repent, feel ashamed, and return to the Dharma, even out of fear, thinking upon the reasons why they committed those grave offences, and knowing that there is nothing other than the true Dharma to help them out of their offences, and that they must uphold the precepts, then they are no longer committing the five grave offences; and therefore, the act of charity for these disciples would be an immeasurable blessing. O Cunda, there was a woman who became pregnant; because of an outbreak of war, when the time of her delivery approached, she escaped to another country. On the way she gave birth to a baby at a shrine where she happened to take a rest. After some time, hearing that things had become quiet in her home country, she started to travel back, taking the child with her. On the way, however, she met with a flooding river and could not cross it with the child on her back. Thus, she thought that it would be better to die with the child, since she could not abandon him, and she was drowned along with her child. Although the nature of this woman was not good, because of her love for the child, she was reborn in heaven after her death. O Cunda, it is the same with the mind determined to uphold the true Dharma, because irrespective of whether one committed evil deeds in the past, because of one's determination to follow the true Dharma, one will be able to become one of the persons most qualified for blessing.

"O Cunda, in having faith in the path, one must not be jealous of others, nor should one be misled by the words of others. Again, one must not be interested in assessing others' conduct as to whether they are in accordance with the rule. It is essential to pay attention to one's own affairs as to what is good and what is not. In this way one can make progress in one's practice. You must discipline your mind; no matter how trivial a matter may be, be not negligent of it." Having heard this, Cunda was filled with delight.

(3) The World-Honored One left Cunda's house accompanied by his disciples and proceeded to the town of Kusinara. Cunda and his family also followed the Buddha and his retinue. Halfway to Kusinara, the World-Honored One had a relapse of his illness. Quietly resting under a roadside tree, the World-Honored One said to Ananda, "I have an acute pain in my back. Will you spread my mat?"

Ananda at once prepared the mat as asked.

After resting on the mat, the World-Honored One summoned Ananda and said, "O Ananda, I feel thirsty. Will you fetch me some clean water from the nearby river?" Ananda replied, "O World-Honored One, a little while ago, merchants with a caravan of five hundred carriages crossed upstream, and the water must still be muddy and unfit for drinking. But, World-Honored One, there is another river Kakuttha not far from here where the water is clear and cool. May we proceed there, where the World-Honored One can drink the water and cool his limbs?" The World-Honored One, however, made his request three times, and in assent, taking a bowl, Ananda went down to the river bank. When he came to the bank, he found that the water already had become clear, and he said, "How marvellous is the great power of the Buddha." He returned to the World-Honored One with the water in the bowl and presented it to him.

At that time, a young man named Pukkusa, a Malla clansman and a disciple of Alara Kalama, was passing along the highroad from Kusinara to the city of Pava. He saw the World-Honored One's holy figure seated at the foot of a tree and went up to the World-Honored One. After reverential greeting, he said, "O Gotama, in the holy path, meditation is the primary practice, through which we control our emotions, discipline our minds, and cut off the sense of alarm and fear. When my teacher Alara Kalama once rested under a roadside tree, and a caravan of fifty carts passed by in front of him, he never broke his silent concentration nor even made the slightest physical move. I was impressed with how noble the practice of meditation is." Then the World-Honored One said, "O Pukkusa, I was once at the village of Atuma and sat under a roadside tree, being mindful of the path. At the time, there passed a caravan of five hundred carts in front of me. Also, when I was once contemplating the life and death of the human world in a farmer's hut in a village, there was a dreadful thunderstorm that shook the entire area, causing the death of two brothers and of four cows of the village. On both occasions, though I was not sleeping, I did not see anything nor hear anything; and the villagers all marvelled." Having listened to the World-Honored One, Pukkusa was deeply impressed, saying, "O World-Honored One, the depth of meditation of the Buddha is beyond my comprehension, and far beyond the capacity of my teacher." The World-Honored One further instructed Pukkusa in detail, and said to him who was in tears, "Those who devote themselves to the Dharma are peaceful and find delight even while they rest in bed. Those wise people whose goal is pure find delight in the practice of the Dharma taught by the Tathagata, and they rely upon his virtue just as all beings rely upon the rains that moisten them all."

(4) When the World-Honored One said this, Pukkusa ordered his attendant, "Go and fetch two robes with golden color; I want to offer them to the World-honored One." With the robes in his hands, Pukkusa said, "O World-Honored One, with your compassion for me, will you accept this offering?" The World-Honored One said, "I shall receive one of them for your sake, and you may offer the other robe to Ananda. He has been serving me day and night, and today he

has taken care of me in my illness. An act of charity to both the sick person and his attendant is the perfection of a great gift." Delightedly Pukkusa presented one of the robes to the World-Honored One and the other to Ananda. Ananda said, "O Pukkusa, this is a beautiful act of charity. You have well followed the word of the great teacher of the world of people. I gladly accept this."

Having made the offering, Pukkusa sat at one side; the World-Honored One continued his teaching of the path. When this was over, Pukkusa said again, "O World-Honored One, I now take refuge in the Buddha, the Dharma, and the Sangha. Please allow me to become a faithful follower of the true Dharma. As long as I live, I am determined to refrain from killing, stealing, sensual indulgence, lying, and drinking." The World-Honored One gave his consent. Pukkusa said, "O World-Honored One, as I am a busy man, may I take leave now? And when the World-Honored One happens to pass the city of Pava at another time, please extend your visit to our village and give instruction to us. I shall be ready to make offerings with whatever food, robes, medicine, and other things I have in my house." Having said this, Pukkusa left in delight.

(5) Soon after, Ananda presented the golden robe to the World-Honored One. Understanding his mind, the World-Honored One at once put it on. At that moment, his sublime figure especially shone forth like blazing flames of fire. Marvelling at this, Ananda said. "O World-Honored One, it has been twenty-five years since I began to accompany you, but there has never been a time when your figure looked so sublime as at this moment. It is marvellous and strange. Will you explain the reason to us?" The World-Honored One replied, "There are two occasions when a buddha's figure looks especially different from the way it looks on most days. The first occasion is the time when a buddha realizes enlightenment, and the second is the time when a buddha is about to enter final nirvana. You must know now that I shall be passing away at midnight tonight without fail."

All those who were present wept. The World-Honored One proceeded to the river Kakuttha, where he washed his body in the water and stepped up to the shade of a tree over the bank. The bright light again shone forth in golden color toward both banks of the river. At that time, Ananda was drying the World-Honored One's robe that was used for bathing, and the World-Honored One asked Cunda to spread his mat and rested on it.

4. Three Types of Incurably Ill Persons

(1) Kasyapa of Uttara questioned the World-Honored One, asking, "Ordinary people have four kinds of poisonous arrows as the causes of sickness. They are greed, anger, ignorance, and conceit. Because of these four, there are many illnesses. The World-Honored One does not have these four, so what is the reason why his back hurts?" The World-Honored One replied, "O Kasyapa, in truth, I am free from all illnesses. From the immemorial past, the Buddha has been totally free from all sickness. O Kasyapa, though the Buddha is said to be a lion among men, in truth, the Buddha is not a lion. The word lion refers to a secret teaching of the Buddha. That I am now supposedly ill is also, in the same way,

nothing but a secret teaching of the Buddha.

"O Kasyapa, there are three kinds of incurably sick people in the world: first, those who slander the Mahayana, second, those who commit the five grave offences, and third, those who cut the roots of merit. These three illnesses are the extremely grave ones that a buddha alone can heal.

"O Kasyapa, a bodhisattva, after renouncing the world, receives the precepts and maintains his proper appearance, peaceful in moving and stopping and fearful even of the most trifling transgression; and he keeps the precepts with the firmness of a diamond. O Kasyapa, a man tried to cross an ocean holding a floating bag, but the Maras of the ocean demanded that he should forsake that float to them. The man knew that if he gave it up, he would surely drown, and therefore he replied, 'Even if you kill me, I shall not give it up to you.' The Maras said, 'If you cannot give the whole thing, then give us just half of it.' But the man still did not agree. Then they said, 'If you cannot give even one-half, then how about one-third? If you reject this idea also, then how about a handful of it, or even a part of it the size of a dust particle.' The man, however, flatly refused and said, 'What you have asked is very little. But I do not know whether my goal is near or far in this ocean. Once I give in to you and give up a little of the bag, it is obvious that all the air in it will go out. Then I shall not be able to make my voyage; probably only death will be waiting for me.' O Kasyapa, it must be the same with the sramana's way of keeping the precepts. When any sramana upholds the precepts, many tempters of human defilements seductively speak to him, saying, 'You can trust me; I shall not deceive you. If you break the four precepts, namely, those against killing, stealing, sensual indulgence, and lying, you still will be able to enter nirvana peacefully.' Every sramana must reply to this as follows, 'Even if I fall into the Avici hell by observing these precepts, I desire not to be born in the heavens by breaking them.' Every sramana must uphold these precepts steadfastly, keep his mind as firm as a diamond, and attach the same value to small and great offenses. In this way every sramana can perfect the fundamental pure precepts. This is the practice of purity, and in this way every sramana can acquire the seven holy treasures, namely, faith, precepts, conscience, knowledge, wisdom, freedom from passions, and finally, sagehood.

(2) "Next, O Kasyapa, every sramana must understand the Four Noble Truths. First is the truth of suffering, which embodies the impending aspect of multiple suffering in the world, and of which birth, old age, sickness, and death are the ones no one can escape. O Kasyapa, suppose there is a beautiful and well-dressed woman who comes to a house. The master asks who she is, to which the woman answers, 'I am Srimahadevi, the goddess of good fortune.' He then asks what she does, and she replies that she gives good fortune wherever she stays. Delightedly, the master invites her to his guest room and entertains her by burning incense and scattering flowers. After a while there comes another woman to the entrance of the house. She looks very ugly in figure as well as in clothing; her skin is ruptured and her clothing all filthy and dirty. To the question as to who she is, the woman replies that she is Kalaratridevi, the goddess of misfortune, and she destroys every good fortune wherever she stays. The

housemaster demands that she leave. With sword in hand, he threatens her life if she refuses to go. Then the woman says, 'How foolish you are! The woman who is staying in your house is my sister. Since I always stay with her, if you force me out, you are forcing my sister out as well.' The man is surprised and rushes into the house to question Srimahadevi. She replies that the ugly woman is correct, and that if he loves her, he must love her sister as well. Thus, the housemaster forces both of them to go out. The two women then next go to some impoverished home where both of them are invited in with delight. O Kasyapa, once born, every person is bound to old age, sickness, and death. Fools love both good fortune and misfortune, whereas the sramana should love neither.

(3) "O Kasyapa, if rain consisted of bits of diamonds, it would surely destroy trees, grass, and everything else but those diamonds. In the same way, the rain that consists of death destroys all people, but it does not destroy those bodhisattvas who abide in the state of nirvana. O Kasyapa, when people die, they go through the fearful place where there is no food to eat; the road is far and distant and on it one has no companion; day and night they proceed with neither rest nor goal whatsoever, in mist and in darkness with no light; indeed, death is the greatest suffering.

"O Kasyapa, the next Noble Truth is the truth of the cause of suffering, which consists of the thirst of love. There are essentially two kinds of love, good and bad. Good love is what bodhisattvas seek, whereas evil love is what common people yearn for. The love of ordinary people is the cause of suffering, but that of bodhisattvas is not. When a king goes out, his retainers all accompany him; wherever the thirst of love proceeds, all defilements accompany it. Just as seedlings grow well in moist earth, the seedlings of defilement grow well wherever the thirst of love moistens. Again, the thirst of love is like the daughter of a devil, because she eats up her baby and even eats up her husband. In the same way, the thirst of love eats up whatever is good immediately after its birth, and even consumes all people. Also, the thirst of love is like a snake hidden in a flowerbed. People love flowers but see no poisonous snakes under them. No sooner does one pick the flower is one bitten to death. People greedily enjoy the five kinds of flowers, namely, the five kinds of desires, and affected by the thirst of love they fall into unhappy destinies. Therefore, a bodhisattva endeavors to extinguish the defiled flame and enter the state of quiescence and ease. When defilements are all extinguished, there will be joy, and no affliction will arise caused by delusion. This is the third Truth, namely that of cessation. Finally, the fourth Truth, that of the noble path, is the Eightfold Noble Path. O Kasyapa, just as we can see things at night by the help of a lamp, so a bodhisattva abides in the Mahayana and relies on the Eightfold Noble Path, whereby he sees everything in the world."

(4) Kasyapa said, "World-Honored One, you taught us previously that the mind of faith is the path, and at another time that non-negligence is the path; in like manner, you told us that endeavor, concentration, contemplation of the impurity of the flesh, reflection on universal impermanence, the upholding of precepts, association with good characters, the practice of compassion, destroying defilements by the power of insight, and so on—every one of these is the path.

The World-Honored One now has introduced the Eightfold Noble Path as the contents of the path. Is it then that all the teachings that the World-Honored One previously taught are false?"

The World-Honored One praised Kasyapa, saying, "Well asked, O, Kasyapa! All these teachings defined as paths are equally included in the truth of the path. O sons of good family, though the path is only one, the Buddha has explained it differently in accordance with the capacities of various people. Even though the nature of fire is one, when it burns wood, we call it a wood fire; when it burns grass, we call it a grass fire. Also, as to one and the same thing, we call it color in the aspect we see, or we call it sound in the aspect we hear. In like manner, whatever we can smell, we call it smell, and whatever we can taste, we call it taste. It is the same with the singular path of the Buddha. Just for the sake of edifying varieties of people, it is explained in a variety of ways, and it is only through these skillful means that countless people can eventually be led to overcome the cause of delusion."

(5) At that time, the Bodhisattva Manjusri said to the World-Honored One, "O World-Honored One, I beg you to explain to us the meaning of the worldly truth that the Buddhas alone experience." The World-Honored One replied, "The worldly truth is identical with the absolute one." "But," Manjusri asked, "are there not two different truths?" The World-Honored One replied, "I have taught two truths in order to accommodate the ordinary faculty of differentiation. O Manjusri, the worldly truth refers to things of which there are only names but no corresponding realities. On the other hand, the absolute truth refers to things of which there are the corresponding objective names and realities. When one's mind is no longer deluded, and when one sees reality as it is, then the content of such insight is called the absolute truth." "Then what is the truth of reality as it is?" Manjusri asked. The World-Honored One replied, "O Manjusri, the truth of things as they are refers to whatever has an objective existence. If things do not have an objective existence, that state of affairs is not called absolute truth; absolute truth is not a deluded state; it has no falsity; and it is called the Mahayana. This is the state that the buddhas alone can speak of, not the tempters. O Manjusri, the truth is the singular path, it is pure, it is not two things, and it is endowed with eternal existence, eternal happiness, eternal self, and eternal purity." Manjusri asked, "Some non-Buddhists also assert the same. Are their assertions also true?" The World-Honored One replied, "In false thought, what is impermanent and incessantly changes is called eternal, but this is wrong and must be corrected as impermanent, because everything arises depending upon causes and conditions and cannot be existent by itself or as itself. Since all phenomena incessantly change and are impermanent, this state of affairs is a form of suffering, having no self, no freedom, and no purity. Therefore it is buddha nature alone that can be described as neither originated nor perishing, neither going nor coming, neither with form nor without form, nor is it like phenomena, such as the physical body, sensations, or objects of sensations, which incessantly change. Buddha nature, indeed, abides forever, hence it must be regarded as eternal happiness, eternal self, the master of freedom, and also

true purity. Many non-Buddhists claim a similar doctrine, but since they do not understand reality as it is, they are actually not teaching the true doctrine of eternal existence, eternal happiness, eternal freedom, and eternal purity; and accordingly, their doctrines cannot at all be identified with the truth of reality as it is."

(6) At that time there was a lay disciple Vimalagarbha in the assembly, who stood up from his seat and reverentially holding his palms together said to the World-Honored One, "O World-Honored One, the wisdom of the Buddhas is limitless, and yet their wisdom is still inferior to this teaching, the doctrine of the buddha nature. For it is only through this teaching that one can realize the true path." The World-Honored One said, "O Vimalagarbha, we have milk from cows, a thick sour milk from milk, a curdled milk from the thick sour milk, butter from the curdled milk, and finally ghee from the butter. The final product is, indeed, the best of all, in which all medicines are inherent. If one drinks this ghee, all illnesses will be cured. It is the same with the Buddha. For there will come various teachings from the Buddha, and finally comes the realization of nirvana, the final product, like ghee. This is also comparable to buddha nature; hence buddha nature actually means the Buddha."

Then Kasyapa said, "O World-Honored One, this doctrine is indeed the highest; from now on, I am determined to write this doctrine down as a scripture, even if I must make paper from my skin, ink from my blood and marrow, and a pen from my bone, and thereby to propagate the meaning of this doctrine all over the world forever. O World-Honored One, when I see a greedy person, I shall first give treasures and then teach this doctrine to him. If a man belongs to high social rank, I shall first use some speech that appeals to his feeling and then teach this doctrine to him. Again, in case of a community of people, I shall first demonstrate my influential power and have them accept this doctrine, or if someone is conceited, I shall first serve him as a servant and then recommend this doctrine to him. If anyone slanders the Buddha's doctrine, I shall persuade him through discussion and then let him learn this doctrine. When a person is already delighted with the Mahayana, I shall visit him to pay tribute and make offerings to him with much praise."

Having listened to this, the World-Honored One praised Kasyapa, "It is beautiful; you are already devoted to the Mahayana. Because of this causal condition, you will be able to realize the path even before innumerable bodhisattvas realize it." Thus the World-Honored One completed his discourse, and then he told the following story.

5. The Price of Half a Verse

(1) "O Kasyapa, in the immemorial past, when no buddha had appeared in this world, I was residing in the Himalayas and was engaged in the bodhisattva practice. On the ground there grew herbal grasses, varieties of birds flocked, brooks were crystal clear, fruits were sweet, and varieties of flowers with exquisite scent were blooming. I was then seeking everywhere for the Mahayana teaching but was still unable to find it. Then many gods thought me strange, and they talked

among themselves. 'This man has well departed from the troubled mind caused by desire and possesses the mind of tranquillity, totally free from all desires. He may be thinking of becoming the god Indra in the next life.' One god then said, 'There is a bodhisattva in the world who practices many things in order to benefit other people but does nothing for his own sake. Such a man understands that human errors are derived from delusion, and even if the earth is filled with treasures, he sees them just as they are, worthless as spittle; and therefore, he does not have any sense of greed. He can discard even his own wife and children, his servants and his own house. Nor does he desire the glory of the gods' world, for he is only concerned with how to realize the highest path and how to accomplish it quickly so that he can benefit all other people. Perhaps he is that Bodhisattva.' Then the god Indra said, 'If he is that Bodhisattva, then he is destined to save all people. O gods, if there is a shade created by the Buddha in this world, in which anyone can rest, the problems of the people will be more easily resolved. If he is to become a buddha, we must protect him by all means. Nevertheless, such things cannot easily be believed. Up to this day, many hundreds of thousands of people have wished to realize the path, but all of them eventually abandoned their goal because of unfavorable conditions. They are like the image of the moon reflected in water, which is easily moved or broken up even by small ripples passing over the surface of the stream. Therefore, I shall now visit him and test how hard his determination may be.' Thus saying, Indra disappeared from his seat and suddenly appeared in the Himalayas, assuming the terrifying form of devil. Quite merrily he sang the song,

> All formations are transitory,
> It is their nature to rise and fall.

(2) "O Kasyapa, listening to this half a verse, I was as delighted as if I were given water to quench my thirst, or suddenly released from imprisonment. This was a precious song, conveying precisely the truth of the world; it must be nothing other than Mahayana doctrine. I stood up from my seat, subduing my leaping heart, and looked around. 'Who has sung this wonderful song? Where is the master of such excellent guidance, whom I have sought for a long time?' But I could not find anybody in sight. The only one whom I saw was a devil with the most terrifying features. I thought, 'Was it this devil who sang this half a verse? No, it cannot be; how could that noble voice of a buddha come out of this being with such ugly features? For it would be like a lotus growing out of fire, or like water springing from a ray of the sun. Nevertheless, other than he, no one is in sight. Perchance it may be that this devil once met a buddha and learnt that verse from him?' Thus thinking, I decided to ask him.

(3) "I approached the devil and asked, 'Where did you learn this noble half a verse?' He answered, 'Do not ask me about that verse. I have not eaten for some days. Looking for food all around, I have not been able to find any. Because of my distress, what came out of my mind was that half a verse. I did not have any particular thought in saying it.' I asked, 'Do not say no. I beg you to teach me the remaining half of the verse, so that I may become your disciple for the rest of my life. The half a verse that you gave is, indeed, a truly noble one, but

because of its being a half, the words as well as their meanings are incomplete. After one offers a treasure, there may be a time when it is destroyed, but not the offering of the Dharma, as people say. Please teach me the remaining half.' The devil then answered, 'You think only of yourself, but not of me. I am totally starved now; how can I think of giving instruction to anyone?' 'What is your kind of food then?' I asked. 'It is better that you do not ask me that. Anyone would be shocked at my answer,' the devil said. I said, 'No one is here, except myself. There is no need of fear. Tell me your kind of food.' 'All right, I shall tell you. My food is warm human flesh and my drink is warm human blood; these are the things on which I depend,' was his answer. 'If that is so, please tell me the remaining half of the verse. My body will die sooner or later and is not of so much use to me. It would be better for my long-cherished wish if my body could be made into an offering to you for the sake of the noble Dharma, rather than be devoured by wild animals such as tigers, wolves, and owls. I am ready to throw away this body that will decay, and I wish instead to obtain the Dharmakaya, firm and unchanging forever.' The devil said, 'Though you have said so, how can anyone believe it?' 'That is a foolish doubt. As one throws away tiles and gravel and picks up a vase made of the seven precious gems, so throwing away this decaying body of flesh, I would acquire a diamond body. If you cannot believe it, I shall swear to all the gods and all the buddhas to witness these words.' To this plea of mine, the devil finally agreed. 'As you are so sincere about what you have said, I shall give you the remaining half.' I spread my clothes on the ground for him to sit on, and I reverently kneeled down to listen to the latter half of the verse. The devil sang,

> Having arisen, they cease;
> Their cessation is happiness.

" 'Now, O Bodhisattva,' the devil said, 'I have given you the whole verse. Your desire must have been fulfilled. If you really intend to benefit all others, why not offer your body to me for my food?'

(4) "O Kasyapa, at that moment, I thoroughly appreciated the meaning of that verse and then wrote it down on rocks and walls, on the bark of trees, and everywhere along the road. After doing so I climbed up to the top of a tree. The tree god asked me what I was intending to do. I answered, 'I am going to offer this body, as I am thankful for the verse I have been taught.' 'What sort of merit is there in such a verse?' asked the tree god. 'This verse conveys the right path of all the buddhas past, present, and future,' I said, adding, 'I want those who are miserly or those who easily become conceited upon making trifling offerings to witness how I throw away my precious body just for the sake of half a verse as though I were throwing away a bundle of grass.' No sooner than saying this, I jumped from the tree top. But before my body touched the ground, the devil changed back into his original godly figure, caught my body in midair, and gently laid it on the ground. And together with many gods, he bowed down at my feet and praised me, saying, 'This is the noblest intention; you are a true bodhisattva. You have already benefitted innumerable people. May you pardon my offence; and after you have accomplished the highest goal you have cherished,

may you extend your teaching to me for the sake of my salvation!' Upon saying this with a reverential gesture at my feet, he disappeared.

"O Kasyapa, in this way I sacrificed my body as the price of half a verse. Since then, through many aeons of time, I continued to practice charity and finally have accomplished the path. O Kasyapa, the immeasurable merit that I have is the reward for my continued practice of charity for the true Dharma of the buddhas. O Kasyapa, you have now aspired for the supreme path. Thereby you have already excelled innumerable bodhisattvas, as many as the sands of the river Ganges."

6. The Four Boundless Minds

(1) The World-Honored One said, "O Kasyapa, know the Dharma and its meaning, time, and contentment, and also know yourself and others, nobility, and ignobility; and practice the four boundless minds, namely, friendliness, compassion, joy, and equanimity.

"O Kasyapa, I shall discipline many who have wrong views through innumerable skillful means. If they are greedy about treasures, I shall transform myself into a holy king and give them whatever they wish to have, and then I shall teach them the supreme path of enlightenment for the sake of their well-being. If they are indulging in the five desires, I shall give them the most satisfactory objects of their desires and then shall lead them to the supreme path of enlightenment for the sake of their well-being. If they are prosperous and self-conceited, I shall become their servant and work hard for them for a long time, and win their hearts; thus shall I induce them to the supreme path of enlightenment for the sake of their well-being. If they are stubborn and self-righteous, I shall reprimand them, advise them, discipline their minds, and make them attain peace by the supreme path of enlightenment. O Kasyapa, all these methods are not false ones. The Buddha is like the lotus flower, because he is not contaminated even though he is in the impure world.

"O Kasyapa, when you practice friendliness, you will be able to destroy the mind of greed; when you practice compassion, you will be able to cut off the mind of anger; when you practice the joy of seeing others happy, you will be able to cut off the mind of suffering, and when you practice equanimity, you will be able to annihilate the minds of greed, anger, and discrimination toward all people.

(2) "O Kasyapa, a bodhisattva sees innumerable people with a mind of equality and does not show the slightest discrimination. This is the realization of the practice of compassion. Nevertheless, this is not by any means the Great Compassion, because such compassion is hard to practice. Just as it is difficult to drill a hole in a well-dried peapod, it is extremely difficult to destroy human defilements when they are thoroughly hardened, even by disciplining the mind against disturbances through one full day and night. Also it is difficult for a man to drive away anger, like a god watching a house; but it is easy for him to lose kindness, like a deer running through the forest. Anger is like a picture inscribed in rock, and compassion is like a picture drawn on the surface of a body of water. Again, the former is like a mass of fire, and the latter a flash of lightning. O Kasyapa, if a bodhisattva maintains no discrimination even to an extreme

villain and does not censure his faults nor raise any anger, he is said to have
Great Compassion.

"O Kasyapa, to eliminate things that are not beneficial to people is
Great Compassion. To give innumerable benefits is the practice of compassion.
To cherish delight toward people is the practice of joy. To see all dharmas in
terms of equality and nondiscrimination, or to throw away one's own enjoyment
and give it to others, is the practice of transcendence or equanimity. These four
practices of infinite mental attitudes are the foundations of all good.

(3) "O Kasyapa, the reason that a bodhisattva practices charity is not fear
or fame or profit, nor is it for deceiving others. Therefore, the bodhisattva must
neither have self-conceit nor expect a return for his acts. When a bodhisattva
practices charity, he does not think of himself; neither does he choose the recipient. Facing all people he shows his compassion as though each of them were his
only child. When he looks at people's suffering, he feels pity just as parents feel
pity for their sick child. When he looks at their happiness he feels joy just as
parents feel joy in seeing their child's recovery. Once a bodhisattva has given
charity, he, like parents letting their grown child freely live his own life, does
not cherish the thought of his former generosity.

(4) "O Kasyapa, when a bodhisattva practices compassion, he can create
immeasurable good. Therefore, his compassion is true and not false. If a man
asks what the root of goodness is, he must reply that it is compassion. O Kasyapa,
because practicing good is a right thought, the right thought is itself compassion. Also, Kasyapa, compassion is the Buddha and the path of enlightenment.
Compassion is the parent that nurtures all people, and such a parent is the
Buddha. O Kasyapa, compassion is the buddha nature inherent in all people.
Because it has been concealed by their defilements, people do not see it, but since
man has this nature and manifests it in his act of compassion, buddha nature is
identical with the Buddha. Hence compassion is also characterized as eternal
existence, eternal happiness, eternal self, and eternal purity. This buddha nature,
namely, the Dharma, is not separate from the Sangha. Hence the Sangha is the
Dharma, the Dharma is the Buddha, and the Buddha is compassion. O Kasyapa,
when compassion is not eternally existent, nor eternally happy, nor eternally
independent, nor eternally pure, such compassion is only a trifle that benefits
only one's self. O Kasyapa, true compassion is beyond the fathoming of ordinary
people. Hence, the Dharma, the Buddha, and the buddha nature, all of these are
beyond ordinary thinking. Because bodhisattvas abide in the nirvana of the
Mahayana, where they live happily and practice this compassion together,
they do not fall into slumber; and because they do not fall asleep, they need not
awaken. There is only incessant endeavor. Since they do no wrong, they are not
disturbed by nightmares while they are asleep. Even if they were born in the
gods' heavens, they would not be entrapped by the kinds of enjoyment that
gods experience. O Kasyapa, the practicing of compassion is filled with such
immeasurable merits.

(5) "O Kasyapa, when a bodhisattva practices compassion, friendliness, and
joy, he is able to live in the loving an only child stage. O Kasyapa, why is this

state called this? O Kasyapa, it is because the state that a bodhisattva achieves through the practice of the four boundless minds can be compared to parents' feelings for their only child. Parents feel joy when they see their child's well-being, and they feel distress in seeing his illness. In like manner, a bodhisattva sees people as his only son and hence feels delight in seeing their diligent practice of good and distress in seeing them afflicted by their defilements, so much so that his blood seeps out from his pores. O Kasyapa, when a baby puts into his mouth feces, mud, or a piece of tile, his parents worry that he will be harmed, and holding his head by the left hand, they will try to get the thing out with the right hand. In like manner, when a bodhisattva achieves that state, he is distressed when people's Dharmakaya does not mature well, and observing their evil actions of body, speech, and thought he tries to eliminate such evil deeds with the hand of his wisdom and wishes them not to wander further through the world of delusion.

"Again, Kasyapa, when a child dies, parents are so saddened that they even want to die with him. A bodhisattva, seeing someone who has severed the good roots of merit falling into hell, hopes that the evil one, while in the state of suffering, will arouse at least one thought of regret. Then the bodhisattva can teach him the Dharma to arouse in his mind at least one thought of good. To do so he is willing to be born in hell with him. Further, O Kasyapa, parents are constantly concerned about their children's conduct, and if they find them doing any wrong, they kindly teach them so that their evils do not aggravate. A bodhisattva, too, is constantly concerned about people, whether they are in the three evil realms or in the celestial worlds, and he is never oblivious of them. Even if they continue to do wrong, he will not nurse his wrath over them or let them augment their evils."

(6) Kasyapa then asked, "O World-Honored One, when nectar is boiled, we can obtain some elements that have different tastes, and when a lump of gold is repeatedly refined, the brilliant beauty of the metal increases. Similarly I have now understood the profound meaning of the doctrine from the World-Honored One's repeated discourses. O World-Honored One, after a bodhisattva practices friendliness, kindness, compassion, and joy and attains the state of loving an only child, what kind of state will he attain?"

The World-Honored One replied, "A bodhisattva will attain the state of equanimity or mental equilibrium like the vacuous sky. O Kasyapa, a bodhisattva abiding in this state will no longer have the kind of love directed to any particular person like a parent, a relative, and so forth; and hence, he will see no difference and make no discrimination toward the objects of the senses or conceptions. His mind will be as impartial as empty space.

"O Kasyapa, a bodhisattva knows all the aspects of the Dharma and their meanings, so that even if there are many different teachings, he knows that they all return to the one truth. Again, he knows all languages; he is capable of teaching people at will. He is, however, not entrapped by his virtues, for if he were, he would no longer be a bodhisattva. For if he clings to his merits, he will no longer be capable of freeing himself from various sufferings. This state of a bodhisattva is called the four non-hindrances, namely, freedom. The four kinds of non-hindrance mean having no objective whatsoever. If one has something to obtain, there will occur some hindrance. Such a hindrance gives rise to wrong views, but a bodhisattva does not have wrong thoughts; and thus, he will not be hindered. Since the bodhisattva does not cling to anything, in this manner he will realize the Mahayana. O Kasyapa, there is no particular object to cling to in what you have asked, nor is there anything in what I am explaining. If you saw something to become attached to in what you have asked about, you would be one of the Maras and not my disciple.

(7) "O Kasyapa, all worldly truth is absolute truth from the Buddha's point of view. For all buddhas teach worldly truth for the sake of absolute truth, and they thereby make all people understand the meaning of absolute truth. If they cannot make them understand it, why should buddhas teach worldly truth? O Kasyapa, when a buddha teaches worldly truth, people think that he teaches absolute truth, and when he teaches absolute truth, they think that he teaches worldly truth. This is the state of the profound insight of the buddhas, which no other beings can see.

"O Kasyapa, the nature or characteristic of the path has neither arisen nor perished and hence cannot be grasped. Also, it has neither color nor form and hence cannot be measured. Nevertheless, the supreme truth has its function. This may be compared to one's mind. One cannot perceive one's mind, but one cannot doubt its function. A bodhisattva can see it directly and clearly.

"O Kasyapa, there are two ways of perceiving, indirect and direct. With the former we infer the existence of fire from the presence of smoke. With the latter we see color with the eye. O Kasyapa, just as a man of clear and perfect eyes sees a mango in his hand, the bodhisattva clearly sees the path, enlightenment, and nirvana. Therefore I once told Sariputra, 'O Sariputra, whatever people in this world know, the Buddha knows, and whatever they do not know, he also knows. Therefore, the Buddha is said to know all things without exception.' "

Chapter 4

THE GREAT DEMISE

1. The Path of the Bodhisattva

(1) At that time, there was a person called Punyaraja in the assembly, who reverentially said to the World-Honored One, "O World-Honored One, by destroying defilements, one realizes nirvana, but does this mean that whoever has not destroyed defilements cannot realize nirvana? If this is so, the nature of nirvana is that it was not existent before the destruction of defilements, and it comes into existence thereafter. It follows that nirvana has a beginning and is therefore finite. How can it be said that it is eternal?"

The World-Honored One replied, "You cannot say that the essence of nirvana did not exist before but now does. Whether a buddha appears or whether he does not, the essence of nirvana is eternal. People cannot see it because it is concealed by their defilements, and hence they say that it is not. Therefore, the Buddha has appeared in this world in order to teach people to see it. It is not that what was originally nonexistent comes into existence. Rather, people are like blind persons who, upon being cured by medical treatment, begin to see the sun and the moon.

"O Punyaraja, when the bodhisattva gives a thing upon a person's request, this is a charity, but it is not of the highest kind. Even when there is no request, if he practices charity with his magnanimous mind, this is called the charity of the highest kind. Moreover, if he practices charity occasionally from time to time, this is not the highest kind of charity. When he practices it at all times, then such charity is called the highest kind of charity. Again, after performing a charity, if he regrets it, this is not the highest kind of charity; doing charity with no regret is the highest kind of charity. When a king performs charity because of his fear of bandits or of the disasters of water and fire, this is not charity of the highest kind; when he does it for pleasure, this is called the highest charity. Practicing charity with some expectation of reward is not the highest kind; the practice of charity with no expectation of reward is the highest kind of charity. If charity is practiced for the sake of fame, family tradition, or self-grandeur, this cannot be said to be of the highest kind. When the bodhisattva practices it without concern for the agent of the charity, its recipient, or its content, without seeing its occasion, without differentiating whether its recipient would be a source of blessing or not, without considering causes and conditions, without considering its result, small or large, pure or impure, without calculating for oneself or others, and moreover without slighting the agent, the recipient, or the gift itself, and if he gives only and exclusively for the sake of nirvana and for the sake of the well-being of all people, then this is the highest kind of charity. The same can be said with regard to the remaining five ways of the bodhisattva.

(2) "O Punyaraja, the fate of a man who cuts the root of good is not entirely determined. If it were predetermined, he would never be able to realize the highest path, but because it is not predetermined, he has a fair chance to realize it. It is the same with those who commit the five grave offences and who slander the true Dharma as well. The bodhisattva does not see any determined form in anything, nor is there any determined form in the Buddha. Though there is no physical form in the Buddha, there is also no lack of physical form in him. He was born in Middle India and stayed at certain times in Sravasti and at other times in Rajagriha, and hence he cannot be said to have been permanently residing anywhere. Nevertheless, he cannot be said to be in one place and not to be in another. Just as there is no place where there is no sky, the Buddha abides everywhere universally. Therefore it cannot be said that he is impermanent either. Now the Buddha shows his entrance into nirvana and hence has no determined form. Nevertheless, since he is eternally existent, eternally happy, eternally independent, and eternally pure, it cannot be said that he has no determined form.

"O Punyaraja, since the Buddha is always engaged in pure practices, there is no outflow of defilement in him. A bodhisattva, too, should perform pure practices in order to cut all the outflow of defilement, always to control the mind, and thereby to guard against greed, anger, ignorance, self-conceit, jealousy, and other defilements.

"O Punyaraja, once upon a time in a certain country, a great number of people were crowded along a long road. The king ordered a retainer to carry a bowl containing oil through the crowd of people and let another man follow him with a sword ready to strike him when even a drop of oil fell out of the container. Because of his fear, the retainer carried it out successfully without a drop falling. It is the same with the bodhisattva; for abiding in the world of delusion, he does not lose insight and refrains from greed over the five kinds of desires; he will maintain the purity of the mind and the practice of the precepts, so as to realize total annihilation, once and for all, of the leaking of defilements.

(3) "O Punyaraja, how can one free himself from the leaking of defilements? If someone practices this doctrine and is mindful of its meaning, he may be freed from the defilements. This person is truly my disciple, having thoroughly received my teaching, and he is what I expect to see and am concerned with. He will clearly know that I shall not perish. Wherever he lives, I shall also abide there and never move away. He who is delighted in his faith in me and upon seeing me and paying respect to me decides to practice the path will go to the person who holds fast to this doctrine and is mindful of its meaning and will respect him, serve him, and make him not lacking anything. When such a man of insight is

visiting from afar, go out at least ten miles to welcome him, because it is very difficult to meet with this teaching, even more difficult than meeting with the blooming of the udumbara tree. In the immemorial past, I sold a part of my flesh every day for money for the sake of this teaching, and I offered it to the Buddha and listened to his teaching, and eventually I gained immeasurable merit. I am certain, therefore, that whoever practices this doctrine will cut the root of defilements without fail.

"O Punyaraja, a bodhisattva must regard his body as a disease, as an enemy, or as a poisoned arrow. The body is the place where all sufferings are concentrated, and from which all evils spring. Nevertheless, he must nourish the body with care, not acting for the sake of greed concerning the body but for the sake of the Dharma, not for the sake of samsara but for the sake of nirvana.

"O Punyaraja, a bodhisattva must always protect his body, for unless he does so he cannot complete his given life. If his life is not fully lived, he cannot fully maintain the doctrine and widely propagate its meaning. O Punyaraja, anyone who wants to cross a river must care for the raft well, and those who travel on land must care for the horse. It is the same with a bodhisattva, for even if he sees impurity in his body, in order to maintain the path he must protect his body so as not to impoverish it.

"Though a bodhisattva need not worry about wild elephants, he must be fearful of evil people who associate with him as friends. Elephants may injure his body, but evil people may injure his mind as well. Again, though elephants may injure the body of flesh, evil friends will injure the body of the Dharma inherent in him. Moreover, even if he is killed by elephants, he will not fall into unhappy destinies, but if he is injured by evil friends, he will surely fall into unhappy destinies.

"O Punyaraja, again, when a bodhisattva wears his clothing, it should not be for his body but for the sake of the Dharma. It must not be for self-grandeur but always for the sake of humbleness and modesty. Clothing is adequate if it protects from heat and cold, rain and wind, and poisonous insects. Again, a bodhisattva must be free from greed in receiving food and drink, for it is not for his body but always for the true Dharma. It should not be for beautifying the skin but for the sake of other people, and not for conceit but for the sake of maintaining physical strength. Again, when the bodhisattva receives a resting place, he must be fully aware that it is not for his greed or self-grandeur but for making his mind the house of enlightenment and for guarding against the enemy of defilements, rain, and wind. Again, in seeking medicines, a bodhisattva must not be greedy or conceited but must do so for the sake of the true Dharma, not for the life of the body but for the sake of eternal life. Wherever or whenever a bodhisattva receives these four kinds of offerings, it is not for his physical life but for the sake of the path, for if he does not receive these charities he cannot maintain his body; if he cannot maintain his health, he cannot endure sufferings; if he cannot endure sufferings, he cannot practice the roots of merit.

(4) "O Punyaraja, once there was a wicked king who put four poisonous snakes into a box and ordered a man to take care of them. He told the man that if he

failed to keep even one of them in control, he would be put to death. Because of his fear, the man ran away, and the king sent five servants after him. These five then tried to deceive him by letting one of the servants befriend him, but the man did not trust anyone and ran away from them to hide in a village. Then there was a voice in midair telling him that no one lived in the village and that six bandits would come there that night, and that if they found him he would surely be killed. Thus, the man ran again from the village and then came to a river with a very swift current, and no ferry was available. So he built a raft out of bits of tree branches and grasses, and thought to himself, 'If I stay here, I shall be killed by poisonous snakes, the king's servants, the deceptive friend, or the six bandits. If I proceed forward and try to cross the stream, I may drown, but if I drown, I at least will not be killed by those snakes or bandits or whomever.' So, jumping into the stream with the raft, he finally made his crossing to the yonder shore where he reached safety.

"O Punyaraja, the body is analogous to the box; the four kinds of physical elements are like the four poisonous snakes. Because of fear of these things, the bodhisattva initially runs away toward the path of saints, but he still faces the danger of the five servants, namely, the five aggregates conditioned by defilements, assuming various forms, such as his own self, trying to capture him. However, the body of a bodhisattva is as firm as diamond, and his mind is as wide as the sky; hence, he will not be destroyed by them. For even if the defiled force of greed and lust tries to seduce him by deception, the bodhisattva will not be so deceived. Observing that the village of the six senses is not a safe place, he will not be terrified by the presence of six kinds of cognitive objects. He proceeds straight in the practice of the path. Moreover, when he meets the rough river of defilements, its depth not fathomable, its yonder shore not visible, many kinds of fish therein destroying people, the bodhisattva contrives a variety of skillful means, such as the raft consisting of the various skillful paths, and thereby he finally reaches the yonder shore of eternal happiness.

"When a bodhisattva practices the path of nirvana, he experiences pain in both his body and his mind. Nevertheless, he thinks that unless he himself endures it, he cannot help others cross the river of defilements, and he endures all sufferings in silence. Since he endures them, there will be no arising of defilements. Since even a bodhisattva has no leaking defilements, how could the Buddha be defiled?"

2. The Great Nirvana

(1) Punyaraja now asked the World-Honored One, "What is the great nirvana?" The World-Honored One answered, "With great compassion, one extends one's pity, treats everyone as his parents, helps them cross the river of life and death, and shows widely the singular path; this is the great nirvana. Also, it is so called because of the great self, for the great self means the truth that nirvana has no self and is absolute freedom. Since nirvana has nothing to grasp at, it can contain every and all dharmas as they are. Since it is everywhere like the sky, though it cannot be seen directly, it can be shown to people at will. Again, since it is

absolute happiness, it is called the great nirvana. Great happiness means neither suffering nor pleasure; it is totally free from all distractions and endowed with perfect insight, its body eternally existing in quiescence. Again, it is called great nirvana because it is pure, clean, and totally bereft of the impurity of the world of delusion, and because its action, body, and mind are all pure.

"O Punyaraja, a bodhisattva knows that every person possesses buddha nature. Because of this buddha nature, even those who have killed the seedling of buddha nature will be able to realize the path of enlightenment if he is capable of overcoming the evil mind. This is, indeed, very difficult to know and can be known only by a buddha.

(2) "O Punyaraja, there are four causes for approaching the great nirvana: first, to associate with good friends; second, to listen to the Dharma with concentration; third, to be mindful of the Dharma; and fourth, to practice the Dharma. O Punyaraja, when a sick man follows his doctor's instructions and drinks a prescribed medicine, he will regain his health. Good friends are like good doctors, and if a bodhisattva follows their teachings, he should be able to eliminate his illness and realize the peace of nirvana.

(3) "O Punyaraja, the state in which defilements do not arise is called nirvana. It is the Buddha whose insight is free of hindrance regardless of whatever object it is directed to. The Buddha is not an ordinary man. His body, his mind, and his insight permeate universally all the countries of the world, transcending boundaries and obstacles eternally and without change.

"O Punyaraja, a bodhisattva holds fast to the one thing and follows the one truth. This one thing means the mind of enlightenment. The bodhisattva preserves this just as a man protects his only son, or just as a one-eyed man protects the remaining eye. For it is through this mind of enlightenment that a bodhisattva attains the path and enters nirvana. Why does he then follow the one truth? He knows that everyone equally relies on the One Vehicle. The One Vehicle means the Mahayana path.

"O Punyaraja, the bodhisattva practices this doctrine and acquires faith and sincerity of mind; he does not censure others' faults, taking care lest his words incite their defilements and lead them to unhappy destinies. Again, he praises people whenever he finds even a little good in them, because good action is buddha nature, and by praising their buddha nature he tries to help them to enter the highest path of enlightenment.

"O Punyaraja, there are five kinds of people who are as rare as the flower of the udumbara tree. The first consists of people who never do anything wrong, and those who repent if they do anything wrong. The second kind consists of people who benefit those through charity and others who think of the benefit they received. The third kind consists of people who receive the Dharma anew and of others who do not forget what they received a long time ago. The fourth kind consists of people who enjoy listening to the Dharma and others who enjoy teaching the Dharma. And the fifth kind consists of people who question well and others who answer well. You are the kind of a person who questions well, whereas I am the kind who answers well. In response to good questions, I can turn, through my teaching, the highest Wheel of the Dharma.

(4) "O Punyaraja, those who cut the roots of merit cannot discard their evil minds whether or not they meet the Buddha. If, however, they begin to seek enlightenment, they will eventually realize the path. O Punyaraja, once when a king heard the sound of a harp and was unable to forget its clear and beautiful sound, he asked his attendants where that sound came from and had them bring the instrument they spoke of. The king ordered this instrument to make a sound, but it made no sound, so he cut its strings off and further broke it into pieces in order to see where that sound came from; all this to no avail. Enraged, the king demanded the sound from his attendants; they replied that no sound can be produced by this method, and that the sound was dependent upon a variety of causes. O Punyaraja, it is the same with buddha nature, because it, too, cannot be seen in any particular location but only through multiple causes and conditions. Since those who cut the roots of merit do not see this buddha nature, how could they cease their transgressions in the unhappy destinies? If, however, they begin to believe in buddha nature, they will not fall back to the previous unhappy destinies. Once this happens, they will no longer be characterized as bereft of good roots. A bodhisattva always praises whatever is good in people and does not speak of their faults. He himself refrains with effort from all evils. If he makes a mistake, he at once regrets it and reports it to his master and colleagues without concealment; and with self-reflection he will not fall into the same error again. Even if it is a trifling error, he regards it as weighty. If others censure him, he clearly admits his fault and keeps his mind straight and believes in the existence of buddha nature. Therefore, he is not a man who has cut the roots of merit; he is a disciple of the Buddha.

(5) "For the sake of attaining the great nirvana, a bodhisattva, embodying all these practices, accomplishes what is difficult to accomplish, endures what is difficult to endure, and gives what is difficult to give. If he is told that by eating only one grain of jute seed every day he will realize the path, a bodhisattva will eat only one grain of jute seed every day. If he is told that by jumping into a fire he can realize the path, a bodhisattva will dwell forever in fire. Again, if someone says that by offering his head, eye, or the like he can attain the path, a bodhisattva will offer all these. Parents give nice clothes to their child, and even if the child behaves mischievously toward them, on account of their love they tolerate it. Moreover, they have no awareness at all that they gave him those clothes. It is the same with a bodhisattva, for he is not conscious of his benevolent acts or that he performs a difficult act of charity. A bodhisattva regards others as he would regard his only child. If a child becomes sick, the parents also feel distressed. It is the same with a bodhisattva, for he feels sympathy with people's sicknesses caused by their defilements; therefore he tries to teach the Dharma to them, so that they may eventually extinguish their defilements. Nevertheless, he is not especially conscious that he helped them to accomplish this. If he does become conscious of such a thought, he will not be able to realize the path.

"O Punyaraja, to all people, I am a good friend. Even those that are held in bondage by grave defilements, if they meet me, I shall help by destroying their defilements with my power."

3. Illness of the World-Honored One

(1) At that time, Cunda was at the side of the World-Honored One, reproaching himself that the World-Honored One's illness might have been caused by the food he had offered to him. As Ananda returned to the World-Honored One's side, Cunda withdrew. The World-Honored One, however, was aware that Cunda was distressed, and he asked Ananda, "Cunda seems to be blaming himself for something, is he not?" "O World-Honored One, Cunda may be blaming himself for the food he offered to the World-Honored One," Ananda replied.

The World-Honored One then said, "O Ananda, you and the others must not blame him. At the time when I realized enlightenment, a maiden called Sujata offered me food, and now, at the time when I am about to leave this life, Cunda offered me food, and the merit of his offering is as great as that of Sujata's. Go to Cunda and tell him that I said that he should not be distressed, that his deed has created great merit, and that he will acquire everlasting happiness." As instructed, Ananda conveyed the message to Cunda.

So delighted was Cunda that he came to the World-Honored One, saying, "O World-Honored One, I feel grateful when I think that my offering has created such merit." The World-Honored One instructed Cunda in verse, saying,

> He who practices charity will acquire merits.
> Such a man of benevolence will prevent evil hatred,
> Will be filled with virtues, will sever the roots of greed, anger, and ignorance,
> And will in the end enter nirvana.

"O Cunda, teach and promote the practice of charity and help those who listen to you to acquire everlasting peace."

(2) The World-Honored One then said to Ananda, "O Ananda, I feel again an acute pain in my back, and I wish to lie down. Lay out my mat." In answer to his wish, Ananda prepared the mat. Laying himself on his right side, the World-Honored One engaged in deep meditation. A while later, he called Ananda, saying, "O Ananda, recite for me the seven limbs of enlightenment." Ananda duly recited them, and the World-Honored One said, "Did you, O Ananda, recite the limb of endeavor?" Ananda said, "Yes;" and the World-Honored One said, "O Ananda, carry out the practice of this discipline and realize the path as promptly as possible." Thus instructing him, the World-Honored One once again entered into deep meditation. One of the disciples, deeply moved, said the following, "Although the World-Honored One is the supreme master of the true Dharma, he has listened to the recitation regarding the path even while enduring the discomfort of his illness. How much more attentively should the rest of us listen to the teaching of the Dharma!"

(3) Now Kalpina came to Ananda and said, "O Ananda, I have some questions to ask the World-Honored One." Ananda replied, "I fear that this cannot

be done now, because it may disturb the World-Honored One while he is suffering discomfort." Having taken notice of this, however, the World-Honored One summoned Ananda, saying, "O Ananda, I have something to say to Kalpina. Summon him here." Thus allowed to do so, Kalpina moved toward the World-Honored One, paying his respects with palms joined together, and the World-Honored One permitted him to ask the question he had on his mind. Kalpina said, "O World-Honored One, the Buddha is the most honored being in heaven and on earth. Why do you not order the gods to fetch medicine and cure your illness?" The World-Honored One replied, "O Kalpina, a long time after its construction, an abode crumbles. The earth, however, is indestructible. My body is just like an old house, whereas my mind is like the earth. My body yields to sickness, but the mind is always at peace." "O World-Honored One," said Kalpina, "the baby swallows are reared by their parents and continue to grow under their protection. If the World-Honored One passes away now, on whom can we rely after your demise?" The World-Honored One then replied, "Throughout different occasions, I have constantly taught you that no one can escape death. O Kalpina, be mindful of the Buddha without fail and seriously practice the precepts." Thus instructed, Kalpina reverentially withdrew from the presence of the World-Honored One.

(4) At that time, the World-Honored One addressed Ananda and said, "O Ananda, let us go to a sala grove by the bank of the river Hiranyavati, outside Kusinagara." The countenance of the World-Honored One looked as calm as the Himalayas. The World-Honored One and his disciples left the bank of the river Krakustha, crossed the river Hiranyavati, and finally arrived at the sala grove.

Then Cunda came forward and said, "O World-Honored One, I am ready to pass away and arrive at the ocean of immeasurable merits where there is neither love nor hate." The World-Honored One replied, "It is the appointed time now, since you have done all that was to be done." Thus, Cunda ended his life in the presence of the World-Honored One just as a candle goes out.

At that time a brahmin of Kusinagara was passing the area on his way to the city of Pava and happened to see the World-Honored One from a distance. Feeling an irresistible impulse of adoration, he approached the World-Honored One and said, "O World-Honored One, my village is not far from here. May the World-Honored One, out of compassion for me, visit my house for an overnight stay. It will be just as easy for the World-Honored One to proceed to the town of Kusinagara after receiving my offering for tomorrow morning." The World-Honored One replied, "Nay, brahmin, but your suggestion is the same as an actual offering." Though three times the brahmin repeated his wish, the World-Honored One likewise did not grant it, and he ordered him to convey his wish to Ananda, who was seated behind the World-Honored One. The brahmin then spoke to Ananda, but his reply, too, was the same, "Nay, O brahmin, you have already made an offering to the World-Honored One, have you not? It is hot now, and your village is far. The World-Honored One is now fatigued and cannot be disturbed any further."

(5) The sala grove was located on the bank of the river Hiranyavati outside Kusinagara and on three sides was surrounded by the river. Looking at the grove, the World-Honored One addressed Ananda and said, "O Ananda, do you see those twin sala trees, standing side by side at the edge of that grove? Go there and spread the mat so that I can lay myself down with my head to the north between the two trees. I am extremely weary, Ananda, and I shall pass away at that spot this night at midnight." Although it was only a few miles from Pava to the grove, the World-Honored One had to rest twenty-five times before he finally reached it.

In tears, Ananda reached the spot below the trees, swept it and cleansed it with sprinkles of water, prepared the mat as instructed, and returned to the World-Honored One, saying, "O World-Honored One, everything is ready as you ordered." The World-Honored One entered the grove accompanied by his disciples. Reaching the spot that had been prepared, the World-Honored One laid himself down quietly, with his head to the north, facing the west, on his right side, and with one leg resting on the other. Now at that time heavenly music rang out and a chorus came swelling up. The twin sala trees bloomed forth with flowers out of season; their color resembled the white of a crane's feathers. Their petals showered down on the World-Honored One like rain.

The World-Honored One asked Ananda, "Have you witnessed how the gods made offerings to me?" With Ananda's affirmative answer, the World-Honored One continued, "Nevertheless, these offerings are not really the way to pay reverence to me nor the way to respond truly to my wishes." "What is the true way to pay reverence to the Buddha and respond to his wishes?" asked Ananda. The World-Honored One replied; "Whether man or woman, whosoever is my disciple must abide in the Dharma, walk with the Dharma, and conduct his or her affairs in accordance with the Dharma; this is the true way for him or her to serve me and pay reverence to me. Accordingly, O Ananda, whosoever wants to follow me and respond to my wishes does not necessarily need to follow the convention of offering incense, flowers, and music. Be mindful and exert yourselves: this will be the best offering to me."

4. The Metaphor of the Treasure Mountain

(1) At that time, the World-Honored One addressed the people that had gathered about him, "If there is any doubt remaining in anyone's mind, you may question me freely, and I shall resolve whatever doubt you might have."

There was a bodhisattva called Simhanada in the assembly, who stood up from his seat and with his palms together said to the World-Honored One, "O World-Honored One, may the World-Honored One, I pray, expound further on the subject of the buddha nature." The World-Honored One responded with the following discourse: "O Simhanada, after being reborn repeatedly through many ages, all will eventually realize the supreme enlightenment, their destined goal. O Simhanada, suppose there is some curdled milk at home. If someone asks whether it is raw cheese, one may answer that it is; for though curdled milk is not raw cheese, the latter can without fail be produced from the former. It is the same with people. All of them possess a mind and on account of this mind are destined for certain to attain supreme enlightenment. Therefore, I always say to everyone that people universally possess buddha nature. This is indeed the One Vehicle in which all can equally ride; it is the mother of all the buddhas. Even when we cannot see the new moon, we cannot say that it is not in the sky. In the same way, we cannot say that people lack buddha nature even though ordinary people cannot see the presence of buddha nature in themselves. Moreover, suppose there is a grass called ksanti in the Himalayas; when cows feed on this grass, they produce ghee, but when they feed on other grasses, they do not produce ghee. However, just because there is no ghee here, one can by no means claim that there is no grass called ksanti in the Himalayas. In the same way one cannot claim that there is no buddha nature because the doctrine of buddha nature has not yet been taught. Again, a piece of black iron glows red when placed in fire, but when removed from the fire it soon becomes cool and black again. In the same way everyone will be able to perceive buddha nature when the fire of defilements is extinguished.

(2) "O Simhanada, nirvana is the state in which the fire of defilements has been extinguished. It is also likened to a room that safely wards off the rain and wind of defilements. Nirvana is the refuge that provides shelter from all kinds of fear. It is also called a beach, because the rampaging waters of desire, existence, wrong views, and ignorance are unable to cast it adrift. It is also called the ultimate refuge, because it enables man to realize ultimate happiness.

"O Simhanada, you are looking with the eyes of human wisdom and therefore this is unclear to you. If you could perceive with the eyes of a buddha, it would become clear to you. Moreover, there are two different ways in the act of perceiving; perceiving through the eye and perceiving through listening. The buddhas perceive buddha nature through the eye just as they see a mango fruit in the palm of the hand. People who perceive only through hearing, on the other hand, are unable to see it clearly. If, however, they arouse faith within, their perceiving will no longer simply be perceiving through hearing. There are two causal factors for the rise of faith, namely, listening to the Dharma and contemplating the Dharma. Faith is dependent upon listening to the Dharma, and listening to the Dharma is dependent on faith.

"O Simhanada, whatever exists arises due to causes and conditions and perishes due to causes and conditions. A person's buddha nature, however, is not destroyed nor does it decay, neither can it be pulled forth nor tied to anything; it is like empty space. Everyone possesses this empty space, and because of the empty nature of this space, ordinary people are unable to see it, and only bodhisattvas have glimpses of it. O Simhanada, this is known only to the buddhas, while ordinary people do not know it; these, therefore, are held in bondage by defilements and suffering in the world of birth and death. If they see buddha nature, they will be able to transcend birth and death and realize nirvana."

(3) Simhanada asked, "O World-Honored One, if all people possess buddha nature, why do their minds suffer retrogression?"

The World-Honored One replied, "O Simhanada, there is no such thing as retrogression of the mind. For if the mind actually did retrogress, no one would be able to realize the path. Only because some are slow to realize it, we speak of retrogression, which occurs when the proper causes and conditions do not coalesce. Therefore, I expound two causal factors, direct causes and indirect causes. The direct cause is buddha nature, while the indirect cause is the arising of the mind of enlightenment. With these two factors, one can realize enlightenment just as one can extract gold from its ore.

"Moreover, O Simhanada, you cannot say that there is no buddha nature just because you experience retrogression of the mind. Suppose two men happened to hear that somewhere in the distance there was a mountain of seven precious gems. In this mountain, there was a spring of longevity, which had water clean and sweet; by arriving at this place one would no longer suffer poverty and one would enjoy longevity by drinking the water. The problem, however, was that the mountain was located in a remote place and the passage leading there was extremely dangerous. The two men nevertheless decided to go together. The one was well prepared for travelling, whereas the other did not take anything at all with him. On the way, they happened to meet with a man who carried much treasure, and to whom they asked, 'Is there really a mountain yonder where there are seven precious gems?' The man answered, 'I have already been there and acquired treasures and drunk the spring water, but the road to that place is precarious, and there are many thieves. There have been only a few who have managed to reach there, although millions have attempted it.' Listening to this, one of the two, having second thoughts, said, 'How could I reach there? I have some wealth. If I were killed on the way, I would be left with neither wealth nor life.' The other, however, thought, 'Since there is someone who has managed to get there, it should not be impossible for me to do the same. If I am able to reach there, I shall acquire treasures and drink the water of the spring of longevity to my heart's desire. And if I am not able, I shall simply die. If I realize the goal of reaching there and return safely, I shall be able to serve my parents well and help my kinfolk prosper also.' So this man sets out by himself. O Simhanada, this mountain of seven treasures denotes great nirvana, the sweet spring, the buddha nature. The one who sets out forthwith is the bodhisattva who does not retrogress, whereas the one who hesitates is the bodhisattva who retrogresses. O Simhanada, the buddha nature of man, like the path, is eternally immutable. One cannot say that it is mutable just because there is someone who had second thoughts and turned back. O Simhanada, in the path of enlightenment, there is no one who really retrogresses. Thus each and every person is positively able to realize the path. Accordingly, I teach that even those who cut the roots of merit by committing the five grave offences are in possession of buddha nature.

"O Simhanada, when a candle is lighted, darkness disappears; when the candle goes out, darkness comes back again. Further, when a seal is pressed onto a mud surface, the seal is taken away and only the impression remains. It is the same with the karmic effects people create, for even while one's mind and body disappear, they continue to reappear in another's body and mind. Nevertheless, all people possess buddha nature. If a poison is mixed with milk, it continues to be poisonous. And the milk cannot be called curd, nor can the curd be called milk, and in this way different names are given to their respective transformations until they become ghee, but the nature of the poison remains the same throughout all the five milk products. Although poison is not mixed in with the final product, if someone drinks it, he will die. It is the same with buddha nature, for even while people live in the five different kinds of existence and are endowed with different bodies, their buddha nature remains the same with no change whatsoever.

(4) "O Simhanada, there is no form in nirvana. Form refers to the characteristics of color, sound, smell, taste, and touch, the characteristics of origination and cessation, the characteristics of male and female. There are none of these forms in nirvana. O Simhanada, he who is attached to these forms subjects himself to the state of ignorance. When he is subject to this state, he creates in himself a thirsting desire; when he experiences this thirsting desire, he is bound to the causal chain; when he is bound to the causal chain, he is subject to birth; and once subject to birth, he is bound to death. If, however, my disciples diligently practice the three disciplines of meditation, insight, and renunciation of the two extremes, they will be able to sever those phenomenal forms. In order to uproot a plant, it is best first to pull it sideways and to then pull it upward; in order to wash clothes, it is best to wash them first with water mixed with ashes and then to rinse them with spring water. Again, a soldier can better fight enemies when he is well protected with armor. It is the same with a bodhisattva, for he must practice those three disciplines. O Simhanada, whenever conceit arises, whether it is after he has experienced pleasure, or after he has taught the Dharma, or after he has received alms, he must practice the discipline of meditation but not that of insight. When he regrets that his utmost exertion does not lead to enlightenment, or that he is unable to control himself as he would like on account of his weak will, or that he is worried that he might transgress the precepts on account of his intense defilements, he must practice the discipline of insight but not that of meditation. If these two disciplines are well balanced, he may proceed to practice the discipline of the renunciation of the two extremes. But if defilement continues to arise while he is engaged in the practice of meditation and insight, he should not proceed to the practice of renunciation but should chant the Sutras as well as be mindful of the buddhas.

(5) "O Simhanada, there is no abode for the Dharmakaya of the Buddha; neither is there an abode for buddha nature. Since all people strive toward this goal without retrogressing, they are able to attain it without fail and are able to perceive it without fail. I say that all people universally possess buddha nature. A king once ordered his minister to bring an elephant to his court and allowed blind people to touch the animal. Then the king summoned those blind people and asked them what kind of thing the animal resembled. The one who touched its tusk replied that the animal was like a radish tail; the one who touched the

ear replied that it was like a winnowing basket; the one who touched its face replied that it was like a rock; the one who touched its leg replied that it was like a wooden mortar; the one who touched its back replied that it was like a bed; the one who touched its belly replied that it was like a huge vat; the one who touched its tail replied that it was like a rope. O Simhanada, the descriptions offered by these blind people are not perfect; on the other hand, they are not totally incorrect. It is the same with people; some claim that buddha nature is the body and the mind, while others claim that it is the self other than the body and the mind. Nevertheless, buddha nature is neither of these, nor is it different from them. O Simhanada, the Buddha is eternal, and his Dharmakaya is free of boundaries and obstructions; it neither comes into being nor perishes; this is called the self. In truth, ordinary people are not in possession of such a self, but they will attain it without fail; and hence, they can be said to be in possession of buddha nature.

(6) "O Simhanada, great loving-kindness and great compassion are called buddha nature. For both always accompany a bodhisattva like a shadow that follows its form. Since all people will necessarily realize both, I say that they all possess buddha nature. Great loving-kindness and great compassion are buddha nature, buddha nature is the Buddha. Great joy and great renunciation are also called buddha nature. For without renouncing the world of delusion, a bodhisattva cannot realize the supreme enlightenment. Since all people will attain both without fail, I teach that they all possess buddha nature. Great joy and great renunciation are buddha nature, and buddha nature is the Buddha. Again, buddha nature is called the mind of great faith, for by means of such faith one can complete the path of the bodhisattva. Since all people will realize this without fail, I say that they all possess buddha nature. Buddha nature is the Buddha. Again, buddha nature is called the state of the only child stage, for it is in this state that the bodhisattva is able to maintain the mind of impartiality toward all. And since all will without fail realize this state, I say that they all possess buddha nature. This state of the only child is buddha nature, and buddha nature is the Buddha.

(7) "O Simhanada, this doctrine is like an ocean, and no one can fathom its depth. Moreover, it has one universal taste and is uniform. Since all equally possess buddha nature, the vehicle through which they strive for emancipation is one and the same. The nature of emancipation is, thus, also one and the same; the beginning and the ending are equally the same; and so is the merit of the state of emancipation. Thus, everything without fail will become eternal, wondrously enjoyable, free and pure. Also, those who firmly hold to this doctrine will never break the precepts even at the risk of their lives, just as the high tide never rises above a fixed water level. Again, this ocean contains immeasurable treasures and buddha merits; hence evil corpses are not to be found there. Since all abide in equality and in the nature of the dharmas, there is neither increase nor decrease, as described in the scripture concerning the state of emancipation."

(8) At this moment, a disciple called Upavana, who had faithfully served the World-Honored One before Ananda had assumed that role, was deeply grieved

upon hearing that the World-Honored One was ill and dying; he approached and stood in front of the World-Honored One. Then the World-Honored One said to Upavana that he should not stand in front of him, and Upavana withdrew to one side.

Ananda felt that this was strange and asked the World-Honored One, "O World-Honored One, I have served you for a long time, but I have yet to hear such words. Moreover, when the World-Honored One is about to enter nirvana, why does he keep Upavana from standing in front of him?" The World-Honored One replied, "O Ananda, it is not that I dislike him. Gods are now vying and rushing here to see me, but because Upavana stands in their way, obstructed by his dignity and virtue, they are unable to approach me."

Ananda then asked, "O World-Honored One, what kind of disciplines did Upavana undertake in order to realize such dignity and virtue?" To this question, the World-Honored One replied, "Long ago, when the Buddha Vipasyin was still in this world, Upavana gladly held a torch in order to illuminate the path of the Buddha. Because of this merit, he has now acquired the great power that even the brilliance of gods cannot equal."

5. The Four Holy Places

(1) Ananda asked, "If the World-Honored One remains in this world, people of virtue and those of diligent practice will all come together to worship the World-Honored One; they will be able to listen to the Dharma and cultivate merits. If, however, the World-Honored One passes away now, those people will not come. What then are we to do?" The World-Honored One replied, "O Ananda, you must not worry. Think of the Lumbini Garden in Kapilavatthu where I was born. Also, think of the foot of the Bodhi Tree, by the river Neranjara, where I attained the supreme enlightenment. Also, think of Deer Park near Baranasi where I gave my first teaching. Moreover, think of this sala tree grove outside Kusinara, where I am about to enter nirvana. By recollecting all these localities, you will accumulate merit.

"O Ananda, if you maintain the mind of faith, recollect the deeds of the Buddha, and offer the Buddha even one stalk of a flower, you will be able to reach nirvana on account of that merit. O Ananda, even if someone only once thinks of the Buddha in his mind, and even if he only once pays reverence to him, he is destined to realize nirvana. O Ananda, again, if someone hears the name of the Buddha, he will be able to enter nirvana on account of that merit. O Ananda, the Buddha is the highest among those whose merits are great. I shall become a refuge for all those who have no refuge, shall be a house for all those who have no house, shall be a light for all those who remain in darkness, and shall be an eye for all those who are blind."

(2) Ananda asked, "We have a disciple whose name is Channa. He is by nature discontented and prone to use abusive words, and he frequently engages in disputes with others. How should we treat him after the World-Honored One passes away?" The World-Honored One answered, "You should refrain from speaking to him. On his own he will feel a sense of shame and reform his own behavior."

Ananda asked, "If a large number of women gather around the disciples and attempt to meet with us, how should we conduct ourselves?" The World-Honored One answered, "You must refrain from meeting them." Ananda asked, "But in case one cannot avoid meeting them, how should one conduct oneself?" The World-Honored One replied, "Refrain from speaking with them." Ananda asked, "But if they request to listen to the Dharma, how should we conduct ourselves?" The World-Honored One replied, "Of course, you should teach them the Dharma. But you must think of elderly women as your own mothers, of older women as your elder sisters, and of younger women as your younger sisters, and be watchful of your actions, words, and thoughts."

Ananda asked, "Is there any difference in regard to merit between making offerings to the World-Honored One while he is alive and making them after he passes away?" The World-Honored One replied, "There is no difference. For the Dharmakaya of the Buddha abides forever. O Ananda, whosoever sees the Buddha sees the Dharma, and whosoever sees the Dharma sees the Sangha; whosoever sees the Sangha sees nirvana. Therefore, one must know that the Three Treasures abide forever and are immutable and become the refuge of all people."

(3) Ananda asked, "After the World-Honored One enters nirvana, how should we perform the funeral rites?" The World-Honored One replied, "You must not worry about that but seek the path alone and exert yourself on your own behalf. Devote the whole of yourself for your own roots of merit. Also, convey to others with delight whatever you have heard from my teachings. There will be many people who will do honor to my remains." Ananda asked, "In what manner will they lay the World-Honored One to rest?" The World-Honored One replied, "As they treat the remains of a king of kings, they will cleanse the body with hot water, wrap it with cotton, place the body in a coffin embellished with gold, pour on scented oil, fill it with good incenses, cremate all this, collect the ashes, and build a stupa over the ashes. Whoever passes by this stupa will worship it, offer flowers and incenses, and acquire merits. This is the way in which a king of kings is to be laid to rest."

Having heard this, Ananda felt distressed and hid himself in a room in the back; leaning against its door, he lamented, "Alas, I remain still at the stage of a learner, one who has not yet realized the state of an arhat. And the World-Honored One is about to abandon me and enter nirvana. When shall I be able to attain emancipation? After his passing away, for whom should I fetch water every morning, prepare the couch every evening; whose face and whose feet should I wash?" Thus thinking to himself, Ananda raised his arms, clung to a branch of a tree and wept from the depths of his heart.

(4) While the disciples were attending the World-Honored One, the World-Honored One asked about the whereabouts of Ananda. They replied that Ananda was weeping under yonder tree. The World-Honored One then sent a disciple to call Ananda. Ananda returned and with a reverential gesture stood by the side of the World-Honored One. The World-Honored One said, "O Ananda, have I not already, on former occasions, said to you that all things are impermanent? It is

in the very nature of things that those who meet are bound to be separated. What are you grieving over? O Ananda, for a long time you have been in my service and you have served me well. Your action, speech, and thoughts were always pure and free of defilements. Be diligent, and the merits that you acquire will be immeasurable.

"O disciples, the reason that I say to Ananda that he should not mourn so is that he will realize his emancipation very soon. O disciples, every buddha of the past had an attendant such as Ananda. Buddhas of the future will also have such attendants. O disciples, Ananda has a firm faith, his mind is upright, his body is free of disease, and he is always diligent and without conceit. His insight is deep and wondrous, and he remembers whatever teaching I have imparted. Furthermore, my disciples, Ananda knows when it is the right time for something. When a visitor arrives and wishes to see me, he first judges whether the time for such a meeting is right for me or not. He always considers first when is the right time for me to meet with my disciples, or to receive lay devotees, or to meet with people of other religions. On account of these wise arrangements, whosoever came to see me or listened to my teaching acquired immeasurable benefit from it. All this is to be credited to Ananda for arranging the right times and for guiding the people to me. O disciples, when people meet a noble king, they are invariably delighted irrespective of whether they listen to the king speaking or whether they observe him remaining silent. When he departs, they cannot help but feel a sense of yearning toward their king, just as a starved man feels an insatiable hunger. It is the same with Ananda, for his personality is full of graceful virtue. When other disciples come to him, he does not fail to inquire about their health; when nuns come to him, he does not fail to advise them to receive the holy precepts as if he were talking to his own sisters. Moreover, when householders visit, he does not fail to encourage them to take refuge in the Three Treasures, to maintain the holy precepts, to respect their parents, and to make offerings to arhats. Everyone delights in listening to his words. If people found him silent, they would ask him the reason. When departing, they feel drawn toward his virtue and reflect on his good will. O disciples, Ananda is endowed with all these excellent virtues.

"Therefore, O Ananda, you must not feel distressed over whether you will have the opportunity to realize emancipation after my passing. Ever since I realized the path, I have continued to teach, and all the Dharma and precepts I have laid down will be your teacher, your guardian, and your refuge. I am the father of the world and its friend. I have accomplished whatever must be accomplished by a father or a friend. From now on, after my passing, you must be mindful of whatever has been taught and diligently practice whatever has been laid down as the precepts; and together with Maha-Kassapa you must guide the world and cultivate the teachings everywhere. O Ananda, you must not trouble your mind to no purpose, for you are destined to realize emancipation, and my true Dharma will spread in all directions and benefit the world."

(5) After listening to the World-Honored One, Ananda was somewhat relieved of his distress and said, "O World-Honored One, my mind has been awakened, and yet there is still one question that I wish to ask. I beseech you to respond to my question."

Granted permission to ask it, Ananda said, "O World-Honored One, there are other great cities not too distant from here, such as Vesali, Rajagaha, Savatthi, Baranasi, and Campa, all of which are prosperous, with their people thriving, and in all of these cities the World-Honored One's teaching is being practiced. Why does the World-Honored One not proceed to one of these cities and enter nirvana there? Why does he wish to pass away in this remote town of Kusinara?" The World-Honored One replied, "O Ananda, speak no more about it. If a king visits a family, even though it be a humble and lowly one, the world will look up to that family. When a medicine, even though it be coarse, cures sickness, or when a corpse, even though it be rotted, can be used as a float at the time of a sudden shipwreck in order to reach the shore, inevitably people will be overjoyed to use it. O Ananda, many wondrous merits embellish this town, for this was the town where buddhas and bodhisattvas of past ages practiced their path. In one of my previous lives, I came here as a king. At that time, the town was prosperous and filled with stately buildings. The king's authority held sway, and the people willingly obeyed his laws. Nevertheless, I could not help thinking that the glory of the world could not endure forever, that the human body was a vessel that would soon decay, that the path alone was true, and that only he who saw this truth would be able to know how to be content with whatever was at hand. Thus thinking, I renounced the throne and single-mindedly devoted myself to the practice of the path. I recollect that this was repeated seven lifetimes. Therefore seven times have I already laid my body down in this land. This land, therefore, has a special relationship to my past lives. The reason that I have come here to enter nirvana is that I wish to make recompense for the benefits that I received during past ages."

After Ananda listened to the World-Honored One, he said, "It is marvellous, O World-Honored One. O World-Honored One, I was not aware of this noble relationship; I shall no longer regard this region as being lowly."

(6) Then the World-Honored One said to Ananda, "Go now, O Ananda, and enter Kusinara and inform the people of Kusinara that this night at midnight the World-Honored One will pass away, and that if they have any doubts, they should promptly come to have them clarified. Tell them that they should not regret their failure to seize this moment." In response to the World-Honored One, Ananda proceeded to the town of Kusinara, accompanied by another disciple.

Now at that time the Mallas, the people of Kusinara, were assembled in the council hall discussing some public affair. Ananda went to the council hall and informed them of the World-Honored One's words. The people were all shocked and grieved, and their lamentation spread into the streets. Their sobbing was heard in the king's palace. The ruler was also shocked by the report brought back by his attendants and dispatched his son Asin to visit the World-Honored

One and ordered him to beseech the World-Honored One to pass away at the palace. Asin rushed to the place where the World-Honored One was and through Ananda conveyed the message of his father. The World-Honored One summoned Asin to appear before him. Asin presented himself, bowed, and said, "People are all submerged in the depth of delusion, and the Buddha alone can rescue them. Your passing away is much too early. O World-Honored One, may the World-Honored One, I pray, move to my father's palace and pass away there rather than in this remote forest. This is my father's wish." The World-Honored One then said, "O Asin, since this world is not real there is nothing in which we can truly delight. The wise invariably wish, therefore, to meet with the Buddha and listen to the Dharma. Basing themselves on their practice of faith, precepts, and charity, they listen and study extensively. Thereby they free themselves from defilements and enjoy prosperity through successive ages. Their renown will be heard afar, and they will eventually enter nirvana. O Asin, return to your father and in my place relay to him that this place has a special affinity to my past lives, and that I, therefore, wish to lay my body down in this part of the country." Asin promptly returned to the palace and conveyed to his father what was said by the World-Honored One. The king, in tears, issued a decree and together with his people rushed to the sala tree grove. It was close to dusk on the fifteenth day of the second month.

(7) Ananda surmised that if these people were allowed to pay their respects one by one, even if they were to do so all night, they would not be able to finish. Believing that it would be better to have them pay their respects together, he gathered the people in a group and said to the World-Honored One that all the Mallas of Kusinara were waiting to see the World-Honored One. The World-Honored One then addressed them warmly expressing his appreciation.

The king then stepped forward and bowing to the ground he said, "O World-Honored One, out of compassion, teach us the Dharma, so that we may surely abide by it." The World-Honored One then said, "People as well as gods are all bound to die. There is no one who is born that does not die. You need not grieve over my passing away. Now I shall go to an endless abode of purity. This abode is always quiescent and forever free of distress. There is no need to grieve for my sake; be mindful of goodness, refrain from evil, rectify past transgressions, practice good for the future, be diligent with virtues, associate with the wise, and when the occasion arises, ponder carefully and refrain from coarse behavior. Human life is difficult to attain. Be sympathetic toward all people. Honor those who are sagacious and pardon those who are foolish; practice charity to those who are destitute, help those who do not have enough, treat the people as if they were your children, govern them with righteousness, and share your wealth and joy with the masses. This is the only path to everlasting happiness. There are many evils in this world. You must be concerned with your own well-being. In this way not only will you be able to see me but also you will be able to free yourself from the net of suffering. The practice of the path depends on one's own mind; one does not necessarily need to see me. A sick man is relieved of his pain without seeing the doctor, as long as he takes the medicine prescribed in the correct manner. If, however, one does not follow my teaching, even if one were to see me, it would be in vain, for even if one were to sit next to me, one would be distant from me. If, however, one were to practice the path, even if one were distant from me, one would, indeed, be very close to me. All of you, control your minds; do not be negligent. There are many evils in the world, and we are surrounded by suffering. Everyone is agitated and no one is at peace. People are like flames flickering in the wind. May all of you enjoy long life and be free from sickness and suffering."

(8) Now at that time Rahula thought to himself, "What joy is there for me in watching the World-Honored One pass away?" He walked out of the forest and went to the north, but thinking of his father he was drowned in tears. He then changed his mind and thought, "When the dawn breaks, I may not be able to see my father, the World-Honored One, who teaches the Dharma surrounded by his disciples just as the full moon is surrounded by the stars." Thus Rahula returned to the grove and sat by the side of the World-Honored One.

The World-Honored One said to Rahula, "O Rahula, be not grieved. You have done whatever had to be done for your father. And I have done whatever had to be done for you. O Rahula, do not trouble your mind. Together with all of you and for the sake of all people, I have diligently and fearlessly endeavored not to create enmity nor to harm anyone. O Rahula, once I enter nirvana, I shall no longer be a father to anyone. It is the same with you. Once you enter nirvana, you will no longer be a son to anyone. You and I together will neither create disorder nor become hateful. O Rahula, the Buddha is eternal. You must renounce whatever is impermanent and earnestly seek emancipation. This is my instruction to you." Rahula and those who were present were all delighted and extolled the wondrous nature of the Buddha.

(9) At that time, in the town of Kusinara, there was an aged mendicant named Subhadda, who was of a different school of thought; he had reached the age of one hundred twenty; being erudite, he was well respected by the people. That evening when he awoke from his sleep, light filled the whole town, but in the house there was darkness, and he could see no one. Then informed that the World-Honored One would enter nirvana that night, Subhadda thought, "It is said in the texts of my religion that the appearance of a buddha is as rare as the blooming of the udumbara tree. Now I have a doubt lodged in my mind, which no one but Gotama can resolve. I must go at once to see him and ask for his teaching. And I must not be late." Thus he hurried to the place where the World-Honored One was.

Subhadda met Ananda outside the forest and said, "I have heard that Gotama is about to enter nirvana; I beseech you to take me to him so that I might ask for his teaching." Ananda replied, "O Subhadda, give up your wish, for the World-Honored One is nearing the end of his life. He must not be disturbed." Subhadda insisted. "O venerable Ananda, the appearance of a buddha is said to be as rare as the blooming of the udumbara tree. I beseech you, only once allow me to bow to Gotama." In this manner he repeated his wish three times, but Ananda did not accede to his request. At that time, however, the World-Honored One heard their exchange and called to Ananda, "O Ananda, you must not block the way of my last disciple. Send Subhadda to me. Subhadda's mind is upright, and his wisdom is clear. He is seeking to resolve his doubt. He did not come in order to argue with me." Following the Buddha's words, Ananda ushered Subhadda into the presence of the World-Honored One.

With overwhelming joy, Subhadda bowed and then said, "O Gotama, I have a question; please allow me to ask this question." With the Buddha's permission, he continued, "O Gotama, there are many scholars, each of whom equally claims that he is the true teacher; for instance, there are Purana Kassapa, Makkali Gosala, Sanjaya Belatthiputta, Ajita Kesakambala, Pakudha Kaccayana, Nigantha Nataputta and others. Each of these scholars claims that his doctrine is the right view and that the others hold wrong views; each calls his practices the causes of emancipation and claims that those of the other schools are the causes of delusion. In this way, they repulse each other and are constantly embroiled in disputations. O Gotama, in reality, which doctrine among them leads to emancipation and which one leads to delusion? Are these teachers cognizant of all the dharmas or are there any of which they are not cognizant? On this matter, please enlighten me."

(10) The World-Honored One instructed Subhadda as follows: "You must not question someone in such a cumbersome manner, for it is useless; but listen carefully. For your sake, I shall now expound the path. O Subhadda, the Eightfold Noble Path is the sole path of emancipation, and to teach otherwise is a cause of delusion. O Subhadda, these teachers harbor wrong views. With regard to deeds performed in this world and their effects on the next lives, some do not believe that one is bound to receive the effects of one's actions. Instead, they seek happiness by enshrining demons or by practicing divination. Some of them harbor evil thoughts that are rooted in desire and anger. They are guilty of offence using evil words; that is, they lie, fawn, slander, and flatter. They commit evil acts, such as indiscriminate killing, stealing, and sensual indulgence. They live evil lives; not seeking refuge in the path, they crave clothing and food. They are guilty of evil exertion, for they do not diligently refrain from evil nor do they perform virtuous acts. They entertain evil thoughts, for they always crave pleasure and abhor the wise. Their discipline of meditation is improper because they are entrapped by greed and do not perceive the value of emancipation. These doctrines, then, all represent wrong views and hence cannot lead to emancipation. O Subhadda, once while I was still at the royal palace, the whole world was led astray by these evil doctrines. I renounced my family, practiced the path, and when I was at the age of thirty-five I realized the Eightfold Noble Path under the Bodhi Tree. Following that, for forty-five years, I perceived and pondered over the way in the right manner. In the right manner I spoke, acted, lived my life, endeavored, thought, and meditated.

"O Subhadda, followers of some of those schools think that when karma is destroyed, the suffering of life also ends, but this is incorrect. When defilements are destroyed, then the suffering caused by karma will end. O Subhadda, if emancipation could be realized only by annihilating the causal conditions of karma, no saintly man would be able to realize emancipation. For the original karma of the immemorial past has no beginning and no end. Nevertheless, the Noble Path is able to stop such fearful karma that has no beginning nor end. If one could realize the path by means of ascetic practices, every animal would be able to realize the path. Therefore, first and foremost, you must know that one must overcome the mind, not the physical body. Here is the true cause of emancipation. O Subhadda, until now I have continued to speak and alone make my way in the three worlds. The Buddha is, indeed, a being of universal wisdom. If you still have any doubts, do not hesitate to question further; I shall not consider it a burden."

Having thus heard, Subhadda said, "O World-Honored One, I have understood it very well, and now I shall discard lowly paths and instead adopt the Noble Path. May the World-Honored One, I pray, out of his compassion, allow me to join the Sangha of his disciples." The World-Honored One then granted his wish.

(11) Subhadda at once shaved his head, donned the robes of a disciple, and with the utmost intentness contemplated the teaching. His mind became as pure as the image of the full moon. For the sake of Subhadda, the World-Honored One again taught the path of the Four Noble Truths. Thus Subhadda attained enlightenment.

At that moment, the World-Honored One said to Ananda, "Once, years ago, at the very outset, I converted Anna Kondanna, and today, at the end, I converted Subhadda. I have thus completed my task in saving whomever is to be saved. From now on, all of you mutually impart the teaching and instruct each other. O Ananda, Subhadda was once a follower of a different school, but because I perceived that the roots of merit had ripened in him, I allowed him to join the Sangha. After I am gone, when followers of other schools come to express their wish to join the order, you must have them undergo a trial period of four months, and grant their wish only upon judging the firmness of their will and observing the quality of their conduct."

Subhadda then said to the World-Honored One, "O World-Honored One, even if I were forced to study the teaching for a period of forty years before being allowed to join the order, I should eagerly accede to that precondition. A mere four months is insignificant indeed to me!" The World-Honored One said, "Well said, O Subhadda, but I know how firm your determination is, and that your speech has no falsity." Then Subhadda said, "O World-Honored One, I am unable to bear the thought of watching the World-Honored One pass away. May the World-Honored One permit me to die before the World-Honored One?" The World-Honored One gave him permission, and Subhadda then ended his life there.

6. The Last Instruction

(1) Now the night gradually deepened. The moon shone brightly; the stars glittered; the wind died down, and the nearby stream flowed quietly. The forest was silent, and not a voice could be heard. For the sake of his disciples, the World-Honored One again taught the essentials of the teaching. "O disciples, you must not think that upon my passing away the true Dharma, too, will forever come

to an end. Till now, I have continued to lay down the norms of conduct and teach the doctrine. From now on after I am gone, you must honor both, and like a man discovering light in the darkness or a poor man finding treasures, you must revere them. Realize that the precepts and the doctrine are your teachers, and safeguard them as if I were still in this world. O disciples, do not accumulate wealth, cultivate land, or practice divination. Control your physical movement, take food at the appointed times, and thus lead a pure life. You must not involve yourself with the affairs of this transient world. You must not carry out orders handed down by kings. You must not perform incantations, delight in wondrous elixirs, or become intimate with those of high rank. You must set your mind right and seek emancipation. Refrain from misleading the public by concealing your faults or performing extraordinary acts. As for your robes, food and drink, bedding, and medicine, you must know how much is sufficient and refrain from acquiring more than you need. These are the essentials for upholding the precepts. Precepts are the causal basis that correctly leads to emancipation, from which, in turn, concentration and insight are born. Therefore, rightly uphold the precepts and be not lax in your efforts. When the precepts are diligently observed, you create goodness, but when they are lacking, neither goodness nor merit is produced. Be aware, therefore, that the precepts are the abode of supreme peace and merit.

(2) "Once you abide by the precepts, you must control the five senses and not fall into the five desires. You must restrain yourselves just as a cowherd drives his cows with a stick so as to keep them from ruining other people's seedlings. If you allow the five senses free rein, not only the five desires but everything will become ungovernable. All will become like an unbridled, untamed wild horse that drags its owner and plunges him into a pitfall. The suffering from misfortunes incurred at a particular time comes to an end at some time, but the misfortunes incurred from the enemy known as the five senses are extremely grave, for down through the ages they assail that individual. Therefore, the wise restrain their senses and do not yield to them. They approach them as if they were the enemy and do not allow them free rein. Even if they sometimes allow them a measure of freedom, before long the wise will destroy them all.

"These five senses depend upon the mind as the master. Hence, you must by all means keep your mind well controlled. The mind is by nature far more dangerous than a poisonous snake, a ferocious animal, or a merciless bandit. Even a raging fire cannot compare to it. An unrestrained mind is like a man who runs and falls down while holding onto a vessel filled to the brim with honey; he does so by paying attention only to the honey and not at all to the deep pits in the ground. A mind is also like an elephant running amok without chains, or like a monkey scampering about on treetops, beyond control. Unlike them, you must restrain yourselves and not be negligent. If you allow your minds to run free, goodness will disappear. Should you, on the other hand, focus your minds on one object, there will not be anything you cannot attain. Therefore, you must actively restrain your mind.

(3) "O disciples, you must accept food as if you were taking medicine. Irrespective of whether it is of good quality or bad, you must not think of it as increasing or decreasing merits. For if it barely sustains your body, and satisfies the sense of hunger and thirst, that is all that is needed. Just as bees collect only the nectar of flowers, but leave their color and scent unharmed, when you receive alms, if they barely satisfy your suffering, that is sufficient. Refrain from spoiling the goodness of the alms-giver by desiring even more or from exhausting the alms-giver's capacity to give, just as the wise man drives his oxen while judging the limits of their strength.

"Lose no time in practicing goodness during the day; neither should you relax this thought whether it is early or late in the evening. By midnight, read the Sutras and then go to rest; but you must not waste away your life in idle sleeping. The fire of impermanence is constantly burning all worlds. Being mindful of this, seek your own salvation. Beware, O disciples, of enemies such as defilements that constantly look for occasions to attack you. How can anyone indulge himself by sleeping and not being on guard? The poisonous snake of defilement sleeps in your mind, like a viper sleeping in your bedroom. At all costs remove the poisonous snake by resorting to the hook of the precepts. Once it is out of the room, you may sleep in peace, but anyone who sleeps where the poisonous snake has not been removed is, indeed, a man without shame. The clothing of shame, inner and outer, is unsurpassed among all adornments. The sense of shame is like an iron hook; it restrains those actions that deviate from the ethical path. Therefore, know shame and do not allow your mind to deviate even for a short while. If anyone should distance himself from the sense of shame, he is bound to lose all of his merits. Good accrues to those who know shame; whereas those who are oblivious of shame are one with the birds and the beasts.

(4) "Even if people hack your body into pieces, you must restrain your mind and never arouse a sense of anger or hate against them. Always watch your words and do not speak ill of them. For evil thoughts and speech harm yourselves rather than others. If you let anger have its way, you will obstruct yourselves in the practice of the path and lose the benefit of your previous merits. The merit of forbearance exceeds the merit derived from the practice of the precepts or of ascetic discipline. We call a man who practices forbearance a great man of strength. Unless one is able to endure the poison of verbal abuses willingly, one cannot be described as one who has entered the path or one who has insight. Anger is the enemy of virtue. It destroys goodness and damages the good name of virtuous people. People do not delight in associating with angry people. Verily, a mind afflicted with anger is more terrifying than a raging fire. Therefore, venerate virtue, do not harbor anger, always be on guard, and refrain from creating openings through which anger might gain entrance. Among enemies that plunder virtues, there is none that is more fearful than anger. It is not good for those who practice the path to harbor anger. This cannot be allowed; like thunder and lightning on a clear day, it is not to be found in the good.

"O disciples, stroke your own heads and you will be reminded that you have shaved off your hair and discarded your hair ornaments; you wear plain garments, and you live on alms received in your bowl. If you feel self-conceit again, you must promptly annihilate it. Even for lay householders is it not good to increase self-conceit, so how much worse it is for you who have renounced the world to practice the path, humbled yourselves for the sake of emancipation, and received alms.

(5) "O disciples, the mind of sycophancy strays from the path. You must rectify such a mind. Verily, flattery is a form of deceiving, which must not be found in anyone who enters the path. Therefore, you should keep your minds direct and honest and, being mindful only of the Dharma, commit no deception.

"O disciples, those beset with many desires are likely to seek many things and hence experience more suffering. Those who have few desires do not seek anything and hence experience little suffering. Anyone who has little desire need not gain the minds of others through flattery, nor is he attracted to those desires of the eyes and ears. His mind is peaceful and free of worry; and even when something serious occurs, he retains his composure and is always fulfilled. Nirvana exists in this state of mind.

"O disciples, if you desire to be free from suffering, you ought to know contentment. The Dharma in which one knows contentment is the abode of wealth, prosperity, and security. Whosoever knows contentment enjoys peace even as he sleeps on the ground, whereas whosoever knows no contentment is not satisfied with a heavenly abode. Whosoever knows contentment is rich even though he is poor, whereas whosoever knows no contentment is poor even though he is prosperous, for he is constantly bound by the five desires.

"If you seek the bliss of quiescence, you must necessarily stay away from noisy places and abide in tranquil ones. Whosoever abides in a tranquil place is a person whom gods revere. Therefore, stay away from the crowd and abide in a solitary and quiet place and meditate on how to annihilate the root of suffering. On the other hand, whoever wishes to be among a large number of people will no doubt experience all sorts of suffering. When a large flock of birds congregates in a tree, no matter how large the tree, it will become diseased and wither away. The world's fetters will cause you to sink into a multitude of sufferings. The world's fetters will plunge you into a predicament from which you will not be able to free yourself, like an aging elephant that is mired in mud and is unable to extricate himself.

(6) "There is no difficulty in any undertaking if you exert yourselves diligently. Even a trickle of water can make a groove in a rock by its incessant flow. Therefore, be diligent at all times. In starting a fire with sticks, if one stops rubbing the sticks before it catches fire, one cannot make the fire after all; it is the same with the man who seeks the path, if his mind is always negligent.

"You must seek right mindfulness. Right mindfulness is your good friend, an excellent protector, for as long as you are rightly engaged in mindfulness, no enemy such as defilements can infiltrate your mind. You must, therefore, maintain right mindfulness. If you lose it, you will lose a variety of merits. If your mindfulness is firm, you will be like someone entering a battlefield well protected by armor; you will have no fear even if you dash into the enemy consisting of the five desires, nor will you be harmed by them in any way.

"O disciples, when the mind is controlled, the mind is in the state of concentration. When it is in a state of concentration, you will see the nature of the origination and cessation of the world of phenomena. Therefore, you must practice meditation at all times. If you attain concentration, the mind will not disperse. Just as one who needs water for irrigation takes good care of the dykes, all of you must take good care of the discipline of meditation so as not to let the water of insight leak away.

"O disciples, whoever possesses insight is free from greed. Always reflect upon this and take heed not to lose this insight. In this way, you will be able to realize emancipation in accordance with the Dharma. If, however, you do not retain this insight, you will be neither a man of the path nor a man of the laity; you will be beyond description. True insight is a sturdy ship that crosses the ocean of birth, old age, sickness, and death; it is the great light that shines brightly in the darkness of ignorance; it is the supreme medicine that cures all illnesses; it is the ax that cuts down the tree of defilements. Therefore, you must nourish yourselves with the insight attained through listening, thinking, and practicing. Insofar as your insight is clear, even if your eye is of the flesh, you are regarded as a man of penetrating insight.

"O disciples, if you engage in meaningless arguments, your minds will become agitated. If this happens, then even though you have left home to attain emancipation you will not succeed. Therefore, you must promptly forsake meaningless arguments and realize the state of bliss in which all the defilements are brought to quiescence.

(7) "You must always single-mindedly exert yourselves and forsake negligence as though you were trying to escape from your enemy. I attained enlightenment through not being negligent. Immeasurable goodness arises from not being negligent. You must diligently maintain the practice of not being negligent. Whether you are in the hills, in a marsh, under the shade of trees, or in a quiet room, you must always be mindful of the Dharma that you have received; you must not be forgetful, and you must diligently practice the Dharma. If you die in vain, you are bound to regret it. I have expounded the teaching like a skillful doctor who diagnoses an illness and prescribes medicine. When the patient is aware of this and yet does not take the medicine, it is not the fault of the doctor. Again, I have been like a skillful guide who shows the people the way to the good path. If travellers hear the guide but do not follow him, it is not the fault of the guide.

"If you still have some doubts as to the Four Noble Truths, promptly question me in order to resolve them. Do not leave your doubts unresolved."

(8) The World-Honored One said this three times. There was not a single person in the whole assembly of the disciples who raised a question. Anuruddha understood the mind of the disciples and said to the World-Honored One, "O World-Honored One, even if one were able to heat the moon or cool the sun,

one could not change the path of the Buddha. The suffering expounded by the Buddha is truly suffering and cannot be regarded as happiness. The cause of suffering is truly the cause and there can be no other cause of suffering. If suffering ceases to be, it is because its cause ceases to be. Thus, if the cause has ceased to be, the effect also ceases to be. The path that leads to the cessation of suffering is indeed the true path and there is no other path. O World-Honored One, all of us gathered here have no doubts whatsoever regarding the Four Noble Truths. However, those of us who have not yet realized enlightenment will no doubt grieve upon witnessing the passing away of the World-Honored One. I believe that those who have entered the path for the first time will hear the teaching and be saved; it will be like men seeing a path by the light shed by a flash of lightning. Those who have already attained enlightenment and have crossed over suffering will wonder why the World-Honored One passes away so swiftly."

After Anuruddha thus spoke to the World-Honored One, the World-Honored one with great compassion for his disciples said, "Be not grieved, all of you. Even if I stay in this world for the duration of a kalpa, it is in the nature of things that those who meet each other are necessarily separated; there is no exception.

"The Dharma through which you bring benefit to yourselves as well as to others is readily available to you. Even if I remained in life longer, there would be no difference. I have rescued whomever was to be rescued, whether he were a heavenly or a human being; and as for those who have not been yet rescued, I have laid down the conditions for their salvation.

"From now on, if you disciples discuss this among yourselves and practice accordingly, it will mean the continuous and imperishable existence of the Dharmakaya of the Buddha.

"One must understand without fail the impermanence of the world. It is in the nature of things that those who meet are necessarily separated. There is no need of grief, for this is the nature of this world. Always seek emancipation with diligence, destroy the darkness of ignorance with the light of insight, and promptly reach the abode where there is no separation.

"This world is verily perilous and fragile, and there is nothing indestructible in it. My passing away is like the removal of a foul sickness. This evil should be discarded. By name we call it the human body. It is immersed in the ocean of birth, old age, sickness, and death. How can the man of insight not be delighted in removing his body, when it is just like slaughtering an enemy?

"All of you, exert yourselves single-mindedly and quickly escape from the fiery pitfall of delusion. Whatever is in this world will decay without exception.

"Be silent, all of you. Speak no more. The time has come; I now enter nirvana. This is my last word."

(9) Thus completing his teaching, the World-Honored One quietly entered meditation and his body moved no more. Then Ananda asked Anuruddha, "O venerable Anuruddha, has the World-Honored One already entered nirvana?" "Nay, Ananda, he has not," answered Anuruddha. By then, the World-Honored One had passed through various states of meditation and had greeted his mother Maya who had quietly come down from heaven. Finally he entered nirvana.

Anuruddha stated that the World-Honored One had gone to nirvana, and Ananda conveyed this to the whole assembly of disciples.

At that moment, the earth trembled, thunder from heaven burst forth, and the blossoms of the sala trees showered down like rain.

7. The Rising Smoke

(1) The disciples could not bear their grief; some pounded their chests and wept, and some fell to the ground mourning in anguish. Everyone was saddened at the thought, "Why so soon has the Eye of the World closed? From today who is going to guide all of us disciples? On whom are we, the disciples, to rely? There are three unhappy destinies that always open up in front of us, but the gate of emancipation is totally closed to us." Anuruddha then exhorted them, "Enough, my brethren, be not grieved nor lament. Has not the World-Honored One, moments ago, taught us that all things are equally impermanent in both their nature and their form?"

(2) The gods in the heavens sang, "By the vow made many ages ago, the World-Honored One was born into this world for our sake, to guide people and gods toward the goal of nirvana. The compassion of the Buddha, like that of a mother, provided milk to all and nurtured them. Now he has gone to nirvana, leaving them to feel that they have lost their refuge. It is a pity that the nectar of the Dharma does not rain down, and that the good seedlings of people are about to decay. May the treasure of the Dharma, and the light of the relics of the Buddha, illumine our path and help us escape from delusion."

Anuruddha knelt down before the World-Honored One and dedicated the following verses to him:

> The foremost among the Buddhas has given us the Dharma milk
> and nourished the Dharma body inherent in us.
> He has now entered nirvana before our Dharma bodies are realized.
> By whom will we who are immersed in suffering and anguish be led?
> The World-Honored One, having undergone much suffering for our
> sake throughout innumerable kalpas, finally realized the supreme
> enlightenment;
> brief has his abiding in this world been, and now he has gone on to
> nirvana forever.
> While we remain in darkness, Maras are taking off their armor in
> delight.
> May the light of the great compassion emanating from the holy relics
> embrace us all,
> and may the Dharma Treasure ever continue to flow and never cease to be.

In tears Ananda dedicated this verse:

> Fortunate was I to be born in the same Sakya clan as the World-Honored
> One;
> fortunate was I to have accompanied the World-Honored One for more
> than two decades.
> Now the World-Honored One has gone to the great nirvana, leaving us
> behind.
> Sad am I, groping my way in the long night of ignorance.

I have not yet disentangled myself from the mesh of delusion, nor have I departed from the shell of ignorance.

Even before breaking the shell with the beak of his insight,
the World-Honored One is now gone, leaving it unbroken.

I am indeed like a newborn babe who has lost its mother and will soon die.

Now I ask the forgiveness of the World-Honored One for my being neglectful and for not having fully attended him as he wished for more than twenty years.

May the World-Honored One, with his great compassion, pour the nectar of his Dharma over me and help me to realize ultimate peace.

May I, until the end of all the worlds to come, be able to see the World-Honored One.

May his great compassion embrace all the world.

Alas, my heart choked, how can I fully express the great benefit the World-Honored One has bestowed upon us?

(3) All those gathered, equally sorrowful in grief, asked Ananda, "O Ananda, allow us to approach and see the World-Honored One, for it will not be possible to be blessed by the appearance of the Buddha again in this world." Ananda thought, "When the World-Honored One was in this world, the number of women who could approach him was limited. Therefore, it is now appropriate for them to pay their respects to the World-Honored One." Thus, he let not only many nuns but also laywomen pay homage to the World-Honored One. They bowed in tears and offered various incenses and flowers.

Among them was a woman nearly one hundred years old and impoverished, who was saddened that she had nothing to offer and cried at the feet of the World-Honored One, wishing, "May I in my next life, wherever I may be born, always be able to worship the Buddha." And her tears accidentally fell on the World-Honored One's feet and moistened them. When all the women withdrew, Ananda allowed other people, too, to pay their respects. They made their offerings and withdrew in grief. Anuruddha and other disciples attended the World-Honored One on both sides and spent the rest of the night discoursing on the Dharma till the morning.

(4) Then Anuruddha said to Ananda, "Go now, O Ananda, into Kusinara and inform the Mallas of Kusinara that the World-Honored One has passed away." Ananda assented and went into the town of Kusinara and informed the Mallas that the World-Honored One had passed away. In sorrow, they all rushed to the sala grove, built a palanquin, laid his remains on it, perfumed it with incense, bedecked it with flowers, and played music that extolled the virtue of the World-Honored One. After the first day was over, the Mallas said to Ananda, "Now the Buddha has entered nirvana. We shall never again have the opportunity to make an offering. Therefore, please allow us to enshrine the World-Honored One's remains for seven days and seven nights, so as to let as many people as possible honor, to their heart's content, the World-Honored One with their offerings and thereby allow all of them to secure their peace during the long night to come." Ananda consulted with Anuruddha on the matter. Anuruddha replied that their wish should be granted. Thus, Ananda conveyed this to the Mallas, who, with much delight, honored the World-Honored One for the following seven days with

abundant offerings. When the seven days were over, according to the instruction Ananda received from the World-Honored One, the Malla youths wrapped the remains with fresh cotton, placed the body into a coffin decorated with gold, poured various kinds of beautiful flowers and perfumes into it, enshrined it on the palanquin, and again honored it with music and songs.

The Mallas said to each other, "The limit of seven days has come, and now the remains must be burnt." They cleansed the streets, sprinkled water over them, and then lifted the palanquin and carried it into the town. Not only the disciples but also the king and the people all followed the procession with banners and canopies. The gods extolled the virtue of the World-Honored One from the skies; in harmony with this, people on earth sang songs of sorrow.

Now there was a daughter of the Mallas called Roja, who always upheld her faith in the path. When the holy palanquin halted for a moment in town, she lifted a golden floral wreath the size of a cartwheel and offered it to the palanquin. Also there was a woman called Mallika. She held up a beautiful piece of cloth and raised her voice, saying, "Fortunate are the Malla people, who have attained great merit. Because the World-Honored One entered nirvana at this place, the Mallas have been able to make offerings to the World-Honored One."

(5) Then the Mallas carried the palanquin, went out of the town, silently crossed the river Hirannavati, and arrived at their shrine, Makutabandhana, and set the palanquin in the main hall. They piled in the courtyard sandalwood and other scented woods, over which they placed the coffin, and they poured scented oil over it. Many disciples and lay believers wept aloud, and the state minister of the Mallas, Roja by name, held a large torch and tried to set fire to it but was unable to do so. Three times he tried to kindle it but failed. The people wondered about it and asked Anuruddha, who answered, "This wondrous event may mean that the World-Honored One is waiting for the arrival of Maha-Kassapa, who is on the way here to pay his final tribute to the World-Honored One. Because of this, I surmise, the World-Honored One is preventing the kindling."

(6) Before the World-Honored One passed away, Maha-Kassapa was teaching the Dharma in the country of Takhagiri; but informed of the World-Honored One's passing away, he was hurrying with a company of five hundred brethren. After having passed through the city of Pava, he approached the town of Kusinara. Around noon he was very tired because of the severe heat and was resting under the shade of a roadside tree, while the company of his brethren were also resting with him and were engaged in Dharma discourse.

At that time, an Ajivaka happened to pass by with a cane in hand and a lotus flower over his head. Kassapa asked him where he came from. The Ajivaka replied that he came from the town of Kusinara. Kassapa asked if he knew anything about his master. The Ajivaka said, "I know that Gotama passed away seven days ago under twin sala trees in the sala grove outside the town of Kusinara, and that the townsmen have been honoring him with offerings. I was given this flower at that place."

Hearing this the disciples fell onto the ground and wept in grief. Kassapa said to them, "Do not lament. All is impermanent. Even the Buddha must pass away; no one can escape. There is no peace in the world of delusion; nirvana alone is the ultimate happiness. You must diligently exert yourselves and free yourselves from the suffering of the world."

There was a disciple called Subhadda who joined the path in his old age and whose mind was not very bright. Once, when the World-Honored One visited Atuma, the people there honored him with offerings. Subhadda tried to boast by making an especially resplendent offering. Foreseeing his intention, the World-Honored One did not accept his offering. Because of this, Subhadda secretly harbored enmity against the World-Honored One. At this time, observing other disciples in grief, he said, "O Brethren, when the World-Honored One was alive, he always admonished us, saying, 'This you may do, that you may not,' so that we could not do whatever we wished to. Since he is gone now, we can do whatever we like. This is much better." Having heard this, Maha-Kassapa was pained. "Only seven days have passed since the World-Honored One's demise, and this man speaks such words. The flower of the true Dharma will soon be scattered by this kind of man, like unstrung flowers that are easily blown away by the wind. When I accompanied the World-Honored One on the last occasion, he exchanged robes with me and allowed me to wear his; he then said to me, 'O Kassapa, after I am gone, transmit the true Dharma that I taught and retain its purity.' Since I have been entrusted, I must call for a gathering of the true disciples and with them decide the true meaning of the Dharma. This is my supreme task." Thereupon he at once expelled Subhadda from the order. (Later, Subhadda repented his behavior and was reaccepted into the order.)

(7) Then Maha-Kassapa urged his brethren, saying, "Get yours robes and bowls ready; we must hurry to the shrine of Makutabandhana and worship the World-Honored One." All the disciples responded to his word, and rushing and crying they reached the Makutabandhana, the shrine of Kusinara.

Upon their arrival, Maha-Kassapa saw the coffin already placed over the pile of wood and could hardly bear his sorrow; yet he reverentially circumambulated the pile thrice in honor of the World-Honored One. At that moment, fire suddenly flared up and burned the coffin, leaving the relics alone. After a while there was rain, which washed the ground. Thus the people grieved more than at the time when the World-Honored One passed away.

The Mallas collected the relics and put them into a golden urn, returned to the town, and placed the urn in the newly built shrine, and they honored the relics by burning incense and offering flowers. After all this was done, the Mallas returned home.

(8) The news that the World-Honored One had passed away spread to all the neighboring countries. Ajatasattu, the king of Magadha, sent a messenger to Kusinara, who said on his behalf, "The World-Honored One was my teacher. May I receive a portion of his relics?" The Sakyas of Kapilavattu also sent a messenger for a portion of the relics, saying, "The World-Honored One was the pride of our clan. May we receive a portion of his relics?" The Bulis of Allakappa, the Koliyas of Ramagama, the brahmins of Vethadipa, the Licchavis of Vesali, and the Mallas of Pava also requested portions of the relics. The Mallas of

Kusinara replied, "The World-Honored One passed away in our city, and we are planning to honor the World-Honored One with our offerings. We shall not give away any part of the relics of the World-Honored One." The messengers of the seven countries were angered and said, "We have made our requests respectfully. If you refuse our requests, then we shall obtain the relics even by the use of force." But the Mallas replied, "If you attempt to do so, we shall respond with force. We have no fear of you."

At that time, there was a brahmin named Dona who was very wise and had faith in the World-Honored One and his path. Observing the situation, he said to the Mallas, "If you engage in battle, you as well as they will be hurt. When the Buddha was still in this world, he taught us to esteem others, and you were directly taught from the World-Honored One to memorize the doctrine and uphold the practices. How can you fight for the remains of the World-Honored One and injure others? If you really intend to honor the Buddha with offerings, you must follow his teaching and practice the virtue of forbearance, how much more so since you as well as they are equally followers of the same Dharma. All his followers must make offerings to the World-Honored One with a common purpose. It is not simply a grave transgression to be attached to treasures; is it not a more grave transgression still to be miserly about the Dharma? Moreover, among the many practices of charity, the offering of the Dharma is the highest. You must not be miserly about sharing the remains; apportion out the remains in an agreeable manner. It is only in this way that your actions will be in accordance with the World-Honored One's teaching, and that you will be able to acquire your well-being." The Mallas understood this advice, put down their arms, and withdrew.

Dona then met with the messengers of the other countries and asked, "For what purpose are you getting ready for war?" They replied, "We have come here to receive a portion of the remains of the World-Honored One." Dona said, "The people of this city are already at peace with you. Bring your treasure jars, and I shall divide the remains." They were all delighted with his offer.

(9) Then Dona divided the relics into eight portions for the people of Kusinara and the seven other countries, and for himself he requested the golden urn that had held the relics of the World-Honored One. And the people of Pipphalivana requested the amber. The Mallas of Kusinara happily agreed with these requests.

The people from the different countries returned home delightedly and honored the remains by building stupas. Thus ten shrines were built, namely, the one in Kusinara, which enshrined the first portion; the one in Pava, which enshrined the second portion; the one in Allakappa, which enshrined the third portion; the one in Ramagama, which enshrined the fourth portion; the one in Vethadipa, which enshrined the fifth portion; the one in Kapilavatthu, which enshrined the sixth portion; the one in Vesali, which enshrined the seventh portion; the one in Magadha, which enshrined the eighth portion; the one of Dona, which enshrined the golden vase; and the one in Pipphalivana, which enshrined the amber.

8. Sequel to the Buddha's Demise

(1) Soon after the World-Honored One passed away, Ananda returned to Rajagaha and stayed in the Bamboo Grove Monastery, of which he had fond memories. Around that time, Ajatasattu, the king of Magadha, was rebuilding the fortresses of the city in preparation for war with King Pajjota. One morning, before setting out for alms begging, Ananda approached the workshop of Gopaka Moggallana, a brahmin. Gopaka prepared a seat for Ananda and said, "O Venerable Ananda, is there someone who is equal to the World-Honored One in always maintaining the Dharma through which the World-Honored One, Gotama, became the Buddha?"

"O brahmin, there is none such. For the World-Honored One was the one who brought into existence the path that had not been in existence before, who made known the path that had not been known, who was the teacher of the path, the knower of the path, and the most skilled in the path; whereas the disciples are merely the ones to be guided on the path and who follow it."

While both were talking, Vassakara, the prime minister of Magadha, came, listened to their conversation, and addressed Ananda, "O Venerable Ananda, is there someone who has been designated by the World-Honored One as the person upon whom the Sangha members may rely?" "Nay, there is no one," replied Ananda. "Then, is there someone whom the members of the Sangha decided to rely upon after the World-Honored One had passed away?" asked Vassakara. "Nay, there is no one," replied Ananda. "O Venerable Ananda, how then can the Sangha members be united in harmony without anyone to rely upon?" "O brahmin, I do not mean that there is not anything to rely on, for we have the Dharma to rely upon. O brahmin, the World-Honored One was the knower, the seer, the arhat, and the realizer of perfect enlightenment; and therefore, he set the course for the members of the Sangha. At the uposatha gathering, all of us, those in one area, gather together to repent and confess, and if there are any transgressions, due punishment is imposed in accordance with the rules."

(2) "Then it is not the members who impose punishment but the law that sanctions punishment. O Venerable Ananda, is there someone in the Sangha whom all of you can respect?" Vassakara asked. "There are some, O brahmin," replied Ananda, "for instance, we respect those who are endowed with the ten delightful achievements: to uphold the precepts rightly; to listen widely and memorize correctly whatever is learned; to know contentment; to enter and leave the various states of meditation at will; to acquire supernatural powers; to acquire the divine faculty of hearing; to acquire the faculty of knowing the minds of others; to acquire the faculty of knowing future destinies; to acquire the divine eye; and to know the state in which all the defilements are destroyed."

At that moment, the prime minister Vassakara said to the general Upananda, "These members of the Sangha revere those who are truly worthy of reverence." Then he asked Ananda, "O Venerable Ananda, where are you staying?" and upon hearing that he was staying at the Bamboo Grove Monastery, Vassakara said, "Since the monastery is well secluded from the villages and is free from any disturbing noises, it is an ideal place for quiet living." "O brahmin," responded Ananda, "it is precisely as you say. Because of your protection as well as Gopaka's, it has become all the more a suitable abode blessed with tranquillity." Vassakara said, "O Ananda, the Bamboo Grove is verily the place of tranquillity, and all of you, venerable ones, enjoy the practice of meditation. Once when I visited the World-Honored One Gotama at the hall of the Great Forest Monastery in Vesali, the World-Honored One spoke to me of different kinds of meditation. The World-Honored One was one who praised different kinds of meditation."

"O brahmin," Ananda said, "the World-Honored One did not praise every type of meditation; he did not praise the kinds that accompany greed, anger, sleepiness, regret, or doubt, but only the four kinds of meditation that one enters when freed from desire and evil thought." Vassakara replied, "O Venerable Ananda, you are right. The World-Honored One criticized the kinds of meditations that are to be criticized and praised those that are to be praised. O Venerable Ananda, we shall now take leave of you."

Vassakara, the prime minister of Magadha, bade farewell and departed. Gopaka then said to Ananda, "O Venerable Ananda, you have not yet answered my question." Ananda replied, "O brahmin, I have already answered that there is no one who is comparable to the World-Honored One, have I not? For we, his disciples, are the followers of his path and are guided by his path."

(3) Once, when Maha-Kaccana was travelling in the forest called Gundavana in the country of Madhura, the king of Madhura, who was a son of the king of Avanti, heard of the high reputation of Kaccana, and went to the forest, riding in his beautiful, well-decorated carriage. Upon meeting Kaccana, he said, "O Venerable Kaccana, the people of the brahmin caste claim that the brahmin class is the highest while all the rest are inferior. They claim that the class of brahmins is pure, because their ancestors were born from the mouth of the god Brahma, and hence they are his descendants. What do you think about their claim?"

"O great king, those words are nothing but sound; they are mere vibrations without any substance. O great king, what do you think; if a kshatriya, in possession of gold, silver, and other treasures, wishes to employ members of other classes, such as the brahmin, vaisya, and sudra, and wishes them to wake up early in the morning, go to bed late at night, and work at all kinds of things, can he do it?" "O Venerable, of course he can." Kaccana continued, "O great king, next, if a brahmin in possession of gold, silver, and other treasures, in like manner, wishes to do the same by employing members of the other three classes, can he do it?" The king answered, "Of course, he can, and it is the same with the vaisya and sudra members."

"O great king, from this it is evident that the four classes are equal and that there are no differences among them. Hence a statement to the effect that the brahmin class is superior is an empty sound. Next, suppose a man from the kshatriya class committed an act of killing, stealing, adultery, deception, slandering, double talk, or sycophancy, or harbored greed, anger, or evil views. O great king, will such a man then fall into hell after his death?" "Of course;

I have heard from ascetics that such is the case, and I myself believe so," answered the king. Kaccana asked, "Then what do you think, O great king, is it the case with a brahmin, a vaisya or a sudra?" The king answered, "Needless to say, it is the same for anyone."

(4) "O great king," asked Kaccana again, "likewise, if anyone from any of the four classes refrains from killing, refrains from stealing, refrains from adultery, refrains from deception, refrains from slandering, refrains from double talk, refrains from sycophancy, and also departs from greed and from anger and holds right views, will he be born in the heavenly world? Again, if anyone from any of the four classes becomes a robber, a highwayman, or a bandit, O great king, regardless of the class to which he belongs, you will surely punish such a man in accordance with the law. O great king, likewise, if anyone from any of the four classes renounces his lay life, practices purity, keeps moral precepts, and thereby becomes a good man, O great king, will you respect such a man?" The king said, "O Venerable, you are right, I shall respect him, honor him, prepare a seat for him, and make offerings to him." Kaccana said, "O great king, for this reason it is evident that the four classes are equal and that there is no difference whatsoever between them."

Thus instructed, the king of Madhura was greatly impressed and said to Kaccana, "O Venerable One, it is indeed excellent. You have beautifully explained the Dharma, uncovering what was covered, showing the way to someone who had lost his way, and bringing light into the darkness so as to let those who have eyes see things as they are. I shall pledge to take my refuge in the Venerable One, the Dharma, and the Sangha, and to become a lay believer as long as I live."

"O great king, you must not take refuge in me, but in the World-Honored One in whom I take my own refuge," replied Kaccana. Then the king asked, "O Venerable One, where is the World-Honored One now?" "O great king," replied Kaccana, "the World-Honored One is hidden away in the cloud of nirvana." The king further said, "O Venerable One, if the World-Honored One were alive, I would visit him no matter how distant it might be, in order to worship him. O Venerable One, I shall take refuge in the World-Honored One who has entered nirvana, the Dharma, and the Sangha. O Venerable One, may you allow me to become a follower."

(5) Kumara-Kassapa, accompanied by five hundred disciples, arrived at the town of Setavya in Kosala and dwelt at the simsapa tree grove located at the north edge of the town. This town was ruled by the governor Payasi as the vassal of the king of Kosala. Payasi followed the wrong view that there is no afterlife, no rebirth, and no effect of good or evil action.

Since the townsmen of Setavya heard of the good name of this samana, renowned as a wise scholar and an excellent orator, they proceeded to the north like a herd and approached the grove of simsapa trees. At that time Payasi was resting in the upper floor of his dwelling; upon viewing all the townsmen moving toward the north, he called his guards and questioned them. After receiving their report, Payasi said, "O guards, I shall also go to the grove along with the townsmen, for Kumara-Kassapa will surely try to convince these ignorant people that there is another world, rebirth, and rewards for good and evil actions."

Thus Payasi, along with the people of Setavya, visited Kumara-Kassapa, and after greeting him said, "O Venerable Kassapa, I hold the view that there is no other world, nor rebirth, nor fruit of good or evil action."

"O governor, I have never seen nor heard of anyone before who entertains such a view, so why, may I ask, do you set forth such a view? Whatever the reason might be, I shall ask you a few questions; please answer as you see fit. O governor, is the moon or sun in this world or in another world, or are they people or gods?" Payasi replied, "O Venerable, both belong to the other world, and both are gods."

(6) "O governor," asked Kumara-Kassapa, "then because of this can I not say that there exists another world, that there is rebirth, and that there is reward for good and evil action?" Payasi then replied, "No, Venerable One, I am not able to agree to what you have just said."

"O governor," Kumara-Kassapa continued, "then, what reason do you have to support your view?" Payasi replied, "O Venerable One, among my relatives and friends, there are many who committed acts of killing, stealing, sexual transgression, deception, flattering, slandering, and double talk, and harbored greed, anger, and wrong views. When they were about to die I asked them at their deathbeds, 'According to those who have renounced lay life, anyone who has committed such evil acts will after death fall into hell. If you fall into hell, please, let me know that there is another world, that there is rebirth, and that there is retribution for good or evil action. As I trust you, I shall believe whatever you tell me.' In this way I have talked to a number of people, but none of them, though they agreed to do so, came to report to me or sent a messenger. Again, I have also talked to those who did not commit any of these ten evil actions, requesting them to report to me if they were reborn in the heavenly world. They, too, have sent me no reply as yet. Therefore, I believe that my view is correct."

"O governor," Kumara-Kassapa said, "Suppose, when a thief is caught and is about to be beheaded at the execution ground south of the city, he asks, 'Please wait, for I have something to report to my relatives. So please wait till I come back.' Will his request be granted?" Payasi said, "Nay, it will not." Then Kassapa continued, "O governor, in like manner, when someone falls into hell, no matter how hard he pleads to the guards of hell by saying, 'Wait, please, I have something to report to my relatives in the human world; wait till I come back from visiting that world,' he will never be allowed to do so. As for someone who is reborn in the heavenly world, suppose a man is stuck in a tub of foul excrement. You pull that man out, brush him off with a bamboo broom, put powder on him to rub off the filth, anoint him with oil, and rub him with scented powder; you have him bathe a number of times, fix his hair, dress him in elegant robes, adorn him with a floral wreath, sprinkle perfume on him, lead him to the upper floors, and entertain him with music. O governor, would this man wish to fall back into the tub of excrement again?" Payasi replied, "O Venerable One, he would not. There is no reason for him to want to go back to a hateful, unclean place that exudes a foul odor."

(7) "O governor," said Kumara-Kassapa, "it is just the same with someone reborn in the heavenly world. The human world is unclean, filled with an odor that they say drives gods away for a distance of over two hundred miles. The human world is a detestable, unpleasant place, so there is no reason for someone who has departed from the human world and has entered heaven to want to return to the human world once again. O governor, the blind see no color like black or white or blue or yellow, nor is there a star or a moon or a sun, and yet it is not correct to say that there is neither black nor white, neither blue nor yellow, neither star nor moon nor sun. Just because human eyes cannot see the heavenly world, it is not correct to deny the existence of such a world."

"O Venerable," insisted Payasi, "I have known that even some ascetics, with their excellent practice of the precepts, wish to live and dislike death, yearn for pleasure and hate suffering. If one knows for certain that his life after death will be fortunate and happy, why will he not try to take his life by drinking poison or thrusting a sword into his body?"

"O governor, suppose a brahmin had two wives; one of them had a son of thirteen or fourteen years of age; the other wife was pregnant. When the brahmin died, the young son went to the other wife and told her that whatever was in the house belonged to him. The woman insisted that if the child in her body were a boy, a part of the wealth would belong to him, and if the child were a girl, she would be in his service. As the woman was pressed repeatedly as to the ownership of the wealth, she finally cut open her abdomen in order to examine whether her child was a boy or a girl. If you seek to find out without resorting to correct methods, you must suffer misfortune and ruin. Everything requires time for maturation. The ascetics who are endowed with excellent virtues live and wait for the time of maturation; in the meantime, they are exerting themselves in the accumulation of merits thus contributing to the happiness and the benefit of the human world."

"O Venerable One," said Payasi, "I often killed criminals and tried to see how their souls left their body, but I failed to see anything. By slicing their bodies into pieces I sought to see where their souls abided, but I failed here also. This is another reason why I insist on my view."

"O governor," Kumara-Kassapa continued, "no matter how much you crush a conch shell, you cannot find the source of its sound, nor can you find the source of fire in the flint and steel no matter how you dissect them into pieces. If, however, you seek for the sound of the conch shell in the right manner it makes wondrous tones; so do the fire-making tools produce fire. O governor, you are trying wrong methods in seeking another world, and have developed wrong views. You must forsake your erroneous views so as not to invite the long night of misfortune and distress."

Thus receiving kind instructions from Kumara-Kassapa, Payasi began to understand the meaning of the teaching, but he was still somewhat attached to his wrong views. Therefore Kassapa continued to expound the right views by resorting to numerous metaphors and eventually brought Payasi to the right views. After receiving this guidance, Payasi became a virtuous man who liked to make offerings.

(8) Around that time, Vakkali was staying in the Bamboo Grove Monastery in Rajagaha. One of his friends from his days as a layman, the naked Kassapa, visited him and after greeting him sat to one side. He asked, "O Vakkali, how long has it been since you left the lay life?" Vakkali answered, "Already eighty years have passed." Kassapa asked, "During those eighty years, how many times have you had relations with women?" Vakkali said, "O Kassapa, you must not ask such a question of me. O Kassapa, you would do better to question me in this way, namely, 'During these years, how many times have you had a lustful thought?' O Kassapa, throughout these years I do not remember having one lustful thought. Nor do I remember, my friend, even once harboring the thought of injuring anyone. O friend, throughout these years, I do not remember harboring the thought of anger. Nor do I remember ever receiving clothing worn by a layman, cutting cloth, sewing with a needle, or dyeing with colors, nor have I helped any of my colleagues to sew clothing. Nor do I remember having been invited or even wishing that someone would invite me, nor do I remember even once having been attracted to pretty women while sitting in the house of a householder and receiving alms. Nor have I taught to women even a verse of four lines. Nor have I visited an abode of nuns nor taught them or novices. Also throughout these eighty years, I do not remember having ordained anyone or made anyone a disciple of the Buddha or rendered help to anyone, or let anyone serve me at meal times or taken a bath, or washed myself with soap or massaged anyone. Nor do I remember falling ill during these years or using medicine, nor do I remember sleeping by leaning on something or by lying on my side. Nor do I remember spending three months of the rainy season in a village or hamlet. O my friend, after being a disciple of the Buddha, I ate alms up to the seventh day with the body of defilements, but by the eighth day, I realized enlightenment."

"O Vakkali," Kassapa said, "I shall remember these things as Vakkali's wondrous deeds. O Vakkali, shall I too be able to become a disciple through the doctrine and discipline such as yours?" Thus the naked Kassapa soon became a disciple by his own wish and soon freed himself from defilements, attained enlightenment, and reached the state of an arhat.

Vakkali then took off his top robe, visited every monastery room, greeting the monks with "O Venerable, advance, advance. Today I shall pass away." He then passed away from the world of delusion. This, then, became also one of Vakkali's wondrous deeds to be widely told among the people.

(9) Accompanying Ananda, Bhadda stayed at the Kukkutarama of Pataliputta. While he practiced meditation and taught the doctrine, he frequently asked Ananda about the path. "O friend, what are defiled practices?" asked Bhadda. "O Bhadda," replied Ananda, "they are wrong view, wrong thought, wrong speech, wrong action, wrong livelihood, wrong mindfulness, and wrong endeavor." Bhadda asked, "Then what are the pure practices?" Ananda replied, "They are the opposite of the former, namely, right view, right thought, right

speech, right action, right livelihood, right mindfulness, and right endeavor." "O friend," asked Bhadda, "what is the purpose of these pure practices?" Ananda replied, "It is to annihilate greed, anger, and ignorance, and thereby to realize nirvana."

"O friend," asked Bhadda, "for what purpose did the World-Honored One set forth the precepts and have his disciples follow them?" Ananda replied, "It was for the sake of having his disciples control themselves by concentrating on objects of mindfulness, such as body, sensation, mind, and dharmas. By the observance of the precepts, one can correctly restrain body and mind; through viewing the body as unclean, sensation as suffering, mind as having no essence, and dharmas as impermanent, one can annihilate greed and anger."

Bhadda asked again, "O friend, since the World-Honored One has entered nirvana, in what way can we make the true Dharma remain in this world for a long time, and how can we prevent it from perishing?" "Well said, friend," Ananda said, "the question is indeed an excellent one. If we directly understand the nature of body, sensation, mind, and dharmas and annihilate greed and anger, the true Dharma will continue in this world for a long time and increase its brightness. If, however, we become negligent in the practice of restraining ourselves by concentrating on objects of mindfulness, body, sensation, mind, and dharmas, the true Dharma will decline."

(10) Having received the punishment called brahmadanda, in which one who commits a minor offence is forbidden to have any conversation with the members of the Sangha, Channa regretted his offence and was in deep distress; upon his repentance, he was pardoned by the Sangha. He seriously practiced the path and sought the mind of quiescence, and he asked one of the elder disciples, "O Venerable, may you teach me so that I can see the Dharma." The elder answered, "O Channa, see that the body is impermanent, so likewise the mind, and that both body and mind are equally without self."

Having listened to this instruction, Channa thought to himself, "I know that the body and mind have no self, and yet my mind does not exhaust the thirst of love, nor become free from desire, nor incline toward the quiescence of defilements or toward enlightenment. If there is no self, then who is this 'I' that see things? Alas, who could ever rescue me, who am so stubborn and reluctant to believe?"

At that time, Channa remembered Ananda, thinking, "The Venerable One served the World-Honored One for a long time and was praised by the World-Honored One. I heard that he was staying in the Ghosita Monastery in Kosambi; I should visit him for instruction." With robe and bowl in hand, Channa at once started his journey to Kosambi, and upon arrival he confided in Ananda. Ananda said, "O Channa, I am truly delighted to know that you have destroyed your stubborn mind. Listen carefully, for you have, indeed, come to desire to know the Dharma."

Delighted with Channa's direct request, Ananda further said to Channa, "O Channa, this is what I heard directly from the World-Honored One, when he taught Kaccana. In this world, there are two extreme views, the views of existence and of nonexistence. When we see that a thing has come to be, the view of nonexistence is confuted; when we see that a thing has perished, the view of existence is confuted. When we are attached to either view, we are deluded. We have the right view when we are free from attachment to things as well as to ourselves; when suffering arises, we see it as arising, and when it perishes, we see it as having perished; we have no doubt or delusion, nor do we depend upon others, for we know it by ourselves. To view things as existent is one extreme, while to view them as nonexistent is another extreme. The Buddha taught the Dharma by staying away from both of these extreme views. Conditioned by ignorance, there arise mental processes; conditioned by mental processes, there arises consciousness; and so on up to conditioned by birth, there arise old age and death. This is the entire process in which the cause of suffering operates. When, on the other hand, ignorance is annihilated completely, mental processes perish; when mental processes perish, then consciousness perishes, and so on up to when birth as well as old age and death are annihilated, the cause of all suffering will also come to cessation." Channa saw the nature of the Dharma by this teaching and was grateful for the compassion of Ananda.

(11) It was when Narada dwelt at the Kukkutarama of Pataliputta that Bhadda died, the beloved queen of King Munda. The grief-stricken king did not take a bath, nor comb his hair, nor take any food, nor conduct the affairs of state; and he held the queen's body day and night. The king summoned the minister of provision Piyaka and ordered him to prepare an iron tub with an iron lid filled with oil to preserve the queen's body, so that he could see her body forever.

Concerned with the king's state of mind, Piyaka thought that there was no other way than to ask someone with higher spiritual powers to remove the king's sorrow. He remembered that the renowned Narada was currently staying at the Kukkutarama. He addressed the king, saying, "O great king, now the well-known and Venerable Narada is staying at the Kukkutarama of Pataliputta. He is endowed with supreme insight and wisdom. He is an aged arhat with excellent skills in explaining the doctrine. If the great king goes to him and requests his instruction, he will be able to pluck the arrow of grief from the mind of the king."

"Then notify the Venerable Narada of my planned visit, for I cannot visit ascetics and brahmins who live in my country without letting them know that I am coming," said the king. "Yes, sire, as you command," replied Piyaka, and he at once visited the Venerable One at the place where he was staying and explained the matter and requested him to rescue the king from his sorrow. As Narada readily accepted the request, the king, helped by Piyaka, visited the Venerable One and received the following teaching.

(12) "O great king, there are five impossibilities in any and every world. They are to halt old age though one is subject to old age, to avoid sickness though one is subject to sickness, to wish to escape from death though one is subject to death, to resist against cessation though one is subject to cessation, and to resist extinction though one is subject to extinction. These five impossibilities no one can change. O great king, when ordinary people, with little wisdom, meet with the inevitable facts, namely that whoever is subject to old age becomes old, that whoever is subject to sickness falls sick, that whoever is

subject to death dies, that whatever is subject to cessation ceases, and that whatever is subject to extinction becomes extinct, they vainly weep and grieve and become lost. The disciples of the Buddha, however, profound in wisdom, think that these events, namely, old age, sickness, and death, are not confined to me alone but extend to all people insofar as repeated births and deaths continue. If I become grief-stricken, tearful, and lost, I shall lose my appetite, my body will weaken and be unable to work, and this will delight my enemies and sadden my own people. Thinking in this manner, I shall overcome my grief. Ordinary people, when shot by poisonous arrows, suffer, while the disciples of the Buddha, who avoid the poisonous arrows, are free of worries and abide in a state of quietude."

Having heard this King Munda said, "O Venerable One, what is the name of this teaching?" Narada replied, "O great king, this is called The Teaching That Plucks Out the Arrow of Grief." The king said, "O Venerable, this is certainly a teaching that plucks out the arrow of grief. By this teaching my sorrows have been completely plucked out." And turning to Piyaka, the king said, "Then cremate the queen's body and erect a stupa in her honor. Beginning today, I shall bathe, comb my hair, take food, and conduct the affairs of state." Thus, King Munda began to hold deep faith in the Dharma of the Buddha, became a saintly king who governed with compassion, and prospered for a long time along with the Dharma.

Glossary

Abhidharma The Buddha's teaching is reflected in the Three Baskets (q.v.) or three collections of works. It includes the Sutras (q.v.) and the Vinaya (q.v.)—these can be called Dharma (q.v.)—extensively and the Abhidharma only in outline. Thus, various schools have elaborated various Abhidharmas. The Abhidharmas are systematizations of the Dharma and consist of the classification, analysis, and explanation of the *dharmas* (q.v.). All things were viewed as falling into five major categories that embraced a total of seventy-five to over one hundred *dharmas* (depending on the school). The five major categories are corporeality, sensation, perception, mental formations, and consciousness. The psychical elements were classified according to their place in a hierarchy of ethical and religious values.

Absolute truth (*paramārtha-satya*) The truth of things as they really are, a truth open only to the insight of the Void or Emptiness (q.v.) (*śūnyatā*), a truth transcending duality of all kinds esp. the duality of self and other; a truth transcending conceptualization. Synonymous with Nirvana (q.v.), Dharma nature (q.v.), and Thusness (q.v). Contrasts with conventional truth.

Action (*saṃskāra*) The second of the twelve links (*nidāna*) of Dependent Origination (q.v.). Denotes all volitional activities initiated by the body (physical acts), mouth (speech), and mind (thoughts). Whether these acts are moral or immoral or neutral, they perpetuate the cycle of rebirth and suffering.

Ādāna-consciousness (*ādāna-vijñāna*) Another name for *ālaya-vijñāna* (q.v.)

Adornment (*alaṃkāra*) Glory, honor, ornament. One form of adornment consists of morality, meditation, and wisdom (the Three learnings, q.v.) and the control of good and evil forces. Twenty-nine forms of adornment are described in sutras on the Pure Land of Amitābha/Amitāyus.

Aggregates, five *See* Five aggregates

Agni   Hindu god of fire and purification.

Ālaya-vijñāna   The fundamental consciousness that underlies the other seven consciousnesses, those of the eye, the ear, the nose, the tongue, the body (tactility), the mano-vijñāna, and the manas (which attaches to the *ālaya-vijñāna* as ego-consciousness). Seeds (germs or potentialities) are deposited in this store (*ālaya*) by the experiences of all the other consciousnesses through a process called perfuming (like fumigating or smoking). These seeds then in turn influence all subsequent cognitions.

Amitābha/Amitāyus Buddha   The Buddha of infinite light (*amitābha*) or infinite life (*amitāyus*). Light symbolizes wisdom and life symbolizes compassion. This Buddha is a Buddha of recompense who fulfills a vow to save all beings, which he can do by the virtue of his accumulation of infinite merits over an infinite time. He establishes a Pure Land to accommodate the beings saved. The only condition for salvation through him is to accept without mistrust the gift of his merits and respond to this gift by reciting his name in gratitude for being about to be made his equal in the next life in the Pure Land.

Anātman   Lacking or lack of an *ātman* (q.v.). Neither within nor outside the phenomena of existence is found a self-existing ego-entity or personality; a basic Buddhist doctrine.

Añjali (**Jpn. gasshō**)   Joining the palms together; a gesture of reverence.

Anuttara-samyak-sambodhi   Highest perfect awakening. The supreme enlightenment realized by the Buddha in meditation under the Bodhi Tree.

Arhat   An epithet of the Buddha and of his enlightened disciples. An Arhat ("worthy") has destroyed defilements and will not be reborn in the world of delusion. In the Mahayana, a distinction is made between the realization of a Buddha and that of the other Arhats.

Asura   A class of warring divinities like the ancient Greek Titans. Rivals of the gods. The world of the asuras is one of the 'six, or five, destinies' (q.v.) (or worlds, or realms).

Ātman   Self, Ego, or soul; permanent and unchangeable nucleus of the individual. Most Buddhist schools reject it as real.

Avalokiteśvara Bodhisattva   The Bodhisattva of compassion, who sees beings in agony and extends his salvific power to them and who has the capacity to save all suffering beings at will and without hindrance.

Avalokiteśvara accompanies Amitābha Buddha, as does his fellow Bodhisattva Mahāsthāmaprāpta, who symbolizes wisdom.

Avīci hell   The lowest and worst hell, where sinners die of the pain and are reborn constantly in the same hell until they work off their transgressions. Also called Uninterrupted (*ānantarya*) for pain is constant.

***Bhikṣu* (Skt); *Bhikkhu* (P)**   Buddhist monk, who has received the precepts (śīla, moral code) of the Vinaya (disciplinary rules of the order, the Sangha).

***Bhikṣuṇī* (Skt); *Bhikkhuni* (P)**   Buddhist nun.

Birth and death (*saṃsāra*)   *See* Transmigration

Bodhi   Enlightenment (q.v.).

Bodhi mind (*bodhicitta*)   The thought of awakening or enlightenment. The mind that aspires to attain enlightenment or Buddhahood, both for one's own sake and for the welfare of all sentient beings.

Bodhimaṇḍa, bodhimaṇḍala   The place where a Bodhisattva attains enlightenment and thus becomes a Buddha: under the Bodhi Tree. Also called the Lion Throne or the Diamond Throne. By extension, a place of teaching, religious practice, worship; a center of the Buddhist world.

Bodhisattva   A being who has the Bodhi mind (q.v.). A being (*sattva*) who aspires to enlightenment (*bodhi*). In a sense, all the Buddha's followers are Bodhisattvas. The Mahayana schools developed the idea of attaining enlightenment not just by oneself alone but together with all others, and not just for oneself alone, but to help others. The Bodhisattva practices the Six Perfections (q.v.) lifetime after lifetime. The stories of the previous lifetimes of the Buddha (called jātakas) show him repeatedly giving up his life for the sake of others. The particular Bodhisattva destined to be the next Buddha of our world is called Maitreya.

Bodhisattva's fifty-two stages to Buddhahood in the T'ien-t'ai school
Ten stages of faith; ten stages of dwelling in the truth of Emptiness (q.v.); ten stages of the practice of altruistic deeds; ten stages of transferring merit to all sentient beings; the Bodhisattva's ten stages to Buddhahood (q.v.), up to and including the stage of the Dharma Clouds (fiftieth stage), in which the Bodhisattva gains untainted wisdom, is able to see the Buddha nature, and guides other beings to attainment; samyak-sambodhi (fifty-first); and Buddhahood, in which all defilements, moral and intellectual, are completely extinct (fifty-second).

Bodhisattva's four activities   (1) Activities grounded in the essential nature of a Bodhisattva, namely, activities that are characterized by straightforwardness, honesty, respectful obedience towards parents, teachers, and elders, and a variety of other virtuous acts; (2) activities stemming from the Bodhisattva's vow to become a Buddha; (3) activities that contribute to spiritual development, namely, the Six Perfections (q.v.); and (4) a variety of activities that contribute to progress on the path to enlightenment such as chanting Sutras (*see* Three Baskets).

Bodhisattva's ten stages to Buddhahood   The stages of (1) Joy, (2) Freedom from All Defilements, (3) Emitting Light, (4) Blazing with Wisdom, (5) Being Victorious over Utmost Adversity, (6) Immediacy (in which the workings of Dependent Origination [q.v.] appear before one's eyes), (7) Transcendence over the World, (8) Immovability (in which all Bodhisattva practices have been perfectly accomplished and in which all subsequent practices are accomplished naturally and without effort), (9) Good Wisdom (in which the Dharma is expounded to all sentient beings), and (10) Dharma Clouds (in which the nectar of the Dharma rains down throughout the world).

Bodily salutation (five point salutation, *pañca-maṇḍala-namaska*)   Prostration (e.g., before the Buddha) in which the head, knees, and elbows touch the ground.

Bondage (bandhana)   Attachment, fetters, or obstacles in the path to emancipation. *See also* Defilement.

Bowl (*pātra*)   Bowl used by monks and nuns to receive alms from lay people. One of the few items, along with the three robes, that monks and nuns can own.

Brahmin (*brāhmaṇ*)   A member of the highest of the four social classes, the priestly caste, of India. His duties include studying and teaching the Vedic texts and to serve as an officiant at Vedic rituals.

Buddha   One who is awakened or enlightened. One who has knowledge of the ultimate truth. Also refers to the historical Buddha Śākyamuni (Gautama Siddhārtha). A Buddha is a human being, possessing omniscience, perfect virtue, Great Compassion, and is often believed to have thirty-two distinguishing physical features such as a golden body (sometimes, with light emanating from every pore). In such forms, numerous Buddhas became objects of worship, rituals, faith, and above all meditation. *See also* Three Bodies of the Buddha

Buddha nature, Buddhahood   The nature of a Buddha is said to exist in all sentient beings, though it is unrealized. This nature is the full potentiality for

Buddhahood, realized when defilements both moral and intellectual are overcome.

Buddhānusmṛti (Jpn. *nembutsu*)   Visualization of the image of the Buddha. In later Pure Land tradition, it is recitation of the name of the Buddha.

Cakravartin (Skt); Cakkavatti (P)   Wheel-Turning King, a king who rules the whole earth by the power he obtains by rotating the magical wheel given him by heaven at his ascension to the throne.

Causes and conditions (*hetu-pratyaya*)   All things come into being (fruition) by virtue of the concurrence of the necessary causes and conditions. See also Dependent Origination, Six direct causes and four indirect causes.

Characteristics of Buddhism (*dharma-uddāna*), three or four   The seals of Buddhist teaching that distinguish it from other teachings. The views (1) that all worldly things are impermanent (*anitya*); (2) that all are without self-nature (*anātman*); (3) that after all contradiction is ovecome, nirvana is ultimate peace; sometimes (4) is added: that all worldly experiences are suffering (because of their impermanent nature).

Cintāmaṇi   *See Maṇi* gem

Circumambulating to the right (*pradakṣiṇa*)   Circumambulating to the right around a person or object, especially a Buddha or a stupa (q.v.), as an expression of reverence.

Compassion (*maitrī, karuṇā*)   The love of a Buddha or a Bodhisattva that gives joy and peace to beings and rescues them from suffering.

Complete precepts (*upasaṃpadā*)   The rules of conduct for monks and nuns. These rules are accepted at ordination. The number of rules differs from school to school; about 250 for monks and 350 for nuns.

Concentration and insight (*samatha-vipaśyanā*)   Involves two integrated acts. The first involves withdrawing, calming, concentration, and the single-minded focusing of the mind on the object of meditation. The second involves analysis and observation and insight into the nature and characteristics of the object of meditation.

Condition (*pratyaya*)   Indirect cause. Direct causes coalesce with conditions or indirect causes and produce their corresponding results. The seed as the direct cause combines with the sun, soil, water, etc., as the conditions to produce a plant. By extension, the whole universe takes part in producing even the smallest result. *See also* Six direct causes and four indirect causes.

Conditioned and unconditioned things (*saṃskṛta, asaṃskṛta*)   A conditioned thing is something that is made. All phenomena that are produced from causes are conditioned. They are subject to the coalescence or dispersal of their causes and conditions and are, therefore, in a state of constant change. They are said to undergo four phases, birth, abiding, change, and extinction. An unconditioned thing is the antithesis of this and is the only goal worth seeking: nirvana, thusness, dharma nature, the dharma world, etc.

Confessional ceremony (*pravāraṇā*)   Confession and repentance for forgiveness by the members of the Sangha (q.v.) for transgressing the rules of the order. This takes place at the end of the rainy season retreat.

Consciousness (*vijñāna*)   The third of the twelve links of Dependent Origination (q.v.). Comes into being at the time when the sentient being first appears in the mother's womb. It is composed of six different consciousnesses, resulting from six sense organs and their respective objects, namely, the eye, ear, nose, tongue, body, and mind, whereby visual consciousness results when the eye perceives form, etc.

Contact (*sparśa*)   The sixth of the twelve links of Dependent Origination (q.v.). Sense organs come into contact with objects at this stage.

Country of Peace and Bliss, Pure Land (*sukhāvatī-kṣetra*)   A land of ultimate bliss. Often it refers to the Pure Land established by Amitābha/Amitāyus in the West, but there are other such lands created by other Buddhas and Bodhisattvas.

Craving, thirst (*tṛṣṇā*)   The eighth of the twelve links of Dependent Origination (q.v.). Intense desire, likened to thirst, arising from sensory impressions or sensations, toward pleasurable things.

Curl of white hair (*ūrṇā-bhrū*)   A curl of white hair in the middle of the forehead. One of the thirty-two distinguishing marks of a Buddha.

Defilement (*kleśa*)   Impurity, depravity. Mental functions that disturb the mind and body and cause suffering. Existing in a hidden or latent stage, defilements exist as potentialities and are actualized within the sphere of the consciousness in response to given situations, that is, to a particular coalescence of causes and conditions. The three primary defilements are greed, anger, and ignorance. At other times, pride, doubt, and false views are added to form a group of six primary defilements. Aside from these primary defilements, there are a number of lesser attendant or derivative defilements such as envy, sloth, negligence, fraudulence, distraction. These groupings expand to number 108 and finally 84,000 defilements.

Delusion, illusion (*māyā, moha, avidyā*)   Not knowing the true aspect or nature of things, being deceived by ignorance as to the true nature of the world.

Delusory thinking (*kalpana, pratikalpana, parikalpana*)   Delusory discriminations between the subject and the object of conception. Because of the mind's attachments, one is unable to perceive the true forms of things, with the result of the wrongful assertion of the ego. Erroneous thought, baseless imagination, false conception, illusion.

Dependent Origination (*pratītya-samutpāda*)   A central concept in Buddhist thought. All phenomena come into being through a process of causation known as Dependent Origination. For example, a cart comes into being (origination) dependent on a number of components such as wheels, axles, sideboards coming together at a particular moment. Thus all phenomenal things come into being and have their temporary existences by virtue of the concurrence of various conditions. Thus when the conditions change, the result itself changes, and when the conditions dissolve, the result itself dissolves. Because all phenomena owe their existences to Dependent Origination, all things are devoid of a permanent, substantive self-nature. In this sense they are empty and without self. The twelve links in the chain of Dependent Origination (*dvādaśāṅga-pratītya-samutpāda*) are intended to explain the causal relations of all phenomena physical and mental. They are (1) ignorance or nescience, the unconscious blindness that is the root of all suffering and gives rise to (2) blind activity, volitional action (q.v.), which gives rise to (3) consciousness, the moment of conception in the mother's womb, which gives rise to (4) name and form, the mind and body, which give rise to (5) the six sense organs, just prior to birth, which give rise to (6) contact, which gives rise to (7) perception, which gives rise to (8) craving, which gives rise to (9) attachment, which gives rise to (10) becoming, or the birth process, which gives rise to (11) birth, which gives rise to (12) old age and death. The first two are of the past life, the next eight are of the present life, while the last two pertain to the future life. The process has gone on indefinitely, again and again like the rotating of a wheel. This is one of the most basic of the Buddha's teachings.

Deva   A heavenly being, literally a 'Radiant One,' invisible to human beings. They are not strictly 'gods' in the absolute sense, because they are not eternal but subject, together with all sentient beings, to the law of rebirth, old age, and death. There are many levels of heavenly beings; and the universe is divided into 3 spheres, or *dhātus*: *kāma-dhātu* (sensual sphere), *rūpadhātu* (form only sphere), and *arūpa-dhātu* (formlessness sphere). The devas inhabit the highest realm of *kāma-dhātu*, which range from the very lowest realm of the various hells, upward through that of ghosts (*pretas*), of animals, of humans, to the various levels of the deities. The devas gain rebirth to higher levels of the 3 spheres according to their merits.

Dhāraṇī   Incantation, spell, mystical or magical formula believed to have beneficial effects for sentient beings. They embody the essence of Buddhism and possess power to help the practitioner on his wayfaring. Recitation of a *dhāraṇī* is a way of concentrating on meditation practice and preventing the influence of evil.

Dharma   The Buddha's teaching as a whole; the Doctrine of the Buddha. Hence it is the ultimate transcendent truth. Sometimes translated as 'law' not in the sense of an ordinance but in the sense of 'natural law' or 'law of nature'. In the sense that this 'law' represents how things really are, it is also called 'truth'.

Dharma nature (*dharmatā*)   The universal and eternal property or essence that is intrinsic to all phenomena as opposed to particular and transient aspects, which are incidental to them. Synonymous with thusness, Emptiness (q.v.), true form, Dharma body (*dharma-kāya*) and Dharma world (*dharma-dhātu*). To be enlightened is to awaken fully to the Dharma nature.

Dharmakāya   *See* Three Bodies of the Buddha

Dharmas   The dharmas are elements out of which things are composed; there are various dharma lists of ultimate realities.

Dhūtaguṇa, dhūtāṅga   A set of twelve practices for ridding oneself of defilements and the desires for food, clothing, and shelter. They are (1) wearing robes made of discarded rags, (2) possessing only three robes, (3) eating at prescribed times only, (4) subsisting on alms begged door to door, (5) eating only once a day, (6) eating a proper amount of food, (7) abiding in a quiet place, (8) meditating in a monastery, (9) meditating under a tree, (10) meditating at a place without a roof, (11) meditating at a proper time, and (12) maintaining lotus position while resting or sleeping.

***Dhyāna* (Skt); *Jhāna* (P)**   To meditate firmly on a given object. Denotes both a system of mental training and a process of progressing from the lower to the higher states of consciousness, from the realm of sense desire to a supramundane state.

Diamond Throne, Bodhi Seat (*vajrāsana, bodhi-maṇḍa*)   The seat on which Śākyamuni Buddha (*see also* Buddha) attained awakening at the foot of the Bodhi Tree at Buddhagayā. Later the term referred to any seat on which a Bodhisattva attained Buddhahood. The diamond is a symbol of indestructibility and steadfastness, especially in relation to defilements. *See also* Buddha

Differentiated wisdom (*savikalpa-jñāna*)   Wisdom, knowledge, or cognition that is based on the bifurcation of subject and object. This form of knowledge is not direct and immediate, since the object so known is influenced by the interpretations on the part of the subject. This form of knowledge can be expressed in language and grasped conceptually; it is analytical, empirical, and relative.

Direct cause (*hetu*)   *See* Six direct causes and four indirect causes.

Direct insight   This is insight without any gradual process of *samādhi* (q.v.). It is one of the three forms of meditation cultivated by the T'ien T'ai school.

Direct knowledge and inferential knowledge (*pratyakṣa, anumāna*)
Direct knowledge is a form of knowing that is prior to the emergence of the subject-object bifurcation. It is prior to both language and concepts. It is instantaneous and momentary. Inferential knowledge is its opposite; it proceeds from the subject-object bifurcation, language, or concepts. It makes use of conditionals (if-then statements), comparisons, analogies, and classifications.

Discipline (*caryā*)   Conduct; to observe and do; to mend one's ways; to cultivate oneself in right practice; to be religious or pious.

Discrimination (*vikalpa, vibhāga, parikalpana*)   A faculty of the mind; its basic function is to judge, interpret, differentiate, bifurcate, dualize. It takes three forms: (1) self-natural or direct discrimination, in which the first five of the six consciousnesses perceive their corresponding sense objects; (2) evaluative discrimination, in which the sixth consciousness discriminates and evaluates these sense-objects; and (3) recollective discrimination, in which past events and experiences are recalled in order to aid the evaluative discrimination. It is held that the ordinary person's vikalpa stems from blind ignorance and is not in accordance with things as they are; therefore it is inferior to right intuitive and transcendental insight or prajñā.

Distinguishing features of a great man (*mahāpuruṣa-lakṣaṇa*)   A great man here is a Buddha or a Cakravartin, a universal monarch. A Buddha possesses thirty-two such marks, such as skin the color of gold, a circle of hair between the eyebrows, a jaw as strong as a lion, very long fingers.

Divine power, superhuman power (*abhijñā*)   Power acquired through profound meditation (*samādhi*). Various lists are mentioned, but the most important one is of five: seeing what the ordinary eye cannot see, hearing what the ordinary ear cannot hear, perceiving the minds of others, recollection of one's previous lives, and the power to go anywhere at will.

Egolessness, nonego (*anātman*)   Non-self. This is based on two characteristics of phenomenal things: that they change constantly, and that all that is transient is liable to suffering. The supreme ātman and the empirical self are alike rejected, but in the Hinayana schools generally the dharmas are still believed to have self-nature. In the Mahayana and in one or two Hinayana schools this notion, too, was rejected and all dharmas were considered to be empty (*śūnya*), i.e., devoid of self-nature.

Egolessness of persons (*pudgala-nairātmya*)   The emptiness or lack of a permanent self. This results from their being the products of Dependent Origination (q.v.)

Egolessness of things (*dharma-nairātmya*)   The emptiness or lack of a self-nature or essence in things (dharma). This results from their being the products of Dependent Origination (q.v.)

Eight awarenesses cultivated by people of great capacity   Bodhisattvas and Buddhas cultivate (1) desirelessness, (2) fulfillment, (3) avoidance of evils, (4) right thought, (5) right meditation, (6) spiritual exertion, (7) right wisdom, and (8) avoidance of gain and meaningless talk.

Eight consciousnesses (*vijñāna*)   Eye consciousness, ear consciousness, nose consciousness, tongue consciousness, body consciousness, *mano-vijñāna* (q.v.), manas (q.v.), and *ālaya-vijñāna* (q.v.).

Eighteen realms   The eye, forms, and eye-consciousness; the ear, sounds, and ear-consciousness; the nose, smells, and nose-consciousness; the tongue, tastes, and tongue-consciousness; the body, tactile sensations, and body-consciousness; and the mind, dharmas, and mind-consciousness.

Eightfold Path (*aṣṭāṅga-mārga*)   Right view, right thought, right speech, right action, right livelihood, right effort, right mindfulness, right concentration. This path is considered the median path or Middle Way between the extremes of hedonism and asceticism.

Emancipation, deliverance, liberation (*vimukti, vimokṣa*)   Release from the samsaric round of birth, misery, and death. Liberation from karmic bondage and the attainment of nirvana. Bondage is primarly internal and mental. There are three kinds of liberation: (1) void emancipation, which is realized by the knowldege of Emptiness (q.v.), (2) wisdom emancipation, which is realized by insight, and (3) mental emancipation, which is realized when the mind is released from the bondage of defilements.

Embracing (*parigraha*)   Receiving and not forsaking; accepting and not forsaking all beings on the part of Amitābha/Amitāyus Buddha.

Emptiness, voidness (*śūnyatā*)   This is not mere nothingness, nor is the associated view a form of nihilism. It is the absence of any substance as abiding entity, but things have a provisional existence as parts of the chain of Dependent Origination (q.v.). They are empty of self-nature; they are not nonexistent. Neither existence nor nonexistence is an absolute. This is the Middle Way in Buddhist philosophy.

Enlightenment (*bodhi*)   The supreme enlightenment or awakening is what was attained by the Buddha and all Buddhas. It is insight and knowledge of the true nature of things. It is emancipation from primal ignorance, or the state of nirvana in which all defilements have been extinguished.

Entrusting the transmission of the Dharma (*nikṣepa, parindanā*)   A master gives the Dharma to a pupil for transmission to his own pupils. The Buddha entrusted the Dharma to his students, who then preserved and spread it in the world for the emancipation of all sentient beings.

Equality (*sāmānya, samatā*)   Objectively, the world is devoid of all differentiations, distinctions, and discriminations. Equality or sameness refers to the absolute truth that permeates the phenomenal world. Subjectively, it is the state of mind that is devoid of all differentiating and discriminatory thoughts or feelings such as those regarding good and evil, likes and dislikes. Ultimately it is the insight into the absolute identity of all apparently differentiated phenomena such as subject and object, enlightenment and defilement, and samsara and nirvana.

Evil paths (*durgati*)   The evil worlds to which sentient beings have to transmigrate as a result of the evil deeds that they have done: hell, the world of ghosts, and the world of animals.

Faith (*śraddhā*)   In Buddhism, faith is a state of mind rather than simple assent to an unproved proposition. It is one of the Five faculties that enable one to attain enlightenment (q.v.). Faith is cultivated through meditation and acts to overcome mental torpor; it purifies the mind and makes it transparent, steadfast, and quiescent. In the Jōdo Shinshū interpretation, faith is the gift of Amitābha/Amitāyus Buddha to the faithful, and one needs but to accept without doubt the True Mind of the Buddha. Such acceptance assures one of birth in the Pure Land where one will attain Buddhahood. The recitation of the name of Amitābha is not prayer but an expression of the gratitude that one feels on becoming one with the Buddha.

False imagination and discrimination (*abhūta-parikalpa*)   Unreal imagination. Taking unreal phenomena for real and making discriminations and judgments about them.

Felloe   The rim of a wheel. Also known as felly.

Fetter (*bandhana*)   Binding, restraining. Another name for Defilement (q.v.).

Field of merit, field of blessing (*puṇya-kṣetra*)   A field of merit is a revered person or group such as the Buddha, the Sangha, or one's parents. Giving to them produces merit for oneself as sowing a field produces crops.

Fire worship, worship of Agni.   The Vedic god Agni (Fire) was worshipped by non-Buddhists as the cleanser of evils.

Five aggregates (*pañca-skandha*)   Form (physical body), sensation, perception, volition, and consciousness. Form (*rūpa*) includes all material objects internal and external. It embraces the four great elements earth, air, fire, and water and their derivatives the sense organs and the sense objects, forms (color and shape), sounds, odors, tastes, and tangible qualities. Sensation (*vedanā*) is what arises when physical and mental organs come into contact with the objects of the external world; sensations are wholesome, unwholesome, or neutral. Perception (*saṃjñā*), like sensation, arises when physical and mental organs come into contact with the objects of the external world; perceptions are wholesome, unwholesome, or neutral. But perception judges the characteristics of the object, determining its color, degree of pleasantness, etc. Volition (*saṃskāra*), mental formations, is what produces karmic effects, as the previous two do not. Karmic effects are produced by such volitions as greed, hatred, and ignorance. Consciousness (*vijñāna*) coordinates the workings of sensation, perception, and volition and perceives and discriminates phenomenal things. The five are always changing. They coalesce to form a given individual, but because they exist in Dependent Origination (q.v.), they have no self-nature and do not constitute a self. The phenomenal ego exists only momentarily, lacks permanence, and thus is not an abiding entity.

Five cardinal transgressions, or grave offences (*pañca-avīci-karma, pañca-ānantarya*)   Patricide, matricide, killing an Arhat, wounding a Buddha so as to cause his blood to flow, and causing disunity in the Sangha. In the Hinayana view, one who commits one of these acts will go to hell.

Five concealments (*pañca-varaṇa*)   Five hindrances that obstruct moral and mental progress: sensuous desires and attachments, ill will and anger, sloth and torpor, restlessness and regret, and doubt and hesitation.

Five deteriorations of devas (q.v.)   Five signs of the approaching death of devas or gods. Withering of the crown of flowers, perspiration of the armpits, defilement of clothing, loss of physical splendor (or frequent blinking of the eyes), and being uncomfortable on one's seat.

Five dharmas (*pañca-dharma*)   All dharmas are grouped into five categories according to the Yogācāra or Vijñaptimātra school: (1) form (all phenomena are produced by causes and conditions), (2) name (the deluded mind perceives appearances, which are mere creations of the mind, as real and gives names to them as really existing), (3) mind (upon perceiving the forms and naming them, the mind imagines them to be objectively existing and makes discriminations), (4) right wisdom (rectifying knowledge that sees the true nature of phenomena), and (5) truth (*tathatā, dharmatā*). The first three of these are subject-object bifurcations of the defiled mind, while the last two are undefiled dharmas (anāsrava-dharma).

Five faculties that enable one to attain enlightenment   Faith, spiritual exertion, mindfulness, meditation, and wisdom.

Five false views (*pañca-mithyā-dṛṣṭi*)   Belief in a substantial self, belief that life is continuous after death or that life is not continuous after death, belief that there is no moral retribution, belief that one's own personal opinions are absolute, and belief that non-Buddhist precepts are efficacious for emancipation.

Five meditations for the ending of the five wrongs (*pañca-smṛty-upasthāna*)   Meditation on the impurity of the human body, to end desire and craving; meditation on compassion for all beings, to end anger; meditation on causal relations, to end stupidity; meditation on the eighteen realms (q.v.) as nothing more than temporary combinations of the five aggregates (q.v.), to end the idea of ego; and meditation by counting breaths, to deepen one's concentration.

Five natures   A classification of people according to the Yogācāra school. The *śrāvakas*, who are destined to become arhats; those who are destined to become pratyekabuddhas; Bodhisattvas, who are destined to become Buddhas; those whose destiny is not yet determined but who can enter the preceding three categories; those who lack the potential to enter any of the first three categories and will be forever unenlightened. These people can, if they observe the precepts and strive to do good deeds, be reborn as gods (which are, however, not enlightened). (Most Mahayana schools reject the doctrine that certain people are destined never to be enlightened, and they maintain that all will eventually reach enlightenment.)

Five pollutions, five impurities (*pañca-kaṣāya*)   Five impurities of the world in the last (dark) age: pollution of the shortening of human life, pollution of prevalent wrong views, pollution of defilements, pollution of sentient beings (deterioration of human qualities), and pollution of the age (epoch).

Five precepts (*pañca-śīla*)   For both monastic and lay Buddhists: not to kill, not to steal, not to lie, not to do sexual misconduct, not to drink, i.e., not to take intoxicants.

Five supramundane powers (*pañca-abhijñāna*)   *See* Divine power

Form   *See* Five aggregates

Four boundless minds (*catur-apramāṇa*)   Benevolence, in which one imparts well-being to sentient beings; compassion, in which one removes the suffering of sentient beings; sympathetic joy, in which one rejoices over the happiness of sentient beings without any trace of envy; and impartiality, in which one imparts benefit to all sentient beings without the attachments of liking or disliking them.

Four fearlessnesses (*catur-nirbhayatā*)   Characteristic of Buddhas and enlightened Buddhists when expounding the Dharma. The conviction that they have attained supreme enlightenment, the conviction that they have expunged all defilements, the conviction that they have revealed the nature of the dharmas that obstruct the way to enlightenment, and the conviction that they have expounded the way to emancipation, enabling them to proclaim unhesitatingly the way that leads to the extinguishing of all defilements.

Four grave offences for the monk (*catur-pārājika*)   The four cardinal offences for the monk are sexual misconduct, theft, killing, and lying. These are grounds for expulsion from the order.

Four Great Kings (*catur-mahārāja*)   These are four gods who dwell by the sides of Mount Meru, one in each of the cardinal directions, and protect Buddhism and the Sangha from malicious attacks of spirits or Asuras (q.v.). In the East, Dhṛtarāṣṭra, in the South, Virūḍhaka, in the West, Virūpākṣa, and in the North, Vaiśravaṇa.

Four kinds of birth (*catur-yoni*)   Sentient beings are classified by manner of birth as viviparous (womb-born), oviparous (egg-born), moisture-born (worms are deemed to be moisture-born), and metamorphically born (being born in the heavens, the hells, etc.).

Four meditations (*catur-dhyāna*)   Four meditative stages that progressively lead to the extinction of delusions, the abandonment of the world of desire, and the attainment of bliss in the world of pure form. (1) A state of passionlessness, joy, happiness, and discursive thought. (2) A state of passionlessness, tranquillity, one-pointedness, joy, happiness, and no discursive thought. (3) A state of passionlessness, tranquillity, one-pointedness, happiness, and no discursive thought or joy. (4) A state of passionlessness, tranquillity, one-pointedness, and no discursive thought or joy or happiness—just pure equanimity and awareness.

The four meditations on formlessness (*catur arūpa-dhyāna*)   Meditation on boundless space, meditation on boundless consciousness, meditation on emptiness (q.v.), and meditation on neither thought nor non-thought. Through the practice of these meditations one progressively attains the state that is free of all physical bondages.

Four meditative ways to superhuman power   Aspiration, effort, mindfulness, and memory.

Four methods of winning over sentient beings (*catur-saṃgraha-vastu*)   Selfless giving, loving words (addressing others with affection and gentleness), imparting benefits to others through virtuous acts, and identifying with others by drawing closer to them, working alongside them, etc.

Four mindfulnesses toward moral conduct (*catur-smṛty-upasthāna*) Mindfulness of the body as impure, mindfulness that all sensations result in suffering, mindfulness that the mind is impermanent, and mindfulness that all phenomenal things are without self-nature.

Four Noble Truths (*catur-ārya-satya*)   The heart of the Buddha's first sermon delivered to the five ascetics with whom he had trained before setting out on his own. In a nutshell, the four are the truths of "suffering, origin, cessation, path" (*duḥkha, samudaya, nirodha, mārga*). Suffering means that all life is susceptible to suffering, which is summed up as the sufferings of birth, old age, illness, death, association with the unpleasant, and separation from the pleasant. All the five aggregates (q.v.) are bound up with suffering. Origin means that the origin of suffering is desire, which is of three types, the desire for the pleasant, the desire for continuance, and the desire for nonexistence. Cessation means that the extinction of suffering is possible through the extinction of its cause: the disease of suffering is curable. Path means the Eightfold Path (q.v.). In short, there is suffering in life; the cause of suffering is desire; suffering can be overcome; and the way to end suffering is the Eightfold Path.

Four non-obstructions (*catur-pratisaṃvid*)   Possessed by Buddhas and some Bodhisattvas: the wisdom of knowing the Dharma, the capacity of understanding the meaning of the Dharma, the knowledge of languages and dialects, and the ability to present the Dharma in logical and intelligible fashion.

Four or six (great) elements (*catur-mahābhūta, ṣaḍ-bhūta*)   Earth (solid matter), water (moisture), fire (heat), wind (motion), and sometimes air (space) and consciousness.

Four paths and four rewards (*catur-pramukha, catur-phala*)   Four spiritual paths and their respective rewards: the stage of the stream-winner (*srota-āpanna*), in which the practitioner enters the stream of cultivation in order to attain enlightenment, having exhausted the intellectual defilements that affect his way of seeing things and the world as they are and attained the state of a sage; the stage of a once-returner (*sakṛd-āgamin*), in which the practitioner returns only once more to the cycle of samsara before attaining enlightenment (he is on his way to the extinction of the emotive and volitional defilements of the world of greed, such as anger and covetousness); the stage of a never-returner (*anāgamin*), in which one has exhausted all the defilements of the world of desire and is destined to be born in a higher realm and never return to this world; and the stage of the Arhat, in which one has completely exhausted the defilements of the three worlds (q.v.).

Four roots of goodness (*catur-kuśala-mūla*)   Here goodness (*kuśala*) refers to the defilement-free insight that is to be realized at the state of darśana-mārga or the Stage of Insight into the nature of dharmas; the four roots are essential and fundamental to the acquisition of that insight. The roots are the state in which the practitioner exercises insight into the sixteen features of the Four Noble Truths, the critical stage in which the practitioner may progress or retrogress, the state in which the practitioner recognizes and is at ease with the truth that dharmas neither arise nor perish, and the state where the practitioner reaches the highest knowledge possible in the phenomenal domain and after which he will enter the state of darśana-mārga.

Four troops (*catur-aṅga-bala-kāya*)   The four types of troops of the army of the Wheel-Turning King: elephants, horses, chariots, and foot soldiers.

Fourteen metaphysical questions (*catur-daśa-avyākṛta-vastu*)   Matters that the Buddha did not pronounce upon because they were irrelevant to attaining enlightenment; questions such as whether the world was finite and whether the Buddha continued to exist after death.

Fruit (*phala*)   Action (*karma*) of good, bad, or neutral moral quality leads inevitably to result or fruit of good, bad, or neutral experience. The action is like a seed or a sprout, and the result is like the fruit.

Fundamental (basic) defilements (*mūla-kleśa*)   Passion (*rāga*), hatred (*pratigha*), stupidity (*mūḍha*), arrogance (*māna*), doubt (*vicikitsā*), and false views (*dṛṣṭi*). (According to the Yogācāra school.)

Gāthā   Verses found in the Buddhist scriptures.

Giving (*dāna*)   Of three kinds, giving of material things, giving of the Dharma, and giving freedom from fear or anxiety to living beings. In pure giving three things are forgotten: the giver, the receiver, and the thing given.

Good friend, friend in goodness (*kalyāṇa-mitra*)   One who leads another in spiritual practice; a guru.

Grasping (*upādāna*)   The ninth of the twelve links of Dependent Origination (q.v.). Craving results in grasping or clinging onto the object of craving. The four kinds of grasping are grasping onto sense desires, false views, wrong rites and ceremonies, and delusory belief in the existence of a permanent substantial self.

Heavens; Celestial worlds (*deva-loka*)   According to Buddhist cosmology, celestial worlds are graded according to the qualities of the gods who dwell in each.

Hinayana (*hīnayāna*)   Deemed a subset of the Buddha's teaching by the Mahayana (q.v.), because it does not follow the bodhisattva ideal that aims for the universal salvation of all sentient beings, not just for one's own liberation. Since 'hinayana' means 'lesser vehicle,' the preferred term for this division of Buddhism is Theravada, the name of its major sect. The Theravada doctrine is less mystical, and its members follow a more empirical and pragmatic teachings of the historical Buddha as recorded in the Pali canonical texts. The Theravada path to enlightenment was first introduced in Ceylon (Sri Lanka) during the third century B.C. and is now also practiced mainly in Burma, Thailand, Cambodia, and Laos.

Icchantika (*icchāntika*)   Variously interpreted as destruction of virtuous roots, non-embodiment of faith, or (usually) ultimate greed or desire. Describes those who supposedly will never reach enlightenment. *See also* Five natures

Ignorance, stupidity (*moha, mūḍha*)   Foolishness, nescience. Delusion and its workings. Ignorance of the Four Noble Truths, of the twelve links of Dependent Origination, or of right view, due to the influence of egocentricity. Ignorance prevents one from attaining right view and enlightenment, and it constitutes the basic source of all other defilements.

Illusory and imagined existence   *See* Three natures

Impermanence (*anityatā*)   Impermanence defines the true nature of all phenomenal beings, which owe their existence to the temporary coalescence of the Five aggregates (q.v.) and to Dependent Origination (q.v.). All phenomenal beings are in a state of constant change from instant to instant, in four phases in each instant: coming into being, remaining, changing, and extinction of breaking-up.

Incomprehensible, inconceivable (*acintya*)   That which cannot be grasped by conceptual thought; that which transcends conceptual thought. Nirvana; a Buddha's divine wisdom and power.

Insight, discernment   A detailed view of the object of meditation with regard

to its characteristics and (especially) its nature, which is essentially impermanent, ill, and without self. Insight has as its goal the extinguishing of ignorance
and, through analytic meditation, of the sense object. Insight also denotes a state
of peace, liberation, freedom from defilements, transcendence over all relative
forms, and emptiness (q.v.).

Insight into the nature of things as they are (*yathābhūta-darśana*)
Insight into thusness (q.v.). To perceive that all phenomenal things are in reality nothing but aggregates of elements both mental and physical, devoid of any
substantive identity that might serve as an object of attachment.

Interdependent origination   *See* Dependent origination

Īśvara   According to the Hindu religion, he is the creator and sustainer of the
world. He is also a mediator who reveals the Absolute (Brahman) to beings in the
phenomenal sphere. The philosophical concept of impersonal Brahman (World
Spirit and Cosmic Essence) became personified as god Īśvara to be worshipped by
the Hindu devotees.

Jātaka   One of a class of Buddhist scriptures. Jātaka tales deal with the previous incarnations of Śākyamuni Buddha (see also Buddha). The central theme
of these tales is compassion manifesting itself in self-sacrifice for the sake of
others.

Jīvaṃjīvaka bird   A certain species of bird with two heads.

Kalaviṅka   A bird with a beautiful voice, said to be found in the Himalayas.

Kalpa   A cosmic cycle lasting a long period of time. According to Hindu cosmology, basic cycle is 4,320 million earthly years. The cosmos passes through
cycles (kalpas) within cycles for all eternity.

Karma   Action, deed. This can be bodily, vocal, or mental, of which the last is
the most important, having the greatest consequences. Actions can be good, bad,
or neutral. Every action brings about its corresponding reward or retribution, in
this life or a following life. Thus, there is a law of moral causation, in which bad
action leads to suffering and good action to happiness. Action can be instantaneous or have the duration of a lifetime. Its force extends from past to present
and into the future. Thus, it bears directly on the process of rebirth. But the doctrine on this matter is not fatalistic because we can always improve ourselves by
efforts in goodness even as we suffer the results of past bad karma. The word
karma is also used somewhat loosely in the sense of "the result of action," i.e., the
retribution or reward of action (*karma-vipāka*, the ripening of action).

Kaṣāya   Faded red color of Buddhist monks' robes.

Kiṃnara   A kind of minor divinity.

Kleśa   *See* Defilement

Lion throne   *See Bodhimaṇḍa.*

Lokanātha   An epithet of the Buddha, meaning Lord of the World.

Loving an only child stage   *See* Only child stage.

Mahāsattva   A Bodhisattva (q.v.).

Mahayana (*mahāyāna*)   Great Vehicle, one of the two major divisions in Buddhism. Contrasts with Little Vehicle, Hinayana (*hīnayāna*). In the Mahayana, more stress is laid upon the idea of the Bodhisattva, who unlike the Arhat renounces nirvana, even though he could attain it at will, so that he can remain in samsara to lead all beings to enlightenment. He is endowed with infinite compassion and uses a variety of means, called skillful means, to teach and help people. Doctrinally, the Mahayana maintains the doctrine of egolessness not only for persons (like the Hinayana) but also for things (dharmas), which are seen as having no self-nature. The Mahayana also sees a plurality of Buddhas at various places and times in the universe. The historical Buddha Śākyamuni (*See also* Buddha) is seen as the earthly manifestation of the Buddha Amitābha/Amitāyus who dwells in the Western Paradise. A Buddha is an absolute and absolutely transcendent being, identical with the Dharma itself (*See also* Three Bodies of the Buddha). Also emphasis is placed on the ideas of salvation by faith, Emptiness (q.v.), suchness, Buddha nature, and the ultimate identity of opposites such as samsara and nirvana. The Great Vehicle is also called the One (Buddha) Vehicle. *See also* Three Vehicles.

Manas   The seventh of the Eight consciousnesses (q.v.) or *vijñānas*. Ego consciousness arises from the six consciousnesses combining to lead an individual to believe in the existence of a separate self.

***Maṇi* gem**   A legendary gem that is said to have the power to dispel misfortune and clear muddy water. The philosopher's stone; the pearl talisman capable of responding to every wish and is said to have been obtained from the dragon king or the head of the great fish Makara or the relics of a Buddha.

Mano-vijñāna   The sixth of the Eight consciousnesses (q.v.) or *vijñānas*. The mind that processes what is sensed by the other five senses into thoughts, feelings, and imagination.

Māra   The devil, the evil one, the destroyer. Attempted to persuade Śākyamuni (*See also* Buddha) not to aim at Buddhahood. Attachment to ego. Sometimes a whole class of māras is mentioned.

Mārga   Path, way. Denotes praxis, practice, as distinguished from theory; moral norm, reasonableness, naturalness. The Buddhist path to enlightenment; also (sometimes) the goal itself. The fourth of the Four Noble Truths (q.v.).

Meaningless arguments (*prapañca*)   Useless sophistry arising from wrong views caused by emotional and intellectual attachment.

Medicine from cows' urine   Monks used to use this for illnesses. One of the few possessions that monks were allowed to own, along with food, robes, and mat for sitting.

Meditation of cessation (*nirodha-samāpatti*)   Meditation in which all mental activities have ceased. The sense faculties remain intact but are in a state of quiescence. Speech, feeling, and perception are stilled.

Meditation of neither thought nor non-thought (*naivasaṃjñānā-saṃjñāyatana-dhyāna*)   A meditation immune to disturbance from the external world; yet traces of defilements, such as the latent craving for existence, remain, so that further refinement is required.

Meditation on boundless space (*ākāśānantyāyatana-dhyāna*)   A form of meditation in which one concentrates on the infinity of space, devoid of all physical objects.

Meditation on the void (*śūnyatā-samādhi*)   In this meditation one perceives that both the self and all phenomenal things are devoid of a permanent and substantive self-nature. Together with the meditations that perceive the essential formlessness of phenomenal things and that in reality nothing exists that can be sought after, the meditation on the void is part of what are known as the three meditations or Three gates of liberation (q.v.).

Merit, virtue (*puṇya*)   Doing meritorious deeds results in the accumulation of merit, and then these merits result in good things that come to one. *See also* Transference of merit.

Middle path (*madhyamā pratipad*)   In the Buddha's first sermon, the Middle Path was the avoidance of the extremes of asceticism on the one hand and sensual indulgence on the other, via the Eightfold Path (q.v.). Philosophically the Middle Path is the avoidance of the extremes of extinction on the one hand and continuity on the other, or the extremes of the absolute reality of phenomena or their absolute unreality.

Mind (*citta, manas, vijñāna*)   In Buddhist texts from various traditions 'mind' is interchangeably called '*citta*' (thought), '*manas*' (ego), or '*vijñāna*' (consciousness). However, the Buddha never considered these terms to be synonymous. He explained the mind to be another sense faculty along with sight, hearing, smelling, taste, and touch. He wanted his disciples to think of the mind simply as a function of mental activity. Otherwise, they might develop an undesirable obsession with an idea of a separate self (ego) existing within the body. Through the doctrine of Five Aggregates (q.v.), which are in constant flux, he explained the non-existence of a permanent spiritual self. Thus, one need not be in bondage to past karma (actions) but is free to change and attain spiritual happiness.

Mind earth   The mind is figuratively described as the earth. The all-producing power of the mind is compared to the character of earth. In Zen, it stands for a mind transmitted from Bodhidharma.

The mind naturally pure (*prakṛti-pariśuddha-citta*)   The doctrine that the mind in its pristine state is originally pure and undefiled. Adventitious defilements cover the mind temporarily and are therefore known as visitors or guests. They are not part of the mind's essential nature.

Mind only (*citta-mātra*)   The view that the Mind (q.v.) is the ultimate reality of all phenomenal existents in the universe. A kind of idealism sometimes compared to the Berkeleian. *See also* Mind naturally pure.

Moment, instant (*kṣaṇa*)   The shortest measure of time (differs by school). It is said that during this time there occurs a cycle of changes in phenomenal things from becoming to being to breakdown and voidness.

Muni   An inspired one, a sage, a solitary, a silent meditator. The supreme muni is, of course, Śākyamuni. *See also* Buddha

Nāga   A serpent, often personified. Associated with water, clouds, or underground regions.

Name and form   Mind and body. *See* Dependent Origination

Nine grades   A Pure Land school classification of people according to their natures and capacities. Their rebirths in the Pure Land differ according to their merits and wisdom. The Jōdo Shin school considers this doctrine provisional and believes that the compassion of Amitābha/Amitāyus Buddha embraces all equally.

Nirvana (*nirvāṇa*)   The state in which the flames of defilement have been blown out. It is described negatively, positively, or by silence. Negatively, it has been described as extinction of ignorance, of desire, of illusion, of hatred. Positively, it is called a refuge, a support, purity, freedom, and so on. Nirvana exists with remainder, i.e., with a physical body, and without remainder. The Buddhas and Arhats have attained nirvana, but the Buddhas do not reside in nirvana, for their Great Compassion leads them to be reborn in the world to teach and help others. Their nirvana is totally unattached so that they are not even attached to nirvana itself.

Nirvana with no fixed abode (*apratiṣṭhita-nirvāṇa*)   Possessed by the Buddhas. They neither settle permanently in nirvana nor are they trapped in samsara (*see* Transmigration). Out of wisdom and compassion they work freely to save sentient beings who remain blinded by delusions and are suffering.

Nirvana with pure self-nature (*citta-prakṛti-pariśuddha-nirvāṇa*)   Nirvana as the original pure mind, identical with the Buddha nature. It is characterized by permanence, joyfulness, enlightened self (which is non-self), and purity.

Non-attachment, indifference, equanimity (*upekṣā*)   One of the Four boundless minds (q.v.). Being indifferent to pleasure and displeasure, not discriminating between likes and dislikes.

Non-birth (*ajātika, anutpanna*)   This depicts the truth of dharmas. Since all things are devoid of substance, there is no becoming, and by extension, no extinction. It is synonymous with emptiness, nirvana, and so on.

Nonexistence of permanent ego and existence of dharmas (*pudgala-nairātmya, dharma-svabhāva*)   Doctrine of the Sarvāstivāda school. The so-called self comes into existence based on the coalescence of component parts and thus possesses no permanent or substantive existence. The dharmas on the other hand really exist, having essence and being.

Nonexistence of self-nature (*niḥsvbhāvatā*)   Denotes the nonexistence of a self-nature that is permanent, substantial, and immutable. It does not mean mere nothingness, which would fly in the face of experience; it does affirm the provisional existence of things in interdependence, but they have no self-nature. Synonymous with emptiness (q.v.).

Non-retrogressive state (*avaivartikā, avinivartanīya*)   The stage from which a practitioner progressing to enlightenment never regresses back to a lower stage. Those who reside in this state are absolutely assured that the wisdom that they have accumulated will always remain with them. Within the fifty-two stages of the Bodhisattva career, this stage is identical with the seventeenth stage; within the Bodhisattva-bhūmi stages it is the seventh.

Non-self (*pudgala-nairātmya, anātman*)   The doctrine that there is no abiding, unchanging essence or entity to be called the self in any phenomenal thing; this includes the personal self. This is a corollary to the doctrine of impermanence. Since all things are in constant flux, there cannot be any identity. Further, since all things are composed of elements, physical and mental, by concurrence of causes and conditions, when these conditions and causes change, what was a momentarily existing self is dissolved. This is one of the basic teachings of Buddhism. There are differences of interpretation of non-self among different schools.

Non-substantiality of dharmas (*dharma-nairātmya*)   Although some schools denied the ultimate existence of a substantial personal self, they still admitted the existence of material things (See Nonexistence of permanent ego and existence of dharmas). In the Mahayana, even the latter are denied any substantiality, as the logical conclusion of the doctrine of Dependent Origination (q.v.). Inasmuch as all things are compositions of elements temporarily put together, they do not have any self-nature.

Nyagrodha (Skt), or nigrodha (P) tree   A fig tree, Ficus benghalensis or Ficus indica; also, called banyan tree.

Obeisance (*vandana*)   Also called Casting the Five Parts of the Body on the Ground. It is an act of respect in which one touches one's knees, elbows, and forehead to the ground at the feet of an honored one, such as the Buddha.

Old age and death (*jarā-maraṇa*)   The twelfth of the twelve links of Dependent Origination (q.v.). The inevitable consequence of birth is death. But this does not mean the end of experience; the whole twelve links are again set into motion. Without the benefit of enlightenment, this process continues again and again.

One Vehicle (*ekayāna*)   Unificatory path. Prior to the rise of "unificatory path," the authors of the early Prajñāparamitā literature describe their religious system as Great Vehicle (Mahayana), claiming that they are superior to earlier Buddhist traditions. According to the temperaments of individuals, one must choose the Mahayana path or those of *śrāvaka* (priests) and *pratyeka-buddha* (hermits). This individualist approach was attached by the authors of the *Lotus Sutra (Saddharma-puṇḍarīka)* who attempted to attract a wider audience by claiming that all paths of Buddhism are incorporated in the One Vehicle. This message was especially welcome in China, and Japan, where the central governments preferred a unified religious principle to control the country as one.

Only child stage   The stage of a Bodhisattva or a Buddha in which one loves all beings as if each one of them were one's only child.

Ordinary man, common person (*pṛthag-jana*)   The ordinary live in ignorance and illusion within the cycle of birth and death.

Outflow and the absence of outflow (*sāsrava, anāsrava*)   A metaphor
for defilement, which is viewed as a discharge from the five sense organs and the
mind or from the six bodily apertures, eye, ear, nose, mouth, urethra, and colon.
The anāsrava is the absence of these, pure and undefiled.

Parinirvana (*parinirvāṇa*)   The demise of a Buddha. The nirvana he enjoys
after his passing, distinguished from the nirvana he attained and enjoyed while
he was alive.

Path of no learning (*aśaikṣa-patha*)   The highest stage of the Arhat. One
who has nothing more to learn and who practices rightly without effort and spontaneously.

Path of the right view (*darśana-mārga*)   The first of the Bodhisattva
stages. The stage at which one is able to discard the defiled view and see the Four
Noble Truths (q.v.). At this stage one is called a sage.

Perception, sensation (*vedanā*)   The seventh of the twelve links of Dependent Origination (q.v.). Arises from contact with the external world.

Perfected in knowledge and conduct (*vidyā-caraṇa-sampanna*)   One
of the ten epithets of the Buddha.

Poṣadha   *See* Uposatha.

Pratyekabuddha   One who attains Buddhahood without the guidance of a
Buddha. The Mahayana regards this realization as less than perfect because of
its lack of universal compassion and altruism for all sentient beings.

Precept (*śīla*)   Buddhist moral norm or system of discipline by the observation of which one is enabled to attain concentration of mind and eventually to
attain true wisdom. The cardinal precepts followed by all Buddhists are five: not
to kill, not to steal, not to commit adultery, not to lie, and not to take intoxicants.
There are other and longer lists of precepts, up to two or three hundred odd for
monks and nuns.

Provisional name, unreal name (*prajñapti*)   All phenomena exist in name
only because they are interdependently existing and are void (without any substantial self-entity).

Punishment (*daṇḍa*)   According to Jaina doctrine, wrong physical acts are the most deserving of punishment, over wrong vocal and mental acts. In Buddhism, mental acts are considered the most heinous. Punishments in the Sangha include brahma-daṇḍa, which is not speaking to the offender, and encouraging self-criticism in the offender.

Pure Land (*sukhāvatī*)   The Land of Peace and Happiness, or the Land of Ultimate Bliss. This is a realm free of defilements, established by the Buddha Amitābha/Amitāyus in the West. Those who have undeviating faith in this Buddha are reborn there and become the equals of a Buddha there.

Pure practice (*brahma-caryā*)   Pure celibate spiritual practice. Faithful observance of the precepts that one has taken on. Broadly speaking, observance of the Eightfold Path, which leads to the extinction of desire. According to the *Nirvāṇa Sūtra*, the removal of suffering from others and the imparting of pleasure to them, accomplished with a pure a mind, is another form of pure practice.

Quieting the mind and seeing clearly (*śamatha, vipaśyanā*)   Two integrated practices. The first involves withdrawal, calming, and concentrating and the single-minded focusing of the mind on the object of meditation. The second involves mindful analysis and observation and insight into the nature and characteristics of the object of meditation.

Rainy season retreat (*vārṣikā*)   The retreat held by the Sangha of monks and nuns during the rainy season, starting either in the middle of April or the middle of May and lasting three months. It was the practice of the Sangha to take shelter in caves or in monastic lodgings during these summer months to engage in the concentrated practices of introspection, meditation, and study.

Recollection, repeated mindfulness (*anusmaraṇa, smṛti*)   Keeping in mind the Buddha, the Dharma, the Sangha, the precepts, charity, the gods, death, the body, breathing, quiescence, or the like, thus purifying the mind and strengthening moral virtues.

Relative and dependent nature   *See* Three natures

Repentance and confession (*kṣama*)   When a monk becomes conscious of his transgressions, he confesses to the Sangha every fortnight on uposatha days or to the Buddha.

Rightly awakened (*samyak-sambuddha*)   One who has obtained perfect enlightenment. One of the epithets of the Buddha.

Robes made of discarded cloth (*pāṃsu-kūla*)   Robes sewn out of bits of discarded cloth pieces. Some Buddhist monks traditionally wrap themselves in robes patched together out of pieces of cloth salvaged from trash heaps.

Rules of the order (*vinaya*)   The Vinaya is the body of rules of the Order (Sangha) that regulate the conduct of monks and nuns. They include prohibitions of wrong acts; prescriptions of proper conduct at ordinations, at rainy season retreats, and in daily conduct. About 250 rules for monks and 350 for nuns.

Samādhi, **concentration**   One-pointedness of mind upon a single object. Samādhi is also the method of inducing calmness and unshaken mental equilibrium or equanimity. It is one of the Eightfold Path (q.v.) and one of the Three learnings (q.v.). It is not, however, the goal but a preparatory stage to the ultimate goal of true insight and compassion.

Samana **(P);** *Śramaṇa* **(Skt)**   A wandering ascetic, often Buddhist.

Samantabhadra   A Bodhisattva who sometimes accompanies the Buddha at one side while Mañjuśrī does so at the other. Mañjuśrī symbolizes the supreme wisdom of the Buddha, while Samantabhadra (All-Good) symbolizes the Dharma, meditation, and practice of the Buddha.

Samsara   *See* Transmigration

Saṃyak-saṃbuddha   *See* Rightly awakened

Sangha (*saṃgha*)   The Buddhist order of monks and nuns, and in a wider sense all Buddhists, monastic and lay. A group of harmonious practitioners of the Dharma. One of the Three Treasures (q.v.).

Secondary delusions, subordinate delusions (*upakleśa*)   Minor evil functions of the mind such as jealousy, parsimony, arrogance that adversely affect the mind.

Self-nature (*svabhāva*)   The fundamental nature, essence, identity, character, or principle of a thing that renders it permanent and immutable. The Dharma denies the existence of self-nature in this sense.

Seven limbs of awakening (*sapta-bodhy-aṅga*)   Seven steps conducive to the attainment of wisdom: (1) mindfulness, (2) awareness of truth and falsity, (3) effort in the Right Dharma, (4) joy in having the Right Dharma, (5) peace and ease attained by discarding encumbrances, (6) concentration of the mind, and (7) an unbiased and indifferent mind.

Śīla   *See* Precept

Six direct causes and four indirect causes (*hetu, pratyaya*)   The direct causes are (1) the general effective cause that helps and does not hinder the arising of dharmas, (2) mutual or coexistent causes like the four elements, (3) mutually supporting or correlated causes such as subject and object, (4) homogeneous causes of which the result is of the same kind, as with kindness and gratitude, (5) the universal cause, which is similar to the homogeneous except that this cause is referred only to defilements, and (6) the heterogeneous cause that produces an effect different in kind, as with overeating that causes sickness. The four indirect causes, or conditions, are (1) the dominant condition, which brings about the fruition of the main cause, (2) the condition for continuity, which is the preceding moment that does not cut off the continuity of cause and effect, (3) the objective cause, like a form that is the object of the eye, and (4) all other conditions that give rise to the effects.

Six non-Buddhist teachers and their teachings   These were at the time of the Buddha. (1) Pūraṇa Kāśyapa, or Purana Kassapa (P), held a form of nihilism with regard to ethics, inasmuch as he denied any idea of a causal relationship between good and evil deeds and their effects (reward or retribution). (2) Maskarin Gośāla, or Makkhali Gosāla (P), can be regarded as a fatalist in that he believed that people had no control over their happiness or suffering; fate and environment were the causes thereof. (3) Sañjaya was an agnostic or skeptic who denied that the causes of suffering were discoverable in this life. (4) Ajita Keśakambala was a materialist and a hedonist. (5) Kātyāyana, or Pakudha Kaccāyana (P), maintained that there was no logical reason for human suffering and that the universe was composed of wind, void, pleasure, pain, and the soul. (6) Nirgrantha Jñātiputra, or Nigantha Nataputta (P), the founder of Jainism, stressed extreme asceticism. His world-view was that of pluralism and relativism. Like the Buddha, he taught ahiṃsa, the doctrine of not harming people or animals. The first five of these doctrines are seen as favoring comfort too much, the sixth as erring on the side of excessive asceticism.

Six objects of cognition   Forms (color and shape), sounds, smells, tastes, tangibles, and dharmas.

Six or five destinies (*gati*)   Hell, the world of the hungry ghosts, the world of animals, the world of people, the world of asuras (q.v.) or titans, and heaven, the world of the gods. Sometimes the last two are considered one, hence the five destinies.

Six Perfections, Ten Perfections (*pāramitās*)   Bodhisattva practices.

The six are (1) selfless giving, (2) observance of precepts, (3) patience or forbearance, (4) exertion or energy, (5) concentration or meditation, and (6) insight or wisdom. The ten start with the six and add (7) skillful means, (8) vows, (9) power, and (10) transcendent cognition.

Skandhas, five   *See* Five aggregates.

Skillful means (*upāya*)   The Bodhisattva knows how to intervene in situations by actions whose meaning may not be entirely understood at the time, to save and help beings to liberation. A classic example is persuading children to leave a burning house by promising to give them three kinds of carts, of differing quality, that are said to stand outside the house, and then, giving all of the children a magnificent cart but not the three inferior kinds, which represent the three differing paths to enlightenment. The magnificent cart represents the One Vehicle (q.v.) available to all beings.

Śrāvaka   One who listens to the Buddha's teachings. A follower who is distinguished from Pratyekabuddhas (q.v.) and Bodhisattvas (q.v.)

Stupa (*stūpa*)   A burial mound for the relics of a Buddha. The pagoda, three or five storied towers, developed from the stupa.

Stupidity, ignorance, nescience (*moha*)   One of the major defilements; being ignorant of the twelve links of the chain of Dependent Origination (q.v.) or of the Four Noble Truths (q.v.). The lack of insight or impartial right view. This mental defilement obstructs one's passage to the right view and insight and hence becomes the basic cause of all evil.

Śūnyatā   *See* Emptiness

Superhuman powers, supernormal powers, supramundane powers (*abhijñā*)   Obtained by one who has attained enlightenment, or by one who has obtained quiescence and wisdom. Include the power to see through obstructions, hear what is not ordinarily heard, know the minds of others, know the destinies of others.

Sutras   Discourses of the Buddha on the doctrine.

Svabhāva   *See* Self-nature.

Taking refuge (*śaraṇa*)   Relying on the Three Treasures (q.v.); becoming a Buddhist.

Tathāgata   An enlightened one who has "gone (*gata*) to thusness (*tathā*)" or who has "come (*āgata*) from thusness (*tathā*)," or who has "come (*āgata*) thus (*tathā*)." One of the epithets of a Buddha.

Tathāgata womb, Tathāgata embryo (*tathāgata-garbha*)   Each being has the Tathāgata womb, which is the store consciousness (*ālaya-vijñāna*), which stores all seeds that influence and shape all subsequent experiences; it is also the container of the potential seed of Buddhahood. Each being is a Tathāgata embryo because of the latent possibility for Buddhahood. When the defilements that cover and conceal the true nature of this Tathāgata embryo are removed through the power of wisdom, then the Tathāgata is able to manifest himself.

Tathāgatagarbha   *See* Tathāgata womb

Ten epithets of the Buddha   Arhat, Rightly and Fully Awakened One, Endowed with Knowledge and Conduct, Well Gone, Knower of the World, Pre-eminent, Leader of Those to be Trained, Teacher of Gods and Men, Buddha, and World-Honored One (*arhat, samyaksaṃbuddha, vidyācaraṇasaṃpanna, sugata, lokavid, anuttara, puruṣadamya-sārathi, śāstṛdevamanuṣyānām, buddha, bhagavān*).

Ten grave prohibitory precepts   (1) Not to kill, (2) not to steal, (3) not to commit adultery, (4) not to lie, (5) not to take intoxicants, (6) not to talk about others' transgressions, (7) not to elevate oneself nor defame others, (8) not to be miserly, (9) not to become angry, and (10) not to malign the Three Treasures.

Ten Perfections   *See* Six Perfections

Ten stages   *See* Bodhisattva's ten stages to Buddhahood

Ten virtuous precepts (*daśa-kuśala-karma-patha*)   Not to kill, not to steal, not to commit adultery, not to lie, not to slander, not to use harsh words, not to talk frivolously, not to be covetous, not to harbor evil thoughts, to have right view.

Thirty-seven conditions conducive to enlightenment (*sapta-trimsad-bodhi-pākṣikā dharmāḥ*)   Also known as the thirty-seven wings of enlightenment. They are four kinds of bodhi, four kinds of effort, four heightened concentrations, five capacities, five superior powers, seven practices to heightened wisdom, and the Noble Eightfold Path.

Thirty-two features of the Buddha (*dvātriṃsad-vara-lakṣaṇa*)   It is said that there were thirty-two special characteristics of the Buddha's body, such as a golden body.

Three aspects of faith   Utmost mind (Jpn. *shishin*), joyful bliss, and aspiration for birth in the Pure Land. Faith with these three aspects is given to sentient beings by Amitābha/Amitāyus Buddha according to the Jōdo Shinshū (True Pure Land Sect).

Three Baskets (*tripiṭaka*) Three collections of Buddhist scriptures, the Sutras (teachings of the Buddha), the Vinaya (rules of conduct for monks and nuns, taught by the Buddha), and the Abhidharma (q.v.).

Three Bodies (*trikāya*) of the Buddha A Buddha has (first) two bodies, the Form Body (*rūpa-kāya*), which can be seen by all (while he lives), and the Dharma Body (*dharma-kāya*), which can only be known in deep and formless meditation by great meditators. The historical Buddha declared that his real nature was the Dharma, not his physical form. "Who sees the Dharma sees the Buddha." The Form Body is (later) divided into two (giving three bodies in all): the Enjoyment Body (*saṃbhoga-kāya*), perceived only in certain kinds of meditation, and the Transformation Body (*nirmāṇa-kāya*), which is perceived by everyone. These bodies are obtained as results of virtuous practice and meditation by the Buddhas.

Three gates of liberation (*vimokṣa-mukha*) The gate of liberation that is Emptiness (q.v.), the gate of liberation that is signless, and the gate of liberation that one is not intent on (*śūnyatā-vimokṣa-mukha, animitta-vimokṣa-mukha, apraṇihita-vimokṣa-mukha*).

Three learnings (*trī-śikṣa*) Morality, meditation, and wisdom (*śīla, samādhi, prajñā*). The first is the practice of the precepts, which prepares one for the second, which is the practice of concentration. This involves ridding oneself of all delusory thoughts and cultivating wisdom. This serves as the preparation for the third and ultimate practice, the practice of wisdom, in which all phenomenal existences are apprehended in their thusness.

Three marks of conditioned existence (1) Impermanent, (2) ill or suffering, (3) selfless (*anitya, duḥkha, anātman*). All phenomena have these three characteristics (but not nirvana, because it is not a phenomenon).

Three meditative states Meditation on Emptiness (q.v.), in which one perceives that both self and that which pertains to it ("I" and "mine") are empty; meditation on formlessness, in which one perceives that all forms are empty and therefore that there exists no differentiated form; meditation on desirelessness, in which one perceives that because forms have no real existence, there is nothing to desire. *See* also Three gates of liberation

Three natures (*trisvabhāva*) Imagined (*parikalpita*), dependent upon other things (*paratantra*), and absolute (*pariniṣpanna*). This triple is a classification of all existents according to the Yogācāra school. They are (1) imagined and illusory existence: what seems to be an existing object is but the reflection of the deluded mind that believes the unreal to be real; (2) relative or dependent existence: since the existent is possible only by the concurrence of certain conditions, there is no permanent entity or reality, since what seems to be objectively real is the creation of the mind, and that mind itself is not independently existing but a temporary conglomeration of causes and conditions; (3) complete and true reality: the absolute and highest reality or noumenon is tathatā (suchness or thusness), upon which the paratantra is dependent. This can be understood only by the untainted insight.

Three periods after the demise of the Buddha   The period of the true Dharma, when teaching, practice, and attainment exist intact; the period of the counterfeit Dharma, when only teaching and practice exist intact, but not attainment; the period of declining Dharma, when only the teaching exists but not the practice or attainment. According to some, the first period lasted five hundred years, the second lasted one thousand, and the third will last ten thousand.

Three robes (*cīvara*)   Three garments permitted to Buddhist monks. A saṃghāti robe, a large robe worn for the daily round of alms begging as well as on the occasions of visiting royal palaces; an uttarāsaṅga robe, an upper garment worn at ceremonies; an antarvāsa robe used for daily chores or sleep.

Three Treasures (*triratna*)   Buddha, Dharma, and Sangha.

Three Vehicles (*triyāna*)   Śrāvaka (q.v.) Vehicle, Pratyekabuddha (q.v.) Vehicle, Bodhisattva (q.v.) Vehicle. Three paths to enlightenment. See also One Vehicle.

Three worlds (*dhātu*)   The world of desire, the world of (pure) form, and the formless world.

Threefold cause of purity (*tri-śuddhi-hetu*)   The three disciplines by which a practitioner can maintain his physical and mental states pure and faultless for the practice of the Dharma: remaining far from evil friends and evil acquaintances; disciplining oneself to desire little and be satisfied with what one has in clothing, food, and bedding; and seeking freedom from defilements.

Thusness, suchness (*tathatā*)   The true reality of things. The ultimate ground of all phenomena. Synonymous with Emptiness (q.v.).

Transference of merit (*puṇya-pariṇāmana*)   Turning over of one's merit, which is accumulated by doing good deeds, to others so that they reap the benefit of them. Mahayana practitioners generally do this. Pure Land schools distinguish between two kinds of transference of merit: that done by the Buddha Amitābha/Amitāyus for our sakes and that done later by ourselves once in the Pure Land. That is, the transference of merit for the sake of birth in the Pure Land is done solely by the absolute power of the Buddha Amitābha/Amitāyus, since we are incapable of doing substantial good ourselves; upon attaining birth in the Pure Land and becoming the equal of the Buddha, we can return to earth to help others attain birth in the Pure Land by sharing our merits with them.

Transformed Buddhas and Bodhisattvas (*nirmāṇakāya-buddha-bod-hisattva*)   The original true body or essence of the Buddha is the truth itself. The Buddha, in order to help beings, manifests himself in a perceptible form, in the form of a human being or in other forms. The same can be said of the great Bodhisattvas. *See also* Three Bodies of the Buddha.

Transmigration (*saṃsāra*)   The cycle of birth, misery, and death that revolves like the wheel of a cart. This transmigratory process takes place in and through the Three worlds (q.v.) and the Six or five destinies (q.v.).

Turning of delusion into enlightenment   The total destruction of delusion and defilements is tantamount to the manifestation of the mind of original purity. The extinction of delusions and defilements that cover over the inherent Buddha nature leads concomitantly to the latter's manifestation.

Turning the Wheel of the Dharma (*dharma-cakra-pravartana*)   A metaphor for the Buddha's teaching activity.

Twelve categories of Buddhist scriptures (*dvādaśāṅga-buddha-vacana*)   (1) Sutras (sūtra), which are the Buddha's discourses, or the prose portions of them; (2) verses that retell the content of the prose discourses in a different literary style; (3) prophesies regarding the future enlightenment of the Buddha's disciples; (4) gāthā or hymns that also record the Buddha's discourses in verse; (5) a collection of utterances initiated by the Buddha and not set forth in response to disciples' questions; (6) records of the historical background for the Sutras and the Vinaya; (7) allegories and parables; (8) accounts of the past lives of Buddhas and disciples not contained in the Jātakas; (9) Jātakas, which recount the Buddha's past lives and spiritual practices; (10) sutras that deal with broad and extensive subject matter; (11) records of the Buddha's wondrous powers and virtues; (12) expositions of the doctrine.

Twelve sense fields (*dvādaśāyatana*)   The six sense organs and their corresponding objects: eye, ear, nose, tongue, body, mind, form, sound, smells, tastes, tangibles, and dharmas.

Two Bodies of the Buddha   *See* Three Bodies of the Buddha

Uḍumbara   A tree that is thought to blossom only once in three thousand years. (Ficus racemosa Linn). A metaphor for the rarity of the Buddha's teaching. Actually, at the time of the Buddha, the disciples gathered under the trees in training, because of the shade provided by the large leaves and also for the fruits that eliminated the necessity to beg. The fig-like fruits contain within the "flowers" which cannot be seen from without; thus, it was believed that this tree did not bloom every year, although in fact it did as part of the fruit.

Undifferentiated wisdom (*nirvikalpa-jñāna*)   Wisdom, knowledge, insight, and intuition that is absolute and free of the bifurcation of subject and object. This form of wisdom is direct and untarnished by differentiation that comes from awareness, judgment, reasoning, or memory. It transcends language, conceptual thinking, and all interpretations. It is identical with the insight of Emptiness (q.v.).

Upāya   *See* Skillful means

Uposatha, upavasatha   A gathering of the Sangha conducted twice a month, on the day of the new moon (fifteenth day of the month by the lunar calendar) and on the day of the full moon (thirtieth day), at which time the monks and nuns read the rules (*prātimokṣa*) of the Order and then confess any transgressions they have committed. Lay followers observe the eight precepts, listen to sermons, and offer food and drink to the monks and nuns.

Utmost mind (Jpn. *shishin*)   One of the Three aspects of faith (q.v.).

Vinaya   Rules of conduct for monks and nuns.

Void   *See* Emptiness

Volitional action (*saṃskāra*)   The second of the twelve links of Dependent Origination (q.v.). Denotes all volitional activity caused by blindness and initiated by the body, speech, and mind. Blindness or ignorance and volitional activities are considered to be the causes created in the immediate past life that bring about birth in this one.

Vow (*praṇidhāna*)   Some people vow to attain nirvana; great Bodhisattvas vow to perfect their practices and save all sentient beings; Buddhas make vows also, for instance Amitābha/Amitāyus Buddha vows to bring all those who have faith in him into his Pure Land, and Bhaiṣajyaguru Buddha vows to cure the sick.

Walking between meditations. (*caṅkramaṇa*)   Walking between sessions of sitting meditation is done to prevent drowsiness and for the sake of health.

White curl (*ūrṇa-bhrū*)   *See* Curl of white hair

Wisdom (*prajñā*)   Insight. Knowledge that is free of all differentiation; that which illuminates the true forms of phenomenal things, destroys delusions and defilements, and actualizes enlightenment. Wisdom manifests itself in two ways. First, it serves as the guiding force to enlightenment. Second, it manifests itself in the phenomenal world of relativity, differentiation, and bifurcation of subject and object. In other words, wisdom embraces both transcendental and worldly knowledge.

World-Honored One (*bhagavat*)   An epithet of the Buddha.

Wrong view (*dṛṣṭi*)   (1) The belief in the existence of a permanent self; (2) attachment to extreme viewpoints, namely, that there is nothing after death or that the self continues after death; (3) denial of the law of cause and effect; (4) attachment to the views of non-Buddhist teachers.

Yama-rāja   The king of the world of the dead. The judge presiding over that world. He examines the conduct of the dead and fixes punishments for wrong deeds.

Yojana   A unit of distance, the distance covered by a bullock cart in a day, approximately 9 miles. A league.

BUDDHA-DHARMA

SCRIPTURAL-SOURCES:
PALI, SANSKRIT, CHINESE

The *Buddha-Dharma* is a translation from the Japanese text of *Shinyaku Bukkyo Seiten*, which consists of simplified or shortened versions (not strict translation) of Buddhist scriptures selected from the *Taishō Shinshū Daizōkyō*, or the Chinese language edition of the Tripitaka. Therefore, the reader will not always find word-for-word correspondence between the text of this book and the sources listed here. Nevertheless, this list may prove helpful to some readers who desire further information or exact wording of the scriptures. Jātakas, Nikāyas, Vinaya, Dhammapada and its commentary, Theragāthā, Therīgāthā, Itivuttaka, and Burmese works are from the Pali unless otherwise noted. Sanskrit and Chinese works identify themselves by their orthography.

Abbreviations

A	Aṅguttara-nikāya(P)		**s.**	sutta (P), sūtra (Skt) or Buddha's discourse
Bk.	Book		**Sc.**	Section
Ch.	Chapter		**Skt**	Sanskrit Version
Chn.	Chinese Version		**Ssc.**	Sub-section
Com.	Commentary or Aṭṭhakathā		**Snip.**	Suttanipāta (P)
D.	Dīgha-nikāya (P)		**Thera G.**	Thera-gāthā (P)
Dhp.	Dhammapada (P)		**Theri G.**	Therī-gāthā (P)
Itiv.	Itivuttaka (P)		**v.**	version
M.	Majjhima-nikāya (P)		**Vin. CV.**	Vinaya-piṭakam Cūḷa-vagga (P)
P.	Pāli version			
p.	parivarta or Chapter (Skt)		**Vin. MV.**	Vinaya-piṭakam Mahā-vagga (P)
S.	Saṃyutta-nikāya (P)			
Sāratha	Sārathappakāsiṇī (P)		**v. v.**	Verses

Introductory Gatha...Ta fang kuang hua yen ching (Chn.) (Mahāvaipulyā-avataṃsaka-sūtra).

Bk.	Ch.	Sc.	Ssc.	Source
I	I	1	1	Jātaka-nidāna (P)
		2		
		3		Fang-kuang-ta-chuang-yen-ching, a Chn. v. of Lalita-vistara (Skt)
		4	1	
		4	2	M. 26 Ariyapariyesana-s. (P)
			3	A. III. 38 Sukhumāla (P)
		4	4	
				Fang-kuang-ta-chuang-yen-ching, a Chn. v. of Lalita-vistara (Skt)
		5		
		6	1-2	M. 85 Bodhirāja-kumāra-s. (P)
			3-4	M. 12 Mahāsīhanāda-s. (P)
	II	1	1-3	Fang-kuang-ta-chuang-yen-ching, a Chn. v. of Lalita-vistara (Skt)
			4	Snip. III, 2 Padhāna-s. (P)
			5	Jātaka-nidāna (P)
			6	Vin. MV. I, 1 (P)
			7	Hua-yen-ching, Shih-ti-p'in, a Chn. version of Avataṃsaka-s, Daśabhūmika-p. (Skt)
		2	1	Hua-yen-ching, Shih-chien-ching-yen-p'in; Hsien-shou-p'in (Chn)
			2	Hua-hen-ching, Lu-shê-na-fo-p'in, a Chn. v. of Avataṃsaka-s., Vairocana-buddha-p. (Skt.)
		2	3	Hua-yen-ching, Ju-lai-ming-hao-p'in, a Chn. v. of Avataṃsaka-s., Tathāgata-nāmadheya-p. (Skt.)
		3		Vin. MV. I, 2-5 (P)
	III	1		Vin. MV. I, 6 (P)
		2		Vin. MV. I, 7-14 (P)
		3	1-2	Vin. MV. I, 15-21 (P)
			3	M. 26 Ariya-paraiyesana-s. (P)
			4	A. III, 101-102 Pubbe (P)
		4		Vin. MV. I, 22 (P)
		5	1-4	Vin. MV. I, 23-4 (P)
			5	M. 74 Dīghanakha-suttānta (P)
		6	1-6	Itiv. 82, 83, 92, 100, 109 (P)
			7	A. III, 134 Uppāda (P)

Bk.	Ch.	Sc.	Ssc.	Source
I	IV	1	1-2	Fo-pên-hsing-chi-ching a Chn. v. of Abhiniṣkramaṇa-s. (Skt)
			3-4	Wu-fên-lü or a Chn. v. of Mahīśāsaka-vinaya (Skt)
		2		S. I, 1, 3-4; 7-9; 1.2.2,9 (P)
		3	1	Jātaka-nidāna (P)
			2-4	Jātaka, 547 (P)
		4	1	Jātaka-nidāna (P)
			2	Jātaka 485 (P)
		5	1-3	Jātaka-nidāna (P)
			4-5	Vin. CV. VII, 1 (P)
		6		Vin. CV. VI, 4-5 (P)
II	I	1	1-2	M. 3 Dhammadāyāda-s. (P)
			3-5	M. 27 Mahā-hatthipadopama-s. (P)
			6	S. 16, 3 Candupamaṃ (P)
			7	A. VII, 68 Aggi (P)
		2	1	S. 3.3.1 Puggala (P)
			2	S. 3.3.5 Pabbatūpama (P)
			3	S. 3.1.1 Daharo (P)
			4	M. 87 Piyajātika-s. (P)
		3	1	S. 21, 8 Nanda (P) — Dhp. Com. (P) — Thera-G. vv. 157-8 (P) — Thera-G. Com. vv. (P)
			2	Thera-G. 159-60 (P)
		4	1-3	Hua-yen-ching, P'u-sa-ming-nan p'in (Chn)
			4	Hua-yen-ching, Ching-hsing-p'in, Chn. v. of Avataṃsaka-s. Viśuddha-carita-p. (Skt)
			5	Hua-yen-ching, Hsien-shou-p'u-sa-p'in (Chn)
	II	1	1	Buddha's Life, Burmese Version, Ch. IX (P)
			2	Thera-G. Com. vv. 1091-1145 (P)
		2		D. 21 Sakka-pañha-suttānta (P)
		3		Dhp. Com. III (P)
		4		M. 141 Sacca-vibhaṅga-s. (P)
		5	1	Jātaka 412-8 (P)
			2	Jātaka 475 (P)
			3	Jātaka 322 (P)
			4	M. 142 Dakkhiṇā-vibhaṅga-s. (P)

Bk.	Ch.	Sc.	Ssc.	Source
II		6	1	Buddha's Life, Burmese Version, Ch. IX (P)
			2-3	Vin. CV. X. I (P)
		7	1-2	A. III, 105, 33 Nidāna (P)
			2-3	Itiv. 39, 42, 40 (P)
			4	A. III, 35 Devadūtā-s. (P)
	III	1		Theri-G. Com vv. 139-144 (P)
		2	1-3	Lêng-ch'ieh-ching, Lo-p'o-na-chüan-ch'ing-p'in, a Chn. v. of Laṅkāvatāra-s., Rāvaṇa-rāja-adhyeṣaṇa-p. (Skt)
		2	4	
		3		Chi-i-ch'ieh-fa-p'in, a Chn. v. of Laṅkāvatāra-s. Samudaya-sarva-dharma-p (Skt)
		4		
		5	1	
			2-5	Lêng-ch'ieh-ching, Wu-ch'ang-p'in, a Chn. v. of Laṅkāvatāra-s., Anitya-p. (Skt)
			6	Lêng-ch'ieh-ching, Ch'a-na-p'in, a Chn. v. of Laṅkāvatāra-s., Kṣaṅika-p. (Skt)
	IV	1	1	Vin. MV. I, 25 (P)
			2	Vin. MV. I, 28-30 (P)
		2	1	Vin. MV. II, 1-2 (P)
			2	Vin. MV. III, 1-2 (P)
		3		Vin. MV. I, 5, 1 (P)
		4		Vin. C.V.V. 8 (P)
		5	1-5	M. 12 Mahāsīhanāda-s. (P)
			6	D. 24 Pāṭika-suttānta (P)
			7	Buddha's Life, Burmese Version Ch. IX (P)
		6	1-3	Fo-shêng-tao-li-tien-wei-mu-shuo-fa-ching(Chn)
			4-5	Ma-kê-ma-yeh-ching (Chn)
			6-7	Fo-shêng-tao-li-tien-wei-mu-shuo-fa-ching(Chn)
			8	Fo-shêng-tao-li-tien-wei-mu-shuo-fa-ching(Chn); Tao-shên-tsu-wu-chi-pien-hua-ching, II, (Chn)
		7	1-2	S. 12, 60 Nidāna, etc. (P)
			3	Dhp. Com. I, 199-203 (P)
			4	Tsêng-i-a-han-ching, a Chn. v. of Ekottarāgama 28-p. (Skt.)
			5	Dhp. Com. III, 224 (P)
		8	1-2	Hsing-ch'i-hsing-ching (Chn)
			3-7	A. III, 61 Tittham (P)
			8	A. III, 63 Venāga (P)
			9	A. III, 79 Gandha (P)

Bk.	Ch.	Sc.	Ssc.	Source
II	IV	9	1	Buddha's Life; Burmese Version, Ch. X
			2-3	A. III, 127-8 Anuruddhā (P)
			4	A. VIII, 30 Anuruddhā (P)
		10	1-6	Jātaka, IV (P)
			7-8	Tsa-a-han-ching, a Chn. v. of Saṃyuktāgama, 43 (Skt)
			9	Tsa-a-han-ching, a Chn. v. of Saṃyuktāgama, 43 (Skt)
III	I	1	1	M. 81 Ghaṭīkāra (P)
		2	1	A. III, 163 Samādhi (P)
			2	A. III, 53 Brāhmaṇā (P)
			3-8	M. 22 Alagaddūpama-s. (P)
		3		Mo-têng-ch'ieh'ching, a Chn. v. of Mātaṅgī-s. (Skt)
		4		Ta-fo-ting-shou-lêng-yen-ching, a Chn. v. of
		5		Mahā-tathāgata-uṣṇīṣa-śūraṅgama-s. (Skt)
	II	1	1	A. III, 68 Aññatitthiya (P)
			2	A. III, 71 Channa (P)
			3-6	A. III, 65 Kesaputtiyā (P)
		2	1	A. III, 90 Paṅkadhā (P)
		2	2-3	A. III, 81-2 Samaṇā, etc. (P)
			4	A. III, 88 Sikkhā (P)
		3	1-2	M. 34 Cūḷa-gopālaka-s. (P)
		3	3-5	M. 31 Cūḷa-gosiṅga-s. (P)
			6-9	A. III, 74-78 Nigaṇṭha, etc. (P)
			10-12	M. 32 Mahā-gosiṅga-s. (P)
		4	1-6	M. 14 Cūḷa-dukkha-khandha-s. (P)
			7-10	M. 18 Madhupiṇḍika-s. (P)
	III	1		M. 5 Anaṅgaṇa-s. (P)
		2		M. 21 Kakacūpama-s. (P)
		3	1	A. III, 34 Āḷavaka (P)
			2	A. III, 72 Ājivaka (P)
		4		D. 31 Siṅgālovāda-suttānta (P)
		5		M. 24 Ratthavinīta-s. (P)

Bk.	Ch.	Sc.	Ssc.	Source
III	III	6	1	S. 1, 4, 6 (10, 12, 10) (P)
			2	S. 2, 1, 6 Kāmada (P)
			3-4	S. 2, 2, 7-8 Subrahmā, etc. (P)
			5	S. 2, 3, 6 Rohita (P)
			7 8 9 10	Ta-fang-kuang-fo-hua-yen-ching, ju-fa-chieh-p'in, a Chn. v. Avataṃsaka-s., Gaṇḍavyūha-p. (Skt)
IV	I	1	1	A. III, 124 Bharaṇḍu (P)
			2	S. 55, 21-2 Mahānāma (P)
			3	S. 55, 37 Mahānāma (P)
			4	S. 55, 54 Gilāyanaṃ (P)
			5	A. III, 121 Kusinārā (P)
			6	A. III, 112-3, 117-8 (P)
			7	A. III, 94 Ājāniya (P)
			8	A. III, 131 Yodhājiva (P)
			9	A. III, 163 Samādhi (P) / A. III, 135 Kesakambala (P)
		2	1-3	D. 6 Mahāli-s.
			4-9	D. 25 Udumbarika-sīhanāda-suttānta (P)
		3	1-6	D. 26 Cakkavatti-sīhanāda-suttānta (P)
			7	A. III, 126 Kaṭuviya (P)
		4	1	Hua-yen, Shih-ming-p'in; Shih-jên-p'in (Chn)
			2	Hua-yen, Shin-jên-p'in (Chn)
			3	Hua-yen, Fo-pu-kê-ssŭ-i-p'in (Chn) / Hua-yen, Fo-hsiao-hsiang-kuang-ming-kung-tê-p'in (Chn)
		4	4	Hua-yen, P'u-hsien-p'u-sa-hsing-p'in, Chn. V. of Avataṃsaka-s., Samantabhadra-bodhisattva-caryā-p. (Skt)
			5-9	Hua-yen, Pao-wang-ju-lai-hsing-ch'i-p'in, Chn. v. of Avataṃsaka-s., Ratnarāja-tathāgata-gotra-saṃbhava-artha-p. (Skt)
			10-13	Hua-yen, Li-shih-chien-p'in, a Chn. v. of Avataṃsaka-s., Loka-niḥsaraṇa-p. (Skt)
		5	1-3	M. 56 Upāli-suttānta (P)
			4-7	D. 4 Soṇadaṇḍa-s. (P)
			8	M. 39 Mahāssapura-s. (P)
			9	M. 40 Cūḷassapura-s. (P)

Bk.	Ch.	Sc.	Ssc.	Source
IV	II	1	1	S. 43, 2-4 Samatho, etc. (P)
			2	S. 35, 85 Suñña (P)
			3	M. 151 Piṇḍapāta-pārisuddhi-s. (P)
			4	M. 121 Cūḷa-suññatā-s. (P)
		2		Chin-kang-pan-jê-po-lo-mi-to-ching, a Chn. v. of Vajracchedikā-prajñāpāramitā-s. (Skt)
		3		Pan-jê-po-lo-mi-to-hsin-ching, a Chn. v. of Prajña-pāramitā-hṛdaya-s. (Skt)
		4		Ta-p'in-pan-jê-po-lo-mi-to-ching, Sa-t'o-po-lun-p'in, Chn. v. of Mahāprajñā-pāramitā-s., Sadāprarudita-p. (Skt)
				Ta-p'in-pan-jê-po-lo-mi-to-ching, T'an-wu-kê-p'in Chn. v. of Mahāprajñā-pāramitā-s., Dharmodgata-p. (Skt)
				Ta-p'in-pan-jê-po-lo-mi-to, Shu-lei-p'in, Chn. v. of Mahāprajñā-pāramitā-s., Parīndanā-p. (Skt)
	III	1	1-4	D. 12 Lohicca-s. (P)
			5-8	D. 13 Tevijja-s. (P)
			9-10	M. 2 Sabbāsava-s. (P)
		2	1-3	M. 67 Cātumā-s.
			4-8	M. 35 Cūḷa-saccaka-s. (P)
			9	M. 36 Mahā-saccaka-s. (P)
		3		Ta-sa-chê-ni-chien-tzü-so-shuo-ching, a Chn. v. of Mahāsātya-Nirgaṇṭhaputra-vyākaraṇa-s. (Skt)
		4		Hua-yen-ching, Ching-kang-t'ung-p'u-sa-hui-hsiang-p'in, a Chn. v. of Avataṃsaka-s. Vajraketu-bodhisattva-pariṇāmanā-p. (Skt)
		5	1	M. 69 Gulissāni-suttānta (P)
			2-3	M. 77 Mahā-sakulūdāyi-s. (P)
			4-6	M. 44 Cūḷa-vedalla-s. (P)
	IV	1		M. 61 Ambalaṭṭhikā-Rāhulovāda-p. (P)
		2		Hua-yen-ching, Shih-ti-p'in, a Chn. v. of Avataṃsaka-s., Daśabhūmīśvara-p. (Skt)
		3	1-2	Wei-mo-ching, Fo-kuo-p'in, a Chn. v. of Vimalakīrti-nirdeśa-s., Buddha-kṣetra-p. (Skt)
			3	Wei-mo-ching, Fang-pien-p'in, a Chn. v. of Vimalakīrti-nirdeśa-s., Abhyupāya-p. (Skt)
			4-7	Wei-mo-ching, Ti-tzu-p'in, a Chn. v. of Vimalakīrti-nirdeśa-s., Śiṣya-p. (Skt)

Bk.	Ch.	Sc.	Ssc.	Source
IV			8-9	Wei-mo-ching, P'u-sa-p'in, Chn. v. of Vimalakīrti-nirdeśa-s., Bodhisattva-p. (Skt)
			10	Wei-mo-ching, Wên-shu-shih-li-wên-chi-p'in, a Chn. v. of Vimalakīrti-nirdeśa-s., Mañjuśrī-saṃstava-p. (Skt)
			11	Wei-mo-ching, Pu-ssu-i-p'in, a Chn. v. of Vimalakīrti-nirdeśa-s., Acintya-p. (Skt)
			12-13	Wei-mo-ching, Kuan-chung-shêng-p'in, a Chn. v. of Vimalakīrti-nirdeśa-s., Sattva-parīkṣā-p. (Skt)
			14	Wei-mo-ching, Fa-tao-p'in, a Chn. v. of Vimalakīrti-nirdeśa-s., Buddha-mārga-p. (Skt)
			15	Wei-mo-ching, Ju-pu-êrh-fa-mên-p'in, a Chn. v. of Vimalakīrti-nirdeśa-s., Advaya-dharma-mukha-p. (Skt)
			16	Wei-mo-ching, P'u-sa-hsing'p'in, a Chn. v. of Vimalakīrti-nirdeśa-s., Bodhisattva-caryā-p. (Skt) Wei-mo-ching, Chien-A-shu-fo-p'in, a Chn. v. of Vimalakīrti-nirdeśa-s., Akṣobhya-buddhadarśana-p. (Skt)
V	I	1	1-2	M. 70 Kiṭāgiri-suttānta (P)
			4-6	M. 76 Sandaka-suttānta (P)
		2		S. 10, 12 Āḷava-sālatha (P)
		3		S. 3 Ambaṭṭha-s. (P)
		4	1-4	M. 9 Sammādiṭṭhi-s (P)
			5-8	M. 77 Mahā-sakulūdayi-s. (P)
			9	M. 4 Bhayabherava-s. (P)
			10	M. 65 Bhaddāli-s. (P)
		5	1	Jātaka 55 (P)
			2-3	Jātaka 92 (P)
				Dhp. Com I (P)
			4-5	Jātaka 417 (P)
		6		Lai-to-hê-lo-ching, a Chn. v. of Rāṣṭrapāla-s. (Skt)
	II	1		Fang-wang-ching, a Chn. v. of Brāhmajālā-s. (Skt)
		2	1-8	Vin. MV. X, 1-2 (P)
			9-10	M. 122 Mahā-suññata-s. (P)
		3	1	Itiv. (P)
		4	1-2	M. 83 Makhādeva (P)
			3	M. 41 Sāleyyaka-s. (P)

Bk.	Ch.	Sc.	Ssc.	Source
V	III	1	1	Tsêng-i-a-han-ching, A Chn. v. of Ekottarāgama 16-p. (P)
			2-4	M. 62 Rāhulovāda-s. (P)
		2	1	A. III, 31 (P)
			2	A. III, 36 (P)
			3	A. III, 37 (P)
			4	A. III, 41-42 (P)
			5	A. III, 62 (P)
			6	A. III, 1, 2, 4 (P)
		3	1	Dhp. Com. I (P)
			2	Yü-yeh-nü-ching (Chn)
			3-6	Yang-chüeh-mo-ching, a Chn. v. of Aṅgulimāla s. (Skt)
		4		D. 27 Aggañña-suttānta (P)
		5	1	A. III, 11-13 (P)
			2	A. III, 14-15 (P)
			3	A. III, 18-20 (P)
		6	1	Chung-a-han-ching, a Chin. v. of Madhyāgama-s. 33 (Skt)
			2-4	M. 51 Kandaraka-s. (P)
	IV	1	1	M. 8 Sallekha-s. (P)
			2	A. III, 51 Janā (P)
			3	A. III, 51 Brāhmaṇā (P)
			4-5	A. III, 60 Saṅgārava (P)
		2	1-2	A. II, 4, 6-7 (P)
			3-4	A. III, 21-22 (P)
			5	A. III, 25 (P)
			6	A. II, 2, 8, (P)
			7	A. II, 3, 10 (P)
			8	A. II, 4, 1-2 (P)
			9	A. II, 1, 2 (P)
			10	A. II, 1, 5 (P)
			11	A. II, 1, 6-8; 2, 1 (P)
		3		A. I (P)
		4	1	Thera-G. vv. 453-458 (P)
			2	A. III, 130 (P)
			3-5	A. III, 98-100 (P)
		5	1	Hua-yen-ching, P'u-sa-yün-chi-shuo-chieh-p'in, (Chn)
			2	Hua-yen-ching, Shih-chu-p'in, a Chn. v. of Avataṃsaka-s., Daśa-sthiti. (Skt)
			3	Hua-yen-ching, Fan-hsing-p'in, a Chn. v. of Avataṃsaka-s., Brāhma-cariya-p. (Skt)

Bk.	Ch.	Sc.	Ssc.	Source
V	IV	5	4	Hua-yen-ching, Ming-fa-p'in, a Chn. v. of Avataṃ-saka-s., Dharma-nirandhakāra-p. (Skt)
			5	Hua-yen-ching, Yeh-mo-tien-kung-p'in, a Chn. v. of Avataṃsaka-s., Yama-rāja-pura-p. (Skt)
VI	I	1	1-3	M. 46 Mahādhamma-samādāna-s. (P)
			4-5	M. 7 Vatthūpama-s. (P)
			6	M. 16 Cetokhila-s. (P)
			7	A. IV, 184 (P)
			8	A. IV, 186 (P)
			9	A. IV, 190 (P)
			10	A. IV, 194 (P)
			11	A. IV, 197 (P)
		2	1	Thera-G. vv 181-2 Com. (P)
			2	A. IV, 185 (P)
			3	A. II, 6, 1-4 (P)
			4	A. II, 3, 2-3 (P)
			5-8	A. II, 6, 8, 11, 2-9 (P)
			9-11	A. V, 32-4 (P)
			12	A. V, 44 (P)
		3	1	A. III, 72 (P)
			2-3	A. V, 4 (P)
			4-6	A. V, 10-12 (P)
			7	A. V, 16 (P)
			8	A. V, 107 (P)
			9	A. III, 73 (P)
			10-11	A. III, 77-8 (P)
		4	1-2	A. V. (P)
			3-4	A. V, 56-7 (P)
			5-7	S. 22, 87 Vakkali (P)
		5		Dhp. (P)
	II	1	1-2	Wu-liang-shou-ching, a Chn. v. of Sukhāvatī-vyūha-s. or Aparimitāyus-s. I (Skt)
			3-5	Wu-liang-shou-ching, a Chn. v. of Sukhāvatī-vyūha-s. or Aparimitāyus-s. II (Skt)

Bk.	Ch.	Sc.	Ssc.	Source
VI	III	1	1	S. 6, 1, 2 Garavo (P)
			2	Itiv. 112 (P)
			3	S. 8, 4 Ānanda (P)
			4	Tsêng-i-a-han-ching, a Chn. v. of Ekottarāgama 35-p. (Skt)
		2	4	S. II (P)
		3	1	M. 25 Nivāpa-s. (P)
			2	M. 6 Ākaṅkheyya-s. (P)
		4		Shêng-man-ching, a Chn. v. of Śrīmālā-devī-
		5		siṃhanāda-s. (Skt)
	IV	1	1-2	M. 50 Māratajjaniya-s. (P)
			3	S. 35, 88 Puṇṇa (P)
		2	1-2	M. 53 Sekha-s. (P)
			3-4	M. 54 Potaliya-s. (P)
			5	Snip. Selasutta (P)
		3		Ssŭ-shih-êrh-chang-ching (Chn)
		4	1	M. 144 Channovāda-s. (P)
			2-3	M. 63 Cūḷa-māluṅkya-s. (P)
		5	1-7	S. 5. 1-8 Bhikkhuṇī-samyutta; Theri-G. Com. (P)
			8-10	M. 146 Nandako-vāda-s. (P)
		6	1	S. 56, 31 Siṃsapā (P)
			2-4	S. 3.3.2 Ayyakā (P)

Bk.	Ch.	Sc.	Ssc.	Source
VII	I	1	1-2	Miao-fa-lien-hua-ching, Hsü-p'in, a Chn. v. of Saddharmapuṇḍarīka-s. Introd. Ch. (Skt)
			3-5	Miao-fa-lien-hua-ching, Fang-pien-p'in, a Chn. v. of Saddharmapuṇḍarīka-s. Upāya-kauśalya-p. (Skt)
		2		Miao-fa-lien-hua-ching, Pi-yü-p'in, a Chn. v. of Saddharmapuṇḍarīka-s. Aupamya-p. (Skt)
		3	1-5	Miao-fa-lien-hua-ching, Hsin-chieh-p'in, a Chn. v. of Saddharmapuṇḍarīka-s. Adhimukti-p. (Skt)
			6	Miao-fa-lien-hua-ching, Yao-ts'ao-yü-p'in, a Chn. v. of Saddharmapuṇḍarīka-s. Oṣadhī-p (Skt)
			7-8	Miao-fa-lien-hua-ching, Hua-ch'eng-yü-p'in, a Chn. v. of Saddharmapuṇḍarīka-s. Pūrvayoga-p. (Skt)
			9	Miao-fa-lien-hua-ching, Fa-shih-p'in, a Chn. v. of Saddharmapuṇḍarīka-s. Dharmabhāṇaka-p. (Skt)
			10	Miao-fa-lien-hua-ching, Chien-fa-ta-p'in, a Chn. v. of Saddharmapuṇḍarīka-s. Stūpasaṃdarśana-p. (Skt)
		4	1-3	Miao-fa-lien-hua-ching, T'i-p'o-ta-to-p'in, Chn. v. of Saddharmapuṇḍarīka-s. Devadatta-p. (Skt)
			4	Miao-fa-lien-hua-ching, Ch'üan-ch'ih-p'in, a Chn. v. of Saddharmapuṇḍarīka-s., Utsāha-p. (Skt)
			5-6	Miao-fa-lien-hua-ching, An-lou-hsing-p'in, a Chn. v. of Saddharmapuṇḍarīka-s. Sukhavihāra-p. (Skt)
			7-8	Miao-fa-lien-hua-ching, P'u-sa-tsung-ti-yu-ch'u-p'in, a Chn. v. of Saddharmapuṇḍarīka-s. Bodhisattva-pṛthivī-vivara-samudgama-p. (Skt)

Bk.	Ch.	Sc.	Ssc.	Source
VII		5	1-2	Miao-fa-lien-hua-ching, Ju-lai-shou-liang-p'in, a Chn. v. Saddharmapuṇḍarīka-s. Tathāgatāyuṣpramāna-p. (Skt)
			3-4	Miao-fa-lien-hua-ching, Fên-pieh-kung-tê-p'in, a Chn. v. of Saddharmapuṇḍarīka-s. Punya-parayāya-p. (skt)
			5	Miao-fa-lien-hua-ching, Fa-shih-kung-tê-p'in, a Chn. v. of Saddharmapuṇḍarīka-s. Dharmabhāṇakānuśaṃsā-p. (Skt)
			6	Miao-fa-lien-hua-ching, Ch'ang-pu-ch'ing-p'u-sa-p'in, a Chn. v. of Saddharmapuṇḍarīka-s. Sadāparibhūta-bodhisattva-p. (Skt)
			7	Miao-fa-lien-hua-ching, Ju-lai-she-li-p'in, a Chn. v. of Saddharmapuṇḍarīka-s.Tathāgatarddhyabhisaṃskāra-p. (Skt)
			8	Miao-fa-lien-hua-ching, Shu-lei-p'in, a Chn. v. of Saddharmapuṇḍarīka-s. Anuparīndanā-p. (Skt)
			9	Miao-fa-lien-hua-ching, Yao-wang-p'u-sa-pên-ti-p'in, a Chn. v. of Saddharmapuṇḍarīka-s. Bhaiṣajyarāja-pūrvayoga-p. (Skt)
			10-11	Miao-fa-lien-hua-ching, Kuan-shi-yin-p'u-sa-p'u-mêp'in, a Chn. v. of Saddharmapuṇḍarīka-s. Avalokiteśvara-bodhisattva-samanthamukha-p. (Skt)
		6	1	M. 28 Mahā-hatthi-padopama-s. (P)
			2	Saṃyuktāgama-s. 35 (Skt)
			3-4	M. 19 Dvedhāvitakka-s. (P)
			5	M. 20 Vitakka-santhāna-s. (P)
	II	1	1	Yu-pu-pi-nai-yeh-po-sêng-shih, Chn. v. of Sarvāstivādin-vinaya-saṃgha-bhedakavastu XIII (Skt)
			2	Wu-fên-lü, a Chn. v. of Mahīśāsaka-vinaya III (Skt)
			3	Yu-pu-pi-nai-yeh-po-seng-shih, a Chn. v. of Sarvāstivādin-vinaya-saṃgha-bhedakavastu XIII (Skt)
			4-5	Wu-fên-lü, a Chn. v. of Mahīśāsaka-vinaya III (Skt)
			6	M. 29 Mahā-sāropama-s. (P)
			7-8	M. 58 Abhayarāja-kumāra-s. (P)
		2	1	Wu-fên-lü, a Chn. v. of Mahīśāsaka-vinaya (Skt)
			2	Wei-shêng-yüan-ching, a Chn. v. of Ajātaśatru-kaukṛyavinodana-s. (Skt)
			3	Kuan-wu-liang-shou-ching, a Chn. v. Amitāyur-dhyāna-s. (Skt)
		3		
		4	1	Ssŭ-fên-lü, A Chn. v. of Dharmagputaka-vinaya IV (Skt)
			2	Wu-Fên-lü, a Chn. v. of Mahīśāsaka-vinaya III (Skt)
			3	Wei-shêng-yüan-ching, a Chn. v. of Ajātaśatru-kaukṛyavinodana-s. (Skt)

Bk.	Ch.	Sc.	Ssc.	Source
VII	II	5	4-14	
			1-4	Ta-pan-nieh-p'an-ching, a Chn. v. of Mahāpari-nirvāṇa-s. (Skt)
			5	Yu-pu-pi-nai-yeh-po-sêng-shih, I, a Chn. v. of Sarvastivādin-vinaya-saṃgha-bhedakavastu I (Skt)
			6	Tsêng-i-a-han-ching, a Chn. v. of Ekottarāgama-s. (Skt)
	III	1		Shou-mo-ti-nü-ching, a Chn. v. of Sumatidārika-paripṛcchā-s. (Skt)
		2		Vin. CV. V. 21 (P)
		3	1	S. 41, 3 Isidatta (P)
			2	S 41. 9 Acela (P)
			3-5	D. 8 Kassapa-sīhanāda-suttānta (P)
			6	S. 41, 5 Kāmabhū (P)
		4	1-12	Tsa-pao-ts'ang-ching (Chn) from Saṃyuktaratna-piṭaka-s. (Skt)
			13-22	Ch'uan-chi-pai-yüan-ching, a Chn. v. of Purṇamukhāvadāna-śatika-s. (Skt)
		5	1-2	M. 23 Vammīka-s. (P)
			3	M. 133 Mahākaccāna-bhaddekaratta-s. (P)
	IV	1	1	A. V. 49 Kosala
			2-5	M. 104 Sāmagāma-s. (P)
		2		A. IV. 35, 183, 187 (P)
		3		Tsêng-i-a-han-ching, a Chn. v. of Ekottarāgama 28-p (Skt)
		4		M. 89 Dhammacetiya-s. (P)
				Tsêng-i-a-han-ching, a Chn. v. of Ekottarāgama 34 (Skt)
		5		Dhp. Com. I (P)
		6	1-3	A-mi-t'o-ching, a Chn. v. of Sukhāvatī-vyūha-s. (Skt)
			4-5	A. I, 14 Etadaggavagga (P)
VIII	I	1	1	
			2	Pan-ni-yüan-ching, a Chn. v. of Parinirvāna-s. I. (Skt)
			3	
			4	Tsêng-i-a-han-ching, a Chn. v. of Ekottarāgama 26 (Skt)
			5	Pan-ni-yüan-ching, a Chn. v. of Parinirvāna-s. (Skt)
	II			Chin-kuang-ming-tsui-shêng-wang-ching,
			1	Fên-pieh-san-shên-p'in, a Chn. v. of Suvarṇa-prabhā sottamarāja-s., Trikāya-p. (Skt)

Bk.	Ch.	Sc.	Ssc.	Source
VIII	II	2		Ssü-tien-wang-hu-kuo-p'in (of the above sütra), a Chn. v. of Cātur-mahārāja-kāyika-devaḥ-p. (Skt) Chin-kuang-ming-ching, Wang-chéng-fa-lun-p'in. a Chn. v. of Suvarṇa-prabhāsa-s., Devendra-samaya-p. (Skt)
		3	1	Chin-kuang-ming-ching, Ch'u-ping-p'in, a Chn. v. of Suvarṇa-prabhāsa-s., Vyādhipraśamaṇa-p. (Skt)
Chn.			2-3	Chin-kuang-ming-ching, Chang-chê-liu-shui-p'in, a v. of Suvarṇa-prabhāsa-s., Jalavāhanasya Mātsya-vaineya-p. (Skt)
			4-6	Shê-shên-p., a Chn. v. of Vyāghrī-p. (Skt)
		4		Ta-p'i-lu-chê-ne-ch'êng-fo-shên-pien-ch'ih-ching, Ju-chên-mên-chu-hsin-p'in, a Chn. v. of Mahāvairocanābhisam bodhi-vikurvitādhiṣṭhana-vaipulyasūtrendrarāja-nāma-dharmaparyāya (Skt)
	III	1		(Hsiao-ch'eng) Ta-pan-nieh-p'an-ching, I, II, a Chn. v. of Mahāparinibbāṇa-s. I, II (P)
		2		Ta-pan-nieh-p'an-ching, a Chn. v. of Mahāparinirvāṇa-s. II-X (Skt)
		3	1-2	Ch'ang-a'han'ching, III, a Chn. v. of Dīrghāgama III (Skt)
			3-5	(Hsiao-ch'eng) Ta-pan-nieh-p'an-ching, a Chn. v. of Mahāparinibbāṇa-s. (P)
		4		Ta-pan-nieh-p'an-ching, a Chn. v. of Mahāparinirvāṇa-s. 11-18 (Skt)
		5		
		6		
	IV	1		Ta-pan-nieh-p'an-ching, a Chn. v. of Mahāparinirvāṇa-s. 21-26 (Skt)
		2		
		3		Pan-ni-yüan-ching, a Chn. v. of Parinirvāṇa-s. II (Skt)
		4	1-7	Ta-pan-nieh-p'an-ching, a Chn. v. of Mahāparinirvāṇa-s. 27-33 (Skt)
		4	8	(Hsiao-ch'eng) Ta-pan-nieh-p'an-ching, a Chn. v. of Mahāparinibbāṇa-s. II (P)
		5	1-7	
			8	Ta-pei-ching, a Chn. v. of Mahākaruṇā-puṇḍarika-s. II (Skt)
			9-11	(Hsiao-ch'eng) Ta-pan-nieh-p'an-ching, II, a Chn. v. of Mahāparinibbāṇa-s. (P)
		6	1-6	Fo-i-chiao-ching (Ch)
			7-8	Ch'ang-a-han-ching, a Chn. v. of Dīrghāgama-s. IV. (Skt)
			9	(Hsiao-ch'eng) Ta-pan-nieh-p'an-ching, a Chn. v. of Mahāparinibbāṇa-s. II (P)
		7		

Bk.	Ch.	Sc.	Ssc.	Source
VIII	IV	8	1-2	M. 108 Gopaka-moggalāna-s. (P)
			3-4	M. 84 Madhuriya-s. (P)
			5-8	D. 23 Pāyāsi-s (P)
			9	S. 47, 21-23 Sīla, etc. (P)
			10	S. 22, 90 Channa (P)
			11-12	A. V, 50 Nārada (P)

PALI AND SANSKRIT WORDS

Pronunciation

At first, readers may be more concerned with understanding the doctrine than with how the foreign words should be pronounced. The Pali and Sanskrit terms that appear in the text are listed here with diacritical marks as transliterated from the original Indian nagari script. The following few simple rules are provided to help readers make approximate sounds of some, not all, of the letters involved so that they could be intelligible in their attempt at pronouncing these complex words.

VOWELS:

a as a in about; e as e in prey, i as i in fill, o as o in go, u as u in full. The macron (ā, ī, ū) indicates a long sound, i.e., ā as a in father, ī as i in police, ū as u in rumor, but o and e are always long. Also, ai and au are always long; i.e., ai as ai in aisle, au as au in Haus (German), or as ow in how.

CONSONANTS:

c as ch in exchange; s, j, y and other letters are like English, ñ as n in singe, or ny; ññ as n-ny; h after b, c, d, g, k, p, t is pronounced, i.e., bh as in abhor; ch as in church hill; dh as in adhere; gh as in foghorn; kh as in sinkhole; ph as in uphill; th as in anthill. Thus, Tathāgata is pronounced Tat-hāgata, not Ta-thāgata. The difference between dotted and undotted letters are difficult to distinguish, but d is like th in this, and ḍ is like d in drum; t as t in water, and ṭ as t in true; n is like n in nut, and ṇ is like n in none, ṅ is like n in sing, king, sink. Dotted s (ṣ) is like sh in ash, and ś is like s in sure. Dotted r (ṛ) is like ri in merrily.

Pali and Sanskrit Words

Abhaya-rajakumara, P and S:
    Abhayarājakumāra

Abhiguna, S: Abhiguṇa

Acala, P and S: Acalā

Aciravati, P: Aciravātī; S: Ajiravatī

Ahimsaka, S: Ahiṃsaka

Ajata, S: Ajāta

Ajatasatru, P: Ajātasattu; S:
    Ajātaśatru

Ajita Kesakambala, S: Ajita
    Keśakambala

Ajivaka, P: Ājīvaka; S: Ājīvika

Akanistha, S: Akaniṣṭha

Aksayamati, S: Akṣayamati

Alamandanda, S: Ālamandanda

Alara Kalama, P: Āḷara Kāḷāma; S:
    Ārāḍa Kālāma

Alavaka, P: Āḷavaka; S: Āṭāvaka

Alavi, P and S: Āḷavī, or S: Āṭavī

alaya-vijnana, S: ālayavijñāna

Alokamukha, S: Ālokamukha

Amalaki, P and S: Āmalakī

Ambagama, P: Ambagāma; S:
    Āmragrāma

Ambalatthika, P: Ambalaṭṭhikā; S:
    Āmrayaṣṭika

Ambasanda, P: Ambasaṇḍā; S:
    Āmbasaṇḍa

Ambattha, P: Ambaṭṭha; S:
    Āmraṣṭha

Amitabha, S: Amitābha

Amitayus, S: Amitāyus

Amragrama, P: Ambagāma; S:
    Āmragrāma

Amrapali, P: Ambapāli; S: Āmrapālī

Ananda, P and S: Ānanda

Anantnacaritra, S: Anantnacāritra

Anathapindika, P: Anāthapiṇḍika; S:
    Anāthapiṇḍada

anatman, P: anatta; S: anātman

Anga, P: Aṅga, S: Aṅga

Angaka (P); S: Aṅgaka

Angulimala, P: Aṅgulimāla; S:
    Aṅgulimāla

Anguttarapa, P: Aṅguttarāpa; S:
    Aṅguttarāpa

Aniruddha (S); P: Anuruddha

Anjana, P and S: Añjana

Anna Kondanna, P: Añña Koṇḍañña;
    S: Ājñāta Kauṇḍinya

Anoma, P: Anomā; S: Anavamā

Anugara, P and S: Anugāra

Anupiya, P: Anūpiya; S: Anupriyā

Anuruddha (P); S: Aniruddha

Apana, P and S: Āpaṇa

Arittha, P: Ariṭṭha; S: Ariṣṭa

Asa, S: Āśā

asoka (P); S: aśoka

Asokasridevata, S: Aśokaśrīdevata

Assaji (P); S: Aśvajit

Assapura (P); S: Aśvapura

Asvaghosa, P: Ashvaghosha; S:
    Aśvaghoṣa

atman, P: atta; S: ātman

Atuma, P and S: Ātumā

Avalokitesvara, S: Avalokiteśvara

Avici, P and S: Avīci

Ayodha, P: Ayojjhā; S: Ayodhā

Bahiya-Daruciriya, P and S:
    Bāhiyadārucīriya

Bahuka, P and S: Bāhukā

Bakkula (P); S: Dvākula

Balaka, P: Bālaka; S: Pālaka

Baliharana, S: Baliharaṇa

Baranasi, P: Bārāṇasi; S: Vārāṇasī

Belatthiputta, P: Belaṭṭhiputta; S:
    Vairaṭṭīputra

Bhadda (P); S: Bhadrā

Bhadda-Kapilani, P: Bhaddā-
    kapilāni; S: Bhadrakapilanī

Bhadda-Kundalakesa, P: Bhaddā-
    Kuṇḍalakesā; S:
    Bhadrakuṇḍalakeśā

Bhaddali, P: Bhaddāli; S:
    Bhadravālin

Bhaddiya (P); S: Bhadrika
Bhagga (P); S: Bhārgā
Bhaggava, (P); S: Bhārgava
Bhagu, (P); S: Bhṛgu
Bhaisajyaraja, S: Bhaiṣajyarāja
Bhanda, P and S: Bhaṇḍa
Bharadvaja, P and S: Bhāradvāja
Bharandu, S: Bharaṇḍu
Bhesakala, P: Bhesakalā: S:
    Bhīsakalā
Bhesika (P); S: Bheśika
Bhismagarjitasvararaja, S:
    Bhīṣmagarjitasvararāja
Bhismottaranirghosa, S:
    Bhīṣmottaranirghoṣa
Bhumu (P); S: Mudū
Bimbisara, P and S: Bimbisāra
birana (P); S: vīriṇa
Brahma, P and S: Brahmā
brahmadanda, S: brahmadaṇḍa
Brahmajala-sutta, P: Brahmajāla-
    sutta; S: Brahmajālasūtra
cakkavatti (P); S: cakravartin
Cala, P and S: Cālā
Campa, P and S: Campā
Canda (P); S: Candra
candala, P: candāla; S: caṇḍāla
Candrasurya-vimalapratibhasri, S:
    Candrasūryavimala-pratibhāśrī
Candrasuryapradipa, S:
    Candrasūryapradīpa
Capala, P and S: Cāpāla
Catuma, P and S: Catumā
Ceti (P); S: Ceḍi
Channa (P); S: Chanda
Chattapani P: Chattapāni; S:
    Chatrapāni
Cinca, S: Ciñcā
cintamani, S: cintāmaṇi
Citta (P); S: Citra
Dabba Malla-putta (P); S:
    Daramallaputra
Dalhanemi (P); S: Dṛḍhanemi

Dandapani, P and S: Daṇḍapani
Dantamati, P and S: Dāntamati
Darupattika (P); S: Dārupatraka
Devaraja, S: Devarāja
Dhammadinna, P: Dhammadinnā; S:
    Dharmadinnā
Dhananjaya, S: Dhanañjaya
dharani, P and S: dhāraṇī
Dharanidhara, S: Dhāraṇīdhara
Dharma-gahanabhyudgata, S:
    Dharmagahanābhy-udgata-rāja
Dharma-padma-srikusala-devata, S:
    Dharmapadma-śrī-kuśala-devata
Dharmadhatu, S: Dharmadhātu
Dharmakara, S: Dharmākara
Dharmakaya, S: Dharmakāya
Dharmavikurvana, S:
    Dharmavikurvaṇa
dhutaguna, S: dhūtaguṇa
Digha (P); S: Dīrgha
Digha-Karayana, P: Dīgha-Kārayāna
Digha-tapassi, P: Dīgha-tapassi; S:
    Dīrghatapasvin
Dighanakha (P); S: Dīrghanakha
Dighavu, P: Dīghāvu; S: Dīrghāyus
Dighiti, P: Dīghīti; S: Dīrghīti
Dipamkara, S: Dīpaṃkara
Dipankara, P: Dīpaṅkara; S:
    Dīpaṅkara
Dona, P: Doṇa; S: Droṇa
Drdha, S: Dṛdhā
Dummuka (P); S: Durmukha
Dunnivittha, P: Dunniviṭṭha; S:
    Durniviṣṭha
Dusin (P); S: Dūṣī
Ekayana, S: Ekayāna
Eleyya, S: Eḷeyya
Gaggara, P: Gaggarā; S: Gargarā
Gandavyuha, S: Gaṇḍavyūha
gandhabba (P); S: gandharva
Gandhara, P and S: Gandhāra
garuda, P and S: garuḍa
Gaya, P: and S: Gayā

Gayasisa, P: Gayāsīsa; S: Gayāśīrṣa

Ghataya, P: Ghatāya; S: Ghṛta

Ghatikara, P and S: Ghaṭīkāra

Ghosita (P); S: Ghosiṭa, or Ghoṣita

Gopa, P and S: Gopā

Gosala, P: Gosāla; S: Gośāla

Gosaliputra, S: Gośālīputra

Gosinga-sala (P); S: Gauśṛṅgaśala

Gotama (P); S: Gautama

Gotami, P: Gotamī; S: Gautamī

Guhyakadhipati, S: Guhyakādhipati

Gulissani (P); S: Guṇisarni

Gunagarbha, S: Guṇagarbha

Gunamukha, S: Guṇamukha

Gunda, P: Gundā; S: Gundrā

Gundavana, P: Gundāvana; S:
    Gundrāvaṇa

Hariti, S: Hārītī

Hatthaka (P); S: Hastaka

Hiranyavati, P: Hiraññavatī; S:
    Hiraṇyavatī

Icchanankala, P: Icchānankalā; S:
    Icchanāṅgela

Indasala, P: Indasāla; S: Indraśāla

Indriyesvara, S: Indriyeśvara

Isana, P: Isāna; S: Īṣāṇa

Isanajarapad, S: Īśānajarapad

Isidatta (P); S: Ṛṣidatta

Isigiri (P); S: Ṛṣigiri

Isipatana (P); S: Ṛṣpatana

Isvara, P: Īssara; S: Īśvara

Jagatimdhara, S: Jagatīṃdhara

Jalavahana, P and S: Jalavāhana

Jali, P and S: Jāli or Jālin

Jaliya, P Jāliya; S: Jālika

Jambu, P and S: Jāmbū

Jambudvipa, P and S: Jambudvīpa

Jambudvipasirsa, S:
    Jāmbudvīpaśīrṣa

Jambugama, P: Jambugāma; S:
    Jambugrāma

Jambunada, P and S: Jāmbūnada

Janussoni, P: Jāṇussoṇi; S:
    Jānukṣīnin

Jataka, P and S: Jātaka

Jatila, P and S: Jaṭilā

Jatindhara, S: Jaṭindhara

Jatiya, P: Jātiyā; S: Jaca

Jayosmayatana, S: Jayoṣmāyatana

Jivaka, P and S: Jīvaka

Jivamjivaka, S: Jīvaṃjīvaka

Jotika (P); S: Jyotika

Jotipala, P: Jotipāla; S: Jyotipāla

Jujaka, P and S: Jūjaka

Kaccana, P Kaccāna; S: Kātyāyana

Kakusandha (P); S: Krakucchanda

Kakuttha, P: Kakuṭṭhā; S:
    Krakuṣṭha

Kalakhemaka, P: Kālākhemaka; S:
    Kālakṣemaka

Kalama, P and S: Kālāma

Kalarajanaka, S: Kalārajanaka

Kalaratridevi, S: Kālarātrīdevī

Kalavinkas, S: Kalaviṅkas

Kali, P and S: Kālī

Kaligodha, P and S: Kāligodhā

Kalinga, P: Kālinga; S: Kaliṅga

Kaludayin, P: Kāḷudāyin (or, Kal-
    Udāyin); S: Kālodāyin

Kamabhu, P and S: Kāmabhū

Kamada, P and S: Kāmada

Kammassadhamma (P); S:
    Kalmāṣadamya

Kandarayana (P); S: Kaṇḍalāyana

Kanha (P); S: Kṛṣṇā

Kanhajali (P); S: Kṛṣṇājinā

Kanhayana (P); S: Kṛṣṇāyana

Kaniska, S: Kaniṣka

Kankha-Revata, P: Kankhā-Revata;
    S: Kāṅkṣārevata

Kannakathala, P: Kaṇṇakathala; S:
    Kṛṇṇakāṣṭhā

Kanthaka, P and S: Kaṇṭhaka

Kapilavatthu (P); S: Kapilavastu

Kappasiya (P); S: Kalpāsiya

Karunayamana, S: Karuṇāyamāna

Kasi, P: Kāsī; S: Kāśī

Kassapa (P); S: Kāśyapa

Kassapa-gotta (P); S: Kāśyapagotra

Katamodrakatisyaka, P: Kaṭamoraka-Tissaka; S: Katamodrakatiṣyaka

Katiyani, P and S: Kātiyānī

Kattakha (P); S: Kāṣṭka

Katyayana, P: Kaccāyana; S: Kātyāyana

Kausiya, S: Kauśiya

Kenika, S: Keṇika

Keniya (P); S: Keṇiya

Kesakambala (P); S: Keśakambala

Kesaputta (P); S: Keśaputra

Khandadeviyaputra, S: Khaṇḍadeviyāputra

Khema (P); S: Kṣema, or Kṣemakā

Khuddarupi, P: Khuddarūpi; S: Kṣudrarūpī

Kiki, P: Kīki; S: Kṛki

kimnaras, S: Kiṃnaras

Kisa Gotami, P: Kisā Gotamī; S: Kṛśā Gautamī

Kisa Sankicca (P); S: Kṛśa Saṅkṛtya

Kitagiri, P: Kīṭagiri; S: Kṛtāgiri

Kokalika, P and S: Kokālika

Kondanna, P: Koṇḍañña; S: Kauṇḍinya

Kora-Khattiya (P); S: Korakṣata

Koravya (P); S: Kauravya

Kosala, P: Kosalā; S: Kauśalā

Kosambi (P); S: Kauśāmbī

Krakustha, P: Kakuṭṭhā; S: Krakuṣṭha

ksanti, S: kṣānti

kshatriya (P); S: kṣatriya

Ksullapanthaka, P: Culla-Panthaka; S: Kṣullapanthaka

Kukkuta (P); S: Kurkuṭa

Kukkutarama, S: Kukkuṭārāma

Kuladevata, S: Kuladevatā

Kumara-Kassapa, P: Kumāra-Kassapa; S: Kumārakāśyapa

Kundadhana, P and S: Kuṇḍadhāna

kusa (P); S: kuśa

Kusana, P: Kusāna; S: Kuṣāṇa

Kusinara: P: Kusinārā, S: Kuśinagara

Kutadanta, P: Kūṭadanta, S: Kuṭadanta

Kutagara, P and S: Kūṭāgāra

Kutigramaka, P: Koṭigāma; S: Kuṭigrāmaka

Lakuntaka-Bhaddiya, P: Lakuṅṭaka-Bhaddiya; S: Lakuṇṭakabhadrika

Lohicca (P); S: Lohitya

Lokayata, S: Lokāyata

Lokesvararaja, S: Lokeśvararāja

Lumbini, P and S: Lumbinī

Macchikasanda, P: Macchikāsaṇḍa, S: Mātsikaṣaṇḍa

Madda (P); S: Madra

Maddi (P); S: Madrī

Madhura, P and S: Madhurā

Magandiya, P and S: Māgandiya

Maha-Cunda, P and S: Mahācunda

Maha-Kaccana, P: Mahā-Kaccāna, S: Mahākātyāyana

Maha-Kaccayana, P: Mahākaccāyana, or Mahākaccāna; S: Mahākātyāyana

Maha-Panthaka, P and S: Mahā-Panthaka

Mahabala, S: Mahābala

Mahabhijna-jnanabhibhu, S: Mahābhijñā-jñānābhibhū

Mahadeva, P and S: Mahādeva

Mahakalpina, P: Mahā-Kappina; S: Mahākalpina

Mahakassapa, P: Mahākassapa; S: Mahākāśyapa

Mahakasyapa, see above

Mahakatayana, P: Mahākaccāyana, S: Mahākātyāyana

Mahakotthita, P: Mahākoṭṭhita, S: Mahākauṣṭila

Mahali, P and S: Mahāli

Mahamati, P and S: Mahāmati

Mahanama, P and S: Mahānāma
Mahapajapati, P: Mahāpajāpatī; S:
    Mahāprajāpatī
Mahaphala, S: Mahāphala
Mahaprabha, S: Mahāprabha
Mahapranada, S: Mahāpraṇāda
Mahapratibhana, S: Mahāpratibhāna
Maharatha, S: Mahāratha
Mahasambhava, S: Mahāsaṃbhava
Mahasammata, S: Mahāsammata
Mahasattvas, S: Mahāsattvas
Mahasthamaprapta, S:
    Mahāsthāmaprāpta
Mahatistha, S: Mahātiṣṭha
Mahavairocana, S: Mahāvairocana
Mahavira, P and S: Mahāvīra
Mahavyuha, S: Mahāvyūha
Mahayana, S: Mahāyāna
Mahissara (P); S: Maheśvara
Maitrayani, S: Maitrāyaṇī
Makkhali Gosala, P: Makkhali
    Gosāla; S: Maskarin Gośālīputra
Makutabhandhana, S:
    Makuṭabandhana
Mallika, P and S: Mallikā
Malunkyaputta, P: Māluṇkyāputta;
    S: Maluṅkyāputra
Manasakata, P: Manasākata; S:
    Manasākṛta
mandarava, P: mandārava; S:
    māndārava
Mandissa (P); S: Maṇḍisya
Manikutaraja, S: Manikūṭarāja
Manjusri, S: Mañjuśrī
Mantani, P: Mantāni; S: Maitrāyaṇi
Mantrausadhi, S: Mantrauṣadhi
Mara, P and S: Māra
Matali, P and S: Mātali
Matangi, P and S: Mātaṅgī
Mathala, S: Māṭhala
Maudgalyayana, P: Moggallāna; S:
    Maudgalyāyana
Maya, P and S: Māyā
Meghasri, S: Meghaśrī

Mendaka, P and S: Meṇḍaka
Migara, P: Migāra; S: Mṛgāra
Mithila, P and S: Mithilā
Moggallana, P: Moggallāna; S:
    Maudgalyāyana
Mogharaja, P: Mogharāja; S:
    Amogharāja
Moliyaphagguna (P); S:
    Mauliyaphalguna
mudra, S: mudrā
Munda, S: Muṇḍa
Nadi, P and S: Nadī
Nadika, P: Nādika; S: Nāḍakantha
Naga, P and S: Nāga
Nagita, P and S: Nāgita
Nairanjama, P: Nerañjarā; S:
    Nairañjanā
Naksatraraja-samkusumitabhijna, S:
    Nakṣatrarāja-saṃkusumitābhijña
Nakula, P and S: Nakulā
Nalanda, P and S: Nālandā
Nalayus, P and S: Nālayus
Nalijangha, S: Naḷijangha
Nanda, P and S: Nandā
Nandihara, P and S: Nandihāra
Nandiya (P); S: Nandika
Nangaraka, P: Naṅgaraka; S:
    Naṅgaraka
Narada: P and S: Nārada
Nataputta, P: Nātaputta; S:
    Jñātiputra
Neranjara, P: Nerañjarā; S:
    Nairañjanā
nibbuta (P); S: nirvṛta
Nigantha Nataputta, P: Nigaṇṭha
    Nātaputta; S: Nigrantha
    Jñātiputra
nigrodha (P); S: nyagrodha
Nigrodha (P); S: Nyagrodha
Okkaka, P: Okkāka; S: Ikṣvāku
Otthaddha, P: Oṭṭhaddha; S:
    Oṣṭhardha
Paccaya (P); S: Pratyaya
Pacetana (P); S: Pracetana

Pacinavamsa, P: Pācīnavaṃsa; S:
 Prācīnavaṃsa
Pajjota (P); S: Pradyota
Pakudha Kaccayana, P: Pakudha
 Kaccāyana; S: Kakuda
 Kātyāyana
Pancala, P and S: Pañcāla
Pancasikha, S: Pañcaśikha
Pandaputta, P: Paṇḍaputta; S:
 Paṇḍaputra
Pandava, P: Paṇḍava; S: Pāṇḍava
Pandita-kumaraka, P and S:
 Paṇḍitākumāraka
Pankadha, P and S: Paṅkadhā
parasamgate, S: parasaṃgate
Parileyyaka, P: Pārileyyaka; S:
 Pārileśyaka
Pasenadi (P); S: Prasenajit
Pataliputra, P: Pāṭaliputta; S:
 Pāṭaliputra
Patikaputta, P: Pāṭikaputta, S:
 Pāthikaputra
Pava, P and S: Pāvā
Pavarana, P: Pavāraṇa; S: Pravāraṇa
Pavarika, P: Pāvārika; S: Prāvārika
Payasi, P and S: Pāyāsi
Pessa (P); S: Preṣya
Phagguna (P); S: Phalguna.
Phusati (P); S: Puṣyatī
Pilindavaccha, P: Piliṇḍavaccha; S:
 Pilindavatsa
Pindola-Bharadvaja, P and S:
 Piṇḍola-Bhāradvāja
Pingiya, P: Piṅgiyāni; S: Piṅgiya
Pippalayana, P and S: Pippalāyana
Pipphalivana (P); S: Pippalavana
Piyaka (P); S: Priyaka
Pokkharasati, P: Pokkharasāti (or,
 Pokkharasādi); S: Puṣkarasāri
posadha, P: uposatha; S: poṣadha
Potaliya (P); S: Potāliya
Potthapada, P: Poṭṭhapada; S:
 Puṣṭapāda
Prabhavyuha, S: Prabhāvyūha

Prabhuta, S: Prabhūtā
Prabhutaratna, S: Prabhūtaratna
Prajna-paramitra Sutra, S:
 Prajñāpāramitā Sūtra
Prajnakuta, S: Prajñākūṭa
pratityasamutpada, S:
 pratītyasamutpāda
Prthurastra, S: Pṛthurāṣṭra
Pukkusa (P); S: Pulkasa
Punabbasuka (P); S: Purnavasu
Punna, P: Puṇṇa; S: Pūrṇa
Punnaji, P: Puṇṇaji; S: Pūrṇajit
Punnavaddhana, P: Puṇṇavaḍḍhana;
 S: Pūrṇavardhana
Punyaraja, S: Puṇyarāja
Purana Kassapa, P: Pūrana Kassapa;
 S: Pūraṇa Kāśyapa
Purna, S: Pūrṇa
Radha, P and S: Rādha
Rahu, P and S: Rāhu
Rahula, P and S: Rāhula
Rajagaha, P: Rājagaha; S: Rājagṛha
Rajakarama, S: Rājakārāma
Rajayatana, P and S: Rājāyatana
Rakkhita (P); S: Rakṣita
Rama, P and S: Rāma
Ramagama, P: Rāmagāma; S:
 Rāmagrāma
Ramaputta, P: Rāmaputta; S:
 Rāmaputra
Ramavaranta, S: Rāmāvarānta
Rammaka (P); S: Rāmyaka
Ratiprabhasasri, S: Ratiprabhāsaśrī
Ratnacuda, S: Ratnacūḍa
Ratnakara, S: Ratnākara
Ratnavisuddha, S: Ratnaviśuddha
Ratnavyuha, S: Ratnavyūha
Ratridevata, S: Rātrīdevata
Ratthapala, P: Raṭṭhapāla; S:
 Rāṣṭrapāla
Ravana, P and S: Rāvaṇa
Revati, S: Revatī
Rgveda, S: Ṛgveda
Rohini, P and S: Rohiṇī

Rohitasva, S: Rohitāśva
Roja, S: Rojā
Rsigiri, P: Isigiri; S: Ṛṣigiri
Sabbakama, P: Sabbakāma; S:
    Sarvakāma
Saccaka (P); S: Satyaka
Sadaparibhuta, S: Sadāparibhūta
Sadaprarudita, S: Sadāprarudita
Saddharma-pundarika, S:
    Saddharma-puṇḍarika
Sagara, P and S: Sāgara
Sagaramegha, S: Sāgaramegha
Sagaramukha, S: Sāgaramukha
Sagaratira, S: Sāgaratīra
Sagata, P: Sāgata; S: Svāgata
Saha, S: Sahā
Saketa, P and S: Sāketa
Sakula, P: Sakulā; S: Śakulā
Sakuludayin, P: Sakuludāyin, S:
    Śakula Udāyin
Sakya, P: Sākya; S: Śākya
Sakyamuni, P: Sākyamunī; S:
    Śākyamuni
Sala, P: Sālā; S : Śālā
sala, P: sālā; S: śālā
Salavatika, P: Sālavatikā; S:
    Śālavatikā
Salhri, P: Sālha, S: Sālhṛ
Sama (P); S: Śyāma
Samagama, P: Sāmagāma; S:
    Śyāmāgrāma
samana, P: samaṇa, S: śramaṇa
Samanamukha, S: Sāmanāmukha
Samantavyuha, S: Samantavyūha
Samavati, P: Sāmāvatī: S: Śyāmāvatī
Samaveda, S: Sāmaveda
Samiddhi (P); S: Samṛddhi
Samkassa (P); S: Sāṃkāśya
Samudrapratisthana, S:
    Samudrapratiṣṭhana
Samudravetadin, Samudravetāḍin
Sandhana, P and S: Samdhāna
Sangarava, P: Sangārava; S:
    Saṅgārava

Sanjaya Belatthiputta, P: Sañjaya
    Belaṭṭhiputta; S: Sañjaya (or,
    Sañjayin) Vairaṭṭīputra
Sanjaya, P and S: Sañjaya
Sanjayin Vairattiputra, see above.
Sanjikaputta, P: Sañjikāputta; S:
    Sañjikaputra
Sanjiva, S: Sañjiva
Sankha (P); S: Śaṅkha
Santendriya, S: Śāntendriya
Saradhvaja, S : Sāradhvaja
Sari, P: Sāri, S: Śāri
Sariputta, P: Sāriputta; S: Śāriputra
Sarvagamin, S: Sarvagāmin
Sarvarupasam-darsana, S:
    Sarvarūpasaṃdarśana
Sarvasattva-priya-darsana, S:
    Sarvasattva-priya-darśana
Sarvasthanu, S: Sarvasthānu
Satagira, S: Śātāgira
Satatasamitabhiyukta, S:
    Satatasamitābhiyukta
Satyaguna, S: Satyaguṇa
Savatthi, P: Sāvatthi, S: Śrāvastī
Savittha, P: Saviṭṭha; S: Saviṣṭha
Sela (P); S: Śaila
Setavya, P and S: Setavyā
Siddhattha (P); S: Śiddhārtha
Sigalakamata, P: Sigālakāmātā; S:
    Singālakamatā
Siha, P: Sīha; S: Siṃha
Sikhandhi, P: Sikhaṇḍhi; S:
    Śikhaṇḍhin
Simhaketu, S: Siṃhaketu
Simhanada, S: Siṃhanāda
Simhapota, S: Siṃhapota
Simhavijrmbhita, S:
    Siṃhavijṛmbhitā
simsapa, P: simsapā; S: śiṃśapā
Singala, P: Siṅgāla; S: Śiṅgāla
Siribadda (P); S: Śrīvardha
Sirima (P); S: Śrīmān
Sisupacala, P: Siṣupacālā; S:
    Śīrṣupacālā

Sivali (P); S: Sīvali

Sivi (P); S: Śibi

Sobhita (P); S: Śobhita

Soma, P and S: Somā

Sona, P: Sonā; S: Śrona

Sona-Kutikanna, P: Sona-Kuṭikaṇṇa;
    S: Śronaviṃśatikoti

Sonadanda (P); S: Śroṇadaṇḍa

sramana, P: samaṇa; S: śramaṇa

Sramanamandala, S:
    Śramaṇamaṇḍala

Sravaka, S: Śrāvaka

Sravasti, P: Sāvatthi; S: Śrāvastī

Srigandha, S: Śrīgandha

Srigarbha, S: Śrīgarbha

Sriguna, S: Śrīguṇa

Srikuta, S: Śrīkūṭa

Srimahadevi, S: Śrīmahādevī

Srimala, S: Śrīmālā

Srimati, S: Śrīmati

Srisambhava, S: Śrīsambhava

Sthila, S: Sthilā

Subhadda (P); S: Subhadra

Subhaparangama, S:
    Śubhapāraṅgama

Subhuti, P and S: Subhūti

Subrahma, S: Subrahmā

Sudarsana, S: Sudarśana

Suddhadhimukti, S: Śuddhādhimukti

Suddhodana (P); S: Śuddhodana

Sugriva, S: Sugrīva

Sujata, P and S: Sujātā

Sujati, S: Sujāti

Sukhavati, S: Sukhāvatī

Sumagadha, S: Sumāgadhā

Sumana, S: Sumanā

Sumati, S: Sumatī

Sumeru-pradiparaja, S:
    Sumerupradīparāja

Sumerudhvaja, S: Sumerudhvajā

Sumsumara, P: Sumsumāra; S:
    Śiśumāra

Sunakkhatta (P); S: Sunakṣatra

Sunaksatra, S: Sunakṣatra

Sunaparantaka, S: Sunāparantaka

Sundari, P and S: Sundarī

Sundarika, P and S: Sundarikā

Sundarinanda, S: Sundarīnandā

Suppabuddha (P); S: Suprabuddha

Suppatittha, P: Supatiṭṭha; S:
    Supratiṣṭha

Suppavasa, P: Suppavāsā; S:
    Supravāsā

Suppiya, P: Suppiyā; S: Supriyā

Suprabha, S: Suprabhā

Supratisthita, P: Suppatiṭṭha; S:
    Supratiṣṭhita

Supratisthitacaritra, S:
    Supratiṣṭhitacāritra

Sura-Ambattha, P: Sūra-Ambaṭṭha

Surupa, P and S: Surūpa

Suryagatraprabha, S:
    Sūryagātraprabha

svaha, S: svāhā

Takkasila, P: Takkasilā; S: Takṣaśilā

Tala, P and S: Tāla

Taladhvaja, S: Tāladvaja

Talaputa, P and S: Talapuṭa

Tapussa (P); S: Trapuṣa

Tarukkha, P: Tārukkha; S: Tārukṣya

Tathagata, P and S: Tathāgata

Tathagata-garbha, S:
    Tathāgatagarbha

Tavatimsa, P: Tāvatiṃsa; S:
    Trāyastriṃśa

Thullakotthita, P: Thullakoṭṭhita; S:
    Sthūlakaṣṭhaka

Tindukkhanu (P); S: Tinduṣṭānu

Tisya, S: Tiṣya

Trayastrimsa, P: Tāvatiṃsa; S:
    Trāyastriṃśa

Tusita (P); S: Tuṣita

Ucchusma, S: Ucchuṣma

Udayin, P and S: Udāyin

Uddaka (P); S: Udraka

Uddaka Ramaputta, P: Uddaka
    Rāmaputta; S: Udraka
    Rāmaputra

Udena (P); S: Udyana
udumbara, P and S: uḍumbara
Udumbarika, S: Uḍumbarikā
Ugga (P); S: Ugra; Ulka
Uggasena (P); S: Ugrasena
Uggata (P); S: Udgata
Ugrasresthin, S: Ugraśreṣṭhin
Ujjeni (P); S: Ujjayanī
Ujunna, P: Ujuññā; S: Ṛjunyā
Ukkala (P); S: Utkala
Ukkattha, P: Ukaṭṭhā; S: Ulkaṣṭha
Upacala, P and S: Upacālā
Upali, P and S: Upāli
Upalivata, S: Upālivata
Upatissa (P); S: Upatiṣya
Upavana, P and: Upavāṇa
uposatha: P: uposatha; S: poṣadha
Uppalavanna, P: Uppalavaṇṇā; S:
    Utpalavarṇā
Uruvela, P: Urevelā; S: Uruvilvā
Uruvilvakasyapa, P: Uruvela-
    Kassapa; S: Uruvilvākāśyapa
Utpala, S: Utpalā
Utpalabhuti, S: Utpalabhūti
Utpalavarna, P: Uppalavaṇṇa; S:
    Utpalavarṇā
Uttara, P and S: Uttarā
Uttaraka, P and S: Uttarakā
Vaccha (P); S: Vatsa
Vacchagotta (P); S: Vatsagotra
Vaidehi, S: Vaidehī
Vaiduryaprabha, S: Vaiḍūryaprabha
Vairattiputra, S: Vairaṭṭīputra
Vaisadya, S: Vaiśadya
Vaisali, P: Vesālī; S: Vaiśālī
Vajji (P); S: Vṛji
Vajra, S: Vajrā
Vajrapani, S: Vajrapāni
Vakkali (P); S: Valkalin
Vamsa (P); S: Vatsa
Vanavasin, S: Vanavāsin
Vanganta, S: Vaṅgantā
Vangisa, P: Vaṇgīsa; S: Vāṅgīśa
Vanka, S: Vaṅka

Vappa (P); S: Vāṣpa
Varana, P: Varanā (or Viranā), S:
    Varaṇa
Varanasi, P: Bārāṇasi; S: Vārāṇasī
Varsakara, P: Vassakara; S:
    Varsakāra
Vasettha, P: Vāseṭṭha; S: Vāsiṣṭha
Vassakara, P: Vassakāra; S:
    Varṣakāra
Vasumitra, S: Vasumitrā
Vedehika (P); S: Vaidehikā
Vedhanna, P: Vedhaññā; S:
    Vaidhnya
Vediyaka (P); S: Vaidya
Vehalinga (P); S: Veruḍiṅga
Venagapura, P: Venāgapura; S:
    Venāgrapura
Venuvagrama, S: Veṇuvagrāma
Venuyastika, S: Veṇuyaṣṭikā
Vepula (P); S: Vipula
Vesali, P: Vesālī; S: Vaiśālī
Vessantara (P); S: Viśvantara
Vessavana (or Vissavana), S:
    Vaiśravaṇa
Vestila, S: Veṣṭhila
Vethadipa, P: Vethadīpa; S:
    Vaiṭhadvīpaka
Vetramulaka, S: Vetramūlaka
Vicitra-saladhvaja-vyuha, S:
    Vicitraśāladhvajavyūha
Vidudabha, P: Vidūdabha; S:
    Virūḍhaka
Vijaya, S: Vijayā
vijnana, S: vijñāna
Vikramasurya-candra-prabha, S:
    Vikrama-sūrya-candra-prabha
Vimala, S: Vimalā
Vimalakirti, S: Vimalakīrti
Vipasyin, P: Vipassin; S: Vipaśyin
Visakha, P: Visākhā; S: Viśākhā
Visarada, S: Viśārada
Visistacaritra, S: Viśiṣṭacāritra
Vissakamma, P: Vissakammā; S:
    Viśvakarmā

Visuddhacaritra, S: Viśuddhacārita
Visvabhu, S: Viśvabhū
Vrji, P: Vajji; S: Vṛji
Vrjian, P: Vajjian; S: Vṛjian
Yajnadatta, S: Yajñadatta

yaksas, S: yakṣas
Yasa (P); S: Yaśas
Yasaskama, S: Yaśaskama
Yasodhara, P: Yasodharā; S:
    Yaśodharā

SUGGESTED READINGS

Numerous books on Buddhism in English, for both general readers and advanced students, have been published, especially in the past 50 years during which period an interest in the religions and cultures of the East has grown quite substantially. Faced with such an overwhelming array, readers may find it difficult to choose books that could provide reliable, yet not too scholarly, explanations of the Buddha-Dharma or a historical biography of the Buddha.

The best choices would be books written in simple English by noted authorities in the field. The following are a few titles of books written by widely known scholars for the general reading public. These will provide an excellent starting point from which the readers' horizons can expand into the various traditions that developed from the simple but profound teaching of the Buddha; that is, the Theravada schools of Southern Asia or the Zen, Pure Land and other schools of the Mahayana in Northern Asia, including the mysterious and fascinating Vajrayana of Tibet. In the process, perhaps the reader can eventually find a suitable spiritual path that would lead to a peaceful, meaningful life in an increasingly complex, stressful world.

Caritas, Michael. *The Buddha.* London: Oxford University Press, 1983.
> A factual account of the life of the Buddha, relating him to the social conditions of the time and examining those elements of his teaching that appealed to the people of many diverse cultures in ancient and modern times.

Harvey, Peter. *An Introduction to Buddhism: Teaching, History & Practices.* Cambridge University Press 1990.
> In this book, Mr. Harvey has not only given a factual accounting of the Buddhist religion, through its philosophy, development and history but he has also shown how these teachings function as a set of life practices for the modern person as well.

Harvey, Peter. *An Introduction to Buddhist Ethics: Foundations, Values and Issues.* Cambridge University Press, 2000.
> A thought provoking book on Buddhist ethics for those who have studied Western ethical theories. This book will inspire the western reader to see

things from a different perspective and offers Buddhist perspectives on contemporary issues.

Lopez, Donald. *Buddhism in Practice*. Princeton University Press, 1995.
    An anthology of forty-eight translated texts, most of which have never appeared in the English language, which describe the vast scope of Buddhist practice in Asia. A part of the Princeton Readings in Religions series, this book also provides substantial introductions to each section by its respective translator.

Mizuno, Kōgen. *The Beginnings of Buddhism*. Translated by Richard L. Gage. Tokyo: Kōsei Publishing Co., 1980.
    Briefly in simple language, Professor Mizuno first describes the political and cultural background of the period in which the Buddha lived. Next, with the general reader in mind, he presents a clear and understandable explanation of the Buddha's teaching. This attractive book includes photographs of the places significant to the life of the Buddha as they now appear in modern India.

Mizuno, Kōgen. *Buddhist Sutras: Origin, Development, Transmission*. English ed. Tokyo: Kōsei Publishing Co., 1982.
    Provides an easy-to-read historical background of how the Buddhist scriptures originated and developed; and how they were translated and introduced to various countries outside of India. Professor Mizuno begins with a simple explanation of the meaning of 'sutra,' and how the form and style first used in ancient Indian Brahmanism were adopted by Buddhists to record the discourses of the Buddha. From a balanced point of view, the author also discusses problems relating to the authenticity of sutras and the controversies that arose due to these problems.

Nakamura, Hajime. *Gotama Buddha*. Los Angeles: Buddhist Books International, 1977.
    From a lifetime study of Buddhism, Dr. Nakamura, the eminent Professor Emeritus of Tokyo University, attempts to provide the general reader with a biography of the Buddha stripped of legendary and mythological stories attributed to him by over enthusiastic scribes in early Buddhist history. He managed to present in this small volume a highly dependable biography based on the earliest Buddhist scriptures and accounts contemporary to the time of the Buddha.

Nyanaponika, Thera. *The Heart of Buddhist Meditation*. New York: Samuel Weiser, Inc., 1969.
    A detailed, clear description of the "mindfulness" meditation (sati) taught by the Theravada Buddhists of Southeast Asia. The book also includes the meditation text on which this form of meditation is based, the Great Discourse of the Foundations of Mindfulness (Mahā-Satipatthāna Sutta), as well as the Thera's description of the practice.

Queen, Christopher S. *Engaged Buddhism in the West.* Somerville: Wisdom Publications, 1999.

> Edited by Christopher S. Queen, this anthology presents Buddhism from a socially engaged context. This book deals with the activism work of Buddhist organizations, temples and members from throughout the world in dealing with issues such as health, commerce, education, the environment, prison reform, gender equality and respect.

Rahula, Walpola. *What the Buddha Taught.* 2nd and enlarged ed. New York: Grove Press, 1974.

> The author, a distinguished scholar of the Theravada (Southern) division of Buddhism, provides the general reader with an authoritative, systematic exposition of the essential and fundamental teaching of the Buddha, including the Four Noble Truths and the Noble Eightfold Path. He also tries to clarify the meanings of many terms that appear in the Pali scriptures.

Robinson, Richard H. and Johnson, Willard L. *The Buddhist Religion.* Belmont, California: Wadsworth Publishing Company, 1982.

> A clear and accurate description of Buddhism as it is found throughout Asia, from India to Korea and Japan, and to the United States. The authors examine all the important teachings as well as Buddhism's role in those societies.

Sangharakshita. *The Eternal Legacy; an Introduction to the Canonical literature of Buddhism.* London: Tharpa Publications, 1985.

> Born in England and ordained as a Buddhist monk, this widely respected author presents "primarily for the student of Buddhism who is not in a position to explore for himself a canonical literature" that encompasses a formidable number of volumes, a discussion of the contents of many of the notable sutras from various traditions of Buddhism. This book is a valuable source of information for the sutra passages that appear in the Buddha-Dharma.

Śāntideva. *Entering the Path of Enlightenment.* The Bodhicaryāvatāra of the Buddhist poet Śāntideva. Translation with guide by Marion L. Matics. New York: The Macmillan Company, 1970.

> Śāntideva, a poet-monk of eighth century C.E. India, describes in verse with wonderful imagery, the steps to be taken to become a bodhisattva, who vows to bring all living beings to enlightenment. Dr. Matics provides not only the translation of this beautiful poem but a helpful introduction to the rise of Mahayana Buddhism and the bodhisattva practice leading to enlightenment.

Streng, Frederick J. *Emptiness: A Study in Religious Meaning.* Nashville: Abingdon Press, 1967.

> The author addresses the question of the religious meaning of the foundational teaching of Mahayana Buddhism, "emptiness" (śunyatā). The emptiness doctrine seems on the surface to be merely a philosophical idea, highly abstract and intangible for the general reader, but the author skillfully opens

the way to a clearer understanding of how the concept of "emptiness" can be applied to one's spiritual life. He begins by explaining how the term originated with Nagarjuna, the Buddhist philosopher in India during the second century C.E., and how it relates to the basic Buddhist concepts.

Thurman, Robert A. F. *Essential Tibetan Buddhism*. San Francisco: Harper, 1996. As one of America's foremost Buddhist scholars and a close confidant of His Holiness, the Dalai Lama, Dr. Thurman has brought together the essential elements of Tibetan Buddhism and traces its development from India. He explains why Tibetan Buddhism is unique, and yet, still able to cope with the world we live in today.

Williams, Paul. *Mahayana Buddhism: The Doctrinal Foundations*. London, New York: Routledge, 1989. A well-written text with many references which provides a thorough introduction to Mahayana Buddhism, incorporating Buddhism's development within a historical context as it spread throughout East Asia.

Wright, A.F. *Buddhism in Chinese History*. Stanford University Press, 1983. An outstanding presentation of the history of Buddhism from the time of its introduction to China to modern day times. Presents some facts and information not found anyplace else.

THE SOCIETY FOR THE PROMOTION OF BUDDHISM

In describing the Society for the Promotion of Buddhism, the sponsoring organization for this project, we must refer to the international industrialist, the late Rev. Dr. Yehan Numata.

Rev. Dr. Numata was born into the family of a Buddhist priest in Hiroshima, Japan. As a young man, he majored in economics at the University of California, Berkeley, working his way though both undergraduate and graduate programs. Returning to Japan, he served as a statistician in the Resource Bureau of the Japanese government.

Rev. Numata had a deep religious experience after conquering a disease of a serious nature during his stay in the United States, which inspired him to resolve to share with others the wonderful messages of the Buddha. To accomplish this he realized that he must be financially independent and not rely on others. He then resigned his post in the Resource Bureau and in 1934 embarked on an enterprise of his own, which developed into what is now Mitutoyo Corporation, the world leader in precision measuring instruments.

Rev. Numata made every effort to introduce people to the great teaching of the Buddha as a means which would lead to the perfection of the human mind. After overseeing his company's operation for more than fifty years, he then incorporated, with his own private funds, the Society for the Promotion of Buddhism (Bukkyo Dendo Kyokai) as an organ to further the cause of Buddhism as a way to contribute to world peace.

One of the Society's goals is to share with others the teachings of the Buddha by every possible means. One such means was to bring about an anthology of Buddhist scriptures which would give the whole of the teaching encompassing all facets of the Dharma and not merely one aspect of Japanese Buddhism represented by sectarianism. This brought about the book "Teaching of Buddha." To date, over 6 million copies, in more than 30 languages have been distributed to hotels, libraries, schools and individuals throughout the world.

Other major undertakings have included the establishment of Numata Chairs in Buddhist Studies at several major universities in the Western Hemisphere and Europe. In order to establish firm bases to share the Buddha's teaching,

Mr. Numata has also built Buddhist temples in several areas of the world where none previously existed.

After a long and meaningful life, the Rev. Dr. Numata passed away at the age of 97 in 1994. Today, the work of the Society is being carried on under the direction of Rev. Numata's first son, the Rev. Toshihide Numata as chairman.

The Society hereby wishes to offer its deep appreciation and thanks to the Rev. Muan Kizu and others who compiled the original Japanese version in concise form from the immensely larger Taisho Daizokyo.

INDEX

Topics are cited by Book number, chapter number, section number, and subsection number, e.g., III, ch.2, 3(6); or, VI, ch.1, 5, #206.

* = where Buddha stayed, or passed by/through (as indicated in the text) to teach disciples, other mendicants, and any other persons. However, entries for places like Rajagaha, Savatthi, and Vesali are too numerous to cite each instance.

A

Abhaya, Ananda's instruction to, about 3 Learnings, III, ch.2, 3(6)

Abhayarajakumara (prince), sent by Nigantha to debate Buddha, VII, ch.2, 1(7)-(8)

Abhiguna (prince), [a Jataka], III, ch.3, 9(3)

Absolute truth, VIII, ch.3, 4(5); VIII, ch.3, 6(7)

Acala (devotee), Sudhana's teacher-guide, III, ch.3, 8(11)

Aciravati River*, IV, ch.3, 1(5)

Acrobat, see Uggasena (acrobat)

Affirmation and negation, the extreme principles of, I, ch.3, 5(5)

After life, VIII, ch.4, 8(7)

Ahimsaka, see Angulimala

Ajatasatru [P: Ajatasattu], birth, VII, ch.2, 2(1); usurps throne and imprisons his father, VII, ch.2, 2(1); concern for son Udaya, VII, ch.2, 4(3); tries to kill his mother, but dissuaded by Jivaka, VII, ch.2, 3(1); illness caused by evil actions, VII, ch.2, 4(4); self-serving state ministers give him advice, VII, ch.2, 4(4)-(9); hears dead father's voice, VII, ch.2, 4(11); Buddha prolongs life for sake of, VII, ch.2, 4(12); abandons plan to attack Vrji, VIII, ch.1, 1(2); his claim for Buddha's relics, VIII, ch.4, 7(8)

Ajita Kesakambala [or, Ajita Kesakambalin] (teacher), II, ch.1, 2(3); IV, ch.3, 5(2); VII, ch.2, 4(7)

Akanistha heaven, VII, ch.1, 1(1)

Aksayamati Bodhisattva, VII, ch.1, 5(10)-(11)

Alamandanda (brahmin), instructed by Maha-Kaccayana, V, ch.4, 2(1)

Alara Kalama (ascetic teacher), I, ch.1, 5(3); his death, I, ch.3, 1(1)

Alavaka (man-eating demon), captures King of Alavi, V, ch.1, 2(1)

Alavi (country)*, III, ch.3, 3(1); where demons inflict suffering, V, ch.1, 2(1)

L

M